PENGUIN REFERENCE

THE PENGUIN THESAURUS OF QUOTATIONS

M. J. Cohen first worked on quotation collecting as a student with his father, the translator, editor and author J. M. Cohen. Together they were responsible for successive editions of *The Penguin Dictionary of Modern Quotations* until J. M. Cohen's death in 1989. The most recent updates of their two complementary books are *The New Penguin Dictionary of Quotations* and *The Penguin Dictionary of Twentieth-Century Quotations*. When not pursuing the quotable, he was for many years an educational publisher. Now a publishing consultant and editor, he lives in north London with his artist wife. They have three daughters.

M J Cohen

THE PENGUIN THESAURUS OF *Quotations*

PENGUIN BOOKS

PENGUIN BOOKS

Published by the Penguin Group
Penguin Books Ltd, 27 Wrights Lane, London W8 5TZ, England
Penguin Putnam Inc., 375 Hudson Street, New York, New York 10014, USA
Penguin Books Australia Ltd, Ringwood, Victoria, Australia
Penguin Books Canada Ltd, 10 Alcorn Avenue, Toronto, Ontario, Canada M4V 3B2
Penguin Books (NZ) Ltd, Private Bag 102902, NSMC, Auckland, New Zealand

Penguin Books Ltd, Registered Offices: Harmondsworth, Middlesex, England

First published as a Penguin hardback 1998
Published in paperback as *The Penguin Thematic Dictionary of Quotations* in
Penguin Books 1999
Reprinted with corrections under the current title 2000
10 9 8 7 6 5 4 3 2 1 0

Set in Monotype Photina
Typeset by Ward Partnership, Saffron Walden, Essex
Printed in England by Clays Ltd, St Ives plc

Contents

Contents

C

Contents

Contents

M

N

O

P

S

T

It is a good thing for an uneducated man to read books of quotations. [(Of himself) Winston Churchill, 1874–1965, *My Early Life*, Ch.9]

Too much traffic with a quotation book begets a conviction of ignorance in a sensitive reader. Not only is there a mass of quotable stuff he never quotes, but an even vaster realm of which he has never heard. [Robertson Davies, 1913–95, *The Enthusiasms of Robertson Davies*]

How do people go to sleep? I'm afraid I've lost the knack. I might try busting myself smartly over the temple with the nightlight. I might repeat to myself, slowly and soothingly, a list of quotations beautiful from minds profound; if I can remember any of the damn things. [Dorothy Parker, 1893–1967, *The Little Hours*]

The taste for quotations [and for the juxtaposition of incongruous quotations] is a Surrealist taste. [Susan Sontag, 1933– , *On Photography*, 'Melancholy Objects']

OSCAR WILDE: I wish I had said that.
WHISTLER: You will, Oscar, you will. [James McNeill Whistler, 1834–1903, in L C Ingleby, *Oscar Wilde*]

To the reader

The Penguin Thematic Dictionary of Quotations gathers quotations under over 800 thematic headings.

Both the two previous Penguin dictionaries, **The New Penguin Dictionary of Quotations** and **The Penguin Dictionary of Twentieth-Century Quotations** have been ransacked, so the sources stretch from the Bible to the Internet. Where its companion volumes are alphabetically arranged under authors, here the organization ensures fascinating juxtapositions. As the authors appear in alphabetical order within each theme, wit and wisdom rub shoulders and Woody Allen's advice on marriage is followed by lines from the Solemnization of Matrimony in *The Book of Common Prayer*.

There should be a line suitable for the occasion, whether to round off your sermon, to start off your speech, to answer a quiz, give authority to your letter or allow you to dip, browse, and flit to other categories. Each theme should prove therefore both a source of reference and an anthology of the familiar and unfamiliar, a mix of lines you remembered, almost remembered and others you find unfamiliar but memorable.

HOW TO USE THE BOOK

If you want to explore a theme, turn to pp. vii–xv. The **Contents** lists more than 800 themes in alphabetical order. Some contain only a few entries, eg two to choose from under **Anthology**. While **Taxation** cheeringly provides eight, compared to twelve for **Tea & Coffee** which follows it. Others, of course, like **Love**, **God**, **Poets: Individual** and **Time** are rich in possibilities.

If you want a specific quotation: Wordsworth on daffodils, Hamlet on suicide: look under **Flowers** and **Suicide** respectively and track alphabetically to the author.

If you are less sure of who said what, or simply wonder whether Alan Bennett or George Orwell has anything apposite about **Society**, then either turn at once to **Society**, or to the index. There, you will find all Bennett's contributions listed in alphabetical order with a signpost pointing to each theme, eg Society 2; under George Orwell, Society 9.

Since categories are interrelated, there are cross-references at the end of each. **Optimism & Pessimism** points you on to **Fatalism**, where you can pick up the paths to **Destiny**; **Resignation**; **Hope**; and to [pure] **Pessimism** itself.

THE QUOTATIONS THEMSELVES

from THE BIBLE

In the Authorized Version, arranged in alphabetical order with the books of the Old Testament followed by the New Testament. The apocryphal books are listed under Bible, Apocrypha.

from SHAKESPEARE

The line references are to the single-volume Oxford University Press edition edited by W J Craig: [*Troilus and Cressida*, I. iii. 109]. If a scene contains prose, however, the line reference is in brackets: *Troilus and Cressida*, III. ii. (17)]. In that case, your own edition may not coincide exactly.

The line references for other English poets are from the Oxford editions of Standard Authors, and again there may be minor variations if you are reading another edition.

To save space, poetry is printed thus: 'If, with the literate, I am / Impelled to try an epigram, / I never seek to take the credit; / We all assume that Oscar said it. [Dorothy Parker, 1893–1967, *Oscar Wilde*]'.

Where an author does not divide his or her book into chapters, eg Thomas Burke's *Reflections on the Revolution in France* or James Joyce's *Ulysses*, a page number has had to do, and it is that of the Penguin edition, where there is one. Sometimes, it has not been possible to find a precise source, but the line is too good to leave out. If readers can help to pin down such floating quotes, sometimes only 'attributed', or fill out birth and death dates, the editor will be delighted to improve the detail in the next edition.

from FOREIGN AUTHORS

The original Latin, French, German, Italian, etc., only appear on the rare occasions when the line is generally known in that form, eg under **Health**, *Orandum est ut sit mens sana in corpore sano*. – Your prayer must be for a sound mind in a sound body. [Juvenal 60–*c*.130 *Satires*, X. 356]. But remember that Gustave Flaubert warned in his *Dictionary of Received Ideas*: 'Beware of quotations in Latin: they always conceal something improper.'

Acknowledgements

Infinitely the most important acknowledgement is to my late father and co-editor, J M Cohen. Many thousands of the entries in this new Dictionary were first gathered by him for one or other of our companion dictionaries of quotations.

Of the many friends and correspondents who helped with suggestions, made good omissions and errors, hunted down lines which appear in this Dictionary I would like to thank: Sally Adams, Brian W Aldiss, Ian Angus, John Armatys, Guy Bellamy, Philippa Bignell, Henry Blyth, Ronald Blythe, Edward Booth-Clibborn of the Design and Art Directors Association of London, Ivan Brown, Dr and Mrs O Buchan, Margaret Busby, G M Byrne, D Campbell, Victor Cappaert, Patrick Carey, Martin Childs, Gerald Cinamon, Charlotte Cohen, Colin Cohen, Margaret Coombs, Ian Crofton, Helena Cronin, John Dacey, Dr Peter Davison, Silvana Dean, Eilís Dillon, Vince Dowd, Wanda Ealing, T Eldridge, Ingrid von Essen, Quentin Falk, Ron Farquhar, Valerie Ferguson, Peter Ford, M Fores, John Fulford, Charles Fyffe, Michael Gilkes, Anna Girvan of the USIS Reference Center, Jonathon Green, Colin Greenland, Frank Hancock, G V Hardyman, J R Hart, Jim Heath of the Performing Rights Society, Donald Hickling, R D Hill, Sunil Hiranandani, Simon Hoggart, Eric Hutton, Philip Kemp, Jenny and Peter Kingsland, Jim Knowlson, Tony Lacey, Phyllis M Lee, J Leeman, Claire L'Enfant, Roselle Le Sauteur, Ellie Ling, K A Llewellyn, Cathy Ludbrook, T J Lustig, Kevin McDermott, Malcolm McEachran, Donald McFarlan, Alan Mackay, Peter Madgwick, John Major, Jonathan Marwil, Peter Matthews, G Miller, Ken Mullen, Christopher Murphy, Lt. Col. N T P Murphy, Neville Osmond, Eric Partridge, H M Paton, R D Pearce, Jeremy Perkins, Frank Pike, Ben Pimlott, Joseph Prescott, Nigel Price, B Ramsay, B Rochester, John M Ross, Ronald Searle, Dennis Sinclair, J Sinclair, Per Skjaeveland, Finbarr Slattery, Geoffrey Smith, Godfrey Smith, R Stanton, Stephen Stirling, Geoffrey Strachan, Melvyn Strong, Elizabeth Teague, Andrew Tems of the Enfield Central Library, W J Thaxter, Vera Thomas, Brian Thompson, Stanley Thornes, Ann Thorp, E Trehern, Glenn Trueman, Richard Usborne, Paul Vaughan, Anne Walmsley, Richard Walters, D Wilson, Anthony Wilttome, Edward Winter, Jon Wynne-Tyson, Igor Zaitsev, and apologize to others, no less helpful, but too numerous to mention.

Thanks too to Esther Sidwell who provided invaluable assistance in editing the text and Martin Toseland at Penguin; also to Kate Barker for preparing the index.

ABILITY

1 Politics and business can be settled by influence, cooks and doctors can only be promoted on their skill. [Penelope Fitzgerald, 1916– , *Innocence*, 16]

2 But above all / we have / the ability / to sort peas, / to cup water in our hands, / to seek / the right screw / under the sofa / for hours. / This / gives us / wings. [Miroslav Holub, 1923–98, *Wings*]

3 From each according to his abilities, to each according to his needs. [Karl Marx, 1818–83, *Criticism of the Gotha Programme*]

4 I used to be able to shoot the rind off an apple stored in a loft at the top of a cast-iron lighthouse. [J B Morton ('Beachcomber'), 1893–1979, *By the Way*, 13 Aug., 'On the Moors: Social Jottings']

5 Competence, like truth, beauty and contact lenses, is in the eye of the beholder. [Laurence J Peter, 1919–90 and Raymond Hull, 1918–85, *The Peter Principle*, Ch. 3]

6 The able man is the one who makes mistakes according to the rules. [Paul Valéry, 1871–1945, *Bad Thoughts and Not So Bad*, 'Q']

7 *Non omnia possumus omnes*. – We are not all capable of everything. [Virgil, 70–19 BC, *Eclogue*, VII, 63]

8 There is probably no man living, though ever so great a fool, that cannot do *something* or other well. [Samuel Warren, 1807–77, *Ten Thousand a Year*, xxviii]

See also POWER

ABROAD

1 I don't hold with abroad and think that foreigners speak English when our backs are turned. [Quentin Crisp, 1908–99, *The Naked Civil Servant*, Ch. 4]

2 Abroad is bloody. [King George VI, 1895–1952, attr., in W H Auden, *A Certain World*]

3 The great and recurrent question about abroad is, is it worth getting there? [Rose Macaulay, 1889–1958, attr.]

4 A man should know something of his own country, too, before he goes abroad. [Laurence Sterne, 1713–68, *Tristram Shandy*, Vol. vii, Ch. 2]

See also FOREIGNERS

ABSENCE

1 Absence makes the heart grow fonder. [anon., from *Davison's Poetical Rhapsody* (1602)]

2 When I came back to Dublin, I was court-martialled in my absence and sentenced to death in my absence, so I said they could shoot me in my absence. [Brendan Behan, 1923–64, *The Hostage*, 1]

3 The heart may think it knows better: the senses know that absence blots people out. We have really no absent friends. [Elizabeth Bowen, 1899–1973, *The Death of the Heart*, II, 2]

4 Absence from whom we love is worse than death. [William Cowper, 1731–1800, *Hope, Like the Short-lived Ray*]

5 The absent are always in the wrong. [Philippe Destouches, 1680–1754, *L'Obstacle imprévu*, 1, vi]

6 As I was going up the stair / I met a man who wasn't there. / He wasn't there again today. / I wish, I wish he'd go away. [Hughes Mearns, 1875–1965, *The Psycho-ed*]

7 I do not love thee! – no! I do not love thee! / And yet when thou art absent I am sad. [Caroline Norton, 1808–77, *I Do Not Love Thee*]

8 Two evils, monstrous either one apart, / Possessed me, and were long and loath at going: / A cry of Absence, Absence, in the heart, / And in the wood the furious winter blowing. [John Crowe Ransom, 1888–1974, *Winter Remembered*]

9 Most of what matters in your life takes place in your absence. [Salman Rushdie, 1937– , *Midnight's Children*, Bk II, 'Alpha and Omega']

10 A certain person may have, as you say, a wonderful presence: I do not know. What I do know is that he has a perfectly delightful absence. [Idries Shah, 1924–96, *Reflections*, 'Presence and Absence']

11 I dote on his very absence. [William Shakespeare, 1564–1616, *The Merchant of Venice*, I, ii (118)]

12 O! never say that I was false of heart, / Though absence seemed my flame to qualify. [*Sonnets*, 109]

13 We shall meet, but we shall miss him, / There will be one vacant chair. [H S Washburn, 1813–1903, *The Vacant Chair*]

See also FAREWELLS

ACADEMICS

1 The Oxford Don: 'I don't feel quite happy about pleasure.' [W H Auden, 1907–73, *The Orators*, 'Journal of an Airman']

2 A professor is one who talks in someone else's sleep. [W H Auden, 1907–73, in Charles Osborne, *W H A: The Life of a Poet*, Ch. 13]

3 Dons admirable! Dons of might! / Uprising on my inward sight / Compact of ancient tales, and port, / And sleep – and learning of a sort. [Hilaire Belloc, 1870–1953, *Lines to a Don*]

4 The true University of these days is a collection of books. [Thomas Carlyle, 1795–1881, *Heroes and Hero-worship*, I, v, 'The Hero as Man of Letters']

5 So, perhaps, I may escape otherwise than by death the last humiliation of an aged scholar, when his juniors conspire to print a volume of essays and offer it to him as a sign that they now consider him senile. [R G Collingwood, 1889–1943, *Autobiography*]

6 Though academics love bickering they hate rows. [Robertson Davies, 1913–95, *The Rebel Angels*, 'The New Aubrey II']

7 Old professors never die, they merely lose their faculties. [Stephen Fry, 1957– , *The Liar*, 2, v]

8 The world's great men have not commonly been scholars, nor its great scholars great men. [Oliver Wendell Holmes, 1809–94, *The Autocrat of the Breakfast Table*, Ch. 6]

9 Mark what ills the scholar's life assail, / Toil, envy, want, the patron, and the jail. [Dr Samuel Johnson, 1709–84, *The Vanity of Human Wishes*, 157]

10 Our American professors like their literature clear and cold and pure and very dead. [Sinclair Lewis, 1885–1951, address on receiving the Nobel Prize, Stockholm, 12 Dec. 1930]

11 The olive-grove of Academe, / Plato's retirement, where the Attic bird / Trills her thick-warbled notes the summer long. [John Milton, 1608–74, *Paradise Regained*, Bk iv, 244]

12 Donsmanship he defines as 'the art of criticizing without actually listening'. [Stephen Potter, 1900–1969, *Lifemanship*, 6]

13 Outwardly he seems stern and unbending, but inwardly he is. [Joseph Prescott, 1913– , *Aphorisms and Other Observations, Second Series*, 'Academicians']

14 To my mind by far the greatest danger in scholarship . . . is not that the individual may fail to master the thought of a school but that a school may succeed in mastering the thought of the individual. [Geoffrey Sampson, 1944– , *Schools of Linguistics*, Preface]

15 He was a scholar, and a ripe and good one; / Exceeding wise, fair-spoken and persuading: / Lofty and sour to them that loved him not; / But to those men that sought him sweet as summer. [William Shakespeare, 1564–1616, *Henry VIII*, IV, ii, 51]

16 To attempt to sustain the attention of rival schools of academics by argument alone is tantamount to constructing a Gothic arch out of junket. [Tom Stoppard, 1937– , *Jumpers*, I]

17 Academism results when the reasons for the rule change, but not the rule. [Igor Stravinsky, 1882–1971, and Robert Craft, 1923– , *Conversations with S*, 'Some Musical Questions']

See also EDUCATION, LEARNING, STUDENTS, TEACHERS, UNIVERSITIES

ACCEPTANCE, see RESIGNATION

ACCIDENTS

1 My only solution for the problem of habitual accidents ... is for everybody to stay in bed all day. Even then, there is always the chance that you will fall out. [Robert Benchley, 1889–1945, *Chips off the Old Benchley*, 'Good Luck']

2 The best laid schemes o' mice an' men / Gang aft a-gley. [Robert Burns, 1759–96, *To a Mouse*]

3 Accidents will occur in the best-regulated families. [Charles Dickens, 1812–70, *David Copperfield*, Ch. 28]

4 'There's been an accident!' they said, / 'Your servant's cut in half: he's dead!' / 'Indeed!' said Mr Jones, 'and please / Send me the half that's got my keys.' [Harry Graham, 1874–1936, *Ruthless Rhymes*, 'Mr Jones']

5 Life is not having been told that the man has just waxed the floor. [Ogden Nash, 1902–71, *You and Me and P. B. Shelley*]

6 Knocked down a doctor? With an ambulance? How could she? It's a contradiction in terms. [N F Simpson, 1919– , *One-way Pendulum*, I]

7 The chapter of accidents is the longest chapter in the book. [John Wilkes, 1727–97, attr. by R Southey in *The Doctor*, Vol. iv, p. 166]

See also CHANCE, DISASTERS, LUCK

ACHIEVEMENT

1 Great things are done when men and mountains meet; / This is not done by jostling in the street. [William Blake, 1757–1827, *Gnomic Verses*]

2 The world is made of people who never quite get into the first team and who just miss the prizes at the flower show. [J Bronowski, 1908–74, *The Face of Violence*, 6]

3 Every achievement is a servitude. It drives us to a higher achievement. [Albert Camus, 1913–60, *Notebooks*, iv: 1942]

4 It is not the clear-sighted who rule the world. Great achievements are accomplished in a blessed, warm fog. [Joseph Conrad, 1857–1924, *Victory*, Pt 2, Ch. 3]

5 Sudanese, called himself a dervish, swallowed a fish-hook, cut himself open, took it out again. If an uneducated savage can do that, you can cut your own hair. [Giles Cooper, 1918–66, radio drama *Mathry Beacon*]

6 Twenty-two acknowledged concubines, and a library of sixty-two thousand volumes, attested the variety of his inclinations; and from the productions which he left behind him, it appears that the former as well as the latter were designed for use rather than ostentation. [Edward Gibbon, 1737–94, *The Decline and Fall of the Roman Empire*, Ch. 7]

7 We never do anything well till we cease to think about the manner of doing it. [William Hazlitt, 1778–1830, *On Prejudice*]

8 Let us, then, be up and doing. / With a heart for any fate; / Still achieving, still pursuing, / Learn to labour and to wait. [H W Longfellow, 1807–82, *A Psalm of Life*]

9 Something attempted, something done, / Has earned a night's repose. [H W Longfellow, 1807–82, *The Village Blacksmith*]

10 For, as I suppose, no man in this world hath lived better than I have done, to achieve that I have done. [Thomas Malory, d. 1471, *Morte d'Arthur*, Bk xvii, Ch. 16]

11 You must always work not just within but below your means. If you can handle three elements, handle only two. If you can handle ten, then handle only five. In that way the ones you do handle, you handle with more ease, more mastery, and you create a feeling of strength in reserve. [Pablo Picasso, 1881–1973, in Françoise Gilot and Carlton Lake, *Life with Picasso*, Pt 2]

12 So many worlds, so much to do, / So little done, such things to be. [Alfred, Lord Tennyson, 1809–92, *In Memoriam*, 73]

13 I myself have accomplished nothing of excellence except a remarkable and, to some of my friends, unaccountable expertness in hitting empty ginger ale bottles with small rocks at a distance of thirty paces. [James Thurber, 1894–1961, *My Life and Hard Times*, Preface]

14 In order to carry out great enterprises, one must live as if one will never have to die. [Marquis de Vauvenargues, 1715–47, *Reflexions and Maxims*, 142]

15 Enough, if something from our hands have power / To live, and act, and serve the future hour; / And if, as toward the silent tomb we go, / Through love, through hope, and faith's transcendent dower, / We feel that we are greater than we know. [William Wordsworth, 1770–1850, *The River Duddon*, 34, 'After-Thought']

See also FAILURE, SUCCESS

ACTING

1 [Film acting] is not so much acting as reacting, doing nothing with tremendous skill. [Michael Caine, 1933– , in *City Limits*, 28 Feb.–6 Mar. 1986]

2 A lot of the time, what acting is really about is meeting someone's eye. [Tom Cruise, 1962– , interview, in *Guardian*, 28 Feb. 1989]

3 Pray to God and say the lines. [Bette Davis, 1908–89, advice to actress Celeste Holm, as quoted by the latter in L Halliwell, *Filmgoer's Book of Quotes*]

4 I mean, the question actors most often get asked is how they can bear saying the same things over and over again night after night, but God knows the answer to *that* is, don't we all *anyway*; might as well get paid for it. [Elaine Dundy, 1927– , *The Dud Avocado*, Ch. 9]

5 Style is knowing what sort of play you are in. [John Gielgud, 1904– , in BBC TV programme *On Acting*, 11 Sept. 1987]

6 All right, you shall be a cauliflower – only be it *gently*. [Joyce Grenfell, 1910–79, *George Don't Do That*, 'Flowers']

7 The important thing in acting is to be able to laugh and cry. If I have to cry, I think of my sex life. If I have to laugh, I think of my sex life. [Glenda Jackson, 1936– , quoted by Kim Basinger in *Playboy*, May 1986]

8 The only thing wrong with performing was that you couldn't phone it in. [Robert Mitchum, 1917–97, quoted by Robert Robinson in *The Sunday Times Magazine*, 11 May 1980]

9 Acting is therefore the lowest of the arts, if it is an art at all. [George Moore, 1852–1933, *Mummer-worship*]

10 [When asked the greatest secret of an actor's success] Sincerity, sincerity. Once you can fake that you can achieve anything. [Laurence Olivier, 1907–89, in Michael Shea, *Influence*, Ch. 15]

11 You can hold a mirror up to nature or a mirror up to art; I don't think you should hold a mirror up to another mirror. [John Peter, 1938– , review of Michael Frayn's play *Look Look* in *The Sunday Times*, 22 Apr. 1990]; see 18

12 Acting is merely the art of keeping a large group of people from coughing. [Ralph Richardson, 1902–83, in *New York Herald Tribune*, 19 May 1946]

13 Acting is to some extent a controlled dream. In one part of your consciousness it really and truly is happening. But, of course, to make it true to the audience all the time, the actor must, at any rate some of the time, believe himself that it is really true. [Ralph Richardson, 1902–83, in Gary O'Connor, *R R: An Actor's Life*, Pt III, Ch. 39]

14 You've got to perform in a role hundreds of times. In keeping it fresh one can become a large, madly humming, demented refrigerator. [Ralph Richardson, 1902–83, in *Time* magazine, 21 Aug. 1978]

15 A woman ought to dance as she moves in a seventeenth-century play, to sail in an eighteenth-century one, to swim in a nineteenth-century dress (with tiny, even steps under crinoline or bustle), and to stride in the twentieth century. [Athene Seyler, 1889–1990, of acting, in obituary, *Guardian*, 14 Sept. 1990]

16 I think the real reason one loves acting lies in this conception of the gesture bound by personality. Even actors who don't admit it actually play much more than the text. They act because they are inventing a character. [Delphine Seyrig, 1932–90, in obituary, *Guardian*, 17 Oct. 1990]

17 Speak the speech, I pray you, as I pronounced it to you, trippingly on the tongue; but if you mouth it as many of your players do, I had as lief the town-crier spoke my lines. Nor do not saw the air too much with your hand, thus; but use all gently. [William Shakespeare, 1564–1616, *Hamlet*, III, ii, 1]

18 The purpose of playing, whose end, both at the first and now, was and is, to hold, as 'twere, the mirror up to nature. [*Hamlet*, III, ii (24)] ; see 11

19 A part to tear a cat in, to make all split. [*Midsummer Night's Dream*, I, ii (32)]

20 Ladies, just a little more virginity, if you don't mind. [(To a 'collection of damsels that had been dragged into the theatre as ladies-in-waiting to the queen' in his production of *Henry VIII*) Herbert Beerbohm Tree, 1853–1917, in Alexander Woollcott, *Shouts and Murmurs*, 'Capsule Criticism']

See also ACTORS, AUDIENCES, PLAYS, PLAYWRIGHTS, THEATRE

ACTION

1 And thou wilt give thyself relief, if thou doest every act of thy life as if it were the last. [Marcus Aurelius, 121–80, *Meditations*, II, 5]

2 But men must know, that in this theatre of man's life it is reserved only for God and angels to be lookers-on. [Francis Bacon, 1561–1626, *The Advancement of Learning*, II, xx, 8]

3 The dreadful burden of having nothing to do. [Nicholas Boileau, 1636–1711, *Epistle* XI, 86]

4 We have to understand the world can only be grasped by action, not by contemplation. The hand is more important than the eye . . . The hand is the cutting edge of the mind. [J Bronowski, 1908–74, *The Ascent of Man*, 3]

5 What's done we partly may compute, / But know not what's resisted. [Robert Burns, 1759–96, *Address to the Unco Guid*, 63]

6 Nothing is ever done until everyone is convinced that it ought to be done, and has been convinced for so long that it is now time to do something else. [F M Cornford, 1874–1943, *Microcosmographia Academica*, 1 (1908)]

7 Deliberation is the work of many men. Action of one alone. [General de Gaulle, 1890–1970, *War Memoirs*, Vol. II : *Unity*, Ch. 5]

8 Everyone knows that it is much harder to turn word into deed than deed into word. [Maxim Gorky, 1868–1936, from 'On Plays', in *USSR in Construction*, Apr. 1937]

9 Clay lies still, but blood's a rover ; / Breath's a ware that will not keep. / Up, lad ; when the journey's over / There'll be time enough for sleep. [A E Housman, 1859–1936, *A Shropshire Lad*, 4, 'Reveille']

10 A categorical imperative would be one which represented an action as objectively necessary in itself, without reference to any other purpose. [Immanuel Kant, 1724–1804, *Fundamental Principles of Morals*, 2]

11 Trust no Future, howe'er pleasant / Let the dead Past bury its dead ! / Act – act in the living Present ! / Heart within, and God o'erhead ! [H W Longfellow, 1807–82, *A Psalm of Life*]

12 Think nothing done while aught remains to do. [Samuel Rogers, 1763–1855, *Human Life*, 49]

13 Trust the man who hesitates in his speech and is quick and steady in action, but beware of long arguments and long beards. [George Santayana, 1863–1952, *Soliloquies in England*, 'The British Character']

14 Between the acting of a dreadful thing / And the first motion, all the interim is / Like a phantasma or a hideous dream: / The genius and the mortal instruments / Are then in council; and the state of man, / Like to a little kingdom, suffers then / The nature of an insurrection. [William Shakespeare, 1564–1616, *Julius Caesar*, II, i, 63]

15 If it were done when 'tis done, then 'twere well / It were done quickly. [*Macbeth*, I, vii, 1]

16 O ! what men dare do ! what men may do ! what men daily do, not knowing what they do ! [*Much Ado About Nothing*, IV, i (19)]

17 Nothing is ever done in this world until men are prepared to kill one another if it is not done. [George Bernard Shaw, 1856–1950, *Major Barbara*, III]

18 Death closes all : but something ere the end, / Some work of noble note, may yet be done, / Not unbecoming men that strove with Gods. [Alfred, Lord Tennyson, 1809–92, *Ulysses*, 51]

19 I always say that if you want a speech made you should ask a man, but if you want something done you should ask a woman. [Margaret Thatcher, 1925– , at AGM of Townswomen's Guild, 26 July 1982]

20 Action is transitory – a step, a blow. / The motion of a muscle – this way or that – / 'Tis done, and in the after-vacancy / We wonder at ourselves like men betrayed: / Suffering is permanent, obscure and dark, / And shares the nature of infinity. [William Wordsworth, 1770–1850, *The Borderers*, III, 1539]

See also BEHAVIOUR

ACTIVITY

1 Now, *here*, you see, it takes all the running *you* can do, to stay in the same place. If you want to get somewhere else, you must run at least twice as fast as that! [Lewis Carroll, 1832–98, *Through the Looking Glass*, Ch. 2]

2 No-wher so bisy a man as he ther nas, / And yet he semed bisier than he was. [Geoffrey Chaucer, 1340?–1400, *Canterbury Tales*, 'Prologue', 321]

3 If a thing is worth doing it is worth doing badly. [G K Chesterton, 1874–1936, *What's Wrong with the World*, 'Folly and Female Education']

4 I love to feel events overlapping each other, crawling over one another like wet crabs in a basket. [Lawrence Durrell, 1912–90, *Balthazar*, Pt I]

5 There are only the pursued, the pursuing, the busy, and the tired. [F Scott Fitzgerald, 1896–1940, *The Great Gatsby*, Ch. 4]

6 Meetings are indispensable when you don't want to do anything. [J K Galbraith, 1908– , *Ambassador's Journal*, Ch. 5]

7 One is always nearer by not keeping still. [Thom Gunn, 1929– , *On the Move*]

8 Busy as a one-armed man with the nettle-rash pasting on wall-paper. [O Henry, 1862–1910, *The Ethics of Pig*]

9 If you must go nowhere, step out. [Percy Wyndham Lewis, 1882–1957, *The Human Age*, Bk I: *The Childermass*, closing words]

10 I wish to preach, not the doctrine of ignoble ease, but the doctrine of the strenuous life. [Theodore Roosevelt, 1858–1919, speech at Chicago, 10 Apr. 1899]

11 Extreme *busyness*, whether at school or college, kirk or market, is a symptom of deficient vitality. [Robert Louis Stevenson, 1850–94, *Virginibus Puerisque*, 'An Apology for Idlers']

12 I was seized by the stern hand of Compulsion, that dark, unseasonable Urge that impels women to clean house in the middle of the night. [James Thurber, 1894–1961, *Alarms and Diversions*, 'There's a Time for Flags']

ACTORS & ACTRESSES IN GENERAL

1 Dear God, send me good actors and send them cheap. [Lilian Baylis, 1874–1937, of 1932 season at the Old Vic, London, in Dame Peggy Ashcroft's obituary, *Guardian*, 15 June 1991]

2 A good actor does not make his entry before the theatre is built. [Jorge Luis Borges, 1899–1986, and Adolfo Bioy Casares, 1914–99, *Six Problems of Don Isidro Parodi*]

3 Never meddle with play-actors, for they're a favoured race. [Miguel Cervantes, 1547–1616, *Don Quixote*, Pt II, Ch. 11]

4 Learn the lines and don't bump into the furniture. [Noël Coward, 1899–1973, advice to a young actor in *Nude with Violin*, attr.]

5 The best actors do not let the wheels show. [Henry Fonda, 1905–82; in *Barnes and Noble Book of Quotations*, ed. Robert I Fitzhenry, 'Acting']

6 Funny without being vulgar. [W S Gilbert, 1836–1911, attr. remark on Irving's *Hamlet*]

7 An actor's a guy who, if you ain't talking about him, ain't listening. [George Glass, 1910–84; *Observer*, 'Sayings of the Year', 1 Jan. 1956. Saying sometimes ascr. to Marlon Brando, with whom it was popular, according to Bob Thomas, *Brando*, Ch. 8]

8 On the stage he was natural, simple, affecting, / 'Twas only that, when he was off, he was acting. [(Of Garrick) Oliver Goldsmith, 1728–74, *Retaliation*, 101]

9 English actresses are mistresses and French ones clever daughters. [Terry Hands, 1941– , attr. in *The Sunday Times Magazine*, 26 Nov. 1978]

10 Actors are cattle. [Alfred Hitchcock, 1899–1980, attr.; in L Halliwell, *Filmgoer's Book of Quotes*. He claimed he had said that actors should be *treated* like cattle]

11 I'll come no more behind your scenes, David; for the silk stockings and white bosoms of your actresses excite my amorous propensities. [Dr Samuel Johnson, 1709–84, in James Boswell, *Life of J*, 1750]

12 His [a player's] conversation usually threatened and announced more than it performed; that he fed you with a continual renovation of hope, to end in a constant succession of disappointment. [Dr Samuel Johnson, 1709–84, in James Boswell, *Life of J*, 1770]

13 I often think that could we creep behind the actor's eyes, we would find an attic of forgotten toys and a copy of the Domesday Book. [Laurence Olivier, 1907–89, in *The New York Times*, 26 Oct. 1986]

14 She ran the whole gamut of her emotions from A to B. [(Of Katharine Hepburn in play *The Lake*, 1933) Dorothy Parker, 1893–1967]

15 The difference between being a director and being an actor is the difference between being the carpenter banging the nails into the wood, and being the piece of wood the nails are being banged into. [Sean Penn, 1960– , interview, *Guardian*, 28 Nov. 1991]

16 When an actor marries an actress they both fight for the mirror. [Burt Reynolds, 1936– , interview, *Guardian*, 12 Mar. 1988]

17 There are lots of reasons why people become actors. Some to hide themselves, and some to show themselves. [Ralph Richardson, 1902–83, interview with Russell Harty on LWT, Sept. 1975, quoted in Kenneth Tynan, *Show People*]

18 They didn't act like people and they didn't act like actors. It's hard to explain. They acted more like they knew they were celebrities and all. I mean they were good, but they were *too* good. [J D Salinger, 1919– , *The Catcher in the Rye*, Ch. 17]

19 They are the abstracts and brief chronicles of the time: after your death you were better have a bad epitaph than their ill report while you live. [William Shakespeare, 1564–1616, *Hamlet*, II, ii (555)]

20 I have thought some of nature's journeymen had made men, and not made them well, they imitated humanity so abominably. [*Hamlet*, III, ii (38)]

21 We're *actors* – we're the opposite of people! [Tom Stoppard, 1937– , *Rosencrantz and Guildenstern are Dead*, II]

22 INTERVIEWER: Why do you prefer movies to the theatre?
VIDAL: I'm embarrassed by live actors. They're always having a much better time than I am. [Gore Vidal, 1925– ; in *Writers at Work*, ed. George Plimpton, Fifth Series]

See also next category, AUDIENCES, FILM STARS, PLAYS, PLAYWRIGHTS, THEATRE

ACTORS & ACTRESSES: INDIVIDUAL (in alphabetical order of subject)

1 Of whom it might be said her soul is showing. [(Of Peggy Ashcroft) Kenneth Tynan, 1927–80; in *Observer* on her eightieth birthday, 20 Dec. 1987]

2 [When asked by Gabriel Byrne why he had made so many films, instead of going back to the theatre] Because I couldn't bear not to have somewhere to go in the mornings. [Richard Burton, 1925–84, interview in *Observer Magazine*, 6 Mar. 1988]

3 Forty years ago he [Noël Coward] was Slightly in *Peter Pan*, and you might say he has been wholly in *Peter Pan* ever since. [Kenneth Tynan, 1927–80, *Curtains*, 1, 'A Tribute to Mr Coward']

4 It's like Edith Evans – she used to open a window to her heart and then slam it shut, so that you'd come back the next night to see more. [Ralph Richardson, 1902–83, in Kenneth Tynan, *Show People*]

5 At Sunday School I was always in demand, especially for our annual Passion Play and Pageant, and I was always given the *meatier* rolls. [Barry Humphries, 1934– , *Dame Edna's Coffee Table Book*, 'My Wonderful Career']

6 I kept wishing he would put on a false nose and be himself again. [(Of Laurence Olivier) Peter Ustinov, 1921– , in *The Sunday Times*, 16 July 1989]

7 Something between bland and grandiose: blandiose perhaps. [(Of Ralph Richardson's voice) Kenneth Tynan, 1927–80, in *Observer Magazine*, 'Tynan on Richardson', 18 Dec. 1977]

8 One went to school, one wanted to act, one started to act, and one's still acting. [Maggie Smith, 1933– , profile, *The Sunday Times*, 1 Jan. 1989]

See also previous categories, AUDIENCES, PLAYS, PLAYWRIGHTS, THEATRE

ADMIRATION, see RESPECT

ADOLESCENCE

1 You don't have to suffer to be a poet. Adolescence is enough suffering for anyone. [John Ciardi, 1916–86, in *Writer's Quotation Book*, ed. James Charlton]

2 Were I to deduce any system from my feelings on leaving Eton, it might be called *The Theory of Permanent Adolescence*. [Cyril Connolly, 1903–74, *Enemies of Promise*, Ch. 24]

3 I think what is happening to me is so wonderful, and not only what can be seen on my body, but all that is taking place inside. I never discuss myself or any of these things with anybody; that is why I have to talk to myself about them. [Anne Frank, 1929–45, *Diary of a Young Girl*, 5 Jan. 1944]

4 They were not long, the days of whine and neuroses. [Kevin Jackson, 1955– , in review of TV programme (subtitled 'A History of the Teenager, 1950–1990'), *Independent*, 21 Feb. 1990]

5 Remember that as a teenager you are at the last stage in your life when you will be happy to hear that the phone is for you. [Fran Lebowitz, ?1948– , *Social Studies*, 'Tips for Teens']

6 In later life we look at things in a more practical way, in full conformity with the rest of society, but adolescence is the only period in which we learn anything. [Marcel Proust, 1871–1922, *Remembrance of Things Past: Within a Budding Grove*, 'Place-names']

7 Oh to become sensible about social advance at seventeen is to be lost. [Stevie Smith, 1902–71, *Parents*]

See also ADULTS, AGE, CHILDHOOD, YOUTH & AGE

ADULTERY

1 Until you start ploughing pertinent wives, you really aren't working. The way to a man's heart is through his wife's belly and don't you forget it. [Edward Albee, 1928– , *Who's Afraid of Virginia Woolf?*, II]

2 It seems so *lazy* to have an affair with your secretary, like always going to the nearest restaurant instead of the best. [Lynn Barber, 1944– , in *Independent on Sunday*, 9 Feb. 1992]

3 What men call gallantry, and gods adultery, / Is much more common where the climate's sultry. [Lord Byron, 1788–1824, *Don Juan*, I, 63]

4 Comus all allows; / Champagne, dice, music or your neighbour's spouse. [Lord Byron, 1788–1824, *English Bards and Scotch Reviewers*, 650]

5 A single sentence will suffice for modern man: he fornicated and read the papers. [Albert Camus, 1913–60, *The Fall*]

6 Sara could commit adultery at one end and weep for her sins at the other, and enjoy both operations at once. [Joyce Cary, 1888–1957, *The Horse's Mouth*, Ch. 8]

7 Annoying to have to lie long after extramarital relations have been broken off. Like hangover without intoxication. [Dulcie Domum, 1946– , in *Weekend Guardian*, 31 Aug.–1 Sept. 1991]

8 Always fornicate / Between clean sheets and spit on a well-scrubbed floor. [Christopher Fry, 1907– , *The Lady's Not for Burning*, II]

9 Adultery in your heart is committed not only when you look with excessive sexual desire at a woman who is not your wife, but also if you look in the same manner at your wife. [Pope John Paul II, 1920– , at Vatican Synod; *Observer*, 'Sayings of the Week', 12 Oct. 1980]

10 BARNARDINE: Thou hast committed –
BARABAS: Fornication? But that was in an other country: and besides, the wench is dead. [Christopher Marlowe, 1564–93, *The Jew of Malta*, IV. i. 40]

11 'Come, come,' said Tom's father, 'at your time of life, / There's no longer excuse for thus playing the rake – / It is time you should think, boy, of taking a wife' – 'Why, so it is, father – whose wife shall I take?' [Thomas Moore, 1779–1852, *A Joke Versified*]

12 It is the cause, it is the cause, my soul; / Let me not name it to you, you chaste stars! / It is the cause. Yet I'll not shed her blood, / Nor scar that whiter skin of hers than snow, / And smooth as monumental alabaster. [William Shakespeare, 1564–1616, *Othello*, V. ii. 1]

13 A lady, if surprised by melancholy, might go to bed with a chap, once; or a thousand times if consumed by passion. But twice, Wagner, *twice* . . . a lady might think she'd be taken for a tart. [Tom Stoppard, 1937– , *Night and Day*, I]

See also INCONSTANCY, SEDUCTION, SEX

ADULTS

1 If this was adulthood, the only improvement she could detect in her situation was that now she could eat dessert without eating her vegetables. [Lisa Alther, 1944– , *Kinflicks*, Ch. 2]

2 The two men seemed to agree about everything, but when grown-ups agree they interrupt each other almost as much as if they were quarrelling. [Rudyard Kipling, 1865–1936, *Rewards and Fairies*, 'The Wrong Thing']

3 Grown-ups never understand anything for themselves, and it is tiresome for children to be always and forever explaining things to them. [Antoine de Saint-Exupéry, 1900–44, *The Little Prince*, Ch. 1]

4 Adults are obsolete children. [Dr Seuss, 1904–91; in L L Levinson, *Bartlett's Unfamiliar Quotations*]

5 A child becomes an adult when he realizes that he has a right not only to be right but also to be wrong. [Thomas Szasz, 1920– , *The Second Sin*, 'Childhood']

See also ADOLESCENCE, AGE, CHILDHOOD

ADVERSITY & PROSPERITY

1 Prosperity is the blessing of the Old Testament, adversity is the blessing of the New. [Francis Bacon, 1561–1626, *Essays*, 5, 'Of Adversity']

2 Prosperity is not without many fears and distastes; and adversity is not without comforts and hopes. [Francis Bacon, 1561–1626, *Essays*, 5, 'Of Adversity']

3 For in all adversity of fortune the worst sort of misery is to have been happy. [Boethius, 480?–524, *The Consolation of Philosophy*, Bk ii, Prose 4]

4 For one man that can stand prosperity, there are a hundred that will stand adversity. [Thomas Carlyle, 1795–1881, *Heroes and Hero-Worship*, v, 'The Hero as Man of Letters']

5 Daughter of Jove, relentless power, / Thou tamer of the human breast, / Whose iron scourge and tort'ring hour / The bad affright, afflict the best. [Thomas Gray, 1716–71, *Hymn to Adversity*]

6 Most of our people have never had it so good. [Harold Macmillan, 1894–1986, speech on financial situation, Bedford, 20 July 1957; originally US presidential election slogan, 1952; reuse attr. to Oliver Poole]

7 Sweet are the uses of adversity, / Which, like the toad, ugly and venomous, / Wears yet a precious jewel in his head; / And this our life, exempt from public haunt, / Finds tongues in trees, books in the running brooks, / Sermons in stones, and good in everything. [William Shakespeare, 1564–1616, *As You Like It*, II. i. 12]

8 Wherein I spake of most disastrous chances, / Of moving accidents by flood and field, / Of hair-breadth 'scapes i' the imminent deadly breach. [*Othello*, I. iii. 134]

See also HAPPINESS, PROBLEMS, SUFFERING, UNHAPPINESS

ADVERTISING

1 You can tell the ideals of a nation by its advertisements. [Norman Douglas, 1868-1952, *South Wind*, Ch. 6]

2 Advertising may be described as the science of arresting the human intelligence long enough to get money from it. [Stephen Leacock, 1869–1944, *Garden of Folly*, 'The Perfect Salesman']

3 I think that I shall never see / A billboard lovely as a tree. / Perhaps unless the billboards fall, / I'll never see a tree at all. [Ogden Nash, 1902–71, *Song of the Open Road*]

4 Half the money I spend on advertising is wasted, and the trouble is I don't know which half. [Lord Leverhulme, 1851–1925, in David Ogilvy, *Confessions of an Advertising Man*, Ch. 3. Quoted by John Wanamaker and sometimes wrongly attr. to him]

5 The consumer isn't a moron; she is your wife. You insult her intelligence if you assume that a mere slogan and a few vapid adjectives will persuade her to buy anything. [David Ogilvy, 1911–99, *Confessions of an Advertising Man*, Ch. 5]

6 Don't Tell My Mother I Work in Advertising – She Thinks I'm a Piano-player in a Brothel. [Jacques Seguela, 1934– , title of book]

ADVICE

1 He [Algren] shunts aside all rules, regulations, and dicta, except for three laws he says a nice old Negro lady once taught him: Never play cards with any man named 'Doc'. Never eat at any place called 'Mom's'. And never, ever, no matter what else you do in your whole life, *never* sleep with anyone whose troubles are worse than your own. [Nelson Algren, 1909–81, in H E F Donohue, *Conversations with Nelson Algren*, Foreword]

2 Where no counsel is, the people fall: but in the multitude of counsellors there is safety. [Bible, OT, *Proverbs* 11:14]

3 Put your trust in God, my boys, and keep your powder dry. [Valentine Blacker, 1778–1823, *Oliver Cromwell's Advice*]

4 Who cannot give good counsel? 'Tis cheap, it costs them nothing. [Robert Burton, 1577–1640, *The Anatomy of Melancholy*, §3, Memb. 3]

5 Advice is seldom welcome; and those who want it the most always like it the least. [Earl of Chesterfield, 1694–1773, letter to his son, 29 Jan. 1748]

6 Don't eat too many almonds; they add weight to the breasts. [Colette, 1873–1954, *Gigi*]

7 Never claim as a right what you can ask as a favour. [John Churton Collins, 1848–1908, in *English Review*, 1914]

8 Never trust a man who, when he's alone in a room with a tea-cosy, doesn't try it on. [Billy Connolly, 1942– , *Gullible's Travels*, 'Thoughts That Sustain Me']

9 Learn the lines and don't bump into the furniture. [Noël Coward, 1899–1973, advice to a young actor in *Nude with Violin*, attr.]

10 Never sign a walentine with your own name. [Charles Dickens, 1812–70, *Pickwick Papers*, Ch. 33]

11 Thrust ivrybody, but cut th' ca-ards. [Finley Peter Dunne, 1867–1936, *Mr Dooley's Opinions*, 'Casual Observations']

12 Beware of bathroom walls that've not been written on. [Bob Dylan, 1941– , song: *Advice for Geraldine on Her Miscellaneous Birthday*]

13 When you're up to your ass in alligators, just stop a moment and ask yourself why you decided to drain the swamp in the first place. [President Lyndon B Johnson, 1908–73, attr.]

14 One gives nothing so freely as advice. [Duc de La Rochefoucauld, 1613–80, *Maxims*, 110]

15 Be nice to people on your way up because you'll meet 'em on your way down. [Wilson Mizner, 1876–1933; in A Johnston, *The Legendary Mizners*, Ch. 4. Also attr. to Jimmy Durante]

16 [When asked at a science-fiction convention, 'What is the best advice you have ever been given?'] On my twenty-first birthday my father said, 'Son, here's a million dollars. Don't lose it.' [Larry Niven, 1938– , attr.]

17 I hope, for his own sake, that he has younger people than me at his disposal if he wishes to ask for bad advice, especially if he means to follow it. [Marcel Proust, 1871–1922, *Remembrance of Things Past: Cities of the Plain*, Pt II, Ch. 1]

18 You will find it a very good practice always to verify your references, sir. [Martin Routh, 1755–1854; attr. by J W Burgon in *Quarterly Review*, July 1878]

19 In baiting a mouse-trap with cheese, always leave room for the mouse. [Saki (H H Munro), 1870–1916, *The Infernal Parliament*]

20 Do not, as some ungracious pastors do, / Show me the steep and thorny way to heaven, / Whiles, like a puffed and reckless libertine, / Himself the primrose path of dalliance treads, / And recks not his own rede. [William Shakespeare, 1564–1616, *Hamlet*, I. iii. 47]

21 I have lived some thirty years on this planet, and I have yet to hear the first syllable of valuable or even earnest advice from my seniors. [H D Thoreau, 1817–62, *Walden*, 'Economy']

22 You might as well fall flat on your face as lean over too far backward. [James Thurber, 1894–1961, *Fables for Our Time*, 'The Bear Who Let It Alone']

23 Everybody who tells you how to act has whisky on their breath. [John Updike, 1932– , *Rabbit, Run*]

See also RULES

AEROPLANES

1 As horrible thoughts, / Loud fluttering aircraft slope above his head / At dusk. The ridiculous empires break like biscuits. [Roy Fuller, 1912–91, *The Middle of a War*]

2 It felt as if angels were pushing. [(On his first flight in a jet aircraft, the Messerschmitt 262, May 1943) Lt.-Gen. Adolf Galland, 1912–96, *The First and the Last*]

3 I'm not allowed to say how many planes joined the raid but I counted them all out and I counted them all back. [Brian Hanrahan, 1949– , on British attack in Falklands War, BBC broadcast, 1 May 1982]

4 Nor law, nor duty bade me fight, / Nor public men, nor cheering crowds, / A lonely impulse of delight / Drove to this tumult in the clouds. [W B Yeats, 1865–1939, *An Irish Airman Foresees His Death*]

AFRICA

1 Mrs Jellyby was looking far away into Africa. [Charles Dickens, 1812–70, *Bleak House*, Ch. 23]

2 This is Africa / Your Africa / That grows again patiently obstinately / And its fruit gradually acquire / The bitter taste of liberty. [David Diop, 1927–60, in Chinua Achebe, *Anthills of the Savannah*, 10]

3 The wind of change is blowing through this Continent, and whether we like it or not, this growth of national consciousness is a political fact. [Harold Macmillan, 1894–1986, speech in Cape Town, 3 Feb. 1960]

4 They say there's good and bad everywhere. There's no good and bad here. They're just Africans. [V S Naipaul, 1932– , *In a Free State*, Ch. 6]

5 *Ex Africa semper aliquid novi.* – There is always something new out of Africa. [Pliny the Elder, 23–79; proverbial adaptation of *Natural History*, viii, 17]

6 When the missionaries first came to Africa they had the Bible and we had the land. They said, 'Let us pray'. We closed our eyes. When we opened them, we had the Bible and they had the land. [Bishop Desmond Tutu, 1931– ; *Observer*, 'Sayings of the Week', 16 Dec. 1984]

AFTERLIFE

1 CLOV: Do you believe in the life to come?
HAMM: Mine was always that. [Samuel Beckett, 1906–89, *Endgame*]

2 That which is the foundation of all our hopes and of all our fears; all our hopes and fears which are of any consideration: I mean a Future Life. [Bishop Joseph Butler, 1692–1752, *The Analogy of Religion*, Introduction]

3 When thou must home to shades of underground, / And there arrived, a new admirèd guest, / The beauteous spirits do engirt thee round, / White Iope, blithe Helen, and the rest. [Thomas Campion, 1567–1620, *When Thou Must Home*]

4 We have no reliable guarantee that the afterlife will be any less exasperating than this one, have we? [Noël Coward, 1899–1973, *Blithe Spirit*, I]

5 Now the labourer's task is o'er; / Now the battle-day is past; / Now upon the further shore / Lands the voyager at last. [John Ellerton, 1826–93, hymn]

6 Work and pray, live on hay. / You'll get pie in the sky when you die. [Joe Hill, 1879–1915, song: *The Preacher and the Slave*]

7 It is wonderful that five thousand years have now elapsed since the creation of the world, and still it is undecided whether or not there has ever been an instance of the spirit of any person appearing after death. All argument is against it; but all belief is for it. [Dr Samuel Johnson, 1709–84, in James Boswell, *Life of J*, 31 Mar. 1778]

8 I wouldn't mind turning into a vermilion goldfish. [(When questioned about the afterlife at the age of eighty) Henri Matisse, 1869–1954; in *Simpson's Contemporary Quotations*]

9 But that I am forbid / To tell the secrets of my prison-house, / I could a tale unfold whose lightest word / Would harrow up thy soul, freeze thy young blood, / Make thy two eyes, like stars, start from their spheres, / Thy knotted and combinèd locks to part, / And each particular hair to stand on end, / Like quills upon the fretful porpentine: / But this eternal blazon must not be / To ears of flesh and blood. [William Shakespeare, 1564–1616, *Hamlet*, I. v. 13]

10 Who would fardels bear, / To grunt and sweat under a weary life, / But that the dread of something after death, / The undiscovered country from whose bourn / No traveller returns, puzzles the will, / And makes us rather bear those ills we have / Than fly to others that we know not of? [*Hamlet*, III. i. 76]

11 Duncan is in his grave; / After life's fitful fever he sleeps well; / Treason has done his worst: not steel, nor poison, / Malice domestic, foreign levy, nothing / Can touch him further. [*Macbeth*, III. ii. 22]

12 CLOWN: What is the opinion of Pythagoras concerning wild fowl?
MALVOLIO: That the soul of our grandam might haply inhabit a bird. [*Twelfth Night*, IV. ii. (55)]

13 For the life to come, I sleep out the thought of it. [*The Winter's Tale*, IV. ii. (30)]

14 My days among the dead are past; / Around me I behold, / Where'er these casual eyes are cast, / The mighty minds of old. [Robert Southey, 1774–1843, *My Days among the Dead*]

15 For tho' from out our bourne of Time and Place / The flood may bear me far, / I hope to see my Pilot face to face / When I have crost the bar. [Alfred, Lord Tennyson, 1809–92, *Crossing the Bar*]

16 I held it truth with him who sings/ To one clear harp in divers tones, / That men may rise on stepping stones / Of their dead selves to higher things. [Alfred, Lord Tennyson, 1809–92, *In Memoriam*, 1]

17 In fact we do not try to picture the afterlife, nor is it ourselves in our nervous tics and optical flecks that we wish to perpetuate; it is the self as the window on the world that we can't bear to think of shutting. [John Updike, 1932– , *Self-consciousness*, Ch. 6]

18 They are all gone into the world of light! / And I alone sit lingering here; / Their very memory is fair and bright, / And my sad thoughts doth clear. [Henry Vaughan, 1622–95, *They are All Gone*]

See also DEATH, ETERNITY, HEAVEN, HEAVEN & HELL, HELL, LIFE & DEATH, LIMBO

AGE

1 Age will not be defied. [Francis Bacon, 1561–1626, *Essays*, 30, 'Of Regimen of Health']

2 A lady of a 'certain age', which means / Certainly aged. [Lord Byron, 1788–1824, *Don Juan*, VI, 69]

3 As a white candle / In a holy place, / So is the beauty / Of an aged face. [Joseph Campbell, 1879–1944, *The Old Woman*]

4 A man is as old as he's feeling, / A woman as old as she looks. [Mortimer Collins, 1827–76, *The Unknown Quantity*]

5 It is better to wear out than to rust out. [Bishop Richard Cumberland, 1631–1718, quoted in G Horne, *The Duty of Contending for the Faith*]

6 'Bob, you know something . . .' Luckman said at last, 'I used to be the same age as everyone else.' 'I think so was I,' Arctor said. 'I don't know what did it . . .' 'Sure, Luckman,' Arctor said, 'you know what did it to all of us.' [Philip K Dick, 1928–82, *A Scanner Darkly*, Ch. 12]

7 Youth is a blunder; Manhood a struggle; Old Age a regret. [Benjamin Disraeli, 1804–81, *Coningsby*, Bk iii, Ch. 1]

8 My thoughtless youth was winged with vain desires, / My manhood, long misled by wandering fires, / Followed false lights; and when their glimpse was gone, / My pride struck out new sparkles of her own. / Such was I, such by nature still I am. / Be thine the glory, and be mine the shame. [John Dryden, 1631–1700, *The Hind and the Panther*, 72]

9 If youth knew, if age could. [Henri Estienne, 1531–98, *Les Prémices*, 191]

10 She stands, I fear, poor thing, now, for something younger than she looks. [Ronald Firbank, 1886–1926, *Valmouth*, Ch. I]

11 One of those men who reach such an acute limited excellence at twenty-one that everything afterward savours of anti-climax. [F Scott Fitzgerald, 1896–1940, *The Great Gatsby*, Ch. 1]

12 A man has every season while a woman only has the right to spring. That disgusts me. [Jane Fonda, 1937– , in *Daily Mail*, 13 Sept. 1989]

13 She may very well pass for forty-three / In the dusk with a light behind her! [W S Gilbert, 1836–1911, *Trial by Jury*]

14 I love everything that's old: old friends, old times, old manners, old books, old wines. [Oliver Goldsmith, 1728–74, *She Stoops to Conquer*, 1]

15 You will recognize, my boy, the first sign of age: it is when you go out into the streets of London and realize for the first time how young the policemen look. [Seymour Hicks, 1871–1949, *Between Ourselves*]

16 Anno domini – that's the most fatal complaint of all in the end. [James Hilton, 1900–54, *Good-bye, Mr Chips*, Ch. 1]

17 Long-expected one and twenty, / Lingering year at length is flown. [Dr Samuel Johnson, 1709–84, *One and Twenty*]

18 How soon hath Time, the subtle thief of youth, / Stoln on his wing my three and twentieth year! [John Milton, 1608–74, sonnet: *On Being Arrived at the Age of Twenty-three*]

19 Age will bring all things, and everyone knows, Madame, that twenty is no age to be a prude. [Molière, 1622–73, *Le Misanthrope*, III. iv]

20 You are as old as the last time you changed your mind. [Tim O'Leary, ?–1991; *Observer*, 'Sayings of the Week', 25 Sept. 1983]

21 So never say to D'Arcy, 'Be your age!' – / He'd shrivel up at once or turn to stone. [William Plomer, 1903–73, *The Playboy of the Demi-world: 1938*]

22 For, as our different ages move, / 'Tis so ordained (would fate but mend it!) / That I shall be past making love / When she begins to comprehend it. [Matthew Prior, 1664–1721, *To a Child of Quality, Five Years Old*]

23 She took to telling the truth; she said she was forty-two and five months. It may have been pleasing to the angels, but her elder sister was not gratified. [Saki (H H Munro), 1870–1916, *Reginald on Besetting Sins*]

24 Though age from folly could not give me freedom, / It does from childishness. [William Shakespeare, 1564–1616, *Antony and Cleopatra*, I. iii. 57]

25 Age cannot wither her, nor custom stale / Her infinite variety; other women cloy / The appetites they feed. [*Antony and Cleopatra*, II. ii. (243)]

26 All the world's a stage, / And all the men and women merely players: / They have their exits and their entrances; / And one man in his time plays many parts, / His acts being seven ages. At first the infant . . . [*As You Like It*, II. vii. (139)]

27 Why came I so untimely forth / Into a world which, wanting thee, / Could entertain us with no worth / Or shadow of felicity? [Edmund Waller, 1606–87, *To a Very Young Lady*]

28 I was twenty-five and too old to be unusual. [James D Watson, 1928– , *The Double Helix*, Ch. 29]

29 We are all American at puberty; we die French. [Evelyn Waugh, 1903–66, *Diaries*, ed. M Davie, 'Irregular Notes', 18 July 1961]

30 I had rather wear out than rust out. [George Whitefield, 1714–70, attr., in Robert Southey, *Life of Wesley*]

31 No woman should ever be quite accurate about her age. It looks so calculating. [Oscar Wilde, 1854–1900, *The Importance of Being Earnest*, III]

32 One should never trust a woman who tells one her real age. A woman who would tell one that would tell one anything. [Oscar Wilde, 1854–1900, *A Woman of No Importance*, I]

33 One that is ever kind said yesterday: / 'Your well-belovèd's hair has threads of grey, / And little shadows come about her eyes.' [W B Yeats, 1865–1939, *The Folly of Being Comforted*]

See also ADOLESCENCE, CHILDHOOD, MIDDLE AGE, OLD AGE, YOUTH & AGE

AGGRESSION & NON-AGGRESSION

1 The lion and the calf shall lie down together but the calf won't get much sleep. [Woody Allen, 1935– , *Without Feathers*, 'The Scrolls']

2 If you can walk over a man once, you can walk over him as often as you like. [Lord Beaverbrook, 1879–1964, quoted by Sir John Junor in interview, *The Sunday Times*, 3 Sept. 1989]

3 Pale Ebenezer thought it wrong to fight, / But Roaring Bill (who killed him) thought it right. [Hilaire Belloc, 1870–1953, 'The Pacifist']

4 Resist not evil: but whosoever shall smite thee on thy right cheek, turn to him the other also. [Bible, NT, *St Matthew* 5:39]

5 Such as do build their faith upon / The holy text of pike and gun. [Samuel Butler, 1612–80, *Hudibras*, 1, i, 193]

6 It's not a slam at *you* when people are rude – it's a slam at the people they've met before. [F Scott Fitzgerald, 1896–1940, *The Last Tycoon*, Ch. 1]

7 What is it that gets loose when you begin to fight, and makes you what you think you're not? . . . Begin as you may, it ends in this – skin game. [John Galsworthy, 1867–1933, *The Skin Game*, III]

8 Non-violence is the first article of my faith. It is also the last article of my creed. [Mahatma Gandhi, 1869–1948, speech in defence against charge of disaffection, etc., at Shahi Bag, India, 18 Mar. 1922]

9 Describe a circle, stroke its back and it turns vicious. [Eugene Ionesco, 1912–94, *The Bald Prima Donna*, I]

10 If you start throwing hedgehogs under me, I shall throw two porcupines under you. [Nikita Khrushchev, 1894–1971 ; *Observer*, 'Sayings of the Week', 10 Nov. 1963]

11 We had no use for the policy of the Gospels: if someone slaps you, just turn the other cheek. We had shown that anyone who slapped us on our cheek would get his head kicked off. [Nikita Khrushchev, 1894–1971, *Khrushchev Remembers*, Vol. II]

12 Quarrels would not last so long if the fault were on only one side. [Duc de La Rochefoucauld, 1613–80, *Maxims*, 496]

13 No absolute is going to make the lion lie down with the lamb unless the lamb is inside. [D H Lawrence, 1885–1930, *The Later D H L*]

14 Quarantine the aggressors. [Franklin D Roosevelt, 1882–1945, speech at Chicago, 5 Oct. 1937]

15 She was a vixen when she went to school: / And though she be but little, she is fierce. [William Shakespeare, 1564–1616, *A Midsummer Night's Dream*, III. ii. 324]

16 No, sir, I do not bite my thumb at you, sir; but I bite my thumb, sir. [*Romeo and Juliet*, I. i. (56)]

17 Thy head is as full of quarrels as an egg is full of meat. [*Romeo and Juliet*, III. i. (23)]

18 Contrary to what clergymen and policemen believe, gentleness is biological and aggression is cultural. [Stefan Themerson, 1910–88, in obituary, *Guardian*, 8 Sept. 1988]

See also ANGER

AGREEMENT & DISAGREEMENT

1 You only find complete unanimity in a cemetery. [Abel Aganbegyan, 1932–   , on Russian economic reforms, in *Guardian*, 27 June 1987]

2 Can two walk together, except they be agreed? [Bible, OT, *Amos* 3:3]

3 Behold, how good and how pleasant it is for brethren to dwell together in unity! It is like the precious ointment upon the head that ran down upon the beard, even Aaron's beard, that went down to the skirts of his garments. [Bible, OT, *Psalms* 133:1]

4 And if a house be divided against itself, that house cannot stand. [Bible, NT, *St Mark* 3:25]

5 Agree with thine adversary quickly, whilst thou art in the way with him. [Bible, NT, *St Matthew* 5:25]

6 Whenever you accept our views we shall be in full agreement with you. [Moshe Dayan, 1915–81, welcoming Cyrus Vance to Israel, in course of Arab–Israeli negotiations; *Observer*, 'Sayings of the Week', 14 Aug. 1977]

7 Most acts of assent require far more courage than most acts of protest, since courage is clearly a readiness to risk self-humiliation. [Nigel Dennis, 1912–89, *Boys and Girls Come Out to Play*]

8 In every age and clime we see, / Two of a trade can ne'er agree. [John Gay, 1685–1732, *Fables*, Pt I, xxi, 43]

9 Disagreement may be the shortest cut between two minds. [Kahlil Gibran, 1883–1931, *Sand and Foam*]

10 His [Joseph M. Schenk's] verbal contract is worth more than the paper it's written on. [Samuel Goldwyn, 1882–1974 (became Goldwynized to: A verbal contract isn't worth the paper it's written on), in Carol Easton, *The Search for Goldwyn*]

11 The two men seemed to agree about everything, but when grown-ups agree they interrupt each other almost as much as if they were quarrelling. [Rudyard Kipling, 1865–1936, *Rewards and Fairies*, 'The Wrong Thing']

12 I agree with everything you say but I would attack to the death your right to say it – Voltaire (the younger). [Tom Stoppard, 1937–   , *Lord Malquist and Mr Moon*, Pt II, 3. Parody of line attr. to Voltaire]; see 13

13 I disapprove of what you say, but I will defend to the death your right to say it. [Attr. to Voltaire in S G Tallentyre, *The Friends of Voltaire* (1906), Ch. 7]

14 Up to a point, Lord Copper. [Evelyn Waugh, 1903–66, *Scoop*, Bk I, Ch. 1, 3]

15 Those who say that I am not in agreement with the [Conservative immigration] policy are, rightly or wrongly, quite wrong. [William Whitelaw, 1918–99, in Simon Hoggart, *On the House*]

16 Ah! don't say you agree with me. When people agree with me I always feel that I must be wrong. [Oscar Wilde, 1854–1900, *The Critic as Artist*, Pt II]

17 If two men on the same job agree all the time, then one is useless. If they disagree all the time, then both are useless. [Darryl F Zanuck, 1902–79; *Observer*, 'Sayings of the Week', 23 Oct. 1949]

AGRICULTURE

1 Cows are my passion. What I have ever sighed for has been to retreat to a Swiss farm, and live entirely surrounded by cows – and china. [Charles Dickens, 1812–70, *Dombey and Son*, Ch. 21]

2 Have it *jest* as you've a mind to, but I've proved it time on time, / If you want to change her nature you have *got* to give her lime. [Rudyard Kipling, 1865–1936, *The Land*]

3 The tawny mowers enter next, / Who seem like Israelites to be / Walking on foot through a green sea. [Andrew Marvell, 1621–78, *Upon Appleton House*, 388]

4 He gave it for his opinion, that whoever could make two ears of corn or two blades of grass to grow upon a spot of ground where only one grew before, would deserve better of mankind, and do more essential service to his country than the whole race of politicians put together. [Jonathan Swift, 1677–1745, *Gulliver's Travels*, 'Voyage to Brobdingnag', Ch. 7]

5 How blest beyond all blessings are farmers, if they but knew their happiness! Far from the clash of arms, the most just earth brings forth from the soil an easy living for them. [Virgil, 70–19 BC, *Georgics*, II, 458]

See also EARTH, LANDS

AMBITIONS

1 Ah, but a man's reach should exceed his grasp, / Or what's a heaven for? [Robert Browning, 1812–89, *Andrea del Sarto*, 96]

2 I have found some of the best reasons I ever had for remaining at the bottom simply by looking at the men at the top. [Frank Moore Colby, 1865–1925, *Essays*, II]

3 How dost thou wear and weary out thy days, / Restless Ambition, never at an end! [Samuel Daniel, 1562–1619, *Philotas*, chorus]

4 Hitch your wagon to a star. [Ralph Waldo Emerson, 1803–82, *Society and Solitude*, 'Civilization']

5 My ambition has been so great it has never seemed to me worth while to try to satisfy it. [Colonel Edward House, 1858–1938, in John Dos Passos, *Mr Wilson's War*, Ch. 1, sect. ii]

6 I would sooner fail than not be among the greatest. [John Keats, 1795–1821, letter to J A Hessey, 9 Oct. 1818]

7 How vainly men themselves amaze, / To win the palm, the oak, or bays; / And their incessant labours see / Crowned from some single herb or tree. [Andrew Marvell, 1621–78, *The Garden*, 1]

8 Rather than be less / Cared not to be at all. [John Milton, 1608–74, *Paradise Lost*, Bk ii, 47]

9 ROLAND MILK, the limp-wristed poet: Before I die I want to do something big and clean in the world.

LADY CABSTANLEIGH: Go and wash an elephant. [J B Morton ('Beachcomber'), 1893–1979, *Beachcomber: The Works of J B M*, ed. Richard Ingrams]

10 Every soldier carries a marshal's baton in his pack [Napoleon]. Yes, but don't let it stick out. [David Ogilvy, 1911–99, *Confessions of an Advertising Man*, Ch. 10]

11 To find something only I can do and do it somewhat. [(Describing the purpose of her life) Rachel Pinney, 1909–95, quoted in her obituary, *Guardian*, 8 Nov. 1995]

12 Ambition first sprung from your bless'd abodes; / The glorious fault of angels and of gods. [Alexander Pope, 1688–1744, *Elegy to the Memory of an Unfortunate Lady*, 13]

13 Fain would I climb, yet fear I to fall. [Sir Walter Raleigh, *c.* 1552–1618, line written on a window-pane. Queen Elizabeth is said to have written under it, 'If the heart fails thee, climb not at all.']

14 Since I was a little girl I always wanted to be Very Decent to People. Other little girls wanted to be nurses and pianists. They were less dissembling. [Philip Roth, 1933– , *Letting Go*, Pt I, Ch. 1]

15 Ambition, / The soldier's virtue. [William Shakespeare, 1564–1616, *Antony and Cleopatra*, III. i. 22]

16 Cromwell, I charge thee, fling away ambition: / By that sin fell the angels. [*Henry VIII*, III. ii. 441]

17 That lowliness is young ambition's ladder, / Whereto the climber-upward turns his face; / But when he once attains the upmost round, / He then unto the ladder turns his back, / Looks in the clouds, scorning the base degrees / By which he did ascend. [*Julius Caesar*, II. i. 22]

18 As Caesar loved me, I weep for him; as he was fortunate, I rejoice at it; as he was valiant, I honour him; but as he was ambitious, I slew him. [*Julius Caesar*, III. ii. (26)]

19 Ambition should be made of sterner stuff. [*Julius Caesar*, III. ii. (98)]

20 What thou wouldst highly, / That wouldst thou holily; wouldst not play false, / And yet wouldst wrongly win. [*Macbeth*, I. v. (21)]

21 I have no spur / To prick the sides of my intent, but only / Vaulting ambition, which o'er-leaps itself / And falls on the other. [*Macbeth*, I. vii. 25]

22 There are two things to aim at in life: first, to get what you want; and, after that, to enjoy it. Only the wisest of mankind achieve the second. [Logan Pearsall Smith, 1865–1946, *Afterthoughts*, 1]

23 I've always wanted to *be* somebody, but now I see I should have been more specific. [Jane Wagner, 1927– , spoken by Lily Tomlin as the Bag-lady in *Search for Signs of Intelligent Life in the Universe*]

24 There is always room at the top. [(When advised not to become a lawyer, since the profession was overcrowded) Daniel Webster, 1782–1852, attr.]

See also INTENTION

AMBIVALENCE

1 I will have nothing to do with a man who can blow hot and cold with the same breath. [Aesop, *fl. c.* 550 BC, *Fables*, 'The Man and the Satyr']

2 The noble Duke of York, / He had ten thousand men, / He marched them up to the top of the hill, / And he marched them down again. / And when they were up, they were up, / And when they were down, they were down, / And when they were only halfway up, / They were neither up nor down. [anon., *The Noble Duke of York*, 18th cent.]

3 We know what happens to people who stay in the middle of the road. They get run over. [Aneurin Bevan, 1897–1960; *Observer*, 'Sayings of the Week', 6 Dec. 1953]

4 Ambivalence, I think, is the chief characteristic of my nation. [(Of Russia) Joseph Brodsky, 1940–96, *Less Than One*, title essay]

5 Like watermen, that row one way and look another. [Robert Burton, 1577–1640, *The Anatomy of Melancholy*, 'Democritus to the Reader']

6 Neither have the hearts to stay, / Nor wit enough to run away. [Samuel Butler, 1612–80, *Hudibras*, III, ii, 569]

7 So they [the Government] go on in strange paradox, decided only to be undecided, resolved to be irresolute, adamant for drift, solid for fluidity, all-powerful for impotence. [Winston Churchill, 1874–1965, speech in House of Commons, 12 Nov. 1936]

8 With affection beaming in one eye, and calculation out of the other. [Charles Dickens, 1812–70, *Martin Chuzzlewit*, Ch. 8]

9 An old Dutch farmer, who remarked to a companion once that it was not best to swap horses when crossing a stream. [Abraham Lincoln, 1809–65, speech, 9 June 1864]

See also CERTAIN, DECISIONS, DOUBT, INDECISION, OBSTINACY, COMPROMISE

AMERICA, see UNITED STATES OF

AMERICANS

1 American women like quiet men: they think they're listening. [anon.]

2 Clean-limbed American boys are not like any others. / Only clean-limbed American boys have mothers. [anon. American, in review, *The Times Literary Supplement*, 1964]

3 Good Americans, when they die, go to Paris. [Thomas Appleton, 1812–84, quoted in O W Holmes, *Autocrat of the Breakfast Table*, Ch. 6. Also used by Oscar Wilde]

4 The combination of a profound hatred of war and militarism with an innocent delight in playing soldiers is one of these apparent contradictions of American life that one has to accept. [Denis Brogan, 1900–74, *The American Character*, Pt 1, Ch. 5]

5 'Th' American nation in th' Sixth Ward is a fine people,' he says. 'They love th' eagle,' he says, 'on th' back iv a dollar.' [Finley Peter Dunne, 1867–1936, *Mr Dooley in Peace and War*, 'Oratory on Politics']

6 There are no second acts in American lives. [F Scott Fitzgerald, 1896–1940, 'Notes']

7 We [Americans] all try to be virtuous. It's our national pastime. [Carlos Fuentes, 1928– , *The Old Gringo*, 17]

8 All American males are failed athletes. [Pete Gent, 1942– , in *Weekend Guardian*, 8–9 July 1989]

9 I don't see much future for the Americans ... Everything about the behaviour of American society reveals that it's half judaized, and the other half negrified. How can one expect a state like that to hold together? [Adolf Hitler, 1889–1945, *Hitler's Secret Conversations*]

10 The American system of rugged individualism. [President Herbert Hoover, 1874–1964, campaign speech in New York, 22 Oct. 1928]

11 I am willing to love all mankind, *except an American*. [Dr Samuel Johnson, 1709–84, in James Boswell, *Life of J*, 15 Apr. 1778]

12 Americans get nervous abroad. As a result they tend either to travel in groups or bomb Libya. [Miles Kington, 1941– , in *Independent*, 29 Mar. 1989]

13 McCarthyism is Americanism with its sleeves rolled. [Senator Joseph McCarthy, 1908–57, speech in Wisconsin, 1952, in R Rovere, *Senator Joe McCarthy*, Ch. 1]

14 An interviewer asked me what book I thought best represented the modern American Woman. All I could think of to answer was: *Madame Bovary*. [Mary McCarthy, 1912–89, *On the Contrary*, 'Characters in Fiction']

15 North Americans have a peculiar bias. They go outside to be alone and they go home to be social. [Marshall McLuhan, 1911–80, in *The Sunday Times Magazine*, 26 Mar. 1978]

16 This generation of Americans has a rendezvous with destiny. [Franklin D Roosevelt, 1882–1945, speech accepting renomination, 27 June 1936]

17 There can be no fifty-fifty Americanism in this country. There is room here for only one hundred per cent Americanism. [Theodore Roosevelt, 1858–1919, speech at Saratoga, New York, 19 July 1918]

18 The world has always felt a long way away to Americans. Its important battles have always been internal, its most feared enemies within. [Salman Rushdie, 1937– , in *Independent on Sunday*, 10 Feb. 1991]

19 That strange blend of the commercial traveller, the missionary, and the barbarian conqueror, which was the American abroad. [Olaf Stapledon, 1886–1950, *Last and First Men*, Ch. 3, sect. i]

20 It would seem that Americans have a kind of resistance to looking closely at society. [Lionel Trilling, 1905–75, *The Liberal Imagination*, 'Manners, Morals and the Novel']

21 Americans have been conditioned to respect newness, whatever it costs them. [John Updike, 1932– , *A Month of Sundays*, Ch. 18]

22 The dream of the American male is for a female who has an essential languor which is not laziness, who is unaccompanied except by himself, and who does not let him down. He desires a beautiful, but comprehensible creature who does not destroy a perfect situation by forming a complete sentence. [E B White, 1899–1985, *The Second Tree from the Corner*, 'Notes on Our Time']

23 There exists in the world today a gigantic reservoir of goodwill toward us, the American people. [Wendell Willkie, 1892–1944, *One World*, Ch. 10]

24 Like so many substantial Americans, he had married young and kept on marrying, springing from blonde to blonde like the chamois of the Alps leaping from crag to crag. [P G Wodehouse, 1881–1975, *Summer Moonshine*, Ch. 2]

See also next category, CANADA, UNITED STATES

AMERICANS & OTHERS

1 The English are polite by telling lies. The Americans are polite by telling the truth. [Malcolm Bradbury, 1932– , *Stepping Westward*, II, 5]

2 Poor Mexico, so far from God and so near to the United States! [Porfirio Diaz, 1830–1915; also attr. to Ambrose Bierce]

3 I decided that Europeans and Americans are like men and women: they understand each other worse, and it matters less, than either of them suppose. [Randall Jarrell, 1914–65, *Pictures from an Institution*, Pt IV, Ch. 10]

4 I do *detest* the Americans. They expect everyone to go to the devil at the same hectic pace as themselves. It takes hundreds of years to do it properly. Look at us [the English]. [John Le Carré, 1931– , *The Tailor of Panama*, Ch. 19]

5 The American character looks always as if it had just had a rather bad haircut, which gives it, in our eyes at any rate, a greater humanity than the European, which even among its beggars has an all too professional air. [Mary McCarthy, 1912–89, *On the Contrary*, 'America the Beautiful']

6 When an American heiress wants to buy a man, she at once crosses the Atlantic. The only really materialistic people I have ever met have been Europeans. [Mary McCarthy, 1912–89, *On the Contrary*, 'America the Beautiful']

7 The immense popularity of American movies abroad demonstrates that Europe is the unfinished negative of which America is the proof. [Mary McCarthy, 1912–89, *On the Contrary*, 'America the Beautiful']

8 We, my dear Mr [Richard] Crossman, are Greeks in the Roman Empire. You will find the Americans much as the Greeks found the Romans – a great big, vulgar, bustling people, more vigorous than we are, but also more idle, with more unspoilt virtues but also more corrupt. [Harold Macmillan, 1894–1986, quoted in obituary, *The Times*, 30 Dec. 1986]

9 In the field of world policy I would dedicate this nation to the policy of the good neighbour. [Franklin D Roosevelt, 1882–1945, first inaugural address, 4 Mar. 1933]

10 An American is either a Jew, or an anti-Semite, unless he is both at the same time. [Jean-Paul Sartre, 1905–80, *Altona*, I]

11 Different cultures. You [the British] are too modest – in a very vain way. We [the Americans] are too busy – in a very humble way, of course. [Gore Vidal, 1925– , interview in *Observer Magazine*, 15 Nov. 1987]

12 We are all American at puberty; we die French. [Evelyn Waugh, 1903–66, *Diaries*, ed. M Davie, 'Irregular Notes', 18 July 1961]

See previous category, INTERNATIONAL RELATIONS, NATIONS, UNITED STATES

ANARCHY

1 Anarchists who love God always fall for Spinoza because he tells them that God doesn't love them. This is just what they need. A poke in the eye. To a real anarchist a poke in the eye is better than a bunch of flowers. It makes him see stars. [Joyce Cary, 1888–1957, *The Horse's Mouth*, 16]

2 When we apply it, you call it anarchy; and when you apply it, I call it exploitation. [G K Chesterton, 1874–1936, *The Scandal of Father Brown*, 'The Crime of the Communist']

3 My political opinions lean more and more to anarchy. The most improper job of any man, even saints, is bossing other men. There is only one bright spot and that is the growing habit of disgruntled men of dynamiting factories and power stations. I hope that, encouraged now as patriotism, may remain a habit. [J R R Tolkien, 1892–1973, letter to his son Christopher (in the RAF), 29 April 1943]

4 Things fall apart; the centre cannot hold; / Mere anarchy is loosed upon the world, / The blood-dimmed tide is loosed, and everywhere / The ceremony of innocence is drowned. [W B Yeats, 1865–1939, *The Second Coming*]

See also CHAOS

ANCESTRY

1 People are thankful to their forebears because they never knew them. [Elias Canetti, 1905–94, *The Human Province*, '1943']

2 No man can cause more grief than that one clinging blindly to the vices of his ancestors.

[William Faulkner, 1897–1962, *Intruder in the Dust*, Ch. 3]

3 My folks didn't come over on the *Mayflower*, but they were there to meet the boat. [Will Rogers, 1879–1935; in *Treasury of Humorous Quotations*, ed. Evan Esar and Nicolas Bentley]

4 Look in the chronicles; we came in with Richard Conqueror. [William Shakespeare, 1564–1616, *The Taming of the Shrew*, Induction, i. (4)]

5 The gardener Adam and his wife / Smile at the claims of long descent. [Alfred, Lord Tennyson, 1809–92, *Lady Clara Vere de Vere*]

See also FAMILY

ANGELS

1 The diffrense from a person and an angel is easy: Most of an angel is in the inside and most of a person on the outside. [Anna, in Fynn, *Mister God, This is Anna*, Ch. 1]

2 And lo, the angel of the Lord came upon them, and the glory of the Lord shone round about them: and they were sore afraid. [Bible, NT, *St Luke* 2:9]

3 Whom but a dusk misfeatured messenger, / No other than the angel of this life, / Whose care is lest men see too much at once. [Robert Browning, 1812–89, *The Ring and the Book*, I, 593]

4 The angels all were singing out of tune, / And hoarse with having little else to do, / Excepting to wind up the sun and moon, / Or curb a runaway young star or two. [Lord Byron, 1788–1824, *The Vision of Judgement*, 2]

5 By many stories, / And true, we learn the angels are all Tories. [Lord Byron, 1788–1824, *The Vision of Judgement*, 26]

6 Angels can fly because they take themselves lightly. [G K Chesterton, 1874–1936, *Orthodoxy*, Ch. 7]

7 You may not be an angel / 'Cause angels are so few, / But until the day that one comes along / I'll string along with you. [Al Dubin, 1891–1945, song: *'I'll String Along with You'*]

8 An angel whose muscles developed no more power weight for weight than those of an eagle or a pigeon would require a breast projecting for about four feet to house the muscles engaged in working its wings, while to economize in weight, its legs would have to be reduced to mere stilts. [J B S Haldane, 1892–1964, *Possible Worlds*, 'On Being the Right Size']

9 Brightest and best of the sons of the morning. / Dawn on our darkness, and lend us Thine aid! [Bishop Heber, 1783–1826, hymn]

10 Around the throne of God, a band / Of glorious angels ever stand. [J M Neale, 1818–66, hymn]

11 Praise the world to the angel, not the untellable. You cannot impress him with the splendour you have felt; in the cosmos where he feels with greater feeling you are a novice. So show him the simple thing. [Rainer Maria Rilke, 1875–1926, *Duino Elegies*, 9]

12 Angels are bright still, though the brightest fell. [William Shakespeare, 1564–1616, *Macbeth*, IV. iii. 22]

13 In heaven an angel is nobody in particular. [George Bernard Shaw, 1856–1950, *Man and Superman*, 'Maxims for Revolutionists', 'Greatness']

14 For adoration all the ranks / Of angels yield eternal thanks, / And David in the midst. [Christopher Smart, 1722–71, *Song to David*, 51]

15 Her angel's face, / As the great eye of heaven, shinèd bright, / And made a sunshine in the shady place. [Edmund Spenser, 1552?–99, *The Faerie Queene*, Bk i, Canto 3, Stanza 6]

16 The brute curiosity of an angel's stare / Turns you like them to stone. [Allen Tate, 1899–1979, *Ode to the Confederate Dead*]

See also HEAVEN

ANGER

1 Anger makes dull men witty, but it keeps them poor. [Francis Bacon, 1561–1626, *Apothegms*, 5, attr. by Bacon to Queen Elizabeth I]

2 A soft answer turneth away wrath: but grievous words stir up anger. [Bible, OT, *Proverbs* 15:1]

3 Be ye angry and sin not: let not the sun go down upon your wrath. [Bible, NT, *Ephesians* 4:26]

4 The tigers of wrath are wiser than the horses of instruction. [William Blake, 1757–1827, *The Marriage of Heaven and Hell*, 'Proverbs of Hell']

5 I was angry with my friend: / I told my wrath, my wrath did end. / I was angry with my foe: / I told it not, my wrath did grow. [William Blake, 1757–1827, *Songs of Experience*, 'A Poison Tree']

6 Life is thorny; and youth is vain; / And to be wroth with one we love / Doth work like madness in the brain. [Samuel Taylor Coleridge, 1772–1834, *Christabel*, Pt II, 413]

7 Heaven has no rage like love to hatred turned, / Nor hell a fury, like a woman scorned. [William Congreve, 1670–1729, *The Mourning Bride*, III. viii]

8 I suppose you're really – an angry young man. [George Fearon, 1901–72 (to John Osborne before the first staging of *Look Back in Anger*, 1956), in J O, *Almost a Gentleman*, Ch. 1]

9 Anger is one of the sinews of the soul; he that wants it hath a maimed mind. [Thomas Fuller, 1608–61, *The Holy State*, Bk iii, Ch. 8]

10 When you get angry, they tell you, count to five before you reply. Why should I count to five? It's what happens *before* you count to five which makes life interesting. [David Hare, 1947– , *Secret Rapture*, vii]

11 Anger is a brief madness. [Horace, 65–8 BC, *Epistles*, I, ii, 62]

12 A woman moved is like a fountain troubled, / Muddy, ill-seeming, thick, bereft of beauty. [William Shakespeare, 1564–1616, *The Taming of the Shrew*, V. ii. 143]

13 O! what a deal of scorn looks beautiful / In the contempt and anger of his lip. [*Twelfth Night*, III. i. (159)]

ANIMALS

1 When people call this beast to mind, / They marvel more and more / At such a little tail behind, / So large a trunk before. [Hilaire Belloc, 1870–1953, *The Bad Child's Book of Beasts*, 'The Elephant']

2 I had an aunt in Yucatan / Who bought a python from a man / And kept it for a pet. / She died, because she never knew / These simple little rules and few: – / The snake is living yet. [Hilaire Belloc, 1870–1953, *More Beasts for Worse Children*, 'The Python']

3 A righteous man regardeth the life of his beast. [Bible, OT, *Proverbs* 12:10]

4 Tyger! Tyger! burning bright / In the forests of the night, / What immortal hand or eye / Could frame thy fearful symmetry? [William Blake, 1757–1827, *Songs of Experience*, 'The Tyger']

5 Little Lamb, who made thee? / Dost thou know who made thee? / Gave thee life, and bid thee feed, / By the stream and o'er the mead; / Gave thee clothing of delight, / Softest clothing, woolly, bright; / Gave thee such a tender voice, Making all the vales rejoice? [William Blake, 1757–1827, *Songs of Innocence*, 'The Lamb']

6 Rats! / They fought the dogs and killed the cats, / And bit the babies in the cradles, / And ate the cheeses out of the vats. [Robert Browning, 1812–89, *The Pied Piper of Hamelin*, 2]

7 Wee, sleekit, cow'rin', tim'rous beastie, / O what a panic's in thy breastie! / Thou need na start awa sae hasty, / Wi' bickering brattle! [Robert Burns, 1759–96, *To a Mouse*]

8 Whenever you observe an animal closely, you feel as if a human being sitting inside were making fun of you. [Elias Canetti, 1905–94, *The Human Province*, '1942']

9 With monstrous head and sickening cry / And ears like errant wings, / The devil's walking parody / On all four-footed things. [G K Chesterton, 1874–1936, *The Donkey*]

10 There is nothing to be pitied in a dumb animal; its dumbness is its salvation, whereas poor man carries the terrible burden of intelligence, and it will surely wipe him out in the not too distant end. The cats and guppies will have the last laugh over the last corpse of the last man: 'If you're so smart, how come you're extinct?' [Alan Coren, 1938– , in *The Times*]

11 If anyone wants to know what elephants are like, they are like people only more so. [Peter Corneille, *Theatreprint*, 1984; in *Animal Quotations*, ed. G F Lamb]

12 He, not unlike the great ones of mankind, / Disfigures earth; and, plotting in the dark, / Toils much to earn a monumental pile, / That may record the mischiefs he has done. [(Of the mole) William Cowper, 1731–1800, *The Task*, Bk 1, 274]

13 The Centipede was happy quite, / Until the Toad in fun / Said, 'Pray which leg goes after which?' / And worked her mind to such a pitch, / She lay distracted in the ditch / Considering how to run. [Mrs Craster, d. 1874, attr.]

14 Nature's great masterpiece, an elephant / The only harmless great thing. [John Donne, 1571?–1631, *The Progress of the Soul*, 381]

15 Animals are such agreeable friends – they ask no questions, they pass no criticisms. [George Eliot, 1819–80, *Scenes of Clerical Life*, 'Mr Gilfil's Love-Story', Ch. 7]

16 Monkeys, who very sensibly refrain from speech, lest they should be set to earn their livings. [Kenneth Grahame, 1859–1932, *The Golden Age*, 'The Magic Ring']

17 Had a look at the alligators. Just floating handbags, really. [Trevor Griffiths, 1935– , *The Comedians*, II]

18 The higher animals are not larger than the lower because they are more complicated. They are more complicated because they are larger. [J B S Haldane, 1892–1964, *Possible Worlds*, 'On Being the Right Size']

19 Mary had a little lamb, / Its fleece was white as snow, / And everywhere that Mary went / The lamb was sure to go. [Sarah Hale, 1788–1879, *Mary's Little Lamb*]

20 I have long held the notion that if a vet can't catch his patient there's nothing much to worry about. [James Herriot, 1916–95, *Vet in Harness*]

21 Nothing to be done really about animals. Anything you do looks foolish. The answer isn't in us. It's almost as if we're put here on earth to show how silly they aren't. [Russell Hoban, 1925– , *Turtle Diary*, Ch. 42]

22 The world rolls under the long thrust of his heel. / Over the cage floor the horizons come. [Ted Hughes, 1930–98, *The Jaguar*]

23 No one can give anyone else the gift of the idyll; only an animal can do so, because only animals were not expelled from Paradise. [Milan Kundera, 1929– , *The Unbearable Lightness of Being*, Pt 7, 4]

24 Creatures that hang themselves up like an old rag, to sleep; / And disgustingly upside down. / Hanging upside down like rows of disgusting old rags / And grinning in their sleep. / Bats! [D H Lawrence, 1885–1930, *Bats*]

25 And so, I missed my chance with one of the lords / Of life. / And I have something to expiate: / A pettiness. [D H Lawrence, 1885–1930, *Snake*]

26 If 'compression is the first grace of style', / you have it. [Marianne Moore, 1887–1972, *To a Snail*]

27 One disadvantage of being a hog is that at any moment some blundering fool may try to make a silk purse out of your wife's ear. [J B Morton ('Beachcomber'), 1893–1979, *By the Way*, Sept., Tail-piece]

28 The camel has a single hump; / The dromedary two; / Or else the other way around. / I'm never sure. Are you? [Ogden Nash, 1902–71, *The Camel*]

29 The cow is of the bovine ilk; / One end is moo, the other, milk. [Ogden Nash, 1902–71, *The Cow*]

30 The turtle lives 'twixt plated decks / Which practically conceal its sex. / I think it clever of the turtle /In such a fix to be so fertile. [Ogden Nash, 1902–71, *The Turtle*]

31 Four legs good, two legs bad. [George Orwell, 1903–50, *Animal Farm*, Ch. 3]

32 Droll rat, they would shoot you if they knew / Your cosmopolitan sympathies / (And God knows what antipathies). [Isaac Rosenberg, 1890–1918, *Break of Day in the Trenches*]

33 God shield us! – a lion among ladies, is a most dreadful thing; for there is not a more fearful wildfowl than your lion living. [William Shakespeare, 1564–1616, *Midsummer Night's Dream*, III. i. (32)]

34 The spirit of the worm beneath the sod / In love and worship, blends itself with God. [P B Shelley, 1792–1822, *Epipsychidion*, 128]

35 An oyster may be crossed in love. [R B Sheridan, 1751–1816, *The Critic*, III. i]

36 Strong is the lion – like a coal / His eyeball – like a bastion's mole / His chest against the foes. [Christopher Smart, 1722–71, *Song to David*, 76]

37 Nowadays we don't think much of a man's love for an animal; we laugh at people who are attached to cats. But if we stop loving animals, aren't we bound to stop loving humans too? [Alexander Solzhenitsyn, 1918– , *Cancer Ward*, Pt I, Ch. 14]

38 The friendly cow, all red and white, / I love with all my heart: / She gives me cream with all her might, / To eat with apple-tart. [Robert Louis

Stevenson, 1850–94, *A Child's Garden of Verses*, 23, 'The Cow']

39 I wonder what it's like to be a tortoise. Not a barrel of laughs, I shouldn't imagine. You can't be frivolous or facetious if you're a tortoise, can you? And think of the danger of being turned into a pair of hair-brushes ... But you do have a home to go to. [Keith Waterhouse, 1929– , *Jeffrey Bernard is Unwell*, I. The play is based on the life and writings of Bernard]

40 I think I could turn and live with animals, they're so placid and self-contained, / I stand and look at them long and long. / They do not sweat and whine about their condition, / They do not lie awake in the dark and weep for their sins, / They do not make me sick discussing their duty to God. [Walt Whitman, 1819–92, *Song of Myself*, 32, 684]

41 While the young lambs bound / As to the tabor's sound. [William Wordsworth, 1770–1850, *Ode, Intimations of Immortality*, 3]

See also CATS, DOGS, HORSES, NATURE

ANSWERS

1 For every why he had a wherefore. [Samuel Butler, 1612–80, *Hudibras*, 1, ii, 132]

2 As long as the answer is right, who cares if the question is wrong? [Norton Juster, 1929– , *The Phantom Tollbooth*, Ch. 14]

3 The first, 'the retort courteous'; the second, 'the quip modest'; the third, 'the reply churlish'; the fourth, 'the reproof valiant'; the fifth, 'the countercheck quarrelsome'; the sixth, 'the lie with circumstance'; the seventh, 'the lie direct'. [William Shakespeare, 1564–1616, *As You Like It*, V. iv. (96)]

See also QUESTIONS

ANTHOLOGY

1 It might well be said of me that here I have merely made up a bunch of other men's flowers, and provided nothing of my own but the string to bind them. [Michel de Montaigne, 1533–92, *Essays*, III, 12]

2 An anthology is like all the plums and orange peel picked out of a cake. [Walter A Raleigh, 1861–1922, letter to Mrs Robert Bridges, 15 Jan. 1915, *Letters*, Vol. II]

ANTICIPATION

1 Don't count your chickens before they are hatched. [Aesop, *fl c.*550 BC, *Fables*, 'The Milkmaid and Her Pail']

2 The scouts' motto is founded on my initials, it is: Be Prepared. [Lord Baden-Powell, 1857–1941, *Scouting for Boys*, Pt 1]

3 It is always wise to look ahead, but difficult to look farther than you can see. [Winston Churchill, 1874–1965; *Observer*, 'Sayings of the Week', 27 July 1952]

4 Never mind about present affliction – any moment may be the next. [Jacqueline du Pré, 1945–87, a favourite quotation of hers; in *With Great Pleasure*, ed. Alec Reid]

5 Some of your hurts you have cured, / And the sharpest you still have survived, / But what torments of grief you endured / From evils which never arrived! [Ralph Waldo Emerson, 1803–82, *Quatrains*, 'Borrowing' (from the French)]

6 It's odd how people waiting for you stand out far less clearly than people you are waiting for. [Jean Giraudoux, 1882–1944, *Tiger at the Gates*, I]

7 Depend upon it, Sir, when a man knows he is to be hanged in a fortnight, it concentrates his mind wonderfully. [Dr Samuel Johnson, 1709–84, in James Boswell, *Life of J*, 19 Sept. 1777]

8 Mary lived by wondering what lay round the corner, I lived by knowing there was no corner. [P J Kavanagh, 1931– , *A Happy Man*, Ch. 12]

9 He told me never to sell the bear's skin before one has killed the beast. [Jean de La Fontaine, 1621–95, *Fables*, V, 20, 'The Bear and the Two Companions']

10 One must always have one's boots on and be ready to go. [Michel de Montaigne, 1533–92, *Essays*, I, 20]

11 Against ill chances men are ever merry, / But heaviness foreruns the good event. [William Shakespeare, 1564–1616, *Henry IV*, IV. ii. 81]

12 O! that a man might know / The end of this day's business ere it come. [*Julius Caesar*, V. i. 123]

13 I am giddy, expectation whirls me round. / The imaginary relish is so sweet / That it enchants my sense. [*Troilus and Cressida*, III. ii. (17)]

14 You must wake and call me early, call me early, mother dear; / To-morrow 'ill be the happiest time of all the glad New-year; / Of all the glad New-year, mother, the maddest merriest day; / For I'm to be Queen o' the May, mother, I'm to be Queen o' the May. [Alfred, Lord Tennyson, 1809–92, *The May Queen*]

APHORISMS, see EPIGRAMS

APOLOGY

1 Never make a defence of apology before you be accused. [Charles I, 1600–1649, letter to Lord Wentworth, 3 Sept. 1636]

2 I should never be allowed out in private. [(Letter to his hostess, apologizing for rudeness) Randolph Churchill, 1911–68, in B Roberts, *Randolph*]

3 Never explain – your friends do not need it and your enemies will not believe you anyway. [Elbert Hubbard, 1856–1915, *Motto Book*]

See also REGRET, EXCUSES

APPEARANCE

1 It is not only fine feathers that make fine birds. [Aesop, *fl c.*550 BC, *Fables*, 'The Jay and the Peacock']

2 If a woman have long hair, it is a glory to her. [Bible, NT, *I Corinthians* 11:15]

3 Judge not according to the appearance. [Bible, NT, *St John* 7:24]

4 A thing may look specious in theory, and yet be ruinous in practice; a thing may look evil in theory and yet be in practice excellent. [Edmund Burke, 1729–97, speech on impeachment of Warren Hastings, 19 Feb. 1788]

5 Maidens, like moths, are ever caught by glare, / And Mammon wins his way where Seraphs might despair. [Lord Byron, 1788–1824, *Childe Harold's Pilgrimage*, I, 9]

6 She looked a million dollars, I must admit, even if in well-used notes. [Angela Carter, 1940–92, *Wise Children*, 5]

7 It was a blonde. A blonde to make a bishop kick a hole in a stained-glass window. [Raymond Chandler, 1888–1959, *Farewell, My Lovely*, Ch. 13]

8 He was as fresh as is the month of May. [Geoffrey Chaucer, 1340?–1400, *Canterbury Tales*, 'Prologue', 92]

9 We tolerate shapes in human beings that would horrify us if we saw them in a horse. [W R Inge, 1860–1954, attr.]

10 Such sweet neglect more taketh me, / Than all the adulteries of art; / They strike mine eyes, but not my heart. [Ben Jonson, 1573–1637, [*Epicoene*, I, i]

11 All I say is, nobody has any business to go around looking like a horse and behaving as if it were all right. You don't catch horses going around looking like people, do you? [Dorothy Parker, 1893–1967, *Horsie*]

12 Philomène was a dainty thing, built somewhat on the order of Lois de Fee, the lady bouncer. She had the rippling muscles of a panther, the solidity of a water buffalo, and the lazy insolence of a shoe salesman. [S J Perelman, 1904–79, *Crazy Like a Fox*, 'Kitchen Bouquet']

13 Every person is destroyed when we cease to see him; after which his next appearance is a new creation, different from that which immediately preceded it, if not from them all. [Marcel Proust, 1871–1922, *Remembrance of Things Past: Within a Budding Grove*, 'Elstir']

14 Things are entirely what they appear to be and *behind* them ... there is nothing. [Jean-Paul Sartre, 1905–80, *Nausea*, Monday]

15 A goodly apple rotten at the heart. / O, what a goodly outside falsehood hath! [William Shakespeare, 1564–1616, *The Merchant of Venice*, I. iii. (102)]

16 Thus ornament is but the guilèd shore / To a most dangerous sea; the beauteous scarf / Veiling an Indian beauty; in a word, / The seeming truth which cunning times put on / To entrap the wisest. [*The Merchant of Venice*, III. i. 97]

17 It is only shallow people who do not judge by appearances. [Oscar Wilde, 1854–1900, *The Picture of Dorian Gray*, Ch. 2]

See also FACES

APPEASEMENT

1 EDWARD MARSH: I'm in favour of kissing him [Roosevelt] on both cheeks.
CHURCHILL: Yes, but not on all four. [Winston Churchill, 1874–1965, attr.]

2 An appeaser is one who feeds a crocodile – hoping that it will eat him last. [Winston Churchill, 1874–1965, in *Reader's Digest*, Dec. 1954]

3 Well, he [Chamberlain] seemed such a nice old gentleman, I thought I would give him my autograph as a souvenir. [Adolf Hitler, 1889–1945 (after Munich), attr.]

See also PEACE

APPLAUSE

1 *Applause*, n. The echo of a platitude. [Ambrose Bierce, 1842–1914, *The Devil's Dictionary*]

2 Applause is a receipt, not a bill. [Artur Schnabel, 1882–1951 (in explanation of his refusal to give encores), in I Kolodin, *Musical Life*]

See also AUDIENCES, ENTHUSIASMS

ARCHITECTURE

1 In my experience, if you have to keep the lavatory door shut by extending your left leg, it's modern architecture. [Nancy Banks-Smith, 1929– , *Guardian*, 20 Feb. 1979]

2 Ghastly Good Taste or, a Depressing Story of the Rise and Fall of English Architecture. [Sir John Betjeman, 1906–84, title and subtitle of book]

3 For Gothic, which is Germanic in spirit although modified by French order and clarity, is all revolt and aspiration. [Gerald Brenan, 1894–1987, *Thoughts in a Dry Season*, 'Art and Architecture']

4 What is proposed is like a monstrous carbuncle on the face of a much-loved and elegant friend. [Prince Charles, 1948– (of a planned extension to the National Gallery, London), speech to Royal Institute of British Architects, Hampton Court, 30 May 1984]

5 This gives French Classical architecture a certain inhumanity. It was the work not of craftsmen, but of wonderfully gifted civil servants. [Kenneth Clark, 1903–83, *Civilization*, Ch. 9]

6 We make buildings for our need, and then, sacrificing our pockets to art, cover them with a mass of purely nonsensical forms which we hope may turn them into fine architecture. [Roger Fry, 1866–1934, letter to *The Times*, 1912, in Virginia Woolf, *R F*, Ch. 8]

7 Architecture cannot lie, and buildings, although inanimate, are to that extent morally superior to men. [John Gloag, 1896–1981, 'The Significance of Historical Research in Architectural and Industrial Design', paper to the Royal Society of Arts, 20 Mar. 1963]

8 I have found among my papers a sheet . . . in which I call architecture frozen music. [Johann Wolfgang von Goethe, 1749–1832, *Conversations with Eckermann*, 23 Mar. 1829; also used by Goethe's contemporary, Friedrich von Schelling, *The Philosophy of Art*, 1807]

9 Large buildings in London and elsewhere today are too often designed in the lift going to lunch. [William Holford, 1907–75; *Observer*, 'Sayings of the Week', 5 June 1960]

10 'Fan vaulting' . . . an architectural device which arouses enormous enthusiasm on account of the difficulties it has all too obviously involved but which from an aesthetic standpoint frequently belongs to the 'Last-supper-carved-on-a-peach-stone' class of masterpiece. [Osbert Lancaster, 1908–86, *Pillar to Post*, 'Perpendicular']

11 Less is more. [Mies van der Rohe, 1886–1969, in *New York Herald Tribune*, 28 June 1959]

12 There was a fence with spaces you / Could look through if you wanted to. / An architect who saw this thing / Stood there one summer evening, / Took out the spaces with great care / And built a castle in the air. [Christian Morgenstern, 1871–1914, *Gallows Songs*, 'The Fence']

13 The challenge for the modern architect is the same as the challenge for all of us in our lives: to make out of the ordinary something out-of-the-ordinary. [Patrick Nuttgens, 1930– , from BBC TV programme *Architecture for Everyman*, in *Listener*, 1 Mar. 1979]

14 Architecture is the most inescapable of the higher arts. [Anthony Quinton, 1925– , from *The Times*, 1982; in *Dictionary of Art Quotations*, comp. Ian Crofton]

15 You hear of me, among others, as a respectable architectural man-milliner; and you send for me that I may tell you the leading fashion. [John Ruskin, 1819–1900, *The Crown of Wild Olive*, 'Traffic', §3]

16 *Si monumentum requiris, circumspice.* – If you seek his monument, look round. [Christopher

Wren, 1632–1723 (inscription in St Paul's Cathedral, written by his son)]

17 The land is the simplest form of architecture. Building upon the land is as natural to man as to other animals, birds or insects. In so far as he was more than an animal, his building became what we call architecture. While he was true to earth his architecture was creative. [Frank Lloyd Wright, 1869–1959, in *New Light's Dictionary of Quotations*, comp. Ved Bhushan]

18 The physician can bury his mistakes, but the architect can only advise his client to plant vines. [Frank Lloyd Wright, 1869–1959, in *The New York Times Magazine*, 4 Oct. 1953]

See also BUILDINGS

ARGUMENT

1 Our disputants put me in mind of the skuttle fish, that when he is unable to extricate himself, blackens all the water about him, till he becomes invisible. [Joseph Addison, 1672–1719, *The Spectator*, 476]

2 A continual dropping in a very rainy day and a contentious woman are alike. [Bible, OT, *Proverbs* 27:15]

3 He could distinguish, and divide / A hair 'twixt south and south-west side. / On either which he would dispute, / Confute, change hands, and still confute. [Samuel Butler, 1612–80, *Hudibras*, 1, i, 63]

4 He's one of those men who argues by increments of noise – so that as you open your mouth he says another, cleverer, louder thing. [A S Byatt, 1936–   , *Possession*, Ch. 15]

5 Dialectics, a kind of false teeth. [Elias Canetti, 1905–94, *The Human Province*, '1970']

6 Great contest follows, and much learned dust / Involves the combatants. [William Cowper, 1731–1800, *The Task*, Bk III, 161]

7 Myself when young did eagerly frequent / Doctor and Saint, and heard great Argument / About it and about: but evermore / Came out by the same Door as in I went. [Edward Fitzgerald, 1809–83, *The Rubá'iyát of Omar Khayyám*, Edn 1, 27]

8 There is no arguing with Johnson; for when his pistol misses fire, he knocks you down with the butt end of it. [Oliver Goldsmith, 1728–74, quoted in James Boswell, *Life of J*, 26 Oct. 1769]

9 My uncle Toby would never offer to answer this by any other kind of argument than that of whistling half a dozen bars of Lillabulero. [Laurence Sterne, 1713–68, *Tristram Shandy*, Vol. I, Ch. 21]

ARISTOCRACY

1 *Ah! ça ira, ça ira, ça ira, ça ira, / Les aristocrates à la lanterne.* – Oh, it'll be, it'll be, it'll be, it'll be, / The aristocrats will hang. [Anon. refrain of the French Revolution. The phrase '*ça ira*' is pre-revolutionary]

2 Nobility of birth commonly abateth industry. [Francis Bacon, 1561–1626, *Essays*, 14, 'Of Nobility']

3 Because you are a great lord, you think you are a great genius! ... You took the trouble to be born, and that is all. [Pierre-Augustin de Beaumarchais, 1732–99, *The Marriage of Figaro*, V. iii]

4 The nobility of England, my lord, would have snored through the Sermon on the Mount. [Robert Bolt, 1924–95, *A Man for All Seasons*, II]

5 Not so her gracious, graceful, graceless Grace. [Lord Byron, 1788–1824, *Don Juan*, XVI, 49]

6 Democracy means government by the uneducated, while aristocracy means government by the badly educated. [G K Chesterton, 1874–1936, in *The New York Times*, 1 Feb. 1931]

7 For the first time I was aware of that layer of blubber which encases an English peer, the sediment of permanent adulation. [Cyril Connolly, 1903–74, *Enemies of Promise*, Ch. 23]

8 The Stately Homes of England, / How beautiful they stand, / To prove the upper classes / Have still the upper hand. [Noël Coward, 1899–1973, *Operette*, I. vii, 'The Stately Homes of England']; see 12

9 He differed from the healthy type that was essentially middle-class – he never seemed to perspire. [F Scott Fitzgerald, 1896–1940, *This Side of Paradise*, Bk I, Ch. 2]

10 All baronets are bad. [W S Gilbert, 1836–1911, *Ruddigore*, I]

11 If human beings could be propagated by cutting, like apple trees, aristocracy would be biologically sound. [J B S Haldane, 1892–1964, *The Inequality of Man*, title essay]

12 The stately homes of England, / How beautiful they stand! [Felicia Hemans, 1793–1835, *The Homes of England*]; see 8

13 *Noblesse oblige.* – Nobility carries its obligations. [Duc de Lévis, 1764–1830, *Maximes et réflexions*, 73]

14 A fully equipped Duke costs as much to keep up as two Dreadnoughts, and Dukes are just as great a terror, and they last longer. [David Lloyd George, 1863–1945, speech on the Budget, 9 Oct. 1909]

15 Thus our democracy was, from an early period, the most aristocratic, and our aristocracy the most democratic in the world. [Lord Macaulay, 1800–1859, *History of England*, I, Ch. 1]

16 Let wealth and commerce, laws and learning die, / But leave us still our old nobility. [Lord John Manners, 1818–1906, *England's Trust*, Pt III, 227]

17 People of quality know everything without learning anything. [Molière, 1622–73, *Les Précieuses ridicules*, ix]

18 Not many of our old families can boast that a Savile Row tailor calls four times a year at their country estate to measure the scarecrows in the fields for new suits. [J B Morton ('Beachcomber'), 1893–1979, *The Best of B*, 9]

19 When I want a peerage, I will pay for it like an honest man. [Lord Northcliffe, 1865–1922, in Reginald Pound and Geoffrey Harmsworth, *Northcliffe*, Ch. 11]

20 I was beginning to learn the exact value of the language, spoken or mute, of aristocratic affability, an affability that is happy to shed balm upon the sense of inferiority of those to whom it is directed, though not to the point of dispelling that inferiority, for in that case it would no longer have any *raison d'être*. [Marcel Proust, 1871–1922, *Remembrance of Things Past: Cities of the Plain*, Pt II, Ch. 1]

21 'Tis only noble to be good. / Kind hearts are more than coronets, / And simple faith than Norman blood. [Alfred, Lord Tennyson, 1809–92, *Lady Clara Vere de Vere*]

22 No little lily-handed Baronet he, / A great broad-shouldered genial Englishman, / A lord of fat prize-oxen and of sheep, / A raiser of huge melons and of pine, / A patron of some thirty charities. [Alfred, Lord Tennyson, 1809–92, *The Princess*, Conclusion, 84]

23 Nothing like blood, sir, in hosses, dawgs, and men. [W M Thackeray, 1811–63, *Vanity Fair*, Ch. 35]

24 You should study the Peerage, Gerald . . . It is the best thing in fiction the English have ever done. [Oscar Wilde, 1854–1900, *A Woman of No Importance*, III]

25 Cads have always a grandmother who is the DUCHESS of BLANK hem hem. They are inclined to cheat at conkers having baked them for 300 years in the ancestral ovens. [Geoffrey Willans, 1911–58, and Ronald Searle, 1920–   , *How to be Topp*, Ch. 4]

26 Unlike the male codfish which, suddenly finding itself the parent of three million five hundred thousand little codfish, cheerfully resolves to love them all, the British aristocracy is apt to look with a somewhat jaundiced eye on its younger sons. [P G Wodehouse, 1881–1975, *Blandings Castle*, 'The Custody of the Pumpkin']

27 We may say what we will against the aristocracy of England . . . but we cannot deny that in certain crises blood will tell. An English peer of the right sort can be bored nearer to the point where mortification sets in, without showing it, than anyone else in the world. [P G Wodehouse, 1881–1975, *Something Fresh*, Ch. 3]

28 Say what you will, there is something fine about our old aristocracy. I'll bet Trotsky couldn't hit a moving secretary with an egg on a dark night. [P G Wodehouse, 1881–1975, *Uncle Fred in the Springtime*, Ch. 11]

29 Those comfortably padded lunatic asylums which are known euphemistically as the stately homes of England. [Virginia Woolf, 1882–1941, *The Common Reader*, First Series, 'Lady Dorothy Nevill']

ARMY

1 This is the army, Mr Jones, / No private rooms or telephones. [Irving Berlin, 1888–1989, song: *This is the Army*]

2 *C'est magnifique, mais ce n'est pas la guerre.* – It is magnificent, but it is not war. [Marshal Bosquet, 1810–61, comment on the Charge of the Light Brigade, 1854]

3 The army is a peasant's idea of order. [Joseph Brodsky, 1940–96, *Less Than One*, title essay]

4 A rapacious and licentious soldiery. [Edmund Burke, 1729–97, speech on Fox's East India Bill, 1 Dec. 1783]

5 I have always regarded the forward edge of the battlefield as the most exclusive club in the world. [Lt Gen. Brian Horrocks, 1895–1985, *A Full Life*]

6 I sometimes think that strategy is nothing but tactics talked through a brass hat! [R V Jones, 1911–97, *Most Secret War*, Ch. 51]

7 The 'eathen in 'is blindness must end where 'e began, / But the backbone of the Army is the Non-commissioned Man! [Rudyard Kipling, 1865–1936, *The 'Eathen*]

8 The conventional army loses if it does not win. The guerrilla wins if he does not lose. [Henry Kissinger, 1923– , *Foreign Affairs*, XIII, 'The Vietnam Negotiations', Jan. 1969]

9 Join a Highland regiment, me boy. The kilt is an unrivalled garment for fornication and diarrhoea. [John Masters, 1914–83, quoting a major of Highlanders, in *Bugles and a Tiger*]

10 *La carrière ouverte aux talents.* – The career open to talents. [Napoleon Bonaparte, 1769–1821, quoted in B E O'Meara, *Napoleon in Exile*]

11 We few, we happy few, we band of brothers; / For he today that sheds his blood with me / Shall be my brother; be he ne'er so vile / This day shall gentle his condition: / And gentlemen in England now a-bed / Shall think themselves accursed they were not here, / And hold their manhoods cheap whiles any speaks / That fought with us upon Saint Crispin's day. [William Shakespeare, 1564–1616, *Henry V*, IV, iii, 60]

12 Half a league, half a league, / Half a league onward. / All in the valley of Death / Rode the six hundred. [Alfred, Lord Tennyson, 1809–92, *The Charge of the Light Brigade*]

13 The chief attraction of military service has consisted and will consist in this compulsory and irreproachable idleness. [Leo Tolstoy, 1828–1910, *War and Peace*, VII, Ch. 1]

14 God is always on the side of the big battalions. [Marshal Turenne, 1611–75; also ascr. to Bussy-Rabutin and Voltaire]

15 An army is a nation within a nation; it is one of the vices of our age. [Alfred de Vigny, 1797–1863, *The Military Necessity*, I, Ch. 2]

16 Ours [our army] is composed of the scum of the earth. [Duke of Wellington, 1769–1852, in conversation 4 Nov. 1831]

See also SOLDIERS

ARROGANCE

1 It was prettily devised of Aesop, 'The fly sat upon the axle-tree of the chariot-wheel and said, What a dust do I raise'. [Francis Bacon, 1561–1626, *Essays*, 54, 'Of Vain-glory']

2 Seest thou a man wise in his own conceit? there is more hope of a fool than of him. [Bible, OT, *Proverbs* 26:12]

3 There, but for the grace of God, goes God. [Winston Churchill, 1874–1965, of Sir Stafford Cripps, in L Kronenberger, *The Cutting Edge*, but also ascr. to H J Mankiewicz on Orson Welles]

4 Looks as he were Lord of humankind. [John Dryden, 1631–1700, *The Spanish Friar*, II, i]

5 He was like a cock who thought the sun had risen to hear him crow. [George Eliot, 1819–80, *Adam Bede*, Ch. 33]

6 It is about time the piano realized it has not written the concerto. [Joseph Mankiewicz, 1909–93, in film *All about Eve*]

7 The bullet that is to kill me has not yet been moulded. [Napoleon Bonaparte, 1769–1821, said in 1814, when the Spanish king asked whether he had ever been hit by a cannon-ball]

See also HUMILITY, PRIDE, AND SMUGNESS

ART

1 The object of art is to give life a shape. [Jean Anouilh, 1910–87, *The Rehearsal*, I. ii]

2 Art is our chief means of breaking bread with the dead. [W H Auden, 1907–73, in *The New York Times*, 7 Aug. 1971]

3 All art is the same – an attempt to fill an empty space. [Samuel Beckett, 1906–89, quoted by Peter Lennon, *Guardian*, 25 Jan. 1990]

4 Art and Religion are, then, two roads by which men escape from circumstance to ecstasy. [Clive Bell, 1881–1964, *Art*, Pt II, 1]

5 It makes us feel that 'life is all right for the time being'. [Elizabeth Bishop, 1911–79, quoted in *New Society*, 22/29 Dec. 1983]

6 For me that is the definition of a great work – a landscape painted so well that the artist disappears in it. [Pierre Boulez, 1925– , in Joan Peyser, *Boulez* Ch. 1]

7 I suppose art is the only thing that can go on mattering once it has stopped hurting. [Elizabeth Bowen, 1899–1973, *The Heat of the Day*, Ch. 16]

8 Art is meant to disturb. Science reassures. [Georges Braque, 1882–1963, *Day and Night: Notebooks*]

9 Art does not imitate life if only for fear of clichés. [Joseph Brodsky, 1940–96, *Less Than One*, 'Keening Muse']

10 It is the glory and the good of Art, / That Art remains the one way possible / Of speaking truth, to minds like mine at least. [Robert Browning, 1812–89, *The Ring and the Book*, XII, 842]

11 The history of art is the history of revivals. [Samuel Butler, 1835–1902, *Notebooks*, Ch. 8, 'Anachronism']

12 Every work of art has one indispensable mark ... the centre of it is simple, however much the fulfilment may be complicated. [G K Chesterton, 1874–1936, *The Innocence of Father Brown*, 'The Queer Feet']

13 There is no more sombre enemy of good art than the pram in the hall. [Cyril Connolly, 1903–74, *Enemies of Promise*, Ch. 14]

14 *Il faut de la religion pour la religion, de la morale pour la morale, de l'art pour l'art.* – We need religion for religion's sake, morality for morality's sake and art for art's sake. [Victor Cousin, 1792–1867, *Cours de philosophie*, Paris lecture 1818, but Benjamin Constant used the last phrase in his journal in 1804]

15 Blest be the art that can immortalize. [William Cowper, 1731–1800, *On the Receipt of My Mother's Picture*, 8]

16 By viewing Nature, Nature's handmaid, art, / Makes mighty things from small beginnings grow. [John Dryden, 1631–1700, *Annus Mirabilis*, 155]

17 Art is the expression of the profoundest thoughts in the simplest way. [Albert Einstein, 1879–1955, in W Neil, *Concise Dictionary of Religious Quotations*]

18 I always said God was against art and I still believe it. [(After the catastrophic first performance of *The Dream of Gerontius*) Edward Elgar, 1857–1934, letter to A J Jaeger, 9 Oct. 1900]

19 Art is a jealous mistress. [Ralph Waldo Emerson, 1803–82, *The Conduct of Life*, 'Wealth']

20 Art is significant deformity. [Roger Fry, 1866–1934, in Virginia Woolf, *R F*, Ch. 8]

21 Yes, the work comes out more beautiful from a material that resists the process, verse, marble, onyx, or enamel. [Théophile Gautier, 1811–72, *L'Art*]

22 In art the best is good enough. [Johann Wolfgang von Goethe, 1749–1832, *Italian Journey*]

23 Art is the only work open to people who can't get along with others and still want to be special. [Alasdair Gray, 1934– , *Lanark*, Bk 3, Ch. 1]

24 Venerate art as art. [William Hazlitt, 1778–1830, *On Patronage*]

25 Art has to move you and design does not, unless it's a good design for a bus. [David Hockney, 1937– , at press conference for his retrospective at Tate Gallery, London, 25 Oct. 1988]

26 We work in the dark – we do what we can – we give what we have. Our doubt is our passion, and our passion is our task. The rest is the madness of art. [Henry James, 1843–1916, *The Middle Years*, 1893]

27 It is art that *makes* life, makes interest, makes importance, for our consideration and application of these things, and I know of no substitute whatever for the force and beauty of its process. [Henry James, 1843–1916, letter to H G Wells, 10 July 1915]

28 We know that the tail must wag the dog, for the horse is drawn by the cart; / But the Devil whoops, as he whooped of old: 'It's clever, but is it Art?' [Rudyard Kipling, 1865–1936, *The Conundrum of the Workshops*]

29 Art does not reproduce what we see. Rather, it makes us see. [Paul Klee, 1879–1940, *Creative Credo*]

30 Science is spectral analysis. Art is light synthesis. [Karl Kraus, 1874–1936, *Half-truths and One-and-a-half Truths*, 'Riddles']

31 Art is not a special sauce applied to ordinary cooking; it is the cooking itself if it is good. [W R

Lethaby, 1857–1931, *Form in Civilization*, 'Art and Workmanship']

32 Human temperaments are too diverse; we can never agree how drunk we like our art to be. [F L Lucas, 1894–1967, *Literature and Psychology*, Ch. 10]

33 The whole of art is an appeal to a reality which is not without us but in our minds. [Desmond MacCarthy, 1877–1952, *Theatre*, 'Modern Drama']

34 In England, pop art and fine art stand resolutely back to back. [Colin MacInnes, 1914–76, *England, Half English*, 'Pop Songs and Teenagers']

35 Art is not a mirror to reflect the world, but a hammer with which to shape it. [Vladimir Mayakovsky, 1893–1930, in *Guardian*, 11 Dec. 1974]

36 To be aristocratic in Art one must avoid polite society. [George Moore, 1852–1933, in Cyril Connolly, *Enemies of Promise*, Ch. 15]

37 All art deals with the absurd and aims at the simple. Good art speaks truth, indeed *is* truth, perhaps the only truth. [Iris Murdoch, 1919–99, *The Black Prince*, 'Bradley Pearson's Foreword']

38 Art comes to you proposing frankly to give nothing but the highest quality to your moments as they pass, and simply for those moments' sake. [Walter Pater, 1839–94, *The Renaissance*, Conclusion]

39 Great art is always an invention that begins as an imitation. [Octavio Paz, 1914–98, *Convergences*]

40 Art is a lie which makes us realize the truth. [Pablo Picasso, 1881–1973, in D Ashton, *Picasso on Art*]

41 I gave the lot up and went in for Art. / I'll wash my own brains, thank you very much. [Fiona Pitt-Kethley, 1954– , '*The Hidden Persuaders*']

42 It's far more difficult to disfigure a great work of art than to create one. [Marcel Proust, 1871–1922, *Remembrance of Things Past: Cities of the Plain*, Pt II, Ch. 1]

43 Conception, my boy, *fundamental brain-work*, is what makes the difference in all art. [Dante Gabriel Rossetti, 1828–82, letter to Hall Caine, quoted in his *Recollections of Rossetti*]

44 Fine art is that in which the hand, the head, and the heart of man go together. [John Ruskin, 1819–1900, *The Two Paths*, Lecture II]

45 Art should be cold. [Arnold Schoenberg, 1874–1951, in Artur Schnabel, *My Life and Music*, Pt II, Ch. 9; but elsewhere ascr. to Stravinsky]

46 Art ... can also in its small way attempt to mend the mistakes of the eternal builder in whose image man was created. [Isaac Bashevis Singer, 1904–91, *Death of Methuselah*, Author's Note]

47 Skill without imagination is craftsmanship and gives us many useful objects such as wickerwork picnic baskets. Imagination without skill gives us modern art. [Tom Stoppard, 1937– , *Artist Descending a Staircase*]

48 I doubt that art needed Ruskin any more than a moving train needs one of its passengers to shove it. [Tom Stoppard, 1937– , in *The Times Literary Supplement*, 3 June 1977]

49 Know that the secret of the arts is to correct nature. [Voltaire, 1694–1778, *A. M. de Verrière*]

50 It is not 'politics' which is the arch-enemy of art, it is neutrality, which robs us of the sense of tragedy. [Orson Welles, 1915–85, letter on the subject of Eugene Ionesco, in *Guardian*, 14 Sept. 1990]

51 Art never expresses anything but itself. [Oscar Wilde, 1854–1900, *The Decay of Lying*]

52 All art is quite useless. [Oscar Wilde, 1854–1900, *The Picture of Dorian Gray*, Preface]

53 When art communicates, a human experience is actively offered and actively received. Below this activity threshold there can be no art. [Raymond Williams, 1921–88, *The Long Revolution*, Pt I, Ch. 1, sect. vi]

54 A work of art is a corner of creation seen through a temperament. [Emile Zola, 1840–1902, *Mes Haines*, 'M. H. Taine, Artiste']

See also next category, PAINTERS, PAINTING, SCULPTURE

ARTISTS

1 About suffering they were never wrong, / The Old Masters. [W H Auden, 1907–73, *Musée des Beaux Arts*]

2 One account, given me by a good artist, is that what he tries to express in a picture is 'a passionate apprehension of form'. [Clive Bell, 1881–1964, *Art*, Pt I, Ch. 3]

3 Let the artist have just enough to eat, and the tools of his trade: ask nothing of him. Materially make the life of the artist sufficiently miserable to be unattractive, and no one will take to art save those in whom the divine daemon is absolute. [Clive Bell, 1881–1964, *Art*, Pt V, Ch. 1]

4 The artist is extremely lucky who is presented with the worst possible ordeal which will not actually kill him. [John Berryman, 1914–72, interview in *Paris Review*, Winter 1972]

5 The worst joke God can play is to make you an artist, but only a mediocre artist. [David Bowie, 1947–   ; in *Wit and Wisdom of Rock and Roll*, ed. Maxim Jakubowski]

6 Every man's work, whether it be literature or music or pictures or architecture or anything else, is always a portrait of himself. [Samuel Butler, 1835–1902, *The Way of All Flesh*, Ch. 14]

7 Remember I'm an artist. And you know what that means in a court of law. Next worst to an actress. [Joyce Cary, 1888–1957, *The Horse's Mouth*, 14]

8 The artistic temperament is a disease that afflicts amateurs. [G K Chesterton, 1874–1936, *Heretics*, 17]

9 An artist will betray himself by some sort of sincerity. [G K Chesterton, 1874–1936, *The Incredulity of Father Brown*, 'The Dagger with Wings']

10 It is closing time in the gardens of the West and from now on an artist will be judged only by the resonance of his solitude or the quality of his despair. [Cyril Connolly, 1903–74, *The Condemned Playground*]

11 That is what the title of artist means: one who perceives more than his fellows, and who records more than he has seen. [Edward Gordon Craig, 1872–1966, *On the Art of the Theatre*, 'The Actor and the Über-Marionette']

12 The more perfect the artist, the more completely separate in him will be the man who suffers and the mind which creates. [T S Eliot, 1888–1965, *Selected Essays*, 'Tradition and the Individual Talent' II]

13 Every artist writes his own autobiography. [Havelock Ellis, 1859–1939, *The New Spirit*, 'Tolstoi', 11]

14 Artists can colour the sky red because they *know* it's blue. Those of us who aren't artists must colour things the way they really are or people might think we're stupid. [Jules Feiffer, 1929–   , *Crawling Arnold*]

15 Beware of the artist who's an intellectual also. The artist who doesn't fit. [F Scott Fitzgerald, 1896–1940, *This Side of Paradise*, Bk I, Ch. 5]

16 The artist in his work ought to be like God in creation, invisible and all powerful; everywhere felt but nowhere visible. [Gustave Flaubert, 1821–80, letter to Mlle de Chantepie, 18 March 1857]

17 Blake is damned good to steal from. [Henry Fuseli, 1741–1825, quoted in Alexander Gilchrist, *Life of Blake*, Ch. 7]

18 The artist is not a special kind of man but every man a special kind of artist. [Eric Gill, 1882–1940, in *Art*, 1942]

19 He had the artistic metempsychosis which is half drunk when sober and looks down on airships when stimulated. [O Henry, 1862–1910, *A Midsummer Masquerade*]

20 If artists do see fields blue they are deranged, and should go to an asylum. If they only pretend to see them blue, they are criminals and should go to prison. [Adolf Hitler, 1889–1945, speech in Munich on occasion of 'Degenerate Art' exhibition, July 1937]

21 We must grant the artist his subject, his idea, his *donné*: our criticism is applied only to what he makes of it. [Henry James, 1843–1916, *The Art of Fiction*, 'Partial Portraits']

22 For it is of the nature of art that the artist cannot suffer alone. [Hans Keller, 1919–85, *Criticism*, Pt 1, Ch. 3]

23 In free society art is not a weapon . . . Artists are not engineers of the soul. [President John F Kennedy, 1917–63, address at dedication of the Robert Frost Library, Amherst College, Massachusetts, 26 Oct. 1963]; see also WRITERS IN GENERAL, 53

24 Only he is an artist who can make a riddle out of a solution. [Karl Kraus, 1874–1936, *Half-truths and One-and-a-half Truths*, 'Riddles']

25 Artists have a right to be modest and a duty to be vain. [Karl Kraus, 1874–1936, *Half-truths and One-and-a-half Truths*, 'Riddles']

26 In other countries, art and literature are left to a lot of shabby bums living in attics and feeding on booze and spaghetti, but in America the successful writer or picture-painter is indistinguishable from any other decent business man. [Sinclair Lewis, 1885–1951, *Babbitt*, Ch. 14]

27 I do not know whether he [Walt Disney] draws a line himself . . . But I assume that his is the direction, the constant aiming after improvement in the new expression . . . it is the direction of a real artist. It makes Disney, not as a draughtsman but as an artist who uses his brains, the most significant figure in graphic art since Leonardo. [David Low, 1891–1963, in R Schickel, *Walt Disney*, Ch. 20]

28 All living artists compete with the towering dead with their nightingales and psalms. [Elisabeth Lutyens, 1906–83, *A Goldfish Bowl*, Ch. 2]

29 The artist's egoism is outrageous; it must be; he is by nature a solipsist and the world exists only for him to exercise upon it his powers of creation. [W Somerset Maugham, 1874–1965, *The Summing Up*, Ch. 61]

30 The great artists of the world are never Puritans, and seldom even ordinarily respectable. [H L Mencken, 1880–1956, *Prejudices*, First Series, 16]

31 The worst sin that can be committted against the artist is to take him at his word, to see in his work a fulfilment instead of an horizon. [Henry Miller, 1891–1980, *The Cosmological Eye*, 'An Open Letter to Surrealists Everywhere']

32 Great artists have no country. [Alfred de Musset, 1810–57, *Lorenzaccio*, I. v]

33 As an artist, a man has no home in Europe save in Paris. [Friedrich Nietzsche, 1844–1900, *Ecce Homo*]

34 An artist should know all about love and learn to live without it. [Anna Pavlova, 1885–1931, in *Guardian*, 5 Oct. 1987]

35 It's the artist's job to create sunshine when there isn't any. [Romain Rolland, 1866–1944, *Jean Christophe: The Market on Change*]

36 The true artist will let his wife starve, his children go barefoot, his mother drudge for his living at seventy, sooner than work at anything but his art. [George Bernard Shaw, 1856–1950, *Man and Superman*, 1]

37 The artist, like the idiot or clown, sits on the edge of the world, and a push may send him over it. [Osbert Sitwell, 1892–1969, *The Scarlet Tree*, Bk IV, Ch. 2]

38 What is an artist? For every thousand people there's nine hundred doing the work, ninety doing well, nine doing good, and one lucky bastard who's the artist. [Tom Stoppard, 1937– , *Travesties*, I. Also used with slightly different wording in *Artist Descending a Staircase*]

39 Too many of the artists of Wales spend too much time talking about the position of the artists of Wales. There is only one position for an artist anywhere: and that is upright. [Dylan Thomas, 1914–53, *Quite Early One Morning*, Pt 2, 'Wales and the Artist']

40 A genius with the IQ of a moron. [(Of Andy Warhol) Gore Vidal, 1925– , in *Observer*, 18 June 1989]

41 An artist is someone who produces things that people don't need to have but that he – for *some reason* – thinks it would be a good idea to give them. [Andy Warhol, 1927–87, *From A to B and Back Again*, 'Atmosphere']

42 A living is made, Mr Kemper, by selling something that everybody needs at least once a year. Yes, sir! And a million is made by producing something that everybody needs every day. You artists produce something that nobody needs at any time. [Thornton Wilder, 1897–1975, *The Matchmaker*, I]

See also previous category, PAINTERS, PAINTING, SCULPTURE

ASSASSINATION

1 An intelligent Russian once remarked to us, 'Every country has its own constitution; ours is absolutism moderated by assassination.' [anon., quoted in Count Münster, *Political Sketches of the State of Europe* (1868)]

2 My name is Dumini, twelve assassinations. [Amerigo Dumini, 1898–1968, in George Seldes, *Sawdust Caesar*, Ch. 17]

3 Assassination should be used as the vote should ideally be used, that is, bearing in mind only the public good and regardless of personal interest. [Edward Hyams, 1910–75, *Killing No Murder*, Ch. 10]

4 Honey, I forgot to duck. [Ronald Reagan, 1911– , to Nancy Reagan on entering hospital after an assassination attempt, 30 Mar. 1981, quoting Jack Dempsey]

5 If it were done when 'tis done, then 'twere well / It were done quickly: if the assassination / Could trammel up the consequence, and catch /With his surcease success; that but this blow / Might be the be-all and the end-all here, / But here, upon this bank and shoal of time, / We'd jump the life to come. [William Shakespeare, 1564–1616, *Macbeth*, I. vii. 1]

6 Assassination is the extreme form of censorship. [George Bernard Shaw, 1856–1950, *The Shewing-up of Blanco Posnet*, 'The Limits of Toleration']

7 It is one of the incidents of the profession. [Umberto I, 1844–1900, after an attempt on his life]

8 I guess it was just being in the wrong place at the right time. That's what assassination is all about. [Andy Warhol, 1927–87, *POPism*, '1968–9']

See also KILLING, MURDER

ASTONISHMENT

1 At the back of our brains there was a forgotten blaze or burst of astonishment at our own existence. The object of the artistic and spiritual life was to dig for this submerged sunrise of wonder. [G K Chesterton, 1874–1936, *Autobiography*, 4]

2 I'm Gormed – and I can't say no fairer than that! [Charles Dickens, 1812–70, *David Copperfield*, Ch. 63]

3 Our hope of salvation lies in our being surprised by the Other. Let us learn always to receive further surprises. [Ivan Illich, 1926– , *Celebration of Awareness*, Ch. 9]

4 There is something about the unexpected that moves us. As if the whole of existence is paid for in some way, except for that one moment, which is free. [Rose Tremain, 1951– , *Sacred Country*, Ch. 14, 'Mary']

5 He felt like a man who, chasing rainbows, has had one of them suddenly turn and bite him in the leg. [P G Wodehouse, 1881–1975, *Beans and Crumpets*, 'Anselm Gets His Chance']

ASTROLOGY

1 You stars that reigned at my nativity, / Whose influence hath allotted death and hell, / Now draw up Faustus, like a foggy mist, / Into the entrails of yon labouring cloud. [Christopher Marlowe, 1564–93, *Doctor Faustus*, 1473]

2 When beggars die, there are no comets seen; / The heavens themselves blaze forth the death of princes. [William Shakespeare, 1564–1616, *Julius Caesar*, II. ii. 30]

3 This is the excellent foppery of the world ... we make guilty of our disasters the sun, the moon and the stars, as if we were villains by necessity, fools by heavenly compulsion, knaves, thieves and treachers by spherical predominance, drunkards, liars and adulterers by an enforced obedience of planetary influence. [*King Lear*, I. ii. (132)]

4 It is the stars, / The stars above us, govern our conditions. [*King Lear*, IV. iii. 34]

5 We are merely the stars' tennis-balls, struck and bandied / Which way please them. [John Webster, 1580?–1625?, *The Duchess of Malfi*, V. iv. 52]

See also next category, STARS

ASTRONOMY

1 'Do you believe in astrology?' 'I don't even believe in astronomy.' [Peter de Vries, 1910–93, *Consenting Adults*, Ch. 4]

2 I knew a man who failing as a farmer / Burned down his farmhouse for the fire insurance, / And spent the proceeds on a telescope / To satisfy a life-long curiosity / About our place among the infinities. / And how was that for other-worldliness? [Robert Frost, 1874–1963, *New Hampshire*]

3 *E pur si muove*. – Yet it does move. [(Attr. saying in 1632, after being forced to recant his doctrine that the earth moves round the sun) Galileo Galilei, 1564–1642]

4 Astronomy teaches the correct use of the sun and the planets. [Stephen Leacock, 1869–1944, *Literary Lapses*, 'A Manual of Education']

See also previous category, STARS

ATHEISM

1 Not only is there no God, but try getting a plumber on weekends. [Woody Allen, 1935– , *Getting Even*, 'My Philosophy']

2 God never wrought miracle to convince atheism, because his ordinary works convince it. [Francis Bacon, 1561–1626, *Essays*, 16, 'Of Atheism']

3 Although he [David Ben-Gurion] did not believe in God himself, he somehow gave the impression that God believed in him. [Chaim Bermant, 1929–98, in *Observer*, 4 Sept. 1983]

4 The fool hath said in his heart, There is no God. [Bible, OT, *Psalms* 14:1 and 53:1]

5 An atheist is a man who has no invisible means of support. [John Buchan, 1875–1940, in H E Fosdick, *On Being a Real Person*, Ch. 10]

6 The Magistrate . . . had the red hair and ginger whiskers of the born atheist. [J G Farrell, 1935–79, *The Siege of Krishnapur*, Pt 1, Ch. 1]

7 A strict observer is one who would be an atheist under an atheistic king. [Jean de La Bruyère, 1645–96, *Characters*, 'Of Fashion', 21]

8 He was an embittered atheist (the sort of atheist who does not so much disbelieve in God as personally dislike him). [George Orwell, 1903–50, *Down and Out in Paris and London*, Ch. 30]

9 It has even been said that the highest praise of God consists in the denial of him by the atheist who finds creation so perfect that he can dispense with a creator. [Marcel Proust, 1871–1922, *Remembrance of Things Past: The Guermantes Way*, Ch. 2]

10 I was told that the Chinese said they would bury me by the Western Lake and build a shrine to my memory. I have some slight regret that this did not happen, as I might have become a god, which would have been very *chic* for an atheist. [Bertrand Russell, 1872–1970, *Autobiography*, Vol. II, Ch. 3]

11 The worst moment for an atheist is when he feels grateful and has no one to thank. [Wendy Ward, in P and J Holton, *Quote and Unquote*]

12 By night an atheist half believes a God. [Edward Young, 1683–1765, *Night Thoughts*, 'Night 5', 176]

See also BELIEF, DOUBT

ATTENTION

1 The only real distinction at this dangerous moment in human history and cosmic development has nothing to do with medals and ribbons. Not to fall asleep is distinguished. Everything else is mere popcorn. [Saul Bellow, 1915– , *Humboldt's Gift*, p. 277]

2 Seeing many things, but thou observest not. [Bible, OT, *Isaiah* 42:20]

3 She looked at him, as one who awakes: / The past was a sleep, and her life began. [Robert Browning, 1812–89, *The Statue and the Bust*, 10]

4 He holds him with his glittering eye. [Samuel Taylor Coleridge, 1772–1834, *The Ancient Mariner*, Pt 1]

5 I neglect God and his Angels, for the noise of a fly, for the rattling of a coach, for the whining of a door. [John Donne, 1571?–1631, *Sermons*, I, 80]

6 All man's life among men is nothing more than a battle for the ears of others. [Milan Kundera, 1929– , *The Book of Laughter and Forgetting*, Pt 4, 1]

7 Every time we really concentrate our attention we destroy some of the evil within. [Simone Weil, 1909–43, *Waiting on God*, 'Reflections on the Right Use of School Studies']

8 To attract attention in the dining-room of the Senior Conservative Club between the hours of one and two-thirty, you have to be a mutton chop, not an earl. [P G Wodehouse, 1881–1975, *Something Fresh*, Ch. 3]

AUDIENCES

1 Long experience has taught me that in England nobody goes to the theatre unless he or she has bronchitis. [James Agate, 1877–1947, *Ego 6*]; see 7

2 If there are cat-calls . . . you are sure at least that the audience is still there. [Caryl Brahms, 1901–82, and S J Simon, 1904–48, *Six Curtains for Stroganova*, Ch. 13]

3 They [American audiences] are so used to getting up and going to the refrigerator that they can't sit still as long as English audiences. [James Coco, 1928– , interview, *Guardian*, 17 June 1982]

4 Will people in the cheaper seats clap your hands? All the rest of you just rattle your jewellery. [John Lennon, 1940–80, at Royal Variety Performance, 15 Nov. 1963]

5 What is an audience to an actor, after all, but a vast tit? [David Mercer, 1928–80, TV play *On the Eve of Publication*]

6 If all the world's a stage, and all the men and women merely players, where do all the audiences come from? [Denis Norden, 1922– , *My Word*, 30 Nov.]

7 I know two kinds of audience only – one coughing and one not coughing. [Artur Schnabel, 1882–1951, *My Life and Music*, Pt II, Ch. 10]; see 1

See also ACTING, MUSIC

AUTOMOBILES, see CARS

AUSTRALIA

1 Being lost in Australia gives you a lovely feeling of security. [Bruce Chatwin, 1940–89, *Songlines*, 10]

2 Earth is here so kind [Australia], that just tickle her with a hoe and she laughs with a harvest. [Douglas Jerrold, 1803–57, *Wit and Opinions*, 'A Land of Plenty']

3 The indifference – the fern-dark indifference of this remote golden Australia. Not to care – from the bottom of one's soul, not to care. [D H Lawrence, 1885–1930, *Kangaroo*, Ch. 10]

4 Australia is not very exclusive . . . On the visa application they still ask if you've been convicted of a felony – although they are willing to give you a visa even if you haven't been. [P J O'Rourke, 1947– , *Holidays in Hell*]

5 As I see it, the little that is subtle in the Australian character comes from the masculine principle in its women, the feminine in its men. [Patrick White, 1912–90, *Flaws in the Glass*, end of section 1]

AUTUMN

1 How well I know what I mean to do / When the long, dark autumn-evenings come. [Robert Browning, 1812–89, *By the Fire Side*, 1]

2 The apples fell and the swallows crossed off the days. [Anthony Carson, *A Rose by Any Other Name*, Ch. 21]

3 I saw old Autumn in the misty morn / Stand shadowless like Silence, listening / To silence. [Thomas Hood, 1799–1845, ode: *Autumn*]

4 Season of mists and mellow fruitfulness, / Close bosom-friend of the maturing sun; / Conspiring with him how to load and bless / With fruit the vines that round the thatch-eaves run. [John Keats, 1795–1821, *To Autumn*, 1]

5 Where are the songs of Spring? Ay, where are they? / Think not of them, thou hast thy music too. [John Keats, 1795–1821, *To Autumn*, 3]

6 The autumn always gets me badly, as it breaks into colours. I want to go south, where there is no autumn, where the cold doesn't crouch over one like a snow-leopard waiting to pounce. The heart of the North is dead, and the fingers are corpse fingers. [D H Lawrence, 1885–1930, letter to J Middleton Murry, 3 Oct. 1924]

7 O wild West Wind, thou breath of Autumn's being, / Thou, from whose unseen presence the leaves dead / Are driven, like ghosts from an enchanter fleeing, / Yellow, and black, and pale, and hectic red, / Pestilence-stricken multitudes. [P B Shelley, 1792–1822, *Ode to the West Wind*, 1]

8 And I rose / In rainy autumn / And walked abroad in a shower of all my days. [Dylan Thomas, 1914–53, *Poem in October*]

9 *Les sanglots longs / Des violons / De l'automne / Blessent mon coeur / D'une langueur / Monotone.* – The long sobs of the autumn violins infect my heart with a monotonous languor. [Paul Verlaine, 1844–96, *Chanson d'automne*]

10 The swallows are making them ready to fly, / Wheeling out on a windy sky: / Goodbye, Summer, goodbye, goodbye. [J G Whyte-Melville, 1821–78, *Goodbye, Summer*]

See also SEASONS, SPRING, SUMMER, WINTER

B

BABIES

1 Never put a hot baby on a cold slab. [anon.]

2 'I have no name: / I am but two days old.' / What shall I call thee? / 'I happy am, / Joy is my name.' / Sweet joy befall thee! [William Blake, 1757–1827, *Songs of Innocence*, 'Infant Joy']

3 There is no finer investment for any community than putting milk into babies. [Winston Churchill, 1874–1965, BBC radio broadcast, 21 Mar. 1943]

4 Weep not, my wanton, smile upon my knee; / When thou art old there's grief enough for thee. / Mother's wag, pretty boy, / Father's sorrow, father's joy. [Robert Greene, 1560?–92, *Sephestia's Song*]

5 A loud noise at one end and no sense of responsibility at the other. [Mgr Ronald Knox, 1888–1957, definition of a baby, quoted by C Blakemore in BBC Reith Lecture, in *Listener*, 9 Dec. 1976]

6 Where did you come from, baby dear? / Out of the everywhere into here. [George Macdonald, 1824–1905, *At the Back of the North Wind*, Ch. 33, Song]

7 You must have been a beautiful baby, / 'Cos baby just look at you now. [Johnny Mercer, 1909–76, song: *You Must Have Been a Beautiful Baby*]

8 A bit of talcum / Is always walcum. [Ogden Nash, 1902–71, *The Baby*]

9 Anybody who hates dogs and babies can't be all bad. [(Of W C Fields) Leo Rosten, 1908–97, at Masquers' Club Dinner, Hollywood, 16 Feb. 1939. Often misquoted as 'children and dogs' and wrongly attr. to Fields]

10 I once knew a chap who had a system of just hanging the baby on the clothes line to dry and he was greatly admired by his fellow citizens for having discovered a wonderful innovation on changing a diaper. [Damon Runyon, 1884–1946, *Short Takes*, 'Diaper Dexterity']

11 How ugly babies are! How heedless / Of all else than their bulging selves – / Like sumo wrestlers, plush with needless / Kneadable flesh – like mutant elves / . . . (A pity that the blubbering blobs / Come unequipped with volume knobs). [Vikram Seth, 1952– , *The Golden Gate*, 13, 47]

12 Baby, sleep a little longer, / Till the little limbs are stronger. [Alfred, Lord Tennyson, 1809–92, *Sea Dreams*, Song]

See also CHILDHOOD

BALDNESS

1 Go up, thou bald head. [Bible, OT, 2 *Kings* 2:23]

2 He had no wool on de top of his head / In de place where de wool ought to grow. [Stephen Foster, 1826–64, *Uncle Ned*]

3 There is more felicity on the far side of baldness than young men can possibly imagine. [Logan Pearsall Smith, 1865–1946, *Last Words*]

BATTLES

1 The combat deepens. On, ye brave, / Who rush to glory, or the grave! / Wave, Munich! all thy banners wave, / And charge with all thy chivalry! [Thomas Campbell, 1777–1844, *Hohenlinden*]

2 *Et le combat cessa, faute de combattants.* – And the battle ended through lack of combatants. [Pierre Corneille, 1606–84, *Le Cid*, IV. iii]

3 I remember Drake ... would call the Enterprise the singeing of the King of Spain's beard. [(Of Cadiz, 1587) Sir Francis Drake, 1540?–96, in F Bacon, *Considerations Touching a War with Spain*]

4 There is plenty of time to win this game, and to thrash the Spaniards too. [Sir Francis Drake, 1540?–96, when the Armada was sighted, 20 July 1588, attr.]

5 One of us two, Herminius, / Shall never more go home. / I will lay on for Tusculum, / And lay thou on for Rome! [Lord Macaulay, 1800–1859, *Lays of Ancient Rome*, 'The Battle of Lake Regillus', 27]

6 It is warm work; and this day may be the last to any of us at a moment. But mark you! I would not be elsewhere for thousands. [(At Battle of Copenhagen) Horatio, Lord Nelson, 1758–1805, in R Southey, *Life of Nelson*, Ch. 7]

7 Don't one of you fire until you see the whites of their eyes. [Israel Putnam, 1715–90, at Bunker Hill, 17 June 1775. Also attr. to W Prescott and others]

8 I am afeard there are few die well that die in a battle; for how can they charitably dispose of anything when blood is their argument? [William Shakespeare, 1564–1616, *Henry V*, IV. i. (149)]

9 What use are cartridges in battle? I always carry chocolate instead. [George Bernard Shaw, 1856–1950, *Arms and the Man*, I]

10 Nothing except a battle lost can be half so melancholy as a battle won. [Duke of Wellington, 1769–1852, dispatch from the field of Waterloo]

11 The battle of Waterloo was won on the playing fields of Eton. [Duke of Wellington, 1769–1852, attr. by Montalembert, *De l'avenir politique de l'Angleterre*]

See ARMY, FIGHTS, SOLDIERS

BEARDS

1 You know it's hard to hear what a bearded man is saying. He can't speak above a whisker. [Herman J Mankiewicz, 1897–1953; in R E Drennan, *Wit's End*]

2 HAMLET: His beard was grizzled, no?
HORATIO: It was, as I have seen it in his life, / A sable silvered. [William Shakespeare, 1564–1616, *Hamlet*, I. ii. 239]

BEAUTY

1 Rugged the breast that beauty cannot tame. [J C Bampfylde, 1754–96, *Sonnet in Praise of Delia*]

2 I am black, but comely, O ye daughters of Jerusalem. [Bible, OT, *Song of Solomon* 1:5]

3 Consider the lilies of the field, how they grow; they toil not, neither do they spin: / And yet I say unto you, that even Solomon in all his glory was not arrayed like one of these. [Bible, NT, *St Matthew* 6:28]

4 For beauty being the best of all we know / Sums up the unsearchable and secret aims / Of nature. [Robert Bridges, 1844–1930, *The Growth of Love*, 8]

5 If you get simple beauty and nought else, / You get about the best thing God invents. [Robert Browning, 1812–89, *Fra Lippo Lippi*, 217]

6 Beauty in distress is much the most affecting beauty. [Edmund Burke, 1729–97, *On the Sublime and Beautiful*, III, ix]

7 She walks in beauty, like the night / Of cloudless climes and starry skies; / And all that's best of dark and bright / Meet in her aspect and her eyes. [Lord Byron, 1788–1824, *Hebrew Melodies*, 'She Walks in Beauty']

8 Nor be, what man should ever be, / The friend of Beauty in distress? [Lord Byron, 1788–1824, *To Florence*]

9 Rose-cheeked Laura, come; / Sing thou smoothly with thy beauty's / Silent music, either other/ Sweetly gracing. [Thomas Campion, 1567–1620, *Laura*]

10 Oh no, it wasn't the aeroplanes. It was Beauty killed the Beast. [James Creelman, 1901–41, and Ruth Rose, final words of film *King Kong*, 1933 version]

11 Look thy last on all things lovely, / Every hour. [Walter de la Mare, 1873–1956, *Fare Well*]

12 Though we travel the world over to find the beautiful, we must carry it with us or we find it not. [Ralph Waldo Emerson, 1803–82, *Essays*, 'Art']

13 Beauty is always the first to hear about the sins of the world. [Jean Giraudoux, 1882–1944, *Duel of Angels*, I]

14 Beauty in things exists in the mind which contemplates them. [David Hume, 1711–76, *Essays*, 'Of Tragedy']

15 Beauty is altogether in the eye of the beholder. [Margaret Hungerford, 1855–97, *Molly Bawn*]

16 Beauty for some provides escape, / Who gain a happiness in eyeing / The gorgeous buttocks of the ape / Or Autumn sunsets exquisitely dying. [Aldous Huxley, 1894–1963, *The Ninth Philosopher's Song*]

17 A thing of beauty is a joy for ever: / Its loveliness increases; it will never / Pass into nothingness. [John Keats, 1795–1821, *Endymion*, Bk i, 1]

18 'Beauty is truth, truth beauty,' – That is all / Ye know on earth, and all ye need to know. [John Keats, 1795–1821, *Ode on a Grecian Urn*, 5]

19 I'm tired of all this nonsense about beauty being only skin-deep. That's deep enough. What do you want – an adorable pancreas? [Jean Kerr, 1923– , *The Snake Has All the Lines*, 'Mirror, Mirror']

20 A woman who cannot be ugly is not beautiful. [Karl Kraus, 1874–1936, *Half-truths and One-and-a-half Truths*, 'Not for Women']

21 How does it feel to be one of the beautiful people, now that you know who you are? [John Lennon, 1940-1980, and Paul McCartney, 1942– , song: *Baby You're a Rich Man*]

22 Oh, thou art fairer than the evening air / Clad in the beauty of a thousand stars. [Christopher Marlowe, 1564–93, *Doctor Faustus*, 1367]

23 She got her good looks from her father – he's a plastic surgeon. [Groucho Marx, 1895–1977, in *New Woman*, Apr. 1989]

24 Euclid alone / Has looked on Beauty bare, Fortunate they / Who, though once only and then but far away, / Have heard her massive sandal set on stone. [Edna St Vincent Millay, 1892–1950, *Euclid Alone Has Looked on Beauty Bare*]

25 Beauty is Nature's brag, and must be shown / In courts, at feasts, and high solemnities. [John Milton, 1608–74, *Comus*, 745]

26 Beauty stands / In the admiration only of weak minds / Led captive. [John Milton, 1608–74, *Paradise Regained*, Bk ii, 220]

27 Yet beauty, though injurious, hath strange power, / After offence returning, to regain / Love once possessed. [John Milton, 1608–74, *Samson Agonistes*, 1003]

28 Beauty is but a flower / Which wrinkles will devour; / Brightness falls from the air, / Queens have died young and fair, / Dust hath closed Helen's eye, / I am sick, I must die. / Lord, have mercy on us! [Thomas Nashe, 1567–1601, *In Plague Time*]

29 The flowers anew, returning seasons bring! / But beauty faded has no second spring. [Ambrose Philips, *c*.1674–1749, *The First Pastoral*, 55]

30 I hate that aesthetic game of the eye and the mind ... played by these connoisseurs, these mandarins who 'appreciate' beauty. What *is* beauty, anyway? There's no such thing. I never 'appreciate', any more than I 'like'. I love or I hate. [Pablo Picasso, 1881–1973, in Françoise Gilot and Carlton Lake, *Life with Picasso*, Pt 6]

31 This is that Lady Beauty, in whose praise / Thy voice and hand shake still, – long known to thee / By flying hair and fluttering hem, – the beat / Following her daily of thy heart and feet, / How passionately and irretrievably, / In what fond flight, how many ways and days! [Dante Gabriel Rossetti, 1828–82, *The House of Life*, 77, 'Soul's Beauty']

32 Remember that the most beautiful things in the world are the most useless; peacocks and lilies for instance. [John Ruskin, 1819–1900, *The Stones of Venice*, I, Ch. 2, §17]

33 I always say beauty is only sin deep. [Saki (H H Munro), 1870–1916, *Reginald's Choir Treat*]

34 Beauty provoketh thieves sooner than gold. [William Shakespeare, 1564–1616, *As You Like It*, I. iii. (113)]

35 She never yet was foolish that was fair. [*Othello*, II. i. 136]

36 O! she doth teach the torches to burn bright. / It seems she hangs upon the cheek of night / Like a rich jewel in an Ethiop's ear. [*Romeo and Juliet*, I. v. (48)]

37 Beauty itself doth of itself persuade / The eyes of men without an orator. [*The Rape of Lucrece*, 29]

38 From fairest creatures we desire increase, / That thereby beauty's rose might never die. [*Sonnets*, 1]

39 Sometimes too hot the eye of heaven shines, / And often is his gold complexion dimmed; / And every fair from fair sometime declines. [*Sonnets*, 18]

40 To me, fair friend, you never can be old, / For as you were when first your eye I eyed, / Such seems your beauty still. [*Sonnets*, 104]

41 For she was beautiful – her beauty made / The bright world dim, and everything beside / Seemed like the fleeting image of a shade. [P B Shelley, 1792–1822, *The Witch of Atlas*, 137]

42 Beauty is momentary in the mind – / The fitful tracing of a portal; / But in the flesh it is immortal. [Wallace Stevens, 1879–1955, *Peter Quince at the Clavier*]

43 For loveliness / Needs not the foreign aid of ornament, / But is, when unadorned, adorned the most. [James Thomson, 1700–1748, *The Seasons*, 'Autumn', 204]

44 If truth is beauty, how come no one has their hair done in the library? [Lily Tomlin, 1939– , in *Was It Good for You Too?* ed. Bob Chieger]; see 18

45 All changed, changed utterly: / A terrible beauty is born. [W B Yeats, 1865–1939, *Easter 1916*]

46 A woman of so shining loveliness / That men threshed corn at midnight by a tress, / A little stolen tress. [W B Yeats, 1865–1939, *The Secret Rose*]

See also UGLINESS

BEDS

1 The cool kindliness of sheets, that soon / Smooth away trouble; and the rough male kiss / Of blankets. [Rupert Brooke, 1887–1915, *The Great Lover*]

2 Lying in bed would be an altogether perfect and supreme experience if only one had a coloured pencil long enough to draw on the ceiling. [G K Chesterton, 1874–1936, *Tremendous Trifles*]

3 Ample make this bed. / Make this bed with awe; / In it wait till judgement break / Excellent and fair. [Emily Dickinson, 1830–86, *Ample Make This Bed*]

4 'Bed,' as the Italian proverb succinctly puts it, 'is the poor man's opera.' [Aldous Huxley, 1894–1963, *Heaven and Hell*]

5 Now deep in my bed / I turn and the world turns on the other side. [Elizabeth Jennings, 1926– , *In the Night*]

6 If God had not meant everyone to be in bed by ten-thirty, He would never have provided the ten o'clock newscast. [Garrison Keillor, 1942– , *Lake Wobegon Days*, 'News']

7 O! it's nice to get up in the mornin', / But it's nicer to stay in bed. [Harry Lauder, 1870–1950, song]

8 No human being believes that any other human being has a right to be in bed when he himself is up. [Robert Lynd, 1879–1949; in *Apt and Amusing Quotations*, ed. G F Lamb, 'Bed']

9 I forget who it was that recommended men for their soul's good to do each day two things they disliked ... it is a precept that I have followed scrupulously; for every day I have got up and I have gone to bed. [W Somerset Maugham, 1874–1965, *The Moon and Sixpence*, Ch. 1]

10 And so to bed. [Samuel Pepys, 1633–1703, *Diary*, 20 Apr. 1660 and *passim*]

11 Not to be a-bed after midnight is to be up betimes. [William Shakespeare, 1564–1616, *Twelfth Night*, II. iii. 1]

12 Only a fool would make the bed every day. [Nancy Spain, 1917–64, in Quentin Crisp, *The Naked Civil Servant*, Ch. 15]

13 In winter I get up at night / And dress by yellow candle-light. / In summer quite the other way, / I have to go to bed by day. [Robert Louis Stevenson, 1850–94, *A Child's Garden of Verses*, 1, 'Bed in Summer']

14 Must we to bed indeed? Well then, / Let us arise and go like men, / And face with an undaunted tread / The long black passage up to bed. [Robert Louis Stevenson, 1850–94, *A Child's Garden of Verses*, 41, 'North-West Passage, 1, Good-Night']

15 I have known couples stay up till three in the morning, each hoping the other would finally give in and make the bed. Perhaps after all our mothers were right, when they warned us that as you lie in your bed, so you must make it. [Katharine Whitehorn, 1926– , in *Observer*, 28 Aug. 1985]

16 Our bed's only MFI; it won't take multiple orgasm. [Victoria Wood, 1953– , stage performance at Strand Theatre, London, Oct. 1990]

See also SLEEPING

BEER

1 Bring us in no browne bred, for that is made of brane, / Nor bring us in no white bred, for therein is no gane, / But bring us in good ale! [anon., *Bring Us in Good Ale*]

2 I feel no pain, dear mother, now / But oh! I am so dry! / Oh, take me to a brewery / And leave me there to die. [anon., sea shanty]

3 O Beer! O Hodgson, Guinness, Allsop, Bass! / Names that should be on every infant's tongue! [C S Calverley, 1831–84, *Beer*]

4 I woke up with an aching head / As usual. / I can't remember going to bed / As usual. / My stomach's feeling very queer, / There's a thunderstorm in my right ear, / It must have been McEwan's beer / As usual. [Billy Connolly, 1942– , *Gullible's Travels*, written by John Murphy]

5 I have fed purely upon ale; I have eat my ale, drank my ale, and I always sleep upon ale. [George Farquhar, 1678–1707, *The Beaux' Stratagem*, I. i]

6 Ale, man, ale's the stuff to drink / For fellows whom it hurts to think. [A E Housman, 1859–1936, *A Shropshire Lad*, 62]

7 Mr Joseph Gibbs finished his half-pint . . . with the slowness of a man unable to see where the next was coming from. [W W Jacobs, 1863–1943, *Ship's Company*, 'Friends in Need']

8 What two ideas are more inseparable than Beer and Britannia? [Sydney Smith, 1771–1845, in H Pearson, *The Smith of Smiths*, Ch. 11]

9 I can not eat but little meat, / My stomach is not good; / But sure I think, that I can drink / With him that wears a hood. / Though I go bare, take ye no care, / I am nothing a-cold; / I stuff my skin, so full within, / Of jolly good ale and old. [William Stevenson, 1546?–75, *Gammer Gurton's Needle*, II, song (authorship is disputed)]

10 Champagne certainly gives one werry gentlemanly ideas, but for a continuance, I don't know but I should prefer mild hale. [R S Surtees, 1803–64, *Jorrocks' Jaunts and Jollities*, No. 9]

11 O plump head-waiter at The Cock, / To which I most resort / How goes the time? 'Tis five o'clock. / Go fetch a pint of port. [Alfred, Lord Tennyson, 1809–92, *Will Waterproof's Lyrical Monologue*, 1]

See also DRINK: STRONG, WINE

BEGINNINGS

1 He would like to start from scratch. Where is scratch? [Elias Canetti, 1905–94, *The Human Province*, '1965']

2 'Begin at the beginning,' the King said, gravely, 'and go on till you come to the end; then stop.' [Lewis Carroll, 1832–98, *Alice in Wonderland*, Ch. 12]

3 It is better to be the lichen on a rock than the President's carnation. Only by avoiding the beginning of things can we escape their ending. [Cyril Connolly, 1903–74, *The Unquiet Grave*, Ch. 1]

4 Distance doesn't matter; it is only the first step that is difficult. [(On the legend that St Denis walked six miles, carrying his head in his hand) Marquise du Deffand, 1697–1780, letter to d'Alembert, 7 July 1763]

5 In my beginning is my end. [T S Eliot, 1888–1965, *Four Quartets*, 'East Coker', I]

6 Large streams from little fountains flow, / Tall oaks from little acorns grow. [David Everett, 1770–1813, *Lines written for a School Declamation*]

7 The first blow is half the battle. [Oliver Goldsmith, 1728–74, *She Stoops to Conquer*, II]

8 He who has begun has half done. Have the courage to be wise. [Horace, 65–8 BC, *Epistles*, I, ii, 40]

9 We stand today on the edge of a new frontier. [President John F Kennedy, 1917–63, speech on his adoption as Democratic presidential candidate, 15 July 1960]

BEHAVIOUR

1 Conduct is three-fourths of our life and its largest concern. [Matthew Arnold, 1822–88, *Literature and Dogma*, Ch. 1, §3]

2 The trouble is, whenever I meet anybody they're always on their best behaviour. And when one is on one's best behaviour one isn't always at one's best. [Alan Bennett, 1934– , *Single Spies*, 'A Question of Attribution']

3 By their fruits ye shall know them. [Bible, NT, *St Matthew* 7:20]

4 How we [the Beats] behave in private is actually the ultimate politics. So the original literary inspiration was to behave in public as we do in private. [Allen Ginsberg, 1926–97, in Barry Miles, *Ginsberg*, Ch. 17]

5 But Fidgety Phil / He won't sit still: / He wriggles / And giggles, / and then, I declare, / Swings backwards and forwards, / And tilts up his chair. [Heinrich Hoffman, 1809–74, *Struwwelpeter*, 'Fidgety Phil']

6 We may give advice, but we can never prompt behaviour. [Duc de La Rochefoucauld, 1613–80, *Masters and Men*, 378]

7 Considering how bad men are, it is wonderful how well they behave. [Salvador de Madariaga, 1886–1978, *Morning without Noon*, Pt 1, Ch. 14]

8 Never descend to the ways of those above you. [George Mallaby, 1902–78, *From My Level*]

9 Go directly, – see what she's doing and tell her she mustn't! [*Punch*, lxiii (1872), 202]

10 You would play upon me; you would seem to know my stops; you would pluck out the heart of my mystery; you would sound me from my lowest note to the top of my compass. [William Shakespeare, 1564–1616, *Hamlet*, III. ii. (387)]

11 Do not do unto others as you would they should do unto you. Their tastes may not be the same. [George Bernard Shaw, 1856–1950, *Man and Superman*, 'Maxims for Revolutionists', The Golden Rule]

12 If people behaved in the way nations do they would all be put in straitjackets. [Tennessee Williams, 1911–83, BBC interview]

See also ACTION

BELIEF

1 Lord, I believe; help thou mine unbelief. [Bible, NT, *St Mark* 9:24]

2 Vain are the thousand creeds / That move men's hearts: unutterably vain. [Emily Brontë, 1818–48, *Last Lines*]

3 *Action will furnish belief*, – but will that belief be the true one? / This is the point, you know. [Arthur Hugh Clough, 1819–61, *Amours de voyage*, V, 2]

4 Man . . . is a being born to believe. [Benjamin Disraeli, 1804–81, speech at Oxford Diocesan Conference, 25 Nov. 1864]

5 The believer will fight another believer over a shade of difference: the doubter fights only with himself. [Graham Greene, 1904–91, *Monsignor Quixote*, Pt 1, Ch. 4]

6 Any stigma, as the old saying is, will serve to beat a dogma. [Philip Guedalla, 1889–1944, *Masters and Men*, 'Ministers of State']

7 As I get older I seem to believe less and less and yet to believe what I do believe more and more. [Rt Revd David Jenkins, 1925– ; *Observer*, 'Sayings of the Week', 6 Nov. 1988]

8 The constant assertion of belief is an indication of fear. [J Krishnamurti, 1895–1986, *The Second Penguin Krishnamurti Reader*, Ch. 14]

9 Credulity is the man's weakness, but the child's strength. [Charles Lamb, 1775–1834, *Essays of Elia*, 'Witches and Other Night Fears']

10 The man who believes in giraffes would swallow anything. [Adrian Mitchell, 1932– , *Loose Leaf Poem*]

11 [When asked if he believed in God] I know more than I can express in words, and the little I can express would not have been expressed, had I not known more. [Vladimir Nabokov, 1899–1977, *Strong Opinions*, Ch. 3]

12 Never believe in mirrors or newspapers. [John Osborne, 1929–94, *Hotel in Amsterdam*, I]

13 He who believes in nothing still needs a girl to believe in him. [Eugen Rosenstock-Huessy, 1888–1959, in W H Auden, *A Certain World*]

14 To die for one's beliefs is to put too high a price on conjecture. [Bertrand Russell, 1872–1970, attr.]

15 I confused things with their names: that is belief. [Jean-Paul Sartre, 1905–80, *Words*, Pt 2]

16 I am a sort of collector of religions; and the curious thing is that I find I can believe in them all. [George Bernard Shaw, 1856–1950, *Major Barbara*, II]

17 Believing where we cannot prove. [Alfred, Lord Tennyson, 1809–92, *In Memoriam*, Prologue]

18 *Credo quia impossibile.* – I believe because it is impossible. [(Usual adapt. of: *Certum est quia impossibile est.* – It is certain ...) Tertullian, c.160–c.220, *De Carne Christi*, 5]

19 Orthodoxy is my doxy; heterodoxy is another man's doxy. [William Warburton, 1698–1779, remark to Lord Sandwich: in Joseph Priestley, *Memoirs*, Vol. 1, p. 372]

20 If there were a verb meaning 'to believe falsely', it would not have any significant first person, present indicative. [Ludwig Wittgenstein, 1889–1951, *Philosophical Investigations*, Pt 2, sect. 10]

See also DOUBT, FAITHS

BELLS

1 In summertime on Bredon / The bells they sound so clear; / Round both the shires they ring them / In steeples far and near, / A happy noise to hear. [A E Housman, 1859–1936, *A Shropshire Lad*, 19]

2 Bells are profane, a tune may be religious. [Ben Jonson, 1573–1637, *The Alchemist*, III. ii]

3 Keeping time, time, time, / In a sort of Runic rhyme, / To the tintinnabulation that so musically wells / From the bells, bells, bells, bells. [Edgar Allan Poe, 1809–49, *The Bells*, 9]

4 The bell invites me. / Hear it not, Duncan; for it is a knell / That summons thee to heaven or to hell. [William Shakespeare, 1564–1616, *Macbeth*, II. i. 62]

5 Ring out, wild bells, to the wild sky ... Ring out the old, ring in the new, / Ring, happy bells, across the snow: / The year is going, let him go;/ Ring out the false, ring in the true. [Alfred, Lord Tennyson, 1809–92, *In Memoriam*, 106]

BEREAVEMENT, see MOURNING

BETRAYAL, see LOYALTY

THE BIBLE

1 No man, who knows nothing else, knows even his Bible. [Matthew Arnold, 1822–88, *Culture and Anarchy*, Ch. 5]

2 He will find one English book and one only, where, as in the *Iliad* itself, perfect plainness of speech is allied with perfect nobleness; and that book is the Bible. [Matthew Arnold, 1822–88, *On Translating Homer*, 3]

3 The white man discovered the Cross by way of the Bible, but the black man discovered the Bible by way of the Cross. [James Baldwin, 1924–87, *Evidence of Things Not Seen*]

4 Both read the Bible day and night, / But thou read'st black where I read white. [William Blake, 1757–1827, *The Everlasting Gospel*, α]

5 In the twentieth century our highest praise is to call the Bible 'the World's Best-Seller'. And it has come to be more and more difficult to say whether we think it is a best-seller because it is great, or vice versa. [Daniel Boorstin, 1914– , *The Image*, 4]

6 The Bible ... is a lesson in how not to write for the movies. [Raymond Chandler, 1888–1959, letter to Edgar Carter, 28 Mar. 1947]

7 Just knows, and knows no more, her Bible true – / A truth the brilliant Frenchman never knew. [William Cowper, 1731–1800, *Truth*, 327]

8 It ain't necessarily so, / It ain't necessarily so – / De t'ings dat yo' li'ble / To read in de Bible – / It ain't necessarily so. [Ira Gershwin, 1896–1983, and Du Bose Heyward, 1885–1940, *Porgy and Bess*, song: 'It Ain't Necessarily So']

9 Abraham ... circumcised himself. Now this is not an easy thing to do – try it sometime and see. [Joseph Heller, 1923–99, *God Knows*, 2]

10 The English Bible, a book which, if everything else in our language should perish, would alone suffice to show the whole extent of its beauty and power. [Lord Macaulay, 1800–1859, *On John Dryden*]

11 The number one book of the ages was written by a committee, and it was called The Bible. [(To writers who complained of changes made to their work) Louis B Mayer, 1885–1957; in L Halliwell, *The Filmgoer's Book of Quotes*]

12 Why do they put the Gideon Bibles only in the bedrooms [of hotels], where it's usually too late? And not in the bar-room downstairs? [Christopher Morley, 1890–1957, *Contribution to a Contribution*]

13 There's a Bible on that shelf there. But I keep it next to Voltaire – poison and antidote.

[Bertrand Russell, 1872–1970, in Kenneth Harris, *K H Talking to . . .*]

14 The Bible is literature, not dogma. [George Santayana, 1863–1952, *Introduction to the Ethics of Spinoza*]

15 I read the Penal Code and the Bible. The Bible is a cruel book. Perhaps the cruellest book ever written. [Georges Simenon, 1903–89, interview in John Mortimer, *In Character*]

16 Jesus loves me – this I know, / For the Bible tells me so. [Susan Warner, 1819–85, *The Love of Jesus*]

See also CHRISTIANITY, GOD, JESUS CHRIST, JEWS

BIOGRAPHY/AUTOBIOGRAPHY

1 A shilling life will give you all the facts. [W H Auden 1907–73, *Who's Who*]

2 Geography is about maps, / But Biography is about chaps. [E C Bentley, 1875–1956, *Biography for Beginners*]

3 Autobiographies tell more lies than all but the most self-indulgent fiction. [A S Byatt, 1936– , *Sugar*, 'The Day That E M Forster Died']

4 In our rampantly secular world, biography is now the only certain form of life after death. [David Cannadine, 1950– , in *Observer*, 21 Apr. 1991]

5 A well-written Life is almost as rare as a well-spent one. [Thomas Carlyle, 1795–1881, *Critical and Miscellaneous Essays*, 'Richter']

6 An autobiography is an obituary in serial form with the last instalment missing. [Quentin Crisp, 1908–99, *The Naked Civil Servant*, Ch. 29]

7 Read no history: nothing but biography, for that is life without theory. [Benjamin Disraeli, 1804–81, *Contarini Fleming*, Pt I, Ch. 23]

8 There is properly no history; only biography. [Ralph Waldo Emerson, 1803–82, *Essays*, 'History']

9 Biography is a very definite region bounded on the north by history, on the south by fiction, on the east by obituary, and on the west by tedium. [Philip Guedalla, 1889–1944; *Observer*, 'Sayings of the Week', 3 Mar. 1929]

10 There is no life that can be recaptured wholly; as it was. Which is to say that all biography is ultimately fiction. [Bernard Malamud, 1914–86, *Dubin's Lives*, 1]

11 The only way biography as an undertaking can recover its main function of good storytelling is to go back to its roots. These roots lie in ancestor worship. [Robert Skidelsky, 1939– , in *The Times Literary Supplement*, 13 Nov. 1987]

12 My problem is that I am not frightfully interested in anything, except myself. And of all forms of fiction autobiography is the most gratuitous. [Tom Stoppard, 1937– , *Lord Malquist and Mr Moon*, Pt II, 3]

13 Only when one has lost all curiosity about the future has one reached the age to write an autobiography. [Evelyn Waugh, 1903–66, *Little Learning*, opening words]

BIOLOGY

1 Biology is the study of complicated things that give the appearance of having been designed for a purpose. Physics is the study of simple things that do not tempt us to invoke design. [Richard Dawkins, 1941– , *The Blind Watchmaker*, Ch. 1]

2 The most important hypothesis in all of biology, for example, is that everything that animals do, atoms do. In other words, there is nothing that living creatures do that cannot be understood from the point of view that they are made of atoms acting according to the laws of physics. [Richard Feynman, 1918–88, *Lectures on Physics*, Vol. 1]

See also MATHEMATICS, PHYSICS, SCIENCE

BIRDS

1 I might have been a farmyard hen, / Scratchin' in the sun, / There might have been a crowd of chicks, / After me to run, / There might have been a cockerel fine, / To pay us his respects, / Instead of sittin' here, / Till someone comes and wrings our necks. [Pam Ayres, 1947– , *Some of Me Poetry*, 'The Battery Hen']

2 A robin redbreast in a cage / Puts all Heaven in a rage. [William Blake, 1757–1827, *Auguries of Innocence*]

3 Ornithology used to be an arcane hobby for embittered schoolmasters, dotty spinsters and lonely little boys but now it is as normal a week-end occupation as rug-making or wife-swapping. [Kyril Bonfiglioli, 1928–85, *Don't Point That Thing at Me*, Ch. 18]

4 That's the wise thrush; he sings each song twice over, / Lest you should think he never could recapture / The first fine careless rapture! [Robert Browning, 1812–89, *Home-thoughts from Abroad*]

5 Thou hast no sorrow in thy song, / No winter in thy year! [Michael Bruce, 1746–67, *To the Cuckoo*. Also attr. to John Logan]

6 A light broke in upon my brain, – / It was the carol of a bird; / It ceased, and then it came again, / The sweetest song ear ever heard. [Lord Byron, 1788–1824, *The Prisoner of Chillon*, 10]

7 Pigeons, those dull, unmysterious city unemployables, dressed in their grey, second-hand suits. [Anthony Carson, *On to Timbuctoo*, 12]

8 Mourn, O Graces and Loves, and all men whom the Graces love. My mistress's sparrow is dead, my mistress's pet, which she loved more than her very eyes. [Catullus, 87–54? BC, *Carmina*, 3]

9 The bisy larke, messager of day. [Geoffrey Chaucer, 1340?–1400, *Canterbury Tales*, 'The Knight's Tale', 633]

10 Take it all in all, I do not believe anybody on earth has a worse time than an Emperor penguin. [Apsley Cherry-Garrard, 1882–1959, *The Worst Journey in the World*, Introduction]

11 And hear the pleasant cuckoo, loud and long – / The simple bird that thinks two notes a song. [W H Davies, 1871–1940, *April's Charms*]

12 It was the Rainbow gave thee birth, / And left thee all her lovely hues. [W H Davies, 1871–1940, *The Kingfisher*]

13 The household bird, with the red stomacher. [John Donne, 1571?–1631, *Epithalamions*, 'On the Lady Elizabeth and Count Palatine', 8]

14 The bird would cease and be as other birds / But that he knows in singing not to sing. / The question that he frames in all but words / Is what to make of a diminished thing. [Robert Frost, 1874–1963, *The Oven Bird*]

15 On a tree by a river a little tomtit / Sang 'Willow, titwillow, titwillow'. [W S Gilbert, 1836–1911, *The Mikado*, II]

16 Save that from yonder ivy-mantled tower, / The moping owl does to the moon complain. [Thomas Gray, 1716–71, *Elegy Written in a Country Churchyard*, 3]

17 So zestfully canst thou sing? / And all this indignity, / With God's consent, on thee! / Blinded ere yet a-wing. [Thomas Hardy, 1840–1928, *The Blinded Bird*]

18 So little cause for carolings / Of such ecstatic sound / Was written on terrestrial things / Afar or nigh around, / That I could think there trembled through / His happy good-night air / Some blessed Hope, whereof he knew / And I was unaware. [Thomas Hardy, 1840–1928, *The Darkling Thrush*]

19 I climbed a hill as light fell short, / And rooks came home in scramble sort, / And filled the trees and flapped and fought / And sang themselves to sleep. [Ralph Hodgson, 1871–1962, *The Song of Honour*]

20 I caught this morning morning's minion, kingdom of daylight's dauphin, dapple-dawn-drawn Falcon. [Gerard Manley Hopkins, 1844–89, *The Windhover*]

21 It took the whole of Creation / To produce my foot, my each feather: / Now I hold creation in my foot. [Ted Hughes, 1930–98, *Hawk Roosting*]

22 The common cormorant or shag / Lays eggs inside a paper bag / The reason you will see no doubt / It is to keep the lightning out / But what these unobservant birds / Have never noticed is that herds / Of wandering bears may come with buns / And steal the bags to hold the crumbs. [Christopher Isherwood, 1904–86, in *The Poet's Tongue*, ed. W H Auden and John Garrett]

23 Thou, light-winged Dryad of the trees, / In some melodious plot / of beechen green, and shadows numberless, / Singest of summer in full-throated ease. [John Keats, 1795–1821, *Ode to a Nightingale*, 1]

24 Thou wast not born for death, immortal Bird! / No hungry generations tread thee down; / The voice I hear this passing night was heard / In ancient days by emperor and clown: / Perhaps the self-same song that found a path / Through the sad heart of Ruth, when, sick for home, / She stood in tears amid the alien corn; / The same that oft-times hath / Charmed magic casements, opening on the foam / Of perilous seas, in faery lands forlorn. [John Keats, 1795–1821, *Ode to a Nightingale*, 6]

25 The red-breast whistles from a garden-croft; / And gathering swallows twitter in the skies. [John Keats, 1795–1821, *To Autumn*, 3]

26 Cuckoos, like noise falling in drops off the leaves. [D H Lawrence, 1885–1930, *Fantasia of the Unconscious*, Ch. 4]

27 Shoot all the bluejays you want, if you can hit 'em, but remember it's a sin to kill a mocking-bird. [Harper Lee, 1926– , *To Kill a Mocking-bird*, II, 10]

28 What bird so sings, yet so does wail? / O 'tis the ravished nightingale. / Jug, jug, jug, jug, tereu, she cries. [John Lyly, *Campaspe*, V, i.]

29 A wonderful bird is the pelican, / His bill will hold more than his belican. / He can take in his beak / Enough food for a week, / But I'm darned if I know how the helican. [Dixon Merritt, 1879–1972, *The Pelican*]

30 Sweet bird, that shunn'st the noise of folly, / Most musical, most melancholy! [(Nightingale) John Milton, 1608–74, *Il Penseroso*, 61]

31 To hear the lark begin his flight, / And singing startle the dull night, / From his watch-tower in the skies, / Till the dappled dawn doth rise. [John Milton, 1608–74, *L'Allegro*, 41]

32 All but the wakeful nightingale; / She all night long her amorous descant sung. [John Milton, 1608–74, *Paradise Lost*, Bk iv, 602]

33 That star-enchanted song falls through the air / From lawn to lawn down terraces of sound, / Darts in white arrows on the shadowed ground; / While all the night you sing. [Harold Monro, 1879–1932, *The Nightingale near the House*]

34 The song of canaries / Never varies, / And when they're moulting / They're pretty revolting. [Ogden Nash, 1902–71, *The Canary*]

35 The north wind doth blow, / And we shall have snow, / And what will poor Robin do then? / Poor thing. / He'll sit in a barn, / And keep himself warm, / And hide his head under his wing, / Poor thing. [Nursery rhyme]

36 Take thy beak from out my heart and take thy form from off my door! / Quoth the Raven, 'Nevermore'. [Edgar Allan Poe, 1809–49, *The Raven*, 17]

37 This guest of summer, / The temple-haunting martlet, does approve / By his loved mansionry that the heaven's breath / Smells wooingly here; no jutty, frieze, / Buttress nor coign of vantage, but this bird / Hath made his pendent bed and procreant cradle: / Where they most breed and haunt, I have observed, / The air is delicate. [William Shakespeare, 1564–1616, *Macbeth*, I. vi. 3]

38 It was the owl that shrieked, the fatal bell-man, / Which gives the stern'st good-night. [*Macbeth*, II. ii. 4]

39 It was the nightingale, and not the lark, / That pierced the fearful hollow of thine ear; / Nightly she sings on yon pomegranate tree. [*Romeo and Juliet*, III. v. 2]

40 The eagle suffers little birds to sing, / And is not careful what they mean thereby. [*Titus Andronicus*, IV. iv. (82)]

41 And now this pale swan in her watery nest / Begins the sad dirge of her certain ending. [*The Rape of Lucrece*, 1611]

42 Hail to thee, blithe spirit! / Bird thou never wert, / That from heaven, or near it, / Pourest thy full heart / In profuse strains of unpremeditated art. [P B Shelley, 1792–1822, *To a Skylark*, 1]

43 And robin redbreast / He shall be the priest / The requiem mass to sing, / softly warbeling. [John Skelton, *c.*1460–1529, *Philip Sparrow*, 399]

44 The merry cuckoo, messenger of spring, / His trumpet shrill hath thrice already sounded. [Edmund Spenser, 1552?–99, *Amoretti*, 19]

45 I heard a bird at dawn / Singing sweetly on a tree, / That the dew was on the lawn, / And the wind was on the lea; / But I didn't listen to him, / For he didn't sing to me. [James Stephens, 1882–1950, *The Rivals*]

46 Ringed with the azure world, he stands. / The wrinkled sea beneath him crawls; / He watches from his mountain walls, / And like a thunderbolt he falls. [Alfred, Lord Tennyson, 1809–92, *The Eagle*]

47 Alone and warming his five wits, / The white owl in the belfry sits. [Alfred, Lord Tennyson, 1809–92, song: *The Owl*]

48 Swallow, Swallow, flying, flying South, / Fly to her, and fall upon her gilded eaves, / And tell her, tell her, what I tell to thee. [Alfred, Lord Tennyson, 1809–92, *The Princess*, IV, third song]

49 'Tis just like a summer bird-cage in a garden;

the birds that are without despair to get in, and the birds that are within despair and are in a consumption for fear they shall never get out. [John Webster, 1580?–1625?, *The White Devil*, I. ii. 47]

50 Caged birds accept each other but flight is what they long for. [Tennessee Williams, 1911–83, *Camino Real*, 7]

51 The pious bird with the scarlet breast, / Our little English robin. [William Wordsworth, 1770–1850, *The Redbreast Chasing the Butterfly*]

52 O blithe new-comer! I have heard, / I hear thee and rejoice. / O cuckoo, shall I call thee bird, / Or but a wandering voice? [William Wordsworth, 1770–1850, *To the Cuckoo*]

53 Ethereal minstrel! pilgrim of the sky! / Dost thou despise the earth where cares abound? [William Wordsworth, 1770–1850, *To a Skylark*, 'Ethereal minstrel!...']

54 Let ... / The swan on still St Mary's Lake / Float double, swan and shadow! [William Wordsworth, 1770–1850, *Yarrow Unvisited*]

55 What tumbling cloud did you cleave, / Yellow-eyed hawk of the mind, / Last evening? that I, who had sat / Dumbfounded before a knave, / Should give to my friend / A pretence of wit. [W B Yeats, 1865–1939, *The Hawk*]

56 Unwearied still, lover by lover, / They paddle in the cold / Companionable streams or climb the air. [W B Yeats, 1865–1939, *The Wild Swans at Coole*]

57 The Swallows twisting here and there / Round unseen corners of the air / Upstream and down so quickly passed / I wondered that their shadows flew as fast. [Andrew Young, 1885–1971, *The Swallows*]

See also ANIMALS

BIRTH

1 In sorrow thou shalt bring forth children. [Bible, OT, *Genesis* 3:16]

2 My mother groaned, my father wept, / Into the dangerous world I leapt; / Helpless, naked, piping loud, / Like a fiend hid in a cloud. [William Blake, 1757–1827, *Songs of Experience*, 'Infant Sorrow']

3 For man's greatest crime is to have been born. [Pedro Calderón de la Barca, 1600–1681, *Life is a Dream*, 1]

4 To be born into this earth is to be born into uncongenial surroundings, hence to be born into a romance. [G K Chesterton, 1874–1936, *Heretics*, 14]

5 We are not born alone. To be born for each man is a getting to know. Every birth is a getting to know. [Paul Claudel, 1868–1955, *Traité de la connaissance du monde*]

6 He not busy being born / Is busy dying. [Bob Dylan, 1941– , song: *It's Alright, Ma (I'm Only Bleeding)*]

7 Man's main task in life is to give *birth* to himself. [Erich Fromm, 1900–1980, *Man for Himself*, Ch. 4]

8 If men could get pregnant abortion would be a sacrament. [Florynce Kennedy, 1916– , in *Ms*, Mar. 1973]

9 I'll simply say here that I was born Beatrice Gladys Lillie at an extremely tender age because my mother needed a fourth at meals. [Beatrice Lillie, 1894–1989, *Every Other Inch a Lady*, Ch. 1]

10 What's this about high birth and and low birth? All births take place at the same height. [Joseph Prescott, 1913– , *Aphorisms and Other Observations*, Second Series, 'Miscellany']

11 I was born because it was a habit in those days, people dident know anything else. [Will Rogers, 1879–1935, *Autobiography*, Ch. 1]

12 When we are born, we cry that we are come / To this great stage of fools. [William Shakespeare, 1564–1616, *King Lear*, IV. vi. (187)]

13 'Do you know who made you?' 'Nobody as I knows on,' said the child, with a short laugh ... 'I 'spect I growed. Don't think nobody never made me.' [Harriet Beecher Stowe, 1811–96, *Uncle Tom's Cabin*, Ch. 20]

14 'Who was your mother?' 'Never had none,' said the child, with another grin. 'Never had any mother? What do you mean? Where were you born?' 'Never was born,' persisted Topsy: 'never had no father, nor mother, nor nothin'. I was raised by a speculator.' [Harriet Beecher Stowe, 1811–96, *Uncle Tom's Cabin*, Ch. 20]

15 Before I knocked and flesh let enter, / With liquid hands tapped on the womb, / I who was shapeless as the water / That shaped the

Jordan near my home / Was brother to Mnetha's daughter / And sister to the fathering worm. [Dylan Thomas, 1914–53, *Before I Knocked*]

16 Some men a forward motion love, / But I by backward steps would move, / And when this dust falls to the urn, / In that state I came, return. [Henry Vaughan, 1622–95, *The Retreat*]

17 I was born there because I wanted to be near my parents. [Max Wall, 1908–90, in obituary, *Guardian*, 23 May 1990]

18 Our birth is but a sleep and a forgetting: / The soul that rises with us, our life's star, / Hath had elsewhere its setting, / And cometh from afar: / Not in entire forgetfulness, / And not in utter nakedness, / But trailing clouds of glory do we come / From God who is our home. [William Wordsworth, 1770–1850, *Ode, Intimations of Immortality*, 5]

See also DEATH, PARENTS

BIRTHDAYS

1 I know there was something, something pretty terrible, too. Not just plain terrible. This was fancy terrible; this was terrible with raisins in it. Ah, yes, I have it. This is my birthday. [Dorothy Parker, 1893–1967, *The Middle or Blue Period*]

2 If one doesn't get birthday presents it can remobilize very painfully the persecutory anxiety which usually follows birth. [Henry Reed, 1914–86, BBC radio drama *The Primal Scene, As It Were*]

3 Because the birthday of my life / Is come, my love is come to me. [Christina Rossetti, 1830–94, *A Birthday*]

4 Birthdays? yes, in a general way; / For the most if not for the best of men: / You were born (I suppose) on a certain day: / So was I: or perhaps in the night: what then? [J K Stephen, 1859–92, *Sincere Flattery of R B*]

5 My birthday began with the water / Birds and the birds of the winged trees flying my name. [Dylan Thomas, 1914–53, *Poem in October*]

BLACK CULTURE

1 Even those who have not been anywhere know that the black man who has spent his life fleeing from himself into whiteness has no power if the white master gives him none. [Ayi Kwei Armah, 1939– , *The Beautyful Ones are Not Yet Born*, Ch. 6]

2 The white man discovered the Cross by way of the Bible, but the black man discovered the Bible by way of the Cross. [James Baldwin, 1924–87, *Evidence of Things Not Seen*]

3 My mother bore me in the southern wild, / And I am black, but O! my soul is white. [William Blake, 1757–1827, *Songs of Innocence*, 'The Little Black Boy']

4 The negroes more philosophy displayed, – / Used to it, no doubt, as eels are to be flayed. [Lord Byron, 1788–1824, *Don Juan*, V, 7]

5 *ma négritude n'est pas une pierre, sa surdité ruée contre la clameur du jour / ma négritude n'est pas une taie d'eau morte sur l'oeil mort de la terre / ma négritude n'est ni une tour ni une cathédrale.* – my negritude is not a stone, its deafness thrown against the clamour of the day / my negritude is not a speck of dead water on the dead eye of earth / my negritude is neither a tower nor a cathedral. [Aimé Césaire, 1913– , *Cahier d'un retour au pays natal*]

6 However painful it may be for me to accept this conclusion, I am obliged to state it: for the black man there is only one destiny. And it is white. [Frantz Fanon, 1925–61, *Black Skin, White Masks*, Introduction]

7 It's hard being black. You ever been black? I was black once – when I was poor. [Larry Holmes, 1949– , quoted by J Bernard in *Spectator*, 11 July 1987]

8 Because just *one* drop of black blood makes a coloured man. *One* drop – you are a Negro! ... Black is powerful. [Langston Hughes, 1902–67, *Simple Takes a Wife*, p. 85]

9 I want to be the white man's brother, not his brother-in-law. [Martin Luther King Jr, 1929–68, in *New York Journal-American*, 10 Sept. 1962]

10 It's just like when you've got some coffee that's too black, which means it's too strong. What do you do? You integrate it with cream, you make it weak ... It used to wake you up, now it puts you to sleep. [(On Black Power and the Civil Rights movement) Malcolm X, 1925–65, *Malcolm X Speaks*, Ch. 14]

11 I'd rather be black than gay because when you're black you don't have to tell your mother. [Charles Pierce, 1926–99; in *Penguin Dictionary of Modern Humorous Quotations*, comp. Fred Metcalf]

BLESSINGS

1 The Lord bless thee, and keep thee. The Lord make his face shine upon thee, and be gracious unto thee. [Bible, OT, *Numbers* 6:24]

2 Blessed are the pure in heart: for they shall see God. Blessed are the peacemakers: for they shall be called the children of God. [Bible, NT, *St Matthew* 5:8]

3 Blessed are the dead which die in the Lord from henceforth: Yea, saith the Spirit, that they may rest from their labours; and their works do follow them. [Bible, NT, *Revelation* 14:13]

4 Lord, dismiss us with Thy blessing, / Thanks for mercies past received. [H J Buckoll, 1803–71, hymn]

5 A spring of love gushed from my heart, / And I blessed them unaware. [Samuel Taylor Coleridge, 1772–1834, *The Ancient Mariner*, Pt IV]

6 'God bless us every one!' said Tiny Tim, the last of all. [Charles Dickens, 1812–70, *A Christmas Carol*, Stave 3]

7 When God at first made man, / Having a glass of blessings standing by, / Let us (said he) pour on him all we can: / Let the world's riches, which dispersèd lie, / Contract into a span. [George Herbert, 1593–1633, *The Pulley*]

8 E'en crosses from his sov'reign hand / Are blessings in disguise. [James Hervey, 1714–58, *Reflections on a Flower-Garden*]

9 The crowning blessing of life – to be born with a bias to some pursuit. [S G Tallentyre, 1868–1919, *The Friends of Voltaire*]

See also PRAYERS

BLINDNESS

1 If the blind lead the blind, both shall fall into the ditch. [Bible, NT, *St Matthew* 15:14]

2 An old man / With an old soul, and both extremely blind. [Lord Byron, 1788–1824, *The Vision of Judgement*, 23]

3 When I consider how my light is spent / Ere half my days in this dark world and wide, / And that one talent which is death to hide, / Lodged with me useless. [John Milton, 1608–74, sonnet: *On His Blindness*]

4 Eyeless in Gaza at the mill with slaves. [John Milton, 1608–74, *Samson Agonistes*, 41]

5 O dark, dark, dark, amid the blaze of noon, / Irrecoverably dark, total eclipse / Without all hope of day! [John Milton, 1608–74, *Samson Agonistes*, 80]

6 I have a right to be blind sometimes ... I really do not see the signal! [(Putting the telescope to his blind eye at the battle of Copenhagen) Horatio, Lord Nelson, 1758–1805, quoted in R Southey, *Life of Nelson*, Ch. 7]

7 You are constantly distracted by the sight of the flowers and the buds bursting. I can sit here and I don't get distracted by flying birds or the sight of a pretty girl going by. Of course ... I can still *hear* a pretty girl go by. [(On the advantages of blindness to a writer) James Thurber, 1894–1961, in Alistair Cooke, *Talk about America*, Ch. 15]

BLOOD

1 Whoso sheddeth man's blood, by man shall his blood be shed. [Bible, OT, *Genesis* 9:6]

2 Will all great Neptune's ocean wash this blood / Clean from my hand? No, this my hand will rather / The multitudinous seas incarnadine, / Making the green one red. [William Shakespeare, 1564–1616, *Macbeth*, II. ii. 61]

3 I am in blood / Stepped in so far that, should I wade no more, / Returning were as tedious as go o'er. [*Macbeth*, III. iv. 136]

4 Yet who would have thought the old man to have had so much blood in him? [*Macbeth*, V. i. (42)]

5 There are two kinds of blood, the blood that flows in the veins and the blood that flows out of them. [Julian Tuwim, 1894–1954, *We, the Polish Jews*]

See also ASSASSINATION, CRIME, KILLING, MURDER, VIOLENCE

THE BODY [HUMAN]

1 I travel light; as light, / That is, as a man can travel who will / Still carry his body around because / Of its sentimental value. [Christopher Fry, 1907– , *The Lady's Not for Burning*, I]

2 As a body everyone is single, as a soul never. [Hermann Hesse, 1877–1962, *Steppenwolf*, 'Treatise on the Steppenwolf']

3 I believe that the struggle against death, the unconditional and self-willed determination to live, is the motive power behind the lives and activities of all outstanding men. [Hermann Hesse, 1877–1962, *Steppenwolf*, 'Treatise on the Steppenwolf']

4 The human body is private property. We have to have a search warrant to look inside, and even then an investigator is confined to a few experimental tappings here and there, some gropings on the party wall, a torch flashed rather hesitantly into some of the dark corners. [Jonathan Miller, 1934– , in BBC TV programme *The Body in Question*, Feb. 1979]

5 Body and soul are not two substances but one. They are man becoming aware of himself in two different ways. [C F von Weizsäcker, 1912– ; in *Hodder Book of Christian Quotations*, comp. Tony Castle]

6 If any thing is sacred the human body is sacred. [Walt Whitman, 1819–92, *I Sing the Body Electric*, 125]

See also next category

BODY PARTS

1 Thy belly is like an heap of wheat set about with lilies. Thy two breasts are like two young roes that are twins. [Bible, OT, *Song of Solomon* 7:2]

2 *Hand*, n. A singular instrument worn at the end of a human arm and commonly thrust into somebody's pocket. [Ambrose Bierce, 1842–1914, *The Devil's Dictionary*]

3 The fingers must be educated, the thumb is born knowing. [Marc Chagall, 1889–1985; in *Barnes and Noble Book of Quotations*, ed. Robert I Fitzhenry, 'Painters']

4 Nobody, not even the rain, has such small hands. [e e cummings, 1894–1962, *W*, LVII]

5 We know the human brain is a device to keep the ears from grating on one another. [Peter de Vries, 1910–93, *Comfort Me with Apples*, Ch. 1]

6 It was not a bosom to repose upon, but it was a capital bosom to hang jewels upon. [Charles Dickens, 1812–70, *Little Dorrit*, Bk 1, Ch. 21]

7 Uncorseted, her friendly bust / Gives promise of pneumatic bliss. [T S Eliot, 1888–1965, *Whispers of Immortality*]

8 Only one thing is wrong with our noses. They are too far off the ground to be much use. [Richard Feynman, 1918–88; in *Independent*, 17 Mar. 1988]

9 Fain would I kiss my Julia's dainty leg, / Which is as white and hairless as an egg. [Robert Herrick, 1591–1674, *Hesperides*, 'On Julia's Legs']

10 I believe / that only what cannot be trimmed / is a head. / There is much promise / in the circumstance / that so many people have heads. [Miroslav Holub, 1923–98, *A Boy's Head*]

11 Hard as hurdle arms, with a broth of goldish flue / Breathed round. [Gerard Manley Hopkins, 1844–89, *Harry Ploughman*]

12 Brought up in an epoch when ladies apparently rolled along on wheels, Mr Quarles was peculiarly susceptible to calves. [Aldous Huxley, 1894–1963, *Point Counter Point*, Ch. 20]

13 I don't suggest that her face has been lifted, but there is a possibility that her body has been lowered. [Clive James, 1939– (of character in BBC TV series *Dallas*), in *Observer*, 19 Apr. 1981]

14 If the creator had a purpose in equipping us with a neck, he surely meant us to stick it out. [Arthur Koestler, 1905–83, in *Encounter*, May 1970]

15 It was Battery Sergeant-Major 'Jumbo' Day. His hair was so shorn his neck seemed to go straight up the back of his hat. [Spike Milligan, 1918– , *Adolf Hitler: My Part in His Downfall*, 'I Join the Regiment']

16 There wanders through the world a knee, / A knee and nothing more. [Christian Morgenstern, 1871–1914, *Galgenlieder*, 'The Knee']

17 He [*Homo sapiens*] is proud that he has the biggest brain of all the primates, but attempts to conceal the fact that he also has the biggest penis. [Desmond Morris, 1928– , *The Naked Ape*, Introduction]

18 To Crystal, hair was the most important thing on earth. She would never get married because you couldn't wear curlers in bed. [Edna O'Brien, 1932– , *Winter's Tales*, 8, 'Come into the Drawing Room, Doris']

19 Man is not, as the vulgarer hedonists seem to suppose, a kind of walking stomach; he has also got a hand, an eye, and a brain. Cease to use your hands, and you have lopped off a huge chunk of your consciousness. [George Orwell, 1903–50, *The Road to Wigan Pier*, Ch. 12]

20 I don't know. I'm never there. [(When asked how long it took to do her hair) Dolly Parton, 1946– ; *Independent*, 'Quote Unquote', 17 Feb. 1990]

21 If the eyes are sometimes the organ through which our intelligence is revealed, the nose is generally the organ in which stupidity is most readily displayed. [Marcel Proust, 1871–1922, *Remembrance of Things Past: Cities of the Plain*, Pt II, Ch. 2]

22 My nose is huge! Vile snub-nose, flat-nosed ass, flat-head, let me inform you that I am proud of such an appendage, since a big nose is the proper sign of a friendly, good, courteous, witty, liberal and brave man, such as I am. [Edmond Rostand, 1868–1918, *Cyrano de Bergerac*, I. i]

BOOKS IN GENERAL

1 Some books are undeservedly forgotten; none are undeservedly remembered. [W H Auden, 1907–73, *The Dyer's Hand*, Pt 1, 'Reading']

2 Books will speak plain when counsellors blanch. [Francis Bacon, 1561–1626, *Essays*, 20, 'Of Counsel']

3 Some books are to be tasted, others to be swallowed, and some few to be chewed and digested. [Francis Bacon, 1561–1626, *Essays*, 50, 'Of Studies']

4 Child! do not throw this book about! / Refrain from the unholy pleasure / Of cutting all the pictures out! [Hilaire Belloc, 1870–1953, *Dedication on the Gift of a Book to a Child*]

5 A book chooses its readers as a play chooses its audience. [Alan Bennett, 1934– , in *With Great Pleasure*, ed. Alec Reid]

6 Of making many books there is no end; and much study is a weariness of the flesh. [Bible, OT, *Ecclesiastes* 12:12]

7 'Tis pleasant, sure, to see one's name in print; / A book's a book, although there's nothing in't. [Lord Byron, 1788–1824, *English Bards and Scotch Reviewers*, 51]

8 'What is the use of a book,' thought Alice, 'without pictures or conversations?' [Lewis Carroll, 1832–98, *Alice in Wonderland*, Ch. 1]

9 Due attention to the inside of books, and due contempt for the outside, is the proper relation between a man of sense and his books. [Earl of Chesterfield, 1694–1773, letter to his son, 10 Jan. 1749]

10 Contemporary books do not keep. The quality in them which makes for their success is the first to go; they turn overnight. [Cyril Connolly, 1903–74, *Enemies of Promise*, Ch. 2]

11 Books cannot always please, however good; / Minds are not ever craving for their food. [George Crabbe, 1754–1832, *The Borough*, Letter 24, 402]

12 Books! Bottled chatter! Things that some other simian has formerly said. [Clarence Day, 1874–1935, *This Simian World*]

13 We know that books are not a way of letting someone else think in our place: on the contrary, they are machines that provoke further thought. [Umberto Eco, 1932– , in *Observer*, 18 June 1995]

14 I feel his books are all written in hotels with the bed unmade at the back of the chair. [Ronald Firbank, 1886–1926, *The Flower beneath the Foot*, Ch. 4]

15 I suggest that the only books that influence us are those for which we are ready, and which have gone a little farther down our particular path than we have yet got ourselves. [E M Forster, 1879–1970, *Two Cheers for Democracy*, 'Books That Influenced Me']

16 Learning hath gained most by those books by which the printers have lost. [Thomas Fuller, 1608–61, *The Holy State*, Bk iii, Ch. 18]

17 A book may be amusing with numerous errors, or it may be very dull without a single absurdity. [Oliver Goldsmith, 1728–74, *The Vicar of Wakefield*, Preface]

18 Even bad books are books and therefore sacred. [Günter Grass, 1927– , *The Tin Drum*, 'Rasputin and the Alphabet']

19 All good books are alike in that they are truer than if they had really happened. [Ernest Hemingway, 1899–1961, in *Esquire* magazine, Dec. 1934]

20 We need the books that affect us like a disaster, that grieve us deeply, like the death of someone we loved more than ourselves, like being banished into forests far from everyone, like suicide. A book must be the axe for the frozen sea inside us. [Franz Kafka, 1883–1924, letter to Oskar Pollack, 27 Jan. 1904]

21 Making books is a skilled trade, like making clocks. [Jean de La Bruyère, 1645–96, *Characters*, 'Of Books', 3]

22 Few books today are forgivable. [R D Laing, 1927–89, *The Politics of Experience*, Introduction]

23 Your *borrowers of books* – those mutilators of collections – spoilers of the symmetry of shelves, and creators of odd volumes. [Charles Lamb, 1775–1834, *Essays of Elia*, 'The Two Races of Men']

24 To every man who struggles with his own soul in mystery, a book that is a book flowers once, and seeds, and is gone. [D H Lawrence, 1885–1930, *Phoenix*, 'A Bibliography of D.H.L.']

25 Never judge a cover by its book. [Fran Lebowitz, ?1948– , *Metropolitan Life*]

26 No book is really worth reading at the age of ten which is not equally (and often far more) worth reading at the age of fifty and beyond. [C S Lewis, 1898–1963; in *The Writer's Quotation Book*, ed. James Charlton]

27 It was a book to kill time for those who like it better dead. [Rose Macaulay, 1889–1958; in *Treasury of Humorous Quotations*, ed. Evan Esar and Nicolas Bentley]

28 Books are not absolutely dead things, but do contain a potency of life in them to be as active as that soul was whose progeny they are; nay they do preserve as in a vial the purest efficacy and extraction of that living intellect that bred them. [John Milton, 1608–74, *Areopagitica*]

29 The principle of procrastinated rape is said to be the ruling one in all the great bestsellers. [V S Pritchett, 1900–1997, *The Living Novel*, 'Clarissa']

30 There is no one thing to be found in books which it is a disgrace not to know. [Walter A Raleigh, 1861–1922, attr.]

31 When a new book is published, read an old one. [Samuel Rogers, 1763–1855, attr.]

32 To burn a book is not to destroy it. One minute of darkness will not make us blind. [Salman Rushdie, 1937– , review of Gabriel García Márquez, *Clandestine in Chile*, in *Weekend Guardian*, 14–15 Oct. 1989]

33 He hath not fed of the dainties that are bred in a book; he hath not eat paper, as it were; he hath not drunk ink. [William Shakespeare, 1564–1616, *Love's Labour's Lost*, IV. ii. (25)]

34 Knowing I loved my books, he furnished me, / From mine own library with volumes that / I prize above my dukedom. [*The Tempest*, I. ii. 166]

35 A best-seller is the gilded tomb of a mediocre talent. [Logan Pearsall Smith, 1865–1946, *Afterthoughts*, 5]

36 No furniture so charming as books. [Sydney Smith, 1771–1845, in Lady Holland, *Memoir*, Vol. i, Ch. 9]

37 Books are good enough in their own way, but they are a mighty bloodless substitute for life. [Robert Louis Stevenson, 1850–94, *Virginibus Puerisque*, 'An Apology for Idlers']

38 A good book is the best of friends, the same today and for ever. [Martin Tupper, 1810–89, *Proverbial Philosophy*, Series I, 'Of Reading']

39 A classic is something that everybody wants to have read and nobody wants to read. [Mark Twain, 1835–1910, speech: 'The Disappearance of Literature']

40 One book's very like another – after all what is it? Something to read and be done with. It's not a thing that matters like print dresses or serviettes – where you either like 'em or don't, and people judge you by. [H G Wells, 1866–1946, *Kipps*, Bk III, Ch. 3, iii]

41 There is no such thing as a moral or an immoral book. Books are well written, or badly written. [Oscar Wilde, 1854–1900, *The Picture of Dorian Gray*, Preface]

42 I would never read a book if it were possible to talk half an hour with the man who wrote it. [Woodrow Wilson, 1856–1924, advice to his students at Princeton, 1900]

See also next category, EDITORS, NOVELISTS, NOVELS, POETRY, POETS, READING

BOOKS: INDIVIDUAL

1 It [his book] also concerns the three most perennially popular subjects currently to be found on the bedside tables of the reading public, viz. golf, cats, and the Third Reich. [Alan Coren, 1938– , *Golfing for Cats*, Foreword]

2 Go, little book, and wish to all / Flowers in the garden, meat in the hall, / A bin of wine, a spice of wit, / A house with lawns enclosing it, / A living river by the door, / A nightingale in the sycamore! [Robert Louis Stevenson, 1850–94, *Underwoods*, I, 1, 'Envoy']

3 'Sartor Resartus' is simply unreadable, and for me that always sort of spoils a book. [Harry Truman, 1884–1972; in *Barnes and Noble Book of Quotations*, ed. Robert I Fitzhenry, 'Books']

4 *Pilgrim's Progress*, about a man who left his family, it didn't say why. The statements was interesting, but tough. [Mark Twain, 1835–1910, *The Adventures of Huckleberry Finn*, Ch. 17]

See also previous category, NOVELISTS, NOVELS, POETRY, POETS, READING

BORES & BOREDOM

1 He's the kind of bore who's here today and here tomorrow. [Binnie Barnes, 1905–98, in *Hammer and Tongues*, ed. Michèle Brown and Ann O'Connor, 'Pessimism']

2 *Bore*, n. A person who talks when you wish him to listen. [Ambrose Bierce, 1842–1914, *The Devil's Dictionary*]

3 I do not object to people looking at their watches when I am speaking. But I strongly object when they start shaking them to make sure they are still going. [Lord Birkett, 1883–1962, in *Observer*, 30 Oct. 1960]

4 Everyone is a bore to someone. That is unimportant. The thing to avoid is being a bore to oneself. [Gerald Brenan, 1894–1987, *Thoughts in a Dry Season*, 'Life']

5 Society is now one polished horde, / Formed of two mighty tribes, the *Bores* and *Bored*. Lord Byron, 1788–1824, *Don Juan*, XIII, 95]

6 There is no such thing on earth as an uninteresting subject; the only thing that can exist is an uninterested person. [G K Chesterton, 1874–1936, *Heretics*, 3]

7 When a man fell into his anecdotage it was a sign for him to retire from the world. [Benjamin Disraeli, 1804–81, *Lothair*, Ch. 28]

8 Millions long for immortality who don't know what to do with themselves on a rainy Sunday afternoon. [Susan Ertz, 1894–1985, *Anger in the Sky*, Ch. 5]

9 'What'll we do with ourselves this afternoon?' cried Daisy, 'and the day after that, and the next thirty years?' [F Scott Fitzgerald, 1896–1940, *The Great Gatsby*, Ch. 7]

9 He is not only dull in himself, but the cause of dullness in others. [Samuel Foote, 1720–77, quoted in James Boswell, *Life of Johnson*, 1783]

10 If you resolve to give up smoking, drinking and loving, you don't actually live longer; it just seems longer. [Cyril Fletcher, 1913–   , quoting 'a third-rate comedian in Sloane Square', in *Observer*, 27 Dec. 1964]

12 We were as nearly bored as enthusiasm would permit. [Edmund Gosse, 1849–1928 (on a Swinburne play), in Christopher Hassall, *Edward Marsh*, Ch. 6]

13 The effect of boredom on a large scale in history is underestimated. It is a main cause of revolutions, and would soon bring to an end all the static Utopias and the farmyard civilization of the Fabians. [W R Inge, 1860–1954, *The End of an Age*, Ch. 6]

14 I've just spent an hour talking to Tallulah [Bankhead] for a few minutes. [Fred Keating, n.d.; in *Woman Talk 2*, comp. Michèle Brown and Ann O'Connor]

15 The capacity of human beings to bore one another seems to be vastly greater than that of any other animals. Some of their most esteemed inventions have no other apparent purpose, for example, the dinner party of more than two, the epic poem, and the science of metaphysics. [H L Mencken, 1880–1956, *Minority Report*, 67]

16 Is not life a hundred times too short for us to bore ourselves? [Friedrich Nietzsche, 1844–1900, *Beyond Good and Evil*, Pt 7, sect. 227]

17 Whether he talked, wrote, or rehearsed – / Still with this dullness was he cursed – / Dull – beyond all conception – dull. [P B Shelley, 1792–1822, *Peter Bell the Third*, 705]

18 A bore is a man who, when you ask him how he is, tells you. [Bert Leston Taylor, 1866–1921, *The So-called Human Race*, p. 163]

19 Boredom is rage spread thin. [Paul Tillich, 1886–1965; in *Barnes and Noble Book of Quotations*, ed. Robert I Fitzhenry, 'Bores']

20 He is an old bore; even the grave yawns for him. [Herbert Beerbohm Tree, 1853–1917; in Hesketh Pearson, *B T*, Ch. 21]

21 A healthy male adult bore consumes each year one and a half times his own weight in other people's patience. [John Updike, 1932– , *Assorted Prose*, 'Confessions of a Wild Bore']

22 A radical theory I had always held but dared not openly formulate: that boredom in the arts can be, under the right circumstances, dull. [Gore Vidal, 1925– , *Myra Breckinridge*, Ch. 21]

BORROWERS & LENDERS

1 Be not made a beggar by banqueting upon borrowing. [Bible, Apocrypha, *Ecclesiasticus* 18:33]

2 Home life ceases to be free and beautiful as soon as it is founded on borrowing and debt. [Henrik Ibsen, 1828–1906, *A Doll's House*, I]

3 The human species, according to the best theory I can form of it, is composed of two distinct races, *the men who borrow* and *the men who lend*. [Charles Lamb, 1775–1834, *Essays of Elia*, 'The Two Races of Men']

4 Neither a borrower, nor a lender be; / For loan oft loses both itself and friend, / And borrowing dulls the edge of husbandry. [William Shakespeare, 1564–1616, *Hamlet*, I. iii. 75]

5 Three things I never lends – my 'oss, my wife, and my name. [R S Surtees, 1803–64, *Hillingdon Hall*, Ch. 33]

6 Who goeth a borrowing / Goeth a sorrowing. / Few lend (but fools) / Their working tools. [Thomas Tusser, 1524?–80, *Five Hundred Points of Good Husbandry*, 'September's Abstract']

7 Let us be happy and live within our means, even if we have to borrer the money to do it with. [Artemus Ward, 1834–67, *Science and Natural History*]

See also DEBT

BOURGEOIS, see MIDDLE CLASS

BOYS

1 A boy does not put his hand into his pocket until every other means of gaining his end has failed. [James Barrie, 1860–1937, *Sentimental Tommy*, Ch. 1]

2 You should not take a fellow eight years old / And make him swear to never kiss the girls. [Robert Browning, 1812–89, *Fra Lippo Lippi*, 224]

3 Ah! happy years! once more who would not be a boy? [Lord Byron, 1788–1824, *Childe Harold's Pilgrimage*, II, 23]

4 Ears like bombs and teeth like splinters: / A blitz of a boy is Timothy Winters. [Charles Causley, 1917– , *Timothy Winters*]

5 Boys do not grow up gradually. They move forward in spurts like the hands of clocks in railway stations. [Cyril Connolly, 1903–74, *Enemies of Promise*, Ch. 21]

6 I've a pretty large experience of boys, and you're a bad set of fellows. Now mind ... you behave yourself! [Charles Dickens, 1812–70, *Great Expectations*, Ch. 11]

7 I only know two sorts of boys, Mealy boys, and beef-faced boys. [Charles Dickens, 1812–70, *Oliver Twist*, Ch. 14]

8 Boys are capital fellows in their own way, among their mates; but they are unwholesome companions for grown people. [Charles Lamb, 1775–1834, *Essays of Elia*, 'The Old and the New Schoolmaster']

9 A boy's will is the wind's will, / And the thoughts of youth are long, long thoughts. [H W Longfellow, 1807–82, *My Lost Youth*]

10 What are little boys made of? / What are little boys made of? / Frogs and snails / And puppy-dogs' tails, / That's what little boys are made of. [Nursery rhyme]

11 Two lads that thought there was no more behind / But such a day tomorrow as today, / And to be boy eternal. [William Shakespeare, 1564–1616, *The Winter's Tale*, I. ii. 63]

12 What money is better bestowed than that of a schoolboy's tip? [W M Thackeray, 1811–63, *The Newcomes*, Ch. 16]

13 And the wild boys innocent as strawberries. [Dylan Thomas, 1914–53, *The Hunchback in the Park*]

14 Begin then, little boy: no one who has not given his mother a smile has ever been thought worthy of his table by a god, or by a goddess of her bed. [Virgil, 70–19 BC, *Eclogue*, IV, 62]

BREVITY

1 But the shortest works are always the best.

[Jean de La Fontaine, 1621–95, *Fables*, X, 15, 'The Rabbits']

2 Brevity is the Soul of Lingerie. [Dorothy Parker, 1893–1967 (caption for a fashion magazine), in Alexander Woollcott, *While Rome Burns*, 'Our Mrs Parker']

3 Brevity is the soul of wit. [William Shakespeare, 1564–1616, *Hamlet*, II. ii. 90]

BRITAIN

1 Land of Hope and Glory, Mother of the Free, / How shall we extol thee, who are born of thee? / Wider still and wider shall thy bounds be set; / God who made thee mighty, make thee mightier yet. [A C Benson, 1862–1925, song set to music by Edward Elgar in *Pomp and Circumstance*]

2 Britannia needs no bulwarks, / No towers along the steep; / Her march is o'er the mountain waves, / Her home is on the deep. [Thomas Campbell, 1777–1844, *Ye Mariners of England*]

3 It is still a puzzle how the natives of this island [Britain] mime almost any form of political barbarism of which geography spares them the immediate experience. [Eric Christiansen, in *Independent*, 5 Nov. 1988]

4 Oh! it's a snug little island, / A right little, tight little island! [Thomas Dibdin, 1771–1841, *The Snug Little Island*]

5 Our day of political pride is over. A great race we are and shall remain; a great power we have been and are no longer. [W R Inge, 1860–1954, *Diary*, Sept. 1914]

6 What is our task? To make Britain a fit country for heroes to live in. [David Lloyd George, 1863–1945, speech, 24 Nov. 1918]

7 Britain has lost its pride but retained its conceit. [Reginald Maudling, 1917–77, in Peter Madgwick *et al.*, *Britain since 1945*, Ch. 1]

8 Methinks I see in my mind a noble and puissant nation rousing herself like a strong man after sleep, and shaking her invincible locks. Methinks I see her as an eagle mewing her mighty youth, and kindling her undazzled eyes at the full midday beam. [John Milton, 1608–74, *Areopagitica*]

9 There be many Caesars / Ere such another Julius. Britain is / A world by itself, and we will nothing pay / For wearing our own noses. [William Shakespeare, 1564–1616, *Cymbeline*, III. i. 11]

10 What two ideas are more inseparable than Beer and Britannia? [Sydney Smith, 1771–1845, in H Pearson, *The Smith of Smiths*, Ch. 11]

11 Everything unknown is taken as marvellous; but now the limits of Britain are laid bare. [Tacitus, *c.*55–*c.*117, *Agricola*, 30]

12 Not once or twice in our rough island-story, / The path of duty was the way to glory. [Alfred, Lord Tennyson, 1809–92, *Ode on the Death of the Duke of Wellington*, 8]

13 When Britain first, at heaven's command, / Arose from out the azure main, / This was the charter of the land, / And guardian angels sung this strain: / 'Rule, Britannia, rule the waves; / Britons never will be slaves.' [James Thomson, 1700–1748, *Alfred: a Masque*, II. v]

See also following categories, ENGLAND, SCOTLAND, WALES

BRITAIN & OTHERS

1 When you think about the defence of England, you no longer think of the chalk cliffs of Dover. You think of the Rhine. That is where our frontier lies today. [Stanley Baldwin, 1867–1947, speech in House of Commons, 30 July 1934]

2 Whereas twenty-five years ago we were an empire, now we are a colony, with the IMF running our financial affairs, the Common Market Commission running our legislation and NATO running our armed forces. [Tony Benn, 1925– (to the Queen), in his diaries, *Conflicts of Interest*, 8 May 1979]

3 England, oh, perfidious England! [Jacques Bénigne Bossuet, 1627–1704. By the time of the French Revolution this had become 'Perfidious Albion']

4 England is a paradise for women, and hell for horses: Italy a paradise for horses, hell for women, as the diverb goes. [Robert Burton, 1577–1640, *The Anatomy of Melancholy*, III, §3, Memb. 1, 2]

5 The Englishman likes to imagine himself at sea, the German in a forest. It is impossible to express the difference of their national identity more concisely. [Elias Canetti, 1905–94, *Crowds and Power*, 'The Crowd in History']

6 In England, the system is benign and the people are hostile. In America, the people are friendly – and the system is brutal! [Quentin Crisp, 1908–99, interview in *Guardian*, 23 Oct. 1985]

7 The Continent will not suffer England to be the workshop of the world. [Benjamin Disraeli, 1804–81, speech in House of Commons, 15 Mar. 1838]

8 [European federation would] mean, if this is the idea, the end of Britain as an independent state ... It means the end of a thousand years of history. [Hugh Gaitskell, 1906–63, speech at Labour Party Conference, Brighton, 3 Oct. 1962]

9 It is, of course, a particularly British characteristic to think that every man is the same under the skin, and that Eskimos are really only would-be old Etonians wearing fur coats. [John Harvey-Jones, 1924– , *Making It Happen*, 6]

10 We are the dirty armpit of Europe. [Ken Livingstone, 1945– ; *Independent*, 'Quote Unquote', 18 Mar. 1989]

11 England is never as great as when she is alone. And France is never France when she fights for herself ... When the French fight for mankind they are wonderful. When they fight for themselves, they are nothing. [André Malraux, 1901–76, in Bruce Chatwin, *What am I Doing Here?*, 'André Malraux']

12 The British tourist is always happy abroad so long as the natives are waiters. [Robert Morley, 1908–92; *Observer*, 'Sayings of the Week', 20 Apr. 1958]

13 England is a nation of shopkeepers. [Napoleon Bonaparte, 1769–1821 (quoting Adam Smith), in B E O'Meara, *Napoleon at St Helena in Exile*]

14 We [the British] have ... elevated servility into one of the fine arts. Yet we make no impact at all on the world we have lost. Britain is a tin can tied to a dog's tail, but a tin can fitted with a silencer. [Edward Pearce, 1939– (of Britain's subservience to the USA on the eve of Gulf War), in *Guardian*, 9 Jan. 1991]

15 England has saved herself by her exertions; and will, as I trust, save Europe by her example. [William Pitt the Younger, 1759–1806, speech in Guildhall, London, 9 Nov. 1805]

16 Your average Frenchman, seeing another Frenchman, assumes he's an enemy unless he proves a friend. In Britain, it's the other way round. [Walter Schwarz, 1930– , in *Guardian Weekly*, 9 Sept. 1984]

17 England and America are two countries separated by the same language. [George Bernard Shaw, 1856–1950, attr. in *Reader's Digest*, Nov. 1942]

18 He [S J Perelman] was too much of an Anglophile to like England greatly. [Paul Theroux, 1941– , introduction to S J P, *The Last Laugh*]

19 Different cultures. You [the British] are too modest – in a very vain way. We [the Americans] are too busy – in a very humble way, of course. [Gore Vidal, 1925– , interview in *Observer Magazine*, 15 Nov. 1987]

20 And the Britons completely isolated from the whole world. [Virgil, 70–19 BC, *Eclogue* 1, 66]

See also previous and following categories, ENGLAND, SCOTLAND, WALES

THE BRITISH

1 There are no countries in the world less known by the British than those selfsame British Islands. [George Borrow, 1803–81, *Lavengro*, Preface]

2 The world is a bundle of hay, / Mankind are the asses who pull; / Each tugs it a different way, / And the greatest of all is John Bull. [Lord Byron, 1788–1824, *Epigram*]

3 The British love permanence more than they love beauty. [Hugh Casson, 1910–99; *Observer*, 'Sayings of the Week', 14 June 1964]

4 They [the British] are the only people who like to be told how bad things are – who like to be told the worst. [Winston Churchill, 1874–1965, speech in House of Commons, 10 June 1941]

5 The thing about the British conscience, you see, is that it really has no more capacity than ... a primitive home computer, if you like. It can only hold two or three things in its memory at a time. [Jonathan Coe, 1961– , *What a Carve Up!*, 'Thomas']

6 To be associated with the British is to be offered the choice of one of two bags tied at the neck with string. One contains a viper, the other a bag of gold. If you are lucky, you will choose the bag of gold, only to find that the British have reserved the right to exchange it for the other without notice. Conversely, ill luck might cause you to pick the bag with the viper, whereupon the British will wait until you have been bitten, and then say, 'We didn't mean it; have this other bag.' [Louis de Bernières, 1955– , *Captain Corelli's Mandolin*, 23]

7 British people have a Socialist mind and a Conservative heart. [Albert Finney, 1936– , in *Evening Standard*, 12 Nov. 1970]

8 She [Dr Lilian Knowles] defined the British genius as 'an infinite capacity for making drains'. [Quoted in Kingsley Martin, 1897–1969, *Father Figures*, Ch. 8]

9 Just at this moment we are suffering a national defeat comparable to any lost military campaign, and what is more it is self-inflicted . . . I think it is about time we pulled our finger out. [Philip, Duke of Edinburgh, 1921– , speech to businessmen in London, 17 Oct. 1961]

10 The trouble is that when you sit around a table with a Britisher he usually gets 80 per cent of the deal and you get what's left. [Franklin D Roosevelt, 1882–1945, in John Morton Blum, *From the Morgenthau Diaries*, Vol. I: *Years of Crisis, 1928–1938*]

11 He is a barbarian, and thinks that the customs of his tribe and island are the laws of nature. [George Bernard Shaw, 1856–1950, *Caesar and Cleopatra*, II]

12 We are a nation of governesses. [George Bernard Shaw, 1856–1950, in *New Statesman*, 12 Apr. 1913]

13 Gorgonized me from head to foot / With a stony British stare. [Alfred, Lord Tennyson, 1809–92, *Maud*, Pt 1, xiii, 2]

14 No more distressing moment can ever face a British government than that which requires it to come to a hard and fast and specific decision. [(Of Aug. 1914) B Tuchman, 1912–89, *The Guns of August*, Ch. 9]

15 Other nations use 'force'; we Britons alone use 'Might'. [Evelyn Waugh, 1903–66, *Scoop*, Bk II, Ch. 5. 1]

BRITISH EMPIRE

1 If all Englishmen were like him we wouldn't have colonized the Isle of Wight. [Guy Bellamy, 1935– , *The Secret Lemonade Drinker*, Ch. 2]

2 Westward the course of empire takes its way; / The four first acts already past, / A fifth shall close the drama with the day: / Time's noblest offspring is the last. [Bishop George Berkeley, 1685–1753, *On the Prospects of Planting Arts and Learning in America*]

3 The English send all their bores abroad, and acquired the Empire as a punishment. [Edward Bond, 1934– , *The Narrow Road to the Deep North*, II, i]

4 I ain't complaining – it's a duty laid down upon us by God – but the Pax Britannia takes a bit of keeping up with – 'arf the world full of savages and 'arf the other 'arf just getting in the way. [Joyce Cary, 1888–1957, *Mister Johnson*]

5 I have not become the King's First Minister in order to preside over the liquidation of the British Empire. [Winston Churchill, 1874–1965, speech in London, 10 Nov. 1942]

6 The sun never sets on Government House. [Noël Coward, 1899–1973, *Words and Music*, 'Planters' Wives']

7 Regions Caesar never knew / Thy posterity shall sway. [William Cowper, 1731–1800, *Boadicea*]

8 In these somewhat troublesome days when the great Mother Empire stands splendidly isolated in Europe. [George Foster, 1847–1931, speech in Canadian House of Commons, 16 Jan. 1896]

9 When we go to meet the foe, / It's the English-speaking race against the world. [Charles Godfrey, d. 1935, song: *We're Brothers of the Selfsame Race*]

10 No doubt but ye are the People – your throne is above the King's. / Whoso speaks in your presence must say acceptable things. [Rudyard Kipling, 1865–1936, *The Islanders*]

11 Take up the White Man's burden – / And reap his old reward: / The blame of those ye better, / The hate of those ye guard. [Rudyard Kipling, 1865–1936, *The White Man's Burden*]

12 It took God longer to write the Bible than it has taken him to build the British Empire. [William MacDonald, *Modern Evangelism*, 1938]

13 'Can't' will be the epitaph of the British Empire – unless we wake up in time. [Oswald

Mosley, 1896–1980, speech at Manchester, 9 Dec. 1937]

14 The Empire is a Commonwealth of Nations. [Earl of Rosebery, 1847–1929, speech at Adelaide, S Australia, 18 Jan. 1884]

15 We seem, as it were, to have conquered and peopled half the world in a fit of absence of mind. [J R Seeley, 1834–95, *The Expansion of England*, Lecture I]

16 To found a great empire for the sole purpose of raising up a people of customers, may at first sight appear a project fit only for a nation of shop-keepers. It is, however, a project altogether unfit for a nation of shopkeepers; but extremely fit for a nation that is governed by shopkeepers. [Adam Smith, 1723–90, *The Wealth of Nations*, Bk iv, Ch. 7, Pt iii]

17 I know why the sun never sets on the British Empire; God wouldn't trust an Englishman in the dark. [Duncan Spaeth, in Gyles Brandreth, *The Last Word*]

18 In my childhood it was said by all: 'A child of ten can go on the road of a town playing with a golden ball in perfect safety under British rule.' [*The Times*]

See also previous categories, EMPIRE, ENGLAND, SCOTLAND, WALES

BUILDINGS

1 It can hardly be a coincidence that no language on earth has ever produced the expression 'as pretty as an airport'. [Douglas Adams, 1952– , *The Long Dark Tea-time of the Soul*, opening words]

2 An airport is a free-range womb. [Brigid Brophy, 1929–95, *In Transit*, sect. I, 4]

3 I disliked buildings, considering them only a stiffer and more ample form of clothing, and no more important. [Annie Dillard, 1945– , *An American Childhood*, Pt 2]

4 He builded better than he knew; – / The conscious stone to beauty grew. [Ralph Waldo Emerson, 1803–82, *The Problem*]

5 Light (God's eldest daughter!) is a principal beauty in a building. [Thomas Fuller, 1608–61, *The Holy State*, Bk ii, Ch. 7]

6 Cinemas and theatres are always bigger inside than they are outside. [Miles Kington, 1941– , in *Independent*, 29 Mar. 1989]

7 How very little, since things were made, / Things have altered in the building trade. [Rudyard Kipling, 1865–1936, *A Truthful Song*]

8 [When asked at a committee what should be done with the Crystal Palace] Put it under a glass case. [Edwin Lutyens, 1869–1944, in Elisabeth Lutyens, *A Goldfish Bowl*, Ch. 2]

9 The decorations are like those of the embassy of a nation about to go into voluntary liquidation. [Colin MacInnes, 1914–76, *England, Half English*, 'See You at Mabel's']

10 You should be able to read a building. It should be what it does. [Richard Rogers, 1933– , in Walter Neurath Memorial Lecture, London University, Mar. 1990]

11 When we build, let us think that we build for ever. [John Ruskin, 1819–1900, *The Seven Lamps of Architecture*, Ch. 5. §10]

12 Even the mice eat next door. [Ronnie Scott, 1927–96 (of his jazz club); in *Ultimate Trivia Quiz Game Book*, ed. M and A Hiron]

See also ARCHITECTURE

BUREAUCRACY, see THE OFFICE

BUSINESS

1 God made the wicked Grocer / For a mystery and a sign, / That men might shun the awful shop / And go to inns to dine. [G K Chesterton, 1874–1936, *The Song against Grocers*]

2 They [corporations] cannot commit treason, nor be outlawed, nor excommunicate, for they have no souls. [Edward Coke, 1552–1634, *Sutton's Hospital Case*]

3 The chief business of the American people is business. [Calvin Coolidge, 1872–1933, speech in Washington, 17 Jan. 1925. Commonly misquoted as 'The business of America is business']

4 Here's the rule for bargains: 'Do other men, for they would do you.' That's the true business precept. [Charles Dickens, 1812–70, *Martin Chuzzlewit*, Ch. 11]

5 Queer Street is full of lodgers just at present.

[Charles Dickens, 1812–70, *Our Mutual Friend*, Bk III, Ch. 1]

6 Business was his pleasure; pleasure was his business. [Maria Edgeworth, 1767–1849, *The Contrast*, Ch. 2]

7 [When asked, 'Which comes first, the words or the music?'] What usually comes first is the contract. [Ira Gershwin, 1896–1983, in *Guardian*, 18 Aug. 1983, at his death]

8 Business is other people's money. [Mme de Girardin, 1804–55, *Marguerites*, Vol. ii, p. 104]

9 Regarded as a means the business man is tolerable; regarded as an end he is not so satisfactory. [John Maynard Keynes, 1883–1946, *Essays in Persuasion*, IV, 'A Short View of Russia']

10 The basic rule of the City was that if you are incompetent you have to be honest, and if you're crooked you have to be clever. The reasoning is that, if you are honest, the chaps will rally round if you make a pig's breakfast out of your business dealings. Conversely, if you are crooked, no one will ask questions so long as you are making substantial profits. [Jonathan Lynn, 1943– , and Antony Jay, 1930– , *Yes Prime Minister*, Vol. 2, 'A Conflict of Interest']

11 He [the businessman] is the only man who is for ever apologizing for his occupation. [H L Mencken, 1880–1956, *Prejudices*, Third Series, 'Types of Men', 7]

12 After all, for mankind as a whole there are no exports. We did not start developing by obtaining foreign exchange from Mars or the moon. Mankind is a closed society. [E F Schumacher, 1911–77, *Small is Beautiful*, Ch. 14]

13 A dinner lubricates business. [William Scott, Lord Stowell, 1745–1836, in James Boswell, *Life of Johnson*, 1781]

14 That smooth-faced gentleman, tickling Commodity, / Commodity, the bias of the world. [William Shakespeare, 1564–1616, *King John*, II. i. 573]

15 A cooperative is private enterprise in a state economy. That's like a newspaper inside a prison. It cannot operate freely. [Oleg Smirnoff, in Hedrick Smith, *The New Russians*, Pt 3, p. 285]

16 People of the same trade seldom meet together, even for merriment and diversion, but the conversation ends in a conspiracy against the public, or in some contrivance to raise prices. [Adam Smith, 1723–90, *The Wealth of Nations*, Vol. ii, Bk i, Ch. 10, Pt ii]

17 Experience has shown that the only sure way to run a small business in Tory Britain is to start with a large one. [David Steel, 1938– , speech at Liberal Party Assembly, Llandudno, Wales, 18 Sept. 1981]

18 Corporations have neither bodies to be punished, nor souls to be condemned; they therefore do as they like. [(Usually quoted as: 'Did you ever expect a corporation to have a conscience, when it has no soul to be damned, and no body to be kicked?') Edward, Lord Thurlow, 1731–1806; in J Poynder, *Literary Extracts*, Vol. i]

19 Safe and sane business management ... reduces itself in the main to a sagacious use of sabotage. [Thorstein Veblen, 1857–1929, *The Nature of Peace*, Ch. 7]

20 Commercialism is doing well that which should not be done at all. [Gore Vidal, 1925– , from BBC TV programme *Success Story*, in *Listener*, 7 Aug. 1975]

21 I remember that a wise friend of mine did usually say, 'that which is everybody's business is nobody's business'. [Izaak Walton, 1593–1683, *The Compleat Angler*, Pt I, Ch. 2]

22 For years I thought what was good for the country was good for General Motors, and vice versa. [Charles E Wilson, 1890–1961, to a Congressional Committee, 15 Jan. 1953. Often misquoted as 'What's good for General Motors is good for the country']

23 Business underlies everything in our national life, including our spiritual life. Witness the fact that in the Lord's Prayer the first petition is for daily bread. No one can worship God or love his neighbour on an empty stomach. [Woodrow Wilson, 1856–1924, speech in New York, 1912]

24 As a rule, from what I've observed, the American captain of industry doesn't do anything out of business hours. When he has put the cat out and locked up the office for the night, he just relapses into a state of coma from which he emerges only to start being a captain of industry again. [P G Wodehouse, 1881–1975, *My Man Jeeves*, 'Leave It to Jeeves']

25 A broker is a man who runs your fortune into a shoestring. [Alexander Woollcott, 1887–1943, in R E Drennan, *Wit's End*]

26 Go to your business, I say, pleasure, whilst I go to my pleasure, business. [William Wycherley, 1640?–1716, *The Country Wife*, II]

See also next category

BUYING & SELLING

1 A nation of shopkeepers are very seldom so disinterested. [Samuel Adams, 1722–1803, speech said to have been made at Philadelphia, 1 Aug. 1776]

2 Like strawberry wives, that laid two or three great strawberries at the mouth of their pot, and all the rest were little ones. [Francis Bacon, 1561–1626, *Apothegms*, 54. Attr. to Queen Elizabeth I]

3 [A good salesman must have] the quality of saying with ten thousand words arousing enthusiasm what others said with ten words causing people to yawn. [Aldo Busi, 1948– , *The Standard Life of a Temporary Pantyhose Salesman*]

4 When a little girl asked me what two and two make, I'm supposed to have answered, 'It depends if you're buying or selling' . . . Not true! [Lew Grade, 1906–98, *Still Dancing*, Ch. 12]

5 When you are skinning your customers, you should leave some skin on to grow so that you can skin them again. [Nikita Khrushchev, 1894–1971, addressing British businessmen; *Observer*, 'Sayings of the Week', 28 May 1961]

6 He was nimble in the calling of selling houses for more than people could afford to pay. [Sinclair Lewis, 1885–1951, *Babbitt*, Ch. 1]

7 He's a man way out there in the blue, riding on a smile and a shoeshine. And when they start not smiling back – that's an earthquake . . . A salesman is got to dream, boy. It comes with the territory. [Arthur Miller, 1915– , *Death of a Salesman*, II, 'Death Requiem']

8 The customer is always right. [H Gordon Selfridge, 1857–1947, shop slogan]

9 To found a great empire for the sole purpose of raising up a people of customers, may at first sight appear a project fit only for a nation of shopkeepers. It is, however, a project altogether unfit for a nation of shopkeepers; but extremely fit for a nation that is governed by shopkeepers. [Adam Smith, 1723–90, *The Wealth of Nations*, Bk iv, Ch. 7, Pt iii]

10 Every one lives by selling something. [Robert Louis Stevenson, 1850–94, *Across the Plains*, 9, 'Beggars']

11 I have heard of a man who had a mind to sell his house, and therefore carried a piece of brick in his pocket, which he showed as a pattern to encourage purchasers. [Jonathan Swift, 1677–1745, *The Drapier's Letters*, No. 2]

C

CALM

1 When the voices of children are heard on the green, / And laughing is heard on the hill, / My heart is at rest within my breast, / And everything else is still. [William Blake, 1757–1827, *Songs of Innocence*, 'Nurse's Song']

2 Thar ain't no sense / In gittin' riled! [Bret Harte, 1836–1902, *Jim*]

3 No stir of air was there, / Not so much life as on a summer's day / Robs not one light seed from the feathered grass, / But where the dead leaf fell, there did it rest. [John Keats, 1795–1821, *Hyperion*, Bk i, 7]

4 Thou still unravished bride of quietness, / Thou foster-child of silence and slow time. [John Keats, 1795–1821, *Ode on a Grecian Urn*, 1]

5 If you can keep your head when all about you are losing theirs, it's just possible you haven't grasped the situation. [Jean Kerr, 1923– , *Please Don't Eat the Daisies*, Introduction]

6 If you can keep your head when all about you / Are losing theirs and blaming it on you. [Rudyard Kipling, 1865–1936, *If–*]

7 Calm was the day, and through the trembling air / Sweet-breathing Zephyrus did softly play. [Edmund Spenser, 1552?–99, *Prothalamion*, 1]

8 Is there any peace / In ever climbing up the climbing wave? [Alfred, Lord Tennyson, 1809–92, *The Lotos-Eaters*, 'Choric Song', 4]

9 The seas are quiet, when the winds give o'er: / So calm are we, when passions are no more. [Edmund Waller, 1606–87, *Of the Last Verses in the Book*]

10 And I shall have some peace there, for peace comes dropping slow, / Dropping from the veils of the morning to where the cricket sings. [W B Yeats, 1865–1939, *The Lake Isle of Innisfree*]

See also PATIENCE, PEACE, RESIGNATION

CAMBRIDGE, see OXFORD

CANADA

1 If the national mental illness of the United States is megalomania, that of Canada is paranoid schizophrenia. [Margaret Atwood, 1939– ; *Barnes and Noble Book of Quotations*, ed. Robert I Fitzhenry, 'Canada']

2 Canada is a country so square that even the female impersonators are women. [Richard Benner, from film *Outrageous*, in *Guardian*, 21 Sept. 1978]

3 At last, fortissimo! [Gustav Mahler, 1860–1911 (on visiting Niagara), in K Blaukopf, *Mahler*, Ch. 8]

4 'I'm world-famous,' Dr Parks said, 'all over Canada.' [Mordechai Richler, 1931– , *The Incomparable Atuk*, Ch. 4]

5 From the lone shieling of the misty island / Mountains divide us and the waste of seas – / Yet still the blood is strong, the heart is Highland, / And we in dreams behold the Hebrides! [Sir Walter Scott, 1771–1832, *Canadian Boat Song* (authorship disputed)]

See also UNITED STATES

CANNIBALS

1 Cannibal – A guy who goes into a restaurant and orders the waiter. [Jack Benny, 1894–1974; in A K Adams, *Cassell's Book of Humorous Quotations*]

2 I won't eat anything that has intelligent life, but I'd gladly eat a network executive or a politician. [Marty Feldman, 1933–83; in *The Cook's Quotation Book*, ed. Maria Polushkin Robbins]

3 Eating people is wrong. [Michael Flanders, 1922–75, song: *The Reluctant Cannibal*]

4 I do wish we could chat longer, Clarice, but I'm having an old friend for dinner. [Anthony Hopkins, 1937– , as Hannibal Lecter in film *The Silence of the Lambs*, scripted by Ted Tally]

5 A converted cannibal is one who, on Friday, eats only fishermen. [Emily Lotney; in Laurence J Peter, *Peter's Quotations*, 'Religion']

6 I have been assured by a very knowing American of my acquaintance in London, that a young healthy child well nursed is at a year old a most delicious, nourishing, and wholesome food, whether stewed, roasted, baked, or boiled, and I make no doubt that it will equally serve in a fricassee, or a ragout. [Jonathan Swift, 1677–1745, *A Modest Proposal*]

7 The better sort of Ishmaelites have been Christian for many centuries and will not publicly eat human flesh uncooked in Lent, without special and costly dispensation from their bishop. [Evelyn Waugh, 1903–66, *Scoop*, Bk II, Ch. 1, 1]

CAPITALISM

1 What is the difference between Capitalism and Communism? Capitalism is the exploitation of man by man; Communism is the reverse. [anon. Polish joke; in R T Tripp, *International Thesaurus of Quotations*]

2 The trouble about a free market economy is that it requires so many policemen to make it work. [Neal Ascherson, 1932– , *Games with Shadows*, 'Policing the Marketplace']

3 Making capitalism out of socialism is like making eggs out of an omelette. [Vadim Bakatin, first candidate in Russian presidential election, 1937– (said in May 1991), in *Hutchinson Gallup Info*, 92]

4 In a community where public services have failed to keep abreast of private consumption things are very different. Here in an atmosphere of private opulence and public squalor, the private goods have full sway. [J K Galbraith, 1908– , *The Affluent Society*, Ch. 18, ii]

5 The private sector is that part of the economy the Government controls and the public sector is the part that nobody controls. [James Goldsmith, 1933–97; *Observer*, 'Sayings of the Week', 25 Mar. 1979]

6 If I had to give a definition of capitalism I would say: the process whereby American girls turn into American women. [Christopher Hampton, 1946– , *Savages*, xvi]

7 It is the unpleasant and unacceptable face of capitalism. [Edward Heath, 1916– (of the Lonrho affair), in House of Commons, 15 May 1973]

8 It is Enterprise which builds and improves the world's possessions ... If Enterprise is afoot, Wealth accumulates whatever may be happening to Thrift; and if Enterprise is asleep, Wealth decays, whatever Thrift may be doing. [John Maynard Keynes, 1883–1946, *Treatise on Money*]

9 If it were necessary to give the briefest possible definition of imperialism, we should have to say that imperialism is the monopoly stage of capitalism. [Vladimir Ilyich Lenin, 1870–1924, *Imperialism, the Highest Stage of Capitalism*, Ch. 7]

10 First of all the Georgian silver goes, and then all that nice furniture that used to be in the saloon. Then the Canalettos go. [Harold Macmillan, 1894–1986 (on privatization), speech to Tory Reform Group, 8 Nov. 1985]

11 Once we [the Poles] had socialism without social justice, now we have capitalism without capital. [Jan Petrzak; *Observer*, 'Sayings of the Week', 15 Apr. 1990]

12 Property is theft [Pierre-Joseph Proudhon, 1809–65, *What is Property?*]

13 Capitalism was doomed ethically before it was doomed economically, a long time ago. [Alexander Solzhenitsyn, 1918– , *Cancer Ward*, Pt II, Ch. 10]

14 It has been well said that the quarrel between capitalism and communism is whether to sit upstairs or downstairs in a bus going the wrong way. [Revd John Stewart, 1909– , letter to the *Listener*, 18 Dec. 1986]

15 Lenin was the first to discover that capitalism 'inevitably' caused war; and he discovered this only when the First World War was already being fought. Of course he was right. Since every great state was capitalist in 1914, capitalism obviously 'caused' the First World War; but just as obviously it had 'caused' the previous generation of Peace. [A J P Taylor, 1906–90, *The Origins of the Second World War*, Ch. 6]

See also COMMUNISM

CARS

1 I think that cars today are almost the exact equivalent of the great Gothic cathedrals: I mean the supreme creation of an era, conceived with passion by unknown artists, and consumed in image if not in usage by a whole population which appropriates them as a purely magical object. [Roland Barthes, 1915–80, *Mythologies*, 'The New Citroën']

2 I have done almost every human activity inside a taxi which does not require main drainage. [Alan Brien, 1925– , in *Punch*, 5 July 1972]

3 The auto, which has made the American the biggest potential rolling army in the world, has also drained us of that plenitude of quiet and patience that makes a people significant in wisdom rather than in waste. [Edward Dahlberg, 1900–1977, *Alms for Oblivion*, 'Randolph Bourne']

4 What is this that roareth thus? / Can it be a Motor Bus? / Yes, the smell and hideous hum / Indicat Motorem Bum. [A D Godley, 1856–1925, *The Motor Bus*]

5 The poetry of motion! The *real* way to travel! The *only way* to travel! Here today – in next week, tomorrow! [(Of the car) Kenneth Grahame, 1859–1932, *The Wind in the Willows*, Ch. 2]

6 When I caught a glimpse of Rita, / Filling in a ticket across her shoulder, made her look a little like a milit'ry man. / Lovely Rita, Meter Maid. [John Lennon, 1940–80, and Paul McCartney, 1942– , song: *Lovely Rita*]

7 To George F. Babbitt ... his motor-car was poetry and tragedy, love and heroism. The office was his pirate ship, but the car his perilous excursion ashore. [Sinclair Lewis, 1885–1951, *Babbitt*, Ch. 3]

8 Stepping into his new Buick convertible he [the American] knows that he would gladly do without it, but imagines that to his neighbour, who is just backing *his* out of the driveway, this car is the motor of life. [Mary McCarthy, 1912–89, *On the Contrary*, 'America the Beautiful']

9 The car has become the carapace, the protective and aggressive shell, of urban and suburban man. [Marshall McLuhan, 1911–80, *Understanding Media*, 22]

10 At sixty miles an hour the loudest noise in this new Rolls-Royce comes from the electric clock. [David Ogilvy, 1911–99, advertisement, in *Confessions of an Advertising Man*, Ch. 6]

11 A car is just a hard shell of aggression, for the soft urban mollusc to secrete itself in. It's a form of disguise. All its parts are hidden. [Stewart Parker, 1941–88, *Spokesong*, II]

12 It is the overtakers who keep the undertakers busy. [William Pitts, 1900–1980; *Observer*, 'Sayings of the Week', 22 Dec. 1963]

13 I've always felt it was the car which went down to the showroom to choose the man, not the other way round, and Volvos like to pick a dentist who is going to send his son to a not quite first-rate public school. [Robert Robinson, 1927– , *Dog Chairman*, 'The Place of the Volvo']

14 Take most people, they're crazy about cars ... and if they get a brand-new car already they start thinking about trading it in for one that's even newer. I don't even like *old* cars. I mean they don't even interest me. I'd rather have a goddam horse. A horse is at least *human*, for God's sake. [J D Salinger, 1919– , *The Catcher in the Rye*, Ch. 17]

CATHOLICS

1 Catholicism – that's die now and pay later. [Woody Allen, 1935– , in film *Hannah and Her Sisters*]

2 He was of the faith chiefly in the sense that the church he currently did not attend was Catholic. [Kingsley Amis, 1922–95, *One Fat Englishman*, Ch. 8]

3 Rome has spoken; the case is concluded. [St Augustine, 354–430, *Sermons*, Bk i]

4 Though Rome's gross yoke / Drops off, no more to be endured, / Her teaching is not so obscured / By errors and perversities, / That no truth shines athwart the lies. [Robert Browning, 1812–89, *Christmas Eve*, 11]

5 What little religion ran in her veins being a condensed Roman Catholicism. [Patrick Gale, 1962– , *Facing the Tank*, 18]

6 Catholics and Communists have committed great crimes, but at least they have not stood aside, like an established society, and been indifferent. I would rather have blood on my hands than water like Pilate. [Graham Greene, 1904–91, *The Comedians*, Pt III, Ch. 4, iv]

7 Truth, for its own sake, had never been a virtue with the Romish clergy. Father Newman informs us that it need not, and on the whole ought not to be; that cunning is the weapon which Heaven has given to the saints wherewith to withstand the brute male force of the wicked world which marries and is given in marriage. Whether his notion be doctrinally correct or not, it is at least historically so. [Charles Kingsley, 1819–75, review of J A Froude's *History of England*, in *Macmillan's Magazine*, Jan. 1864]

8 We know these new English Catholics. They are the last words in Protest. They are Protestants protesting against Protestantism. [D H Lawrence, 1885–1930, review of Eric Gill's *Art Nonsense*]

9 She [the Roman Church] thoroughly understands what no other Church has ever understood, how to deal with enthusiasts. [Lord Macaulay, 1800–1859, *Historical Essays*, 'Von Ranke']

10 The Catholic and the Communist are alike in assuming that an opponent cannot be both honest and intelligent. [George Orwell, 1903–50, *Collected Essays*, 'The Prevention of Literature']

11 I was fired from there [her convent school], finally, for a lot of things, among them my insistence that the Immaculate Conception was spontaneous combustion. [Dorothy Parker, 1893–1967, in *Writers at Work*, ed. Malcolm Cowley, First Series]

12 Protestant women may take the Pill. Roman Catholic women must keep taking the *Tablet*. [Irene Thomas, 1920–94?, attr. in conversation]

13 'God knows how you Protestants can be expected to have any sense of direction,' she said. 'It's different with us. I haven't been to mass for years, I've got every mortal sin on my conscience, but I know when I'm doing wrong. I'm still a Catholic.' [Angus Wilson, 1913–91, *The Wrong Set*, 'Significant Experience']

See also CHURCH OF ENGLAND, PAPACY, PROTESTANTS

CATS

1 It [the Cheshire Cat] vanished quite slowly, beginning with the end of the tail, and ending with the grin, which remained some time after the rest of it had gone. [Lewis Carroll, 1832–98, *Alice in Wonderland*, Ch. 6]

2 He always has an alibi, and one or two to spare: / At whatever time the deed took place – Macavity wasn't there! [T S Eliot, 1888–1965, *Macavity: The Mystery Cat*]

3 What female heart can gold despise? / What cat's averse to fish? [Thomas Gray, 1716–71, *Ode on the Death of a Favourite Cat*]

4 I have noticed that what cats most appreciate in a human being is not the ability to produce food which they take for granted – but his or her entertainment value. [Geoffrey Household, 1900–1988, *Rogue Male*]

5 The Cat. He walked by himself, and all places were alike to him. [Rudyard Kipling, 1865–1936, *Just So Stories*, 'The Cat That Walked by Himself']

6 Cat: one Hell of a nice animal, frequently mistaken for a meatloaf. [B Kliban, 1935–90, *Cat*]

7 When the tea is brought at five o'clock, / And all the neat curtains are drawn with care, / The little black cat with bright green eyes / Is suddenly purring there. [Harold Monro, 1879–1932, *Milk for the Cat*]

8 When I play with my cat, who knows whether she is not amusing herself with me more than I with her. [Michel de Montaigne, 1533–92, *Essays*, II, 12]

9 The trouble with a kitten is / THAT / Eventually it becomes a / CAT. [Ogden Nash, 1902–71, *The Kitten*]

10 I love little pussy, / Her coat is so warm, / And if I don't hurt her,/ She'll do me no harm. [Nursery rhyme]

11 The greater cats with golden eyes / Stare out between the bars. [Victoria Sackville-West, 1892–1962, *The King's Daughter*, II, 1]

12 A harmless necessary cat. [William Shakespeare, 1564–1616, *The Merchant of Venice*, IV. i. 55]

13 Vengeance I ask and cry, / By way of exclamation, / On all the whole nation / Of cattes wild and tame: / God send them sorrow and shame! [John Skelton, *c.*1460–1529, *Philip Sparrow*, 273]

14 I will consider my Cat Jeoffry. / For he is the servant of the Living God, duly and daily serving him. [Christopher Smart, 1722–71, *Jubilate Agno*, XIX, 51]

15 Q: We have cats the way most people have mice [Signed] Mrs C. L. FOOTLOOSE
A: I see you have. I can't tell from your communication whether you wish advice or are just boasting. [James Thurber, 1894–1961, *The Owl in the Attic*]

See also ANIMALS, DOGS

CAUTION

1 *Quidquid agas, prudenter agas, et respice finem.* – Whatever you do, do cautiously, and look to the end. [anon. chronicle *Gesta Romanorum*, cap. 103]

2 He was cautious, but he was careful not to show it. [Frederic Raphael, 1931– , *Oxbridge Blues*, 'The Muse']

3 Of all forms of caution, caution in love is perhaps the most fatal to true happiness. [Bertrand Russell, 1872–1970, *The Conquest of Happiness*, Ch. 12]

4 It is the bright day that brings forth the adder: / And that craves wary walking. [William Shakespeare, 1564–1616, *Julius Caesar*, II. i. 14]

CENSORSHIP

1 Would you allow your wife or your servant to read this book? [Mervyn Griffith-Jones, 1909–79, presenting the case for the prosecution of *Lady Chatterley's Lover*, 20 Oct. 1960, at Old Bailey, London]

2 It's red hot, mate. I hate to think of this sort of book getting into the wrong hands. As soon as I've finished this, I shall recommend they ban it. [Tony Hancock, 1924–68, BBC TV comedy series *Hancock's Half Hour*, 'The Missing Page', scripts by Ray Galton and Alan Simpson]

3 Wherever they burn books they will also end up burning people. [(Used as inscription on memorial at Dachau concentration camp) Heinrich Heine, 1797–1856, *Almansor*]

4 As good almost kill a man as kill a good book; who kills a man kills a reasonable creature, God's image; but he who destroys a good book, kills reason itself, kills the image of God, as it were in the eye. [John Milton, 1608–74, *Areopagitica*]

5 Hell must be a place where you are only allowed to read what you agree with. [John Mortimer, 1923– (on the furore over Salman Rushdie's *Satanic Verses*), in *The Sunday Times*, 5 Mar. 1989]

6 To burn a book is not to destroy it. One minute of darkness will not make us blind. [Salman Rushdie, 1937– , review of Gabriel García Márquez, *Clandestine in Chile*, in the *Weekend Guardian*, 14–15 Oct. 1989]

7 It is not difficult to censor foreign news, / What is hard today is to censor one's own thoughts, – / To sit by and see the blind man / On the sightless horse, riding into the bottomless abyss. [Arthur Waley, 1889–1965, *Censorship*]

CERTAIN & UNCERTAIN

1 If a man will begin with certainties, he shall end in doubts; but if he will be content to begin with doubts, he shall end in certainties. [Francis Bacon, 1561–1626, *The Advancement of Learning*, I, v, 8]

2 Nothing more certain than incertainties; / Fortune is full of fresh variety: / Constant in nothing but inconstancy. [Richard Barnfield, 1574–1627, *The Shepherd's Content*, xi]

3 What is now proved was once only imagined. [William Blake, 1757–1827, *The Marriage of Heaven and Hell*, 'Proverbs of Hell']

4 The man who has made up his mind for all contingencies will often be too quick for one who tries to understand. [Pieter Geyl, 1887–1966, *Debates with Historians*, 'Ranke in the Light of the Catastrophe']

5 I'll give you a definite maybe. [Samuel Goldwyn, 1882–1974, attr.]

6 Has it occurred to you that the lust for certainty may be a sin? [Archbishop John Habgood, 1927– , in BBC TV Programme *On the Record*, 8 Dec. 1988]

7 Negative Capability, that is, when a man is capable of being in uncertainties, mysteries, doubts, without any irritable reaching after fact and reason. [John Keats, 1795–1821, letter to G and T Keats, 21 Dec. 1817]

8 I had nothing to offer anybody except my own confusion. [Jack Kerouac, 1922–69, *On the Road*, Pt II, 3]

9 Ah, what a dusty answer gets the soul / When hot for certainties in this our life. [George Meredith, 1828–1909, *Modern Love*, 50]

10 'This one's going to be a real winner,' said C.J. 'I didn't get where I am today without knowing a real winner when I see one.' [David Nobbs, 1935– , in BBC TV series, 1976–80, *The Fall and Rise of Reginald Perrin*, 'Thursday', and running catchphrase]

11 On the subject of confused people, I liked the store detective who said he'd seen a lot of people so confused that they'd stolen things, but never one so confused that they'd paid twice. [Norah Phillips, 1910–92, in *Sunday Telegraph*, 14 Aug. 1977]

12 He combined scepticism of everything with credulity about everything ... and I am convinced this is the true Shakespearean way wherewith to take life. [John Cowper Powys, 1872–1963, *Autobiography*, Introduction]

13 What men really want is not knowledge but certainty. [Bertrand Russell, 1872–1970, quoted by G M Carstairs, in *Listener*, 30 July 1964]

14 Be sure of it; give me the ocular proof. [William Shakespeare, 1564–1616, *Othello*, III. iii. 361]

15 In what concerns divine things, belief is not fitting. Only certainty will do. Anything less than certainty is not worthy of God. [Simone Weil, 1909–43, *Waiting on God*, 'Forms of the Implicit Love of God']

See also AMBIVALENCE, BELIEF, DOUBT

CHANCE

1 So they cast lots, and the lot fell upon Jonah. [Bible, OT, *Jonah* 1:7]

2 And a certain man drew a bow at a venture, and smote the king of Israel between the joints of the harness. [Bible, OT, *I Kings* 22:34]

3 But for the grace of God, there goes John Bradford. [John Bradford, 1510?–55, on seeing some criminals led to execution]

4 Crass Casualty obstructs the sun and rain, / And dicing Time for gladness casts a moan ... / These purblind Doomsters had as readily strown / Blisses about my pilgrimage as pain. [Thomas Hardy, 1840–1928, *Hap*]

5 That power / Which erring men call Chance. [John Milton, 1608–74, *Comus*, 587]

6 He either fears his fate too much, / Or his deserts are small, / That puts it not unto the touch / To win or lose it all. [Marquis of Montrose, 1612–50, *My Dear and Only Love*]

7 If Cleopatra's nose had been shorter, the whole face of the earth would have changed. [Blaise Pascal, 1623–62, *Pensées*, II, 162]

8 O! many a shaft, at random sent / Finds mark the archer little meant! / And many a word, at random spoken, / May soothe or wound a heart that's broken! [Sir Walter Scott, 1771–1832, *The Lord of the Isles*, V, 28]

See also ACCIDENTS, DESTINY, LUCK

CHANGE

1 *Tempora mutantur, et nos mutamur in illis.* – Times change, and we change with them. [anon., quoted in Harrison, *Description of Britain* (1577), Pt III, Ch. iii]

2 Remember that to change your mind and follow him who sets you right is to be none the less free than you were before. [Marcus Aurelius, 121–80, *Meditations*, VIII, 16]

3 But we breathe, we change! We lose our hair, our teeth! Our bloom! Our ideas! [Samuel Beckett, 1906–89, *Endgame*]

4 Can the Ethiopian change his skin, or the leopard his spots? [Bible, OT, *Jeremiah* 13:23]

5 The world's a scene of changes, and to be / Constant, in Nature were inconstancy. [Abraham Cowley, 1618–67, *Inconstancy*]

6 A man so various that he seemed to be / Not one, but all mankind's epitome. / Stiff in opinions, always in the wrong; / Was everything by starts and nothing long: / But, in the course of one revolving moon, / Was chemist, fiddler, statesman, and buffoon. [John Dryden, 1631–1700, *Absalom and Achitophel*, Pt I, 545]

7 He believed in sudden conversion, a belief which may be right, but which is peculiarly attractive to the half-baked mind. [E M Forster, 1879–1970, *Howards End*, Ch. 6]

8 People change and forget to tell each other. [Lillian Hellman, 1905–84, *Toys in the Attic*, III]

9 All is flux, nothing stays still. [Heraclitus, *c.*544–483 BC, in H Diels and W Kranz, *Fragments of the Pre-Socratics*]

10 You cannot step twice into the same river. [Heraclitus, *c.*544–483 BC, in H Diels and W Kranz, *Fragments of the Pre-Socratics*]

11 Alteration though it be from worse to better hath in it inconveniences, and those weighty. [Richard Hooker, 1554?–1600, *Of the Laws of Ecclesiastical Polity*, Bk 4, §14]

12 When our first parents were driven out of Paradise, Adam is believed to have remarked to Eve: 'My dear, we live in an age of transition.' [W R Inge, 1860–1954, *Assessments and Anticipations*, 'Work']

13 *Plus ça change, plus c'est la même chose.* – The more things change, the more they are the same. [Alphonse Karr, 1808–90, *Les Guêpes*, Jan. 1849]

14 If we want things to stay as they are, things will have to change. [Guiseppe di Lampedusa, 1896–1957, *The Leopard*, Ch. 1]

15 Nothing is settled, everything can still be altered. What was done but turned out wrong, can be done again. 'The Golden Age, which blind superstition had placed behind [or ahead of] us, is *in us*.' [Claude Lévi-Strauss, 1908– , *Tristes Tropiques*, Ch. 38]

16 Change and decay in all around I see; / O Thou, who changest not, abide with me! [H F Lyte, 1793–1847, hymn]

17 There is, in public affairs, no state so bad, provided it has age and stability on its side, that it is not preferable to change and disturbance. [Michel de Montaigne, 1533–92, *Essays*, II, 17]

18 The dropping of rain hollows out a stone, a ring is worn by use. [Ovid, 43BC–AD17, *Epistulae ex Ponto*, IV, x, 5]

19 Our life passes in transformation. [Rainer Maria Rilke, 1875–1926, *Duino Elegies*, 7]

20 Man's yesterday may ne'er be like his morrow; / Nought may endure but Mutability. [P B Shelley, 1792–1822, *Mutability*]

21 The old order changeth, yielding place to new, / And God fulfils Himself in many ways, / Lest one good custom should corrupt the world. [Alfred, Lord Tennyson, 1809–92, *Idylls of the King*, 'The Passing of Arthur', 408]

22 Let the great world spin for ever down the ringing grooves of change. [Alfred, Lord Tennyson, 1809–92, *Locksley Hall*, 812]

23 The stone that is rolling can gather no moss; / For master and servant oft changing is loss. [Thomas Tusser, 1524?–80, *Five Hundred Points of Good Husbandry*, 'Housewifely Admonitions']

24 First let me insist on what our opponents habitually ignore, and indeed, they seem intellectually incapable of understanding, namely the inevitable gradualness of our scheme of change. [Sidney Webb, 1859–1947, presidential speech at Labour Party Conference, London, 26 June 1923]

See also EVOLUTION, PROGRESS, REVOLUTIONS

CHAOS

1 She had the air of a born unpacker – swift and firm, yet withal tender . . . She was one of those born to make chaos cosmic. [Max Beerbohm, 1872–1956, *Zuleika Dobson*, Ch. 2]

2 There is nothing stable in the world; uproar's your only music. [John Keats, 1795–1821, letter to G and T Keats, 13 Jan. 1818]

3 Religion blushing veils her sacred fires, / And unawares morality expires. / Nor public flame, nor private, dares to shine; / Nor human spark is left nor glimpse divine! / Lo! thy dread empire, Chaos! is restored; / Light dies before thy uncreating word; / Thy hand, great Anarch! lets the curtain fall / And universal darkness buries all. [Alexander Pope, 1688–1744, *The Dunciad*, Bk iv, 649]

See also ANARCHY

CHARACTER

1 My Trouble is I lack what the English call character. By which they mean the power to refrain. [Alan Bennett, 1934– , *Single Spies*, 'An Englishman Abroad']

2 On ev'ry hand it will allow'd be, / He's just – nae better than he should be. [Robert Burns, 1759–96, *A Dedication to Gavin Hamilton*, 25]

3 She was a blonde nearly-young American woman of such dynamism that the tideless waves struggled to get farther up the beach. [Anthony Carson, *A Rose by Any Other Name*, Ch. 10]

4 Considering all the time you took forming yourself, Elsie, I'm surprised you're not a nicer little girl than you are. [Noël Coward, 1899–1973, *Fumed Oak*, II. ii]

5 All my life I have held that you can class people according to how they may be imagined behaving to King Lear. [Isak Dinesen, 1885–1962, *Out of Africa*, 'Farah and I Sell Out']

6 A man so various that he seemed to be / Not one, but all mankind's epitome. / Stiff in opinions, always in the wrong; / Was everything by starts and nothing long: / But, in the course of one revolving moon, / Was chemist, fiddler, statesman, and buffoon. [John Dryden, 1631–1700, *Absalom and Achitophel*, Pt I, 545]

7 'Character,' says Novalis, in one of his questionable aphorisms – 'character is destiny.' [George Eliot, 1819–80, *The Mill on the Floss*, Bk vi, Ch. 6]

8 A character, no more than a fence, can be strengthened by whitewash. [Paul Frost, 1938– ; in *Hodder Book of Christian Quotations*, comp. Tony Castle]

9 There are people whose external reality is generous because it is transparent, because you can read everything, accept everything, understand everything about them: people who carry their own sun with them. [Carlos Fuentes, 1928– , *The Old Gringo*, 6]

10 Talent is formed in quiet, character in the stream of human life. [Johann Wolfgang von Goethe, 1749–1832, *Torquato Tasso*, I, ii]

11 In a devious way I am uncomplicated. [Günter Grass, 1927– , *From the Diary of a Snail*, Ch. 8]

12 Having a character that consists mainly of defects, I try to correct them one by one, but there are limits to the altitude that can be attained by hauling on one's own boot-straps. [Clive James, 1939– , *Unreliable Memoirs*, Ch. 3]

13 She had indeed no sense of humour and, with her pretty way of holding her head on one side, was one of those persons whom you want, as the phrase is, to shake, but who have learnt Hungarian by themselves. [Henry James, 1843–1916, *The Figure in the Carpet*, V]

14 She's the sort of woman who does a tremendous lot for her old governesses. [Marcel Proust, 1871–1922, *Remembrance of Things Past: The Guermantes Way*, Ch. 1]

15 You can tell a lot about a fellow's character by his way of eating jelly beans. [Ronald Reagan, 1911– , in *The New York Times*, 15 Jan. 1981]

16 He looked like the kind of a guy that wouldn't talk to you much unless he wanted something off you. He had a lousy personality. [J D Salinger, 1919– , *The Catcher in the Rye*, Ch. 11]

17 Give me that man / That is not passion's slave, and I will wear him / In my heart's core, ay, in my heart of heart, / As I do thee. [William Shakespeare, 1564–1616, *Hamlet*, III. ii (76)]

18 There was a star danced, and under that was I born. [*Much Ado About Nothing*, II. i. (351)]

19 My nature is subdued / To what it works in, like the dyer's hand. [*Sonnets*, 111]

20 Though her mien carries much more invitation than command, to behold her is an immediate check to loose behaviour; to love her is a liberal education. [Richard Steele, 1672–1729, *The Tatler*, 49]

CHARITY

1 The living need charity more than the dead. [George Arnold, 1834–65, *The Jolly Old Pedagogue*]

2 We are all here on earth to help others; what on earth the others are here for I don't know. [W H Auden, 1907–73; in *Barnes and Noble Book of Quotations*, ed. Robert I Fitzhenry, 'Goodness']

3 In charity there is no excess. [Francis Bacon, 1561–1626, *Essays*, 13, 'Of Goodness and Goodness of Nature']

4 Blessed is he that considereth the poor: the

Lord will deliver him in time of trouble. [Bible, OT, *Psalms* 41:1]

5 Knowledge puffeth up, but charity edifieth. [Bible, NT, *1 Corinthians* 8:1]

6 Though I speak with the tongues of men and of angels, and have not charity, I am become as sounding brass, or a tinkling cymbal. [Bible, NT, *1 Corinthians* 13:1]

7 And now abideth faith, hope, charity, these three; but the greatest of these is charity. [Bible, NT, *1 Corinthians* 13:13]

8 Charity shall cover the multitude of sins. [Bible, NT, *1 Peter* 4:8]

9 And there came a certain poor widow, and she threw in two mites. [Bible, NT, *St Mark* 12:42]

10 When thou doest alms, let not thy left hand know what thy right hand doeth. [Bible, NT, *St Matthew* 6:3]

11 A man who sees another man on the street corner with only a stump for an arm will be so shocked the first time he'll give him sixpence. But the second time it'll only be a threepenny bit. And if he sees him a third time, he'll have him cold-bloodedly handed over to the police. [Bertolt Brecht, 1898–1956, *The Threepenny Opera*, I. i]

12 Too many people have decided to do without generosity in order to practise charity. [Albert Camus, 1913–60, *The Fall*]

13 Charity is the power of defending that which we know to be indefensible. Hope is the power of being cheerful in circumstances which we know to be desperate. [G K Chesterton, 1874–1936, *Heretics*, 12]

14 Subscribe to our noble society for providing the infant negroes in the West Indies with flannel waistcoats and moral pocket handkerchiefs. [Charles Dickens, 1812–70, *Pickwick Papers*, Ch. 27]

15 True generosity consists precisely in fighting to destroy the causes which nourish false charity. [Paulo Freire, 1921–97, *Pedagogy of the Oppressed*, Ch. 1]

16 Far other aims his heart had learned to prize, / More skilled to raise the wretched than to rise. / His house was known to all the vagrant train, / He chid their wanderings, but relieved their pain. [Oliver Goldsmith, 1728–74, *The Deserted Village*, 147]

17 There are people who can never forgive a beggar for their not having given him anything. [Karl Kraus, 1874–1936, *Half-truths and One-and-a-half Truths*, 'Lord, Forgive the . . .']

18 [Of charitable donations] It's rather like trying to mop up the oceans of the world with a box of Kleenex, but it keeps compassion fatigue at bay. [David Lodge, 1935– , *Therapy* 1, p. 6]

19 The organized charity, scrimped and iced, / In the name of a cautious, statistical Christ. [J B O'Reilly, 1844–90, *In Bohemia*]

20 In faith and hope the world will disagree, / But all mankind's concern is charity. [Alexander Pope, 1688–1744, *An Essay on Man*, III, 303]

21 *Inopi beneficium bis dat qui dat celeriter*. – He gives the poor twice as much good who gives quickly. [Publilius Syrus, 1st cent. BC, *Maxims*, 6. Becomes proverb: *Bis dat qui cito dat* – He gives twice who gives promptly]

22 No one would remember the Good Samaritan if he'd only had good intentions. He had money as well. [Margaret Thatcher, 1925– , TV interview, 6 Jan. 1986]

23 I try to give to the poor people what the rich could get for money. No, I wouldn't touch a leper for a thousand pounds; yet I would willingly cure him for the love of God. [Mother Teresa, 1910–97, *A Gift for God*, 'Riches']

24 Give all thou canst; high Heaven rejects the lore / Of nicely-calculated less or more. [William Wordsworth, 1770–1850, *Ecclesiastical Sonnets*, III, 43, 'Inside of King's College Chapel, Cambridge']

CHARM

1 It's a sort of bloom on a woman. If you have it, you don't need to have anything else; and if you don't have it, it doesn't much matter what else you have. [James Barrie, 1860–1937, *What Every Woman Knows*, I]

2 You know what charm is: a way of getting the answer yes without having asked any clear question. [Albert Camus, 1913–60, *The Fall*]

3 All charming people have something to conceal, usually their total dependence on the appreciation of others. [Cyril Connolly, 1903–74, *Enemies of Promise*, Ch. 16]

4 The most winning woman I ever knew was hanged for poisoning three little children for their insurance money. [Arthur Conan Doyle, 1859–1930, *The Sign of Four*, Ch. 2]

5 Whate'er he did was done with so much ease, / In him alone 'twas natural to please. [John Dryden, 1631–1700, *Absalom and Achitophel*, Pt I, 27]

6 People were not charmed with Eglantine because she herself was charming, but because she was charmed. [Ada Leverson, 1865–1936, *Love at Second Sight*]

CHASTITY

1 Give me chastity and continency, but not yet. [St Augustine, 354–430, *Confessions*, VIII, 7]

2 'Tis Chastity, my brother, Chastity: / She that has that is clad in complete steel. [John Milton, 1608–74, *Comus*, 420]

3 How happy is the blameless vestal's lot! / The world forgetting, by the world forgot. [Alexander Pope, 1688–1744, *Elegy to the Memory of an Unfortunate Lady*, 207]

4 Your old virginity is like one of our French withered pears; it looks ill, it eats drily. [William Shakespeare, 1564–1616, *All's Well that Ends Well*, I. i. (176)]

5 Chaste as the icicle / That's curdied by the frost from purest snow, / And hangs on Dian's temple. [*Coriolanus*, V. iii. 65]

6 Be thou as chaste as ice, as pure as snow, thou shalt not escape calumny. [*Hamlet*, III. i. (142)]

7 A man whose blood / Is very snow-broth; one who never feels / The wanton stings and motions of the sense. [*Measure for Measure*, I. iv. 57]

8 Why should a man whose blood is warm within, / Sit like his grandsire cut in alabaster? [*The Merchant of Venice*, I. i. 83]

See also PURITY

CHILDHOOD & CHILDREN

1 I am an only child. I have one sister. [Woody Allen, 1935– , in Adler and Feinman, *WA: Clown Prince of American Humor*, Ch. 2]

2 It was no wonder that people were so horrible when they started life as children. [Kingsley Amis, 1922–95, *One Fat Englishman*, 14]

3 Only those in the last stage of disease could believe that children are true judges of character. [W H Auden, 1907–73, 'Journal of an Airman']

4 Children sweeten labours; but they make misfortunes more bitter. [Francis Bacon, 1561–1626, *Essays*, 7, 'Of Parents and Children']

5 Being constantly with children was like wearing a pair of shoes that were expensive and too small. She couldn't bear to throw them out, but they gave her blisters. [Beryl Bainbridge, 1934– , *Injury Time*, Ch. 4]

6 Were we closer to the ground as children or is the grass emptier now? [Alan Bennett, 1934– , *Forty Years On*, I]

7 Childhood is measured out by sounds and smells / And sights, before the dark of reason grows. [John Betjeman, 1906–84, *Summoned by Bells*, Ch. 4]

8 Out of the mouth of babes and sucklings hast thou ordained strength. [Bible, OT, *Psalms* 8:2]

9 Happy is the man that hath his quiver full of them. [Bible, OT, *Psalms* 127:5]

10 When I was a child, I spake as a child, I understood as a child, I thought as a child: but when I became a man, I put away childish things. [Bible, NT, *1 Corinthians* 13:11]

11 Suffer the little children to come unto me, and forbid them not: for of such is the kingdom of heaven. [Bible, NT, *St Mark* 10:14]

12 He who shall teach the child to doubt / The rotting grave shall ne'er get out. [William Blake, 1757–1827, *Auguries of Innocence*]

13 Perfect little body, without fault or stain on thee. [Robert Bridges, 1844–1930, *On a Dead Child*]

14 Do you hear the children weeping, O my brothers, / Ere the sorrow comes with years? [Elizabeth Barrett Browning, 1806–61, *The Cry of the Children*]

15 Cornelia kept her in talk till her children came from school, and these, said she, are my jewels. [Robert Burton, 1577–1640, *Anatomy of Melancholy*, III, §2, Memb. 2, 3]

16 As soon as I stepped out of my mother's womb on to dry land, I realized that I had made a mistake – that I shouldn't have come, but the trouble with children is that they are not returnable. [Quentin Crisp, 1908–99, *The Naked Civil Servant*, Ch. 2]

17 I think I can say my childhood was as

unhappy as the next braggart's. [Peter de Vries, 1910–93, *Comfort Me with Apples*, Ch. 1]

18 Language was not powerful enough to describe the infant phenomenon. [Charles Dickens, 1812–70, *Nicholas Nickleby*, Ch. 23]

19 Young children have no sense of wonder. They bewilder well but few things surprise them. [Annie Dillard, 1945– , *An American Childhood*, Pt 2]

20 [When asked whether he liked children] I do if they're properly cooked! [W C Fields, 1879–1946, in *Fields for President*, Ch. 7]

21 *Les enfants terribles.* – The embarrassing young. [Gavarni, 1804–66, title of a series of prints]

22 STEVE: What have you got against having children?

SIMON: Well, Steve, in the first place there isn't enough room. In the second place they seem to start by mucking up their parents' lives, and then go on in the third place to muck up their own. In the fourth place it doesn't seem right to bring them into a world like this in the fifth place and in the sixth place I don't like them very much in the first place. OK? [Simon Gray, 1936– , *Otherwise Engaged*, II]

23 Where once my careless childhood strayed, / A stranger yet to pain. [Thomas Gray, 1716–71, *Ode on a Distant Prospect of Eton College*, 2]

24 There is always one moment in childhood when the door opens and lets the future in. [Graham Greene, 1904–91, *The Power and the Glory*, Pt I, Ch. i]

25 Childhood's a risk we all take. [David Hughes, 1930– , *The Pork Butcher*, p. 114]

26 The proper time to influence the character of a child is about a hundred years before he is born. [W R Inge, 1860–1954; in *Observer*, 21 July 1929]

27 Children do not give up their innate imagination, curiosity, dreaminess easily. You have to love them to get them to do that. [R D Laing, 1927–89, *The Politics of Experience*, Ch. 3]

28 I hear in the chamber above me / The patter of little feet. [H W Longfellow, 1807–82, *The Children's Hour*]

29 Looking after children is one way of looking after yourself. [Ian McEwan, 1948– , *Black Dogs*, Preface]

30 Who can foretell for what high cause / This darling of the Gods was born? [Andrew Marvell, 1621–78, *The Picture of Little T.C. in a Prospect of Flowers*]

31 In those days, as a little child, I was living in Paradise, and had no need of the arts, that at best are only a shadow of Paradise. [John Masefield, 1878–1967, *So Long to Learn*]

32 The childhood shows the man, / As morning shows the day. Be famous then / By wisdom; as thy empire must extend, / So let extend thy mind o'er all the world. [John Milton, 1608–74, *Paradise Regained*, Bk iv, 220]

33 I love children – especially when they cry and somebody takes them away. [Nancy Mitford, 1904–73; in *Dictionary of Outrageous Quotations*, comp. C R S Marsden]

34 Perhaps a child, like a cat, is so much inside of himself that he does not see himself in the mirror. [Anaïs Nin, 1903–77, *Diary of A N*, Vol. 2, Mar. 1937]

35 I could see that childhood was an invention of grown-ups, a fiction we were required to take on trust in case we demanded something better. [Philip Oakes, 1938– ; in *Listener*, 9 Mar. 1989]

36 The modern child will answer you back before you've said anything. [Laurence J Peter, 1919–90, *Peter's Quotations*, 'Childhood']

37 The old Adam in this Child may be so buried, that the new man may be raised up in him. [*The Book of Common Prayer*, Public Baptism of Infants, Blessing]

38 Who will show a child as it really is? Who will place it in its constellation and put the measure of distance in its hand? [Rainer Maria Rilke, 1875–1926, *Duino Elegies*, 4]

39 Anybody who hates dogs and babies can't be all bad. [(Of W C Fields) Leo Rosten, 1908–97, at Masquers' Club Dinner, Hollywood, 16 Feb. 1939. Often misquoted as 'children and dogs' and wrongly attr. to Fields]

40 Grown-ups never understand anything for themselves, and it is tiresome for children to be always and forever explaining things to them. [Antoine de Saint-Exupéry, 1900–1944, *The Little Prince*, Ch. 1]

41 Children don't read to find their identity, to free themselves from guilt, to quench the thirst for rebellion or to get rid of alienation. They have no use for psychology. They detest sociology. They still believe in God, the family, angels, devils, witches, goblins, logic, clarity, punctuation, and other such obsolete stuff ... [Isaac Bashevis Singer, 1904–91, speech on receiving the Nobel Prize for Literature, in *Observer*, 17 Dec. 1978]

42 My parents kept me from children who were rough / And who threw words like stones and who wore torn clothes. [Stephen Spender, 1909–95, *My Parents Kept Me from Children Who Were Rough*]

43 A child should always say what's true / And speak when he is spoken to, / And behave mannerly at table: / At least as far as he is able. [Robert Louis Stevenson, 1850–94, *A Child's Garden of Verses*, 5, 'Whole Duty of Children']

44 A child becomes an adult when he realizes that he has a right not only to be right but also to be wrong. [Thomas Szasz, 1920– , *The Second Sin*, 'Childhood']

45 A child's / Forgotten mornings when he walked with his mother / Through the parables / Of sun light / And the legends of the green chapels. [Dylan Thomas, 1914–53, *Poem in October*]

46 Among these Mr Quiverful, the rector of Puddingdale, whose wife still continued to present him from year to year with fresh pledges of her love. [Anthony Trollope, 1815–82, *Barchester Towers*, Ch. 7]

47 Happy those early days! when I / Shined in my angel-infancy. / Before I understood this place / Appointed for my second race, / Or taught my soul to fancy aught / But a white celestial thought. [Henry Vaughan, 1622–95, *The Retreat*]

48 Never have children, only grandchildren. [Gore Vidal, 1925– , *Two Sisters*]

49 Birds in their little nests agree; / And 'tis a shameful sight, / When children of one family / Fall out, and chide, and fight. [Isaac Watts, 1674–1748, *Divine Songs for Children*, 17, 'Love between Brothers and Sisters']

50 Heaven lies around us in our infancy!/ Shades of the prison-house begin to close. / Upon the growing boy. [William Wordsworth, 1770–1850, *Ode, Intimations of Immortality*, 5]

51 Behold the child among his new-born blisses, / A six-years' darling of a pigmy size! [William Wordsworth, 1770–1850, *Ode, Intimations of Immortality*, 7]

52 The child is father of the man; / And I could wish my days to be / Bound each to each by natural piety. [William Wordsworth, 1770–1850, *My Heart Leaps Up*]

53 Sweet childish days, that were as long / As twenty days are now. [William Wordsworth, 1770–1850, *To a Butterfly, I've Watched You Now*]

54 – A simple child, / That lightly draws its breath, / And feels its life in every limb, / What should it know of death? [William Wordsworth, 1770–1850, *We are Seven*]

See also BOYS, GIRLS, PARENTS

CHINA & CHINESE

1 Almost one out of every four people in the world is Chinese, you know, even though many of them might not look it. [Joseph Heller, 1923–99, *Good as Gold*, 5]

2 Even the Hooligan was probably invented in China centuries before we thought of him. [Saki (H H Munro), 1870–1916, *Reginald on House-parties*]

3 A black sun has appeared in the sky of my motherland. [(Of the violent suppression of demonstration in Tiananmen Square, Beijing) Wuer Kaixi; *Observer*, 'Sayings of the Week', 2 July 1989]

CHIVALRY

1 Even nowadays a man can't step up and kill a woman without feeling just a bit unchivalrous. [Robert Benchley, 1889–1945, *Chips off the Old Benchley*, 'Down in Front']

2 But the age of chivalry is gone. That of sophisters, economists, and calculators, has succeeded; and the glory of Europe is extinguished for ever. [Edmund Burke, 1729–97, *Reflections on the Revolution in France*, Penguin edn, p. 170]

3 He was a verray parfit, gentil knight. [Geoffrey Chaucer, 1340?–1400, *Canterbury Tales*, 'Prologue', 72]

4 Some say that the age of chivalry is past, that the spirit of romance is dead. The age of chivalry is never past, so long as there is a wrong left unredressed on earth. [Charles Kingsley, 1819–75, quoted in Mrs C Kingsley, *Life*, ii, Ch. 28]

5 And much more am I sorrier for my good knights' loss than for the loss of my fair queen; for queens I might have enough, but such a fellowship of good knights shall never be together in no company. [Thomas Malory, d. 1471, *Morte d'Arthur*, Bk xx, Ch. 9]

6 So faithful in love, and so dauntless in war, / There never was knight like the young Lochinvar. [Sir Walter Scott, 1771–1832, *Marmion*, V, 12]

7 Now all the youth of England are on fire, / And silken dalliance in the wardrobe lies; / Now thrive the armourers, and honour's thought / Reigns solely in the breast of every man: / They sell the pasture now to buy the horse, / Following the mirror of all Christian kings, / With wingèd heels. [William Shakespeare, 1564–1616, *Henry V*, II. Chorus, 1]

8 To reverence the King, as if he were / Their conscience, and their conscience as their King, / To break the heathen and uphold the Christ, / To ride abroad redressing human wrongs, / To speak no slander, no, or listen to it, / To honour his own word as if his God's. [Alfred, Lord Tennyson, 1809–92, *Guinevere*, 465]

CHOICE

1 *L'embarras des richesses.* – Too much to choose from. [Abbé d'Allainval, 1700–1753, title of play]

2 Variety is the soul of pleasure. [Aphra Behn, 1640–89, *The Rover*, Pt II, I]

3 White shall not neutralize the black, nor good / Compensate bad in man, absolve him so: / Life's business being just the terrible choice. [Robert Browning, 1812–89, *The Ring and the Book*, X, 1235]

4 Variety's the very spice of life, / That gives it all its flavour. [William Cowper, 1731–1800, *The Task*, Bk II, 606]

5 Any colour, so long as it's black. [Henry Ford, 1863–1947, advertisement for Model-T Ford car, attr. in Allan Nevins, *Ford*, Vol. 2, Ch. 15]

6 I shall be telling this with a sigh / Somewhere ages and ages hence: / Two roads diverged in a wood, and I – / I took the one less travelled by, / And that has made all the difference. [Robert Frost, 1874–1963, *The Road Not Taken*]

7 Decisions are easier, you know, when there are no choices left. [P V Narasimha Rao, 1921– , first interview as Indian Prime Minister with foreign journalist, in *Observer*, 7 July 1991]

8 Choose an author as you choose a friend. [Earl of Roscommon, 1637–88, *Essay on Translated Verse*, 96]

9 There's small choice in rotten apples. [William Shakespeare, 1564–1616, *The Taming of the Shrew*, I. i. (137)]

10 Why every one as they like; as the good woman said when she kissed her cow. [Jonathan Swift, 1677–1745, *Polite Conversation*, Dialogue 1]

11 Where to elect there is but one, / 'Tis Hobson's choice, – take that or none. [Thomas Ward, 1577–1639, *England's Reformation*, Ch. 4]

12 Services are voluntary – that is to say, you must either attend all or none. [Evelyn Waugh, 1903–66, *Decline and Fall*, III, 1]

CHRISTIANITY

1 Half of Christendom worships a Jew, and the other half a Jewess. [anon.; in H L Mencken, *New Dictionary of Quotations*]

2 Onward, Christian soldiers, / Marching as to war, / With the Cross of Jesus / Going on before. [S Baring-Gould, 1834–1924, hymn]

3 God so loved the world, that he gave his only begotten Son, that whosoever believeth in him should not perish, but have everlasting life. [Bible, NT, *St John* 3:16]

4 I dare, without usurpation, assume the honourable style of a Christian. [Sir Thomas Browne, 1605–82, *Religio Medici*, Pt I, 1]

5 How very hard it is / To be a Christian! [Robert Browning, 1812–89, *Easter-Day*, 1]

6 Christians have burnt each other, quite persuaded / That all the Apostles would have done as they did. [Lord Byron, 1788–1824, *Don Juan*, I, 83]

7 But Cristes lore and his apostles twelve, / He taughte, but first he folwed it himselve. [Geoffrey Chaucer, 1340?–1400, *Canterbury Tales*, 'Prologue', 527]

8 'The Christian ideal,' it is said, 'has not been tried and found wanting; it has been found difficult and left untried.' [G K Chesterton, 1874–1936, *What's Wrong with the World*, 'The Unfinished Temple']

9 *In hoc signo vinces*. – Beneath this sign thou shalt conquer. [Emperor Constantine, 288?–337, words heard in a vision]

10 The Cross alone has flown the wave. / But since the Cross sank, much that's warped and cracked / Has followed in its name, has heaped its grave. [Hart Crane, 1899–1932, *The Mermen*]

11 A local cult, called Christianity. [Thomas Hardy, 1840–1928, *The Dynasts*, 1, vi]

12 Christianity promises to make men free; it never promises to make them independent. [W R Inge, 1860–1954, *The Philosophy of Plotinus*]

13 Christianity is good news: not good advice. [W R Inge, 1860–1954, in *Geoffrey Madan's Notebooks*, ed. J A Gere and John Sparrow, 'Livres sans nom']

14 To my own Gods I go. / It may be they shall give me greater ease / Than your cold Christ and tangled Trinities. [Rudyard Kipling, 1865–1936, *Plain Tales from the Hills*, 'Lisbeth', epigraph]

15 Christian! dost thou see them / On the holy ground, / How the troops of Midian / Prowl and prowl around? / Christian! up and smite them. / Counting gain but loss; / Smite them by the merit / Of the Holy Cross! [J M Neale, 1818–1866, hymn]

16 People may say what they like about the decay of Christianity; the religious system that produced green Chartreuse can never really die. [Saki (H H Munro), 1870–1916, *Reginald on Christmas Presents*]

17 How like a fawning publican he looks! / I hate him for he is a Christian. / But more for that in low simplicity / He lends out money gratis, and brings down / The rate of usance here with us in Venice. [William Shakespeare, 1564–1616, *The Merchant of Venice*, I. iii. (42)]

18 The Christian Church is the one organization in the world that exists purely for the benefit of non-members. [Archbishop William Temple, 1881–1944; in *Hodder Book of Christian Quotations*, comp. Tony Castle]

19 See how these Christians love one another. [Tertullian, *c*.160–*c*.220, *Apologeticus*, 39]

20 Donald is considerably to the right of our Lord and Saviour Jesus Christ! [John Updike, 1932– , *A Month of Sundays*, Ch. 18]

21 Lord, I ascribe it to Thy grace, / And not to chance, as others do, / That I was born of Christian race, / And not a Heathen or a Jew. [Isaac Watts, 1674–1748, *Divine Songs for Children*, 6, 'Praise for the Gospel']

22 Christianity really is a man's religion: there's not much in it for women except docility, obedience, who-sweeps-a-room-as-for-thy-cause, downcast eyes and death in childbirth. For the men it's better: all power and money and fine robes, the burning of heretics – fun, fun, fun! – and the Inquisition fulminating from the pulpit. [Fay Weldon, 1931– , *The Heart of the Country*, 'Love Your Enemy']

23 'You're a Christian?' 'Church of England,' said Mr Polly. 'Mm,' said the employer, a little checked. 'For good all round business work, I should have preferred a Baptist.' [H G Wells, 1866–1946, *The History of Mr Polly*, Ch. III, Pt 1]

24 Much in sorrow, oft in woe, / Onward, Christians, onward go. [Henry Kirke White, 1785–1806, hymn. Altered by Dr W B Collyer to 'Oft in danger, oft in woe']

25 Scratch the Christian and you find the pagan – spoiled. [Israel Zangwill, 1864–1926, *Children of the Ghetto*, II, 6]

See also ATHEISM, etc.

CHRISTMAS

1 I have often thought, says Sir Roger, it happens very well that Christmas should fall out in the middle of winter. [Joseph Addison, 1672–1719, *The Spectator*, 269]

2 Once in royal David's city / Stood a lowly cattle shed, / Where a Mother laid her Baby / In a manger for His bed: / Mary was that Mother mild, / Jesus Christ her little Child. [Mrs C F Alexander, 1818–95, hymn]

3 God rest you merry, gentlemen, / Let nothing you dismay; / Remember Christ our Saviour, / Was born on Christmas Day. [anon. carol: *God Rest You*]

4 I'm dreaming of a white Christmas, / Just like the ones I used to know. [Irving Berlin, 1888–1989, song: *White Christmas*, in musical *Holiday Inn*]

5 And is it true? And is it true, / This most tremendous tale of all, / Seen in a stained-glass window's hue, / A Baby in an ox's stall? [John Betjeman, 1906–84, *Christmas*]

6 Christians awake, salute the happy morn, / Whereon the Saviour of the world was born. [John Byrom, 1692–1763, hymn for Christmas Day]

7 He who begins by loving Christianity better than Truth will proceed by loving his own sect or church better than Christianity, and end by loving himself better than all. [Samuel Taylor Coleridge, 1772–1834, *Aids to Reflection, Moral and Religious Aphorisms*, 25]

8 A cold coming we had of it, / Just the worst time of the year / For a journey. [T S Eliot, 1888–1965, *Journey of the Magi*]

9 The established English custom of dropping the national mantle of self-consciousness at Christmastime and revealing the horrible likeness of the charade underneath. [Richard Gordon, 1921– , *Doctor in the House*, Ch. 10]

10 If someone said on Christmas Eve, / 'Come see the oxen kneel . . .' / I should go with him in the gloom, / Hoping it might be so. [Thomas Hardy, 1840–1928, *Oxen*]

11 Cassiopeia was over / Cassidy's hanging hill, / I looked and three whin bushes rode across / The horizon – the Three Wise Kings. [Patrick Kavanagh, 1905–67, *Christmas Childhood*]

12 This is the month and this the happy morn. [John Milton, 1608–74, *On the Morning of Christ's Nativity*, 1]

13 Good King Wenceslas looked out, / On the Feast of Stephen; / When the snow lay round about, / Deep and crisp and even. [J M Neale, 1818–66, carol]

14 Heap on more wood! the wind is chill; / But let it whistle as it will. / We'll keep our Christmas merry still. [Sir Walter Scott, 1771–1832, *Marmion*, VI, Introduction]

15 It came upon the midnight clear, / That glorious song of old, / From Angels bending near the earth / To touch their harps of gold; / 'Peace on the earth; good will to man / From Heaven's all gracious King.' / The world in solemn stillness lay / To hear the angels sing. [E H Sears, 1810–76, *That Glorious Song of Old*, carol]

16 As I in hoary winter's night stood shivering in the snow, / Surprised I was with sudden heat which made my heart to glow; / And lifting up a fearful eye to view what fire was near, / A pretty Babe all burning bright did in the air appear. [Robert Southwell, 1561?–95, *The Burning Babe*]

17 While shepherds watched their flocks by night / All seated on the ground, / The angel of the Lord came down / And glory shone around. [Nahum Tate, 1652–1715, and Nicholas Brady, 1659–1726, hymn]

18 At Christmas play and make good cheer, / For Christmas comes but once a year. [Thomas Tusser, 1524?–80, *Five Hundred Points of Good Husbandry*, 'The Farmer's Daily Diet']

19 To perceive Christmas through its wrapping becomes more difficult with every year. [E B White, 1899–1985, *The Second Tree from the Corner*, 'Time Present']

CHURCHES

1 The nearer the Church the further from God. [Lancelot Andrewes, 1565–1626, *Sermon on the Nativity* (1622)]

2 There is no salvation outside the Church. [St Augustine, 354–430, *De Bapt.*, IV, 17]

3 The Church's Restoration / In eighteen-eighty-three / Has left for contemplation / Not what there used to be. [John Betjeman, 1906–84, hymn]

4 Thou art Peter, and upon this rock I will build my church; and the gates of hell shall not prevail against it. [Bible, NT, *St Matthew* 16:18]

5 My house shall be called the house of prayer; but ye have made it a den of thieves. [Bible, NT, *St Matthew* 21:13]

6 But if at the Church they would give us some ale, / And a pleasant fire our souls to regale, / We'd sing and we'd pray all the livelong day, / Nor ever once wish from the Church to stray. [William Blake, 1757–1827, *Songs of Experience*, 'The Little Vagabond']

7 Every day people are straying away from the church and going back to God. Really. [Lenny Bruce, 1923–66, *The Essential Lenny Bruce*, ed. J Cohen, 'Religions Inc']

8 There's some are fou o' love divine, / There's some are fou o' brandy. [Robert Burns, 1759–96, *The Holy Fair*, 239]

9 Not a religion for gentlemen. [Charles II, 1630–85 (of Presbyterianism), in Bishop Burnet, *History of his Own Times*, Vol. i, Bk ii, Ch. 2]

10 What is a church? – Our honest sexton tells, / 'Tis a tall building, with a tower and bells. [George Crabbe, 1754–1832, *The Borough*, Letter 2, 11]

11 Our church is, I believe, the first split-level church in America. It has five rooms and two baths downstairs ... There is a small worship area at one end. [Peter de Vries, 1910–93, *The Mackerel Plaza*, Ch. 1]

12 Wherever God erects a house of prayer, / The Devil always builds a chapel there; / And 'twill be found, upon examination, / The latter has the largest congregation. [Daniel Defoe, 1661?–1731, *The True-Born Englishman*]

13 Our cathedrals are like abandoned computers now, but they used to be prayer factories once. [Lawrence Durrell, 1912–90, in *Listener*, 20 Apr. 1978]

14 The hippopotamus's day / Is passed in sleep; at night he hunts; / God works in a mysterious way – / The Church can feed and sleep at once. [T S Eliot, 1888–1965, *The Hippopotamus*]

15 I like the silent church before the service begins better than any preaching. [Ralph Waldo Emerson, 1803–82, *Essays*, 'Self-Reliance']

16 The three kinds of services you generally find in the Episcopal churches. I call them either low-and-lazy, broad-and-hazy, or high-and-crazy. [Willa Gibbs, 1917– , *The Dean*, Pt 1, Ch. 9]

17 There's nowt'll replace the formative intellectual matrices of a really well-run Sunday School. By Christ. [Trevor Griffiths, 1935– , *The Party*, II]

18 A serious house on serious earth it is. [Philip Larkin, 1922–85, *Church-going*]

19 There are many who stay away from church these days because you hardly ever mention God any more. [Arthur Miller, 1915– , *The Crucible*, I]

20 With antique pillars massy proof, / And storied windows richly dight, / Casting a dim religious light. / There let the pealing organ blow, / To the full-voiced quire below. [John Milton, 1608–74, *Il Penseroso*, 158]

21 The Churches grow old but do not grow up. [Doris Langley Moore, 1902–89, *The Vulgar Heart*, Ch. 2]

22 To church; and with my mourning, very handsome, and new periwig, make a great show. [Samuel Pepys, 1633–1703, *Diary*, 31 Mar. 1667]

23 As some to church repair, / Not for the doctrine, but the music there. [Alexander Pope, 1688–1744, *An Essay on Criticism*, 342]

24 A church can be so broadened that the roof falls in. [Michael Schmidt, 1947– , in *PN Review*, No. 61, 1988, Editorial]

25 The Church's one foundation / Is Jesus Christ her Lord; / She is His new creation / By water and the Word. [Samuel J Stone, 1839–1901, hymn]

26 I believe in the Church. One Holy, Catholic and Apostolic, and I regret that it nowhere exists. [Archbishop William Temple, 1881–1944, attr.]

27 In general the churches, visited by me too often on weekdays ... bore for me the same relation to God that billboards did to Coca-Cola: they promoted thirst without quenching it. [John Updike, 1932– , *A Month of Sundays*, Ch. 2]

28 Any God I ever felt in church I brought in with me. And I think all the other folks did too. They come to church to *share* God not find God. [Alice Walker, 1944– , *The Color Purple*, p. 165]

29 I have noticed again and again since I have been in the Church that lay interest in ecclesiastical matters is often a prelude to insanity. [Evelyn Waugh, 1903–66, *Decline and Fall*, I, 8]

30 'You're a Christian?' 'Church of England,' said Mr Polly. 'Mm,' said the employer, a little checked. 'For good all round business work, I should have preferred a Baptist.' [H G Wells, 1866–1946, *The History of Mr Polly*, Ch. III, Pt 1]

31 I look upon all the world as my parish. [John Wesley, 1703–91, *Journal*, 11 June 1739]

32 Tax not the royal Saint with vain expense. [William Wordsworth, 1770–1850, *Ecclesiastical Sonnets*, III, 43, 'Inside of King's College Chapel, Cambridge']

33 The Church complains of persecution when it is not allowed to persecute. [Luis de Zulueta, speech in the Spanish parliament, 1936]

CHURCH OF ENGLAND

1 [Of the parallels between the railways and the Church] Both had their heyday in the mid nineteenth century; both own a great deal of Gothic-style architecture which is expensive to maintain; both are regularly assailed by critics; and both are firmly convinced that they are the best means of getting man to his ultimate destination. [Revd W Awdry, 1911–97, creator of *Thomas the Tank Engine* children's books; quoted in his obituary in *Independent*, 22 Mar. 1997]

2 A little skill in antiquity inclines a man to Popery; but depth in that study brings him about again to our religion. [Thomas Fuller, 1608–61, *The Holy State*, Bk ii, Ch. 6]

3 I sometimes think that if the Lord Jesus returned today, the Church of England would ask him to set out his ideas on a single sheet of A4. [David Hare, 1947– , *Racing Demon*, I. iv]

4 We have just buried the Church of England. [Revd Joseph McCullough, 1908–90 (to David Edwards at the funeral of Archbishop William Temple), in obituary in *Guardian*, 7 Mar. 1990]

5 It is hard to tell where MCC ends and the Church of England begins. [J B Priestley, 1894–1984, in *New Statesman*, 20 July 1962]

6 The Church should go forward along the path of progress and be no longer satisfied only to represent the Conservative Party at prayer. [Maude Royden, 1876–1956, speech at Queen's Hall, London, 16 July 1917]

7 'The Church of England,' I said . . . 'is no doubt a compromise.' [J H Shorthouse, 1834–1903, *John Inglesant*, Ch. 39]

8 I have, alas, only one illusion left, and that is the Archbishop of Canterbury. [Sydney Smith, 1771–1845, in Lady Holland, *Memoir*, Vol. I, Ch. 9]

9 Becoming an Anglo-Catholic must surely be a sad business – rather like becoming an amateur conjurer. [John Strachey, 1901–63, *The Coming Struggle for Power*, Pt III, Ch. 11]

WINSTON CHURCHILL

1 Then comes Winston with his hundred-horse-power mind and what can I do? [Stanley Baldwin, 1867–1947, in G M Young, *Stanley Baldwin*, Ch. 11]

2 He is a man suffering from petrified adolescence. [Aneurin Bevan, 1897–1960, in Vincent Brome, *Aneurin Bevan*, Ch. 11]

3 To have been alive with him [Winston Churchill] was to have dined at the table of history. ['Cassandra', 1909–67, in *Daily Mirror*]

4 It was a nation and race dwelling all around the globe that had the lion's heart. I had the luck to be called upon to give the roar. [Winston Churchill, 1874–1965, speech at Palace of Westminster on his eightieth birthday, 30 Nov. 1954]

5 W.C. [Winston Churchill] is a bigger danger than the Germans by a long way in what is just now imminent in the Dardanelles. [Admiral John Fisher, 1841–1920, letter to Bonar Law, 17 May 1915, in Robert Blake, *The Unknown Prime Minister*, Ch. 15]

6 Winston [Churchill] would go up to his Creator and say that he would very much like to meet His Son, about Whom he had heard a great deal and, if possible, would like to call on the Holy Ghost. Winston *loved* meeting people. [David Lloyd George, 1863–1945, in A J Sylvester, *Diary*, 2 Jan. 1937]

7 He mobilized the English language and sent it into battle to steady his fellow countrymen and hearten those Europeans upon whom the long dark night of tyranny had descended. [Edward R Murrow, 1908–65, broadcast, 30 Nov. 1954]

8 It is fun to be in the same decade with you. [Franklin D Roosevelt, 1882–1945 (to Churchill, in answer to congratulations on his sixtieth birthday), in Winston S Churchill, *The Hinge of Fate*, Ch. 4]

9 Simply a radio personality who outlived his prime. [Evelyn Waugh, 1903–66, in Christopher Sykes, *E W*]

CINEMA, see FILM

CITY

1 *Fourmillante cité, cité pleine de rêves, / Où le spectre en plein jour raccroche le passant! / Les mystères partout coulent comme des sèves / Dans les canaux étroits du colosse puissant.* – Swarming city, city full of dreams, where a ghost in daylight clutches a passer-by! Mysteries everywhere flow like sap in the narrow channels of the great giant. [Charles Baudelaire, 1821–67, *Les Sept Vieillards*]

2 Invoke the philologic pen / To show you that a Citizen / Means Something in the City. [G K Chesterton, 1874–1936, *Songs of Education*, 4, 'Citizenship']

3 No city should be too large for a man to walk out of in a morning. [Cyril Connolly, 1903–74, *The Unquiet Grave*, Ch. 1]

4 God the first garden made, and the first city Cain. [Abraham Cowley, 1618–67, *The Garden*]

5 American life, in large cities at any rate, is a perpetual assault on the senses and the nerves; it is out of asceticism, out of unworldliness, precisely, that we bear it. [Mary McCarthy, 1912–89, *On the Contrary*, 'America the Beautiful']

6 Towered cities please us then / And the busy hum of men. [John Milton, 1608–74, *L'Allegro*, 117]

7 Clearly, then, the city is not a concrete jungle, it is a human zoo. [Desmond Morris, 1928– , *The Human Zoo*, Introduction]

8 In the city time becomes visible. [Lewis Mumford, 1895–1990: *The Culture of Cities*, Introduction]

9 City government is of the people, by the rascals, for the rich. [Lincoln Steffens, 1866–1936, in *The Times*, 18 July 1977]

10 The City is of Night; perchance of Death, / But certainly of Night. [James Thomson, 1834–82, *The City of Dreadful Night*, 1]

11 A great city is that which has the greatest men and women. [Walt Whitman, 1819–92, *Song of the Broad-Axe*, 108]

See also COUNTRY, LONDON, NEW YORK, PARIS, ROME

CIVIL SERVICE

1 You know it's the best machine in the world, but you're not quite sure what to do with it. [R A Butler, 1902–82 (comparing Whitehall to a Rolls-Royce), in *The Sunday Times*, 8 Jan. 1989]

2 The Civil Service is profoundly deferential – 'Yes, Minister! No, Minister! If you wish it, Minister!' [Richard Crossman, 1907–74, *Diaries of a Cabinet Minister*, 22 Oct. 1964]

3 A difficulty for every solution. [Herbert Samuel, 1870–1963, attr.]

4 You can always tell employees of the government by the total vacancy which occupies the space where most other people have faces. [John Kennedy Toole, 1937–69, *A Confederacy of Dunces*, IX, 1]

5 Britain has invented a new missile. It's called the civil servant – it doesn't work and it can't be fired. [Walter Walker, 1912– ; *Observer*, 'Sayings of the Year', 3 Jan. 1982]

See also OFFICE

CIVIL WAR

1 From hence, let fierce contending nations know / What dire effects from civil discord flow. [Joseph Addison, 1672–1719, *Cato*, V. iv. 111]

2 When civil dudgeon first grew high, / And men fell out they knew not why. [Samuel Butler, 1612–80, *Hudibras*, I, i, 1]

3 As it will be the right of all, so it will be the duty of some, definitely to prepare for a separation, amicably if they can, violently if they must. [Josiah Quincy Jr, 1772–1864, speech in US House of Representatives, 14 Jan. 1811]

4 In a civil war, a general must know – and I'm afraid it's a thing rather of instinct than of practice – he must know exactly when to move over to the other side. [Henry Reed, 1914–86, BBC radio drama *Not a Drum was Heard: The War Memoirs of General Gland*]

See also REBELLION, REVOLUTION, WARS

CIVILIZATION

1 Civilizations are remembered by their artefacts, not their bank rates. [Stephen Bayley, 1951– , in *Guardian*, 31 Dec. 1987]

2 Suddenly, we have this mentality now, that if we destroy a building the past will be destroyed, and we will have no roots any more. A strong civilization is one that can replace things. [Pierre Boulez, 1925– , interview in *Guardian*, 13 Jan. 1989]

3 The three great elements of modern civilization, Gunpowder, Printing, and the Protestant Religion. [Thomas Carlyle, 1795–1881, *Critical and Miscellaneous Essays*, 'The State of German Literature']

4 And now, what will become of us without barbarians? Those people were a kind of solution.

[Constantine Cavafy, 1863–1933, *Waiting for the Barbarians*]

5 The civilization of one epoch becomes the manure of the next. Everything over-ripens in the same way. The disasters of the world are due to its inhabitants not being able to grow old simultaneously. [Cyril Connolly, 1903–74, *The Unquiet Grave*, Ch. 1]

6 In essence the Renaissance was simply the green end of one of civilization's hardest winters. [John Fowles, 1926– , *The French Lieutenant's Woman*, Ch. 10]

7 The principal task of civilization, its actual *raison d'être*, is to defend us against nature. [Sigmund Freud, 1856–1939, *The Future of an Illusion*]

8 We believe that civilization has been built up, *under the pressure of the struggle for existence*, by sacrifices in gratification of the primitive impulses. [Sigmund Freud, 1856–1939, *Introductory Lectures*]

9 [When asked by an interviewer what he thought of Western civilization] I think it would be a good idea. [Mahatma Gandhi, 1869–1948, attr. in E F Schumacher, *Good Work*, Ch. 2]

10 The resources of civilization are not yet exhausted. [W E Gladstone, 1809–98, speech at Leeds, 7 Oct. 1881]

11 Only in a decaying and doomed civilization did people imagine that they could eat their cake and have it; and that was precisely why they were doomed. [Arthur Koestler, 1905–83, *The Age of Longing*, Pt ii, Ch. 2]

12 The degree of a nation's civilization is marked by its disregard for the necessities of existence. [W Somerset Maugham, 1874–1965, *Our Betters*, I]

13 Civilization consists in the attempt to reduce violence to the *ultima ratio*, the final argument. [José Ortega y Gasset, 1883–1955, *The Revolt of the Masses*, Ch. 8]

14 Civilization has made the peasantry its pack animal. [Leon Trotsky, 1874–1940, *History of the Russian Revolution*, Pt III, Ch. 1]

15 Civilization advances by extending the number of important operations which we can perform without thinking about them. [A N Whitehead, 1861–1947, *An Introduction to Mathematics*, Ch. 5]

16 Civilization is hooped together, brought / under a rule, under the semblance of peace / By manifold illusion. [W B Yeats, 1865–1939, *Supernatural Songs*, 'Meru']

See also CULTURE

CLASS

1 He was a wight of high renown, / And thou art but of low degree; / 'Tis pride that pulls the country down; / Then take thine auld cloak about thee! [anon., *The Old Cloak*, sung in *Othello*, II. iii]

2 Sex you can get anywhere in the world. But class, I mean, real class, you can only get in Britain. [Malcolm Bradbury, 1932– , TV play, *Love on a Gunboat*]

3 Whatever crimes the Proletariat commits / It can't be beastly to the Children of the Ritz. [Noël Coward, 1899–1973, *Words and Music*, 'Children of the Ritz']

4 I never knew that the lower classes had such white skins. [Lord Curzon, 1859–1925 (when seeing troops bathing), attr. in K Rose, *Superior Person*, Ch. 12]

5 Oh let us love our occupations, / Bless the squire and his relations, / Live upon our daily rations, / And always know our proper stations. [Charles Dickens, 1812–70, *The Chimes*, Second Quarter]

6 I was told that the Privileged and the People formed Two Nations. [Benjamin Disraeli, 1804–81, *Sybil*, Bk iv, Ch. 8]

7 Class v. class, bitter as before, / The unending violence of US and THEM, / personified in 1984 / by Coal Board MacGregor and the NUM. [Tony Harrison, 1937– , *V*]

8 The essence of a class system is not that the privileged are conscious of their privileges, but that the deprived are conscious of their deprivation. [Clive James, 1939– , *Unreliable Memoirs*, Ch. 12]

9 You may be the most liberal Liberal Englishman, and yet you cannot fail to see the categorical difference between the responsible and the irresponsible classes. [D H Lawrence, 1885–1930, *Kangaroo*, Ch. 1]

10 The one class you do *not* belong to and are not proud of at all is the lower-middle class. No one ever describes himself as belonging to the lower-middle class. [George Mikes, 1912–87, *How to be an Alien*]

11 What a beautiful morning it's been out on deck ... Only on the third class tourist class passengers' deck was it a sultry overcast dull morning, but then if you do things on the cheap you must expect these things. [Spike Milligan, 1918– , *A Dustbin of Milligan*, 'Letters to Harry Secombe', I]

12 It is brought home to you ... that it is only because miners sweat their guts out that superior persons can remain superior. [George Orwell, 1903–50, *The Road to Wigan Pier*, Ch. 2]

13 This business of petty inconvenience and indignity, of being kept waiting about, of having to do everything at other people's convenience is inherent in working-class life. A thousand influences constantly press a working man into a *passive* role. He does not act, he is acted upon. [George Orwell, 1903–50, *The Road to Wigan Pier*, Ch. 3]

14 Comrade X, it so happens, is an old Etonian. He would be ready to die on the barricades, in theory anyway, but you notice that he still leaves his bottom waistcoat button undone. [George Orwell, 1903–50, *The Road to Wigan Pier*, Ch. 8]

15 The vulgar boil, the learned roast an egg. [Alexander Pope, 1688–1744, *Satires and Epistles of Horace Imitated*, Epistle II, 85]

16 Swann, who behaved simply and casually with a duchess, would tremble for fear of being despised, and would instantly begin to pose, when in the presence of a housemaid. [Marcel Proust, 1871–1922, *Remembrance of Things Past: Swann's Way*, 'Swann in Love']

17 I have defined Ladies as people who did not do things themselves. [Gwen Raverat, 1885–1957, *Period Piece*, Ch. 7]

18 The hand of little employment hath the daintier sense. [William Shakespeare, 1564–1616, *Hamlet*, IV. vii. (75)]

19 We must be thoroughly democratic, and patronize everybody without distinction of class. [George Bernard Shaw, 1856–1950, *John Bull's Other Island*, II]

20 Titles distinguish the mediocre, embarrass the superior, and are disgraced by the inferior. [George Bernard Shaw, 1856–1950, *Man and Superman*, 'Maxims for Revolutionists', Titles]

21 A simple maiden in her flower / Is worth a hundred coats-of-arms. [Alfred, Lord Tennyson, 1809–92, *Lady Clara Vere de Vere*]

22 Really, if the lower orders don't set us a good example, what on earth is the use of them? [Oscar Wilde, 1854–1900, *The Importance of Being Earnest*, I]

CLEANLINESS & UNCLEANLINESS

1 He that toucheth pitch shall be defiled therewith. [Bible, Apocrypha, *Ecclesiasticus* 13:1]

2 Bath twice a day to be really clean, once a day to be passably clean, once a week to avoid being a public menace. [Anthony Burgess, 1917–93, *Inside Mr Enderby*, Pt 1, Ch. 2, i]

3 To employ an English charwoman is a compromise between having a dirty house and cleaning it yourself. [George Mikes, 1912–87, *How to be an Alien*]

4 I used your soap two years ago; since then I have used no other. [*Punch*, lxxxvi (1884), 197]

5 Let it be observed, that slovenliness is no part of religion; that neither this, nor any text of Scripture, condemns neatness of apparel. Certainly this is a duty, not a sin. 'Cleanliness is, indeed, next to godliness.'* [John Wesley, 1703–91, *Sermon* XCIII, 'On Dress'. *This phrase is probably Hebrew in origin]

6 Style is the dress of thought; a modest dress, / Neat, but not gaudy, will true critics please. [Samuel Wesley, 1662–1735, *An Epistle to a Friend concerning Poetry*]

7 Have you ever taken anything out of the clothes basket because it had become, relatively, the cleaner thing? [Katharine Whitehorn, 1926– , in *Observer*, 1964, 'On Shirts']

CLERGY

1 In good King Charles's golden days, / When loyalty no harm meant; / A furious High-Churchman I was, / And so I gained preferment. [anon., song, *The Vicar of Bray*]

2 I always like to associate with a lot of priests because it makes me understand anti-clerical things so well. [Hilaire Belloc, 1870–1953, letter to E S P Haynes, 9 Nov. 1909, in Robert Speaight *Life of Hilaire Belloc*, Ch. 17]

3 And priests in black gowns were walking their

rounds, / And binding with briars my joys and desires. [William Blake, 1757–1827, *Songs of Experience*, 'The Garden of Love']

4 As for the British churchman, he goes to church as he goes to the bathroom, with the minimum of fuss and no explanation if he can help it. [Ronald Blythe, 1922– , *The Age of Illusion*, Ch. 12]

5 And spectral dance, before the dawn, / A hundred Vicars down the lawn; / Curates, long dust, will come and go / On lissom, clerical, printless toe; / And oft between the boughs is seen / The sly shade of a Rural Dean. [Rupert Brooke, 1887–1915, *The Old Vicarage, Grantchester*]

6 Cleric before, and Lay behind; / A lawless linsy-woolsy brother, / Half of one order, half another. [Samuel Butler, 1612–80, *Hudibras*, 1, iii, 1226]

7 This noble ensample to his sheep he yaf, That first he wroghte, and afterward he taughte. [Geoffrey Chaucer, 1340?–1400, *Canterbury Tales*, 'Prologue', 496]

8 Himself a wanderer from the narrow way, / His silly sheep, what wonder if they stray? [William Cowper, 1731–1800, *The Progress of Error*, 118]

9 The parson knows enough who knows a duke. [William Cowper, 1731–1800, *The Task*, Bk VI, 403]

10 Pray remember, Mr Dean, no dogma, no Dean. [Benjamin Disraeli, 1804–81, quoted in F Monypenny and G E Buckle, *Life*, Vol. iv, p. 368]

11 It is no accident that the symbol of a bishop is a crook, and the sign of an archbishop is a double-cross. [Dom Gregory Dix, 1901–52, quoted by Francis Brown in a letter to *The Times*, 3 Dec. 1977]

12 For clergy are men as well as other folks. [Henry Fielding, 1707–54, *Joseph Andrews*, Bk ii, Ch. 6]

13 I remember the average curate at home was something between a eunuch and a snigger. [Ronald Firbank, 1886–1926, *The Flower beneath the Foot*, Ch. 4]

14 Checkin' the crazy ones, coaxin' onaisy ones, / Liftin' the lazy ones on wid the stick. [A P Graves, 1846–1931, *Father O'Flynn*]

15 Lord, how can man preach thy eternal word? / He is a brittle crazy glass: / Yet in thy Temple thou dost him afford / This glorious and transcendent place, / To be a window, through thy grace. [George Herbert, 1593–1633, *Windows*]

16 People expect the clergy to have the grace of a swan, the friendliness of a sparrow, the strength of an eagle and the night hours of an owl – and some people expect such a bird to live on the food of a canary. [Revd Edward Jeffrey; *Observer*, 'Sayings of the Week', 14 June 1964]

17 Bishops vary just as much as books. Some are like eagles, soaring high above us, bearing important messages; others are nightingales, who sing God's praises in a marvellous way; and others are poor wrens. [Pope John Paul I, 1912–78, *Illustrissimi*, 'Letter to Mark Twain']

18 Annie couldn't see why religion has nothing to do with bishops so I explained to her that they are basically managers in fancy dress. [Jonathan Lynn, 1943– , and Anthony Jay, 1930– , *Yes Prime Minister*, Vol. I, 'The Bishop's Gambit']

19 A nun, at best, is only half a woman, just as a priest is only half a man. [H L Mencken, 1880–1956, *Minority Report*, 221]

20 New Presbyter is but old Priest writ large. [John Milton, 1608–74, sonnet: *On the New Forcers of Conscience*]

21 In the nineteenth century the average length of life for clergymen was eighty-one years, for politicians seventy-seven years and for atheists and sceptics sixty-four years. [David Ogg, 1887–1965, from *Europe of the Ancien Régime*; quoted in Gerald Brenan, *Thoughts in a Dry Season*, 'Religion', who comments, 'So it paid then to believe in God']

22 To happy convents, bosomed deep in vines, / Where slumber abbots, purple as their wines. [Alexander Pope, 1688–1744, *The Dunciad*, Bk iv, 301]

23 To rest, the cushion and soft dean invite, / Who never mentions hell to ears polite. [Alexander Pope, 1688–1744, *Moral Essays*, Epistle IV, 149]

24 Preachers say, Do as I say, not as I do. [John Selden, 1584–1654, *Table Talk*, 111]

25 To live a barren sister all your life, / Chanting faint hymns to the cold fruitless moon. [William Shakespeare, 1564–1616, *A Midsummer Night's Dream*, I. i. 72]

26 Don't you know, as the French say, there are three sexes – men, women, and clergymen? [Revd Sydney Smith, 1771–1845, in Lady Holland, *Memoir*, Vol. i, Ch. 9]

27 It is clearly absurd that it should be possible for a woman to qualify as a saint with direct access to the Almighty while she may not qualify as a curate. [Mary Stocks, 1891–1975, *Still More Commonplace*]

28 I never saw, heard, nor read, that the clergy were beloved in any nation where Christianity was the religion of the country. Nothing can render them popular but some degree of persecution. [Jonathan Swift, 1677–1745, *Thoughts on Religion*]

29 There is a species of person called a 'Modern Churchman' who draws the full salary of a beneficed clergyman and need not commit himself to any religious belief. [Evelyn Waugh, 1903–66, *Decline and Fall*, II, 4]

30 I asked why he was a priest, and he said if you have to work for anybody an absentee boss is best. [Jeanette Winterson, 1959– , *The Passion*, 1]

31 Nuns fret not at their convent's narrow room; / And hermits are contented with their cells. [William Wordsworth, 1770–1850, *Miscellaneous Sonnets*, I, 1]

CLEVERNESS

1 I never heard tell of any clever man that came of entirely stupid people. [Thomas Carlyle, 1795–1881, Rectorial Address at Edinburgh University, 2 Apr. 1886]

2 It's easy to be brilliant if you are not bothered about being right. [(Of Richard Crossman) Denis Healey, 1917– , *The Time of My Life*, Ch. 5]

3 Let us not be so difficult; the most accommodating are the cleverest. [Jean de La Fontaine, 1621–95, *Fables*, VII, 4, 'The Heron']

4 It takes great cleverness to be able to conceal one's cleverness. [Duc de La Rochefoucauld, 1613–80, *Maxims*, 245]

5 Tell me, is he bright enough to find / that memo pad you call your mind? [Craig Raine, 1944– , *Rich*, 'Attempt at Jealousy']

6 A smart girl is one who knows how to play tennis, piano and dumb. [Lynn Redgrave, 1943– , in *Guardian*, 22 May 1992]

7 'Fair youth, do you know what I'd do with you if you was my sun?' 'No,' sez he. 'Wall,' sez I, 'I'd appint your funeral tomorrow arternoon & the *korps should be ready*! You're too smart to live on this yearth.' [Artemus Ward, 1834–67, *A W His Book*, 'Edwin Forrest as Othello']

8 If I ever felt inclined to be timid as I was going into a room full of people, I would say to myself, 'You're the cleverest member of one of the cleverest families in the cleverest class of the cleverest nation in the world, why should you be frightened?' [Beatrice Webb, 1858–1943, in Bertrand Russell, *Portraits from Memory*, VIII]

9 If all the good people were clever, / And all clever people were good, / The world would be nicer than ever / We thought that it possibly could./

But somehow, 'tis seldom or never / The two hit it off as they should; / The good are so harsh to the clever, / The clever so rude to the good! [Elizabeth Wordsworth, 1840–1932, *Good and Clever*]

CLOTHES

1 A gee-string of very respectable dimensions, more of a gee-gee string, would have kept a horse decent. [Angela Carter, 1940–92, *Wise Children*, 2]

2 Any man may be in good spirits and good temper when he's well dressed. There an't much credit in that. [Charles Dickens, 1812–70, *Martin Chuzzlewit*, Ch. 5]

3 I have heard with admiring submission the experience of the lady who declared that the sense of being well-dressed gives a feeling of inward tranquillity which religion is powerless to bestow. [Ralph Waldo Emerson, 1803–82, *Social Aims*]

4 It's the sort of suit you walk into a tailor's in and ask for the cheapest suit in the shop and he says you're wearing it. [Trevor Griffiths, 1935– , *The Comedians*, I]

5 Englishwomen's shoes look as if they had been made by someone who had often heard shoes described, but had never seen any. [Margaret Halsey, 1910– , *With Malice Toward Some*, Pt 2]

6 I have always said that the best clothes are invisible ... they make you notice the person.

[Katharine Hamnett, 1952– ; *Independent*, 'Quote Unquote', 11 Mar. 1989]

7 A man is about thirty-eight before he stock-piles enough socks to be able to get one truly matching pair. [Merrily Harpur, 1948– , in *Femail on Sunday*, 7 July 1985]

8 Those who make their dress a principal part of themselves, will, in general, become of no more value than their dress. [William Hazlitt, 1778–1830, *On the Clerical Character*]

9 A sweet disorder in the dress / Kindles in clothes a wantonness. [Robert Herrick, 1591–1674, *Hesperides*, 'Delight in Disorder']

10 Whenas in silks my Julia goes, / Then, then (methinks) how sweetly flows / That liquefaction of her clothes. [Robert Herrick, 1591–1674, *Hesperides*, 'Upon Julia's Clothes']

11 Mind my duvetyne dress above all! It's golded silvy, the newest sextones with princess effect. For Rutland blue's got out of passion. [James Joyce, 1882–1941, *Finnegans Wake*, Pt 1, p. 148]

12 The pocket was the first instinct of humanity and was used long years before the human race had a trousers between them – the quiver for arrows is one example and the pouch of a kangaroo is another. [Flann O'Brien, 1911–66, *At Swim-Two-Birds*, Ch. 1]

13 Where's the man could ease a heart, / Like a satin gown? [Dorothy Parker, 1893–1967, *The Satin Dress*]

14 Brevity is the Soul of Lingerie. [Dorothy Parker, 1893–1967 (caption for a fashion magazine), in Alexander Woollcott, *While Rome Burns*, 'Our Mrs Parker']

15 If you give a girl an inch nowadays she will make a dress of it. [Dr H R Pickard; *Observer*, 'Sayings of the Week', 7 Oct. 1928]

16 Shirts like these don't go far in the winter-time. I mean that's one thing I know for a fact. No, what I need is a kind of a shirt with stripes, a good solid shirt, with stripes going down. [Harold Pinter, 1930– , *The Caretaker*, II]

17 Curious how much more room dirty clothes take up than clean ones, when you're packing – quite out of proportion to the amount of dirt they contain. [Claude Russell, 1919– , in Edward Marsh, *A Number of People*]

18 His socks compelled one's attention without losing one's respect. [Saki (H H Munro), 1870–1916, *Ministers of Grace*]

19 Costly thy habit as thy purse can buy, / But not expressed in fancy; rich, not gaudy; / For the apparel oft proclaims the man. [William Shakespeare, 1564–1616, *Hamlet*, I. iii. 65]

20 Every true man's apparel fits your thief. [*Measure for Measure*, IV. ii. (46)]

21 See, where she comes apparelled like the spring. [*Pericles*, I. i. 12]

22 I scramble into my clothes – whatever's lying in a heap on the floor. I do, however, put on a clean pair of underpants each morning – by Friday I've got seven pairs on. [Pamela Stephenson, 1950– , in *The Sunday Times Magazine*, 13 Jun. 1982]

23 She wears her clothes, as if they were thrown on her with a pitchfork. [Jonathan Swift, 1677–1745, *Polite Conversation*, Dialogue 1]

24 Beware of all enterprises that require new clothes. [H D Thoreau, 1817–62, *Walden*, 'Economy']

25 That which her slender waist confined / Shall now my joyful temples bind; / No monarch but would give his crown / His arms might do what this has done. [Edmund Waller, 1606–87, *On a Girdle*]

26 The tulip and the butterfly / Appear in gayer coats than I: / Let me be dressed fine as I will, / Flies, worms, and flowers exceed me still. [Isaac Watts, 1674–1748, *Divine Songs for Children*, 22, 'Against Pride in Clothes']

27 Let it be observed, that slovenliness is no part of religion; that neither this, nor any text of Scripture, condemns neatness of apparel. Certainly this is a duty, not a sin. 'Cleanliness is, indeed, next to godliness.'* [John Wesley, 1703–91, *Sermon* XCIII, 'On Dress'. *This phrase is probably Hebrew in origin]

28 You can say what you like about long dresses, but they cover a multitude of shins. [Mae West, 1892–1980, in J Weintraub, *Peel Me a Grape*]

29 What can you expect of a girl who was allowed to wear black satin at her coming-out ball? [Edith Wharton, 1862–1937, *The Age of Innocence*, Bk I, Ch. 5]

30 Hats divide generally into three classes: offensive hats, defensive hats, and shrapnel.

[Katharine Whitehorn, 1926– ; in *Shouts and Murmurs*, a selection from the *Observer*, 1962–3, 'How to Wear Hats']

CLUB

1 The *rules* of a club are occasionally in favour of the poor member. The drift of a club is always in favour of the rich one. [G K Chesterton, 1874–1936, *Orthodoxy*, Ch. 9]

2 Please accept my resignation. I don't want to belong to any club that will accept me as a member. [Groucho Marx, 1895–1977, *Groucho and Me*, Ch. 26]

3 Since my daughter is only half-Jewish, could she go in the water up to her knees? [Groucho Marx, 1895–1977 (when excluded from a smart Californian beach club on racial grounds), in obituary by Philip French, *Observer*, 21 Aug. 1977]

COFFEE, see TEA

COLD, see HOT

COLD WAR

1 An iron curtain has descended across the Continent. [Winston Churchill, 1874–1965, address at Westminster College, Fulton, USA, 5 Mar. 1946]; see 3, 9

2 If you are scared to go to the brink, you are lost. [John Foster Dulles, 1888–1959, interview in *Life* magazine, 16 Jan. 1956]

3 An iron curtain would at once descend on this territory. [Josef Goebbels, 1897–1945, *Das Reich*, 25 Feb. 1945]; see 1, 9

4 Whether you like it or not, history is on our side. We will bury you. [Nikita Khrushchev, 1894–1971, at Moscow reception, 18 Nov. 1956]

5 They talk about who won and who lost. Human reason won. Mankind won. [Nikita Khrushchev, 1894–1971 (on the Cuban crisis), in *Observer*, 11 Nov. 1962]

6 The superpowers often behave like two heavily-armed blind men feeling their way around a room, each believing himself in mortal peril from the other, whom he assumes to have perfect vision. [Henry Kissinger, 1923– ; *Observer*, 'Sayings of the Week', 30 Sept. 1979]

7 For the sake of the achievement of a specific political goal, it is possible to sacrifice half mankind. [Mao Zedong, 1893–1976, speech at meeting in Moscow, Nov. 1957, in *Pravda*, 26 Aug. 1973]

8 Communism is like prohibition, it's a good idea but it won't work. [Will Rogers, 1879–1935, *Autobiography*, Nov. 1927]

9 With a rumble and a roar, an iron curtain is descending on Russian history. [Vasili Rozanov, 1856–1919, *Apocalypse of Our Time*, 1918]; see 1, 3

10 We're eyeball to eyeball, and the other fellow just blinked. [Dean Rusk, 1909–94, on the Cuban missile crisis, 24 Oct. 1962]

See also INTERNATIONAL RELATIONS

COLOUR

1 So in the simple blessing of a rainbow, / in the bevelled edge of a sunlit mirror, / I have seen, visible, Death's artifact / like a soldier's ribbon on a tunic tacked. [Dannie Abse, 1923– , *The Pathology of Colours*]

2 All colours will agree in the dark. [Francis Bacon, 1561–1626, *Essays*, 3, 'Of Unity in Religion']

3 Why make so much of fragmentary blue / In here and there a bird, or butterfly, / Or flower, or wearing-stone, or open eye, / When heaven presents in sheets the solid hue? [Robert Frost, 1874–1963, *Fragmentary Blue*]

4 *Verde que te quiero verde. / Verde viento. Verde ramas. / El barco sobre el mar / y el caballo en la montaña.* – Green how I love you green. Green wind. Green boughs. The ship on the sea and the horse on the mountain. [Federico García Lorca, 1899–1936, *Romance sonambulo*]

5 *A noir, E blanc, I rouge, U vert, O bleu, voyelles.* – A black, E white, I red, U green, O blue, vowels. [Arthur Rimbaud, 1854–91, *Voyelles*]

6 The purest and most thoughtful minds are those which love colour the most. [John Ruskin, 1819–1900, *The Stones of Venice*, I, Ch. 5, §30]

7 With hue like that when some great painter dips / His pencil in the gloom of earthquake and eclipse. [P B Shelley, 1792–1822, *The Revolt of Islam*, V, 1925]

8 Pink is the navy blue of India. [Diana Vreeland, 1903–89, attr. in *Rolling Stone*, 11 Aug. 1977]

COMEDY

1 Comedy is tragedy interrupted. [Alan Ayckbourn, 1939– , interview]

2 Farce . . . is the theatre of the surrealist body. [Eric Bentley, 1916– , *The Life of Drama*, Ch. 7]

3 Tragedy is if I cut my finger . . . Comedy is if you walk into an open sewer and die. [Mel Brooks, 1926– , in Kenneth Tynan, *Show People*]

4 All tragedies are finished by a death, / All comedies are ended by a marriage. [Lord Byron, 1788–1824, *Don Juan*, III, 9]

5 All I need to make a comedy is a park, a policeman and a pretty girl. [Charlie Chaplin, 1889–1977, *My Autobiography*, Ch. 10]

6 I remain just one thing and one thing only – and that is a clown. It places me on a far higher plane than any politician. [Charlie Chaplin, 1889–1977; *Observer*, 'Sayings of the Week', 17 June 1960]

7 Farce is the essential theatre. Farce refined becomes high comedy: farce brutalized becomes tragedy. But at the roots of all drama farce is to be found. [Edward Gordon Craig, 1872–1966, *Index to the Story of My Days*]

8 Nobody should try to play comedy unless they have a circus going on inside. [Michael Curtiz, 1888–1962, in David Niven, *The Moon's a Balloon*, Ch. 11]

9 Comedy, like sodomy, is an unnatural act. [Marty Feldman, 1933–83, in *The Times*, 9 June 1969]

10 But then people don't usually laugh unless there's something serious at stake. What makes farce funny is seeing someone experience on the stage the terror and panic you feel inside yourself. [Michael Frayn, 1933– , interview in *Observer*, 17 Sept. 1989]

11 We mustn't complain too much of being comedians – it's an honourable profession. If only we could be good ones the world might gain at least a sense of style. We have failed – that's all. We are bad comedians, we aren't bad men. [Graham Greene, 1904–91, *The Comedians*, Pt II, Ch 1, i]

12 I think avoiding humiliation is the core of tragedy and comedy. [John Guare, 1938– , in *Independent*, 17 Oct. 1988]

13 Sometimes they ask you to crack a joke for them when you meet them on the street. But if I was walking along with a couple of pipes and met a passing welder I wouldn't ask him to weld the pipes. [Lenny Henry, 1958– , interview in *Guardian*, 31 Aug. 1988]

14 I think most broken-hearted clowns would be much more broken-hearted if they weren't clowns; and the only really broken-hearted clowns that I know are those that are not working or [are] unemployed. [Frankie Howerd, 1922–92, interview on BBC Radio 4, in *Listener*, 21 May 1987]

15 We participate in a tragedy; at a comedy we only look. [Aldous Huxley, 1894–1963, *The Devils of Loudun*, Ch. 11]

16 The root of the comic is to be sought in the sensations resulting from the observations of a thing behaving like a person. But from that point of view all men are necessarily comic; for they are all things, or physical bodies, behaving as persons. [Percy Wyndham Lewis, 1882–1957, *The Wild Body*]

17 Farce . . . a form of drama which seems to me often more true to the facts of life as we know them than many great tragedies. [John Mortimer, 1923– , *Clinging to the Wreckage*, 23]

18 Comedy, we may say, is society protecting itself – with a smile. [J B Priestley, 1894–1984, *George Meredith*]

19 A comedian can only last till he either takes himself serious or his audience takes him serious. [Will Rogers, 1879–1935, newspaper article, 1931]

20 The most lamentable comedy, and most cruel death of Pyramus and Thisby. [William Shakespeare, 1564–1616, *A Midsummer Night's Dream*, I. ii. (11)]

21 I have a technical objection to making sexual infatuation a tragic theme. Experience proves that it is only effective in the comic spirit. [George Bernard Shaw, 1856–1950, *Three Plays for Puritans*, Preface]

22 It's hard enough to write a good drama, it's much harder to write a good comedy, and it's hardest of all to write drama with comedy. [Mark Steyn, in *Independent*, 21 Feb. 1990]

23 In the best comedy, there is clearly something wrong, but it is secret and unstated – not even implied. Comedy is the public version of a private darkness. [Paul Theroux, 1941– , *My Secret History*, V, 7]

24 And killing time is perhaps the essence of comedy, just as the essence of tragedy is killing eternity. [Miguel de Unamuno, 1864–1937, *San Manuel Bueno*, Prologue]

25 A monstrous aunt can be funny. A monstrous mother would be tragic. [Richard Usborne, 1907– , *Wodehouse at Work to the End*, Ch. 2]

26 The world is a comedy to those that think, a tragedy to those that feel. [Horace Walpole, 1717–97, letter to the Countess of Upper Ossory, 16 Aug. 1776]

See also LAUGHTER, THEATRE, TRAGEDY

COMFORT

1 It's grand, and ye canna expect to be baith grand and comfortable. [James Barrie, 1860–1937, *The Little Minister*, Ch. 10]

2 Comfort came in with the middle classes. [Clive Bell, 1881–1964, *Civilization*, Ch. 4]

3 Comfort ye, comfort ye my people, saith your God. [Bible, OT, *Isaiah* 40:1]

4 As one whom his mother comforteth, so will I comfort you. [Bible, OT, *Isaiah* 66:13]

5 Miserable comforters are ye all. [Bible, OT, *Job* 16:2]

6 I love it, I love it; and who shall dare / To chide me for loving that old arm-chair? [Eliza Cook, 1818–89, *The Old Arm-Chair*]

7 The English have adopted Central Heating like some kind of cargo cult . . . All the English seem to know is they're supposed to have these sharp-looking metal objects scattered around the walls – they're not interested in heat. [Lucy Ellmann, 1956– , *Sweet Desserts*, 'Banana Split']

8 One should comfort the afflicted, but verily, also one should afflict the comfortable, and especially when they are comfortably, contentedly, even happily wrong. [J K Galbraith, 1908– , in *Guardian*, 28 July 1989]

9 Be comforted. You would not be seeking Me if you had not found Me. [Blaise Pascal, 1623–62, *Pensées*, VII, 552]

10 Stretched on the rack of a too easy chair. [Alexander Pope, 1688–1744, *The Dunciad*, Bk v, 342]

11 He receives comfort like cold porridge. [William Shakespeare, 1564–1616, *The Tempest*, II. i. (10)]

12 Two loves I have of comfort and despair, / Which like two spirits do suggest me still: / The better angel is a man right fair, / The worser spirit a woman coloured ill. [*Sonnets*, 144]

13 It is hard, of course, to console or advise professional consolers and advisers; rote phrases, professional sympathy, even an emphatic patience are brusquely shunted aside. At a convention of masseurs no one turns his back. [John Updike, 1932– , *A Month of Sundays*, Ch. 25]

14 When they ask for bread don't give them crackers as does the Church, and don't, like the State, tell them to eat cake. Explain that man cannot live by bread alone, and give them stones. [Nathanael West, 1903–40, *Miss Lonelyhearts*, 'Miss Lonelyhearts and the Dead Pan']

COMMERCE, see BUSINESS

COMMITMENT

1 I'm not just involved in tennis but committed. Do you know the difference between involvement and commitment? Think of ham and eggs. The chicken is involved. The pig is committed. [Martina Navratilova, 1956– , in *International Herald Tribune*, 3 Sept. 1982]

2 Give me my scallop-shell of quiet, / My staff of faith to walk upon, / My scrip of joy, immortal diet, / My bottle of salvation, / My gown of glory, hope's true gage, / And thus I'll take my pilgrimage. [Sir Walter Raleigh, *c.*1552–1618, *The Passionate Man's Pilgrimage*]

3 I made no vows, but vows / Were then made for me; bond unknown to me / Was given, that I should be, else sinning greatly, / A dedicated spirit. [William Wordsworth, 1770–1850, *The Prelude*, IV, 334]

COMMITTEES

1 A conference is a gathering of important people who singly can do nothing, but together can decide that nothing can be done. [Fred Allen, 1894–1956, in Jonathon Green, *The Cynic's Lexicon*]

2 A camel is a horse designed by a committee. [anon.; sometimes ascribed to Sir Alec Issigonis, designer]

3 To get something done a committee should consist of no more than three men, two of whom are absent. [Robert Copeland; in *Penguin Dictionary of Modern Humorous Quotations*, comp. Fred Metcalf]

4 A committee is an animal with four back legs. [John Le Carré, 1931– , *Tinker, Tailor, Soldier, Spy*, Pt III, Ch. 34]

5 Oh for just / one / more conference / regarding the eradication of all conferences! [Vladimir Mayakovsky, 1893–1930, *In re Conferences*]

6 The number one book of the ages was written by a committee, and it was called The Bible. [(To writers who complained of changes made to their work) Louis B Mayer, 1885–1957; in L Halliwell, *The Filmgoer's Book of Quotes*]

7 A meeting is an occasion when people gather together, some to say what they do not think, and others not to say what they really do. [(Of the USSR) Vladimir Voinovich, 1932– , in *Listener*, 10 Nov. 1988]

See also OFFICE

COMMUNICATION

1 All those who have something to say are deeply divided, and therefore tormented men or women – that is, they are both innocent children and devils. [Manning Clark, 1915–91, *A Discovery of Australia*, 'Being an Historian']

2 Only connect! [E M Forster, 1879–1970, *Howards End*, epigraph]

3 If we felt in our heart that we were *always* doctoring our experiences, our attempts to reach others would all be at bottom forms of salesmanship, not attempts to tell things as we think they really are. [Richard Hoggart, 1918– , BBC Reith Lectures, in *Listener*, Dec. 1971]

4 There's no fixed connection with the Castle, no central exchange which transmits our calls further. When anybody calls up the Castle from here the instruments in all the subordinate departments ring, or rather they would ring if practically all the departments ... didn't leave their receivers off. [Franz Kafka, 1883–1924, *The Castle*, Ch. 5]

5 The new electronic interdependence recreates the world in the image of a global village. [Marshall McLuhan, 1911–80, *The Gutenberg Galaxy*]

6 The art of dialling has replaced the art of dialogue. [Gita Mehta, 1943– , *Karma Cola*, VIII, 2]

7 People talking without speaking, / People listening without hearing, / People writing songs that voices never shared. / No one dared. [Paul Simon, 1942– , song: *The Sound of Silence*]

8 Well, if I called the wrong number, why did you answer the phone? [James Thurber, 1894–1961, *Men, Women and Dogs*, cartoon caption]

9 He would have liked to sit down and talk with someone about the flat things, as blameless as paper, about which it is necessary to talk. It is not possible with parents, any more than with corkscrews. His mother would bore right in, hoping to draw something out. [Patrick White, 1912–90, *The Tree of Man*, Ch. 16]

10 The interest in life does not lie in what people do, nor even in their relations to each other, but largely in the power to communicate with a third party, antagonistic, enigmatic, yet perhaps persuadable, which one may call life in general. [Virginia Woolf, 1882–1941, *The Common Reader*, First Series, 'On Not Knowing Greek']

See also SPEECH, TALK, TELEVISION

COMMUNISM

1 Lenin was an admirable man, possessed by a terribly wrong idea. It was terribly wrong because it was only partly right. And it was so absolutely punitive that it needed to be absolutely right. [Robert Bolt, 1924–95, *State of Revolution*, Introduction]

2 We might have a two-party system, but one of the two parties would be in office and the other in prison. [Nikolai A Bukharin, 1888–1938, attr. in Isaac Deutscher, *The Prophet Armed, Trotsky: 1879–1921*]

3 From now on the Party line is that there is no Party line. [(Of Yugoslav Communist Party, 1951) Milovan Djilas, 1911–95, in Fitzroy Maclean, *Disputed Barricade*, 15]

4 What is a communist? One who hath yearnings / For equal division of unequal earnings. [Ebenezer Elliott, 1781–1849, *Epigram*]

5 Look at the Paris Commune. That was the Dictatorship of the Proletariat. [Friedrich Engels, 1820–95, Preface to Karl Marx, *The Civil War in France* (1891 edn)]

6 Catholics and Communists have committed great crimes, but at least they have not stood aside, like an established society, and been indifferent. I would rather have blood on my hands than water like Pilate. [Graham Greene, 1904–91, *The Comedians*, Pt III, Ch. 4, iv]

7 My interest in the photocopier was philosophical really. Beyond a shadow of doubt, it's that technology that brought down communism. [David Hockney, 1937– , in *Guardian*, 13 Sept. 1990]

8 If anyone believes our smiles involve the abandonment of the teaching of Marx, Engels, and Lenin he deceives himself poorly. Those who wait for that must wait until a shrimp learns to whistle. [Nikita Khrushchev, 1894–1971, impromptu speech at Moscow dinner for East German visitors, 17 Sept. 1955]

9 Every year humanity takes a step towards Communism. Maybe not you, but at all events your grandson will surely be a Communist. [Nikita Khrushchev, 1894–1971, in conversation with Sir William Hayter, June 1956]

10 Communism is Soviet power plus the electrification of the whole country. [Vladimir Ilyich Lenin, 1870–1924, slogan promoting the electrification programme; at Congress of Soviets, 22 Dec. 1920]

11 We Communists are dead men on leave. [Eugen Leviné (at his trial), in R Leviné-Meyer, *Leviné: The Life of a Revolutionary*, Ch. 3]

12 Said Marx: 'Don't be snobbish, we seek to abolish / The 3rd Class, not the 1st.' [Christopher Logue, 1932– , *C L's A B C*, 'M']

13 They [the Soviets] are Communists just as the Victorians were Christians. They attend CP meetings and lectures on Marxism-Leninism at regular intervals in exactly the same way as the Victorians attended church on Sunday ... And they apply the principles of Marxism in their private lives to just about the same extent as the Victorians applied the principles of the Sermon on the Mount. Neither more nor less. [Fitzroy Maclean, 1911–96, *Back to Bokhara*]

14 But whenever there's a snatch of talk / it turns to the Kremlin mountaineer, / the ten thick worms his fingers, / his words like measures of weight, / the huge laughing cockroaches on his top lip, / The glitter of his boot-rims. [Osip Mandelstam, 1891–1938, *Poems*, No. 286, *Stalin Epigram*]

15 A spectre is haunting Europe – the spectre of Communism. [Karl Marx, 1818–83, and Friedrich Engels, 1820–95, *The Communist Manifesto*, opening words]

16 Unlike a classical dictatorship, in which the lines of conflict run between government and the governed, in modern Communist societies this line runs through each person, for everyone in his or her own way is both a victim and a supporter of the system. [Profile of Vaclav Havel, *Observer*,29 Jan. 1989]

17 The Catholic and the Communist are alike in assuming that an opponent cannot be both honest and intelligent. [George Orwell, 1903–50, *Collected Essays*, 'The Prevention of Literature']

18 It has been well said that the quarrel between capitalism and communism is whether to sit upstairs or downstairs in a bus going the wrong way. [Revd John Stewart, 1909– , letter to *Listener*, 18 Dec. 1986]

19 Communism continued to haunt Europe as a spectre – a name men gave to their own fears and blunders. But the crusade against Communism was even more imaginary than the spectre of Communism. [A J P Taylor, 1906–90, *The Origins of the Second World War*, Ch. 2]

20 It seems to me that I am more to the left than you, Mr Stalin. [H G Wells, 1866–1946, interview with Stalin in *New Statesman*, 27 Oct. 1934]

See also CAPITALISM

COMPARISONS

1 Though analogy is often misleading, it is the least misleading thing we have. [Samuel Butler, 1835–1902, *Notebooks*, Ch. 7, 'Thought and Word', 2]

2 She and comparisons are odious. [John Donne, 1571?–1631, *Elegies*, 8, 'The Comparison', 54]; see 6

3 We have mastered a destiny which broke another man [Napoleon] a hundred and thirty years ago. [Adolf Hitler, 1889–1945, speech to the Reichstag, 26 Apr. 1942, in A Bullock, *Hitler*, Pt XII, 3]

4 What woman has this old cat's graces? / What boy can sing as the thrush sings? [Francis Meynell, 1891–1975, *Man and Beast*]

5 So excellent a king; that was, to this, / Hyperion to a satyr. [William Shakespeare, 1564–1616, *Hamlet*, I. ii. 139]

6 Comparisons are odorous. [*Much Ado About Nothing*, III. v. (18)]; see 2

7 Shall I compare thee to a summer's day? / Thou art more lovely and more temperate: / Rough winds do shake the darling buds of May, / And summer's lease hath all too short a date. / Sometimes too hot the eye of heaven shines, / And often is his gold complexion dimmed; / And every fair from fair sometime declines. [*Sonnets*, 18]

8 No caparisons, miss, if you please. Caparisons don't become a young woman. [R B Sheridan, 1751–1816, *The Rivals*, IV. ii]

9 Individual human beings are so subtly developed through the centuries that it is strictly impermissible to compare any two men who are not contemporaries – that is to say are taken from two quite different times. [Pierre Teilhard de Chardin, 1881–1955, *The Appearance of Man*, Ch. 17, sect. ii]

10 If one may measure small things by great. [Virgil, 70–19 BC, *Georgics*, IV. 176]

11 Go, lovely rose, / Tell her that wastes her time and me, / That now she knows, / When I resemble her to thee, / How sweet and fair she seems to be. [Edmund Waller, 1606–87, song]

COMPETITION

1 We're number two. We try harder. [Advertisement for Avis car rental, 1960s, ascr. to Doyle, Dane and Bernbach agency]

2 If you think squash is a competitive activity try flower-arranging. [Alan Bennett, 1934– , *Talking Heads*, 'Bed among the Lentils']

3 Thou shalt not covet, but tradition / Approves all forms of competition. [Arthur Hugh Clough, 1819–61, *The Latest Decalogue*]

4 Keeping up with the Joneses was a full-time job with my mother and father. It was not until many years later when I lived alone that I realized how much cheaper it was to drag the Joneses down to my level. [Quentin Crisp, 1908–99, *The Naked Civil Servant*, Ch. 1]

5 Nice guys finish last. [(Of New York Giants) Leo Durocher, 1906–91. According to P F Boller Jr and J George, *They Never Said It*, he really said, 'Nice guys. Finish last', 6 July 1946]

6 In every age and clime we see, / Two of a trade can ne'er agree. [John Gay, 1685–1732, *Fables*, Pt I, xxi, 43]

7 We need the free competition of minds. [Mikhail Gorbachev, 1931– , speech to the Central Committee of the Communist Party, Feb. 1988]

8 The rod produces an effect which terminates in itself. A child is afraid of being whipped, and gets his task, and there's an end on't; whereas by exciting emulation and comparisons of superiority, you lay the foundation of lasting mischief; you make brothers and sisters hate each other. [(On Mr Hunter, his headmaster) Dr Samuel Johnson, 1709–84, in James Boswell, *Life of J*, Introductory]

9 Man is a gaming animal. He must always be trying to get the better in something or other. [Charles Lamb, 1775–1834, *Essays of Elia*, 'Mrs Battle's Opinions on Whist']

10 Our very business in life is not to get ahead of others, but to get ahead of ourselves. [Thomas L Monson, 1954– , attr.]

11 *How to be one up* – how to make the other man feel that something has gone wrong, however slightly. [Stephen Potter, 1900–1969, *Lifemanship*, 1]

12 The thing is, it's really hard to be roommates with people if your suitcases are much better than theirs – if yours are really good ones and theirs aren't. You think if they're intelligent and all, the other person, and have a good sense of humour, that they don't give a damn whose suitcases are better, but they do. [J D Salinger, 1919– , *The Catcher in the Rye*, Ch. 15]

COMPLAINT

1 It is a general popular error to imagine the loudest complainers for the public to be the most anxious for its welfare. [Edmund Burke, 1729–97, *Observations on 'The Present State of the Nation'*]

2 When late I attempted your pity to move, / Why seemed you so deaf to my prayers? / Perhaps it was right to dissemble your love, / But – why did you kick me downstairs? [J P Kemble, 1757–1823, *The Panel*, I. i (an adaptation of Isaac Bickerstaffe's comedy *'Tis Well 'tis no Worse*)]

3 If there was one thing he hated more than another it was the way she had of waking him in the morning ... It was her way of establishing her grievance for the day. [Katherine Mansfield, 1888–1923, *Bliss*, 'Mr Reginald Peacock's Day']

COMPOSERS IN GENERAL

1 Let us reserve the term 'advanced' for those [composers] who deserve it – dead these five centuries or alive now. [Robert Simpson, 1921–97, talk on BBC radio, 1976]

2 A good composer does not imitate; he steals. [Igor Stravinsky, 1882–1971; in Peter Yates, *Twentieth Century Music*, Pt 1, Ch. 8]

COMPOSERS: INDIVIDUAL (in alphabetical order of subject)

1 If Bach wriggles, Wagner writhes. [Samuel Butler, 1835–1902, *Notebooks*, Ch. 8, 'Musical Criticism']

2 Bach almost persuades me to be a Christian. [Roger Fry, 1866–1934, in Virginia Woolf, *R F*, Ch. 11]

3 Beethoven's Fifth Symphony is the most sublime noise that has ever penetrated into the ear of man. [E M Forster, 1879–1970, *Howards End*, Ch. 5]

4 It [the last movement of Beethoven's Ninth Symphony] is the song of the angels sung by earth spirits. [E H W Meyerstein, 1889–1952, letter to his mother, 21 Oct. 1908]

5 Beethoven's Fifth Symphony may be Fate – or Kate – knocking at the door. That is up to you. [C B Rees, in *Penguin Music Magazine*, 1946]

6 A Brahms, for all his grumbling and grizzling, had never guessed what it felt like to be suspected of stealing an umbrella. [E M Forster, 1879–1970, *Howards End*, Ch. 5]

7 I have already heard it [Debussy's music]. I had better not go: I will start to get accustomed to it and finally like it. [Nikolai Rimsky-Korsakov, 1844–1908; in Igor Stravinsky and Robert Craft, *Conversations with S*]

8 [When asked, 'Why do you write?'] Because I cannot swim. [Frederick Delius, 1862–1934, from *Pourquoi écrivez-vous?*, quoted in *The Sunday Times*, 7 Apr. 1985]

9 The odd and pleasant taste of a pink sweet filled with snow. [Claude Debussy, 1862–1918 (of Grieg's music), from *Gil Blas*, 1903; in *Dictionary of Musical Quotations*, comp. I Crofton and D Fraser]

10 Some say, that Signor Bononcini, / Compared to Handel's a mere ninny; / Others aver, to him, that Handel / Is scarcely fit to hold a candle. / Strange! that such high dispute should be / 'Twixt Tweedledum and Tweedledee. [John Byrom, 1692–1763, *Epigram on the Feuds between Handel and Bononcini*]

11 Never compose anything unless the not composing of it becomes a positive nuisance to you. [Gustav Holst, 1874–1934, letter to W G Whittaker, 1921; in Nat Shapiro, *Encyclopedia of Quotations about Music*]

12 Whether the angels play only Bach in praising God I am not quite sure: I am sure, however, that *en famille* they play Mozart. [Karl Barth, 1886–1968, quoted in obituary in *The New York Times*, 11 Dec. 1968]

13 It is a sobering thought that when Mozart was my age he had been dead for two years. [Tom Lehrer, 1928– ; in Nat Shapiro, *Encyclopedia of Quotations about Music*]

14 The sonatas of Mozart are unique; they are too easy for children, and too difficult for artists. [Artur Schnabel, 1882–1951; in Nat Shapiro, *Encyclopedia of Quotations about Music*]

15 He [Puccini] wrote marvellous operas, but dreadful music. [Dimitri Shostakovich, 1906–75, in conversation with Benjamin Britten, in Lord Harewood, *The Tongs and the Bones*]

16 Rachmaninov's immortalizing totality was his scowl. He was a six-and-a-half-foot-tall scowl.

[Igor Stravinsky, 1882–1971, and Robert Craft, *Conversations with S*]

17 M. Ravel has refused the Légion d'Honneur but all his music accepts it. [Erik Satie, 1866–1925, in James Harding, *E S*, Ch. 21]

18 Give me a laundry-list and I'll set it to music. [Giachino Rossini, 1792–1868; quoted in Evan Esar, ed., *Treasury of Humorous Quotations*]

19 It is time to consider how Domenico Scarlatti / condensed so much music into so few bars. [Basil Bunting, 1900–1985, *Briggflatts*, 4]

20 [When told his violin concerto needed a soloist with six fingers] Very well, I can wait. [Arnold Schoenberg, 1874–1951, attr.; in Nat Shapiro, *Encyclopedia of Quotations about Music*. Another version is: 'I want the little finger to become longer. I can wait']

21 Schumann's our music-maker now; / Has his march-movement youth and mouth? Ingres's the modern man that paints; / Which will lean on me, of his saints? / Heine for songs; for kisses, how? [Robert Browning, 1812–89, *Dîs Aliter Visum*, 8]

22 Creative reply of a Soviet artist to just criticism. [Dimitri Shostakovich, 1906–75, epigraph to his Fifth Symphony]

23 Musicians did not like the piece [Strauss's *Elektra*] at all. One eminent British composer on leaving the theatre was asked what he thought of it. 'Words fail me,' he replied, 'and I'm going home at once to play the chord of C major twenty times over to satisfy myself that it still exists.' [Thomas Beecham, 1879–1961, *A Mingled Chime*, Ch. 18]

24 For Strauss the composer I take off my hat. For Strauss the man I put it on again. [Arturo Toscanini, 1867–1957, in Antony Storr, *The School of Genius*]

25 His [Stravinsky's] music used to be original. Now it is aboriginal. [Ernest Newman, 1868–1959, from *Musical Times*, 1921; in *Dictionary of Musical Quotations*, comp. I Crofton and D Fraser]

26 My music is best understood by children and animals. [Igor Stravinsky, 1882–1971; *Observer*, 'Sayings of the Week', 8 Oct. 1961]

27 I like listening to it [Tchaikovksy's Fifth] just as I like looking at a fuchsia drenched with rain. [James Agate, 1877–1947, *Ego 8*, 1947]

28 If I died tomorrow, I wouldn't be afraid to meet the composer. [Paul Tortelier, 1914–90 (of his special affection for playing Tchaikovsky's Rococo Variations), in obituary in *Guardian*, 19 Dec. 1990]

29 I don't know whether I like it [his own Fourth Symphony], but it is what I meant. [Ralph Vaughan Williams, 1872–1958, quoted by Adrian Boult in broadcast, 1 Aug. 1965]

30 A beautiful sunset that was mistaken for a dawn. [(Of Wagner's music) attr. Claude Debussy, 1862–1918]

31 Wagner is the Puccini of music. [J B Morton ('Beachcomber'), 1893–1979, attr.]

32 [When asked by Gillian Widdicombe what he remembered of a week under intensive care, just after his eightieth birthday] It was very quiet. Didn't see a soul, not even Ben Britten's. Then there was a fanfare, but it wasn't one of mine. Bliss, I suppose. [William Walton, 1902–83, in obituary in *Observer*, 13 Mar. 1983]

COMPROMISE

1 All government, indeed every human benefit and enjoyment, every virtue, and every prudent act, is founded on compromise and barter. [Edmund Burke, 1729–97, speech on conciliation with America, 22 Mar. 1775]

2 If you cannot catch a bird of paradise, better take a wet hen. [Nikita Khrushchev, 1894–1971, in *Time* magazine, 6 Jan. 1958]

3 Of course heaven forbids certain pleasures, but one finds means of compromise. [Molière, 1622–73, *Tartuffe*, IV. v]

4 *Medio tutissimus ibis.* – You will go most safely in the middle. [Ovid, 43 BC–AD 17, *Metamorphoses*, II, 137]

See also AMBIVALENCE, INDECISION

CONFIDENCE, see PRIDE, SMUGNESS

CONFORMITY

1 When in Rome, live as the Romans do; when elsewhere, live as they live elsewhere. [St Ambrose, 337–97, advice to St Augustine; quoted by Jeremy Taylor, *Ductor Dubitantium*, I, i, 5]

2 I think the reward for conformity is that everyone likes you except yourself. [Rita Mae Brown, 1944– , *Bingo*, Ch. 35]

3 Take the tone of the company you are in. [Earl of Chesterfield, 1694–1773, letter to his son, 9 Oct. 1747]

4 Whoso would be a man must be a nonconformist. [Ralph Waldo Emerson, 1803–82, *Essays*, 'Self-reliance']

5 Why do you have to be a nonconformist like everybody else? [Stan Hunt, cartoon caption in the *New Yorker*. Often wrongly attr. to James Thurber]

6 All change in history, all advance, comes from nonconformity. If there had been no trouble-makers, no dissenters, we should still be living in caves. [A J P Taylor, 1906–90, *The Trouble-makers*, 1]

CONSCIENCE

1 A conscience void of offence toward God, and toward men. [Bible, NT, *Acts of the Apostles* 24:16]

2 I cannot and will not cut my conscience to fit this year's fashions. [Lillian Hellman, 1905–84, letter to House Committee of un-American Activities, 19 May 1952]

3 People talk about the conscience, but it seems to me one must just bring it up to a certain point and leave it there. You can let your conscience alone if you're nice to the second housemaid. [Henry James, 1843–1916, *The Awkward Age*, VI, 23]

4 Conscience was the barmaid of the Victorian soul . . . Once the appointed limit was reached, conscience would rap on the bar of the soul. 'Time's up, gentlemen,' she would say, 'we close at ten-thirty.' [C E M Joad, 1891–1953, *Under the Fifth Rib*, Ch. 9]

5 The English have a proverb: 'Conscience makes cowboys of us all.' [Saki (H H Munro), 1870–1916, *Wratislav*]

6 Leave her to heaven, / And to those thorns that in her bosom lodge, / To prick and sting her. [William Shakespeare, 1564–1616, *Hamlet*, I. v. 86]

7 The play's the thing / Wherein I'll catch the conscience of the king. [*Hamlet*, II. ii. (641)]

8 A peace above all earthly dignities, / A still and quiet conscience. [*Henry VIII*, III. ii. 380]

9 My conscience hath a thousand several tongues, / And every tongue brings in a several tale, / And every tale condemns me for a villain. [*Richard III*, V. ii. 194]

CONSCIOUSNESS

1 Rational consciousness, as we call it, is but one special type of consciousness, whilst all about it, parted from it by the filmiest of screens, there lie potential forms of consciousness entirely different. [William James, 1842–1910, *The Varieties of Religious Experience*, Lectures 16–17]

2 The whole drift of my education goes to persuade me that the world of our present consciousness is only one of many worlds of consciousness that exist. [William James, 1842–1910, *The Varieties of Religious Experience*, Lecture 20]

3 The highest activities of consciousness have their origins in physical occurrences of the brain just as the loveliest melodies are not too sublime to be expressed by notes. [W Somerset Maugham, 1874–1965, *A Writer's Notebook*, 1902]

4 I regard consciousness as fundamental. I regard matter as derivative from consciousness. We cannot get behind consciousness. [Max Planck, 1858–1947, interview with J W N Sullivan, in Kenneth Walker, *The Circle of Life*, Pt II, Ch. 3]

5 Thus conscience does make cowards of us all; / And thus the native hue of resolution / Is sicklied o'er with the pale cast of thought, / And enterprises of great pith and moment / With this regard their currents turn awry, / And lose the name of action. [William Shakespeare, 1564–1616, *Hamlet*, III. i. 83]

CONSERVATIVES (with capital or small c)

1 No attempt at ethical or social seduction can eradicate from my heart a deep burning hatred for the Tory Party . . . So far as I am concerned they are lower than vermin. [Aneurin Bevan, 1897–1960, speech at Manchester, 4 July 1948]

2 Tories are not always wrong, but they are always wrong at the right moment. [Violet

Bonham-Carter, 1887–1969; *Observer*, 'Sayings of the Week', 26 Apr. 1964]

3 By many stories, / And true, we learn the angels are all Tories. [Lord Byron, 1788–1824, *The Vision of Judgement*, 26]

4 All conservatism is based upon the idea that if you leave things alone you leave them as they are. But you do not. If you leave a thing alone you leave it to a torrent of change. [G K Chesterton, 1874–1936, *Orthodoxy*, Ch. 7]

5 We now are, as we always have been, decidedly and conscientiously attached to what is called the Tory, and which might with more propriety be called the Conservative, party. [J W Croker, 1780–1857, *Quarterly Review*, Jan. 1830]

6 A Conservative government is an organized hypocrisy. [Benjamin Disraeli, 1804–81, speech in House of Commons, 17 Mar. 1838]

7 A sound Conservative government ... Tory men and Whig measures. [Benjamin Disraeli, 1804–81, *Coningsby*, Bk ii, Ch. 6]

8 Men are conservatives when they are least vigorous, or when they are most luxurious. They are conservatives after dinner. [Ralph Waldo Emerson, 1803–82, *Essays*, 'New England Reformers']

9 A Conservative is only a Tory who is ashamed of himself. [John Hookham Frere, 1769–1846, attr.]

10 Vote Labour and you build castles in the air. Vote Conservative and you can live in them. [David Frost, 1939– , BBC TV programme *That Was the Week That Was*, 31 Dec. 1962; in *Simpson's Contemporary Quotations*]

11 I often think it's comical / How Nature always does contrive / That every boy and every gal, / That's born into the world alive, / Is either a little Liberal, / Or else a little Conservative! [W S Gilbert, 1836–1911, *Iolanthe*, II]

12 Conservatives do not believe that political struggle is the most important thing in life . . . The simplest among them prefer fox-hunting – the wisest religion. [Lord Hailsham, 1907– , *The Case for Conservatism*, p. 10]

13 The conservative has but little to fear from the man whose reason is the servant of his passions, but let him beware of him in whom reason has become the greatest and most terrible of passions. [J B S Haldane, 1892–1964, *Daedalus or Science and the Future*]

14 The party of the state owners has become the party of the estate agents. [Denis Healey, 1917– , in *Financial Times*, 28 Nov. 1990]

15 [Of the Conservative Party] They are nothing else but a load of kippers, two-faced with no guts. [Eric Heffer, 1922–91, said in House of Commons, n.d.]

16 A study of the history of opinion is a necessary preliminary to the emancipation of the mind. I do not know which makes a man more conservative – to know nothing but the present, or nothing but the past. [John Maynard Keynes, 1883–1946, *The End of Laissez-faire*, Pt 1]

17 [Of the Conservative Party] If these people ever travelled the road to Damascus, they would only do so on a return ticket. [Neil Kinnock, 1942– ; *Independent*, 'Quote Unquote', 20 Apr. 1991]

18 What is conservatism? Is it not adherence to the old and tried, against the new and untried? [Abraham Lincoln, 1809–65, speech, 27 Feb. 1860]

19 Most of our people have never had it so good. [Harold Macmillan, 1894–1986, speech on financial situation, Bedford, 20 July 1957; originally US presidential election slogan, 1952; reuse attr. to Oliver Poole]

20 Too much thinking, in my opinion, is not becoming to Toryism. It ought not to be encouraged. Thought is a Socialist temptation, not a Tory one. [Shiva Naipaul, 1945–85, in *Spectator*, 28 May 1983]

21 You can't teach an old dogma new tricks. [Dorothy Parker, 1893–1967; in R E Drennan, *Wit's End*]

22 A radical is a man with both feet planted firmly in the air. A reactionary is a somnambulist walking backwards. A conservative is a man with two perfectly good legs who, however, has never learned how to walk forward. A liberal is a man who uses his legs and his hands at the behest of his head. [Franklin D Roosevelt, 1882–1945, radio address, 26 Oct. 1939]

23 Ideologically, in its craving for authority figures, it [the Conservative Party] has replaced the Altar and the Throne by the police. [Ralph Samuel, 1934–96, in *Guardian*, 2 Dec. 1985]

24 The staid, conservative, / Came-over-with-the-Conqueror type of mind. [William Watson, 1858–1935, *A Study in Contrasts*, I, i, 42]

See also LIBERALS, SOCIALISTS

CONSISTENCY & INCONSISTENCY

1 A man so various that he seemed to be / Not one, but all mankind's epitome. / Stiff in opinions, always in the wrong; / Was everything by starts and nothing long: / But, in the course of one revolving moon, / Was chemist, fiddler, statesman, and buffoon. [John Dryden, 1631–1700, *Absalom and Achitophel*, Pt I, 545]

2 A foolish consistency is the hobgoblin of little minds, adored by little statesmen and philosophers and divines. [Ralph Waldo Emerson, 1803–82, *Essays*, 'Self-reliance']

3 Consistency is contrary to nature, contrary to life. The only completely consistent people are the dead. [Aldous Huxley, 1894–1963, *Do What You Will*, 'Wordsworth in the Tropics']

4 Some praise at morning what they blame at night; / But always think the last opinion right. [Alexander Pope, 1688–1744, *An Essay on Criticism*, 430]

5 Do I contradict myself? / Very well then I contradict myself, / (I am large, I contain multitudes). [Walt Whitman, 1819–92, *Song of Myself*, 51, 1324]

CONSTANCY & INCONSTANCY

1 Whither thou goest, I will go; and where thou lodgest, I will lodge: thy people shall be my people, and thy God my God. [Bible, OT, *Ruth* 1:16]

2 That household virtue, most uncommon, / Of constancy to a bad, ugly woman. [Lord Byron, 1788–1824, *The Vision of Judgement*, 12]

3 The world's a scene of changes, and to be / Constant, in Nature were inconstancy. [Abraham Cowley, 1618–67, *Inconstancy*]

4 I never will desert Mr Micawber. [(Mrs Micawber) Charles Dickens, 1812–70, *David Copperfield*, Ch. 12]

5 I have been faithful to thee, Cynara! in my fashion. [Ernest Dowson, 1867–1900, *Non Sum Qualis Eram*]

6 We only part to meet again. / Change, as ye list, ye winds; my heart shall be / The faithful compass that still points to thee. [John Gay, 1685–1732, *Sweet William's Farewell*]

7 But I'm always true to you, darlin', in my fashion, / Yes, I'm always true to you, darlin', in my way. [Cole Porter, 1891–1964, song: *Always True to You in My Fashion*, in musical *Kiss Me, Kate*]

8 If I, by miracle, can be / This live-long minute true to thee, / 'Tis all that heaven allows. [Earl of Rochester, 1647–80, *Love and Life, A Song*]

9 When change itself can give no more, / 'Tis easy to be true. [Charles Sedley, 1639?–1701, *Not, Celia, That I Juster Am*]

10 An ill-favoured thing, sir, but mine own. [William Shakespeare, 1564–1616, *As You Like It*, V. iv. (60)]

11 Constant you are; / But yet a woman. [1 *Henry IV*, II. iii. (113)]

12 But I am constant as the northern star, / Of whose true fixed and resting quality / There is no fellow in the firmament. [*Julius Caesar*, III. i. 60]

13 Sigh no more, ladies, sigh no more, / Men were deceivers ever; / One foot in sea, and one on shore, / To one thing constant never. [*Much Ado About Nothing*, II. iii. (65)]

14 O! swear not by the moon, the inconstant moon, / that monthly changes in her circled orb, / Lest that thy love prove likewise variable. [*Romeo and Juliet*, II. ii. 109]

15 O heaven! were man / But constant, he were perfect. [*The Two Gentlemen of Verona*, V. iv. 110]

16 The fickleness of the women I love is only equalled by the infernal constancy of the women who love me. [George Bernard Shaw, 1856–1950, *The Philanderer*, II]

17 Time shall moult away his wings, / Ere he shall discover / In the whole wide world again / Such a constant lover. [John Suckling, 1609–42, *A Poem with the Answer*]

18 To love one maiden only, cleave to her, / And worship her by years of noble deeds, / Until they won her. [Alfred, Lord Tennyson, 1809–92, *Idylls of the King*, 'Guinevere', 472]

See also INCONSTANCY, LOYALTY, TRUST

CONSTITUTIONS

1 An intelligent Russian once remarked to us, 'Every country has its own constitution; ours is absolutism moderated by assassination.' [anon., quoted Count Münster, *Political Sketches of the State of Europe* (1868)]

2 The principles of a free constitution are irrevocably lost when the legislative power is nominated by the executive. [Edward Gibbon, 1737–94, *The Decline and Fall of the Roman Empire*, Ch. 3]

CONSUMERS, see MATERIALISM

CONTENTMENT

1 And if, the following day, he chance to find / A new repast, or an untasted spring, / Blesses his stars, and thinks it luxury. [Joseph Addison, 1672–1719, *Cato*, I. iv. 68]

2 Live with the gods. And he does so who constantly shows them that his soul is satisfied with what is assigned to him. [Marcus Aurelius, 121–80, *Meditations*, V, 27]

3 I have learned, in whatsoever state I am, therewith to be content. [Bible, NT, *Philippians* 4:11]

4 Contented wi' little, and cantie wi' mair. [Robert Burns, 1759–96, *Contented wi' Little*]

5 Don't let's ask for the moon. We have the stars. [Bette Davis, 1908–89, in film *Now, Voyager*, screenplay by Casey Robinson, from novel by Olive Prouty]

6 Here with a Loaf of Bread beneath the Bough, / A Flask of Wine, a Book of Verse – and Thou / Beside me singing in the Wilderness – / And Wilderness is Paradise enow. [Edward Fitzgerald, 1809–83, *The Rubá'iyát of Omar Khayyám*, Edn 1, 11]

7 A man he was, to all the country dear, / And passing rich with forty pounds a year; / Remote from towns he ran his godly race, / Nor e'er had changed, nor wished to change his place. [Oliver Goldsmith, 1728–74, *The Deserted Village*, 141]

8 Think to yourself that every day is your last; the hour to which you do not look forward will come as a welcome surprise. As for me, when you want a good laugh, you will find me, in a fine state, fat and sleek, a true hog of Epicurus' sty. [Horace, 65–8BC, *Epistles*, I, iv, 13]

9 The toad beneath the harrow knows / Exactly where each tooth-point goes; / The butterfly upon the road / Preaches contentment to that toad. [Rudyard Kipling, 1865–1936, *Pagett M P*]

10 The value of life lies, not in the length of days, but in the use we make of them; a man may live long, yet live very little. Satisfaction in life depends not on the number of your years, but on your will. [Michel de Montaigne, 1533–92, *Essays*, I, 20]

11 He [James Anderton] had the look of deep and complacent satisfaction which men assume when they speak of having been beaten in childhood. [John Mortimer, 1923– , *In Character*, 'An Ironside Reborn']

12 I've been the whole hog plenty of times. Sometimes . . . you can be happy . . . and not go the whole hog. Now and again . . . you can be happy . . . without going any hog. [Harold Pinter, 1930– , *The Homecoming*, II]

13 Who doth ambition shun, / And loves to live i' the sun, / Seeking the food he eats, / And pleased with what he gets. [William Shakespeare, 1564–1616, *As You Like It*, V. i. (38)]

14 He is well paid that is well satisfied. [*The Merchant of Venice*, IV. i. (416)]

15 That content surpassing wealth / The sage in meditation found / And walked with inward glory crowned. [P B Shelley, 1792–1822, *Stanzas Written in Dejection*]

16 I often wished that I had clear, / For life, six hundred pounds a-year, / A handsome house to lodge a friend; / A river at my garden's end, / A terrace walk, and half a rood / Of land set out to plant a wood. [Jonathan Swift, 1677–1745, *Imitation of Horace*, II, vi, 1]

17 An elegant sufficiency, content, / Retirement, rural quiet, friendship, books, / Ease and alternate labour, useful life, / Progressive virtue, and approving Heaven! [James Thomson, 1700–1748, *The Seasons*, 'Spring', 1161]

See also HAPPINESS, PLEASURE

CONTRACEPTION

1 Vasectomy means not ever having to say you're sorry. [Larry Adler, 1914– (parody of line from E Segal, *Love Story*), in BBC programme *Quote . . . Unquote*, and recorded in book of selections from the programme, ed. N Rees]

2 I want to tell you a terrific story about oral contraception. I asked this girl to sleep with me and she said 'no'. [Woody Allen, 1935– , in Adler and Feinman, *W A: Clown Prince of American Humor*, Ch. 2]

3 The best contraceptive is a glass of cold water: not before or after, but instead. [anon. Pakistani delegate at International Planned Parenthood Federation Conference]

4 There's a proposal to install contraceptive machines in the students' cloakrooms at college ... It's a very special machine, designed for Catholics ... You put contraceptives in and get money out. [David Lodge, 1935– , *How Far Can You Go?*, Ch. 3]

5 Where are the children I might have had? You may suppose I might have wanted them. Drowned to the accompaniment of the rattling of a thousand douche bags. [Malcolm Lowry, 1909–57, *Under the Volcano*, Ch. 10]

6 It is now quite lawful for a Catholic woman to avoid pregnancy by a resort to mathematics, though she is still forbidden to resort to physics and chemistry. [H L Mencken, 1880–1956, *Minority Report*, 62]

7 Contraceptives should be used on every conceivable occasion. [Spike Milligan, 1918– , *The Last Goon Show of All*]

8 Skullion had little use for contraceptives at the best of times. Unnatural, he called them, and placed them in the lower social category of things along with elastic-sided boots and made-up bow ties. Not the sort of attire for a gentleman. [Tom Sharpe, 1928– , *Porterhouse Blue*, Ch. 9]

CONVERSATION

1 How often you and I / Had tired the sun with talking and sent him down the sky. [W J Cory, 1823–92, *Heraclitus*]

2 He believed that the art of conversation was dead. His own small talk, at any rate, was bigger than most people's large. [Peter de Vries, 1910–93, *Comfort Me with Apples*, Ch. 1]

3 Encounters with people of so many different kinds and on so many different psychological levels have been for me incomparably more important than fragmentary conversations with celebrities. The finest and most significant conversations of my life were anonymous. [C G Jung, 1875–1961, *Memories, Dreams, Reflections*, Ch. 4]

4 Conversation is like playing tennis with a ball made of Krazy Putty that keeps coming back over the net in a different shape. [David Lodge, 1935– , *Small World*, Pt 1, 1]

5 I find it quite remarkable, don't you, how people always take offence when a conversation ceases to be personal? [Frederic Raphael, 1931– , *The Glittering Prizes*, 'An Academic Life']

6 Conversation is imperative if gaps are to be filled, and old age, it is the last gap but one. [Patrick White, 1912–90, *The Tree of Man*, Ch. 22]

See also GOSSIP, SPEECH, TALK

COOKERY

1 Bouillabaisse is only good because cooked by the French, who, if they cared to try, could produce an excellent and nutritious substitute out of cigar stumps and empty matchboxes. [Norman Douglas, 1868–1952, *Siren Land*, 'Rain on the Hills']

2 The French cook; we open tins. [John Galsworthy, 1867–1933; in *Treasury of Humorous Quotations*, ed. Evan Esar and Nicolas Bentley]

3 Serve up in a clean dish, and throw the whole out of the window as fast as possible. [Edward Lear, 1812–88, *To Make an Amblongus Pie*]

4 Kissing don't last: cookery do! [George Meredith, 1828–1909, *The Ordeal of Richard Feverel*, Ch. 28]

5 I never see any home cooking. All I get is fancy stuff. [Philip, Duke of Edinburgh, 1921– ; *Observer*, 'Sayings of the Week', 28 Oct. 1962]

6 The cook was a good cook, as cooks go; and as cooks go she went. [Saki (H H Munro), 1870–1916, *Reginald on Besetting Sins*]

7 'Tis an ill cook that cannot lick his own fingers. [William Shakespeare, 1564–1616, *Romeo and Juliet*, IV. ii. (6)]

8 Mother doesn't cook ... she burns. [John Kennedy Toole, 1937–69, *A Confederacy of Dunces*, I, 3]

See also FOOD

CORRUPTION

1 Corruption, the most infallible symptom of constitutional liberty. [Edward Gibbon, 1737–

94, *The Decline and Fall of the Roman Empire*, Ch. 21]

2 I have often noticed that a bribe ... has that effect – it changes a relation. The man who offers a bribe gives away a little of his own importance; the bribe once accepted, he becomes the inferior, like a man who has paid for a woman. [Graham Greene, 1904–91, *The Comedians*, Pt 1, Ch. 4, iii]

3 I am against government by crony. [Harold L Ickes, 1874–1952, on resigning as US Secretary of the Interior, Feb. 1946]

4 Something is rotten in the state of Denmark. [William Shakespeare, 1564–1616, *Hamlet*, I. iv. 90]

COSMOS, see UNIVERSE

COUNTRY & TOWN

1 I have never understood why anybody agreed to go on being a rustic after about 1400. [Kingsley Amis, 1922–95, *The Green Man*, 'Dr Thomas Underhill']

2 We'd both been to the country and found it disappointingly empty. [Julian Barnes, 1946– , *Metroland*, Pt 1, 4]

3 An industrial worker would sooner have a £5 note but a countryman must have praise. [Ronald Blythe, 1922– , *Akenfield*, Ch. 5, 'Christopher Falconer']

4 For what were all these country patriots born? / To hunt, and vote, and raise the price of corn? [Lord Byron, 1788–1824, *The Age of Bronze*, 14]

5 I live not in myself, but I become / Portion of that around me; and to me / High mountains are a feeling, but the hum / Of human cities torture. [Lord Byron, 1788–1824, *Childe Harold's Pilgrimage*, III, 72]

6 I nauseate walking; 'tis a country diversion, I loathe the country. [William Congreve, 1670–1729, *The Way of the World*, IV. iv]; see 15

7 God made the country, and man made the town. [William Cowper, 1731–1800, *The Task*, Bk I, 749]

8 It is my belief, Watson, founded upon my experience, that the lowest and vilest alleys of London do not present a more dreadful record of sin than does the smiling and beautiful countryside. [Arthur Conan Doyle, 1859–1930, *The Adventures of Sherlock Holmes*, 'The Copper Beeches']

9 There is nothing good to be had in the country, or, if there is, they will not let you have it. [William Hazlitt, 1778–1830, *Observations on Mr Wordsworth's 'Excursion'*]

10 I do not think there is anything deserving the name of society to be found out of London. [William Hazlitt, 1778–1830, *On Coffee-House Politicians*]

11 When I am in the country I wish to vegetate like the country. [William Hazlitt, 1778–1830, *On Going a Journey*]

12 This was what I prayed for: a plot of land not too large, containing a garden, and near the house a fresh spring of water, and a bit of forest to complete it. [Horace, 65–8 BC, *Satires*, vi, 1]

13 To one who has been long in city pent, / 'Tis very sweet to look into the fair / And open face of heaven. [John Keats, 1795–1821, sonnet: *To One Who Has Been Long in City Pent*]

14 I dislike being in the country in August, because my legs get so bitten by barristers. [Lydia Lopokova, 1891–1981, attr. in Robert L Heilbroner *The Worldly Philosophers*, Ch. 9]

15 I don't like going for walks in the country because it's so easy to turn round and go home again that you can't help wondering whether it's worthwhile setting out in the first place. [Robert Robinson, 1927– , *Dog Chairman*, 'Aiming, Shooting and Missing']; see 6

16 Under the greenwood tree / Who loves to lie with me, / And turn his merry note / Unto the sweet bird's throat, / Come hither, come hither, come hither: / Here shall he see / No enemy / But winter and rough weather. [William Shakespeare, 1564–1616, *As You Like It*, II. v. 1]

17 I have no relish for the country; it is a kind of healthy grave. [Sydney Smith, 1771–1845, letter to Miss G Harcourt, 1838]

18 It is a place with only one post a day ... In the country I always fear that creation will expire before tea-time. [Sydney Smith, 1771–1845, in H Pearson, *The Smith of Smiths*, Ch. 5]

19 In the highlands, in the country places, / Where the old plain men have rosy faces. [Robert Louis Stevenson, 1850–94, *Songs of Travel*, 16]

20 I will arise and go now, and go to Innisfree, / And a small cabin build there, of clay and wattles made: / Nine bean-rows will I have there, a hive for the honey-bee, / And live alone in the bee-loud glade. [W B Yeats, 1865–1939, *The Lake Isle of Innisfree*]

See also CITY

COURAGE

1 Distrust yourself, and sleep before you fight. / 'Tis not too late tomorrow to be brave. [John Armstrong, 1709–79, *Art of Preserving Health*, IV, 457]

2 In civil business; what first? Boldness; what second, and third? Boldness. And yet boldness is a child of ignorance and baseness. [Francis Bacon, 1561–1626, *Essays*, 12, 'Of Boldness']

3 No coward soul is mine, / No trembler in the world's storm-troubled sphere: / I see Heaven's glories shine, / And faith shines equal, arming me from fear. [Emily Brontë, 1818–48, *Last Lines*]

4 To dry one's eyes and laugh at a fall, / And, baffled, get up and begin again. [Robert Browning, 1812–89, *Life in a Love*]

5 Tomorrow let us do or die! [Thomas Campbell, 1777–1844, *Gertrude of Wyoming*, Pt III, 37]

6 And though hard be the task, / 'Keep a stiff upper lip.' [Phoebe Cary, 1824–71, *Keep a Stiff Upper Lip*]

7 How sleep the brave, who sink to rest, / By all their country's wishes blest! [William Collins, 1721–59, *Ode Written in the Year 1746*]

8 Boldness, more boldness, and perpetual boldness! [Georges Danton, 1759–94, speech in the Legislative Assembly, Paris, 2 Sept. 1792]

9 None but the brave deserves the fair. [John Dryden, 1631–1700, *Alexander's Feast*, 15]

10 Heart of oak are our ships, / Heart of oak are our men: / We always are ready; / Steady, boys, steady; / We'll fight and we'll conquer again and again. [David Garrick, 1717–79, *Heart of Oak*]

11 Life is mostly froth and bubble, / Two things stand like stone, / Kindness in another's trouble, / Courage in your own. [Adam Lindsay Gordon, 1833–70, *Ye Wearie Wayfarer*, Fytte 8]

12 DOROTHY PARKER: Exactly what do you mean by 'guts'?

HEMINGWAY: I mean grace under pressure. [Ernest Hemingway, 1899–1961, interview with Parker in *New Yorker*, 30 Nov. 1929; quoted in J F Kennedy, *Profiles in Courage*, Ch. 1]

13 If people bring so much courage to this world, the world has to kill them ... It kills the very good and very gentle and the very brave impartially. [Ernest Hemingway, 1899–1961, in Arthur M Schlesinger Jr, *A Thousand Days*]

14 One man with courage makes a majority. [President Andrew Jackson, 1767–1845, ascr. by Robert Kennedy in his foreword to his brother's *Profiles in Courage*]

15 An' for all 'is dirty 'ide / 'E was white, clear white inside / When 'e went to tend the wounded under fire. [Rudyard Kipling, 1865–1936, *Gunga Din*]

16 If the creator had a purpose in equipping us with a neck, he surely meant us to stick it out. [Arthur Koestler, 1905–83; in *Encounter*, May 1970]

17 Courage is not simply *one* of the virtues but the form of every virtue at the testing point, which means at the point of highest reality. [C S Lewis, 1898–1963, in 'Palinurus' (Cyril Connolly), *The Unquiet Grave*, Ch. 3]

18 No man in the world has more courage than the man who can stop after eating one peanut. [Channing Pollock, 1880–1946, in Jonathon Green, *Consuming Secrets*]

19 Boldness be my friend! [William Shakespeare, 1564–1616, *Cymbeline*, I. vi. 18]

20 The better part of valour is discretion. [1 *Henry IV*, V. iv. (120)]

21 Cowards die many times before their deaths; / The valiant never taste of death but once. [*Julius Caesar*, II. ii. 32]

22 For courage mounteth with occasion. [*King John*, II. i. 82]

23 I dare do all that may become a man; / Who dares do more is none. [*Macbeth*, I. vii. 46]

24 And as she looked about, she did behold, / How over that same door was likewise writ, / Be bold, be bold, and everywhere, Be bold. [Edmund Spenser, 1552?–99, *The Faerie Queene*, Bk ii, Canto 11, stanza 54]

See also COWARDICE

COURTESY, see MANNERS

COURTSHIP

1 Oh Bernard muttered Ethel this is so sudden. No no cried Bernard and taking the bull by both horns he kissed her violently on her dainty face. My bride to be he murmered several times. [Daisy Ashford, 1881–1972, *The Young Visiters*, 9]

2 If you want to win her hand, / Let the maiden understand / That she's not the only pebble on the beach. [Harry Braisted, 19th cent., *You're Not the only Pebble on the Beach*]

3 The trouble with some women is they get all excited about nothing – and then marry him. [Cher, 1946– , in *Hammer and Tongues*, ed. Michèle Brown and Ann O'Connor, 'Husbands']

4 Courtship to marriage, as a very witty prologue to a very dull play. [William Congreve, 1670–1729, *The Old Bachelor*, V. x]

5 Marriage is to courtship as humming is to singing. [Peter de Vries, 1910–93, *Consenting Adults*, Ch. 6]

6 His designs were strictly honourable, as the saying is; that is, to rob a lady of her fortune by way of marriage. [Henry Fielding, 1707–54, *Tom Jones*, Bk xi, 4]

7 Effie M. was a monster. Six foot high and as strong as a farm horse. No sooner had she decided that she wanted Uncle Tom than she knocked him off his bicycle and told him. [Laurie Lee, 1914–97, *Cider with Rosie*, 'The Uncles']

8 Marry me, and you'll be farting through silk. [Robert Mitchum, 1917–97 (when proposing to his future wife), ascr. in interview in *Guardian*, 23 June 1984]

9 It were all one / That I should love a bright particular star / And think to wed it, he is so above me. [William Shakespeare, 1564–1616, *All's Well that Ends Well*, I. i. (97)]

10 Men are April when they woo, December when they wed: maids are May when they are maids, but the sky changes when they are wives. [*As You Like It*, IV. i (153)]

11 For these fellows of infinite tongue, that can rhyme themselves into ladies' favours, they do always reason themselves out again. [*Henry V*, V. ii. (162)]

12 She's beautiful and therefore to be wooed; / She is a woman, therefore to be won. [1 *Henry VI*, V. iii. 78]

13 My story being done, / She gave me for my pains a world of sighs; / She swore, in faith, 'twas strange, 'twas passing strange; / 'Twas pitiful, 'twas wondrous pitiful: / She wished she had not heard it, yet she wished / That heaven had made her such a man; she thanked me, / And bade me, if I had a friend that loved her, / I should but teach him how to tell my story, / And that would woo her. Upon this hint I spake. [*Othello*, I. ii. 158]

14 Was ever woman in this humour wooed? / Was ever woman in this humour won? [*Richard III*, I. ii. 229]

15 Women are angels, wooing: / Things won are done; joy's soul lies in the doing: / That she beloved knows nought that knows not this: / Men prize the thing ungained more than it is. [*Troilus and Cressida*, I. ii. (310)]

16 Make me a willow cabin at your gate, / And call upon my soul within the house; / Write loyal cantons of contemnèd love, / And sing them loud even in the dead of night; / Holla your name to the reverberate hills. [*Twelfth Night*, I. v. (289)]

COWARDICE

1 Only cowards insult dying majesty. [Aesop, *fl. c.*550 BC, *Fables*, 'The Sick Lion']

2 I'm really a timid person – I was beaten up by Quakers. [Woody Allen, 1935– , in film *Sleeper*, scripted with Marshall Brickman]

3 A sober man may become a drunkard through being a coward. A brave man may become a coward through being a drunkard. [G K Chesterton, 1874–1936, *Charles Dickens*, 8]

4 Probably a fear we have of facing up to the real issues. Could you say we were guilty of Noel Cowardice? [Peter de Vries, 1910–93, *Comfort Me with Apples*, Ch. 15]

5 In the army *they shot cowards*. Homoeopathy, surely, carried to its wildest extreme. [Alice Thomas Ellis, 1932– , *The 27th Kingdom*, Ch. 15]

6 The coward's weapon, poison. [Phineas Fletcher, 1582–1650, *Sicelides*, V, iii]

7 Call out the Boys of the Old Brigade, / Who made Old England free – / Send out my Mother, my Sister and my Brother, / But for God's sake don't send me! [Alfred Lester, 1874–1925, *Conscientious Objector's Lament*]

8 Cowards' hearts beat faster than heroes' but last longer. [Zarko Petan, in *The Times*, 15 June 1977]

9 Most men are cowards, all men should be knaves. [Earl of Rochester, 1647–80, *A Satire against Mankind*, 158]

10 We'll have a swashing and a martial outside, / As many other mannish cowards have / That do outface it with their semblances. [William Shakespeare, 1564–1616, *As You Like It*, I. iii. (123)]

11 Cowards die many times before their deaths; / The valiant never taste of death but once. [*Julius Caesar*, II. ii. 32]

12 As an old soldier I admit the cowardice: it's as universal as sea sickness, and matters just as little. [George Bernard Shaw, 1856–1950, *Man and Superman*, III]

13 My valour is certainly going! – it is sneaking off! – I feel it oozing out as it were at the palms of my hands! [R B Sheridan, 1751–1816, *The Rivals*, V, iii]

See also COURAGE

CREATION

1 The Hand that made us is divine. [Joseph Addison, 1672–1719, *The Spectator*, 465, Ode]

2 All things bright and beautiful, / All creatures great and small, / All things wise and wonderful, / The Lord God made them all. [Mrs C F Alexander, 1818–95, hymn]

3 There is no need to look for a purpose behind it all: energy has just gone on spreading, and the spreading has happened to generate elephants and enthralling opinions. [P W Atkins, 1940– , *The Creation*, 'Why Things Change']

4 In the beginning God created the heaven and the earth. And the earth was without form, and void; and darkness was upon the face of the deep. [Bible, OT, *Genesis* 1:1]

5 And God saw everything that he had made, and, behold, it was very good. [Bible, OT, *Genesis* 1:31]

6 For, behold, I create new heavens and a new earth. [Bible, OT, *Isaiah* 65:17]

7 Every creature of God is good. [Bible, NT, *1 Timothy* 4:4]

8 When the stars threw down their spears, / And watered heaven with their tears, / Did he smile his work to see? / Did he who made the Lamb make thee? [William Blake, 1757–1827, *Songs of Experience*, 'The Tyger']

9 Creation purged o' the miscreate, man redeemed, / A spittle wiped off from the face of God! [Robert Browning, 1812–89, *The Ring and the Book*, VI, 1478]

10 Thou madest man, he knows not why. [Alfred, Lord Tennyson, 1809–92, *In Memoriam*, Prologue]

11 God made the woman for the man, / And for the good and increase of the world. [Alfred, Lord Tennyson, 1809–92, *Edwin Morris*, 43]

12 The art of creation / is older than the art of killing. [Andrei Voznesensky, 1933– , *Poem with a Footnote*]

13 The distance between the necessary and the good is the distance between the creature and the creator. [Simone Weil, 1909–43; in Auden and Kronenberger, *The Faber Book of Aphorisms*]

CREATIVITY

1 I must Create a System, or be enslaved by another Man's; / I will not Reason and Compare; my business is to Create. [William Blake, 1757–1827, *Jerusalem*, f.10, 20]

2 Produce! Produce! Were it but the pitifullest infinitesimal fraction of a product, produce it in God's name! 'Tis the utmost thou hast in thee: out with it, then. [Thomas Carlyle, 1795–1881, *Sartor Resartus*, Bk ii, Ch. 9]

3 Birds build – but not I build; no, but strain, / Time's eunuch, and not breed one work that wakes. / Mine, O thou lord of life, send my roots rain. [Gerard Manley Hopkins, 1844–89, *Thou art Indeed Just, Lord*]

4 I had to keep you waiting till the strain of composition had worn off my face. [George Moore, 1852–1933, in O St John Gogarty, *As I Was Going Down Sackville Street*, Ch. 17]

5 Vitality in a woman is a blind fury of creation. She sacrifices herself to it. [George Bernard Shaw, 1856–1950, *Man and Superman*, I]

6 The worst crime is to leave a man's hands empty. / Men are born makers, with that primal simplicity / In every maker since Adam. [Derek Walcott, 1930– , *Omeros*, Ch. xxviii, 2]

7 I said, 'A line will take us hours maybe; / Yet if it does not seem a moment's thought, / Our stitching and unstitching has been naught.' [W B Yeats, 1865–1939, *Adam's Curse*]

See also ORIGINALITY

CRICKET

1 It's more than a game. It's an institution. [Thomas Hughes, 1822–96, *Tom Brown's Schooldays*, Pt II, Ch. 7]

2 Cricket is first and foremost a dramatic spectacle. It belongs with the theatre, ballet, opera and the dance. [C L R James, 1901–89, *Beyond a Boundary*, Ch. 16]

3 There'a a breathless hush in the Close tonight – / Ten to make and the match to win – / A bumping pitch and a blinding light, / An hour to play and the last man in. / And it's not for the sake of a ribboned coat, / Or the selfish hope of a season's fame, / But his Captain's hand on his shoulder smote – / 'Play up! play up! and play the game!' [Henry Newbolt, 1862–1938, *Vitae Lampada*]

4 It's a funny kind of month, October. For the really keen cricket fan it's when you discover that your wife left you in May. [Denis Norden, 1922– , in *She* magazine, Oct. 1977]

5 It is hard to tell where MCC ends and the Church of England begins. [J B Priestley, 1894–1984; *New Statesman*, 20 July 1962]

6 [When asked by Ben Travers what bowling to Hobbs and Sandham had been like] It's like trying to bowl to God on concrete. [R C Robertson-Glasgow, 1901–65, in Ben Travers, *94 Declared*]

7 Personally, I have always looked on cricket as organized loafing. [Archbishop William Temple, 1881–1944, remark to parents when Headmaster of Repton School]

8 And I look through my tears on a soundless-clapping host / As the run-stealers flicker to and fro, / To and fro:– / O my Hornby and my Barlow long ago! [Francis Thompson, 1859–1907, *At Lord's*]

See also FOOTBALL, GOLF, SPORTS

CRIME

1 Society already understands that the criminal is not he who washes our dirty linen in public, but he who dirties the linen. [Vladimir Bukovsky, 1942– , said on 5 Jan. 1972: *Radio Times*, 19 Sept. 1977]

2 How many crimes committed merely because their authors could not endure being wrong! [Albert Camus, 1913–60, *The Fall*]

3 The probation service have found out that there are two types of person appearing before the courts – those who have problems – and those who are problems. [Simon Cohen, 1931– , *Magistrate*, June 1983]

4 Like all art and politics, gangsterism is a very important avenue of assimilation into society. [E L Doctorow, 1931– ; *Observer*, 'Sayings of the Week', 7 Oct. 1990]

5 Singularity is almost invariably a clue. The more featureless and commonplace a crime is, the more difficult it is to bring it home. [Arthur Conan Doyle, 1859–1930, *The Adventures of Sherlock Holmes*, 'The Boscombe Valley Mystery']

6 He [Professor Moriarty] is the Napoleon of crime. [Arthur Conan Doyle, 1859–1930, *The Memoirs of Sherlock Holmes*, 'The Final Problem']

7 Oh let us not be condemned for what we are. / It is enough to account for what we do. / Save us from the judge who says: You are your father's son, / One of your father's crimes – your crime is you. [James Fenton, 1949– , *Children in Exile*]

8 It was beautiful and simple as all truly great swindles are. [O Henry, 1862–1910, *The Octopus Marooned*]

9 Brandy for the Parson, / 'Baccy for the Clerk; / Laces for a lady, letters for a spy, / Watch the wall, my darling, while the Gentlemen go by! [Rudyard Kipling, 1865–1936, *A Smuggler's Song*]

10 Crimes are created by Parliament; it needs a policeman to make a criminal. You don't become a criminal by breaking the law, but by getting found out. [Edmund Leach, 1910–89, *Runaway World*, Ch. 3]

11 'Irregularity' means there's been a crime but you can't prove it. 'Malpractice' means there's been a crime and you can prove it. [Jonathan Lynn, 1943– , and Antony Jay,

1930– , *Yes Prime Minister*, Vol. 2, 'A Conflict of Interest']

12 Crime is only a left-handed form of human endeavour. [In film *The Asphalt Jungle*, script by Ben Maddow, 1909–92, and John Huston, 1906–87, from novel of W R Burnett]

13 My house has been broken open on the most scientific principles. [T L Peacock, 1785–1866, *Crotchet Castle*, Ch. 17]

14 Crime, like virtue, has its degrees. [Jean Racine, 1639–99, *Phèdre*, IV. ii. 1096]

15 Much as he is opposed to lawbreaking, he is not bigoted about it. [Damon Runyon, 1884–1946, attr.]

16 Really premeditated crimes are those that are not committed. [Leonardo Sciascia, 1921–89, *1912=1*]

17 If he's a criminal, he's in plain clothes – that's all I can say. [N F Simpson, 1919– , *A Resounding Tinkle*, I, i]

18 Hark ye, Clinker, you are a most notorious offender. You stand convicted of sickness, hunger, wretchedness, and want. [Tobias Smollett, 1721–71, *Humphrey Clinker*, letter to Sir Watkin Phillips, 24 May]

19. Crime and its components have always been an unselfconscious adjunct of show-business. [John Stalker, 1939– , in *The Sunday Times*, 22 Apr. 1990]

20 I came to the conclusion many years ago that almost all crime is due to the repressed desire for aesthetic expression. [Evelyn Waugh, 1903–66, *Decline and Fall*, III, 1]

21 Arson, after all, is an artificial crime ... A large number of houses deserve to be burnt. [H G Wells, 1866–1946, *The History of Mr Polly*, Ch. x, Pt 1]

See also EVIL, JUSTICE, LAW, WICKEDNESS

CRITICS & CRITICISM

1 I am bound by my own definition of criticism: a disinterested endeavour to learn and propagate the best that is known and thought in the world. [Matthew Arnold, 1822–88, *Essays in Criticism*, 'The Function of Criticism at the Present Time']

2 There is less of this than meets the eye. [Tallulah Bankhead, 1903–68, in Alexander Woollcott, *Shouts and Murmurs*, 'Capsule Criticism']

3 I will try to account for the degree of my aesthetic emotion. That, I conceive, is the function of the critic. [Clive Bell, 1881–1964, *Art*, II, 3]

4 The art of the critic in a nutshell: to coin slogans without betraying ideas. [Walter Benjamin, 1892–1940, *One-way Street*, 'Chinese Curios']

5 To many people dramatic criticism must seem like an attempt to tattoo soap bubbles. [John Mason Brown, 1900–1969, in Frank Muir, *Frank Muir Book*]

6 A man must serve his time to every trade / Save censure – critics all are ready made. [Lord Byron, 1788–1824, *English Bards and Scotch Reviewers*, 63]

7 As soon / Seek roses in December – ice in June; / Hope constancy in wind, or corn in chaff; / Believe a woman or an epitaph, / Or any other thing that's false, before / You trust in critics. [Lord Byron, 1788–1824, *English Bards and Scotch Reviewers*, 75]

8 It is not enough for a critic to be right, since he will occasionally be wrong. It is not enough for him to give colourable reasons. He must create a reasonable world into which his reader may enter blindfold and feel his way to the chair by the fire without barking his shins on the unexpected dust mop. [Raymond Chandler, 1888–1959, letter to Frederick Lewis Allen, 7 May 1948]

9 The great critics, of whom there are piteously few, build a home for the truth. [Raymond Chandler, 1888–1959, letter to Frederick Lewis Allen, 7 May 1948]

10 A great deal of contemporary criticism reads to me like a man saying: 'Of course I do not like green cheese: I am very fond of brown sherry.' [G K Chesterton, 1874–1936, *All I Survey*, 'On Jonathan Swift']

11 Either criticism is no good at all (a very defensible position) or else criticism means saying about an author the very things that would have made him jump out of his boots. [G K Chesterton, 1874–1936, *Charles Dickens*, 10]

12 Though by whim, envy, or resentment led, / They damn those authors whom they never read. [Charles Churchill, 1731–64, *The Candidate*, 57]

13 Reviewers are usually people who would have been poets, historians, biographers, etc., if they could; they have tried their talents at one or at the other, and have failed; therefore they turn critics. [Samuel Taylor Coleridge, 1772–1834, *Lectures on Shakespeare and Milton*, I]

14 A good critic is one who narrates the adventures of his mind among masterpieces. [Anatole France, 1844–1924, *La Vie littéraire*, I, Preface]

15 The plot was designed in a light vein that somehow became varicose. [David Gardner, in Bennett Cerf, *Try and Stop Me*]

16 Asking a working writer what he thinks about critics is like asking a lamp-post how it feels about dogs. [Christopher Hampton, 1946– , in *The Sunday Times Magazine*, 16 Oct. 1977]

17 Parodies and caricatures are the most penetrating of criticisms. [Aldous Huxley, 1894–1963, *Point Counter Point*, Ch. 28]

18 Oscar Williams's new book is pleasanter and a little quieter than his old, which gave the impression of having been written on a typewriter by a typewriter. [Randall Jarrell, 1914–65, quoted in *The Times Literary Supplement*, 11 July 1986]

19 The father of English criticism. [Dr Samuel Johnson, 1709–84, *The Lives of the English Poets*, 'Dryden']

20 Censure acquits the raven, but pursues the dove. [Juvenal, 60–*c.*130, *Satires*, I, ii, 63]

21 The pleasure of criticizing robs us of the pleasure of being moved by some very fine things. [Jean de La Bruyère, 1645–96, *Characters*, 'Of Books', 20]

22 The only way to escape misrepresentation is never to commit oneself to any critical judgement that makes an impact – that is, never *say* anything. [F R Leavis, 1895–1978, *The Great Tradition*, Ch. 1]

23 I cried all the way to the bank. [Liberace, 1919–87 (reaction to hostile criticism in 1954), in Bob Thomas, *L: The True Story*]

24 People who like this sort of thing will find this the sort of thing they like. [(Of a book) Abraham Lincoln, 1809–65, in G W E Russell, *Collections and Recollections*, Ch. 30]

25 A wise scepticism is the first attribute of a good critic. [James Russell Lowell, 1819–91, *Among My Books*, 'Shakespeare Once More']

26 Naming the parts does not show us what makes the gun go off. [Molly Mahood, 1919– , *Shakespeare's Wordplay*, p. 19]

27 I was so long writing my review that I never got around to reading the book. [Groucho Marx, 1895–1977; in Laurence J Peter, *Peter's Quotations*]

28 This is not a novel to be tossed aside lightly. It should be thrown with great force. [Dorothy Parker, 1893–1967, book review]

29 Nor in the critic let the man be lost. [Alexander Pope, 1688–1744, *An Essay on Criticism*, 523]

30 In the pathology of nervous diseases, a doctor who doesn't talk too much nonsense is a half-cured patient, just as a critic is a poet who has stopped writing verse and a policeman a burglar who has retired from practice. [Marcel Proust, 1871–1922, *Remembrance of Things Past: The Guermantes Way*, Ch. 1, 'Decline and Death of My Grandmother']

31 For whom, then, do they [aesthetic laws] exist? For the critic? He who can distinguish a good fruit from a bad with his palate does not have to be able to express the distinction through a chemical formula and does not need the formula to recognize the distinction. [Arnold Schoenberg, 1874–1951, *The Theory of Harmony*, Ch. 22]

32 Yes, sir, puffing is of various sorts: the principal are, the puff direct – the puff preliminary – the puff collateral – the puff collusive, and the puff oblique, or puff by implication. [R B Sheridan, 1751–1816, *The Critic*, I. ii]

33 Pay no attention to what the critics say; no statue has ever been put up to a critic. [Jean Sibelius, 1865–1957, in B de Törne, *Sibelius: A Close-up*, Ch. 2]

34 What can we know in this world? It is as if you were to ask a bookworm crawling inside *War and Peace* whether it is a good novel or a bad one. He is sitting on one little letter trying to get some nourishment. How can he be a critic of Tolstoy? [Isaac Bashevis Singer, 1904–91, quoted by Norman Lebrecht, 'Singer, Late in Summer', *Adam International Review*, Vol. 46, Nos. 452–4, 1984]

35 I never read a book before reviewing it, it prejudices a man so. [Sydney Smith, 1771–1845, in H Pearson, *The Smith of Smiths*, Ch. 3]

36 Their teacher had advised them not to read Tolstoy's novels, because they were very long and would easily confuse the clear ideas which they had learned from reading critical studies of him. [Alexander Solzhenitsyn, 1918– , *The First Circle*, Ch. 40]

37 Of all the cants which are canted in this canting world, – though the cant of hypocrites may be the worst, – the cant of criticism is the most tormenting! [Laurence Sterne, 1713–68, *Tristram Shandy*, Vol. iii, Ch. 12]

38 I doubt that art needed Ruskin any more than a moving train needs one of its passengers to shove it. [Tom Stoppard, 1937– , in *The Times Literary Supplement*, 3 June 1977]

39 I had another dream the other day about music critics. They were small and rodent-like with padlocked ears, as if they had stepped out of a painting by Goya. [Igor Stravinsky, 1882–1971, in *Evening Standard*, 29 Oct. 1969]

40 As learned commentators view / In Homer more than Homer knew. [Jonathan Swift, 1677–1745, *On Poetry*, 103]

41 The prudent critic will try himself by his achievements rather than by his ideals, and his neighbours, living and dead alike, by their ideals not less than by their achievements. [R H Tawney, 1880–1962, *Religion and the Rise of Capitalism*, Ch. v]

42 O you chorus of indolent reviewers. [Alfred, Lord Tennyson, 1809–92, *Experiments in Quantity*, 'Milton, Hendecasyllabics']

43 A louse in the locks of literature. [(Of Churton Collins) Alfred, Lord Tennyson, 1809–92, in Evan Charteris, *Life and Letters of Sir Edmund Gosse*, Ch. 14]

44 [When asked his opinion of a play] It had only one fault. It was kind of lousy. [James Thurber, 1894–1961, in P G Wodehouse, *Performing Flea*, 1947–52]

45 A critic is a man who knows the way but can't drive the car. [Kenneth Tynan, 1927–80, in *The New York Times Magazine*, 9 Jan. 1966]

46 How commentators each dark passage shun, / And hold their farthing candle to the sun. [Edward Young, 1683–1765, *Love of Fame*, Satire VII, 97]

See also LITERATURE

CRUELTY

1 Cruelty has a human heart, / And Jealousy a human face; / Terror the human form divine, / And Secrecy the human dress. [William Blake, 1757–1827, *Appendix to the Songs of Innocence and of Experience*, 'A Divine Image']

2 Man's inhumanity to man / Makes countless thousands mourn! [Robert Burns, 1759–96, *Man was Made to Mourn*, 55]

3 I would not enter on my list of friends / (Though graced with polished manners and fine sense, / Yet wanting sensibility) the man / Who needlessly sets foot upon a worm. [William Cowper, 1731–1800, *The Task*, Bk VI, 560]

4 The aim of sadism is to transform a man into a thing, something animate into something inanimate, since by complete and absolute control the living loses one essential quality of life – freedom. [Erich Fromm, 1900–1980, *The Heart of Man*]

5 Those who harm simple / people and who laugh at their / injuries will not be safe. / For the poet remembers. [Czeslaw Milosz, 1911, inscription at the martyrs' monument, Gdansk shipyard, Poland]

6 Let me be cruel, not unnatural; / I will speak daggers to her but use none. [William Shakespeare, 1564–1616, *Hamlet*, III. ii. (420)]

7 I must be cruel only to be kind. [*Hamlet*, III. iii. 178]

8 Unsex me here, / And fill me from the crown to the toe top full / Of direst cruelty! [*Macbeth*, I. v. (42)]

See also KINDNESS

CULTURE

1 Culture being a pursuit of our total perfection by means of getting to know, on all the matters which most concern us, the best which has been thought and said in the world. [Matthew Arnold, 1822–88, *Culture and Anarchy*, Preface]

2 Philistine must have originally meant, in the mind of those who invented the nickname, a strong, dogged, unenlightened opponent of the chosen people, of the children of light. [Matthew Arnold, 1822–88, *Essays in Criticism*, First Series, 'Heinrich Heine']

3 This great society is going smash; / They

cannot fool us with how fast they go, / How much they cost each other and the gods! / A culture is no better than its woods. [W H Auden, 1907–73, *Winds*]

4 In cultural matters, it is not demand that creates supply, it is the other way round. [Joseph Brodsky, 1940–96, *On Grief and Reason*]

5 A culture which leaves unsatisfied and drives to rebelliousness so large a number of its members neither has a prospect of continued existence nor deserves it. [Sigmund Freud, 1856–1939, *The Future of an Illusion*]

6 When I hear the word 'gun' I reach for my culture. [I J Good, 1916– , *The Scientist Speculates*]; see 7

7 When I hear anyone talk of culture, I reach for my revolver. [Hanns Johst, 1890–1978, *Schlageter*. The German actually reads 'I reach for the safety catch on my Browning.' Usually attr. wrongly to Hermann Goering]; see 6

8 Two half-truths do not make a truth, and two half-cultures do not make a culture. [Arthur Koestler, 1905–83 (on the 'Two Cultures'), *The Ghost in the Machine*, Preface]

9 Don't be sucked in by the su-superior, / don't swallow the culturebait. [D H Lawrence, 1885–1930, *Don'ts*]

10 We should know how to inherit, because inheriting is culture. [Thomas Mann, 1875–1955, quoted by Hans Werner Henze in *Music and Politics*]

11 One of those 'Two Cultures' is really nothing but utilitarian technology; the other is B-grade novels, ideological fiction, popular art. Who cares if there exists a gap between such 'physics' and such 'humanities'? [Vladimir Nabokov, 1899–1977, *Strong Opinions*, Ch. 6]

12 Culture come when you buck up / on you'self. / It start when you' body make shadow / on the lan', / an' you know say / that you standin' up into mirror / underneat' you. [Andrew Salkey, 1928–95, *Jamaica: A Long Poem*]

13 All my wife has ever taken from the Mediterranean – from that whole vast intuitive culture – are four bottles of Chianti to make into lamps, and two china condiment donkeys labelled Sally and Peppy. [Peter Shaffer, 1926– , *Equus*, I. xviii]

14 Instead of dirt and poison we have rather chosen to fill our hives with honey and wax; thus furnishing mankind with the two noblest of things, which are sweetness and light. [Jonathan Swift, 1677–1745, *The Battle of the Books*]

15 Culture . . . is an instrument manipulated by teachers for manufacturing more teachers, who, in their turn, will manufacture still more teachers. [Simone Weil, 1909–43, *The Need for Roots*, Pt 2, 'Uprootedness in the Towns']

16 One of the ladies who pursue Culture in bands, as though it were dangerous to meet it alone. [Edith Wharton, 1862–1937, *Xingu and Other Stories*, 'Xingu']

See also CIVILIZATION

CURIOSITY

1 Be not curious in unnecessary matters: for more things are shewed unto thee than men understand. [Bible, Apocrypha, *Ecclesiasticus* 3:23]

2 For lust of knowing what should not be known, / We take the Golden Road to Samarkand. [James Elroy Flecker, 1884–1915, *Hassan*, V. ii]

3 An Elephant's Child – who was full of 'satiable curtiosity. [Rudyard Kipling, 1865–1936, *Just So Stories*, 'The Elephant's Child']

4 People die when curiosity goes. People have to find out, people have to know. How can there be any true revolution till we know what we're made of? [Graham Swift, 1949– , *Waterland*, 27]

CURSES

1 In holy anger, and pious grief, / He solemnly cursed that rascally thief! / He cursed him at board, he cursed him in bed; / From the sole of his foot to the crown of his head; / He cursed him in sleeping, that every night / He should dream of the devil, and wake in a fright. [Revd R H Barham, 1788–1845, *The Jackdaw of Rheims*]

2 There's a great text in Galatians, / Once you trip on it, entails / Twenty-nine distinct damnations, / One sure if another fails. [Robert Browning, 1812–89, *Soliloquy of the Spanish Cloister*]

3 Ruin seize thee, ruthless King! / Confusion on thy banners wait; / Though fanned by Conquest's crimson wing, / They mock the air with idle state. [Thomas Gray, 1716–71, *The Bard*, I, 1]

4 A plague o' both your houses! / They have made worms' meat of me. [William Shakespeare, 1564–1616, *Romeo and Juliet*, III. i. (112)]

5 You taught me language; and my profit on't / Is, I know how to curse; the red plague rid you, / For learning me your language! [*The Tempest*, I. ii. 363]

6 Curses are like young chickens, they always come home to roost. [Robert Southey, 1774–1843, *The Curse of Kehama*, motto]

7 She has heard a whisper say, / A curse is on her if she stay / To look down to Camelot. [Alfred, Lord Tennyson, 1809–92, *The Lady of Shalott*, 2]

See also SWEARING

CUSTOM, see HABIT

CYNICS

1 Wot's the good of Hanyfink? – Why – Nuffink! [Albert Chevalier, 1861–1923, music-hall refrain]

2 Only a great cynic would be an optimist these days. [Milan Kundera, 1929– , interview in *The Sunday Times Magazine*, 20 May 1984]

3 Cynicism is intellectual dandyism. [George Meredith, 1828–1909, *The Egoist*, Ch. 7]

4 All those men have their price. [(Reference to pretended patriots) Robert Walpole, 1676–1745, *Walpoliana*, Vol. I, p. 88]

5 Cynicism is humour in ill-health. [H G Wells, 1866–1946, *Short Stories*, 'The Last Trump']

6 What is a cynic? A man who knows the price of everything and the value of nothing. [Oscar Wilde, 1854–1900, *Lady Windermere's Fan*, III]

D

DANCE & DANCING

1 There's threesome reels, and foursome reels, / There's hornpipes and strathspeys, man; / But the ae best dance e'er cam to our lan', / Was – the De'il's awa' wi' the Exciseman. [Robert Burns, 1759–96, *The De'il's awa' wi' the Exciseman*]

2 Did ye not hear it? – No; 'twas but the wind, / Or the car rattling o'er the stony street; / On with the dance! let joy be unconfined; / No sleep till morn, when Youth and Pleasure meet / To chase the glowing Hours with flying feet. [Lord Byron, 1788–1824, *Childe Harold's Pilgrimage*, III, 22]

3 Will you, won't you, will you, won't you, will you join the dance? [Lewis Carroll, 1832–98, *Alice in Wonderland*, Ch. 10]

4 Dance, then, wherever you may be; / I am the Lord of the Dance, said he, / And I'll lead you all, wherever you may be, / And I'll lead you all in the Dance, said he. [Sydney Carter, 1915– , gospel song: *Lord of the Dance*]

5 Mind you, Hugh Gaitskell was a very good dancer. And to me, that is more important than politics in a man. [Barbara Castle, 1911– ; *Independent*, 'Quote Unquote', 21 Sept. 1996]

6 Dance, dance, dance little lady, / Leave tomorrow behind. [Noël Coward, 1899–1973, *This Year of Grace*, II, 'Dance Little Lady']

7 My own personal reaction is that most ballets would be quite delightful if it were not for the dancing. [*Evening Standard*, in M Bateman, *This England*, selections from the *New Statesman*, Pt I]

8 I've danced with a man, who's danced with a girl, who's danced with the Prince of Wales. [Herbert Farjeon, 1887–1945, *Picnic*]

9 My men like satyrs grazing on the lawns, / Shall with their goat-feet dance an antic hay. [Christopher Marlowe, 1564–93, *Edward II*, I. i. 59]

10 He capers nimbly to a lady's chamber / To the lascivious pleasing of a lute. [William Shakespeare, 1564–1616, *Richard II*, I. i. 12]

11 A perpendicular expression of a horizontal desire. [George Bernard Shaw, 1856–1950, in *New Statesman*, 23 Mar. 1962]

12 O body swayed to music, O brightening glance, / How can we know the dancer from the dance? [W B Yeats, 1865–1939, *Among School Children*, 8]

DANGERS

1 Dangers by being despised grow great. [Edmund Burke, 1729–97, speech on the Petition of the Unitarians, 1792]

2 A man's most dangerous moment . . . is when he's getting into his shirt. Then he puts his head in a bag. [D H Lawrence, 1885–1930, *Lady Chatterley's Lover*, Ch. 15]

3 I was much too far out all my life. / And not waving but drowning. [Stevie Smith, 1902–71, *Not Waving but Drowning*]

See also SECURITY

DAUGHTERS & SONS

1 Fame is rot; daughters are the thing. [James Barrie, 1860–1937, *Dear Brutus*, II]

2 A wise son maketh a glad father: but a foolish son is the heaviness of his mother. [Bible, OT, *Proverbs* 10:1]

3 Our Polly is a sad slut! nor heeds what we have taught her. / I wonder any man alive will ever rear a daughter! [John Gay, 1685–1732, *The Beggar's Opera*, I. viii]

4 Your children are not your children. They are the sons and daughters of Life's longing for itself . . . you may strive to be like them, but seek not to make them like you. [Kahlil Gibran, 1883–1931, *The Prophet*, 'Of Children']

5 LEONTINE: An only son, sir, might expect more indulgence.
CROAKER: An only father, sir, might expect more obedience. [Oliver Goldsmith, 1728–74, *The Good-Natured Man*, 1]

6 For so the game is ended / That should not have begun. / My father and my mother / They had a likely son, / And I have none. [A E Housman, 1859–1936, *Last Poems*, 14]

7 My son – and what's a son? A thing begot / Within a pair of minutes, thereabouts, / A lump bred up in darkness. [Thomas Kyd, 1557–95?, *The Spanish Tragedy*, III. xi, anonymous additions]

8 It is no wonder, he thinks, that God sent his only son to earth and not his only daughter. She would have really fucked up everything: arbitrarily deciding not to go about her father's business because it seemed too nebulous; refusing to walk on water because she didn't want to take her shoes off, getting her feet wet, look like a fool; [Dyan Sheldon, 1946– , *Victim of Love*, 3]

DAWN

1 The lark now leaves his watery nest / And climbing, shakes his dewy wings; / He takes this window for the east; / And to implore your light, he sings, / Awake, awake, the morn will never rise, / Till she can dress her beauty at your eyes. [William Davenant, 1606–68, *Song*]

2 Morning has broken / Like the first morning, / Blackbird has spoken / Like the first bird. [Eleanor Farjeon, 1881–1965, hymn, from poem *Morning Song*]

3 Awake! for Morning in the Bowl of Night / Has flung the Stone that puts the Stars to Flight: / And Lo! the Hunter of the East has caught / The Sultan's Turret in a Noose of Light. [Edward Fitzgerald, 1809–83, *The Rubá'iyát of Omar Khayyám*, Edn 1, 1]

4 The breezy call of incense-breathing Morn, / The swallow twittering from the straw-built shed, / The cock's shrill clarion, or the echoing horn, / No more shall rouse them from their lowly bed. [Thomas Gray, 1716–71, *Elegy Written in a Country Churchyard*, 5]

5 As soon as Dawn with her rose-tinted hands had lit the East. [Homer, *c.*900 BC, *Odyssey*, II, 1]

6 'Tis always morning somewhere in the world. [Richard Henry Horne, 1803–84, *Orion*, Bk iii, Canto 2]

7 While the cock with lively din, / Scatters the rear of darkness thin, / And to the stack, or the barn door, / Stoutly struts his dames before. [John Milton, 1608–74, *L'Allegro*, 49]

8 Ere the blabbing Eastern scout, / The nice Morn on th' Indian steep / From her cabined loop-hole peep. [John Milton, 1608–74, *Comus*, 138]

9 Now morn her rosy steps in th' eastern clime / Advancing, sowed the earth with orient pearl. [John Milton, 1608–74, *Paradise Lost*, Bk v, 1]

10 Till morning fair / Came forth with pilgrim steps in amice grey. [John Milton, 1608–74, *Paradise Regained*, Bk iv, 426]

11 Hark! hark! the lark at heaven's gate sings, / And Phoebus 'gins arise, / His steeds to water at those springs / On chaliced flowers that lies; / And winking Mary-buds begin / To ope their golden eyes; / With everything that pretty is, / My lady sweet, arise. [William Shakespeare, 1564–1616, *Cymbeline*, II. iii. (22)]

12 But look, the morn, in russet mantle clad, / Walks o'er the dew of yon high eastern hill. [*Hamlet*, I. i. 166]

13 The glow-worm shows the matin to be near, / And 'gins to pale his uneffectual fire. [*Hamlet*, I. v. 89]

14 The wolves have preyed; and look, the gentle day, / Before the wheels of Phoebus, round about / Dapples the drowsy east with spots of grey. [*Much Ado About Nothing*, V. iii. 25]

15 Night's candles are burnt out, and jocund day / Stands tiptoe on the misty mountain tops. [*Romeo and Juliet*, III. v. 9]

16 Full many a glorious morning have I seen / Flatter the mountain tops with sovereign eye, / Kissing with golden face the meadows green, / Gilding pale streams with heavenly alchemy. [*Sonnets*, 33]

17 On the bald street breaks the blank day. [Alfred, Lord Tennyson, 1809–92, *In Memoriam*, 7]

18 I said to Dawn: Be sudden – to Eve: Be soon. [Francis Thompson, 1859–1907, *The Hound of Heaven*, 30]

19 The meek-eyed Morn appears, mother of dews. [James Thomson, 1700–1748, *The Seasons*, 'Summer', 47]

20 Down the long and silent street, / The dawn, with silver-sandalled feet, / Crept like a frightened girl. [Oscar Wilde, 1854–1900, *The Harlot's House*]

21 For what human ill does not dawn seem to be an alleviation? [Thornton Wilder, 1897–1975, *The Bridge of San Luis Rey*, Ch. 3]

22 I would be ignorant as the dawn / That has looked down / On that old queen measuring a town / With the pin of a brooch. [W B Yeats, 1865–1939, *The Dawn*]

See also DAYS, LIGHT, NIGHT

DAYS

1 I believe the twenty-four hour day has come to stay. [Max Beerbohm, 1872–1956, *Christmas Garland*, 'Perkins and Mankind']

2 Sweet day, so cool, so calm, so bright, / The bridal of the earth and sky, / The dew shall weep thy fall to-night; / For thou must die. [George Herbert, 1593–1633, *Virtue*]

3 Monday is parson's holiday. [Jonathan Swift, 1677–1745, *Journal to Stella*, 3 Mar. 1712]

See also DAWN, LIGHT, NIGHT

DEAFNESS

1 I'm not so deaf as the man who said family prayers kneeling on the cat. [Sir William Ridgeway, 1853–1926, attr. in *Letters of A. E. Housman*, ed. H Maas, p. 427]

2 It is not the hearing that one misses but the over-hearing. [David Wright, 1920–94, *Deafness: A Personal Account*]

DEATH

1 It's not that I'm afraid to die. I just don't want to be there when it happens. [Woody Allen, 1935– , *Without Feathers*, 'Death (A Play)']

2 Death is an acquired trait. [Woody Allen, 1935– , in E Lax, *W A and His Comedy*, Ch. 11]

3 Only we die in earnest, that's no jest. [anon., from 'On the Life of Man', from Orlando Gibbons, *First Set of Madrigals and Motets*]

4 *Et in Arcadia ego.* – Even in Arcadia I [death] am present. [anon. inscription on tomb, the subject of paintings by Nicolas Poussin and others]; see also UTOPIAS, 1

5 Man dies when he wants, as he wants, of what he chooses [Jean Anouilh, 1910–87, attr.]

6 Truth sits upon the lips of dying men. [Matthew Arnold, 1822–88, *Sohrab and Rustum*, 656]

7 I have often thought upon death, and I find it the least of all evils. [Francis Bacon, 1561–1626, *An Essay on Death*]

8 Men fear death, as children fear to go in the dark; and as that natural fear in children is increased with tales, so is the other. [Francis Bacon, 1561–1626, *Essays*, 2, 'Of Death']

9 It is as natural to die as to be born; and to a little infant, perhaps, the one is as painful as the other. [Francis Bacon, 1561–1626, *Essays*, 2 'Of Death']

10 Life! we've been long together, / Through pleasant and through cloudy weather; / 'Tis hard to part when friends are dear, / Perhaps 'twill cost a sigh, a tear; / Then steal away, give little warning; / Choose thine own time; / Say not 'Good-night'; but in some brighter clime / Bid me 'Good-morning'. [Anna Laetitia Barbauld, 1743–1825, *Ode to Life*]

11 To die will be an awfully big adventure. [James Barrie, 1860–1937, *Peter Pan*, III]

12 *Mort, vieux capitaine, il est temps! levons l'ancre!* – Death, old captain, it is time, let us raise anchor! [Charles Baudelaire, 1821–67, *Le Voyage*]

13 You find when you are giving up the ghost, / That those who loved you best despised you most. [Hilaire Belloc, 1870–1953, *Discovery*]

14 The dead are the imagination of the living. [John Berger, 1926– , *And Our Faces, My Heart, Brief as Photos*]

15 But I'm dying now and done for, / What on earth was all the fun for? / For I'm old and ill and terrified and tight. [John Betjeman, 1906–84, *Sun and Fun*]

16 Set thine house in order: for thou shalt die. [Bible, OT, *Isaiah* 38:1]

17 He slept with his fathers. [Bible, OT, *I Kings* 14:20]

18 Yea, though I walk through the valley of the shadow of death, I will fear no evil: for thou art with me; thy rod and thy staff they comfort me. [Bible, OT, *Psalms* 23:4]

19 Through envy of the devil came death into the world. [Bible, Apocrypha, *Wisdom of Solomon* 2:24]

20 The last enemy that shall be destroyed is death. [Bible, NT, *1 Corinthians* 15:26]

21 O death, where is thy sting? O grave, where is thy victory? [Bible, NT, *1 Corinthians* 15:55]

22 Behold, a pale horse: and his name that sat on him was Death. [Bible, NT, *Revelation* 6:8]

23 Death hath no more dominion over him. [Bible, NT, *Romans* 6:9]

24 Let the dead bury their dead. [Bible, NT, *St Matthew* 8:22]

25 The angel of death has been abroad throughout the land; you may almost hear the beating of his wings. [John Bright, 1811–89, speech in House of Commons, 23 Feb. 1855]

26 And the worst friend and enemy is but Death. [Rupert Brooke, 1887–1915, *Peace*]

27 Oh! Death will find me long before I tire / Of watching you; and swing me suddenly / Into the shade and loneliness and mire / Of the last land! [Rupert Brooke, 1887–1915, sonnet: *Oh! Death Will Find Me*]

28 We all labour against our own cure; for death is the cure of all diseases. [Sir Thomas Browne, 1605–82, *Religio Medici*, Pt II, 9]

29 How he lies in his rights of a man! / Death has done all death can. [Robert Browning, 1812–89, *After*]

30 For I say, this is death, and the sole death, / When a man's loss comes to him from his gain, / Darkness from light, from knowledge ignorance, / And lack of love from love made manifest. [Robert Browning, 1812–89, *A Death in the Desert*, 482]

31 So he passed over, and all the trumpets sounded for him on the other side. [(Of Mr Valiant-for-Truth)] John Bunyan, 1628–88, *The Pilgrim's Progress*, Pt II]

32 No one owns life, but anyone who can pick up a frying-pan owns death. [William Burroughs, 1914–97, in Adrian Henri, *Adrian Henri's Last Will and Testament*]

33 And know, whatever thou hast been, / 'Tis something better not to be. [Lord Byron, 1788–1824, *Euthanasia*]

34 To circumvent death, to evade it, is one of the oldest and strongest desires of rulers. [Elias Canetti, 1905–94, *Crowds and Power*, 'The Crowd in History']

35 Now he is treading that dark road to the place from which they say no one has ever returned. [Catullus, 84–?54 BC, *Carmina*, 3]

36 Well, now, there's a remedy for everything except death. [Miguel Cervantes, 1547–1616, *Don Quixote*, Pt II, Ch. 10]

37 He could not die when trees were green, / For he loved the time too well. [John Clare, 1793–1864, *The Dying Child*]

38 Still are thy pleasant voices, thy nightingales, awake; / For Death, he taketh all away, but them he cannot take. [W J Cory, 1823–92, *Heraclitus*]

39 what i want to know is / how do you like your blueeyed boy / Mister Death. [e e cummings, 1894–1962, *Collected Poems*, 1938, 31]

40 When I lie where shades of darkness / Shall no more assail mine eyes. [Walter de la Mare, 1873–1956, *Fare Well*]

41 He is the Ancient Tapster of this Hostel, / To him at length even we all keys must resign. [Walter de la Mare, 1873–1956, *Hospital*]

42 He'd make a lovely corpse. [Charles Dickens, 1812–70, *Martin Chuzzlewit*, Ch. 25]

43 It was not death, for I stood up, / And all the dead lie down; / It was not night, for all the bells / Put out their tongues, for noon. [Emily Dickinson, 1830–86, *It was Not Death, for I Stood Up*]

44 When I die I want to decompose in a barrel of porter and have it served in all the pubs in Dublin. I wonder would they know it was me? [J P Donleavy, 1926– , *The Ginger Man*, Ch. 31]

45 This is my play's last scene, here heavens appoint / My pilgrimage's last mile. [John Donne, 1571?–1631, *Holy Sonnets*, 6]

46 Death be not proud, though some have called thee / Mighty and dreadful, for, thou art not so, / For, those whom thou think'st, thou dost overthrow / Die not, poor death. [John Donne, 1571?–1631, *Holy Sonnets*, 10]

47 Since I am coming to that holy room, / Where, with thy quire of Saints for evermore, / I shall be made thy Music; As I come / I tune the instrument here at the door, / And what I must do then, think here before. [John Donne, 1571?–1631, *Hymn to God in My Sickness*]

48 As virtuous men pass mildly away, / And whisper to their souls to go, / Whilst some of their sad friends do say, / The breath goes now, and some say no. [John Donne, 1571?–1631, *Valediction: Forbidding Mourning*]

49 Remember me when I am dead / And simplify me when I'm dead. [Keith Douglas, 1920–44, *Simplify Me when I'm Dead*]

50 Th' dead ar-re always pop'lar. I knowed a society wanst to vote a monyment to a man an' refuse to help his fam'ly, all in wan night. [Finley Peter Dunne, 1867–1936, *Mr Dooley in Peace and War*, 'On Charity']

51 Death is my neighbour now. [Edith Evans, 1888–1976, BBC radio interview, a week before her death, 14 Oct. 1976]

52 Ranulphe says he [King Henry I] took a surfeit by eating of a lamprey, and thereof died. [Robert Fabyan, d. 1513, *Chronicles*, 229. Ranulphe did not, in fact, specify]

53 The Duke of Clarence ... a prisoner in the Tower, was secretly put to death and drowned in a barrel of Malmesey wine. [Robert Fabyan, d. 1513, *Chronicles*, 1477. Early edns give 'malvesye']

54 A direful death indeed they had / That would put any parent mad / But she was more than usual calm / She did not give a singel dam. [Marjorie Fleming, 1803–11, *Journal*, 1]

55 My dear, I'm always nervous about doing something for the first time. [Gwen Ffrangcon-Davies, 1891–1992, on facing death at 101; *Observer*, 'Sayings of the Week', 2 Feb. 1992]

56 Why should the dead be wiser than the living? The dead know only this – that it was better to be alive. [James Elroy Flecker, 1884–1915, *Hassan*, V, i]

57 All perfect republics are perfect nonsense. The craving to risk death is our last great perversion. We come from night, we go into night. Why live in night? [John Fowles, 1926– , *The Magus*, rev. edn, Ch. 19]

58 Man always dies before he is fully born. [Erich Fromm, 1900–1980, *Man for Himself*, Ch. 3]

59 When a Forsyte died – but no Forsyte had as yet died – death being contrary to their principles, they took precautions against it. [John Galsworthy, 1867–1933, *The Forsyte Saga: The Man of Property*, Pt I, Ch. 1]

60 Lady Bullock, who had been at death's door for so long now that one might have been pardoned for mistaking her for its knocker. [Leon Garfield, 1921–96, *The Prisoners of September*, Ch. 29]

61 Death is the greatest kick of all, that's why they save it for last. [In Robert Reisner, *Graffiti*]

62 To bring the dead to life / Is no great magic. / Few are wholly dead: / Blow on a dead man's embers / And a live flame will start. [Robert Graves, 1895–1985, *To Bring the Dead to Life*]

63 I had to do everything to stay alive and succeeded almost completely by dedicating myself to a precise programme which is summarized in my slogan 'I will not die even if they kill me.' [Giovanni Guareschi, 1908–68, *The Little World of Don Camillo*, 'How I Got Like This']

64 All her shining keys will be took from her, and her cupboards opened, and things a' didn't wish seen, anybody will see; and her little wishes and ways will all be as nothing. [Thomas Hardy, 1840–1928, *The Mayor of Casterbridge*, Ch. 18]

65 Death is still working like a mole, / And digs my grave at each remove. [George Herbert, 1593–1633, *Grace*]

66 Death is nothing at all. I have only slipped away into the next room. I am I and you are you. [Revd Henry Scott Holland, 1847–1914, sermon in St Paul's Cathedral, London, 15 May 1910]

67 Pale Death knocks with impartial foot at poor men's hovels and kings' palaces. [Horace, 65–8 BC, *Odes*, I, iv, 13]

68 Death ... It's the only thing we haven't succeeded in completely vulgarizing. [Aldous Huxley, 1894–1963, *Eyeless in Gaza*, Ch. 31]

69 There are more dead people than living. And their numbers are increasing. The living are getting rarer. [Eugene Ionesco, 1912–94, *Rhinoceros*, III]

70 What could the thing that was to happen to him be, after all, but just this thing that had begun to happen? Her dying, her death, his consequent solitude – *that* was what he had figured as the beast in the jungle. [Henry James, 1843–1916, *The Beast in the Jungle*]

71 I am able to follow my own death step by step. Now I move softly towards the end. [Pope John XXIII, 1881–1963 (said two days before his death), in *Guardian*, 3 June 1963]

72 Darkling I listen; and, for many a time / I have been half in love with easeful death, / Called him soft names in many a musèd rhyme, / To take into the air my quiet breath; / Now more than ever it seems rich to die, / To cease upon the midnight with no pain, / While thou art pouring forth thy soul abroad / In such an ecstasy! / Still wouldst thou sing, and I have ears in vain – / To thy high requiem become a sod. [John Keats, 1795–1821, *Ode to a Nightingale*, 5]

73 Verse, Fame and Beauty are intense indeed, / But Death intenser – Death is Life's high meed. [John Keats, 1795–1821, sonnet: *Why Did I Laugh To-night?*]

74 Everyone's afraid of dying but no one is afraid of being dead. [Mgr Ronald Knox, 1888–1957, quoted by Cardinal Basil Hume in interview in John Mortimer, *In Character*]

75 O pity the dead that are dead, but cannot make / the journey, still they moan and beat / against the silvery adamant walls of life's exclusive city. [D H Lawrence, 1885–1930, *The Houseless Dead*]

76 There is a Reaper whose name is Death, / And, with his sickle keen, / He reaps the bearded grain at a breath, / And the flowers that grow between. [H W Longfellow, 1807–82, *The Reaper and the Flowers*]

77 This is death / To die and know it. This is the Black Widow, death. [Robert Lowell, 1917–77, *Mr Edwards and the Spider*]

78 Let me die a youngman's death / not a clean & inbetween / the sheets holy-water death / not a famous-last-words / peaceful out of breath death. [Roger McGough, 1937– , *Let Me Die a Youngman's Death*]

79 It is the only disease you don't look forward to being cured of. [Herman J Mankiewicz, 1897–1953, and Orson Welles, 1915–85, in film *Citizen Kane*]

80 Blessed be death that cuts in marble / What would have sunk in dust. [Edna St Vincent Millay, 1892–1950, *Keen*]

81 My race of glory run, and race of shame, / And I shall shortly be with them that rest. [John Milton, 1608–74, *Samson Agonistes*, 597]

82 One only dies once – but one is dead so long! [Molière, 1622–73, *Le Dépit amoureux*, V, iii]

83 It's not pining, it's passed on. This parrot is no more. It's ceased to be. It's expired. It's gone to meet its maker. This is a late parrot. It's a stiff. Bereft of life it rests in peace. It would be pushing up the daisies if you hadn't nailed it to the perch. It's rung down the curtain and joined the choir invisible. It's an ex-parrot. [*Monty Python's Flying Circus*, 1969–1974, BBC TV comedy series, programme 14, Dec. 1969]

84 He did not die in the night, / He did not die in the day, / But in the morning twilight / His spirit passed away. [William Morris, 1834–96, *Shameful Death*]

85 And in the happy no-time of his sleeping / Death took him by the heart. [Wilfred Owen, 1893–1918, *Asleep*]

86 *Abiit ad plures.* – He has joined the great majority. [Petronius, d. *c.*66, *Trimalchio's Feast*, 42, 5]

87 Dying / Is an art, like everything else. / I do it exceptionally well. [Sylvia Plath, 1932–63, *Lady Lazarus*]

88 I mount! I fly! / O grave! where is thy victory? / O death! where is thy sting? [Alexander Pope, 1688–1744, *The Dying Christian to His Soul*]

89 O eloquent, just, and mighty Death! whom none could advise, thou hast persuaded; what none hath dared, thou hast done; and whom all the world hath flattered, thou only hast cast out of the world and despised; thou hast drawn together all the far-stretched greatness, all the pride, cruelty, and ambition of man, and covered it all over with these two narrow words. *Hic jacet* [Here lies]. [Sir Walter Raleigh, *c.*1552–1618, *A History of the World*, Bk v, Ch. 6]

90 Death could drop from the dark / As easily as song. [Isaac Rosenberg, 1890–1918, *Returning, We Hear the Larks*]

91 When I am dead, my dearest, / Sing no sad songs for me; / Plant thou no roses at my head, / Nor shady cypress tree; / Be the green grass above me / With showers and dewdrops wet; / And if thou wilt, remember, / And if thou wilt, forget. [Christina Rossetti, 1830–94, song: *When I am Dead, My Dearest*]

92 Waldo is one of those people who would be enormously improved by death. [Saki (H H Munro), 1870–1916, *The Feast of Nemesis*]

93 Dying is not everything: you have to die in time. [Jean-Paul Sartre, 1905–80, *Words*, Pt 1]

94 And come he slow, or come he fast, / It is but Death who comes at last. [Sir Walter Scott, 1771–1832, *Marmion*, II, 30]

95 I have a rendezvous with Death / At some disputed barricade. [Alan Seeger, 1888–1916, *I Have a Rendezvous with Death*]

96 Not that it is a disservice to a man to be made mindful of his death, but, at three o'clock in the morning, it is less than philosophy. [Richard Selzer, 1928– , *Confessions of a Knife*, 'The Surgeon as Priest']

97 But I will be / A bridegroom in my death, and run into 't / As to a lover's bed. [William Shakespeare, 1564–1616, *Antony and Cleopatra*, IV. xii. 99]

98 Her clothes spread wide, / And, mermaid-like, awhile they bore her up; / Which time she chanted snatches of old tunes, / As one incapable of her own distress, / Or like a creature native and indued / Unto that element; but long it could not be / Till that her garments, heavy with their drink, / Pulled the poor wretch from her melodious lay / To muddy death. [(Of Ophelia) *Hamlet*, IV. vii. (176)]

99 This fell sergeant, death, / Is strict in his arrest. [*Hamlet*, V. ii. (350)]

100 A man can die but once; we owe God a death. [*2 Henry IV*, III. ii. (253)]

101 Vex not his ghost: O! let him pass; he hates him / That would upon the rack of this tough world / Stretch him out longer. [*King Lear*, V. iii. (314)]

102 Nothing in his life / Became him like the leaving it; he died / As one that had been studied in his death / To throw away the dearest thing he owed, / As 'twere a careless trifle. [*Macbeth*, I. iv. 7]

103 Duncan is in his grave; / After life's fitful fever he sleeps well; / Treason has done his worst: not steel, nor poison, / Malice domestic, foreign levy, nothing / Can touch him further. [*Macbeth*, III. ii. 22]

104 The sense of death is most in apprehension, / And the poor beetle, that we tread upon, / In corporal sufferance finds a pang as great / As when a giant dies. [*Measure for Measure*, III. i. 75]

105 Ay, but to die, and go we know not where; / To lie in cold obstruction and to rot; / This sensible warm motion to become / A kneaded clod; and the delighted spirit / To bathe in fiery floods, or to reside / In thrilling region of thick-ribbèd ice; / To be imprisoned in the viewless winds, / And blown with restless violence round about / The pendant world! [*Measure for Measure*, III. i. 116]

106 The worst is death, and death will have his day. [*Richard II*, III. ii. 103]

107 Lord, Lord! methought what pain it was to drown: / What dreadful noise of water in mine ears! / What sights of ugly death within mine eyes! [*Richard III*, I. iv. 21]

108 How oft when men are at the point of death / Have they been merry! [*Romeo and Juliet*, V. iii. 88]

109 He that dies pays all debts. [*The Tempest*, III. ii. (143)]

110 So shalt thou feed on Death, that feeds on men, / And Death once dead, there's no more dying then. [*Sonnets*, 146]

111 I saw a man this morning / Who did not wish to die: / I ask, and cannot answer, / If otherwise would I. [Patrick Shaw-Stewart, 1888–1917, *Poem*, 1916]

112 To that high capital, where kingly Death / Keeps his pale court in beauty and decay, / He came. [P B Shelley, 1792–1822, *Adonais*, 55]

113 How wonderful is Death, / Death and his brother Sleep! [P B Shelley, 1792–1822, *The Daemon of the World*, i, 1]

114 It is a modest creed, and yet / Pleasant if one considers it, / To own that death itself must be, / Like all the rest, a mockery. [P B Shelley, 1792–1822, *The Sensitive Plant*, III, 126]

115 I cannot forgive my friends for dying: I do not find these vanishing acts of theirs at all amusing. [Logan Pearsall Smith, 1865–1946, *Afterthoughts*, 2]

116 Death is one of two things. Either it is annihilation, and the dead have no consciousness of anything; or, as we are told, it is really a change: a migration of the soul from this place to another. [Socrates, 469–399BC, quoted in Plato, *Apology*, 41]

117 Give them not praise. For, deaf, how should they know / It is not curses heaped on each gashed head? [Charles Sorley, 1895–1915, *When You See Millions of the Mouthless Dead*]

118 I shall be like that tree, I shall die at the top. [Jonathan Swift, 1677–1745, attr. in Sir Walter Scott, *Life of Swift*]

119 As a god self-slain on his own strange altar, / Death lies dead. [A C Swinburne, 1837–1909, *A Forsaken Garden*, 10]

120 'Twere best at once to sink to peace, / Like birds the charming serpent draws, / To drop head-foremost in the jaws / Of vacant darkness and to cease. [Alfred, Lord Tennyson, 1809–92, *In Memoriam*, 34]

121 Trust that those we call the dead / Are breathers of an ampler day. [Alfred, Lord Tennyson, 1809–92, *In Memoriam*, 118]

122 A day less or more / At sea or ashore, / We die – does it matter when? [Alfred, Lord Tennyson, 1809–92, *The Revenge*, 11]

123 Then comes the check, the change, the fall, / Pain rises up, old pleasures pall, / There is one remedy for all. [Alfred, Lord Tennyson, 1809–92, *The Two Voices*, 55]

124 As the last bell struck, a peculiar sweet smile shone over his face, and he lifted up his head a little, and quickly said, 'Adsum!' and fell back. It was the word we used at school, when names were called; and lo, he, whose heart was as that of a little child, had answered to his name, and stood in the presence of The Master. [W M Thackeray, 1811–63, *The Newcomes*, Ch. 80]

125 Do not go gentle into that good night. / Rage, rage against the dying of the light. [Dylan Thomas, 1914–53, *Do Not Go Gentle into That Good Night*]

126 We only die when we fail to take root in others. [Leon Trotsky, 1874–1940, in Trevor Griffiths, *The Party*, II]

127 Go and try to disprove death. Death will disprove you, and that's all! [Ivan Turgenev, 1818–83, *Fathers and Sons*, Ch. 27]

128 Dear, beauteous death! the jewel of the just, / Shining no where, but in the dark. [Henry Vaughan, 1622–95, *They are All Gone*]

129 One owes respect to the living: but to the dead one owes nothing but the truth. [Voltaire, 1694–1778, *Lettres sur Oedipe*, i, note]

130 I know death hath ten thousand several doors / For men to take their exits. [John Webster, 1580?–1625?, *The Duchess of Malfi*, IV. ii. 222]

131 They say I died in 1974, but I have racked my brain and cannot recall anything untoward happening that year. [Emlyn Williams, 1905–87 (on the premature announcement of his death), in obituary in *Guardian*, 26 Sept. 1987]

132 Nothing is stronger than the position of the dead among the living. [Virginia Woolf, 1882–1941, quoted by Penelope Lively, *The Sunday Times*, 2 Apr. 1989]

DEBT

1 I swear by all the orders of chivalry in the world to pay you every single *real*, and perfumed into the bargain. [Miguel Cervantes, 1547–1616, *Don Quixote*, Pt I, Ch. 4]

2 If there's anyone listening to whom I owe *money*, I'm prepared to forget it if you are. [Errol Flynn, 1909–59, in broadcast before leaving Australia; in L Halliwell, *Filmgoer's Book of Quotes*]

3 A judge said not long ago – that all his experience both as Counsel and Judge had been spent in sorting out the difficulties of people who, upon the recommendation of people they did not know, signed documents which they did not read, to buy goods they did not need, with money they had not got. [Gilbert Harding, 1907–60 (TV answer to question on subject of hire purchase), in *G H and His Friends*]

4 Home life ceases to be free and beautiful as soon as it is founded on borrowing and debt. [Henrik Ibsen, 1828–1906, *A Doll's House*, I]

5 To John I owed great obligation; / But John, unhappily, thought fit / To publish it to all the nation: / Sure John and I are more than quit. [Matthew Prior, 1664–1721, *Epigram*]

6 Not everyone is a debtor who wishes to be; not everyone who wishes makes creditors. [François Rabelais, *c.*1492–1553, *Pantagruel*, Bk III, Ch. 3]

7 Some people say a man is made out of mud, / A poor man's made out of muscle and blood. / Muscle and blood and skin and bone / A mind that's weak and a back that's strong . . . I owe my soul to the company store. [Merle Travis, 1917–83, song: *Sixteen Tons*, 1947, sung by Tennessee Ernie Ford]

8 I don't owe a penny to a single soul – not counting tradesmen, of course. [P G Wodehouse, 1881–1975, *My Man Jeeves*, 'Jeeves and the Hard-boiled Egg']

See also BORROWERS

DECEIT & DECEPTION

1 Early one morning, just as the sun was rising, / I heard a maid singing in the valley below: / 'Oh, don't deceive me; Oh, never leave me! / How could you use a poor maiden so?' [anon. song, *Early One Morning*]

2 That other principle of Lysander, 'That children are to be deceived with comfits, and men with oaths'. [Francis Bacon, 1561–1626, *The Advancement of Learning*, II, xxiii, 45]

3 A game which a sharper once played with a dupe, entitled, 'Heads I win, tails you lose.' [J W Croker, 1780–1857, *Croker Papers*]

4 Things are seldom what they seem, / Skim milk masquerades as cream. [W S Gilbert, 1836–1911, *HMS Pinafore*, 11]

5 Even when he cheated he couldn't win, because the people he cheated against were always better at cheating too. [Joseph Heller, 1923–99, *Catch-22*, Ch. 4]

6 The best grafts in the world are built up on copybook maxims and psalms and proverbs and Esau's fables. They seem to kind of hit off human nature. [O Henry, 1862–1910, *A Tempered Wind*]

7 It's a double pleasure to trick the trickster. [Jean de La Fontaine, 1621–95, *Fables* I, 15, 'The Cock and the Fox']

8 You can fool all the people some of the time, and some of the people all the time, but you cannot fool all the people all the time. [Abraham Lincoln, 1809–65, attr. words in speech at Clinton, Illinois, 8 Sept. 1858. Also attr. to P T Barnum]; see 16 and POLITICIANS IN GENERAL, 1

9 An' you've gut to git up airly / Ef you want to take in God. [James Russell Lowell, 1819–91, *The Biglow Papers*, First Series, 1]

10 Though his tongue / Dropt manna, and could make the worse appear / The better reason. [John Milton, 1608–74, *Paradise Lost*, Bk ii, 112]

11 Wisest men / Have erred, and by bad women been deceived; / And shall again, pretend they ne'er so wise. [John Milton, 1608–74, *Samson Agonistes*, 210]

12 I do not approve of guys using false pretences on dolls, except, of course, when nothing else will do. [Damon Runyon, 1884–1946, *Take It Easy*, 'It Comes Up Mud']

13 O, what a tangled web we weave, / When first we practise to deceive! [Sir Walter Scott, 1771–1832, *Marmion*, VI, 17]

14 Look like the innocent flower, / But be the serpent under 't. [William Shakespeare, 1564–1616, *Macbeth*, I. v. 66]

15 The world is still deceived with ornament. / In law, what plea so tainted and corrupt / But, being seasoned with a gracious voice, / Obscures the show of evil? [*The Merchant of Venice*, III. i. 74]

16 You can fool too many of the people too much of the time. [James Thurber, 1894–1961, *Fables for Our Time*, 'The Owl Who Was God']; see 8

DECISIONS

1 The die is cast. [Julius Caesar, 102?–44 BC (at the crossing of the Rubicon), in Suetonius, *The Twelve Caesars*, J C, 32]

2 I'll give you a definite maybe. [Samuel Goldwyn, 1882–1974, attr.]

3 The man who is denied the opportunity of taking decisions of importance begins to regard as important the decisions he is allowed to take. He becomes fussy about filing, keen on seeing that pencils are sharpened, eager to ensure that the windows are open (or shut) and apt to use two or three different-coloured inks. [C Northcote Parkinson, 1909–93, *Parkinson's Law*, Ch. 10]

4 Decisions are easier, you know, when there are no choices left. [P V Narasimha Rao, 1921– , first interview as Indian Prime Minister with foreign journalist, in *Observer*, 7 July 1991]

DEDICATIONS

1 I dedicate these pages to my Guardian Angel, impressing upon him that I'm only fooling and warning him to see to it that there is no misunderstanding when I go home. [Flann O'Brien, 1911–66, *The Dalkey Archive*, dedication]

2 To the only begetter of these insuing sonnets. [William Shakespeare, 1564–1616, *Sonnets*, dedication]

3 To the Happy Few [Stendhal, 1783–1842, *Le Rouge et le noir*, epigraph]

4 To My Daughter, LEONORA, without whose never-failing sympathy and encouragement this book would have been finished in half the time. [P G Wodehouse, 1881–1975, *The Heart of a Goof*, dedication]

DEFEAT

1 How are the mighty fallen in the midst of the battle! [Bible, OT, *2 Samuel* 1:25]

2 I know your cause is lost, but in the heart / Of all right causes is a cause that cannot lose. [Christopher Fry, 1907– , *The Dark is Light Enough*, III]

3 We was robbed! [Joe Jacobs, 1896–1940, after Max Schmeling (whose manager he was) was declared loser in heavyweight boxing title fight with Jack Sharkey, 21 June 1932]

4 *Vae victis*. – Woe to the vanquished. [Livy, 59 BC–AD 17, *History*, V, 48]

5 The quickest way of ending a war is to lose it. [George Orwell, 1903–50, *Shooting an Elephant*, 'Second Thoughts on James Burnham']

6 Winning isn't everything, but losing isn't anything. [(Charlie Brown) Charles M Schulz 1922– ; quoted by Salman Rushdie in *Observer*, 4 May 1997]

7 We are not interested in the possibilities of defeat. [Queen Victoria, 1819–1901, to A J Balfour, Dec. 1899]

See also VICTORY

DEFINITIONS

1 *Lexicographer*. A writer of dictionaries, a harmless drudge. [Dr Samuel Johnson, 1709–84, *Dictionary of the English Language*]

2 In the beginning and in the end the only decent / Definition is tautology: man is man, / Woman woman, and tree tree. [Louis MacNeice, 1907–63, *Plain Speaking*]

3 Last night Cocklecarrot exclaimed, with his customary lucidity, that if a cow with handlebars is a bicycle, within the meaning of the Act, then a bicycle with four legs instead of two wheels is a cow. [J B Morton ('Beachcomber'), 1893–1979, *The Best of B*, 17]

4 A radical – one who not only knows all the answers but keeps on thinking up new questions. [in *New Statesman*, undated]

5 A circle is the longest distance to the same point. [Tom Stoppard, 1937– , *Every Good Boy Deserves Favour*]

See also NAMES

DELAY, see LATENESS, PROCRASTINATION

DEMOCRACY

1 Democracy means government by discussion but it is only effective if you can stop people talking. [Clement Attlee, 1883–1967, speech at Oxford, 14 June 1957]

2 [The party system] is merely a convenient device to enable the majority to have their way and the minority to have their say. [S D Bailey, 1916–95, *The British Party System*]

3 The trouble in modern democracy is that men do not approach to leadership until they have lost the desire to lead anyone. [Lord Beveridge, 1879–1963; *Observer*, 'Sayings of the Week', 15 Apr. 1934]

4 A perfect democracy is therefore the most

shameless thing in the world. [Edmund Burke, 1729–97, *Reflections on the Revolution in France*, Penguin edn, p. 191]

5 Democracy means government by the uneducated, while aristocracy means government by the badly educated. [G K Chesterton, 1874–1936, in *The New York Times*, 1 Feb. 1931]

6 No one pretends that democracy is perfect or all-wise. Indeed, it has been said that democracy is the worst form of government except all those other forms that have been tried from time to time. [Winston Churchill, 1874–1965, speech in House of Commons, 11 Nov. 1947]

7 Very little is dependable in the politics of a going democracy except the people's conviction that one world-saver at a time is enough. [Alistair Cooke, 1908– , *America*, Ch. 10]

8 One with the law is a majority. [Calvin Coolidge, 1872–1933, speech of acceptance as Republican vice-presidential candidate, 27 July 1920]; see 18

9 Democracy is the refuge for your cousin or your uncle that failed in the peanut business. [William Faulkner, 1897–1962, speech, 1957, in *Guardian*, 26 Sept. 1988]

10 So Two cheers for Democracy: one because it admits variety and two because it permits criticism. Two cheers are quite enough; there is no occasion to give three. Only Love the Beloved Republic deserves that. [E M Forster, 1879–1970, *Two Cheers for Democracy*, 'What I Believe'. Final sentence quotes Swinburne]

11 In an autocracy, one person has his way; in an aristocracy, a few people have their way; in a democracy, no one has his way. [Celia Green, 1935– , *The Decline and Fall of Science*, 'Aphorisms']

12 I called democracy a superstition and a fetish: and I repeat that it is plainly both. [W R Inge, 1860–1954, *The Church and the Age*, Preface]

13 Universal suffrage almost inevitably leads to government by mass bribery, an auction of the worldly goods of the unrepresented minority. [W R Inge, 1860–1954, *The End of an Age*, Ch. 1]

14 Democracy is a *state* which recognizes the subordination of the minority to the majority, i.e. an organization for the systematic use of force by one class against another, by one section of the population against another. [Vladimir Ilyich Lenin, 1870–1924, *Imperialism, The State and Revolution*, Ch. 4, sect. vi]

15 That this nation, under God, shall have a new birth of freedom; and that government of the people, by the people, and for the people, shall not perish from the earth. [Abraham Lincoln, 1809–65, Gettysburg Address, 19 Nov. 1863]

16 Thus our democracy was, from an early period, the most aristocratic, and our aristocracy the most democratic in the world. [Lord Macaulay, 1800–1859, *History of England*, I, Ch. 1]

17 Man's capacity for evil makes democracy necessary and man's capacity for good makes democracy possible. [Reinhold Niebuhr, 1892–1971, *The Children of Light and the Children of Darkness*, Foreword]

18 One, on God's side, is a majority. [Wendell Phillips, 1811–84, speech at Brooklyn, 1 Nov. 1859]; see 8

19 Democracy passes into despotism. [Plato, *c.*428–347 BC, *Republic*, Bk viii, 562]

20 We must be the great arsenal of democracy. [Franklin D Roosevelt, 1882–1945, *Fireside Chat*, radio address, 29 Dec. 1940]

21 Democracy is like a hobby-horse: it will carry you nowhere unless you use your own legs. [Herbert Samuel, 1870–1963; *Observer*, 'Sayings of the Week', 27 Mar. 1927]

22 We must be thoroughly democratic, and patronize everybody without distinction of class. [George Bernard Shaw, 1856–1950, *John Bull's Other Island*, II]

23 Democracy substitutes election by the incompetent many for appointment by the corrupt few. [George Bernard Shaw, 1856–1950, *Man and Superman*, 'Maxims for Revolutionists', Democracy]

24 It's not the voting that's democracy, it's the counting. [Tom Stoppard, 1937– , *Jumpers*, I]

25 What we need is not a perfect saviour but a perfect democratic system . . . Rather ten devils to check each other than one mandarin with absolute power. [Tiananmen Declaration, issued in Tiananmen Square, Beijing, 2 June 1989, by Liu Xiaobo, Zhou Duo, Hou Dejian and Gao Xin]

26 There is a limit to the application of democratic methods. You can inquire of all the passengers as to what type of car they like to ride in, but it is impossible to question them as to whether to apply the brakes when the train is at full speed and accident threatens. [Leon Trotsky, 1874–1940, *History of the Russian Revolution*, Pt III, Ch. 6]

27 The difference between an ordinary democracy and a people's democracy is that in a people's democracy opinion cannot be freely expressed and therefore goes unheeded, whereas in an ordinary democracy like those in the West, opinion can be freely expressed and therefore goes unheeded. [Peter Ustinov, 1921– , rectorial address, University of Dundee, 17 Oct. 1968]

28 Democracy is the recurrent suspicion that more than half the people are right more than half of the time. [E B White, 1899–1985, *The Wild Flag*]

29 The world must be made safe for democracy. [Woodrow Wilson, 1856–1924, address to Congress, 2 Apr. 1917]

See also ELECTIONS, PARLIAMENT, POLITICS

DEPRESSION

1 Take no heaviness to heart: drive it away, and remember the last end. [Bible, Apocrypha, *Ecclesiasticus* 38:20]

2 One of the depressing things about depression is knowing that there are lots of people in the world with far more reason to feel depressed than you have, and finding that, so far from making you snap out of your depression, it only makes you despise yourself more and thus feel more depressed. [David Lodge, 1935– , *Therapy*, 1, p. 107]

3 I have not that alacrity of spirit, / Nor cheer of mind, that I was wont to have. [William Shakespeare, 1564–1616, *Richard III*, V. iii. 73]

DESIRES

1 Those who restrain Desire, do so because theirs is weak enough to be restrained. [William Blake, 1757–1827, *The Marriage of Heaven and Hell*, 'Those who restrain Desire . . .']

2 He who desires but acts not breeds pestilence. [William Blake, 1757–1827, *The Marriage of Heaven and Hell*, 'Proverbs of Hell']

3 Man's Desires are limited by his Perceptions; none can desire what he has not perceived. [William Blake, 1757–1827, *There is No Natural Religion*]

4 The man's desire is for the woman; but the woman's desire is rarely other than for the desire of the man. [Samuel Taylor Coleridge, 1772–1834, *Table Talk*, 23 July 1823]

5 Modern man lives under the illusion that he knows what he wants, while he actually wants what he is supposed to want. [Erich Fromm, 1900–1980, *The Fear of Freedom*, 8]

6 You have wants the way other people have toothache. Kind of dull and general. [Christopher Hampton, 1946– , *Treats*, vi]

7 Our capacity for disgust, let me observe, is in proportion to our desires; that is in proportion to the intensity of our attachment to the things of this world. [Thomas Mann, 1875–1955, *The Confessions of Felix Krull*, Pt I, Ch. 5]

8 The countries which we long for occupy, at any given moment, a far larger place in our actual life than the country in which we happen to be. [Marcel Proust, 1871–1922, *Remembrance of Things Past: Swann's Way*, 'Swann in Love']

9 To be forced by desire into any unwarrantable belief is a calamity. [I A Richards, 1893–1979, *Principles of Literary Criticism*]

10 Why, she would hang on him, / As if increase of appetite had grown / By what it fed on. [William Shakespeare, 1564–1616, *Hamlet*, I. ii. 143]

11 Is it not strange that desire should so many years outlive performance? [*2 Henry IV*, II. iii. (283)]

12 Though statisticians in our time have never kept the score, / Man wants a great deal here below and Woman even more. [James Thurber, 1894–1961, *Further Fables for Our Time*, 'The Godfather and His Godchild']

DESPAIR

1 The name of the slough was Despond. [John Bunyan, 1628–88, *The Pilgrim's Progress*, Pt I]

2 I tell you naught for your comfort, / Yea, naught for your desire, / Save that the sky grows darker yet / And the sea rises higher. [G K Chesterton, 1874–1936, *The Ballad of the White Horse*, 1]

3 In a real dark night of the soul it is always three o'clock in the morning, day after day. [F Scott Fitzgerald, 1896–1940, *The Crack-up*, 'March 1936 Handle with Care']

4 No worst, there is none. Pitched past pitch of grief, / More pangs will, schooled at forepangs, wilder wring. / Comforter, where, where is your comforting? [Gerard Manley Hopkins, 1844–89, *No Worst, There is None*]

5 *Nil desperandum Teucro duce et auspice Teucro.* – With Teucer as leader and under Teucer's star, never despair. [Horace, 65–8 BC, *Odes*, vii, 27]

6 Don't despair, not even over the fact that you don't despair. [Franz Kafka, 1883–1924, *The Diaries of F K*, 21 July 1913]

7 From the cheerful ways of men / Cut off, and for the book of knowledge fair / Presented with a universal blank / Of nature's works to me expunged and razed, / And wisdom at one entrance quite shut out. [John Milton, 1608–74, *Paradise Lost*, Bk iii, 46]

8 'Strange friend,' I said, 'here is no cause to mourn.' / 'None,' said the other, 'save the undone years, / The hopelessness. Whatever hope is yours / Was my life also; I went hunting wild / After the wildest beauty in the world.' [Wilfred Owen, 1893–1918, *Strange Meeting*]

9 People think bleakness is despair, but it's not. There is always that last place. [Dennis Potter, 1935–94, profile in *Listener*, 20 Nov. 1986]

10 Only on the firm foundation of unyielding despair can the soul's edifice henceforth be built. [Bertrand Russell, 1872–1970, *Philosophical Essays*, 2]

11 Human life begins on the other side of despair. [Jean-Paul Sartre, 1905–80, *The Flies*, III. ii]

12 I 'gin to grow aweary of the sun, / And wish the estate o' the world were now undone. [William Shakespeare, 1564–1616, *Macbeth*, V. v. 49]

13 Two loves I have of comfort and despair, / Which like two spirits do suggest me still: / The better angel is a man right fair, / The worser spirit a woman coloured ill. [*Sonnets*, 144]

14 Yet now despair itself is mild, / Even as the winds and waters are; / I could lie down like a tired child, / And weep away the life of care / Which I have borne and yet must bear. [P B Shelley, 1792–1822, *Stanzas Written in Dejection*]

15 I was much too far out all my life. / And not waving but drowning. [Stevie Smith, 1902–71, *Not Waving but Drowning*]

16 The mass of men lead lives of quiet desperation. [H D Thoreau, 1817–62, *Walden*, 'Economy']

17 I can endure my own despair, / But not another's hope. [William Walsh, 1663–1708, song: *Of All the Torments*]

See also COMFORT, DEPRESSION, HOPE

DESTINY

1 It's not the bullet with my name on it that worries me. It's the one that says 'to whom it may concern'. [anon. Belfast resident; *Observer*, 'Sayings of the Week', 20 Oct. 1991]

2 The universe is transformation; our life is what our thoughts make it. [Marcus Aurelius, AD 121–80, *Meditations*, IV, 3]

3 Whatever may happen to you was prepared for you from all eternity; and the implication of causes was from eternity spinning the thread of your being. [Marcus Aurelius, AD 121–80, *Meditations*, X, 5]

4 The die is cast. [Julius Caesar, 102?–44 BC (at the crossing of the Rubicon), in Suetonius, *The Twelve Caesars*, J C, 32]

5 I felt as if I were walking with destiny, and that all my past life had been but a preparation for this hour and this trial . . . I was sure I should not fail. Therefore, although impatient for the morning, I slept soundly and had no need for cheering dreams. Facts are better than dreams. [Winston Churchill, 1874–1965, *The Second World War*, Vol. 1, closing words, 38]

6 'There's a Providence in it all,' said Sam. 'O' course there is,' replied his father with a nod of grave approval. 'Wot 'ud become o' the undertakers vithout it, Sammy?' [Charles Dickens, 1812–70, *Pickwick Papers*, Ch. 52]

7 'Tis all a Chequer-board of Nights and Days / Where Destiny with Men for Pieces plays / Hither and thither moves, and mates, and slays, / And one by one back in the Closet lays. [Edward Fitzgerald, 1809–83, *The Rubá'iyát of Omar Khayyám*, Edn 1, 49]

8 O Thou who didst with Pitfall and with Gin / Beset the Road I was to wander in, / Thou wilt not with Predestination round / Enmesh me, and impute my Fall to Sin? [Edward Fitzgerald, 1809–83, *The Rubá'iyát of Omar Khayyám*, Edn 1, 57]

9 I don't know Who – or what – put the question, I don't know when it was put. I don't even remember answering. But at some moment I did answer *Yes* to Someone – or Something – and from that hour I was certain that existence is meaningful and that, therefore, my life, in self-surrender, had a goal. [Dag Hammarskjöld, 1905–61, *Markings*, 'Whitsunday 1961']

10 The Immanent Will that stirs and urges everything. [Thomas Hardy, 1840–1928, *The Convergence of the Twain*]

11 There once was a man who said, 'Damn! / It is borne in upon me I am / An engine that moves / In predestinate grooves, / I'm not even a bus, I'm a tram.' [Maurice E Hare, 1886–1967]

12 I go the way that Providence dictates with the assurance of a sleepwalker. [Adolf Hitler, 1889–1945, speech at Munich, 15 Mar. 1936, after successful reoccupation of the Rhineland]

13 BELLING: And what, if I may ask, is your destiny?
GREGERS: To be the thirteenth at table. [Henrik Ibsen, 1828–1906, *The Wild Duck*, V]

14 Must helpless man, in ignorance sedate, / Roll darkling down the torrent of his fate? [Dr Samuel Johnson, 1709–84, *The Vanity of Human Wishes*, 345]

15 Long years ago we made a tryst with destiny, and now the time comes when we shall redeem our pledge, not wholly, or in full measure. [Jawaharlal Nehru, 1889–1964, in *Guardian*, 8 Dec. 1984]

16 My time has not yet come either; some are born posthumously. [Friedrich Nietzsche, 1844–1900, *Ecce Homo*]

17 We may become the makers of our fate when we have ceased to pose as its prophets. [Karl Popper, 1902–94, *The Open Society and Its Enemies*, Introduction]

18 There is a tide in the affairs of men, / Which, taken at the flood, leads on to fortune; / Omitted, all the voyage of their life / Is bound in shallows and in miseries. [William Shakespeare, 1564–1616, *Julius Caesar*, IV. iii. 217]

19 Hanging and wiving goes by destiny. [*The Merchant of Venice*, II. ix. 83]

20 He hath no drowning mark upon him; his complexion is perfect gallows. [*The Tempest*, I. i. (33)]

21 O that 'twere possible / After long grief and pain / To find the arms of my true love / Round me once again! [Alfred, Lord Tennyson, 1809–92, *Maud*, Pt II, iv, 1]

22 Yes, I am a fatal man, Madame Fribsbi. To inspire hopeless passion is my destiny. [(Mirobolant) W M Thackeray, 1811–63, *Pendennis*, Ch. 23]

23 Every bullet has its billet. [William III, 1650–1702, quoted by John Wesley, *Journal*, 6 June 1765]

24 Whether we be young or old, / Our destiny, our being's heart and home, / Is with infinitude, and only there; / With hope it is, hope that can never die, / Effort, and expectation, and desire, / And something evermore about to be. [William Wordsworth, 1770-1850 *The Prelude*, VI, 603]

See also CHANCE, LUCK

DESTRUCTION

1 That which the palmerworm hath left hath the locust eaten. [Bible, OT, *Joel* 1:4]

2 Wide is the gate, and broad is the way, that leadeth to destruction. [Bible, NT, *St Matthew* 7:13]

3 Whom God wishes to destroy, he first makes mad. [Euripides, 480–406 BC, *Fragments*. Exists in many forms; the Latin version '*Quos deus vult perdere, prius dementat*' is quoted in Boswell, *Life of Johnson*]; see 8

4 It is not what they built. It is what they knocked down. / It is not the houses. It is the spaces between the houses. [James Fenton, 1949– , *A German Requiem*]

5 Some say the world will end in fire, / Some say in ice. / From what I've tasted of desire / I hold with those who favour fire, / But if I had to perish twice, / I think I know enough of hate / To say that for destruction ice / Is also great / And would suffice. [Robert Frost, 1874–1963, *Fire and Ice*]

6 The man of power is ruined by power, the man of money by money, the submissive man by subservience, the pleasure seeker by pleasure.

[Hermann Hesse, 1877–1962, *Steppenwolf*, 'Treatise on the Steppenwolf']

7 When smashing monuments, save the pedestals – they always come in handy. [Stanislaw Lec, 1909–66, *Unkempt Thoughts*, p. 50]

8 Whom the mad would destroy they first make Gods. [(Of Mao Zedong, 1967) Bernard Levin, 1928– , in *The Times*; in *Dictionary of Contemporary Quotations*, ed. J Green]; see 3

9 Crumbling between the fingers, under the feet, / Crumbling behind the eyes, / Their world gives way and dies / And something twangs and breaks at the end of the street. [Louis MacNeice, 1907–63, *Débâcle*]

10 What the wrong gods established / no army can ever save. [Tom Paulin, 1949– , *A Partial State*]

DETECTIVES

1 Detectives are only policemen with smaller feet. [Marlene Dietrich, 1901–92, in Hitchcock film *Stage Fright*, script by Whitfield Cook *et al.* from S Jepson's *Man Running*]

2 'Is there any point to which you would wish to draw my attention?' 'To the curious incident of the dog in the night-time.' 'The dog did nothing in the night-time.' 'That was the curious incident,' remarked Sherlock Holmes. [Arthur Conan Doyle, 1859–1930, *The Memoirs of Sherlock Holmes*, 'Silver Blaze']

See also POLICE

THE DEVIL

1 The Devil, having nothing else to do, / Went off to tempt my Lady Poltagrue. / My Lady, tempted by a private whim, / To his extreme annoyance, tempted him. [Hilaire Belloc, 1870–1953, *Epigrams*, 'On Lady Poltagrue']

2 How art thou fallen from heaven, O Lucifer, son of the morning! [Bible, OT, *Isaiah* 14:12]

3 And the Lord said unto Satan, Whence comest thou? Then Satan answered the Lord, and said, From going to and fro in the earth, and from walking up and down in it. [Bible, OT, *Job* 1:7]

4 Be sober, be vigilant; because your adversary the devil, as a roaring lion, walketh about, seeking whom he may devour. [Bible, NT, *1 Peter* 5:8]

5 The devil is come down unto you, having great wrath, because he knoweth that he hath but a short time. [Bible, NT, *Revelation* 12:12]

6 Get thee behind me, Satan. [Bible, NT, *St Matthew* 16:23]

7 Truly, my Satan, thou art but a dunce, / And dost not know the garment from the man; / Every harlot was a virgin once, / Nor canst thou ever change Kate into Nan. [William Blake, 1757–1827, *The Gates of Paradise*, Prologue]

8 Thus the devil played at chess with me, and yielding a pawn, thought to gain a queen of me, taking advantage of my honest endeavours. [Sir Thomas Browne, 1605–82, *Religio Medici*, Pt 1, 18]

9 An apology for the Devil – it must be remembered that we have only heard one side of the case. God has written all the books. [Samuel Butler, 1835–1902, *Notebooks*, Ch. 14, 'An Apology for the Devil']

10 But fare you weel, auld Nickie-ben! / O wad ye tak a thought an' men'! / Ye aiblins might – I dinna ken – / Still hae a stake: / I'm wae to think upo' yon den, / Ev'n for your sake! [Robert Burns, *Address to the Deil*, 121]

11 Satan met his ancient friend / With more hauteur, as might an old Castilian / Poor noble meet a mushroom rich civilian. [Lord Byron, 1788–1824, *The Vision of Judgement*, 36]

12 I think if the devil doesn't exist, but man has created him, he has created him in his own image and likeness. [Fyodor Dostoyevsky, 1821–81, *Brothers Karamazov*, Pt II, Bk v, Ch. 4]

13 Satan . . . is a hard boss to work for . . . When other people are having their vacation is when he keeps you the busiest. As old Dr Watts or St Paul or some other diagnostician says: 'He always finds somebody for idle hands to do.' [O Henry, 1862–1910, *A Midsummer Masquerade*]

14 The devil mostly speaks a language called Bellsybabble which he makes up himself as he goes along but when he is very angry he can speak quite bad French very well though some who have heard him say that he has a strong Dublin accent. [James Joyce, 1882–1941, *The Cat and the Devil*]

15 It is so stupid of modern civilization to have given up believing in the devil when he is the only explanation of it. [Mgr Ronald Knox, 1888–1957, *Let Dons Delight*, Ch. 8]

16 It is no good casting out devils. They belong to us, we must accept them and be at peace with them. [D H Lawrence, 1885–1930, *Phoenix*, 'The Reality of Peace']

17 Unhappy spirits that fell with Lucifer, / Conspired against our God with Lucifer, / And are for ever damned with Lucifer. [Christopher Marlowe, 1564–93, *Doctor Faustus*, 310]

18 When night / Darkens the streets, then wander forth the sons / Of Belial, flown with insolence and wine. [John Milton, 1608–74, *Paradise Lost*, Bk i, 500]

19 His form had yet not lost / All her original brightness, nor appeared / Less than archangel ruined, and th' excess / Of glory obscured. [John Milton, 1608–74, *Paradise Lost*, Bk i, 591]

20 The devil was sick, the devil a monk wou'd be: / The devil was well, and the devil a monk he'd be. [Peter Motteux, 1660–1718, trans. of Rabelais, *Gargantua and Pantagruel*, Bk iv, Ch. 24]

21 The fallacy of the liberal mind is to see good in everything. That has been of great assistance to the devil. [Malcolm Muggeridge, 1903–90, interview in John Mortimer, *In Character*]

22 *Courage, l'ami, le diable est mort.* – Courage, my friend, the devil is dead. [Charles Reade, 1814–84, *The Cloister and the Hearth*, Ch. 24]

23 The prince of darkness is a gentleman. [William Shakespeare, 1564–1616, *King Lear*, III. iv. (148)]

24 The devil can cite Scripture for his purpose. [*The Merchant of Venice*, I. iii. (99)]

25 Sometimes / The Devil is a gentleman. [P B Shelley, 1792–1822, *Peter Bell the Third*, 81]

26 From his brimstone bed, at break of day / A walking the Devil is gone, / To look at his little snug farm of the World, / And see how his stock went on. [Robert Southey, 1774–1843, *The Devil's Walk* (a poem written in collaboration with Coleridge)]

See also EVIL, HELL, WICKEDNESS

DIARIES

1 Let diaries, therefore, be brought in use. [Francis Bacon, 1561–1626, *Essays*, 18, 'Of Travel']

2 It [Beatrice Webb's diary] could just as well have been composed by an intelligent cockroach. [John Carey, 1934– , *Original Copy*, 'The Last of Beatrice']

3 I never travel without my diary. One should always have something sensational to read in the train. [Oscar Wilde, 1854–1900, *The Importance of Being Earnest*, II]

DIFFERENCES

1 He shall separate them one from another, as a shepherd divideth his sheep from the goats. [Bible, NT, *St Matthew* 25:32]

2 There's as much difference between us and ourselves as between us and others. [Michel de Montaigne, 1533–92, *Essays*, II, 1]

DIFFICULTIES, see PROBLEMS

DIPLOMACY

1 Diplomacy ... means the art of nearly deceiving all your friends, but not quite deceiving all your enemies. [Kofi Busia, 1913–78, interview, 2 Feb. 1970; in *Simpson's Contemporary Quotations*]

2 Diplomacy is the art of saying 'Nice Doggie!' till you can find a rock. [Wynn Catlin, 1930– , in *Kiss Me Hardy*, ed. Roger Kilroy]

3 Talking jaw-jaw is always better than war-war. [Winston Churchill, 1874–1965, speech in White House, Washington, 26 June 1954]; see 9

4 A diplomat is a man who always remembers a woman's birthday but never remembers her age. [Robert Frost, 1874–1963; in *Treasury of Humorous Quotations*, ed. Evan Esar and Nicolas Bentley]

5 Diplomacy – lying in state. [Oliver Herford, 1863–1935; in Laurence J Peter, *Peter's Quotations*]

6 Let us never negotiate out of fear. But let us never fear to negotiate. [President John F Kennedy, 1917–63, inaugural address as President, 20 Jan. 1961]

7 There cannot be a crisis next week. My schedule is already full. [Henry Kissinger, 1923– , in *The New York Times Magazine*, 1 June 1969]

8 The only decent diplomat is a deaf Trappist. [John Le Carré, 1931– , *A Perfect Spy*, 3]

9 Jaw-jaw is better than war-war. [Harold Macmillan, 1894–1986, said at Canberra, 30 Jan. 1958]; see 3

10 If an ambassador says yes, it means perhaps; if he says perhaps, it means no; if he ever said no, he would cease to be an ambassador. [K M Panikkar, 1895–1963; in *New Light's Dictionary of Quotations*, comp. Ved Bhushan]

11 Diplomacy is letting someone else have your way. [Lester Pearson, 1897–1972, in *Observer*, 18 Mar. 1965]

12 A diplomat these days is nothing but a head-waiter who's allowed to sit down occasionally. [Peter Ustinov, 1921– , *Romanoff and Juliet*, I]

13 An ambassador is an honest man sent to lie abroad for the good of his country. [Henry Wotton, 1568–1639, written in Christopher Fleckmore's album and quoted in Izaak Walton, *Life of H W*]

See also POLITICS, TACT

DISABILITIES

1 I'm a coloured, one-eyed Jew – do I need anything else? [Sammy Davis Jr, 1925–90, *Yes I Can*]

2 Deformed, unfinished, sent before my time / Into this breathing world, scarce half made up, / And that so lamely and unfashionable / That dogs bark at me as I halt by them. [William Shakespeare, 1564–1616, *Richard III*, I. i. 20]

DISAGREEMENT, see AGREEMENT

DISAPPOINTMENTS

1 The glory dropped from their youth and love, / And both perceived they had dreamed a dream. [Robert Browning, 1812–89, *The Statue and the Bust*, 51]

2 Now the peak of summer's past, the sky is overcast / And the love we swore would last for an age seems deceit. [C Day Lewis, 1904–72, *Hornpipe*]

3 As for disappointing them, I should not so much mind; but I can't abide to disappoint myself. [Oliver Goldsmith, 1728–74, *She Stoops to Conquer*, 1]

4 *Parturient montes, nascetur ridiculus mus.* – Mountains will be in labour, and the birth will be an absurd little mouse. [Horace, 65–8 BC, *Ars Poetica*, 139]

5 We for a certainty are not the first / Have sat in taverns while the tempest hurled / Their hopeful plans to emptiness, and cursed / Whatever brute and blackguard made the world. [A E Housman, 1859–1936, *Last Poems*, 9]

6 Like Dead Sea fruits, that tempt the eye, / But turn to ashes on the lips! [Thomas Moore, 1779–1852, *Lalla-Rookh*, 'Fire-Worshippers', i, 484]

7 'Blessed is the man who expects nothing, for he shall never be disappointed' was the ninth beatitude. [Alexander Pope, 1688–1744, letter to Fortescue, 23 Sept. 1725]

8 Disillusionment in living is the finding out nobody agrees with you not those that are fighting for you. Complete disillusionment is when you realize that no one can for they can't change. [Gertrude Stein, 1874–1946, *The Making of Americans*]

DISASTERS

1 When struck by a thunderbolt it is unnecessary to consult the Book of Dates as to the precise meaning of the omen. [Ernest Bramah, 1868–1942, *The Wallet of Kai Lung*, 'Transmutation of Ling']

2 The civilization of one epoch becomes the manure of the next. Everything over-ripens in the same way. The disasters of the world are due to its inhabitants not being able to grow old simultaneously. [Cyril Connolly (Palinurus), 1903–74, *The Unquiet Grave*, Ch. 1]

3 Beautiful Railway Bridge of the Silv'ry Tay! / Alas, I am very sorry to say / That ninety lives have been taken away / On the last Sabbath day of 1879, / Which will be remember'd for a very long time. [William McGonagall, 1825–1902, *The Tay Bridge Disaster*]

4 From the sublime to the ridiculous there is only one step. [Napoleon Bonaparte, 1769–1821, to De Pradt, the Polish ambassador after the retreat from Moscow, 1812]

5 A man may surely be allowed to take a glass of wine *by his own fireside*. [(Refreshing himself at the Piazza Coffee House as his theatre in Drury Lane went up in flames, 24 Feb. 1809)

R B Sheridan, 1751–1816, quoted in Thomas Moore, *Memoirs of the Life of Sheridan*, Vol. ii, Ch. 20]

See also ACCIDENTS, CHANCE

DISCOVERY & EXPLORATION

1 *Eureka!* – I have found it! [(On making a discovery) Archimedes, 287–212 BC]

2 They are ill discoverers that think there is no land, when they can see nothing but sea. [Francis Bacon, 1561–1626, *The Advancement of Learning*, I, vii, 5]

3 Polar exploration is at once the cleanest and most isolated way of having a bad time which has been devised. [Apsley Cherry-Garrard, 1882–1959, *The Worst Journey in the World*, Introduction]

4 It has not escaped our notice that the specific pairing we have postulated immediately suggests a possible copying mechanism for the genetic material. [Francis Crick, 1916– , and James D Watson, 1928– , paper announcing discovery of DNA in *Nature*, 1953]

5 One day, about noon, going towards my boat, I was exceedingly surprised with the print of a man's naked foot on the shore, which was very plain to be seen in the sand. [Daniel Defoe, 1661?–1731, *Robinson Crusoe*, Pt I]

6 We are the Pilgrims, master; we shall go / Always a little further; it may be / Beyond that last blue mountain barred with snow / Across that angry or that glimmering sea. [James Elroy Flecker, 1884–1915, *Hassan*, V. iii]

7 *Où penchés – l'avant des blanches caravelles, / Ils regardaient monter en un ciel ignoré / Du fond de l'Océan des étoiles nouvelles.* – Where leaning over the prow of white four-masters, they saw new stars climb from the depths of the ocean into an unknown sky. [J M de Hérédia, 1842–1905, *Les Conquérants*]

8 Explorers have to be ready to die lost. [Russell Hoban, 1925– , interview in *The Times*, 1975]

9 Then felt I like some watcher of the skies/ When a new planet swims into his ken; / Or like stout Cortez, when with eagle eyes / He stared at the Pacific – and all his men / Looked at each other with a wild surmise – / Silent, upon a peak in Darien. [John Keats, 1795–1821, sonnet: *On First Looking into Chapman's Homer*]

10 Something lost behind the Ranges. Lost and waiting for you. Go! [Rudyard Kipling, 1865–1936, *The Explorer*]

11 I do not know what I may appear to the world, but to myself I seem to have been only like a boy playing on the sea-shore, and diverting myself in now and then finding a smoother pebble or a prettier shell than ordinary, whilst the great ocean of truth lay all undiscovered before me. [Isaac Newton, 1642–1727, in D Brewster, *Memoirs of N*, II, Ch. 27]

12 Anyone who tells you he has discovered something new is a fool, or a liar or both. [Mack Sennett, 1880–1960, in James Agee, *Agee on Film*, Vol. 1]

13 Discovery consists of seeing what everybody has seen and thinking what nobody has thought. [Albert Szent-Györgyi, 1893–1986, in I J Good, *The Scientist Speculates*, p. 15]

DISCRETION

1 Between thirty and forty a man may have reached the height of discretion without having tumbled over the top into the feather-bed of correctitude. [Arnold Bennett, 1867–1931, in *Evening Standard Years*, 29 May 1930]

2 Open not thine heart to every man, lest he requite thee with a shrewd turn. [Bible, Apocrypha, *Ecclesiasticus* 8:19]

3 Curse not the king, no not in thy thought; and curse not the rich in thy bedchamber: for a bird of the air shall carry the voice, and that which hath wings shall tell the matter. [Bible, OT, *Ecclesiastes* 10:20]

4 As a jewel of gold in a swine's snout, so is a fair woman which is without discretion. [Bible, OT, *Proverbs* 11:22]

5 Set a watch, O Lord, before my mouth, keep the door of my lips. [Bible, OT, *Psalms* 141:3]

6 But still keep something to yoursel / Ye scarcely tell to ony. [Robert Burns, 1759–96, *Epistle to a Young Friend*, 35]

7 Mum's the word. [George Colman the Younger, 1762–1836, *The Battle of Hexham*, II, i]

8 It does not always pay to have a golden tongue unless one has the ability to hold it. [(Of Lord Curzon) Paul Johnson, 1928– , in *Listener*, 5 June 1986]

9 How hard it is for women to keep counsel. [William Shakespeare, 1564–1616, *Julius Caesar*, II. iv. 9]

10 I shall not say why and how I became, at the age of fifteen, the mistress of the Earl of Craven. [Harriette Wilson, 1789–1846, *Memoirs*, first sentence]

See also GOSSIP, SCANDAL, TACT

DIVERSITY

1 Glory be to God for dappled things – / For skies of couple-colour as a brindled cow; / For rose-moles all in stipple upon trout that swim. [Gerard Manley Hopkins, 1844–89, *Pied Beauty*]

2 All things counter, original, spare, strange; / Whatever is fickle, freckled (who knows how?) / With swift, slow; sweet, sour; adazzle, dim; / he fathers-forth whose beauty is past change. / Praise him. [Gerard Manley Hopkins, 1844–89, *Pied Beauty*]

3 Now it is the virtue of design, pattern, or inscape to be distinctive and it is the vice of distinctiveness to become queer. [Gerard Manley Hopkins, 1844–89, letter to Robert Bridges, 15 Feb. 1879]

4 Letting a hundred flowers blossom and a hundred schools of thought contend is the policy for promoting the progress of the arts and the sciences. [Mao Zedong, 1893–1976, *On the Correct Handling of Contradictions*, 27 Feb. 1957]

5 Not chaos-like, together crushed and bruised, / But, as the world harmoniously confused: / Where order in variety we see, / And where, though all things differ, all agree. [Alexander Pope, 1688–1744, *Windsor Forest*, 13]

DIVORCE

1 It was partially my fault we got divorced . . . I had a tendency to place my wife under a pedestal. [Woody Allen, 1935– , in Chicago nightclub, Mar. 1964]

2 For a while we pondered whether to take a vacation or get a divorce. My wife got the house, the car, the bank account, and if I marry again and have children, she gets them too. [Woody Allen, 1935– , in *Was It Good for You Too?*, ed. Bob Chieger]

3 Alimony is like buying oats for a dead horse. [Arthur 'Bugs' Baer, 1897–1975, from *New York American*, in Jonathon Green, *Cynic's Lexicon*]

4 Divorce is a system whereby two people make a mistake and one of them goes on paying for it. [Len Deighton, 1929– , in A Alvarez, *Life after Marriage*]

5 No *divorcées* were included, except those who had shown signs of penitence by being remarried to the very wealthy. [Edith Wharton, 1862–1937, *The House of Mirth*, Bk I, Ch. 5]

6 Divorce is / the sign of knowledge in our time. [William Carlos Williams, 1883–1963, *Patterson*, I, Preface]

See also MARRIAGE

DOCTORS & NURSES

1 I am dying with the help of too many physicians. [Alexander the Great, 356–323 BC; quoted in Evan Esar, ed., *Treasury of Humorous Quotations*]

2 Lord Dawson was not a good doctor: King George V himself told me that he would never have died, had he had another doctor! [Margot Asquith, 1865–1945, quoted in *Observer*, 20 Dec. 1981]

3 They answered, as they took their fees, / 'There is no cure for this disease'. [Hilaire Belloc, 1870–1953, *Cautionary Tales*, 'Henry King']

4 Honour a physician with the honour due unto him for the uses which you may have of him: for the Lord hath created him. [Bible, Apocrypha, *Ecclesiasticus* 38:1]

5 Is there no balm in Gilead; is there no physician there? [Bible, OT, *Jeremiah* 8:22]

6 Physician, heal thyself. [Bible, NT, *St Luke* 4:23]

7 Never go to a doctor whose office plants have died. [Erma Bombeck, 1927– , in *Hammer and Tongues*, ed. Michèle Brown and Ann O'Connor, 'Medicine']

8 The wounded surgeon plies the steel / That questions the distempered part. [T S Eliot, 1888–1965, *Four Quartets*, 'Burnt Norton', IV]

9 Every physician almost hath his favourite disease. [Henry Fielding, 1707–54, *Tom Jones*, Bk ii. Ch. 9]

10 The resistance of the patient to the doctor is the objective of every treatment. [Georg Groddeck, 1866–1934, *The Book of the It*, Letter 14]

11 [Feeling patient's pulse] Either he's dead, or my watch has stopped. [Groucho Marx, 1895–1987 in film *A Day at the Races*, screenplay by Robert Pirosh, George Seaton and George Oppenheimer]

12 He must have killed a lot of men to have made so much money. [Molière, 1622–73, *Le Malade imaginaire*, I. v]

13 GÉRONTE: I think you are locating them in the wrong places. The heart is on the left and the liver on the right.

SGANARELLE: Yes, that was so in the old days. But we have changed all that. [Molière, 1622–73, *Le Médecin malgré lui*, II. iv]

14 Who shall decide when doctors disagree? [Alexander Pope, 1688–1744, *Moral Essays*, Epistle III, 1]

15 Cured yesterday of my disease, / I died last night of my physician. [Matthew Prior, 1664–1721, *The Remedy Worse than the Disease*]

16 In the pathology of nervous diseases, a doctor who doesn't talk too much nonsense is a half-cured patient, just as a critic is a poet who has stopped writing verse and a policeman a burglar who has retired from practice. [Marcel Proust, 1871–1922, *Remembrance of Things Past: The Guermantes Way*, Ch. 1, 'Decline and Death of My Grandmother']

17 First they [physicians] get *on*, then they get *honour*, then they get *honest*. [Humphry Davy Rolleston, 1862–1944, in David Ogilvy, *Confessions of an Advertising Man*, Ch. 2]

18 Diseases desperate grown, / By desperate appliance are relieved, / Or not at all. [William Shakespeare, 1564–1616, *Hamlet*, IV. iii. 9]

19 Canst thou not minister to a mind diseased, / Pluck from the memory a rooted sorrow, / Raze out the written troubles of the brain, / And with some sweet oblivious antidote / Cleanse the stuffed bosom of that perilous stuff / Which weighs upon the heart? [*Macbeth*, V. ii. 40]

20 There are worse occupations in this world than feeling a woman's pulse. [Laurence Sterne, 1713–68, *A Sentimental Journey*, 'The Pulse. Paris']

21 Yet her conception of God was certainly not orthodox. She felt towards Him as she might have felt towards a glorified sanitary engineer; and in some of her speculations she seems hardly to distinguish between the Deity and the Drains. [Lytton Strachey, 1880–1932, *Eminent Victorians*, 'Florence Nightingale']

See also HEALTH, ILLNESS, MEDICINE

DOGS

1 It's the one species I wouldn't mind seeing vanish from the face of the earth. I wish they were like the White Rhino – six of them left in the Serengeti National Park, and all males. [Alan Bennett, 1934– , *Getting On*, I]

2 A dog starved at his master's gate / Predicts the ruin of the State. [William Blake, 1757–1827, *Auguries of Innocence*]

3 His lockèd, letter'd, braw brass collar, / Shew'd him the gentleman and scholar. [Robert Burns, 1759–96, *The Twa Dogs*, 13]

4 I am cursed with a right leg that arouses the desire of any male dog that happens to be passing. I used to think that this only happened to me but I've discovered that many people have the same problem. They have a *femme fatale* limb. [Jasper Carrott, 1945– , *Sweet and Sour Carrott*, p. 44]

5 Jacob is a German Shepherd. (I have never understood why they aren't called German sheepdogs. What do the Germans call shepherds?) [Alan Coren, 1938– , *Seems Like Old Times*, 'January']

6 Shaggy, and lean, and shrewd, with pointed ears, / And tail cropped short, half lurcher and half cur. [William Cowper, 1731–1800, *The Task*, Bk V, 45]

7 Has anybody seen my Mopser? – / A comely dog is he, / With hair the colour of a Charles the Fifth, / And teeth like ships at sea. [Walter de la Mare, 1873–1956, *The Bandog*]

8 The dog, to gain some private ends, / Went mad and bit the man ... / The man recovered of the bite, / The dog it was that died. [Oliver Goldsmith, 1728–74, *The Vicar of Wakefield*, Ch. 17, 'An Elegy on the Death of a Mad Dog']

9 Brothers and Sisters, I bid you beware / Of giving your heart to a dog to tear. [Rudyard Kipling, 1865–1936, *The Power of the Dog*]

10 Me or the Mexican who comes to chop wood / All the same, / All humanity is jam to you. [D H Lawrence, 1885–1930, *Bibbles*]

11 Dogs, like horses, are quadrupeds. That is to say, they have four rupeds, one at each corner, on which they walk. [Frank Muir, 1920–98, in Frank Muir and Denis Norden, *You Can't Have Your Kayak and Heat It*, 'Ta-ra-ra-boom-de-ay!']

12 Old Mother Hubbard / Went to the cupboard, / To get her poor dog a bone; / But when she got there, / The cupboard was bare, / And so the poor dog had none. [Nursery rhyme]

13 I am his Highness' dog at Kew; / Pray tell me, sir, whose dog are you? [Alexander Pope, 1688–1744, *On the Collar of a Dog which I Gave to his Royal Highness*]

14 Anybody who hates dogs and babies can't be all bad. [(Of W C Fields) Leo Rosten, 1908–97, at Masquers' Club Dinner, Hollywood, 16 Feb. 1939. Often misquoted as 'children and dogs' and wrongly attr. to Fields]

15 That's the only dog I know who can smell someone just *thinking* about food. [Charles Schulz, 1922– , in *Peanuts* strip cartoon]

16 The more I see of men, the more I admire dogs. [Mme de Sévigné, 1626–96, attr.]

17 My hounds are bred out of the Spartan kind, / So flewed, so sanded; and their heads are hung / With ears that sweep away the morning dew; / Crook-kneed, and dew-lapped like Thessalian bulls; / Slow in pursuit, but matched in mouth like bells. [William Shakespeare, 1564–1616, *A Midsummer Night's Dream*, IV. i. (125)]

18 I loathe people who keep dogs. They are cowards who haven't got the guts to bite people themselves. [August Strindberg, 1849–1912, *A Madman's Diary*]

See also ANIMALS, CATS

DOUBT

1 I do not believe in the afterlife, although I am bringing a change of underwear. [Woody Allen, 1935– , in *Time* Magazine, 3 July 1972]

2 If a man will begin with certainties, he shall end in doubts; but if he will be content to begin with doubts, he shall end in certainties. [Francis Bacon, 1561–1626, *The Advancement of Learning*, I, v, 8]

3 Oh! let us never, never doubt / What nobody is sure about! [Hilaire Belloc, 1870–1953, *More Beasts for Worse Children*, 'The Microbe']

4 How long halt ye between two opinions? [Bible, OT, *1 Kings* 18:21]

5 Lord, I believe; help thou mine unbelief. [Bible, NT, *St Mark* 9:24]

6 If the Sun and Moon should doubt, / They'd immediately go out. [William Blake, 1757–1827, *Auguries of Innocence*]

7 He who shall teach the child to doubt / The rotting grave shall ne'er get out. [William Blake, 1757–1827, *Auguries of Innocence*]

8 All we have gained then by our unbelief / Is a life of doubt diversified by faith, / For one of faith diversified by doubt: / We called the chess-board white, – we call it black. [Robert Browning, 1812–89, *Bishop Blougram's Apology*, 209]

9 A castle, called Doubting Castle, the owner whereof was Giant Despair. [John Bunyan, 1628–88, *The Pilgrim's Progress*, Pt I]

10 And like all self-possessed people he was prey to doubt. [Bruce Chatwin, 1940–89, *What am I Doing Here?*, 'Heavenly Horses']

11 My mind is in a state of philosophical doubt. [Samuel Taylor Coleridge, 1772–1834, *Table Talk*, 30 Apr. 1830]

12 'Do you believe in astrology?' 'I don't even believe in astronomy.' [Peter de Vries, 1910–93, *Consenting Adults*, Ch. 4]

13 I am the doubter and the doubt, / And I the hymn the Brahmin sings. [Ralph Waldo Emerson, 1803–82, *Brahma*]

14 Of that there is no manner of doubt – / No probable, possible shadow of doubt – / No possible doubt whatever. [W S Gilbert, 1836–1911 *The Gondoliers*, I]

15 The believer will fight another believer over a shade of difference: the doubter fights only with himself. [Graham Greene, 1904–91, *Monsignor Quixote*, Pt 1, Ch. 4]

16 His doubts are better than most people's certainties. [Earl of Hardwicke, 1690–1764, reference to Dirleton's *Doubts*; quoted in Boswell, *Life of Johnson*, 1791]

17 We work in the dark – we do what we can – we give what we have. Our doubt is our passion, and our passion is our task. The rest is the madness of art. [Henry James, 1843–1916, *The Middle Years*, 1893]

18 Truth, Sir, is a cow, which will yield such people [sceptics] no more milk, and so they are gone to milk the bull. [Dr Samuel Johnson, 1709–84, in James Boswell, *Life of J*, 21 July 1763]

19 The only limit to our realization of tomorrow will be our doubts of today. [Franklin D Roosevelt, 1882–1945, address written for Jefferson Day dinner to have been given 13 Apr. 1945. He died on the 12th]

20 She believed in nothing; only her scepticism kept her from being an atheist. [Jean-Paul Sartre, 1905–80, *Words*, Pt 1]

21 Doubt thou the stars are fire; / Doubt that the sun doth move; / Doubt truth to be a liar; / But never doubt I love. [William Shakespeare, 1564–1616, *Hamlet*, II. ii. (115)]

22 Our doubts are traitors, / And make us lose the good we oft might win, / By fearing to attempt. [*Measure for Measure*, I. iv. 77]

23 Cleave ever to the sunnier side of doubt. [Alfred, Lord Tennyson, 1809–92, *The Ancient Sage*, 68]

24 There lives more faith in honest doubt, / Believe me, than in half the creeds. [Alfred, Lord Tennyson, 1809–92, *In Memoriam*, 96]

25 *La vida es duda, / y la fe sin la duda es sólo muerte.* – Life is doubt, and faith without doubt is nothing but death. [Miguel de Unamuno, 1864–1937, *Poesías*, 1907]

26 Another sort of doubt which I venture to call 'philosophical', though I cannot here present all the excuses for stretching the word to cover all doubts of this sort. Examples of this sort are, 'Can a man keep a promise by mistake?', 'Is a zebra without stripes a zebra?' [John Wisdom, 1905–93, *Other Minds*]

27 The best lack all conviction, while the worst / Are full of passionate intensity. [W B Yeats, 1865–1939, *The Second Coming*]

See also CERTAIN, FAITHS

DREAMS

1 Dreams and predictions ought to serve but for winter talk by the fireside. [Francis Bacon, 1561–1626, *Essays*, 35, 'Of Prophecies']

2 It was a dream of perfect bliss, / Too beautiful to last. [T H Bayly, 1797–1839, *It was a Dream*]

3 If there were dreams to sell, / What would you buy? / Some cost a passing bell; / Some a light sigh, / That shakes from Life's fresh crown / Only a roseleaf down. [T L Beddoes, 1798–1851, *Dream-Pedlary*]

4 'Father, O father! what do we here / In this land of unbelief and fear? / The Land of Dreams is better far, / Above the light of the morning star.' [William Blake, 1757–1827, *The Land of Dreams*]

5 Dreams out of the ivory gate, and visions before midnight. [Sir Thomas Browne, 1605–82, *On Dreams*]

6 If someone were to tell me I had twenty years left, and ask me how I'd like to spend them, I'd reply: 'Give me two hours a day of activity, and I'll take the other 22 in dreams . . . provided I can remember them.' [Luis Buñuel, 1900–1983, *My Last Breath*, Ch. 9]

7 For I see now that I am asleep that I dream when I am awake. [Pedro Calderón de la Barca, 1600–1681, *Life is a Dream*, II]

8 No psychoanalyst has knocked / The bottom out of Bottom's dream. [G K Chesterton, 1874–1936, *The Apology of Bottom the Weaver*]

9 I do not know whether I was then a man dreaming I was a butterfly, or whether I am now a butterfly dreaming I am a man. [Chuang Tsu, *c.*369–286 BC, *On Levelling All Things*, 2]

10 Last night I dreamt I ate a ten-pound marshmallow. When I woke up the pillow was gone. [Tommy Cooper, 1921–84, gag in variety act; in John Fisher, *Funny Way to be a Hero*, 'Just a Wolf in Sheep's Clothing']

11 (dreaming, / et / cetera, of / Your smile eyes knees and of your Etcetera) [e e cummings 1894–1962, *Collected Poems*, 1938, 148]

12 Very old are we men: / Our dreams are tales / Told in dim Eden / By Eve's nightingales. [Walter de la Mare, 1873–1956, *All That's Past*]

13 Dear love, for nothing less than thee / Would I have broke this happy dream, / It was a theme / For reason, much too strong for fantasy, / Therefore thou waked'st me wisely; yet / My dream thou brok'st not, but continued'st it. [John Donne, 1571?–1631, *The Dream*]

14 I'll let you be in my dreams if I can be in

yours. [Bob Dylan, 1941– , song: *Talkin' World War III Blues*]

15 Dreaming when Dawn's Left Hand was in the sky / I heard a Voice within the Tavern cry: / 'Awake, my Little ones, and fill the Cup / Before Life's Liquor in its Cup be dry.' [Edward Fitzgerald, 1809–83, *The Rubá'iyát of Omar Khayyám*, Edn 1, 2]

16 I dream of Jeanie with the light brown hair. [Stephen Foster, 1826–64, song: *Jeanie with the Light Brown Hair*]

17 Real are the dreams of Gods, and smoothly pass / Their pleasures in a long immortal dream. [John Keats, 1795–1821, *Lamia*, I, 127]

18 All men dream: but not equally. Those who dream by night in the dusty recesses of their minds wake in the day to find that it was vanity: but the dreamers of the day are dangerous men, for they may act their dream with open eyes, to make it possible. [T E Lawrence, 1888–1935, *Seven Pillars of Wisdom*, Ch. 1]

19 Another difference between me and Samuel Taylor Coleridge is more massive in design: / People used to interrupt him while he was dreaming his dreams, but they interrupt me while I am recounting mine. [Ogden Nash, 1902–71, *I Can Hardly Wait for the Sandman*]

20 All that we see or seem / Is but a dream within a dream. [Edgar Allan Poe, 1809–49, *A Dream within a Dream*]

21 Deep into the darkness peering, long I stood there, wondering, fearing, / Doubting, dreaming dreams no mortal ever dared to dream before [Edgar Allan Poe, 1809–49, *The Raven*, 5]

22 I dream quite a bit, myself. Only when I'm asleep, of course. Curious thing is it's always the same dream ... Not that I mind, of course, I'm not one to hanker after change the whole time. [Henry Reed, 1914–86, BBC radio drama *The Primal Scene, As It Were*]

23 In a dream you are never eighty. [Anne Sexton, 1928–74, *All My Pretty Ones*, 'Old']

24 I could be bounded in a nutshell, and count myself a king of infinite space, were it not that I have bad dreams. [William Shakespeare, 1564–1616, *Hamlet*, II. ii. (264)]

25 The eye of man hath not heard, the ear of man hath not seen, man's hand is not able to taste, his tongue to conceive, nor his heart to report, what my dream was. [*A Midsummer Night's Dream*, IV. i. (218)]

26 O, I have passed a miserable night, / So full of ugly sights, of ghastly dreams, / That, as I am a Christian faithful man, / I would not spend another such a night, / Though 'twere to buy a world of happy days, / So full of dismal terror was the time! [*Richard III*, I. iv. 2]

27 Thus have I had thee, as a dream doth flatter, / In sleep a king, but, waking, no such matter. [*Sonnets*, 87]

28 Many's the long night I've dreamed of cheese – toasted, mostly. [Robert Louis Stevenson, 1850–94, *Treasure Island*, Ch. 15]

29 Dreams are true while they last, and do we not live in dreams? [Alfred, Lord Tennyson, 1809–92, *The Higher Pantheism*]

30 The boys are dreaming wicked or of the bucking ranches of the night and the jolly-rodgered sea. [Dylan Thomas, 1914–53, *Under Milk Wood*]

31 One can write, think and pray exclusively of others; dreams are all egocentric. [Evelyn Waugh, 1903–66, *Diaries*, ed. M Davie, 'Irregular Notes', 5 Oct. 1962]

32 I have spread my dreams under your feet; / Tread softly because you tread on my dreams. [W B Yeats, 1865–1939, *He Wishes for the Cloths of Heaven*]

See also IMAGINATION

DRINK: STRONG

1 If drink; / Good wine, a friend, or being dry, / Or lest we should be by and by all be true that I do think, / There are five reasons we should; / Or any other reason why. [Henry Aldrich, 1647–1710, *A Catch*]

2 Little nips of whisky, little drops of gin, / Make a lady wonder where on earth she's bin. [anon.]

3 Wine is a mocker, strong drink is raging. [Bible, OT, *Proverbs* 20:1]

4 Sherry ... a sickly compound, the use of which will transform a nation, however bold and warlike by nature, into a race of sketchers, scribblers and punsters, in fact into what Englishmen are at the present day. [George Borrow, 1803–81, *Wild Wales*, Ch. 28]

5 We'll tak a cup o' kindness yet, / For auld lang syne. [Robert Burns, 1759–96, *Auld Lang Syne*]

6 Freedom and Whisky gang thegither! [Robert Burns, 1759–96, *The Author's Earnest Cry and Prayer*, 185]

7 'You can tell a man who boozes from the company he chooses.' / And the pig got up and slowly walked away. [B H Burt, 1880–1950, song: *The Pig Got Up . . .*]

8 There's nought, no doubt, so much the spirit calms / As rum and true religion. [Lord Byron, 1788–1824, *Don Juan*, II, 34]

9 I am willing to taste any drink once. [James Branch Cabell, 1879–1958, *Jurgen*, Ch. 2]

10 Of course you can get a quart into a pint pot – you can get a couple of gallons into it, if you stay till closing time. [Patrick Skene Catling, 1925– , review of J A Simpson's *Concise Oxford Dictionary of Proverbs* in *Spectator*, 8 Jan. 1983]

11 'If I had a water thirst,' replied Sancho, 'there are wells on the road where I could have quenched it.' [Miguel Cervantes, 1547–1616, *Don Quixote*, Pt II, Ch. 24]

12 No animal ever invented anything so bad as drunkenness – or so good as drink. [G K Chesterton, 1874–1936, *All Things Considered*, 'Wine When It is Red']

13 A sober man may become a drunkard through being a coward. A brave man may become a coward through being a drunkard. [G K Chesterton, 1874–1936, *Charles Dickens*, 8]

14 The French tipple all the time and kill their livers, and the Scots drink in bouts and kill their neighbours. [John Crofton, 1912– , at press conference, launching report 'Health Education in the Prevention of Alcohol-related Problems', Edinburgh, 18 Jan. 1985]

15 For why / Should every creature drink but I, / Why, man of morals, tell me why? [Abraham Cowley, 1618–67, *Anacreontic: Drinking*]

16 Then trust me, there's nothing like drinking / So pleasant on this side the grave; / It keeps the unhappy from thinking, / And makes e'en the valiant more brave. [Charles Dibdin, 1745–1814, *Nothing like Grog*]

17 It came like magic in a pint bottle; it was not ecstasy but it was comfort. [Charles Dickens, 1812–70, *Little Dorrit*, Bk 1, Ch. 24]

18 'Mrs Harris,' I says, 'leave the bottle on the chimley-piece, and don't ask me to take none, but let me put my lips to it when I am so dispoged.' [Charles Dickens, 1812–70, *Martin Chuzzlewit*, Ch. 19]

19 Drinking is the soldier's pleasure. [John Dryden, 1631–1700, *Alexander's Feast*, 57]

20 I hate champagne more than anything in the world next to Seven-up. [Elaine Dundy, 1927– , *The Dud Avocado*, Ch. 1]

21 Imagine waking up in the morning and knowing that's as good as you're going to feel all day. [(Of teetotallers) Jimmy Durante, 1893–1980, in S Hoggart, *On the House*, p. 132]

22 I was in love with a beautiful blonde once, dear. She drove me to drink. That's the one thing I'm indebted to her for. [W C Fields, 1879–1946, in *Never Give a Sucker an Even Break*]

23 When he buys his ties he has to ask if gin will make them run. [F Scott Fitzgerald, 1896–1940, *Notebooks*, 'E']

24 First you take a drink, then the drink takes a drink, then the drink takes you. [F Scott Fitzgerald, 1896–1940, in Jules Feiffer, *Ackroyd*, '1964, May 7'. Elsewhere attr. to Sinclair Lewis]

25 A medium vodka dry martini – with a slice of lemon peel. Shaken and not stirred. [Ian Fleming, 1908–64, *Dr No*, Ch. 14]

26 We can drink till all look blue. [John Ford, 1586–1639?, *The Lady's Trial*, IV. ii]

27 A taste for drink, combined with gout, / Had doubled him up for ever. [W S Gilbert, 1836–1911, *The Gondoliers*, 1]

28 Let schoolmasters puzzle their brain, / With grammar, and nonsense, and learning, / Good liquor, I stoutly maintain, / Gives genius a better discerning. [Oliver Goldsmith, 1728–74, *She Stoops to Conquer*, I, song]

29 Another little drink wouldn't do us any harm. [Clifford Grey, 1887–1941, song in musical *The Bing Boys*, 1916]

30 Glass of brandy and water! That is the current but not the appropriate name: ask for a glass of liquid fire and distilled damnation. [Robert Hall, 1764–1831, Gregory, *Life*]

31 Licker talks mighty loud w'en it git loose from de jug. [Joel Chandler Harris, 1848–1908, *Nights with Uncle Remus*, Ch. 34]

32 There are two times when you never can tell what is going to happen. One is when a man takes his first drink; and the other is when a woman takes her latest. [O Henry, 1862–1910, *The Octopus Marooned*]

33 Drink not the third glass which thou canst not tame / When once it is within thee. [George Herbert, 1593–1633, *Church Porch*, 5]

34 Man wants but little drink below, / But wants that little strong. [Oliver Wendell Holmes, 1809–94, *A Song of Other Days* (parody of Goldsmith)]

35 Now is the time for drinking, now the time to beat the earth with unfettered foot. [Horace, 65–8BC, *Odes*, xxxvii, 1]

36 Malt does more than Milton can / To justify God's ways to man. [A E Housman, 1859–1936, *A Shropshire Lad*, 62]

37 Claret is the liquor for boys; port for men; but he who aspires to be a hero ... must drink brandy. [Dr Samuel Johnson, 1709–84, in James Boswell, *Life of J*, 7 Apr. 1779]

38 I've made it a rule never to drink by daylight and never to refuse a drink after dark. [H L Mencken, 1880–1956, in *New York Post*, 18 Sept. 1945]

39 I was born below par to th' extent of two whiskies. [C E Montague, 1867–1928, *Fiery Particles*, 'A Propos des Bottes']

40 It's a long time between drinks. [J M Morehead, 1796–1866, said to the Governor of South Carolina, when Morehead was Governor of North Carolina, and quoted in R L Stevenson, *The Wrong Box*, Ch. 8]

41 Candy is dandy, / But liquor is quicker. [Ogden Nash, 1902–71, *Reflections on Ice-breaking*]

42 Three highballs, and I think I'm St Francis of Assisi. [Dorothy Parker, 1893–1967, *Just a Little One*]

43 I drink for the thirst to come. [François Rabelais, *c.*1492–1553, *Gargantua*, Ch. 5]

44 *Trink* is a panomphaean word. It speaks oracles, that is to say, in all languages. [François Rabelais, *c.*1492–1553, *Pantagruel*, Bk V, Ch. 46]

45 O God! that men should put an enemy in their mouths to steal away their brains. [William Shakespeare, 1564–1616, *Othello*, II. iii. (293)]

46 I'm only a beer teetotaller, not a champagne teetotaller. [George Bernard Shaw, 1856–1950, *Candida*, III]

47 Alcohol is a very necessary article ... It enables Parliament to do things at eleven at night that no sane person would do at eleven in the morning. [George Bernard Shaw, 1856–1950, *Major Barbara*, II]

48 Gin was mother's milk to her. [George Bernard Shaw, 1856–1950, *Pygmalion*, III]

49 There are two things that will be believed of any man whatsoever, and one of them is that he has taken to drink. [Booth Tarkington, 1869–1946, *Penrod*, Ch. 10]

50 Dylan himself once defined an alcoholic as a man you don't like who drinks as much as you do. [Dylan Thomas, 1914–53, in Constantine Fitzgibbon, *Life of D T*, Ch. 6]

51 'I think this calls for a drink' has long been one of our national slogans. [James Thurber, 1894–1961, *Alarms and Diversions*, 'Merry Christmas']

52 Liquor and love / rescue the cloudy sense / banish its despair / give it a home. [William Carlos Williams, 1883–1963, *The World Narrowed to a Point*]

53 It was my Uncle George who discovered that alcohol was a food well in advance of modern medical thought. [P G Wodehouse, 1881–1975, *The Inimitable Jeeves*, Ch. 16]

54 Though in silence, with blighted affection, I pine, / Yet the lips that touch liquor must never touch mine! [George W Young, 1846–1919, *The Lips That Touch Liquor*]

See also BEER, DRUNKENNESS, WINE

DRINK: WEAK

1 Tea, although an Oriental, / Is a gentleman at least; / Cocoa is a cad and coward, / Cocoa is a vulgar beast. [G K Chesterton, 1874–1936, *The Song of Right and Wrong*]

2 [When asked why he never drank water] Fish fuck in it. [W C Fields, 1879–1946; in L Halliwell, *The Filmgoer's Book of Quotes*]

3 I was a little exhausted when I arrived [at the War Office] ... and asked the tall ex-Guards soldier in attendance for a glass of water. 'Certainly, sir: Irish or Scotch?' [Viscount

Haldane, 1856–1928, letter, in Dudley Sommer, *Haldane of Cloan*, Ch. 8]

4 No poems can please for long or live that are written by water-drinkers. [Horace, 65–8 BC, *Epistles*, I, xix, 2]

5 It's not the taste of water I object to. It's the after-effects. [Mgr Ronald Knox, 1888–1957, in *Geoffrey Madam's Notebooks*, ed. J A Gere and John Sparrow, 'Extracts and Summaries']

See also TEA, WATER

DRUGS

1 Cocaine isn't habit-forming. I should know – I've been using it for years. [Tallulah Bankhead, 1903–68; in Lillian Hellman, *Pentimento*, 'Theatre']

2 I'll die young, but it's like kissing God. [Lenny Bruce, 1923–66 (of his drug-taking), in R Neville, *Playpower*]

3 I was seeing what Adam had seen on the morning of his creation – the miracle, moment by moment, of naked existence. [Aldous Huxley, 1894–1963, *The Doors of Perception*]

4 Every form of addiction is bad, no matter whether the narcotic be alcohol or morphine or idealism. [C G Jung 1875–1961, *Memories, Dreams, Reflections*, Ch. 12]

5 If you take the game of life seriously, if you take your nervous system seriously, if you take your sense organs seriously, if you take the energy process seriously, you must turn on, tune in, and drop out. [Timothy Leary, 1920–96, *The Politics of Ecstasy*, Ch. 21]

6 He gives the kids free samples, / Because he knows full well / That today's young innocent faces / Are tomorrow's clientele. [Tom Lehrer, 1928– , song: *The Old Dope Pedlar*]

7 Or have we eaten of the insane root / That takes the reason prisoner? [William Shakespeare, 1564–1616, *Macbeth*, I. iii. 84]

8 Not poppy, nor mandragora, / Nor all the drowsy syrups of the world, / Shall ever medicine thee to that sweet sleep / Which thou owedst yesterday. [*Othello*, III. iii. 331]

9 Stimulate the phagocytes. Drugs are a delusion. [George Bernard Shaw, 1856–1950, *The Doctor's Dilemma*, I]

10 Grass will carry you through times of no money better than money through times of no dope. [Gilbert Shelton, 1939– , motto in strip cartoon 'Fabulous Furry Freak Brothers']

DRUNKENNESS

1 Man, being reasonable, must get drunk; / The best of life is but intoxication. [Lord Byron, 1788–1824, *Don Juan*, II, 179]

2 No animal ever invented anything so bad as drunkenness – or so good as drink. [G K Chesterton, 1874–1936, *All Things Considered*, 'Wine When It is Red']

3 'Tis your country bids! / Gloriously drunk, obey th' important call! [William Cowper, 1731–1800, *The Task*, Bk IV, 509]

4 Of seeming arms to make a short essay, / Then hasten to be drunk, the business of the day. [John Dryden, 1631–1700, *Cymon and Iphigenia*, 407]

5 I've been drunk for about a week now, and I thought it might sober me up to sit in a library. [F Scott Fitzgerald, 1896–1940, *The Great Gatsby*, Ch. 3]

6 There is always hope for a man who, when sober, will not concede or acknowledge that he was ever drunk. [O Henry, 1862–1910, *The Rubaiyat of a Scotch Highball*]

7 A branch of the sin of drunkenness, which is the root of all sins. [King James I, 1566–1625, *A Counterblast to Tobacco*]

8 You know you've had a few too many when you come home and find cold scrambled eggs on top of last night's lamb chops. [Ring Lardner, 1885–1933, in R E Drennan, *Wit's End*]

9 You're not drunk if you can lie on the floor without holding on. [Dean Martin, 1917–95, in Paul Dickson, *Official Rules*]

10 Better sleep with a sober cannibal than a drunken Christian. [Herman Melville, 1819–91, *Moby Dick*, Ch. 3]

11 Not drunk is he who from the floor / Can rise alone and still drink more; / But drunk is he, who prostrate lies, / Without the power to drink or rise. [T L Peacock, 1785–1866, *The Misfortunes of Elphin*, Ch. 3, heading]

12 For sixpence he can get drunk / And be a torero, the government, or a saint. [Peter Redgrove, 1932– , *Malagueño*]

13 But I'm not so think as you drunk I am. [J C Squire, 1884–1958, *Ballade of Soporific Absorption*]

See also DRINK : STRONG

DUTY

1 Fear God, and keep his commandments: for this is the whole duty of man. [Bible, OT, *Ecclesiastes* 12:13]

2 Render therefore unto Caesar the things which are Caesar's; and unto God the things that are God's. [Bible, NT, *St Matthew* 22:21]

3 I know of only one duty, and that is to love. [Albert Camus, 1913–60, *Notebooks*, 1935–42]

4 'Do the duty that lies nearest thee', which thou knowest to be a duty! Thy second duty will already have become clearer. [Thomas Carlyle, 1795–1881, *Sartor Resartus*, Bk ii, Ch. 9]

5 *Faites votre devoir, et laissez faire aux dieux.* – Do your duty, and leave the rest to the gods. [Pierre Corneille, 1606–84, *Horace*, II. viii]

6 Property has its duties as well as its rights. [Thomas Drummond, 1797–1840, letter to Earl of Donoughmore, 22 May 1838]

7 So nigh is grandeur to our dust, / So near is God to man, / When Duty whispers low, *Thou must*, / The youth replies, *I can*. [Ralph Waldo Emerson, 1803–82, *Voluntaries*, 3]

8 Duty is what no one else will do at the moment. [Penelope Fitzgerald, 1916– , *Offshore*, 1]

9 The job of a citizen is to keep his mouth open. [Günter Grass, 1927– ; in *Contradictory Quotations*, ed. M Rogers]

10 A man's gotta do what a man's gotta do. [In film *Shane*, screenplay by A B Guthrie Jr, from novel by Jack Schaefer, but J Steinbeck, *Grapes of Wrath*, Ch. 18, predates]

11 If we believe a thing to be bad, and if we have a right to prevent it, it is our duty to try to prevent it and to damn the consequences. [Lord Milner, 1854–1925, speech in Glasgow, 26 Nov. 1909]

12 Eye Nature's walks, shoot folly as it flies, / And catch the manners living as they rise; / Laugh where we must, be candid where we can; / But vindicate the ways of God to man. [Alexander Pope, 1688–1744, *An Essay on Man*, I, 13]

13 Such duty as the subject owes the prince, / Even such a woman oweth to her husband. [William Shakespeare, 1564–1616, *The Taming of the Shrew*, V. ii. 156]

14 When a stupid man is doing something he is ashamed of, he always declares that it is his duty. [George Bernard Shaw, 1856–1950, *Caesar and Cleopatra*, III]

15 The toppling crags of Duty scaled / Are close upon the shining table-lands / To which our God Himself is moon and sun. [Alfred, Lord Tennyson, 1809–92, *Ode on the Death of the Duke of Wellington*, 8]

16 O hard, when love and duty clash! [Alfred, Lord Tennyson, 1809–92, *The Princess*, I, 273]

17 Stern Daughter of the Voice of God! / O Duty! if that name thou love / Who art a light to guide, a rod / To check the erring and reprove. [William Wordsworth, 1770–1850, *Ode to Duty*]

E

EARS, see LISTENING

EARTH

1 One outstandingly important fact regarding Spaceship Earth, and that is that no instruction book came with it. [Buckminster Fuller, 1895–1983, *Operating Manual for Spaceship Earth*, Ch. 4]

2 Let me enjoy the earth no less / Because the all-enacting Might / That fashioned forth its loveliness / Had other aims than my delight. [Thomas Hardy, 1840–1928, *Let Me Enjoy*]

3 I like terra firma – the more firma, the less terra. [George S Kaufman, 1889–1961; in *Barnes and Noble Book of Quotations*, ed. Robert I Fitzhenry]

4 Above the smoke and stir of this dim spot, / Which men call earth. [John Milton, 1608–74, *Comus*, 5]

5 The earth is nobler than the world we have put upon it. [J B Priestley, 1894–1984, *Johnson over Jordan*, III]

6 This earth is the honey of all beings; all beings the honey of this earth. [Upanishads, 7th cent. BC, *Famous Debates in the Forest*, V]

7 Earth fills her lap with pleasures of her own: / Yearnings she hath in her own natural kind. [William Wordsworth, 1770–1850, *Ode, Intimations of Immortality*, 6]

See also ENVIRONMENT, WORLD

ECCENTRICS

1 All the world is queer save thee and me, and even thou art a little queer. [Robert Owen, 1771–1858, attr., when ending his partnership with William Allen, 1828]

2 Nature hath framed strange fellows in her time: / Some that will evermore peep through their eyes / And laugh like parrots at a bag-piper: / And other of such vinegar aspect / That they'll not show their teeth in way of smile, / Though Nestor swear the jest be laughable. [William Shakespeare, 1564–1616, *The Merchant of Venice*, I. i. 51]

3 Ali . . . could often not purchase a toothbrush without making the act appear eccentric. [Barbara Trapido, 1941– , *Noah's Ark*, 8]

ECONOMICS & THE ECONOMY

1 Our funds are low. We have a deficit to bring down. We have more will than wallet. [George Bush, 1924– , inaugural presidential address, Washington, 20 Jan. 1989]

2 Respectable Professors of the Dismal Science (Of political economy) Thomas Carlyle, 1795–1881, *Latter Day Pamphlets*, 1, 'The Present Time']

3 This would, at a stroke, reduce the rise in prices, increase productivity and reduce unemployment. [Conservative Party, release distributed at press conference, 16 June 1970. Wrongly attr. to Edward Heath at the conference, according to D Butler and A Sloman, *British Political Facts 1900–1975*]

4 Everybody is always in favour of general economy and particular expenditure. [Anthony Eden, 1897–1977; *Observer*, 'Sayings of the Week', 17 June 1956]

5 A completely planned economy ensures that when no bacon is delivered, no eggs are delivered at the same time. [Leo Frain, in *Sunday Telegraph*, Jan. 1965]

6 All races have produced notable economists, with the exception of the Irish who doubtless can protest their devotion to higher arts. [J K Galbraith, 1908– , *The Age of Uncertainty*, Ch. 1]

7 Trickle down theory: the less than elegant metaphor that if one feeds the horse enough oats, some will pass through to the road for the sparrows. [J K Galbraith, 1908– , *The Culture of Contentment*, Ch. 8]

8 Economy is going without something you do want in case you should, some day, want something you probably won't want. [Anthony Hope, 1863–1933, *The Dolly Dialogues*, 12]

9 The Economic Problem, as one may call it for short, the problem of want and poverty and the economic struggle between classes and nations, is nothing but a frightful muddle, a transitory and *unnecessary* muddle. [John Maynard Keynes, 1883–1946, *Essays in Persuasion*, Preface]

10 If the Treasury were to fill old bottles with banknotes, bury them at suitable depths in disused coalmines which are then filled up to the surface with town rubbish, and leave it to private enterprise on well-tried principles of *laissez-faire* to dig the notes up again ... there need be no more unemployment and, with the help of the repercussions, the real income of the community ... would probably become a good deal larger than it actually is. [John Maynard Keynes, 1883–1946, *The General Theory of Employment*, Bk iii, Ch. 10]

11 The ideas of economists and political philosophers, both when they are right and when they are wrong, are more powerful than is commonly understood. Indeed the world is ruled by little else. Practical men, who believe themselves to be quite exempt from any intellectual influences, are usually the slaves of some defunct economist. [John Maynard Keynes, 1883–1946, *The General Theory of Employment*, Bk vi, Ch. 24]

12 'Sound' finance may be right psychologically; but economically it is a depressing influence. [John Maynard Keynes, 1883–1946; *Observer*, 'Sayings of Our Times', 1932]

13 I'm afraid he's at an even greater disadvantage in understanding economics, Prime Minister. He's an economist. [Jonathan Lynn, 1943– , and Antony Jay, 1930– , *Yes Prime Minister*, Vol. 1, 'A Real Partnership']

14 'How do you treat a cold?' One nanny said, 'Feed a cold' – she was a neo-Keynesian. Another nanny said, 'Starve a cold' – she was a monetarist. [Harold Macmillan, 1894–1986, maiden speech in House of Lords at age of ninety, 13 Nov. 1984]

15 A nation is not in danger of financial disaster merely because it owes itself money. [Andrew Mellon, 1855–1937, said in 1933; *Observer*, 'Sayings of Our Times', 31 May 1953]

16 It is an economic axiom as old as the hills that goods and services can be paid for only with goods and services. [A J Nock, 1873–1945, *Memoirs of a Superfluous Man*, III, Ch. 3]

17 Recession is when you have to tighten the belt. Depression is when there is no belt to tighten. We are probably in the next degree of collapse when there are no trousers as such. [Boris Pankin, 1931– ; *Independent*, 'Quote Unquote', 25 July 1992]

18 I have found that people are usually much more moved by economics than by morals. [Norah Phillips, 1910–92; in *Independent*, 'Quote Unquote', 30 Mar. 1991]

19 Being innocent of mathematics, I had to think. [Joan Robinson, 1903–83 (of her economics), in obituary in *New Statesman*, 19 Aug. 1983]

20 Small is Beautiful. [E F Schumacher, 1911–77, title of book subtitled 'A Study of Economics as if People Mattered']

21 If all economists were laid end to end, they would not reach a conclusion. [George Bernard Shaw, 1856–1950, attr.]

22 I was in search of a one-armed economist so that the guy could never make a statement and then say 'on the other hand ...' [Harry Truman, 1884–1972, in *Time* magazine, 30 Jan. 1989]

See also BUSINESS, MONEY, WEALTH

EDEN

1 Adam lay I-bowndyn, bowndyn in a bond, / Fowre thowsand wynter thowt he not to long; / And al was for an appil, an appil that he tok, / As clerkis fyndin wretyn in here book. [anon., *Bless the Time the Apple was Taken!*, 15th cent.]

2 Of Man's first disobedience, and the fruit / Of that forbidden tree, whose mortal taste / Brought death into the world, and all our woe, / With loss of Eden. [John Milton, 1608–74, *Paradise Lost*, Bk i, 1]

3 Some natural tears they dropped, but wiped them soon; / The world was all before them, where to choose / Their place of rest, and Providence their guide: / They hand in hand with wandering steps and slow / Through Eden took their solitary way. [John Milton, 1608–74, *Paradise Lost*, Bk xii, 645]

4 Some flow'rets of Eden ye still inherit, / But the trail of the serpent is over them all! [Thomas Moore, 1779–1852, *Lalla-Rookh*, 'Paradise and the Peri', 206]

5 I sometimes think that if Adam and Eve had been merely engaged, she would not have talked with the serpent; and the world had been saved an infinity of misery. [H G Wells, 1866–1946, *Select Conversations with an Uncle*]

See also HEAVEN, SINS

EDITORS & PUBLISHERS

1 Some said, 'John, print it'; others said, 'Not so.' / Some said, 'It might do good'; others said, 'No'. [John Bunyan, 1628–88, *The Pilgrim's Progress*, Apology for His Book]

2 Now Barabbas was a publisher. [Thomas Campbell, 1777–1844, attr, in Samuel Smiles, *A Publisher and His Friends*. Often also attr. to Byron]

3 He loved to quote the axiom, 'Trust your editor, and you'll sleep on straw.' [John Cheever, 1912–82, in Susan Cheever, *Home before Dark*, Ch. 11]

4 It turned out that, following the Crucifixion, far and away the most commercially successful area of publishing was religious books! Up until 33 AD it had been gardening and desk diaries, but since the Resurrection it had been religion, definitely. [Alan Coren, 1938–   , *The Cricklewood Diet*, 'The Holy Grail']

5 An editor: a person who knows precisely what he wants – but isn't quite sure. [Walter Davenport, 1889–1971, quoted by Bennett Cerf in *Saturday Review Reader*, No. 2]

6 What I have crossed out I didn't like. What I haven't crossed out I'm dissatisfied with. [Cecil B de Mille, 1881–1959 (of a script): attr. in L Halliwell, *The Filmgoer's Book of Quotes*]

7 My own motto is publish and be sued. [Richard Ingrams, 1937–   (as editor of *Private Eye*), in BBC radio programme, 4 May 1977]

8 I respect Millar: he has raised the price of literature. [Dr Samuel Johnson, 1709–84, in James Boswell, *Life of J*, 1755]

9 Read over your compositions, and where ever you meet with a passage which you think is particularly fine, strike it out. [(Quoting a college tutor) Dr Samuel Johnson, 1709–84, in James Boswell, *Life of J*, 30 Apr. 1773]

10 A publisher who writes is like a cow in a milk bar. [Arthur Koestler, 1905–83 (to Anthony Blond); in *The Wit of Publishing*, ed. R Huggett]

11 Publishers can get their minds halfway round anything. [John Le Carré, 1931–   , *The Russia House*, Ch. 5]

12 Gutenberg made everybody a reader. Xerox makes everybody a publisher. [Marshall McLuhan, 1911–80 (from interview in the *Washington Post*), in *Guardian Weekly*, 12 June 1977]

13 Damn it, man, I could cut the Lord's Prayer! [Leonard Rees, 1856–1932, in James Agate, *Ego 1*]

14 The longest-lived editor is the one least distinguishable from his average reader. [Robert Robinson, 1927–   , *Dog Chairman*, 'Our Betters']

15 I don't believe in publishers who wish to butter their bannocks on both sides while they'll hardly allow an author to smell treacle. I consider they are too grabby together and like Methodists they love to keep the Sabbath and everything else they can lay their hands on. [Amanda Ros, 1860–1939, letter to Lord Ponsonby, 1910]

16 On one of Mr Benchley's manuscripts he [Ross] wrote in the margin opposite 'Andromache', 'Who he?' Mr Benchley wrote back. 'You keep out of this.' [Harold Ross, 1892–1951, quoted by Dorothy Parker in *Writers at Work*, ed. Malcolm Cowley, First Series]

17 Publish and be damned. [Duke of

Wellington, 1769–1852 (of Harriette Wilson's *Autobiography*), attr. in Elizabeth Longford, Wellington, *The Years of the Sword*, Ch. 10]

See also BOOKS, LITERATURE

EDUCATION

1 More will mean worse. [Kingsley Amis, 1922–95 (of expansion of higher education), in *Encounter*, July 1960]

2 I had a good education but it never went to my head, somehow. It should be a journey ending up with you at a different place. It didn't take with me. My degree was a kind of inoculation. I got just enough education to make me immune from it for the rest of my life. [Alan Bennett, 1934– , *Getting On*, I]

3 The real struggle is not between East and West, or capitalism and communism, but between education and propaganda. [Martin Buber, 1878–1961, in A Hodes, *Encounter with Martin Buber*]

4 Education makes a people easy to lead, but difficult to drive; easy to govern but impossible to enslave. [Lord Brougham, 1778–1868, attr.]

5 There's a new tribunal now, / Higher than God's – the educated man's! [Robert Browning, 1812–89, *The Ring and the Book*, X, 1975]

6 'Reeling and Writhing, of course, to begin with,' the Mock Turtle replied; 'and then the different branches of Arithmetic – Ambition, Distraction, Uglification, and Derision.' [Lewis Carroll, 1832–98, *Alice in Wonderland*, Ch. 9]

7 Education is a sieve as well as a lift. [Sid Chaplin, 1916–86, *The Day of the Sardine*, Ch. 2]

8 Education is simply the soul of a society as it passes from one generation to another. [G K Chesterton, 1874–1936; *Observer*, 'Sayings of the Week', 6 July 1924]

9 Certainly the prolonged education indispensable to the progress of society is not natural to mankind. [Winston Churchill, 1874–1965, *My Early Life*, Ch. 3]

10 Examinations are formidable even to the best prepared, for the greatest fool may ask more than the wisest man can answer. [Charles Colton, 1780?–1832, *Lacon*, 322]

11 C-l-e-a-n, clean, verb active, to make bright, to scour. W-i-n, win, d-e-r, der, winder, a casement. When the boy knows this out of the book, he goes and does it. [Charles Dickens, 1812–70, *Nicholas Nickleby*, Ch. 8]

12 Education is a state-controlled manufactory of echoes. [Norman Douglas, 1868–1952, *How about Europe?*, p. 29]

13 By education most have been misled; / So they believe, because they so were bred. / The priest continues what the nurse began, / And thus the child imposes on the man. [John Dryden, 1631–1700, *The Hind and the Panther*, 1, 389]

14 Education is the process of casting false pearls before real swine. [Irwin Edman, 1896–1954, in Frank Muir, *Frank Muir Book*]

15 There is much to be said for apathy in education. [E M Forster, 1879–1970, *Maurice*, Ch. 1]

16 'But we don't want to teach 'em,' replied the Badger. 'We want to learn 'em ...' [Kenneth Grahame, 1859–1932, *The Wind in the Willows*, Ch. 11]

17 The aim of education is the knowledge not of fact but of values. [W R Inge, 1860–1954, *The Church in the World*, Oct. 1932]

18 If you educate a man you educate a person, but if you educate a woman you educate a family. [Ruby Manikan (echoing Bishop Fénélon's *Treaty on the Education of Girls*); *Observer*, 'Sayings of the Week', 30 Mar. 1947]

19 Education must have an end in view, for it is not an end in itself. [Sybil Marshall, 1913– , *An Experiment in Education*, Ch. 4]

20 Education costs money, but then so does ignorance. [Claus Moser, 1922– , speech at British Association, Swansea, 20 Aug. 1990]

21 Discussion in class, which means letting twenty young blockheads and two cocky neurotics discuss something that neither their teacher nor they know. [Vladimir Nabokov, 1899–1977, *Pnin*, Ch. 6, x]

22 *All* education is, in a sense, vocational, vocational for living. [John Newsom, 1910–71, 'The Education Women Need', *Observer*, 6 Sept. 1964]

23 He was sent, as usual, to a public school, where a little learning was painfully beaten into him, and from thence to the university, where it was carefully taken out of him. [T L Peacock, 1785–1866, *Nightmare Abbey*, Ch. 1]

24 'Tis education forms the common mind, / Just as the twig is bent, the tree's inclined. [Alexander Pope, 1688–1744, *Moral Essays*, Epistle I, 149]

25 Real education must ultimately be limited to men who insist on knowing, the rest is mere sheep-herding. [Ezra Pound, 1885–1972, *ABC of Reading*, Ch. 8]

26 The well-meaning people who talk about education as if it were a substance distributable by coupon in large or small quantities never exhibit any understanding of the truth that you cannot teach anybody anything that he does not want to learn. [George Sampson, 1873–1950, *Seven Essays*, I, xix]

27 An unlessoned girl, unschooled, unpractised; / Happy in this, she is not yet so old / But she may learn. [William Shakespeare, 1564–1616, *The Merchant of Venice*, III. i. 160]

28 Education: In the holidays from Eton. [Osbert Sitwell, 1892–1969, entry in *Who's Who*, 1929]

29 Education is what survives when what has been learnt has been forgotten. [B F Skinner, 1904–90, in *New Scientist*, 21 May 1964]

30 Education has for its object the formation of character. [Herbert Spencer, 1820–1903, *Social Statics*, II, Ch. 4]

31 Soap and education are not as sudden as a massacre, but they are more deadly in the long run. [Mark Twain, 1835–1910, *The Facts Concerning the Recent Resignation*]

32 Human history becomes more and more a race between education and catastrophe. [H G Wells, 1866–1946, *The Outline of History*, Ch. 15]

33 I can't do with any more education. I was full up years ago. [P G Wodehouse, 1881–1975, *The Code of the Woosters*, Ch. 1]

See also ACADEMICS, SCHOOLS, STUDENTS

EFFICIENCY

1 I do not consider that efficiency need be mated to extreme delicacy or precision of touch . . . It should possess a sweeping gesture – even if that gesture may at moments sweep the ornaments from the mantelpiece. [Harold Nicolson, 1886–1968, *Small Talk*, 'On Being Efficient']

2 There are only two qualities in the world: efficiency and inefficiency; and only two sorts of people: the efficient and the inefficient. [George Bernard Shaw, 1856–1950, *John Bull's Other Island*, IV]

EFFORT

1 The struggle itself towards the heights is enough to fill a man's heart. One must imagine Sisyphus happy. [Albert Camus, 1913–60, *The Myth of Sisyphus*, title essay]

2 Our motto: Life is too short to stuff a mushroom. [Shirley Conran, 1932– , *Superwoman*, epigraph]

3 *Wer immer strebend sich bemüht, / Den können wir erlösen.* – If a man makes continuous efforts, we can save him. [Johann Wolfgang von Goethe, 1749–1832, *Faust*, Pt II, V]

4 'Does the road wind up-hill all the way?' / 'Yes, to the very end.' / 'Will the day's journey take the whole long day?' / 'From morn to night, my friend.' [Christina Rossetti, 1830–94, *Up-Hill*]

5 Don't tell me how talented you are. Tell me how hard you work. [Artur Rubinstein, 1887–1982, in David Dubal, *Evenings with Horowitz*, Ch. 43]

EGO & EGOTISM

1 So take your proper share man, of / Dope and drink: / Aren't you the Chairman of / Ego, Inc? [W H Auden, 1907–73, *Song of the Devil*]

2 Certainly it is the nature of extreme self-lovers, as they will set an house on fire, and it were but to roast their eggs. [Francis Bacon, 1561–1626, *Essays*, 'Of Wisdom for a Man's Self']; see 6

3 *Egotist*, n. A person of low taste, more interested in himself than in me. [Ambrose Bierce, 1842–1914, *The Devil's Dictionary*]

4 It's 'Damn you, Jack – I'm all right!' with you chaps. [Sir David Bone, 1874–1959, *The Brassbounder*, Ch. 3]

5 The land self-interest groans from shore to shore, / For fear that plenty should attain the poor. [Lord Byron, 1788–1824, *The Age of Bronze*, 14]

6 The proud, the cold untroubled heart of stone, / That never mused on sorrow but its own. [Thomas Campbell, 1777–1844, *Pleasures of Hope*, 1, 185]

7 Someone said of a very great egotist: 'He would burn your house down to cook himself a couple of eggs.' [Nicolas-Sébastien Chamfort, 1741–94, *Characters and Anecdotes*]; see 2

8 And therfore, at the kinges court, my brother, / Ech man for him-self, ther is non other. [Geoffrey Chaucer, 1340?–1400, *Canterbury Tales*, 'The Knight's Tale', 323]

9 He never wants anything but what's right and fair; only when you come to settle what's right and fair, it's everything that he wants and nothing that you want. [Thomas Hughes, 1822–96, *Tom Brown's Schooldays*, Pt II, Ch. 2]

10 Shyness is just egoism out of its depth. [Penelope Keith, 1940– ; *Observer*, 'Sayings of the Week', 3 July 1988]

11 You haf too much Ego in your Cosmos. [Rudyard Kipling, 1865–1936, *Life's Handicap*, 'Bertran and Bimi']

12 He's been true to *one* party – an' thet is himself. [James Russell Lowell, 1819–91, *The Biglow Papers*, First Series, 2]

13 No healthy male ever really thinks or talks of anything save himself. [H L Mencken, 1880–1956, *Prejudices*, Fourth Series, 'Reflections on Monogamy', 8]

14 For all the fruitful altruisms of Nature develop in an egotistical mode; human altruism which is not egoism is sterile, it is that of a writer who interrupts his work to receive a friend who is unhappy, to accept some public function or to write propaganda articles. [Marcel Proust, 1871–1922, *Remembrance of Things Past: Time Regained*, Ch. 2]

15 The wretch, concentred all in self, / Living, shall forfeit fair renown, / And, doubly dying, shall go down / To the vile dust from whence he sprung, / Unwept, unhonoured, and unsung. [Sir Walter Scott, 1771–1832, *The Lay of the Last Minstrel*, VI, 1]

See also SELF

ELECTIONS

1 The accursed power which stands on Privilege / (And goes with Women, and Champagne, and Bridge) / Broke – and Democracy resumed her reign: / (Which goes with Bridge, and Women, and Champagne). [Hilaire Belloc, 1870–1953, 'On a General Election']

2 The ballot is stronger than the bullet. [Abraham Lincoln, 1809–65, speech, 19 May 1856]

3 One day the don't-knows will get in, and then where will we be? [(On results of a pre-election poll) Spike Milligan, 1918– , attr.]

4 Indeed, you won the elections, but I won the count. [(To an opponent who accused him of rigging the elections) Anastasio Somoza, 1925–80, in *Guardian*, 17 June 1977]

5 It's not the voting that's democracy, it's the counting. [Tom Stoppard, 1937– , *Jumpers*, I]

6 A candidate should not mean but be. [Gore Vidal, 1925– , *The Best Man*]

7 He stood twice for Parliament, but so diffidently that his candidature passed almost unnoticed. [Evelyn Waugh, 1903–66, *Decline and Fall*, III, 1]

8 I do not aspire to advise my sovereign in her choice of servants. [(On why he didn't vote at elections) Evelyn Waugh, 1903–66, in *A Little Order*, ed. D Gallagher]

9 They [Labour Ministers] are going about the country stirring up complacency. [William Whitelaw, 1918–99 (during 1974 election), in Simon Hoggart, *On the House*, p. 38. Sometimes misquoted as 'stirring up apathy']

10 Never murder a man who is committing suicide. [(Of Governor Hughes's election campaign) Woodrow Wilson, 1856–1924, in John Dos Passos, *Mr W's War*, Pt II, Ch. 10, sect. X]

See also DEMOCRACY, GOVERNMENT, PARLIAMENT, POLITICS

EMBARRASSMENT

1 They are the most embarrassed people in the world, the English. You cannot look each other in the face ... Is there anyone not embarrassed in England? The Queen perhaps. She is not embarrassed. With the rest it's 'I won't make you feel bad as long as you don't make me feel bad.' That is the social contract. Society is making each other feel better. [Alan Bennett, 1934– , *The Old Country*, I

2 Now I am ashamed of confessing that I have nothing to confess. [Fanny Burney, 1752–1840, *Evelina*, letter 59]

3 The question [with Mr Podsnap] was, would it bring a blush into the cheek of the young person? [Charles Dickens, 1812–70, *Our Mutual Friend*, Bk 1, Ch. 11]

4 Ordinary men . . . / Put up a barrage of common sense to baulk / Intimacy but by mistake interpolate / Swear-words like roses in their talk. [Louis MacNeice, 1907–63, *Conversation*]

5 The more things a man is ashamed of, the more respectable he is. [George Bernard Shaw, 1856–1950, *Man and Superman*, I]

6 Into the face of the young man who sat on the terrace of the Hotel Magnifique at Cannes there had crept a look of furtive shame, the shifty, hangdog look which announces that an Englishman is about to talk French. [P G Wodehouse, 1881–1975, *The Luck of the Bodkins*, Ch. 1]

See also GUILT

EMOTIONS

1 We cannot kindle when we will / The fire which in the heart resides, / The spirit bloweth and is still, / In mystery our soul abides. [Matthew Arnold, 1822–88, *Morality*]

2 Those who would make us feel, must feel themselves. [Charles Churchill, 1731–64, *The Rosciad*, 962]

3 If you could see my legs when I take my boots off, you'd form some idea of what unrequited affection is. [Charles Dickens, 1812–70, *Dombey and Son*, Ch. 48]

4 Undisciplined squads of emotion. [T S Eliot, 1888–1965, *Four Quartets*, 'East Coker', V]

5 The only way of expressing emotion in the form of art is by finding an 'objective correlative'; in other words, a set of objects, a situation, a chain of events which shall be the formula of that *particular* emotion. [T S Eliot, 1888–1965, *Selected Essays*, 'Hamlet']

6 But we, how shall we turn to little things / And listen to the birds and winds and streams / Made holy by their dreams / Nor feel the heartbreak in the heart of things? [W W Gibson, 1878–1962, *A Lament*]

7 O for a life of sensations rather than of thoughts! [John Keats, 1795–1821, letter to Benjamin Bailey, 22 Nov. 1817]

8 One may not regard the world as a sort of metaphysical brothel for emotions. [Arthur Koestler, 1905–83, *Darkness at Noon*, 'The Second Hearing', 7]

9 First feelings are always the most natural. [Louis XIV, 1638–1715, reported by Mme de Sévigné]

10 When the heart dictates the line / it sends a slave on to the stage / and there's an end of art and there's / a breath of earth and destiny. [Boris Pasternak, 1890–1960, *Oh, Had I Known*]

11 The young man who has not wept is a savage, and the old man who will not laugh is a fool. [George Santayana, 1863–1952, *Dialogues in Limbo*, Ch. 3]

12 I realized afterwards that it is possible to know everything about our affections except their strength; that is to say, their sincerity. [Jean-Paul Sartre, 1905–80, *Words*, Pt 1]

13 Words may be false and full of art; / Sighs are the natural language of the heart. [Thomas Shadwell, 1642?–92, *Psyche*, III]

14 I wish thar was winders to my Sole, sed I, so that you could see some of my feelins. [Artemus Ward, 1834–67, *A W His Book*, 'The Showman's Courtship']

15 It is so many years before one can believe enough in what one feels even to know what the feeling is. [W B Yeats, 1865–1939, *Autobiographies*, 'Reveries XXX']

See also PASSIONS

EMPIRE

1 The reluctant obedience of distant provinces generally costs more than it is worth. [Lord Macaulay, 1800–1859, *Historical Essays*, 'Lord Mahon's War of the Succession']

2 An empire founded by war has to maintain itself by war. [Baron de Montesquieu, 1689–1755, *Considérations sur les causes de la grandeur des Romains et de leur décadence*, Ch. 8]

3 The sun does not set in my dominions. [(Philip II) Friedrich von Schiller, 1759–1805, *Don Carlos*, I, vi]

4 This agglomeration which was called and still calls itself the Holy Roman Empire was neither holy, nor Roman, nor an empire in any way. [Voltaire, 1694–1778, *Essai sur le moeurs et l'esprit des nations*, lxx]

5 There are two kinds of imperialists – imperialists and bloody imperialists. [Rebecca West, 1892–1983, review in first issue of the *Freewoman*, 23 Nov. 1911]

6 We have fought for our place in the sun and won it. Our future is on the water. [Kaiser Wilhelm II, 1859–1941, speech at Elbe regatta, Hamburg, 18 June 1901, but phrase of earlier origin]

See also BRITISH EMPIRE

ENDS & ENDING

1 Better is the end of a thing than the beginning thereof. [Bible, OT, *Ecclesiastes* 7:8]

2 I am Alpha and Omega, the beginning and the end, the first and the last. [Bible, NT, *Revelation* 22:13]

3 The opera ain't over till the fat lady sings. [Dan Cook, 1926– (from baseball commentary on US TV, Apr. 1978), in *Washington Post*, 11 June 1978. Often wrongly ascr. to Dick Motta, coach of Washington Bullets, who adopted it]

4 Judge not the play before the play be done. [John Davies, 1569–1626, *Respice Finem*]

5 Suppose that we, to-morrow or the next day, / Came to an end – in storm the shafting broken, / Or a mistaken signal, the flange lifting – / Would that be premature, a text for sorrow? [C Day Lewis, 1904–72, *Suppose That We*]

6 In my end is my beginning. [T S Eliot, 1888–1965, *Four Quartets*, 'East Coker', V]

7 This is the way the world ends / Not with a bang but a whimper. [T S Eliot, 1888–1965, *The Hollow Men*, V]

8 The time-honoured bread-sauce of the happy ending. [Henry James, 1843–1916, *Theatricals*, Second Series]

9 On the other square, to the left, was elegantly engraved in capital letters this sentence. ALL THINGS MOVE TO THEIR END. [François Rabelais, *c.*1492–1553, *Pantagruel*, Bk V, Ch. 37]

10 Here is my journey's end, here is my butt, / And very sea-mark of my utmost sail. [William Shakespeare, 1564–1616, *Othello*, V. ii. 266]

11 The end crowns all, / And that old common arbitrator, Time, / Will one day end it. [*Troilus and Cressida*, IV. v. 223]

12 The end may justify the means as long as there is something that justifies the end. [Leon Trotsky, 1874–1940, in A Pozzolini, *Antonio Gramsci: An Introduction to His Thought*, Preface]

ENDURANCE

1 Nothing happens to any man that he is not formed by nature to bear. [Marcus Aurelius, AD 121–80, *Meditations*, V, 18]

2 Where I am, I don't know, I'll never know, in the silence you don't know, you must go on, I can't go on, I'll go on. [Samuel Beckett, 1906–89, *The Unnamable*, last words]

3 He that endureth to the end shall be saved. [Bible, NT, *St Matthew* 10:22]

4 I would say to the House, as I said to those who have joined this Government, 'I have nothing to offer but blood, toil, tears and sweat.' [Winston Churchill, 1874–1965, first speech in House of Commons as Prime Minister, 13 May 1940]

5 Under the bludgeonings of chance / My head is bloody, but unbowed. [W E Henley, 1849–1903, *Invictus*]

6 Tis a lesson you should heed, / Try, try again. / If at first you don't succeed, / Try, try again. [William Edward Hickson, 1803–70, *Try and Try Again*]

7 He saw the cities of many peoples and learnt their ways. He suffered many hardships on the high seas in his struggles to preserve his life and bring his comrades home. [Homer, *c.*900 BC, *Odyssey*, I, 4]

8 The troubles of our proud and angry dust / Are from eternity, and shall not fail. / Bear them we can, and if we can we must. / Shoulder the sky, my lad, and drink your ale. [A E Housman, 1859–1936, *Last Poems*, 9]

9 Always do that, wild duck. Stick at the bottom. Deep as they can get ... And so they never come up again. [Henrik Ibsen, 1828–1906, *The Wild Duck*, II]

10 When the going gets tough, the tough get going. [Joseph Kennedy, 1888–1969, in J H Cutler, *Honey Fitz*, p. 291]

11 Sorrow and silence are strong, and patient endurance is godlike. [H W Longfellow, 1807–82, *Evangeline*, II, 1]

12 Men must endure / Their going hence, even as their coming hither: / Ripeness is all. [William Shakespeare, 1564–1616, *King Lear*, V. ii. 9]

13 Perseverance, dear my lord, / Keeps honour bright: to have done, is to hang / Quite out of fashion, like a rusty mail / In monumental mockery. [*Troilus and Cressida*, III. iii. 150]

14 'Tis known by the name of perseverance in a good cause, – and of obstinacy in a bad one. [Laurence Sterne, 1713–68, *Tristram Shandy*, Vol. 1, Ch. 17]

15 Tho' / We are not now that strength that in old days / Moved earth and heaven: that which we are, we are; / One equal temper of heroic hearts, / Made weak by time and fate, but strong in will / To strive, to seek, to find, and not to yield. [Alfred, Lord Tennyson, 1809–92, *Ulysses*, 65]

16 Endure, and preserve yourselves for better things. [Virgil, 70–19 BC, *Aeneid*, I, 207]

See also FATALISM

ENEMIES

1 [When told a Labour colleague was his own worst enemy] Not while I'm alive, he ain't! [Ernest Bevin, 1881–1951 (there are various candidates for the insult), in Michael Foot, *Aneurin Bevan*, Vol. 2, Ch. 1]

2 Love your enemies. [Bible, NT, *St Matthew* 5:8, 5:44]

3 I wish my deadly foe no worse / Than want of friends, and empty purse. [Nicholas Breton, 1545?–1626?, *A Farewell to Town*]

4 But what if I should discover that the enemy himself is within me, that I myself am the enemy that must be loved – what then? [C G Jung, 1875–1961, attr.]

5 We have met the enemy, and he is us. [Walter Kelly, 1913–73, in strip cartoon 'Pogo', parodying Captain Oliver Hazard Perry (1785–1819), 'We have met the enemy and he is ours', at Battle of Lake Erie, 10 Sept. 1813]; see 4

6 Even a paranoid can have enemies. [Henry Kissinger, 1923– , in *Time* magazine, 24 Jan. 1977. Also ascr. to Delmore Schwartz]

7 The enemy advances, we retreat; the enemy camps, we harass; the enemy tires, we attack; the enemy retreats, we pursue. [Mao Zedong, 1893–1976, letter, 5 Jan. 1930, but in fact quoting a letter from the Front Committee to the Central Committee of the Chinese Communist Party]

8 'Was it a friend or foe that spread these lies?' / 'Nay, who but infants question in such wise? / 'Twas one of my most intimate enemies.' [Dante Gabriel Rossetti, 1828–82, *Fragment*]

9 And the stern joy which warriors feel / In foemen worthy of their steel. [Sir Walter Scott, 1771–1832, *The Lady of the Lake*, V, 10]

10 Heat not a furnace for your foe so hot / That it do singe yourself. [William Shakespeare, 1564–1616, *Henry VIII*, I. i. 140]

11 I have not got a single enemy I would not want. [Norman Tebbit, 1931– ; *Independent*, 'Quote Unquote', 16 Feb. 1991]

12 I'm lonesome. They are all dying. I have hardly a warm personal enemy left. [James McNeill Whistler, 1834–1903, in D C Seitz, *W Stories*]

13 A man cannot be too careful in the choice of his enemies. [Oscar Wilde, 1854–1900, *The Picture of Dorian Gray*, Ch. 1]

See also FRIENDS

ENGLAND IN GENERAL

1 Philistinism! – We have not the expression in English. Perhaps we have not the word because we have so much of the thing. [Matthew Arnold, 1822–88, *Essays in Criticism*, First Series, 'Heinrich Heine']

2 For England, home, and beauty. [Samuel J Arnold, 1774–1852, *The Death of Nelson*]

3 Within these breakwaters English is spoken: without / Is the immense, improbable atlas. [W H Auden, 1907–73, *Dover*]

4 England! awake! awake! awake! / Jerusalem thy sister calls! / Why wilt thou sleep the sleep of death, / And close her from thy ancient walls? [William Blake, 1757–1827, *Jerusalem*, f. 77]

5 I will not cease from mental fight, / Nor shall my sword sleep in my hand, / Till we have built Jerusalem / In England's green and pleasant land. [William Blake, 1757–1827, *Milton*, Preface]

6 Oh, to be in England, / Now that April's there. [Robert Browning, 1812–89, *Home-Thoughts from Abroad*]

7 There are in England sixty different religious sects, but only one sauce. [Attr. to Prince Francesco Caracciolo, 1752–99]

8 In rural England, people live wrapped tight in a cocoon; only their eyes move to make sure that nobody gets more than themselves. [J L Carr, 1912–94, *How Steeple Sinderby Wanderers Won the FA Cup*, Pt 2]

9 And they that rule in England, / In stately conclave met, / Alas, alas for England / They have no graves as yet. [G K Chesterton, 1874–1936, *Elegy in a Country Churchyard*]

10 Be England what she will, / With all her faults, she is my country still. [Charles Churchill, 1731–64, *The Farewell*, 27]

11 This could have occurred nowhere but in England, where men and sea interpenetrate, so to speak. [Joseph Conrad, 1857–1924, *Youth*]

12 England, with all thy faults, I love thee still – / My country! [William Cowper, 1731–1800, *The Task*, Bk II, 206]

13 England is the paradise of women, the purgatory of men, and the hell of horses. [John Florio, 1553?–1625, *Second Fruits*]

14 It will be said of this generation that it found England a land of beauty and left it a land of beauty spots. [C E M Joad, 1891–1953; *Observer*, 'Sayings of Our Times', 31 May 1953]

15 Happy is England, sweet her artless daughters: / Enough their simple loveliness for me. [John Keats, 1795–1821, sonnet: *Happy is England*]

16 Winds of the World, give answer! They are whimpering to and fro – / And what should they know of England who only England know? [Rudyard Kipling, 1865–1936, *The English Flag*]

17 What stands if Freedom fall? / Who dies if England live? [Rudyard Kipling, 1865–1936, *For All We Have and Are*]

18 Attend, all ye who list to hear our noble England's praise; / I tell of the thrice-noble deeds she wrought in ancient days. [Lord Macaulay, 1800–1859, *The Armada*]

19 The history of England is emphatically the history of progress. [Lord Macaulay, 1800–1859, *Historical Essays*, 'Sir J. Mackintosh's History of the Revolution']

20 England is the only country where food is more dangerous than sex. [Jackie Mason, 1931– , *The World According to Me*]

21 In England there is only silence or scandal. [André Maurois, 1885–1967, attr.]

22 In England it is bad manners to be clever, to assert something confidently. It may be your personal view that two and two make four, but you must not state it in a self-assured way, because this is a democratic country and others may be of a different opinion. [George Mikes, 1912–87, *How to be an Alien*]

23 In a world where England is finished and dead: / I do not wish to live. [Alice Duer Miller, 1874–1942, *The White Cliffs*]

24 There is such relish in England for anything that doesn't succeed. [Jonathan Miller, 1934– , interview, in *The Sunday Times*, 4 Dec. 1988]

25 England expects every man will do his duty. [(At the battle of Trafalgar) Horatio, Lord Nelson, 1758–1805, quoted in Robert Southey, *Life of Nelson*, Ch. 9]

26 A family with the wrong members in control – that, perhaps, is as near as one can come to describing England in a phrase. [George Orwell, 1903–50, *The Lion and the Unicorn*, 'The Ruling Class']

27 This is a letter of hate. It is for you my countrymen. I mean those men of my country who have defiled it . . . I only hope it (my hate) will keep me going. I think it will. I think it will sustain me in the last few months. Till then, damn you England. [John Osborne, 1929–94, letter to *Tribune*, 18 Aug. 1961]

28 There'll always be an England / While there's a country lane, / Wherever there's a cottage small / Beside a field of grain. [Ross Parker, 1914–74, and Hughie Charles, 1907–95, song: *There'll Always be an England*]

29 England is the paradise of individuality, eccentricity, heresy, anomalies, hobbies, and humours. [George Santayana, 1863–1952, *Soliloquies in England*, 'The British Character']

30 This England never did, nor never shall, / Lie at the proud foot of a conqueror, / But when it first did help to wound itself: / Now these her princes are come home again, / Come the three corners of the world in arms, / And we shall shock them. Nought shall make us rue / If England to itself do rest but true. [William Shakespeare, 1564–1616, *King John*, V. vii. 112]

31 This royal throne of kings, this sceptered isle, / This earth of majesty, this seat of Mars, / This other Eden, demi-paradise, / This fortress built by Nature for herself / Against infection and the hand of war, / This happy breed of men, this little world, / This precious stone set in the silver sea, / Which serves it in the office of a wall, / Or as a moat defensive to a house, / Against the envy of less happier lands. / This blessed plot, this earth, this realm, this England. [*Richard II*, II. i. 40]

32 England, we love thee better than we know. [R V Trench, 1807–86, *Gibraltar*]

33 In England life is not governed by ideas, ideas are born from life. [Richard von Weizsäcker, 1920– ; *Observer*, 'Sayings of the Week', 6 July 1986]

See next categories, BRITAIN, BRITAIN & OTHERS

ENGLAND: PARTICULAR PLACES

1 One has no great hopes from Birmingham. I always say there is something direful in the sound. [Jane Austen, 1775–1817, *Emma*, 36]

2 When I am living in the Midlands / That are sodden and unkind. [Hilaire Belloc, 1870–1953, *The South Country*]

3 Bournemouth is one of the few English towns that one can safely call 'her'. [John Betjeman, 1906–84, *First and Last Loves*]

4 Come, friendly bombs, and fall on Slough. / It isn't fit for humans now. [John Betjeman, 1906–84, *Slough*]

5 The folk that live in Liverpool, their heart is in their boots; / They go to hell like lambs, they do, because the hooter hoots. [G K Chesterton, 1874–1936, *Me Heart*]

6 Kent, sir – everybody knows Kent – apples, cherries, hops and women. [Charles Dickens, 1812–70, *Pickwick Papers*, 2]

7 God gives all men all earth to love, / But, since man's heart is small, / Ordains for each one spot shall prove / Belovèd over all. / Each to his choice, and I rejoice / The lot has fallen to me / In a fair ground – in a fair ground – / Yea, Sussex by the Sea! [Rudyard Kipling, 1865–1936, *Sussex*]

8 In Cornwall it's Saturday before you realize it's Thursday. [Wilfred Pickles, 1904–78]

9 I am a stranger here in Gloucestershire: / These high wild hills and rough uneven ways / Draw out our miles and make them wearisome. [William Shakespeare, 1564–1616, *Richard II*, II. iii. 3]

See also previous and next categories, BRITAIN, BRITAIN & OTHERS

THE ENGLISH

1 Of all nations in the world the English are perhaps the least a nation of pure philosophers. [Walter Bagehot, 1826–77, *The English Constitution*, Ch. 2]

2 Northerners ... don't live in the north, because the north already lives in them. Penny Lane is in their ears and in their eyes. [(On the death of Russell Harty) Nancy Banks-Smith, 1929– , in *Guardian*, 9 June 1988]

3 I've always said, if you want to outwit an Englishman, touch him when he doesn't want to be touched. [Julian Barnes, 1946– , *Talking It Over*, 7]

4 I haven't been abroad in so long that I almost speak English without an accent. [Robert Benchley, 1889–1945, *Inside Benchley*, 'The Old Sea Rover Speaks']

5 They are the most embarrassed people in the world, the English. You cannot look each other in the face ... Is there anyone not embarrassed in England? The Queen perhaps. She is not embarrassed. With the rest it's 'I won't make you feel bad as long as you don't make me feel bad.' That is the social contract. Society is making each other feel better. [Alan Bennett, 1934– , *The Old Country*, I]

6 I like the English. They have the most rigid code of immorality in the world. [Malcolm Bradbury, 1932– , *Eating People is Wrong*, Ch. 5]

7 The English are polite by telling lies. The Americans are polite by telling the truth. [Malcolm Bradbury, 1932– , *Stepping Westward*, II, 5]

8 Cool, and quite English, imperturbable. [Lord Byron, 1788–1824, *Don Juan*, XIII, 14]

9 An Englishman, / Being flattered, is a lamb;

threatened, a lion. [George Chapman, 1559?–1634, *Alphonsus*, I, ii]

10 Smile at us, pay us, pass us; but do not quite forget. / For we are the people of England, that never have spoken yet. [G K Chesterton, 1874–1936, *The Secret People*]

11 The English never draw a line without blurring it. [Winston Churchill, 1874–1965, speech in House of Commons, 16 Nov. 1948]

12 But mad dogs and Englishmen go out in the midday sun. [Noël Coward, 1899–1973, *Words and Music*, 'Mad Dogs and Englishmen']; see 36

13 It is said, I believe, that to behold the Englishman at his *best* one should watch him play tip-and-run. [Ronald Firbank, 1886–1926, *The Flower Beneath the Foot*, Ch. 14]

14 It is not that the Englishman can't feel – it is that he is afraid to feel. He has been taught at his public school that feeling is bad form. He must not express great joy or sorrow, or even open his mouth too wide when he talks – his pipe might fall out if he did. [E M Forster, 1879–1970, *Abinger Harvest*, 'Notes on the English Character']

15 To an Englishman something is what it is called: to a Scotsman something is what it is. [Epigraph to Lewis Grassic Gibbon and Hugh MacDiarmid, *Scottish Scene*]

16 He is an Englishman! / For he himself has said it, / And it's greatly to his credit, / That he is an Englishman! . . . For he might have been a Roosian, / A French, or Turk, or Proosian, / Or perhaps Ital-ian! / But in spite of all temptations / To belong to other nations, / He remains an Englishman! [W S Gilbert, 1836–1911, *HMS Pinafore*, I, i]

17 If it weren't for his good manners, Leopold could easily pass for an Englishman. [Norman Ginsbury, 1902– , *The First Gentleman*, II, i]

18 *Responsum est, quod Angli vocarentur. At ille: 'Bene,' inquit; 'nam et angelicam habent faciem, et tales angelorum in caelis decet esse coherides.'* – The reply was that they were Angles. 'It is well,' said he, 'for they have the faces of angels, and such should be the co-heirs of the angels in heaven.' [Gregory I, 540–604 (traditionally quoted as '*Non Angli sed Angeli*' – 'Not Angles but Angels'), in The Venerable Bede, *Ecclesiastical History*, II, i]

19 An Englishman is a man who lives on an island in the North Sea governed by Scotsmen. [Philip Guedalla, 1889–1944, *Supers and Supermen*, 'Some More Frenchmen']

20 The English are very good at hiding emotions, but without suggesting there is anything passionate to hide. [David Hare, 1947– , in *Observer Magazine*, 26 May 1989]

21 The English (it must be owned) are rather a foul-mouthed nation. [William Hazlitt, 1778–1830, *On Criticism*]

22 The English don't raise their voices, Arthur, although they may have other vulgarities. [Lillian Hellman, 1905–84, *Pentimento*, 'Arthur W A Cowan']

23 According to the English there are two countries in the world today which are led by adventurers: Germany and Italy. But England, too, was led by adventurers when she built her Empire. Today she is ruled merely by incompetents. [Adolf Hitler, 1889–1945 (to Ciano), in A Bullock, *Hitler*, Pt VI, 6]

24 The men, the young and the clever ones, find it a house . . . with intellectual elbow-room, with freedom of talk. Most English talk is a quadrille in a sentry-box. [Henry James, 1843–1916, *The Awkward Age*, V, 19]

25 When two Englishmen meet, their first talk is of the weather. [Dr Samuel Johnson, 1709–84, *The Idler*, 11]

26 As thorough an Englishman as ever coveted his neighbour's goods. [Charles Kingsley, 1819–75, *The Water Babies*, Ch. 4]

27 It was not preached to the crowd, / It was not taught by the State. / No man spoke it aloud, / When the English began to hate. [Rudyard Kipling, 1865–1936, *The Beginnings*]

28 For Allah created the English mad – the maddest of all mankind! [Rudyard Kipling, 1865–1936, *Kitchener's School*]

29 We do not regard Englishmen as foreigners. We look on them only as rather mad Norwegians. [Halvard Lange, 1902–70; *Observer*, 'Sayings of the Week', 9 Mar. 1957]

30 The English people on the whole are surely the *nicest* people in the world, and everyone makes everything so easy for everybody else, that there is almost nothing to resist at all. [D H Lawrence, 1885–1930, *Dull London*]

31 I do *detest* the Americans. They expect everyone to go to the devil at the same hectic pace as themselves. It takes hundreds of years to do it properly. Look at us [the English]. [John Le Carré, 1931– , *The Tailor of Panama*, Ch. 19]

32 An Englishman's way of speaking absolutely classifies him. / The moment he talks he makes some other Englishman despise him. [Alan Jay Lerner, 1918–86, *My Fair Lady*, I. i, music by Frank Loewe]

33 Of all the sarse that I can call to mind, / England does make the most onpleasant kind: / It's you're the sinner 'ollers, she's the saint; / Wut's good's all English, all thet isn't ain't. [James Russell Lowell, 1819–91, *The Biglow Papers*, Second Series, 2]

34 Here is one of the points about this planet which should be remembered; into every penetrable corner of it, and into most of the impenetrable corners, the English will penetrate. [Rose Macaulay, 1889–1958, *Crewe Train*, Pt 1, Ch. 1]

35 If an Englishman gets run down by a truck he apologizes to the truck. [Jackie Mason, 1931– ; *Observer*, 'Sayings of the Week', 23 Sept. 1990]

36 By midday in Colombo, the heat is so unbearable that the streets are empty save for thousands of Englishmen taking mad dogs for walks. [Spike Milligan, 1918– , *A Dustbin of Milligan*, 'Letters to Harry Secombe', III]; see 12

37 God is decreeing to begin some new and great period in His Church, even to the reforming of the Reformation itself. What does he then but reveal Himself to His servants, and as His manner is, first to His Englishmen? [John Milton, 1608–74, *Areopagitica*]

38 It's one thing being British / but you need a white skin to be English / then you can shout things in public places / at kids with a different complexion. [Tom Paulin, 1949– , *Chucking It Away* (after Heinrich Heine)]

39 But Lord! to see the absurd nature of Englishmen that cannot forbear laughing and jeering at everything that looks strange. [Samuel Pepys, 1633–1703, *Diary*, 27 Nov. 1662]

40 Remember that you are an Englishman, and have consequently won first prize in the lottery of life. [Cecil Rhodes, 1853–1902, in Peter Ustinov, *Dear Me*, Ch. 4]

41 It was always yet the trick of our English nation, if they have a good thing, to make it too common. [William Shakespeare, 1564–1616, *2 Henry IV*, I. ii. (244)]

42 And you, good yeomen, / Whose limbs were made in England, show us here / The mettle of your pasture. [*Henry V*, III. i. 25]

43 Your pious English habit of regarding the world as a moral gymnasium built expressly to strengthen your character in. [George Bernard Shaw, 1856–1950, *Man and Superman*, I]

44 An Englishman thinks he is moral when he is only uncomfortable. [George Bernard Shaw, 1856–1950, *Man and Superman*, III]

45 There is nothing so bad or so good that you will not find an Englishman doing it; but you will never find an Englishman in the wrong. He does everything on principle. He fights you on patriotic principles; he robs you on business principles; he enslaves you on imperial principles. [George Bernard Shaw, 1856–1950, *The Man of Destiny*]

46 How can what an Englishman believes be heresy? It is a contradiction in terms. [George Bernard Shaw, 1856–1950, *St Joan*, IV]

47 As an Englishman does not travel to see Englishmen, I retired to my room. [Laurence Sterne, 1713–68, *A Sentimental Journey*, 'Preface, In the Desobligeant']

48 The English take their pleasures sadly after the fashion of their country. [Duc de Sully, 1559–1641, *Memoirs*]

49 You never find an Englishman among the underdogs – except in England of course. [Evelyn Waugh, 1903–66, *The Loved One*]

50 We must be free or die, who speak the tongue / That Shakespeare spake; the faith and morals hold / Which Milton held. [William Wordsworth, 1770–1850, *National Independence and Liberty*, 1, 16]

See also previous category, BRITAIN, BRITAIN & OTHERS

ENTHUSIASMS

1 It is unfortunate, considering that enthusiasm moves the world, that so few enthusiasts can be trusted to speak the truth. [A J Balfour, 1848–1930, letter to Mrs Drew, 19 May 1891]

2 Nothing great was ever achieved without enthusiasm. [Ralph Waldo Emerson, 1803–82, *Essays*, 'Circles']

3 Tell me what you like, and I'll tell you what you are. [John Ruskin, 1819–1900, quoted by Dennis Potter in *With Great Pleasure*, Vol. II]

4 So long as a man rides his hobby-horse peaceably and quietly along the king's highway, and neither compels you or me to get up behind him, – pray, Sir, what have either you or I to do with it? [Laurence Sterne, 1713–68, *Tristram Shandy*, Vol. I, Ch. 7]

5 In every enthusiast there lurks a false enthusiast; in every lover a feigned lover; in every man of genius a pseudo-genius. [Paul Valéry, 1871–1945, *Suite*, 'Duties']

ENVIRONMENT

1 Think globally, act locally. [anon. ecological slogan quoted by Fritjof Capra]

2 Heredity is just environment stored. [Luther Burbank, 1849–1926; in *A Dictionary of Scientific Quotations*, ed. A L Mackay]

3 If we can stop the sky turning into a microwave oven, we still face the prospect of living in a garbage dump. [Prince Charles, 1948– ; *Independent*, 'Quote Unquote', 11 Mar. 1989]

4 Man is preceded by forest, followed by desert. [Graffito in France during the student revolt, 1968]

5 You talk about walking in the wilderness, but what else *is* the world but that, and besides, aren't we all walking in one kind of wilderness or another, since only we can make them. [James Hanley, 1901–85, *A Walk in the Wilderness*, title story]

6 The world is an increasingly treeless jungle. [Fenella Harrison, 1944– , '"Words of Wisdom" for an Unborn Child'; *The Times*, 21 Apr. 1988]

7 What would the world be, once bereft / Of wet and of wildness? Let them be left, / O let them be left, wildness and wet; / Long live the weeds and the wilderness yet. [Gerard Manley Hopkins, 1844–89, *Inversnaid*]

8 [Environment is] a big, booming, buzzing confusion. [William James, 1842–1910, in Peter F Smith, *The Dynamics of Urbanism*, Ch. 2]

9 President Robbins was so well adjusted to his environment that sometimes you could not tell which was the environment and which was President Robbins. [Randall Jarrell, 1914–65, *Pictures from an Institution*, Pt I, Ch. 4]

10 We should see ourselves as members of a very democratic planetary community and remember that, in a democracy, we can be voted out. [James Lovelock, 1919– , interview in *The Sunday Times*, 1 Oct. 1989]

11 I am I plus my surroundings, and if I do not preserve the latter, I do not preserve myself. [José Ortega y Gasset, 1883–1955, *Meditations of Quixote*, 'To the Reader']

12 Perhaps the immobility of the things that surround us is forced upon them by our conviction that they are themselves and not anything else, by the immobility of our conception of them. [Marcel Proust, 1871–1922, *Remembrance of Things Past: Swann's Way*, 'Overture']

13 The atmosphere knows no boundaries, and the winds carry no passports. [Crispin Tickell, 1930– (on the greenhouse effect); *Independent*, 'Quote Unquote', 13 May 1989]

ENVY

1 I am sure the grapes are sour. [Aesop, *fl c.*550 BC, 'The Fox and the Grapes']

2 Envy and wrath shorten the life. [Bible, Apocrypha, *Ecclesiasticus* 30:24]

3 Thou shalt not covet, but tradition / Approves all forms of competition. [Arthur Hugh Clough, 1819–61, *The Latest Decalogue*]

4 Some folks rail against other folks, because other folks have what some folks would be glad of. [Henry Fielding, 1707–54, *Joseph Andrews*, iv, 6]

5 Oh! how bitter a thing it is to look into happiness through another man's eyes. [William Shakespeare, 1564–1616, *As You Like It*, V. ii. (48)]

6 He hath a daily beauty in his life / That makes me ugly. [*Othello*, V. i. 19]

7 An envious fever / Of pale and bloodless emulation. [*Troilus and Cressida*, I. iii. 133]

See also COMPETITION, JEALOUSY

EPIGRAMS

1 One cannot dictate an aphorism to a typist. It would take far too long. [Karl Kraus, 1874–1936, *Half-truths and One-and-a-half Truths*, 'Riddles']

2 An aphorism never coincides with the truth: it is either a half-truth or one-and-a-half truths. [Karl Kraus, 1874–1936, *Half-truths and One-and-a-half Truths*, 'Riddles']

3 There are aphorisms that, like airplanes, stay up only while they are in motion. [Vladimir Nabokov, 1899–1977, *The Gift*, Ch. 1]

4 If, with the literate, I am / Impelled to try an epigram, / I never seek to take the credit; / We all assume that Oscar said it. [Dorothy Parker, 1893–1967, *Oscar Wilde*]

5 A proverb is one man's wit and all men's wisdom. [Lord John Russell, 1792–1878, attr. in R J Mackintosh, *Sir James Macintosh*, Vol. 2, Ch. 7]

EPITAPHS

1 Here lies Fred, / Who was alive and is dead: / Had it been his father, / I had much rather; / Had it been his brother, / Still better than another; / Had it been his sister, / No one would have missed her; / Had it been the whole generation, / Still better for the nation: / But since 'tis only Fred, / Who was alive and is dead, – / There's no more to be said. [anon., quoted in Horace Walpole, *Memoirs of George II*]

2 Little Willie from his mirror / Licked the mercury right off, / Thinking in his childish error, / It would cure the whooping cough. / At the funeral his mother / Smartly said to Mrs Brown: / 'Twas a chilly day for Willie / When the mercury went down.' [anon., *Willie's Epitaph*]

3 A very gallant gentleman. [E L Atkinson, 1882–1929, and Apsley Cherry-Garrard, 1866–1959, inscription on the burial-place of Captain Oates in the Antarctic, 1912]

4 Of this bad world the loveliest and best / Has smiled and said 'Good Night', and gone to rest. [Hilaire Belloc, 1870–1953, 'On a Dead Hostess']

5 When I am dead, I hope it may be said: / 'His sins were scarlet, but his books were read.' [Hilaire Belloc, 1870–1953, 'On His Books']

6 When Sir Joshua Reynolds died / All Nature was degraded; / The King dropped a tear in the Queen's ear, / And all his pictures faded. [William Blake, 1757–1827, *On Art and Artists*]

7 I never gave away anything without wishing I had kept it; nor kept anything without wishing I had given it away. [(Suggesting her own epitaph) Louise Brooks, 1908–85, in Kenneth Tynan, *Show People*]

8 Underneath this sable hearse / Lies the subject of all verse: / Sidney's sister, Pembroke's mother: / Death, ere thou hast slain another, / Fair, and learned, and good as she, / Time shall throw a dart at thee. [William Browne, 1590?–1643, *Epitaph on the Dowager Countess of Pembroke*]

9 Here lie Willie Michie's banes; / O Satan, when ye tak him, / Gie him the schoolin' of your weans, / For clever deils he'll mak them! [Robert Burns, 1759–96, *Epitaph on a Schoolmaster*]

10 With death doomed to grapple, / Beneath this cold slab, he / Who lied in the chapel / Now lies in the Abbey. [Lord Byron, 1788–1824, *Epitaph for William Pitt*]

11 Oh! snatched away in beauty's bloom, / On thee shall press no ponderous tomb. [Lord Byron, 1788–1824, 'Oh! Snatched Away']

12 Betwixt the stirrup and the ground / Mercy I asked, mercy I found. [William Camden, 1551–1623, *Epitaph for a Man Killed by Falling from His Horse*]

13 Good to the poor, to kindred dear, / To servants kind, to friendship clear, / To nothing but herself severe. [Thomas Carew, 1595?–1639, *Inscription on the Tomb of Lady Mary Wentworth*]

14 Here, a sheer hulk, lies poor Tom Bowling, / The darling of our crew . . . Faithful, below, he did his duty; / But now he's gone aloft. [Charles Dibdin, 1745–1814, *Tom Bowling*]

15 Here lies my wife: here let her lie! / Now she's at rest, and so am I. [John Dryden, 1631–1700, *Epitaph Intended for His Wife*]

16 Under this stone, reader, survey / Dead Sir John Vanbrugh's house of clay. / Lie heavy on him, Earth! For he / Laid many heavy loads on thee! [Abel Evans, 1679–1737, *Epitaph*]

17 On the whole I would rather be in Philadelphia. [W C Fields, 1879–1946, supposed epitaph, in *Vanity Fair*, June 1925]

18 Dere's no more work for poor old Ned, / He's gone whar de good niggers go. [Stephen Foster, 1826–64, *Old Ned*]

19 I would have written of me on my stone: / I had a lover's quarrel with the world. [Robert Frost, 1874–1963, *Epitaph*]

20 Here lies Nolly Goldsmith, for shortness called Noll, / Who wrote like an angel, but talked like poor Poll. [David Garrick, 1717–79, *Impromptu Epitaph*]

21 Life is a jest; and all things show it. / I thought so at once; but now I know it. [John Gay, 1685–1732, *My Own Epitaph*]

22 The king himself has followed her, – / When she has walked before. [Oliver Goldsmith, 1728–74, *Elegy on Mrs Mary Blaize*]

23 Too poor for a bribe, and too proud to importune, / He had not the method of making a fortune. [Thomas Gray, 1716–71, *Sketch of His Own Character*]

24 When the Present has latched its postern behind my tremulous stay, / And the May month flaps its glad green leaves like wings, / Delicate-filmed as new-spun silk, will the neighbours say, / 'He was a man who used to notice such things'? [Thomas Hardy, 1840–1928, *Afterwards*]

25 God give me work while I may live and life till my work is done. [Winifred Holtby, 1898–1935, inscription on her grave]

26 His foe was folly and his weapon wit. [Anthony Hope, 1863–1933, inscription on tablet to Sir W S Gilbert]

27 Their shoulders held the skies suspended; / They stood, and earth's foundations stay; / What God abandoned, these defended, / And saved the sum of things for pay. [A E Housman, 1859–1936, *Last Poems*, 37, 'Epitaph on an Army of Mercenaries']

28 His fall was destined to a barren strand, / A petty fortress, and a dubious hand; / He left the name, at which the world grew pale, / To point a moral, or adorn a tale. [Dr Samuel Johnson, 1709–84, *The Vanity of Human Wishes*, 219]

29 In lapidary inscriptions a man is not upon oath. [Dr Samuel Johnson, 1709–84, in James Boswell, *Life of J*, 1775]

30 Oliver Goldsmith, poet, naturalist, and historian, who left hardly any style of writing untouched, and touched nothing that he did not adorn. [(epitaph) Dr Samuel Johnson, 1709–84, in James Boswell, *Life of J*, 22 June 1776]

31 Underneath this stone doth lie / As much beauty as could die. [Ben Jonson, 1573–1637, *Epitaph on Elizabeth L. H.*]

32 God finally caught his eye. [George S Kaufman, 1889–1961, mock epitaph on a waiter; in *Portable Curmudgeon*, comp. J Winokur, but also used in poem by D McCord, 1935]

33 Here lies one whose name was writ in water. [John Keats, 1795–1821, epitaph, written by himself]

34 They rest awhile in Zion, / Sit down and smile in Zion; / Ay, even jest in Zion; / In Zion, at their ease. [Rudyard Kipling, 1865–1936, *Zion, 1914–18*]

35 I cannot be grasped in this world, for I am as much at home with the dead as with the yet unborn – a little closer to the heart of creation than is usual, if still not close enough. [Paul Klee, 1879–1940, extract from *Diary*, inscribed on his grave as an epitaph]

36 Commit no thesis. [John Knappswood, 1903–89, inscription for a poet's tomb]

37 Riddle of destiny, who can show / What thy short visit meant, or know / What thy errand here below? [Charles Lamb, 1775–1834, *On an Infant Dying as soon as Born*]

38 Child of a day, thou knowest not / The tears that overflow thy urn. [Walter Savage Landor, 1775–1864, *Child of a Day*]

39 De mortuis nil nisi bunkum. [Harold Laski, 1893–1950, attr.]

40 Jack chose death, or shall we say another form of rebirth. He went like a conqueror, not the vanquished. He went with the illuminated smile of one who has chosen well. [Charmian London (epitaph on her husband's suicide), quoted in Alex Kershaw, *Jack London: A Life*]

41 By those white cliffs I never more must see, / By that dear language which I spake like thee, / Forget all feuds, and shed one English tear / O'er English dust. A broken heart lies here. [Lord Macaulay, 1800–1859, *A Jacobite's Epitaph*]

42 A cheat, a thief, a swearer and blasphemer, who smelt of the rope from a hundred yards away, but for the rest the best lad in the world. [Clément Marot, 1499–1544, *Epîtres*, XXIX]

43 As long as he lived, he was the guiding-star of a whole brave nation, and when he died the little children cried in the streets. [(William the Silent) J L Motley, 1814–77, *The Rise of the Dutch Republic*, Pt VI, Ch. 7]

44 Beneath this slab / John Brown is stowed. / He watched the ads, / And not the road. [Ogden Nash, 1902–71, *Lather as You Go*]

45 For all the Brothers were valiant, and all the Sisters virtuous. [Margaret, Duchess of Newcastle, 1624?–73, her epitaph in Westminster Abbey]

46 He lies below, correct in cypress wood, / And entertains the most exclusive worms. [Dorothy Parker, 1893–1967, *Epitaph for a Very Rich Man*]

47 This is on me. [(Suggested epitaph for her own tombstone) Dorothy Parker, 1893–1967, in J Keats, *You Might as Well Live*, Pt 1, Ch. 5]

48 Excuse my dust. [(Alternative epitaph) Dorothy Parker, 1893–1967, in Alexander Woollcott, *While Rome Burns*, 'Our Mrs Parker']

49 In wit a man; simplicity a child. [Alexander Pope, 1688–1744, *Epitaph on Gay*]

50 Nobles and heralds, by your leave, / Here lies what once was Matthew Prior; / The son of Adam and of Eve, / Can Bourbon or Nassau go higher? [Matthew Prior, 1664–1721, *Epitaph on Himself*]

51 Do not despair / For Johnny Head-in-Air. / He sleeps as sound / As Johnny Underground. [John Pudney, 1909–77, lines scribbled on an envelope during an air raid in 1941, and later used for film *The Way to the Stars*]

52 Here lies a lady of beauty and high degree. / Of chills and fevers she died, of fever and chills. [John Crowe Ransom, 1888–1974, *Here Lies a Lady*]

53 Here lies our sovereign lord the king / Whose promise none relies on; / He never said a foolish thing, / Nor ever did a wise one. [Earl of Rochester, 1647–80, *Epitaph on Charles II*. Various forms exist]

54 Oh! she was good as she was fair. / None – none on earth above her! / As pure in thought as angels are, / To know her was to love her. [Samuel Rogers, 1763–1855, *Jacqueline*, I, 68]

55 Now boast thee, death, in thy possession lies / A lass unparalleled. [(Of Cleopatra) William Shakespeare, 1564–1616, *Antony and Cleopatra*, V. ii. (317)]

56 He was a man, take him for all in all, / I shall not look upon his like again. [*Hamlet*, I. ii. 187]

57 What! old acquaintance! could not all this flesh / Keep in a little life? Poor Jack, farewell / I could have better spared a better man. [(Of Falstaff) *1 Henry IV*, V. iv. (102)]

58 This was the noblest Roman of them all. / All the conspirators save only he / Did that they did in envy of great Caesar. [(Of Brutus) *Julius Caesar*, V. v. 68]

59 His life was gentle, and the elements / So mixed in him that Nature might stand up, / And say to all the world, 'This was a man!' [(Of Brutus) *Julius Caesar*, V. v. 73]

60 Good friend, for Jesu's sake forbear / To dig the dust enclosèd here. / Blest be the man that spares these stones, / And curst be he that moves my bones. [William Shakespeare, 1564–1616, his epitaph]

61 He went, unterrified, / Into the gulf of death; but his clear sprite / Yet reigns o'er earth; the third among the sons of light. [(Of Keats) P B Shelley, 1792–1822, *Adonais*, 34]

62 Through the unheeding many he did move, / A splendour among shadows, a bright blot / Upon this gloomy scene, a spirit that strove / For truth, and like the preacher found it not. [P B Shelley, 1792–1822, sonnet: *Lift not the Painted Veil*]

63 Go, tell the Spartans, thou who passest by, / That here obedient to their laws we lie. [Simonides, *c.*556–468 BC, on the Spartan dead at the Battle of Thermopylae, 480 BC]

64 She [Eleanor Roosevelt] would rather light candles than curse the darkness, and her glow has warmed the world. [Adlai Stevenson, 1900–1965, address to the United Nations General Assembly, 7 Nov. 1962, on her death]

65 Under the wide and starry sky, / Dig the grave and let me lie. / Glad did I live and gladly die, / And I laid me down with a will. / This be the verse you grave for me: / 'Here he lies where he longed to be; / Home is the sailor, home from sea, / And the hunter home from the hill.' [Robert Louis Stevenson, 1850–94, *Underwoods*, 21, 'Requiem']

66 *Ubi saeva indignatio ulterius cor lacerare*

nequit. – Where fierce indignation can no longer tear his heart. [Jonathan Swift, 1677–1745, his epitaph]

67 Bury the Great Duke / With an empire's lamentation. [Alfred, Lord Tennyson, 1809–92, *Ode on the Death of the Duke of Wellington*, 1]

68 This is where the real fun starts. [Ben Travers, 1886–1980, suggested epitaph, in *Listener*, 31 Dec. 1981]

69 Lovely Pamela, who found / One sure way to get around / Goes to bed beneath this stone / Early, sober, and alone. [Richard Usborne, 1907– , *Epitaph on a Party Girl*]

70 Of this blest man, let his just praise be given, / Heaven was in him before he was in heaven. [Izaak Walton, 1593–1683, written in Dr Richard Sibbes, *Returning Backslider*]

71 I always thought I'd like my tombstone to be blank. No epitaph, and no name. Well, actually I'd like it to say 'figment'. [Andy Warhol, 1927–87, *America*]

72 ... my epitaph. That, when the time comes, will manifestly have to be: 'I told you so. You *damned* fools.' (The italics are mine.) [H G Wells, 1866–1946, in *The War of the Worlds*, Preface (1941; originally written 1907)]

73 [When asked what she wanted to be remembered for] Everything. [Mae West, 1892–1980, in *Observer*, 30 Nov. 1969]

74 The rapt one, of the godlike forehead, / The heaven-eyed creature sleeps in earth: / And Lamb, the frolic and the gentle, / Has vanished from his lonely hearth. [William Wordsworth, 1770–1850, *Extempore Effusion upon the Death of James Hogg*]

75 Three years she grew in sun and shower, / Then Nature said, 'A lovelier flower / On earth was never sown; / This child I to myself will take: / She shall be mine, and I will make / A Lady of my own.' [William Wordsworth, 1770–1850, *Three Years She Grew*]

76 He first deceased; she for a little tried / To live without him: liked it not, and died. [Henry Wotton, 1568–1639, *Upon the Death of Sir Albert Morton's Wife*]

EQUALITY

1 His lordship may compel us to be equal upstairs, but there will never be equality in the servants' hall. [James Barrie, 1860–1937, *The Admirable Crichton*, I]

2 All service ranks the same with God – / With God, whose puppets, best and worst, / Are we: there is no last or first. [Robert Browning, 1812–89, *Pippa Passes*, IV, 113]

3 All places are distant from heaven alike. [Robert Burton, 1577–1640, *The Anatomy of Melancholy*, II, §2, Memb. 3]

4 Never mind, dear, we're all made the same, though some more than others. [Noël Coward, 1899–1973, *Collected Sketches and Lyrics*, 'The Café de la Paix']

5 The trouble with treating people as equals is that the first thing you know they may be doing the same thing to you. [Peter de Vries, 1910–93, *The Prick of Noon*, Ch. 1]

6 When the Lord sent me forth into the world, He forbade me to put off my hat to any, high or low. [George Fox, 1624–90, *Journal*, 1649]

7 When everyone is somebodee, / Then no one's anybody. [W S Gilbert, 1836–1911, *The Gondoliers*, II]

8 Pale Death knocks with impartial foot at poor men's hovels and kings' palaces. [Horace, 65–8 BC, *Odes*, iv, 13]

9 We hold these truths to be sacred and undeniable; that all men are created equal and independent, that from that equal creation they derive rights inherent and inalienable, among which are the preservation of life, and liberty, and the pursuit of happiness. [Thomas Jefferson, 1743–1826, original draft for the American Declaration of Independence]

10 Your levellers wish to level *down* as far as themselves; but they cannot bear levelling *up* to themselves. [Dr Samuel Johnson, 1709–84, in James Boswell, *Life of J*, 21 July 1763]

11 i do not care / what a dogs / pedigree may be . . . / millionaires and / bums taste / about alike to me [Don Marquis, 1878–1937, *archy and mehitabel*, XII, 'certain maxims of archy']

12 All animals are equal, but some animals are more equal than others. [George Orwell, 1903–50, *Animal Farm*, Ch. 10]

13 I believe in equality. Bald men should marry bald women. [Fiona Pitt-Kethley, 1954– , interview in *Guardian*, 21 Nov. 1990]

14 The poorest he that is in England hath a life to live as the greatest he. [Thomas Rainborowe, 1598–1648, *Army Debates at Putney*, 29 Oct. 1647]

15 The self-same sun that shines upon his court / Hides not his visage from our cottage, but / Looks on alike. [William Shakespeare, 1564–1616, *The Winter's Tale*, IV. iii. (457)]

16 We who are liberal and progressive know that the poor are our equals in every sense except that of being equal to us. [Lionel Trilling, 1905–75, *The Liberal Imagination*, 'Princess Casamassima']

17 The constitution does not provide for first and second class citizens. [Wendell Willkie, 1892–1944, *An American Programme*, Ch. 2]

18 Everybody should have an equal chance – but they shouldn't have a flying start. [Harold Wilson, 1916–95; *Observer*, 'Sayings of the Year', 1963]

19 Brothers all / In honour, as in one community, / Scholars and gentlemen. [William Wordsworth, 1770–1850, *The Prelude*, IX, 227]

See also INEQUALITY

EQUANIMITY

1 He was outwardly decent and managed to preserve his aquarium, but inside he was impromptu and full of unexpectedness. [O Henry, 1862–1910, *The Octopus Marooned*]

2 Remember, when life's path is steep, to keep an even mind. [Horace, 65–8 BC, *Odes*, II, iii, 1]

3 You're like a pay toilet, aren't you? You don't give a shit for nothing. [Howard Hughes, 1905–76 (to Robert Mitchum), quoted by Mitchum in interview in *Observer*, 5 Feb. 1989]

4 A man that fortune's buffets and rewards / Hast ta'en with equal thanks; and blessed are those / Whose blood and judgement are so well co-mingled / That they are not a pipe for fortune's finger / To sound what stop she please. [William Shakespeare, 1564–1616, *Hamlet*, III. ii (72)]

See also CALM, PATIENCE

ETERNITY

1 'Tis heaven itself, that points out an hereafter, / And intimates eternity to man. / Eternity! thou pleasing, dreadful thought! [Joseph Addison, 1672–1719, *Cato*, V. i. 8]

2 For a thousand years in thy sight are but as yesterday when it is past, and as a watch in the night. [Bible, OT, *Psalms* 90:4]

3 Eternity is in love with the productions of time. [William Blake, 1757–1827, *The Marriage of Heaven and Hell*, 'Proverbs of Hell']

4 Spend in pure converse our eternal day; / Think each in each, immediately wise; / Learn all we lacked before; hear, know, and say / What this tumultuous body now denies; / And feel, who have laid our groping hands away; / And see, no longer blinded by our eyes. [Rupert Brooke, 1887–1915, sonnet: *Not with Vain Tears*]

5 He said, 'What's time? Leave Now for dogs and apes! / Man has Forever.' [Robert Browning, 1812–89, *A Grammarian's Funeral*, 83]

6 Little drops of water, little grains of sand, / Make the mighty ocean, and the pleasant land. / So the little minutes, humble though they be, / Make the mighty ages of eternity. [Julia Carney, 1823–1908, *Little Things*. Wrongly attr. to various other writers]

7 Our journey had advanced; / Our feet were almost come / To that odd fork in Being's road, / Eternity by term. [Emily Dickinson, 1830–86, *Our Journey Had Advanced*]

8 That is the road we all have to take – over the Bridge of Sighs into eternity [Søren Kierkegaard, 1813–55, in W H Auden, *A Kierkegaard Anthology*, p. 23]

9 And here we have, incidentally, lighted upon the cause of the Circuit of the All; it is a movement which seeks perpetuity by way of futurity. [Plotinus, AD 205–70, *Enneads*, III, 7]

10 In the sweet by-and-by, / We shall meet on that beautiful shore. [Ira D Sankey, 1840–1908, 'Sweet By-and-by']

11 The one remains, the many change and pass; / Heaven's light forever shines, earth's shadows fly; / Life, like a dome of many-coloured glass, / Stains the white radiance of eternity. [P B Shelley, 1792–1822, *Adonais*, 460]

12 We feel and know that we are eternal. [Benedict Spinoza, 1632–77, *Ethics*, Pt V, 23, note]

13 Eternity is a terrible thought. I mean,

where's it going to end? [Tom Stoppard, 1937– , *Rosencrantz and Guildenstern are Dead*, II]

14 I dimly guess what Time in mists confounds; / Yet ever and anon a trumpet sounds / From the hid battlements of Eternity. [Francis Thompson, 1859–1907, *The Hound of Heaven*, 143]

15 The corn was orient and immortal wheat, which never should be reaped, nor was ever sown. I thought it had stood from everlasting to everlasting. [Thomas Traherne, 1637?–74, *Centuries of Meditations*, iii, 3]

16 I saw Eternity the other night / Like a great ring of pure and endless light, / All calm, as it was bright, / And round beneath it, Time in hours, days, years, / Driv'n by the spheres / Like a vast shadow moved; in which the world / And all her train were hurled. [Henry Vaughan, 1622–95, *The World*]

17 And pluck till time and times are done / The silver apples of the moon, / The golden apples of the sun. [W B Yeats, 1865–1939, *The Song of Wandering Aengus*]

See also IMMORTALITY, INFINITY

ETHICS, see MORALS

EUROPE

1 We must build a kind of United States of Europe. [Winston Churchill, 1874–1965, speech in Zürich, 19 Sept. 1946]

2 *Europe des patries.* – Europe of the fatherlands. [Michel Debré, 1912–96, speech on taking office as Prime Minister of France, 15 Jan. 1959. Often falsely ascr. to General de Gaulle]

3 The Continent will not suffer England to be the workshop of the world. [Benjamin Disraeli, 1804–81, speech in House of Commons, 15 Mar. 1838]

4 What else is Europe but a conglomeration of mistakes? Mistakes that are so diverse that they complement and balance one another. Taken separately, we're each unbearable in our own way. [Hans Magnus Enzensberger, 1929– , *Europe, Europe*, 'Polish Incidents']

5 Their [the Conservatives'] Europeanism is nothing but imperialism with an inferiority complex. [Denis Healey, 1917– ; *Observer*, 'Sayings of the Week', 7 Oct. 1962]

6 I decided that Europeans and Americans are like men and women: they understand each other worse, and it matters less, than either of them suppose. [Randall Jarrell, 1914–65, *Pictures from an Institution*, Pt IV, Ch. 10]

7 When an American heiress wants to buy a man, she at once crosses the Atlantic. The only really materialistic people I have ever met have been Europeans. [Mary McCarthy, 1912–89, *On the Contrary*, 'America the Beautiful']

8 The immense popularity of American movies abroad demonstrates that Europe is the unfinished negative of which America is the proof. [Mary McCarthy, 1912–89, *On the Contrary*, 'America the Beautiful']

9 What happened at Brussels yesterday was bad, bad for us, bad for Europe and bad for the whole free world. [(On General de Gaulle's vetoing Britain's entry to the European Community) Harold Macmillan, 1894–1986, TV broadcast, 15 Jan. 1963]

10 The only places John likes on the Continent are those in which it's only by an effort of the imagination that you can tell you're not in England. [W Somerset Maugham, 1874–1965, *The Constant Wife*, III]

11 England has saved herself by her exertions; and will, as I trust, save Europe by her example. [William Pitt the Younger, 1759–1806, speech in Guildhall, London, 9 Nov. 1805]

12 Roll up that map [of Europe]; it will not be wanted these ten years. [William Pitt the Younger, 1759–1806, said in Dec. 1805, after Napoleon's victory at Austerlitz]

13 It [Europe] will be a gay world. There will be lights everywhere except in the minds of men, and the fall of the last civilization will not be heard above the din. [Herbert Read, 1893–1968, in Richard Hoggart and Douglas Johnson, *An Idea of Europe*]

14 In America everything goes and nothing matters, while in Europe nothing goes and everything matters. [Philip Roth, 1933– , interview in *Time* magazine, Nov. 1983]

15 We are part of the community of Europe and we must do our duty as such. [Lord Salisbury, 1830–1903, speech at Caernarvon, 10 Apr. 1888]

16 Better fifty years of Europe than a cycle of Cathay. [Alfred, Lord Tennyson, 1809–92, *Locksley Hall*, 184]

17 That Europe's nothin' on earth but a great big auction, that's all it is. [Tennessee Williams, 1911–83, *Cat on a Hot Tin Roof*, I]

See also individual European countries

EVENING

1 *Voici le soir charmant, ami du criminel ; / Il vient comme un complice, – pas de loup.* – Here is the charming evening, the criminal's friend. It comes like an accomplice, with stealthy tread. [Charles Baudelaire, 1821–67, *Le Crépuscule du soir*]

2 Where the quiet-coloured end of evening smiles, / Miles and miles. [Robert Browning, 1812–89, *Love among the Ruins*, 1]

3 Rise up, lads, the evening is coming. The evening star is just raising his long-awaited light in heaven. [Catullus, 87–54 ? BC, *Carmina*, 62]

4 While now the bright-haired sun / Sits in yon western tent, whose cloudy skirts, / With brede ethereal wove, / O'erhang his wavy bed : / Now air is hushed, save where the weak-eyed bat, / With short shrill shriek flits by on leathern wing, / Or where the beetle winds / His small but sullen horn. [William Collins, 1721–59, *Ode to Evening*]

5 When the evening is spread out against the sky / Like a patient etherised upon a table. [T S Eliot, 1888–1965, *Love Song of J. Alfred Prufrock*]

6 The curfew tolls the knell of parting day, / The lowing herd winds slowly o'er the lea, / The ploughman homeward plods his weary way, / And leaves the world to darkness and to me. [Thomas Gray, 1716–71, *Elegy Written in a Country Churchyard*, 1]

7 Day has put on his jacket, and around / His burning bosom buttoned it with stars. [Oliver Wendell Holmes, 1809–94, *Evening*]

8 Queen and huntress, chaste and fair, / Now the sun is laid to sleep, / Seated in thy silver chair, / State in wonted manner keep : / Hesperus entreats thy light, / Goddess, excellently bright. [Ben Jonson, 1573–1637, *Cynthia's Revels*, V. iii]

9 Between the dark and the daylight, / When the night is beginning to lower, / Comes a pause in the day's occupations, / That is known as the Children's Hour. [H W Longfellow, 1807–82, *The Children's Hour*]

10 The cares that infest the day / Shall fold their tents, like the Arabs, / And as silently steal away. [H W Longfellow, 1807–82, *The Day is Done*]

11 When the grey-hooded Ev'n / Like a sad votarist in palmer's weed, / Rose from the hindmost wheels of Phoebus' wain. [John Milton, 1608–74, *Comus*, 188]

12 Sweet the coming on / Of grateful evening mild ; then silent night / With this her solemn bird and this fair moon, / And these the gems of heaven, her starry train. [John Milton, 1608–74, *Paradise Lost*, Bk iv, 646]

13 I said to Dawn : Be sudden – to Eve : Be soon. [Francis Thompson, 1859–1907, *The Hound of Heaven*, 30]

See also NIGHT

EVIL

1 Evil is not . . . wholly evil ; it is misplaced good. [Samuel Alexander, 1859–1938, *Space, Time and Deity*]

2 The fearsome word-and-thought-defying banality of evil. [(Referring to revelations of the trial in 1961) Hannah Arendt, 1906–75, *Eichmann in Jerusalem*, Ch. 15]

3 There is no peace, saith the Lord, unto the wicked. [Bible, OT, *Isaiah* 48 :22]

4 Their feet run to evil, and they make haste to shed innocent blood. [Bible, OT, *Isaiah* 59 :7]

5 Often the fear of one evil leads us into a worse. [Nicholas Boileau, 1636–1711, *L'Art poétique*, 1, 64]

6 What we call evil is simply ignorance bumping its head in the dark. [Henry Ford, 1863–1947 ; *Observer*, 'Sayings of the Week', 16 Mar. 1930]

7 All ideologies are relative ; the only absolute is the torment that men inflict on each other . . . [Yevgenia Ginzberg, 1906–77, in Eric de Mauny, *Russian Prospect*]

8 Don't let's make imaginary evils, when you know we have so many real ones to encounter. [Oliver Goldsmith, 1728–74, *The Good-Natured Man*, 1]

9 Evil, what is evil ? / There is only one evil, to deny life / As Rome denied Etruria / And mechanical America Montezuma still. [D H Lawrence, 1885–1930, *Cypresses*]

10 More safe I sing with mortal voice, unchanged / To hoarse or mute though fall'n on evil days, / On evil days though fall'n, and evil tongues; / In darkness, and with dangers compassed round, / And solitude. [John Milton, 1608–74, *Paradise Lost*, Bk vii, 24]

11 Evil is even, truth is an odd number and death is a full stop. [Flann O'Brien, 1911–66, *At Swim-Two-Birds*, Ch. 1]

12 No man is justified in doing evil on the ground of expediency. [Theodore Roosevelt, 1858–1919, *The Strenuous Life*, 'Latitude and Longitude among Reformers']

13 Evil is the product of the ability of humans to make abstract that which is concrete. [Jean-Paul Sartre, 1905–80, in *New Society*, 31 Dec. 1970]

14 And oftentimes, to win us to our harm, / The instruments of darkness tell us truths, / Win us with honest trifles, to betray's / In deepest consequence. [William Shakespeare, 1564–1616, *Macbeth*, I. iii. 123]

15 To mourn a mischief that is past and gone, / Is the next way to draw new mischief on. [*Othello*, I. iii. 204]

16 But let the wrong cry out as raw as wounds / This Time forgets and never heals, far less transcends. [Stephen Spender, 1909–95, *In Railway Halls*]

17 Every time we really concentrate our attention we destroy some of the evil within. [Simone Weil, 1909–43, *Waiting on God*, 'Reflections on the Right Use of School Studies']

18 Between two evils, I always pick the one I never tried before. [Mae West, 1892–1980, in film *Klondike Annie*]

19 The fact of the instability of evil is the moral order of the world. [A N Whitehead, 1861–1947, in Victor Gollancz, *A Year of Grace*, Intro.]

See also GOOD, WICKEDNESS

EVOLUTION

1 That series of inventions, by which man from age to age has remade his environment, is a different kind of evolution – not biological, but cultural evolution. I call that brilliant sequence of cultural peaks *The Ascent of Man*. [J Bronowski, 1908–74, *The Ascent of Man*, Ch. 1]

2 It has, I believe, been often remarked that a hen is only an egg's way of making another egg. [Samuel Butler, 1835–1902, *Life and Habit*, Ch. 8]

3 I have called this principle, by which each slight variation, if useful, is preserved, by the term of Natural Selection. [Charles Darwin, 1809–82, *The Origin of Species*, Ch. 3]

4 The expression often used by Mr Herbert Spencer of the Survival of the Fittest is more accurate, and is sometimes equally convenient. [Charles Darwin, 1809–82, *The Origin of Species*, Ch. 3]

5 The evolution of the human race will not be accomplished in the ten thousand years of tame animals, but in the million years of wild animals, because man is and will always be a wild animal. [Charles Galton Darwin, 1887–1962, *The Next Million Years*, Ch. 7]

6 Natural selection . . . has no purpose in mind. It has no mind and no mind's eye. It does not plan for the future. It has no vision, no foresight, no sight at all. If it can be said to play the role of watchmaker in nature, it is the blind watchmaker. [Richard Dawkins, 1941– , *The Blind Watchmaker*, Ch. 1]

7 Is man an ape or an angel? Now I am on the side of the angels. [Benjamin Disraeli, 1804–81, speech at Oxford Diocesan Conference, 25 Nov. 1864]

8 Life is a copiously branching bush, continually pruned by the grim reaper of extinction, not a ladder of predictable progress. [(On evolution) Stephen J Gould, 1941– , *Wonderful Life*, Ch. 1]

9 Evolution is far more important than living. [Ernst Jünger, 1895– , in Albert Camus, *The Rebel*, Ch. 3]

10 From an evolutionary point of view, man has stopped moving, if he ever did move. [Pierre Teilhard de Chardin, 1881–1955, *The Phenomenon of Man*, Postscript]

11 We are the products of editing, rather than authorship. [George Wald, 1906–97, in *Annals of New York Academy of Sciences*, Vol. 19, 1957]

12 There is no reason whatever to believe that the order of nature has any greater bias in favour of man than it had in favour of the ichthyosaur or the pterodactyl. [H G Wells, 1866–1946, in Sagittarius and D George, *The Perpetual Pessimist*]

See also PROGRESS

EXAGGERATION & EXCESS

1 Nothing to excess. [anon. Greek written up in the temple at Delphi, according to Plato's *Protagoras*]

2 The road of excess leads to the palace of wisdom. [William Blake, 1757–1827, *The Marriage of Heaven and Hell*, 'Proverbs of Hell']

3 The best things carried to excess are wrong. [Charles Churchill, 1731–64, *The Rosciad*, 1039]

4 He lacked ... the light hand with which Corvick had gilded the gingerbread – he laid on the tinsel in splotches. [Henry James, 1843–1916, *The Figure in the Carpet*, XI]

5 An orgy looks particularly alluring seen through the mists of righteous indignation. [Malcolm Muggeridge, 1903–90, *The Most of M M*, 'Dolce Vita in a Cold Climate']

6 'Tis not the eating, nor 'tis not the drinking, that is to be blamed, but the excess. [John Selden, 1584–1654, *Table Talk*, 54]

7 It out-herods Herod. [William Shakespeare, 1564–1616, *Hamlet*, III. ii (16)]

8 Forty thousand brothers / Could not, with all their quantity of love, / Make up my sum. [*Hamlet*, V. i. 291)]

9 I have peppered two of them; two I am sure I have paid, two rogues in buckram suits. I tell thee what, Hal, if I tell thee a lie, spit in my face, call me horse. Thou knowest my old ward; here I lay, and thus I bore my point. Four rogues in buckram let drive at me. [*Henry IV*, II. iv. (214)]

10 To gild refinèd gold, to paint the lily, / To throw a perfume on the violet, / To smooth the ice, or add another hue / Unto the rainbow, or with taper-light / To seek the beauteous eye of heaven to garnish, / Is wasteful and ridiculous excess. [*King John*, V. ii. 11]

11 Superfluity comes sooner by white hairs, but competency lives longer. [*The Merchant of Venice*, I. ii (9)]

12 The superfluous, a very necessary thing. [Voltaire, 1694–1778, *Le Mondain*, 22]

See also MODERATION

EXCUSES, EXCUSES

1 Forgetting that several excuses are always less convincing than one. [Aldous Huxley, 1894–1963, *Point Counter Point*, Ch. 1]

2 I am one of those unfortunates to whom death is less hideous than explanations. [D B Wyndham Lewis, 1891–1961, *Welcome to All This*]

3 *Qui s'accuse s'excuse.* [Christopher Ricks 1933– , *Dickens and the Twentieth Century*, 'Great Expectations']

See also APOLOGY

EXERCISE

1 As men / Do walk a mile, women should talk an hour, / After supper. 'Tis their exercise. [Francis Beaumont, 1584–1616, and John Fletcher, 1579–1625, *Philaster*, II. iv]

2 Exercise is bunk. If you are healthy, you don't need it: if you are sick, you shouldn't take it. [Henry Ford, 1863–1947, attr.]

3 To cure the mind's wrong bias, Spleen, / Some recommend the bowling-green; / Some, hilly walks; all, exercise; / Fling but a stone, the giant dies. / Laugh and be well. [Matthew Green, 1696–1737, *The Spleen*, 89]

4 I never did like working out - it bears the same relationship to real sport as masturbation does to real sex. [David Lodge, 1935– , *Therapy*, 1, p. 25]

See also HEALTH, SPORTS

EXILES

1 For I must to the green-wood go / Alone, a banished man. [ballad: *The Nut Brown Maid*]

2 Adieu, adieu! my native shore / Fades o'er the waters blue. [Lord Byron, 1788–1824, *Childe Harold's Pilgrimage*, I, 13]

3 I have loved justice and hated iniquity; therefore I die in exile. [Gregory VII, 1020–85, attr. last words, in Salerno]

4 This must my comfort be, / That sun that warms you here shall shine on me. [William Shakespeare, 1564–1616, *Richard II*, I. iii. 144]

5 They have learnt nothing and forgotten

nothing. [(Of the exiled émigrés in 1796) Charles-Maurice de Talleyrand, 1754–1838, quoted by Chevalier de Panat in letter to Mallet du Pan]

EXISTENCE

1 And we are here as on a darkling plain / Swept with confused alarms of struggle and flight, / Where ignorant armies clash by night. [Matthew Arnold, 1822–88, *Dover Beach*]

2 It is upon the flaws of Nature, not the laws of Nature, that the possibility of our existence hinges. [John D Barrow, 1952– , *The Artful Universe*, 'Gravity's Rainbow']

3 The isness of things is well worth studying; but it is their whyness that makes life worth living. [William Beebe, 1877–1962, in Konrad Lorenz, *On Aggression*, Ch. 2]

4 Perhaps every breath you take is someone else's last. [Elias Canetti, 1905–94, *The Human Province*, '1950']

5 I am: yet what I am none cares, or knows. [John Clare, 1793–1864, *I am*]

6 Be as a page that aches for a word / Which speaks on a theme that is timeless. [Neil Diamond, 1941– , song: *Be*]

7 Into this Universe, and *Why* not knowing / Nor *Whence*, like Water willy-nilly flowing: / And out of it, as Wind along the Waste, / I know not *Whither*, willy-nilly blowing. [Edward Fitzgerald, 1809–83, *The Rubá'iyát of Omar Khayyám*, Edn 1, 29]

8 We are too late for the gods, too early for Being. Being's poem, just begun, is man. [Martin Heidegger, 1889–1976, *Poetry, Language and Thought*, 1]

9 You had better be a round peg in a square hole than a square peg in a square hole. The latter is in for life, while the first is only an indeterminate sentence. [Elbert Hubbard, 1856–1915, in W H Auden and L Kronenberger, *Faber Book of Aphorisms*]

10 Life exists in the universe only because the carbon atom possesses certain exceptional properties. [James Jeans, 1887–1946, *The Mysterious Universe*, Ch. 1]

11 As far as we can discern, the sole purpose of human existence is to kindle a light in the darkness of mere being. [C G Jung, 1875–1961, *Memories, Dreams, Reflections*, Ch. 11]

12 The perpetual struggle for room and food. [Thomas Malthus, 1766–1834, *On Population*, Ch. 31]

13 This is the old Platonic riddle of nonbeing. Nonbeing must in some sense be, otherwise what is it that there is not? This tangled doctrine might be nicknamed Plato's beard; historically it has proved tough, frequently dulling the edge of Occam's razor. [Willard Quine, 1908– , *From a Logical Point of View*, 'On What There is']

14 To be and not to be, that is the answer. [Michael Rubinstein, 1920– , in conversation]

15 Matter ... a convenient formula for describing what happens where it isn't. [Bertrand Russell, 1872–1970, *An Outline of Philosophy*]

16 I know perfectly well that I don't want to do anything; to do something is to create existence – and there's quite enough existence as it is. [Jean-Paul Sartre, 1905–80, *Nausea*, 'One Hour Later']

17 Unless all existence is a medium of revelation, no particular revelation is possible. [Archbishop William Temple, 1881–1944, *Nature, Man and God*]

See also LIFE

EXPERIENCE

1 You should make a point of trying every experience once, except incest and folk-dancing. [Sir Arnold Bax, 1883–1953 (quoting 'sympathetic Scot'), *Farewell to My Youth*, 'Cecil Sharp']

2 You will think me lamentably crude: my experience of life has been drawn from life itself. [Max Beerbohm, 1872–1956, *Zuleika Dobson*, Ch. 7]

3 I have been young, and now am not too old; / And I have seen the righteous forsaken, / His health, his honour and his quality taken, / This is not what we were formerly told. [Edmund Blunden, 1896–1974, *Report on Experience*]

4 Experience isn't interesting till it begins to repeat itself – in fact, till it does that, it hardly *is* experience. [Elizabeth Bowen, 1899–1973, *The Death of the Heart*, Pt I, Ch. 1]

5 Example is the school of mankind, and they will learn at no other. [Edmund Burke, 1729–97, *Letters on a Regicide Peace*, 1]

6 *You* have not had thirty years' experience ... *You* have had one year's experience ... *You* have had one year's experience thirty times. [J L Carr, 1912–94, *The Harpole Report*, Ch. 21]

7 I was thinking that we all learn by experience, but some of us have to go to summer school. [Peter de Vries, 1910–93, *The Tunnel of Love*, Ch. 14]

8 Experientia does it – as papa used to say. [(Mrs Micawber) Charles Dickens, 1812–70, *David Copperfield*, Ch. 11]

9 It is not you or I that is important, neither what sort we might be nor how we came to be each where we are. What is important is anyone's coming awake and discovering a place ... What is important is the moment of opening a life and feeling it touch – with an electric hiss and cry – this speckled mineral sphere, our present world. [Annie Dillard, 1945– , *An American Childhood*, 'Epilogue']

10 What deeply affects every aspect of a man's experience of the world is his perception that *things could be otherwise*. [Michael Frayn, 1933– , *Constructions*, 42]

11 Life should serve up its feast of experience in a series of courses. [William Golding, 1911–93, *Close Quarters*, 17]

12 Example is always more efficacious than precept. [Dr Samuel Johnson, 1709–84, *Rasselas*, Ch. 29]

13 I compare human life to a large mansion of many apartments, two of which I can only describe, the doors of the rest being as yet shut upon me. [John Keats, 1795–1821, letter to J H Reynolds, 3 May 1818]

14 If you want knowledge, you must take part in the practice of changing reality. If you want to know the taste of a pear, you must change the pear by eating it yourself. [Mao Zedong, 1893–1976, *On Practice*, July 1937]

15 Till old experience do attain / To something like prophetic strain. [John Milton, 1608–74, *Il Penseroso*, 173]

16 I have twenty-five years' experience equals I have one year's experience, and it is twenty-four years old. [Claus Moller, in BBC TV programme *Business Matters*, 11 Apr. 1988]

17 Experience dulls the edges of all our dogmas. [Gilbert Murray, 1866–1957, attr.]

18 The more acute the experience the less articulate its expression. [Harold Pinter, 1930– , programme note to *The Room* and *The Dumb Waiter*]

19 All craftsmen share a knowledge. They have held / Reality down fluttering to a bench. [Victoria Sackville-West, 1892–1962, *The Land*, 'Summer']

20 All experience is an arch wherethro' / Gleams that untravelled world, whose margin fades / For ever and for ever when I move. [Alfred, Lord Tennyson, 1809–92, *Ulysses*, 19]

21 No man ... who has wrestled with a self-adjusting card table can ever quite be the man he once was. [James Thurber, 1894–1961, *Let Your Mind Alone*, 'Sex *ex* Machina']

22 Experience is the name every one gives to their mistakes. [Oscar Wilde, 1854–1900, *Lady Windermere's Fan*, III]

EXPERTS

1 An expert is a man who has made all the mistakes which can be made, in a very narrow field. [Niels Bohr, 1885–1962, quoted by Edward Teller, 10 Oct. 1972; in *Dictionary of Scientific Quotations*, ed. A L Mackay]

2 Too bad all the people who know how to run the country are busy driving taxi cabs and cutting hair. [George Burns, 1896–1996, in *Life* magazine, Dec. 1979]

3 An expert is one who knows more and more about less and less. [Nicholas Murray Butler, 1862–1947, Commencement Address, Columbia University]; see 6

4 All other men are specialists, but his specialism is omniscience. [Arthur Conan Doyle, 1859–1930, *His Last Bow*, 'The Bruce-Partington Plans']

5 An expert is someone who knows some of the worst mistakes that can be made in his subject, and how to avoid them. [Werner Heisenberg, 1901–76, *Physics and Beyond*, Ch. 17]

6 Specialist – a man who knows more and more

about less and less. [Charles Mayo, 1865–1939, in *Modern Hospital*, Sept. 1938, but he did not claim it as his own]; see 3

7 The time comes when you realize that you haven't merely been specializing in something – something has been specializing in you. [Arthur Miller, 1915– , *The Price*, II]

See also KNOWLEDGE

EXPLOITATION

1 What is the difference between Capitalism and Communism? Capitalism is the exploitation of man by man; Communism is the reverse. [anon. Polish joke; in R T Tripp, *International Thesaurus of Quotations*]

2 You shall not press down upon the brow of labour this crown of thorns, you shall not crucify mankind upon a cross of gold. [W J Bryan, 1860–1925, speech at the Democratic National Convention, Chicago, 8 July 1896]

3 Such hath it been – shall be – beneath the sun / The many still must labour for the one! [Lord Byron, 1788–1824, *The Corsair*, I, 8]

4 When we apply it, you call it anarchy; and when you apply it, I call it exploitation. [G K Chesterton, 1874–1936, *The Scandal of Father Brown*, 'The Crime of the Communist']

5 Fool that I was, upon my eagle's wings / I bore this wren till I was tired with soaring, / And now he mounts above me. [John Dryden, 1631–1700, *All for Love*, II. i]

6 Exploitation without work of man by man. [Prosper Enfantin, 1796–1864, *Oeuvres de Saint Simon et Enfantin*]

7 The oppressors do not perceive their monopoly of *having more* as a privilege which dehumanizes others and themselves. [Paulo Freire, 1921–97, *Pedagogy of the Oppressed*, Ch. 1]

8 Development in the Third World usually means the over-development of objects and the underdevelopment of people. [Richard Gott, 1938– , in *Guardian*, 30 Nov. 1976]

9 He was the only man I knew who came back from Dunkirk with two women ... Well it's too far for one to row, isn't it? [Tony Hancock, 1924–68, BBC TV comedy series *Hancock's Half Hour*, 'The Reunion Party', scripts by Ray Galton and Alan Simpson]

10 Men who call women ladies generally treat them as maids. [Aidan Mathews, 1956– , *Lipstick on the Host*, title story]

11 Men of England, wherefore plough / For the lords who lay ye low? [P B Shelley, 1792–1822, *Song to the Men of England*]

See also COMPETITION, WORK

EXPLORATION, see DISCOVERY

EXTRAVAGANCE

1 Dreading that climax of all human ills, / The inflammation of his weekly bills. [Lord Byron, 1788–1824, *Don Juan*, III, 34]

2 In squandering wealth was his peculiar art: / Nothing went unrewarded but desert. / Beggared by fools, whom still he found too late: / He had his jest, and they had his estate. [John Dryden, 1631–1700, *Absalom and Achitophel*, Pt I, 559]

3 My problem lies in reconciling my gross habits with my net income. [Errol Flynn, 1909–59, in Jane Mercer, *Great Lovers of the Movies*]

4 We're overpaying him but he's worth it. [Samuel Goldwyn, 1882–1974; attr. in A K Adams, *Cassell's Book of Humorous Quotations*]

5 My candle burns at both ends; / It will not last the night; / But, ah, my foes, and oh, my friends – / It gives a lovely light. [Edna St Vincent Millay, 1892–1950, *A Few Figs from Thistles*, 'First Fig']

6 All decent people live beyond their incomes nowadays, and those who aren't respectable live beyond other people's. A few gifted individuals manage to do both. [Saki (H H Munro), 1870–1916, *The Match-Maker*]

7 'Ah, well then,' said Oscar, 'I suppose that I shall have to die beyond my means.' [(Oscar Wilde, when asked a very large sum for an operation) R H Sherard, *Life of W*, Ch. 18]

See also MONEY, WEALTH

EXTREMES & EXTREMISM

1 This woman did not fly to extremes; she lived there. [Quentin Crisp, 1908–99, *The Naked Civil Servant*, Ch. 3]

2 So over-violent, or over-civil, / That every man, with him, was God or Devil. [John Dryden, 1631–1700, *Absalom and Achitophel*, Pt I, 557]

3 I would remind you that extremism in the defence of liberty is no vice. And let me remind you also that moderation in the pursuit of justice is no virtue. [Barry Goldwater, 1909–98, speech on accepting Republican nomination, San Francisco, 16 July 1964, but he attr. it to Cicero]

4 'Extremes meet', as the whiting said with its tail in its mouth. [Thomas Hood, 1799–1845, *The Doves and the Crows*]

5 I'll ha'e nae hauf-way hoose, but aye be whaur / Extremes meet – it's the only way I ken / To dodge the curst conceit o' bein' richt / That damns the vast majority o' men. [Hugh MacDiarmid, 1892–1978, *A Drunk Man Looks at the Thistle*, 141–4]

6 *Les extrèmes se touchent*. – Extremes meet. [Louis-Sébastien Mercier, 1740–1814, *Tableau de Paris*, Vol. IV, Ch. 348, heading]

EYES

1 Eyes too expressive to be blue, / Too lovely to be grey. [Matthew Arnold, 1822–88, *Faded Leaves*, 4]

2 It is not possible to look and listen with equal attention and, in any competition, the eyes have it. [Nancy Banks-Smith, 1929– , in *Guardian*, 23 Mar. 1990]

3 If thine eye offend thee, pluck it out. [Bible, NT, *St Matthew* 18:9]

4 Paradys stood formed in hir yën. [Geoffrey Chaucer, 1340?–1400, *Troilus and Criseyde*, V, 817]

5 He had but one eye and the popular prejudice runs in favour of two. [Charles Dickens, 1812–70, *Nicholas Nickleby*, Ch. 4]

6 'Yes I have a pair of eyes,' replied Sam, 'and that's just it. If they wos a pair o' patent double million magnifyin' gas microscopes of hextra power, p'raps I might be able to see through a flight o' stairs and a deal door; but bein' only eyes, you see, my wision's limited.' [Charles Dickens, 1812–70, *Pickwick Papers*, Ch. 34]

7 Send home my long strayed eyes to me, / Which, Oh, too long have dwelt on thee. [John Donne, 1571?–1631, *The Message*]

8 Love's tongue is in his eyes. [Phineas Fletcher, 1582–1650, *Piscatory Eclogues*, V, xiii]

9 Keep your eye clear / as the bleb of the icicle, / trust the feel of what nubbed treasure / your hands have known. [Seamus Heaney, 1939– , *North*]

10 Her eyes the glow-worm lend thee, / The shooting-stars attend thee; / And the elves also, / Whose little eyes glow, / Like the sparks of fire, befriend thee. [Robert Herrick, 1591–1674, *Hesperides*, 'The Night-Piece, to Julia']

11 His eyes look as if he's pawned his real ones and is wearing paste. [Russell Hoban, 1925– , *Turtle Diary*, Ch. 2]

12 Look at yourself with one eye, listen to yourself with the other. [Eugene Ionesco, 1912–94, *Improvisation*]

13 She looked at me the way you'd look at a chessman if it made its own move. [Randall Jarrell, 1914–65, *Pictures from an Institution*, Pt II, Ch. 1]

14 The light, that lies / In woman's eyes, / Has been my heart's undoing. [Thomas Moore, 1779–1852, *Irish Melodies*, 'The Time I've Lost']

15 I prefer to forget both pairs of glasses and pass my declining years saluting strange women and grandfather clocks. [Ogden Nash, 1902–71, *Peekaboo, I Almost See You*]

16 Why has not man a microscopic eye? / For this plain reason, man is not a fly. [Alexander Pope, 1688–1744, *An Essay on Man*, I, 193]

17 If the eyes are sometimes the organ through which our intelligence is revealed, the nose is generally the organ in which stupidity is most readily displayed. [Marcel Proust, 1871–1922, *Remembrance of Things Past: Cities of the Plain*, Pt II, Ch. 2]

18 In a dark time the eye begins to see. [Theodore Roethke, 1908–63, *In a Dark Time*]

19 From women's eyes this doctrine I derive: / They sparkle still the right Promethean fire; / They are the books, the arts, the academes, / That show, contain, and nourish all the world. [William Shakespeare, 1564–1616, *Love's Labour's Lost*, IV. iii. (350)]

20 The fringèd curtains of thine eye advance, / And say what thou seest yond. [*The Tempest*, I. ii. 405]

21 My mistress' eyes are nothing like the sun. [*Sonnets*, 130]

22 Gorgonised me from head to foot / With a stony British stare. [Alfred, Lord Tennyson, 1809–92, *Maud*, Pt 1, xiii, 2]

23 How sweet are looks that ladies bend / On whom their favours fall! [Alfred, Lord Tennyson, 1809–92, *Sir Galahad*, 2]

24 Some circumstantial evidence is very strong, as when you find a trout in the milk. [H D Thoreau, 1817–62, *Journal*, 11 Nov. 1854]

25 But optics sharp it needs, I ween, / To see what is not to be seen. [John Trumbull, 1750–1831, *McFingal*, Canto 1, 67]

26 Big chap with a small moustache and the sort of eye that can open an oyster at sixty paces. [P G Wodehouse, 1881–1975, *The Code of the Woosters*, Ch. 2]

27 The fishy glitter in his eye became intensified. He looked like a halibut which had been asked by another halibut to lend it a couple of quid till next Wednesday. [P G Wodehouse, 1881–1975, *A Few Quick Ones*, 'The Word in Season']

28 It was one of those cold, clammy, accusing sort of eyes – the kind that makes you reach up to see if your tie is straight: and he looked at me as if I were some sort of unnecessary product which Cuthbert the Cat had brought in after a ramble among the local ash-cans. [P G Wodehouse, 1881–1975, *The Inimitable Jeeves*, Ch. 10]

29 Processions that lack high stilts have nothing that catches the eye. [W B Yeats, 1865–1936, *High Talk*]

See also FACES, SIGHT, VISIONS

F

FACES

1 There is a garden in her face, / Where roses and white lilies grow. [Richard Alison, *fl. c.*1606, *An Hour's Recreation in Music*]

2 He thought what a pity it was that all his faces were designed to express rage or loathing. Now that something had happened that really deserved a face, he'd none to celebrate it with. As a kind of token, he made his Sex Life in Ancient Rome face. [Kingsley Amis, 1922–95, *Lucky Jim*, Ch. 25]

3 I have no face, only two profiles clapped together. [Margot Asquith, 1865–1945; in *Hammer and Tongues*, ed. Michèle Brown and Ann O'Connor, 'Appearance']

4 Private faces in public places / Are wiser and nicer / Than public faces in private places. [W H Auden, 1907–73, *Marginalia*]

5 A merry heart maketh a cheerful countenance. [Bible, OT, *Proverbs* 15:13]

6 As a white candle / In a holy place, / So is the beauty / Of an aged face. [Joseph Campbell, 1879–1944, *The Old Woman*]

7 There is a garden in her face, / Where roses and white lilies grow; / A heavenly paradise is that place, / Wherein all pleasant fruits do flow. / There cherries grow which none may buy, / Till 'Cherry-ripe' themselves do cry. [Thomas Campion, 1567–1620, *There is a Garden in Her Face*]

8 Alas, after a certain age every man is responsible for his face. [Albert Camus, 1913–60, *The Fall*]

9 At fifty you have the choice of keeping your face or your figure and it's *much* better to keep your face. [Barbara Cartland, 1904– , interview in *Daily Mail*, 10 July 1981]

10 That hadde a fyr-reed cherubinnes face. [Geoffrey Chaucer, 1340?–1400, *Canterbury Tales*, 'Prologue', 624]

11 Frances is as plain as it is possible to be without requiring a licence to enter a public place. [Alan Coren, 1938– , *Seems Like Old Times*, 'August']

12 No spring, nor summer beauty hath such grace, / As I have seen in one autumnal face. [John Donne, 1571?–1631, *Elegies*, 9, 'The Autumnal', 1]

13 Her pure and eloquent blood / Spoke in her cheeks, and so distinctly wrought, / That one might almost say, her body thought. [John Donne, 1571?–1631, *The Second Anniversary*, 244]

14 In an experience of women that extends over many nations and three separate continents, I have never looked upon a face which gave a clearer promise of a refined and sensitive nature. [(Dr Watson) Arthur Conan Doyle, 1859–1930, *The Sign of Four*, Ch. 2]

15 As a beauty I'm not a great star. / Others are handsomer far; / But my face – I don't mind it / Because I'm behind it; / It's the folk out in front that I jar. [Anthony Euwer, 1877–1955, limerick]

16 There is a lady sweet and kind, / Was never face so pleased my mind; / I did but see her passing by, / And yet I love her till I die. [Thomas Ford, 1580?–1648, *There is a Lady*]

17 There is a great difference between painting a face and not washing it. [Thomas Fuller, 1608–61, *Church History*, Bk vii, sect. i, 32]

18 It is sometimes said that face-to-face you don't see the other person's face. [Mikhail Gorbachev, 1931– , after his second summit meeting with President Reagan, Oct. 1986]

19 I am the family face; / Flesh perishes, I live on, / Projecting trait and trace / Through time to times anon, / And leaping from place to place / Over oblivion. [Thomas Hardy, 1840–1928, *Heredity*]

20 It was an oddity of Mrs Lowder's that her face in speech was like a lighted window at night, but that silence immediately drew the curtain. [Henry James, 1843–1916, *The Wings of the Dove*, Bk II, 2]

21 A face on him as long as a late breakfast. [James Joyce, 1882–1941, *Ulysses*, Penguin edn, 1992, p. 420]

22 Her eyes, nose, mouth, skin, all might have been designed in committee to meet the barest requirements of feasibility. [Ian McEwan, 1948– , *The Comfort of Strangers*, Ch. 6]

23 Was this the face that launched a thousand ships, / And burnt the topless towers of Ilium? / Sweet Helen, make me immortal with a kiss! / Her lips suck forth my soul: see, where it flies! – / Come, Helen, come give me my soul again. / Here will I dwell, for heaven be in these lips, / And all is dross that is not Helena. [Christopher Marlowe, 1564–93, *Doctor Faustus*, 1354]

24 I never forget a face, but I'll make an exception in your case. [Groucho Marx, 1895–1977, in *Guardian*, 18 June 1965]

25 My face is my fortune, sir, she said. [Nursery rhyme]

26 At fifty, everyone has the face he deserves. [George Orwell, 1903–50, *Notebook*, 17 Apr. 1949]

27 If to her share some female errors fall, / Look on her face, and you'll forget 'em all. [Alexander Pope, 1688–1744, *The Rape of the Lock*, II, 17]

28 The human face is indeed, like the face of the God of some oriental theogony, a whole cluster of faces, juxtaposed on different planes so that one does not see them all at once. [Marcel Proust, 1871–1922, *Remembrance of Things Past: Within a Budding Grove*, 'Elstir']

29 And so when studying faces, we do indeed measure them, but as painters, not as surveyors. [Marcel Proust, 1871–1922, *Remembrance of Things Past: Within a Budding Grove*, 'Elstir']

30 If the eyes are sometimes the organ through which our intelligence is revealed, the nose is generally the organ in which stupidity is most readily displayed. [Marcel Proust, 1871–1922, *Remembrance of Things Past: Cities of the Plain*, Pt II, Ch. 2]

31 My nose is huge! Vile snub-nose, flat-nosed ass, flat-head, let me inform you that I am proud of such an appendage, since a big nose is the proper sign of a friendly, good, courteous, witty, liberal, and brave man, such as I am. [Edmond Rostand, 1868–1918, *Cyrano de Bergerac*, I, i]

32 I have heard of your paintings too, well enough. God hath given you one face, and you make yourselves another. [William Shakespeare, 1564–1616, *Hamlet*, III. i. (150)]

33 There's no art / To find the mind's construction in the face; / He was a gentleman on whom I built / An absolute trust. [*Macbeth*, I. iv. 11]

34 Your face, my thane, is as a book where men / May read strange matters. [*Macbeth*, I. v. (63)]

35 There are a sort of men whose visages / Do cream and mantle like a standing pond. [*The Merchant of Venice*, I. i 88]

36 *Item*, Two lips, indifferent red; *Item*, Two grey eyes with lids to them; *Item*, One neck, one chin, and so forth. [*Twelfth Night*, I. v. (268)]

37 'I grant you that he's not two-faced,' I said. 'But what's the use of that when the one face he has got is so peculiarly unpleasant?' [C P Snow, 1905–80, *The Affair*, Ch. 4]

38 She developed a persistent troubled frown which gave her the expression of someone who is trying to repair a watch with his gloves on. [James Thurber, 1894–1961, *The Beast in Me and Other Animals*, 'Look Homeward, Jeannie']

39 The 50s face was angry, the 60s face was well-fed, the 70s face was foxy. Perhaps it was the right expression: there was a lot to be wary about. [Keith Waterhouse, 1929– , in *Observer Magazine*, 30 Dec. 1979]

40 He had the face of a saint, but he had rendered this generally acceptable by growing side-whiskers. [H G Wells, 1866–1946, *Short Stories*, 'The Last Trump']

See also APPEARANCE, EYES

FACTS

1 But Facts are chiels that winna ding, / An' downa be disputed. [Robert Burns, 1759–96, *A Dream*, 30]

2 Now, what I want is Facts . . . Facts alone are wanted in life. [Charles Dickens, 1812–70, *Hard Times*, Bk i, Ch. 1]

3 I find myself in the position of denying non-existent facts. [Michael Dukakis, 1933– , in *Independent*, 10 Sept. 1988]

4 It's a fact the whole world knows, / That Pobbles are happier without their toes. [Edward Lear, 1812–88, *Nonsense Songs*, 'The Pobble Who Has No Toes']

5 'But I can do nothing unless I am in complete possession of the facts.' 'Obviously you can't cook them unless you have them.' [W Somerset Maugham, 1874–1965, *Cakes and Ale*, Ch. 9]

6 And so he comes to the conclusion / The whole affair was an illusion. / 'For look,' he cries triumphantly, / 'What's not permitted CANNOT be!' [Christian Morgenstern, 1871–1914, *Palmström*, 'Impossible Facts']

7 Gently my eyelids close; / I'd rather be good than clever; / And I'd rather have my facts all wrong / Than have no facts whatever. [Ogden Nash, 1902–71, *Who Did Which?*]

8 Comment is free but facts are sacred. [C P Scott, 1846–1932, in *Manchester Guardian*, 5 May 1921]

9 Matters of fact, which as Mr Budgell somewhere observes, are very stubborn things. [Matthew Tindal, 1657–1733, *Will of M T*]

See also TRUTH

FAILURE

1 I coulda had class! I coulda been a contender! I coulda been somebody! Instead of a bum, which is what I am! [Marlon Brando, 1924– , in film *On the Waterfront*, screenplay by Budd Schulberg. Echoed by Robert de Niro in film *Raging Bull*]

2 I'm a connoisseur of failure. I can smell it, roll it round my mouth, tell you the vintage and the side of the hill that grew it. [Giles Cooper, 1918–66, radio drama *Unman, Wittering and Zigo*]

3 She knows there's no success like failure / And that failure's no success at all. [Bob Dylan, 1941– , song: *Love Minus Zero/No Limit*]

4 If at first you don't succeed, try again. Then quit. No use being a damn fool about it. [W C Fields, 1879–1946; in L Halliwell, *The Filmgoer's Book of Quotes*]

5 Half the failures in life arise from pulling in one's horse as he is leaping. [Julius and Augustus Hare, 1795–1855 and 1792–1834, *Guesses at Truth*, 1st series, p. 156]

6 So have I loitered my life away, reading books, looking at pictures, going to plays, hearing, thinking, writing on what pleased me best. I have wanted only one thing to make me happy, but wanting that have wanted everything. [William Hazlitt, 1778–1830, *My First Acquaintance with Poets*]

7 He was a self-made man who owed his lack of success to nobody. [Joseph Heller, 1923–99, *Catch-22*, Ch. 3]

8 Generally it is our failures that civilize us. Triumph confirms us in our habits. [Clive James, 1939– , *Unreliable Memoirs*, Ch. 6]

9 Four be the things I'd been better without: / Love, curiosity, freckles, and doubt. [Dorothy Parker, 1893–1967, *Inventory*]

10 MACBETH: If we should fail –
LADY MACBETH: We fail! / But screw your courage to the sticking place, / And we'll not fail. [William Shakespeare, 1564–1616, *Macbeth*, I. vii. 59]

11 Never having been able to succeed in the world, he took his revenge by speaking ill of it. [Voltaire, 1694–1778, *Zadig*, Ch. 4]

See also SUCCESS

FAIRIES

1 Up the airy mountain, / Down the rushy glen, / We daren't go a-hunting, / For fear of little men. [William Allingham, 1828–89, *The Fairies*]

2 Every time a child says, 'I don't believe in fairies,' there's a little fairy somewhere that falls down dead. [James Barrie, 1860–1937, *Peter Pan*, 1]

3 Farewell rewards and fairies, / Good housewives now may say, / But now foul sluts in dairies / Do fare as well as they, / And though they sweep their hearths no less / Than maids were wont to do, / Yet who of late for cleanliness, / Finds sixpence in her shoe? [Richard Corbet, 1582–1635, *The Fairies' Farewell*]

4 There are fairies at the bottom of our garden. [Rose Fyleman, 1877–1957, *Fairies*]

5 Nobody Loves a Fairy When She's Forty. [Arthur W D Henley, n.d., title of song (1934)]

6 I met a lady in the meads / Full beautiful, a faery's child; / Her hair was long, her foot was light, / And her eyes were wild. [John Keats, 1795–1821, *La Belle Dame sans Merci*, 3]

7 Fairy elves, / Whose midnight revels, by a forest side / Or fountain, some belated peasant sees, / Or dreams he sees, while overhead the moon / Sits arbitress. [John Milton, 1608–74, *Paradise Lost*, Bk i, 781]

8 O! then, I see, Queen Mab hath been with you . . . / She is the fairies' midwife, and she comes / In shape no bigger than an agate-stone / On the fore-finger of an alderman, / Drawn with a team of little atomies / Athwart men's noses as they lie asleep. [William Shakespeare, 1564–1616, *Romeo and Juliet*, I. iii. 53]

9 Ye elves of hills, brooks, standing lakes and groves; / And ye, that on the sands with printless foot / Do chase the ebbing Neptune and do fly him / When he comes back. [*The Tempest*, V. i. 33]

10 The land of faery, / Where nobody gets old and godly and grave, / Where nobody gets old and crafty and wise, / Where nobody gets old and bitter of tongue. [W B Yeats, 1865–1939, *The Land of Heart's Desire*]

FAITHS

1 The Sea of Faith / Was once, too, at the full and round earth's shore / Lay like the folds of a bright girdle furled. / But now I only hear / Its melancholy, long, withdrawing roar, / Retreating, to the breath / Of the night-wind, down the vast edges drear / And naked shingles of the world. [Matthew Arnold, 1822–88, *Dover Beach*]

2 A faith is something you die for; a doctrine is something you kill for: there is all the difference in the world. [Tony Benn, 1925–   : *Observer*, 'Sayings of the Week', 16 Apr. 1989]

3 *Faith*, n. Belief without evidence in what is told by one who speaks without knowledge, of things without parallel. [Ambrose Bierce, 1842–1914, *The Devil's Dictionary*]

4 The Lord is my shepherd; I shall not want. He maketh me to lie down in green pastures: He leadeth me beside the still waters. [Bible, OT, *Psalms* 23:1]

5 He only is my rock and my salvation: he is my defence; I shall not be moved. [Bible, OT, *Psalms* 62:6]

6 The Lord shall preserve thy going out, and thy coming in, from this time forth, and even for evermore. [Bible, OT, *Psalms* 121:8]

7 We walk by faith, not by sight. [Bible, NT, *2 Corinthians* 5:7]

8 Faith is the substance of things hoped for, the evidence of things not seen. [Bible, NT, *Hebrews* 11:1]

9 Faith without works is dead. [Bible, NT, *James* 2:20]

10 Ask, and it shall be given you; seek, and ye shall find; knock, and it shall be opened unto you. [Bible, NT, *St Matthew* 7:7]

11 If ye have faith as a grain of mustard seed, ye shall say unto this mountain, Remove hence to yonder place; and it shall remove. [Bible, NT, *St Matthew* 17:20]

12 I have fought a good fight, I have finished my course, I have kept the faith. [Bible, NT, *1 Timothy* 4:7]

13 To believe only possibilities is not faith, but mere philosophy. [Sir Thomas Browne, 1605–82, *Religio Medici*, Pt 1, 48]

14 He who would valiant be / 'Gainst all disaster / Let him in constancy / Follow the Master. / There's no discouragement / Shall make him once relent, / His first avowed intent / To be a pilgrim. [John Bunyan, 1628–88, *The Pilgrim's Progress*, Pt II (*English Hymnal* version)]

15 Reason is itself a matter of faith. It is an act of faith to assert that our thoughts have any relation to reality at all. [G K Chesterton, 1874–1936, *Orthodoxy*, Ch. 3]

16 The faith that stands on authority is not faith. [Ralph Waldo Emerson, 1803–82, *Essays*, 'The Over-Soul']

17 Somebody Up There Likes Me. [Rocky Graziano, 1922–90, catchphrase and title of autobiography]

18 We're all unbelievers within our own faiths. [Graham Greene, 1904–91; *Observer*, 'Sayings of the Week', 9 Sept. 1984]

19 And I said to the man who stood at the gate of the year: 'Give me a light that I may tread safely into the unknown.' And he replied: 'Go out into the darkness and put your hand into the hand of God. That shall be to you better than light and safer than a known way.' [Minnie Haskins, 1875–1957, *The Desert*, Introduction. Quoted by King George VI in his Christmas Broadcast, 1939]

20 [When asked if he believed in God] I do not believe ... I know. [C G Jung, 1875–1961, in Laurens van der Post, *Jung and the Story of Our Time*]

21 Booth died blind and still by faith he trod, / Eyes still dazzled by the ways of God. [Vachel Lindsay, 1879–1931, *General William Booth Enters Heaven*]

22 Be a sinner and strong in your sins, but be stronger in your faith and rejoice in Christ. [Martin Luther, 1483--1546, letter to Melanchthon, 1521]

23 Faith may be defined briefly as an illogical belief in the occurrence of the improbable. [H L Mencken, 1880–1956, *Prejudices*, Third Series, 'Types of Men', 3]

24 Be comforted. You would not be seeking Me if you had not found Me. [Blaise Pascal, 1623–62, *Pensées*, VII, 552]

25 For modes of faith let graceless zealots fight; / His can't be wrong whose life is in the right. [Alexander Pope, 1688–1744, *An Essay on Man*, III, 303]

26 When love begins to sicken and decay, / It useth an enforcèd ceremony! / There are no tricks in plain and simple faith. [William Shakespeare, 1564–1616, *Julius Caesar*, IV. ii. 20]

27 Faith has need of the whole truth. [Pierre Teilhard de Chardin, 1881–1955, *The Appearance of Man*]

28 Faith is the state of being ultimately concerned. [Paul Tillich, 1886–1965, *Dynamics of Faith*, Ch. 1]

29 My work ... is to shatter the faith of men here, there and everywhere, faith in affirmation, faith in negation, and faith in abstention from faith, and this for the sake of faith in faith itself. [Miguel de Unamuno, 1864–1937, *The Tragic Sense of Life*, Conclusion]

30 Some have no faith, and the others have faith exclusively in one religion and only bestow upon the others the sort of attention we give to strangely shaped shells. [Simone Weil, 1909–43, *Waiting on God*, 'Forms of the Implicit Love of God']

31 One in whom persuasion and belief / Had ripened into faith, and faith become / A passionate intuition. [William Wordsworth, 1770–1850, *The Excursion*, IV, 1293]

See also BELIEF

FAME

1 A celebrity is a person who works hard all his life to become known, then wears dark glasses to avoid being recognized. [Fred Allen, 1894–1956, *Treadmill to Oblivion*]

2 My name has gotten to be a household word – at least in certain households. I think there are now people who know my name, but don't know what I do. I'm famous for being famous. [John Ashbery, 1927– , interview in *PN Review*, No. 46, 1985]

3 Fame is like a river, that beareth up things light and swollen, and drowns things weighty and solid. [Francis Bacon, 1561–1626, *Essays*, 53, 'Of Praise']

4 Bellow says he spent the first third of his life absorbing material, the second third trying to make himself famous, and the last third trying to avoid fame. [Saul Bellow, 1915– , in Edward Hoagland, *Learning to Eat Soup*]

5 They liked celebrity in those days; they thought it was catching. [Terence Blacker, 1948– , *Fixx*, p. 107]

6 The celebrity is a person who is known for his well-knownness. [Daniel Boorstin, 1914– , *The Image*, Ch. 2]

7 I awoke one morning and found myself famous. [Lord Byron, 1788–1824 (on instantaneous success of *Childe Harold*), quoted in T Moore, *Life of Byron*, 1, 347]

8 Being a personality is not the same as having a personality. [Alan Coren, 1938– , in *Mail on Sunday*, 12 Mar. 1989]

9 (When asked whether a boxer was a household name in Belfast) He's not even a household name in his own living-room. [Ian Dark, 1950– , from BBC radio programme *Today*: *Listener*, 'Out Takes of the Year', 17/24 Dec. 1987]

10 A legend is an old man with a cane known for what he used to do: I'm still doing it. [Miles Davis, 1926–91; *Observer*, 'Sayings of the Week', 21 July 1991]

11 How dreary to be somebody! / How public, like a frog / To tell your name the livelong day / To an admiring bog! [Emily Dickinson, 1830–86, *Life*]

12 What is fame? an empty bubble; / Gold? a transient, shining trouble. [James Grainger, 1721?–66, *Solitude*, 96]

13 Fame is a powerful aphrodisiac. [Graham Greene, 1904–91, in *Radio Times*, 10 Sept. 1964]

14 It is a mark of many famous people that they cannot part with their brightest hour. [Lillian Hellman, 1905–84, *Pentimento*, 'Theatre']

15 Fame is the spur that the clear spirit doth raise / (That last infirmity of noble mind) / To scorn delights, and live laborious days; / But the fair guerdon when we hope to find, / And think to burst out into sudden blaze, / Comes the blind Fury with th' abhorrèd shears, / And slits the thin-spun life. [John Milton, 1608–74, *Lycidas*, 70]

16 I'm never going to be famous. My name will never be writ large on the roster of Those Who Do Things. I don't do anything. Not one single thing. I used to bite my nails, but I don't even do that any more. [Dorothy Parker, 1893–1967, *The Little Hours*]

17 So young, and already so unknown? [(Of another scientist) Wolfgang Pauli, 1900–1958, in E Regis, *Who Got Einstein's Office?*]

18 What rage for fame attends, both great and small! / Better be damned than mentioned not at all! [Peter Pindar, 1738–1819, *To the Royal Academicians*, 8]

19 Nor fame I slight, nor for her favours call; / She comes unlooked for, if she comes at all. [Alexander Pope, 1688–1744, *The Temple of Fame*, 513]

20 A dead writer can at least be illustrious without any strain on himself. [Marcel Proust, 1871–1922, *Remembrance of Things Past: The Guermantes Way*, Ch. 2]

21 Today's superstars may be more famous than God (and have more reliable agents). [Frederic Raphael, 1931– , in *The Sunday Times*, 22 May 1988]

22 It is easier to gain fame than to retain it. [Artur Schnabel, 1882–1951, *My Life and Music*, Pt II, Ch. 4]

23 He lives in fame that died in virtue's cause. [William Shakespeare, 1564–1616, *Titus Andronicus*, I. i. 390]

24 The pilgrim of eternity, whose fame / Over his living head like Heaven is bent, / An early, but enduring monument. [P B Shelley, 1792–1822, *Adonais*, 264]

25 To famous men all the earth is a sepulchre. [Thucydides, *c.*471–*c.*400 BC, *History*, II, 43, iii]

26 The only man who wasn't spoilt by being lionized was Daniel. [Herbert Beerbohm Tree, 1853–1917, in Hesketh Pearson, *B T*, Ch. 12]

27 In these days a man is nobody unless his biography is kept so far posted up that it may be ready for the national breakfast-table on the morning after his demise. [Anthony Trollope, 1815–82, *Doctor Thorne*, Ch. 25]

28 It's the place where my prediction from the sixties finally came true: 'In the future everyone will be famous for fifteen minutes.' [Andy Warhol, 1927–87, *A W's Exposures*, 'Studio 54']

See also REPUTATION

FAMILIARITY

1 Where's the face / One would meet in every place? / Where's the voice, however soft, / One would hear so very oft? [John Keats, 1795–1821, *Fancy*, 73]

2 Old friends are best. King James used to call for his old shoes; they were easiest for his feet. [John Selden, 1584–1654, *Table Talk*, 47]

3 I'd know his way of spitting, and he astride the moon. [J M Synge, 1871–1909, *The Playboy of the Western World*, III]

4 Familiarity breeds contempt – and children. [Mark Twain, 1835–1910, *Notebooks*, p. 237]

FAMILY

1 He that hath wife and children, hath given hostages to fortune; for they are impediments to great enterprises, either of virtue, or mischief. [Francis Bacon, 1561–1626, *Essays*, 8, 'Of Marriage and Single Life']

2 They were a little less than 'kin', and rather more than 'kind'. [Revd R H Barham, 1788–1845, *Nell Cook*]; see 17

3 To make a happy fire-side clime / To weans and wife, / That's the true pathos and sublime / Of human life. [Robert Burns, 1759–96, *To Dr Blacklock*]

4 It is a melancholy truth that even great men have their poor relations. [Charles Dickens, 1812–70, *Bleak House*, Ch. 28]

5 Our family is not yet so good as to be degenerating. [Kurt Ewald, *My Little Boy*]

6 Good families are generally worse than any others. [Anthony Hope, 1863–1933, *The Prisoner of Zenda*, Ch. 1]

7 All my relations are muscle-bound from jumping to conclusions. [Danny Kaye, 1913–87, in film *The Secret Life of Walter Mitty*, script by Ken Englund and Everett Freeman]

8 A poor relation – is the most irrelevant thing in nature. [Charles Lamb, 1775–1834, *Last Essays of Elia*, 'Poor Relations']

9 Far from being the basis of the good society, the family, with its narrow privacy and tawdry secrets, is the source of all our discontents. [Edmund Leach, 1910–89, *Runaway World*, Ch. 3]

10 He's an uncle on my father's side. And if he's on my father's side, I'll fight on my mother's. [Groucho Marx, 1895–1977, in radio show *Flywheel, Shyster and Flywheel*, 1933, scripts ed. Michael Barson]

11 Every man sees in his relatives, and especially in his cousins, a series of grotesque caricatures of himself. [H L Mencken, 1880–1956, *Prejudices*, Third Series, 'Types of Men', 12]

12 One would be in less danger / From the wiles of the stranger / If one's own kin and kith / Were more fun to be with. [Ogden Nash, 1902–71, *Family Court*]

13 All men are brothers, but thank God, they aren't all brothers-in-law. [Anthony Powell, 1905– , *At Lady Molly's*, Ch. 4]

14 For there is no friend like a sister / In calm or stormy weather. [Christina Rossetti, 1830–94, *Goblin Market*, 1, 562]

15 Families naturally prefer widows to unmarried mothers, but only just. [Jean-Paul Sartre, 1905–80, *Words*, Pt 1]

16 The family that prays together stays together. [Al Scalpone, 1913– (slogan of Roman Catholic Rosary Crusade, first broadcast 6 Mar. 1947), in Father Patrick Peyton, *All for Her*]

17 A little more than kin, and less than kind. [William Shakespeare, 1564–1616, *Hamlet*, I. ii. 65]; see 2

18 When our relatives are at home, we have to think of all their good points or it would be impossible to endure them. But when they are away, we console ourselves for their absence by dwelling on their vices. [George Bernard Shaw, 1856–1950, *Heartbreak House*, I]

19 As a rule there is only one person an English girl hates more than she hates her eldest sister; and thats her mother. [George Bernard Shaw, 1856–1950, *Man and Superman*, II]

20 He that loves not his wife and children, feeds a lioness at home and broods a nest of sorrows. [Jeremy Taylor, 1613–53, *Sermons*, 'Married Love']

21 We have become a grandmother. [Margaret Thatcher, 1925– , on TV, 3 Mar. 1989]

22 All happy families resemble one another, each unhappy family is unhappy in its own way. [Leo Tolstoy, 1828–1910, *Anna Karenina*, I, Ch. 1]

23 It is no use telling me that there are bad aunts and good aunts. At the core they are all alike. Sooner or later, out pops the cloven hoof. [P G Wodehouse, 1881–1975, *The Code of the Woosters*, Ch. 2]

24 I'm not lugged into Family Rows. On the occasions when Aunt is calling to Aunt like mastodons bellowing across primeval swamps and Uncle James's letter about Cousin Mabel's peculiar behaviour is being shot round the family circle ('Please read this carefully and send it on to Jane'), the clan has a tendency to ignore me. [P G Wodehouse, 1881–1975, *The Inimitable Jeeves*, Ch. 16]

FANATICS

1 Just as every conviction begins as a whim so does every emancipator serve his apprenticeship as a crank. A fanatic is a great leader who is just entering the room. [Heywood Broun, 1888–1939, in *New York World*, 6 Feb. 1928]

2 A fanatic is a man that does what he thinks th' Lord wud do if He knew th' facts iv th' case. [Finley Peter Dunne, 1867–1936, *Mr Dooley's Opinions*, 'Casual Observations']

3 Fanatics have their dreams, wherewith they weave / A paradise for a sect. [John Keats, 1795–1821, *The Fall of Hyperion*, Bk i, 1]

4 When people are fanatically dedicated to political or religious faiths or any other kind of dogmas or goals, it's always because these dogmas or goals are in doubt. [Robert M Pirsig, 1928– , *Zen and the Art of Motorcycle Maintenance*, Pt II, Ch. 13]

5 Fanaticism consists of redoubling your effort when you have forgotten your aim. [George Santayana, 1863–1952, *The Life of Reason*, Vol. 1, Introduction]

6 The best lack all conviction, while the worst / Are full of passionate intensity. [W B Yeats, 1865–1939, *The Second Coming*]

FAREWELLS

1 Fare thee well, for I must leave thee, / Do not let this parting grieve thee, / And remember that the best of friends must part. [anon. song, *There is a Tavern in the Town*]

2 Come, dear children, let us away; / Down and away below. [Matthew Arnold, 1822–88, *The Forsaken Merman*, 1]

3 To throw away the key and walk away, / Not abrupt exile, the neighbours asking why, / But following a line with left and right, / An altered gradient at another rate. [W H Auden, 1907–73, *The Journey*]

4 Ae fond kiss, and then we sever! [Robert Burns, 1759–96, *Ae Fond Kiss*]

5 Fare thee well! and if for ever, / Still for ever, fare thee well. [Lord Byron, 1788–1824, *Fare Thee Well*]

6 When we two parted / In silence and tears, / Half broken-hearted / To sever for years, / Pale grew thy cheek and cold, / Colder thy kiss; / Truly that hour foretold / Sorrow to this. [Lord Byron, 1788–1824, *When We Two Parted*]

7 Parting is all we know of heaven, / And all we need of hell. [Emily Dickinson, 1830–86, *Parting*]

8 When I died last, and, Dear, I die / As often as from thee I go, / Though it be but an hour ago, / And lovers' hours be full eternity. [John Donne, 1571?–1631, *The Legacy*]

9 Sweetest love, I do not go, / For weariness of thee, / Nor in hope the world can show / A fitter Love for me; / But since that I / Must die at last, 'tis best / To use myself in jest, / Thus by feigned deaths to die. [John Donne, 1571?–1631, song: *Sweetest Love . . .*]

10 Since there's no help, come let us kiss and part. [Michael Drayton, 1563–1631, *The Parting*, 1]

11 Farewell, too little and too lately known, / Whom I began to think and call my own. [John Dryden, 1631–1700, *To the Memory of Mr Oldham*]

12 In every parting there is an image of death. [George Eliot, 1819–80, *Scenes of Clerical Life*, 'Amos Barton', Ch. 10]

13 Not fare well, / But fare forward, voyagers. [T S Eliot, 1888–1965, *Four Quartets*, 'Dry Salvages', III]

14 *Partir c'est mourir un peu, / C'est mourir à ce qu'on aime.* – To part is to die a little, to die to what one loves. [Edmond Haraucourt, 1856–1941, *Seul*, 'Rondel de l'Adieu']

15 Only a little more / I have to write, / Then I'll give o'er, / And bid the world good-night. [Robert Herrick, 1591–1674, *Hesperides*, 'His Poetry his Pillar']

16 I'm going into the next room to pack my bags and you'll never see me again, except at mealtimes and at odd moments during the day and night for a cup of tea and a bun. [Eugene Ionesco, 1912–94, *Jacques or Obedience*]

17 With all my will, but much against my heart, / We two now part, / My Very Dear, / Our solace is, the sad road lies so clear. [Coventry Patmore, 1823–96, *The Unknown Eros*, Bk i, 16, 'A Farewell']

18 My soul, sit thou a patient looker-on; / Judge not the play before the play is done; / Her plot hath many changes; every day / Speaks a new scene; the last act crowns the play. [Francis Quarles, 1592–1644, epigram: *Respice Finem*]

19 God be with you till we meet again; / By His counsels guide, uphold you, / With His sheep securely fold you. [J E Rankin, 1828–1904, hymn]

20 Thus we live, for ever taking leave. [Rainer Maria Rilke, 1875–1926, *Duino Elegies*, 8]

21 Be ahead of all farewells, as if they were behind you, like the winter that is just departing. [Rainer Maria Rilke, 1875–1926, *Sonnets to Orpheus*, II, 12]

22 My name is Might-have-been; / I am also called No-more, Too-late, Farewell. [Dante Gabriel Rossetti, 1828–82, *The House of Life*, 97, 'A Superscription']

23 A man never knows how to say goodbye; a woman never knows when to say it. [Helen Rowland, 1875–1950, *Reflections of a Bachelor Girl*]

24 Every parting is a foretaste of death; every reunion a foretaste of resurrection. [Arthur Schopenhauer, 1788–1860, *Aphorisms*, 'On Psychology', 4]

25 Like the dew on the mountain, / Like the foam on the river, / Like the bubble on the fountain, / Thou art gone, and for ever. [Sir Walter Scott, 1771–1832, *The Lady of the Lake*, III, 16]

26 I do desire we may be better strangers. [William Shakespeare, 1564–1616, *As You Like It*, III. ii (276)]

27 Now cracks a noble heart. Good-night, sweet prince, / And flights of angels sing thee to thy rest! [*Hamlet*, V. ii. (373)]

28 For ever, and for ever, farewell, Cassius! / If we do meet again, why we shall smile! / If not, why then, this parting was well made. [*Julius Caesar*, V. i. 117]

29 Good-night, good-night! parting is such sweet sorrow / That I shall say good-night till it be morrow. [*Romeo and Juliet*, II. ii. 184]

30 Farewell! thou art too dear for my possessing, / And like enough thou know'st thy estimate. [*Sonnets*, 87]

31 Sir, you have tasted two whole worms: you have hissed all my mystery lectures and been caught fighting a liar in the quad; you will leave Oxford by the next town drain. [Revd W A Spooner, 1844–1930, attr. but apocryphal]

32 Shall I strew on thee rose or rue or laurel, / Brother, on this that was the veil of thee? / Or quiet sea-flower moulded by the sea, / Or simplest growth of meadow-sweet or sorrel? [A C Swinburne, 1837–1909, *Ave atque Vale*, 1]

33 I remember the way we parted, / The day and the way we met: / You hoped we were both broken-hearted, / And knew we should both forget. [A C Swinburne, 1837–1909, *An Interlude*]

34 Thy voice is on the rolling air; / I hear thee where the waters run; / Thou standest in the rising sun, / And in the setting thou art fair. [Alfred, Lord Tennyson, 1809–92, *In Memoriam*, 130]

35 And closing the door with the delicate caution of one brushing flies off a sleeping Venus, he passed out of my life. [P G Wodehouse, 1881–1975, *Very Good, Jeeves!*, 'Jeeves and the Old School Chum']

See also GREETINGS

FARMS, see AGRICULTURE

FASCISM

1 Fascism is not in itself a new order of society. It is the future refusing to be born. [Aneurin Bevan, 1897–1960, quoted in Michael Foot, *A B*, Vol. I, Ch. 10]

2 The destiny of history has united you with myself and the Duce in an indissoluble way. [General Franco, 1892–1975, letter to Adolf Hitler]

3 *Kraft durch Freude*. – Strength through joy. [Robert Ley, 1890–1945, German Labour Front slogan, first used 2 Dec. 1933]

4 In politics, as in grammar, one should be able to tell the substantives from adjectives. Hitler was a substantive; Mussolini only an adjective. Hitler was a nuisance; Mussolini was bloody. Together a bloody nuisance. [Salvador de Madariaga, 1886–1978, attr.]

5 I am not, and never have been, a man of the right. My position was on the left and is now in the centre of politics. [Oswald Mosley, 1896–1980, letter to *The Times*, 26 Apr. 1968]

6 Fascism is not an article for export. [Benito Mussolini, 1883–1945 (German press report, 1932), in George Seldes, *Sawdust Caesar*, Ch. 24]

7 I should be pleased, I suppose, that Hitler has carried out a revolution on our lines. But they are Germans. So they will end by ruining our idea. [Benito Mussolini, 1883–1945, in Christopher Hibbert, *B M*, Pt II, Ch. 1]

8 In Germany, the Nazis came for the Communists and I didn't speak up because I was not a Communist. Then they came for the Jews and I didn't speak up because I was not a Jew. Then they came for the trade unionists and I didn't speak up because I was not a trade unionist. Then they came for the Catholics and I was a Protestant so I didn't speak up. Then they came for me . . . By that time there was no one to speak up for anyone. [Martin Niemöller, 1892–1984, attr. in *Congressional Record*, 14 Oct. 1968]

9 It is usual to speak of the Fascist objective as the 'beehive state', which does a grave injustice to bees. A world of rabbits ruled by stoats would be nearer the mark. [George Orwell, 1903–50, *The Road to Wigan Pier*, Ch. 12]

See also HITLER, TYRANTS

FASHION

1 The trick of wearing mink is to look as though you are wearing a cloth coat. The trick of wearing a cloth coat is to look as though you are wearing a mink. [Pierre Balmain, 1914–82; *Observer*, 'Sayings of the Week', 13 Feb. 1955]

2 One had as good be out of the world, as out of the fashion. [Colley Cibber, 1671–1757, *Love's Last Shift*, II]

3 'Mrs Boffin, Wegg,' said Boffin, 'is a highflyer at Fashion.' [Charles Dickens, 1812–70, *Our Mutual Friend*, Bk 1, Ch. 5]

4 If you see a bandwagon, it's too late. [James Goldsmith, 1933–97, in Jeffrey Robinson, *The Risk Takers*]

5 With other fashionable topics, such as pictures, taste, Shakespeare, and the musical glasses. [Oliver Goldsmith, 1728–74, *The Vicar of Wakefield*, Ch. 9]

6 Trendy is emulating your children while they emulate your parents. [Bill Greenwell, in *New Statesman*, 18 June 1982]

7 English women are elegant until they are ten years old, and perfect on grand occasions. [Nancy Mitford, 1904–73; in L and M Cowan, *The Wit of Women*]

8 Be not the first by whom the new are tried, / Nor yet the last to lay the old aside. [Alexander Pope, 1688–1744, *An Essay on Criticism*, 335]

9 But now, God knows, / Anything goes. [Cole Porter, 1891–1964, song: *Anything Goes*, and also title of musical]

10 Her frocks are built in Paris, but she wears them with a strong English accent. [Saki (H H Munro), 1870–1916, *Reginald on Worries*]

11 It is charming to totter into vogue. [Horace Walpole, 1717–97, letter to G A Selwyn, 2 Dec. 1765]

See also TASTE

FAT & THIN

1 Outside every fat man there is an even fatter man trying to close in. [Kingsley Amis, 1922–95, *One Fat Englishman*, Ch. 3]; see 3, 7, 11, 12

2 I was quite fat by this time and all fat women look the same, they all look forty-two. [Margaret Atwood, 1939– , *Lady Oracle*, Ch. 4]

3 Imprisoned in every fat man a thin one is wildly signalling to be let out. [Cyril Connolly, 1903–74, *The Unquiet Grave*, Ch. 1]; see 1, 7, 11, 12

4 She was so thin you could have recognized her skeleton. [Randall Jarrell, 1914–65, *Pictures from an Institution*, Pt II, Ch. 3]

5 It is not growing like a tree / In bulk, doth make men better be. [Ben Jonson, 1573–1637, *Ode on the Death of Sir H. Morison*]

6 Fat is a Feminist Issue. [Susie Orbach, 1946– , title of book]

7 I'm fat, but I'm thin inside. Has it ever struck you that there's a thin man inside every fat man, just as they say there's a statue inside every block of stone? [George Orwell, 1903–50, *Coming up for Air*, I, 3]; see 1, 3, 11, 12

8 Do I not bate? do I not dwindle? Why, my skin hangs about me like an old lady's loose gown; I am withered like an old apple-john. [William Shakespeare, 1564–1616, *1 Henry IV*, III. iii. (2)]

9 I have more flesh than another man, and therefore more frailty. [*1 Henry IV*, III. iii. (187)]

10 Let me have men about me that are fat; / Sleek-headed men and such as sleep o' nights; / Yond Cassius has a lean and hungry look; / He thinks too much: such men are dangerous. [*Julius Caesar*, I. ii. 191]

11 Enclosing every thin man, there's a fat man demanding elbow-room. [Evelyn Waugh,

1903–66, *Officers and Gentlemen*, Interlude]: see 1, 3, 7, 12

12 In answer to: Inside every thin woman there's a fat woman trying to get out, I always think it's: Outside every thin woman there's a fat man trying to get in. [Katharine Whitehorn, 1926– , in BBC radio programme *Quote, Unquote*, 27 July 1985]; see 1, 3, 7, 11

13 One can never be too thin or too rich. [Duchess of Windsor, 1896–1986, attr.]

14 As is so often the case with butlers, there was a good deal of Beach. Julius Caesar, who liked to have men about him who were fat, would have taken to him at once. He was a man who had made two chins grow where only one had been before, and his waistcoat swelled like the sail of a racing yacht. [P G Wodehouse, 1881–1975, *Galahad at Blandings*, Ch. 2]

15 She fitted into my biggest armchair as if it had been built round her by someone who knew they were wearing armchairs tight about the hips that season. [P G Wodehouse, 1881-1975, *My Man Jeeves*, 'Jeeves and the Unbidden Guest']

16 The Right Hon. was a tubby little chap who looked as if he had been poured into his clothes and had forgotten to say 'When!' [P G Wodehouse, 1881–1975, *Very Good, Jeeves!*, 'Jeeves and the Impending Doom']

FATALISM

1 The best of men cannot suspend their fate: / The good die early, and the bad die late. [Daniel Defoe, 1661?–1731, *Character of the Late Dr S. Annesley*]

2 The troubles of our proud and angry dust / Are from eternity, and shall not fail. / Bear them we can, and if we can we must. / Shoulder the sky, my lad, and drink your ale. [A E Housman, 1859–1936, *Last Poems*, 9]

3 I'm not a fatalist; even if I were, what could I do about it? [Emo Philips, in TV programme, *Saturday Live*, 8 Mar. 1986]

4 Not a whit, we defy augury; there's a special providence in the fall of a sparrow. If it be now, 'tis not to come; if it be not to come, it will be now; if it be not now, yet it will come: the readiness is all. [William Shakespeare, 1564–1616, *Hamlet*, V. ii. (232)]

5 Things without all remedy / Should be without regard: what's done is done. [*Macbeth*, III. ii. 11]

6 Things past redress are now with me past care. [*Richard II*, II. iii. 171]

7 Adversity's sweet milk, philosophy. [*Romeo and Juliet*, III. iii. 54]

See also DESTINY, RESIGNATION

FATHERS

1 After all I'm your father. It's true if it hadn't been me it would have been someone else. But that's no excuse. [Samuel Beckett, 1906–89, *Endgame*]

2 Happy is the man that hath his quiver full of them [children]. [Bible, OT, *Psalms* 127:5]

3 I'll meet the raging of the skies, / But not an angry father. [Thomas Campbell, 1777–1844, *Lord Ullin's Daughter*]

4 Investigations into paternity are forbidden. [Code Napoléon, 1804, Article 340]

5 LEONTINE: An only son, sir, might expect more indulgence.

CROAKER: An only father, sir, might expect more obedience. [Oliver Goldsmith, 1728–74, *The Good-Natured Man*, 1]

6 Sefton wasn't excessively or unreasonably Oedipal – he didn't want his father entirely out of the way; but it wouldn't do any harm if he just moved to one side a bit. [Howard Jacobson, 1942– , *Coming from Behind*, Ch. 10]

7 It's all any reasonable child can expect if the dad is present at the conception. [Joe Orton, 1933–67, *Entertaining Mr Sloane*, III]

8 PRENTICE: You did have a father?

GERALDINE: Oh, I'm sure I did. My mother was frugal in her habits, but she'd never economize unwisely. [Joe Orton, 1933–67, *What the Butler Saw*, I]

9 Men are more careful of the breed of their horses and dogs than of their children. [William Penn, 1644–1718, *Reflexions and Maxims*, i, 85]

10 My heart belongs to Daddy / 'Cause my Daddy, he treats me so well. [Cole Porter, 1891–1964, song: *My Heart Belongs to Daddy*, in musical *Leave It to Me*]

11 It is a wise father that knows his own child. [William Shakespeare, 1564–1616, *The Merchant of Venice*, II. i. (83)]

12 Fathers, from hence trust not your daughters' minds / By what you see them act. [*Othello*, I. i. (171)]

13 The only thing that prevented a father's love from faltering was the fact that there was in his possession a photograph of himself at the same early age, in which he, too, looked like a homicidal fried egg. [P G Wodehouse, 1881–1975, *Eggs, Beans and Crumpets*, 'Sonny Boy']

See also CHILDHOOD, MOTHERS, PARENTS

FAULTS

1 *Elles doivent avoir les défauts de leurs qualités.* – They must have the defects of their qualities. [Honoré de Balzac, 1799–1850, *Le Lys dans la vallée*]

2 And e'en his failings leaned to Virtue's side. [Oliver Goldsmith, 1728–74, *The Deserted Village*, 164]

3 If we had no faults we should not take so much pleasure in noticing them in others. [Duc de La Rochefoucauld, 1613–80, *Maxims*, 31]

4 We only confess our little faults to persuade people that we have no large ones. [Duc de La Rochefoucauld, 1613–80, *Maxims*, 327]

5 *O felix culpa, quae talem ac tantum meruit habere Redemptorem.* – O happy fault, which has earned the possession of such, and so great a Redeemer. [Missal, *Exsultet*, on Holy Saturday]

6 People often say that, by pointing out to a man the faults of his mistress, you succeed only in strengthening his attachment to her, because he does not believe you; yet how much more if he does! [Marcel Proust, 1871–1922, *Remembrance of Things Past: Swann's Way*, 'Swann in Love']

7 Every one fault seeming monstrous till his fellow-fault came to match it. [William Shakespeare, 1564–1616, *As You Like It*, III. ii. (377)]

8 And oftentimes excusing of a fault / Doth make the fault the worse by the excuse. [*King John*, IV. ii. 30]

9 They say best men are moulded out of faults, / And for the most, become much more the better / For being a little bad. [*Measure for Measure*, V. i. (440)]

10 Roses have thorns, and silver fountains mud; / Clouds and eclipses stain both moon and sun. [*Sonnets*, 35]

11 It is the little rift within the lute, / That by and by will make the music mute. [Alfred, Lord Tennyson, 1809–92, *Idylls of the King*, 'Merlin and Vivien', 388]

12 'We all have flaws,' he said, 'and mine is being wicked.' [James Thurber, 1894–1961, *The Thirteen Clocks*, Ch. 8]

See also FAILURE, MISTAKES

FEAR

1 *Oderint, dum metuant.* – Let them hate so long as they fear. [Lucius Accius, *c.*170–85 BC, quoted in Cicero's *Philippic*, I, 14]

2 Alone, alone, about the dreadful wood / Of conscious evil runs a lost mankind, / Dreading to find its Father. [W H Auden, 1907–73, *For the Time Being*, 'Chorus']

3 Can she who shines so calm be fear? / What poison pours she in slumber's ear? [Edmund Blunden, 1896–1974, *Evening Mystery*]

4 Where he stands, the Arch Fear in a visible form, / Yet the strong man must go. [Robert Browning, 1812–89, *Prospice*]

5 No passion so effectually robs the mind of all its powers of acting and reasoning as fear. [Edmund Burke, 1729–97, *On the Sublime and Beautiful*, II, ii]

6 Fear has many eyes and can see things underground. [Miguel Cervantes, 1547–1616, *Don Quixote*, Pt I, Ch. 20]

7 Like one that on a lonesome road / Doth walk in fear and dread, / And having once turned round walks on, / And turns no more his head; / Because he knows, a frightful fiend / Doth close behind him tread. [Samuel Taylor Coleridge, 1772–1834, *The Ancient Mariner*, Pt vi]

8 Perfect fear casteth out love. [Cyril Connolly, 1903–74 (to Philip Toynbee during the Blitz), in obituary in the *Observer*, 1 Dec. 1974]

9 I wants to make your flesh creep. [(The Fat Boy) Charles Dickens, 1812–70, *Pickwick Papers*, Ch. 8]

10 And I have seen the eternal Footman hold my coat, and snicker, / And in short, I was afraid. [T S Eliot, 1888–1965, *Love Song of J. Alfred Prufrock*]

11 And I will show you something different from either / Your shadow at morning striding behind you / Or your shadow at evening rising to meet you; / I will show you fear in a handful of dust. [T S Eliot, 1888–1965, *The Waste Land*, 27]

12 There is no terror in a bang, only in the anticipation of it. [Alfred Hitchcock, 1899–1980; in L Halliwell, *The Filmgoer's Book of Quotes*]

13 Only a certain number of things can happen and whatever can happen *will* happen. The differences in scale and costume do not alter the event. Oedipus went to Thebes, Peter Rabbit into Mr McGregor's garden, but the story is essentially the same: life points only towards the terror. [Russell Hoban, 1925–   , *Turtle Diary*, Ch. 12]

14 I think of all the corpses / Worm-eaten in the shade; / I cannot chew my peanuts / Or drink my lemonade: / Good God, I am afraid! [Samuel Hoffenstein, 1890–1947, *The Shropshire Lad's Cousin*]

15 I, a stranger and afraid / In a world I never made. [A E Housman, 1859–1936, *Last Poems*, 12]

16 'Twas only fear first in the world made gods. [Ben Jonson, 1573–1637, *Sejanus*, II, ii]

17 Dread is a sympathetic antipathy and an antipathetic sympathy. [Søren Kierkegaard, 1813–55, in W H Auden, *A Kierkegaard Anthology*, p. 134]

18 Through the Jungle very softly flits a shadow and a sigh – / He is Fear, O Little Hunter, he is Fear! [Rudyard Kipling, 1865–1936, *The Song of the Little Hunter*]

19 Gratitude looks to the past and love to the present; fear, avarice, lust and ambition look ahead. [C S Lewis, 1898–1963, *The Screwtape Letters*, 15]

20 Let me assert my firm belief that the only thing we have to fear is fear itself. [Franklin D Roosevelt, 1882–1945, first presidential inaugural address, 4 Mar. 1933]

21 Why do I yield to that suggestion / Whose horrid image doth unfix my hair / And make my seated heart knock at my ribs, / Against the use of nature? Present fears / Are less than horrible imaginings. [William Shakespeare, 1564–1616, *Macbeth*, I. iii. 134]

22 Infirm of purpose! / Give me the daggers. The sleeping and the dead / Are but as pictures; 'tis the eye of childhood / That fears a painted devil. [*Macbeth*, II. ii. 53]

23 The time has been my senses would have cooled / To hear a night-shriek, and my fell of hair / Would at a dismal treatise rouse and stir / As life were in't. [*Macbeth*, V. v. 10]

24 Or in the night, imagining some fear, / How easy is a bush supposed a bear! [*A Midsummer Night's Dream*, V. i. 21]

25 Anything scares me, anything scares anyone but really after all considering how dangerous everything is nothing is really very frightening. [Gertrude Stein, 1874–1946, *Everybody's Autobiography*, Ch. 2]

26 Hope thou not much, and fear thou not at all. [A C Swinburne, 1837–1909, *Hope and Fear*]

27 Her own mother lived the latter years of her life in the horrible suspicion that electricity was dripping invisibly all over the house. [James Thurber, 1894–1961, *My Life and Hard Times*, Ch. 2]

28 My apprehensions come in crowds; / I dread the rustling of the grass; / The very shadows of the clouds / Have power to shake me as they pass. [William Wordsworth, 1770–1850, *The Affliction of Margaret*]

FEMINISM

1 You can have a men's novel with no women in it except possibly the landlady / or the horse, but you can't have a women's novel with no men in it. / Sometimes men put women in men's novels / but they leave out some of the parts; / the heads, for instance. [Margaret Atwood, 1939–   , *Poem*, in Resa Dudovitz, *The Myth of Superwoman*]

2 Women were brought up to believe that men were the answer. They weren't. They weren't even one of the questions. [Julian Barnes, 1946–   , *Staring at the Sun*, Pt 2]

3 Feminism is an insurrection, not a coffee morning. [Geraldine Bedell, 1956–   , in *Independent*, 14 Nov. 1988]

4 Anything You Can Do, I Can Do Better. [Irving Berlin, 1888–1989, title of song in musical *Annie Get Your Gun*, II]

5 Of course I'm a feminist. You have to be these days – it's the only way to pull the chicks. [Ben Elton, 1959– , Rick Mayall, 1958– , and Lise Meyer, from TV programme *The Young Ones*, in *Observer*, 24 Apr. 1988]

6 All men are rapists, and that's all they are. They rape us with their eyes, their laws, and their codes. [Marilyn French, 1929– , *The Women's Room*, Bk 5, Ch. 19]

7 It's hard to fight an enemy with outposts in your head. [Sally Kempton, ?1943– (of feminism), in *Esquire* magazine, July 1970]

8 I'm furious about the Women's Liberationists. They keep getting up on soap-boxes and proclaiming that women are brighter than men. That's true, but it should be kept very quiet or it ruins the whole racket. [Anita Loos, 1893–1981; *Observer*, 'Sayings of the Year', 30 Dec. 1973]

9 The vote, I thought, means nothing to women. We should be armed. [Edna O'Brien, 1932– , epigraph to Erica Jong, *Fear of Flying*, Ch. 16]

10 We have to free half of the human race, the women, so that they can help to free the other half. [Emmeline Pankhurst, 1858–1928, quoted in Naim Attallah, *Women*]

11 Men will often admit other women are oppressed but not you. [Sheila Rowbotham, 1943– , *Woman's Consciousness, Man's World*]

12 The one point on which all women are in furious secret rebellion against the existing law is the saddling of the right to a child with the obligation to become the servant of a man. [George Bernard Shaw, 1856–1950, *Getting Married*, Preface]

13 Womanist is to feminist as purple is to lavender. [Alice Walker, 1944– , in *Guardian*, 17 May 1986]

14 The thought could not be avoided that the best home for a feminist was in another person's lab. [James D Watson, 1928– , *The Double Helix*, Ch. 2]

15 I didn't set out to be a feminist writer. I just look at the sheep out of the window and watch their behaviour. [Fay Weldon, 1931– , interview in *Observer*, 30 Apr. 1989]

16 I only know that people call me a feminist whenever I express sentiments that differentiate me from a doormat or a prostitute. [Rebecca West, 1892–1983 (said in 1913), in *Observer*, 25 July 1982]

17 Women have always been the guardians of wisdom and humanity which makes them natural, but usually secret, rulers. The time has come for them to rule openly, but together with and not against men. [Charlotte Wolff, 1904–86, *Bisexuality: A Study*, Ch. 2]

18 I do not wish them to have power over men: but over themselves. [(Of women) Mary Wollstonecraft, 1759–97, *A Vindication of the Rights of Women*, 4]

See also WOMEN

FICTION, see NOVELS, PROSE, STORIES

FIGHTS & FIGHTING

1 He that fights and runs away / May live to fight another day. [anon., *Musarum Deliciae*, 17th cent.]

2 Thrice is he armed that hath his quarrel just, / But four times he who gets his blow in fust. [Josh Billings, 1818–85, *J B, his Sayings*]

3 I was ever a fighter, so – one fight more, / The best and the last! [Robert Browning, 1812–89, *Prospice*]

4 Liberty's in every blow! / Let us do or die! [Robert Burns, 1759–96, *Scots, Wha Hae*]

5 But brawling leads to laryngitis. [Jean Cocteau, 1889–1963, *Les Enfants terribles*]

6 'Tis better to have fought and lost, / Than never to have fought at all. [Arthur Hugh Clough, 1819–61, *Peschiera*]

7 Fought all his battles o'er again; / And thrice he routed all his foes; and thrice he slew the slain. [John Dryden, 1631–1700, *Alexander's Feast*, 67]

8 It's not what men fight for. They fight in the last resort to impress their mothers. [Gabriel Fielding, 1916–86, *The Birthday King*, Ch. 3]

9 And he is dead who will not fight, / And who dies fighting has increase. [Julian Grenfell, 1888–1915, *Into Battle*]

10 Our swords shall play the orators for us. [Christopher Marlowe, 1564–93, *Tamburlaine the Great*, Pt I, I. ii. 132]

11 Never fight fair with a stranger, boy. You'll never get out of the jungle that way. [Arthur Miller, 1915– , *Death of a Salesman*, 1]

12 The stubborn spear-men still made good / Their dark impenetrable wood, / Each stepping where his comrade stood, / The instant that he fell. [Sir Walter Scott, 1771–1832, *Marmion*, VI, 34]

13 Shall we fight or shall we fly? / Good Sir Richard, tell us now, / For to fight is but to die! / There'll be little of us left by the time this sun is set. [Alfred, Lord Tennyson, 1809–92, *The Revenge*, 9]

See also BATTLES, VICTORY, WARS

FILM

1 The great art of films does not consist of descriptive movement of face and body but in the movements of thought and soul, transmitted in a kind of intense isolation. [Louise Brooks, 1908–85, in Kenneth Tynan, *Show People*]

2 Theatre is like operating with a scalpel. Film is operating with a laser. [Michael Caine, 1933– , in BBC TV programme *Acting*, 28 Aug. 1987]

3 I made mistakes in drama. I thought drama was when actors cried. But drama is when the audience cries. [Frank Capra, 1897–1991, on French TV, Feb. 1983; in *Chambers Film Quotes*, comp. Tony Crawley]

4 The cinema has become more and more like the theatre, it's all mauling and muttering. [Shelagh Delaney, 1939– , *A Taste of Honey*, II. ii]

5 Photography is truth. And cinema is truth twenty-four times a second. [Jean-Luc Godard, 1930– , in film *Le Petit Soldat*]

6 GEORGE FRANJU: Movies should have a beginning, a middle and an end.
GODARD: Certainly, but not necessarily in that order. [Jean-Luc Godard, 1930– , in *Time* magazine, 14 Sept. 1981]

7 Why should people go out and pay money to see bad films when they can stay at home and see bad television for nothing? [Samuel Goldwyn, 1882–1974; *Observer*, 'Sayings of the Week', 9 Sept. 1956]

8 What we want is a story that starts with an earthquake and works its way up to a climax. [Samuel Goldwyn, 1882–1974; in L Halliwell, *Filmgoer's Book of Quotes*]

9 Film is not the art of scholars but of illiterates. Film culture is not analysis but agitation of the mind. [Werner Herzog, 1942– , in *Guardian*, 8 Sept. 1977]

10 For me the cinema is not a slice of life, but a piece of cake. [Alfred Hitchcock, 1899–1980, in *The Sunday Times Magazine*, 6 Mar. 1977]

11 They are doing things on the screen these days that the French don't even put on post-cards. [Bob Hope, 1903– ; in L Halliwell, *The Filmgoer's Book of Quotes*]

12 You ain't heard nothin' yet. [Al Jolson, 1886–1950, in first talking film, *The Jazz Singer*, July 1927]

13 When I see those ads with the quote 'You'll have to see this picture twice', I know it's the kind of picture I don't want to see once. [Pauline Kael, 1919– , *Deeper into Movies*, 'Waiting for Orgy']

14 The words 'Kiss Kiss Bang Bang', which I saw on an Italian movie poster, are perhaps the briefest statement imaginable of the basic appeal of movies. This appeal is what attracts us and ultimately what makes us despair when we begin to understand how seldom movies are more than this. [Pauline Kael, 1919– , *Kiss Kiss Bang Bang*, 'A Note on the Title']

15 Film is the least realistic of art forms. [David Mamet, 1947– , interview in *Guardian*, 16 Feb. 1989]

16 Sticks Nix Hick Pix. [(On Midwestern reaction to films about poor hillbillies) headline in *Variety*, 17 July 1935. Also ascribed to Abel Green, 1900–1973]

17 Some of the worst films of all time have been made by people who think too much. [Steven Soderbegh, 1963– , interview in *Guardian*, 7 Sept. 1989]

18 We fight wars which we lose, then we make films showing how we won them and the films make more money than the war lost. [Gore Vidal, 1925– , in *Weekend Guardian*, 4–5 Nov. 1989]

19 I wouldn't say when you've seen one Western you've seen the lot; but when you've seen the lot you get the feeling you've seen one. [Katharine Whitehorn, 1926– , *Sunday Best*, 'Decoding the West']

20 It [D W Griffith's film *Birth of a Nation*] is like writing history with lightning and my only regret is that it is all so terribly true. [President Woodrow Wilson, 1856–1924, in D J Boorstin, *The Image*, Ch. 4]

FILM DIRECTORS & WRITERS

1 It [film making] is the business of turning money into light and then back into money again. [John Boorman, 1933– , quoted by Tom Stoppard in *The Sunday Times*, 20 Jan. 1980]

2 The director of a film is treated by his staff the way a group of passengers would treat a psychotic ship's captain during a typhoon; namely, with respect and apprehension. [Marshall Brickman, 1941– , interview in *Guardian*, 13 Sept. 1980]

3 Bring on the empty horses! [Michael Curtiz, 1888–1962, attr. during filming of *The Charge of the Light Brigade*. David Niven used it for the title of second volume of his autobiography]

4 If I had to define myself I'd say I am 'a painter of letters' as one would say that there are 'men of letters'. [Jean-Luc Godard, 1930– , in Jay Leyda, *Voices of Film Experience*]

5 You can't make a 'Hamlet' without breaking a few egos. [William Goldman, 1931– (of the screenwriter's problems over the star system), in *Observer*, 8 Apr. 1984]

6 Chaplin is no business man – all he knows is that he can't take anything less. [Samuel Goldwyn, 1882–1974, in Charles Chaplin, *My Autobiography*, Ch. 19]

7 How'm I gonna do decent pictures when all my good writers are in jail? . . . Don't misunderstand me, they all ought to be hung. [Samuel Goldwyn, 1882–1974, quoted by Dorothy Parker in *Writers at Work*, ed. Malcolm Cowley, First Series]

8 Every director bites the hand that lays the golden egg. [Samuel Goldwyn, 1882–1974, attr. in Alva Johnston, *The Great Goldwyn*, Ch. 1]

9 De Mille made small-minded pictures on a big scale – they're about as Promethean as a cash register. [Pauline Kael, 1919– , *Kiss Kiss Bang Bang*, 'Epics']

10 I do not know whether he [Walt Disney] draws a line himself. But I assume that his is the direction, the constant aiming after improvement in the new expression . . . it is the direction of a real artist. It makes Disney, not as a draughtsman but as an artist who uses his brains, the most significant figure in graphic art since Leonardo. [David Low, 1891–1963, in R Schickel, *Walt Disney*, Ch. 20]

11 That man [a fellow scriptwriter] is so bad he shouldn't be left alone in a room with a typewriter. [Herman J Mankiewicz, 1897–1953, attr.]

12 The difference between being a director and being an actor is the difference between being the carpenter banging the nails into the wood, and being the piece of wood the nails are being banged into. [Sean Penn, 1960– , interview in *Guardian*, 28 Nov. 1991]

13 The man who cut my picture [*Greed*] had nothing on his mind but a hat. [Erich von Stroheim, 1885–1957, in Kevin Brownlow, *Hollywood: The Pioneers*, Ch. 22]

14 I'm just in love with making movies. Not very fond of movies – I don't go to them much. I think it's very harmful for movie-makers to see movies, because you either imitate them or worry about not imitating them. [Orson Welles, 1915–85, from TV programme *Arena*, in *Listener*, 17 Oct. 1985]

15 A team effort is a lot of people doing what I say. [Michael Winner, 1935– , in *Observer Magazine*, 8 May 1983]

FILM STARS IN GENERAL

1 As far as the film-making process is concerned, stars are essentially worthless and absolutely essential. [William Goldman, 1931– , *Adventures in the Screen Trade*, Pt 1, Ch. 1]

2 Starlet is a name for any woman under thirty not actively employed in a brothel. [Ben Hecht, 1893–1964, in *Hollywood Anecdotes*, ed. Paul F Boller Jr and Kristin Thompson]

3 HOLDEN: You used to be in silent pictures, you used to be big!
SWANSON: I am *still* big. It's the pictures that got small. [Billy Wilder, 1906– , in film *Sunset Boulevard*, scripted with Charles Brackett and D M Marshman]

FILM STARS: INDIVIDUAL (in alphabetical order of subject)

1 Working with her [Julie Andrews] is like being hit over the head with a Valentine card. [Christopher Plummer, 1927– , in *Utterly Trivial Knowledge: The Music Game*, ed. John Denny]

2 He gave her class and she gave him sex. [Katharine Hepburn, 1907– (of Fred Astaire and Ginger Rogers on former's death), in *Guardian*, 23 June 1987]

3 I've just spent an hour talking to Tallulah [Bankhead] for a few minutes. [Fred Keating, in *Woman Talk 2*, comp. Michèle Brown and Ann O'Connor]

4 She [Brigitte Bardot] was the type of flower that one waters but does not cut. [Roger Vadim, 1928– , *Bardot, Deneuve and Fonda*, quoted in *The Sunday Times*, 6 Apr. 1986]

5 He [Marlon Brando] is our greatest actor, our noblest actor, and he is also our national lout. [Norman Mailer, 1923– , in *Observer*, 1 Jan. 1989]

6 I can't once remember him [Charlie Chaplin] still. He was always standing up as he sat down and going out as he came in. [Louise Brooks, 1908–85, in Kenneth Tynan, *Show People*]

7 People never sat at his [Charlie Chaplin's] feet. He went to where people were sitting and stood in front of them. [Herman J Mankiewicz, 1897–1953, in Kenneth Tynan, *Show People*, 'Louise Brooks']

8 The audience didn't realize how odd he [Charlie Chaplin] was because he was so near to reality in his madness. [Ralph Richardson, 1902–83, in BBC TV programme *The Michael Parkinson Show*, 13 Dec. 1980]

9 Being a star has made it possible for me to get insulted in places where the average Negro could never hope to get insulted. [Sammy Davis Jr, 1925–90, *Yes I Can*]

10 I've been around so long I can remember Doris Day before she was a virgin. [Groucho Marx, 1895–1977; in L Halliwell, *Filmgoer's Book of Quotes*. Also ascr. to Oscar Levant]

11 Douglas [Fairbanks] had always faced a situation the only way he knew how, by running away from it. [Mary Pickford, 1893–1979, *Sunshine and Shadow*]

12 Anybody who hates dogs and babies can't be all bad. [(Of W C Fields) Leo Rosten, 1908–96, at Masquers' Club Dinner, Hollywood, 16 Feb. 1939. Often misquoted as 'children and dogs' and wrongly attr. to Fields]

13 She [Zsa-Zsa Gabor] not only worships the Golden Calf, she barbecues it. [Oscar Levant, 1906–72, attr.]

14 The whole set-up has taken on a very weathered look, dry and draughty, like an abandoned temple, something lost in the jungles at Angkor Wat. [(Of Greta Garbo) Truman Capote, 1924–84, *Answered Prayers*, III]

15 She [Greta Garbo] gave cinema the sacredness of mass. [Federico Fellini, 1920–93, on her death; *Independent*, 'Quote Unquote', 21 Apr. 1990]

16 (When asked by David Niven, 'Why *did* you give up the movies?') I had made enough faces. [Greta Garbo, 1905–90, in David Niven, *Bring on the Empty Horses*, 'Two Queens']

17 What, when drunk, one sees in other women, one sees in Garbo sober. [Kenneth Tynan, 1927–80, *Curtains*, 2, 'Garbo']

18 I've made so many movies playing a hooker that they don't pay me in the regular way any more. They leave it on the dresser. [Shirley Maclaine, 1934– , in *New Woman*, July 1989]

19 She had a heart. It photographed. [Victor Saville, 1897–1979, of Jessie Matthews (who appeared in the film *Evergreen*, directed by Saville) in her obituary in *Guardian*, 21 Aug. 1981]

20 He [Paul Newman] has the attention span of a bolt of lightning. [Robert Redford, 1937– , in *The New York Times*, 28 Sept. 1986]

21 She looked as though butter wouldn't melt in her mouth – or anywhere else. [Elsa Lanchester, 1902–86, of Maureen O'Hara; *News Summaries*, 30 Jan. 1950]

22 There, but for the Grace of God, goes God. [Herman J Mankiewicz, 1897–1953 (Of Orson Welles, during the making of the film *Citizen Kane*), in *The Citizen Kane Book*. Also ascr. to Winston Churchill on Stafford Cripps]

23 A plumber's idea of Cleopatra. [W C Fields, 1879–1946 (of Mae West in her films), in Louise Brooks, *Lulu in Hollywood*, 'The Other Face of W. C. Fields']

24 She stole everything but the cameras. [George Raft, 1895–1980, as Mae West's co-star on her film début; in L Halliwell, *Filmgoer's Book of Quotes*]

See also previous categories

FIRE

1 All things, oh priests, are on fire . . . The eye is on fire; forms are on fire; eye-consciousness is on fire; impressions received by the eye are on fire. [Buddha, *c.*563–483 BC, *The Fire Sermon*]

2 When our brother Fire was having his dog's day / Jumping the London streets with millions of tin cans / Clanking at his tail, we heard some shadow say / 'Give the dog a bone.' [Louis MacNeice, 1907–1963, *Brother Fire*]

3 A little fire is quickly trodden out, / Which being suffered, rivers cannot quench. [William Shakespeare, 1564–1616, *3 Henry VI*, IV. viii. 7]

4 Prometheus stole fire from Heaven so that we could not only cook dinner but one another. [Gore Vidal, 1925– , in *Observer Review*, 27 Aug. 1989]

FISH & FISHING

1 And nigh this toppling reed, still as the dead / The great pike lies, the murderous patriarch, / Watching the water-pit shelving and dark / Where through the plash his lithe bright vassals tread. [Edmund Blunden, 1896–1974, *The Pike*]

2 Thy lot thy brethren of the slimy fin / Would envy, could they know that thou wast doomed / To feed a bard, and to be praised in verse. [William Cowper, 1731–1800, *To the Immortal Memory of the Halibut on which I Dined*]

3 Ann, Ann! / Come! quick as you can! / There's a fish that *talks* / In the frying pan. [Walter de la Mare, 1873–1956, *Alas, Alack*]

4 And now the salmon-fishers moist / Their leathern boats begin to hoist; / And like Antipodes in shoes, / Have shod their heads in their canoes. [Andrew Marvell, 1621–78, *Upon Appleton House*, 769]

5 Dr Strabismus (Whom God Preserve) of Utrecht is carrying out research work with a view to crossing salmon with mosquitoes. He says it will mean a bite every time for fishermen. [J B Morton ('Beachcomber'), 1893–1979, *By the Way*, Jan., tail-piece]

6 Wha'll buy my caller herrin'? / They're bonnie fish and halesome farin'. [Lady Nairne, 1766–1845, *Caller Herring*]

7 Who wants my jellyfish? / I'm not sellyfish. [Ogden Nash, 1902–71, *The Jellyfish*]

8 Tell me, O Octopus, I begs, / Is those things arms, or is they legs? / I marvel at thee, Octopus; / If I were thou, I'd call me Us. [Ogden Nash, 1902–71, *The Octopus*]

9 Was he the only fisherman left in the world / using the old ways, who believed his work was prayer, / who caught only enough, since the sea had to live. [Derek Walcott, 1930– , *Omeros*, Ch. lx]

10 As no man is born an artist, so no man is born an angler. [Izaak Walton, 1593–1683, *The Compleat Angler*, 'Epistle to the Reader']

FLATTERY

1 It is happy for you that you possess the talent of flattering with delicacy. May I ask whether these pleasing attentions proceed from the impulse of the moment, or are the result of previous study? [Jane Austen, 1775–1817, *Pride and Prejudice*, 14]

2 The arch-flatterer, with whom all the petty flatterers have intelligence, is a man's self. [Francis Bacon, 1561–1626, *Essays*, 10, 'Of Love']

3 Every woman is infallibly to be gained by every sort of flattery, and every man by one sort or other. [Earl of Chesterfield, 1694–1773, letter to his son, 16 Mar. 1752]

4 And, of all lies (be that one poet's boast) / The lie that flatters I abhor the most. [William Cowper, 1731–1800, *Table Talk*, 87]

5 We authors, Ma'am. [Benjamin Disraeli, 1804–81 (remark to Queen Victoria, attr.); quoted in F Monypenny and G E Buckle, *Life*, Vol. v, p. 49]

6 Everyone likes flattery; and when you come to Royalty you should lay it on with a trowel. [Benjamin Disraeli, 1804–81 (remark to Matthew Arnold, attr.), quoted in G W E Russell, *Collections and Recollections*, Ch. 23]

7 Be advised that all flatterers live at the expense of those who listen to them. [Jean de La Fontaine, 1621–95, *Fables*, 'The Crow and the Fox']

8 Flattery is false coin that is only current thanks to our vanity. [Duc de La Rochefoucauld, 1613–80, *Maxims*, 158]

9 But when I tell him he hates flatterers, / He says he does, being then most flattered. [William Shakespeare, 1564–1616, *Julius Caesar*, II. i. 207]

10 What really flatters a man is that you think him worth flattering. [George Bernard Shaw, 1856–1950, *John Bull's Other Island*, IV]

11 Flattery is all right – if you don't inhale. [Adlai Stevenson, 1900–1965, speech, 1 Feb. 1961]

12 'Tis an old maxim in the schools, / That flattery's the food of fools; / Yet now and then your men of wit. / Will condescend to take a bit. [Jonathan Swift, 1677–1745, *Cadenus and Vanessa*, 758]

FLOWERS

1 The desert shall rejoice, and blossom as the rose. [Bible, OT, *Isaiah* 35:1]

2 Ah, Sun-flower! weary of time, / Who countest the steps of the sun; / Seeking after that sweet golden clime, / Where the traveller's journey is done;

Where the Youth pined away with desire, / And the pale Virgin shrouded in snow, / Arise from their graves, and aspire / Where my Sun-flower wishes to go. [William Blake, 1757–1827, *Songs of Experience*, 'Ah! Sun-flower']

3 O Rose, thou art sick! / The invisible worm, / That flies in the night, / In the howling storm, / Has found out thy bed / Of crimson joy; / And his dark secret love / Does thy life destroy. [William Blake, 1757–1827, *Songs of Experience*, 'The Sick Rose']

4 Here tulips bloom as they are told; / Unkempt about those hedges blows / An English unofficial rose; / And there the unregulated sun / Slopes down to rest when day is done. [Rupert Brooke, 1887–1915, *The Old Vicarage, Grantchester*]

5 It was roses, roses, all the way, / With myrtle mixed in my path like mad. [Robert Browning, 1812–89, *The Patriot*]

6 Wee modest crimson-tippèd flow'r. [Robert Burns, 1759–96, *To a Mountain Daisy*]

7 As a flower springs up secretly in a fenced garden, known to no cattle, bruised by no plough, caressed by the winds, strengthened by the sun, and drawn up by the shower, so many a boy and many a girl desire it. [Catullus, 87–54? BC, *Carmina*, 62]

8 Of alle the floures in the mede, / Than love I most these floures whyte and rede, / Swiche as men callen daysies in our toun. [Geoffrey Chaucer, 1340?–1400, *The Legend of Good Women*, Prologue, 36 (second version, 41)]

9 For the flowers of the forest are withered away. [Alison Cockburn, 1713–94, *The Flowers of the Forest*]

10 The bud may have a bitter taste, / But sweet will be the flower. [William Cowper, 1731–1800, *Olney Hymns*, 35]

11 Oh, no man knows / Through what wild centuries / Roves back the rose. [Walter de la Mare, 1873–1956, *All That's Past*]

12 I sometimes think that never blows so red / The Rose as where some buried Caesar bled; / That every Hyacinth the Garden wears / Dropt in her Lap from some once lovely Head. [Edward Fitzgerald, 1809–83, *The Rubá'iyát of Omar Khayyám*, Edn 1, 18]

13 Sweet as the primrose peeps beneath the thorn. [Oliver Goldsmith, 1728–74, *The Deserted Village*, 330]

14 Fair daffodils, we weep to see / You haste away so soon: / As yet the early-rising sun / Has not attained his noon. [Robert Herrick, 1591–1674, *Hesperides*, 'To Daffodils']

15 Gather ye rosebuds while ye may, / Old Time is still a-flying: / And this same flower that smiles to-day, / To-morrow will be dying. [Robert Herrick, 1591–1674, *Hesperides*, 'To Virgins, to Make Much of Time']

16 You buy some flowers for your table; / You tend them tenderly as you're able; / You fetch them water from hither and thither – / What thanks do you get for it all? They wither. [Samuel Hoffenstein, 1890–1947, *Poems in Praise of Practically Nothing*, Second Series]

17 Here are sweet-peas, on tip-toe for a flight: / With wings of gentle flush o'er delicate white, / And taper fingers catching at all things, / To bind them all about with tiny rings. [John Keats, 1795–1821, '*I Stood Tip-toe*', 57]

18 Mid-May's eldest child, / The coming musk-rose, full of dewy wine, / The murmurous haunt of flies on summer eves. [John Keats, 1795–1821, *Ode to a Nightingale*, 5]

19 Throw hither all your quaint enamelled eyes / That on the green turf suck the honied showers, / And purple all the ground with vernal flowers. / Bring the rathe primrose that forsaken dies, / The tufted crow-toe and pale jessamine, / The white pink, and the pansy freaked with jet, / The glowing violet, / The muskrose and the well-attired woodbine, / With cowslips wan that hang the pensive head, / And every flower that sad embroidery wears: / Bid amaranthus all his beauty shed, / And daffadillies fill their cups with tears, / To strew the laureate hearse where Lycid lies. [John Milton, 1608–74, *Lycidas*, 139]

20 O fairest flower, no sooner blown but blasted, / Soft silken primrose fading timelessly. [John Milton, 1608–74, *On the Death of a Fair Infant*, 1]

21 As the sun-flower turns on her god, when he sets, / The same look which she turned, when he rose. [Thomas Moore, 1779–1852, *Irish Melodies*, 'Believe Me, If All . . .']

22 Daffy-down-dilly is new come to town, / With a yellow petticoat, and a green gown. [Nursery rhyme]

23 Say it with flowers. [Patrick O'Keefe, 1872–1934, slogan for Society of American Florists, 1917]

24 Thou shalt not lack / The flower that's like thy face, pale primrose, nor / The azured hare-bell, like thy veins. [William Shakespeare, 1564–1616, *Cymbeline*, IV. ii. 220]

25 But earthlier happy is the rose distilled, / Than that which withering on the virgin thorn, / Grows, lives, and dies, in single blessedness. [*A Midsummer Night's Dream*, I. i. 76]

26 Yet marked I where the bolt of Cupid fell; / It fell upon a little western flower, / Before milk-white, now purple with love's wound, / And maidens call it Love-in-idleness. [*A Midsummer Night's Dream*, II. i. 165]

27 I know a bank whereon the wild thyme blows, / Where oxlips and the nodding violet grows / Quite over-canopied with luscious woodbine, / With sweet musk-roses, and with eglantine. [*A Midsummer Night's Dream*, II. i. 249]

28 O Proserpina! / For the flowers now that frighted thou let'st fall / From Dis's waggon! daffodils, / That come before the swallow dares, and take / The winds of March with beauty; violets dim, / But sweeter than the lids of Juno's eyes / Or Cytherea's breath; pale primroses, / That die unmarried ere they can behold / Bright Phoebus in his strength – a malady / Most incident to maids; bold oxlips and / The crown imperial; lilies of all kinds, / The flower-de-luce being one. [*The Winter's Tale*, IV. iii. 116]

29 For sweetest things turn sourest by their deeds; / Lilies that fester smell far worse than weeds. [*Sonnets*, 94]

30 There grew pied wind-flowers and violets, / Daisies, those pearled Arcturi of the earth, / The constellated flower that never sets; / Faint oxslips; tender bluebells, at whose birth / The sod scarce heaved. [P B Shelley, 1792–1822, *The Question*]

31 And is there any moral shut / Within the bosom of the rose? [Alfred, Lord Tennyson, 1809–92, *The Day-Dream*, 'Moral', 7]

32 All night have the roses heard / The flute, violin, bassoon; / All night has the casement jessamine stirred / To the dancers dancing in tune; / Till a silence fell with the waking bird, / And a hush with the setting moon. [Alfred, Lord Tennyson, 1809–92, *Maud*, Pt 1, xxii, 3]

33 Summer set lip to earth's bosom bare, / And left the flushed print in a poppy there. [Francis Thompson, 1859–1907, *The Poppy*]

34 Now the jonquil o'ercomes the feeble brain; / We faint beneath the aromatic pain. [Anne Finch, Countess of Winchelsea, 1661–1720, *The Spleen*]

35 I wandered lonely as a cloud / That floats on high o'er vales and hills, / When all at once I saw a crowd, / A host, of golden daffodils. [William Wordsworth, 1770–1850, *I Wandered Lonely as a Cloud*]

36 To me the meanest flowers that blow can give / Thoughts that do often lie too deep for tears. [William Wordsworth, 1770–1850, *Ode, Intimations of Immortality*, 11]

37 A primrose by a river's brim / A yellow primrose was to him, / And it was nothing more. [William Wordsworth, 1770–1850, *Peter Bell*, I, 248]

38 A violet by a mossy stone / Half hidden from the eye! / – Fair as a star, when only one / Is shining in the sky. [William Wordsworth, 1770–1850, *She Dwelt among the Untrodden Ways*]

39 Thou unassuming common-place / Of Nature. [William Wordsworth, 1770–1850, *To the Daisy*, 'With little here to do . . .']

40 Pleasures newly found are sweet / When they lie about our feet. [William Wordsworth, 1770–1850, *To the Small Celandine*, 'Pleasures newly found . . .']

41 Far-off, most secret and inviolate Rose, / Enfold me in my hour of hours. [W B Yeats, 1865–1939, *The Secret Rose*]

FOOD

1 You know the kind of thing – the salad was decorated with the Lord's Prayer in beetroot. [(Of Lady Desborough's 'fussy and over-elaborate food') Margot Asquith, 1865–1945, quoted in *Observer*, 20 Dec. 1981]

2 There is no such thing as a little garlic. [Arthur 'Bugs' Baer, 1897–1975, in Frank Muir, *Frank Muir Book*]

3 His meat was locusts and wild honey. [Bible, NT, *St Matthew* 3:4]

4 It is not meet to take the children's bread, and to cast it to dogs. [Bible, NT, *St Matthew* 15:26]

5 Tell me what you eat: I will tell you what you are. [Jean-Anthelme Brillat-Savarin, 1755–1826, *The Physiology of Taste*, Aphorisms IV]

6 So munch on, crunch on, take your nuncheon, / Breakfast, supper, dinner, luncheon! [Robert Browning, 1812–89, *The Pied Piper of Hamelin*, 7]

7 Fair fa' your honest sonsie face, / Great chieftain o' the puddin'-race! / Aboon them a' ye tak your place, / Painch, tripe, or thairm: / Weel are ye worthy o' a grace / As lang's my arm. [Robert Burns, 1759–96, *To a Haggis*]

8 The healthy stomach is nothing if not conservative. Few radicals have good digestions. [Samuel Butler, 1835–1902, *Notebooks*, Ch. 6, 'Indigestion']

9 That all-softening, overpowering knell, / The tocsin of the soul – the dinner-bell. [Lord Byron, 1788–1824, *Don Juan*, V, 49]

10 A cheap but wholesome salad from the brook. [William Cowper, 1731–1800, *The Task*, Bk VI, 304]

11 I can't abear a Butcher, / I can't abide his meat. [Walter de la Mare, 1873–1956, *I Can't Abear*]

12 It's a very odd thing – / As odd as can be – / That whatever Miss T. eats / Turns into Miss T. [Walter de la Mare, 1873–1956, *Miss T.*]

13 I wished now that I had gone to the restaurant across the street where the food had at least the merit of being tasteless. [Peter de Vries, 1910–93, *Comfort Me with Apples*, Ch. 18]

14 Oliver Twist has asked for more! [Charles Dickens, 1812–70, *Oliver Twist*, Ch. 2]

15 Ranulphe says he [King Henry I] took a surfeit by eating of a lamprey, and thereof died. [Robert Fabyan, d.1513, *Chronicles*, 229. (Ranulphe did not, in fact, specify)]

16 A man is what he eats. [Ludwig Feuerbach, 1804–72, *Blätter für Literarische Unterhaltung*, 12 Nov. 1850]

17 The holes in your Swiss cheese are somebody else's Swiss cheese. [Melvin Fishman, in *The Times Higher Education Supplement*, 15 Jan. 1982]

18 Take the soup away! / O take the nasty soup away! / I won't have any soup today. [Heinrich Hoffman, 1809–74, *Struwwelpeter*, 'Augustus']

19 I look upon it, that he who does not mind his belly, will hardly mind anything else. [Dr Samuel Johnson, 1709–84, in James Boswell, *Life of J*, 5 Aug. 1763]

20 A cucumber should be well sliced, and dressed with pepper and vinegar, and then thrown out, as good for nothing. [Dr Samuel Johnson, 1709–84, in James Boswell, *Tour of the Hebrides*, 5 Oct. 1773]

21 A heap / Of candied apple, quince, and plum, and gourd; / With jellies soother than the creamy curd, / And lucent syrops tinct with cinnamon. [John Keats, 1795–1821, *The Eve of St Agnes*, 30]

22 C – [Coleridge] holds that a man cannot have a pure mind who refuses apple-dumplings. [Charles Lamb, 1775–1834, *Essays of Elia*, 'Grace before Meat']

23 Food is an important part of a balanced diet. [Fran Lebowitz, ?1948– , *Metropolitan Life*, 'Food for Thought and Vice Versa']

24 a / whole scuttleful of chef douvres what / you mean is hors douvres mehitabel i / told her what i mean is grub [Don Marquis, 1878–1937, *archy and mehitabel*, XI, 'why mehitabel jumped']

25 England is the only country where food is more dangerous than sex. [Jackie Mason, 1931– , *The World According to Me*]

26 Time for a little something. [A A Milne, 1882–1956, *Winnie-the-Pooh*, Ch. 6]

27 What do you experience with your first mouthful of hot fudge sundae? It's not surprising that we carry it over to describe the intensity of love and sex. [Dr S Mintz, 1922– , in *Weekend Guardian*, 29–30 Dec. 1990]

28 Isn't there any other part of a matzo you can eat? [Marilyn Monroe, 1926–62 (on having matzo balls for dinner for the third time at Arthur Miller's parents), quoted by Laurence Olivier in BBC TV programme]

29 No man is lonely while eating spaghetti. [Robert Morley, 1908–92, in Jonathon Green, *Consuming Passions*]

30 The English have three vegetables and two of them are cabbage. [Walter Page, 1855–1918, in Jonathon Green, *Consuming Passions*]

31 *L'appétit vient en mangeant*. – Appetite comes with eating. [François Rabelais, *c.*1492–1553, *Gargantua*, Ch. 5]

32 The national dish of America is menus. [Robert Robinson, 1927– , in BBC TV programme *Robinson's Travels*, Aug. 1977]

33 Does the Spearmint Lose Its Flavour on the Bedpost Overnight? [Billy Rose, 1899–1996, title of song, 1924, in musical *Be Yourself*, written with Marty Bloom]

34 I believe I once considerably scandalized her by declaring that clear soup was a more important factor in life than a clear conscience. [Saki (H H Munro), 1870–1916, *The Blind Spot*]

35 My advice if you insist on slimming: Eat as much as you like – just don't swallow it. [Harry Secombe, 1921– , in *Daily Herald*, 5 Oct. 1962]

36 The liver, doted upon by the French, assaulted by the Irish, disdained by the Americans, and chopped up with egg, onion, and chicken fat by the Jews. [Richard Selzer, 1928– , *Confessions of a Knife*, 'Liver']

37 The food that to him now is as luscious as locusts shall be to him shortly as bitter as coloquintida. [William Shakespeare, 1564–1616, *Othello*, I. iii. (354)]

38 I eat merely to put food out of my mind. [N F Simpson, 1919– , *The Hole*]

39 Bad men live to eat and drink, whereas good men eat and drink in order to live. [Socrates, 469–399BC, quoted in Plutarch, *Moralia*, 'How a Young Man Ought to Hear Poems', 4]

40 The shiny stuff is tomatoes. / The salad lies in a group. / The curly stuff is potatoes. / The stuff that moves is soup. / Anything that is white is sweet. / Anything that is brown is meat. / Anything that is grey, don't eat. [(On airways food) Stephen Sondheim, 1930– , song: *Do I Hear a Waltz?*]

41 I enjoyed the mealtimes more than the meals. [Muriel Spark, 1918– , *The Only Problem*, 8]

42 The human desire for food and sex is relatively equal. If there are armed rapes why should there not be armed hot dog thefts? [John Kennedy Toole, 1937–69, *A Confederacy of Dunces*, VII, 1]

43 Cauliflower is nothing but cabbage with a college education. [Mark Twain, 1835–1910, *Pudd'nhead Wilson*, Ch. 5, epigraph]

44 This dish of meat is too good for any but anglers, or very honest men. [Izaak Walton, 1593–1683, *The Compleat Angler*, Pt I, Ch. 8]

45 Try the Andy Warhol New York City Diet: when I order in a restaurant, I order everything I don't want, so I have a lot to play around with while everyone else eats. [Andy Warhol, 1927–87, *From A to B and Back Again*, 'Beauty']

46 Yes, cider and tinned salmon are the staple diet of the agricultural classes. [Evelyn Waugh, 1903–66, *Scoop*, Bk I, Ch. 1, 4]

47 This is just to say / I have eaten / the plums / that were in / the icebox / and which / you were probably / saving / for breakfast. / Forgive me / they were delicious / so sweet / and so cold. [William Carlos Williams, 1883–1963, *This is Just to Say*]

48 If I had the choice between smoked salmon and tinned salmon, I'd have it tinned. With vinegar. [Harold Wilson, 1916–95, in *Observer*, 11 Nov. 1962]

49 'Have you ever seen Spode eat asparagus?' 'No.' 'Revolting. It alters one's whole conception of Man as Nature's last word.' [P G Wodehouse, 1881–1975, *The Code of the Woosters*, Ch. 4]

See also FRUIT

FOOLS & FOLLY

1 There is in human nature generally more of the fool than of the wise [Francis Bacon, 1561–1626, *Essays*, 12, 'Of Boldness']

2 There's a sucker born every minute. [Phineas T Barnum, 1810–91, attr., but in fact coined by 'Paper-collar Joe', according to A H Saxon, *P T B: The Legend and the Man*]

3 The dullard's envy of brilliant men is always assuaged by the suspicion that they will come to a bad end. [Max Beerbohm, 1872–1956, *Zuleika Dobson*, Ch. 4]

4 Make little weeping for the dead, for he is at rest: but the life of the fool is worse than death. [Bible, Apocrypha, *Ecclesiasticus* 22:11]

5 Answer not a fool according to his folly, lest thou also be like unto him. Answer a fool according to his folly, lest he be wise in his own conceit. [Bible, OT, *Proverbs* 26:4]

6 God hath chosen the foolish things of the world to confound the wise. [Bible, NT, *1 Corinthians* 1:27]

7 A fool sees not the same tree that a wise man sees. [William Blake, 1757–1827, *The Marriage of Heaven and Hell*, 'Proverbs of Hell']

8 If the fool would persist in his folly he would become wise. [William Blake, 1757–1827, *The Marriage of Heaven and Hell*, 'Proverbs of Hell']

9 *Un sot trouve toujours un plus sot qui l'admire.* – A fool always finds a greater fool to admire him. [Nicholas Boileau, 1636–1711, *L'Art poétique*, 1, 232]

10 There's a more hateful form of foolery – / The social sage's, Solomon of saloons / And philosophic diner-out, the fribble / Who wants a doctrine for a chopping-block / To try the edge of his faculty upon. [Robert Browning, 1812–89, *Mr Sludge 'the Medium'*, 772]

11 If honest nature made you fools, / What sairs your grammars? [Robert Burns, 1759–96, *Epistle to John Lapraik*, 63]

12 But human bodies are sic fools, / For a' their colleges and schools, / That when nae real ills perplex them, / They make enow themselves to vex them. [Robert Burns, 1759–96, *The Twa Dogs*, 195]

13 I sometimes wonder if the manufacturers of foolproof items keep a fool or two on their payroll to test things. [Alan Coren, 1938– , *Seems Like Old Times*, 'August']

14 A fool must now and then be right, by chance. [William Cowper, 1731–1800, *Conversation*, 96]

15 A fool with judges, amongst fools a judge: / He says but little, and that little said / Owes all its weight, like loaded dice, to lead. / His wit invites you by his looks to come, / But when you knock, it never is at home. [William Cowper, 1731–1800, *Conversation*, 300]

16 I am two fools, I know, / For loving, and for saying so, / In whining Poetry. [John Donne, 1571?–1631, *The Triple Fool*]

17 A fool and his money are soon parted. What I want to know is how they got together in the first place. [Cyril Fletcher, 1913– , in BBC radio programme, 28 May 1969]

18 *Da steh' ich nun, ich armer Tor! / Und bin so klug als wie zuvor.* – There I am, a poor fool, and am no wiser than I was before. [Johann Wolfgang von Goethe, 1749–1832, *Faust*, Pt I, 'Nacht']

19 In my time, the follies of the town crept slowly among us, but now they travel faster than a stagecoach. [Oliver Goldsmith, 1728–74, *She Stoops to Conquer*, I]

20 Not huffy or stuffy, not tiny or tall, / But fluffy, just fluffy, with no brains at all. [A P Herbert, 1890–1971, *I Like Them Fluffy*]

21 There's Bardus, a six-foot column of fop, / A lighthouse without any light atop. [Thomas Hood, 1799–1845, *Miss Kilmansegg*, 'Her First Step']

22 Mingle some brief folly with your wisdom. To forget it in due place is sweet. [Horace, 65–8 BC, *Odes*, III, xii, 27]

23 That fellow seems to me to possess but one idea, and that is a wrong one. [(Of a dull fellow) Dr Samuel Johnson, 1709–84, in James Boswell, *Life of J*, 1770]

24 But a fool must follow his natural bent / (Even as you and I!). [Rudyard Kipling, 1865–1936, *The Vampire*]

25 Music-hall songs provide the dull with wit, just as proverbs provide them with wisdom. [W Somerset Maugham, 1874–1965, *A Writer's Notebook*, 1892]

26 A fellow who is always declaring he's no fool

usually has his suspicions. [Wilson Mizner, 1876–1933, in A Johnston, *The Legendary Mizners*, Ch. 4]

27 I assure you that a learned fool is more foolish than an ignorant fool. [Molière, 1622–73, *Les Femmes savantes*, IV. iii]

28 You beat your pate, and fancy wit will come: / Knock as you please, there's nobody at home. [Alexander Pope, 1688–1744, epigram: *An Empty House*]

29 No creature smarts so little as a fool. [Alexander Pope, 1688–1744, *Epistle to Dr Arbuthnot*, 84]

30 For fools rush in where angels fear to tread. [Alexander Pope, 1688–1744, *An Essay on Criticism*, 625]

31 Alas! 'tis true I have gone here and there, / And made myself a motley to the view. [William Shakespeare, 1564–1616, *Sonnets*, 110]

32 All matches are unwise. It's unwise to be born; it's unwise to be married; it's unwise to live; and it's unwise to die. [George Bernard Shaw, 1856–1950, *You Never Can Tell*, IV]

33 Hated by fools, and fools to hate / Be that my motto and my fate. [Jonathan Swift, 1677–1745, *To Dr Delaney, On the Libels*, 171]

34 Ninety-nine per cent of the people in the world are fools and the rest of us are in great danger of contagion. [Thornton Wilder, 1897–1975, *The Matchmaker*, I]

35 But there comes a moment in everybody's life when he must decide whether he'll live among human beings or not – a fool among fools or a fool alone. [Thornton Wilder, 1897–1975, *The Matchmaker*, IV]

36 Be wise with speed; / A fool at forty is a fool indeed. [Edward Young, 1683–1765, *Love of Fame*, Satire II, 281]

FOOTBALL

1 Doctor Livingstone thought that football was God in the same way as his fellow Glaswegians. All the rules are the same as those of God. Would God allow us to be off-side? Of course not. To molest the unprotected goalkeeper? Never. [David Pownall, 1938– , *The Raining Tree War*, Ch. 5]

2 For when the One Great Scorer comes / To write against your name. / He marks – not that you won or lost – / But how you played the game. [Grantland Rice, 1880–1954, *Alumnus Football*]

3 Some people think football is a matter of life and death. I don't like that attitude. I can assure them it is much more serious than that. [Bill Shankly, 1914–81, in *The Sunday Times*, 4 Oct. 1981]

4 Football combines the two worst things about America: it is violence punctuated by committee meetings. [George F Will, 1941– , in *International Herald Tribune*, Paris, 7 May 1990]

See also CRICKET, GOLF, SPORTS

FORCE

1 This policy cannot be achieved through speeches, shooting matches and songs . . . it can be achieved only through blood and iron. [Otto von Bismarck, 1815–98, speech in Prussian Chamber, 28 Jan. 1886. 'Iron and blood' used by him, 29 Sept. 1862]

2 Force is not a remedy. [John Bright, 1811–89, speech at Birmingham, 16 Nov. 1880]

3 The use of force alone is but *temporary*. It may subdue for a moment; but it does not remove the necessity of subduing again; and a nation is not governed, which is perpetually to be conquered. [Edmund Burke, 1729–97, speech on conciliation with America, 22 Mar. 1775]

4 Brute force without wisdom falls by its own weight. [Horace, 65–8 BC, *Odes*, III, iv, 65]

5 Who overcomes / By force, hath overcome but half his foe. [John Milton, 1608–74, *Paradise Lost*, Bk i, 648]

See also POWER, VIOLENCE

FOREIGNERS

1 Magda was foreign – so foreign, indeed, that it was only possible to place her low down in the Balkans. [Patrick Campbell, 1913–80, 'The Crime in the Cloakroom']

2 'Can you always tell whether a stranger is your friend?' 'Yes.' 'Then you are an Oriental.' [E M Forster, 1879–1970, *A Passage to India*, Ch. 36]

3 He spoke with the faintest foreign accent and it was difficult to determine whether he was Jewish or of an ancient English family. He gave the impression that very many cities had rubbed him smooth. [Graham Greene, 1904–91, *A Gun for Sale*, Ch. 4, sect. iii]

4 All the people like us are We, / And every one else is They. [Rudyard Kipling, 1865–1936, *We and They*]

5 By foreign hands thy dying eyes were closed, / By foreign hands thy decent limbs composed, / By foreign hands thy humble grave adorned. / By strangers honoured, and by strangers mourned! [Alexander Pope, 1688–1744, *Elegy to the Memory of an Unfortunate Lady*, 51]

6 'Who's 'im, Bill?' 'A stranger!' ''Eave 'arf a brick at 'im'. [*Punch* (1854), xxvi, 82]

7 They spell it Vinci and pronounce it Vinchy; foreigners always spell better than they pronounce. [Mark Twain, 1835–1910, *Innocents Abroad*, Ch. 19]

See also INTERNATIONAL RELATIONS, NATIONALISM, NATIONS

FORGETTING

1 And we forget because we must / And not because we will. [Matthew Arnold, 1822–88, *Absence*]

2 But the iniquity of oblivion blindly scattereth her poppy, and deals with the memory of men without distinction to merit of perpetuity. [Sir Thomas Browne, 1605–82, *Urn Burial*, Ch. 5]

3 I cannot sing the old songs now! / It is not that I deem them low; / 'Tis that I can't remember how / They go. [C S Calverley, 1831–84, *Changed*]

4 Oon ere it herde, at the other out it wente. [Geoffrey Chaucer, 1340?–1400, *Troilus and Criseyde*, iv, 434]

5 The pyramids themselves, doting with age, have forgotten the names of their founders. [Thomas Fuller, 1608–61, *The Holy State*, Bk iii, Ch. 14]

6 You were the sort that men forget; / Though I – not yet! – / Perhaps not ever. [Thomas Hardy, 1840–1928, *You were the Sort That Men Forget*]

7 Brooding o'er the gloom, spins the brown eve-jar. / Darker grows the valley, more and more forgetting: / So were it with me if forgetting could be willed. [George Meredith, 1828–1909, *Love in the Valley*, 5]

8 And if I drink oblivion of a day, / So shorten I the stature of my soul. [George Meredith, 1828–1909, *Modern Love*, 12]

9 Do you know my friend Mr Betts? / I wish I could remember as accurately as he forgets. [Ogden Nash, 1902–71, *Mr Betts's Mind a Kingdom Is*]

10 Better by far you should forget and smile / Than that you should remember and be sad. [Christina Rossetti, 1830–94, *Remember*]

11 But men are men; the best sometimes forget. [William Shakespeare, 1564–1616, *Othello*, II. iii. (243)]

12 Time hath, my lord, a wallet at his back, / Wherein he puts alms for oblivion, / A great-sized monster of ingratitudes: / Those scraps are good deeds past: which are devoured / As fast as they are made, forgot as soon / As done. [*Troilus and Cressida*, III. iii. 145]

13 When the lamp is shattered / The light in the dust lies dead – / When the cloud is scattered / The rainbow's glory is shed. / When the lute is broken, / Sweet tones are remembered not: / When the lips have spoken, / Loved accents are soon forgot. [P B Shelley, 1792–1822, *Lines: When the Lamp is Shattered*]

14 I've a grand memory for forgetting, David. [Robert Louis Stevenson, 1850–94, *Kidnapped*, Ch. 18]

15 There are three things I always forget. Names, faces, and – the third I can't remember. [Italo Svevo, 1861–1928, attr.]

16 One forgets words as one forgets names. One's vocabulary needs constant fertilizing or it will die. [Evelyn Waugh, 1903–66, *Diaries*, ed. M Davie, 'Irregular Notes', 25 Dec. 1962]

17 Forget not yet the tried intent / Of such a truth as I have meant, / My great travail so gladly spent / Forget not yet. [Sir Thomas Wyatt, 1503?–42, *Forget Not Yet*]

See also MEMORY

FORGIVENESS

1 You ought certainly to forgive them, as a Christian, but never to admit them in your sight, or allow their names to be mentioned in your hearing. [(Mr Collins) Jane Austen, 1775–1817, *Pride and Prejudice*, 57]

2 Mutual Forgiveness of each vice, / Such are the Gates of Paradise. [William Blake, 1757–1827, *The Gates of Paradise*, Prologue]

3 He kept turning the other cheek until they stuck a medal on it. [Elias Canetti, 1905–94, *The Human Province*, '1955']

4 Once a woman has forgiven her man, she must not reheat his sins for breakfast. [Marlene Dietrich, 1901–92, *Marlene Dietrich's ABC*, 'Forgiveness']

5 Wilt thou forgive that sin, where I begun, / Which is my sin, though it were done before? / Wilt thou forgive those sins through which I run / And do them still, though still I do deplore? / When thou hast done, thou hast not done, / For I have more. [John Donne, 1571?–1631, *Hymn to God the Father*]

6 Forgiveness to the injured does belong; / For they ne'er pardon, who have done the wrong. [John Dryden, 1631–1700, *The Conquest of Granada*, Pt II, I, ii]

7 God may pardon you, but I never can. [Queen Elizabeth I, 1533–1603 (to the Countess of Nottingham), in David Hume, *History of England under the House of Tudor*, Vol. ii, Ch. 7]

8 Oh, Thou, who Man of baser Earth didst make, / And who with Eden didst devise the Snake; / For all the Sin wherewith the Face of Man / Is blackened. Man's Forgiveness give – and take! [Edward Fitzgerald, 1809–83, *The Rubá'iyát of Omar Khayyám*, Edn 1, 58]

9 At length I heard a ragged noise and mirth / Of thieves and murderers: there I him espied, / Who straight, 'Your suit is granted,' said, and died. [George Herbert, 1593–1633, *Redemption*]

10 Nobody ever forgets where he buried a hatchet. ['Kin' Hubbard, 1868–1930, *Indianapolis News*, 4 Jan. 1925]

11 Jews ask forgiveness of man, not God, which is rough on us because man is a harder con than God any day. [John Le Carré, 1931– , *The Tailor of Panama*, Ch. 6]

12 A woman can forgive a man for the harm he does her . . . but she can never forgive him for the sacrifices he makes on her account. [W Somerset Maugham, 1874–1965, *The Moon and Sixpence*, Ch. 41]

13 And love th' offender, yet detest th' offence. [Alexander Pope, 1688–1744, *Elegy to the Memory of an Unfortunate Lady*, 192]

14 To err is human, to forgive, divine. [Alexander Pope, 1688–1744, *An Essay on Criticism*, 525]

15 And forgive us our trespasses, As we forgive them that trespass against us. [*The Book of Common Prayer*, Lord's Prayer]

16 The stupid neither forgive nor forget; the naïve forgive and forget; the wise forgive but do not forget. [Thomas Szasz, 1920– , *The Second Sin*, 'Personal Conduct']

See also PITY

FORTUNE, see CHANCE, DESTINY

FRANCE & THE FRENCH

1 In the nineteenth century the Germans painted their dream and the outcome was invariably vegetable. The French needed only to paint a vegetable and it was already a dream. [Theodor Adorno, 1903–69, *Minima Memoralia*, Pt 1, 29]

2 France, famed in all great arts, in none supreme. [Matthew Arnold, 1822–88, *To a Republican Friend*]

3 The French are wiser than they seem, and the Spaniards seem wiser than they are. [Francis Bacon, 1561–1626, *Essays*, 26, 'Of Seeming Wise']

4 The whole of Gaul is divided into three parts. [Julius Caesar, 102?–44 BC, *De Bello Gallico*, I, i]

5 France was long a despotism tempered by epigrams. [Thomas Carlyle, 1795–1881, *French Revolution*, Pt I, Bk i, Ch. 1]

6 Oh the Germans classify, but the French arrange. [Willa Cather, 1873–1947, *Death Comes to the Archbishop*, 'Prologue']

7 And Frensh she spak ful faire and fetisly, / After the scole of Stratford atte Bowe, / For Frensh of Paris was to hir unknowe. [Geoffrey Chaucer, 1340?–1400, *Canterbury Tales*, 'Prologue', 122]

8 The Almighty in His infinite wisdom did not see fit to create Frenchmen in the image of Englishmen. [Winston Churchill, 1874–1965, speech in House of Commons, 10 Dec. 1942]

9 Trust the French to touch the nerve of the national spirit, or, as they prefer to say about any country but their own, the problem. [Alistair Cooke, 1908– , *Talk about America*, Ch. 14]

10 There's always something fishy about the French! [Noël Coward, 1899–1973, *Conversation Piece*, I, vi]

11 The erroneous but almost universally held idea that culture belongs to France and that for a Frenchman to exhibit talent is a kind of patriotism. [Quentin Crisp, 1908–99, *The Wit and Wisdom of Q C*, ed. Guy Kettelhack, Pt 5]

12 Bouillabaisse is only good because cooked by the French, who, if they cared to try, could produce an excellent and nutritious substitute out of cigar stumps and empty matchboxes. [Norman Douglas, 1868–1952, *Siren Land*, 'Rain on the Hills']

13 *France, mère des arts, des armes et des lois.* – France, mother of the arts, of arms and of law. [Joachim Du Bellay, 1515–60, *Les Regrets*, 9]

14 If the French were to play cricket they would all want to be 'batsmen' – the cynosure of all eyes – at the same time, just as nearly all of them want to be Prime Minister. [Jean Fayard; in *Strangers' Gallery*, ed. A Synge]

15 *Toute ma vie je me suis fait une certaine idée de la France.* – All my life I have thought of France in a certain way. [General de Gaulle, 1890–1970, *War Memoirs*, Vol. I: *The Call to Honour*, Ch. 1]

16 You cannot ignore a country with 265 varieties of cheese. [General de Gaulle, 1890–1970, in *Newsweek*, 1 Oct. Often misquoted as 'You cannot govern ...' and dates of first use vary]

17 I hate the French because they are all slaves, and wear wooden shoes. [Oliver Goldsmith, 1728–74, *Essays*, 24, 'Distresses of a Common Soldier']

18 Fifty million Frenchmen can be wrong. [Texas Guinan, 1884–1933, attr. in *New York World-Telegram*, 21 Mar. 1931, when denied entry into France]

19 He was confined to heavings and shruggin's and copious *Mong Jews*! The French are very badly fitted with relief-valves. [Rudyard Kipling, 1865–1936, *A Diversity of Creatures*, 'The Horse Marines']

20 England is never as great as when she is alone. And France is never France when she fights for herself ... When the French fight for mankind they are wonderful. When they fight for themselves, they are nothing. [André Malraux, 1901–76, in Bruce Chatwin, *What am I Doing Here?* 'André Malraux']

21 We are part of the continent of Europe, not just a balcony overlooking the Atlantic. [François Mitterrand, 1916–96, in *Libération*, Nov. 1988]

22 A little of everything and nothing thoroughly, after the French fashion. [Michel de Montaigne, 1533–92, *Essays*, I, 26]

23 France has for centuries blocked our way to Europe. Before the invention of the aeroplane we had to step over it to get anywhere. [Robert Morley, 1908–92; in *Apt and Amusing Quotations*, ed. G F Lamb, 'France']

24 Every French soldier carries in his cartridge-pouch the baton of a marshal of France. [Napoleon Bonaparte, 1769–1821, quoted in E Blaze, *La Vie militaire sous l'empire*. Also attr. to Louis XVIII]

25 You must hate a Frenchman as you hate the devil. [Lord Nelson, 1758–1805, quoted in R Southey, *Life of N*, Ch. 3]

26 There's something Vichy about the French. [Ivor Novello, 1893–1951, in Edward Marsh, *Ambrosia and Small Beer*, Ch. 4]

27 *Ce qui n'est pas clair n'est pas français.* – What is not clear is not French. [Antoine de Rivarol, 1753–1801, *De l'universalité de la langue française*]

28 Your average Frenchman, seeing another Frenchman, assumes he's an enemy unless he proves a friend. In Britain, it's the other way round. [Walter Schwarz, 1930– , in *Guardian Weekly*, 9 Sept. 1984]

29 But Normans don't joke until they've known you for twenty years, and then never about food. [Walter Schwarz, 1930– , in *Guardian Weekly*, 9 Sept. 1984]

30 That sweet enemy, France. [Sir Philip Sidney, 1554–86, *Astrophel and Stella*, Sonnet 41]

31 They order, said I, this matter better in France. [Laurence Sterne, 1713–68, *A Sentimental Journey*, opening]

32 We are all American at puberty; we die

French. [Evelyn Waugh, 1903–66, *Diaries*, ed. M Davie, 'Irregular Notes', 18 July 1961]

33 France is a country where the money falls apart in your hands and you can't tear the toilet paper. [Billy Wilder, 1906– ; in L Halliwell, *The Filmgoer's Book of Quotes*]

See also BRITAIN, ENGLAND, GERMANY, INTERNATIONAL RELATIONS, ITALY, NATIONALISM, NATIONS, SPAIN, SWITZERLAND

FREEDOM, see LIBERTY

FRENCH REVOLUTION

1 *Liberté! Égalité! Fraternité!* – Liberty! Equality! Fraternity! [anon. phrase used in the French Revolution, but actually earlier in origin]

2 I prefer people who chop off heads to people who celebrate people who chop off heads. [(Of the Revolution's bicentenary) Pierre Boulez, 1925– , interview in *Guardian*, 13 Jan. 1989]

3 An event has happened, upon which it is difficult to speak, and impossible to be silent. [Edmund Burke, 1729–97, on the impeachment of Warren Hastings, 5 May 1789]

4 Whenever our neighbour's house is on fire, it cannot be amiss for the engines to play a little on our own. [Edmund Burke, 1729–97, *Reflections on the Revolution in France*, Penguin edn, p. 92]

5 It was the best of times, it was the worst of times. [Charles Dickens, 1812–70, *A Tale of Two Cities*, opening words]

6 'It is possible that it may not come, during our lives. We shall not see the triumph.' 'We shall have helped it,' returned madame. [Charles Dickens, 1812–70, *A Tale of Two Cities*, II, 16]

7 How much the greatest event it is that ever happened in the world! and how much the best! [(The fall of the Bastille) Charles James Fox, 1749–1806, letter to Richard Fitzpatrick, 30 July 1789]

8 LOUIS XVI: *C'est une révolte?* – Is it a revolt?
THE DUKE: No, Sire, it's a revolution. [Duc de La Rochefoucauld-Liancourt, 1747–1827, on hearing of the Fall of the Bastille, July 1789]

9 *J'ai vécu.* – I lived. [Abbé Sieyès, 1748–1836, reply when asked what he had done during the Terror]

10 Even tho' thrice again / The red fool-fury of the Seine / Should pile her barricades with dead. [Alfred, Lord Tennyson, 1809–92, *In Memoriam*, 127]

11 There was reason to fear that, like Saturn, the Revolution might devour each of its children in turn. [Pierre Vergniaud, 1753–93, Lamartine, *Histoire des Girondins*, Bk xxxviii, Ch. 20]

12 We invented the Revolution / but we don't know how to run it. [Peter Weiss, 1916–82, *The Marat / Sade*, xv]

13 Bliss was it in that dawn to be alive, / But to be young was very heaven! [(Of the Revolution) William Wordsworth, 1770–1850, *The Prelude*, XI, 108]

14 [When asked what he thought of it] It is too early to say. [Zhou Enlai, 1898–1976 (at the bicentenary of the Revolution), in *Guardian*, 2 May 1989]

See also REVOLUTIONS, RUSSIAN REVOLUTION

FRIENDS

1 Even your best friends won't tell you. [Advertisement for Listerine mouthwash, 1920s]

2 There is little friendship in the world, and least of all between equals. [Francis Bacon, 1561–1626, *Essays*, 48, 'Of Followers']

3 A faithful friend is the medicine of life. [Bible, Apocrypha, *Ecclesiasticus* 6:16]

4 Forsake not an old friend; for the new is not comparable to him; a new friend is as new wine; when it is old, thou shalt drink it with pleasure. [Bible, Apocrypha, *Ecclesiasticus* 9:10]

5 There is a friend that sticketh closer than a brother. [Bible, OT, *Proverbs* 18:24]

6 Saul and Jonathan were lovely and pleasant in their lives, and in their death they were not divided. [Bible, OT, *2 Samuel* 1:23]

7 While your friend holds you affectionately by both your hands you are safe, because you can watch both his. [Ambrose Bierce, 1842–1914, *The Devil's Dictionary*, entry under 'Epigram']

8 Thy friendship oft has made my heart to ache: / Do be my enemy – for friendship's sake. [William Blake, 1757–1827, *To Hayley*]

9 I don't trust him. We're friends. [Bertolt Brecht, 1898–1956, *Mother Courage*, iii]

10 Should auld acquaintance be forgot, / And never brought to min'? [Robert Burns, 1759–96, *Auld Lang Syne*]

11 Friendship is Love without his wings! [Lord Byron, 1788–1824, *Hours of Idleness*, 'L'Amitié']

12 But of all plagues, good Heaven, thy wrath can send, / Save me, oh, save me, from the candid friend! [George Canning, 1770–1827, *New Morality*, 209]

13 A man's friend likes him but leaves him as he is: his wife loves him and is always trying to turn him into somebody else. [G K Chesterton, 1874–1936, *Orthodoxy*, Ch. 5]

14 O the pious friendships of the female sex! [William Congreve, 1670–1729, *The Way of the World*, II, iii]

15 The man that hails you Tom or Jack, / And proves by thumps upon your back / How he esteems your merit, / Is such a friend, that one had need / Be very much his friend indeed / To pardon or to bear it. [William Cowper, 1731–1800, *Friendship*, 163]

16 There is nothing in the world I wouldn't do for Hope, and there is nothing he wouldn't do for me . . . We spend our lives doing nothing for each other. [Bing Crosby, 1901–77; *Observer*, 'Sayings of the Week', 7 May 1950]

17 Fate chooses your relations, you choose your friends. [Jacques Delille, 1738–1813, *Malheur et pitié*, I]

18 'Wal'r, my boy,' replied the Captain, 'in the Proverbs of Solomon you will find the following words, "May we never want a friend in need, nor a bottle to give him!" When found, make a note of.' [Charles Dickens, 1812–70, *Dombey and Son*, Ch. 15]

19 The falling out of faithful friends, renewing is of love. [Richard Edwardes, 1523?–66, *Amantium Irae*]

20 A friend is a person with whom I may be sincere. Before him I may think aloud. [Ralph Waldo Emerson, 1803–82, *Essays*, 'Friendship']

21 Friendship is a disinterested commerce between equals; love, an abject intercourse between tyrants and slaves. [Oliver Goldsmith, 1728–74, *The Good-Natured Man*, 1]

22 A fav'rite has no friend. [Thomas Gray, 1716–71, *Ode on the Death of a Favourite Cat*]

23 Judd remained for him the Oldest Friend whom one definitely dislikes. [Aldous Huxley, 1894–1963, *Brief Candles*, 'After the Fireworks']

24 If a man does not make new acquaintance as he advances through life, he will soon find himself alone. A man, Sir, should keep his friendship *in constant repair*. [Dr Samuel Johnson, 1709–84, in James Boswell, *Life of J*, 1755]

25 We tiptoed around each other like heartbreaking new friends. [Jack Kerouac, 1922–69, *On the Road*, Pt I, Ch. 1]

26 Friends are God's apology for relations. [Hugh Kingsmill, 1889–1949, *The Best of Hugh Kingsmill*, ed. Michael Holroyd, Introduction]

27 Everyone calls himself a friend, but only a fool relies on it; nothing is commoner than the name, nothing rarer than the thing. [Jean de La Fontaine, 1621–95, *Fables*, IV, 17, 'The Wisdom of Socrates']

28 It is more shameful to distrust one's friends than to be deceived by them. [Duc de La Rochefoucauld, 1613–80, *Maxims*, 84]

29 In the misfortunes of our best friends, we find something that is not unpleasing. [Duc de La Rochefoucauld, 1613–80, *Suppressed Maxims*, 583]

30 I get by with a little help from my friends. [John Lennon, 1940–80, and Paul McCartney, 1942– , song: *With a Little Help from My Friends*]

31 Levin wanted friendship and got friendliness; he wanted steak and they offered spam. [Bernard Malamud, 1914–86, *A New Life*, sect. vi]

32 The best friend of a boy is his mother, of a man his horse; only it's not clear when the transition takes place. [Joseph Mankiewicz, 1909–93; in A Andrews, *Quotations for Speakers and Writers*]

33 My dear, she's been my greatest friend for fifteen years, I know her through and through, and I tell you that she hasn't got a single redeeming quality. [W Somerset Maugham, 1874–1965, *Our Betters*, III]

34 Fellowship is heaven, and lack of fellowship is hell; fellowship is life, and lack of fellowship is death; and the deeds that ye do upon the earth, it is for fellowship's sake that ye do them. [William Morris, 1834–96, *The Dream of John Ball*, Ch. 4]

35 He's an oul' butty o' mine – oh, he's a darlin' man, a daarlin' man. [Sean O'Casey, 1880–1964, *Juno and the Paycock*, I]

36 True friendship's laws are by this rule expressed, / Welcome the coming, speed the parting guest. [Alexander Pope, 1688–1744, *Homer's Odyssey*, XV, 83]

37 Friends / To borrow my books and set wet glasses on them. [Edwin Arlington Robinson, 1869–1935, *Captain Craig*, II]

38 To like and dislike the same things, that is indeed true friendship. [Sallust, 86–34 BC, *Catiline*, 20]

39 A friend in need is a friend to be avoided. [Herbert Samuel, 1870–1963, in *Sunday Telegraph Magazine*, 27 Nov. 1977]

40 Friendship is almost always the union of a part of one mind with a part of another; people are friends in spots. [George Santayana, 1863–1952, *Soliloquies in England*, 'Friendships']

41 My friends were poor but honest. [William Shakespeare, 1564–1616, *All's Well that Ends Well*, I. iii. (203)]

42 Be thou familiar, but by no means vulgar. / Those friends thou hast, and their adoption tried, / Grapple them to thy soul with hoops of steel. [*Hamlet*, I. iii. 61]

43 Give me that man / That is not passion's slave, and I will wear him / In my heart's core, ay, in my heart of heart, / As I do thee. [*Hamlet*, III. ii (76)]

44 A friend should bear his friend's infirmities, / But Brutus makes mine greater than they are. [*Julius Caesar*, IV. iii. 85]

45 Never come such division 'tween our souls! [*Julius Caesar*, IV. iii. 234]

46 So we grew together, / Like to a double cherry, seeming parted, / But yet an union in partition; / Two lovely berries moulded on one stem. [*A Midsummer Night's Dream*, III. ii. 208]

47 Friendship is constant in all other things / Save in the office and affairs of love. [*Much Ado About Nothing*, II. i. (184)]

48 I count myself in nothing else so happy / As in a soul remembering my good friends. [*Richard II*, II. iii. 46]

49 But if the while I think on thee, dear friend, / All losses are restored and sorrows end. [*Sonnets*, 30]

50 We need two kinds of acquaintances, one to complain to, while we boast to the others. [Logan Pearsall Smith, 1865–1946, *Afterthoughts*, 4]

51 Some great misfortune to portend, / No enemy can match a friend. [Jonathan Swift, 1677–1745, *On the Death of Dr Swift*, 119]

52 He makes no friend who never made a foe. [Alfred, Lord Tennyson, 1809–92, *Idylls of the King*, 'Lancelot and Elaine', 1082]

53 Softly, thro' a vinous mist, / My college friendships glimmer. [Alfred, Lord Tennyson, 1809–92, *Will Waterproof's Lyrical Monologue*, 5]

54 I do not believe that friends are necessarily the people you like best, they are merely the people who got there first. [Peter Ustinov, 1921– , *Dear Me*, Ch. 5]

55 There are two forms of friendship; meeting and separation. They are indissoluble. [Simone Weil, 1909–43, *Waiting on God*, 'The Love of God']

56 They are not quite my friends, but I know them better than many who are; they aren't related to me, but they might as well be. They are the close friends of *my* close friends – my friends-in-law. [Katharine Whitehorn, 1926– , *Sunday Best*, 'Best Friend Once Removed']

57 I have lost friends, some by death . . . others through sheer inability to cross the street. [Virginia Woolf, 1882–1941, *The Waves*]

See also ENEMIES

FRUIT

1 Doubtless God could have made a better berry [than the strawberry], but doubtless God never did. [William Butler, 1535–1618, quoted in Izaac Walton, *The Compleat Angler*, Pt I, Ch. 5]

2 He hangs in shades the orange bright, / Like golden lamps in a green night. [Andrew Marvell, 1621–78, *Bermudas*, 17]

See also FOOD

FUNERALS

1 Strew on her roses, roses, / And never a spray of yew. / In quiet she reposes: / Ah! would that I did too! [Matthew Arnold, 1822–88, *Requiescat*]

2 When we attend the funerals of our friends we grieve for them, but when we go to those of other people it is chiefly our own deaths that we mourn for. [Gerald Brenan, 1894–1987, *Thoughts in a Dry Season*, 'Death']

3 And by my grave you'd pray to have me back, / So I could see how well you looked in black. [Marco Carson, *To Any Woman*]

4 'If you don't go to other men's funerals,' he told Father stiffly, 'they won't go to yours.' [Clarence Day, 1874–1935, *Life with Father*, 'Father Interferes']

5 I've a great fancy to see my own funeral afore I die. [Maria Edgeworth, 1767–1849, *Castle Rackrent*, 'Continuation of Memoirs']

6 She chose her bearers before she died / From her fancy-men. [Thomas Hardy, 1840–1928, *Julie-Jane*]

7 They say such nice things about people at their funerals that it makes me sad to realize I'm going to miss mine by just a few days. [Garrison Keillor, 1942– , *Lake Wobegon Days*, 'Lecture in San Francisco', 13 Dec. 1984]

8 Along the avenue of cypresses, / All in their scarlet cloaks and surplices / Of linen, go the chanting choristers, / The priests in gold and black, the villagers. [D H Lawrence, 1885–1930, *Giorno dei Morti*]

9 Why should I go [to Marilyn Monroe's funeral]? She won't be there. [Arthur Miller, 1915– , attr.]

10 I have nothing against undertakers personally. It's just that I wouldn't want one to bury my sister. [Jessica Mitford, 1917–96, attr. in *Saturday Review*, 1 Feb. 1964]

11 We therefore commit his body to the ground; earth to earth; ashes to ashes; dust to dust; in sure and certain hope of the Resurrection to eternal life. [*The Book of Common Prayer*, The Burial of the Dead, 'Committal']

12 Over this damp grave I speak the words of my love; / I, with no rights in this matter, / Neither father nor lover. [Theodore Roethke, 1908–63, *Elegy for Jane*]

13 Not a drum was heard, not a funeral note, / As his corse to the rampart we hurried. [Charles Wolfe, 1791–1823, *The Burial of Sir John Moore*, 1]

See also DEATH, GRAVE

THE FUTURE

1 Years hence, perhaps, may dawn an age, / More fortunate, alas! than we, / Which without hardness will be sage, / And gay without frivolity. [Matthew Arnold, 1822–88, *The Grande Chartreuse*, 157]

2 Boast not thyself of to-morrow; for thou knowest not what a day may bring forth. [Bible, OT, *Proverbs* 27:1]

3 Take therefore no thought for the morrow: for the morrow shall take thought for the things of itself. Sufficient unto the day is the evil thereof. [Bible, NT, *St Matthew* 6:34]

4 *Future*, n. That period of time in which our affairs prosper, our friends are true and our happiness is assured. [Ambrose Bierce, 1842–1914, *The Devil's Dictionary*]

5 I can face anything except the future, and certain parts of the past and present. [Ashley Brilliant, 1933– , *Pot-Shots*, #1698]

6 For some reason, the past doesn't radiate such immense monotony as the future does. Because of its plenitude, the future is propaganda. So is grass. [Joseph Brodsky, 1940–96, *Less Than One*, title essay]

7 You can never plan the future by the past. [Edmund Burke, 1729–97, *Letter to a Member of the National Assembly*]

8 I have seen the Future – and it was being Repaired. [Mel Calman, 1931–94, cartoon caption in *The Times*, 30 Dec. 1986]; see also RUSSIAN REVOLUTION, 6

9 One should never place one's trust in the future. It doesn't deserve it. [André Chamson, 1900–1983, *On ne voit pas les coeurs*, II. 1]

10 Still you can't worry too much about the future. Life is not a rehearsal. [Billy Connolly, 1942– , *Gullible's Travels*, 'Scotland']

11 *To-morrow?* – Why, To-morrow I may be / Myself with Yesterday's Sev'n Thousand Years. [Edward Fitzgerald, 1809–83, *The Rubá'iyát of Omar Khayyám*, Edn 1, 20]

12 The only certain thing about the future is that it will surprise even those who have seen furthest into it. [Eric Hobsbawm, 1917– , *The Age of Empire, 1875–1914*, final sentence]

13 But this *long run* is a misleading guide to current affairs. *In the long run* we are all dead.

[John Maynard Keynes, 1883–1946, *A Tract on Monetary Reform*, Ch. 3]

14 The only reason people want to be masters of the future is to change the past. [Milan Kundera, 1929– , *The Book of Laughter and Forgetting*, Pt 1, 17]

15 One would expect people to remember the past and to imagine the future. But in fact ... they imagine ... [history] in terms of their own experience, and when trying to gauge the future they cite supposed analogies from the past: till, by a double process of repetition, they imagine the past and remember the future. [Lewis Namier, 1888–1969, *Conflicts*, pp. 69–70]

16 He is a bad man who does not pay to the future at least as much as he has received from the past. [A W Pollard, 1859–1944; *Observer*, 'Sayings of the Week', 31 July 1927]

17 They think about Tomorrow, in other words simply about another today; towns have only one day at their disposal which comes back exactly the same every morning. [Jean-Paul Sartre, 1905–80, *Nausea*, 'Tuesday at Bouville']

18 Shall I tell you the signs of a New Age coming? / It is a sound of drubbing and sobbing / Of people crying, We are old, we are old / And the sun is going down and becoming cold. [Stevie Smith, 1902–71, *The New Age*]

19 ANDERSON: Tomorrow is another day, McKendrick.

MCKENDRICK: Tomorrow, in my experience, is usually the same day. [Tom Stoppard, 1937– , *Professional Foul*]

G

GAMBLING

1 As I walk along the Bois Bou-long, / With an independent air, / You can hear the girls declare, / 'He must be a millionaire'; / You can hear them sigh and wish to die, / You can see them wink the other eye / At the man who broke the Bank at Monte Carlo. [Fred Gilbert, 1850–1903, *The Man Who Broke the Bank at Monte Carlo*]

2 It [poker] exemplifies the worst aspects of capitalism that have made our country so great. [Walter Matthau, 1920– , in A Alvarez, *The Biggest Game in Town*]

3 If there was two birds sitting on a fence, he would bet you which one would fly first. [Mark Twain, 1835–1910, *The Celebrated Jumping Frog*]

GAMES

1 Life's too short for chess. [Henry J Byron, 1834–84, *Our Boys*, I]

2 Poets do not go mad; but chess-players do. [G K Chesterton, 1874–1936, *Orthodoxy*, Ch. 2]

3 With spots quadrangular of diamond form, / Ensanguined hearts, clubs typical of strife, / And spades, the emblem of untimely graves. [William Cowper, 1731–1800, *The Task*, Bk IV, 217]

4 A game to subdue the turbulent spirit, or to worry a tranquil mind. [William Hartston, 1947– , *The Kings of Chess*, Ch. I]

5 When in doubt, win the trick. [Edmond Hoyle, 1672–1769, *Hoyle's Games*, 'Whist: Twenty-four Short Rules for Learners']

6 I am sorry I have not learnt to play at cards. It is very useful in life: it generates kindness, and consolidates society. [Dr Samuel Johnson, 1709–84, in James Boswell, *Tour of the Hebrides*, 11 Nov. 1773]

7 [When asked by a poor bridge partner, 'How should I have played that hand?'] Under an assumed name. [George S Kaufman, 1889–1961, in Scott Meredith, *G S K and the Algonquin Round Table*]

8 Men are as chancy as children in their choice of playthings. [Rudyard Kipling, 1865–1936, *Kim*, Ch. 10]

9 'A clear fire, a clean hearth, and the rigour of the game.' This was the celebrated wish of old Sarah Battle (now with God), who, next to her devotions, loved a good game at whist. [Charles Lamb, 1775–1834, *Essays of Elia*, 'Mrs Battle's Opinions on Whist']

10 A professor of anatomy once declared that there are only fourteen types of woman – young women, women who are really wonderful all things considered, and the twelve most famous women in history – and the same applies to Bridge partners. Over and above this, they are usually either so good that you lose all your self-confidence, or so bad that you lose all your money. [W D H McCullough, 1901–78, and 'Fougasse', 1887–1965, *Aces Made Easy*]

11 I shall never forget my mother's horror and my father's cry of joy when, for the first time in my life, I said angrily to my father, 'That's not the hand I dealt you, Dad.' [J B Morton ('Beachcomber'), 1893–1979, *The Best of B*, 11]

12 Gamesmanship or, The Art of Winning Games without Actually Cheating. [Stephen Potter, 1900–1969, title of book]

13 It was remarked to me ... that to play billiards was the sign of an ill-spent youth. [Herbert Spencer, 1820–1903, quoted in David Duncan, *Life and Letters of S*, Ch. 20]

14 Solitaire is the only thing in life that demands absolute honesty. [Hugh Wheeler, 1912– , in musical *A Little Night Music*]

15 Poker shouldn't be played in a house with women. [Tennessee Williams, 1911–83, *A Streetcar Named Desire*, II. iii]

See also CRICKET, FOOTBALL, GOLF, SPORTS

GARDENS & GARDENING

1 I value my garden more for being full of blackbirds than of cherries, and very frankly give them fruit for their songs. [Joseph Addison, 1672–1719, *The Spectator*, 477]

2 Gardening is not a rational act. What matters is the immersion of the hands in the earth, that ancient ceremony of which the Pope kissing the tarmac is merely a pallid vestigial remnant. [Margaret Atwood, 1939– , *Bluebeard's Egg*, 'Unearthing Suite']

3 God Almighty first planted a garden; and, indeed, it is the purest of human pleasures. [Francis Bacon, 1561–1626, *Essays*, 46, 'Of Gardens']

4 A garden is a lovesome thing, God wot! [T E Brown, 1830–97, *My Garden*]

5 God the first garden made, and the first city Cain. [Abraham Cowley, 1618–67, *The Garden*]

6 Who loves a garden loves a greenhouse too. [William Cowper, 1731–1800, *The Task*, Bk III, 566]

7 As a matter of fact, you know I am rather sorry you should see the garden now, because, alas! it is not looking at its best. Oh, it doesn't *compare* to what it was last year. [Ruth Draper, 1889–1956, *Showing the Garden*]

8 What is a weed? A plant whose virtues have not yet been discovered. [Ralph Waldo Emerson, 1803–82, *Fortune of the Republic*]

9 The kiss of the sun for pardon. / The song of the birds for mirth. / One is nearer God's Heart in a garden / Than anywhere else on earth. [Dorothy Gurney, 1858–1932, *God's Garden*]

10 Everything in the Garden's Lovely! [J P Harrington, b.1865, and George Le Brun, d.1905, title of music-hall song, sung by Marie Lloyd]

11 Oh, Adam was a gardener, and God who made him sees / That half a proper gardener's work is done upon his knees. [Rudyard Kipling, 1865–1936, *The Glory of the Garden*, 8]

12 The nectarine, and curious peach, / Into my hands themselves do reach; / Stumbling on melons, as I pass, / Ensnared with flowers, I fall on grass. [Andrew Marvell, 1621–78, *The Garden*, 37]

13 I know a little garden close / Set thick with lily and red rose, / Where I would wander if I might / From dewy dawn to dewy night. / And have one with me wandering. [William Morris, 1834–96, *The Life and Death of Jason*, IV, 577]

14 It is only to the gardener that time is a friend, giving each year more than he steals. [Beverley Nichols, 1899–1983, *Merry Hall*, Feb. 1957]

15 Few and signally blest are those whom Jupiter has destined to be cabbage-planters. For they've always one foot on the ground, and the other not far from it. [François Rabelais, *c.*1492–1553, *Pantagruel*, Bk IV, Ch. 18]

16 A sensitive plant in a garden grew, / And the young winds fed it with silver dew. [P B Shelley, 1792–1822, *The Sensitive Plant*, I, 1]

17 In a coign of the cliff between lowland and highland, / At the sea-down's edge between windward and lee, / Walled round with rocks as an inland island, / The ghost of a garden fronts the sea. [A C Swinburne, 1837–1909, *A Forsaken Garden*, 1]

18 Come into the garden, Maud, / For the black bat, night, has flown, / Come into the garden, Maud, / I am here at the gate alone; / And the woodbine spices are wafted abroad, / And the musk of the rose is blown. [Alfred, Lord Tennyson, 1809–92, *Maud*, Pt 1, xxii, 1]

19 Nothing grows in our garden, only washing. And babies. [Dylan Thomas, 1914–53, *Under Milk Wood*]

20 *Cela est bien dit, répondit Candide, mais il faut cultiver notre jardin.* – That's true enough, said Candide, but we must go and work in the garden. [Voltaire, 1694–1778, *Candide*, Ch. 30]

GENERATIONS

1 Vanity of vanities, saith the Preacher, vanity of vanities; all is vanity. / What profit hath a man of all his labour which he taketh under the sun? / One generation passeth away, and another generation cometh. [Bible, OT, *Ecclesiastes* 1:2]

2 The fathers have eaten sour grapes, and the children's teeth are set on edge. [Bible, OT, *Ezekiel* 18:2]

3 Any given generation gives the next generation advice that the given generation should have been given by the previous one but now it's too late. [Roy Blount Jr, 1941– , from 'Don't Anybody Steal These', in *Antaeus: Journals, Notebooks and Diaries*, ed. D Halpern, p. 50]

4 I saw the best minds of my generation destroyed by madness, starving hysterical naked. [Allen Ginsberg, 1926–97, *Howl*]

5 Men in their generations are like the leaves of the trees. The wind blows and one year's leaves are scattered on the ground; but the trees burst into bud and put on fresh ones when the spring comes around. [Homer, *c*.900BC, *Iliad*, I, 146]

6 Let the word go forth from this time and place, to friend and foe alike, that the torch has been passed to a new generation of Americans – born in this century, tempered by war, disciplined by a hard and bitter peace. [President John F Kennedy, 1917–63, inaugural address, 20 Jan. 1961]

7 The generations of living things pass in a short time, and like runners hand on the torch of life. [Lucretius, 99–55BC, *On the Nature of the Universe*, II, 78]

8 Every generation revolts against its fathers and makes friends with its grandfathers. [Lewis Mumford, 1895–1990, *The Brown Decades*, Ch. 1]

9 The rapid, blind / And fleeting generations of mankind. [P B Shelley, 1792–1822, *The Witch of Atlas*, 615]

10 That's what you all are . . . All of you young people who served in the war. You are a lost generation. [Gertrude Stein, 1874–1946, in Ernest Hemingway, *A Moveable Feast*, 3]; see 11

11 'You are all a lost generation,' Gertrude Stein said to Hemingway. We weren't lost. Knew where we were, all right, but we wouldn't go home. Ours was the generation that stayed up all night. Indeed we spent so little time in bed most of us had only one child. [James Thurber, 1894–1961, *Selected Letters from J T*, ed. Helen Thurber and Edward Weeks, letter to Frances Glennon, June 1959, PPS]; see 10

GENEROSITY

1 Liberality lies less in giving liberally than in the timeliness of the gift. [Jean de La Bruyère, 1645–96, *Characters*, 'Of the Heart', 47]

2 Send two dozen roses to Room 424 and put 'Emily, I love you' on the back of the bill. [Groucho Marx, 1895–1977, in film *A Day at the Races*, screenplay by Robert Pirosh et al.]

3 There are only two classes of people, the magnanimous, and the rest. [Marcel Proust, 1871–1922, *Remembrance of Things Past: Swann's Way*, 'Swann in Love']

4 There's nothing in Christianity or Buddhism that quite matches the sympathetic unselfishness of an oyster. [Saki (H H. Munro), 1870–1916, *The Match-Maker*]

5 For his bounty, / There was no winter in't; an autumn 'twas / That grew the more by reaping . . . [William Shakespeare, 1564–1616, *Antony and Cleopatra*, V. ii. 86]

See also CHARITY

GENIUS

1 Talent is what a man possesses and genius what possesses man. [Isaac Stern quoting 'a famous English writer' in BBC TV Bernard Levin interview, in *Listener*, 9 June 1983]

2 Geniuses are the luckiest of mortals because what they must do is the same as what they most wanted to do. [W H Auden, 1907–73, foreword to Dag Hammarskjöld, *Markings*]

3 We see the contrast between the genius which does what it must and the talent which does what it can. [Maurice Baring, 1874–1945 (on Pushkin's *Mozart and Salieri*), in *Outline of Russian Literature*, Ch. 3]

4 We define genius as the capacity for productive reaction against one's training. [Bernard Berenson, 1865–1959, *The Decline of Art*]

5 If we could all live a thousand years . . . we would each, at least once during that period, be considered a genius. Not because of our great age, but because one of our gifts or aptitudes, however slight in itself, would coincide with what people at that particular moment took to be the mark of genius. [John Berger, 1926– , *And Our Faces, My Heart, Brief as Photos*, 6]

6 And he [John von Neumann] was a genius, in the sense that a genius is a man who has *two* great ideas. [J Bronowski, 1908–74, *The Ascent of Man*, 13]

7 Since when was genius found respectable? [Elizabeth Barrett Browning, 1806–61, *Aurora Leigh*, Bk vi]

8 *Le génie n'est qu'une grande aptitude – la patience.* – Genius is nothing but a great aptitude for patience. [George-Louis de Buffon, 1707–88, attr. in Hérault de Séchelles, *Voyage à Montbar*]

9 Genius (which means transcendent capacity of taking trouble, first of all). [Thomas Carlyle, 1795–1881, *Frederick the Great*, Bk iv, Ch. 3]

10 Genius is of no country; her pure ray / Spreads all abroad, as general as the day. [Charles Churchill, 1731–64, *The Rosciad*, 207]

11 Genius is one per cent inspiration and ninety-nine per cent perspiration. [Thomas Edison, 1847–1931, newspaper interview, 1903, in *Life*, Ch. 24]

12 There sit the sainted sage, the bard divine, / The few, whom genius gave to shine / Through every unborn age, and undiscovered clime. [Thomas Gray, 1716–71, *Ode to Music*]

13 The true genius is a mind of large general powers, accidentally determined to some particular direction. [Dr Samuel Johnson, 1709–84, *The Lives of the English Poets*, 'Cowley']

14 She [Dr Lilian Knowles] defined the British genius as 'an infinite capacity for making drains'. [Quoted in Kingsley Martin, 1897–1969, *Father Figures*, Ch. 8]

15 Genius does what it must, and Talent does what it can. [Owen Meredith, 1831–91, *Last Words of a Sensitive Second-rate Poet*]

16 Just as priests, having the widest experience of the human heart, are best able to pardon the sins which they do not themselves commit, so genius, having the widest experience of the human intelligence, can best understand the ideas most directly in opposition to those which form the foundations of its own works. [Marcel Proust, 1871–1922, *Remembrance of Things Past: Within a Budding Grove*, 'Madame Swann at Home']

17 Talent without genius comes to little. Genius without talent is *nothing*. [Paul Valéry, 1871–1945, *At Moments*, 'The Beautiful is Negative']

18 Genius is in the planet's blood. / You're either a poet or a Lilliputian. [Andrei Voznesensky, 1933– , *Who Are We?*]

19 I have nothing to declare except my genius. [Oscar Wilde, 1854–1900 (at the New York Customs House, 1882), quoted in F Harris, *Oscar Wilde*, p. 75]

See also TALENT

GENTLEMEN

1 A gentleman is any man who wouldn't hit a woman with his hat on. [Fred Allen, 1894–1956; in Laurence J Peter, *Peter's Quotations*]

2 I am parshial to ladies if they are nice I suppose it is my nature. I am not quite a gentleman but you would hardly notice it but cant be helped anyhow. [Daisy Ashford, 1881–1972, *The Young Visiters*, Ch. 1]

3 I am a gentleman, though spoiled i' the breeding. The Buzzards are all gentlemen. We came in with the Conqueror. [Richard Brome, 1590?–1625?, *The English Moor*, III. ii]

4 The best of men / That e'er wore earth about him, was a sufferer, / A soft, meek, patient, humble, tranquil spirit, / The first true gentleman that ever breathed. [Thomas Dekker, 1572?–1632, *The Honest Whore*, Pt I, I. ii]

5 Once a gentleman, and always a gentleman. [Charles Dickens, 1812–70, *Little Dorrit*, Bk 11, Ch. 28]

6 When we began this fight, we had clean hands – are they clean now? What's gentility worth if it can't stand fire? [John Galsworthy, 1867–1933, *The Skin Game*, III]

7 He was so particularly the English gentleman and the fortunate settled normal person ... He had kind safe eyes and a voice which, for all its clean fullness, told the quiet tale of its having never had once to raise itself. [Henry James, 1843–1916, *The Wings of the Dove*, Bk I, Ch. 1]

8 For he's one of Nature's Gentlemen, the best of every time. [W J Linton, 1812–98, *Nature's Gentleman*]

9 Gentlemen always seem to remember blondes. [Anita Loos, 1893–1981, *Gentlemen Prefer Blondes*, Ch. 1]

10 A gentleman need not know Latin, but he should at least have forgotten it. [Brander Matthews, 1852–1929, advice to Dr Joseph Shipley]

11 It's only if a man's a gentleman that he won't hesitate to do an ungentlemanly thing. Mortimer is on the boundary line and it makes him careful. [W Somerset Maugham, 1874–1965, *The Constant Wife*, II]

12 It is almost a definition of a gentleman to say that he is one who never inflicts pain. [Cardinal Newman, 1801–90, *The Idea of a University*, 'Knowledge and Religious Duty']

13 I am of the opinion that had your father spent more of your mother's immoral earnings on your education you would not even then have been a gentleman. [Frank Otter, in Seymour Hicks, *Vintage Years*]

14 Since every Jack became a gentleman / There's many a gentle person made a Jack. [William Shakespeare, 1564–1616, *Richard III*, I. iii. 72]

15 MENDOZA: I am a brigand. I live by robbing the rich.

TANNER: I am a gentleman. I live by robbing the poor. [George Bernard Shaw, 1856–1950, *Man and Superman*, III]

16 He's a gentleman: look at his boots. [George Bernard Shaw, 1856–1950, *Pygmalion*, I]

17 The only infallible rule we know is, that the man who is always talking about being a gentleman never is one. [R S Surtees, 1803–64, *Ask Mamma*, Ch. 1]

18 He was a gentleman who was generally spoken of as having nothing a-year, paid quarterly. [R S Surtees, 1803–64, *Mr Sponge's Sporting Tour*, Ch. 24]

19 The English gentleman of gentlemen was he who had land, and family title-deeds, and an old family place, and family portraits, and family embarrassments, and a family absence of any useful employment. [Anthony Trollope, 1815–82, *The Way We Live Now*, Ch. 13]

20 A true gentleman is a man who knows how to play the bagpipes – but doesn't. [*Wall Street Journal*, quoted in *Reader's Digest*, Mar. 1976]

21 For generations the British bourgeoisie have spoken of themselves as gentlemen, and by that they have meant, among other things, a self-respecting scorn of irregular perquisites. It is the quality that distinguishes the gentleman from both the artist and the aristocrat. [Evelyn Waugh, 1903–66, *Decline and Fall*, I, 6]

22 He [Michael Arlen] is every other inch a gentleman. [Rebecca West, 1892–1983, in V Glendinning, *R W*, Pt 3, Ch. 5. Also ascr. to Alexander Woollcott]

GERMANY & THE GERMANS

1 In the nineteenth century the Germans painted their dream and the outcome was invariably vegetable. The French needed only to paint a vegetable and it was already a dream. [Theodor Adorno, 1903–69, *Minima Memoralia*, Pt 1, 29]

2 A German is someone who cannot tell a lie without believing it himself. [Theodor Adorno, 1903–69, *Minima Memoralia*, Pt 2, 70]

3 Hamelin Town's in Brunswick, / By famous Hanover city; / The river Weser, deep and wide, / Washes its wall on the southern side; / A pleasanter spot you never spied. [Robert Browning, 1812–89, *The Pied Piper of Hamelin*, 1]

4 The Englishman likes to imagine himself at sea, the German in a forest. It is impossible to express the difference of their national identity more concisely. [Elias Canetti, 1905–94, *Crowds and Power*, 'The Crowd in History']

5 Oh the Germans classify, but the French arrange. [Willa Cather, 1873–1947, *Death Comes to the Archbishop*, 'Prologue']

6 Don't let's be beastly to the Germans. [Noël Coward, 1899–1973, lyric: *Don't Let's be Beastly to the Germans*]

7 One of the mistakes the Germans made, in this century and also in the time before, was that they were not brave enough to be afraid. [Günter Grass, 1927– , in Channel 4 TV programme *Voices*, 27 June 1985]

8 We shall never be rough and heartless when it is not necessary, that is clear. We Germans, who are the only people in the world who have a decent attitude towards animals, will also assume a decent attitude towards these human animals. [Heinrich Himmler, 1900–1945, speech, 4 Oct. 1943]

9 How appallingly thorough these Germans always managed to be, how emphatic! In sex no less than in war – in scholarship, in science. Diving deeper than anyone else and coming up muddier. [Aldous Huxley, 1894–1963, *Time Must Have a Stop*, 6]

10 If the French were German in their essence, then how the Germans would admire them! [Franz Kafka, 1883–1924, *The Diaries of F K*, 17 Dec. 1910]

11 All free men, wherever they may live, are citizens of Berlin. And therefore, as a free man, I take pride in the words: '*Ich bin ein Berliner*.' [President John F Kennedy, 1917–63, speech at West Berlin City Hall, 26 June 1963]

12 Heinrich Heine so loosened the corsets of the German language that today even little salesmen can fondle her breasts. [Karl Kraus, 1874–1936, *Half-truths and One-and-a-half Truths*, 'Riddles']

13 It is as if the life had retreated eastwards. As if the Germanic life were slowly ebbing away from contact with western Europe, ebbing to the deserts of the east. [D H Lawrence, 1885–1930, *A Letter from Germany*, 1924]

14 Once all the Germans were warlike and mean / But that couldn't happen again. / We taught them a lesson in 1918, / And they've hardly bothered us since then. [Tom Lehrer, 1928– , song: *Sleep, Baby, Sleep*]

15 War is Prussia's national industry. [attr. to Comte Mirabeau, 1749–91, by Albert Sorel, but probably a misquotation of a longer passage in his *Monarchie prussienne*]

16 I should be pleased, I suppose, that Hitler has carried out a revolution on our lines. But they are Germans. So they will end by ruining our idea. [Benito Mussolini, 1883–1945, in Christopher Hibbert, *B M*, Pt II, Ch. 1]

17 This is all a German racket designed to take over the whole of Europe. It has to be thwarted. This rushed take-over by the Germans on the worst possible basis, with the French behaving like poodles to the Germans, is absolutely intolerable. [Nicholas Ridley, 1929–93, interview in *Spectator*, 14 July 1990]

18 Ah, a German and a genius! a prodigy, admit him! [(when Handel was announced) Jonathan Swift, 1677–1745, attr.]

19 The English and French bourgeoisie created a new society after their own image. The Germans came later, and they were compelled to live for a long time on the pale gruel of philosophy. [Leon Trotsky, 1874–1940, *History of the Russian Revolution*, Pt 1, Ch. 10]

20 America ... is the prize amateur nation of the world. Germany is the prize professional nation. [Woodrow Wilson, 1856–1924, speech to officers of the fleet, Aug. 1917]

See also NATIONS

GHOSTS & SPIRITS

1 Miss Erikson looked more peculiar than ever this morning. Is her spiritualism getting worse? [Noël Coward, 1899–1973, *Present Laughter*, I]

2 you want to know / whether i believe in ghosts / of course i do not believe in them / if you had known / as many of them as i have / you would not / believe in them either [Don Marquis, 1878–1937, *archy and mehitabel*, XXXIII, 'ghosts']

3 There must be crowds of ghosts among the trees, – / Not people killed in battle – they're in France / But horrible shapes – old men who died / Slow natural deaths – old men with ugly souls, / Who wore their bodies out with nasty sins. [Siegfried Sassoon, 1886–1967, *Repression of War Experience*]

4 Then it started like a guilty thing / Upon a fearful summons. [William Shakespeare, 1564–1616, *Hamlet*, I. i. 148]

5 Angels and ministers of grace defend us! / Be thou a spirit of health or goblin damned, / Bring with thee airs from heaven or blasts from hell, / Be thy intents wicked or charitable, / Thou com'st in such a questionable shape / That I will speak to thee. [*Hamlet*, I. iv. 39]

6 I do not set my life at a pin's fee; / And for my soul, what can it do to that, / Being a thing immortal as itself? [*Hamlet*, I. iv. 65]

7 The times have been, / That when the brains were out, the man would die, / And there an end; but now they rise again, / With twenty mortal murders on their crowns, / And push us from our stools. [*Macbeth*, III. iv. 78]

8 I seemed to move among a world of ghosts, / And feel myself the shadow of a dream. [Alfred, Lord Tennyson, 1809–92, *The Princess*, I, 17]

9 The ghost that got into our house on the night of November 17, 1915, raised such a hullabaloo of misunderstandings that I am sorry I didn't just let it keep on walking, and go to bed. [James Thurber, 1894–1961, *My Life and Hard Times*, Ch. 4]

GIRLS

1 Who needs a whole girl if you've got her knee? [Joseph Brodsky, 1940–96 (one-line poem), in interview in *Poetry Review*, Spring 1988]

2 Of all the girls that are so smart / There's none like pretty Sally, / She is the darling of my heart, / And she lives in our alley. [Henry Carey, 1693?–1743, song: *Sally in our Alley*]

3 A damsel with a dulcimer / In a vision once I saw: / It was an Abyssinian maid, / And on her dulcimer she played, / Singing of Mount Abora. [Samuel Taylor Coleridge, 1772–1834, *Kubla Khan*]

4 If girls aren't ignorant, they're cultured ... You can't avoid suffering. [William Cooper, 1910– , *Scenes from Provincial Life*, Pt III, 2]

5 a pretty girl who naked is / is worth a million statues [e e cummings, 1894–1962, *Collected Poems*, 1938, 133]

6 A man says to another man: 'I'd certainly like to steal your girl.' Second man: 'I'd give her to you, but she's part of a set.' [F Scott Fitzgerald, 1896–1940, *Notebooks*, 'E']

7 Don't you think it's better for a girl to be preoccupied with sex than occupied? [F Hugh Herbert, 1897–1935, said by Maggie McNamara in film *The Moon is Blue*]

8 'Boys will be boys –' 'And even that wouldn't matter if we could only prevent girls from being girls.' [Anthony Hope, 1863–1933, *The Dolly Dialogues*, 16]

9 Oh, she's a splendid girl. Wonderfully pneumatic. [Aldous Huxley, 1894–1963, *Brave New World*, Ch. 3]

10 There was a little girl / Who had a little curl / Right in the middle of her forehead; / And when she was good / She was very, very good, / But when she was bad she was horrid. [H W Longfellow, 1807–82, *There was a Little Girl*]

11 I like the girls who do, / I like the girls who don't; / I hate the girl who says she will / And then she says she won't. / But the girl that I like best of all / And I think you'll say I'm right – / Is the one who says she never has / But looks as though she ... / 'Ere listen ... [Max Miller, 1895–1963, from song: *The Girls Who Do*, in *The Max Miller Blue Book*]

12 What are little girls made of? / What are little girls made of? / Sugar and spice / And all things nice, / That's what little girls are made of. [Nursery rhyme]

13 He who believes in nothing still needs a girl to believe in him. [Eugen Rosenstock-Huessy, 1888–1959, in W H Auden, *A Certain World*]

14 The blessed damozel leaned out / From the gold bar of heaven; / Her eyes were deeper than the depth / Of waters stilled at even; / She had three lilies in her hand / And the stars in her hair were seven. [Dante Gabriel Rossetti, 1828–82, *The Blessed Damozel*, 1]

15 I was about half in love with her by the time we sat down. That's the thing about girls. Every time they do something pretty, even if they're not much to look at, or even if they're sort of stupid, you fall half in love with them, and then you never know *where* you are. [J D Salinger, 1919– , *The Catcher in the Rye*, Ch. 10]

16 The trouble with girls is, if they like a boy, no matter how big a bastard he is, they'll say he has an inferiority complex, and if they *don't* like him, no matter how nice a guy he is, or how big an inferiority complex he has, they'll say he's conceited. Even smart girls do it. [J D Salinger, 1919– , *The Catcher in the Rye*, Ch. 18]

17 'American girls do have regrets,' Amy said. 'That is what distinguishes them from French girls.' [Amanda Vail, 1921–66, *Love Me Little*, Ch. 10]

18 I loved a lass, a fair one, / As fair as e'er was seen; / She was indeed a rare one, / Another Sheba queen. [George Wither, 1588–1667, *A Love Sonnet*]

19 She dwelt among the untrodden ways / Beside the springs of Dove, / A maid whom there were none to praise / And very few to love. [William Wordsworth, 1770–1850, *She Dwelt among the Untrodden Ways*]

GIVING & TAKING

1 It is more blessed to give than to receive. [Bible, NT, *Acts of the Apostles* 20:35]

2 God loveth a cheerful giver. [Bible, NT, *2 Corinthians* 9:7]

3 Unto every one that hath shall be given, and he shall have abundance: but from him that hath not shall be taken away even that which he hath. [Bible, NT, *St Matthew* 25:29]

4 He ne'er considered it, as loath / To look a gift-horse in the mouth. [Samuel Butler, 1612–80, *Hudibras*, 1, i, 483]

5 She for him had given / Her all on earth, and more than all in heaven! [Lord Byron, 1788–1824, *The Corsair*, III, 17]

6 The good received, the giver is forgot. [William Congreve, 1670–1729, *Epistle to Lord Halifax*, 40]

7 For to the noble mind / Rich gifts wax poor when givers prove unkind. [William Shakespeare, 1564–1616, *Hamlet*, III. i. 100]

8 We do not obtain the most precious gifts by going in search of them but by waiting for them. [Simone Weil, 1909–43, *Waiting on God*, 'Reflections on the Right Use of School Studies']

9 Behold, I do not give lectures or a little charity, / When I give I give myself. [Walt Whitman, 1819–92, *Song of Myself*, 40, 994]

GLORY

1 The boast of heraldry, the pomp of power, / And all that beauty, all that wealth e'er gave, / Awaits alike th' inevitable hour, / The paths of glory lead but to the grave. [Thomas Gray, 1716–71, *Elegy Written in a Country Churchyard*, 9]

2 *O quam cito transit gloria mundi*. – Oh, how swiftly the glory of the world passes away! [Thomas à Kempis, *c.*1380–1471, *The Imitation of Christ*, 3. (*Sic transit gloria mundi* – Thus passes the glory of the world – is used at the enthronement of a new pope and is proverbial)]

3 Sound, sound the clarion, fill the fife, / Throughout the sensual world proclaim, / One crowded hour of glorious life / Is worth an age without a name. [Thomas Mordaunt, 1730–1809, *Verses Written during the War 1756–63*]

4 The final event to himself [Mr Burke] has been, that as he rose like a rocket, he fell like the stick. [Thomas Paine, 1737–1809, *Letter to the Addressers on the Late Proclamation*]

5 'Come cheer up my lads, 'tis to glory we steer' – As the soldier remarked whose post lay in the rear. [Christina Rossetti, 1830–94, *Couplet*]

6 Vain pomp and glory of this world, I hate ye: / I feel my heart new opened. O! how wretched / Is that poor man that hangs on princes' favours! / There is, betwixt that smile we would aspire to, / That sweet aspect of princes, and their ruin, / More pangs and fears than wars or women have; / And when he falls, he falls like Lucifer, / Never to hope again. [William Shakespeare, 1564–1616, *Henry VIII*, III. ii. 365]

7 Glorious the northern lights astream; / Glorious the song, when God's the theme; / Glorious the thunder's roar. [Christopher Smart, 1722–71, *Song to David*, 85]

8 May God deny you peace but give you glory! [Miguel de Unamuno, 1864–1937, *The Tragic Sense of Life*, closing words]

9 Glories like glow-worms, afar off shine bright, / But looked to near, have neither heat nor light. [John Webster, 1580?–1625?, *The Duchess of Malfi*, IV. ii. 148]

10 The rainbow comes and goes, / And lovely is the rose, / The moon doth with delight / Look round her when the heavens are bare. / Waters on a starry night / Are beautiful and fair; / The sunshine is a glorious birth; / But yet I know, where'er I go, / That there hath past away a glory from the earth. [William Wordsworth, 1770–1850, *Ode, Intimations of Immortality*, 2]

GLUTTONY

1 In the land of Egypt, when we sat by the flesh pots, and when we did eat bread to the full. [Bible, OT, *Exodus* 16:3]

2 Gluttony is an emotional escape, a sign something is eating us. [Peter de Vries, 1910–93, *Comfort Me with Apples*, Ch. 15]

3 When Rabbit said, 'Honey or condensed milk with your bread?' he was so excited that he said, 'Both,' and then, so as not to seem greedy, he added, 'But don't bother about the bread, please.' [A A Milne, 1882–1956, *Winnie-the-Pooh*, Ch. 2]

4 These citizens are always willing to bet that what Nicely-Nicely dies of will be over-feeding and never anything small like pneumonia, for Nicely-Nicely is known far and wide as a character who dearly loves to commit eating. [Damon Runyon, 1884–1946, *Take It Easy*, 'Lonely Heart']

5 They are as sick that surfeit with too much, as they that starve with nothing. [William Shakespeare, 1564–1616, *The Merchant of Venice*, I. ii. (5)]

6 He is a very valiant trencherman. [*Much Ado About Nothing*, I. i. (52)]

7 Serenely full, the epicure would say, / Fate cannot harm me, I have dined to-day. [Sydney Smith, 1771–1845, in Lady Holland, *Memoir*, Vol. i, Ch. 11]

See also GREED

GOD

1 And if it turns out that there is a God, I don't believe that he is evil. The worst that can be said is that he's an under-achiever. [Woody Allen, 1935–   , in film *Love and Death*]

2 Then Job fell to his knees and cried to the Lord, 'Thine is the kingdom and the power and the glory. Thou hast a good job. Don't blow it.' [Woody Allen, 1935–   , *Without Feathers*, 'The Scrolls']

3 God don't come when you want Him but He's right on time. [anon. jazz historian, in Tennessee Williams, *Memoirs*]

4 Thou hast created us for Thyself, and our heart is not quiet until it rests in Thee. [St Augustine, 354–430, *Confessions*, I, 1]

5 For none deny there is a God, but those for whom it maketh that there were no God. [Francis Bacon, 1561–1626, *Essays*, 16 'Of Atheism']

6 It were better to have no opinion of God at all, than such an opinion as is unworthy of him. [Francis Bacon, 1561–1626, *Essays*, 17, 'Of Superstition']

7 If the concept of God has any validity or use, it can only be to make us larger, freer, and more loving. If God cannot do this, then it is time we got rid of Him. [James Baldwin, 1924–87, *The Fire Next Time*, 'Down at the Cross']

8 If the light of a thousand suns suddenly arose in the sky, that splendour might be compared to the radiance of the Supreme Spirit. [(Epigraph to Robert Jungk, *Brighter than A Thousand Suns*, used to describe the first atomic explosions) *The Bhagavad Gita*, Ch. 11, 12]

9 And God said unto Moses, I AM THAT I AM. [Bible, OT, *Exodus* 3:14]

10 Have we not all one father? hath not one God created us? [Bible, OT, *Malachi* 2:10]

11 God is a righteous Judge, strong and patient: and God is provoked every day. [Bible, OT, *Psalms* 7:12 (*Book of Common Prayer* version)]

12 God is our refuge and strength, a very present help in trouble. [Bible, OT, *Psalms* 46:1]

13 A father of the fatherless, and a judge of the widows, is God in his holy habitation. [Bible, OT, *Psalms* 68:5]

14 God is no respecter of persons. [Bible, NT, *Acts of the Apostles* 10:34]

15 It is a fearful thing to fall into the hands of the living God. [Bible, NT, *Hebrews* 10:31]

16 He that loveth not knoweth not God; for God is love. [Bible, NT, *1 John* 4:8]

17 If God be for us, who can be against us? [Bible, NT, *Romans* 8:31]

18 In the beginning was the Word, and the Word was with God, and the Word was God. [Bible, NT, *St John* 1:1]

19 God is a Spirit; and they that worship him must worship him in spirit and in truth. [Bible, NT, *St John* 4:24]

20 The kingdom of God is within you. [Bible, NT, *St Luke* 17:21]

21 He maketh his sun rise on the evil and on the good, and sendeth rain on the just and on the unjust. [Bible, NT, *St Matthew* 5:45]

22 With God all things are possible. [Bible, NT, *St Matthew* 19:26]

23 Tho' thou art worshipped by the names divine / Of Jesus and Jehovah, thou art still / The Son of Morn in weary Night's decline, / The lost traveller's dream under the hill. [William Blake, 1757–1827, *The Gates of Paradise*, Epilogue]

24 The pride of the peacock is the glory of God. / The lust of the goat is the bounty of God. / The wrath of the lion is the wisdom of God. / The nakedness of woman is the work of God. [William Blake, 1757–1827, *The Marriage of Heaven and Hell*, 'Proverbs of Hell']

25 Now that it has come of age, the world is more godless, and perhaps it is for that very reason nearer to God than ever before. [Dietrich Bonhoeffer, 1906–45, *Letters and Papers from Prison*, letter 18 July 1944]

26 A God who let us prove his existence would

be an idol. [Dietrich Bonhoeffer, 1906–45, *No Rusty Swords*, Pt 2, Ch. 1]

27 God's gifts put man's best gifts to shame. [Elizabeth Barrett Browning, 1806–61, *Sonnets from the Portuguese*, 26]

28 God is the perfect poet, / Who in his person acts his own creations. [Robert Browning, 1812–89, *Paracelsus*, II]

29 God must be glad one loves His world so much. [Robert Browning, 1812–89, *Pippa Passes*, Pt III, 73]

30 A touch divine – / And the scaled eyeball owns the mystic rod; / Visibly through his garden walketh God. [Robert Browning, 1812–89, *Sordello*, 1]

31 God was still ... the best of the dramatic poets, though shapeless and uneconomical. A bit like Charles Dickens. God was good on the physical and emotional sides and a great one for hate. He generously spilled his own hate into his dearest creation. [Anthony Burgess, 1917–93, *Enderby's Dark Lady*, 7]

32 As you know, God is usually on the side of the big battalions against the small. [Comte de Bussy-Rabutin, 1618–93, letter to the Comte de Limoges, 18 Oct. 1677]; see 97, 102

33 An honest God's the noblest work of man. [Samuel Butler, 1835–1902, *Notebooks: Further Extracts*, Vol. i, 'An Honest God' (reversing a saying of Pope)]; see 64

34 We plough the fields, and scatter / The good seed on the land, / But it is fed and watered / By God's Almighty Hand. He sends the snow in winter, / The warmth to swell the grain, / The breezes and the sunshine, / And soft refreshing rain. [Jane Montgomery Campbell, 1817–78, hymn]

35 God was a mistake. But it is hard to decide whether too early or too late. [Elias Canetti, 1905–94, *The Human Province*, '1948']

36 You must understand, James, that their English God is not so dominant a business institution as ours [the American God]. [J L Carr, 1912–94, *The Battle of Pollocks Crossing*, p. 155]

37 And almost every one when age, / Disease, or sorrows strike him, / Inclines to think there is a God, / Or something very like Him. [Arthur Hugh Clough, 1819–61, *Dipsychus*, I, v]

38 Thou shalt have one God only; who / Would be at the expense of two? [Arthur Hugh Clough, 1819–61, *The Latest Decalogue*]

39 Even bein' Gawd ain't a bed of roses. [Marc Connelly, 1890–1980, *Green Pastures*, vi]

40 Oh for a closer walk with God, / A calm and heavenly frame; / A light to shine upon the road / That leads me to the Lamb! [William Cowper, 1731–1800, *Olney Hymns*, 1]

41 God moves in a mysterious way, / His wonders to perform; / He plants his footsteps in the sea, / And rides upon the storm. [William Cowper, 1731–1800, *Olney Hymns*, 35]

42 God, from whose territory I had withdrawn my ambassadors at the age of fifteen. It had become obvious that he was never going to do a thing I said. [Quentin Crisp, 1908–99, *The Naked Civil Servant*, Ch. 16]

43 It is the final proof of God's omnipotence that he need not exist in order to save us. [Peter de Vries, 1910–93, *The Mackerel Plaza*, Ch. 2]

44 Thou hast made me, and shall thy work decay? [John Donne, 1571?–1631, *Holy Sonnets*, 1]

45 It's not God that I don't accept, Alyosha, only I most respectfully return Him the ticket. [Fyodor Dostoyevsky, 1821–81, *Brothers Karamazov*, Pt II, 5, 4]

46 The Lord God is subtle but he is not malicious. [Albert Einstein, 1879–1955, quip first made in May 1921, later carved in German above the fireplace of Fine Hall, the Mathematical Institute of Princeton University]

47 I cannot believe that God plays dice with the cosmos. [Albert Einstein, 1879–1955, in letter to Max Born, 4 Dec. 1926]; see 58

48 God is a circle whose centre is everywhere and whose circumference is nowhere. [Empedocles, 5th cent. BC, attr.]

49 My God, how wonderful Thou art, / Thy majesty how bright, / How beautiful Thy mercy-seat / In depths of burning light! [F W Faber, 1814–63, hymn]

50 I can't help feeling sceptical about the Bible's claim that God made man in his own image. What? Two solemn little Jehovahs to gaze back at him with fathomless wisdom and benevolence? What would have been the fun in that? He could have achieved *that* simply by creating a couple of mirrors, or a closed-circuit television. [Michael Frayn, 1933– , *Constructions*, 157]

51 At bottom God is nothing more than an exalted father. [Sigmund Freud, 1856–1939, *Totem and Taboo*, Ch. 4, sect. v]

52 Forgive, O Lord, my little jokes on Thee / And I'll forgive Thy great big one on me. [Robert Frost, 1874–1963, *Cluster of Faith*]

53 God is not Dead but Alive and Well and working on a Much Less Ambitious Project. [Graffito in a Greenwich pub, in *Guardian*, 'London Letter', 27 Nov. 1975]

54 O worship the King, all glorious above! / O gratefully sing his power and his love! / Our Shield and Defender – the Ancient of Days, / Pavilioned in splendour, and girded with praise. [Robert Grant, 1779–1838, hymn]

55 A gaping silken dragon, / Puffed by the wind, suffices us for God. [Robert Graves, 1895–1985, *The Cuirassiers of the Frontier*]

56 I'm not very conscious of His presence, but I hope that He is still dogging my footsteps. [Graham Greene, 1904–91; *Observer*, 'Sayings of the Week', 9 Sept. 1984]

57 O man-projected Figure, of late / Imaged as we, thy knell who shall survive? / Whence came it we were tempted to create / One whom we can no longer keep alive? [Thomas Hardy, 1840–1928, *God's Funeral*]

58 God not only plays dice. He also sometimes throws the dice where they cannot be seen. [Stephen Hawking, 1942– , in *Nature* (1975), 257, 362]; see 47

59 Good God, how much reverence can you have for a Supreme Being who finds it necessary to include such phenomena as phlegm and tooth-decay in His divine system of Creation? [Joseph Heller, 1923–99, *Catch-22*, Ch. 18]

60 Mine eyes have seen the glory of the coming of the Lord: / He is trampling out the vintage where the grapes of wrath are stored. [Julia Ward Howe, 1819–1910, *Battle Hymn of the American Republic*]

61 *Car le mot, c'est le Verbe, et le Verbe, c'est Dieu.* – For words are the Word, and the Word is God. [Victor Hugo, 1802–85, *Les Contemplations*, I, i, 8]

62 Operationally, God is beginning to resemble not a ruler but the last fading smile of a cosmic Cheshire cat. [Julian Huxley, 1887–1975, *Religion without Revelation*, Ch. 3]

63 Many people believe that they are attracted by God or by nature, when they are only repelled by man. [W R Inge, 1860–1954, *More Lay Thoughts of a Dean*, Pt IV, 1]; see 33

64 An honest God is the noblest work of man. [R G Ingersoll, 1833–99, *Gods*, Pt I]

65 If God exists, what's the good of literature? If God does not exist, what's the point of writing? [Eugene Ionesco, 1912–94, interview in *Guardian*, 14 Sept. 1990]

66 I wouldn't put it past God to arrange a virgin birth if he wanted to, but I very much doubt if he would – because it seems to be contrary to the way in which he deals with persons and brings his wonders out of natural personal relationships. [Rt Revd David Jenkins, 1925– , in *Church Times*, 4 May 1984]

67 Man proposes but God disposes. [Thomas à Kempis *c.*1380–1471, *The Imitation of Christ*, 19]

68 Though Thy Power brings / All skill to naught, Ye'll understand a man must think o' things. [Rudyard Kipling, 1865–1936, *McAndrew's Hymn*]

69 There once was a man who said, 'God / Must find it exceedingly odd / If he finds that this tree / Continues to be / When there's no one about in the quad.' [Mgr Ronald Knox, 1888–1957]

70 God seems to have left the receiver off the hook, and time is running out. [Arthur Koestler, 1905–83, *The Ghost in the Machine*, Ch. 18]

71 God is love but get it in writing. [Gypsy Rose Lee, 1914–70, catchphrase]

72 He's vulgar, Wormwood. He has a bourgeois mind. [C S Lewis, 1898–1963, *The Screwtape Letters* (of God), 22]

73 *Ein' feste Burg ist unser Gott, / Ein' gute Wehr und Waffen.* – A safe stronghold our God is still, / A trusty shield and weapon. [Martin Luther, 1483–1546, *Ein' feste Burg*, trans. T Carlyle]

74 The dramatist changes the props but keeps the players. The Almighty does the reverse. [Thomas McKeown, 1912–88, in *Perspectives in Biology and Medicine*, Spring 1983]

75 Why assume so glibly that the God who

presumably created the universe is still running it? It is certainly perfectly conceivable that He may have finished it and then turned it over to lesser gods to operate. [H L Mencken, 1880–1956, *Minority Report*, 298]

76 Just are the ways of God, / And justifiable to men; Unless there be who think not God at all. [John Milton, 1608–74, *Samson Agonistes*, 293]

77 [Ferndean School Report] Progress and conduct: I am afraid that I am severely disappointed in God's works. All three of Him have shown no tendency to improve and He merely sits at the back of the class talking to himselves. He has shown no interest in Rugger, asked to be excused Prayers, and moves in a mysterious way. [Monty Python's Flying Circus, 1969–74, *The Brand New Monty Python Book*]

78 God seems to me to be an artist ... rather than a judge. He has created the drama, and the parts of the play that are wicked and dreadful may be necessary to the whole creation in a way we can't understand. Life is a drama and not a progress. [Malcolm Muggeridge, 1903–90, interview in John Mortimer, *In Character*]

79 God is really only another artist. He invented the giraffe, the elephant, and the cat. He has no real style. He just goes on trying other things. [Pablo Picasso, 1881–1973, in Françoise Gilot and Carlton Lake, *Life with Picasso*, Pt 1]

80 God's a rumour if you like. [Dennis Potter, 1935–94, *Seeing the Blossom*, an interview with Melvyn Bragg, TV Channel 4, April 1994]

81 Whose service is perfect freedom. [*Book of Common Prayer*, Morning Prayer, *Second Collect* (for Peace)]

82 Not three Gods: but one God. [*Book of Common Prayer*, Morning Prayer, *Athanasian Creed* (Quicunque Vult)]

83 I think God is groovy. He had a great publicity agent. [P J Proby, 1938– ; Jonathan Green, *Book of Rock Quotes*]

84 It has even been said that the highest praise of God consists in the denial of him by the atheist who finds creation so perfect that he can dispense with a creator. [Marcel Proust, 1871–1922, *Remembrance of Things Past: The Guermantes Way*, Ch. 2]

85 God is very economical, don't you think? Wastes nothing. Yet also the opposite. [Ralph Richardson, 1902–83, in Kenneth Tynan, *Show People*]

86 *Was wirst du tun, Gott, wenn ich sterbe? / Ich bin dein Krug (wenn ich zerscherbe?)* – What will you do, God, if I die? I am your pitcher (if I break?). [Rainer Maria Rilke, 1875–1926, *Book of Hours*, 'What will you do, God?']

87 Now I, to comfort him, bid him a' should not think of God, I hoped there was no need to trouble himself with any such thoughts yet. [William Shakespeare, 1564–1616, *Henry V*, II. iii. (20)]

88 The only excuse for God is that he does not exist. [Stendhal, 1783–1842, quoted in J Hick, *Evil and the God of Love*, 'Preface']

89 It is a mistake to suppose that God is only, or even chiefly, concerned with religion. [Archbishop William Temple, 1881–1944, in R V C Bodley, *In Search of Serenity*, Ch. 12]

90 Closer is He than breathing, and nearer than hands and feet. [Alfred, Lord Tennyson, 1809–92, *The Higher Pantheism*]

91 I found Him in the shining of the stars, / I marked Him in the flowering of His fields, / But in His ways with men I find Him not. [Alfred, Lord Tennyson, 1809–92, *Idylls of the King*, 'The Passing of Arthur', 9]

92 That God, which ever lives and loves, / One God, one law, one element, / And one far-off divine event, / To which the whole creation moves. [Alfred, Lord Tennyson, 1809–92, *In Memoriam*, Conclusion]

93 I fled Him, down the nights and down the days; / I fled Him, down the arches of the years; / I fled him, down the labyrinthine ways / Of my own mind; and in the mist of tears / I hid from Him, and under running laughter. [Francis Thompson, 1859–1907, *The Hound of Heaven*, 1]

94 You must forget everything traditional that you have learned about God, perhaps even the word itself. [Paul Tillich, 1886–1965, *The Shaking of the Foundations*, 'The Depth of Existence']

95 If God were not a necessary Being of himself, He might almost seem to be made for the use and benefit of mankind. [John Tillotson, 1630–94, *Sermon*, 93]

96 God is a sort of burglar. As a young man you knock him down; as an old man you try to conciliate him, because he may knock you down. [Herbert Beerbohm Tree, 1853–1917, in Hesketh Pearson, *B T*, Ch. 21]

97 God is always on the side of the big battalions. [Marshal Turenne, 1611–75]; see 32, 102

98 For none can thee secure, / But one, who never changes, / Thy God, thy life, thy cure. [Henry Vaughan, 1622–95, *Peace*]

99 The true God, the mighty God, is the God of ideas. [Alfred de Vigny, 1797–1863, *La Bouteille à la mer*]

100 If God did not exist, it would be necessary to invent Him. [Voltaire, 1694–1778, *A l'auteur du livre des trois imposteurs*]

101 If God made us in His image, we have certainly returned the compliment. [Voltaire, 1694–1778, *Le Sottisier*, xxxii]

102 It is said that God is always on the side of the big battalions. [Voltaire, 1694–1778, letter to M. le Riche, 6 Feb. 1770]; see 32, 97

103 When I found out I thought God was white, and a man, I lost interest. [Alice Walker, 1944– , *The Color Purple*, p. 166]

104 I think it pisses God off if you walk by the color purple in a field somewhere and don't notice it. What it do when it pissed off? I ast. Oh, it make something else. People think pleasing God is all God care about. But any fool living in the world can see it always trying to please us back. [Alice Walker, 1944– , *The Color Purple*, p. 167]

105 Our God, our help in ages past, / Our hope for years to come, / Our shelter from the stormy blast, / And our eternal home. [Isaac Watts, 1674–1748, *Psalms*, xc. First line altered by John Wesley to 'O God . . .']

106 It is not my business to think about myself. My business is to think about god. It is for god to think about me. [Simone Weil, 1909–43, *Waiting on God*, Letter 1]

107 (Of God) I don't care what they people say, He's been perfectly sweet to me. [Godfrey Winn, quoted in *Guardian*, 17 Dec. 1996]

108 A God all mercy is a God unjust. [Edward Young, 1683–1765, *Night Thoughts*, 'Night 4', 233]

See also FAITHS, RELIGION

GODS

1 Heartily know, / When half-gods go, / The gods arrive. [Ralph Waldo Emerson, 1803–82, *Give All to Love*]

2 God of the golden bow, / And of the golden lyre, / And of the golden hair, / And of the golden fire, / Charioteer / Of the patient year, / Where – where slept thine ire? [John Keats, 1795–1821, *Hymn to Apollo*]

3 Deep in the shady sadness of a vale / Far sunken from the healthy breath of morn, / Far from the fiery noon, and eve's one star, / Sat gray-haired Saturn, quiet as a stone. [John Keats, 1795–1821, *Hyperion*, Bk i, 1]

4 O latest born and loveliest vision far / Of all Olympus' faded hierarchy. [John Keats, 1795–1821, *Ode to Psyche*, 24]

5 Judas is the last god, and, by heaven, the most potent. [D H Lawrence, 1885–1930, *St Mawr*]

6 Gods are no more likely to achieve their private ambitions than are mere men who suffer the slings and arrows of outrageous fortune, but gods have much more fun. [Edmund Leach, 1910–89, *Runaway World*, Ch. 6]

7 Alas, I do not rule the world and that, I am afraid, is the story of my life – always a godmother, never a God. [Fran Lebowitz, ?1948– , *Metropolitan Life*, 'Digital Clocks and Pocket Calculators']

8 There is a very good saying that if triangles invented a god, they would make him three-sided. [Baron de Montesquieu, 1689–1755, *Lettres persanes*, 59]

9 When men heard thunder on the left the gods had somewhat of special advertisement to impart. [Sir Eustace Peachtree, 17th cent., *The Dangers of This Mortal Life*]

10 Man never found the deities so kindly / As to assure him that he'd live tomorrow. [François Rabelais, *c.*1492–1553, *Pantagruel*, Bk III, Ch. 2]

11 He wants nothing of a god but eternity and a heaven to throne in. [William Shakespeare, 1564–1616, *Coriolanus*, V. iv. (25)]

12 There's a divinity that shapes our ends, / Rough-hew them how we will. [*Hamlet*, V. ii. 10]

13 As flies to wanton boys, are we to the gods; / They kill us for their sport. [*King Lear*, IV. i. 36]

14 The gods are just, and of our pleasant vices /

Make instruments to plague us. [*King Lear*, V. iii. (172)]

15 This wimpled, whining, purblind, wayward boy, / This senior-junior, giant-dwarf, Dan Cupid; / Regent of love rhymes, lord of folded arms, / The anointed sovereign of sighs and groans, / Liege of all loiterers and malcontents. [*Love's Labour's Lost*, III. i. (189)]

16 Yea, is not even Apollo, with hair and harpstring of gold, / A bitter God to follow, a beautiful God to behold? [A C Swinburne, 1837–1909, *Hymn to Proserpine*]

17 The Gods themselves cannot recall their gifts. [Alfred, Lord Tennyson, 1809–92, *Tithonus*, 49]

GOLF

1 It's not in support of cricket but as an earnest protest against golf. [(On subscribing a shilling to W G Grace's Testimonial) Max Beerbohm, 1872–1956; in *Carr's Dictionary of Extraordinary English Cricketers*]

2 It [golf] is the unthinkable in pursuit of the unsinkable. [Douglas Watkinson, *Dragon's Tail*]

See also CRICKET, FOOTBALL, SPORTS

GOOD & EVIL

1 Speechless Evil / Borrowed the language of Good / And reduced it to noise. [W H Auden, 1907–73, *The Cave of Making*, Postscript]

2 Good can imagine Evil, but Evil cannot imagine Good. [W H Auden, 1907–73, *A Certain World*, 'Imagination']

3 Ye shall be as gods, knowing good and evil. [Bible, OT, *Genesis* 3:5]

4 Woe unto them that call evil good, and good evil. [Bible, OT, *Isaiah* 5:20]

5 Eschew evil, and do good: seek peace, and ensue it. [Bible, OT, *Psalms* 34:14 (*Book of Common Prayer* version)]

6 For the good that I would I do not: but the evil which I would not, that I do. [Bible, NT, *Romans* 7:19]

7 My own hope is, a sun will pierce / The thickest cloud earth ever stretched; / That, after Last returns the First, / Though a wide compass round be fetched; / That what began best can't end worst, / Nor what God blessed once, prove accurst. [Robert Browning, 1812–89, *Apparent Failure*]

8 'Wouldn't it be terrible to be bad?' he says to her right hip. 'You'd never know what a relief it was to stop being good.' [Michael Frayn, 1933– , *Sweet Dreams*, p. 75]

9 Who holds that if way to the Better there be, it exacts a full look at the Worst. [Thomas Hardy, 1840–1928, *In Tenebris*, II]

10 What though the spicy breezes / Blow soft o'er Ceylon's isle, / Though every prospect pleases, / And only man is vile. / In vain with lavish kindness / The gifts of God are strown, / The heathen in his blindness / Bows down to wood and stone. [Bishop Heber, 1783–1826, hymn]

11 There is so much good in the worst of us, / And so much bad in the best of us, / That it hardly becomes any of us / To talk about the rest of us. [Edward Wallis Hoch, 1849–1925, *Good and Bad*. Authorship not absolutely certain]

12 Good is that which makes for unity; Evil is that which makes for separateness. [Aldous Huxley, 1894–1963, *Ends and Means*, Ch. 15]

13 I am coming to feel that the people of ill will have used time much more effectively than the people of goodwill. We will have to repent in this generation not merely for the vitriolic words and actions of the bad people, but for the appalling silence of the good people. [Martin Luther King Jr, 1929–68, letter from Birmingham City Jail, Alabama, 16 Apr. 1963]

14 He that has light within his own clear breast / May sit i' th' centre, and enjoy bright day, / But he that hides a dark soul, and foul thoughts / Benighted walks under the midday sun. [John Milton, 1608–74, *Comus*, 381]

15 And out of good still to find means of evil. [John Milton, 1608–74, *Paradise Lost*, Bk i, 165]

16 We have seen / Good men made evil wrangling with the evil, / Straight minds grown crooked fighting crooked minds. / Our peace betrayed us; we betrayed our peace. / Look at it well. This was the good town once. [Edwin Muir, 1887–1959, *The Good Town*]

17 Every positive value has its price in negative terms, and you never see anything very great which is not, at the same time, horrible in some respect. The genius of Einstein leads to

Hiroshima. [Pablo Picasso, 1881–1973, in Françoise Gilot and Carlton Lake, *Life with Picasso*, Pt 2]

18 Ask you what provocation I have had? / The strong antipathy of good to bad. [Alexander Pope, 1688–1744, *Epilogue to the Satires*, Dialogue II, 197]

19 One of the worst things about life is not how nasty the nasty people are. You know that already. It is how nasty the nice people can be. [Anthony Powell, 1905– , *Hearing Secret Harmonies*, Ch. 7]

20 The web of our life is of a mingled yarn, good and ill together. [William Shakespeare, 1564–1616, *All's Well that Ends Well*, IV. iii. (83)]

21 There is nothing either good or bad, but thinking makes it so. [*Hamlet*, II. ii. (259)]

22 Wisdom and goodness to the vile seem vile; / Filths savour but themselves. [*King Lear*, IV. ii. 38]

23 How far that little candle throws his beams! / So shines a good deed in a naughty world. [*The Merchant of Venice*, V. i. 90]

24 The good want power, but to weep barren tears. / The powerful goodness want: worse need for them. / The wise want love; and those who love want wisdom; / And all best things are thus confused with ill. [P B Shelley, 1792–1822, *Prometheus Unbound*, I, 625]

25 A nice man is a man of nasty ideas. [Jonathan Swift, 1677–1745, *Thoughts on Various Subjects*]

26 For good ye are and bad, and like to coins, / Some true, some light, but every one of you / Stamped with the image of the King. [Alfred, Lord Tennyson, 1809–92, *Idylls of the King*, 'The Holy Grail', 25]

27 Oh yet we trust that somehow good / Will be the final goal of ill. [Alfred, Lord Tennyson, 1809–92, *In Memoriam*, 54]

28 This truth within thy mind rehearse, / That in a boundless universe / Is boundless better, boundless worse. [Alfred, Lord Tennyson, 1809–92, *The Two Voices*, 9]

29 BELINDA: Ay, but you know we must return good for evil.
LADY BRUTE: That may be a mistake in the translation. [John Vanbrugh, 1664–1726, *The Provoked Wife*, I. I]

30 When I'm good I'm very good, but when I'm bad I'm better. [Mae West, 1892–1980, in film *I'm No Angel*]

See also next category

GOOD & GOODNESS

1 Men have never been good, they are not good, they never will be good. [Karl Barth, 1886–1968, *Christian Community*, p. 36]

2 I have always heard, Sancho, that doing good to base fellows is like throwing water into the sea. [Miguel Cervantes, 1547–1616, *Don Quixote*, Pt I, Ch. 23]

3 He tried the luxury of doing good. [George Crabbe, 1754–1832, *Tales of the Hall*, III, 'Boys at School', 139]

4 It's easy to see the faults in people I know; it's hardest to see the good. Especially when the good isn't there. [Will Cuppy, 1884–1949, attr.]

5 Grief never mended no broken bones, and as good people's wery scarce, what I says is, make the most on 'em. [Charles Dickens, 1812–70, *Sketches by Boz*, 'Scenes', Ch. 22, 'Gin-Shops']

6 And learn the luxury of doing good. [Oliver Goldsmith, 1728–74, *The Traveller*, 22]

7 And leave us leisure to be good. [Thomas Gray, 1716–71, *Hymn to Adversity*]

8 Good, but not religious-good. [Thomas Hardy, 1840–1928, *Under the Greenwood Tree*, I, Ch. 2]

9 Be good, sweet maid, and let who will be clever; / Do noble things, not dream them, all day long; / And so make Life, and Death, and that For Ever, / One grand sweet song. [Charles Kingsley, 1819–75, *A Farewell. To C.E.G.*]

10 The greatest pleasure I know is to do a good action by stealth, and to have it found out by accident. [Charles Lamb, 1775–1834, 'Table Talk by the Late Elia', *The Athenaeum*, 4 Jan. 1834]

11 They're always throwin' goodness at you / But with a little bit of luck / A man can duck! [Alan Jay Lerner, 1918–86, *My Fair Lady*, I. ii]

12 Abashed the devil stood, / And felt how awful goodness is. [John Milton, 1608–74, *Paradise Lost*, Bk iv, 846]

13 People will endlessly conceal from themselves that good is only good if one is good for nothing. The whole history of philosophy, the whole theology, is the act of concealment. [Iris Murdoch, 1919–99, *The Time of the Angels*, Ch. 17]

14 Everything is good when it leaves the Creator's hands; everything degenerates in the hands of man. [Jean-Jacques Rousseau, 1712–78, *Emile*, I, i]

15 If to do were as easy as to know what were good to do, chapels had been churches, and poor men's cottages princes' palaces. [William Shakespeare, 1564–1616, *The Merchant of Venice*, I. ii. (13)]

16 Nothing can harm a good man, either in life or after death. [Socrates, 469–399 BC, quoted in Plato, *Apology*, 42]

17 I believe in an ultimate decency of things. [Robert Louis Stevenson, 1850–94, letter, 23 Aug. 1893]

18 Hold thou the good: define it well: / For fear divine philosophy / Should push beyond her mark and be / Procuress to the Lords of Hell. [Alfred, Lord Tennyson, 1809–92, *In Memoriam*, 53]

19 'Tis only noble to be good. / Kind hearts are more than coronets, / And simple faith than Norman blood. [Alfred, Lord Tennyson, 1809–92, *Lady Clara Vere de Vere*]

20 But my life now, my whole life, independently of anything that can happen to me, every minute of it is no longer meaningless as it was before, but has a positive meaning of goodness with which I have the power to invest it. [Leo Tolstoy, 1828–1910, *Anna Karenina*, VII, Ch. 19]

21 Death said: 'The good is one thing, the pleasant another; these two, having different objects, chain a man. It is well with him who clings to the good; he who chooses the pleasant misses his end.' [Upanishads, 7th cent. BC, *Katha Upanishad*, ii]

22 The best is the enemy of the good. [Voltaire, 1694–1778, *Dictionnaire philosophique*, 'Art dramatique']

23 He was quite sure that he had been wronged. Not to be wronged is to forgo the first privilege of goodness. [H G Wells, 1866–1946, *Bealby*, Pt IV, 1]

24 Goodness, what beautiful diamonds!

WEST: Goodness had nothing to do with it, dearie! [Mae West, 1892–1980, in film *Night after Night*, script by Vincent Lawrence]

25 If all the good people were clever, / And all clever people were good, / The world would be nicer than ever / We thought that it possibly could.

But somehow, 'tis seldom or never / The two hit it off as they should; / The good are so harsh to the clever, / The clever so rude to the good! [Elizabeth Wordsworth, 1840–1932, *Good and Clever*]

26 The good die first, / And they whose hearts are dry as summer dust / Burn to the socket. [William Wordsworth, 1770–1850, *The Excursion*, I, 500]

GOSSIP

1 It's not the party of life in the end that's important. It's the comment in the bedroom. [Enid Bagnold, 1889–1981, *The Loved and the Envied*, Ch. 26]

2 He that repeateth a matter separateth very friends. [Bible, OT, *Proverbs* 17:9]

3 So loud each tongue, so empty was each head, / So much they talked, so very little said. [Charles Churchill, 1731–64, *The Rosciad*, 549]

4 It will be a beautiful family talk, mean and worried and full of sorrow and spite and excitement. I cannot be asked to miss it in my weak state. I should only fret. [Ivy Compton-Burnett, 1884–1969, *A Family and a Fortune*, Ch. 10]

5 Where village statesmen talked with looks profound, / And news much older than their ale went round. [Oliver Goldsmith, 1728–74, *The Deserted Village*, 223]

6 Borrit ... once spoke of the Masai tribe holding, as a tenet of faith, that all cows in the world belong to them. Ada, in similar manner, arrogated to herself all the world's gossip, sources other than her own a presumption. [Anthony Powell, 1905– , *Temporary Kings*, Ch. 3]

7 So live that you wouldn't be ashamed to sell the family parrot to the town gossip. [Will Rogers, 1879–1935; in *Treasury of Humorous Quotations*, ed. Evan Esar and Nicolas Bentley]

8 Teas, / Where small talk dies in agonies. [P B Shelley, 1792–1822, *Peter Bell the Third*, 204]

9 There is only one thing in the world worse than being talked about, and that is not being talked about. [Oscar Wilde, 1854–1900, *The Picture of Dorian Gray*, Ch. 1]

See also SCANDAL, TALK

GOVERNMENT

1 The four pillars of government . . . (which are religion, justice, counsel, and treasure). [Francis Bacon, 1561–1626, *Essays*, 15, 'Of Seditions and Troubles']

2 Every government carries a health warning. [Badge slogan, 1976]

3 There are two ways to get into government – one is to crawl into a government and the other is to kick your way in. [Aneurin Bevan, 1897–1960, quoted in BBC radio programme *The Week in Westminster*, 15 July 1989]

4 The people / Had forfeited the confidence of the government / And could win it back only / By redoubled efforts. Would it not be easier / In that case for the government / To dissolve the people / And elect another? [Bertolt Brecht, 1898–1956, *The Solution*]

5 Government is a contrivance of human wisdom to provide for human *wants*. Men have a right that these wants should be provided for by this wisdom. [Edmund Burke, 1729–97, *Reflections on the Revolution in France*, Penguin edn, p. 15]

6 If any ask me what a free government is, I answer, that for any practical purpose, it is what the people think so. [Edmund Burke, 1729–97, *Letter to the Sheriffs of Bristol*]

7 The only good government . . . is a bad one in a hell of a fright. [Joyce Cary, 1888–1957, *The Horse's Mouth*, 32]

8 The Government [of Clement Attlee] paid for its programme on tick – the tick of a time bomb, as it turned out. [Peter Clarke, 1942– , *A Question of Leadership*, 9]

9 England does not love coalitions. [Benjamin Disraeli, 1804–81, speech in House of Commons, 16 Dec. 1852]

10 A government that is big enough to give you all you want is big enough to take it all away. [Barry Goldwater, 1909–98, speech at West Chester, Pennsylvania, 21 Oct. 1964]

11 Th' applause of listening senates to command, / The threats of pain and ruin to despise, / To scatter plenty o'er a smiling land, / And read their history in a nation's eyes. [Thomas Gray, 1716–71, *Elegy Written in a Country Churchyard*, 16]

12 The Treasury operates like one of those First World War howitzers that landed their shells on targets that gunners never saw. Home Office policy is hand to hand fighting. [Roy Hattersley, 1932– , in *Guardian*, 18 July 1987]

13 The Treasury are never happy; even in Paradise they will be worried about excessive imports. [A P Herbert, 1890–1971; *Observer*, 'Sayings of the Week', 19 Apr. 1964]

14 Thinking is an area where the Government has made one of its most spectacular economies. It is now done by a very small number of people. Often by one person (who has to double up by running the country as well). [Victor Keegan, 1940– , in *Guardian*, 13 Feb. 1989]

15 We give the impression of being in office but not in power. [Norman Lamont, 1942– , speech from back benches in House of Commons, 9 June 1993]

16 Every cook has to learn how to govern the state. [Vladimir Ilyich Lenin, 1870–1924, *Will the Bolsheviks Retain Government Power?*]

17 We're all equals . . . A team. Like the Cabinet, except that we're all on the same side. [Jonathan Lynn, 1943– , and Antony Jay, 1930– , *Yes Prime Minister*, Vol. 1, 'Party Games']

18 The point about government is that no one has control. Lots of people have the power to stop something happening – but almost nobody has the power to *make* anything happen. We have a system of government with the engine of a lawn-mower and the brakes of a Rolls-Royce. [Jonathan Lynn, 1943– , and Antony Jay, 1930– , *Yes Prime Minister*, Vol. 1, 'A Real Partnership']

19 It is the duty of Her Majesty's government . . . neither to flap nor to falter. [Harold Macmillan, 1894–1986; *Observer*, 'Sayings of the Week', 19 Nov. 1961]

20 The government burns down whole cities while the people are forbidden to light lamps. [Mao Zedong, 1893–1976, attr.]

21 To govern is to choose. [Pierre Mendès-France, 1907–82, attr.]

22 Do you not know, my son, with how little wisdom the world is governed? [Count Oxenstierna, 1583–1654, letter to his son, 1648]

23 Government, even in its best state, is but a necessary evil; in its worst state, an intolerable one. [Thomas Paine, 1737–1809, *Common Sense*, Ch. 1]

24 You may call it a coalition, you may call it the accidental and fortuitous concurrence of atoms. [Lord Palmerston, 1784–1865, speech in House of Commons, 5 Mar. 1857]

25 Despotism tempered by assassination. [Lord Reith, 1889–1971 (on the best form of government), in *Observer*, 12 Nov. 1972]

26 I don't make jokes – I just watch the government and report the facts. [Will Rogers, 1879–1935, in *Saturday Review*, 25 Aug. 1962, 'A Rogers Thesaurus']

27 It would be desirable if every Government, when it comes into power, should have its old speeches burned. [Philip Snowden, 1864–1937, in C E Bechofer Roberts ('Ephesian'), *Philip Snowden*, Ch. 12]

28 To govern is not to write resolutions and distribute directives; to govern is to control the implementation of the directives. [Joseph Stalin, 1879–1953, in N McInnes, *The Communist Parties of Western Europe*, Ch. 3]

29 City government is of the people, by the rascals, for the rich. [Lincoln Steffens, 1866–1936, in *The Times*, 18 July 1977]

30 Experience shows that the most dangerous moment for a bad government is usually just as it's starting on reform. [Alexis de Tocqueville, 1805–59, *The Ancien Régime and the Revolution*, Bk iii, Ch. 4]

31 Many people consider the things which government does for them to be social progress, but they consider the things government does for others as socialism. [Earl Warren, 1891–1974; in Laurence J Peter, *Peter's Quotations*]

See also OPPOSITION, PARLIAMENT, POLITICS

GRATITUDE & INGRATITUDE

1 Maybe the only thing worse than having to give gratitude constantly all the time, is having to accept it. [William Faulkner, 1897–1962, *Requiem for a Nun*, II. i]

2 One's over-great haste to repay an obligation is a kind of ingratitude. [Duc de La Rochefoucauld, 1613–80, *Maxims*, 226]

3 Gratitude looks to the past and love to the present; fear, avarice, lust and ambition look ahead. [C S Lewis, 1898–1963, *The Screwtape Letters*, 15]

4 Has God then forgotten what I have done for him? [Louis XIV, 1638–1715, attr. (after the battle of Malplaquet)]

5 'My esteemed chums,' murmured Hurree Jamset Ram Singh. 'This is not an occasion for looking the gift horse in the mouthfulness.' [Frank Richards, 1876–1961, *Bunter's Last Fling*, Ch. 5]

6 Blow, blow, thou winter wind, / Thou art not so unkind / As man's ingratitude: / Thy tooth is not so keen, / Because thou art not seen, / Although thy breath be rude. [William Shakespeare, 1564–1616, *As You Like It*, II. vii. 174]

7 How sharper than a serpent's tooth it is / To have a thankless child! [*King Lear*, I. iv. (312)]

8 For it so falls out / That what we have we prize not to the worth / Whiles we enjoy it, but being lacked and lost, / Why then we rack the value. [*Much Ado About Nothing*, IV. i. (219)]

9 Evermore thanks, the exchequer of the poor. [*Richard II*, II. iii. 65]

10 I hate ingratitude more in a man / Than lying, vainness, babbling drunkenness, / Or any taint of vice whose strong corruption / Inhabits our frail blood. [*Twelfth Night*, III. iv. (390)]

THE GRAVE

1 Personally I have no bone to pick with graveyards. [Samuel Beckett, 1906–89, *First Love*]

2 As a rule Corde avoided cemeteries and never went near the graves of his parents. He said it was just as easy for your dead to visit you, only by now he would have to hire a hall. [Saul Bellow, 1915– , *The Dean's December*, 15]

3 Cold in the earth – and the deep snow piled above thee, / Far, far, removed, cold in the dreary grave! [Emily Brontë, 1818–48, *Remembrance*]

4 For there is good news yet to hear and fine things to be seen, / Before we go to Paradise by way of Kensal Green. [G K Chesterton, 1874–1936, *The Rolling English Road*]

5 That corpse you planted last year in your garden, / Has it begun to sprout? Will it bloom this year? [T S Eliot, 1888–1965, *The Waste Land*, 71]

6 Each in his narrow cell for ever laid, / The rude forefathers of the hamlet sleep. [Thomas Gray, 1716–71, *Elegy Written in a Country Churchyard*, 4]

7 His landmark is a kopje-crest / That breaks the veldt around; / And foreign constellations west / Each night above his mound. [Thomas Hardy, 1840–1928, *Drummer Hodge*]

8 Lovers lying two by two / Ask not whom they sleep beside, / And the bridegroom all night through / Never turns him to the bride. [A E Housman, 1859–1936, *A Shropshire Lad*, 12]

9 Teach me to live, that I may dread / The grave as little as my bed. [Bishop Thomas Ken, 1637–1711, *An Evening Hymn*]

10 We have fed our sea for a thousand years / And she calls us, still unfed, / Though there's never a wave of all her waves / But marks our English dead. [Rudyard Kipling, 1865–1936, *The Coastwise Lights*]

11 They died / When time was open-eyed, / Wooden and childish; only bones abide / There, in the nowhere, where their boats were tossed / Sky-high, where mariners had fabled news / of IS, the whited monster. [Robert Lowell, 1917–77, *The Quaker Graveyard in Nantucket*]

12 He gets the odd villain. / A couple of revolutionaries / Whose graves keep catching fire / But mostly they're a decent mob, the dead. [Adrian Mitchell, 1932– , *Please Keep Off the Dead*]

13 In the most high and palmy state of Rome / A little ere the mightiest Julius fell, / The graves stood tenantless and the sheeted dead / Did squeak and gibber in the Roman streets. [William Shakespeare, 1564–1616, *Hamlet*, I. i. 113]

14 Let's talk of graves, of worms and epitaphs; / Make dust our paper, and with rainy eyes / Write sorrow on the bosom of the earth; / Let's choose executors and talk of wills. [*Richard II*, III. ii. 145]

15 The cemetery is an open space among the ruins, covered in winter with violets and daisies. It might make one in love with death, to think that one should be buried in so sweet a place. [P B Shelley, 1792–1822, *Adonais*, Preface]

16 Peace is in the grave. / The grave hides all things beautiful and good: / I am a God and cannot find it there. [P B Shelley, 1792–1822, *Prometheus Unbound*, I, 638]

17 Autumn is desolation in the plot / Of a thousand acres, where these memories grow / From the inexhaustible bodies that are not/ Dead, but feed the grass, row after rich row. [Allen Tate, 1899–1979, *Ode to the Confederate Dead*]

18 Where blew a flower may a flower no more / Lift its head to the blows of the rain; / Though they be mad and dead as nails, / Heads of the characters hammer through daisies; / Break in the sun till the sun breaks down, / And death shall have no dominion. [Dylan Thomas, 1914–53, *And Death Shall Have No Dominion*]

19 When you find grass uncut in a village cemetery you know it is a bad village. If they don't look after the dead, they won't look after the living. [Omar Torrijos Herrera, 1929–81, in Graham Greene, *Getting to Know the General*, Pt 1, 3]

20 But keep the wolf far thence, that's foe to men, / For with his nails he'll dig them up again. [John Webster, 1580?–1625?, *The White Devil*, V. iv. 108]

21 Tread lightly, she is near / Under the snow, / Speak gently, she can hear / The daisies grow. [Oscar Wilde, 1854–1900, *Requiescat*]

22 It is a fact that, up north, cemeteries are a way of life. [Jeanette Winterson, 1959– , in *Guardian*, 7 Aug. 1991]

See also FUNERALS

GREATNESS

1 No great man lives in vain. The history of the world is but the biography of great men. [Thomas Carlyle, 1795–1881, *Heroes and Hero-Worship*, i, 'The Hero as Divinity']

2 There is a great man who makes every man feel small. But the real great man is the man who makes every man feel great. [G K Chesterton, 1874–1936, *Charles Dickens*, Ch. 1]

3 To be great is to be misunderstood. [Ralph Waldo Emerson, 1803–82, *Essays*, 'Self-Reliance']

4 A big man has no time really to do anything but just sit and be big. [F Scott Fitzgerald, 1896–1940, *This Side of Paradise*, Bk III, Ch. 2]

5 He can be called a remarkable man who stands out from those around him by the resourcefulness of his mind, and who knows how to be restrained in the manifestations which proceed from his nature, at the same time conducting himself justly and tolerantly towards the weakness of others. [George Gurdjieff, 1868–1949, *Meetings with Remarkable Men*, Introduction]

6 He [T E Lawrence] is one of those great men for whom one feels intensely sorry, because he was nothing but a great man. [Aldous Huxley, 1894–1963, letter to Victoria Ocampo, 12 Dec. 1946]

7 You could not stand five minutes with that man [Edmund Burke] beneath a shed while it rained, but you must be convinced you had been standing with the greatest man you had ever yet seen. [Dr Samuel Johnson, 1709–84, in Mrs Piozzi, *Anecdotes of J*. Also quoted by Boswell]

8 The great man ... walks across his century and leaves the marks of his feet all over it, ripping out the dates on his goloshes as he passes. [Stephen Leacock, 1869–1944, *Literary Lapses*, 'The Life of John Smith']

9 The heights by great men reached and kept / Were not attained by sudden flight, / But they, while their companions slept, / Were toiling upward in the night. [H W Longfellow, 1807–82, *The Ladder of St Augustine*]

10 Lives of great men all remind us / We can make our lives sublime, / And, departing, leave behind us / Footprints on the sands of time. [H W Longfellow, 1807–82, *A Psalm of Life*]

11 It's great to be great but it's greater to be human. [Will Rogers, 1879–1935, *Autobiography*, Ch. 15]

12 But you must fear, / His greatness weighed, his will is not his own. For he himself is subject to his birth. [William Shakespeare, 1564–1616, *Hamlet*, I. iii. 16]

13 Rightly to be great / Is not to stir without great argument, / But greatly to find quarrel in a straw / When honour's at the stake. [*Hamlet*, IV. iv. 53]

14 Farewell! a long farewell, to all my greatness! / This is the state of man: today he puts forth / The tender leaves of hope; tomorrow blossoms, / And bears his blushing honours thick upon him; / The third day comes a frost, a killing frost. [*Henry VIII*, III. ii. 351]

15 Be not afraid of greatness: some men are born great, some achieve greatness, and some have greatness thrust upon them. [*Twelfth Night*, II. v. (158)]

16 I think continually of those who were truly great. / Who, from the womb, remembered the soul's history / Through corridors of light. [Stephen Spender, 1909–95, *I Think Continually of Those*]

17 Great events do not necessarily have great causes. [A J P Taylor, 1906–90, in obituary in *Independent*, 8 Sept. 1990]

18 Pray God our greatness may not fail / Thro' craven fears of being great. [Alfred, Lord Tennyson, 1809–92, *Hands All Round*]

19 The great man dies twice; once as a man and once as a great man. [Paul Valéry, 1871–1945, 'Notebook B (1910)']

GREECE & THE GREEKS

1 The governing idea of Hellenism is spontaneity of consciousness; that of Hebraism, strictness of conscience. [Matthew Arnold, 1822–88, *Culture and Anarchy*, Ch. 4]

2 For all the Athenians and strangers which were there spent their time in nothing else, but either to tell, or to hear some new thing. [Bible, NT, *Acts of the Apostles* 17:21]

3 The isles of Greece, the isles of Greece! / Where burning Sappho loved and sung, / Where grew the arts of war and peace, / Where Delos rose, and Phoebus sprung! / Eternal summer gilds them yet, / But all, except their sun, is set. [Lord Byron, 1788–1824, *Don Juan*, III, 86, 1]

4 The Muse gave the Greeks genius and the art of the well-turned phrase. [Horace, 65–8 BC, *Ars Poetica*, 323]

5 Greek, Sir, ... is like lace; every man gets as much of it as he can. [Dr Samuel Johnson, 1709–84, in James Boswell, *Life of J*, 1780]

6 Athens, the eye of Greece, mother of arts / And eloquence. [John Milton, 1608–74, *Paradise Regained*, Bk iv, 240]

7 Thy Naiad airs have brought me home / To the glory that was Greece. / And the grandeur that was Rome. [Edgar Allan Poe, 1809–49, *To Helen*]

8 The people of Crete unfortunately make more history than they can consume locally. [Saki (H H Munro), 1870–1916, *The Jesting of Arlington Stringham*]

9 Nobody can say a word against Greek: it stamps a man at once as an educated gentleman. [George Bernard Shaw, 1856–1950, *Major Barbara*, I]

10 The world's great age begins anew, / The golden years return, / The earth doth like a snake renew / Her winter weeds outworn: / Heaven smiles, and faiths and empires gleam, / Like wrecks of a dissolving dream. [P B Shelley, 1792–1822, *Hellas*, 1060]

11 Another Athens shall arise, / And to remoter time / Bequeath, like sunset to the skies, / The splendour of its prime. [P B Shelley, 1792–1822, *Hellas*, 1084]

12 *Timeo Danaos et dona ferentes.* – I fear the Greeks, even though they offer gifts. [Virgil, 70–19 BC, *Aeneid*, II, 49]

GREED

1 Thinking to get at once all the gold that the goose could give, he killed it, and opened it only to find – nothing. [Aesop, *fl c.*550 BC, 'The Goose with the Golden Eggs']

2 The horseleach hath two daughters, crying, Give, give. [Bible, OT, *Proverbs* 30:15]

3 Not greedy of filthy lucre. [Bible, NT, *1 Timothy* 3:3]

4 So for a good old-gentlemanly vice, / I think I must take up with avarice. [Lord Byron, 1788–1824, *Don Juan*, I, 216]

5 Avarice, the spur of industry. [David Hume, 1711–76, *Essays*, 'Of Civil Liberty']

6 He was for ever carrying one well-kept Italian hand to his heart and plunging the other straight into her pocket, which, as she had instantly observed him to recognize, fitted it like a glove. [Henry James, 1843–1916, *The Wings of the Dove*, Bk VII, 3]

7 Good morning to the day: and next, my gold! – / Open the shrine that I may see my saint. [Ben Jonson, 1573–1637, *Volpone*, I. i]

8 You yourself / Are much condemned to have an itching palm. [William Shakespeare, 1564–1616, *Julius Caesar*, IV. iii. 9]

9 To what cannot you compel the hearts of men, O cursed lust for gold! [Virgil, 70–19 BC, *Aeneid*, III, 56]

See also GLUTTONY

GREETINGS

1 Hail Caesar, those about to die salute you. [anon.; gladiators' salute on entering the arena]

2 If I should meet thee / After long years, / How should I greet thee? / With silence and tears. [Lord Byron, 1788–1824, *When We Two Parted*]

3 He would answer to 'Hi!' or to any loud cry, / Such as 'Fry me!' or 'Fritter my wig!' / To 'What-you-may-call-um!' or 'What-was-his-name!' / But especially 'Thing-um-a-jig!' [Lewis Carroll, 1832–98, *The Hunting of the Snark*, Fit 1]

4 *Nunc tamen interea haec prisco quae more parentum / Tradita sunt tristi munere ad inferias, / Accipe fraterno multum manantia fletu. / Atque in perpetuum, frater, ave atque vale.* – But now meanwhile take these offerings, according to the old custom of our fathers, the tribute of sorrow, for a funeral sacrifice. Take them, wet with many a tear of your brother's. And for ever, brother, hail and farewell. [Catullus, 84–54? BC, *Carmina*, 101]

5 Wery glad to see you, indeed, and hope our acquaintance may be a long 'un, as the gen'l'm'n said to the fi' pun' note. [Charles Dickens, 1812–70, *Pickwick Papers*, Ch. 25]

6 Do you suppose I could buy back my introduction to you? [Groucho Marx, 1895–1977, in film *Monkey Business*, script by S J Perelman *et al.*]

7 I step over to his table and give him a medium hello, and he looks up and gives me a medium hello right back, for, to tell the truth, Maury and I are never bosom friends. [Damon Runyon,

1884–1946, *Runyon à la Carte*, 'A Light in France']

8 Dr Livingstone, I presume. [H M Stanley, 1841–1904, *How I Found Livingstone*, Ch. 11]

See also FAREWELLS

GRIEF

1 I tell you, hopeless grief is passionless. [Elizabeth Barrett Browning, 1806–61, sonnet: *Grief*]

2 Grief is itself a med'cine. [William Cowper, 1731–1800, *Charity*, 159]

3 Nessun maggior dolore / Che ricordarsi del tempo felice / Nella miseria. – There is no greater grief than to recall a time of happiness when in misery. [Dante Alighieri, 1265–1321, *The Divine Comedy*, 'Inferno', v, 121]

4 They are the silent griefs which cut the heart-strings. [John Ford, 1586–1639?, *The Broken Heart*, V. iii]

5 In all the silent manliness of grief. [Oliver Goldsmith, 1728–74, *The Deserted Village*, 384]

6 Of all the griefs that harass the distressed, / Sure the most bitter is a scornful jest. [Dr Samuel Johnson, 1709–84, *London*, 166]

7 Now you can reach forty and get no nearer a real grief than the television news. [P J Kavanagh, 1931– , *People and Weather*, 4]

8 Grief fills the room up of my absent child, / Lies in his bed, walks up and down wih me, / Puts on his pretty looks, repeats his words, / Remembers me of all his gracious parts, / Stuffs out his vacant garments with his form. [William Shakespeare, 1564–1616, *King John*, III. iv. 93]

9 Give sorrow words: the grief that does not speak / Whispers the o'er-fraught heart, and bids it break. [*Macbeth*, IV. iii. 209]

10 Well, every one can master a grief but he that has it. [*Much Ado About Nothing*, III. ii. (28)]

11 You may my glories and my state depose, / But not my griefs; still am I king of those. [*Richard II*, IV. i. 192]

12 What's gone and what's past help / Should be past grief. [*The Winter's Tale*, III. ii. (223)]

13 Winter is come and gone, / But grief returns with the revolving year. [P B Shelley, 1792–1822, *Adonais*, 154]

14 Many a green isle needs must be / In the deep wide sea of Misery. [P B Shelley, 1792–1822, *Lines Written among the Euganean Hills*, 1]

15 Grief for a while is blind, and so was mine. / I wish no living thing to suffer pain. [P B Shelley, 1792–1822, *Prometheus Unbound*, I, 304]

16 I have submitted to a new control: / A power is gone, which nothing can restore; / A deep distress hath humanised my soul. [William Wordsworth, 1770–1850, *Elegiac Stanzas, Suggested by a Picture of Peele Castle*]

See also REGRET, SORROW, SUFFERING, UNHAPPINESS, WORRY

GUESTS, see HOSPITALITY

GUILT

1 Feeling a tremendous rakehell, and not liking myself much for it, and feeling rather a good chap for not liking myself much for it, and not liking myself at all for feeling rather a good chap. [Kingsley Amis, 1922–95, *That Uncertain Feeling*, Ch. 7]

2 Remorse, the fatal egg by Pleasure laid / In every bosom where her nest is made. [William Cowper, 1731–1800, *The Progress of Error*, 239]

3 *Denn alle Schuld rächt sich auf Erden.* – For all guilt is punished on earth. [Johann Wolfgang von Goethe, 1749–1832, *Wilhelm Meister*, ii, 13]

4 I am suspicious of guilt in myself and in other people: it is usually a way of not thinking, or of announcing one's own fine sensibilities the better to be rid of them fast. [Lillian Hellman, 1905–84, *Scoundrel Time*]

5 'But I am not guilty,' said K.; 'it's a misunderstanding. And if it comes to that, how can any man be called guilty?' [Franz Kafka, 1883–1924, *The Trial*, Ch. 9]

6 We all piss in the swimming-pool. Because I piss from the diving-board, I am guilty? [Jan Kalina (said to the Czech secret police, who answered yes), reported in BBC TV programme *Tiny Revolutions*, 22 Sept. 1981]

7 For years I worried because my penis hangs slightly to the left, and finally read in a book that this is within the realm of the normal, but then wondered, what sort of person would read books like that? [Garrison Keillor, 1942– , *Lake Wobegon Days*, 'News']

8 Guilt is of course not an emotion in the Celtic countries, it is simply a way of life – a kind of gleefully painful social anaesthetic. [A L Kennedy, 1960– , *So I Am Glad*, p. 36]

9 It's always tricky, humiliating a masochist – and so hard to tell when you're done. [A L Kennedy, 1960– , *So I Am Glad*, p. 102]

10 True guilt is guilt at the obligation one owes to oneself to be oneself. False guilt is guilt felt at not being what other people feel one ought to be or assume that one is. [R D Laing, 1927–89, *The Self and Others*, Ch. 10]

11 You will put on a dress of guilt / and shoes with broken high ideals. [Roger McGough, 1937– , *Comeclose and Sleepnow*]

12 When a man points a finger at someone else, he should remember that four of his fingers are pointing at himself. [Louis Nizer, 1902–94, *My Life in Court*]

13 'Tis one thing to be tempted, Escalus, / Another thing to fall. I do not deny, / The jury, passing on the prisoner's life, / May in the sworn twelve have a thief or two / Guiltier than him they try. [William Shakespeare, 1564–1616, *Measure for Measure*, II. i. 17]

14 O ill-starred wench! / Pale as thy smock! when we shall meet at compt, / This look of thine will hurl my soul from heaven, / And fiends will snatch at it. [*Othello*, V. ii. 271]

HABIT

1 Custom reconciles us to everything. [Edmund Burke, 1729–97, *On the Sublime and Beautiful*, IV, xviii]

2 Habit with him was all the test of truth, / 'It must be right: I've done it from my youth.' [George Crabbe, 1754–1832, *The Borough*, Letter 3, 138]

3 Custom, that unwritten law, / By which the people keep even kings in awe. [Charles Davenant, 1656–1714, *Circe*, II, iii]

4 Custom, then, is the great guide of human life. [David Hume, 1711–76, *An Enquiry Concerning Human Understanding*, sect. v, Pt I]

5 If habit is a second nature it prevents us from knowing whose cruelties it lacks as well as its enchantments. [Marcel Proust, 1871–1922, *Remembrance of Things Past: Cities of the Plain*, Pt II, Ch. 1]

6 But to my mind, – though I am native here, / And to the manner born, – it is a custom / More honoured in the breach than the observance. [William Shakespeare, 1564–1616, *Hamlet*, I. iv. 14]

7 How use doth breed a habit in a man! [*The Two Gentlemen of Verona*, V. iv. 1]

8 Familiar acts are beautiful through love. [P B Shelley, 1792–1822, *Prometheus Unbound*, IV, 403]

9 Rigid, the skeleton of habit alone upholds the human frame. [Virginia Woolf, 1882–1941, *Mrs Dalloway*]

See also TRADITION

HAPPINESS

1 The greatest happiness of the greatest number is the foundation of morals and legislation. [Jeremy Bentham, 1748–1832, *The Commonplace Book*]

2 It is only possible to live happily ever after on a day-to-day basis. [Margaret Bonanno, 1950– , *A Certain Slant of Light*]

3 Breathless, we flung us on the windy hill, / Laughed in the sun, and kissed the lovely grass. [Rupert Brooke, 1887–1915, *The Hill*]

4 Certainly there is no happiness within this circle of flesh, nor is it in the optics of these eyes to behold felicity. The first day of our jubilee is death. [Sir Thomas Browne, 1605–82, *Religio Medici*, Pt 1, 43]

5 What though my wingèd hours of bliss have been, / Like angel-visits, few and far between? [Thomas Campbell, 1777–1844, *Pleasures of Hope*, 1, 377]

6 The happy people are failures because they are on such good terms with themselves that they don't give a damn. [Agatha Christie, 1890–1976, *Sparkling Cyanide*]

7 Happy the man, and happy he alone, / He, who can call to-day his own: / He who, secure within, can say, / To-morrow do thy worst, for I have lived to-day. [John Dryden, 1631–1700, trans. of Horace, *Odes*, III, xxix]

8 Never contradict. Never explain. Never apologize. (Those are the secrets of a happy life!) [Admiral John Fisher, 1841–1920, letter to *The Times*, 5 Sept. 1919]

9 He recognizes that there is a real divergence of

expert opinion between those that believe that men are happy because they are miserable, and those that believe that men are miserable because they are happy; and wisely arrives at a synthesis of both views. [Michael Frayn, 1933– , *Sweet Dreams*, p. 88]

10 Anyone happy in this age and place / is daft or corrupt. Better to abdicate / From a material and spiritual terrain / Fit only for barbarians. [Roy Fuller, 1912–91, *Translation*]

11 How wide the limits stand / Between a splendid and an happy land. [Oliver Goldsmith, 1728–74, *The Deserted Village*, 267]

12 Still to ourselves in every place consigned, / Our own felicity we make or find. [Oliver Goldsmith, 1728–74, *The Traveller*, 431]

13 So have I loitered my life away, reading books, looking at pictures, going to plays, hearing, thinking, writing on what pleased me best. I have wanted only one thing to make me happy, but wanting that have wanted everything. [William Hazlitt, 1778–1830, *My First Acquaintance with Poets*]

14 Happy the man who, far from business schemes, like the early race of mortals, ploughs and reploughs his ancestral land, with oxen of his own breeding, and no slavish yoke round his neck. [Horace, 65–8 BC, *Epodes*, II, 1]

15 *Nihil est ab omni / Parte beatum.* – No lot is in all respects happy. [Horace, 65–8 BC, *Odes*, II xvi, 27]

16 That action is best which procures the greatest happiness for the greatest numbers. [Francis Hutcheson, 1694–1746, *Inquiry into the Original of Our Ideas of Beauty and Virtue*, II, iii]

17 I can sympathize with people's pains, but not with their pleasures. There is something curiously boring about somebody else's happiness. [Aldous Huxley, 1894–1963, *Limbo*, 'Cynthia']

18 Happiness is like coke – something you get as a by-product in the process of making something else. [Aldous Huxley, 1894–1963, *Point Counter Point*, Ch. 30]

19 I shall long to see the miseries of the world, since the sight of them is necessary to happiness. [Dr Samuel Johnson, 1709–84, *Rasselas*, Ch. 3]

20 Happiness is not an ideal of reason but of imagination. [Immanuel Kant, 1724–1804, *Fundamental Principles of the Metaphysics of Ethics*, sect. 2]

21 It is a flaw / In happiness to see beyond our bourn, – / It forces us in summer skies to mourn, / It spoils the singing of the nightingale. [John Keats, 1795–1821, *Epistle to J. H. Reynolds*, 82]

22 Happiness comes uninvited; and the moment you are conscious that you are happy, you are no longer happy. [J Krishnamurti, 1895–1986, *The Penguin Krishnamurti Reader*, 'Questions and Answers']

23 Best trust the happy moments. What they gave / Makes man less fearful of the certain grave, / And gives his work compassion and new eyes. / The days that make us happy make us wise. [John Masefield, 1878–1967, *Biography*]

24 Cheerfulness is a quiet condition; glee, on the other hand, is only desperation on a good day. [Aidan Mathews, 1956– , *Lipstick on the Host*, title story]

25 Ask yourself whether you are happy, and you cease to be so. [John Stuart Mill, 1806–73, *Autobiography*, Ch. 5]

26 And feel that I am happier than I know. [John Milton, 1608–74, *Paradise Lost*, Bk vii, 282]

27 Our predicament is not the difficulty of attaining happiness, but the difficulty of avoiding the misery to which the pursuit of happiness exposes us. [Michael Oakeshott, 1901–90, in obituary in *Guardian*, 22 Dec. 1990]

28 O happiness! our being's end and aim! / Good, pleasure, ease, content! whate'er thy name: / That something still which prompts th' eternal sigh, / For which we bear to live, or dare to die. [Alexander Pope, 1688–1744, *An Essay on Man*, IV, 1]

29 Happy the man whose wish and care / A few paternal acres bound, / Content to breathe his native air, / In his own ground. [Alexander Pope, 1688–1744, *Ode on Solitude*]

30 Not to admire, is all the art I know / To make men happy, and to keep them so. [Alexander Pope, 1688–1744, *Trans. of Horace, Epistle I, vi*]

31 Happiness is beneficial for the body, but it is grief that develops the powers of the mind. [Marcel Proust, 1871–1922, *Remembrance of Things Past: Time Regained*, Ch. 2]

32 Amnesia is not knowing who one is and wanting desperately to find out. Euphoria is not knowing who one is and not caring. Ecstasy is knowing exactly who one is – and still not caring. [Tom Robbins, 1936– , *Another Roadside Attraction*]

33 Happiness: a good bank account, a good cook, and a good digestion. [Jean-Jacques Rousseau, 1712–78; in Nat Shapiro, ed., *An Encyclopedia of Quotations about Music*]

34 To be without some of the things you want is an indispensable part of happiness. [Bertrand Russell, 1872–1970, *The Conquest of Happiness*, Ch. 8]

35 Really high-minded people are indifferent to happiness, especially other people's. [Bertrand Russell, 1872–1970, *The Impact of Science on Society* (1952), Ch. 7]

36 Happiness is the only sanction of life; where happiness fails, existence remains a mad lamentable experiment. [George Santayana, 1863–1952, *The Life of Reason*, Vol. I, Ch. 10]

37 O God! methinks it were a happy life, / To be no better than a homely swain; / To sit upon a hill, as I do now, / To carve out dials, quaintly, point by point, / Thereby to see the minutes how they run, / How many make the hour full complete; / How many hours bring about the day; / How many days will finish up the year; / How many years a mortal man may live. [William Shakespeare, 1564–1616, *3 Henry VI*, II. v. 21]

38 Haply I think on thee – and then my state, / Like to the lark at break of day arising / From sullen earth, sings hymns at heaven's gate; / For the sweet love remembered such wealth brings / That then I scorn to change my state with kings. [*Sonnets*, 29]

39 We have no more right to consume happiness without producing it than to consume wealth without producing it. [George Bernard Shaw, 1856–1950, *Candida*, I]

40 A lifetime of happiness! No man alive could bear it: it would be hell on earth. [George Bernard Shaw, 1856–1950, *Man and Superman*, I]

41 Call no man happy till he dies, he is at best fortunate. [Solon, *c*.640–*c*.558 BC, quoted in Herodotus, *Histories*, I, 32]

42 Almost all our misfortunes in life come from the wrong notions we have about the things that happen to us. To know men thoroughly, to judge events sanely is, therefore, a great step towards happiness. [Stendhal, 1783–1842, *Journal*, 10 Dec. 1801]

43 The world is so full of a number of things, / I'm sure we should all be as happy as kings. [Robert Louis Stevenson, 1850–94, *A Child's Garden of Verses*, 24, 'Happy Thought']

44 There is no duty we so much underrate as the duty of being happy. [Robert Louis Stevenson, 1850–94, *Virginibus Puerisque*, 'An Apology for Idlers']

45 Happiness is an imaginary condition, formerly often attributed by the living to the dead, now usually attributed by adults to children, and by children to adults. [Thomas Szasz, 1920– , *The Second Sin*, 'Emotions']

46 What interests me isn't the happiness of every man, but that of each man. [Boris Vian, 1920–59, *Moon Indigo*]

47 Miss Farish, who was accustomed, in the way of happiness, to such scant light as shone through the cracks of other people's lives. [Edith Wharton, 1862–1937, *The House of Mirth*, Bk I, Ch. 14]

48 Happiness is no laughing matter. [Archbishop Whately of Dublin, 1787–1863, *Apothegms*]

49 I was happy but happy is an adult word. You don't have to ask a child about happy, you see it. They are or they are not. Adults talk about being happy because largely they are not. [Jeanette Winterson, 1959– , *The Passion*, 1]

50 That blessed mood, / In which the burthen of the mystery, / In which the heavy and the weary weight, / Of all this unintelligible world, / Is lightened. [William Wordsworth, 1770–1850, *Lines Composed a Few Miles above Tintern Abbey*, 37]

51 Not in Utopia, – subterranean fields, – / Or some secreted island, Heaven knows where! / But in the very world, which is the world / Of all of us, – the place where, in the end, / We find our happiness, or not at all! [(Of French Revolution) William Wordsworth, 1770–1850, *The Prelude*, XI, 140]

52 How happy is he born and taught, / That serveth not another's will; / Whose armour is his honest thought, / And simple truth his utmost skill! [Henry Wotton, 1568–1639, *The Character of a Happy Life*]

53 The hell with it. Who never knew / the price of happiness will not be happy. [Yevgeny Yevtushenko, 1933– , *Lies*]

See also JOY, PLEASURE, UNHAPPINESS

HASTE

1 Celerity is never more admired / Than by the negligent. [William Shakespeare, 1564–1616, *Antony and Cleopatra*, III. vii. 24]

2 It is too rash, too unadvised, too sudden; / Too like the lightning, which doth cease to be / Ere one can say it lightens. [*Romeo and Juliet*, II. ii. 118]

3 Wisely and slow; they stumble that run fast. [*Romeo and Juliet*, II. iii. 94]

4 Though I am always in haste, I am never in a hurry. [John Wesley, 1703–91, letter to a member of the Society, 10 Dec. 1777]

HATE

1 Gr-r-r – there go, my heart's abhorrence! / Water your damned flower-pots, do! / If hate killed men, Brother Lawrence, / God's blood, would not mine kill you! [Robert Browning, 1812–89, *Soliloquy of the Spanish Cloister*]

2 Now hatred is by far the longest pleasure; / Men love in haste, but they detest at leisure. [Lord Byron, 1788–1824, *Don Juan*, XIII, 6]

3 It was a case of dislike before first sight. [Winston Churchill, 1874–1965 (describing Kitchener's reaction to him), attr.]

4 She once used me with that insolence, that in revenge I took her to pieces; sifted her, and separated her failings; I studied 'em, and got 'em by rote. The catalogue was so large, that I was not without hopes, one day or other to hate her heartily. [William Congreve, 1670–1729, *The Way of the World*, I. iii]

5 I never hated a man enough to give him diamonds back. [Zsa Zsa Gabor, 1919– ; *Observer*, 'Sayings of the Week', 28 Aug. 1957]

6 What we need is hatred. From it are our ideas born. [Jean Genet, 1910–86, *The Negroes*, epigraph]

7 We can scarcely hate anyone that we know. [William Hazlitt, 1778–1830, *Why Distant Objects Please*]

8 If you hate a person, you hate something in him that is part of yourself. What isn't part of ourselves doesn't disturb us. [Hermann Hesse, 1877–1962, *Demian*, Ch. 6]

9 Dear Bathurst ... was a man to my very heart's content: he hated a fool, and he hated a rogue, and he hated a Whig; he was a very good hater. [Dr Samuel Johnson, 1709–84, in Mrs Piozzi, *Anecdotes of J*]

10 There's no hate lost between us. [Thomas Middleton, 1570?–1627, *The Witch*, IV, ii]

11 Anybody who hates dogs and babies can't be all bad. [(Of W C Fields) Leo Rosten, 1908–97, at Masquers' Club Dinner, Hollywood, 16 Feb. 1939. Often misquoted as 'children and dogs' and wrongly attr. to Fields]

12 Few people can be happy unless they hate some person, nation or creed. [Bertrand Russell, 1872–1970, attr.]

13 As a rule there is only one person an English girl hates more than she hates her eldest sister; and thats her mother. [George Bernard Shaw, 1856–1950, *Man and Superman*, II]

14 A hater he came and sat by a ditch, / And he took an old cracked lute; / And he sang a song that was more of a screech / 'Gainst a woman that was a brute. [P B Shelley, 1792–1822, *A Hate-Song*]

15 Malice is like a game of poker or tennis; you don't play it with anyone who is manifestly inferior to you. [Hilde Spiel, 1911– , *The Darkened Room*]

16 It is a characteristic of the human mind to hate the man one has injured. [Tacitus, *c.*55–*c.*117, *Agricola*, 45]

17 She has kissed her way into society. I don't like her. But don't misunderstand me: my dislike is purely platonic. [(Of an actress who was better as a lover than on the stage) Herbert Beerbohm Tree, 1853–1917, in Hesketh Pearson, *B T*, Ch. 12]

18 Hatred is like vitamins, you do feel better. [Kurt Vonnegut, 1922– (in conversation with Heinrich Böll on TV programme *Voices*), in *Listener*, 4 July 1985]

19 I love him not, but show no reason can / Wherefore, but this, I *do not love* the man.

[Rowland Watkyns, *c.*1616–64, *Flamma sine fumo*, 'Antipathy']

20 An intellectual hatred is the worst. [W B Yeats, 1865–1939, *A Prayer for My Daughter*]

See also LOVE, LOVE & HATE

HEALTH

1 Better to hunt in fields, for health unbought, / Than fee the doctor for a nauseous draught. / The wise, for cure, on exercise depend; / God never made his work for man to mend. [John Dryden, 1631–1700, *Epistle to John Driden of Chesterton*, 92]

2 Christian Science is so often therapeutically successful because it lays stress on the patient's believing in his or her own health rather than in Noah's Ark or the Ascension. [J B S Haldane, 1892–1964, *Possible Worlds*, 'Duty of Doubt']

3 *Orandum est ut sit mens sana in corpore sano.* – Your prayer must be for a sound mind in a sound body. [Juvenal, 60–*c.*130, *Satires*, X, 356]

4 Health is an episode between two illnesses. [Dr Ted Kaptchuk, 1947– , interview in *Guardian*, 2 July 1986]

5 Get your room full of good air, then shut up the windows and keep it. It will keep for years. Anyway, don't keep using your lungs all the time. Let them rest. [Stephen Leacock, 1869–1944, *Literary Lapses*, 'How to Live to be 200']

6 Gentlemen know that fresh air should be kept in its proper place – out of doors – and that, God having given us indoors and out-of-doors, we should not attempt to do away with this distinction. [Rose Macaulay, 1889–1958, *Crewe Train*, Pt 1, Ch. 5]

7 Life is not living, but being in health. [Martial, *c.*40–*c.*104, *Epigrams*, VI, 70]

8 Health is infinite and expansive in mode, and reaches out to be filled with the fullness of the world; whereas disease is finite and reductive in mode, and endeavours to reduce the world to itself. [Oliver Sacks, 1933– , *Awakenings*, 'Perspectives']

9 The liver, doted upon by the French, assaulted by the Irish, disdained by the Americans, and chopped up with egg, onion, and chicken fat by the Jews. [Richard Selzer, 1928– , *Confessions of a Knife*, 'Liver']

10 I am convinced digestion is the great secret of life. [Sydney Smith, 1771–1845, letter to Arthur Kinglake, 30 Sept. 1837]

11 We are all ill: but even a universal sickness implies an idea of health. [Lionel Trilling, 1905–75, *The Liberal Imagination*, 'Art and Neurosis']

12 Look to your health; and if you have it, praise God, and value it next to a good conscience; for health is the second blessing that we mortals are capable of; a blessing that money cannot buy. [Izaak Walton, 1593–1683, *The Compleat Angler*, Pt I, Ch. 21]

See also DOCTORS, ILLNESS

HEART

1 I said to Heart, 'How goes it?' Heart replied: / 'Right as a Ribstone Pippin!' But it lied. [Hilaire Belloc, 1870–1953, *Epigrams*, 'The False Heart']

2 No longer can we be satisfied with a life where the heart has its reasons which reason cannot know. Our hearts must know the world of reason, and must be guided by an informed heart. [Bruno Bettelheim, 1903–90, in *Guardian* at his death, 15 Mar. 1990]

3 The heart is deceitful above all things, and desperately wicked. [Bible, OT, *Jeremiah* 17:9]

4 I watched my foolish heart expand / In the lazy glow of benevolence, / O'er the various modes of man's belief. [Robert Browning, 1812–89, *Christmas Eve*, 20]

5 She had / A heart – how shall I say? – too soon made glad, / Too easily impressed. [Robert Browning, 1812–89, *My Last Duchess*]

6 His heart was one of those which most enamour us, / Wax to receive, and marble to retain. [Lord Byron, 1788–1824, *Beppo*, 34]

7 His heart runs away with his head. [George Colman, the Younger, 1762–1836, *Who Wants a Guinea?*, I. i]

8 'There are strings . . . in the human heart that had better not be wibrated.' [(Simon Tappertit) Charles Dickens, 1812–70, *Barnaby Rudge*, Ch. 22]

9 The day breaks not, it is my heart. [John Donne, 1571?–1631, *Break of Day*. (Also attributed to John Dowland)]

10 When I was one-and-twenty / I heard a wise man say, / 'Give crowns and pounds and guineas / But not your heart away.' [A E Housman, 1859–1936, *A Shropshire Lad*, 13]

11 My heart is a lonely hunter that hunts on a lonely hill. [Fiona Macleod, 1856–1905, *The Lonely Hunter*, vi]

12 The heart has its reasons, which are quite unknown to the head. [Blaise Pascal, 1623–62, *Pensées*, IV, 277]

13 'With every pleasing, every prudent part, / Say, what can Chloe want?' – She wants a heart. [Alexander Pope, 1688–1744, *Moral Essays*, Epistle II, 159]

14 They shift the moving toyshop of their heart. [Alexander Pope, 1688–1744, *The Rape of the Lock*, I, 100]

15 My heart is like a singing bird / Whose nest is in a watered shoot; / My heart is like an apple-tree / Whose boughs are bent with thickset fruit; / My heart is like a rainbow shell / That paddles in a halcyon sea; My heart is gladder than all these / Because my love is come to me. [Christina Rossetti, 1830–94, *A Birthday*]

16 It is only with the heart that one can see rightly; what is essential is invisible to the eye. [Antoine de Saint-Exupéry, 1900–1944, *The Little Prince*, Ch. 21]

17 Oh lift me from the grass! / I die! I faint! I fail! / Let thy love and kisses rain / On my lips and eyelids pale. / My cheek is cold and white, alas! / My heart beats loud and fast; – / Oh! press it to thine own again, / Where it will break at last. [P B Shelley, 1792–1822, *The Indian Serenade*]

18 My true love hath my heart and I have his, / By just exchange one for another given. [Sir Philip Sidney, 1554–86, *Arcadia*, Bk iii]

19 A process in the weather of the heart / Turns damp to dry; the golden shot / Storms in the freezing tomb. [Dylan Thomas, 1914–53, *A Process in the Weather of the Heart*]

20 The chambers of the mansion of my heart, / In every one whereof thine image dwells, / Are black with grief eternal for thy sake. [James Thomson, 1834–82, *The City of Dreadful Night*, 10]

21 O heart! O heart! if she'd but turn her head, / You'd know the folly of being comforted. [W B Yeats, 1865–1939, *The Folly of Being Comforted*]

22 Out-worn heart, in a time out-worn, / Come clear of the nets of wrong and right. [W B Yeats, 1865–1939, *Into the Twilight*]

23 We had fed the heart on fantasies, / The heart's grown brutal from the fare. [W B Yeats, 1865–1939, *Meditations in Time of Civil War*, VI]

See also EMOTIONS

HEAVEN

1 For a day in thy courts is better than a thousand. I had rather be a doorkeeper in the house of my God, than to dwell in the tents of wickedness. [Bible, OT, *Psalms* 84:10]

2 In my Father's house are many mansions. [Bible, NT, *St John* 14:2]

3 Except ye be converted, and become as little children, ye shall not enter into the kingdom of heaven. [Bible, NT, *St Matthew* 18:3]

4 I give you the end of a golden string; / Only wind it into a ball, / It will lead you in at Heaven's gate, / Built in Jerusalem's wall. [William Blake, 1757–1827, *Jerusalem*, f. 77]

5 Unfading moths, immortal flies, / And the worm that never dies. / And in that Heaven of all their wish, / There shall be no more land, say fish. [Rupert Brooke, 1887–1915, *Heaven*]

6 Hatred and cark and care, what place have they / In yon blue liberality of heaven? [Robert Browning, 1812–89, *Aristophanes' Apology*, 52]

7 I knew you once: but in Paradise, / If we meet, I will pass nor turn my face. [Robert Browning, 1812–89, *The Worst of It*, 19]

8 The desert were a paradise, / If thou wert there, if thou wert there. [Robert Burns, 1759–96, *O, Wert Thou in the Cauld Blast*]

9 Saint Peter sat by the celestial gate: / His keys were rusty, and the lock was dull. [Lord Byron, 1788–1824, *The Vision of Judgement*, 1]

10 I try to make the here and now as heavenly as possible in case there isn't one to ascend into when we're done. [Michael Caine, 1933– ; *Independent*, 'Quote Unquote', 5 Oct. 1996]

11 All the way to heaven is *heaven*. [St Catherine of Siena, 1347–80, quoted in *Weekend Guardian*, 1–2 July 1989]

12 If a man could pass through Paradise in a dream, and have a flower presented to him as a pledge that his soul had really been there, and if he found that flower in his hand when he awoke – Aye, and what then? [Samuel Taylor Coleridge, 1772–1834, *Anima Poetae* (1816)]

13 All Paradise opens! Let me die eating ortolans to the sound of soft music! [Benjamin Disraeli, 1804–81, *The Young Duke*, Bk i, Ch. 10]

14 I don't know, but I've been told / That the streets of heaven have all been sold. [Arlo Guthrie, 1947– , song]

15 'Twould ring the bells of Heaven / The wildest peal for years, / If Parson lost his senses / And people came to theirs. [Ralph Hodgson, 1871–1962, *The Bells of Heaven*]

16 I have desired to go / Where springs not fail, / To fields where flies no sharp and sided hail / And a few lilies blow. [Gerard Manley Hopkins, 1844–89, *Heaven-Haven*]

17 It was that verse about becoming again as a little child that caused the first sharp waning of my Christian sympathies. If the Kingdom of Heaven could be entered only by those fulfilling such a condition I knew I should be unhappy there. [Philip Larkin, 1922–85, *Required Writing*, 'The Savage Seventh']

18 They paved paradise / And put up a parking lot. [Joni Mitchell, 1943– , song: *Big Yellow Taxi*]

19 If you go to Heaven without being naturally qualified for it, you will not enjoy yourself there. [George Bernard Shaw, 1856–1950, *Man and Superman*, III]

20 Heaven, as conventionally conceived, is a place so inane, so dull, so useless, so miserable, that nobody has ever ventured to describe a whole day in heaven, though plenty of people have described a day at the seaside. [George Bernard Shaw, 1856–1950, *Misalliance*, Preface]

21 —'s idea of heaven is, eating *pâté de foie gras* to the sound of trumpets. [Sydney Smith, 1771–1845, in Hesketh Pearson, *The Smith of Smiths*, Ch. 10]

22 O world invisible, we view thee, / O world intangible, we touch thee, / O world unknowable, we know thee. [Francis Thompson, 1859–1907, *The Kingdom of God*]

23 Look for me in the nurseries of Heaven. [Francis Thompson, 1859–1907, *To my God-child*]

24 My soul, there is a country / Far beyond the stars, / Where stands a wingèd sentry / All skilful in the wars: / There, above noise and danger, / Sweet peace sits crowned with smiles, / And one born in a manger / Commands the beauteous files. [Henry Vaughan, 1622–95, *Peace*]

25 There is a land of pure delight / Where saints immortal reign; / Infinite day excludes the night, / And pleasures banish pain. [Isaac Watts, 1674–1748, hymn]

26 There is a happy land, / Far, far away, / Where saints in glory stand, / Bright, bright as day. [Andrew Young, 1807–89, hymn]

See also next category, HELL

HEAVEN & HELL

1 *Heaven* is where / the police are British / the cooks are French / the engineers are German / the administrators are Swiss / and the lovers are Italian.

Hell is where / the police are German / the cooks are British / the engineers are Italian / the administrators are French / and the lovers are Swiss. [anon. letter in *Independent*, 2 June 1990]

2 If it's heaven for climate, it's hell for company. [James Barrie, 1860–1937, *The Little Minister*, Ch. 3]

3 He did not think . . . that it was necessary to make a hell of this world to enjoy paradise in the next. [William Beckford, 1759–1844, *Vathek*]

4 Then I saw that there was a way to Hell, even from the gates of heaven. [John Bunyan, 1628–88, *The Pilgrim's Progress*, Pt I]

5 There is only one post fit for you, and that is the office of perpetual president of the Heaven and Hell Amalgamation Society. [Thomas Carlyle, 1795–1881, remark to Lord Houghton, quoted in T E Wemyss Reid, *Life of Lord H*]

6 Hell is paved with good intentions, but heaven goes in for something more dependable. Solid gold. [Joyce Cary, 1888–1957, *The Horse's Mouth*, 22]

7 The fear of hell is hell itself, and the longing for paradise is paradise itself. [Kahlil Gibran, 1883–1931, *Spiritual Sayings*]

8 The doors of heaven and hell are adjacent and identical: both green, both beautiful. [Nikos Kazantzakis, 1883–1957, *The Last Temptation*, Ch. 18]

9 Heaven and earth are ruthless and treat the myriad creatures as straw dogs. [Lao Tzu, *c.*604–531 BC, *Tao te Ching*, 4, trans. D C Lau, 5]

10 Better to reign in hell than serve in heav'n. [John Milton, 1608–74, *Paradise Lost*, Bk i, 263]

11 I don't believe in heaven or hell, they're here; you choose which one you're going to be a lodger in. [Tony Parker, 1923–96, quoting keeper describing his life in *Lighthouse*, Ch. 20]

12 Hell is paved with good intentions, not with bad ones. [George Bernard Shaw, 1856–1950, *Man and Superman*, 'Maxims for Revolutionists', Good Intentions]

13 Neither Heaven nor Hell are hereafter. Hell is time arrested within and refusing to join in the movement of wind and stars. Heaven is the boulder rock unrolled to let new life out: it is man restored to all four of his seasons rounding for eternity. [Laurens van der Post, 1906–96, *The Seed and the Sower*]

14 Heaven and Hell are Just One Breath Away. [Andy Warhol, 1927–87, title of last picture]

See also previous and following categories

HELL

1 All sin tends to be addictive, and the terminal point of addiction is what is called damnation. [W H Auden, 1907–1973, 'Hell']

2 That's what hell must be like, small chat to the babbling of Lethe about the good old days when we wished we were dead. [Samuel Beckett, 1906–89, *Embers*]

3 He considered it essential to believe in the existence of hell but unnecessary to believe that there was anybody in it. [Patricia Beer, 1924–99, *Moon's Ottery*, Ch. 6]

4 *Lasciate ogni speranza voi ch'entrate.* – All hope abandon, ye who enter here. [Dante Alighieri, 1265–1321, *The Divine Comedy*, 'Inferno', iii, 9]

5 There is wishful thinking in Hell as well as on earth. [C S Lewis, 1898–1963, *The Screwtape Letters*, Preface]

6 Hell hath no limits, nor is circumscribed / In one self place; for where we are is hell, / And where hell is, there must we ever be. [Christopher Marlowe, 1564–93, *Doctor Faustus*, 560]

7 Yet from those flames / No light, but rather darkness visible / Served only to discover sights of woe, / Regions of sorrow, doleful shades where peace / And rest can never dwell, hope never comes / That comes to all. [John Milton, 1608–74, *Paradise Lost*, Bk i, 62]

8 Me miserable! which way shall I fly / Infinite wrath, and infinite despair? / Which way I fly is hell; myself am hell; / And in th' lowest deep a lower deep / Still threatening to devour me opens wide, / To which the hell I suffer seems a heav'n. [John Milton, 1608–74, *Paradise Lost*, Bk iv, 73]

9 It is, we believe, / Idle to hope that the simple stirrup-pump / Can extinguish hell. [Henry Reed, 1914–86, *A Map of Verona*, Chard Whitlow (Mr Eliot's Sunday Evening Postscripts)]

10 Hell is other people. [Jean-Paul Sartre, 1905–80, *Huis clos* (*In Camera*), v]

11 In whatever circle of hell we live, I think that we are free to break it. And if people do not break it, then they stay there of their own free will. So they put themselves in hell freely. [Jean-Paul Sartre, 1905–80, in *L'Express*, 11–17 Oct. 1965]

12 The primrose way to the everlasting bonfire. [William Shakespeare, 1564–1616, *Macbeth*, II. iii. (22)]

13 Were't not for gold and women, there would be no damnation. [Cyril Tourneur, 1575?–1626, *The Revenger's Tragedy*, II. i]

14 The way down to hell is easy. The gates of black Dis stand open night and day. But to retrace one's steps and escape to the upper air – that is toil, that is labour. [Virgil, 70–19BC, *Aeneid*, VI, 126]

15 There is a dreadful Hell, / And everlasting pains; / There sinners must with devils dwell / In darkness, fire, and chains. [Isaac Watts, 1674–1748, *Divine Songs for Children*, 11, 'Heaven and Hell']

See also HEAVEN, HEAVEN & HELL

HELP

1 But what is past my help is past my care. [Francis Beaumont, 1584–1616, and John Fletcher, 1579–1625, *The Double Marriage*, I. i]

2 Do the work that's nearest, / Though it's dull at whiles, / Helping, when we meet them, / Lame dogs over stiles. [Charles Kingsley, 1819–75, *Letter to Thomas Hughes*]

3 God helps them who help themselves. [Jean de La Fontaine, 1621–95, *Fables*, VI, 18, 'The Carter in Trouble']

4 Long is the way / and hard, that out of hell leads up to light. [John Milton, 1608–74, *Paradise Lost*, Bk ii, 432]

5 My dear boy, you may help a lame dog over a stile but he is still a lame dog on the other side. [Ernest Newman, 1868–1959, to Peter Heyworth in answer to the suggestion that Newman should do something to encourage young composers]

6 Throw out the life-line, throw out the life-line, / Someone is sinking today. [Edward Smith Ufford, 1851–1928, revivalist hymn]

HEROISM

1 Some talk of Alexander, and some of Hercules; / Of Hector and Lysander, and such great names as these; / But of all the world's brave heroes, there's none that can compare / With the tow, row, row, row, row, row, row, for the British Grenadier [anon. song *The British Grenadier*]

2 No hero is mortal till he dies. [W H Auden, 1907–73, *A Short Ode to a Philologist*]

3 Unhappy the land that has no heroes ... No. Unhappy the land that is in need of heroes. [Bertolt Brecht, 1898–1956, *The Life of Galileo*, 13]

4 In short, he was a perfect cavaliero, / And to his very valet seemed a hero. [Lord Byron, 1788–1824, *Beppo*, 33]; see 6

5 Down these mean streets a man must go who is not himself mean. [Raymond Chandler, 1888–1959, *Pearls are a Nuisance*, 'The Simple Art of Murder']

6 No man is a hero to his valet. [Mme de Cornuel, 1605–94, *Lettres de Mlle Aïssé*, 13 Aug. 1728]; see 4

7 Every hero becomes a bore at last. [Ralph Waldo Emerson, 1803–82, *Representative Men*, 'Uses of Great Men']

8 Show me a hero and I will write you a tragedy. [F Scott Fitzgerald, 1896–1940, *Notebooks*, 'E']

9 Heroes are men who glorify a life which they can't bear any longer. [Jean Giraudoux, 1882–1944, *Duel of Angels*, III]

10 Some village Hampden, that with dauntless breast / The little tyrant of his fields withstood; / Some mute inglorious Milton here may rest, / Some Cromwell guiltless of his country's blood. [Thomas Gray, 1716–71, *Elegy Written in a Country Churchyard*, 15]

11 The boy stood on the burning deck – / Whence all but he had fled. [Felicia Hemans, 1793–1835, *Casabianca*]

12 [When asked how he became a war hero] It was involuntary. They sank my boat. [President John F Kennedy, 1917–63, in Arthur M Schlesinger Jr, *A Thousand Days*, Ch. 4]

13 He never loved the frenzy of the sun / Nor the clear seas. / He came with hero's arms and bullock's eyes / Afraid of nothing but his nagging gods. [Sidney Keyes, 1922–43, *Dido's Lament for Aeneas*]

14 A Lady with a Lamp shall stand / In the great history of the land. / A noble type of good, / Heroic womanhood. [H W Longfellow, 1807–82, *Santa Filomena*]

15 Then out spake brave Horatius, / The Captain of the Gate: / 'To every man upon this earth / Death cometh soon or late. / And how can man die better / Than facing fearful odds, / For the ashes of his fathers, / And the temples of his Gods?' [Lord Macaulay, 1800–1859, *Lays of Ancient Rome*, 'Horatius', 27]

16 Ultimately a hero is a man who would argue with the Gods, and awakens devils to contest his vision. [Norman Mailer, 1923– , *The Presidential Papers*, Special Preface]

17 They were singularly brave men, these Prussian machine-gunners, but the extreme of heroism, alike in foe or friend, is indistinguishable from despair. [Frederic Manning, 1887–1935, *Her Privates We*, 1]

18 I'm a hero wid coward's legs, I'm a hero from the waist up. [Spike Milligan, 1918– , *Puckoon*, Ch. 2]

19 See, the conquering hero comes! / Sound the trumpets, beat the drums! [Thomas Morell, 1703–84, *Joshua*, Pt III]

20 The sand of the desert is sodden red, – Red with the wreck of a square that broke; – / The gatling's jammed and the colonel dead, / And the regiment blind with the dust and smoke. / The river of death has brimmed its banks / And England's far and honour a name, / But the voice of a schoolboy rallies the ranks: / 'Play up! play up! and play the game!' [Henry Newbolt, 1862–1938, *Vitae Lampada*]

21 Our great-grandchildren, when they learn how we began this war by snatching glory out of defeat . . . may also learn how the little holiday steamers made an excursion to hell and came back glorious. [J B Priestley, 1894–1984, *Postscripts*, 'On Dunkirk', BBC radio broadcast, 5 June 1940]

22 The hero is strangely akin to those who die young. [Rainer Maria Rilke, 1875–1926, *Duino Elegies*, 6]

23 Being a hero is about the shortest-lived profession on earth. [Will Rogers, 1879–1935, in *Saturday Review*, 25 Aug. 1962, 'A Rogers Thesaurus']

24 Had we lived, I should have had a tale to tell of the hardihood, endurance and courage of my companions which would have stirred the heart of every Englishman. These rough notes and our dead bodies must tell the tale. [Robert Falcon Scott, 1868–1912, 'Message to the Public', *Journal*, Mar. 1912]

25 *Arma virumque cano, Troiae qui primus ab oris / Italiam fato profugus Lavinaque venit / Litora.* – I sing of arms and of the hero who first came from the shores of Troy, exiled by Fate, to Italy and its Lavinian shore. [Virgil, 70–19BC, *Aeneid*, I, 1]

26 Obviously, in a plutocracy / the natural hero / is the man who robs a bank. [William Carlos Williams, 1883–1963, *Childe Harold to the Round Tower Came*]

HIDING

1 Where does a wise man kick a pebble? On the beach. Where does a wise man hide a leaf? In the forest. [G K Chesterton, 1874–1936, *The Innocence of Father Brown*, 'The Broken Sword']

2 I have done one braver thing / Than all the Worthies did, / And yet a braver thence doth spring, / Which is to keep that hid. [John Donne, 1571?–1631, *The Undertaking*]

3 Addresses are given to us to conceal our whereabouts. [Saki (H H Munro), 1870–1916, *Cross Currents*]

HIERARCHIES

1 The rich man in his castle, / The poor man at his gate, / God made them, high or lowly, / And ordered their estate. [Mrs C F Alexander, 1818–95, hymn]

2 If we lived in a featureless desert, we would learn to place the individual grains of sand in a moral and aesthetic hierarchy. [Michael Frayn, 1933– , *Constructions*, 10]

3 *The Peter Principle*: In a Hierarchy Every Employee Tends to Rise to his Level of Incompetence. [Laurence J Peter, 1919–90, and Raymond Hull, 1918–85, *The Peter Principle*, Ch. 1]

4 'I believe I take precedence,' he said coldly; 'you are merely the club Bore: I am the club Liar.' [Saki (H H Munro), 1870–1916, *A Defensive Diamond*]

5 Members rise from CMG (known sometimes in Whitehall as 'Call me God') to the KCMG ('Kindly Call me God') to . . . the GCMG ('God Calls me God'). [Anthony Sampson, 1926– , *Anatomy of Britain*, Ch. 18]

6 So, naturalists observe, a flea / Hath smaller fleas that on him prey; / And these have smaller fleas to bite 'em, / And so proceed *ad infinitum*. [Jonathan Swift, 1677–1745, *On Poetry*, 337]

See also CLASS, ORDER

HISTORY & HISTORIANS

1 History is, strictly speaking, the study of questions; the study of answers belongs to anthropology and sociology. [W H Auden, 1907–73, *The Dyer's Hand*, 3, 'Hic et Ille', sect. B]

2 Man is a history-making creature who can neither repeat his past nor leave it behind. [W H Auden, 1907–73, *The Dyer's Hand*, 5, 'D. H. Lawrence']

3 Bournemouth is one of the few English towns that one can safely call 'her'. [John Betjeman, 1906–84, *First and Last Loves*]

4 History is an art which must not neglect the known facts. [Bernard Berenson, 1865–1959, attr.]

5 They [Thucydides and Xenophon] maintained the dignity of history. [Henry St John, Viscount Bolingbroke, 1678–1751, *On the Study of History*, 5]

6 English history is all about men liking their fathers, and American history is all about men hating their fathers and trying to burn down everything they ever did. [Malcolm Bradbury, 1932– , *Stepping Westward*, Bk II, Ch. 5]

7 A typical historian. You people raise hindsight to the status of a profession. [Malcolm Bradbury, 1932– , and Christopher Bigsby, 1941– , TV play *After Dinner Game*]

8 People think too historically. They are always living half in a cemetery. [Aristide Briand, 1862–1932; in H L Mencken, *New Dictionary of Quotations*]

9 History is in the shit sense. You have left it behind you. Fiction is piss: a stream of past events but not behind you, because they never really happened. [Brigid Brophy, 1929–95, *In Transit*, sect. I, 1]

10 In history, there seems to be only a negative learning. One notes what one has done to others in order to hold it against them. [Elias Canetti, 1905–94, *The Human Province*, '1969']

11 Of necessity, the more contemporary history becomes the more it becomes contemporary hearsay. [David Cannadine, 1950– , in *New Society*, 6 Dec. 1984]

12 History is the essence of innumerable biographies. [Thomas Carlyle, 1795–1881, *Critical and Miscellaneous Essays*, 'On History']

13 Happy the people whose annals are blank in history books! [Thomas Carlyle, 1795–1881, *Frederick the Great*, Bk xvi, Ch. 1]

14 All history is the history of thought. [R G Collingwood, 1889–1943, Autobiography, Ch. 10]

15 We are never completely contemporaneous with our present. History advances in disguise; it appears on stage wearing the mask of the receding scene, and we tend to lose the meaning of the play. [Régis Debray, 1941– , *Revolution in the Revolution?*, Ch. 1]

16 History is philosophy drawn from examples. [Dionysius of Halicarnassus, *c*.40–8 BC, *Ars Rhetorica*, 11, 2]

17 History is the endless repetition of the wrong way of living, and it'll start again tomorrow, if it's moved from here today. [Lawrence Durrell, 1912–90, in *Listener*, 20 Apr. 1978]

18 After such knowledge, what forgiveness? Think now / History has many cunning passages, contrived corridors / And issues. [T S Eliot, 1888–1965, *Gerontion*]

19 A good historian is timeless; although he is a patriot, he will never flatter his country in any respect. [François de Fénelon, 1651–1715, letter to the Academy]

20 Men wiser and more learned than I have discerned in history a plot, a rhythm, a predetermined pattern. These harmonies are concealed from me. I can see only one emergency following on another. [H A L Fisher, 1856–1940, *A History of Europe*, Preface]

21 History is more or less bunk. [Henry Ford, 1863–1947, interview in the *Chicago Tribune*, 25 May 1916]

22 Many historians have heard the music of the past but have transcribed it for penny whistle. [Peter Gay, 1923– , *Freud for Historians*, Ch. 2, 3]

23 His reign is marked by the rare advantage of furnishing very few materials for history; which is, indeed, little more than the register of the crimes, follies and misfortunes of mankind. [Edward Gibbon, 1737–94, *The Decline and Fall of the Roman Empire*, Ch. 3]

24 It was Quintilian or Max Beerbohm who said, 'History repeats itself: historians repeat each other.' [Philip Guedalla, 1889–1944, *Supers and Supermen*, 'Some Historians']

25 Once in a lifetime / The longed-for tidal wave / Of justice can rise up, / And hope and history rhyme. [Seamus Heaney, 1939– , *The Cure at Troy*, p. 77]

26 What experience and history teach is this – that people and governments never have learnt anything from history, or acted on principles deduced from it. [Georg Hegel, 1770–1831, *Philosophy of History*, Introduction]

27 History has to use second-hand timber when she builds a new edifice – like those awkward post-war chickenhouses people build out of bits of army huts and old ammo-boxes, with 'W.D.' stamped all over them and costly enigmatical fittings too much trouble to unscrew. [Richard Hughes, 1900–1976, *The Fox in the Attic*, Bk III, 31]

28 Histories do not break off clean, like a glass rod; they fray, stretch, and come undone, like a rope. [Robert Hughes, 1938– , *The Shock of the New*, Ch. 8]

29 The historian, essentially, wants more documents than he can really use; the dramatist only wants more liberties than he can really take. [Henry James, 1843–1916, *The Aspern Papers*, Preface to 1909 edn]

30 History, Stephen said, is a nightmare from which I am trying to awake. [James Joyce, 1882–1941, *Ulysses*, Penguin edn, 1992, p. 42]

31 History generally, and the history of revolutions in particular, is always richer in content, more varied, more many-sided, more lively and more 'subtle' than even the best parties and the most class-conscious vanguards of the most advanced classes imagine. [Vladimir Ilyich Lenin, 1870–1924, *'Left-wing' Communism*, Ch. 10]

32 Some [historians] should be labelled parachutists: the others might more fittingly be called truffle hunters. [Emmanuel Le Roy Ladurie, 1929– , quoted in *Guardian*, 6 Nov. 1987]

33 The anthropologist respects history, but he does not accord it a special value. He conceives it as a study complementary to his own: one of them unfurls the range of human societies in time, the other in space. [Claude Lévi-Strauss, 1908– , *The Savage Mind*]

34 For history's a twisted root / With art its small, translucent fruit / And never the other way round. [Archibald Macleish, 1892–1982, *Ars Poetica*]

35 History, like a badly constructed concert hall, has occasional dead spots where the music can't be heard. [Archibald Macleish, 1892–1982; *Observer*, 'Sayings of the Week', 12 Feb. 1967]

36 History is too serious to be left to historians. [Iain Macleod, 1913–70; *Observer*, 'Sayings of the Week', 16 July 1961]

37 Hegel says somewhere that all great events and personalities in world history reappear in one way or another. He forgot to add: the first time as tragedy, the second as farce. [Karl Marx, 1818–83, *The Eighteenth Brumaire of Louis Napoleon*, Pt I]

38 Those who make history can afford to forget or retain nostalgic memories of it, those made by it daily live in this shadow. [Bhiku Parekh, 1935– , in *New Statesman and Society*, 9 Sept. 1988]

39 There is no history of mankind, there is only an indefinite number of histories of all kinds of aspects of human life. And one of these is the history of political power. This is elevated into the history of the world. [Karl Popper, 1902–94, *The Open Society and Its Enemies*, 25]

40 Civilization gets the historians it deserves. [Roy Porter, 1946– , in *Observer*, 30 Oct. 1988]

41 And even I can remember / A day when the historians left blanks in their writings, / I mean for things they didn't know. [Ezra Pound, 1885–1972, *Cantos*, XIII]

42 The people of Crete unfortunately make more history than they can consume locally. [Saki (H H Munro), 1870–1916, *The Jesting of Arlington Stringham*]

43 Historians are left forever chasing shadows, painfully aware of their inability ever to construct a dead world in its completeness however thorough or revealing their documentation ... We are doomed to be forever hailing someone who has just gone round the corner and out of earshot. [Simon Schama, 1945– , *Dead Certainties*, Afterword]

44 World history is the world's court of judgement. [Friedrich von Schiller, 1759–1805, *Resignation*]

45 A historian is a prophet in reverse. [Friedrich von Schlegel, 1772–1829, *The Athenaeum, I*, 'Fragments']

46 World history is a conspiracy of diplomats against common sense. [Arthur Schnitzler, 1862–1931, in *Practical Wisdom*, ed. Frederick Ungar]

47 There is a history in all men's lives. [William Shakespeare, 1564–1616, *2 Henry IV*, III. i. 80]

48 Life is one tenth Here and Now, nine-tenths a history lesson. For most of the time the Here and Now is neither now nor here. [Graham Swift, 1949– , *Waterland*, 8]

49 History gets thicker as it approaches recent times. [A J P Taylor, 1906–90, *English History, 1914–1945*, Bibliography]

50 He [Napoleon III] was what I often think is a dangerous thing for a statesman to be – a student of history; and like most of those who study history, he learned from the mistakes of the past how to make new ones. [A J P Taylor, 1906–90, in *Listener*, 6 June 1963]

51 Historians are like deaf people who go on answering questions that no one has asked them. [Leo Tolstoy, 1828–1910, in Manning Clark, *A Discovery of Australia*, 'Being an Historian']

52 History is just the portrayal of crimes and misfortunes. [Voltaire, 1694–1778, *L'Ingénu*, Ch. 10]

53 All our ancient history, as one of our wits remarked, is no more than accepted fiction. [Voltaire, 1694–1778, *Jeannot et Colin*]

54 He had no idea how time could be reworded / Which is the historian's task. [Derek Walcott, 1930– , *Omeros*, Ch. xviii, 1]

55 Anything but history, for history must be false. [Robert Walpole, 1676–1745 (remark to his son, who offered to read to him), *Walpoliana*, Vol. I, p. 60]

56 History is lived forward but it is written in retrospect. [C V Wedgwood, 1910–97, in Salman Rushdie, *The Jaguar Smile*, Epilogue]

57 Now it is on the whole more convenient to keep history and theology apart. [H G Wells, 1866–1946, *A Short History of the World*, Ch. 37]

58 It is sometimes very hard to tell the difference between history and the smell of a skunk. [Rebecca West, 1892–1983, epigraph to *Voices from the Great War*, ed. Peter Vansittart]

See also PAST, TRADITION

HITLER

1 The people Hitler never understood, and whose actions continued to exasperate him to the end of his life, were the British. [Alan Bullock, 1914– , *Hitler*, Pt VIII, 5]

2 Whatever may be the reason – whether it was that Hitler thought he might get away with what he had got without fighting for it, or whether it was that after all the preparations were not sufficiently complete – however, one thing is certain: he missed the bus. [Neville Chamberlain, 1869–1940, speech to Conservative and Unionist Associations, 4 Apr. 1940]

3 Hitlerism is almost entirely of Jewish origin. [G K Chesterton, 1874–1936; *Observer*, 'Sayings of the Week', 23 July 1933]

4 You [Hitler] do your worst, and we will do our best. [Winston Churchill, 1874–1965, speech at Civil Defence Services' Luncheon, 14 July 1941]

5 I have only one purpose, the destruction of Hitler, and my life is much simplified thereby. If Hitler invaded Hell I would make at least a favourable reference to the Devil in the House of Commons. [Winston Churchill, 1874–1965, *The Second World War*, Vol. 3, 20]

6 Bolshaw approved of Hitler in so much as he approved of the principle of the Führer's function while feeling that he could fulfil it better himself. [William Cooper, 1910– , *Scenes from Provincial Life*, Pt I, Ch. 3]

7 We're going to string old Hitler / From the very highest bough / Of the biggest aspidistra in the world. [Gracie Fields, 1898–1979, song: *The Biggest Aspidistra*, words and music by J Harper *et al.*]

8 He disapproved of Adolf Hitler, who had done such a great job of combating un-American activities in Germany. [Joseph Heller, 1923–99, *Catch-22*, Ch. 4]

9 A racing tipster who only reached Hitler's level of accuracy would not do well for his clients. [A J P Taylor, 1906–90, *The Origins of the Second World War*, Ch. 7]

See also FASCISM, WORLD WAR 2

HOLIDAYS

1 A good holiday is one spent among people whose notions of time are vaguer than yours. [J B Priestley, 1894–1984; in *Penguin Dictionary of Modern Humorous Quotations*, comp. Fred Metcalf]

2 If all the year were playing holidays, / To sport would be as tedious as to work. [William Shakespeare, 1564–1616, *1 Henry IV*, I. ii (226)]

See also LEISURE

HOLLYWOOD

1 If music be the breakfast food of love, kindly do not disturb until lunch time. [James Agee, 1909–55 (on Hollywood musicals), in *Agee on Film*]

2 All that sun and the streets are so clean. Have you ever considered why? All the garbage is on television. [Woody Allen, 1935– , in *New Woman*, Mar. 1989, variant in film *Annie Hall*]

3 Real cities have something else, some bony structure under the muck. Los Angeles has Hollywood – and hates it. It ought to consider itself damn lucky. Without Hollywood it would be a mail order city. Everything in the catalogue you could get better somewhere else. [Raymond Chandler, 1888–1959, *The Little Sister*, Ch. 13]

4 If my books had been any worse, I should not have been invited to Hollywood, and if they had been any better, I should not have come. [Raymond Chandler, 1888–1959, letter to Charles Morton, assoc. ed. of *Atlantic Monthly*, 12 Dec. 1945]

5 I think people need something to look up to, and Hollywood was the only Royalty that America ever had. [Bette Davis, 1908–89, interview in *The Sunday Times*, 20 Sept. 1987]

6 I'm a product of Hollywood. Fantasy is not unnatural to me: it's my reality. Hollywood people are like everyone else, only more so. They depict reality as opposed to living it. [Carrie Fisher, 1956– , interview in *Weekend Guardian*, 12–13 Jan. 1991]

7 I was born at the age of twelve on a Metro-Goldwyn-Mayer lot. [Judy Garland, 1922–69; *Observer*, 'Sayings of the Week', 18 Feb. 1951]

8 Deep below the glitter, it's all solid tinsel. [Samuel Goldwyn, 1882–1974, attr. *Guardian*, 11 Apr. 1984]; see 10

9 We [Hollywood people] are the croupiers in a crooked gambling house. [Samuel Hoffenstein, 1890–1947, in Lillian Ross, *Picture*, 'Throw the Little Old Lady down the Stairs!']

10 Strip the phoney tinsel off Hollywood and you'll find the real tinsel underneath. [Oscar Levant, 1906–72, *Memoirs of an Amnesiac*]; see 8

11 It's the place where the sky is always blue and so are the screenwriters. Where the story line is accepted on Monday by the twenty-four-year-old head of a studio, and rejected on the Thursday by his sixteen-year-old replacement. [(Of Los Angeles) Maureen Lipman, 1946– , *How was it for You?*, 'Travels with Me aren't']

12 Back to the mink-lined rut. [(On being forced back to Hollywood after the Wall Street crash) Anita Loos, 1893–1981, in obituary in *Guardian*, 20 Aug. 1981]

13 A trip through a sewer in a glass-bottomed boat. [(Of Hollywood) Wilson Mizner, 1876–1933, in A Johnston, *The Legendary Mizners*, Ch. 4]

14 Working for Warner Bros is like fucking a porcupine: it's a hundred pricks against one. [Wilson Mizner, 1876–1933, in David Niven, *Bring on the Empty Horses*, 'Degrees of Friendliness']

15 Hollywood money isn't money. It's congealed snow, melts in your hand, and there you are. [Dorothy Parker, 1893–1967, in *Writers at Work*, ed. Malcolm Cowley, First Series]

16 In Hollywood, if you don't have happiness you send out for it. [Rex Reed, 1938– , in J R Colombo, *Colombo's Hollywood*, 'Hollywood the Bad']

17 Hollywood people are afraid to leave Hollywood. Out in the world, they are frightened ... Every one of us thinks, You know, I really don't deserve a swimming pool. [Gottfried Reinhardt, 1913–94, in Lillian Ross, *Picture*, 'Throw the Little Old Lady down the Stairs!']

18 The lunatics have taken over the asylum. [(When United Artists was taken over by Chaplin, Pickford, Fairbanks and Griffith) Richard Rowland, 1881–1947; in L Halliwell, *The Filmgoer's Book of Quotes*]

19 Czar of all the rushes. [(Of Louis B Mayer, head of MGM) B P Schulberg, 1892–1957; in L Halliwell, *The Filmgoer's Book of Quotes*]

20 The trouble, Mr Goldwyn, is that you are only interested in art and I am only interested in money. [George Bernard Shaw, 1856–1950 (when declining to sell Goldwyn the screen rights of his plays), in Philip French, *The Movie Moguls*, Ch. 4]

See also FILM, FILM DIRECTORS, FILM STARS, UNITED STATES: PARTICULAR PLACES

HOME & HOUSES

1 Houses are built to live in and not to look on. [Francis Bacon, 1561–1626, *Essays*, 45, 'Of Building']

2 Except the Lord build the house, they labour in vain that build it. [Bible, OT, *Psalms* 127:1]

3 Had I but plenty of money, money enough and to spare, / The house for me, no doubt, were a house in the city-square. [Robert Browning, 1812–89, *Up at a Villa – Down in the City*, 1]

4 For a man's house is his castle. [Edward Coke, 1552–1634, *Institutes*, III, 73]

5 Home is only where you go to when you've nowhere to go. [Bette Davis, 1908–89, quoted by Katharine Whitehorn in *Observer*, 20 Sept. 1987]; see 24

6 I'm not frightened of the darkness outside. It's the darkness inside houses I don't like. [Shelagh Delaney, 1939– , *A Taste of Honey*, I. i]

7 Many a man who thinks to found a home discovers that he has merely opened a tavern for his friends. [Norman Douglas, 1868–1952, *South Wind*, 24]

8 How does it feel / To be without a home / Like a complete unknown / Like a rolling stone? [Bob Dylan, 1941– , song: *Like a Rolling Stone*]

9 'Home is the place where, when you have to go there, / They have to take you in.' / 'I should have called it / Something you somehow haven't to deserve.' [Robert Frost, 1874–1963, *The Death of the Hired Man*]; see 20

10 I am a marvellous housekeeper. Every time I leave a man, I keep his house. [Zsa Zsa Gabor, 1919– , in *Was It Good for You Too?*, ed. Bob Chieger]

11 Long ago, the Englishman's castle was his home; then that went, and his home became his castle. Now his castle is the nation's and his home is the bank's. [Leon Garfield, 1921–96, in *Children's Literature in Education*, Ch. 2]

12 Oh give me a home where the buffalo roam, / Where the deer and the antelope play, / Where seldom is heard a discouraging word / And the skies are not cloudy all day. [Brewster Higley, 19th cent., song: *Home on the Range*]

13 I want a house that has got over all its troubles; I don't want to spend the rest of my life bringing up a young and inexperienced house. [Jerome K Jerome, 1859–1927, *They and I*]

14 A house is a machine for living in. [Le Corbusier, 1887–1965, *Vers une architecture*]

15 A man's home may seem to be his castle on the outside; inside, it is more often his nursery. [Clare Boothe Luce, 1903–87, in *Bulletin of Baldwin School, Pennsylvania*, Sept. 1974]

16 A man travels the world over in search of what he needs and returns home to find it. [George Moore, 1852–1933, *The Brook Kerith*, Ch. 11]

17 Have nothing in your houses that you do not know to be useful, or believe to be beautiful. [William Morris, 1834–96, *The Beauty of Life*]

18 'Mid pleasures and palaces though we may roam, / Be it ever so humble, there's no place like home. [J H Payne, 1792–1852, *Clari, the Maid of Milan*, 'Home, Sweet Home']

19 They're all made out of ticky-tacky, and they all look just the same. [Malvina Reynolds, 1900–1978, song: *Little Boxes*, about the tract houses in the hills south of San Francisco, sung by Pete Seeger]

20 Home is where you go and they have to let you in. [George Sanders, 1906–72, in film *Uncle Harry* (1944), script by Stephen Longstreet and Keith Winter]; see 9

21 Home is the girl's prison and the woman's workhouse. [George Bernard Shaw, 1856–1950, *Man and Superman*, 'Maxims for Revolutionists', Women in the Home]

22 Sated with home, of wife, of children tired. / The restless soul is driven abroad to roam; / Sated abroad, all seen and all admired, / The restless soul is driven to ramble home. [James and Horace Smith, 1775–1839, and 1779–1849, *Rejected Addresses*, 'Cui Bono?']

23 An English home – gray twilight poured / On dewy pastures, dewy trees, / Softer than sleep – all things in order stored, / A haunt of ancient Peace. [Alfred, Lord Tennyson, 1809–92, *The Palace of Art*, 22]

24 Home is where you come to when you have nothing better to do. [Margaret Thatcher, 1925– ; *Independent*, 'Quote Unquote', 11 May 1991. Misquoted as her attitude to domesticity, rather than a reference to children's attitudes]; see 5

25 I had three chairs in my house: one for solitude, two for friendship, three for society. [H D Thoreau, 1817–62, *Walden*, 'Visitors']

26 Some respite to husbands the weather may send, / But housewives' affairs have never an end. [Thomas Tusser, 1524?–80, *Five Hundred Points of Good Husbandry*, 'Preface to the Book of Housewifery']

27 Three addresses always inspire confidence, even in tradesmen. [Oscar Wilde, 1854–1900, *The Importance of Being Earnest*, III]

28 But with love brooding there, why, no place can compare / With my little grey home in the west. [D Eardley Wilmot, 19th cent., *My Little Grey Home*]

HOMOSEXUALS

1 I became one of the stately homos of England. [Quentin Crisp, 1908–99, *The Naked Civil Servant*, Ch. 24]

2 [When asked by a US immigration official if he was a practising homosexual] Practising? Certainly not. I'm absolutely perfect. [Quentin Crisp, 1908–99, quoted by Ray Connolly in *The Sunday Times*, 20 Jan. 1980]

3 Gay men want to be happy; lesbians only want to be right. Gay men like real women; lesbians hate real men. [Quentin Crisp, 1908–99, in *Guardian*, 18 Oct. 1996]

4 When asked whether, as a member of the Bloomsbury Group, he did not have homosexual leanings] More leant-upon than leanings, I'd have thought. [David Garnett, 1892–1981, quoted by John Pearson in *The Sunday Times*, 16 Mar. 1980]

5 America, I'm putting my queer shoulder to the wheel. [Allen Ginsberg, 1926–97, *America*]

6 All women are Lesbians, except those who don't know it yet. [Jill Johnston, 1929– , from *Dialogue on Women's Liberation*]

7 The rest of the world goes on out there, all around us [gays under the threat of AIDS], as if nothing is happening, going on with their own lives and not knowing what it's like, what we're going through. We're living through war, but where they're living it's peacetime, and we're all in the same country. [Larry Kramer, 1935– , *The Normal Heart*, II. 11]

8 This sort of thing may be tolerated by the French, but we are British – thank God. [Field-Marshal Montgomery, 1887–1976, on Homosexuality Bill, in House of Lords, 24 May 1965]

9 In the old-fashioned forties, when the West End was ruled by glossy revivals and homosexual managers, a young actor was asked at an audition if he wasn't, perhaps, heterosexual. 'Well yes,' he admitted and added eagerly, 'but it doesn't show from the front.' [John Mortimer, 1923– , *Clinging to the Wreckage*, 19]

10 Homosexuals, like Jews, often find themselves numbered among their enemies' best friends. [Frederic Raphael, 1931– , in *3: Radio Three Magazine*, Oct. 1982]

See also LOVE: HOMOSEXUAL

HONESTY & DISHONESTY

1 Everybody's honest in one way or another. The trouble is, there's only one official way. [Jean Anouilh, 1910–87, *Dinner with the Family*, III]

2 The social, friendly, honest man, / Whate'er he be, / 'Tis he fulfils great Nature's plan, / And none but he! [Robert Burns, 1759–96, *Epistle to Lapraik*, No. 2, 87]

3 The man of life upright,/ whose guiltless life is free/ From all dishonest deeds / Or thought of vanity. [Thomas Campion, 1567–1620, *The Man of Life Upright*]

4 An honest woman and a broken leg are best at home, and for an honest girl a job of work's her holiday. [Miguel Cervantes, 1547–1616, *Don Quixote*, Pt II, Ch. 5]

5 An honest man, close-buttoned to the chin, / Broadcloth without, and a warm heart within. [William Cowper, 1731–1800, *Epistle to Joseph Hill*]

6 A few honest men are better than numbers. [Oliver Cromwell, 1599–1658, letter to Sir W Spring, Sept. 1643]

7 But to live outside the law, you must be honest. [Bob Dylan, 1941– , song: *Absolutely Sweet Marie*]

8 Everyone suspects himself of at least one of the cardinal virtues, and this is mine: I am one of the few honest people that I have ever known. [F Scott Fitzgerald, 1896–1940, *The Great Gatsby*, Ch. 3]

9 Honesty is praised and starves. [Juvenal, 60–*c*.130, *Satires*, I, 74]

10 Though I be poor, I'm honest. [Thomas Middleton, 1570?–1627, *The Witch*, III. ii]

11 An honest man's the noblest work of God. [Alexander Pope, 1688–1744, *An Essay on Man*, IV, 248]

12 To be honest, as this world goes, / Is to be one man picked out of ten thousand. [William Shakespeare, 1564–1616, *Hamlet*, II. ii. (179)]

13 Corruption wins not more than honesty. / Still in thy right hand carry gentle peace, / To silence envious tongues: be just, and fear not. / Let all the ends thou aim'st at be thy country's, / Thy God's, and truth's. [*Henry VIII*, III. ii. 443]

14 I am as honest as any man living that is an old man and no honester than I. [*Much Ado About Nothing*, III. v. (15)]

15 An honest tale speeds best being plainly told. [*Richard III*, IV. iv. 359]

16 Though I am not naturally honest, / I am so sometimes by chance. [*The Winter's Tale*, IV. iii. (734)]

See also INTEGRITY, TRUTH

HONOUR

1 Let us honour if we can / The vertical man / Though we value none/ But the horizontal one. [W H Auden, 1907–73, *Epigraph*]

2 Leave not a stain in thine honour. [Bible, Apocrypha, *Ecclesiasticus* 33:22]

3 Honour has come back, as a king, to earth, / And paid his subjects with a royal wage; / And Nobleness walks in our ways again; / And we have come into our heritage. [Rupert Brooke, 1887–1915, *The Dead*]

4 That chastity of honour, that felt a stain like a wound. [Edmund Burke, 1729–97, *Reflections on the Revolution in France*, Penguin edn, p. 170]

5 Honour is a luxury for aristocrats, but it is a necessity for hall-porters. [G K Chesterton, 1874–1936, *Heretics*, 13]

6 The louder he talked of his honour, the faster we counted our spoons. [Ralph Waldo Emerson, 1803–82, *The Conduct of Life*, 'Wealth']

7 All is lost save honour. [(On the loss of the battle of Pavia; and in slightly different form in a letter to his mother) Francis I, King of France, 1494–1547, 23 Feb. 1525]

8 Purity is the feminine, Truth the masculine, of Honour. [Julius and Augustus Hare, 1795–1855, and 1792–1834, *Guesses at Truth*, Ist Series, p. 180]

9 Honour is flashed off exploit, so we say. [Gerard Manley Hopkins, 1844–89, *St Alphonsus Rodriguez*]

10 Yet this inconstancy is such, / As you too shall adore; / I could not love thee, Dear, so much / Loved I not honour more. [Richard Lovelace, 1618–58, *To Lucasta, Going to the Wars*]

11 Remember, men, we're fighting for this woman's honour; which is probably more than she ever did. [Groucho Marx, 1895–1977, in film *Duck Soup*, script by Bert Kalmar, *et al.*]

12 To set the cause above renown, / To love the game beyond the prize, / To honour, while you strike him down, / The foe that comes with fearless eyes. [Henry Newbolt, 1862–1938, *Clifton Chapel*]

13 Rightly to be great / Is not to stir without great argument, / But greatly to find quarrel in a straw / When honour's at the stake. [William Shakespeare, 1564–1616, *Hamlet*, IV. iv. 53]

14 By heaven methinks it were an easy leap / To pluck bright honour from the pale-faced moon, / Or dive into the bottom of the deep, / Where fathom-line could never touch the ground, / And pluck up drownèd honour by the locks. [*1 Henry IV*, I. iii. 201]

15 Honour pricks me on. Yea, but how if honour prick me off when I come on? – how then? ... What is honour? A word. What is that word, honour? Air. A trim reckoning! Who hath it? He that died o' Wednesday. Doth he feel it? No. Doth he hear it? No. It is insensible then? Yea, to the dead. But will it not live with the living? No. Why? Detraction will not suffer it. Therefore I'll none of it: honour is a mere scutcheon: and so ends my catechism. [*1 Henry IV*, V. i. (131)]

16 If we are marked to die, we are enow / To do our country loss; and if to live, / The fewer men, the greater share of honour. [*Henry V*, IV. iii. 20]

17 Well, honour is the subject of my story. / I cannot tell what you and other men / Think of this life: but, for my single self, / I had as lief not be as live to be / In awe of such a thing as I myself. [*Julius Caesar*, I. ii. 92]

18 For Brutus is an honourable man; / So are they all, all honourable men. [*Julius Caesar*, III. ii. (88)]

19 For new-made honour doth forget men's names. [*King John*, I. i. 87]

20 A jewel in a ten-times-barred-up chest / Is a bold spirit in a loyal breast. / Mine honour is my life; both grow in one; / Take honour from me, and my life is done. [*Richard II*, I. i. 180]

21 And as the sun breaks through the darkest clouds, / So honour peereth in the meanest habit. [*The Taming of the Shrew*, IV. iii. (175)]

22 His honour rooted in dishonour stood, / And faith unfaithful kept him falsely true. [Alfred, Lord Tennyson, 1809–92, *Idylls of the King*, 'Lancelot and Elaine', 871]

HOPE

1 Still nursing the unconquerable hope, / Still clutching the inviolable shade. [Matthew Arnold, 1822–88, *The Scholar-Gypsy*, 211]

2 The heart less bounding at emotion new, / The hope, once crushed, less quick to spring again. [Matthew Arnold, 1822–88, *Thyrsis*, 139]

3 Hope is a good breakfast, but it is a bad supper. [Francis Bacon, 1561–1626, *Apothegms*, 36]

4 Hope deferred maketh the heart sick. [Bible, OT, *Proverbs* 13:12]

5 Charity is the power of defending that which we know to be indefensible. Hope is the power of being cheerful in circumstances which we know to be desperate. [G K Chesterton, 1874–1936, *Heretics*, 12]

6 It is perfection, to be without hope. [Douglas Dunn, 1942– , *The Dilemma*]

7 Because I do not hope to turn again / Because I do not hope / Because I do not hope to turn. [T S Eliot, 1888–1965, *Ash Wednesday*, I]

8 The Worldly Hope men set their Hearts upon / Turns Ashes – or it prospers; and anon, / Like Snow upon the Desert's dusty face, / Lighting a little Hour or two – is gone. [Edward Fitzgerald, 1809–83, *The Rubá'iyát of Omar Khayyám*, Edn 1, 14]

9 He that lives upon hope will die fasting. [Benjamin Franklin, 1706–90, *Poor Richard's Almanac*, Preface, 1758]

10 It's not the despair, Laura. I can stand the despair. It's the hope. [Michael Frayn, 1933– , screenplay of film *Clockwise*, cix]

11 'While there is life, there's hope,' he cried; / 'Then why such haste?' so groaned and died. [John Gay, 1685–1732, *Fables*, Pt I, xxvii, 49]

12 Hope, like the gleaming taper's light, / Adorns and cheers our way; / And still, as darker grows the night, / Emits a brighter ray. [Oliver Goldsmith, 1728–74, *The Captivity*, II]

13 Not, I'll not, carrion comfort, Despair, not feast on thee; / Not untwist – slack they may be – these last strands of man / In me ór, most weary, cry *I can no more*. I can; / Can something, hope, wish day come, not choose not to be. [Gerard Manley Hopkins, 1844–89, *Carrion Comfort*]

14 We must rediscover the distinction between hope and expectation. [Ivan Illich, 1926– , *Deschooling Society*, 7]

15 So farewell hope, and with hope farewell fear, / Farewell remorse: all good to me is lost; / Evil be thou my Good. [John Milton, 1608–74, *Paradise Lost*, Bk iv, 108]

16 Hope springs eternal in the human breast; / Man never is, but always to be blessed. [Alexander Pope, 1688–1744, *An Essay on Man*, I, 95]

17 For hope is but the dream of those that wake. [Matthew Prior, 1664–1721, *Solomon*, III, 102]

18 Hope to catch larks if the heavens fell. [François Rabelais, *c.*1492–1553, *Gargantua*, Ch. 11]

19 The miserable hath no other medicine / But only hope. [William Shakespeare, 1564–1616, *Measure for Measure*, III. i. 2]

20 True hope is swift, and flies with swallow's wings; / Kings it makes gods, and meaner creatures kings. [*Richard III*, V. ii. 23]

21 Hope thou not much, and fear thou not at all. [A C Swinburne, 1837–1909, *Hope and Fear*]

See also ANTICIPATION, DESPAIR, OPTIMISM

HORSES & RACING

1 The libel laws ... have always made it virtually impossible to write a really good racing book about anything but the horses. [Jeffrey Bernard, 1932–97, in *Spectator*, 29 Mar. 1986]

2 One stiff blind horse, his every bone a-stare, / Stood stupefied, however he came there: / Thrust out past service from the devil's stud! [Robert Browning, 1812–89, *Childe Roland to the Dark Tower Came*, 13]

3 Ascot is so exclusive that it is the only racecourse in the world where the horses own the people. [Art Buchwald, 1925– , *I Chose Caviar*, 'Ordeal at Ascot']

4 As lene was his hors as is a rake. [Geoffrey Chaucer, 1340?–1400, *Canterbury Tales*, 'Prologue', 287]

5 Before the gods that made the gods / Had seen their sunrise pass, / The White Horse of the White Horse Vale / Was cut out of the grass. [G K Chesterton, 1874–1936, *The Ballad of the White Horse*, 1]

6 And here I say to parents, especially wealthy parents, 'Don't give your son money. As far as you can afford it, give him horses.' [Winston Churchill, 1874–1965, *My Early Life*, Ch. 4]

7 Some farrier should prescribe his proper course, / Whose only fit companion is his horse. [William Cowper, 1731–1800, *Conversation*, 411]

8 A *dark* horse, which had never been thought of . . . rushed past the grand stand to sweeping triumph. [Benjamin Disraeli, 1804–81, *The Young Duke*, Bk ii, Ch. 5]

9 Dangerous at both ends and uncomfortable in the middle. [(Attr. description of the horse) Ian Fleming, 1908–64, in *The Sunday Times*, 9 Oct. 1966]

10 Oh! doodah day! / Gwine to run all night! / Gwine to run all day! / I bet my money on the bobtail nag. / Somebody bet on the bay. [Stephen Foster, 1826–64, *Camptown Races*]

11 Four things greater than all things are, – / Women and Horses and Power and War. [Rudyard Kipling, 1865–1936, *The Ballad of the King's Jest*]

12 There are no handles to a horse, but the 1910 model has a string to each side of its face for turning its head when there is anything you want it to see. [Stephen Leacock, 1869–1944, *Literary Lapses*, 'Reflections on Riding']

13 He flung himself from the room, flung himself upon his horse and rode madly off in all directions. [Stephen Leacock, 1869–1944, *Nonsense Novels*, 'Gertrude the Governess']

14 It will be Eclipse first, the rest nowhere. [Dennis O'Kelly, 1720?–87, at Epsom, 3 May 1769]

15 I know two things about the horse / And one of them is rather coarse. [Naomi Royde-Smith, ?1875–1964, in Frances and Vera Meynell, *Weekend Book*]

16 Take most people, they're crazy about cars . . . and if they get a brand-new car already they start thinking about trading it in for one that's even newer. I don't even like *old* cars. I mean they don't even interest me. I'd rather have a goddam horse. A horse is at least *human*, for God's sake. [J D Salinger, 1919–   , *The Catcher in the Rye*, Ch. 17]

17 To confess that you are totally Ignorant about the Horse, is social suicide: you will be despised by everybody, especially the horse. [W C Sellar, 1898–1951, and R J Yeatman, 1897–1968, *Horse Nonsense*]

18 A horse! a horse! my kingdom for a horse! [William Shakespeare, 1564–1616, *Richard III*, V. iv. 7]

19 Go anywhere in England where there are natural, wholesome, contented, and really nice English people: and what do you always find? That the stables are the real centre of the household. [George Bernard Shaw, 1856–1950, *Heartbreak House*, III]

20 We attended stables, as we attended church, in our best clothes, thereby no doubt showing the degree of respect due to horses, no less than to the deity. [Osbert Sitwell, 1892–1969, *The Scarlet Tree*, Bk IV, Ch. 2]

21 There is no secret so close as that between a rider and his horse. [R S Surtees, 1803–64, *Mr Sponge's Sporting Tour*, Ch. 31]

22 My horses understand me tolerably well; I converse with them at least four hours every day. They are strangers to bridle or saddle; they live in great amity with me, and friendship to each other. [Jonathan Swift, 1677–1745, *Gulliver's Travels*, 'Voyage to the Houyhnhnms', Ch. 11]

See also HUNTING

HOSPITALITY

1 Let brotherly love continue. / Be not forgetful to entertain strangers: for thereby some have entertained angels unawares. [Bible, NT, *Hebrews* 13:1]

2 I was an hungered, and ye gave me meat: I was thirsty, and ye gave me drink: I was a stranger, and ye took me in. [Bible, NT, *St Matthew* 25:35]

3 Hospitality is a wonderful thing. If people really want you, they'll have you even if the cook has just died in the house of smallpox. [F Scott Fitzgerald, 1896–1940, *Notebooks*, 'E']

4 I entertained on a cruising trip that was so much fun that I had to sink my yacht to make my guests go home. [F Scott Fitzgerald, 1896–1940, *Notebooks*, 'K']

5 The best number for a dinner party is two – myself and a dam' good head waiter. [Nubar Gulbenkian, 1896–1972, in *Daily Telegraph*, 14 Jan. 1965]

6 This was a good dinner enough, to be sure; but it was not a dinner to *ask* a man to. [Dr Samuel Johnson, 1709–84, in James Boswell, *Life of J*, 5 Aug. 1763]

7 Nor was he insincere in saying, 'Make my house / your inn.' / Inns are not residences. [Marianne Moore, 1887–1972, *Silence*]

8 And mighty proud I am (and ought to be thankful to God Almighty) that I am able to have a spare bed for my friends. [Samuel Pepys, 1633–1703, *Diary*, 8 Aug. 1666]

9 Dinner at the Huntercombes' possessed 'only two dramatic features – the wine was a farce and the food a tragedy'. [Anthony Powell, 1905– , *The Acceptance World*, Ch. 4]

10 A free-loader is a confirmed guest. He is the man who is always willing to come to dinner. [Damon Runyon, 1884–1946, *Short Takes*, 'Free-loading Ethics']

11 Unbidden guests / Are often welcomest when they are gone. [William Shakespeare, 1564–1616, *1 Henry VI*, II. ii. 55]

12 My father is a very hospitable man: he keeps six hotels. [George Bernard Shaw, 1856–1950, *Arms and the Man*, I]

See also HOTELS, PUB

HOT & COLD

1 The crawling glaciers pierce me with the spears / Of their moon-freezing crystals, the bright chains / Eat with their burning cold into my bones. [P B Shelley, 1792–1822, *Prometheus Unbound*, I, 31]

2 Heat, ma'am! It was so dreadful here that I found there was nothing left for it but to take off my flesh and sit in my bones. [Sydney Smith, 1771–1845, in Lady Holland, *Memoir*, Vol. i, Ch. 9]

HOTELS

1 We cannot have single gentlemen to come into this establishment and sleep like double gentlemen without paying extra for it ... an equal quantity of slumber was never got out of one bed and bedstead, and if you want to sleep in that way, you must pay for a double-bedded room. [Charles Dickens, 1812–70, *The Old Curiosity Shop*, Ch. 35]

2 A single room is that which has no parts and no magnitude. [Stephen Leacock, 1869–1944, *Literary Lapses*, 'Boarding-house Geometry']

3 I am not the type who wants to go back to the land; I am the type who wants to go back to the hotel. [Fran Lebowitz, ?1948– , *Social Studies*, 'Things']

4 I prefer temperance hotels – although they sell worse liquor than any other kind of hotels. [Artemus Ward, 1834–67, *A W's Lecture*]

See also HOSPITALITY, PUB

HOUSEWORK

1 You cannot have everything and certainly cannot dust everything. To cite Conran's Law of Housework – it expands to fill the time available plus half an hour: so obviously it is never finished ... Keep housework in its place, which, you will remember, is underfoot. [Shirley Conran, 1932– , *Superwoman 2*]

2 There was no need to do any housework at all. After the first four years the dirt doesn't get any worse. [Quentin Crisp, 1908–99, *The Naked Civil Servant*, Ch. 15]

HUMAN BEINGS

1 The miracle of man is not how far he has sunk but how magnificently he has risen. We are known among the stars by our poems, not our corpses. [Robert Ardrey, 1908–80, *African Genesis*; quoted by John Julius Norwich in *Christmas Crackers* (1972)]

2 It is a sorry business to inquire into what men think, when we are every day only too uncomfortably confronted with what they do. [Michael Arlen, 1895–1956, *The Three Cornered Moon*]

3 A wanderer is man from his birth. / He was born in a ship / On the breast of the river of Time. [Matthew Arnold, 1822–88, *The Future*]

4 If men were as much lizards as lizards / They'd

be worth looking at. [W H Auden, 1907–73, *The Dyer's Hand*, 5, 'D. H. Lawrence', epigraph]

5 *Boire sans soif et faire l'amour en tout temps, Madame ; il n'y a que ça qui nous distingue des autres bêtes.* – Drinking when we are not thirsty and making love at all seasons, madam: that is all there is to distinguish us from the other animals. [Pierre-Augustin de Beaumarchais, 1732–99, *The Marriage of Figaro*, II. xxi]

6 Did you know that hamsters mate one day in three and fight two days in three? Just like human beings. [Guy Bellamy, 1935– , *I Have a Complaint to Make*, Ch. 7]

7 Man doth not live by bread only, but by every word that proceedeth out of the mouth of the Lord doth man live. [Bible, OT, *Deuteronomy* 8:3; also *St Matthew* 4:4 and *St Luke* 4:4 (with 'alone' for 'only')]

8 And the Lord God formed man of the dust of the ground, and breathed into his nostrils the breath of life; and man became a living soul. [Bible, OT, *Genesis* 2:7]

9 Man is born unto trouble, as the sparks fly upward. [Bible, OT, *Job* 5:7]

10 Thou hast made him a little lower than the angels. [Bible, OT, *Psalms* 8:5]

11 I am fearfully and wonderfully made. [Bible, OT, *Psalms* 139:14]

12 Every creature of God is good. [Bible, NT, *1 Timothy* 4:4]

13 We carry with us the wonders we seek without us: there is all Africa and her prodigies in us. [Sir Thomas Browne, 1605–82, *Religio Medici*, Pt 1, 15]

14 Man is a noble animal, splendid in ashes, and pompous in the grave. [Sir Thomas Browne, 1605–82, *Urn Burial*, Ch. 5]

15 Thus we are men and we know not how: there is something in us that can be without us, and will be after us. [Sir Thomas Browne, 1605–82, *Religio Medici*, I, 35]

16 We mortals cross the ocean of this world / Each in his average cabin of a life. [Robert Browning, 1812–89, *Bishop Blougram's Apology*, 100]

17 I hate 'Humanity' and all such abstracts: but I love *people*. Lovers of 'Humanity' generally hate *people and children*, and keep parrots or puppy dogs. [Roy Campbell, 1902–57, *Light on a Dark Horse*, Ch. 13]

18 The human race, to which so many of my readers belong, has been playing at children's games from the beginning, and will probably do it till the end, which is a nuisance for the few people who grow up. [G K Chesterton, 1874–1936, *The Napoleon of Notting Hill*, Bk I, Ch. 1]

19 Mankind is not a tribe of animals to which we owe compassion. Mankind is a club to which we owe our subscription. [G K Chesterton, 1874–1936, in *Daily News*, 10 Apr. 1906]

20 Humanity i love you / because you would rather black the boots of / success than enquire whose soul dangles from his / watch-chain which would be embarrassing for both / parties and because you / unflinchingly applaud all / songs containing the words country home and / mother when sung at the old howard [e e cummings, 1894–1962, *Collected Poems* (1938), 107]

21 Humanity i love you because you / are perpetually putting the secret of / life in your pants and forgetting / it's there and sitting down / on it [e e cummings, 1894–1962, *XLI Poems* (1925), 'La Guerre, II']

22 Unless above himself he can / Erect himself, how poor a thing is man. [Samuel Daniel, 1562–1619, *To the Lady Margaret, Countess of Cumberland*, 12]

23 Man with all his noble qualities, with sympathy that feels for the most debased, with benevolence which extends not only to other men but to the humblest living creature, with his god-like intellect which has penetrated into the movements and constitution of the solar system – with all these exalted powers – still bears in his bodily frame the indelible stamp of his lowly origin. [Charles Darwin, 1809–82, *The Descent of Man*, Conclusion]

24 The evolution of the human race will not be accomplished in the ten thousand years of tame animals, but in the million years of wild animals, because man is and will always be a wild animal. [Charles Galton Darwin, 1887–1962, *The Next Million Years*, Ch. 7]

25 What is man, when you come to think upon him, but a minutely set, ingenious machine for turning, with infinite artfulness, the red wine of Shiraz into urine? [Isak Dinesen, 1885–1962, *Seven Gothic Tales*, 'The Dreamers']

26 How many roads must a man walk down / Before you call him a man ? [Bob Dylan, 1941– , song : *Blowin' in the Wind*]

27 I am a little world made cunningly / Of elements, and an angelic spright. [John Donne, 1571 ?–1631, *Holy Sonnets*, 5]

28 This is the porcelain clay of humankind. [John Dryden, 1631–1700, *Don Sebastian*, I. i]

29 People are inexterminable – like flies and bed-bugs. There will always be some that survive in cracks and crevices – that's us. [Robert Frost, 1874–1963 ; *Observer*, 'Sayings of the Week', 29 Mar. 1959]

30 As an archaeology of our thought easily shows, man is an invention of recent date. And one perhaps nearing its end. [Michel Foucault, 1926–84, *The Order of Things*, Ch. 10, sect. vi]

31 The diffrense from a person and an angel is easy : Most of an angel is in the inside and most of a person on the outside. [Anna, in Fynn, *Mister God, This Is Anna*, Ch. 1]

32 Consider that human beings are made up of a small and very unimpressive array of raw materials. They are 80 per cent water and the market value of the chemicals in their production is not much in excess of one pound. [Edward Goldsmith, 1928– , *The Great U-turn*, Ch. 7]

33 Perhaps we are all fictions, father, in the mind of God. [Graham Greene, 1904–91, *Monsignor Quixote*, Pt 1, Ch. 1]

34 Oh wearisome condition of humanity ! / Born under one law, to another bound : / Vainly begot, and yet forbidden vanity ; / Created sick, commanded to be sound. [Fulke Greville, 1554–1628, *Mustapha*, V, iv]

35 The condition of man ... is a condition of war of everyone against everyone. [Thomas Hobbes, 1588–1679, *Leviathan*, Pt I, Ch. 4]

36 The fact that the Matthew Passion, for example, the Hammerklavier Sonata, had had human authors was a source of hope. It was just conceivable that humanity might some day and somehow be made a little more John-Sebastian-like. [Aldous Huxley, 1894–1963, *Eyeless in Gaza*, Ch. 22]

37 We need words to keep us human. Being human is an accomplishment like playing an instrument. It takes practice. [Michael Ignatieff, 1947– , *The Needs of Strangers*, Ch. 4]

38 Cats and monkeys, monkeys and cats – all human life is there. [Henry James, 1843–1916, *The Madonna of the Future*]

39 Men are like wine. Some turn to vinegar, but the best improve with age. [Pope John XXIII, 1881–1963, in Gerald Brenan, *Thoughts in a Dry Season*, 'Life']

40 Humanity does not pass through phases as a train passes through stations : being alive, it has the privilege of always moving yet never leaving anything behind. [C S Lewis, 1898–1963, *The Allegory of Love*, Ch. 1]

41 The long-sought missing link between animals and the really humane being is ourselves. [Konrad Lorenz, 1903–89, on Epigraph to Christa Wolf, *Accident*]

42 What am I, Life ? A thing of watery salt / Held in cohesion by unresting cells, / Which work they know not why, which never halt, / Myself unwitting where their master dwells ? [John Masefield, 1878–1967, *Lollingdon Downs*, Sonnet 37]

43 I'll give you my opinion of the human race in a nutshell ... Their heart's in the right place, but their head is a thoroughly inefficient organ. [W Somerset Maugham, 1874–1965, *The Summing Up*, Ch. 55]

44 People who need people are the luckiest people in the world. [Bob Merrill, 1921–98, song : *People Who Need People*, in musical *Funny Girl*]

45 A human being : an ingenious assembly of portable plumbing. [Christopher Morley, 1890–1957, *Human Being*, Ch. 11]

46 There are one hundred and ninety-three living species of monkeys and apes. One hundred and ninety-two of them are covered with hair. The exception is a naked ape self-named *Homo sapiens*. [Desmond Morris, 1928– , *The Naked Ape*, Introduction]

47 I teach you the superman. Man is something that is to be surpassed. [Friedrich Nietzsche, 1844–1900, *Thus Spake Zarathustra*, Prologue, Ch. 3]

48 Man is the only creature that consumes without producing. [George Orwell, 1903–50, *Animal Farm*, Ch. 1]

49 Man, as he is, is not a genuine article. He is an imitation of something, and a very bad imitation. [P D Ouspensky, 1878–1947, *The Psychology of Man's Possible Evolution*, Ch. 2]

50 Man is no more than a reed, the weakest in nature. But he is a thinking reed. [Blaise Pascal, 1623–62, *Pensées*, VI, 347]

51 Every human being is a whole colony. [Pablo Picasso, 1881–1973, in Françoise Gilot and Carlton Lake, *Life with Picasso*, Pt 1]

52 Chaos of thought and passion, all confused; / Still by himself abused, or disabused; / Created half to rise, and half to fall; / Great Lord of all things, yet a prey to all; / Sole judge of truth, in endless error hurled: / The glory, jest, and riddle of the world! [Alexander Pope, 1688–1744, *An Essay on Man*, II, 13]

53 Human beings are simply archaic, ivy-covered ruins, preserved by the connoisseur, and they stand out oddly in the new world of the masses. [V S Pritchett, 1900–1997, *New Writing and Daylight*, 'The Future of Fiction']

54 Man is the measure of all things. [Protagoras, *c.*485–415 BC, quoted by Plato in *Theaetetus*, 160D]

55 I wish I loved the Human Race; / I wish I loved its silly face; / I wish I liked the way it walks; / I wish I liked the way it talks; / And when I'm introduced to one / I wish I thought *What Jolly Fun!* [Walter A Raleigh, 1861–1922, *Laughter from a Cloud*, 'Wishes of an Elderly Man']

56 Human beings were invented by water as a device for transporting itself from one place to another. [Tom Robbins, 1936– , *Another Roadside Attraction*, Pt I]

57 I'd be a dog, a monkey, or a bear, / Or anything but that vain animal, / Who is so proud of being rational. [Earl of Rochester, 1647–80, *A Satire against Mankind*, 5]

58 Broadly speaking, we are in the middle of a race between human skill as to means and human folly as to ends. [Bertrand Russell, 1872–1970, *The Impact of Science on Society* (1952), Ch. 7]

59 Man is a useless passion. [Jean-Paul Sartre, 1905–80, *Being and Nothingness*, Pt IV, Ch. 2]

60 *Alle Menschen werden Brüder.* – All men become brothers. [Friedrich von Schiller, 1759–1805, *An die Freude*]

61 What is man, the son of man, asks the biochemist, but a container of salt solution in a state of more or less saturation? [Richard Selzer, 1928– , *Confessions of a Knife*, 'Stone']

62 The more I see of men, the more I admire dogs. [Mme de Sévigné, 1626–96, attr.]

63 What a piece of work is a man! How noble in reason! how infinite in faculty! in form, in moving, how express and admirable! in action how like an angel! in apprehension how like a god! the beauty of the world! the paragon of animals! And yet, to me, what is this quintessence of dust? man delights not me; no, nor woman neither. [William Shakespeare, 1564–1616, *Hamlet*, II. ii. (323)]

64 Unaccommodated man is no more but such a poor, bare, forked animal as thou art. [*King Lear*, III. iv. (109)]

65 But man, proud man, / Drest in a little brief authority, / Most ignorant of what he's most assured, / His glassy essence, like an angry ape, / Plays such fantastic tricks before high heaven / As make the angels weep. [*Measure for Measure*, II. ii. 117]

66 Lord, what fools these mortals be! [*A Midsummer Night's Dream*, III. ii. 115]

67 How beauteous mankind is! O brave new world, / That has such people in't! [*The Tempest*, V. i. 183]

68 Wonders are many, and none is more wonderful than man. [Sophocles, 495–406 BC, *Antigone*, 322]

69 Anything one is remembering is a repetition, but existing as a human being, that is being, listening and hearing is never repetition. [Gertrude Stein, 1874–1946, in David Lodge, *Changing Places*, Ch. 5]

70 Man, unlike any other thing organic or inorganic in the universe, grows beyond his work, walks up the stairs of his concepts, emerges ahead of his accomplishments. [John Steinbeck, 1902–68, *The Grapes of Wrath*, Ch. 14]

71 People are getting to be a disgrace to the planet. [Robert Stone, 1937– , *A Flag for Sunrise*, Ch. 6]

72 Glory to Man in the highest! for Man is the master of things. [A C Swinburne, 1837–1909, *Hymn of Man*, last line]

73 Men, my brothers, men the workers, ever reaping something new: / That which they have done but earnest of the things that they shall do. [Alfred, Lord Tennyson, 1809–92, *Locksley Hall*, 117]

74 I am a man, and reckon nothing human alien to me. [Terence, *c.*195–159 BC, *The Self-tormentor*, I, i]

75 As a species, taking all in all, we are still too young, too juvenile, to be trusted. [Lewis Thomas, 1913–93, *Late Night Thoughts*, 'Seven Wonders']

76 Humankind must at last grow up. We must recognize that the Other is ourselves. [E P Thompson, 1924–93, *Beyond the Cold War*]

77 Man is only man at the surface. Remove his skin, dissect, and immediately you come to machinery. [Paul Valéry, 1871–1945, in W H Auden, *A Certain World*]

78 Man is the shuttle, to whose winding quest / And passage through these looms / God ordered motion, but ordained no rest. [Henry Vaughan, 1622–95, *Man*]

79 The children of God should not have any other country here below but the universe itself, with the totality of all the reasoning creatures it ever has contained, contains, or ever will contain. That is the native city to which we owe our love. [Simone Weil, 1909–43, *Waiting on God*, Letter VI]

See also next category

HUMAN NATURE

1 Nature is often hidden; sometimes overcome; seldom extinguished. [Francis Bacon, 1561–1626, *Essays*, 38, 'Of Nature in Men']

2 A man's nature runs either to herbs, or to weeds; therefore let him seasonably water the one, and destroy the other. [Francis Bacon, 1561–1626, *Essays*, 38, 'Of Nature in Men']

3 Human Beings are an untidy lot. They'd lose their arms and legs if they weren't joined on right. [Elisabeth Beresford, *The Wombles*, Ch. 1]

4 Watch and pray, that ye enter not into temptation: the spirit indeed is willing, but the flesh is weak. [Bible, NT, *St Matthew* 26:41]

5 Man partly is and wholly hopes to be. [Robert Browning, 1812–89, *A Death in the Desert*, 588]

6 'Well, of course, people are only human,' said Dudley to his brother, 'but it really does not seem much for them to be.' [Ivy Compton-Burnett, 1884–1969, *A Family and a Fortune*, Ch. 2]

7 Mortals, whose pleasures are their only care, / First wish to be imposed on, and then are. [William Cowper, 1731–1800, *The Progress of Error*, 289]

8 I got disappointed in human nature as well and gave it up because I found it too much like my own. [J P Donleavy, 1926– , *Fairy Tales of New York*, 2]

9 Things are in the saddle, / And ride mankind. [Ralph Waldo Emerson, 1803–82, *Ode, Inscribed to W. H. Channing*]

10 Man cannot live on the human plane, he must be either above or below it. [Eric Gill, 1882–1940, *Autobiography*, Conclusion]

11 We need more understanding of human nature, because the only real danger that exists is man himself... We know nothing of man, far too little. His psyche should be studied because we are the origin of all coming evil. [C G Jung, 1875–1961, in BBC TV 'Face to Face' interview with John Freeman, 22 Oct. 1959]

12 Scenery is fine – but human nature is finer. [John Keats, 1795–1821, letter to Benjamin Bailey, 13 Mar. 1818]

13 Man's ultimate love for man? Yes, yes, but only in the separate darkness of man's love for the present, unknowable God. [D H Lawrence, 1885–1930, *Kangaroo*, Ch. 17]

14 Man, false man, smiling, destructive man. [Nathaniel Lee, 1655–92, *Theodosius*, III, ii]

15 Men have an extraordinarily erroneous opinion of their position in nature; and the error is ineradicable. [W Somerset Maugham, 1874–1965, *A Writer's Notebook*, 1896]

16 Man is always worse than most people suspect, but also generally better than most people dream. [Reinhold Niebuhr, 1892–1971, in *Guardian*, 15 July 1988]

17 We strive all the time to give our life its form, but we do so by copying willy-nilly, like a drawing, the features of the person we are and not of the person we should like to be. [Marcel Proust, 1871–1922, *Remembrance of Things Past: The Guermantes Way*, Ch. 1]

18 Quite a common observation is: 'It takes all sorts to make a world.' This may well be true: but if it is – where are they all? [Idries Shah, 1924–

96, *Reflections*, 'The Difference between Saying and Doing']

19 To suffer woes which hope thinks infinite; / To forgive wrongs darker than death or night; / To defy power, which seems omnipotent; / To love, and bear; to hope till hope creates / From its own wreck the thing it contemplates; /Neither to change, nor falter, nor repent; / This, like thy glory, Titan, is to be / Good, great and joyous, beautiful and free; / This is alone life, joy, empire, and victory. [P B Shelley, 1792–1822, *Prometheus Unbound*, IV, 570]

20 I no more like people personally than I like dogs. When I meet people I am only apprehensive whether they will bite me, which is reasonable and sensible. [Stanley Spencer, 1891–1959, in Maurice Collis, *Stanley Spencer, a Biography*, Ch. 17]

21 Man is a social animal. [Benedict Spinoza, 1632–77, *Ethics*, Pt IV, 35, note]

22 It is not the ape, nor the tiger in man that I fear, it is the donkey. [Archbishop William Temple, 1881–1944, attr.]

23 I loathe the expression 'What makes him tick' . . . A person not only ticks, he also chimes and strikes the hour, falls and breaks and has to be put together again, and sometimes stops like an electric clock in a thunderstorm. [James Thurber, 1894–1961, *Selected Letters from J T*, ed. Helen Thurber and Edward Weeks, letter to Frances Glennon, June 1959, PS]

24 A man is more complex, infinitely more so, than his thoughts. [Paul Valéry, 1871–1945, *Odds and Ends*, VII]

25 Instead of this absurd division into sexes they ought to class people as static and dynamic. [Evelyn Waugh, 1903–66, *Decline and Fall*, III, 7]

26 In or about December, 1910, human *character* changed. [Virginia Woolf, 1882–1941, *The Common Reader*, First Series, 'Mr Bennett and Mrs Brown']

See also previous category

HUMILITY

1 I haven't the humility to find anything beneath me. [Beryl Bainbridge, 1934– , *An Awfully Big Adventure*, 3]

2 Whose shoe's latchet I am not worthy to unloose. [Bible, NT, *St John* 1:27]

3 Go and sit down in the lowest room; that when he that bade thee cometh, he may say to thee, Friend, go up higher. [Bible, NT, *St Luke* 14:10]

4 Whosoever shall exalt himself shall be abased; and he that shall humble himself shall be exalted. [Bible, NT, *St Matthew* 23:12]

5 Humility is only doubt, / And does the sun and moon blot out. [William Blake, 1757–1827, *The Everlasting Gospel*, γ]

6 We are so very 'umble. [(Uriah Heep) Charles Dickens, 1812–70, *David Copperfield*, Ch. 17]

7 The meek shall inherit the earth, but not the mineral rights. [Paul Getty, 1892–1976, attr.]

8 Do good by stealth, and blush to find it fame. [Alexander Pope, 1688–1744, *Epilogue to the Satires*, Dialogue I, 136]

9 I do not know that Englishman alive / With whom my soul is any jot at odds / More than the infant that is born tonight: / I thank my God for my humility. [William Shakespeare, 1564–1616, *Richard III*, II. i. 70]

10 I have often wished I had time to cultivate modesty . . . But I am too busy thinking about myself. [Edith Sitwell, 1887–1964; *Observer*, 'Sayings of the Week', 30 Apr. 1950]

11 Not only humble but umble, which I look upon to be the comparative, or, indeed, superlative degree. [Anthony Trollope, 1815–82, *Doctor Thorne*, Ch. 4]

See also ARROGANCE, MODESTY, PRIDE

HUMOUR

1 I have a fine sense of the ridiculous, but no sense of humour. [Edward Albee, 1928– , *Who's Afraid of Virginia Woolf?*, 1]

2 If it bends, it's funny; if it breaks, it's not funny. [Woody Allen, 1935– , in film *Crimes and Misdemeanours*]

3 Intermingle . . . jest with earnest. [Francis Bacon, 1561–1626, *Essays*, 32, 'Of Discourse']

4 Only a humorist could take humour apart, and he has too much humour to do it. [Robert Benchley, 1889–1945, quoted by James Thurber in *Selected Letters*, ed. Helen Thurber and Edward Weeks, letter to Frances Glennon, 24 June 1959]

5 People should be taught what is, not what should be. All my humour is based on destruction and despair. If the whole world were tranquil, without disease and violence, I'd be standing in the breadline – right back of J. Edgar Hoover. [Lenny Bruce, 1923–66, epigraph to *The Essential Lenny Bruce*, ed. J Cohen]

6 The absurd is born of this confrontation between the human need and the unreasonable silence of the world. [Albert Camus, 1913–60, *The Myth of Sisyphus*, 'Absurd Walls']

7 The absurd is sin without God. [Albert Camus, 1913–60, *The Myth of Sisyphus*, 'Philosophical Suicide']

8 Men will confess to treason, murder, arson, false teeth, or a wig. How many of them will own up to a lack of humour? [Frank Moore Colby, 1865–1925, *Essays*, I, 'Satire and Teeth']

9 Humorists are not happy men. Like Beachcomber or Saki or Thurber they burn while Rome fiddles. [Cyril Connolly, 1903–74, *Enemies of Promise*, Ch. 16]

10 I think there's a terrific merit in having no sense of humour, no sense of irony, practically no sense of anything at all. If you're born with these so-called defects you have a very good chance of getting to the top. That's what's enabled her [Mrs Thatcher] to turn Britain into a cross between Singapore and Telford. [Peter Cook, 1937–95, in *Guardian*, 23 July 1988]

11 The comic is the perception of the opposite; humour is the feeling of it. [Umberto Eco, 1932– , *Travels in Hyperreality*]

12 Funny peculiar, or funny ha-ha? [Ian Hay, 1876–1952, *The Housemaster*, III (catchphrase appears but does not originate here)]

13 And since, I never dare to write / As funny as I can. [Oliver Wendell Holmes, 1809–94, *The Height of the Ridiculous*]

14 Everybody likes a kidder, but nobody lends him money. [Arthur Miller, 1915– , *Death of a Salesman*, I]

15 Everything is funny as long as it's happening to somebody else. [Will Rogers, 1879–1935, *The Illiterate Digest*]

16 Where be your gibes now? your gambols? your songs? your flashes of merriment, that were wont to set the table in a roar? [(Of Yorick) William Shakespeare, 1564–1616, *Hamlet*, IV. vii. (207)]

17 I like humour dry. Charles's splashes. [C P Snow, 1905–80, *The Search*, Pt III, Ch. 2]

18 They [humorists] lead, as a matter of fact, an existence of jumpiness and apprehension. They sit on the edge of the chair of Literature. In the house of Life they have the feeling that they have never taken off their overcoats. [James Thurber, 1894–1961, *My Life and Hard Times*, Preface]

19 Humour . . . is emotional chaos remembered in tranquillity. [James Thurber, 1894–1961, in *New York Post*, 29 Feb. 1960]

20 Humour is counterbalance. Laughter need not be cut out of anything, since it improves anything. The power that created the poodle, the platypus and people has an integrated sense of both comedy and tragedy. [James Thurber, 1894–1961, *Selected Letters*, ed. Helen Thurber and Edward Weeks, letter to Frances Glennon, June 1959]

21 The difficulty with humorists is that they will mix what they believe with what they don't; whichever seems likelier to win an effect. [John Updike, 1932– , *Rabbit, Run*]

See also COMEDY, JOKES, LAUGHTER, WIT

HUNGER

1 Hunger is the best sauce in the world. [Miguel Cervantes, 1547–1616, *Don Quixote*, Pt II, Ch. 5]

2 The war against hunger is truly mankind's war of liberation. [President John F Kennedy, 1917–63, speech at opening of World Food Congress, 4 June 1963]

3 Within a decade no child will go to bed hungry . . . no family will fear for its next day's bread. [Henry Kissinger, 1923– , at World Food Conference, June 1974]

4 A hungry stomach has no ears. [Jean de La Fontaine, 1621–95, *Fables*, IX, 18, 'The Kite and the Nightingale']

5 I have known what it was like to be hungry, but I always went right to a restaurant. [Ring Lardner, 1885–1933, *The Lardners: My Family Remembered*]

6 You cannot feed the hungry on statistics. [David Lloyd George, 1863–1945 (speech on Tariff Reform, 1904), in Malcolm Thomson, *David Lloyd George*, Ch. 8]

7 *Qu'ils mangent de la brioche.* – Let them eat

cake. [Queen Marie-Antoinette, 1755–93, attr., on being told that the people could not afford bread. In fact pre-dated by reference in Rousseau, *Confessions*, Bk vi]

8 You can say that this Administration will have the first complete, far-reaching attack on the problem of hunger in history. Use all the rhetoric, so long as it doesn't cost money. [President Nixon, 1913–94, from official minutes of White House meeting, 17 Mar. 1969]

9 Old Mother Hubbard / Went to the cupboard, / To get her poor dog a bone; / But when she got there, / The cupboard was bare, / And so the poor dog had none. [Nursery rhyme]

10 If this little doll is sitting in your joint all afternoon . . . the best thing to do right now is to throw a feed into her as the chances are her stomach thinks her throat is cut. [Damon Runyon, 1884–1946, *Furthermore*, 'Little Miss Marker']

11 I have two enemies in all the world, / two twins inseparably fused: / the hunger of the hungry and the fullness of the full. [Marina Tsvetayeva, 1892–1941, *If the Soul were Born with Pinions*]

12 Business underlies everything in our national life, including our spiritual life. Witness the fact that in the Lord's Prayer the first petition is for daily bread. No one can worship God or love his neighbour on an empty stomach. [Woodrow Wilson, 1856–1924, speech in New York, 1912]

See also FOOD, GLUTTONY

HUNTING

1 He yaf not of that text a pulled hen, / That seith that hunters been nat holy men. [Geoffrey Chaucer, 1340?–1400, *Canterbury Tales*, 'Prologue', 177]

2 Detested sport, / That owes its pleasures to another's pain. [William Cowper, 1731–1800, *The Task*, Bk III, 326]

3 Three jolly gentlemen, / In coats of red, / Rode their horses / Up to bed. [Walter de la Mare, 1873–1956, *The Huntsmen*]

4 There is a passion for hunting something deeply implanted in the human breast. [Charles Dickens, 1812–70, *Oliver Twist*, Ch. 10]

5 The hounds all join in glorious cry, / The huntsman winds his horn: / And a-hunting we will go. [Henry Fielding, 1707–54, *A-Hunting We Will Go*]

6 D'ye ken John Peel with his coat so gay? / D'ye ken John Peel at the break of the day? / D'ye ken John Peel when he's far far away / With his hounds and his horn in the morning? [J W Graves, 1795–1886, song: *John Peel*]

7 Most of their discourse was about hunting, in a dialect I understand very little. [Samuel Pepys, 1633–1703, *Diary*, 22 Nov. 1663]

8 Hunting he loved, but love he laughed to scorn. [William Shakespeare, 1564–1616, *Venus and Adonis*, 4]

9 The chase, the sport of kings; / Image of war, without its guilt. [William Somerville, 1675–1742, *The Chase*, I, 13]

10 Women never look so well as when one comes in wet and dirty from hunting. [R S Surtees, 1803–64, *Mr Sponge's Sporting Tour*, Ch. 21]

11 *J'aime le son du cor, le soir, au fond des bois.* – I love the sound of the horn, at evening, from the depths of the woods. [Alfred de Vigny, 1797–1863, *Le Cor*]

12 The English country gentleman galloping after a fox – the unspeakable in full pursuit of the uneatable. [Oscar Wilde, 1854–1900, *A Woman of No Importance*, I]

13 It was a confusion of ideas between him and one of the lions he was hunting in Kenya that had caused A. B. Spottsworth to make the obituary column. He thought the lion was dead, and the lion thought it wasn't. [P G Wodehouse, 1881–1975, *Ring for Jeeves*, Ch. 1]

14 Whoso list to hunt, I know where is an hind, / But as for me, alas, I may no more. [Sir Thomas Wyatt, 1503?–42, *Whoso List to Hunt*]

See also HORSES

HUSBANDS

1 Being a husband is a whole-time job. That is why so many husbands fail. They cannot give their entire attention to it. [Arnold Bennett, 1867–1931, *The Title*, I]

2 Husbands, love your wives, and be not bitter against them. [Bible, NT, *Colossians* 3:19]

3 Ah, gentle dames! It gars me greet / To think how mony counsels sweet, / How mony lengthen'd sage advices, / The husband frae the wife despises! [Robert Burns, 1759–96, *Tam o' Shanter*, 33]

4 She was a worthy womman al hir lyve: / Housbondes at chirche-dore she hadde fyve, / Withouten other companye in youthe. [Geoffrey Chaucer, 1340?–1400, *Canterbury Tales*, 'Prologue', 459]

5 An archaeologist is the best husband any woman can have: the older she gets, the more interested he is in her. [Agatha Christie, 1890–1976, ascr. in news report, 9 Mar. 1954]

6 If I marry, Sir Sampson, I'm for a good estate with any man, and for any man with a good estate. [William Congreve, 1670–1729, *Love for Love*, III. v]

7 Composed that monstrous animal a husband and wife. [Henry Fielding, 1707–54, *Tom Jones*, Bk xv, 9]

8 [When asked how many husbands she had had] You mean apart from my own? [Zsa Zsa Gabor, 1919– , on US TV, 1985; in *Chambers Film Quotes*, comp. Tony Crawley]

9 In that moment it burst upon me that I had been living here these eight years with a strange man, and had borne him three children. [Henrik Ibsen, 1828–1906, *A Doll's House*, III]

10 It's not the seven deadly virtues that make a man a good husband, but the three hundred pleasing amiabilities. [W Somerset Maugham, 1874–1965, *The Constant Wife*, I]

11 JOHN: Do you think I can't be a lover as well as a husband?

CONSTANCE: My dear, no one can make yesterday's cold mutton into tomorrow's lamb cutlets. [W Somerset Maugham, 1874–1965, *The Constant Wife*, III]

12 He tells you when you've got on / too much lipstick, / And helps you with your girdle / when your hips stick. [Ogden Nash, 1902–71, *The Perfect Husband*]

13 A husband is what is left of the lover after the nerve has been extracted. [Helen Rowland, 1875–1950, *A Guide to Men*, 'Prelude']

14 A young man married is a man that's marred. [William Shakespeare, 1564–1616, *All's Well that Ends Well*, II. iii. (315)]

15 For a light wife doth make a heavy husband. [*The Merchant of Venice*, V. i. 130]

16 I could not endure a husband with a beard on his face: I had rather lie in the woollen. [*Much Ado About Nothing*, II. i. (31)]

17 In marriage, a man becomes slack and selfish, and undergoes a fatty degeneration of his moral being. [Robert Louis Stevenson, 1850–94, *Virginibus Puerisque*, I, 1]

18 He will hold thee, when his passion shall have spent its novel force, / Something better than his dog, a little dearer than his horse. [Alfred, Lord Tennyson, 1809–92, *Locksley Hall*, 49]

19 Chumps always make the best husbands. When you marry, Sally, grab a chump. Tap his forehead first, and if it rings solid, don't hesitate. All the unhappy marriages come from the husbands having brains. What good are brains to a man? They only unsettle him. [P G Wodehouse, 1881–1975, *The Adventures of Sally*, Ch. 10]

See also MARRIAGE, WIVES

HYPOCRISY

1 It is the wisdom of the crocodiles, that shed tears when they would devour. [Francis Bacon, 1561–1626, *Essays*, 23, 'Of Wisdom for a Man's Self']

2 The words of his mouth were smoother than butter, but war was in his heart: his words were softer than oil, yet were they drawn swords. [Bible, OT, *Psalms* 55:21]

3 Which devour widows' houses, and for a pretence make long prayers. [Bible, NT, *St Mark* 12:40]

4 Ye are like unto whited sepulchres, which indeed appear beautiful outward, but are within full of dead men's bones, and of all uncleanness. [Bible, NT, *St Matthew* 23:27]

5 Compound for sins, they are inclined to / By damning those they have no mind to. [Samuel Butler, 1612–80, *Hudibras*, 1, i, 213]

6 That vice pays homage to virtue is notorious; we call it hypocrisy. [Samuel Butler, 1835–1902, *The Way of All Flesh*, Ch. 19]; see 14

7 'I weep for you,' [the oysters he was about to eat] the Walrus said: / 'I deeply sympathize.' / With sobs and tears he sorted out / Those of the largest size, / Holding his pocket-handkerchief / Before his streaming eyes. [Lewis Carroll, 1832–98, *Through the Looking Glass*, Ch. 4]

8 The carl spak oo thing, but he thoghte another. [Geoffrey Chaucer, 1340?–1400, *Canterbury Tales*, 'The Friar's Tale', 270]

9 The smyler with the knyf under the cloke. [Geoffrey Chaucer, 1340?–1400, *Canterbury Tales*, 'The Knight's Tale', 1141]

10 We ought to see far enough into a hypocrite to see even his sincerity. [G K Chesterton, 1874–1936, *Heretics*, 5]

11 Though we all disguise our feelings pretty well, / What we mean by 'Very good' is 'Go to hell'. [Noël Coward, 1899–1973, *Bitter Sweet*, I. ii]

12 The true hypocrite is the one who ceases to perceive his deception, the one who lies with sincerity. [André Gide, 1869–1951, *Journal of 'The Counterfeiters'*, Second Notebook, Aug. 1921]

13 My dear friend, clear your *mind* of cant. [Dr Samuel Johnson, 1709–84, in James Boswell, *Life of J*, 15 May 1783]

14 Hypocrisy is the homage paid by vice to virtue. [Duc de La Rochefoucauld, 1613–80, *Maxims*, 218]; see 6

15 Hypocrisy is the most difficult and nerve-racking vice that any man can pursue; it needs an unceasing vigilance and a rare detachment of spirit. It cannot, like adultery or gluttony, be practised at spare moments; it is a whole time job. [W Somerset Maugham, 1874–1965, *Cakes and Ale*, Ch. 1]

16 Cover that bosom. I must not see it. Souls are wounded by such things, and they arouse wicked thoughts. [Molière, 1622–73, *Tartuffe*, III. ii]

17 With devotion's visage / And pious action we do sugar o'er / The devil himself. [William Shakespeare, 1564–1616, *Hamlet*, III. i. 47]

18 And thus I clothe my naked villany / With odd old ends stol'n forth of holy writ, / And seem a saint when most I play the devil. [*Richard III*, I. iii. 336]

19 There is plenty of humbug in hell. [George Bernard Shaw, 1856–1950, *Man and Superman*, III]

20 Making the world safe for hypocrisy. [Thomas Wolfe, 1900–1938, *Look Homeward, Angel*, Pt III, Ch. 36]

See also HONESTY, INTEGRITY

I

IDEALS

1 Give Mr Bast money and don't worry about his ideals. He'll pick up those for himself. [E M Forster, 1879–1970, *Howards End*, Ch. 15]

2 Oh, life would be all right if we didn't have to put up with these damned creditors who keep pestering us with the demands of their ideals. [Henrik Ibsen, 1828–1906, *The Wild Duck*, V]

3 Whenever one comes to close grips with so-called idealism, as in war time, one is shocked by its rascality. [H L Mencken, 1880–1956, *Minority Report*, 223]

4 There aren't any good, brave causes left. [John Osborne, 1929–94, *Look Back in Anger*, III. i]

5 We are all in the gutter, but some of us are looking at the stars. [Oscar Wilde, 1854–1900, *Lady Windermere's Fan*, II]

IDEAS

1 Nothing is more dangerous than an idea when that's the only one you have got. [Alain, 1868–1951, *Propos sur la religion*, 74]

2 Between the idea / And the reality / Between the motion / And the act / Falls the Shadow. [T S Eliot, 1888–1965, *The Hollow Men*, V]

3 I maintain that ideas are events. It is more difficult to make them interesting, I know, but if you fail the style is at fault. [Gustave Flaubert, 1821–80, letter to Louise Colet, 15 Jan. 1853]

4 It is better to entertain an idea than to take it home to live with you for the rest of your life. [Randall Jarrell, 1914–65, *Pictures from an Institution*, Pt IV, Ch. 9]

5 It is with ideas as with umbrellas, if left lying about they are peculiarly liable to change of ownership. [Thomas Kettle, 1880–1916, from his wife's memoir; in *Book of Irish Quotations*, ed. Sean McMahon. There are other claimants]

6 In a war of ideas it is people who get killed. [Stanislaw Lec, 1909–66, *Unkempt Thoughts*, p. 105]

7 'Dying for an idea,' again, sounds well enough, but why not let the idea die instead of you? [Percy Wyndham Lewis, 1882–1957, *The Art of Being Ruled*, Pt I, Ch. 1]

8 An idea isn't responsible for the people who believe in it. [Don Marquis, 1878–1937, *New York Sun*, 'The Sun Dial']

9 When you are a Bear of Very Little Brain, and you Think of Things, you find sometimes that a Thing which seemed very Thingish inside you is quite different when it gets out into the open and has other people looking at it. [A A Milne, 1882–1956, *House at Pooh Corner*, Ch. 6]

10 A powerful idea communicates some of its power to the man who contradicts it. [Marcel Proust, 1871–1922, *Remembrance of Things Past: Within a Budding Grove*, 'Madame Swann at Home']

11 You can't massacre an idea, you cannot run tanks over hope. [Ronald Reagan, 1911– (of Chinese repression of student demonstrations), Churchill Lecture at Guildhall, London, 13 June 1989]

12 Delightful task! to rear the tender thought, / To teach the young idea how to shoot. [James Thomson, 1700–1748, *The Seasons*, 'Spring', 1152]

13 Ideas that enter the mind under fire remain there securely and for ever. [Leon Trotsky, 1874–1940, *My Life*, Ch. 35]

14 A serious man has few ideas. A man of many ideas cannot be serious. [Paul Valéry, 1871–1945, *Analects*, I]

See also JUDGEMENT, OPINIONS, THINKING

IDLENESS, see LAZINESS

IGNORANCE

1 Where people wish to attach, they should always be ignorant. To come with a well informed mind, is to come with an inability of administering to the vanity of others, which a sensible person would always wish to avoid. A woman especially, if she have the misfortune of knowing any thing, should conceal it as well as she can. [Jane Austen, 1775–1817, *Northanger Abbey*, Ch. 14]

2 Spontaneity is only a term for man's ignorance of the gods. [Samuel Butler, 1835–1902, *Erewhon*, 25]

3 In fact, I'm about as useful as Linda Lovelace with lockjaw. [Prince Charles, 1948– (at a private dinner, confessing his ignorance of the subject under discussion), in S Hoggart, *On the House*, p. 96]

4 Mr Kremlin himself was distinguished for ignorance, for he had only one idea, – and that was wrong. [Benjamin Disraeli, 1804–81, *Sybil*, Bk iv, 5]

5 Thought would destroy their paradise. / No more; where ignorance is bliss, / 'Tis folly to be wise. [Thomas Gray, 1716–71, *Ode on a Distant Prospect of Eton College*, 10]

6 Ignorance alone makes monsters or bugbears; our actual acquaintances are all very common-place people. [William Hazlitt, 1778–1830, *Why Distant Objects Please*]

7 Ignorance, Madam, pure ignorance. [(On being asked how, in his *Dictionary*, he came to define *Pastern* as the knee of a horse) Dr Samuel Johnson, 1709–84, in James Boswell, *Life of J*, 1755]

8 Education costs money, but then so does ignorance. [Claus Moser, 1922– , speech at British Association, Swansea, 20 Aug. 1990]

9 Our knowledge can only be finite, while our ignorance must necessarily be infinite. [Karl Popper, 1902–94, *Conjectures and Refutations*]

10 Everybody is ignorant, only on different subjects. [Will Rogers, 1879–1935, *The Illiterate Digest*, 'Defending My Soup Plate']

11 What you don't know would make a great book. [Sydney Smith, 1771–1845, in Lady Holland, *Memoir*, Vol. i, Ch. 11]

12 The most powerful weapon of ignorance – the diffusion of printed material. [Leo Tolstoy, 1828–1910, *War and Peace*, Epilogue, Pt II, Ch. 8]

13 Harold Ross, a man who knew nothing ... and had a contempt for anything he didn't understand, which was practically everything. [Alexander Woollcott, 1887–1943, in James Thurber, *The Years with Ross*, Ch. 15]

See also KNOWLEDGE, STUPIDITY

ILLEGITIMACY

1 If you please, ma'am, it was a very little one. [(Excusing an illegitimate baby) Captain Marryat, 1792–1848, *Midshipman Easy*, Ch. 31]

2 Why brand they us / With base? with baseness? bastardy? base, base? / ... Edmund the base / Shall top the legitimate:–I grow, I prosper; / Now, gods stand up for bastards! [William Shakespeare, 1564–1616, *King Lear*, I. ii. 9 and 20]

3 He is always breaking the law. He broke the law when he was born: his parents were not married. [George Bernard Shaw, 1856–1950, *Major Barbara*, I]

ILLNESS & CURE

1 My sore throats are always worse than anyone's. [Jane Austen, 1775–1817, *Persuasion*, Ch. 18]

2 Cure the disease and kill the patient. [Francis Bacon, 1561–1626, *Essays*, 27, 'Of Friendship']

3 They that be whole need not a physician, but they that are sick. [Bible, NT, *St Matthew* 9:12]

4 I've just learnt about his illness; let's hope it's nothing trivial. [Irvin S Cobb, 1876–1944; in *Treasury of Humorous Quotations*, ed. Evan Esar and Nicolas Bentley. Elsewhere attr. to Winston Churchill on Aneurin Bevan]

5 *Tous les jours, à tous points de vue, je vais de mieux en mieux.* – Every day, in every way, I'm getting better and better. [Emil Coué, 1857–1926, formula of his faith-cures]

6 The nurse sleeps sweetly, hired to watch the sick, / Whom, snoring, she disturbs. [William Cowper, 1731–1800, *The Task*, Bk I, 'The Sofa', 89]

7 And *so* poorly and *so* run down. She says her blood is nothing but rose-water. [Ronald Firbank, 1886–1926, *Valmouth*, Ch. 4]

8 Much of the world's work, it has been said, is done by men who do not feel quite well. Marx is a case in point. [J K Galbraith, 1908– , *The Age of Uncertainty*, Ch. 3]

9 Hungry Joe collected lists of fatal diseases and arranged them in alphabetical order so that he could put his finger without delay on any one he wanted to worry about. [Joseph Heller, 1923–99, *Catch-22*, Ch. 17]

10 I never read a patent medicine advertisement without being impelled to the conclusion that I am suffering from the particular disease therein dealt with in its most virulent form. [Jerome K Jerome, 1859–1927, *Three Men in a Boat*, Ch. 1]

11 It is a curious fact, but nobody ever is sea-sick – on land. [Jerome K Jerome, 1859–1927, *Three Men in a Boat*, Ch. 1]

12 I've a head like a concertina, I've a tongue like a button-stick, / I've a mouth like an old potato, and I'm more than a little sick. [Rudyard Kipling, 1865–1936, *Cells*]

13 How sickness enlarges the dimensions of a man's self to himself. [Charles Lamb, 1775–1834, *Last Essays of Elia*, 'The Convalescent']

14 I am only half there when I am ill, and so there is only half a man to suffer. To suffer in one's whole self is so great a violation, that it is not to be endured. [D H Lawrence, 1885–1930, letter to Catherine Carswell, 16 Apr. 1916]

15 In the good old days, you got ill, you were poor, you died. Today, everyone seems to think they have the right to be cured. Result of this sloppy socialist thinking? More poor people. [Laurence Marks, 1948– , and Maurice Gran, 1949– , YTV series, *New Statesman*, 'Sex is Wrong']

16 Illness is in part what the world has done to a victim, but in a larger part it is what the victim has done with his world, and with himself. [Karl Menninger, 1893–1990, quoted in Susan Sontag, *Illness as Metaphor*, Ch. 6]

17 It's only a little cold I have; there's nothing derogatory wrong with me. [Sean O'Casey, 1880–1964, *The Plough and the Stars*, I]

18 She sighs for ever on her pensive bed, / Pain at her side, and Megrim at her head. [Alexander Pope, 1688–1744, *The Rape of the Lock*, IV, 23]

19 Illness is the most heeded of doctors: to kindness and wisdom we make promises only; pain we obey. [Marcel Proust, 1871–1922, *Remembrance of Things Past: Cities of the Plain*, Pt II, Ch. 1]

20 [George Mandel:] 'He's [Joseph Heller's] got something called Guillain-Barré.' 'My God,' Mario blurted out. 'That's terrible.' A surprised George murmured, 'Hey, Mario, you know about Guillain-Barré?' 'No, I never heard nothing about it,' Mario replied. 'But when they name any disease after two guys, it's got to be terrible.' [Mario Puzo, 1920–99, in Joseph Heller and Speed Vogel, *No Laughing Matter*, p. 44]

21 Health is infinite and expansive in mode, and reaches out to be filled with the fullness of the world; whereas disease is finite and reductive in mode, and endeavours to reduce the world to itself. [Oliver Sacks, 1933– , *Awakenings*, 'Perspectives']

22 At the time, a refined family had to include at least one delicate child. I was a perfect subject because I had some thought of dying at birth. [Jean-Paul Sartre, 1905–80, *Words*, Pt 1]

23 Illness is the night-side of life, a more onerous citizenship. Everyone who is born holds dual citizenship, in the kingdom of the well and in the kingdom of the sick. Although we all prefer to use only the good passport, sooner or later each of us is obliged, at least for a spell, to identify ourselves as citizens of that other place. [Susan Sontag, 1933– , *Illness as Metaphor*, opening words]

24 In home-sickness you must keep moving – it is the only disease that does not require rest. [H de Vere Stacpoole, 1863–1951, *The Bourgeois*]

25 We are so fond of one another, because our ailments are the same. [Jonathan Swift, 1677–1745, *Journal to Stella*, 1 Feb. 1711]

26 Most of the time we think we're sick, it's all in the mind. [Thomas Wolfe, 1900–1938, *Look Homeward, Angel*, Pt I, Ch. 1]

See also DOCTORS, HEALTH

ILLUSION

1 Beware that you do not lose the substance by grasping at the shadow. [Aesop, *fl* *c*.550 BC, *Fables*, 'The Dog and the Shadow']

2 I saw the sunlit vale, and the pastoral fairy-tale; / The sweet and bitter scent of the may drifted by; / But it looked like a lie, / Like a kindly meant lie. [Edmund Blunden, 1896–1974, *The Sunlit Vale*]

3 Take care, your worship, those things over there are not giants but windmills. [Miguel Cervantes, 1547–1616, *Don Quixote*, Pt I, Ch. 8]

4 If the red slayer thinks he slays, / Or if the slain think he is slain, / They know not well the subtle ways / I keep, and pass, and turn again. [Ralph Waldo Emerson, 1803–82, *Brahma*]

5 *Alles Vergängliche / Ist nur ein Gleichnis.* – All that is transitory is only an image. [Johann Wolfgang von Goethe, 1749–1832, *Faust*, Pt 2, V]

6 I was never much displeased with those harmless delusions that tend to make us more happy. [Oliver Goldsmith, 1728–74, *The Vicar of Wakefield*, Ch. 3]

7 Not all that tempts your wand'ring eyes / And heedless hearts, is lawful prize; / Nor all that glisters, gold. [Thomas Gray, 1716–71, *Ode on the Death of a Favourite Cat*]

8 Deprive the average human being of his life-lie, and you rob him of his happiness. [Henrik Ibsen, 1828–1906, *The Wild Duck*, V]

9 That white horse you see in the park could be a zebra synchronized with the railings. [Ann Jellicoe, 1927– , *The Knack*, III]

10 Hence, vain deluding joys, / The brood of Folly without father bred. [John Milton, 1608–74, *Il Penseroso*, 1]

11 [Burke] is not affected by the reality of distress touching his heart, but by the showy resemblance of it striking his imagination. He pities the plumage, but forgets the dying bird. [Thomas Paine, 1737–1809 (of *Reflections on the Revolution in France*), *The Rights of Man*, Pt I]

12 Here we are again with both feet firmly planted in the air. [Hugh Scanlon, 1913– , on his union's attitude to the Common Market; in *Observer*, 'Sayings of the Year', 30 Dec. 1973]

13 The earth hath bubbles, as the water has, / And these are of them. [William Shakespeare, 1564–1616, *Macbeth*, I. iii. 79]

14 Is this a dagger which I see before me, / The handle toward my hand? Come, let me clutch thee: / I have thee not, and yet I see thee still, / Art thou not, fatal vision, sensible / To feeling as to sight? or art thou but / A dagger of the mind, a false creation, / Proceeding from the heat-oppressèd brain? [*Macbeth*, II. i. 33]

15 Our revels now are ended. These our actors, / As I foretold you, were all spirits and / Are melted into air, into thin air: / And, like the baseless fabric of this vision, / The cloud-capped towers, the gorgeous palaces, / The solemn temples, the great globe itself, / Yea, all which it inherit, shall dissolve / And, like this insubstantial pageant faded, / Leave not a rack behind. [*The Tempest*, IV. i. 148]

See also next category, DREAMS, VISIONS

IMAGINATION

1 A lady's imagination is very rapid; it jumps from admiration to love, from love to matrimony in a moment. [Jane Austen, 1775–1817, *Pride and Prejudice*, 6]

2 Just when we are safest, there's a sunset-touch, / A fancy from a flower-bell, someone's death, / A chorus-ending from Euripides, – / And that's enough for fifty hopes and fears / As old and new at once as nature's self, / To rap and knock and enter in our soul. [Robert Browning, 1812–89, *Bishop Blougram's Apology*, John Murray edn, Vol. I, 531, 17]

3 Imagination droops her pinion [Lord Byron, 1788–1824, *Don Juan*, IV, 3]

4 The primary imagination I hold to be the living power and prime agent of all human perception, and as a repetition in the finite mind of the eternal act of creation in the infinite I AM. [Samuel Taylor Coleridge, 1772–1834, *Biographia Literaria*, Ch. 13]

5 The Fancy is indeed no other than a mode of memory emancipated from the order of time and space. [Samuel Taylor Coleridge, 1772–1834, *Biographia Literaria*, Ch. 13]

6 Where there is no imagination there is no horror. [Arthur Conan Doyle, 1859–1930, *A Study in Scarlet*, Ch. 5]

7 The imagination of a boy is healthy, and the mature imagination of a man is healthy; but there is a space of life between, in which the soul is in a ferment, the character undecided, the way of life uncertain, the ambition thick-sighted: thence proceeds mawkishness. [John Keats, 1795–1821, *Endymion*, Preface]

8 All the gardener Fancy e'er could feign, / Who breeding flowers, will never breed the same. [John Keats, 1795–1821, *Ode to Psyche*, 62]

9 I am certain of nothing but the holiness of the heart's affections and the truth of the imagination. – What the imagination seizes as beauty must be truth. [John Keats, 1795–1821, letter to Benjamin Bailey, 22 Nov. 1817]

10 The life of nations no less than that of men is lived largely in the imagination. [Enoch Powell, 1912–98, said in 1946, epigraph to Martin J Wiener, *English Culture and the Decline of the Industrial Spirit, 1850–1980*]

11 My imaginations are as foul / As Vulcan's stithy. [William Shakespeare, 1564–1616, *Hamlet*, III. ii (88)]

12 Give me an ounce of civet, good apothecary, to sweeten my imagination. [*King Lear*, IV. vi. (133)]

13 Tell me where is fancy bred, / Or in the heart or in the head? How begot, how nourishèd? [*The Merchant of Venice*, III. ii. 63]

14 The lunatic, the lover, and the poet, / Are of imagination all compact. [*A Midsummer Night's Dream*, V. i. 7]

15 As imagination bodies forth / The forms of things unknown, the poet's pen / Turns them to shapes, and gives to airy nothing / A local habitation and a name. [*A Midsummer Night's Dream*, V. i. 14]

16 So full of shapes is fancy, / That it alone is high fantastical. [*Twelfth Night*, I. i. 9]

17 Skill without imagination is craftsmanship and gives us many useful objects such as wickerwork picnic baskets. Imagination without skill gives us modern art. [Tom Stoppard, 1937– , *Artist Descending a Staircase*]

18 Hence in a season of calm weather / Though inland far we be, / Our souls have sight of that immortal sea / Which brought us hither, / Can in a moment travel thither, / And see the children sport upon the shore, / And hear the mighty waters rolling evermore. [William Wordsworth, 1770–1850, *Ode, Intimations of Immortality*, 9]

See also previous category, DREAMS, VISIONS

IMITATION

1 The advantage of having imitators is that at last they cure you of yourself. [Jorge Luis Borges, 1899–1986, quoted by Philip Roth in interview in *Independent*, 2 Sept. 1990]

2 Every man is a borrower and a mimic, life is theatrical and literature a quotation. [Ralph Waldo Emerson, 1803–82, *Society and Solitude*, 'Success']

3 When people are free to do as they please, they usually imitate each other. [Eric Hoffer, 1902–83, *The Passionate State of Mind*, aphorism 33]

4 It is to what I have called the Apes of God that I am drawing your attention – *those prosperous mountebanks who alternately imitate and mock at and traduce those figures they at once admire and hate*. [Percy Wyndham Lewis, 1882–1957, *The Apes of God*, Pt III]

5 As to the rest, I am no more guilty of imitating 'real life' than 'real life' is responsible for plagiarizing me. [Vladimir Nabokov, 1899–1977, *Nabokov's Dozen*, Bibliographical Note]

6 JENNY: What was known as art silk –
TIM: Like art cinema –
JENNY: It wasn't really silk at all. [John Osborne, 1929–94, *Look under Plain Cover*]

7 He was indeed the glass / Wherein the noble youth did dress themselves. [William Shakespeare, 1564–1616, *2 Henry IV*, II. iii. 21]

IMMORTALITY

1 I don't want to achieve immortality through my work ... I want to achieve it through not dying. [Woody Allen, 1935– , in E Lax, *W A and His Comedy*, Ch. 12]

2 Because we all have been for all time: I and thou, and those kings of men. And we all shall be from all time, we all for ever and ever.

As the Spirit of our mortal body wanders on in childhood, and youth and old age, the Spirit wanders on to a new body: of this the sage has no doubts. [*Bhagavad Gita*, 2nd millenium BC, Ch. 2, 12]

3 There is not room for Death, / Nor atom that his might could render void: / Thou – Thou art Being and Breath, / And what Thou art may never be destroyed. [Emily Brontë, 1818–48, *Last Lines*]

4 The secret of my universe: to imagine God without human mortality. [Albert Camus, 1913–60, *Notebooks*, iv: 1942]

5 Because I could not stop for Death, / He kindly stopped for me; / The carriage held but just ourselves / And Immortality. [Emily Dickinson, 1830–86, *The Chariot*]

6 If you were to destroy in mankind the belief in immortality, not only love but every living force maintaining the life of the world would at once be dried up. Moreover, nothing then would be immortal, everything would be permissible, even cannibalism. [Fyodor Dostoyevsky, 1821–81, *Brothers Karamazov*, Pt I, Bk i, Ch. 6]

7 Oh may I join the choir invisible / Of those immortal dead who live again / In minds made better by their presence. [George Eliot, 1819–80, *Poems*, 'Oh May I Join the Choir Invisible']

8 He had decided to live for ever or die in the attempt. [Joseph Heller, 1923–99, *Catch-22*, Ch. 3]

9 *Exegi monumentum aere perennius.* – I have completed a monument more lasting than brass. [Horace, 65–8 BC, *Odes*, III, xxx, 1]

10 She cannot fade, though thou hast not thy bliss, / For ever wilt thou love and she be fair. [John Keats, 1795–1821, *Ode on a Grecian Urn*, 2]

11 Thou wast not born for death, immortal Bird! / No hungry generations tread thee down; / The voice I hear this passing night was heard / In ancient days by emperor and clown: / Perhaps the self-same song that found a path / Through the sad heart of Ruth, when, sick for home, / She stood in tears amid the alien corn; / The same that oft-times hath / Charmed magic casements, opening on the foam / Of perilous seas, in faery lands forlorn. [John Keats, 1795–1821, *Ode to a Nightingale*, 6]

12 The immortality of the soul! What a boring conception! Can't think of anything worse than living for infinity in a great transcendental hotel, with nothing to do in the evenings. [John Mortimer, 1923– , *A Voyage round My Father*, II]

13 All our calm is in that balm – / Not lost but gone before. [Caroline Norton, 1808–77, *Not Lost But Gone Before*]

14 Stuck with placards for 'Deathless', that bitter beer that tastes sweet to its drinkers. [Rainer Maria Rilke, 1875–1926, *Duino Elegies*, 10]

15 Here was the world's worst wound. And here with pride / 'Their name liveth for ever,' the Gateway claims. / Was ever an immolation so belied / As these intolerably nameless names? [Siegfried Sassoon, 1886–1967, *On Passing the New Menin Gate*]

16 Give me my robe, put on my crown; I have / Immortal longings in me. [William Shakespeare, 1564–1616, *Antony and Cleopatra*, V. ii. (282)]

17 But thy eternal summer shall not fade. [*Sonnets*, 18]

18 He has outsoared the shadow of our night; / Envy and calumny and hate and pain, / And that unrest which men miscall delight, / Can touch him not and torture not again; / From the contagion of the world's slow stain / He is secure. [P B Shelley, 1792–1822, *Adonais*, 352]

19 We feel and know that we are eternal. [Benedict Spinoza, 1632–77, *Ethics*, Pt V, 23, note]

20 But felt through all this fleshly dress / Bright shoots of everlastingness. [Henry Vaughan, 1622–95, *The Retreat*]

21 But the race remains immortal, the star of their house is constant through many years, and the grandfather's grandfathers are numbered in the roll. [Virgil, 70–19 BC, *Georgics*, IV, 208]

22 Dust as we are, the immortal spirit grows / Like harmony in music; there is a dark / Inscrutable workmanship that reconciles / Discordant elements. [William Wordsworth, 1770–1850, *The Prelude*, I, 340]

See also DEATH, ETERNITY, LIFE & DEATH, LIMBO

IMPOSSIBILITY & POSSIBILITY

1 A plausible impossibility is always preferable to an unconvincing possibility. [Aristotle, 384–322 BC, *Poetics*, 24]

2 Go, and catch a falling star, / Get with child a mandrake root, / Tell me, where all past years are, / Or who cleft the Devil's foot. [John Donne, 1571?–1631, song: *Go and Catch* . . .]

3 In two words: im-possible. [Samuel Goldwyn, 1882–1974 (attr. – by Charles Chaplin? – but apocryphal), in Alva Johnston, *The Great Goldwyn*]

4 The difficult is what takes a little time; the impossible is what takes a little longer. [Fridtjof Nansen, 1861–1930. Also attr. to others. Variant form was motto placarded at South-East Asia HQ in 1939–45 war]; see 6

5 The world is the sum-total of our vital possibilities. [José Ortega y Gasset, 1883–1955, *The Revolt of the Masses*, Ch. 4]

6 Difficult things take a long time, the impossible takes a little longer. [Chaim Weizmann, 1874–1952, in V Weizmann, *The Impossible Takes Longer*]; see 4

7 Possible? Is anything impossible? Read the newspapers. [Duke of Wellington, 1769–1852, quoted in *Words of W*]

8 'Alf Todd,' said Ukridge, soaring to an impressive burst of imagery, 'has about as much chance as a one-armed blind man in a dark room trying to shove a pound of melted butter into a wild cat's left ear with a red-hot needle.' [P G Wodehouse, 1881–1975, *Ukridge*, Ch. 5]

IMPROVEMENT

1 It was a pity he couldna be hatched o'er again, an' hatched different. [George Eliot, 1819–80, *Adam Bede*, Ch. 18]

2 Ah Love! Could thou and I with Fate conspire / To grasp this sorry Scheme of Things entire, / Would not we shatter it to bits – and then / Re-mould it nearer to the Heart's Desire! [Edward Fitzgerald, 1809–83, *The Rubá'iyát of Omar Khayyám*, Edn 1, 73]

3 Everything better is purchased at the price of something worse. [C G Jung, 1875–1961, quoted by W L Webb in *Guardian*, 27 Dec. 1984]

4 It is a stupidity second to none, to busy oneself with the correction of the world. [Molière, 1622–73, *Le Misanthrope*, I. i]

5 Striving to better, oft we mar what's well. [William Shakespeare, 1564–1616, *King Lear*, I. iv. (370)]

INCONSTANCY

1 Frankie and Johnny were lovers, my gawd, how they could love, / Swore to be true to each other, true as the stars above; / He was her man, but he done her wrong. [anon., *Frankie and Johnny*]

2 Though she were true, when you met her, / And last, till you write your letter, / Yet she / Will be / False, ere I come, to two, or three. [John Donne, 1571?–1631, song: *Go and Catch* . . .]

3 *Je t'aimais inconstant, qu'aurais-je fait fidèle?* – I loved you when you were inconstant. What should I have done if you had been faithful? [Jean Racine, 1639–99, *Andromaque*, IV. v. 1365]

4 A man worth having is true to his wife, or can be true to his wife, or ever was, or ever will be so. [John Vanburgh, 1664–1726, *The Relapse*, I. ii]

See also CONSTANCY, LOYALTY

INDECISION

1 When love once pleads admission to our hearts, / In spite of all the virtue we can boast, / The woman that deliberates is lost. [Joseph Addison, 1672–1719, *Cato*, IV. i. 29]

2 How happy could I be with either, / Were t'other dear charmer away! / But while ye thus tease me together, / To neither a word will I say. [John Gay, 1685–1732, *The Beggar's Opera*, II. xiii]

3 There is no more miserable human being than one in whom nothing is habitual but indecision. [William James, 1842–1910, *The Principles of Psychology*, Ch. 4]

See also AMBIVALENCE, COMPROMISE

INDEPENDENCE

1 They do most by Books, who could do much without them, and he that chiefly owes himself unto himself, is the substantial Man. [Sir Thomas Browne, 1605–82, *Christian Morals*, II, 11]

2 Peace, commerce, and honest friendship with all nations – entangling alliances with none. [Thomas Jefferson, 1743–1826, first presidential inaugural address, 4 Mar. 1801]

3 It's one of those irregular verbs, isn't it? 'I have an independent mind, you are eccentric, he is round the twist'? [Jonathan Lynn, 1943– , and Antony Jay, 1930– , *Yes Prime Minister*, Vol. 1, 'The Bishop's Gambit']

4 Every man paddle his own canoe. [Captain Marryat, 1792–1848, *Settlers in Canada*, Ch. 8]

5 The greatest thing in the world is to know how to be self-sufficient. [Michel de Montaigne, 1533–92, *Essays*, I, 39]

6 The proverb warns that, 'You should not bite the hand that feeds you.' But maybe you should, if it prevents you from feeding yourself. [Thomas Szasz, 1920– , *The Second Sin*, 'Control and Self-control']

7 MISTRESS: Do you mind if we have separate bills? You see, I don't sleep with him any more. [Keith Waterhouse, 1929– , *Jeffrey Bernard is Unwell*, I. The play is based on the life and writings of Bernard]

8 Lord of himself, though not of lands, / And having nothing, yet hath all. [Henry Wotton, 1568–1639, *The Character of a Happy Life*]

See also INTERDEPENDENCE, SELF-PRESERVATION

INDIA

1 India is a geographical term. It is no more a united nation than the Equator. [Winston Churchill, 1874–1965, speech in Royal Albert Hall, 18 Mar. 1931]

2 One does not own to the possession of money in India. [Rudyard Kipling, 1865–1936, *Kim*, Ch. 11]

3 They [the Nabobs] raised the price of everything in their neighbourhood, from fresh eggs to rotten boroughs. [Lord Macaulay, 1800–1859, *Historical Essays*, 'Lord Clive']

4 You've no idea what it costs to keep the old man [Mahatma Gandhi] in poverty. [Lord Louis Mountbatten, 1900–1979; in *Utterly Trivial Knowledge: The Pure Trivia Game*, ed. Margaret Hickey]

5 The saying is that Madras is hot for ten months of the year and hotter for two. [R K Narayan, 1906– , *The Bachelor of Arts*, Ch. 7]

6 No one looks more like a displaced person than an Indian in an overcoat. [Paul Theroux, 1941– , *My Secret History*, IV, 1]

INDIFFERENCE

1 Nothing is so fatal to religion as indifference, which is, at least, half infidelity. [Edmund Burke, 1729–97, letter to William Smith, 29 Jan. 1795]

2 Sir, I view the proposal to hold an international exhibition at San Francisco with an equanimity bordering on indifference. [W S Gilbert, 1836–1911, quoted in Hesketh Pearson, *G, His Life and Strife*, Ch. 19]

3 The worst sin towards our fellow creatures is not to hate them, but to be indifferent to them: that's the essence of inhumanity. [George Bernard Shaw, 1856–1950, *The Devil's Disciple*, II]

4 I regard you with an indifference closely bordering on aversion. [Robert Louis Stevenson, 1850–94, *New Arabian Nights*, 'Story of the Bandbox']

See also OBJECTIVITY

THE INDIVIDUAL

1 Nature made him, and then broke the mould. [Ludovico Ariosto, 1474–1533, *Orlando Furioso*, X, 84]

2 O! why was I born with a different face? / Why was I not born like the rest of my race? [William Blake, 1757–1827, *To Thomas Butts*]

3 Every man's the son of his own deeds; and since I am a man I can become pope. [Miguel Cervantes, 1547–1616, *Don Quixote*, Pt I, Ch. 47]

4 We boil at different degrees. [Ralph Waldo Emerson, 1803–82, *Society and Solitude*, 'Eloquence']

5 I'd always assumed I was the central character in my own story but now it occurred to me I might in fact be only a minor character in someone else's. [Russell Hoban, 1925– , *Turtle Diary*, Ch. 51]

6 Comrades! We must abolish the cult of the individual decisively, once and for all. [Nikita Khrushchev, 1894–1971, speech to secret session of 20th Congress of Communist Party, 25 Feb. 1956. Often becomes 'the cult of personality']

7 The definition of the individual was: a multitude of one million divided by one million. [Arthur Koestler, 1905–83, *Darkness at Noon*, 'The Grammatical Fiction', 2]

8 No, I am no one's contemporary – ever. / That would have been above my station ... / How I loathe that other with my name. / He certainly never was me. [Osip Mandelstam, 1891–1938, *Poems*, No. 141]

See also SELF

INEQUALITY

1 When Adam delved and Eve span, / Who was then the gentleman? [John Ball, d.1381, text for sermon at outbreak of Peasants' Revolt. Adapted from poem by Richard Rolle of Hampole]

2 [Today's world is] like a ship in which the steerage passengers report the stern is sinking, to receive the reply from those in the first class lounge that they'll consider helping, but first they must deal with the rise in the price of fillet steak. [William Clark, 1916–85, in B Whitaker, *A Bridge of People*, Ch. 9]

3 By no endeavour, / Can magnet ever / Attract a silver churn! [W S Gilbert, 1836–1911, *Patience*, II]

4 Subordination tends greatly to human happiness. Were we all upon an equality, we should have no other enjoyment than mere animal pleasure. [Dr Samuel Johnson, 1709–84, in James Boswell, *Life of J*, 20 July 1763]

5 No two people can be half an hour together, but one shall acquire an evident superiority over the other. [Dr Samuel Johnson, 1709–84, in James Boswell, *Life of J*, 15 Feb. 1766]

6 We need inequality in order to eliminate poverty. [Sir Keith Joseph, 1918–94, in Audrey Hilton, *This England, 74–78*, 'Political Persuasion']

7 Remember, no one can make you feel inferior without your consent. [Eleanor Roosevelt, 1884–1962, in *Catholic Digest*, Aug. 1960]

8 As ridiculous to approve of property and let a few men have a grossly unfair share of it, as say you are all for marriage, and then let one man have all the wives. [Katharine Whitehorn, 1926– , in *Observer*, 29 June 1986]

9 There is something utterly nauseating about a system of society which pays a harlot 25 times as much as it pays its Prime Minister, 250 times as much as it pays its Members of Parliament, and 500 times as much as it pays some of its ministers of religion. [Harold Wilson, 1916–95 (on the case of Christine Keeler), speech in House of Commons, June 1963]

10 Gow has an inferiority complex about other people. [D A Winstanley, 1877–1947, in *Geoffrey Madan's Notebooks*, ed. J A Gere and John Sparrow, 'Anecdotes']

See also EQUALITY

INFIDELITY, see INCONSTANCY

INFINITY

1 If the doors of perception were cleansed, everything would appear to man as it is, infinite. [William Blake, 1757–1827, *The Marriage of Heaven and Hell*, 'The ancient tradition ...']

2 Infinity is a dreadfully poor place. They can never manage to make ends meet. [Norton Juster, 1929– , *The Phantom Tollbooth*, Ch. 16]

3 I cannot help it; – in spite of myself, infinity torments me. [Alfred de Musset, 1810–57, *L'Espoir en Dieu*, 9]

See also ETERNITY, IMMORTALITY

INFLUENCE

1 When bad men combine, the good must associate; else they will fall, one by one, an unpitied sacrifice in a contemptible struggle. [Edmund Burke, 1729–97, *Thoughts on the Cause of the Present Discontents*]

2 Only in constant action was his constant certainty found. / He will throw a longer shadow as time recedes. [John Cornford, 1915–36, in *J C, A Memoir*, ed. Pat Sloan, Pt 2, sect. vii, 'Sergei Mironovich Kirov']

3 Charming women can true converts make, / We love the precepts for the teacher's sake. [George Farquhar, 1678–1707, *The Constant Couple*, V. iii]

4 He told me his object in life is to influence people for good, but he can't make up his mind whether to spread out his influence thin over 'millions' or give it in strong doses to a small circle of intimates. [Edward Marsh, 1874–1953, letter, in Christopher Hassall, *E M*, Ch. 7]

5 I should always prefer influence to power. [Kingsley Martin, 1897–1969, *Father Figures*, Ch. 8]

See also POWER

INHERITANCE

1 Esau selleth his birthright for a mess of pottage. [Bible, OT, *Genesis* 25. Chapter heading in *Genevan Bible*]

2 For we brought nothing into this world, and it is certain we can carry nothing out. [Bible, NT, *1 Timothy* 6:7]

3 And all to leave, what with this toil he won, / To that unfeathered, two-legged thing, a son. [John Dryden, 1631–1700, *Absalom and Achitophel*, Pt I, 169]

4 All heiresses are beautiful. [John Dryden, 1631–1700, *King Arthur*, I. i]

5 We should know how to inherit, because inheriting is culture. [Thomas Mann, 1875–1955, quoted by Hans Werner Henze in *Music and Politics*]

6 For one person who dreams of making fifty thousand pounds, a hundred people dream of being left fifty thousand pounds. [A A Milne, 1882–1956, *If I May*, 'The Future']

7 'Poor deer,' quoth he, 'thou makest a testament / As worldlings do, giving thy sum of more. / To that which had too much.' [William Shakespeare, 1564–1616, *As You Like It*, II. i. 47]

8 O what a world of vile ill-favoured faults / Looks handsome in three hundred pounds a year! [*The Merry Wives of Windsor*, III. iv. (32)]

9 *Item*, I give unto my wife my second best bed. [William Shakespeare, 1564–1616, will]

10 An unforgiving eye and a damned disinheriting countenance! [R B Sheridan, 1751–1816, *The School for Scandal*, IV. I]

INNOCENCE

1 Be ye therefore wise as serpents, and harmless as doves. [Bible, NT, *St Matthew* 10:16]

2 She feared no danger for she knew no sin. [John Dryden, 1631–1700, *The Hind and the Panther*, I, 4]

3 Your innocence is on at such a rakish angle / It gives you quite an air of iniquity. [Christopher Fry, 1907– , *The Lady's Not for Burning*, I]

4 Ralph wept for the end of innocence, the darkness of man's heart, and the fall through the air of the true, wise friend called Piggy. [William Golding, 1911–93, *Lord of the Flies*, Ch. 12]

5 The punishment of a criminal is an example to the rabble; but every decent man is concerned if an innocent person is condemned. [Jean de La Bruyère, 1645–96, *Characters*, 'Of Certain Customs', 52]

6 I'd the upbringing a nun would envy and that's the truth. Until I was fifteen I was more familiar with Africa than my own body. [Joe Orton, 1933–67, *Entertaining Mr Sloane*, I]

7 We are innocent, as we have proclaimed and maintained from the time of our arrest. This is the whole truth. To forsake this truth is to pay too high a price even for the priceless gift of life – for life thus purchased we could not live out in dignity and self-respect. [Ethel (1916–53) and Julius (1918–53) Rosenberg, petition for clemency filed 19 Jan. 1953 before execution for espionage]

8 We were as twinned lambs that did frisk i' the sun, / And bleat the one at the other: what we changed / Was innocence for innocence: we knew not / The doctrine of ill-doing, no, nor dreamed / That any did. [William Shakespeare, 1564–1616, *The Winter's Tale*, I. ii. 67]

See also GUILT

INNOVATION

1 He that will not apply new remedies must expect new evils; for time is the greatest innovator. [Francis Bacon, 1561–1626, *Essays*, 24, 'Of Innovations']

2 To innovate is not to reform [Edmund Burke, 1729–97, *A Letter to a Noble Lord*, 1796]

3 It was I who introduced bottled water into India. [Barbara Cartland, 1904– ; *Independent*, 'Quote Unquote', 18 Mar. 1989]

INSECTS

1 Ye country comets, that portend / No war nor prince's funeral, / Shining unto no higher end / Than to presage the grass's fall. [Andrew Marvell, 1621–78, *The Mower to the Glow Worms*]

2 God in His wisdom made the fly / And then forgot to tell us why. [Ogden Nash, 1902–71, *The Fly*]

3 Busy, curious, thirsty fly / Drink with me, and drink as I. [William Oldys, 1696–1761, *Busy, Curious, Thirsty Fly*]

4 O joy of the gnat, that still leaps inwards even in the act of wedding; for womb is all! [Rainer Maria Rilke, 1875–1926, *Duino Elegies*, 8]

5 'I'll not hurt a hair of thy head: – Go,' says he, lifting up the sash and opening his hand as he spoke, to let it [a fly] escape; – 'go poor devil, get thee gone, why should I hurt thee? – This world surely is wide enough to hold both thee and me.' [Laurence Sterne, 1713–68, *Tristram Shandy*, Vol. ii, Ch. 12]

6 They form a line, and drive out the idle bands of drones from the hives. [Virgil, 70–19 BC, *Georgics*, IV, 167]

7 How doth the little busy bee / Improve each shining hour, / And gather honey all the day / From every opening flower! [Isaac Watts, 1674–1748, *Divine Songs for Children*, 20, 'Against Idleness and Mischief']

INSPIRATION

1 We have watered our horses in Helicon. [George Chapman, 1559?–1634, *May-Day*, III. iii]

2 You can't direct it and it refuses to come. It's as tiring as constipation. It might start tomorrow. [(Of writing poetry) Lawrence Durrell, 1912–90, interview in *Guardian*, 28 May 1985]

3 Your battles inspired me – not the obvious material battles but those that were fought and won behind your forehead. [James Joyce, 1882–1941, letter to Henrik Ibsen, March 1901]

4 'Well, I sort of made it up,' said Pooh ... 'it comes to me sometimes.' 'Ah!' said Rabbit, who never let things come to him, but always went and fetched them. [A A Milne, 1882–1956, *House at Pooh Corner*, Ch. 5]

5 What in me is dark / Illumine, what is low raise and support; / That to the height of this great argument / I may assert eternal Providence, / And justify the ways of God to men. [John Milton, 1608–74, *Paradise Lost*, Bk i, 22]

See also CREATIVITY

INSTITUTIONS

1 An institution is the lengthened shadow of one man. [Ralph Waldo Emerson, 1803–82, *Essays*, 'Self Reliance']

2 Is an institution always a man's shadow shortened in the sun, the lowest common denominator of everybody in it? [Randall Jarrell, 1914–65, *Pictures from an Institution*, Pt V, Ch. 9]

3 I hear it was charged against me that I sought to destroy institutions, / But really I am neither for nor against institutions. [Walt Whitman, 1819–92, *I Hear It was Charged against Me*]

INSULTS & PUT-DOWNS

1 ABBE GUYOT DESFONTAINES: (excusing himself for having written a libellous pamphlet): *Il faut que je vive.* – But I must live.
D'ARGENSON: *Je n'en vois pas la nécessité.* – I do not see the necessity. [Comte d'Argenson, 1652–1721, quoted in Voltaire, *Alzire*, 'Discours préliminaire']

2 I mock thee not, though I by thee am mocked; / Thou call'st me madman, but I call thee blockhead. [William Blake, 1757–1827, *To Flaxman*]

3 Her [Lady Diana Cooper's] capacity for abstract thought seems to have been roughly that of a strawberry mousse. [John Carey, 1934– , in *The Sunday Times*, 20 Sept. 1981]

4 An injury is much sooner forgotten than an insult. [Earl of Chesterfield, 1694–1773, letter to his son, 9 Oct. 1746]

5 In defeat unbeatable; in victory unbearable. [Winston Churchill, 1874–1965 (of Field-Marshall Montgomery), in Edward Marsh, *Ambrosia and Small Beer*, Ch. 5, sect. ii]

6 She [Victoria Sackville-West] looked like Lady Chatterley above the waist and the game-keeper below. [Cyril Connolly, 1903–74; in *Oh, What an Awful Thing to Say!*, comp. W Cole and L Phillips]

7 I never snub anybody accidentally. [Norman Ginsbury, 1902– , *Viceroy Sarah*, I. ii]

8 Like the radish, red outside, white inside, and always on the side the bread is buttered. [Eric Hobsbawm, 1917– (of the leaders of the French Third Republic), *The Invention of Tradition*, ed. Eric Hobsbawm and Terence Ranger]

9 Anyone who extends to him [Mayor La Guardia] the right hand of fellowship is in danger of losing a couple of fingers. [Alva Johnston, 1880–1950, in Arthur M Schlesinger Jr, *The Politics of Upheaval*, Pt I, Ch. 8, sect. iii]

10 [When asked by Andrew Lloyd Webber, 'Hey, why do people take an instant dislike to me?'] Because it saves time. [Alan Jay Lerner, 1918–86, in *Observer*, 30 Apr. 1989]

11 I'll bet your father spent the first year of your life throwing rocks at the stork. [Groucho Marx, 1895–1977, in film *The Marx Brothers at the Circus*, script by Irving Brecher]

12 She has a Rolls body and a Balham mind. [J B Morton ('Beachcomber'), 1893–1979, *The Best of B*, 9]

13 [When told someone was very nice to her inferiors] Where does she find them? [Dorothy Parker, 1893–1967, in letter of Rupert Hart-Davis, 22 Jan. 1956, *Lyttelton–Hart-Davis Letters*, Vol. 1]

14 Let Sporus tremble. – What? that thing of silk, / Sporus, that mere white curd of ass's milk? / Satire or sense, alas! can Sporus feel? / Who breaks a butterfly upon a wheel? [Alexander Pope, 1688–1744, *Epistle to Dr Arbuthnot*, 305]

15 You knew that château-bottled shit Widmerpool. [Anthony Powell, 1905– , *Hearing Secret Harmonies*, Ch. 7]

16 I can't see that she could have found anything nastier to say if she'd thought it out with both hands for a fortnight. [Dorothy L Sayers, 1893–1957, *Busman's Holiday*, 'Prothalamion']

17 Thou whoreson zed! thou unnecesssary letter! [William Shakespeare, 1564–1616, *King Lear*, II. ii. (68)]

18 JUDGE: You are offensive, sir.
SMITH: We both are; the difference is that I'm trying to be and you can't help it. [F E Smith, Earl of Birkenhead, 1872–1930, in C E Bechofer Roberts ('Ephesian'), *Lord Birkenhead*, Ch. 3]

19 'The best confidential report I ever heard of,' said Lord Wavell, 'was also the shortest. It was by one Horse Gunner of another, and ran, "Personally I would not breed from this officer."' [Lord Wavell, 1883–1950; in Gilbert Harding, *Treasury of Insult*]

20 The guy's no good – he never was any good . . . his mother should have thrown *him* away and kept the stork. [Mae West, 1892–1980; in *Hammer and Tongues*, ed. Michèle Brown and Ann O'Connor, 'Men']

21 You have Van Gogh's ear for music. [Billy Wilder, 1906– , to Cliff Osmond, attr.]

22 If I had had to choose between him and a cockroach as a companion for a walking-tour, the cockroach would have had it by a short head. [P G Wodehouse, 1881–1975, *Very Good, Jeeves!*, 'The Spot of Art']

INSURANCE

1 The Act of God designation on all insurance policies; which means, roughly, that you cannot be insured for the accidents that are most likely to happen to you. If your ox kicks a hole in your neighbour's Maserati, however, indemnity is instantaneous. [Alan Coren, 1938– , *The Lady from Stalingrad Mansions*, 'A Short History of Insurance']

2 I detest life-insurance agents; they always argue that I shall some day die, which is not so. [Stephen Leacock, 1869–1944, *Literary Lapses*, 'Insurance up to Date']

INTEGRITY

1 Be so true to thyself, as thou be not false to others. [Francis Bacon, 1561–1626, *Essays*, 23, 'Of Wisdom for a Man's Self']

2 For the men no lords can buy or sell, / They sit not easy when all goes well. [G K Chesterton, 1874–1936, *The Song of Defeat*]

3 You lose more of yourself than you redeem / Doing the decent thing. [Seamus Heaney, 1939– , *Station Island*, XII]

4 Do all things like a man, not sneakingly: / Think the King sees thee still; for his King does. [George Herbert, 1593–1633, *Church Porch*, 21]

5 *Integer vitae scelerisque purus.* – The man of upright life, unstained by guilt. [Horace, 65–8 BC, *Odes*, I, xxii, 1]

6 The man who is tenacious of purpose in a rightful cause is not shaken from his firm resolve by the frenzy of his fellow citizens clamouring for what is wrong, or by the tyrant's threatening face. [Horace, 65–8 BC, *Odes*, III, iii, 1]

7 I'm afraid of losing my obscurity. Genuineness only thrives in the dark. Like celery. [Aldous Huxley, 1894–1963, *Those Barren Leaves*, Pt 1, Ch. 1]

8 What do the facts we know *about* a man amount to? Only two things we can know of him, and this by pure soul-intuition: we can know if he is true to the flame of life and love which is inside his heart, or if he is false to it. [D H Lawrence, 1885–1930, *Kangaroo*, Ch. 7]

9 *Hier stehe ich, ich kann nicht anders.* – Here I stand, I cannot do otherwise. [Martin Luther, 1483–1546, speech at the Diet of Worms, 18 Apr. 1521]

10 So absolute she seems / And in herself complete, so well to know / Her own, that what she wills to do or say, / Seems wisest, virtuousest, discreetest, best. [John Milton, 1608–74, *Paradise Lost*, Bk vii, 547]

11 For modes of faith let graceless zealots fight; / His can't be wrong whose life is in the right. [Alexander Pope, 1688–1744, *An Essay on Man*, III, 303]

12 This above all: to thine own self be true, / And it must follow, as the night the day, / Thou canst not then be false to any man. [William Shakespeare, 1554–1616, *Hamlet*, I. iii. 78]

See also HONESTY, SELF, SIMPLICITY, SINCERITY

INTELLECT

1 Intellect deteriorates after every surrender as folly, unless we consciously resist, the nonsense does not pass by but into us. [Jacques Barzun, 1907– , *The House of Intellect*, Ch. 9]

2 I care not whether a man is good or evil; all that I care / Is whether he is a wise man or a fool. Go! put off holiness, / And put on intellect. [William Blake, 1757–1827, *Jerusalem*, f. 91, 54]

3 The intellect is always fooled by the heart. [Duc de La Rochefoucauld, 1613–80, *Maxims*, 102]

4 For who would lose, / Though full of pain, this intellectual being, / Those thoughts that wander through eternity, / To perish rather, swallowed up and lost / In the wide womb of uncreated night, / Devoid of sense and motion? [John Milton, 1608–74, *Paradise Lost*, Bk ii, 146]

5 Intellect is invisible to the man who has none. [Arthur Schopenhauer, 1788–1860, *Aphorisms*, 'On Philosophy and the Intellect']

6 He's the very incarnation of intellect. You can hear his mind working. [George Bernard Shaw, 1856–1950, *You Never Can Tell*, IV]

See also INTELLIGENCE, MIND, THINKING

INTELLECTUALS

1 An intellectual – one educated beyond the bounds of common sense. [anon.; in P and J Holton, *Quote and Unquote*]

2 To the man-in-the-street, who, I'm sorry to say, / Is a keen observer of life, / The word 'Intellectual' suggests straight away / A man who's untrue to his wife. [W H Auden, 1907–73, *The Orators*, epigraph]

3 Intellectuals are people who believe that ideas are of more importance than values. That is to say, their own ideas and other people's values. [Gerald Brenan, 1894–1987, *Thoughts in a Dry Season*, 'Life']

4 But – Oh! ye lords of ladies intellectual, / Inform us truly, have they not hen-pecked you all? [Lord Byron, 1788–1824, *Don Juan*, I, 22]

5 An intellectual is someone whose mind watches itself. [Albert Camus, 1913–60, *Notebooks, 1935–42*]

6 We should take care not to make the intellect our god; it has, of course, powerful muscles, but no personality. [Albert Einstein, 1879–1955, *Out of My Later Years*, Ch. 51]

7 The native intellectual, who takes up arms to defend his nation's legitimacy and who wants to bring proofs to bear out that legitimacy, who is willing to strip himself naked to study the history of his body, is obliged to dissect the heart of his body. [Frantz Fanon, 1925–61, *The Wretched of the Earth*, Ch. 4]

8 The intellectual's problem is not vision, it's commitment. You enjoy biting the hand that feeds you, but you'll never bite it off. [Trevor Griffiths, 1935– , *The Party*, I]

9 In France intellectuals are usually incapable of opening an umbrella. [André Malraux, 1901–76, in Bruce Chatwin, *What am I Doing Here*, 'André Malraux']

10 Every intellectual attitude is latently political. [Thomas Mann, 1875–1955, in *Observer*, 11 Aug. 1974]

11 Those Eggheads are terrible Philistines. A real good head is not oval but round. [Vladimir Nabokov, 1899–1977, *Strong Opinions*, Ch. 6]

12 All intellectuals should suffer a certain amount of persecution as early in life as possible. Not too much. That is bad for them. But a certain amount. [Bertrand Russell, 1872–1970, in Kenneth Harris, *K H Talking to . . .*]

13 'Hullo! friend,' I call out. 'Won't you lend us a hand?' 'I am an intellectual and don't drag wood about,' came the answer. 'You're lucky,' I reply. 'I too wanted to become an intellectual, but I didn't succeed.' [Albert Schweitzer, 1875–1965, *More from the Primeval Forest*, Ch. 5]

14 Do you think it pleases a man when he looks into a woman's eyes and sees a reflection of the British Museum Reading Room? [Muriel Spark, 1918– ; in L and M Cowan, *The Wit of Women*]

15 The man or woman of thoroughbred intelligence who rides his mind at a gallop across country in pursuit of an idea. [(Definition of a highbrow) Virginia Woolf, 1882–1941, *The Death of the Moth*, 'Middlebrow']

16 A reasoning, self-sufficing thing, / An intellectual all-in-all. [William Wordsworth, 1770–1850, *A Poet's Epitaph*]

INTELLIGENCE

1 The intelligent are to the intelligentsia what a gentleman is to a gent. [Stanley Baldwin, 1867–1947, in G M Young, *S B*, Ch. 13]

2 Intelligence is almost useless to someone who has no other quality. [Alexis Carrel, 1873–1944, *Man the Unknown*, Ch. 4, 6]

3 Is there intelligent life on earth? Yes, but I'm only visiting. [Graffito in Cambridge, quoted by Norman Shrapnel in *Guardian*, 17 Oct. 1970]

4 You never see animals going through the absurd and often horrible fooleries of magic and religion ... Only man behaves with such gratuitous folly. It is the price he has to pay for being intelligent but not, as yet, quite intelligent enough. [Aldous Huxley, 1894–1963, *Texts and Pretexts*, 'Amor Fati']

5 If he was the sole entrant in an intelligence contest, he'd come third. [Jonathan Lynn, 1943– , and Antony Jay, 1930– , *Yes Prime Minister*, Vol. 1, 'Party Games']

6 Military intelligence is a contradiction in terms. [Groucho Marx, 1895–1977, in A Spiegelman and B Schneider, *Whole Grains*]

7 You know, there are three kinds of intelligence – the intelligence of man, the intelligence of the animal, and the intelligence of the military. In that order. [Gottfried Reinhardt, 1913–94, in Lillian Ross, *Picture*, 'Piccolos under Your Name, Strings under Mine']

INTENTION

1 'Then you should say what you mean,' the March Hare went on. 'I do,' Alice hastily replied; 'at least – at least I mean what I say – that's the same thing, you know.' [Lewis Carroll, 1832–98, *Alice in Wonderland*, Ch. 7]

2 The will is never free – it is always attached to an object, a purpose. It is simply the engine in the car – it can't steer. [Joyce Cary, 1888–1957, in *Writers at Work*, ed. Malcolm Cowley, First Series]

3 Th' entente is al, and nought the lettres space. [Geoffrey Chaucer, 1340?–1400, *Troilus and Criseyde*, v, 1630]

4 Constantly to seek the purpose of life is one of the odd escapes of man. If he finds what he seeks it will not be worth that pebble on the path. [J Krishnamurti, 1895–1986, *The Second Penguin Krishnamurti Reader*, Ch. 14]

5 With malice toward none; with charity for all; with firmness in the right, as God gives us to see the right, let us strive on to finish the work we are in. [Abraham Lincoln, 1809–65, second presidential inaugural address, 4 Mar. 1865]

6 My purpose holds / To sail beyond the sunset, and the baths / Of all the western stars, until I die. / It may be that the gulfs will wash us down; / It may be we shall touch the Happy Isles / And see the great Achilles, whom we knew. [Alfred, Lord Tennyson, 1809–92, *Ulysses*, 59]

INTERDEPENDENCE

1 Am I my brother's keeper? [Bible, OT, *Genesis* 4:9]

2 We are members one of another. [Bible, NT, *Ephesians* 4:25]

3 I am you and you are me and what have we done to each other? [Richard Condon, 1915–96, *The Manchurian Candidate*, 'The Keener's Manual', epigraph]

4 No man is an Island, entire of itself; every man is a piece of the Continent, a part of the main. [John Donne, 1571?–1631, *Devotions*, 17]

5 Any man's death diminishes me, because I am involved in Mankind; And therefore never send to know for whom the bell tolls; it tolls for thee. [John Donne, 1571?–1631, *Devotions*, 17]

6 *Tous pour un, un pour tous.* – All for one, one for all. [Alexandre Dumas, 1803–70, *The Three Musketeers*, motto]

7 Yes, we must, indeed, all hang together or, most assuredly, we shall all hang separately. [Benjamin Franklin, 1706–90, remark at signing of Declaration of Independence, 4 July 1776]

8 People must help one another; it is nature's law. [Jean de La Fontaine, 1621–95, *Fables*, VIII, 17, 'The Ass and the Dog']

9 What will God say to us if some of us go to him without the others? [Charles Péguy, 1873–1914; in W Neil, *Concise Dictionary of Religious Quotations*]

10 The fifth province is not anywhere here or there, north or south, east or west. It is a place within each of us – that place that is open to the other, that swinging door which allows us to venture out and others to venture in. [Mary Robinson, 1944– , in *Independent*, 19 May 1991]

11 We – are we not formed, as notes of music are, / For one another, though dissimilar? [P B Shelley, 1792–1822, *Epipsychidion*, 142]

12 The fountains mingle with the river / And the rivers with the ocean, / The winds of heaven mix for ever / With a sweet emotion; / Nothing in the world is single; / All things by a law divine / In one spirit meet and mingle. / Why not I with thine? [P B Shelley, 1792–1822, *Love's Philosophy*]

13 No one can be perfectly free till all are free; no one can be perfectly moral till all are moral; no one can be perfectly happy till all are happy. [Herbert Spencer, 1820–1903, *Social Statics*, IV, 30, 16]

14 I think we must all learn to be guests of each other. [George Steiner, 1929– , interview in *Guardian*, 19 May 1981]

15 We're all in this together by ourselves. [Lily Tomlin, 1939– ; in *Hammer and Tongues*, ed. Michèle Brown and Ann O'Connor, 'Life']

See also INDEPENDENCE

INTERNATIONAL RELATIONS

1 I said that the world must be made safe for at least fifty years. If it was only for fifteen to twenty years then we should have betrayed our soldiers. [Winston Churchill, 1874–1965, *The Second World War*, Vol. 5, 20]

2 If EDC [European Defence Community] should fail, the United States might be compelled to make an 'agonizing reappraisal' of its basic policy. [John Foster Dulles, 1888–1959, speech at North Atlantic Council, Paris, 14 Dec. 1953]

3 Oh, East is East, and West is West, and never the twain shall meet, / Till Earth and Sky stand presently at God's great Judgment Seat; / But there is neither East nor West, Border, nor Breed, nor Birth, / When two strong men stand face to face, though they come from the ends of the earth! [Rudyard Kipling, 1865–1936, *The Ballad of East and West*]

4 *La cordiale entente qui existe entre mon gouvernement et le sien* [Great Britain]. – The cordial understanding that exists between our two governments. [Louis-Philippe, 1773–1850, speech, 27 Dec. 1843]

5 Our desire is to be friendly to every country in the world, but we have no desire to have a friendly country choosing our enemies for us. [President Nyerere, 1921–99; in Robert Andrews, *Routledge Dictionary of Quotations*, 'Alliances']

6 In the field of world policy I would dedicate this nation to the policy of the good neighbour. [Franklin D Roosevelt, 1882–1945, first inaugural address, 4 Mar. 1933]

7 Speak softly and carry a big stick: you will go far. [Theodore Roosevelt, 1858–1919, speech at Chicago, 2 Apr. 1903]

8 There are four sides to every issue: your side, my side, the right side and the United Nations' side. [Gerald Segal, 1953– , in *The Sunday Times*, 19 June 1988]

9 Ten hostages is terrorism; / A million, and it's strategy. / To ban books is fanaticism; / To threaten in totality / All culture and all civilization, / All humankind and all creation, / This is a task of decorous skill / And needs high statesmanship and will. [Vikram Seth, 1952– , *The Golden Gate*, 7, 31]

10 An ally has to be watched just like an enemy. [Leon Trotsky, 1874–1940, in A Ulam, *Expansion and Coexistence*]

11 It is our true policy to steer clear of permanent alliance with any portion of the foreign world. [George Washington, 1732–99, farewell address, 17 Sept. 1796]

See also COLD WAR, NATIONALISM

INTOLERANCE

1 Whoever shall say, Thou fool, shall be in danger of hell fire. [Bible, NT, *St Matthew* 5:8, 5:22]

2 When old settlers say 'One has to understand the country,' what they mean is, 'You have to get used to our ideas about the native.' They are saying, in effect, 'Learn our ideas, or otherwise get out; we don't want you.' [Doris Lessing, 1919– , *The Grass is Singing*, Ch. 1]

3 All his faults, observed, / Set in a notebook, learned, and conned by rote, / To cast into my teeth. [William Shakespeare, 1564–1616, *Julius Caesar*, I. iii. 96]

See also CRITICS, TOLERANCE

INVENTIONS

1 One invention still lacking: how to reverse explosions. [Elias Canetti, 1905–94, *The Human Province*, '1945']

2 Inventions that are not made, like babies that are not born, are rarely missed. [J K Galbraith, 1908– , *The Affluent Society*, Ch. 9, iii]

3 There is no great invention, from fire to flying, which has not been hailed as an insult to some god. [J B S Haldane, 1892–1964, *Daedalus or Science and the Future*]

4 Few have heard of Fra Luca Parioli, the inventor of double-entry book-keeping; but he has probably had much more influence on human life than has Dante or Michelangelo. [Herbert J Muller, 1905–80, *The Uses of the Past*, Ch. 8]

5 When younger he [Sir George Sitwell] had invented many other things; at Eton, for example, a musical toothbrush which played 'Annie Laurie' as you brushed your teeth and a small revolver for killing wasps. [Osbert Sitwell, 1892–1969, *The Scarlet Tree*, Bk IV, Ch. 1]

6 If you took away everything in the world that had to be invented, there'd be nothing left except a lot of people getting rained on. [Tom Stoppard, 1937– , *Enter a Free Man*, I]

7 He had been eight years upon a project for extracting sunbeams out of cucumbers, which were to be put into phials hermetically sealed, and let out to warm the air in raw inclement summers. [Jonathan Swift, 1677–1745, *Gulliver's Travels*, 'Voyage to Laputa', Ch. 5]

See also DISCOVERY

INVITATIONS

1 Come in the evening, or come in the morning, / Come when you're looked for, or come without warning. [T O Davis, 1814–45, *The Welcome*]

2 'Will you walk into my parlour?' said a spider to a fly: / 'Tis the prettiest little parlour that ever you did spy.' [Mary Howitt, 1799–1888, *The Spider and the Fly*]

3 Why don't you come up some time, see me? [Usually misquoted as 'Come up and see me sometime' [Mae West, 1892–1980, in film *She Done Him Wrong*, from West's play *Diamond Lil*]

4 Why don't you slip out of those wet clothes and into a dry Martini. [Billy Wilder, 1906– , in film *The Major and the Minor*, 1942, scripted with Charles Brackett. Line spoken by Robert Benchley, who sometimes is given credit; but ascr. also to Mae West in film *Every Day's a Holiday* (1937) and Alexander Woollcott]

See also HOSPITALITY

IRELAND & THE IRISH

1 For they're hangin' men and women there for the wearin' o' the Green. [anon., *The Wearin' o' the Green*, Irish street ballad]

2 The Irish don't know what they want and won't be happy till they get it. [anon. infantry officer, 1975]

3 PAT: He was an Anglo-Irishman.
MEG: In the blessed name of God, what's that?
PAT: A Protestant with a horse. [Brendan Behan, 1923–64, *The Hostage*, 1]

4 Other people have a nationality. The Irish and the Jews have a psychosis. [Brendan Behan, 1923–64, *Richard's Cork Leg*, I]

5 We Irish had the right word on the tip of our tongue, but the imperialist got at that. What should trip off it we trip over. [Brigid Brophy, 1929–95, *In Transit*, sect. I, 6]

6 For the great Gaels of Ireland / Are the men that God made mad, / For all their wars are merry, / And all their songs are sad. [G K Chesterton, 1874–1936, *The Ballad of the White Horse*, 2]

7 Ulster will fight; Ulster will be right. [Lord Randolph Churchill, 1849–94, letter, 7 May 1886]

8 The grass grows green on the battlefield, but never on the scaffold. [Winston Churchill, 1874–1965, on Irish Rebellion, 1916, attr.]

9 Jesus must have been an Irishman. After all, He was unmarried, thirty-two years old, lived at home, and His mother thought He was God. [Shane Connaughton, 1951– , *Divisions at the Oscar*]

10 The men of the Emerald Isle. [William Drennan, 1754–1820, *Erin*]

11 The English and the Irish are very much alike, except that the Irish are more so. [Mgr James Dunne, 1859–1934, in conversation, during the Irish Troubles]

12 All races have produced notable economists, with the exception of the Irish who doubtless can protest their devotion to higher arts. [J K Galbraith, 1908– , *The Age of Uncertainty*, Ch. 1]

13 BOSWELL: Is not the Giant's Causeway worth seeing?
JOHNSON: Worth seeing? yes; but not worth going to see. [Dr Samuel Johnson, 1709–84, in James Boswell, *Life of J*, 12 Oct. 1779]

14 Ireland is the old sow that eats her farrow. [James Joyce, 1882–1941, *A Portrait of the Artist as a Young Man*, Ch. 5]

15 I belong to the *faubourg Saint-Patrice* called Ireland for short. [James Joyce, 1882–1941, *Ulysses*, Penguin edn, 1992, p. 748]

16 In Ireland there's a precedent for everything. Except commonsense. [Benedict Kiely, 1919– , *Nothing Happens in Carmincross*, 'The Landing']

17 The problem with Ireland is that it's a country full of genius, but with absolutely no talent. [Hugh Leonard, 1926– , interview in *The Times*, Aug. 1977]

18 'Tis Ireland gives England her soldiers, her generals too. [George Meredith, 1828–1909, *Diana of the Crossways*, Ch. 2]

19 It [Dublin] is a city where you can see a sparrow fall to the ground, and God watching it. [Conor Cruise O'Brien, 1917– , attr.]

20 An Englishman thinks seated; a Frenchman, standing; an American, pacing; an Irishman afterward. [Austin O'Malley, 1858–1932; in A Andrews, *Quotations for Speakers and Writers*]

21 That's this country [Ireland] all over! Not content with a contradiction in terms, it must go on to an antithesis in ideas. 'Temperance Hotel'! You might as well speak of a celibate kip [brothel]! [George Tyrrell, 1861–1909, in O St John Gogarty, *As I Was Going Down Sackville Street*, Ch. 25]

22 Romantic Ireland's dead and gone, / It's with O'Leary in the grave. [W B Yeats, 1865–1939, *September 1913*]

IRONY

1 You have delighted us long enough. [Jane Austen, 1775–1817, *Pride and Prejudice*, 18]

2 Sarcasm I now see to be, in general, the language of the devil. [Thomas Carlyle, 1795–1881, *Sartor Resartus*, Bk ii, Ch. 4]

3 I don't deserve any credit for turning the other cheek as my tongue is always in it. [Flannery O'Connor, 1925–64, from *The Habit of Being*, letter to Alice Morris, 10 June 1955]

4 I bet you could get into the subway without using anybody's name. [Dorothy Parker, 1893–1967, *Just a Little One*]

5 In this country we find it pays to shoot an admiral from time to time to encourage the others. [Voltaire, 1694–1778, *Candide*, Ch. 23]

ISLAM

1 The deadlands of the mullahs / Where young men dream of laws / As simple as the gallows. [Tom Paulin, 1949– , *Song for February*]

2 Unlike Christianity, which preached a peace that is never achieved, Islam unashamedly came with a sword. [Steven Runciman, 1903– , *A History of the Crusades*, 'The First Crusade']

See also RELIGION

ISRAEL

1 His Majesty's Government views with favour the establishment in Palestine of a national home for the Jewish people, and will use its best endeavours to facilitate the achievement of this object, it being clearly understood that nothing shall be done that may prejudice the civil and religious rights of non-Jewish communities in Palestine. [A J Balfour, 1848–1930, letter to Lord Rothschild, 2 Nov. 1917, the so-called Balfour Declaration]

2 I saw all Israel scattered upon the hills, as sheep that have not a shepherd. [Bible, OT, *I Kings* 22:17]

3 Can there any good thing come out of Nazareth? [Bible, NT, *St John* 1:46]

4 When Arthur Balfour launched his scheme for peopling Palestine with Jewish immigrants, I am credibly informed that he did not know there were Arabs in the country. [W R Inge, 1860–1954, from *Evening Standard*; in M Bateman, *This England*, selections from the *New Statesman*, Pt I]

5 I will tell you that this nation [Israel] of four million citizens is really an uneasy coalition of four million prime ministers, if not four million self-appointed prophets and messiahs. [Amos Oz, 1939– , *Granta*, 17, 'Israel']

6 Most of them [Israeli observers who study overseas systems] are like the lawyer who appeared before the jury and said: 'The following are the conclusions on which I base my facts.' [Shimon Peres, 1923– , attr.]

7 We, like you, are people – people who want to build a home, plant a tree, to love, to live side by side with you in dignity and empathy, as human beings, as free men. We are today giving peace a chance, and saying again to you: enough. [Yitzakh Rabin, 1922–95, speech on signing of Israel–Palestine Declaration, Washington, 13 Sept. 1993]

8 In Israel it's enough to live – you don't have to do anything else and you go to bed exhausted. Have you ever noticed that Jews shout? Even one ear is more than you need. [Philip Roth, 1933– , *The Counterlife*, 2]

9 In those holy fields / Over whose acres walked those blessed feet / Which fourteen hundred years ago were nailed / For our advantage on the bitter cross. [William Shakespeare, 1564–1616, *1 Henry IV*, I. i. 24]

See also JEWS

ITALY & THE ITALIANS

1 For wheresoe'er I turn my ravished eyes, / Gay gilded scenes and shining prospects rise, / Poetic fields encompass me around, / And still I seem to tread on classic ground. [Joseph Addison, 1672–1719, *Letter from Italy*]

2 Open my heart and you will see / Graved inside of it, 'Italy'. [Robert Browning, 1812–89, '*De Gustibus* –']

3 Travelling is the ruin of all happiness! There's no looking at a building here after seeing Italy. [Fanny Burney, 1752–1840, *Cecilia*, IV, 2]

4 England is a paradise for women, and hell for horses: Italy a paradise for horses, hell for women, as the diverb goes. [Robert Burton, 1577–1640, *Anatomy of Melancholy*, III, §3, Memb. 1, 2]

5 I stood in Venice, on the Bridge of Sighs; / A palace and a prison on each hand. [Lord Byron, 1788–1824, *Childe Harold's Pilgrimage*, IV, 1]

6 Venice is like eating an entire box of chocolate liqueurs at one go. [Truman Capote, 1924–84; *Observer*, 'Sayings of the Week', 26 Nov. 1961]

7 Sirmio, little eye of peninsulas and islands. [Catullus, 87–54? BC, *Carmina*, 31]

8 A man who has not been in Italy, is always conscious of an inferiority. [Dr Samuel Johnson, 1709–84, in James Boswell, *Life of J*, 11 Apr. 1776]

9 Is it the secret of the long-nosed Etruscans? / The long-nosed, sensitive footed, subtly-smiling Etruscans, / Who made so little noise outside the cypress groves? [D H Lawrence, 1885–1930, *Cypresses*]

10 Giotto's tower, / The lily of Florence blossoming in stone. [H W Longfellow, 1807–82, *Giotto's Tower*]

11 Italy is a geographical expression. [Prince Metternich, 1773–1859, letter to Lord Palmerston, 6 Aug. 1847]

12 Thou Paradise of exiles, Italy! [P B Shelley, 1792–1822, *Julian and Maddalo*, 57]

13 Sun-girt City, thou hast been / Ocean's child, and then his queen ; / Now is come a darker day, / And thou soon must be his prey. [(Venice) P B Shelley, 1792–1822, *Lines Written among the Euganean Hills*, 115]

14 Lump the whole thing ! Say that the Creator made Italy from designs by Michael Angelo ! [Mark Twain, 1835–1910, *Innocents Abroad*, Ch. 27]

15 Once did she hold the gorgeous east in fee ; / And was the safeguard of the west . . . Venice, the eldest child of Liberty. [William Wordsworth, 1770–1850, *On the Extinction of the Venetian Republic*]

J

JAZZ

1 I've felt that the only way to survive was with dignity, pride and courage. I heard that in certain forms of music, and I heard it most of all in the blues, because it was always an individual. It was one man and his guitar against the world. [Eric Clapton, 1954– , in ITV programme *The South Bank Show*, 1987]

2 He [Charlie Parker] always filled me with a kind of despair, because he played the way I would have liked to write, and this wasn't possible for me or anyone else. He made poetry seem word-bound. [P J Kavanagh, 1931– , *The Perfect Stranger*, Ch. 5]

3 On me your voice falls as they say love should, / Like an enormous yes. [Philip Larkin, 1922–85, *For Sidney Bechet*]

4 The basic difference between classical music and jazz is that in the former the music is always greater than its performance – whereas the way jazz is performed is always more important than what is being played. [André Previn, 1929– , in *The Times*, 1967]

See also MUSIC, MUSICIANS

JEALOUSY

1 The ear of jealousy heareth all things. [Bible, Apocrypha, Wisdom of Solomon, 1:10]

2 Set me as a seal upon thine heart, as a seal upon thine arm; for love is strong as death; jealousy is cruel as the grave. [Bible, OT, *Song of Solomon* 8:6]

3 When Eve saw her reflection in a pool, she sought Adam and accused him of infidelity. [Ambrose Bierce, 1842–1914, *The Devil's Dictionary*]

4 Jealousy is no more than feeling alone among smiling enemies. [Elizabeth Bowen, 1899–1973, *The House in Paris*, II, 8]

5 She looks at other women as though she would inhale them. [Ronald Firbank, 1886–1926, *The Flower Beneath the Foot*, Ch. 5]

6 Man is jealous because of his *amour propre*; woman is jealous because of her lack of it. [Germaine Greer, 1939– , *The Female Eunuch*, 'Egotism']

7 When I told my missis once I should never dream of being jealous of *her*, instead of up and thanking me for it, she spoilt the best frying-pan we ever had. [W W Jacobs, 1863–1943, *Ship's Company*, 'Good Intentions']

8 Should such a man, too fond to rule alone, / Bear, like the Turk, no brother near the throne, / View him with scornful, yet with jealous eyes, / And hate for arts that caused himself to rise; / Damn with faint praise, assent with civil leer, / And, without sneering, teach the rest to sneer; / Willing to wound, and yet afraid to strike, / Just hint a fault, and hesitate dislike. [(Of Addison) Alexander Pope, 1688–1744, *Epistle to Dr Arbuthnot*, 193]

9 For what we suppose to be our love or our jealousy is never a single, continuous and indivisible passion. It is composed of an infinity of successive loves, of different jealousies, each of which is ephemeral, although by their uninterrupted multiplicity they give us the impression of continuity, the illusion of unity. [Marcel Proust,

1871–1922, *Remembrance of Things Past: Swann's Way*, 'Swann in Love']

10 Two stars keep not their motion in one sphere. [William Shakespeare, 1564–1616, *1 Henry IV*, V. iv. 65]

11 Why, man, he doth bestride the narrow world / Like a Colossus; and we petty men / Walk under his huge legs, and peep about / To find ourselves dishonourable graves. [*Julius Caesar*, I. ii. 134]

12 O! beware, my lord, of jealousy; / It is the green-eyed monster which doth mock / The meat it feeds on. [*Othello*, III. iii. 165]

13 Trifles light as air / Are to the jealous confirmations strong / As proofs of holy writ. [*Othello*, III. iii. 323]

See also ENVY

JESUS CHRIST

1 Jesus calls us; o'er the tumult / Of our life's wild, restless sea. [Mrs C F Alexander, 1818–95, hymn]

2 But there remains the question: what righteousness really is. The method and secret and sweet reasonableness of Jesus. [Matthew Arnold, 1822–88, *Literature and Dogma*, Ch. 12, §2]

3 The only son who ever told the truth about his father was Jesus Christ – and there are doubts about him. [Alan Bennett, 1934– , *Kafka's Dick*, II]

4 For unto us a child is born, unto us a son is given: and the government shall be upon his shoulder: and his name shall be called Wonderful, Counsellor, The mighty God, The everlasting Father, The Prince of Peace. [Bible, OT, *Isaiah* 9:6]

5 He is despised and rejected of men; a man of sorrows, and acquainted with grief. [Bible, OT, *Isaiah* 53:3]

6 Jesus Christ the same yesterday, and to day, and for ever. [Bible, NT, *Hebrews* 13:8]

7 The foxes have holes, and the birds of the air have nests; but the Son of man hath not where to lay his head. [Bible, NT, *St Matthew* 8:20]

8 The Vision of Christ that thou dost see / Is my vision's greatest enemy. [William Blake, 1757–1827, *The Everlasting Gospel*, α]

9 Because I'm Jewish, a lot of people ask why I killed Christ. What can I say? It was an accident. It was one of those parties that got out of hand. [Lenny Bruce, 1923–66, *The Essential L B*, ed. J Cohen, 'The Dirty Word Concept']

10 If Jesus Christ were to come to-day, people wouldn't even crucify him. They would ask him to dinner, and hear what he had to say, and make fun of it. [Thomas Carlyle, 1795–1881, remark, quoted in D A Wilson, *Cat His Zenith*]

11 Conquering kings their titles take / From the foes they captive make: / Jesu, by a nobler deed, / From the thousands He hath freed. [John Chandler, 1806–76, hymn]

12 Show me, dear Christ, thy spouse, so bright and clear. [John Donne, 1571?–1631, *Holy Sonnets*, 18]

13 Done is a battell on the dragon blak, / Our campioun Christ confountet hes his force; / The yettis of hell ar brokin with a crak, / The signe triumphall rasit is of the croce. [William Dunbar, 1460?–1520?, *On the Resurrection of Christ*]

14 In the juvescence of the year / Came Christ the tiger. [T S Eliot, 1888–1965, *Gerontion*]

15 Christ died for our sins. Dare we make his martydrom meaningless by not committing them? [Jules Feiffer, 1929– ; in Laurence J Peter, *Peter's Quotations*]

16 One was left, too, with a gap in Christianity: the canonical gospels do not record that Christ laughed or played. Can a man be perfect if he never laughs or plays? Krishna's jokes may be vapid, but they bridge a gap. [E M Forster, 1879–1970, *The Hill of Devi*, 'Gokul Ashtami']

17 Christ of his gentleness, / Thirsting and hungering / Walked in the wilderness; / Soft words of grace he spoke / Unto lost desert-folk / That listened wondering. [Robert Graves, 1895–1985, *In the Wilderness*]

18 Have you been to Jesus for the cleansing power? / Are you washed in the blood of the Lamb? [Elisha B Hoffman, 1776–1822, hymn]

19 For all the Saints who from their labours rest, / Who Thee by faith before the world confessed, / Thy name, O Jesu, be for ever blest. / Alleluia! [Bishop W How, 1823–97, hymn]

20 The Head that once was crowned with

thorns / Is crowned with glory now. [Thomas Kelly, 1769–1854, hymn]

21 When Jesus came to Birmingham, they simply passed him by, / They never hurt a hair of him, they only let him die. [G A Studdert Kennedy, 1883–1929, *The Unutterable Beauty*, 'Indifference']

22 It's hard to see Christ for priests. That happens when / A poet engenders generations of advertising men. [Adrian Mitchell, 1932– , *Quite Apart from the Holy Ghost*]

23 Hail holy light, offspring of heav'n first-born, / Or of th' Eternal co-eternal beam. [John Milton, 1608–74, *Paradise Lost*, Bk iii, 1]

24 How sweet the name of Jesus sounds / In a believer's ear! [John Newton, 1725–1807, 'The Name of Jesus']

25 All hail, the power of Jesus' name! / Let angels prostrate fall. [Edward Perronet, 1726–92, hymn]

26 Sally said I was a sacrilegious atheist. I probably am. The thing Jesus *really* would've liked would be the guy that plays the kettle drums in the orchestra. [J D Salinger, 1919– , *The Catcher in the Rye*, Ch. 18]

27 Whether you think Jesus was God or not, you must admit that he was a first-rate political economist. [George Bernard Shaw, 1856–1950, *Androcles and the Lion*, Preface, 'Jesus as Economist']

28 How can one believe in the divinity of Our Lord . . . when he was so unconscionably rude to His mother? [Revd F A Simpson, quoted by Revd Eric James in *Listener*, 30 Oct. 1980]

29 Who dreamed that Christ has died in vain? / He walks again on the Seas of Blood, He comes in the terrible Rain. [Edith Sitwell, 1887–1964, *The Shadow of Cain*]

30 But He was never, well, / What I call / A Sportsman; / For forty days / He went out into the desert / – And never shot anything. [Osbert Sitwell, 1892–1969, *Old Fashioned Sportsmen*]

31 Thou hast conquered, O pale Galilean; the world has grown grey from thy breath; / We have drunken of things Lethean, and fed on the fullness of death. [A C Swinburne, 1837–1909, *Hymn to Proserpine*]

32 And so the Word had breath, and wrought / With human hands the creed of creeds / In loveliness of perfect deeds, / More strong than all poetic thought. [Alfred, Lord Tennyson, 1809–92, *In Memoriam*, 36]

33 When I survey the wondrous Cross, / On which the Prince of Glory died, / My richest gain I count but loss / And pour contempt on all my pride. [Isaac Watts, 1674–1748, hymn]

34 Jesu, lover of my soul, / Let me to thy bosom fly, / While the nearer waters roll, / While the tempest still is high; / Hide me, O my Saviour, hide, / Till the storm of life is past: / Safe into the haven guide, / O receive my soul at last. [Charles Wesley, 1707–88, hymn]

See also CATHOLICS, CHRISTIANITY, CHRISTMAS, CHURCHES, CHURCH OF ENGLAND, PROTESTANTS

JEWELLERY

1 Don't ever wear artistic jewellery; it wrecks a woman's reputation. [Colette, 1873–1954, *Gigi*]

2 Often I don't recognize faces, but I always recognize the jewellery. [Jean Giraudoux, 1882–1944, *Tiger at the Gates*, I]

3 Kissing your hand may make you feel very good but a diamond and safire bracelet lasts forever. [Anita Loos, 1893–1981, *Gentlemen Prefer Blondes*, Ch. 1]

4 Rich and rare were the gems she wore, / And a bright gold ring on her hand she bore. [Thomas Moore, 1779–1852, *Irish Melodies*, 'Rich and Rare']

5 Diamonds are a Girl's Best Friend. [Leo Robin, 1900–1984, title of song in musical *Gentlemen Prefer Blondes*]

JEWS

1 The governing idea of Hellenism is spontaneity of consciousness; that of Hebraism, strictness of conscience. [Matthew Arnold, 1822–88, *Culture and Anarchy*, Ch. 4]

2 As everyone knows, where there are two Jews there are three opinions. [Rabbi Anthony Bayfield, 1946– , in *Guardian*, 31 Dec. 1987]

3 The poor darlings [the Jews], I'm awfully fond of them and I'm awfully sorry for them, but it's their own silly fault – they ought to have let God alone. [Hilaire Belloc, 1870–1953, letter to Robert Speaight in Speaight's *Life of H B*, Ch. 19]

4 Says Hyam to Moses, / 'Let's cut off our noses.' / Says Moses to Hyam, / 'Ma tear, who vould buy 'em?' [Shirley Brooks, 1816–74, *A Practical Answer*]

5 How odd / Of God / To choose / The Jews. [W N Ewer, 1885–1976, *How Odd*]

6 *Jedes Land hat die Juden, die es verdient.* – Every country has the Jews that it deserves. [Karl Emil Franzos, 1848–1904, *Schlüssel zur neueren Geschichte der Juden*]

7 I herewith commission you to carry out all preparations with regard to . . . a *total solution* of the Jewish question in those territories of Europe which are under German influence. [Hermann Goering, 1893–1946 (instructions to Heydrich, 31 July 1941), in W L Shirer, *The Rise and Fall of the Third Reich*, Bk v, Ch. 27]

8 It is extremely difficult for a Jew to be converted, for how can he bring himself to believe in the divinity of – another Jew? [Heinrich Heine, 1797–1856, attr.]

9 He had been brought up to spot a gentile as someone who ordered pints in pubs. [Howard Jacobson, 1942– , *Coming from Behind*, Ch. 7]

10 For me this is a vital litmus test: no intellectual society can flourish where a Jew feels even slightly uneasy. [Paul Johnson, 1928– , in *The Sunday Times Magazine*, 6 Feb. 1977]

11 Jews ask forgiveness of man, not God, which is rough on us because man is a harder con than God any day. [John Le Carré, 1931– , *The Tailor of Panama*, Ch. 6]

12 I decide who is a Jew. [Karl Lueger, 1844–1910, in A Bullock, *Hitler*, Pt I, 1. Sometimes wrongly attr. to Goering]

13 Pessimism is a luxury that a Jew never can allow himself. [Golda Meir, 1898–1978; *Observer*, 'Sayings of the Year', 29 Dec. 1974]

14 I'm not really a Jew; just Jew-ish, not the whole hog. [Jonathan Miller, 1934– , *Beyond the Fringe*]

15 The old jibe is that Jews are like everyone else, only more so; British Jews, they like to think, are like other Jews, only less so. [Frederic Raphael, 1931– , in *Listener*, 20 Apr. 1989]

16 I saw my first porno film recently – a Jewish porno film – one minute of sex and nine minutes of guilt. [Joan Rivers, 1933– ; in *Hammer and Tongues*, ed. Michèle Brown and Ann O'Connor, 'Guilt']

17 It's a family joke that when I was a tiny child I turned from the window out of which I was watching a snowstorm, and hopefully asked, 'Momma, do we believe in winter?' [Philip Roth, 1933– , *Portnoy's Complaint*, 'Cunt Crazy']

18 A Jewish man with parents alive is a fifteen-year-old boy, and will remain a fifteen-year-old boy till they die. [Philip Roth, 1933– , *Portnoy's Complaint*, 'Cunt Crazy']

19 For sufferance is the badge of all our tribe. [William Shakespeare, 1564–1616, *The Merchant of Venice*, I. iii. (111)]

20 If you prick us, do we not bleed? If you tickle us, do we not laugh? If you poison us, do we not die? and if you wrong us, shall we not revenge? [*The Merchant of Venice*, III. i. (69)]

21 I believe that the Jews have made a contribution to the human condition out of all proportion to their numbers: I believe them to be an immense people. Not only have they supplied the world with two leaders of the stature of Jesus Christ and Karl Marx, but they have even indulged in the luxury of following neither one nor the other. [Peter Ustinov, 1921– , *Dear Me*, Ch. 16]

22 No Jew was ever fool enough to turn Christian unless he was a clever man. [Israel Zangwill, 1864–1926, *Children of the Ghetto*, I, 7]

23 The law of dislike for the unlike will always prevail. And whereas the unlike is normally situated at a safe distance, the Jews bring the unlike into the heart of *every milieu*, and must there defend a frontier line as large as the world. [Israel Zangwill, 1864–1926, *Speeches, Articles and Letters*, 'The Jewish Race']

See also ISRAEL

JOKES

1 The marvellous thing about a joke with a double meaning is that it can only mean one thing. [Ronnie Barker, 1929– , *Sauce*, 'Daddie's Sauce']

2 The aim of a joke is not to degrade the human being but to remind him that he is already degraded. [George Orwell, 1903–50, *Collected Essays*, 'Funny but Not Vulgar']

3 A jest's prosperity lies in the ear / Of him that hears it, never in the tongue / Of him that makes it. [William Shakespeare, 1564–1616, *Love's Labour's Lost*, V. ii. (869)]

4 My way of joking is to tell the truth. It's the funniest joke in the world. [George Bernard Shaw, 1856–1950, *John Bull's Other Island*, II]

5 It requires a surgical operation to get a joke well into a Scotch understanding. [Sydney Smith, 1771–1845, in Lady Holland, *Memoir*, Vol. I, Ch. 2]

6 Guides cannot master the subtleties of the American joke. [Mark Twain, 1835–1910, *Innocents Abroad*, Ch. 19]

See also COMEDY, HUMOUR, SATIRE, WIT

JOURNALISM

1 Good prose is the selection of the best words; poetry is the best words in the best order; and journalese is any old words in any old order. [anon., quoted by Adam Brewer in letter to *The Times*, 21 Aug. 1987]

2 Christianity naturally, but why journalism? [(To Frank Harris, who claimed that the two greatest curses of civilization were Christianity and journalism) A J Balfour, 1848–1930, in Margot Asquith, *Autobiography*, Ch. 10]

3 When the legend becomes fact, print the legend. [James Warner Bellah, 1899–1976, and Willis Goldbeck, 1899–1979, in film *The Man Who Shot Liberty Valance*]

4 Reporters don't believe in anything, vicar. It's an article of faith. [Guy Bellamy, 1935– , *A Village Called Sin*, Ch. 15]

5 Journalists say a thing that they know isn't true, in the hope that if they keep on saying it long enough it *will* be true. [Arnold Bennett, 1867–1931, *The Title*, II]

6 Journalism could be described as turning one's enemies into money. [Craig Brown, 1957– , in *Daily Telegraph*, 28 Sept. 1990]

7 The making of evanescent bricks with ephemeral straw. [(Definition of journalism) James Cameron, 1911–85, in *Independent*, 28 July 1991]

8 Burke said that there were Three Estates in Parliament; but, in the Reporters' Gallery yonder, there sat a *Fourth Estate*, more important far than they all. [Thomas Carlyle, 1795–1881, *Heroes and Hero-Worship*, v, 'The Hero as Man of Letters']; see 19

9 By his standards anyone who noticed how many walls the room had would be observant. [Raymond Chandler (of an interviewer who got things wrong), from *Selected Letters*, ed. F MacShane, quoted in *The Sunday Times*, 29 Nov. 1981]

10 Journalism largely consists in saying 'Lord Jones Dead' to people who never knew Lord Jones was alive. [G K Chesterton, 1874–1936, *The Wisdom of Father Brown*, 'The Purple Wig']

11 If you are Editor [of *The Times*] you can never get away for an evening. It's worse than a herd of dairy cows. [Alan Clark, 1928–99, *Diaries*, 6 June 1984]

12 Literature is the art of writing something that will be read twice; journalism what will be grasped at once. [Cyril Connolly, 1903–74, *Enemies of Promise*, Ch. 3]

13 There is a painful difference, often obscured by popular prejudice, between reporting something and making it up. [Michael Frayn, 1933– , *Clouds*, I. i]

14 I call journalism everything that will interest less tomorrow than it does today. [André Gide, 1869–1951, attr.]

15 I'll tell you briefly what I think of newspapermen: the hand of God reaching down into the mire couldn't elevate one of them to the depths of degradation – not by a million miles. [Ben Hecht, 1893–1964, screenplay of film *Nothing Sacred*]

16 Journalism allows its readers to witness history; fiction gives its readers an opportunity to live it. [John Hersey, 1914–96, in *Time*, 13 Mar. 1950]

17 Journalists write because they have nothing to say, and have something to say because they write. [Karl Kraus, 1874–1936, *Half-truths and One-and-a-half Truths*, 'In Hollow Heads']

18 The man must have a rare recipe for melancholy, who can be dull in Fleet Street. [Charles Lamb, 1775–1834, letter to T Manning, 15 Feb. 1802]

19 The gallery in which the reporters sit has become a fourth estate of the realm. [Lord

Macaulay, 1800–1859, *Historical Essays*, 'Hallam's Constitutional History']; see 8

20 Journalists are more attentive to the minute hand of history than to the hour hand. [Desmond MacCarthy, 1877–1952, in Kenneth Tynan, *Curtains*, Pt 2]

21 A reporter is a man who has renounced everything in life but the world, the flesh, and the devil. [David Murray, 1888–1962; in *Observer*, 'Sayings of the Week', 5 July 1931]

22 It is hard news that catches readers. Features hold them. [Lord Northcliffe, 1865–1922, in T Clarke, *My Northcliffe Diary*]

23 For casual reading – in your bath, for instance, or late at night when you are too tired to go to bed, or in the odd quarter of an hour before lunch – there is nothing to touch a back number of the *Girl's Own Paper*. [George Orwell, 1903–50, in *Fortnightly Review*, Nov. 1936]

24 In America, journalism is apt to be regarded as an extension of history: in Britain, as an extension of conversation. [Anthony Sampson, 1926– , *Anatomy of Britain Today*, Ch. 9]

25 A foreign correspondent is someone who lives in foreign parts and corresponds, usually in the form of essays containing no new facts. Otherwise he's someone who flies around from hotel to hotel and thinks the most interesting thing about any story is the fact that he has arrived to cover it. [Tom Stoppard, 1937– , *Night and Day*, I]

26 You cannot hope / To bribe or twist, / Thank God! the / British journalist. / But, seeing what / the man will do / unbribed, there's / no occasion to. [Humbert Wolfe, 1886–1940, *The Uncelestial City*, Bk 1, 'Over the Fire']

27 Rock journalism is people who can't write interviewing people who can't talk for people who can't read. [Frank Zappa, 1940–93, in *Rolling Stone*, 1970]

See also MEDIA, NEWSPAPERS

JOY

1 Weeping may endure for a night, but joy cometh in the morning. [Bible, OT, *Psalms* 30:5]

2 Energy is eternal delight! [William Blake, 1757–1827, *The Marriage of Heaven and Hell*, 'The Voice of the Devil']

3 He who binds to himself a Joy / Doth the wingèd life destroy; / But he who kisses the Joy as it flies / Lives in Eternity's sunrise. [William Blake, 1757–1827, *Gnomic Verses*, 'Several Questions Answered']

4 Oh, the wild joys of living! the leaping from rock up to rock, / The strong rending of boughs from the fir-tree, the cool silver shock / Of the plunge in a pool's living water. [Robert Browning, 1812–89, *Saul*, 9]

5 There's not a joy the world can give like that it takes away. [Lord Byron, 1788–1824, *Stanzas for Music*, 'There's Not a Joy']

6 So, if I dream I have you, I have you, / For all our joys are but fantastical. [John Donne, 1571?–1631, *Elegies*, 10, 'The Dream', I, 13]

7 And, e'en while fashion's brightest arts decoy, / The heart distrusting asks, if this be joy. [Oliver Goldsmith, 1728–74, *The Deserted Village*, 263]

8 The meanest flowret of the vale, / The simplest note that swells the gale, / The common sun, the air, and skies, / To him are opening paradise. [Thomas Gray, 1716–71, *Ode on the Pleasure Arising from Vicissitude*]

9 From the heart of the fountain of delight rises a jet of bitterness that tortures us among the very flowers. [Lucretius, 99–55 BC, *On the Nature of the Universe*, IV, 1133]

10 Our planet / is poorly equipped / for delight / One must snatch / gladness / from the days that are. / In this life / it's not difficult to die. / To make life / is more difficult by far. [Vladimir Mayakovsky, 1893–1930, *Sergei Yesenin*]

11 *Freude, schöner Götterfunken, / Tochter aus Elysium.* – Joy, lovely radiance of the god, thou daughter of Elysium. [Friedrich von Schiller, 1759–1805, *An die Freude*]

12 Eternity was in our lips and eyes, / Bliss in our brows bent. [William Shakespeare, 1564–1616, *Antony and Cleopatra*, I. iii. 35]

13 Rarely, rarely, comest thou, / Spirit of Delight! [P B Shelley, 1792–1822, song: *Rarely, Rarely, Comest Thou*]

14 We are not sure of sorrow, / And joy was never sure. [A C Swinburne, 1837–1909, *The Garden of Proserpine*, 10]

15 You never enjoy the world aright, till the sea itself floweth in your veins, till you are clothed with the heavens, and crowned with the stars.

[Thomas Traherne, 1637?–74, *Centuries of Meditations*, i, 29]

16 I have felt / A presence that disturbs me with the joy / Of elevated thoughts; a sense sublime / Of something far more deeply interfused, / Whose dwelling is the light of setting suns, / And the round ocean and the living air, / And the blue sky, and in the mind of man. [William Wordsworth, 1770–1850, *Lines Composed a Few Miles above Tintern Abbey*, 93]

17 Surprised by joy – impatient as the wind / I turned to share the transport. [William Wordsworth, 1770–1850, *Miscellaneous Sonnets*, 1, 27]

See also HAPPINESS, PLEASURE

JUDGEMENT, legal and otherwise

1 The verdict of the world is final. [St Augustine, 354–430, *Contra Epistolam Parmeniani*, III, 24]

2 Judge none blessed before his death. [Bible, Apocrypha, *Ecclesiasticus* 11:28]

3 MENE, MENE, TEKEL, UPHARSIN ... Thou art weighed in the balances, and art found wanting. Thy kingdom is divided, and given to the Medes and Persians. [The Bible, OT, *Daniel* 5:25]

4 Out of thine own mouth will I judge thee. [Bible, NT, *St Luke* 19:22]

5 Judge not, that ye be not judged. [Bible, NT, *St Matthew* 7:1]

6 No man can justly censure or condemn another, because indeed no man truly knows another. [Sir Thomas Browne, 1605–82, *Religio Medici*, Pt II, 4]

7 'I'll be judge, I'll be jury,' said cunning old Fury: / 'I'll try the whole cause, and condemn you to death.' [Lewis Carroll, 1832–98, *Alice in Wonderland*, Ch. 3]

8 Sentence first – verdict afterwards. [Lewis Carroll, 1832–98, *Alice in Wonderland*, Ch. 12]

9 I'll let you in on a secret about my son Solomon: he was dead serious when he proposed cutting the baby in half, that *putz*. I swear to God. The dumb son of a bitch was trying to be fair, not shrewd. [Joseph Heller, 1923–99, *God Knows*, 1]

10 Christ says, 'Judge not,' *but we must judge*. [W R Inge, 1860–1954, attr.]

11 Everyone complains of his memory, but no one complains of his judgement. [Duc de La Rochefoucauld, 1613–80, *Maxims*, 89]

12 I have already told you, here [Paris] they hang a man first and try him afterwards. [Molière, 1622–73, *Monsieur de Pourceaugnac*, III. I]

13 'Tis with our judgements as our watches, none / Go just alike, yet each believes his own. [Alexander Pope, 1688–1744, *An Essay on Criticism*, 9]

14 The hungry judges soon the sentence sign, / And wretches hang that jurymen may dine. [Alexander Pope, 1688–1744, *The Rape of the Lock*, III, 21]

15 The dice of judgement ... the same dice as you gentlemen use in this supreme court of yours. [François Rabelais, *c.*1492–1553, *Pantagruel*, Bk III, Ch. 39]

16 It is much more difficult to judge oneself than to judge others. [Antoine de Saint-Exupéry, 1900–1944, *The Little Prince*, Ch. 10]

17 Commonly we say a judgement falls on a man for something in him we cannot abide. [John Selden, 1584–1654, *Table Talk*, 67]

18 O judgment! thou art fled to brutish beasts, / And men have lost their reason. [William Shakespeare, 1564–1616, *Julius Caesar*, III. ii. (110)]

19 See how yond justice rails upon yond simple thief. Hark in thine ear: change places; and handy-dandy, which is the justice, which is the thief? [*King Lear*, IV. vi. (156)]

20 How would you be, / If He, which is the top of judgement, should / But judge you as you are? [*Measure for Measure*, II. ii. 75]

21 A Daniel come to judgement! yea! a Daniel! / O wise young judge, how I do honour thee! [*The Merchant of Venice*, IV. i. (223)]

22 I say she used to be no better than she ought to be, but she is now. [James Thurber, 1894–1961, *Men, Women and Dogs*, cartoon caption]

See also INNOCENCE, JUSTICE, LAW, LAWYERS, PUNISHMENT

JUDGMENT DAY

1 Every idle word that men shall speak, they shall give account thereof in the day of judgement. [Bible, NT, *St Matthew* 12:36]

2 Don't wait for the Last Judgement. It takes place every day. [Albert Camus, 1913–60, *The Fall*]

3 At the round earth's imagined corners, blow / Your trumpets, Angels, and arise, arise / From death, you numberless infinities / Of souls. [John Donne, 1571?–1631, *Holy Sonnets*, 7]

4 What if this present were the world's last night? [John Donne, 1571?–1631, *Holy Sonnets*, 13]

5 On the Last Day the wrecks will surface over the / sea. [Gavin Ewart, 1916–95, *Resurrection*]

6 Some say the world will end in fire, / Some say in ice. / From what I've tasted of desire / I hold with those who favour fire, / But if I had to perish twice, / I think I know enough of hate / To say that for destruction ice / Is also great / And would suffice. [Robert Frost, 1874–1963, *Fire and Ice*]

7 There's not a modest maiden elf / But dreads the final Trumpet, / Lest half of her should rise herself, / And half some sturdy strumpet! [Thomas Hardy, 1840–1928, *The Levelled Churchyard*]

8 Oh, war shill we go w'en de great day comes, / Wid de blowin' er de trumpits en de bangin' er de drums? / How many po' sinners'll be kotched out late / En find no latch ter de golden gate? [Joel Chandler Harris, 1848–1908, *Uncle Remus: His Songs*, I]

9 Though the mills of God grind slowly, yet they grind exceeding small; / Though with patience He stands waiting, with exactness grinds He all. [H W Longfellow, 1807–82, *Retribution* (trans. of Friedrich von Logau)]

10 That day of wrath, that dreadful day, / When heaven and earth shall pass away. [Sir Walter Scott, 1771–1832, *The Lay of the Last Minstrel*, VI, 31]

11 Doomsday is near; die all, die merrily. [William Shakespeare, 1564–1616, *1 Henry IV*, IV. i. 134]

12 Till the sun grows cold, / And the stars are old, / And the leaves of the Judgement Book unfold. [Bayard Taylor, 1825–78, *Bedouin Song*]

13 *Dies irae, dies illa / Solvet saeclum in favilla, / Teste David cum Sibylla.* – Day of wrath and doom impending, / David's word with Sibyl's blending, / Heaven and earth in ashes ending. [Thomas of Celano, *c.*1219–60, *Analecta Hymnica*, trans. in *The English Hymnal*]

14 And what rough beast its hour come round at last, / Slouches towards Bethlehem to be born? [W B Yeats, 1865–1939, *The Second Coming*]

JUSTICE & INJUSTICE

1 The law doth punish man or woman / That steals the goose from off the common, / But lets the greater felon loose, / That steals the common from the goose. [(On enclosures) anon., 18th cent.]

2 Military justice is to justice as military music is to music. [anon., in Max Ophuls's film *The Memory of Justice*]

3 Acts of injustice done / Between the setting and the rising sun / In history lie like bones, each one. [W H Auden, 1907–73, and Christopher Isherwood, 1904–86, *The Ascent of F6*, II. v]

4 The place of justice is a hallowed place. [Francis Bacon, 1561–1626, *Essays*, 56, 'Of Judicature']

5 With what measure ye mete, it shall be measured to you. [Bible, NT, *St Mark* 4:24]

6 It is better that ten guilty persons escape than one innocent suffer. [William Blackstone, 1723–80, *Commentary on the Laws of England*, Bk iv, 27]

7 The rain it raineth on the just / And also on the unjust fella: / But chiefly on the just, because / The unjust steals the just's umbrella. [Lord Bowen, 1835–94, quoted in Walter Sichel, *Sands of Time*, Ch. 4]

8 You want justice, but do you want to pay for it, hm? When you go to a butcher you know you have to pay, but you people go to a judge as if you were off to a funeral supper. [Bertolt Brecht, 1898–1956, *The Caucasian Chalk Circle*, V]

9 Give both the infinitudes their due – / Infinite mercy, but, I wish, / As infinite a justice too. [Robert Browning, 1812–89, *The Heretic's Tragedy*]

10 When one has been threatened with a great injustice, one accepts a smaller as a favour. [Jane Welsh Carlyle, 1795–1881, *Journal*, 21 Nov. 1855]

11 Trial by jury itself . . . will be a delusion, a mockery, and a snare. [Lord Denman, 1779–1854, judgement in *O'Connell* v. *The Queen*, 4 Sept. 1844]

12 *Fiat justitia et pereat mundus.* – Let justice be done, though the world perish. [Emperor Ferdinand I, 1503–64, motto]

13 Justice, I firmly believe, is so subtle a thing that to interpret it one has only need of a heart. [José García Oliver, 1901–80, in Hugh Thomas, *The Spanish Civil War*, Ch. 43]

14 'Justice' was done, and the President of the Immortals, in Aeschylean phrase, had ended his sport with Tess. [Thomas Hardy, 1840–1928, *Tess of the D'Urbervilles*, Ch. 59]

15 A long line of cases shows that it is not merely of some importance, but it is of fundamental importance, that justice should not only be done, but should manifestly and undoubtedly be seen to be done. [Lord Justice Hewart, 1870–1943, *Rex* v. *Sussex Justices*, 9 Nov. 1923]

16 Thou art indeed just, Lord, if I contend / With thee; but, sir, so what I plead is just. / Why do sinners' ways prosper? and why must / Disappointment all I endeavour end? [Gerard Manley Hopkins, 1884–89, *Thou art Indeed Just, Lord*]

17 A lawyer has no business with the justice or injustice of the cause which he undertakes, unless his client asks his opinion, and then he is bound to give it honestly. The justice or injustice of the cause is to be decided by the judge. [Dr Samuel Johnson, 1709–84, in James Boswell, *Tour of the Hebrides*, 15 Aug. 1773]

18 The injustice done to an individual is sometimes of service to the public. [Junius, 18th cent., *Letters*, 41]

19 You may object that it is not a trial at all; you are quite right, for it is only a trial if I recognize it as such. [Franz Kafka, 1883–1924, *The Trial*, Ch. 2, 'First Interrogation']

20 Love of justice in most men is no more than the fear of suffering injustice. [Duc de La Rochefoucauld, 1613–80, *Maxims*, 78]

21 Justice is such a fine thing that we cannot pay too dearly for it. [Alain René Lesage, 1668–1747, *Crispin rival de son maître*, IX]

22 I'm arm'd with more than complete steel – / The justice of my quarrel. [Christopher Marlowe, 1564–93, *Lust's Dominion*, IV. iii (authorship of play doubtful)]

23 Oh, Elizabeth, your justice would freeze beer! [Arthur Miller, 1915– , *The Crucible*, II]

24 Poetic Justice, with her lifted scale, / Where, in nice balance, truth with gold she weighs, / And solid pudding against empty praise. [Alexander Pope, 1688–1744, *The Dunciad*, Bk i, 52]

25 If you give me six lines written by the most honest man, I will find something in them to hang him. [Cardinal Richelieu, 1585–1642, attr. in various forms and to other authors]

26 A man who is good enough to shed his blood for his country is good enough to be given a square deal afterwards. More than that no man is entitled to, and less than that no man shall have. [Theodore Roosevelt, 1858–1919, speech at Springfield, Illinois, 4 June 1903]

27 Use every man after his desert and who would 'scape whipping? [William Shakespeare, 1564–1616, *Hamlet*, II. ii. (561)]

28 What stronger breastplate than a heart untainted! / Thrice is he armed that hath his quarrel just, / And he but naked, though locked up in steel, / Whose conscience with injustice is corrupted. [*2 Henry VI*, III. ii. 232]

29 Though justice be thy plea, consider this, / That in the course of justice none of us / Should see salvation: we do pray for mercy, / And that same prayer doth teach us all to render / The deeds of mercy. [*The Merchant of Venice*, IV. i. (198)]

30 Are you going to hang him *anyhow* – and try him afterward? [Mark Twain, 1835–1910, *Innocents at Home*, Ch. 5]

31 The supernatural virtue of justice consists of behaving exactly as though there were equality when one is the stronger in an unequal relationship. [Simone Weil, 1909–43, *Waiting on God*, 'Forms of the Implicit Love of God']

See also GUILT, INNOCENCE, JUDGEMENT, LAW, LAWYERS, PUNISHMENTS

K

KILLING

1 If any man thinks he slays, and if another thinks he is slain, neither knows the ways of truth. The Eternal in man cannot kill: the Eternal in man cannot die. [*Bhagavad Gita*, 2:19]

2 Saul hath slain his thousands, and David his ten thousands. [Bible, OT, *I Samuel* 18:7]

3 I've been accused of every death except the casualty list of the World War. [Al Capone, 1899–1947, in Kenneth Allsop, *The Bootleggers*, Ch. 11]

4 Thou shalt not kill; but needst not strive / Officiously to keep alive. [Arthur Hugh Clough, 1819–61, *The Latest Decalogue*]

5 Killing / Is the ultimate simplification of life. [Hugh MacDiarmid, 1892–1978, *England's Double Knavery*]

6 Put out the light and then put out the light. / If I quench thee, thou flaming minister, / I can again thy former light restore, / Should I repent me; but once put out thy light, / Thou cunning'st pattern of excelling nature, / I know not where is that Promethean heat / That can thy light relume. [William Shakespeare, 1564–1616, *Othello*, V. ii. 7]

7 Yet each man kills the thing he loves, / By each let this be heard, / Some do it with a bitter look, / Some with a flattering word. / The coward does it with a kiss, / The brave man with a sword! [Oscar Wilde, 1854–1900, *The Ballad of Reading Gaol*, Pt I, 7]

See also BLOOD, DEATH, MURDER

KINDNESS

1 Every man who will not have softening of the heart must at last have softening of the brain. [G K Chesterton, 1874–1936, *Orthodoxy*, Ch. 3]

2 Life is mostly froth and bubble, / Two things stand like stone, / Kindness in another's trouble, / Courage in your own. [Adam Lindsay Gordon, 1833–70, *Ye Wearie Wayfarer*, Fytte 8]

3 I shall pass through this world but once. If, therefore, there be any kindness I can show, or any good thing I can do, let me do it now; let me not defer it or neglect it, for I shall not pass this way again. [Stephen Grellet, 1773–1855. Also attr. to others]

4 In the West people make free with words like 'freedom' and 'the spirit' but few ever think to ask a man whether he has enough money for lunch. [Czeslaw Milosz, 1911– , *Visions from San Francisco Bay*]

5 Contrary to what clergymen and policemen believe, gentleness is biological and aggression is cultural. [Stefan Themerson, 1910–88, in obituary in *Guardian*, 8 Sept. 1988]

6 So many gods, so many creeds, / So many paths that wind and wind, / While just the art of being kind / Is all the sad world needs. [Ella Wheeler Wilcox, 1855–1919, *The World's Need*]

7 I have always depended on the kindness of strangers. [Tennessee Williams, 1911–83, *A Streetcar Named Desire*, Blanche's final words in II. xi]

8 That best portion of a good man's life, / His little, nameless, unremembered acts / Of kindness and of love. [William Wordsworth, 1770–1850, *Lines Composed a Few Miles above Tintern Abbey*, 33]

See also GENEROSITY, GOOD

KINGS & QUEENS IN GENERAL

1 *Il ne faut pas être plus royaliste que le roi.* – You must not be more royalist than the king. [anon. phrase current in the reign of Louis XVI; in Chateaubriand, *De la monarchie selon la charte*, Ch. 81]

2 *Le roi est mort, vive le roi.* – The king is dead, long live the king. [anon. phrase used by the heralds to proclaim the death of one French king and the accession of his successor. First used in 1461]

3 What I say is what dose it matter we cant all be of the Blood royal can we. [Daisy Ashford, 1881–1972, *The Young Visiters*, 5]

4 He [Cromwell] gart kings ken they had a lith [joint] in their neck. [Alexander Boswell, Lord Auchinleck, 1706–82, quoted in James Boswell, *Tour of the Hebrides*, note, 6 Nov. 1773]

5 The best reason why Monarchy is a strong government is that it is an intelligible government. The mass of mankind understand it, and they hardly anywhere in the world understand any other. [Walter Bagehot, 1826–77, *The English Constitution*, Ch. 2]

6 Put not your trust in princes, nor in the son of man, in whom there is no help. [Bible, OT, *Psalms* 146:3]

7 That the king can do no wrong is a necessary and fundamental principle of the English constitution. [William Blackstone, 1723–80, *Commentary on the Laws of England*, Bk iii, 17]

8 Such grace had kings when the world begun! [Robert Browning, 1812–89, *Pippa Passes*, Pt III, 1222]

9 Kings will be tyrants from policy, when subjects are rebels from principle. [Edmund Burke, 1729–97, *Reflections on the Revolution in France*, Penguin edn, p. 172]

10 Somebody has said, that a king may make a nobleman, but he cannot make a gentleman. [Edmund Burke, 1729–97, letter to William Smith, 29 Jan. 1795]

11 God save our gracious king! / Long live our noble king! / God save the king! [Henry Carey, 1693?–1743, *God Save the King*]

12 Courts and camps are the only places to learn the world in. [Earl of Chesterfield, 1694–1773, letter to his son, 2 Oct. 1747]

13 A dying monarchy is always one that has too much power, not too little; a dying religion always interferes more than it ought, not less. [G K Chesterton, 1874–1936, in *Daily News*, 11 Mar. 1911]

14 Everyone likes flattery; and when you come to Royalty you should lay it on with a trowel. [Benjamin Disraeli, 1804–81 (attr. remark to Matthew Arnold), quoted in G W E Russell, *Collections and Recollections*, Ch. 23]

15 There will soon be only five kings left – the Kings of England, Diamonds, Hearts, Spades and Clubs. [King Farouk of Egypt, 1920–65, to Lord Boyd-Orr at Cairo Conference, 1948]

16 Oh, 'tis a glorious thing, I ween, / To be a regular Royal Queen! / No half-and-half-affair, I mean, / But a right-down regular Royal Queen! [W S Gilbert, 1836–1911, *The Gondoliers*, 1]

17 The tourists who come to our island take in the Monarchy along with feeding the pigeons in Trafalgar Square. [Willie Hamilton, 1917– , *My Queen and I*, Ch. 9]

18 It was not for me to bandy civilities with my Sovereign. [Dr Samuel Johnson, 1709–84, in James Boswell, *Life of J*, Feb. 1767]

19 Whoso pulleth out this sword of this stone and anvil is rightwise king born of all England. [Thomas Malory, d. 1471, *Morte d'Arthur*, Bk. i, Ch. 4]

20 The King asked / The Queen, and / The Queen asked / The Dairymaid: / 'Could we have some butter for / The Royal slice of bread?' [A A Milne, 1882–1956, *When We Were Very Young*, 'The King's Breakfast']

21 The right divine of kings to govern wrong. [Alexander Pope, 1688–1744, *The Dunciad*, Bk iv, 188]

22 A king is a thing men have made for their own sakes, for quietness' sake. Just as if in a family one man is appointed to buy the meat. [John Selden, 1584–1654, *Table Talk*, 71]

23 There's such divinity doth hedge a king, / That treason can but peep to what it would.

[William Shakespeare, 1564–1616, *Hamlet*, IV. v. (123)]

24 Uneasy lies the head that wears a crown. [*2 Henry IV*, III. i. 31]

25 O polished perturbation! golden care! / That keep'st the ports of slumber open wide / To many a watchful night! [*2 Henry IV*, IV. v. 22]

26 And what have kings that privates have not too, / Save ceremony, save general ceremony? [*Henry V*, IV. i. (258)]

27 Nice customs curtsey to great kings. [*Henry V*, V. ii. (291)]

28 Gives not the hawthorn bush a sweeter shade / To shepherds looking on their silly sheep, / Than doth a rich embroidered canopy / To kings that fear their subjects' treachery? [*3 Henry VI*, II. v. 42]

29 I swear 'tis better to be lowly born, / And range with humble livers in content, / Than to be perked up in a glistering grief, / And wear a golden sorrow. [*Henry VIII*, II. iii. 19]

30 We were not born to sue, but to command. [*Richard II*, I. i. 96]

31 Not all the water in the rough rude sea / Can wash the balm from an anointed king; / The breath of worldly men cannot depose / The deputy elected by the Lord. [*Richard II*, III. ii. 54]

32 For God's sake, let us sit upon the ground / And tell sad stories of the death of kings: / How some have been deposed, some slain in war, / Some haunted by the ghosts they have deposed; / Some poisoned by their wives, some sleeping killed; / All murdered: for within the hollow crown / That rounds the mortal temples of a king / Keeps Death his court. [*Richard II*, III. ii. 155]

33 God save the king! Will no man say, amen? [*Richard II*, IV. i. 172]

34 To know nor faith, nor love, nor law; to be / Omnipotent but friendless is to reign. [P B Shelley, 1792–1822, *Prometheus Unbound*, II. iv. 47]

35 Authority forgets a dying king. [Alfred, Lord Tennyson, 1809–92, *Idylls of the King*, 'The Passing of Arthur', 289]

36 All kings is mostly rapscallions. [Mark Twain, 1835–1910, *The Adventures of Huckleberry Finn*, Ch. 23]

37 The monarchy is a labour-intensive industry. [Harold Wilson, 1916–95; *Observer*, 'Sayings of the Week', 13 Feb. 1977]

38 The king reigns, but does not govern. [Jan Zamoyski, 1541–1605, speech in Polish Parliament, 1605]

See also next category

KINGS & QUEENS: INDIVIDUALS (in alphabetical order of subject)

1 He nothing common did, or mean, / Upon that memorable scene, / But with his keener eye / The axe's edge did try. [(Of Charles I) Andrew Marvell, 1621–78, *An Horatian Ode upon Cromwell's Return from Ireland*, 57]

2 A merry monarch, scandalous and poor. [Earl of Rochester, 1647–80, *A Satire on King Charles II*]

3 I suppose the Prince of Wales feels extra sympathy towards those who've got no job because, in a way, he's got no job. [(Of Prince Charles) Norman Tebbit, 1931– , in BBC TV programme *Panorama*, Nov. 1987]

4 A cut-purse of the empire and the rule, / That from a shelf the precious diadem stole, / And put it in his pocket! [(Of Claudius) William Shakespeare, 1564–1616, *Hamlet*, III. iii. 99]

5 How different, how very different from the home life of our own dear Queen! [anon. (alleged remark of a Victorian matron during a performance of *Antony and Cleopatra*), quoted in Irvin S Cobb, *A Laugh a Day*]

6 The barge she sat in, like a burnished throne, / Burned on the water; the poop was beaten gold, / Purple the sails, and so perfumed, that / The winds were lovesick with them, the oars were silver / Which to the tune of flutes kept stroke, and made / The water which they beat to follow faster, / As amorous of their strokes. For her own person, / It beggared all description. [(Of Cleopatra) William Shakespeare, 1564–1616, *Antony and Cleopatra*, II. ii. (199)]

7 There's a bloody sight more pox than pax about that boyo. [(Of Edward VII) James Joyce, 1882–1941, *Ulysses*, Penguin edn, 1992, p. 429]

8 A telephone exchange without enough subscribers. [(Of Edward VII) Rebecca West, 1892–1983, in *The Times Educational Supplement*, 8 May 1987]

9 The most damning epitaph you can compose about Edward [VIII] – as a prince, as a king, as a man – is one that all comfortable people should cower from deserving: he was at his best only when the going was good. [Alistair Cooke, 1908– , *Six Men*, Pt II]

10 But you must believe me when I tell you that I have found it impossible to carry the heavy burden of responsibility and to discharge my duties as King as I would wish to do, without the help and support of the woman I love. [Edward VIII, 1894–1972, abdication speech, 11 Dec. 1936]

11 He [Edward VIII] will go from resort to resort getting more tanned and more tired. [(On the king's abdication) Westbrook Pegler, 1894–1969, in Alistair Cooke, *Six Men*, Pt II]

12 I know I have the body of a weak and feeble woman, but I have the heart and stomach of a king, and of a king of England too. [Elizabeth I, 1533–1603, speech at Tilbury, on the approach of the Spanish Armada, 1588]

13 I think everybody really will concede that on this, of all days, I should begin my speech with the words 'My husband and I'. [Elizabeth II, 1926– , speech at Silver Wedding banquet, Guildhall, London, 20 Nov. 1972. The phrase was used as far back as her Christmas Broadcast, 1953]

14 Britain's two female figureheads are a woman who can't tell a joke and a woman who can't understand one. [Germaine Greer, 1939– , in *The Sunday Times Magazine*, 19 Jan. 1986]

15 Pity our poor dear queen. She finds herself increasingly the head of not so much the royal family as the royal one-parent family. [(On the break-up of the marriage of the Duke and Duchess of York) Melanie Phillips, 1951– , in *Guardian*, 21 Mar. 1992]

16 If Her Majesty stood for Parliament – if the Tory Party had any sense and made Her its leader instead of that grammar school twit Heath – us Tories, mate, would win every election we went in for. [Spoken by Johnny Speight, 1920–98, in BBC TV comedy series *Till Death Us Do Part*, 'I Can Give It Up']

17 In order that he might rob a neighbour whom he had promised to defend, black men fought on the coast of Coromandel, and red men scalped each other by the Great Lakes of North America. [Lord Macaulay, 1800–1859, *Historical Essays*, 'Frederic the Great']

18 George the First was always reckoned / Vile, but viler George the Second; / And what mortal ever heard / Any good of George the Third? / When from earth the Fourth descended / God be praised, the Georges ended! [Walter Savage Landor, 1775–1864, *Epigram*]

19 A better farmer ne'er brushed dew from lawn, / A worse king never left a realm undone! [(Of George III) Lord Byron, 1788–1824, *The Vision of Judgement*, 8]

20 An old, mad, blind, despised, and dying king. [(Of George III) P B Shelley, 1792–1822, sonnet: *England in 1819*]

21 I can't understand it. I'm really quite an ordinary sort of chap. [King George V, 1865–1936, attr. at his jubilee in May 1935]

22 The wisest fool in Christendom. [(Of James I) Henri IV of France, 1553–1610, attr. also to Sully]

23 [James I] remained an omniscient umpire whom no one consulted. [Hugh Trevor-Roper, 1914– , *Archbishop Laud*, Ch. 1]

24 The king of France's horses are better housed than I. [Ernst August, elector of Hanover, 1629–98, on seeing Louis XIV's stables at Versailles]

25 This [Buckingham Palace] isn't ours. It's a tied cottage. [Philip, Duke of Edinburgh, 1921– ; in *Royal Quotes*, sel. Noel St George]

26 It little profits that an idle king, / By this still hearth, among these barren crags, / Matched with an aged wife, I mete and dole / Unequal laws unto a savage race. [Alfred, Lord Tennyson, 1809–92, *Ulysses*, 1]

27 'Ave you 'eard o' the Widow at Windsor / With a hairy gold crown on 'er 'ead? [(Of Queen Victoria) Rudyard Kipling, 1865–1936, *The Widow at Windsor*]

28 The Faery [Queen Victoria], he determined, should henceforth wave her wand for him [Disraeli] alone. [Lytton Strachey, 1880–1932, *Queen Victoria*, Ch. 8, iii]

29 At every crisis he [the Kaiser Wilhelm II] crumpled. In defeat, he fled; in revolution, he abdicated; in exile, he remarried. [Winston Churchill, 1874–1965, in *Geoffrey Madan's*

Notebooks, ed. J A Gere and John Sparrow, 'Livres sans nom']

See also previous category

KISSING

1 Let him kiss me with the kisses of his mouth: for thy love is better than wine. [Bible, OT, *Song of Solomon* 1:2]

2 The moth's kiss, first! / Kiss me as if you made believe / You were not sure, this eve, / How my face, your flower, had pursed / Its petals up. [Robert Browning, 1812–89, *In a Gondola*]

3 What of soul was left, I wonder, when the kissing had to stop? [Robert Browning, 1812–89, *A Toccata of Galuppi's*, 14]

4 Gin a body meet a body / Coming through the rye; / Gin a body kiss a body, / Need a body cry? [Robert Burns, 1759–96, *Coming through the Rye*]

5 O fie miss, you must not kiss and tell. [William Congreve, 1670–1729, *Love for Love*, II. x]

6 So, so, break off this last lamenting kiss, / Which sucks two souls, and vapours both away, / Turn thou ghost that way, and let me turn this, / And let our selves benight our happiest day. [John Donne, 1571?–1631, *The Expiration*]

7 If you want to kiss me any time during the evening, Nick, just let me know and I'll be glad to arrange it for you. Just mention my name. [F Scott Fitzgerald, 1896–1940, *The Great Gatsby*, Ch. 6]

8 I dare not ask a kiss; / I dare not beg a smile; / Lest having that, or this, / I might grow proud the while. [Robert Herrick, 1591–1674, *Hesperides*, 'To Electra']

9 You must remember this; / A kiss is just a kiss, / A sigh is just a sigh – / The fundamental things apply / As time goes by. [Herman Hupfeld, 1894–1951, song: *As Time Goes By*, used in film *Casablanca*]

10 Yeah, you remember kissing. It used to come between saying '*Hi*' and fucking. I'm an old-fashioned guy. [David Lodge, 1935– , *Small World*, Pt 2, 2]

11 And she gave me a sisterly kiss. Older sister. [Norman Mailer, 1923– , *The Deer Park*]

12 [When caught by his wife, kissing a chorus girl] I wasn't kissing her, I was whispering in her mouth. [Chico Marx, 1891–1961, in Groucho Marx and R J Anobile, *Marx Brothers Scrapbook*, Ch. 24]

13 Some men kiss and do not tell, some kiss and tell; but George Moore tells and does not kiss. [Susan Langstaff Mitchell, 1866–1926, in O St John Gogarty, *As I Was Going down Sackville Street*, Ch. 7]

14 Had she come all the way for this, / To part at last without a kiss? [William Morris, 1834–96, *The Haystack in the Floods*]

15 Personally, I consider a taxicab much more convenient and less expensive than an old-fashioned victoria if you wish to get to some place, but of course guys and dolls engaged in a little offhand guzzling never wish to get any place in particular, or at least not soon. [Damon Runyon, 1884–1946, *Furthermore*, 'Princess O'Hara']

16 We have kissed away / Kingdoms and provinces. [William Shakespeare, 1564–1616, *Antony and Cleopatra*, III. viii. 17]

17 I understand thy kisses and thou mine, / And that's a feeling disputation. [*1 Henry IV*, III. i. (204)]

18 I kissed thee ere I killed thee. [*Othello*, V. ii. 357]

19 But in Paris, as none kiss each other but the men, I did what amounted to the same thing – I bid God bless her. [Laurence Sterne, 1713–68, *A Sentimental Journey*, 'The Fille de Chambre, Paris']

20 Dear as remembered kisses after death. [Alfred, Lord Tennyson, 1809–92, *The Princess*, IV, second song]

21 ... kissed her once by the pigsty when she wasn't looking and never kissed her again although she was looking all the time. [Dylan Thomas, 1914–53, *Under Milk Wood*]

22 Kissing is a means of getting two people so close together that they can't see anything wrong with each other. [Gene Yasenak, in *Was It Good for You Too?*, ed. Bob Chieger]

See also LOVE, SEX

KNOWLEDGE

1 [Knowledge is] a rich storehouse for the glory of the Creator, and the relief of man's estate.

[Francis Bacon, 1561–1626, *The Advancement of Learning*, I. v. 11]

2 For knowledge itself is power. [Francis Bacon, 1561–1626, *Religious Meditations*, 'Of Heresies']

3 It might be said of these two boys that Shovel knew everything but Tommy knew other things. [James Barrie, 1860–1937, *Sentimental Tommy*, Ch. 3]

4 In much wisdom is much grief: and he that increaseth knowledge increaseth sorrow. [Bible, OT, *Ecclesiastes* 1:18]

5 It is better to know nothing than to know what ain't so. [Josh Billings, 1818–85, *Proverb*]

6 I was in a Printing-house in Hell, and saw the method in which knowledge is transmitted from generation to generation. [William Blake, 1757–1827, *The Marriage of Heaven and Hell*, 'A Memorable Fancy': I was in a Printing-house . . .]

7 General knowledges are those knowledges which idiots possess. To particularize is the alone distinction of merit. [William Blake, 1757–1827, annotation to Joshua Reynolds, *Discourses*, II]

8 Well didst thou speak, Athena's wisest son! / 'All that we know is, nothing can be known.' [Lord Byron, 1788–1824, *Childe Harold's Pilgrimage*, II, 7]

9 Everything he knows is always present to him. He knocks on all doors and enters nowhere. Having knocked, he thinks he has been there. [Elias Canetti, 1905–94, *The Human Province*, '1962']

10 But I'm such a bad scholar, I feel like a man with a white cane knocking into knowledge. [Peter Carey, 1943– , interview in *The Sunday Times*, 20 Mar. 1988]

11 Grace is given of God, but knowledge is born in the market. [Arthur Hugh Clough, 1819–61, *Amours de voyage*, IV, 81]

12 All other men are specialists, but his specialism is omniscience. [Arthur Conan Doyle, 1859–1930, *His Last Bow*, 'The Bruce-Partington Plans']

13 It is better to be un-informed than ill-informed. [Keith Duckworth, 1933– , in Graham Robson, *Cosworth: The Search for Power*]

14 We used to think that if we knew one, we knew two, because one and one are two. We are finding that we must learn a great deal more about 'and'. [Arthur Eddington, 1882–1944; in *Dictionary of Scientific Quotations*, ed. A L Mackay]

15 One thing in any case is certain: man is neither the oldest nor the most constant problem that has been posed for human knowledge. [Michel Foucault, 1926–84, *The Order of Things*, Ch. 10, sect. vi]

16 In arguing too, the parson owned his skill, / For e'en though vanquished, he could argue still; / While words of learned length, and thundering sound, / Amazed the gazing rustics ranged around; / And still they gazed, and still the wonder grew, / That one small head could carry all he knew. [Oliver Goldsmith, 1728–74, *The Deserted Village*, 211]

17 I saw that lack of love contaminates. / You know I know you know I know you know. [Thom Gunn, 1929– , *Carnal Knowledge*]

18 'Who can know anybody?' said the bookshop owner. 'Every person is like thousands of books. New, reprinting, in stock and out of stock, fiction, non-fiction, poetry, rubbish. The lot. Different every day. One's lucky to be able to put his hand on the one that's wanted, let alone know it.' [Russell Hoban, 1925– , *The Lion of Boaz-Jachin and Jachin-Boaz*, Ch. 32]

19 There was never an age in which useless knowledge was more important than in our own. [C E M Joad, 1891–1953; *Observer*, 'Sayings of the Week', 30 Sept. 1951]

20 Knowledge is of two kinds. We know a subject ourselves, or we know where we can find information upon it. [Dr Samuel Johnson, 1709–84, in James Boswell, *Life of J*, 18 Apr. 1775]

21 If it rained knowledge, I'd hold out my hand; but I would not give myself the trouble to go in quest of it. [Dr Samuel Johnson, 1709–84, in James Boswell, *Life of J*, 12 May 1778]

22 So that means you need to know things even when you don't need to know them. You need to know them not because you need to know them but because you need to know whether or not you need to know. And if you don't need to know you still need to know so that you know that there was no need to know. [Jonathan Lynn, 1943– , and Antony Jay, 1930– , *Yes Prime Minister*, Vol. 2, 'Man Overboard']

23 Every schoolboy knows who imprisoned Montezuma, and who strangled Atahualpa.

[Lord Macaulay, 1800–1859, *Historical Essays*, 'Lord Clive']

24 Nonetheless, I am wary of intuition, the wisdom of globe-trotters: true knowledge is sedentary. [François Mitterrand, 1916–96, *The Wheat and the Chaff*, Pt 2, 8 Dec. 1975]

25 I am sufficiently proud of my knowing something to be modest about my not knowing all. [Vladimir Nabokov, 1899–1977, *Lolita*]

26 In other words, apart from the known and the unknown, what else is there? [Harold Pinter, 1930– , *The Homecoming*, II]

27 The bookful blockhead, ignorantly read, / With loads of learned lumber in his head. [Alexander Pope, 1688–1744, *An Essay on Criticism*, 612]

28 All craftsmen share a knowledge. They have held / Reality down fluttering to a bench. [Victoria Sackville-West, 1892–1962, *The Land*, 'Summer']

29 Children with Hyacinth's temperament don't know better as they grow older; they merely know more. [Saki (H H Munro), 1870–1916, *Hyacinth*]

30 In his brain, – / Which is as dry as the remainder biscuit / After a voyage, – he hath strange places crammed / With observation, the which he vents / In mangled forms. [William Shakespeare, 1564–1616, *As You Like It*, II. vii. 37]

31 'Whewell's forte is science,' said someone. 'Yes, and his foible is omni-science,' added Sydney. [Sydney Smith, 1771–1845, in H Pearson, *The Smith of Smiths*, Ch. 11]

32 Taste all, and hand the knowledge down. [Gary Snyder, 1930– , *Turtle Island*, 'Ethnobotany']

33 This gray spirit yearning in desire / To follow knowledge like a sinking star, / Beyond the utmost bound of human thought. [Alfred, Lord Tennyson, 1809–92, *Ulysses*, 30]

34 I am this world and I eat this world. Who knows this, knows. [Upanishads, 7th cent. BC, *Taittireeya Upanishad*, III, 10]

35 Happy is he who has been able to learn the causes of things. [Virgil, 70–19 BC, *Georgics*, II, 490]

36 All the business of war, and indeed all the business of life, is to endeavour to find out what you don't know from what you do; that's what I called 'guessing what was at the other side of the hill'. [Duke of Wellington, 1769–1852, *Croker Papers*, Vol. iii]

37 Knowledge does not keep any better than fish. [A N Whitehead, 1861–1947, *The Aims of Education*, Pt III, Ch. 4]

38 I have drunk ale from the Country of the Young / And weep because I know all things now. [W B Yeats, 1865–1939, *He Thinks of His Past Greatness*]

See also CURIOSITY, EXPERIENCE, IGNORANCE, LEARNING

L

LANDS & LANDSCAPE

1 Any landscape is a condition of the spirit. [Henri Fréderic Amiel, 1821–81, *Journal*, 31 Oct. 1852]

2 When I try to imagine a faultless love / Or the life to come, what I hear is the murmur / Of underground streams, what I see is a limestone landscape. [W H Auden, 1907–73, *In Praise of Limestone*]

3 'Tis distance lends enchantment to the view, / And robes the mountain in its azure hue. [Thomas Campbell, 1777–1844, *Pleasures of Hope*, 1, 7]

4 The land was ours before we were the land's. / She was our land more than a hundred years / Before we were her people. / Such as we were we gave ourselves outright / (The deed of gift was many deeds of war) / To the land vaguely realizing westward, / But still unstoried, artless, unenhanced, / Such as she was, such as she has become. [Robert Frost, 1874–1963, *The Gift Outright*]

5 *Kennst du das Land wo die Zitronen blühn?* – Do you know the land where the lemon-trees flower? [Johann Wolfgang von Goethe, 1749–1832, *Mignonslied*]

6 There are plenty of ruined buildings in the world but no ruined stones. [Hugh MacDiarmid, 1892–1978, *On a Raised Beach*]

7 Meadows trim with daisies pied, / Shallow brooks and rivers wide, / Towers, and battlements it sees / Bosomed high in tufted trees, / Where perhaps some beauty lies, / The cynosure of neighbouring eyes. [John Milton, 1608–74, *L'Allegro*, 75]

8 If landscapes were sold like the sheets of characters of my boyhood, one penny plain and twopence coloured, I should go the length of twopence every day of my life. [Robert Louis Stevenson, 1850–94, *Travels with a Donkey*, 'Father Apollinaris']

See also EARTH, ENVIRONMENT, MOUNTAINS, NATURE

LANGUAGE

1 He was full of cliché, but then a cliché is not a cliché if you have never heard it before; and our ordinary reader clearly had not and so was ready to greet each one with the same ecstasy it must have produced when it was first coined. For Cliché is but pauperized Ecstasy. [Chinua Achebe, 1930– , *Anthills of the Savannah*, 1]

2 Would you convey my compliments to the purist who reads your proofs and tell him or her that I write in a sort of broken-down patois which is something like the way a Swiss waiter talks, and that when I split an infinitive, God damn it, I split it so it will stay split. [Raymond Chandler, 1888–1959, letter to Edward Weeks, ed. of the *Atlantic Monthly*, 18 Jan. 1947]

3 Colourless green ideas sleep furiously. [Sentence to illustrate grammatical structure as independent of meaning] Naom Chomsky, 1928– , *Syntactic Structures*, 2, 3]

4 Thus I got into my bones the essential structure of the ordinary British sentence – which is a noble thing. [Winston Churchill, 1874–1965, *My Early Life*, Ch. 2]

5 This is the sort of English up with which I will not put. [Winston Churchill, 1874–1965 (marginal comment on state document), in Sir Ernest Gowers, *Plain Words*]

6 As anyone who has ever forked out for a quarter-pound of mixed metaphors will testify, once a bastion falls, the flood-gates open and before you know where you are you're up to the neck in wrung withers. [Alan Coren, 1938– , in *Punch*, 16 Feb. 1972]

7 You can't be happy with a woman who pronounces both d.s in Wednesday. [Peter de Vries, 1910–93, *Sauce for the Goose*]

8 Language is fossil poetry. [Ralph Waldo Emerson, 1803–82, *Essays*, 'The Poet']

9 Language is like a cracked kettle on which we beat out tunes for bears to dance to, while all the time we long to move the stars to pity. [Gustave Flaubert, 1821–80, *Madame Bovary*, Pt 1, Ch. 12]

10 What do I mean by a phrase? A clutch of words that gives you a clutch at the heart. [Robert Frost, 1874–1963, interview in *Saturday Evening Post*, 16 Nov. 1960]

11 Let's have some new clichés. [Samuel Goldwyn, 1882–1974; *Observer*, 'Sayings of the Week', 24 Oct. 1948]

12 It is when I struggle to be brief that I become obscure. [Horace, 65–8 BC, *Ars Poetica*, 25]

13 Language is a form of human reason and has its reasons which are unknown to man. [Claude Lévi-Strauss, 1908– , *The Savage Mind*, Ch. 9]

14 Grammar, which can govern even kings. [Molière, 1622–73, *Les Femmes savantes*, II. vi]

15 The great enemy of clear language is insincerity. [George Orwell, 1903–50, *Collected Essays*, 'Politics and the English Language']

16 Any general statement is like a cheque drawn on a bank. Its value depends on what is there to meet it. [Ezra Pound, 1885–1972, *ABC of Reading*, Ch. 1]

17 Statements are sentences, but not all sentences are statements. [Willard Quine, 1908– , *Elementary Logic*, opening sentence]

18 Duplicity lies at the heart of language: only Trappists avoid the trap. [Frederic Raphael, 1931– , in *The Sunday Times*, 31 May 1987]

19 Taffeta phrases, silken terms precise, / Three-piled hyperboles, spruce affectation, / Figures pedantical. [William Shakespeare, 1564–1616, *Love's Labour's Lost*, V. ii. 407]

20 Here will be an old abusing of God's patience and the king's English. [*The Merry Wives of Windsor*, I. iv. (5)]

21 An aspersion upon my parts of speech! was ever such a brute! Sure, if I reprehend anything in this world, it is the use of my oracular tongue, and a nice derangement of epitaphs! [R B Sheridan, 1751–1816, *The Rivals*, III. iii]

22 Well, your natives have that. They have *sounds* for things, but it's not language. I mean, a dog barks but it's not language. I mean, yer Jocks an' yer Irish they've got that, they've got sounds. Yer Gaelic ... but it's no good to 'em 'cept for talking among themselves. They wanna talk to other people, they've got to learn English. [Spoken by Johnny Speight, 1920–98, BBC TV comedy series *Till Death Us Do Part*, 'The Bird Fancier']

See also LANGUAGES, SPEECH, TALK, WRITERS, WRITING

LANGUAGES

1 The knowledge of the ancient languages is mainly a luxury. [John Bright, 1811–89, letter in *Pall Mall Gazette*, 30 Nov. 1886]

2 The various languages you ought to have: one for your mother, which you will subsequently never speak again; one which you only read but never dare to write; one in which you pray but without understanding a single word; one in which you do arithmetic and to which all money matters belong; one in which you write (but no letters); one in which you travel, and in this you can also write your letters. [Elias Canetti, 1905–94, *The Human Province*, '1942']

3 I said it in Hebrew – I said it in Dutch – / I said it in German and Greek; / But I wholly forgot (and it vexes me much) / That English is what you speak! [Lewis Carroll, 1832–98, *The Hunting of the Snark*, Fit 4]

4 I speak Spanish to God, Italian to women, French to men, and German to my horse. [Emperor Charles V, 1500–1558, attr.]

5 We exchanged many frank words in our respective languages. [Peter Cook, 1937–95, *Beyond the Fringe*]

6 Imagine the Lord talking French! Aside from a few odd words in Hebrew, I took it completely for granted that God had never spoken anything but the most dignified English. [Clarence Day, 1874–1935, *Life with Father*, 'Father Interferes']

7 'I hear it's the Hebrew in Heaven, sir – Spanish is seldom spoken,' he exclaimed seraphically. [Ronald Firbank, 1886–1926, *The Eccentricities of Cardinal Pirelli*, Ch. 8]

8 My English text is chaste, and all licentious passages are left in the decent obscurity of a learned language. [Edward Gibbon, 1737–94, *Autobiography*]

9 After all, when you come right down to it, how many people speak the same language even when they speak the same language? [Russell Hoban, 1925– , *The Lion of Boaz-Jachin and Jachin-Boaz*, Ch. 27]

10 I am always sorry when any language is lost, because languages are the pedigree of nations. [Dr Samuel Johnson, 1709–84, in James Boswell, *Tour of the Hebrides*, 18 Sept. 1773]

11 He spoke and wrote trade-English – a toothsome amalgam of Americanisms and epigrams. [Rudyard Kipling, 1865–1936, 'The Village That Voted the Earth was Flat']

12 The English language no longer belongs to the English. It's an export reject. [George Lamming, 1927– , in BBC radio programme *Third World*, on Caribbean writing, 1958]

13 If the English language had been properly organized ... then there would be a word which meant both 'he' and 'she', and I could write, 'If John or May comes, heesh will want to play tennis,' which would save a lot of trouble. [A A Milne, 1882–1956, *The Christopher Robin Birthday Book*]

14 One tongue is sufficient for a woman. [John Milton, 1608–74, attr., when asked whether he would instruct his daughters in foreign languages]

15 American is the language in which people say what they mean as Italian is the language in which they say what they feel. English is the language in which what a character means or feels has to be deduced from what he or she says, which may be quite the opposite. [John Mortimer, 1923– , in *Mail on Sunday*, 26 Mar. 1989]

16 I include 'pidgin-English' ... even though I am referred to in that splendid language as 'Fella belong Mrs Queen'. [Philip, Duke of Edinburgh, 1921– , speech at English-speaking Union Conference, Ottawa, 29 Oct. 1958]

17 They have been at a great feast of languages, and stolen the scraps. [William Shakespeare, 1564–1616, *Love's Labour's Lost*, V. i. (39)]

18 Speaks three or four languages word for word without book. [*Twelfth Night*, I. iii. (28)]

19 I am the Roman Emperor, and am above grammar. [Emperor Sigismund, 1368–1437 (reply to prelate who had criticized his Latin)]

20 A language is a dialect that has an army and a navy. [Max Weinreich, in Leo Rosten, *The Joys of Yiddish*, Preface]

21 Into the face of the young man who sat on the terrace of the Hotel Magnifique at Cannes there had crept a look of furtive shame, the shifty, hangdog look which announces that an Englishman is about to talk French. [P G Wodehouse, 1881–1975, *The Luck of the Bodkins*, Ch. 1]

See LANGUAGE, SPEECH, TALK

LAST WORDS

1 See in what peace a Christian can die. [Joseph Addison, 1672–1719, dying words, quoted in E Young, *Conjectures on Original Composition*]

2 This is my final word. It is time for me to become an apprentice once more. I have not settled in which direction. But somewhere, sometime, soon. [(His last public statement) Lord Beaverbrook, 1879–1964, speech at Dorchester Hotel, London on 25 May 1964, his 85th birthday]

3 [When asked by Leonard Bernstein on her deathbed if she was hearing music in her skull and, if so, which composer] One music ... with no beginning, no end. [Nadia Boulanger, 1887–1979, in Bruno Monsaingeon, *Mademoiselle*]

4 *Et tu, Brute?* – You also, Brutus? [Julius Caesar, 102?–44 BC, alleged dying words, for which there is no authority]

5 I realize that patriotism is not enough. I must have no hatred or bitterness towards anyone. [Edith Cavell, 1865–1915, last words, 12 Oct. 1915]

6 Let not poor Nelly starve. [Charles II, 1630–85 (of Nell Gwynn, on his deathbed, 5 Feb. 1685, to his brother James), quoted in Bishop Burnet, *History of His Own Times*, Vol. I, Bk ii, Ch. 17]

7 He had been, he said, an unconscionable time dying; but he hoped that they would excuse it.

[Charles II, 1630–85, Lord Macaulay, *History of England*, Vol. i, Ch. 4]

8 It is not my design to drink or to sleep, but my design is to make what haste I can to be gone. [Oliver Cromwell, 1599–1658, quoted in J Morley, *Life*, v, Ch. 10]

9 Farewell my friends. I am going to glory. [Isadora Duncan, 1878–1927 (last words before her scarf became fatally caught in car wheel), in M Desti, *Isadora Duncan's End*, Ch. 25]

10 Dear, this is the hardest bloody part I've ever played. [Eithne Dunne, Irish actress, 1917–88 (at her death), in obituary in *Guardian*, 28 Dec. 1988]

11 All my possessions for a moment of time. [Elizabeth I, 1533–1603, last words]

12 I have no pain, dear mother, now; but oh! I am so dry: / Just moisten poor Jim's lips once more; and, mother, do not cry! [Edward Farmer, 1809?–76, *The Collier's Dying Child*]

13 Now I'll have *eine kleine Pause*. [Kathleen Ferrier, 1912–53, in Gerald Moore, *Am I Too Loud?*, Ch. 19. They were the last words he heard her speak, not long before her death]

14 Why fear death? It is the most beautiful adventure in life. [Charles Frohman, 1860–1915, last words before going down in the *Lusitania*, 7 May 1915]

15 How is the Empire? [George V, official last words, as quoted in *The Times*, 21 June 1936, but letter from Lord Wigram, 31 Jan. 1936, in *Oxford Dictionary of Modern Quotations*, ed. Tony Augarde, describes the King saying it when reading the 'Imperial and Foreign' page of *The Times*]

16 Bugger Bognor! [King George V, 1865–1936, attr. dying words when told by his physician he would soon be convalescing in Bognor]

17 One day, when the going is tough and the big game is hanging in the balance, ask the team to win one for the Gipper. I don't know where I'll be, Rock, but I'll know about it and I'll be happy. [George Gipp, 1895–1920, last words, 14 Dec. 1920, to coach Knute Rockne. Gipp was a legendary football player from Notre Dame University and his pledge became the subject of a film in 1940, with Ronald Reagan as 'The Gipper']

18 *Mehr Licht!* – More light! [Johann Wolfgang von Goethe, 1749–1832, reported dying words. Actually he asked for the second shutter of his window to be opened so that more light could come in]

19 I have loved justice and hated iniquity; therefore I die in exile. [Gregory VII, 1020–85, attr. last words, in Salerno]

20 *Dieu me pardonnera, c'est son métier.* – God will pardon me, it is His trade. [Heinrich Heine, 1797–1856, last words, quoted in Edmond and Charles Goncourt, *Journal*, 23 Feb. 1863]

21 Turn up the lights, I don't want to go home in the dark. [O Henry, 1862–1910, 5 June 1910, quoting popular song]

22 Don't waste any time mourning – organize! [Joe Hill, 1879–1915, letter to W D Haywood, the day before being shot by firing squad, Utah State Penitentiary, 19 Nov. 1915]

23 I am about to take my last voyage, a great leap in the dark. [Thomas Hobbes, 1588–1679, in John Watkins, *Anecdotes of Men of Learning*]

24 I'll tell that story on the golden floor. [A E Housman, 1859–1936 (on being told a joke when he was dying), attr. by the Revd J Plowden-Wardlaw, vicar of St Edward the Great, Cambridge]

25 *O sancta simplicitas!* – O holy simplicity! [John Huss, 1373–1415, at the stake, on seeing a peasant bringing a faggot to throw on the pile]

26 So here it is at last, the distinguished thing! [(Said by a 'voice' heard as he suffered his first stroke, often wrongly described as his last words.) Henry James, 1843–1916, in Edith Wharton, *A Backward Glance*, Ch. 14]

27 Tell the boys to follow, to be faithful, to take me seriously. [Henry James, 1843–1916 (said to Alice James), in H Montgomery Hyde, *Henry James at Home*, Ch. 7, iv]

28 *Vicisti, Galilaee.* – Thou hast conquered, O Galilean. [Emperor Julian the Apostate, *c.*331–63, Latin translation of alleged dying words]

29 Do not hack me as you did my Lord Russell. [Duke of Monmouth, 1649–85 (words to his executioner), quoted in Lord Macaulay, *The History of England*, Vol. i, Ch. 5]

30 I pray you, Master Lieutenant, see me safe up, and for my coming down let me shift for myself. [Sir Thomas More, 1478–1535, on mounting the scaffold, 7 July 1535]

31 Kiss me, Hardy. [(At Battle of Trafalgar) Horatio, Lord Nelson, 1758–1805, quoted in Robert Southey, *Life of Nelson*, Ch. 9]

32 What an artist dies in me! [Emperor Nero, 37–68, dying words, quoted by Suetonius, *Life of Nero*, 49]

33 I am just going outside, and may be some time. [Captain Lawrence Oates, 1880–1912, 16 Mar. 1912, in R F Scott's diary, *Scott's Last Expedition*, Ch. 20]

34 Die, my dear Doctor, that's the last thing I shall do! [Lord Palmerston, 1784–1865, attr. in E Latham, *Famous Sayings and their Authors*]

35 And so I betake myself that course, which is almost as much as to see myself go into my grave; for which, and all the discomforts that will accompany my being blind, the good God prepare me. [Samuel Pepys, 1633–1703, *Diary*, final entry]

36 In a few minutes I am going out to shape all the singing tomorrows. [(Letter, July 1942, before his execution by the Germans) Gabriel Péri, 1902–42]

37 *Tirez le rideau, la farce est jouée.* – Ring down the curtain, the farce is over. [François Rabelais, *c.*1492–1553, attr.]

38 *Je m'en vais chercher un grand peut-être.* – I am going in search of a great perhaps. [François Rabelais, *c.*1492–1553, alternative attr. last words]

39 So the heart be right, it is no matter which way the head lieth. [Sir Walter Raleigh, *c.*1552–1618, when laying his head on the block]

40 So little done, so much to do. [Cecil Rhodes, 1853–1902, in Lewis Michell, *Life of Rhodes*, Vol. 2, Ch. 39]

41 [When asked if he had any last request before he was shot] Why yes – a bullet-proof vest! [James W Rodgers, d.1960; in Jonathon Green, *Famous Last Words*]

42 If thou didst ever hold me in thy heart, / Absent thee from felicity awhile, / And in this harsh world draw thy breath in pain, / To tell my story. [William Shakespeare, 1564–1616, *Hamlet*, V. ii. (360)]

43 O! here / Will I set up my everlasting rest, / And shake the yoke of inauspicious stars / From this world-wearied flesh. Eyes look your last! / Arms, take your last embrace! [*Romeo and Juliet*, V. iii. 109]

44 'You, Clutterbuck, come, stir your stumps, / Why are you in such doleful dumps? / A fireman and afraid of bumps! – / What are they feared on? fools! 'od rot 'em!' / Were the last words of Higginbottom. [James and Horace Smith, 1775–1839 and 1779–1849, *Rejected Addresses*, 'A Tale of Drury Lane, The Burning']

45 Crito, we ought to offer a cock to Asclepius. See to it, and don't forget. [Socrates, 469–399 BC, quoted in Plato, *Phaedo*, 118]

46 Just before she died she asked, 'What *is* the answer?' No answer came. She laughed and said, 'In that case what is the question?' Then she died. [Gertrude Stein, 1874–1946, in D Sutherland, *G S: A Biography of Her Work*, Ch. 6]

47 If this is dying, I don't think much of it. [Lytton Strachey, 1880–1932, in Michael Holroyd, *L S*, Pt V, Ch. 17, sect. viii]

48 God bless ... God damn! [James Thurber, 1894–1961, quoted by Paul Theroux in *The Sunday Times*, 31 Jan. 1982, who comments, 'As a judgement on the world it is very nearly perfect.']

See also EPITAPHS

LATENESS

1 I have been five minutes too late all my lifetime! [Hannah Cowley, 1743–1809, *The Belle's Stratagem*, I. i]

2 It's but little good you'll do a-watering the last year's crop. [George Eliot, 1819–80, *Adam Bede*, Ch. 18]

3 I have noticed that the people who are late are so often much jollier than the people who have to wait for them. [E V Lucas, 1868–1938, *365 Days and One More*]

4 Three o'clock is always too late or too early for anything you want to do. [Jean-Paul Sartre, 1905–80, *Nausea*, Friday]

5 Ah! the clock is always slow; / It is later than you think. [Robert Service, 1874–1958, *It is Later Than You Think*]

6 Delays have dangerous ends. [William Shakespeare, 1564–1616, *1 Henry VI*, III. ii. 33]

7 Too swift arrives as tardy as too slow. [*Romeo and Juliet*, II. vi. 15]

LAUGHTER & SMILES

1 I force myself to laugh at everything, for fear of being compelled to weep. [Pierre-Augustin de Beaumarchais, 1732–99, *The Barber of Seville*, I. ii]

2 From quiet homes and first beginning, / Out to the undiscovered ends, / There's nothing worth the wear of winning, / But laughter and the love of friends. [Hilaire Belloc, 1870–1953, *Dedicatory Ode*]

3 And if I laugh at any mortal thing, / 'Tis that I may not weep. [Lord Byron, 1788–1824, *Don Juan*, IV, 4]

4 No man who has once heartily and wholly laughed can be altogether irreclaimably bad. [Thomas Carlyle, 1795–1881, *Sartor Resartus*, Bk i, Ch. 4]

5 There is nothing sillier than a silly laugh. [Catullus, 87–54 ? BC, *Carmina*, 39]

6 The most wasted of all days is that on which one has not laughed. [Nicolas-Sébastien Chamfort, 1741–94, *Maxims and Considerations*]

7 She gave me a smile I could feel in my hip pocket. [Raymond Chandler, 1888–1959, *Farewell My Lovely*, Ch. 18]

8 I am sure that since I have had the full use of my reason, nobody has ever heard me laugh. [Earl of Chesterfield, 1694–1773, letter to his son, 9 Mar. 1748]

9 He who laughs last is generally the last to get the joke. [Terry Cohen ; in P and J Holton, *Quote and Unquote*]

10 She is not fair to outward view / As many maidens be ; / Her loveliness I never knew / Until she smiled on me. [Hartley Coleridge, 1796–1849, song : *She is Not Fair*]

11 There is nothing more unbecoming a man of quality than to laugh ; 'tis such a vulgar expression of the passion ! [William Congreve, 1670–1729, *The Double Dealer*, I. iv]

12 My smile falls heavily among the *bric-à-brac*. [T S Eliot, 1888–1965, *Portrait of a Lady*]

13 The loud laugh that spoke the vacant mind. [Oliver Goldsmith, 1728–74, *The Deserted Village*, 121]

14 When you're smiling the whole world smiles with you. [Joe Goodwin, 1889–1943, and Larry Shay, 1897–1988, song : *When You're Smiling*]

15 A solitary laugh is often a laugh of superiority. [Graham Greene, 1904–91, *Monsignor Quixote*, Pt 1, Ch. 9]

16 And he smiled a kind of sickly smile, and curled up on the floor, / And the subsequent proceedings interested him no more. [Bret Harte, 1836–1902, *The Society upon the Stanislaus*]

17 Sudden glory is the passion which maketh those grimaces called laughter. [Thomas Hobbes, 1588–1679, *Leviathan*, Pt I, Ch. 6]

18 I had also mastered the art of laughing at myself a fraction of a second before anybody else did. [Clive James, 1939– , *Unreliable Memoirs*, Ch. 10]

19 Their smiles, / Wan as primroses gathered at midnight / By chilly-fingered Spring. [John Keats, 1795–1821, *Endymion*, 969]

20 One must laugh before one is happy, or one may die without ever laughing at all. [Jean de La Bruyère, 1645–96, *Characters*, 'Of the Heart', 63]

21 Anything awful makes me laugh. I misbehaved once at a funeral. [Charles Lamb, 1775–1834, letter to Southey, 9 Aug. 1815]

22 There is a kind of laughter people laugh at public events, as if a joke were a charity auction and they want to be seen to be bidding. [William McIlvanney, 1936– , *The Big Man*, Ch. 1]

23 He stands, smiling encouragement, like a clumsy dentist. [Katherine Mansfield, 1888–1923, *The Garden Party*, 'Bank Holiday']

24 Laugh and be merry, remember, better the world with a song. / Better the world with a blow in the teeth of a wrong. [John Masefield, 1878–1967, *Laugh and be Merry*]

25 Haste thee, nymph, and bring with thee / Jest and youthful jollity, / Quips and cranks, and wanton wiles, / Nods, and becks, and wreathèd smiles. [John Milton, 1608–74, *L'Allegro*, 5]

26 A smile that glowed / Celestial rosy red, love's proper hue. [John Milton, 1608–74, *Paradise Lost*, Bk vii, 618]

27 Laughter is serious. More complicated, more serious than tears. [Toni Morrison, 1931– , *Jazz*, p. 113]

28 A good laugh is the best pesticide. [Vladimir Nabokov, 1899–1977, *Strong Opinions*, 9]

29 Laughter is pleasant, but the exertion is too much for me. [(Hon. Mr Listless) T L Peacock, 1785–1866, *Nightmare Abbey*, Ch. 5]

30 Eternal smiles his emptiness betray, / As shallow streams run dimpling all the way. [Alexander Pope, 1688–1744, *Epistle to Dr Arbuthnot*, 315]

31 My lungs began to crow like chanticleer, / That fools should be so deep-contemplative, / And I did laugh sans intermission / An hour by his dial. [William Shakespeare, 1564–1616, *As You Like It*, II. vii. 30]

32 Seldom he smiles, and smiles in such a sort / As if he mocked himself, and scorned his spirit, / That could be moved to smile at anything. [*Julius Caesar*, I. ii. 204]

33 I was irrevocably betrothed to laughter, the sound of which has always seemed to me the most civilized music in the world. [Peter Ustinov, 1921– , *Dear Me*, Ch. 3]

34 We are not amused. [Queen Victoria, 1819–1901, *Notebooks of a Spinster Lady*, 2 Jan. 1900]

35 I love such mirth as does not make friends ashamed to look upon one another next morning. [Izaak Walton, 1593–1683, *The Compleat Angler*, Pt I, Ch. 5]

See also COMEDY, HUMOUR, JOKES, TEARS, WIT

LAW

1 One of the Seven was wont to say: 'That laws were like cobwebs; where the small flies were caught, and the great brake through.' [Francis Bacon, 1561–1626, *Apothegms*, 181]

2 Let it be written among the laws of the Persians and the Medes, that it be not altered. [Bible, OT, *Esther* 1:19]

3 All things are lawful for me, but all things are not expedient. [Bible, NT, *1 Corinthians* 10:23]

4 Where no law is, there is no transgression. [Bible, NT, *Romans* 4:15]

5 There is but one law for all, namely, that law which governs all law, the law of our Creator, the law of humanity, justice, equity – the law of nature, and of nations. [Edmund Burke, 1729–97, speech, 28 May 1794]

6 When you break the big laws, you do not get liberty; you do not even get anarchy. You get the small laws. [G K Chesterton, 1874–1936, in *Daily News*, 29 July 1905]

7 The good of the people is the chief law. [Cicero, 106–43 BC, *De Legibus*, III, iii]

8 *Cui bono?* – To whose profit? [Cicero, 106–43 BC, *Pro Milone*, XII, xxxii]

9 How long soever it hath continued, if it be against reason, it is of no force in law. [Edward Coke, 1552–1634, *Institutes*, 'Commentary upon Littleton', I, 80]

10 The lawcourts of England are open to all men like the doors of the Ritz Hotel. [Mr Justice Darling, 1849–1936; also attr. to Lord Justice Sir James Matthew and Judge Sturgess]

11 'If the law supposes that . . . the law is a ass – a idiot.' [Charles Dickens, 1812–70, *Oliver Twist*, Ch. 51]

12 After all, that is the beauty of the common law; it is a maze and not a mortuary. [Lord Diplock, 1907–66, in *Morris* v. *C W Martin and Sons Ltd.* (1966); in *Dictionary of Legal Quotations*, comp. Simon James and Chantal Stebbings]

13 The law's made to take care o' raskills. [George Eliot, 1819–80, *The Mill on the Floss*, Bk iii, Ch. 4]

14 The Law is the true embodiment / Of everything that's excellent. / It has no kind of fault or flaw, / And I, my lords, embody the Law. [W S Gilbert, 1836–1911, *Iolanthe*, I]

15 Laws grind the poor, and rich men rule the law. [Oliver Goldsmith, 1728–74, *The Traveller*, 386]

16 I have come to regard the law courts [in the Strand] not as a cathedral but rather as a casino. [Richard Ingrams, 1937– , in *Guardian*, 30 July 1977]

17 Seven hours to law, to soothing slumber seven, / Ten to the world allot, and all to heaven. [William Jones, 1746–94, *Lines in Substitution for Those of Sir Edward Coke*]

18 The Law and Morality are, naturally enough, brothers-in-law rather than natural brothers. [Hans Keller, 1919–85, *Criticism*, Pt 1, Ch. 3]

19 Keep ye the Law – be swift in all obedience – / Clear the land of evil, drive the road and bridge the ford. [Rudyard Kipling, 1865–1936, *A Song of the English*]

20 Yours the lawlessness / of something simple that has lost its law. [Robert Lowell, 1917–77, *Caligula*]

21 No brilliance is needed in the law. Nothing but common sense, and relatively clean finger nails. [John Mortimer, 1923– , *A Voyage round My Father*, I]

22 Since twelve honest men have decided the cause, / And were judges of fact, tho' not judges of laws. [William Pulteney, Earl of Bath, 1684–1764, *The Honest Jury*, 3]

23 MRS BERTRAM: That sounds like nonsense, my dear.

MR BERTRAM: May be so, my dear; but it may be very good law for all that. [Sir Walter Scott, 1771–1832, *Guy Mannering*, Ch. 9]

24 Ignorance of the law excuses no man: not that all men know the law, but because 'tis an excuse every man will plead, and no man can tell how to refute him. [John Selden, 1584–1654, *Table Talk*, 77]

25 But there is a higher law than the Constitution. [W H Seward, 1801–72, speech in US Senate, 11 Mar. 1850]

26 Old father antick the law. [William Shakespeare, 1564–1616, *1 Henry IV*, I. ii. (69)]

27 The law hath not been dead, though it hath slept. [*Measure for Measure*, II. ii. 90]

28 Still you keep o' the windy side of the law. [*Twelfth Night*, III. iv. (183)]

29 In sentencing a man for one crime, we may well be putting him beyond the reach of the law in respect of those crimes which he has not yet had an opportunity to commit. The law, however, is not to be cheated in this way. I shall therefore discharge you. [N F Simpson, 1919– , *One-way Pendulum*, I]

30 Fresh from brawling courts / And dusty purlieus of the law. [Alfred, Lord Tennyson, 1809–92, *In Memoriam*, 89]

31 It ain't no sin to crack a few laws now and then, just so long as you don't break any. [Mae West, 1892–1980, in film *Every Day's a Holiday*]

32 Yale [Law School] is terrific for anything you wanna do, so long as it don't involve people with sneakers, guns, dope, or sloth. [Tom Wolfe, 1931– , *The Bonfire of the Vanities*, Ch. 16]

See also JUDGEMENT, JUSTICE, LAWYERS

LAWYERS

1 Old lawyers never die – they just lose their appeal. [anon., on a mug belonging to John Mortimer, in *Observer*, 20 Feb. 1983]

2 Then, shifting his side (as a lawyer knows how). [William Cowper, 1731–1800, *The Report of an Adjudged Case*]

3 Battledore and shuttlecock's a wery good game, vhen you an't the shuttlecock and two lawyers the battledores, in which case it gets too excitin' to be pleasant. [Charles Dickens, 1812–70, *Pickwick Papers*, Ch. 20]

4 There's no better way of exercising the imagination than the study of law. No poet ever interpreted nature as freely as a lawyer interprets truth. [Jean Giraudoux, 1882–1944, *Tiger at the Gates*, I]

5 When there's a rift in the lute, the business of the lawyer is to widen the rift and gather the loot. [Arthur Garfield Hays, 1879–1954; in A Andrews, *Quotations for Speakers and Writers*]

6 Lawyers earn their bread in the sweat of their browbeating. [James Huneker, 1860–1921, from *Painted Veils*; in *Quotable Lawyer*, ed. D Shrager and E Frost]

7 A lawyer has no business with the justice or injustice of the cause which he undertakes, unless his client asks his opinion, and then he is bound to give it honestly. The justice or injustice of the cause is to be decided by the judge. [Dr Samuel Johnson, 1709–84, in James Boswell, *Tour of the Hebrides*, 15 Aug. 1773]

8 A dog who thinks he is man's best friend is a dog who obviously has never met a tax lawyer. [Fran Lebowitz, ?1948– , *Social Studies*, 'Things']

9 Barristers may be gentlemen trying to be lawyers, and solicitors are lawyers trying to be gentlemen. But . . . neither is very good at either. [Austin Mitchell, 1934– , in *Guardian*, 6 June 1990]

10 The first thing we do, let's kill all the lawyers. [William Shakespeare, 1564–1616, *2 Henry VI*, IV. ii. (86)]

See also JUDGEMENT, JUSTICE, LAW

LAZINESS

1 Woe to the idle shepherd that leaveth the flock! [Bible, OT, *Zechariah* 11:17]

2 Go to the ant, thou sluggard, consider her ways, and be wise. [Bible, OT, *Proverbs* 6:6]

3 The sluggard is wiser in his own conceit than seven men that can render a reason. [Bible, OT, *Proverbs* 26:16]

4 The foul sluggard's comfort: 'It will last my time.' [Thomas Carlyle, 1795–1881, *Critical and Miscellaneous Essays*, 'Count Cagliostro. Flight Last']

5 Idleness is only the refuge of weak minds. [Earl of Chesterfield, 1694–1773, letter to his son, 20 July 1749]

6 I make no secret of the fact that I would rather lie on a sofa than sweep beneath it. But you have to be efficient if you're going to be lazy. [Shirley Conran, 1932– , *Superwoman*, 'The Reason Why']

7 How various his employments, whom the world / Calls idle; and who justly, in return, / Esteems that busy world an idler too! [William Cowper, 1731–1800, *The Task*, Bk III, 352]

8 God's pampered people whom, debauched with ease, / No king could govern, nor no God could please. [John Dryden, 1631–1700, *Absalom and Achitophel*, Pt I, 47]

9 To live at ease, and not be bound to think. [John Dryden, 1631–1700, *The Medal*, 236]

10 Says little, thinks less, and does – nothing at all, faith. [George Farquhar, 1678–1707, *The Beaux' Stratagem*, I. i.]

11 A fox may steal your hens, sir, / ... If lawyer's hand is fee'd sir, / He steals your whole estate. [John Gay, 1685–1732, *The Beggar's Opera*, 1, x]

12 Lounjun' 'round en suffer'n. [Joel Chandler Harris, 1848–1908, *Nights with Uncle Remus*, Ch. 12]

13 Lazy fokes' stummucks don't git tired. [Joel Chandler Harris, 1848–1908, *Nights with Uncle Remus*, Ch. 34]

14 It is impossible to enjoy idling thoroughly unless one has plenty of work to do. [Jerome K Jerome, 1859–1927, *Idle Thoughts of an Idle Fellow*, 'On Being Idle']

15 If you are idle, be not solitary; if you are solitary, be not idle. [(Letter to Boswell) Dr Samuel Johnson, 1709–84, in James Boswell, *Life of J*, 27 Oct. 1779]

16 I have, all my life long, been lying till noon; yet I tell all young men, and tell them with great sincerity, that nobody who does not rise early will ever do any good. [Dr Samuel Johnson, 1709–84, in James Boswell, *Tour of the Hebrides*, 14 Sept. 1773]

17 Laziness is the supreme virtue. [Hans Keller, 1919–85, in *The Sunday Times Review*, 23 Feb. 1986]

18 My only hobby is laziness, which naturally rules out all the others. [Granni Nazzano, attr.]

19 I killin' meself workin', an' he sthruttin' about from mornin' till night like a paycock! [Sean O'Casey, 1880–1964, *Juno and the Paycock*, 1]

20 It's not 'cause I wouldn't / It's not 'cause I shouldn't / And, Lord knows, it's not 'cause I couldn't, / It's simply because I'm the laziest gal in town. [Cole Porter, 1891–1964, song: *The Laziest Gal in Town*, in musical *Stage Fright* (sung by Marlene Dietrich)]

21 I know you all, and will awhile uphold / The unyoked humour of your idleness. [William Shakespeare, 1564–1616, *1 Henry IV*, I. ii (217)]

22 The insupportable labour of doing nothing. [Richard Steele, 1672–1729, *The Tatler*, 54]

23 'Courage!' he said, and pointed toward the land, / 'This mounting wave will roll us shoreward soon.' / In the afternoon they came unto a land / In which it seemèd always afternoon. [Alfred, Lord Tennyson, 1809–92, *The Lotos-Eaters*, 1]

24 Surely, surely, slumber is more sweet than toil, the shore / Than labour in the deep mid-ocean, wind and wave and oar; / Oh rest ye, brother mariners, we will not wander more. [Alfred, Lord Tennyson, 1809–92, *The Lotos-Eaters*, 'Choric Song', 4]

25 It is better to have loafed and lost than never to have loafed at all. [James Thurber, 1894–1961, *Fables for Our Time*, 'The Courtship of Arthur and Al']

26 For Satan finds some mischief still / For idle hands to do. [Isaac Watts, 1674–1748, *Divine Songs for Children*, 20, 'Against Idleness and Mischief']

27 'Tis the voice of the sluggard: I heard him complain, / 'You have waked me too soon, I must slumber again.' [Isaac Watts, 1674–1748, *Moral Songs*, 1, 'The Sluggard']

See also ACTIVITY

LEADERSHIP

1 At last we have a leader who can lie. [Richard Crossman, 1907–74 (on Harold Wilson's becoming Labour Party leader in succession to Gaitskell), *Diaries of a Cabinet Minister*]

2 A born leader of men is somebody who is afraid to go anywhere by himself. [Clifford Hanley, 1922–99, in conversation; in *Scottish Quotations*, comp. Alan Bold]

3 The art of leadership . . . consists in consolidating the attention of the people against a single adversary and taking care that nothing will split up that attention. [Adolf Hitler, 1889–1945, *Mein Kampf*, Ch. 3]

4 The true leader is always led. [C G Jung, 1875–1961, in *Guardian Weekly*, 30 Oct. 1976]

5 I am their leader, I really should be following them. [Alexandre Auguste Ledru-Rollin, 1807–74, in E de Mirecourt, *Les Contemporains*, Vol. 14]

6 I am opposed to Titanic seamanship in politics and as an old mariner I would not drive the ship on to the ice floes that have drifted into our seas from the frozen wastes of the Tory past. [David Lloyd George, 1863–1945, quoted by Dingle Foot in *Guardian*, 17 Jan. 1963]

See also GOVERNMENT, POLITICS

LEARNING

1 Studies serve for delight, for ornament, and for ability. [Francis Bacon, 1561–1626, *Essays*, 50, 'Of Studies']

2 Histories make men wise; poets, witty; the mathematics, subtle; natural philosophy, deep; moral, grave; logic and rhetoric, able to contend. [Francis Bacon, 1561–1626, *Essays*, 50, 'Of Studies']

3 Beauty and the lust for learning have yet to be allied. [Max Beerbohm, 1872–1956, *Zuleika Dobson*, Ch. 7]

4 Gie me ae spark o' Nature's fire, / That's a' the learning I desire. [Robert Burns, 1759–96, *Epistle to John Lapraik*, 73]

5 With various readings stored his empty skull, / Learn'd without sense, and venerably dull. [Charles Churchill, 1731–64, *The Rosciad*, 591]

6 No, I'm no enemy to learning; it hurts not me. [William Congreve, 1670–1729, *The Way of the World*, III. xiii]

7 Vether it's worth goin' through so much, to learn so little, as the charity-boy said ven he got to the end of the alphabet, is a matter o' taste. [Charles Dickens, 1812–70, *Pickwick Papers*, Ch. 27]

8 When house and land are gone and spent, / Then learning is most excellent. [Samuel Foote, 1720–77, *Taste*, I, i]

9 You will hear more good things on the outside of a stagecoach from London to Oxford than if you were to pass a twelve-month with the undergraduates, or heads of colleges, of that famous university. [William Hazlitt, 1778–1830, *On the Ignorance of the Learned*]

10 I am quite agreeable that a woman shall be informed about everything, but I cannot allow her the shocking passion for acquiring learning in order to be learned. When she is asked questions, I like her often to know how not to know the things she does know. [Molière, 1622–73, *Les Femmes savantes*, I. iii]

11 He intended, he said, to devote the rest of his life to learning the remaining twenty-two letters of the alphabet. [George Orwell, 1903–50, *Animal Farm*, Ch. 9]

12 A little learning is a dang'rous thing; / Drink deep, or taste not the Pierian spring: / There shallow draughts intoxicate the brain, / And drinking largely sobers us again. [Alexander Pope, 1688–1744, *An Essay on Criticism*, 215]

13 Study is like the heaven's glorious sun, / That will not be deep-searched with saucy looks; / Small have continuous plodders ever won, / Save base authority from others' books. [William Shakespeare, 1564–1616, *Love's Labour's Lost*, I. i. 84]

14 But I grow old always learning many things. [Solon, *c.*640–*c.*558 BC, quoted in Plutarch, *Solon*, xxxi]

15 Wearing all that weight / Of learning lightly like a flower. [Alfred, Lord Tennyson, 1809–92, *In Memoriam*, Conclusion]

See also EDUCATION, KNOWLEDGE, STUDENTS

LEISURE

1 What is this life if, full of care, / We have no time to stand and stare? [W H Davies, 1871–1940, *Leisure*]

2 Leisure is work you volunteer for. [Robert Robinson, 1927– , *Dog Chairman*, 'Try a Grasshopper']

3 The secret of being miserable is to have leisure to bother about whether you are happy or not. [George Bernard Shaw, 1856–1950, *Misalliance*, Preface]

4 A god gave us this leisure. [Virgil, 70–19 BC, *Eclogue*, I, 6]

See also SPORTS, WORK

LENDING, see BORROWERS

LETTERS

1 When he wrote a letter, he would put that which was most material in the postscript, as if it had been a by-matter. [Francis Bacon, 1561–1626, *Essays*, 22, 'Of Cunning']

2 Only with those in verse, Mr Witwoud. I never pin up my hair with prose. [William Congreve, 1670–1729, *The Way of the World*, I. iv]

3 'That's rather a sudden pull up, ain't it, Sammy?' inquired Mr Weller. 'Not a bit on it,' said Sam; 'she'll vish there wos more, and that's the great art o' letter writin'.' [Charles Dickens, 1812–70, *Pickwick Papers*, Ch. 30]

4 I want those letters to be sincere letters. I want them filled up with lots of personal details so there'll be no doubt I mean every word you say. [Joseph Heller, 1923–99, *Catch-22*, Ch. 25]

5 They teach the morals of a whore, and the manners of a dancing-master. [(Of Lord Chesterfield's *Letters*) Dr Samuel Johnson, 1709–84, in James Boswell, *Life of J*, 1754]

6 There is more knowledge of the heart in one letter of Richardson's, than in all *Tom Jones*. [Dr Samuel Johnson, 1709–84, in James Boswell, *Life of J*, 6 Apr. 1772]

7 You don't know a woman until you've had a letter from her. [Ada Leverson, 1865–1936, *Tenterhooks*, Ch. 7]

8 The inmate of a lunatic asylum was writing a letter. A man looked over his shoulder and asked: 'To whom are you writing?' The inmate replied: 'I am writing to myself.' 'What are you saying?' asked the other man. 'Oh, I shan't know till I get it tomorrow,' said the inmate. [George Robey, 1869–1954, in A E Wilson, *The Prime Minister of Mirth*, Ch. 12]

See also COMMUNICATION, WRITING

LIBERALS

1 A liberal is a conservative who has been arrested. [anon., in Tom Wolfe, *The Bonfire of the Vanities*, Ch. 24]

2 Every Briton is at heart a Tory – especially every British Liberal. [Arnold Bennett, 1867–1931, *Journal*, Dec. 1929]

3 You Liberals think that goats are just sheep from broken homes. [Malcolm Bradbury, 1932– , and Christopher Bigsby, 1941– , TV play *After Dinner Game*]

4 If God had been a Liberal there wouldn't have been ten commandments, there would have been ten suggestions. [Malcolm Bradbury, 1932– , and Christopher Bigsby, 1941– , TV play *After Dinner Game*]

5 I am for 'Peace, retrenchment and reform', the watchword of the great Liberal party thirty years ago. [John Bright, 1811–89, speech at Birmingham, 28 Apr. 1859]

6 It [the Social Democratic Party] promises them [its supporters] a better yesterday. [Ralf Dahrendorf, 1929– , in *Observer*, 10 Oct. 1982]

7 To be absolutely honest, what I feel really bad about is that I don't feel worse. There's the ineffectual liberal's problem in a nutshell. [Michael Frayn, 1933– , in *Observer*, 8 Aug. 1965]

8 A liberal is a man too broad-minded to take his own side in a quarrel. [Robert Frost, 1874–1963; in *Portable Curmudgeon*, comp. J Winokur, 'Quotes on L']

9 I often think it's comical / How Nature always does contrive / That every boy and every gal, / That's born into the world alive, / Is either a little Liberal, / Or else a little Conservative! [W S Gilbert, 1836–1911, *Iolanthe*, II]

10 I have always said, the first Whig was the Devil. [Dr Samuel Johnson, 1709–84, in James Boswell, *Life of J*, 28 Apr. 1778]

11 A pleasant old buffer, nephew to a lord, / Who believed that the bank was mightier than the sword, / And that an umbrella might pacify barbarians abroad: / Just like an old liberal / Between the wars. [William Plomer, 1903–73, *Father and Son: 1939*]

12 A radical is a man with both feet planted firmly in the air. A reactionary is a somnambulist walking backwards. A conservative is a man with two perfectly good legs who, however, has never learned how to walk forward. A liberal is a man who uses his legs and his hands at the behest of his head. [Franklin D Roosevelt, 1882–1945, radio address, 26 Oct. 1939]

13 I can't think of anyone more susceptible to the Rad–Lib philosophy: 'No problem is insoluble given a big enough plastic bag.' [Tom Stoppard, 1937– , *Jumpers*, I]

See also CONSERVATIVES, SOCIALISTS

LIBERTY

1 It is a strange desire to seek power and to lose liberty. [Francis Bacon, 1561–1626, *Essays*, 11, 'Of Great Place']

2 A! fredome is a noble thing! / Fredome mayse man to haiff liking. / Fredome al solace to man giffis; / He levys at eas that frely levys. [John Barbour, 1316?–95, *The Bruce*, 225]

3 Freedom is nothing but the distance / between the hunter and the hunted. [Bei Dao, *The August Sleeper*]

4 Only reason can convince us of those three fundamental truths without a recognition of which there can be no effective liberty: that what we believe is not necessarily true; that what we like is not necessarily good; and that all questions are open. [Clive Bell, 1881–1964, *Civilization*, 5]

5 The Cause of Freedom is the cause of God! [W L Bowles, 1762–1850, *Edmund Burke*, 78]

6 Abstract liberty, like other mere abstractions, is not to be found. [Edmund Burke, 1729–97, speech on conciliation with America, 22 Mar. 1775]

7 Hereditary bondsmen! know ye not / Who would be free themselves must strike the blow? [Lord Byron, 1788–1824, *Childe Harold's Pilgrimage*, II, 76]

8 Yet, Freedom! yet thy banner, torn, but flying, / Streams like the thunder-storm *against* the wind. [Lord Byron, 1788–1824, *Childe Harold's Pilgrimage*, IV, 98]

9 For Freedom's battle once begun, / Bequeathed by bleeding Sire to Son, / Though baffled oft is ever won. [Lord Byron, 1788–1824, *The Giaour*, 123]

10 Eternal Spirit of the chainless Mind! / Brightest in dungeons, Liberty! thou art. [Lord Byron, 1788–1824, *Sonnet on Chillon*]

11 Deliver me from myself! Deliver my being from its condition! I am free, deliver me from liberty! [Paul Claudel, 1868–1955, *Cinq grandes odes*, II, 'L'esprit et l'eau']

12 Magna Charta is such a fellow, that he will have no sovereign. [Edward Coke, 1552–1634, on the Lords' Amendment to the Petition of Right, 17 May 1628]

13 Like a bird on a wire, like a drunk in a midnight choir, / I have tried, in my way, to be free. [Leonard Cohen, 1934– , song: *Bird on a Wire*]

14 Slaves cannot breathe in England; if their lungs / Receive our air, that moment they are free; / They touch our country, and their shackles fall. [William Cowper, 1731–1800, *The Task*, Bk II, 40]

15 'then shall the voices of liberty be mute?' / He spoke. And drank rapidly a glass of water. [e e cummings, 1894–1962, *is* 5, 'Two, III']

16 The condition upon which God hath given liberty to man is eternal vigilance. [John Philpot Curran, 1750–1817, speech on the right of election of Lord Mayor of Dublin, 10 July 1790]; see 51, 53

17 I only ask to be free. The butterflies are free. [(Harold Skimpole) Charles Dickens, 1812–70, *Bleak House*, Ch. 6]

18 I am as free as nature first made man, / Ere the base laws of servitude began, / When wild in woods the noble savage ran. [John Dryden, 1631–1700, *The Conquest of Granada*, Pt I, I. i]

19 Yes, 'n' how many years can some people exist / Before they're allowed to be free? / Yes, 'n' how many times can a man turn his head, / Pretending he just doesn't see? / The answer, my friend, is blowin' in the wind. [Bob Dylan, 1941– , song: *Blowin' in the Wind*]

20 Liberation, a human phenomenon, cannot be achieved by semi-humans. [Paulo Freire, 1921–97, *Pedagogy of the Oppressed*, Ch. 1]

21 Man has achieved *freedom from* – without yet having *freedom to* – to be himself, to be productive, to be fully awake. [Erich Fromm, 1900–1980, *The Fear of Freedom*, 4]

22 The aim of sadism is to transform a man into a thing, something animate into something inanimate, since by complete and absolute control the living loses one essential quality of life – freedom. [Erich Fromm, 1900–1980, *The Heart of Man*]

23 If society fits you comfortably enough, you call it freedom. [Robert Frost, 1874–1963, in *Esquire* magazine, 1965]

24 O Freedom, what liberties are taken in thy name! [Daniel George, 1890–1967, and Sagittarius (Olga Katzin), 1896–1987, *The Perpetual Pessimist*]

25 *Laissez faire, laissez passer.* – Liberty of action, liberty of movement. [Vincent de Gournay, 1712–59, speech, Sept. 1758. Also attr. to Marquis d'Argenson and François Quesnay]

26 When the people contend for their liberty, they seldom get anything by their victory but new masters. [Marquis of Halifax, 1663–95, *Moral Thoughts and Reflections*, 'Of Prerogative, Power and Liberty']

27 I know not what course others may take; but as for me, give me liberty or give me death. [Patrick Henry, 1736–99, speech to Virginia Convention, 23 Mar. 1775, but not recorded until forty years later by William Wirt, so wording in some doubt]

28 I struck the board, and cried, 'No more; / I will abroad.' / What, shall I ever sigh and pine? / My lines and life are free; free as the road, / Loose as the wind, as large as store. [George Herbert, 1593–1633, *The Collar*]

29 Only very slowly and late have men come to realize that unless freedom is universal it is only extended privilege. [Christopher Hill, 1912– , *The Century of Revolution*, Ch. 20]

30 One should never put on one's best trousers to go out to battle for freedom and truth. [Henrik Ibsen, 1828–1906, *An Enemy of the People*, V]

31 Man must choose whether to be rich in things or in the freedom to use them. [Ivan Illich, 1926– , *Deschooling Society*, Ch. 4]

32 The enemies of Freedom do not argue; they shout and they shoot. [W R Inge, 1860–1954, *The End of an Age*, Ch. 4]

33 The tree of liberty must be refreshed from time to time with the blood of patriots and tyrants. It is its natural manure. [Thomas Jefferson, 1743–1826, letter to W S Smith, 13 Nov. 1787]

34 They took away my liberty, not my freedom. [Brian Keenan, 1950– (describing his captivity in Lebanon), at Dublin news conference after his release, 30 Aug. 1990]

35 Freedom's just another word for nothin' left to lose, / And nothin' ain't worth nothin' but it's free. [Kris Kristofferson, 1936– , and Fred L Foster, song: *Me and Bobby McGee*]

36 We were a self-centred army without parade or gesture, devoted to freedom, the second of man's creeds, a purpose so ravenous that it devoured all our strength, a hope so transcendent that our earlier ambitions faded in its glare. [T E Lawrence, 1888–1935, *Seven Pillars of Wisdom*, Ch. 1]

37 So long as the state exists there is no freedom. When there is freedom there will be no state. [Vladimir Ilyich Lenin, 1870–1924, *The State and Revolution*, Ch. 5, iv]

38 It is true that liberty is precious – so precious that it must be rationed. [Vladimir Ilyich Lenin, 1870–1924, in Sidney and Beatrice Webb, *Soviet Communism*, Ch. 12]

39 I intend no modification of my oft-expressed personal wish that all men everywhere could be free. [Abraham Lincoln, 1809–65, letter, 22 Aug. 1862]

40 Freedom is always and exclusively freedom for the one who thinks differently. [Rosa Luxemburg, 1871–1919, *The Russian Revolution*, sect. 4]

41 There is only one cure for the evils which newly acquired freedom produces; and that is freedom. [Lord Macaulay, 1800–1859, *Literary Essays*, 'Milton']

42 A professor said, 'People are not interested in freedom but in ham and eggs.' To which I retorted, 'Ten years in prison with only ham and eggs for breakfast would cure that.' [Salvador de Madariaga, 1886–1978, in BBC TV programme *Viewpoint*, 14 Oct. 1969]

43 There is no easy walk to freedom. [Nelson Mandela, 1918– , quoted by Donald Woods in *Observer*, 8 Jan. 1978]

44 I am not a number – I am a free man! [George Markstein, 1929–87, and David Tomblin, catchphrase in TV series *The Prisoner*, 1967]

45 The liberty of the individual must be thus far limited; he must not make himself a nuisance to other people. [John Stuart Mill, 1806–73, *On Liberty*, Ch. 3]

46 Liberty consists in doing what one desires. [John Stuart Mill, 1806–73, *On Liberty*, Ch. 5]

47 The mountain nymph, sweet Liberty. [John Milton, 1608–74, *L'Allegro*, 36]

48 Freely we serve / Because we freely love, as in our will / To love or not; in this we stand or fall. [John Milton, 1608–74, *Paradise Lost*, Bk v, 538]

49 Licence they mean when they cry liberty. [John Milton, 1608–74, sonnet: *On the Detraction . . .*]

50 Liberty is the right to do everything which the laws allow. [Baron de Montesquieu, 1689–1755, *L'Esprit des lois*, XI, 3]

51 I sometimes think that the price of liberty is not so much eternal vigilance as eternal dirt. [George Orwell, 1903–50, *The Road to Wigan Pier*, Ch. 4]; see 16, 53

52 If liberty means anything at all, it means the right to tell people what they do not want to hear. [George Orwell, 1903–50, 'The Freedom of the Press', proposed preface to *Animal Farm*]

53 Eternal vigilance is the price of liberty – power is ever stealing from the many to the few. [Wendell Phillips, 1811–84, speech in Boston, Mass., 28 Jan. 1852. This sometimes has been considered a quotation by Phillips from Jefferson, but without justification. Also attr. to Patrick Henry]; see 16, 51

54 We must plan for freedom, and not only for security, if for no other reason than that only freedom can make security secure. [Karl Popper, 1902–94, *The Open Society and Its Enemies*, 21]

55 *En leur reigle n'estoit que ceste clause: Fais ce que voudras.* – In their rules there was only one clause: Do what you will. [François Rabelais, *c.*1492–1553, *Gargantua*, Ch. 57]

56 O Liberty, Liberty, what crimes are committed in your name! [(On passing a statue of Liberty, on her way to the scaffold) Mme Roland, 1754–93, quoted in A de Lamartine, *Histoire des Girondins*, Bk 51, Ch. 8]

57 A world founded upon four essential freedoms. The first is freedom of speech and expression – everywhere in the world. The second is freedom of every person to worship God in his own way – everywhere in the world. The third is freedom from want . . . everywhere in the world. The fourth is freedom from fear . . . anywhere in the world. [Franklin D Roosevelt, 1882–1945, speech, 6 Jan. 1941]

58 Man was born free, and everywhere he is in chains. [Jean-Jacques Rousseau, 1712–78, *The Social Contract*, Ch. 1]

59 First you have to liberate the children (because they're the future) and then you have to liberate the men (because they've been so deformed by the system) and then if there's any liberation left you can take it into the kitchen and eat it. [Joanna Russ, 1937– , *On Strike against God*, p. 84]

60 Man is condemned to be free. [Jean-Paul Sartre, 1905–80, *Existentialism is a Humanism*]

61 Liberty in my view is conforming to majority opinion. [Hugh Scanlon, 1913– , in BBC TV interview, 7 Aug. 1977]

62 I must have liberty / Withal, as large a charter as the wind, / To blow on whom I please. [William Shakespeare, 1564–1616, *As You Like It*, II. vii. 47]

63 Rise like lions after slumber / In unvanquishable number, / Shake your chains to earth like dew / Which in sleep had fallen on you – / Ye are many – they are few. [P B Shelley, 1792–1822, *The Mask of Anarchy*, 151]

64 You took my freedom away a long time ago and you can't give it back because you haven't got it yourself. [Alexander Solzhenitsyn, 1918– , *The First Circle*, Ch. 17]

65 My definition of a free society is a society where it is safe to be unpopular. [Adlai Stevenson, 1900–1965, speech in Detroit, 7 Oct. 1952]

66 It is by the goodness of God that in our country we have those three unspeakably precious things: freedom of speech, freedom of conscience, and the prudence never to practise either of them. [Mark Twain, 1835–1910, *Following the Equator*, Ch. 20]

67 I disapprove of what you say, but I will defend to the death your right to say it. [Attr. to Voltaire in S G Tallentyre, *The Friends of Voltaire* (1906), Ch. 7]

68 Afoot and light-hearted I take to the open road, / Healthy, free, the world before me. [Walt Whitman, 1819–92, *Song of the Open Road*, 1, 1]

69 Freedom is an indivisible word. If we want to enjoy it, and fight for it, we must be prepared to extend it to everyone, whether they are rich or poor, whether they agree with us or not, no matter what their race or the colour of their skin. [Wendell Willkie, 1892–1944, *One World*, Ch. 13]

70 Me this unchartered freedom tires; / I feel the weight of chance-desires: / My hopes no more must change their name, / I long for a repose that ever is the same. [William Wordsworth, 1770–1850, *Ode to Duty*]

71 Two voices are there; one is of the sea, / One of the mountains; each a mighty voice: / In both from age to age thou didst rejoice, / They were thy chosen music, Liberty! [William Wordsworth, 1770–1850, *On the Subjugation of Switzerland*]

See also SLAVERY, TYRANTS

LIBRARIES

1 A man should keep his little brain attic stocked with all the furniture that he is likely to use, and the rest he can put away in the lumber-room of his library, where he can get it if he wants it. [Arthur Conan Doyle, 1859–1930, *The Adventures of Sherlock Holmes*, 'Five Orange Pips']

2 Between the enormous fluted Ionic columns / There seeps from heavily jowled or hawk-like foreign faces / The guttural sorrow of the refugees. [Louis MacNeice, 1907–63, *The British Museum Reading Room*]

3 A library is thought in cold storage. [Herbert Samuel, 1870–1963, in his *Book of Quotations*, 'Books']

4 My library / Was dukedom large enough. [William Shakespeare, 1564–1616, *The Tempest*, I. ii. 109]

5 Come, and take choice of all my library, / And so beguile thy sorrow. [*Titus Andronicus*, IV. i. 34]

6 A circulating library in a town is as an evergreen tree of diabolical knowledge! It blossoms through the year! [R B Sheridan, 1751–1816, *The Rivals*, I. ii]

7 It is a librarian's duty to distinguish between poetry and a sort of belle-litter. [Tom Stoppard, 1937– , *Travesties*, I]

8 There is in the British Museum an enormous mind. Consider that Plato is there cheek by jowl with Aristotle; and Shakespeare with Marlowe. This great mind is hoarded beyond the power of any single mind to possess it. [Virginia Woolf, 1882–1941, *Jacob's Room*, Ch. 9]

See also BOOKS

LIES & LYING

1 Ettie [Lady Desborough] tells enough white lies to ice a cake. [Margot Asquith, 1865–1945, quoted by Lord David Cecil in *Observer*, 20 Dec. 1981]

2 A mixture of a lie doth ever add pleasure. [Francis Bacon, 1561–1626, *Essays*, 1, 'Of Truth']

3 It is not the lie that passeth through the mind, but the lie that sinketh in and settleth in it, that doth the hurt. [Francis Bacon, 1561–1626, *Essays*, 1, 'Of Truth']

4 Matilda told such dreadful lies, / It made one gasp and stretch one's eyes; / Her aunt, who, from her earliest youth, / Had kept a strict regard for truth, / Attempted to believe Matilda: / The effort very nearly killed her. [Hilaire Belloc, 1870–1953, *Cautionary Tales*, 'Matilda']

5 I said in my haste, All men are liars. [Bible, OT, *Psalms* 116:11]

6 Truth exists; only lies are invented. [Georges Braque, 1882–1963, *Pensées sur l'art*]

7 There's a real love of a lie, / Liars find ready-made for lies they make, / As hand for glove, or tongue for sugar-plum. [Robert Browning, 1812–89, *Mr Sludge 'the Medium'*, 689]

8 And, after all, what is a lie? 'Tis but / The truth in masquerade. [Lord Byron, 1788–1824, *Don Juan*, XI, 37]

9 A lie can be half-way round the world before the truth has got its boots on. [James Callaghan, 1912– , speech in House of Commons, 1 Nov. 1976, quoting a proverb]

10 A person I knew used to divide human beings into three categories: those who prefer having nothing to hide rather than being obliged to lie, those who prefer lying to having nothing to hide, and finally those who like both lying and the hidden. [Albert Camus, 1913–60, *The Fall*]

11 It cannot in the opinion of His Majesty's Government be classified as slavery in the extreme acceptance of the word without some risk of terminological inexactitude. [Winston Churchill, 1874–1965, speech in House of Commons, 22 Feb. 1906]

12 I am a lie who always speaks the truth. [Jean Cocteau, 1889–1963, *Opéra : le paquet rouge*]

13 What's the good of a lie if it's seen through? When I tell a lie no one can tell it from the gospel truth. Sometimes I can't even tell it myself. [Graham Greene, 1904–91, *The Captain and the Enemy*, Pt 1, Ch. 1]

14 You see, always divide people into two groups. Those who live by what they know to be a lie, and those who live by what they believe, falsely, to be the truth. [Christopher Hampton, 1946– , *The Philanthropist*, vi]

15 Dare to be true: nothing can need a lie; / A fault, which needs it most, grows two thereby. [George Herbert, 1593–1633, *Church Porch*, 13]

16 The broad masses of the people ... will more easily fall victims to a big lie than to a small one. [Adolf Hitler, 1889–1945, *Mein Kampf*, Ch. 10]

17 The lie in the Soul is a true lie. [Benjamin Jowett, 1817–93, from the Introduction to his trans. of Plato's *Republic*]

18 The habitual liar always imagines that his lie rings true. No miracle of belief can equal his childlike faith in the credulity of the people who listen to him; and so it comes to pass that he fools nobody as completely as he fools himself. [Gerald Kersh, 1911–68, *Night and the City*, Ch. 1]

19 In the long run a harmful truth is better than a useful lie. [Thomas Mann, 1875–1955, quoted by Arthur Koestler on leaving the Communist Party; in Koestler's obituary in *Guardian*, 4 Mar. 1983]

20 Unless a man feels he has a good enough memory, he should never venture to lie. [Michel de Montaigne, 1533–92, *Essays*, I, 9]; see 27

21 By the time you swear you're his, / Shivering and sighing, / And he vows his passion is / Infinite, undying – / Lady, make a note of this: / One of you is lying. [Dorothy Parker, 1893–1967, *Unfortunate Coincidence*]

22 He would, wouldn't he? [Mandy Rice-Davies, 1944– , when told Lord Astor had denied any involvement with her, at trial of Stephen Ward, 28 June 1963]

23 Lord, Lord, how this world is given to lying! [William Shakespeare, 1564–1616, *1 Henry IV*, V. iv. (148)]

24 They have committed false report; moreover, they have spoken untruths; secondarily, they are slanders; sixth and lastly, they have belied a lady; thirdly, they have verified unjust things; and to conclude, they are lying knaves. [*Much Ado About Nothing*, V. i. (224)]

25 Let me have no lying: it becomes none but tradesmen. [*The Winter's Tale*, IV. iii. (747)]

26 Lying hardly describes it. I overdo it. I get carried away in an ecstasy of mendacity. [George Bernard Shaw, 1856–1950, *Man and Superman*, II]

27 Liars ought to have good memories. [Algernon Sidney, 1622–83, *Discourses Concerning Government*, Ch. 2, xv]; see 20

28 In our country the lie has become not just a moral category but a pillar of the State. [Alexander Solzhenitsyn, 1918– ; *Observer*, 'Sayings of the Year', 29 Dec. 1974]

29 A lie is an abomination unto the Lord, and a very present help in trouble. [Adlai Stevenson, 1900–1965, speech, Springfield, Illinois, Jan. 1951]

30 I would make a proposition to my Republican friends ... That if they will stop telling lies about the Democrats, we will stop telling the truth about them. [Adlai Stevenson, 1900–1965, campaign remark, Fresno, California, 10 Sept 1952; in *Respectfully Quoted*, ed. Suzy Platt. Described as a favourite line of Stevenson; it in fact reverses original of Senator Chauncey Depew]

31 The cruellest lies are often told in silence. [Robert Louis Stevenson, 1850–94, *Virginibus Puerisque*, I, 4, 'Truth of Intercourse']

32 Why are you bothering to lie to me? You are like a man on a desert island refusing to admit to his companion that he ate the last coconut. [Tom Stoppard, 1937– , *Artist Descending a Staircase*]

33 I said the thing which was not. [Jonathan Swift, 1677–1745, *Gulliver's Travels*, 'Voyage to the Houyhnhnms', Ch. 3]

34 He will lie even when it is inconvenient, the

sign of a true artist. [Gore Vidal, 1925– , *Two Sisters*]

35 I can't tell a lie, Pa ... I did cut it with my little hatchet. [George Washington, 1732–99, attr. in M L Weems, *Life of G W*, Ch. 2]

36 This is an operative statement. The others are inoperative. [Ronald L Ziegler, 1939– , statement to White House press corps, 1973, admitting the untruth of earlier denials of government involvement in Watergate]

See also TRUTH

LIFE & DEATH

1 Life is very sweet, brother; who would wish to die? [George Borrow, 1803–81, *Lavengro*, 25]

2 Life, that dares send / A challenge to his end, / And when it comes say, 'Welcome, friend!' [Richard Crashaw, 1613?–49, *Wishes to His Supposed Mistress*, 85]

3 I'm quite hopeful about life after death. It's life before death I'm not terribly cheerful about. [Alice Thomas Ellis, 1932– , interview in *Observer*, 1 Feb. 1987]

4 But life and death / Is cat and dog in this double-bed of a world. [Christopher Fry, 1907– , *A Phoenix Too Frequent*]

5 Is life a boon? / If so, it must befall / That death, whene'er he call, / Must call too soon. [W S Gilbert, 1836–1911, *The Yeomen of the Guard*, I]

6 A useless life is an early death. [Johann Wolfgang von Goethe, 1749–1832, *Iphigenia*, I. ii]

7 And until you have grasped this: 'Die and be transformed!' you will be nothing but a sombre guest on the sorry earth. [Johann Wolfgang von Goethe, 1749–1832, *Ecstasy and Desire*]

8 For who to dumb Forgetfulness a prey, / This pleasing anxious being e'er resigned, / Left the warm precincts of the cheerful day / Nor cast one longing ling'ring look behind? [Thomas Gray, 1716–71, *Elegy Written in a Country Churchyard*, 22]

9 In the last analysis, it is our conception of death which decides our answers to all the questions that life puts to us. [Dag Hammarskjöld, 1905–61, *Diaries*, 1958]

10 *Gut ist der Schlaf, der Tod ist besser – freilich / Das beste wäre, nie geboren sein.* – Sleep is good, death is better; but of course, the best thing would be never to have been born at all. [Heinrich Heine, 1797–1856, *Morphine*]

11 No arts; no letters; no society; and which is worst of all, continual fear and danger of violent death; and the life of man, solitary, poor, nasty, brutish, and short. [Thomas Hobbes, 1588–1679, *Leviathan*, Pt I, Ch. 13]

12 Put me on earth again, and I would rather be a serf in the house of some landless man ... than king of all these dead men that have done with life. [Homer, *c.*900BC, *Odyssey*, XI, 489]

13 All / Life death does end and each day dies with sleep. [Gerard Manley Hopkins, 1844–89, *No Worst, There is None*]

14 It matters not how a man dies, but how he lives. The act of dying is not of importance, it lasts so short a time. [Dr Samuel Johnson, 1709–84, in James Boswell, *Life of J*, 26 Oct. 1769]

15 I rent everything, other than the gift of life itself, which was given to me without any predictable lease, a gift that can be withdrawn at any time. [Jerzy Kosinski, 1933–91, in interview three days before committing suicide, in *Weekend Guardian*, 25–6 May 1991]

16 Alas, solitude is not very likely, there is so little of it in life, so what can we expect after death! After all, the dead far outnumber the living! [Milan Kundera, 1929– , *Immortality*, Pt 1, 3]

17 There are only three events in a man's life; birth, life, and death; he is not conscious of being born, he dies in pain, and he forgets to live. [Jean de La Bruyère, 1645–96, *Characters*, 'Of Man', 48]

18 I strove with none; for none was worth my strife; / Nature I loved, and, next to Nature, Art; / I warmed both hands before the fire of life; / It sinks, and I am ready to depart. [Walter Savage Landor, 1775–1864, *I Strove with None*]

19 Many men would take the death-sentence without a whimper to escape the life-sentence which fate carries in her other hand. [T E Lawrence, 1888–1935, *The Mint*, Pt I, Ch. 4]

20 He was pleasantly surprised to find himself so reconciled to death. If he ever lived his life again, he decided, he would insist on a brand new actor in the leading role. [John Le Carré, 1931– , *The Tailor of Panama*, Ch. 22]

21 My grandmother made dying her life's work. [Hugh Leonard, 1926– , *Home before Night*, opening sentence]

22 The continuous labour of your life is to build the house of death. [Michel de Montaigne, 1533–92, *Essays*, I, 20]

23 When a man dies, he does not just die of the disease he has: he dies of his whole life. [Charles Péguy, 1873–1914; in W H Auden, and L Kronenberger, *The Faber Book of Aphorisms*, 'The Professions']

24 The fever called 'Living' / Is conquered at last. [Edgar Allan Poe, 1809–49, *For Annie*]

25 To contain the whole of death so gently even before life has begun, and not be angry – this is beyond description. [Rainer Maria Rilke, 1875–1926, *Duino Elegies*, 4]

26 To die, to sleep; / To sleep: perchance to dream: ay, there's the rub. / For in that sleep of death what dreams may come / When we have shuffled off this mortal coil, / Must give us pause. There's the respect / That makes calamity of so long life; / For who would bear the whips and scorns of time, / The oppressor's wrong, the proud man's contumely, / The pangs of disprized love, the law's delay, / The insolence of office, and the spurns / That patient merit of the unworthy takes, / When he himself might his quietus make / With a bare bodkin? who would fardels bear, / To grunt and sweat under a weary life, / But that the dread of something after death, / The undiscovered country from whose bourn / No traveller returns, puzzles the will, / And makes us rather bear those ills we have / Than fly to others that we know not of? [William Shakespeare, 1564–1616, *Hamlet*, III. i. 64]

27 Why he that cuts off twenty years of life / Cuts off so many years of fearing death. [*Julius Caesar*, III. i. 101]

28 She should have died hereafter: / There would have been a time for such a word. / To-morrow, and to-morrow, and to-morrow, / Creeps in this petty pace from day to day, / To the last syllable of recorded time; / And all our yesterdays have lighted fools / The way to dusty death. Out, out, brief candle! / Life's but a walking shadow, a poor player / That struts and frets his hour upon the stage, / And then is heard no more: it is a tale / Told by an idiot, full of sound and fury, / Signifying nothing. [*Macbeth*, V. v. 17]

29 Be absolute for death; either death or life / Shall thereby be the sweeter. Reason thus with life: / If I do lose thee, I do lose a thing / That none but fools would keep: a breath thou art, / Servile to all the skyey influences. [*Measure for Measure*, III. i. 5]

30 The weariest and most loathèd worldly life / That age, ache, penury and imprisonment / Can lay on nature is a paradise / To what we fear of death. [*Measure for Measure*, III. i. 127]

31 Death is the veil which those who live call life: / They sleep, and it is lifted. [P B Shelley, 1792–1822, *Prometheus Unbound*, III. iii. 113]

32 The whole of his life had prepared Podduyev for living, not for dying. [Alexander Solzhenitsyn, 1918– , *Cancer Ward*, Pt I, Ch. 8]

33 A life that moves to gracious ends / Thro' troops of unrecording friends, / A deedful life, a silent voice. [Alfred, Lord Tennyson, 1809–92, *To —, after Reading a Life and Letters*]

34 Whatever crazy sorrow saith, / No life that breathes with human breath / Has ever truly longed for death. [Alfred, Lord Tennyson, 1809–92, *The Two Voices*, 132]

35 Every moment dies a man, / Every moment one is born. [Alfred, Lord Tennyson, 1809–92, *The Village of Sin*, 4]

36 All say, 'How hard it is that we have to die' – a strange complaint to come from the mouths of people who have had to live. [Mark Twain, 1835–1910, *Pudd'nhead Wilson*, Ch. 10]

37 But life is, what none can express, / A quickness, which my God hath kissed. [Henry Vaughan, 1622–95, *Quickness*]

38 Live? Our servants will do that for us. [Auguste Villiers de l'Isle-Adam, 1838–89, *Axel*, IV. ii]

39 LORD ILLINGWORTH: The Book of Life begins with a man and a woman in a garden.

MRS ALLONBY: It ends with Revelations. [Oscar Wilde, 1854–1900, *A Woman of No Importance*, I]

40 Death and life were not / Till man made up the whole, / Made lock, stock and barrel / Out of his bitter soul. [W B Yeats, 1865–1939, *The Tower*, 3]

See also next two categories, DEATH, EXISTENCE

LIFE & LIVING

1 The food in this place is really terrible. Yes, and such small portions. That's essentially how I feel about life. [Woody Allen, 1935– , in film *Annie Hall*, scripted with Marshall Brickman]

2 Life loves the liver of it. [Maya Angelou, 1928– , in *Conversations with M A*, ed. Jeffrey M Elliot]

3 Is it so small a thing / To have enjoyed the sun, / To have lived light in the spring, / To have loved, to have thought, to have done? [Matthew Arnold, 1822–88, *Empedocles on Etna*, I, ii, 397]

4 Remember that no man loses any other life than this which he now lives, nor lives any other than this which he now loses. [Marcus Aurelius, AD 121–80, *Meditations*, II, 14]

5 Life is rather like a tin of sardines – we're all of us looking for the key. [Alan Bennett, 1934– , *Beyond the Fringe*]

6 I thought life was going to be like Brahms, do you know? Instead it's, well, it's been Eric Coates. And very nice, too. But not Brahms. [Alan Bennett, 1934– , *Getting On*, II]

7 For everything that lives is holy, life delights in life. [William Blake, 1757–1827, *America*, 71]

8 There's night and day, brother, both sweet things; sun, moon, and stars, brother, all sweet things; there's likewise a wind on the heath. [George Borrow, 1803–81, *Lavengro*, Ch. 25]

9 Life is Just a Bowl of Cherries. [Lew Brown, 1893–1958, title of song in musical *Scandals*]

10 Love, we are in God's hand. / How strange now, looks the life he makes us lead. / So free we seem, so fettered fast we are! [Robert Browning, 1812–89, *Andrea del Sarto*, 49]

11 For life, with all its yields of joy and woe, / And hope and fear, – believe the aged friend – / Is just a chance o' the prize of learning love. [Robert Browning, 1812–89, *A Death in the Desert*, 245]

12 At last awake / From life, that insane dream we take / For waking now. [Robert Browning, 1812–89, *Easter-Day*, 14]

13 I count life just a stuff / To try the soul's strength on. [Robert Browning, 1812–89, *In a Balcony*, 651]

14 Life is one long process of getting tired. [Samuel Butler, 1835–1902, *Notebooks*, Ch. 1, 'Life', 7]

15 Life is the art of drawing sufficient conclusions from insufficient premises. [Samuel Butler, 1835–1902, *Notebooks*, Ch. 1, 'Life', 9]

16 To live is like to love – all the reason is against it, and all healthy instinct for it. [Samuel Butler, 1835–1902, *Notebooks*, Ch. 14 'Life and Love']

17 Life is a tragedy when seen in close-up, but a comedy in long-shot. [Charlie Chaplin, 1889–1977, in obituary in *Guardian*, 28 Dec. 1977]

18 If life had a second edition, how I would correct the proofs. [John Clare, 1793–1864, letter to a friend]

19 Life is a maze in which we take the wrong turning before we have learnt to walk. [Cyril Connolly (Palinurus), 1903–74, *The Unquiet Grave*, Ch. 1]

20 To me life is just a novitiate eternity. [Dame Felicitas Corrigan, 1908– , in *Observer*, 28 July 1991]

21 But boldly say each night, / To-morrow let my sun his beams display, / Or in clouds hide them; I have lived to-day. [Abraham Cowley, 1618–67, *Of Myself*]

22 His faith perhaps in some nice tenets might / Be wrong; his life, I'm sure, was always in the right. [Abraham Cowley, 1618–67, *On the Death of Mr Crashaw*]

23 Life is an incurable disease. [Abraham Cowley, 1618–67, *To Dr Scarborough*]

24 Life was a funny thing that happened to me on the way to the grave. [Quentin Crisp, 1908–99, *The Naked Civil Servant*, Ch. 18]

25 I have measured out my life with coffee spoons. [T S Eliot, 1888–1965, *Love Song of J. Alfred Prufrock*]

26 Birth, and copulation, and death. / That's all the facts when you come to brass tacks. [T S Eliot, 1888–1965, *Sweeney Agonistes*, 'Fragment of an Agon']

27 Yet we have gone on living, / Living and partly living. [T S Eliot, 1888–1965, *Murder in the Cathedral*, I]

28 We are always getting ready to live, but never living. [Ralph Waldo Emerson, 1803–82, *Journals*, 13 Apr. 1834]

29 His life was a sort of dream, as are most lives with the mainspring left out. [F Scott Fitzgerald, 1896–1940, *Notebooks*, 'C']

30 One thing I know. If living isn't a seeking for the grail it may be a damned amusing game. [F Scott Fitzgerald, 1896–1940, *This Side of Paradise*, Bk II, Ch. 5]

31 Life's a pudding full of plums. [W S Gilbert, 1836–1911, *The Gondoliers*, 1]

32 That is the art of living that your price shall suit everybody. [James Hanley, 1901–85, *Drift*, Ch. 2]

33 There was Life – pale and hoar; / And slow it said to me, / 'Twice-over cannot be!' [Thomas Hardy, 1840–1928, *A Second Attempt*]

34 Life is made up of marble and mud. [Nathaniel Hawthorne, 1804–64, *The House of the Seven Gables*, Ch. 2]

35 Men to whom life had appeared as a reversible coat – seamy on both sides. [O Henry, 1862–1910, *The Hiding of Black Bill*]

36 It may be life, but ain't it slow? [A P Herbert, 1890–1971, *It May be Life*]

37 I slept and dreamed that life was beauty; / I woke and found that life was duty. [Ellen Sturgis Hooper, 1816–41, *Beauty and Duty*]

38 Life is an abnormal business. [Eugene Ionesco, 1912–94, *Rhinoceros*, I]

39 W. R. RODGERS: What do you think of life? JOHN: There's nothing more terrifying. [Augustus John, 1878–1961, in *The Sunday Times*, 1 Dec. 1963]

40 Human life is everywhere a state in which much is to be endured and little to be enjoyed. [Dr Samuel Johnson, 1709–84, *Rasselas*, Ch. 11]

41 Life is a pill which none of us can bear to swallow without gilding. [Dr Samuel Johnson, 1709–84, in Mrs Piozzi, *Anecdotes of J*]

42 If there is a transmigration of souls, then I am not yet on the bottom rung. My life is a hesitation before birth. [Franz Kafka, 1883–1924, *The Diaries of F K*, 24 Jan. 1922]

43 A man's life of any worth is a continual allegory – and very few eyes can see the mystery of his life – a life like the scriptures – figurative. [John Keats, 1795–1821, letter to G and G Keats, 14 Feb. – 3 May 1819]

44 Good for a shaking experience or two, though, isn't it – life? I think it means no harm, it's just too big not to be brutal from time to time. [A L Kennedy, 1960– , *So I Am Glad*, p. 108]

45 Life is a cheap *table d'hôte* in a rather dirty restaurant, with time changing the plates before you've had enough of anything. [Thomas Kettle, 1880–1916, from his wife's memoir; in *Book of Irish Quotations*, ed. Sean McMahon]

46 Life makes no absolute statement. It is all Call and Answer. [D H Lawrence, 1885–1930, *Kangaroo*, Ch. 10]

47 Life is like a sewer. What you get out of it depends on what you put into it. [Tom Lehrer, 1928– , preamble to song *We Will All Go Together When We Go*]

48 Life is what happens to us while we're making other plans. [John Lennon, 1940–80, song: *Beautiful Boy*]

49 Life would be tolerable, were it not for its amusements. [George Cornewall Lewis, 1806–63, in *The Times*, 18 Sept. 1872]

50 Life is real! Life is earnest! / And the grave is not its goal. / Dust thou art, to dust returnest, / Was not spoken of the soul. [H W Longfellow, 1807–82, *A Psalm of Life*]

51 live so that you / can stick out your tongue / at the insurance / doctor [Don Marquis, 1878–1937, *archy and mehitabel*, XII, 'certain maxims of archy']

52 Life's battle is a conquest for the strong; / The meaning shows in the defeated thing. [John Masefield, 1878–1967, *The Wanderer*]

53 It is not true that life is one damn thing after another – it is one damn thing over and over. [Edna St Vincent Millay, 1892–1950, *Letters of E M*, letter to A D Fiske, 24 Oct. 1930]

54 Nor love thy life, nor hate; but what thou liv'st, / Live well, how long or short permit to heav'n. [John Milton, 1608–74, *Paradise Lost*, Bk xi, 553]

55 I've looked at life from both sides now / From win and lose and still somehow / It's life's illusions I recall / I really don't know life at all. [Joni Mitchell, 1943– , song: *Both Sides Now*]

56 To know how to live is my trade and my art. [Michel de Montaigne, 1533–92, *Essays*, II, 6]

57 Life is a dream; when we sleep we are awake, and when awake we sleep. [Michel de Montaigne, 1533–92, *Essays*, II, 12]

58 There are three ingredients in the good life: learning, earning and yearning. [Christopher Morley, 1890–1957, *Parnassus on Wheels*, Ch. 10]

59 Life is a foreign language: all men mispronounce it. [Christopher Morley, 1890–1957, *Thunder on the Left*, Ch. 14]

60 Most of what's most interesting in life goes on below the belt. [John Mortimer, 1923– , *Summer's Lease*, Ch. 9]

61 The life of every man is an endlessly repeated performance of the life of man. [Edwin Muir, 1887–1959, *An Autobiography*, Ch. 1]

62 Live every day as if it was your last, but think as if you will live for ever. [Benito Mussolini, 1883–1945, quoted in address by Gianfranco Fini, the Italian neo-Fascist leader, at the funeral of two Fascist veterans, Rome, 24 May 1988]

63 Our lives are merely strange dark interludes in the electric display of God the Father. [Eugene O'Neill, 1888–1953, *Strange Interlude*, ix]

64 This long disease, my life. [Alexander Pope, 1688–1744, *Epistle to Dr Arbuthnot*, 132]

65 'In fact,' Sam the Gonoph says, 'I long ago came to the conclusion that all life is six to five against.' [Damon Runyon, 1884–1946, *More Than Somewhat*, 'A Nice Price']

66 There is no cure for birth and death save to enjoy the interval. [George Santayana, 1863–1952, *Soliloquies in England*, 'War Shrines']

67 Life is not a spectacle or a feast; it is a predicament. [George Santayana, 1863–1952, in Sagittarius and D George, *The Perpetual Pessimist*]

68 Life is nothing until it is lived; but it is yours to make sense of, and the value of it is nothing other than the sense you choose. [Jean-Paul Sartre, 1905–80, *Existentialism is a Humanism*]

69 There must be more to life than having everything! [Maurice Sendak, 1928– , *Higglety Pigglety Pop!*, Ch. 1]

70 Life is as tedious as a twice-told tale, / Vexing the dull ear of a drowsy man. [William Shakespeare, 1564–1616, *King John*, III. iv. 108]

71 If life were a candy bar, she'd eat the wrapper. [Dyan Sheldon, 1946– , *Dreams of an Average Man*, 7]

72 Those poor slaves . . . / Who travel to their home among the dead / By the broad highway of the world, and so / With one chained friend, perhaps a jealous foe, / The dreariest and the longest journey go. [P B Shelley, 1792–1822, *Epipsychidion*, 155]

73 Lift not the painted veil which those who live / Call life. [P B Shelley, 1792–1822, sonnet: *Lift Not the Painted Veil*]

74 The unexamined life is not worth living. [Socrates, 469–399 BC, quoted in Plato, *Apology*, 38]

75 Different living is not living in different places / But creating in the mind a map. [Stephen Spender, 1909–95, *Different Living*]

76 Life is a gamble, at terrible odds – if it was a bet, you wouldn't take it. [Tom Stoppard, 1937– , *Rosencrantz and Guildenstern are Dead*, III]

77 I will drink / Life to the lees. [Alfred, Lord Tennyson, 1809–92, *Ulysses*, 6]

78 When all is done, human life is, at the greatest and the best, but like a froward child, that must be played with and humoured a little to keep it quiet till it falls asleep, and then the care is over. [Sir William Temple, 1628–99, *Essay on Poetry*]

79 Oh, isn't life a terrible thing, thank God? [Dylan Thomas, 1914–53, *Under Milk Wood*]

80 For life is but a dream whose shapes return, / Some frequently, some seldom, some by night / And some by day. [James Thomson, 1834–82, *The City of Dreadful Night*, 1]

81 Unfortunately, life is an offensive, directed against the repetitious mechanism of the Universe. [A N Whitehead, 1861–1947, *Adventures of Ideas*, Ch. 5]

82 A dead Nature aims at nothing. It is the essence of life that it exists for its own sake, as the intrinsic reaping of value. [A N Whitehead, 1861–1947, *Nature and Life*, Ch. 1]

83 I spent the afternoon musing on Life. If you come to think of it, what a queer thing Life is! So unlike anything else, don't you know, if you see what I mean. [P G Wodehouse, 1881–1975, *My Man Jeeves*, 'Rallying round Old George']

84 Life is not a series of gig lamps symmetrically arranged: life is a luminous halo, a semi-transparent envelope surrounding us from the beginning of consciousness to the end. [Virginia Woolf, 1882–1941, *The Common Reader*, First Series, 'Modern Fiction']

85 Life itself, every moment of it, every drop of it, here, this instant, now, in the sun, in Regent's

Park, was enough. Too much, indeed. [Virginia Woolf, 1882–1941, *Mrs Dalloway*]

See also previous and next categories, BIRTH, DEATH

LIFE IS FLEETING

1 What is our life? a play of passion, / Our mirth the music of derision, / Our mothers' wombs the tiring houses be, / Where we are dressed for this short comedy. [anon. poem *On the Life of Man*, from Orlando Gibbons, *First Set of Madrigals and Motets*]

2 The bloom is gone, and with the bloom go I. [Matthew Arnold, 1822–88, *Thyrsis*, 60]

3 Everything is only for a day, both that which remembers and that which is remembered. [Marcus Aurelius, AD 121–80, *Meditations*, IV, 35]

4 The world's a bubble; and the life of man, / Less than a span. [Francis Bacon, 1561–1626, *The World*]

5 They give birth astride of a grave, the light gleams an instant, then it's night once more. [Samuel Beckett, 1906–89, *Waiting for Godot*, 1]

6 When we compare the present life of man with that time of which we have no knowledge, it seems to me like the swift flight of a lone sparrow through the banqueting-hall where you sit in the winter months ... This sparrow flies swiftly in through one door of the hall, and out through another ... Similarly, man appears on earth for a little while, but we know nothing of what went on before this life, and what follows. [The Venerable Bede, 673–735, *History of the English Church and People*, 2, Ch. 13]

7 Human life is mainly a process of filling in time until the arrival of death, or Santa Claus, with very little choice, if any, of what kind of business one is going to transact during the long wait. [Eric Berne, 1910–70, *Games People Play*, Ch. 18]

8 Let us crown ourselves with rosebuds, before they be withered. [Bible, Apocrypha, *Wisdom of Solomon* 2:8]

9 Whatsoever thy hand findeth to do, do it with thy might; for there is no work, nor device, nor knowledge, nor wisdom, in the grave whither thou goest. [Bible, OT, *Ecclesiastes* 9:10]

10 All flesh is grass, and all the goodliness thereof is as the flower of the field. The grass withereth, the flower fadeth: because the spirit of the Lord bloweth upon it: surely the people is grass. [Bible, OT, *Isaiah* 40:6 (cf. *1 Peter* 1:24)]

11 Naked came I out of my mother's womb, and naked shall I return thither: the Lord gave, and the Lord hath taken away; blessed be the name of the Lord. [Bible, OT, *Job* 1:21]

12 Thou makest his beauty to consume away, like as it were a moth fretting a garment: every man therefore is but vanity. [Bible, OT, *Psalms* 39:12 (*Book of Common Prayer* version)]

13 Their inward thought is, that their houses shall continue for ever, and their dwelling-places to all generations; they call their lands after their own names. Nevertheless, man being in honour abideth not: he is like the beasts that perish. [Bible, OT, *Psalms* 49:11]

14 We spend our years as a tale that is told. The days of our years are threescore years and ten; and if by reason of strength they be fourscore years, yet is their strength labour and sorrow; for it is soon cut off, and we fly away. [Bible, OT, *Psalms* 90:9]

15 Let us eat and drink; for to morrow we die. [Bible, NT, *1 Corinthians* 15:32 (cf. *Isaiah* 22:13)]

16 He that loves a rosy cheek, / Or a coral lip admires, / Or, from star-like eyes, doth seek / Fuel to maintain his fires; / As old Time makes these decay, / So his flames must waste away. [Thomas Carew, 1595?–1639, *Disdain Returned*]

17 Days and moments quickly flying, / Blend the living with the dead; / Soon will you and I be lying / Each within our narrow bed. [Edward Caswell, 1814–78, hymn]

18 Let us live, my Lesbia, and love, and not give a farthing for the talk of censorious old men. Suns may set and rise again. As for us, when the brief light has once set, we must sleep one endless night. [Catullus, 87–54? BC, *Carmina*, 5]

19 This world nis but a thurghfare ful of wo, / And we been pilgrimes, passinge to and fro; / Deeth is an ende of every worldly sore. [Geoffrey Chaucer, 1340?–1400, *Canterbury Tales*, 'The Knight's Tale', 1989]

20 Ye, farewel al the snow of ferne yere! [Geoffrey Chaucer, 1340?–1400, *Troilus and Criseyde*, v, 1176]

21 What argufies pride and ambition? / Soon or late death will take us in tow: / Each bullet has got its commission, / And when our time's come we must go. [Charles Dibdin, 1745–1814, *Each Bullet Has Its Commission*]

22 They are not long, the days of wine and roses: / Out of a misty dream / Our path emerges for a while, then closes / Within a dream. [Ernest Dowson, 1867–1900, *Vita Summa Brevis*]

23 All human things are subject to decay, / And when fate summons, monarchs must obey. [John Dryden, 1631–1700, *Mac Flecknoe*, 1]

24 Our plesance heir is all vain glory, / This fals warld is bot transitory, / The flesche is brukle, the Fend is sle; / *Timor mortis conturbat me.* [William Dunbar, 1460?–1520?, *Lament for the Makaris*]

25 A little rule, a little sway, / A sunbeam in a winter's day, / Is all the proud and mighty have / Between the cradle and the grave. [John Dyer, 1700–1758, *Grongar Hill*, 89]

26 The Wine of Life keeps oozing drop by drop, / The Leaves of Life keep falling one by one. [Edward Fitzgerald, 1809–83, *The Rubá'iyát of Omar Khayyám*, Edn 1, 8]

27 One thing is certain, that Life flies; / One thing is certain, and the Rest is Lies; / The Flower that once has blown for ever dies. [Edward Fitzgerald, 1809–83, *The Rubá'iyát of Omar Khayyám*, Edn 1, 26]

28 One Moment in Annihilation's Waste, / One Moment, of the Well of Life to taste – / The Stars are setting and the Caravan / Starts for the Dawn of Nothing – Oh, make haste! [Edward Fitzgerald, 1809–83, *The Rubá'iyát of Omar Khayyám*, Edn 1, 38]

29 For one night or the other night / Will come the Gardener in white, and gathered flowers are dead, Yasmin. [James Elroy Flecker, 1884–1915, *Hassan*, I. ii]

30 *Alles Vergängliche / Ist nur ein Gleichnis.* – All that is transitory is only an image. [Johann Wolfgang von Goethe, 1749–1832, *Faust*, Pt Two, V]

31 Take your delight in momentariness, / Walk between dark and dark – a shining space / With the grave's narrowness, though not its peace. [Robert Graves, 1895–1985, *Sick Love*]

32 Death borders upon our birth, and our cradle stands in the grave. [Joseph Hall, 1574–1656, *Epistles*, 2]

33 Fair daffodils, we weep to see / You haste away so soon: / As yet the early-rising sun / Has not attained his noon. [Robert Herrick, 1591–1674, *To Daffodils*]

34 The life so short, the craft so long to learn. [Hippocrates, *c.*460–357 BC, *Aphorisms*, I, i, trans. Chaucer. Often quoted in Latin: *Ars longa, vita brevis*]

35 Babies haven't any hair; / Old men's heads are just as bare; – / Between the cradle and the grave / Lies a haircut and a shave. [Samuel Hoffenstein, 1890–1947, *Songs of Faith in the Year after Next*, 8]

36 *Vitae summa brevis spem nos vetat incohare longam.* – Life's short span forbids our embarking on far-reaching hopes. [Horace, 65–8 BC, *Odes*, I, iv, 15]

37 *Carpe diem, quam minimum credula postero.* – Seize today, and put as little trust as you can in the morrow. [Horace, 65–8 BC, *Odes*, I, xi, 8]

38 *Eheu fugaces, Postume, Postume, / Labuntur anni.* – Alas Postumus, Postumus, the fleeting years are slipping by. [Horace, 65–8 BC, *Odes*, II, xiv, 1]

39 Tomorrow, more's the pity, / Away we both must hie, / To air the ditty / And to earth I. [A E Housman, 1859–1936, *Last Poems*, 41]

40 This life at best is but an inn, / And we the passengers. [James Howell, 1594?–1666, *Familiar Letters*, Bk i, 73]

41 Stop and consider! life is but a day; / A fragile dew-drop on its perilous way / From a tree's summit; a poor Indian's sleep / While his boat hastens to the monstrous steep / Of Montmorenci. [John Keats, 1795–1821, *Sleep and Poetry*, 85]

42 Redeem thy mis-spent time that's past; / Live this day, as if 'twere thy last. [Bishop Thomas Ken, 1637–1711, *A Morning Hymn*]

43 But at my back I always hear / Time's wingèd chariot hurrying near, / And yonder all before us lie / Deserts of vast eternity. / Thy beauty shall no more be found, / Nor, in thy marble vaults, shall sound / My echoing song; then worms shall try / That long-preserved virginity, / And your quaint honour turn to dust, / And into ashes all my lust: / The grave's a fine and private place, / But none, I think, do there embrace. [Andrew Marvell, 1621–78, *To His Coy Mistress*]

44 *La vie est vaine : / Un peu d'amour, / Un peu de haine . . . / Et puis – bonjour !*
La vie est brève : / Un peu d'espoir, / Un peu de rêve / Et puis – bon soir !
Life is fruitless : a little love, a little hate . . . and then – good morning.
Life is brief : a little hope, a little dream and then – good night ! [Léon Montenaeken, b.1859, *Peu de chose*]

45 Beauty is but a flower / Which wrinkles will devour ; / Brightness falls from the air, / Queens have died young and fair, / Dust hath closed Helen's eye, / I am sick, I must die. / Lord, have mercy on us ! [Thomas Nashe, 1567–1601, *In Plague Time*]

46 That the play is the tragedy 'Man', / And its hero the Conqueror Worm. [Edgar Allan Poe, 1809–49, *The Conqueror Worm*]

47 The blossoms of the apricot / blow from the east to the west, / And I have tried to keep them from / falling. [Ezra Pound, 1885–1972, *Cantos*, XIII]

48 In the midst of life we are in death. [*The Book of Common Prayer*, The Burial of the Dead, Anthem]

49 Darling, let us go to see if the rose, which this morning had spread her purple robe to the sun, has not this evening lost the folds of her purple robe and her colour, that is like yours. [Pierre de Ronsard, 1524–85, *Odes*, 'To Cassandre', 17]

50 Brief and powerless is Man's life ; on him and all his race the slow, sure doom falls pitiless and dark. [Bertrand Russell, 1872–1970, *Mysticism and Logic*, 'A Free Man's Worship']

51 The bright day is done, / And we are for the dark. [William Shakespeare, 1564–1616, *Antony and Cleopatra*, V. ii. 192]

52 And so, from hour to hour we ripe and ripe, / And then from hour to hour we rot and rot, / And thereby hangs a tale. [*As You Like It*, II. vii. 26]

53 The time of life is short ; / To spend that shortness basely were too long. [*1 Henry IV*, V. ii. 81]

54 We are such stuff / As dreams are made on, and our little life / Is rounded with a sleep. [*The Tempest*, IV. i. 156]

55 He weaves, and is clothed with derision ; / Sows, and he shall not reap ; / His life is a watch or a vision / Between a sleep and a sleep. [A C Swinburne, 1837–1909, *Atalanta in Calydon*, Chorus, 'Before the Beginning of Years']

56 Time driveth onward fast, / And in a little while our lips are dumb. / Let us alone. What is it that will last ? / All things are taken from us, and become / Portions and parcels of the dreadful Past. [Alfred, Lord Tennyson, 1809–92, *The Lotos-Eaters*, 'Choric Song', 4]

57 My days have crackled and gone up in smoke, / Have puffed and burst as sun-starts on a stream. / Yea, faileth now even dream / The dreamer, and the lute the lutanist. [Francis Thompson, 1859–1907, *The Hound of Heaven*, 122]

58 Though nothing can bring back the hour / Of splendour in the grass, of glory in the flower. [William Wordsworth, 1770–1850, *Ode, Intimations of Immortality*, 10]

59 There's not a nook within this solemn pass / But were an apt confessional for one / Taught by his summer spent, his autumn gone, / That life is but a tale of morning grass / Withered at eve. [William Wordsworth, 1770–1850, *Yarrow Revisited*, 6, 'The Trossachs']

See also AGE, DEATH, LIFE & DEATH, MORTALITY, PAST, TIME

LIGHT

1 And God said, Let there be light : and there was light. [Bible, OT, *Genesis* 1 :3]

2 The people that walked in darkness have seen a great light : they that dwell in the land of the shadow of death, upon them hath the light shined. [Bible, OT, *Isaiah* 9 :2]

3 The light shineth in darkness ; and the darkness comprehended it not. [Bible, NT, *St John* 1 :5]

4 But yet the light that led astray / Was light from Heaven. [Robert Burns, 1759–96, *The Vision*, 239]

5 And not by eastern windows only, / When daylight comes, comes in the light, / In front the sun climbs slow, how slowly, / But westward, look, the land is bright. [Arthur Hugh Clough, 1819–61, *Say Not the Struggle Naught Availeth*]

6 There's a certain slant of light, / On winter afternoons, / That oppresses, like the weight / Of cathedral tunes. [Emily Dickinson, 1830–86, *There's a Certain Slant of Light*]

7 Light (God's eldest daughter!) is a principal beauty in a building. [Thomas Fuller, 1608–61, *The Holy State*, Bk ii, Ch. 7]

8 'Let there be Licht,' said God, and there was / A little. [Hugh MacDiarmid, 1892–1978, *A Drunk Man Looks at the Thistle*, 2100]

9 Swift as a shadow, short as any dream, / Brief as the lightning in the collied night, / That, in a spleen, unfolds both heaven and earth, / And ere a man hath power to say, 'Behold!' / The jaws of darkness do devour it up: / So quick bright things come to confusion. [William Shakespeare, 1564–1616, *A Midsummer Night's Dream*, I. i. 144]

10 Light breaks where no sun shines; / Where no sea runs, the waters of the heart / Push in their tides. [Dylan Thomas, 1914–53, *Light Breaks Where No Sun Shines*]

11 The light that never was, on sea or land, / The consecration, and the poet's dream. [William Wordsworth, 1770–1850, *Elegiac Stanzas, Suggested by a Picture of Peele Castle*]

See also DAWN, NIGHT

LIMBO

1 Eternal nothingness is OK if you're dressed for it. [Woody Allen, 1935– , *Getting Even*, 'My Philosophy']

2 Wandering between two worlds, one dead, / The other powerless to be born. [Matthew Arnold, 1822–88, *The Grande Chartreuse*, 85]

3 Into a Limbo large and broad, since called / The paradise of fools, to few unknown. [John Milton, 1608–74, *Paradise Lost*, Bk iii, 495]

4 BRICK: Well, they say nature hates a vacuum, Big Daddy.

BIG DADDY: That's what they say, but sometimes I think that a vacuum is a hell of a lot better than some of the stuff that nature replaces it with. [Tennessee Williams, 1911–83, *Cat on a Hot Tin Roof*, II]

See also AFTERLIFE, NOTHING

LISTENING

1 Oh – I listen a lot and talk less. You can't learn anything when you're talking. [Bing Crosby, 1901–77, BBC TV interview with Michael Parkinson, 1975]

2 Look at yourself with one eye, listen to yourself with the other. [Eugene Ionesco, 1912–94, *Improvisation*]

3 All man's life among men is nothing more than a battle for the ears of others. [Milan Kundera, 1929– , *The Book of Laughter and Forgetting*, Pt 4, 1]

4 Not many sounds in life, and I include all urban and rural sounds, exceed in interest a knock at the door. [Charles Lamb, 1775–1834, *Essays of Elia*, 'Valentine's Day']

5 You can exclude noise by soundproofing your mind. [Harold Ross, 1892–1951 (quoting anonymous authority), in James Thurber, *The Years with Ross*, Ch. 3]

6 Thurber is the greatest unlistener I know. [Harold Ross, 1892–1951, in James Thurber, *The Years with Ross*, Ch. 5]

7 But I did not remove my glasses, for I had not asked for her company in the first place, and there is a limit to what one can listen to with the naked eye. [Muriel Spark, 1918– , *Voices at Play*, 'The Dark Glasses']

8 There's nothing like eavesdropping to show you that the world outside your head is different from the world inside your head. [Thornton Wilder, 1897–1975, *The Matchmaker*, III]

See also ATTENTION, SILENCE

LITERACY

1 It is better to be able neither to read nor write than to be able to do nothing else. [William Hazlitt, 1778–1830, *On the Ignorance of the Learned*]

2 The ratio of literacy to illiteracy is constant, but nowadays the illiterates can read and write. [Alberto Moravia, 1907–90, quoted by Mary McCarthy in *Observer*, 14 Oct. 1979]

3 If you're born in India, you're bilingual. And if you're bilingual, you can't read. Not so well. [Mary Norton, 1903–92, *The Borrowers*, Ch. 9]

4 To be a well-favoured man is the gift of fortune; but to write and read comes by nature. [William Shakespeare, 1564–1616, *Much Ado About Nothing*, III. iii. (14)]

5 Education . . . has produced a vast population able to read but unable to distinguish what is worth reading. [G M Trevelyan, 1876–1962, *English Social History*, Ch. 18]

6 A good listener is not someone who has nothing to say. A good listener is a good talker with a sore throat. [Katharine Whitehorn, 1926– ; in Herbert V Prochnow, *The Public Speaker's Treasure Chest*]

See also BOOKS, READING, WRITING

LITERATURE

1 Classics – and in particular modern classics – are the books one thinks one ought to read, thinks one has read. [Alan Bennett, 1934– , *Kafka's Dick*, Introduction]

2 A losing trade, I assure you, sir: literature is a drug. [George Borrow, 1803–81, *Lavengro*, 30]

3 Literary men are ... a perpetual priesthood. [Thomas Carlyle, 1795–1881, *Critical and Miscellaneous Essays*, 'The State of German Literature']

4 He set out seriously to describe the indescribable. That is the whole business of literature, and it is a hard row to hoe. [G K Chesterton, 1874–1936, *All I Survey*, 'On Literary Cliques']

5 Nothing can permanently please, which does not contain in itself the reason why it is so, and not otherwise. [Samuel Taylor Coleridge, 1772–1834, *Biographia Literaria*, Ch. 14]

6 Literature is the art of writing something that will be read twice; journalism what will be grasped at once. [Cyril Connolly, 1903–74, *Enemies of Promise*, Ch. 3]

7 It is our business, as readers of literature, to know what we like. It is our business as Christians, as *well* as readers of literature, to know what we ought to like. It is our business as honest men not to assume that what we like is what we ought to like. [T S Eliot, 1888–1965, *Selected Essays*, 'Charles Whibley']

8 National literature no longer means very much, the age of world literature is due. [Johann Wolfgang von Goethe, 1749–1832, *Conversations with Eckermann*, 31 Jan. 1827]

9 All modern American literature comes from one book by Mark Twain called *Huckleberry Finn*. [Ernest Hemingway, 1899–1961, *The Green Hills of Africa*, Ch. 1]

10 Literature flourishes best when it is half a trade and half an art. [W R Inge, 1860–1954, *The Victorian Age*, p. 49]

11 If God exists, what's the good of literature? If God does not exist, what's the point of writing? [Eugene Ionesco, 1912–94, interview in *Guardian*, 14 Sept. 1990]

12 Symbols drove Sefton to distraction. To him they were like fleas in the double bed of literature. He was aware that they might be in there somewhere but he could never find them himself. [Howard Jacobson, 1942– , *Coming from Behind*, Ch. 8]

13 It takes a great deal of history to produce a little literature. [Henry James, 1843–1916, *Hawthorne*, Ch. 1]

14 Literature is mostly about having sex and not much about having children; life is the other way round. [David Lodge, 1935– , *The British Museum is Falling Down*, Ch. 4]

15 I can't remember a single masculine figure created by a woman who is not, at bottom, a booby. [H L Mencken, 1880–1956, *In Defence of Women*, Ch. 1, sect. i]

16 Every man with a belly full of the classics is an enemy of the human race. [Henry Miller, 1891–1980, *Tropic of Cancer*, 'Dijon']

17 All art is full of magic and trickery, but in a novel the whole thing can subside into an ocean of reflection and continuous thought – at least in a traditional novel – whereas in theatre you are really jumping from place to place like a mountain goat. [Iris Murdoch, 1919–99, interview in *Weekend Guardian*, 22–23 Apr. 1989]

18 Literature is news that *stays* news. [Ezra Pound, 1885–1972, *ABC of Reading*, Ch. 2]

19 Great Literature is simply language charged with meaning to the utmost possible degree. [Ezra Pound, 1885–1972, *How to Read*, Pt II]

20 If evil does not exist, what is going to happen to literature? [V S Pritchett, 1900–1997, *Mr Beluncle*, 23]

21 Life deceives us so much that we come to believing that literature has no relation with it and we are astonished to observe that the wonderful ideas books have presented to us are gratuitously exhibited in everyday life, without risk of being spoilt by the writer. [Marcel Proust,

1871–1922, *Remembrance of Things Past: Time Regained*, Ch. 2]

22 Literature is the one place in any society where, within the secrecy of our own heads, we can hear *voices talking about everything in every possible way*. [Salman Rushdie, 1937– , lecture 'Is Nothing Sacred?', at Institute of Contemporary Arts, London, 6 Feb. 1990]

23 A literary movement: five or six people who live in the same town and hate each other. [George W Russell (AE), 1867–1935; attr. in *Book of Irish Quotations*, ed. Sean McMahon]

24 The world could get along very well without literature; it could get along even better without man. [Jean-Paul Sartre, 1905–80, *What is Literature?*]

25 Hemingway, remarks are not literature. [Gertrude Stein, 1874–1946, *Autobiography of Alice B. Toklas*, Ch. 7]

26 Romanticism is the art of presenting people with the literary works which are capable of affording them the greatest possible pleasure in the present state of their customs and beliefs. Classicism, on the other hand, presents them with the literature that gave the greatest possible pleasure to their great-grandfathers. [Stendhal, 1783–1842, *Racine and Shakespeare*, Ch. 3]

27 *Et tout le reste est littérature.* – And everything else is just literature. [Paul Verlaine, 1844–96, *L'Art poétique*, 36]

28 I don't think literature is ever finished in any country which has more prizes than it has writers. [Gore Vidal, 1925– ; *Observer*, 'Sayings of the Week', 27 Sept. 1987]

29 He [the dog] is unhappy and wants to tell us about it, which, after all, is all that most literature is. [Arthur Waugh, 1866–1943, in *Waugh on Women*, ed. Jacqueline McDonnell]

30 Particularly against books the Home Secretary is. If we can't stamp out literature in the country, we can at least stop it being brought in from outside. [Evelyn Waugh, 1903–66, *Vile Bodies*, Ch. 2]

31 '*Language*, man!' roared Parsons; 'why, it's LITERATURE!' [H G Wells, 1866–1946, *The History of Mr Polly*, Ch. I, Pt 3]

See also BOOKS, POETRY, PROSE, WRITERS, WRITING

LOGIC

1 Logic is the art of going wrong with confidence. [anon., in W H Auden, *A Certain World*]

2 'Contrariwise,' continued Tweedledee, 'if it was so, it might be; and if it were so, it would be: but as it isn't, it ain't. That's logic.' [Lewis Carroll, 1832–98, *Through the Looking Glass*, Ch. 4]

3 Good are the Ethics, I wis; good absolute, not for me, though; / Good, too, Logic, of course; in itself, but not in fine weather. [Arthur Hugh Clough, 1819–61, *Amours de voyage*, II, 225]

4 Crime is common. Logic is rare. Therefore it is upon the logic rather than upon the crime that you should dwell. [Arthur Conan Doyle, 1859–1930, *The Adventures of Sherlock Holmes*, 'The Copper Beeches']

5 The conclusion of your syllogism, I said lightly, is fallacious, being based upon licensed premises. [Flann O'Brien, 1911–66, *At Swim-Two-Birds*, Ch. 1]

6 Everything that can be said can be said clearly. [Ludwig Wittgenstein, 1889–1951, *Tractatus Logico-philosophicus*, 4, 116]

See also PHILOSOPHY

LONDON

1 Every city has a sex and age which have nothing to do with demography. Rome is feminine . . . London is a teen-ager and urchin, and, in this, hasn't changed since the time of Dickens. Paris, I believe, is a man in his twenties in love with an older woman. [John Berger, 1926– , in *Guardian*, 27 Mar. 1987]

2 What a place to plunder! [Marshal Blücher, 1742–1814, alleged remark on seeing London in 1814]

3 You have to give this much to the Luftwaffe: when it knocked down our buildings, it didn't replace them with anything more offensive than rubble. *We* did that. [Prince Charles, 1948– (of redevelopment around St Paul's), speech at Mansion House, London, 1 Dec. 1987]

4 The great wen of all. [William Cobbett, 1762–1835, *Rural Rides* (1821)]

5 We didn't find that it come up to its likeness in the red bills – it is there drawd too architectooralooral. [Charles Dickens, 1812–70, *Great Expectations*, Ch. 27]

6 London is a modern Babylon. [Benjamin Disraeli, 1804–81, *Tancred*, Bk v, Ch. 5]

7 London, thou art the flour of cities all! [William Dunbar, 1460?–1520?, *London*]

8 Unreal City, / Under the brown fog of a winter dawn, / A crowd flowed over London Bridge, so many, / I had not thought death had undone so many. [T S Eliot, 1888–1965, *The Waste Land*, 60]

9 Crowds without company, and dissipation without pleasure. [Edward Gibbon, 1737–94, *Autobiography*]

10 Ye towers of Julius, London's lasting shame, / With many a foul and midnight murther fed. [Thomas Gray, 1716–71, *The Bard*, II, 3]

11 London doesn't love the latent or the lurking, has neither time, nor taste, nor sense for anything less discernible than the red flag in front of the steam-roller. It wants cash over the counter and letters ten feet high. [Henry James, 1843–1916, *The Awkward Age*, I, 2]

12 She was all for scenery – yes; but she wanted it human and personal, and all she could say was that there would be in London – wouldn't there? – more of that kind than anywhere else. [Henry James, 1843–1916, *The Wings of the Dove*, Bk III, 2]

13 Here falling houses thunder on your head, / And here a female atheist talks you dead. [Dr Samuel Johnson, 1709–84, *London*, 17]

14 When a man is tired of London he is tired of life; for there is in London all that life can afford. [Dr Samuel Johnson, 1709–84, in James Boswell, *Life of J*, 20 Sept. 1777]

15 The main reason Londoners are slow to adulate is that they believe that anyone who is world-famous cannot be all that good at what he does. [Irma Kurtz, 1935– , *Dear London: Notes from the Big City*]

16 I thought of London spread out in the sun, / Its postal districts packed like squares of wheat. [Philip Larkin, 1922–85, *The Whitsun Weddings*]

17 When it's three o'clock in New York, it's still 1938 in London. [Bette Midler, 1945– , from *The Times*, 1978; in *The Penguin Dictionary of Modern Humorous Quotations*, comp. Fred Metcalf]

18 If one must have a villa in summer to dwell, / Oh give me the sweet shady side of Pall Mall! [Charles Morris, 1745–1838, *The Contrast*, last lines]

19 It was a saying of Lord Chatham, that the parks were the lungs of London. [William Pitt, the Elder (Earl of Chatham), 1708–78, as quoted by W Windham in speech in House of Commons, 30 June 1808]

20 In fact when somebody from Hampstead is drowning, all their previous furniture passes in front of them. [Alexei Sayle, 1952– , from BBC TV programme *Comic Roots*, in *Listener*, 1 Sept. 1983]

21 Hell is a city much like London – / A populous and a smoky city. [P B Shelley, 1792–1822, *Peter Bell the Third*, 147]

22 At length they all to merry London came, / To merry London, my most kindly nurse, / That to me gave this life's first native source: / Though from another place I take my name, / An house of ancient fame. [Edmund Spenser, 1552?–99, *Prothalamion*, 127]

23 Earth has not anything to show more fair: / Dull would he be of soul who could pass by / A sight so touching in its majesty: / This city now doth, like a garment, wear / The beauty of the morning; silent, bare, / Ships, towers, domes, theatres, and temples lie / Open unto the fields, and to the sky; / All bright and glittering in the smokeless air. [William Wordsworth, 1770–1850, *Miscellaneous Sonnets*, II, 36, 'Upon Westminster Bridge']

See also CITY, NEW YORK, PARIS, ROME

LONELINESS

1 Woe to him that is alone when he falleth, for he hath not another to help him up. [Bible, OT, *Ecclesiastes* 4:10]

2 What is the worst of woes that wait on age? / What stamps the wrinkle deeper on the brow? / To view each loved one blotted from life's page. / And be alone on earth, as I am now. [Lord Byron, 1788–1824, *Childe Harold's Pilgrimage*, II, 98]

3 If you are afraid of loneliness, don't marry. [Anton Chekhov, 1860–1904, quoted in Roger Hall, *Conjugal Rites*]

4 Alone, alone, all, all alone, / Alone on a wide, wide sea! [Samuel Taylor Coleridge, 1772–1834, *The Ancient Mariner*, Pt IV]

5 Men's legs have a terribly lonely life – standing in the dark in your trousers all day. [Ken Dodd, 1927– , in *Guardian*, 7 Apr. 1973]

6 Pray that your loneliness may spur you into finding something to live for, great enough to die for. [Dag Hammarskjöld, 1905–61, *Diaries*, 1951]

7 On stage I make love to twenty-five thousand people; then I go home alone. [Janis Joplin, 1943–70; in *Barnes and Noble Book of Quotations*, ed. Robert I Fitzhenry, 'Acting']

8 All the lonely people, where do they all come from? / All the lonely people, where do they all belong? [John Lennon, 1940–80, and Paul McCartney, 1942– , song: *Eleanor Rigby*]

9 But when he's gone / Me and them lonesome blues collide. / The bed's too big. / The frying pan's too wide. [Joni Mitchell, 1943– , song: *My Old Man*]

10 I feel like one / Who treads alone / Some banquet-hall deserted, / Whose lights are fled, / Whose garlands dead / And all but he departed! [Thomas Moore, 1779–1852, *National Airs*, 'Oft in the Stilly Night']

11 Never less alone than when alone, / Those whom he loved so long and sees no more, / Loved and still loves – not dead – but gone before, / He gathers round him. [Samuel Rogers, 1763–1855, *Human Life*, 755]

12 To be adult is to be alone. [Jean Rostand, 1894–1977, *Thoughts of a Biologist*, 6]

13 People tell me there are a lot of guys like me, which doesn't explain why I'm lonely. [Mort Sahl, 1926– , in E Lax, *Woody Allen and His Comedy*, Ch. 12]

See also SOLITUDE

LOSS

1 Friends who set forth at our side, / Falter, are lost in the storm. / We, we only, are left! [Matthew Arnold, 1822–88, *Rugby Chapel*, 102]

2 I-chabod, saying, The glory is departed from Israel. [Bible, OT, *1 Samuel* 4:21]

3 'Tis better to have loved and lost than never to have lost at all. [Samuel Butler, 1835–1902, *The Way of All Flesh*, Ch. 77]; see also LOVE, 62, 106

4 To lose the touch of flowers and women's hands is the supreme separation. [Albert Camus, 1913–60, in *Guardian*, 30 Sept. 1974]

5 For 'tis a truth well known to most, / That whatsoever thing is lost – / We seek it, ere it come to light, / In every cranny but the right. [William Cowper, 1731–1800, *The Retired Cat*, 95]

6 Everything that is found is always lost again, and nothing that is found is ever lost again. [Russell Hoban, 1925– , *The Lion of Boaz-Jachin and Jachin-Boaz*, Ch. 2]

7 You've got to be missing for forty-eight hours before you're missing. The worst he could be is lost. [Neil Simon, 1927– , *The Odd Couple*, I, and said by Walter Matthau in film of same title]

8 No man can lose what he never had. [Izaak Walton, 1593–1683, *The Compleat Angler*, Pt I, Ch. 5]

LOVE

1 It is good to be merry and wise, / It is good to be honest and true, / It is best to be off with the old love, / Before you are on with the new. [anon., *Songs of England and Scotland* (1835)]

2 It's love that makes the world go round. [anon. French song, translation]

3 Tomorrow may he love who never loved before, and may he who has loved love too. [anon., *Pervigilium Veneris*]

4 Love is, above all, the gift of oneself. [Jean Anouilh, 1910–87, *Ardèle*, II]

5 There is no such thing as the State / And no one exists alone; / Hunger allows no choice / To the citizen or the police; / We must love one another or die. [W H Auden, 1907–73, *September 1, 1939*]

6 Next to being married, a girl likes to be crossed in love a little now and then. [Jane Austen, 1775–1817, *Pride and Prejudice*, 24]

7 Nuptial love maketh mankind; friendly love perfecteth it; but wanton love corrupteth and embaseth it. [Francis Bacon, 1561–1626, *Essays*, 10, 'Of Love']

8 Love ceases to be a pleasure, when it ceases to be a secret. [Aphra Behn, 1640–89, *The Lover's Watch*, 'Four o'Clock']

9 In expressing love we belong among the undeveloped countries. [Saul Bellow, 1915– ; in *Lover's Quotation Book*, ed. Helen Handley]

10 Stay me with flagons, comfort me with apples: for I am sick of love. [Bible, OT, *Song of Solomon* 2:5]

11 Many waters cannot quench love, neither can the floods drown it. [Bible, OT, *Song of Solomon* 8:7]

12 Love is the fulfilling of the law. [Bible, NT, *Romans* 13:10]

13 There is no fear in love; but perfect love casteth out fear. [Bible, NT, *1 John* 4:18]

14 A new commandment I give unto you, That ye love one another. [Bible, NT, *St John* 13:34]

15 Thou shalt love thy neighbour as thyself. [Bible, NT, *St Matthew* 19:19; also *Leviticus* 19:18]

16 Never seek to tell thy love, / Love that never told can be; / For the gentle wind does move / Silently, invisibly. [William Blake, 1757–1827, *Never Seek to Tell Thy Love*]

17 Love seeketh not itself to please, / Nor for itself hath any care, / But for another gives its ease, / And builds a Heaven in Hell's despair. [William Blake, 1757–1827, *Songs of Experience*, 'The Clod and the Pebble']

18 For Mercy has a human heart, / Pity a human face, / And Love, the human form divine, / And Peace, the human dress. [William Blake, 1757–1827, *Songs of Innocence*, 'The Divine Image']

19 Such ever was love's way; to rise, it stoops. [Robert Browning, 1812–89, *A Death in the Desert*, 134]

20 Flower o' the broom, / Take away love, and our earth is a tomb! [Robert Browning, 1812–89, *Fra Lippo Lippi*, 53]

21 O lyric Love, half angel and half bird / And all a wonder and a wild desire. [Robert Browning, 1812–89, *The Ring and the Book*, I, 1391]

22 To see her is to love her, / And love but her for ever: / For Nature made her what she is, / And never made anither! [Robert Burns, 1759–96, *Bonnie Lesley*]

23 Man's love is of man's life a thing apart, / 'Tis woman's whole existence. [Lord Byron, 1788–1824, *Don Juan*, I, 194]

24 In her first passion woman loves her lover, / In all the others all she loves is love. [Lord Byron, 1788–1824, *Don Juan*, III, 3]

25 The Summer hath his joys, / And Winter his delights. / Though Love and all his pleasures are but toys, / They shorten tedious nights. [Thomas Campion, 1567–1620, *Now Winter Nights Enlarge*]

26 Then fly betimes, for only they / Conquer Love that run away. [Thomas Carew, 1595?–1639, song: *Conquest by Flight*]

27 It is difficult suddenly to put aside a long-standing love; it is difficult, but somehow you must do it. [Catullus, 84–54? BC, *Carmina*, 76]

28 Love, in present-day society, is just the exchange of two imaginary pictures, and the contact of one epidermis with another. [Nicolas-Sébastien Chamfort, 1741–94, *Maxims and Considerations*]

29 Love wol nat ben constreyned by maistrye; / Whan maistrie comth, the God of Love anon / Beteth his winges, and farewel! he is gon! [Geoffrey Chaucer, 1340?–1400, *Canterbury Tales*, 'The Franklin's Tale', 36]

30 The lyf so short, the craft so long to lerne, / Th' assay so hard, so sharp the conquering, / The dredful joye, alway that slit so yerne; / All this mene I by love. [Geoffrey Chaucer, 1340?–1400, *The Parliament of Fowls*, 1]

31 Many a man has fallen in love with a girl in a light so dim he would not have chosen a suit by it. [Maurice Chevalier, 1888–1972, *News Summaries*, 17 July 1955]

32 Love lies beyond / The tomb, the earth, which fades like dew! / I love the fond, / The faithful, and the true. [John Clare, 1793–1864, *Love Lies beyond the Tomb*]

33 All thoughts, all passions, all delights, / Whatever stirs this mortal frame, / All are but ministers of Love, / And feed his sacred flame. [Samuel Taylor Coleridge, 1772–1834, *Love*]

34 If one wished to be perfectly sincere, one would have to admit there are two kinds of love – well-fed and ill-fed. The rest is pure fiction. [Colette, 1873–1954; in *Lover's Quotation Book*, ed. Helen Handley]

35 Love's but the frailty of the mind, – When 'tis not with ambition joined. [William Congreve, 1670–1729, *The Way of the World*, III. xii]

36 Love, thou art absolute sole Lord / Of life and death. [Richard Crashaw, 1613?–49, *Hymn to Saint Teresa*, 1]

37 Love is a sickness full of woes, / All remedies refusing; / A plant that with most cutting grows, / Most barren with best using. / Why so? / More we enjoy it, more it dies; / If not enjoyed, it sighing cries, / Hey ho. [Samuel Daniel, 1562–1619, *Hymen's Triumph*, I, v]

38 *L'amor che move il sole e l'altre stelle.* – Love that moves the sun and the other stars. [Dante Alighieri, 1265–1321, *The Divine Comedy*, 'Paradiso', xxxiii, 145]

39 We must love one another, yes, yes, that's all true enough, but nothing says we have to like each other. [Peter de Vries, 1910–93, *The Glory of the Hummingbird*, Ch. 1]

40 It has been said that love robs those who have it of their wit, and gives it to those who have none. [Denis Diderot, 1713–84, *Paradoxe sur le comédien*]

41 Is love eternal, indestructible: does it, like throw-away plastic packaging, endure beyond the grave? Own experience suggests that though love can initially degrade, it does, in the end, usefully biodegrade. [Dulcie Domum, 1946– , in *Weekend Guardian*, 10–11 Mar. 1990]

42 Only our love hath no decay; / This, no tomorrow hath, nor yesterday, / Running it never runs from us away, / But truly keeps his first, last, everlasting day. [John Donne, 1571?–1631, *The Anniversary*]

43 For love, all love of other sights controls, / And makes one little room, an everywhere. [John Donne, 1571?–1631, *The Good-Morrow*]

44 Love all alike, no season knows, nor clime, / Nor hours, days, months, which are the rags of time. [John Donne, 1571?–1631, *The Sun Rising*]

45 And love's the noblest frailty of the mind. [John Dryden, 1631–1700, *The Indian Emperor*, II. ii]

46 Men love women, women love children, children love hamsters, hamsters don't love anybody. [Alice Thomas Ellis, 1932– , in BBC TV programme *Bookmark*, 16 Dec. 1987]

47 Love is like linen often changed, the sweeter. [Phineas Fletcher, 1582–1650, *Sicelides*, III. v]

48 *The affirmation of one's own life, happiness, growth, freedom is rooted in one's capacity to love*, i.e. in care, respect, responsibility, and knowledge. If an individual is able to love productively, he loves himself too; if he can love *only* others, he cannot love at all. [Erich Fromm, 1900–1980, *The Art of Loving*, Ch. 2, sect. 3d]

49 Earth's the right place for love; / I don't know where it's likely to go better. [Robert Frost, 1874–1963, *Birches*]

50 This as it will be seen is other far / Than with brooks taken otherwhere in song. / We love the things we love for what they are. [Robert Frost, 1874–1963, *Hyla Brook*]

51 Time was when Love and I were well acquainted. [W S Gilbert, 1836–1911, *The Sorcerer*, I]

52 Friendship is a disinterested commerce between equals; love, an abject intercourse between tyrants and slaves. [Oliver Goldsmith, 1728–74, *The Good-Natured Man*, 1]

53 Yet love survives, the word carved on the sill / Under antique dread of the headsman's axe. [Robert Graves, 1895–1985, *End of Play*]

54 Love is a universal migraine / A bright stain on the vision / Blotting out reason. [Robert Graves, 1895–1985, *Symptoms of Love*]

55 Love is a fanclub with only two fans. [Adrian Henri, 1932– , *Love is . . .*]

56 You say, to me-wards your affection's strong; / Pray love me little, so you love me long. [Robert Herrick, 1591–1674, *Hesperides*, 'Love Me Little, Love Me Long']

57 It's easier to love humanity as a whole than to love one's neighbour. [Eric Hoffer, 1902–83, in *The New York Times Magazine*, 15 Feb. 1959]

58 There isn't any formula or method. You learn to love by loving – by paying attention and doing what one thereby discovers has to be done. [Aldous Huxley, 1894–1963, *Time Must Have a Stop*, 30]

59 Love is like the measles; we all have to go through it. [Jerome K Jerome, 1859–1927, *Idle Thoughts of an Idle Fellow*, 'On Being in Love']

60 Love is the wisdom of the fool and the folly of the wise. [Dr Samuel Johnson, 1709–84, in William Cooke, *Life of Samuel Foote*]

61 Love in a hut, with water and a crust, / Is – Love forgive us! – cinders, ashes, dust. [John Keats, 1795–1821, *Lamia*, II, 1]

62 It is better to have loved a short man, than never to have loved a tall. [Miles Kington, 1941– , 'cod' Albanian proverb, in *Independent*, 27 Dec. 1991]; see 106 and LOSS, 3

63 How alike are the groans of love to those of the dying. [Malcolm Lowry, 1909–57, *Under the Volcano*, Ch. 12]

64 Who ever loved, that loved not at first sight? [Christopher Marlowe, 1564–93, *Hero and Leander*, I, 176]

65 Love that so desires would fain keep her changeless; / Fain would fling the net, and fain have her free. [George Meredith, 1828–1909, *Love in the Valley*, 6]

66 If I were pressed to say why I loved him, I feel that my only reply could be: 'Because it was he, because it was I'. [Michel de Montaigne, 1533–92, *Essays*, I, 28]

67 No, there's nothing half so sweet in life / As love's young dream. [Thomas Moore, 1779–1852, *Irish Melodies*, 'Love's Young Dream']

68 Love is enough: though the world be a-waning, / And the woods have no voice but the voice of complaining. [William Morris, 1834–96, *Love is Enough*]

69 Love then, and even later, was the whole concern of everyone's life. That is always the fate of leisured societies. [Napoleon Bonaparte, 1769–1821, quoted by F L Lucas in *Tragedy*]

70 Love is not the dying moan of a distant violin – it's the triumphant twang of a bedspring. [S J Perelman, 1904–79, in A Andrews, *Quotations for Speakers and Writers*]

71 Love set you going like a fat gold watch. [Sylvia Plath, 1932–63, *Morning Song*]

72 Is it, in heav'n, a crime to love too well? [Alexander Pope, 1688–1744, *Elegy to the Memory of an Unfortunate Lady*, 6]

73 Birds do it, bees do it, / Even educated fleas do it. / Let's do it, let's fall in love. [Cole Porter, 1891–1964, song: *Let's Do It*, in musical *Paris*; these words added later]

74 With the wisdom invariably shown by people who, not being in love themselves, feel that a clever man should only be unhappy about a person who is worth his while, which is rather like being astonished that anyone should condescend to die of cholera at the bidding of so insignificant a creature as the comma bacillus. [Marcel Proust, 1871–1922, *Remembrance of Things Past: Swann's Way*, 'Swann in Love']

75 There can be no peace of mind in love, since the advantage one has secured is never anything but a fresh starting-point for further desires. [Marcel Proust, 1871–1922, *Remembrance of Things Past: Within a Budding Grove*, 'Madame Swann at Home']

76 The most exclusive love for a person is always a love for something else. [Marcel Proust, 1871–1922, *Remembrance of Things Past: Within a Budding Grove*, 'Place-names']

77 Love rules the court, the camp, the grove, / And men below, and saints above; / For love is heaven, and heaven is love. [Sir Walter Scott, 1771–1832, *The Lay of the Last Minstrel*, III, 2]

78 Love still has something of the sea / From whence his mother rose. [Charles Sedley, 1639?–1701, *Love Still Has Something*]

79 Love means never having to say you're sorry. [Eric Segal, 1937– , last line of film *Love Story* and novel, Ch. 13]

80 There's beggary in the love that can be reckoned. [William Shakespeare, 1564–1616, *Antony and Cleopatra*, I. ii. 15]

81 If thou remember'st not the slightest folly / That ever love did make thee run into, / Thou has not loved. [*As You Like It*, II. iv. (34)]

82 Men have died from time to time, and worms have eaten them, but not for love. [*As You Like It*, IV. i (110)]

83 It is to be all made of faith and service / . . . It is to be all made of fantasy, / All made of passion and all made of wishes, / All adoration, duty and observance, / All humbleness, all patience and impatience, / All purity, all trial, all obeisance. [*As You Like It*, V. ii. (96)]

84 OPHELIA: 'Tis brief, my lord.
HAMLET: As woman's love. [*Hamlet*, III. ii (165)]

85 When Love speaks, the voice of all the gods / Makes heaven drowsy with the harmony. [*Love's Labour's Lost*, IV. iii. (344)]

86 For aught that ever I could read, / Could ever hear by tale or history, / The course of true love never did run smooth. [*A Midsummer Night's Dream*, I. i. 123]

87 Swift as a shadow, short as any dream, / Brief as the lightning in the collied night, / That, in a spleen, unfolds both heaven and earth, / And ere a man hath power to say, 'Behold!' / The jaws of darkness do devour it up: / So quick bright things come to confusion. [*A Midsummer Night's Dream*, I. i. 144]

88 Love looks not with the eyes, but with the

mind, / And therefore is winged Cupid painted blind. [*A Midsummer Night's Dream*, I. i. 234]

89 Then must you speak / Of one that loved not wisely but too well. [*Othello*, V. ii. 342]

90 For stony limits cannot hold love out. [*Romeo and Juliet*, II. ii. 67]

91 Love goes toward love, as schoolboys from their books; / But love from love, toward school with heavy looks. [*Romeo and Juliet*, II. ii. 156]

92 This is the monstruosity in love, lady, that the will is infinite and the execution confined. [*Troilus and Cressida*, III. ii. (85)]

93 O spirit of love! how quick and fresh art thou, / That notwithstanding thy capacity / Receiveth as the sea, nought enters there, / Of what validity and pitch soe'er, / But falls into abatement and low price, / Even in a minute: so full of shapes is fancy, / That it alone is high fantastical. [*Twelfth Night*, I. i. 9]

94 Love sought is good, but giv'n unsought is better. [*Twelfth Night*, III. i. (170)]

95 How wayward is this foolish love / That, like a testy babe, will scratch the nurse / And presently all humbled kiss the rod! [*The Two Gentlemen of Verona*, I. ii. 55]

96 So true a fool is love that in your will, / Though you do anything, he thinks no ill. [*Sonnets*, 57]

97 Let me not to the marriage of true minds / Admit impediments. Love is not love / Which alters when it alteration finds, / Or bends with the remover to remove: / O, no! it is an ever-fixèd mark. [*Sonnets*, 116]

98 Bid me discourse, I will enchant thine ear, / Or like a fairy, trip upon the green, / Or like a nymph, with long dishevelled hair, / Dance on the sands, and yet no footing seen: / Love is a spirit all compact of fire, / Not gross to sink, but light, and will aspire. [*Venus and Adonis*, 145]

99 O Love! who bewailest / The frailty of all things here, / Why choose you the frailest / For your cradle, your home, and your bier? [P B Shelley, 1792–1822, *Lines: When the Lamp is Shattered*]

100 All love is sweet, / Given or returned. Common as light is love, / And its familiar voice wearies not ever. [P B Shelley, 1792–1822, *Prometheus Unbound*, II. v. 39]

101 One word is too often profaned / For me to profane it, / One feeling too falsely disdained / For thee to disdain it. [P B Shelley, 1792–1822, *To —, One Word is Too Often Profaned*]

102 And all for love, and nothing for reward. [Edmund Spenser, 1552?–99, *The Faerie Queene*, Bk ii, Canto 8, stanza 2]

103 When love gets to be important to someone, it means that he hasn't been able to manage something else. Falling in love seems to me an almost sure sign of failure. Except for the very few who have a talent for it. [Richard G Stern, 1928– , *Golk*, Ch. 2, iii]

104 He who wants to do good knocks at the gate; he who loves finds the door open. [Rabrindranath Tagore, 1861–1941, *Stray Birds*, 83]

105 We needs must love the highest when we see it. [Alfred, Lord Tennyson, 1809–92, 'Guinevere', 655]

106 I hold it true, whate'er befall; / I feel it when I sorrow most; / 'Tis better to have loved and lost / Than never to have loved at all. [Alfred, Lord Tennyson, 1809–1892, *In Memoriam*, 27]; see 62 and LOSS, 3

107 Such a one do I remember, whom to look at was to love. [Alfred, Lord Tennyson, 1809–92, *Locksley Hall*, 72]

108 We love being in love, that's the truth on't. [W M Thackeray, 1811–63, *Henry Esmond*, Bk ii, Ch. 15]

109 If love is the answer, could you rephrase the question? [Lily Tomlin, 1939– ; in Barbara Rowes, *Book of Quotes*]

110 Sometimes I wish I could fall in love. Then at least you know who your opponent is! [Peter Ustinov, 1921– , *Romanoff and Juliet*, II]

111 *Omnia vincit Amor: et nos cedamus Amori.* – Love carries all before him: we too must yield to Love. [Virgil, 70–19 BC, *Eclogue*, X, 69]

112 The most exciting attractions are between two opposites that never meet. Fantasy love is much better than reality love. Never doing it is very exciting. [Andy Warhol, 1927–87, *From A to B and Back Again*, Ch. 3]

113 He spake of love, such love as spirits feel / In worlds whose course is equable and pure; / No fears to beat away – no strife to heal, – / The past unsighed for, and the future sure. [William Wordsworth, 1770–1850, *Laodamia*, 97]

114 You must love him, ere to you / He will seem worthy of your love. [William Wordsworth, 1770–1850, *A Poet's Epitaph*]

115 A man falls in love through his eyes, a woman through her ears. [Woodrow Wyatt, 1919–97, *To the Point*, p. 107]

116 We have gone round and round / In the narrow theme of love / Like an old horse in a pound. [W B Yeats, 1865–1939, *Solomon to Sheba*]

117 Love fled / And paced upon the mountains overhead / And hid his face amid a crowd of stars. [W B Yeats, 1865–1939, *When You are Old*]

See also next two categories, HATE, LOVERS, LUST

LOVE: HOMOSEXUAL

1 He was my North, my South, my East, my West, / My working week and my Sunday rest, / My noon, my midnight, my talk, my song; / I thought that love would last for ever: I was wrong. [W H Auden, 1907–73, *Stop All the Clocks, Cut Off the Telephone*]

2 Thy love to me was wonderful, passing the love of women. [Bible, OT, *2 Samuel* 1:26]

3 I am the Love that dare not speak its name. [Lord Alfred Douglas, 1870–1945, *Two Loves*]

See also the next and previous categories, HOMOSEXUALS, LOVERS, LUST

LOVE & HATE

1 Better is a dinner of herbs where love is, than a stalled ox and hatred therewith. [Bible, OT, *Proverbs* 15:17]

2 Give me more love or more disdain; / The torrid or the frozen zone. [Thomas Carew, 1595?–1639, *Mediocrity in Love Rejected*]

3 *Odi et amo: quare id faciam, fortasse requiris. / Nescio, sed fieri sentio et excrucior.* – I hate and love. You may ask why I do so. I do not know, but I feel it and am in torment. [Catullus, 84–54? BC, *Carmina*, 85]

4 Everybody hates me because I'm so universally liked. [Peter de Vries, 1910–93, *The Vale of Laughter*, Pt 1, Ch. 1]

5 Violent antipathies are always suspicious, and betray a secret affinity. [William Hazlitt, 1778–1830, *On Vulgarity and Affectation*]

6 If one judges love by the majority of its effects, it is more like hatred than like friendship. [Duc de La Rochefoucauld, 1613–80, *Maxims*, 72]

7 Who would be loved / If he could be feared and hated, yet still / Enjoy his lust, eat well and play the flute? [Peter Porter, 1929– , *Soliloquy at Potsdam*]

8 *Ah! je l'ai trop aimé pour ne le point haïr!* – Oh, I have loved him too much to feel no hate for him. [Jean Racine, 1639–99, *Andromaque*, II. i. 416]

9 But we, when we are entirely intent on one thing, can feel the pull of another. Hostility comes easiest to us. [Rainer Maria Rilke, 1875–1926, *Duino Elegies*, 4]

10 My only love sprung from my only hate! [William Shakespeare, 1564–1616, *Romeo and Juliet*, I. v. (142)]

See also HATE, LOVE, LOVERS, LUST

LOVE OF GOD

1 Love, and do what you will. [St Augustine, 354–430, *In Epist. Ioann. Tract.*, VIII, 7]

2 He that loveth not his brother whom he hath seen, how can he love God whom he hath not seen? [Bible, NT, *1 John* 4:20]

3 How do I love thee? Let me count the ways. / I love thee to the depth and breadth and height / My soul can reach, when feeling out of sight / For the ends of Being and ideal Grace. [Elizabeth Barrett Browning, 1806–61, *Sonnets from the Portuguese*, 43]

4 And smite upon that thick cloud of unknowing with a sharp dart of longing love; and go not thence for thing that befalleth. [*The Cloud of Unknowing*, 14th cent., Ch. 6]

5 Love is swift of foot; / Love's a man of war, / And can shoot, / And can hit from far. [George Herbert, 1593–1633, *Discipline*]

6 'You must sit down,' says Love, 'and taste my meat.' / So I did sit and eat. [George Herbert, 1593–1633, *Love*]

7 Love is God, and to die means that I, a particle of love, shall return to the general and eternal source. [Leo Tolstoy, 1828–1910, *War and Peace*, VII, Ch. 16]

8 It is only necessary to know that love is a direction and not a state of the soul. [Simone

Weil, 1909–43, *Waiting on God*, 'The Love of God']

See also FAITHS, GOD, RELIGION

LOVERS

1 Escape me? / Never – / Beloved! / While I am I, and you are you, / So long as the world contains us both, / Me the loving and you the loth, / While the one eludes, must the other pursue. [Robert Browning, 1812–89, *Life in a Love*]

2 O, my Luve's like a red red rose / That's newly sprung in June: / O, my Luve's like the melodie / That's sweetly play'd in tune. [Robert Burns, 1759–96, *My Love is like a Red Red Rose*]

3 Oh! that the Desert were my dwelling-place, / With one fair Spirit for my minister, / That I might all forget the human race, / And, hating no one, love but only her! [Lord Byron, 1788–1824, *Childe Harold's Pilgrimage*, IV, 177]

4 To abuse a man is a lover-like thing and gives him rights. [Joyce Cary, 1888–1957, *Herself Surprised*, Ch. 35]

5 But what a woman says to her desirous lover should be written in wind and swift-flowing water. [Catullus, 87–54? BC, *Carmina*, 70]

6 For we wear each other out with our wakefulness. / For he makes me feel like a light-bulb that cannot switch itself off. [Wendy Cope, 1945– , *My Lover*]

7 Come live with me, and be my love, / And we will some new pleasures prove / Of golden sands and crystal brooks / With silken lines, and silver hooks. [John Donne, 1571?–1631, *The Bait*]

8 Whoever loves, if he do not propose / The right true end of love, he's one that goes / To sea for nothing but to make him sick. [John Donne, 1571?–1631, *Elegies*, 18, 'Love's Progress', 1]

9 I wonder by my troth, what thou, and I / Did, till we loved? were we not weaned till then, / But sucked on country pleasures, childishly / Or snorted we in the seven sleepers' den? [John Donne, 1571?–1631, *The Good-Morrow*]

10 All mankind love a lover. [Ralph Waldo Emerson, 1803–82, *Essays*, 'Love']

11 She who has never loved has never lived. [John Gay, 1685–1732, *Captives*, II. i]

12 For a woman to have a *liaison* is almost always pardonable, and occasionally, when the lover chosen is sufficiently distinguished, even admirable; but in love as in sport, the amateur status must be strictly maintained. [Robert Graves, 1895–1985, *Occupation: Writer*, 'Lars Porsena']

13 I'm a great lover. I can make sex last ... ooh ... twenty minutes. That includes going out to dinner first, of course. [Andy Greenhalgh, ?1945– , in *Guardian*, 14 July 1987]

14 Proud word you never spoke, but you will speak / Four not exempt from pride some future day. / Resting on one white hand a warm wet cheek / Over my open volume you will say, / 'This man loved *me*!' then rise and trip away. [Walter Savage Landor, 1775–1864, *Proud Word You Never Spoke*]

15 Through this same man and me hath all this war been wrought, and the death of the most noblest knights of the world; for through our love that we have loved together is my most noble lord slain. [Thomas Malory, d.1471, *Morte d'Arthur*, Bk xxi, Ch. 9]

16 Come live with me and be my love, / And we will all the pleasures prove / That hills and valleys, dales and fields, / Woods, or steepy mountain yields. [Christopher Marlowe, 1564–93, *The Passionate Shepherd to His Love*]

17 She whom I love is hard to catch and conquer, / Hard, but O the glory of the winning were she won! [George Meredith, 1828–1909, *Love in the Valley*, 2]

18 Here's my strength and my weakness, gents, / I loved them until they loved me. [Dorothy Parker, 1893–1967, *Ballade at Thirty-Five*]

19 Whose love is given over-well / Shall look on Helen's face in hell, / Whilst they whose love is thin and wise / May view John Knox in paradise. [Dorothy Parker, 1893–1967, *Partial Comfort*]

20 Love's perfect blossom only blows / Where noble manners veil defect. / Angels may be familiar; those / Who err each other must respect. [Coventry Patmore, 1823–96, *The Angel in the House*, Bk i, 11, Prelude 2]

21 Ye gods! annihilate but space and time, / And make two lovers happy. [Alexander Pope, 1688–1744, *The Art of Sinking in Poetry*, 11]

22 It is easier to keep half a dozen lovers guessing than to keep one lover after he has stopped guessing. [Helen Rowland, 1875–1950, *A Guide to Men*, 'Third Interlude']

23 We that are true lovers run into strange capers. [William Shakespeare, 1564–1616, *As You Like It*, II. iv. (53)]

24 It adds a precious seeing to the eye; / A lover's eyes will gaze an eagle blind; / A lover's ear will hear the lowest sound. [*Love's Labour's Lost*, IV. iii. (333)]

25 But love is blind, and lovers cannot see / The pretty follies that themselves commit. [*The Merchant of Venice*, II. vi. 36]

26 At lovers' perjuries, / They say, Jove laughs. [*Romeo and Juliet*, II. ii. 92]

27 How silver-sweet sound lovers' tongues by night, / Like softest music to attending ears! [*Romeo and Juliet*, II. ii. 165]

28 Then let thy love be younger than thyself, / Or thy affection cannot hold the bent. [*Twelfth Night*, II. iv. 36]

29 Gallons of ink and miles of typewriter ribbon expended on the misery of the unrequited lover; not a word about the utter tedium of the unrequiting. [Tom Stoppard, 1937– , *The Real Thing*, I. iv]

30 Why so pale and wan, fond lover? / Prithee, why so pale? / Will, when looking well can't move her, / Looking ill prevail? / Prithee, why so pale? [John Suckling, 1609–42, *Aglaura*, IV. i, song]

31 O that 'twere possible / After long grief and pain / To find the arms of my true love / Round me once again! [Alfred, Lord Tennyson, 1809–92, *Maud*, Pt II, iv, 1]

32 MISTRESS: Do you mind if we have separate bills? You see, I don't sleep with him any more. [Keith Waterhouse, 1929– , *Jeffrey Bernard is Unwell*, I. The play is based on the life and writings of Bernard]

33 'But you said they were like a couple of love-birds.' 'Quite. But even with love-birds circumstances can arise which will cause the female love-bird to get above herself and start throwing her weight about.' [P G Wodehouse, 1881–1975, *Eggs, Beans and Crumpets*, 'All's Well with Bingo']

34 But one man loved the pilgrim soul in you, / And loved the sorrows of your changing face. [W B Yeats, 1865–1939, *When You are Old*]

See also HATE, LOVE, LOVE: HOMOSEXUAL, LOVE & HATE, LUST

LOYALTY & DISLOYALTY

1 He that is not with me is against me. [Bible, NT, *St Luke* 11:23]

2 Before the cock crow, thou shalt deny me thrice. [Bible, NT, *St Matthew* 26:34]

3 If I had to choose between betraying my *country* and betraying my *friend*, I hope I should have the guts to betray my *country*. [E M Forster, 1879–1970, *Two Cheers for Democracy*, 'What I Believe']

4 I don't want loyalty. I want *loyalty*. I want him to kiss my ass in Macy's window at high noon and tell me it smells like roses. I want his pecker in my pocket. [President Lyndon B Johnson, 1908–73, in D Halberstam, *The Best and the Brightest*, Ch. 20]

5 He ... felt towards those whom he had deserted that peculiar malignity which has, in all ages, been characteristic of apostates. [Lord Macaulay, 1800–1859, *History of England*, I, Ch. 1]

6 The seraph Abdiel, faithful found, / Among the faithless, faithful only he. [John Milton, 1608–74, *Paradise Lost*, Bk v, 893]

7 I don't care a damn for your loyal service when you think I am right; when I really want it most is when you think I am *wrong*. [General John Monash, 1865–1931, attr. in Colin MacInnes, *England, Half English*, 'Joshua Reborn']

8 Better lo'ed ye canna be, / Will ye no come back again? [Lady Nairne, 1766–1845, *Bonnie Charlie's Now Awa!*]

9 O good old man! how well in thee appears / The constant service of the antique world, / When service sweat for duty, not for meed! / Thou art not for the fashion of these times, / Where none will sweat but for promotion. [William Shakespeare, 1564–1616, *As You Like It*, II. i. 56]

10 To hell, allegiance! vows to the blackest devil! / Conscience and grace to the profoundest pit! / I dare damnation. [*Hamlet*, IV. v. (130)]

11 CARDINAL WOLSEY: Had I but served my God with half the zeal / I served my king, he would not in mine age / Have left me naked to mine enemies. [*Henry VIII*, III. ii. 456]; see 17

12 Unthread the bold eye of rebellion, / And welcome home again discarded faith. [*King John*, V. iv. 11]

13 When I forget my sovereign, may God forget me! [Edward, Lord Thurlow, 1731–1806, speech in House of Lords, 15 Dec. 1778]

14 I can take no allegiance to a flag if I don't know who's holding it. [Peter Ustinov, 1921– , *Dear Me*, Ch. 16]

15 It is easier for a man to be loyal to his club than to his planet; the by-laws are shorter, and he is personally acquainted with the other members. [E B White, 1899–1985, *One Man's Meat*]

16 This book is about the organization man . . . I can think of no other way to describe the people I am talking about. They are not workers, nor are they the white-collar people in the usual, clerk sense of the word. These people only work for the Organization. The ones I am talking about *belong* to it as well. [William H Whyte, 1917– , *The Organization Man*, Ch. 1]

17 Had I but served God as diligently as I have served the King, he would not have given me over in my gray hairs. [Cardinal Wolsey, 1475?–1530, to Sir William Kingston]; see 11

See also CONSTANCY, INCONSTANCY, TRUST

LUCK

1 Nothing more certain than incertainties; / Fortune is full of fresh variety: / Constant in nothing but inconstancy. [Richard Barnfield, 1574–1627, *The Shepherd's Content*, xi]

2 The race is not to the swift, nor the battle to the strong. [Bible, OT, *Ecclesiastes* 9:11]

3 She was dealt a high card in life, but it was the wrong suit. [John Carswell, 1918–97, *The Exile: A Life of Ivy Litvinov*, last para.]

4 In the long run, in spite of everything, I have been very lucky. I asked for bread and was given a stone. It turned out to be precious. [Quentin Crisp, 1908–99, *How to Become a Virgin*, 1]

5 'Tis a gross error, held in schools, / That Fortune always favours fools. [John Gay, 1685–1732, *Fables*, II. xii. 119]

6 Some luck lies in not getting what you thought you wanted but getting what you have, which once you have it you may be smart enough to see is what you would have wanted had you known. [Garrison Keillor, 1942– , *Lake Wobegon Days*, 'Revival']

7 I never had a piece of toast / Particularly long and wide / But fell upon the sandy floor / And always on the buttered side. [James Payn, 1830–98, 'Parody', in *Chambers' Journal* (1884)]

8 Let us sit and mock the good housewife Fortune from her wheel, that her gifts may henceforth be bestowed equally. [William Shakespeare, 1564–1616, *As You Like It*, I. ii. (35)]

9 When Fortune means to men most good, / She looks upon them with a threatening eye. [*King John*, III. iv. 119]

See also CERTAIN, CHANCE, DESTINY

LUST

1 They were as fed horses in the morning: every one neighed after his neighbour's wife. [Bible, OT, *Jeremiah* 5:8]

2 I've looked on a lot of women with lust. I've committed adultery in my heart many times. This is something God recognizes I will do – and I have done it – and God forgives me for it. [Jimmy Carter, 1924– , interview in *Playboy*, Nov. 1976]

3 Lolita, light of my life, fire of my loins. My sin, my soul, Lo-lee-ta: the tip of the tongue taking a trip of three steps down the palate to tap, at three, on the teeth. Lo. Lee. Ta. [Vladimir Nabokov, 1899–1977, *Lolita*, opening sentences]

4 The expense of spirit in a waste of shame / Is lust in action; and till action, lust / Is perjured, murderous, bloody, full of blame, / Savage, extreme, rude, cruel, not to trust. [William Shakespeare, 1564–1616, *Sonnets*, 129]

See also ADULTERY, PROMISCUITY, SINS

LUXURY

1 It snewed in his hous of mete and drinke. [Geoffrey Chaucer, 1340?–1400, *Canterbury Tales*, 'Prologue', 345]

2 Merrily taking twopenny ale and cheese with a pocket knife; / But these were luxuries not for him who went for the Simple Life. [G K Chesterton, 1874–1936, *The Good Rich Man*]

3 It's no go the merrygoround, it's no go the rickshaw, / All we want is a limousine and a ticket for the peepshow. / Their knickers are made of crêpe-de-chine, their shoes are made of python, / Their halls are lined with tiger rugs and their walls with heads of bison. [Louis MacNeice, 1907–63, *Bagpipe Music*]

4 Give us the luxuries of life, and we will dispense with its necessities. [J L Motley, 1814–77, quoted in O W Holmes, *The Autocrat of the Breakfast Table*, Ch. 6]

5 Every luxury was lavished on you – atheism, breast-feeding, circumcision. I had to make my own way. [Joe Orton, 1933–67, *Loot*, I]

See also COMFORT, WEALTH

M

MACHINES, see TECHNOLOGY

MADNESS & SANITY

1 The rewards for being sane may not be very many but knowing what's funny is one of them. [Kingsley Amis, 1922–95, *Stanley and the Women*, Pt 2]

2 Blessed are the cracked, for they shall let in the light. [anon., in David Weeks, with Kate Ward, *Eccentrics: The Scientific Investigation*, 3]

3 We all are born mad. Some remain so. [Samuel Beckett, 1906–89, *Waiting for Godot*, II]

4 A knight errant who turns mad for a reason deserves neither merit nor thanks. The thing is to do it without cause. [Miguel Cervantes, 1547–1616, *Don Quixote*, Pt I, Ch. 25]

5 All the physicians and authors in the world could not give a clear account of his madness. He is mad in patches, full of lucid intervals. [Miguel Cervantes, 1547–1616, *Don Quixote*, Pt. II, Ch. 18]

6 The madman is not the man who has lost his reason. The madman is the man who has lost everything except his reason. [G K Chesterton, 1874–1936, *Orthodoxy*, Ch. 2]

7 He is crazed with the spell of far Arabia, / They have stolen his wits away. [Walter de la Mare, 1873–1956, *Arabia*]

8 It's ten years since I went out of my mind. I'd never go back. [Ken Dodd, 1927– , in M Billington, *How Tickled I Am*, Ch. 4]

9 There is a pleasure sure / In being mad, which none but madmen know! [John Dryden, 1631–1700, *The Spanish Friar*, II. i]

10 Don't let the sound of your own wheels drive you crazy. [Jacqueline du Pré, 1945–87 (a favourite quotation of hers), in *With Great Pleasure*, ed. Alec Reid]

11 Whom God wishes to destroy, he first makes mad. [Euripides, 480–406 BC, *Fragments*. Exists in many forms; the Latin version, '*Quos deus vult perdere, prius dementat*', is quoted in James Boswell, *Life of Johnson*]

12 Oh! he [General Wolfe] is mad, is he? Then I wish he would *bite* some other of my generals. [King George II, 1683–1760, quoted F Thackeray, *History of William Pitt*]

13 To be mad is not easy, / Will earn him no money, / But a niche in the news. [Robert Graves, 1895–1985, *The Halls of Bedlam*]

14 Insanity is a kind of innocence. [Graham Greene, 1904–91, *The Quiet American*, Pt III, Ch. 2, ii]

15 There was only one catch and that was Catch-22, which specified that a concern for one's own safety in the face of dangers that were real and immediate was the process of a rational mind. [Joseph Heller, 1923–99, *Catch-22*, Ch. 5]

16 Show me a sane man and I will cure him for you. [C G Jung, 1875–1961, quoted by Vincent Brome in *Observer*, 19 July 1975]

17 Madness need not be all breakdown. It may also be breakthrough. It is potential liberation and renewal as well as enslavement and existential death. [R D Laing, 1927–89, *The Politics of Experience*, Ch. 6]

18 Sanity is not being caught by a psychiatrist. [Fiona Pitt-Kethley, 1954– , in *Guardian*, 8 May 1991]

19 As soon as he ceased to be mad he became merely stupid. There are maladies which we must not seek to cure because they alone protect us from others that are more serious. [Marcel Proust, 1871–1922, *Remembrance of Things Past: The Guermantes Way*, Ch. 1]

20 It's the little questions from women about tappets that finally push men over the edge. [Philip Roth, 1933– , *Letting Go*, Pt I, Ch. 1]

21 For, to define true madness, / What is't but to be nothing else but mad. [*Hamlet*, II. ii. 93]

22 Though this be madness, yet there is method in't. [William Shakespeare 1564-1616 *Hamlet*, II. ii. (211)]

23 I am but mad north-north-west; when the wind is southerly I know a hawk from a handsaw. [*Hamlet*, II. ii. (405)]

24 O, what a noble mind is here o'erthrown: / The courtier's, soldier's, scholar's eye, tongue, sword; / The expectancy and rose of the fair state, / The glass of fashion, and the mould of form, / The observed of all observers, quite, quite down! [*Hamlet*, III. i. (159)]

25 Mad world! mad kings! mad composition! [*King John*, II. i. 561]

26 O! Let me not be mad, not mad, sweet heaven! / Keep me in temper; I would not be mad. [*King Lear*, I. v. (51)]

27 I am a very foolish, fond old man, / Fourscore and upward, not an hour more or less; / And, to deal plainly, / I fear I am not in my perfect mind. [*King Lear*, IV. vii. 60]

28 Why this is very midsummer madness. [*Twelfth Night*, III. iv. (62)]

29 *Enter Tilburina stark mad in white satin, and her confidant stark mad in white linen.* [R B Sheridan, 1751–1816, *The Critic*, III. i. (stage direction)]

30 If you talk to God, you are praying; if God talks to you, you have schizophrenia. If the dead talk to you, you are a spiritualist; if God talks to you, you are a schizophrenic. [Thomas Szasz, 1920– , *The Second Sin*, 'Schizophrenia']

31 I shudder and I sigh to think / That even Cicero / And many-minded Homer were / *Mad as the mist and snow*. [W B Yeats, 1865–1939, *Mad as the Mist and Snow*]

See also ILLNESS, MIND, NEUROSIS, PSYCHIATRY

MAGIC SPELLS

1 And all should cry, Beware! Beware! / His flashing eyes, his floating hair! / Weave a circle round him thrice, / And close your eyes with holy dread, / For he on honey-dew hath fed, / And drunk the milk of Paradise. [Samuel Taylor Coleridge, 1772–1834, *Kubla Khan*]

2 Double, double, toil and trouble; / Fire burn and cauldron bubble. [William Shakespeare, 1564–1616, *Macbeth*, IV. i. 10]

3 You spotted snakes with double tongue, / Thorny hedge-hogs, be not seen. [*A Midsummer Night's Dream*, II. ii. 9]

4 Full fathom five thy father lies; / Of his bones are coral made: / Those are pearls that were his eyes: / Nothing of him that doth fade, / But doth suffer a sea-change / Into something rich and strange. [*The Tempest*, I. ii. 394]

5 I'll break my staff, / Bury it certain fathoms in the earth, / And, deeper than did ever plummet sound, / I'll drown my book. [*The Tempest*, V. i. 54]

See also FAIRIES, ILLUSION

MAJORITIES, see DEMOCRACY

MANAGERS & MANAGEMENT

1 This island is almost made of coal and surrounded by fish. Only an organizing genius could produce a shortage of coal and fish in Great Britain at the same time. [Aneurin Bevan, 1897–1960, speech at Blackpool, 18 May 1945]

2 The world is disgracefully managed, one hardly knows to whom to complain. [Ronald Firbank, 1886–1926, *Vainglory*, 10]

3 The silliest woman can manage a clever man; but it needs a very clever woman to manage a fool. [Rudyard Kipling, 1865–1936, 'Three and – an Extra']

4 The power to get other people to do things has been the prerogative of the harlot throughout the ages – and of the manager. [Katharine Whitehorn, 1926– , in *Observer*, 26 May 1985]

See also OFFICE, POWER

MANKIND, see HUMAN BEINGS, HUMAN NATURE

MANNERS

1 If a man be gracious and courteous to strangers, it shows he is a citizen of the world. [Francis Bacon, 1561–1626, *Essays*, 13, 'Of Goodness and Goodness of Nature']

2 Evil communications corrupt good manners. [Bible, NT, *1 Corinthians* 15:33]

3 The three great stumbling-blocks in a girl's education, she says, are *homard – l'Américaine*, a boiled egg and asparagus. Shoddy table manners, she says, have broken up many a happy home. [Colette, 1873–1954, *Gigi*]

4 To Americans English manners are far more frightening than none at all. [Randall Jarrell, 1914–65, *Pictures from an Institution*, Pt I, Ch. 5]

5 My father used to say, / 'Superior people never make long visits.' [Marianne Moore, 1887–1972, *Silence*]

6 She had only taken one bite out of the tiny piece of bread and butter on her plate, and her little finger was like a hook on which to hang a whole system of genteel behaviour. [William Plomer, 1903–73, *I Speak of Africa*, 'Saturday, Sunday, Monday']

7 We could not lead a pleasant life, / And 'twould be finished soon, / If peas were eaten with the knife, / And gravy with the spoon. / Eat slowly; only men in rags / And gluttons old in sin / Mistake themselves for carpet bags / And tumble victuals in. [Walter A Raleigh, 1861–1922, *Laughter from a Cloud*, 'Stans puer ad mensam']

8 'How did you think I managed at dinner, Clarence?' 'Capitally!' 'I had a knife and two forks left at the end,' she said regretfully. [W Pett Ridge, 1857–1930, *Love at Paddington Green*, Ch. 6]

9 Why what a candy deal of courtesy / This fawning greyhound then did proffer me! [William Shakespeare, 1564–1616, *1 Henry IV*, I. iii. 251]

10 The gentle mind by gentle deeds is known: / For a man by nothing is so well bewrayed, / As by his manners. [Edmund Spenser, 1552?–99, *The Faerie Queene*, Bk vi, Canto 3, Stanza 1]

11 The Japanese have perfected good manners and made them indistinguishable from rudeness. [Paul Theroux, 1941– , *The Great Railway Bazaar*, Ch. 28]

12 Manners are especially the need of the plain. The pretty can get away with anything. [Evelyn Waugh, 1903–66; *Observer*, 'Sayings of the Year', 1962]

See also BEHAVIOUR, CLASS, SNOBS

MARRIAGE

1 Well, I'm old-fashioned. I don't believe in extramarital relationships. I think people should mate for life, like pigeons or Catholics. [Woody Allen, 1935– , in film *Manhattan*, scripted with Marshall Brickman]

2 Bigamy is having one husband too many. Monogamy is the same. [anon. woman, epigraph to Erica Jong, *Fear of Flying*, Ch. 1]

3 Marriage is an attempt to change a night owl into a homing pigeon. [anon.]

4 I married beneath me. All women do. [Nancy, Viscountess Astor, 1879–1964, speech at Oldham, 1951]

5 He was reputed one of the wise men that made answer to the question, when a man should marry? 'A young man not yet, an elder man not at all.' [Francis Bacon, 1561–1626, *Essays*, 8, 'Of Marriage and Single Life']

6 Marriage always demands the greatest understanding of the art of insincerity possible between two human beings. [Vicki Baum, 1888–1960, *Results of an Accident*, p. 140]

7 I'm not going to make the same mistake once. [(Of marriage) Warren Beatty, 1937– , in *Was It Good for You Too?*, ed. Bob Chieger]

8 There is much to be said for exotic marriages. If your husband is a bore, it takes years longer to discover it. [Saul Bellow, 1915– , *Mr Sammler's Planet*, Ch. 6]

9 All weddings are similar but every marriage is different. Death comes to everyone but one mourns alone. [John Berger, 1926– , *The White Bird*, 'The Storyteller']

10 Therefore shall a man leave his father and his mother, and shall cleave unto his wife: and they shall be one flesh. [Bible, OT, *Genesis* 2:24]

11 It is better to marry than to burn. [Bible, NT, *1 Corinthians* 7:9]

12 What therefore God hath joined together, let not man put asunder. [Bible, NT, *St Matthew* 19:6]

13 *Marriage*, n. The state or condition of a community consisting of a master, a mistress and two slaves, making in all two. [Ambrose Bierce, 1842–1914, *The Devil's Dictionary*]

14 When you're young, you think of marriage as a train you simply have to catch. You run and run until you've caught it, and then you sit back and look out of the window and realize you're bored. [Elizabeth Bowen, 1899–1973, said to Molly Keane, who quoted it in *The Sunday Times*, 11 Sept. 1988]

15 'We stay together, but we distrust one another.' 'Ah, yes . . . but isn't that a definition of marriage?' [Malcolm Bradbury, 1932– , *The History Man*, Ch. 3]

16 In a happy marriage it is the wife who provides the climate, the husband the landscape. [Gerald Brenan, 1894–1987, *Thoughts in a Dry Season*, 'Marriage']

17 Eventually he asked her to marry him. In this he showed sense; it is best to marry for purely selfish reasons. [Anita Brookner, 1938– , *A Start in Life*, 22]

18 One was never married, and that's his hell; another is, and that's his plague. [Robert Burton, 1577–1640, *Anatomy of Melancholy*, Memb. 4, 7]

19 Taking numbers into account, I should think more mental suffering had been undergone in the streets leading from St George's, Hanover Square, than in the condemned cells of Newgate. [Samuel Butler, 1835–1902, *The Way of All Flesh*, Ch. 13]

20 For no one cares for matrimonial cooings, / There's nothing wrong in a connubial kiss: / Think you, if Laura had been Petrarch's wife, / He would have written sonnets all his life? [Lord Byron, 1788–1824, *Don Juan*, III, 8]

21 Why don't they knead two virtuous souls for life / Into that moral centaur, man and wife? [Lord Byron, 1788–1824, *Don Juan*, V, 158]

22 Though women are angels, yet wedlock's the devil. [Lord Byron, 1788–1824, 'To Eliza']

23 I shall marry in haste and repeat at leisure. [James Branch Cabell, 1879–1958, *Jurgen*, Ch. 16]

24 Love and marriage, love and marriage, / Go together like a horse and carriage. [Sammy Cahn, 1913–93, song: *Love and Marriage*, in musical *Our Town*]

25 The deep, deep peace of the double-bed after the hurly-burly of the chaise-longue. [(Of her marriage) Mrs Patrick Campbell, 1865–1940, in Alexander Woollcott, *While Rome Burns*, 'The First Mrs Tanqueray']

26 KING [replying to Queen Caroline's deathbed injunctions to marry again]: – No, I will take mistresses.

QUEEN CAROLINE: But, goodness me, that won't prevent you! [John Hervey, *Memoirs of George II*, Vol. 2]

27 What is marriage but prostitution to one man instead of many? [Angela Carter, 1940–92, *Nights at the Circus*, 'London 2']

28 If you are afraid of loneliness, don't marry. [Anton Chekhov, 1860–1904, Notebooks 1894–1902, p. 49, Roger Hall, *Conjugal Rites*]

29 Medieval marriages were entirely a matter of property, and, as everyone knows, marriage without love means love without marriage. [Kenneth Clark, 1903–83, *Civilization*, Ch. 3]

30 I am not against hasty marriages, where a mutual flame is fanned by an adequate income. [Wilkie Collins, 1824–89, *No Name*, IV, Ch. 8]

31 Let us be very strange and well-bred: Let us be as strange as if we had been married a great while; and as well-bred as if we were not married at all. [William Congreve, 1670–1729, *The Way of the World*, IV. v]

32 Marriage is a wonderful invention; but, then again, so is a bicycle repair kit. [Billy Connolly, 1942– , in Duncan Campbell, *B C the Authorized Version*, 'Music']

33 Marriage is not all bed and breakfast. [R Coulson, *Reflections*]

34 Wedlock, indeed, hath oft comparèd been / To public feasts, where meet a public rout; / Where they that are without would fain go in. / And they that are within would fain go out. [John Davies, 1569–1626, *A Contention betwixt a Wife, A Widow and a Maid*, 196]; see 66

35 The value of marriage is not that adults produce children but that children produce adults. [Peter de Vries, 1910–93, *The Tunnel of Love*, Ch. 8]

36 There were three of us in this marriage, so it was a bit crowded. [(Of Charles, Prince of Wales and his continuing relationship with Camilla Parker-Bowles) Diana, Princess of Wales, 1961–97, on BBC programme *Panorama*, 20 Nov. 1995]

37 The wictim o' connubiality, as Blue Beard's domestic chaplain said, with a tear of pity, ven he buried him. [Charles Dickens, 1812–70, *Pickwick Papers*, Ch. 20]

38 I pray thee, good Lord, that I may not be married. But if I am to be married, that I may not be a cuckold. But if I am to be a cuckold, that I may not know. But if I am to know, that I may not mind. [Isak Dinesen, 1885–1962, *Seven Gothic Tales*, 'The Poet'. A saying described as 'the bachelors' prayer']

39 Every woman should marry – and no man. [Benjamin Disraeli, 1804–81, *Lothair*, Ch. 30]

40 I am to be married within these three days: married past redemption. [John Dryden, 1631–1700, *Marriage à la Mode*, I. i]

41 And all the young ladies said that a love-match was the only thing for happiness, where the parties could anyway afford it. [Maria Edgeworth, 1767–1849, *Castle Rackrent*, 'Continuation of Memoirs']

42 I would not marry God. [(Cable when her engagement was rumoured) Maxine Elliott, 1867–1940, in D Forbes Robertson, *Maxine*]

43 If you're looking for monogamy, you'd better marry a swan. [Nora Ephron, 1941– , in screenplay of film *Heartburn*]

44 Hanging and marriage, you know, go by Destiny. [George Farquhar, 1678–1707, *The Recruiting Officer*, III. ii]

45 A man in love is incomplete until he has married. Then he's finished. [Zsa Zsa Gabor, 1919– , in *Newsweek*, 28 Mar. 1960]

46 I haven't known any open marriages, though quite a few have been ajar. [Zsa Zsa Gabor, 1919– , in *Hammer and Tongues*, ed. Michèle Brown and Ann O'Connor, 'Marriage']

47 The problem with marriage is that it ends every night after making love, and it must be rebuilt every morning before breakfast. [Gabriel García Márquez, 1928– , *Love in the Time of Cholera*, p. 209]

48 You were born together, and together you shall be for evermore . . . but let there be spaces in your togetherness. And let the winds of the heavens dance between you. [Kahlil Gibran, 1883–1931, *The Prophet*, 'Of Marriage']

49 The life of a wife and husband who love each other is never at rest. Whether the marriage is true or false, the marriage portion is the same: elemental discord. [Jean Giraudoux, 1882–1944, *Tiger at the Gates*, II]

50 When you marry your mistress you create a job vacancy. [James Goldsmith, 1933–97, in *Independent Magazine*, 22 Apr. 1989. He did not claim to have originated the saying]

51 Why have such scores of lovely, gifted girls / Married impossible men? [Robert Graves, 1895–1985, *A Slice of Wedding Cake*]

52 How To Be Happy though Married. [Revd E J Hardy, 1849–1920, title of book (1910)]

53 If men knew how women pass the time when they are alone, they'd never marry. [O Henry, 1862–1910, *Memoirs of a Yellow Dog*]

54 The critical period in matrimony is breakfast time. [A P Herbert, 1890–1971, *Uncommon Law*, 'Is Marriage Lawful?']

55 A gentleman who had been very unhappy in marriage, married immediately after his wife died: Johnson said, it was the triumph of hope over experience. [Dr Samuel Johnson, 1709–84, in James Boswell, *Life of J*, 1770]

56 Sir, it is so far from being natural for a man and a woman to live in a state of marriage, that we find all the motives that they have for remaining in that connection, and the restraints which civilized society imposes to prevent separation, are hardly sufficient to keep them together. [Dr Samuel Johnson, 1709–84, in James Boswell, *Life of J*, 31 Mar. 1772]

57 I would advise no man to marry, Sir, . . . who is not likely to propagate understanding. [Dr Samuel Johnson, 1709–84, in Mrs Piozzi, *Anecdotes of J*]

58 You may carve it on his tombstone, you may cut it on his card, / That a young man married is a young man marred. [Rudyard Kipling, 1865–1936, *The Story of the Gadsbys*]; see 82

59 [When asked, 'Would you still have married your wife if she hadn't had two million pounds?'] I would have married her if she had only had one million pounds! [Harold Lever, 1914–95, in S Hoggart, *Back in the House*, p. 6]

60 It's a commonplace that you can always tell

which couples in a restaurant are married to each other because they're eating in silence ... It's not that they have nothing to say to each other, but that it doesn't have to be said. Being happily married means that you don't have to perform marriage, you just live in it like a fish lives in the sea. [David Lodge, 1935– , *Therapy*, 1, p. 128]

61 Both my marriages were failures! Number one departed and number two stayed. [Gustav Mahler, 1860–1911, quoted on Swiss radio, Dec. 1987]

62 Emily, I've a little confession to make. I really am a horse doctor. But marry me, and I'll never look at any other horse. [Groucho Marx, 1895–1977, in film *A Day at the Races*, screenplay by Robert Pirosh, George Seaton and George Oppenheimer]

63 No man is genuinely happy, married, who has to drink worse gin than he used to drink when he was single. [H L Mencken, 1880–1956, *Prejudices*, Fourth Series, 'Reflections on Monogamy', 14]

64 Hail wedded love, mysterious law, true source / Of human offspring, sole propriety / In Paradise of all things common else. [John Milton, 1608–74, *Paradise Lost*, Bk iv, 750]

65 There was an old party of Lyme, / Who married three wives at one time, / When asked, 'Why the third?' / He replied, 'One's absurd, / And bigamy, sir, is a crime!' [Cosmo Monkhouse, 1840–1901]

66 It [marriage] is like a cage; one sees the birds outside desperate to get in, and those inside equally desperate to get out. [Michel de Montaigne, 1533–92, *Essays*, III, 5]; see 34

67 Matrimony and murder both carry a mandatory life sentence. [John Mortimer, 1923– , *Rumpole for the Defence*, 'Rumpole and the Boat People']

68 'We aren't getting anywhere. You know that as well as I do.' 'One doesn't have to get anywhere in a marriage. It's not a public conveyance.' [Iris Murdoch, 1919–99, *A Severed Head*, Ch. 3]

69 Why have hamburger out when you've got steak at home? That doesn't always mean it's tender. [Paul Newman, 1925– , of marriage; *Observer*, 'Sayings of the Week', 11 Mar. 1984, but earlier variants on this line]

70 Jack Sprat could eat no fat, / His wife could eat no lean; / And so between them both, you see, / They licked the platter clean. [Nursery rhyme]

71 Strange to say what delight we married people have to see these poor fools decoyed into our condition. [Samuel Pepys, 1633–1703, *Diary*, 25 Dec. 1665]

72 Those whom God hath joined together let no man put asunder. [*The Book of Common Prayer*, Solemnization of Matrimony]

73 Advice to persons about to marry. – Don't. [*Punch*, Vol. VIII (1845), p. 1]

74 My husband Lorenzo says he can't live more than a few weeks with me because I take up all the oxygen. [Mirella Ricciardi, in *Guardian*, 31 Mar. 1982]

75 I hold this to be the highest function of the bond between two people: that each protects the other's solitude. [Rainer Maria Rilke, 1875–1926, letter to Paula Modersohn-Becker, 12 Feb. 1902]

76 It doesn't much signify whom one marries, for one is sure to find next morning that it was someone else. [Samuel Rogers, 1763–1855, *Table Talk*]

77 Men who have a pierced ear are better prepared for marriage – they've experienced pain and bought jewellery. [Rita Rudner, 1956– , on Channel 4 TV, 5 Dec. 1989]

78 The main purpose of marriage is rearing children and when that's done you should be free to renew your option – about twenty years seems like a reasonable term to me. [Willy Russell, 1947– , interview in *Guardian*, 20 Oct. 1987]

79 Marriage? It's like asparagus eaten with vinaigrette or hollandaise, a matter of taste but of no importance. [Françoise Sagan, 1935– , in *Guardian*, 21 June 1988]

80 Marriage is nothing but a civil contract. [John Selden, 1584–1654, *Table Talk*, 85]

81 The hind that would be mated by the lion / Must die for love. [William Shakespeare, 1564–1616, *All's Well that Ends Well*, I. i. (103)]

82 A young man married is a man that's marred. [*All's Well that Ends Well*, III. i. (103)]; see 58

83 I will do anything, Nerissa, ere I will be married to a sponge. [*The Merchant of Venice*, I. ii. (105)]

84 Jack shall have Jill; / Nought shall go ill; / The man shall have his mare again, / And all shall be well. [*Midsummer Night's Dream*, III. ii. 461]

85 In time the savage bull doth bear the yoke. [*Much Ado About Nothing*, I. i. (271)]

86 O curse of marriage! / That we can call these delicate creatures ours, / And not their appetites. I had rather be a toad, / And live upon the vapour of a dungeon, / Than keep a corner in the thing I love / For others' uses. [*Othello*, III. iii. 268]

87 Many a good hanging prevents a bad marriage. [*Twelfth Night*, I. v. (20)]

88 What God hath joined together no man shall ever put asunder: God will take care of that. [George Bernard Shaw, 1856–1950, *Getting Married*]

89 It is a woman's business to get married as soon as possible, and a man's to keep unmarried as long as he can. [George Bernard Shaw, 1856–1950, *Man and Superman*, II]

90 Those who talk most about the blessings of marriage and the constancy of its vows are the very people who declare that if the chain were broken and the prisoners left free to choose, the whole social fabric would fly asunder. You cannot have the argument both ways. If the prisoner is happy, why lock him in? If he is not, why pretend that he is? [George Bernard Shaw, 1856–1950, *Man and Superman*, III]

91 Marriage is popular because it combines the maximum of temptation with the maximum of opportunity. [George Bernard Shaw, 1856–1950, *Man and Superman*, 'Maxims for Revolutionists', Marriage]

92 'Tis safest in matrimony to begin with a little aversion. [R B Sheridan, 1751–1816, *The Rivals*, I. ii]

93 Twelve years doesn't mean you're a *happy* couple. It just means you're a *long* couple. [Neil Simon, 1927– , *The Odd Couple*, I]

94 [Of marriage] A pair of shears, so joined that they cannot be separated; often moving in opposite directions, yet always punishing anyone who comes between them. [Sydney Smith, 1771–1845, in Lady Holland, *Memoir*, Vol. i, Ch. 11]

95 It's not talk of God / And the decade ahead / That allows you to get through the worst. / It's 'you do' and 'I don't' and 'nobody said that' / And 'who brought the subject up first?' [Stephen Sondheim, 1930– , song: *It's the Little Things*, in musical *Company*]

96 Marriage is like life in this – that it is a field of battle, and not a bed of roses. [Robert Louis Stevenson, 1850–94, *Virginibus Puerisque*, I, 2]

97 The reason why so few marriages are happy is because young ladies spend their time in making nets, not in making cages. [Jonathan Swift, 1677–1745, *Thoughts on Various Subjects*]

98 Remember, it is as easy to marry a rich woman as a poor woman. [W M Thackeray, 1811–63, *Pendennis*, Ch. 28]

99 This I set down as a positive truth. A woman with fair opportunities and without a positive hump, may marry whom she likes. [W M Thackeray, 1811–63, *Vanity Fair*, Ch. 4]

100 Every night of her married life she has been late for school. [Dylan Thomas, 1914–53, *Under Milk Wood*]

101 We are an ideal couple and have not had a harsh word in the seven weeks of our married life. [James Thurber, 1894–1961, letter to Herman and Dorothy Miller, Aug. 1935, *Selected Letters*, ed. Helen Thurber and Edward Weeks]

102 Every marriage tends to consist of an aristocrat and a peasant. Of a teacher and a learner. [John Updike, 1932– , *Couples*, Ch. 1]

103 In married life three is company and two is none. [Oscar Wilde, 1854–1900, *The Importance of Being Earnest*, I]

104 Marriage is a bribe to make a housekeeper think she's a householder. [Thornton Wilder, 1897–1975, *The Matchmaker*, I]

105 Most everybody in the world climbs into their graves married. [Thornton Wilder, 1897–1975, *Our Town*, II]

106 I'm not living with you. We occupy the same cage. [Tennessee Williams 1911–83, *Cat on a Hot Tin Roof*, I]

107 So that is marriage, Lily thought, a man and a woman looking at a girl throwing a ball. [Virginia Woolf, 1882–1941, *To the Lighthouse*, Ch. 13]

See also DIVORCE, HUSBANDS, UNMARRIED, WEDDINGS, WOMEN & MEN

MARTYRS

1 Damn it all, you can't have the crown of thorns and the thirty pieces of silver. [Aneurin Bevan, 1897–1960, in Michael Foot, *Aneurin Bevan*, Vol. 2, Ch. 1]

2 Precious in the sight of the Lord is the death of his saints. [Bible, OT, *Psalms* 116:15]

3 Martyrs do not build churches: they are the mortar, or the alibi. They are followed by the priests and bigots. [Albert Camus, 1913–60, *The Rebel*, Ch. 2]

4 And therefore I tell you (and I pray God it be not laid to your charge) that I am the Martyr of the People. [Charles I, 1600–1649, speech on the scaffold, 30 Jan. 1649]

5 This hand hath offended. [Thomas Cranmer, 1489–1556, said at his burning, of the hand that had signed a recantation, 21 Mar. 1556]

6 Be of good comfort, Master Ridley, and play the man. We shall this day light such a candle by God's grace in England, as (I trust) shall never be put out. [Bishop Latimer, 1485?–1555, said when he and Ridley were about to be burned, 16 Oct. 1555]

7 Avenge, O Lord, thy slaughtered saints, whose bones / Lie scattered on the Alpine mountains cold; / Even them who kept thy truth so pure of old / When all our fathers worshipped stocks and stones. [John Milton, 1608–74, sonnet: *On the Late Massacre in Piedmont*]

8 Martyrdom is the only way in which a man can become famous without ability. [George Bernard Shaw, 1856–1950, in Preface to 1908 reprint of *Fabian Essays*]

9 The blood of the martyrs is the seed of the Church. [Tertullian, *c.*160–*c.*220, *Apologeticus*, 50]

10 He [Professor Dodwell] has set his heart on being a martyr, and I have set mine on disappointing him. [William III, 1650–1702, attr. remark on a Jacobite]

See also SACRIFICE

MASSES

1 *Nec audiendi sunt qui solent dicere, 'Vox populi, vox dei'; quum tumultuositas vulgi semper insaniae proxima sit.* – Nor should we listen to those who say, 'The voice of the people is the voice of God', for the turbulence of the mob is always close to insanity. [Alcuin, 735–804, *Epistolae*, 166, §9]

2 You cannot make a man by standing a sheep on its hind legs. But by standing a flock of sheep in that position you can make a crowd of men. [Max Beerbohm, 1872–1956, *Zuleika Dobson*, Ch. 9]

3 A great multitude, which no man could number, of all nations, and kindreds, and people, and tongues. [Bible, NT, *Revelation* 7:9]

4 I love the people with their simple straightforward minds. It's only that their smell brings on my migraine. [Bertolt Brecht, 1898–1956, *The Caucasian Chalk Circle*, V]

5 The multitude: that numerous piece of monstrosity, which, taken asunder, seem men, and the reasonable creatures of God; but, confused together, make but one great beast, and a monstrosity more hideous than Hydra. [Sir Thomas Browne, 1605–82, *Religio Medici*, Pt II, 1]

6 Having first looked to government for bread, on the very first scarcity they will turn and bite the hand that fed them [Edmund Burke, 1729–97, *Thoughts and Details on Scarcity*]

7 The Public is an old woman. Let her maunder and mumble. [Thomas Carlyle, 1795–1881, *Journal*, 1835]

8 The machinery of science must be individualistic and isolated. A mob can shout round a palace; but a mob cannot shout down a telephone. The specialist appears, and democracy is half spoilt at a stroke. [G K Chesterton, 1874–1936, *What's Wrong with the World*, 'The Unfinished Temple']

9 Whatever crimes the Proletariat commits / It can't be beastly to the Children of the Ritz. [Noël Coward, 1899–1973, *Words and Music*, 'Children of the Ritz']

10 'It's always best on these occasions to do what the mob do.' 'But suppose there are two mobs?' suggested Mr Snodgrass. 'Shout with the largest,' replied Mr Pickwick. [Charles Dickens, 1812–70, *Pickwick Papers*, Ch. 13]

11 Nor is the people's judgement always true; / The most may err as grossly as the few. [John Dryden, 1631–1700, *Absalom and Achitophel*, Pt I, 781]

12 All the world over, I will back the masses

against the classes. [W E Gladstone, 1809–98, speech at Liverpool, 28 June 1886]

13 There is not a more mean, stupid, dastardly, pitiful, selfish, spiteful, envious, ungrateful animal than the Public. It is the greatest of cowards, for it is afraid of itself. [William Hazlitt, 1778–1830, *On Living to One's Self*]

14 Only constant repetition will finally succeed in imprinting an idea on the memory of the crowd. [Adolf Hitler, 1889–1945, *Mein Kampf*, Ch. 6]

15 The broad masses of the people . . . will more easily fall victims to a big lie than to a small one. [Adolf Hitler, 1889–1945, *Mein Kampf*, Ch. 10]

16 About things on which the public thinks long it commonly attains to think right. [Dr Samuel Johnson, 1709–84, *The Lives of the English Poets*, 'Addison']

17 In every age the vilest specimens of human nature are to be found among demagogues. [Lord Macaulay, 1800–1859, *History of England*, I, Ch. 5]

18 The people need poetry that will be their own secret / To keep them awake forever, / And bathe them in the bright-haired wave / Of its breathing. [Osip Mandelstam, 1891–1938, *Poems*, No. 287]

19 The dictatorship of the proletariat. [Karl Marx, 1818–83, letter to Weydemeyer, 5 Mar. 1852]

20 The masters have been abolished; the morality of the common man has triumphed. [Friedrich Nietzsche, 1844–1900, *Genealogy of Morals*, Aphorism 9]

21 Minorities are individuals or groups of individuals especially qualified. The masses are the collection of people not especially qualified. [José Ortega y Gasset, 1883–1955, *The Revolt of the Masses*, Ch. 1]

22 The proles are not human beings. [George Orwell, 1903–50, *1984*, Pt 1, Ch. 5]

23 The people's voice is odd, / It is, and it is not, the voice of God. [Alexander Pope, 1688–1744, *Epistle*, I, 89]

24 I can't help feeling wary when I hear anything said about the masses. First you take their faces from 'em by calling 'em the masses and then you accuse 'em of not having any faces. [J B Priestley, 1894–1984, *Saturn over the Water*, Ch. 2]

25 The multitude is always in the wrong. [Earl of Roscommon, 1637–88, *Essay on Translated Verse*, 183]

26 The people will live on. / The learning and blundering people will live on. / They will be tricked and sold and again sold / And go back to the nourishing earth for rootholds. [Carl Sandburg, 1878–1967, *The People, Yes*]

27 He himself stuck not to call us the many-headed multitude. [William Shakespeare, 1564–1616, *Coriolanus*, II. iii. 18]

28 You common cry of curs! whose breath I hate / As reek o' the rotten fens, whose loves I prize / As the dead carcasses of unburied men / That do corrupt my air. [*Coriolanus*, III. iii. 118]

29 Once the people begin to reason, all is lost. [Voltaire, 1694–1778, letter to Damilaville, 1 Apr. 1766]

30 The century on which we are entering – the century which will come out of this war – can be and must be the century of the common man. [Vice-President Henry Wallace, 1888–1965, speech, 8 May 1942]

31 Our supreme governors, the mob. [Horace Walpole, 1717–97, letter to Horace Mann, 7 Sept. 1743]

See also CLASS, DEMOCRACY, MIDDLE CLASS

MATERIALISM

1 Make to yourselves friends of the mammon of unrighteousness. [Bible, NT, *St Luke* 16:9]

2 Where your treasure is, there will your heart be also. [Bible, NT, *St Matthew* 6:21]

3 No man can serve two masters . . . Ye cannot serve God and mammon. [Bible, NT, *St Matthew* 6:24]

4 Man must choose whether to be rich in things or in the freedom to use them. [Ivan Illich, 1926–   , *Deschooling Society*, Ch. 4]

5 The almighty dollar, that great object of universal devotion throughout our land, seems to have no genuine devotees in these peculiar villages. [Washington Irving, 1783–1859, *Wolfert's Roost*, 'The Creole Village']

6 When an American heiress wants to buy a man, she at once crosses the Atlantic. The only really materialistic people I have ever met have been Europeans. [Mary McCarthy, 1912–89, *On the Contrary*, 'America the Beautiful']

7 Painful though it was, / I cut my last winter rose for her. / She turned it inside out / To see who the manufacturer was. [Spike Milligan, 1918– , *Open Heart University*, 'Trust']

8 Go out and fight so life shouldn't be printed on dollar bills. [Clifford Odets, 1906–63, *Awake and Sing*, I]

9 As if a woman of education bought things because she wanted 'em. [John Vanburgh, 1664–1726, *The Confederacy*, II. i]

10 Conspicuous consumption of valuable goods is a means of reputability to the gentleman of leisure. [Thorstein Veblen, 1857–1929, *The Theory of the Leisure Class*, Ch. 4]

11 The world is too much with us; late and soon, / Getting and spending, we lay waste our powers: / Little we see in Nature that is ours; / We have given our hearts away, a sordid boon! / The sea that bares her bosom to the moon; / The winds that will be howling at all hours, / And are up-gathered now like sleeping flowers; / For this, for everything, we are out of tune. [William Wordsworth, 1770–1850, *Miscellaneous Sonnets*, 33]

See also CAPITALISM, COMMUNISM

MATHEMATICS

1 Multiplication is vexation, / Division is as bad; / The Rule of three doth puzzle me, / And Practice drives me mad. [anon. Elizabethan MS (1570)]

2 What is algebra exactly; is it those three-cornered things? [James Barrie, 1860–1937, *Quality Street*, II]

3 I never could make out what those damn dots meant. [(Of the decimal point) Lord Randolph Churchill, 1849–94, quoted by Winston Churchill, *Lord R C*, Vol. ii, p. 184]

4 As far as the laws of mathematics refer to reality, they are not certain, and as far as they are certain, they do not refer to reality. [Albert Einstein, 1879–1955, in F Capra, *The Tao of Physics*, Ch. 2]

5 Equations are important to me, because politics is for the present, but an equation is something for eternity. [Albert Einstein, 1879–1955, in Stephen Hawking, *A Brief History of Time*, 'Albert Einstein']

6 I don't believe in mathematics. [Albert Einstein, 1879–1955 (to Gustave Ferrière), in Carl Seelig, *A E*, Ch. 5]

7 MORIARTY: How are you at Mathematics? SECOMBE: I speak it like a native. [Spike Milligan, 1918– , radio programme *The Goon Show*, 'Dishonoured']

8 One geometry cannot be more true than another; it can only be more *convenient*. Geometry is not true, it is advantageous. [Henri Poincaré, 1854–1912, *Science and Hypothesis*, Ch. 3]

9 Mathematics possesses not only truth, but supreme beauty – a beauty cold and austere, like that of sculpture. [Bertrand Russell, 1872–1970, *Mysticism and Logic*, Ch. 4]

10 Mathematics may be defined as the subject in which we never know what we are talking about, nor whether what we are saying is true. [Bertrand Russell, 1872–1970, *Mysticism and Logic*, Ch. 4]

11 Algebra and money are essentially levellers; the first intellectually, the second effectively. [Simone Weil, 1909–43, *Gravity and Grace*, 'Algebra']

See also LOGIC, SCIENCE

MATURITY

1 At sixteen I was stupid, confused, insecure and indecisive. At twenty-five I was wise, self-confident, prepossessing and assertive. At forty-five I am stupid, confused, insecure and indecisive. Who would have supposed that maturity is only a short break in adolescence? [Jules Feiffer, 1929– , caption to drawing in *Observer*, 3 Feb. 1974]

2 The mark of the immature man is that he wants to die nobly for a cause, while the mark of the mature man is that he wants to live humbly for one. [Wilhelm Stekel, 1868–1940, in J D Salinger, *The Catcher in the Rye*, Ch. 24]

3 Men come of age at sixty, women at fifteen. [James Stephens, 1882–1950; *Observer*, 'Sayings of the Week', 1 Oct. 1944]

4 Maturity is the assimilation of the features of every ancestor. [Derek Walcott, 1930– , *Is Massa Dead?*, 'The Muse of History']

5 I have always said about Tony [Benn] that he immatures with age. [Harold Wilson, 1916–95, from BBC TV programme *Pebble Mill*, in Jad Williams, *Tony Benn*, Ch. 37]

See also ADOLESCENCE, AGE, MIDDLE AGE

MEANNESS

1 We could have saved sixpence. We have saved fivepence. (*Pause*) But at what cost? [Samuel Beckett, 1906–89, *All That Fall*]

2 I am not yet a very mean old man, but I am moving in that direction. I view with increasing distaste those guests who can leave an inch or so of good wine in their glasses. [J B Priestley, 1894–1984, in obituary in *The Times*, 16 Aug. 1984]

3 Mun, a had na' been the-erre abune twa hoours when – *bang* – went *saxpence*!! [*Punch*, LV (1868), 235]

4 There are some meannesses which are too mean even for man – woman, lovely woman alone, can venture to commit them. [W M Thackeray, 1811–63, *A Shabby-Genteel Story*, Ch. 3]

5 The vice of meanness, condemned in every other country, is in Scotland translated into a virtue called 'thrift'. [David Thomson, 1914–88, *Nairn in Darkness and Light*, p. 70]

See also ENVY, GREED, MONEY, THRIFT

MEDIA

1 The medium is the message. This is merely to say that the personal and social consequences of any medium ... result from the new scale that is introduced into our affairs by each extension of ourselves or by any new technology. [Marshall McLuhan, 1911–80, *Understanding Media*, Ch. 1]

2 A hot medium is one that extends one single sense in 'high definition'. High definition is the state of being well filled with data. A photograph is, visually, 'high definition' ... Telephone is a cool medium or one of low definition, because the ear is given a meagre amount of information. [Marshall McLuhan, 1911–80, *Understanding Media*, Ch. 2]

3 The media. It sounds like a convention of spiritualists. [Tom Stoppard, 1937– , *Night and Day*, I]

See also JOURNALISM, NEWSPAPERS, TELEVISION

MEDICINE

1 Medicinal discovery, / It moves in mighty leaps, / It leapt straight past the common cold / And gave it us for keeps. [Pam Ayres, 1947– , '*Oh, No, I Got a Cold*']

2 Some fell by laudanum, and some by steel, / And death in ambush lay in every pill. [Samuel Garth, 1661–1719, *The Dispensary*, IV, 62]

3 Extreme remedies are most appropriate for extreme diseases. [Hippocrates, *c*.460–357 BC, *Aphorisms*, I, vi]

4 Throw physic to the dogs; I'll none of it. [William Shakespeare, 1564–1616, *Macbeth*, V. ii. 47]

See also DOCTORS, HEALTH, ILLNESS

MEDIOCRITY

1 Mediocrity knows nothing higher than itself, but talent instantly recognizes genius. [Arthur Conan Doyle, 1859–1930, *The Sign of Four*, Ch. 1]

2 Some men are born mediocre, some men achieve mediocrity, and some men have mediocrity thrust upon them. With Major Major it had been all three. [Joseph Heller, 1923–99, *Catch-22*, Ch. 9]

3 We bring to one dead level ev'ry mind. [Alexander Pope, 1688–1744, *The Dunciad*, Bk iv, 268]

4 It isn't evil that's running the earth, but mediocrity. The crime is not that Nero played while Rome burned, but that he played badly. [Ned Rorem, 1923– , *Final Diary*]

See also ORDINARY

MEMORY

1 Apart from my amnesia, my memory's very good. [Jean Anouilh, 1910–87, *Traveller without Luggage*, II. i]

2 *Les souvenirs sont cors de chasse / Dont meurt le bruit parmi le vent.* – Memories are hunting-horns, whose noise dies away in the wind. [Guillaume Apollinaire, 1880–1918, *Cors de chasse*]

3 *J'ai plus de souvenirs que si j'avais mille ans.* – I have more memories than if I were a thousand years old. [Charles Baudelaire, 1821–67, *Spleen*]

4 The biological (if not the aesthetic) value of remembering is not that it allows one to reminisce about the past but that it permits one to calculate coldly about the unknown future. [Colin Blakemore, 1944– (from BBC Reith lectures), in *Listener*, 2 Dec. 1976]

5 Our memories are card-indexes consulted and then returned in disorder by authorities whom we do not control. [Cyril Connolly, 1903–74, *The Unquiet Grave*, Ch. 3]

6 In plucking the fruit of memory one runs the risk of spoiling its bloom. [Joseph Conrad, 1857–1924, *Arrow of Gold*, Author's Note]

7 A memory is what is left when something happens and does not completely unhappen. [Edward de Bono, 1933– , *The Mechanism of Mind*]

8 Lord knows what incommunicable small terrors infants go through, unknown to all. We disregard them, we say they forget, because they have not the words to make us remember ... By the time they learn to speak they have forgotten the details of their complaints, and so we never know. They forget so quickly, we say, because we cannot contemplate the fact that they never forget. [Margaret Drabble, 1939– , *The Millstone*, p. 127]

9 Footfalls echo in the memory / Down the passage which we did not take / Towards the door we never opened / Into the rose-garden. [T S Eliot, 1888–1965, *Four Quartets*, 'Burnt Norton', 1]

10 And when Thyself with shining Foot shall pass / Among the Guests Star-scattered on the Grass, / And in thy joyous Errand reach the Spot / Where I made one – turn down an empty Glass! [Edward Fitzgerald, 1809–83, *The Rubá'iyát of Omar Khayyám*, Edn 1, 75]

11 Everyone seems to remember with great clarity what they were doing on November 22nd, 1963, at the precise moment they heard President Kennedy was dead. [Frederick Forsyth, 1938– , *The Odessa File*, opening words]

12 'There,' he said. 'You'll remember this day, my girl. For the rest of your life.' 'I already have,' said Mary. [Alan Garner, 1934– , *The Stone Book*]

13 O Memory! thou fond deceiver, / Still importunate and vain, / To former joys recurring ever, / And turning all the past to pain! [Oliver Goldsmith, 1728–74, song: *O Memory*]

14 With rue my heart is laden / For golden friends I had, / For many a rose-lipt maiden / And many a lightfoot lad. [A E Housman, 1859–1936, *A Shropshire Lad*, 54]

15 It is not what old men forget that shadows their senescence, but what they remember. [George Lyttelton, 1883–1962, *Lyttelton–Hart-Davis Letters*, Vol. 2, letter of 27 Oct. 1955]

16 Flocks of the memories of the day draw near / The dovecot doors of sleep. [Alice Meynell, 1847–1922, *At Night*]

17 Oft in the stilly night, / Ere Slumber's chain has bound me, / Fond Memory brings the light / Of other days around me; / The smiles, the tears, / Of boyhood's years, / The words of love then spoken; / The eyes that shone, / Now dimmed and gone, / The cheerful hearts now broken! [Thomas Moore, 1779–1852, *National Airs*, 'Oft in the Stilly Night']

18 The richness of life lies in the memories we have forgotten. [Cesare Pavese, 1908–50, *This Business of Living: A Diary, 1935–1950*, 13 Feb. 1944]

19 Memory is not what we remember, but that which remembers us. Memory is a present that never stops passing. [Octavio Paz, 1914–98, *The Curse*]

20 I think we should always look back on our own past with a sort of tender contempt. [Dennis Potter, 1935–94, *Seeing the Blossom*, an interview with Melvyn Bragg, TV Channel 4, April 1994]

21 The taste was that of the little piece of madeleine which on Sunday mornings at Combray ... when I went to say good morning to her in her bedroom, my aunt Léonie used to give me, dipping it first in her own cup of tea or tisane. [Marcel Proust, 1871–1922, *Remembrance of Things Past: Swann's Way*, 'Overture']

22 Remember me when I am gone away, / Gone far away into the silent land. [Christina Rossetti, 1830–94, *Remember*]

23 I have been here before, / But when or how I cannot tell: / I know the grass beyond the door, / The sweet keen smell, / The sighing sound, the lights around the shore. [Dante Gabriel Rossetti, 1828–82, *Sudden Light*]

24 Praising what is lost / Makes the remembrance dear. [William Shakespeare, 1564–1616, *All's Well that Ends Well*, V. iii. 19]

25 While memory holds a seat / In this distracted globe. Remember thee! / Yea from the table of my memory / I'll wipe away all trivial fond records. [*Hamlet*, I. v. 96]

26 There's rosemary, that's for remembrance; pray, love, remember: and there is pansies, that's for thoughts. [*Hamlet*, IV. v. (174)]

27 Old men forget: yet all shall be forgot, / But he'll remember with advantages / What feats he did that day. Then shall our names, / Familiar in his mouth as household words, / Harry the King, Bedford and Exeter, / Warwick and Talbot, Salisbury and Gloucester, / Be in their flowing cups freshly remembered. [*Henry V*, IV. iii. 49]

28 That memory, the warder of the brain, / Shall be a fume. [*Macbeth*, I. vii. 65]

29 And thou in this shalt find thy monument, / When tyrants' crests and tombs of brass are spent. [*Sonnets*, 107]

30 Yet leaving here a name, I trust, / That will not perish in the dust. [Robert Southey, 1774–1843, *My Days among the Dead*]

31 I remembered your name perfectly, but I just can't think of your face. [Revd W A Spooner, 1844–1930, attr., but apocryphal]

32 The memories of men are too frail a thread to hang history on. [John Still, *The Jungle Tide*, 1930, Ch. 5]

33 I shall remember while the light lives yet / And in the night time I shall not forget. [A C Swinburne, 1837–1909, *Erotion*]

34 Till life forget and death remember, / Till thou remember and I forget. [A C Swinburne, 1837–1909, *Itylus*, 5]

35 As a perfume doth remain / In the folds where it hath lain, / So the thought of you, remaining / Deeply folded in my brain, / Will not leave me: all things leave me: / You remain. [Arthur Symons, 1865–1945, *Memory*]

36 Yes. I remember Adlestrop – / The name, because one afternoon / Of heat the express-train drew up there / Unwontedly. It was late June. [Edward Thomas, 1878–1917, *Adlestrop*]

37 Definition of a slogan: a form of words for which memorability has been *bought*. [Richard Usborne, 1907– , in letter to editors, 1964]

38 Perhaps one day this too will be pleasant to remember. [Virgil, 70–19 BC, *Aeneid*, I, 203]

39 O joy! that in our embers / Is something that doth live, / That nature yet remembers / What was so fugitive! / The thought of our past years in me doth breed / Perpetual benediction. [William Wordsworth, 1770–1850, *Ode, Intimations of Immortality*, 9]

See also FORGETTING, PAST

MEN

1 A man is two people, himself and his cock. A man always takes his friend to the party. Of the two, the friend is the nicer, being more able to show his feelings. [Beryl Bainbridge, 1934– , in *Observer*, 17 Oct. 1982]

2 Bloody men are like bloody buses – / You wait for about a year / And as soon as one approaches your stop / Two or three others appear. [Wendy Cope, 1945– , *Bloody Men*]

3 Men are but children of a larger growth. [John Dryden, 1631–1700, *All for Love*, IV. i]

4 I can eat a man, but I'm not sure of the fibre content. [Jenny Eclair, 1960– , interview in *The Times*, 16 Nov. 1985]

5 Men's men: gentle or simple, they're much of a muchness. [George Eliot, 1819–80, *Daniel Deronda*, Bk iv, Ch. 21]

6 Men like war: they do not hold much sway over birth, so they make up for it with death. Unlike women, men menstruate by shedding other people's blood. [Lucy Ellmann, 1956– , in *Observer Magazine*, 4 Oct. 1992]

7 What would ye, ladies? It was ever thus. / Men are unwise and curiously planned. [James Elroy Flecker, 1884–1915, *Hassan*, V, ii]

8 A man ... is *so* in the way in the house! [Elizabeth Gaskell, 1810–65, *Cranford*, Ch. 1]

9 Man's a ribald – Man's a rake, / Man is Nature's sole mistake. [W S Gilbert, 1836–1911, *The Pirates of Penzance*, II]

10 When God created man, she was only experimenting. I always thought men were a phallusy. [Graffito in ladies' lavatory]

11 The tragedy of machismo is that a man is never quite man enough. [Germaine Greer, 1939– , *The Madwoman's Underclothes*, 'My Mailer Problem']

12 If you can fill the unforgiving minute / With sixty seconds' worth of distance run, / Yours is the Earth and everything that's in it, / And – which is more – you'll be a Man, my son! [Rudyard Kipling, 1865–1936, *If*]

13 Why can't a woman be more like a man? / Men are so honest, so horribly square; / Eternally noble, historically fair. [Alan Jay Lerner, 1918–86, *My Fair Lady*, I. iv]

14 The male sex still constitute in many ways the most obstinate vested interest one can find. [Lord Longford, 1905– , speech in House of Lords, 23 June 1963]

15 There was nothing more fun than a man. [Dorothy Parker, 1893–1967, *The Little Old Lady in Lavender Silk*]

16 I like men to behave like men – strong and childish. [Françoise Sagan, 1935– ; in *Dictionary of Contemporary Quotations*, ed. Jonathon Green]

17 Men are so romantic, don't you think? They look for a perfect partner when what they should be looking for is perfect love. [Fay Weldon, 1931– , interview in *The Sunday Times*, 6 Sept. 1987]

18 A man in the house is worth two in the street. [Mae West, 1892–1980, in film *Belle of the Nineties*]

19 It's not the men in my life but the life in my men. [Mae West, 1892–1980, in film *I'm no Angel*]

20 There is, of course, no reason for the existence of the male sex except that one sometimes needs help with moving the piano. [Rebecca West, 1892–1983, in V Glendinning, *R W*, Pt 6, Ch. 5]

21 I don't hate men, I just wish they'd try harder. They all want to be heroes and all we want is for them to stay at home and help with the housework and the kids. That's not the kind of heroism they enjoy. [Jeanette Winterson, 1959– , *Sexing the Cherry*, p. 127]

See also HUMAN BEINGS, HUMAN NATURE, WOMEN, WOMEN & MEN

MERCY, see PITY

MIDDLE AGE

1 At fifty you have the choice of keeping your face or your figure and it's *much* better to keep your face. [Barbara Cartland, 1904– , interview in the *Daily Mail*, 10 July 1981]

2 *Nel mezzo del cammin di nostra vita.* – In the mid-course of our life. [Dante Alighieri, 1265–1321, *The Divine Comedy*, 'Inferno', i, 1]

3 So here I am, in the middle way, having had twenty years – / Twenty years largely wasted, the years of *l'entre deux guerres*. [T S Eliot, 1888–1965, *Four Quartets*, 'East Coker', V]

4 There is a compensation for being over forty . . . I now do my crossword puzzles in ink. [Cyril Fletcher, 1913– , in BBC radio programme *Does the Team Think?*]; see OPTIMISM, 22

5 A contemporary comforted me with the observation that it's nice, as one approaches fifty, to discover what one wants to be when one grows up. [George V Higgins, 1939–99, in *Guardian*, 17 June 1988]

6 The forties are the old age of youth and the fifties the youth of old age. [Edward Hoagland, 1932– , *Learning to Eat Soup*]

7 Nature is as wasteful of promising young men as she is of fish-spawn. It's not just getting them killed in wars: mere middle age snuffs out ten times more talent than ever wars and sudden death do. [Richard Hughes, 1900–1976, *The Fox in the Attic*, Bk I, Ch. 18]

8 I think middle age is the best time, if we can escape the fatty degeneration of the conscience which often sets in at about fifty. [W R Inge, 1860–1954; *Observer*, 'Sayings of the Week', 8 June 1930]

9 Middle-aged life is merry, and I love to lead it. [Ogden Nash, 1902–71, *Peekaboo, I Almost See You*]

10 At fifty, everyone has the face he deserves. [George Orwell, 1903–50, *Notebook*, 17 Apr. 1949]

11 A man not old, but mellow, like good wine. [Stephen Phillips, 1864–1915, *Ulysses*, III. ii]

12 When forty winters shall besiege thy brow, / And dig deep trenches in thy beauty's field. [William Shakespeare, 1564–1616, *Sonnets*, 2]

13 Every man over forty is a scoundrel. [George Bernard Shaw, 1856–1950, *Man and Superman*, 'Maxims for Revolutionists', Stray Sayings]

14 Life Begins at Forty. [Sophie Tucker, 1884–1966, title of song, written by Jack Yellen]

15 Every twenty years the middle-aged

celebrate the decade of their youth. [Gore Vidal, 1925– , in *Observer*, 27 Aug. 1989]

See also ADOLESCENCE, AGE, OLD AGE, YOUTH & AGE

MIDDLE CLASS

1 *Philistine* gives the notion of something particularly stiff-necked and perverse in the resistance to light and its children; and therein it specially suits our middle-class. [Matthew Arnold, 1822–88, *Culture and Anarchy*, Ch. 3]

2 He bade me observe it, and I should always find, that the calamities of life were shared among the upper and lower part of mankind; but that the middle station had the fewest disasters. [Daniel Defoe, 1661?–1731, *Robinson Crusoe*, Pt I]

3 What fools middle-class girls are to expect other people to respect the same gods as themselves and E. M. Forster. [Margaret Drabble, 1939– , *A Summer Bird-cage*, Ch. 11]

4 The bourgeois is consequently by nature a creature of weak impulses, anxious, fearful of giving himself away and easy to rule. Therefore, he has substituted majority for power, law for force, and the polling booth for responsibility. [Hermann Hesse, 1877–1962, *Steppenwolf*, 'Treatise on the Steppenwolf']

5 '*Bourgeois*,' I observed, 'is an epithet which the riff-raff apply to what is respectable, and the aristocracy to what is decent.' [Anthony Hope, 1863–1933, *The Dolly Dialogues*, 17]

6 The class in which one half wouldn't be seen dead with the other. [Anthony Jay, 1936– (of the middle class), quoted by Robert Robinson in *The Sunday Times Magazine*, 11 May 1980]

7 How beastly the bourgeois is especially the male of the species. [D H Lawrence, 1885–1930, *How Beastly the Bourgeois is*]

8 That is the worst thing about being a middle-class woman ... you have more knowledge of yourself and the world; you are equipped to make choices, but there are none left to make. [Alison Lurie, 1926– , *The War between the Tates*, 3]

9 We of the sinking middle class ... may sink without further struggles into the working class where we belong, and probably when we get there it will not be so dreadful as we feared, for, after all, we have nothing to lose but our aitches. [George Orwell, 1903–50, *The Road to Wigan Pier*, Ch. 13]

10 These modest yet proud middle-class people considered beauty above their means or below their condition; they allowed it to titled women and prostitutes. [Jean-Paul Sartre, 1905–80, *Words*, Pt 1]

11 The English and French bourgeoisie created a new society after their own image. The Germans came later, and they were compelled to live for a long time on the pale gruel of philosophy. [Leon Trotsky, 1874–1940, *History of the Russian Revolution*, Pt 1, Ch. 10]

See also ARISTOCRACY, CLASS, MASSES, SNOBS

MILLIONAIRES

1 All millionaires love a baked apple. [Ronald Firbank, 1886–1926, *Vainglory*, 13]

2 He was not the frock-coated and impressive type of millionaire which has become so frequent since the war. He was rather the 1910 model – a sort of cross between Henry VIII and 'our Mr Jones will be in Minneapolis on Friday'. [F Scott Fitzgerald, 1896–1940, *Notebooks*, 'H']

3 Paul Getty, who had always been vastly, immeasurably wealthy, and yet went about looking like a man who cannot quite remember whether he remembered to turn the gas off before leaving home. [Bernard Levin, 1928– , *The Pendulum Years*, Ch. 1]

4 Who wants to be a millionaire? I don't. [Cole Porter, 1891–1964, song: *Who Wants to be a Millionaire?*, in musical *High Society*]

5 I am a Millionaire. That is my religion. [George Bernard Shaw, 1856–1950, *Major Barbara*, II]

See also MONEY, RICH, WEALTH

MIND

1 My brain: it's my second favourite organ. [Woody Allen, 1935– , in film *Sleeper*, scripted with Marshall Brickman]

2 *Brain*, n. An apparatus with which we think that we think. [Ambrose Bierce, 1842–1914, *The Devil's Dictionary*]

3 If the cells and fibre in one human brain were all stretched out end to end, they would certainly reach to the moon and back. Yet the fact that they are not arranged end to end enabled man to go there himself. The astonishing tangle within our heads makes us what we are. [Colin Blakemore, 1944– (from BBC Reith Lectures), in *Listener*, 25 Nov. 1976]

4 His mind is open. Yes, it is so open that nothing is retained. Ideas simply pass through him. [F H Bradley, 1846–1924, *Aphorisms*, 59]

5 The march of the human mind is slow. [Edmund Burke, 1729–97, speech on conciliation with America, 22 Mar. 1775]

6 Of its own beauty is the mind diseased, / And fevers into false creation. [Lord Byron, 1788–1824, *Childe Harold's Pilgrimage*, IV, 122]

7 The object of opening the mind, as of opening the mouth, is to shut it again on something solid. [G K Chesterton, 1874–1936, quoted by Katharine Whitehorn in *Observer*, 28 Dec. 1986]

8 The empires of the future are the empires of the mind. [Winston Churchill, 1874–1965, speech at Harvard University, 16 Sept. 1943]

9 lady will you come with me into / the extremely little house of / my mind. [e e cummings, 1894–1962, *Collected Poems* (1938), 230]

10 A man should keep his little brain attic stocked with all the furniture that he is likely to use, and the rest he can put away in the lumber-room of his library, where he can get it if he wants it. [Arthur Conan Doyle, 1859–1930, *The Adventures of Sherlock Holmes*, 'Five Orange Pips']

11 My mind to me a kingdom is, / Such present joys therein I find, / That it excels all other bliss / That earth affords or grows by kind. [Edward Dyer, 1540–1607, *My Mind to Me a Kingdom is*]

12 The brain is a wonderful organ; it starts working the moment you get up in the morning and doesn't stop until you get into the office. [Robert Frost, 1874–1963; in *Executive's Quotation Book*, ed. James Charlton]

13 It is slavery to live in the mind unless it has become part of the body. [Kahlil Gibran, 1883–1931, *Spiritual Sayings*]

14 The remarkable thing about the human mind is its range of limitations. [Celia Green, 1935– , *The Decline and Fall of Science*, 'Aphorisms']

15 He had a mind like a beautiful Clapham Junction, through which lines slid off at every sort of tangent. [Jo Grimond, 1913–93 (of an Oxford friend killed in the war), contribution to book *My Oxford*]

16 On earth there is nothing great but man; in man there is nothing great but mind. [William Hamilton, 1788–1856, *Lectures on Metaphysics*]

17 There is an unseemly exposure of the mind, as well as of the body. [William Hazlitt, 1778–1830, *On Disagreeable People*]

18 O the mind, mind has mountains; cliffs of fall / Frightful, sheer, no-man-fathomed. Hold them cheap / May who ne'er hung there. [Gerard Manley Hopkins, 1844–89, *No Worst, There is None*]

19 Little minds are interested in the extraordinary; great minds in the commonplace. [Elbert Hubbard, 1856–1915; in *Roycroft Dictionary and Book of Epigrams*]

20 I think you will practically recognize the two types of mental make-up that I mean if I head the columns by the titles 'tender-minded' and 'tough-minded' respectively. [William James, 1842–1910, *Pragmatism*, Lecture 10]

21 A fellow who makes no figure in company, and has a mind as narrow as the neck of a vinegar cruet. [Dr Samuel Johnson, 1709–84, in James Boswell, *Tour of the Hebrides*, 30 Sept. 1773]

22 The pendulum of the mind oscillates between sense and nonsense, not between right and wrong. [C G Jung, 1875–1961, *Memories, Dreams, Reflections*, 5]

23 Four seasons fill the measure of the year; / There are four seasons in the mind of man. [John Keats, 1795–1821, sonnet: *The Human Seasons*]

24 The only means of strengthening one's intellect is to make up one's mind about nothing – to let the mind be a thoroughfare for all thoughts. [John Keats, 1795–1821, letter to G and G Keats, 17–27 Sept. 1819]

25 To make the mind an absolute ruler is as good as making a Cook's tourist-interpreter a king and a god, because he can speak several languages and make an Arab understand that an Englishman wants fish for supper. [D H Lawrence, 1885–1930, *Fantasia of the Unconscious*, Ch. 11]

26 The highest function of *mind* is its function of messenger. [D H Lawrence, 1885–1930, *Kangaroo*, Ch. 16]

27 So this gentleman said a girl with brains ought to do something else with them besides think. [Anita Loos, 1893–1981, *Gentlemen Prefer Blondes*, Ch. 1]

28 The mind, that ocean where each kind / Does straight its own resemblance find; / Yet it creates, transcending these, / Far other worlds, and other seas, / Annihilating all that's made / To a green thought in a green shade. [Andrew Marvell, 1621–78, *The Garden*, 41]

29 It's all in the mind, you know. [Spike Milligan, 1918– , running gag in BBC radio comedy series *The Goon Show*, 1950s]

30 I wrote somewhere once that the third-rate mind was only happy when it was thinking with the majority, the second-rate mind was only happy when it was thinking with the minority, and the first-rate mind was only happy when it was thinking. [A A Milne, 1882–1956, *War with Honour*]

31 A mind not to be changed by place or time. / The mind is its own place, and in itself / Can make a heav'n of hell, a hell of heav'n. [John Milton, 1608–74, *Paradise Lost*, Bk i, 253]

32 The mind's a razor / on the body's strop. [Paul Muldoon, 1951– , *Meeting the British*, 'The Soap-pig']

33 Do you think my mind is maturing late, / Or simply rotted early? [Ogden Nash, 1902–71, *Lines on Facing Forty*]

34 That's the classical mind at work, runs fine inside but looks dingy on the surface. [Robert M Pirsig, 1928– , *Zen and the Art of Motorcycle Maintenance*, Pt III, Ch. 25]

35 Grant but as many sorts of mind as moss. [Alexander Pope, 1688–1744, *Moral Essays*, Epistle I, 18]

36 Be to her virtues very kind; / Be to her faults a little blind; / Let all her ways be unconfined; / And clap your padlock – on her mind. [Matthew Prior, 1664–1721, *An English Padlock*]

37 The life which, of all the various lives we lead concurrently, is the most episodic, the most full of vicissitudes; I mean the life of the mind. [Marcel Proust, 1871–1922, *Remembrance of Things Past: Swann's Way*, 'Combray']

38 What a waste it is to lose one's mind – or not to have a mind. [Vice-President Daniel Quayle, 1947– (speech to United Negro College Fund, whose motto is 'A mind is a terrible thing to waste'), in *Observer*, 8 Oct. 1989]

39 As for the brain, it is all mystery and memory and electricity. [Richard Selzer, 1928– , *Confessions of a Knife*, 'Liver']

40 My mind is troubled, like a fountain stirred; / And I myself see not the bottom of it. [William Shakespeare, 1564–1616, *Troilus and Cressida*, III. iii. (314)]

41 The thought that my mind is really nothing but an empty sieve – often this, too, disconcerts me. [Logan Pearsall Smith, 1865–1946, *Trivia*, I, 'Dissatisfaction']

42 A short neck denotes a good mind ... You see, the messages go quicker to the brain because they've shorter to go. [Muriel Spark, 1918– , *The Ballad of Peckham Rye*, Ch. 7]

43 It is the mind that maketh good or ill, / That maketh wretch or happy, rich or poor. [Edmund Spenser, 1552?–99, *The Faerie Queene*, Bk vi, Canto 9, stanza 30]

44 Once we are destined to live out our lives in the prison of our mind, our one duty is to furnish it well. [Peter Ustinov, 1921– , *Dear Me*, Ch. 20]

45 The mind can also be an erogenous zone. [Raquel Welch, 1940– , in J R Colombo, *Colombo's Hollywood*]

46 Then, sir, you will turn it over once more in what you are pleased to call your mind. [Lord Westbury, 1800–1873, in T A Nash, *Life of Lord W*, Bk ii, Ch. 12]

47 Minds like beds always made up, / (more stony than a shore) / unwilling or unable. [William Carlos Williams, 1883–1963, *Patterson*, I, Preface]

48 Huge and mighty forms, that do not live / Like living men, moved slowly through the mind / By day, and were a trouble to my dreams. [William Wordsworth, 1770–1850, *The Prelude*, I, 398]

49 Bring the balloon of the mind / That bellies and drags in the wind / Into its narrow shed. [W B Yeats, 1865–1939, *The Balloon of the Mind*]

See also IDEAS, INTELLIGENCE, THINKING

MINORITY

1 I love small nations. I love small numbers. The world will be saved by the few. [André Gide, 1869–1951, in *The Times Higher Education Supplement*, 15 Jan. 1982]

2 The minority is always right. [Henrik Ibsen, 1828–1906, *An Enemy of the People*, IV]

3 Minorities are individuals or groups of individuals especially qualified. The masses are the collection of people not especially qualified. [José Ortega y Gasset, 1883–1955, *The Revolt of the Masses*, Ch. 1]

MIRACLES

1 Behold, the bush burned with fire, and the bush was not consumed. [Bible, OT, *Exodus* 3:2]

2 Rise, take up thy bed, and walk. [Bible, NT, *St John* 5:8]

3 It was a miracle of rare device, / A sunny pleasure-dome with caves of ice! [Samuel Taylor Coleridge, 1772–1834, *Kubla Khan*]

4 I do not think our successes can compete with those of Lourdes. There are so many more people who believe in the miracles of the Blessed Virgin than in the existence of the unconscious. [Sigmund Freud, 1856–1939, *New Introductory Lectures*, Lecture 34]

5 But for the miracles, I should consider Nero the ideal man. [Bishop Charles Gore, 1853–1932, attr.]

6 Picasso insisted everything was miraculous. It was miraculous, he said, 'that one did not melt in one's bath'. [Pablo Picasso, 1881–1973, attr. by Jean Cocteau]

7 They say miracles are past. [William Shakespeare, 1564–1616, *All's Well that Ends Well*, II. iii. 1]

MISANTHROPY

1 I want to be understood; to be quite frank, the friend of the human race is not in the least my role. [Molière, 1622–73, *Le Misanthrope*, I. i]

2 I cannot but conclude the bulk of your natives to be the most pernicious race of little odious vermin that nature ever suffered to crawl upon the surface of the earth. [Jonathan Swift, 1677–1745, *Gulliver's Travels*, 'Voyage to Brobdingnag', Ch. 6]

3 Principally I hate and detest that animal called man; although I heartily love John, Peter, Thomas, and so forth. [Jonathan Swift, 1677–1745, letter to Pope, 29 Sept. 1725]

See also HATE, HUMAN BEINGS, HUMAN NATURE

MISFORTUNES

1 *Calamity*, n. Calamities are of two kinds: misfortune to ourselves, and good fortune to others. [Ambrose Bierce, 1842–1914, *The Devil's Dictionary*]

2 For of fortunes sharp adversitee / The worst kinde of infortune is this, / A man to have ben in prosperitee, / And it remembren, whan it passed is. [Geoffrey Chaucer, 1340?–1400, *Troilus and Criseyde*, iii, 1625]

3 Some people are born in circumstances which resemble being saddled in the enclosure at Epsom when the race is at Ripon. [Tom Crabtree, ?1924–   , in *Guardian*, 8 Sept. 1977]

4 'I am a lone lorn creetur',' were Mrs Gummidge's words ... 'and everythink goes contrairy with me.' [Charles Dickens, 1812–70, *David Copperfield*, Ch. 3]

5 One is never as fortunate or as unfortunate as one imagines. [Duc de La Rochefoucauld, 1613–80, *Maxims*, 49]

6 The misfortunes hardest to bear are those which never come. [James Russell Lowell, 1819–91, speech in Birmingham, England, 6 Oct. 1884]

7 There's one thing to be said for inviting trouble: it generally accepts. [Mae Maloo, in *Reader's Digest*, Sept. 1976]

8 there is always / a comforting thought / in time of trouble when / it is not our trouble [Don Marquis, 1878–1937, *archy does his part*, 'comforting thoughts']

9 now and then / there is a person born / who is so unlucky / that he runs into accidents / which started out to happen / to somebody else [Don Marquis, 1878–1937, *archys life of mehitabel*, XLI, 'archy says']

10 I never knew any man in my life who could not bear another's misfortunes perfectly like a Christian. [Alexander Pope, 1688–1744, *Thoughts on Various Subjects*]

11 Bad luck was always / As welcome as / A sandy foreskin. [Oliver Reynolds, 1957– , *Acholba*]

12 Misery acquaints a man with strange bedfellows. [William Shakespeare, 1564–1616, *The Tempest*, II. ii. (42)]

13 still small voice spake unto me, / 'Thou art so full of misery, / Were it not better not to be?' [Alfred, Lord Tennyson, 1809–92, *The Two Voices*, 1]

See also LUCK, HAPPINESS

MISTAKES

1 If you board the wrong train, it is no use running along the corridor in the other direction. [Dietrich Bonhoeffer, 1906–45, *The Way to Freedom*]

2 It is worse than a crime, it is a blunder. [Boulay de la Meurthe, 1761–1840, comment on the execution of the Duc d'Enghien, 21 Mar. 1804. Also attr. to Talleyrand]

3 A man looking at a hippopotamus may sometimes be tempted to regard a hippopotamus as an enormous mistake; but he is also bound to confess that a fortunate inferiority prevents him personally from making such mistakes. [G K Chesterton, 1874–1936, *Charles Dickens*, 10]

4 There are so many kinds of awful men – / One can't avoid them all. She often said / She'd never make the same mistake again: / She always made a new mistake instead. [Wendy Cope, 1945– , *Rondeau Redoublé*]

5 I beseech you, in the bowels of Christ, think it possible you may be mistaken. [Oliver Cromwell, 1599–1658, letter to the Church of Scotland, 3 Aug. 1650]

6 As she frequently remarked when she made any such mistake, it would be all the same a hundred years hence. [Charles Dickens, 1812–70, *Nicholas Nickleby*, Ch. 9]

7 *Es irrt der Mensch, so lang er strebt.* – Man errs so long as he strives. [Johann Wolfgang von Goethe, 1749–1832, *Faust*, Pt I, 'Prologue in Heaven']

8 Error of opinion may be tolerated where reason is left free to combat it. [Thomas Jefferson, 1743–1826, first inaugural address, 4 Mar. 1801]

9 I make mistakes; I'll be the second to admit it. [Jean Kerr, 1923– , *The Snake Has All the Lines*, 'I Was a Sand Crab']

10 All men are liable to error; and most men are, in many points, by passion or interest, under temptation to it. [John Locke, 1632–1704, *Essay on the Human Understanding*, Ch. 20, 17]

11 The man who makes no mistakes does not usually make anything. [E J Phelps, 1822–1900, speech at Mansion House, 24 Jan. 1899]

12 If this be error, and upon me proved, / I never writ, nor no man ever loved. [William Shakespeare, 1564–1616, *Sonnets*, 116]

13 We often discover what *will* do, by finding out what will not do; and probably he who never made a mistake never made a discovery. [Samuel Smiles, 1812–1904, *Self-Help*, Ch. 11]

See also FAILURE, FAULTS

MODERATION

1 Nothing to excess. [anon. Greek written up in the temple at Delphi, according to Plato's *Protagoras*]

2 I know that many have been taught to think that moderation, in a case like this, is a sort of treason. [Edmund Burke, 1729–97, *Letter to the Sheriffs of Bristol*]

3 By God, Mr Chairman, at this moment I stand astonished at my own moderation! [Robert Clive, 1725–74, reply during Parliamentary inquiry, March 1773]

4 The innocent word 'Trimmer' signifies no more than this, that if men are together in a boat, and one part of the company would weigh it down on one side, another would make it lean as much to the contrary. [Marquis of Halifax, 1663–95, *Character of a Trimmer*, Preface]

5 Thou shalt not carry moderation unto excess. [Arthur Koestler, 1905–83 (last entry in his final notebook), in George Mikes, *A K: The Story of a Friendship*]

See also EXAGGERATION

MODERN AGE

1 In the space age the most important space is between the ears. [Anne Armstrong, 1927– , in *Guardian*, 30 Jan. 1974]

2 This strange disease of modern life. [Matthew Arnold, 1822–88, *The Scholar-Gypsy*, 203]

3 There is only one way left to escape the alienation of present day society: *to retreat ahead of it.* [Roland Barthes, 1915–80, *Mythologies, The Pleasure of the Text*, 'Modern']

4 The modern world seems to have no notion of preserving different things side by side, of allowing its proper and proportionate place to each, of saving the whole varied heritage of culture. It has no notion except that of simplifying something by destroying nearly everything. [G K Chesterton, 1874–1936, *All I Survey*, 'On Love']

5 *O tempora, O mores!* – What times! What habits! [Cicero, 106–43 BC, *In Catilinam*, I, I]

6 The modern world lacks not only hiding-places, but certainties. [Salman Rushdie, 1937– , 'Outside the Whale', *Granta*, 11]

See also INNOVATION, TWENTIETH CENTURY

MODESTY

1 All modesty is false, otherwise it's not modesty. [Alan Bennett, 1934– , *Kafka's Dick*, I]

2 She just wore / Enough for modesty – no more. [R W Buchanan, 1841–1901, *White Rose and Red*, I. v. 60]

3 And of his port as meke as is a mayde. [Geoffrey Chaucer, 1340?–1400, *Canterbury Tales*, 'Prologue', 69]

4 A womman cast hir shame away, / Whan she cast of her smok. [Geoffrey Chaucer, 1340?–1400, *Canterbury Tales*, 'The Wife of Bath's Prologue', 782]

5 Shyness is just egoism out of its depth. [Penelope Keith, 1940– ; *Observer*, 'Sayings of the Week', 3 July 1988]

6 Be plain in dress, and sober in your diet; / In short, my deary! kiss me, and be quiet. [Lady Mary Wortley Montagu, 1689–1762, *Summary of Lord Lyttelton's Advice*]

7 The daughter-in-law of Pythagoras said that a woman who goes to bed with a man ought to lay aside her modesty with her skirt, and put it on again with her petticoat. [Michel de Montaigne, 1533–92, *Essays*, I, 21]

8 I'm very modest. I tend to hide my light under a peck. [Ken Mullen, 1943– , in conversation]

9 If you want people to think well of you, do not speak well of yourself. [Blaise Pascal, 1623–62, *Pensées*, I, 44]

10 Has she no faults then (Envy says), Sir? / Yes she has one, I must aver; / When all the world conspires to praise her, / The woman's deaf and does not hear. [Alexander Pope, 1688–1744, *On a Certain Lady at Court*]

11 The nuns who never take a bath without wearing a bathrobe all the time. When asked why, since no man can see them, they reply 'Oh, but you forget the good God.' [Bertrand Russell, 1872–1970, *The Basic Writings*, Pt II, Ch. 7]

12 A maiden never bold; / Of spirit so still and quiet, that her motion / Blushed at herself. [William Shakespeare, 1564–1616, *Othello*, I. iii. 94]

See also ARROGANCE, HUMILITY, PRIDE

MONARCHY, see KINGS, etc.

MONEY

1 Money is better than poverty, if only for financial reasons. [Woody Allen, 1935– , *Without Feathers*, 'The Early Essays']

2 Business, you know, may bring money, but friendship hardly ever does. [Jane Austen, 1775–1817, *Emma*, 34]

3 Money is like muck, not good except it be spread. [Francis Bacon, 1561–1626, *Essays*, 15, 'Of Seditions and Troubles']

4 If you would know what the Lord God thinks of money, you have only to look at those to whom He gives it. [Maurice Baring, 1874–1945, quoted by Dorothy Parker in *Writers at Work*, ed. Malcolm Cowley, First Series]

5 Money speaks sense in a language all nations understand. [Aphra Behn, 1640–89, *The Rover*, Pt Two, III. i]

6 I'm tired of Love: I'm still more tired of Rhyme. / But Money gives me pleasure all the time. [Hilaire Belloc, 1870–1953, 'Fatigue']

7 Wine maketh merry: but money answereth all things. [Bible, OT, *Ecclesiastes* 10:19]

8 The love of money is the root of all evil. [Bible, NT, *1 Timothy* 6:10]

9 It has been said that the love of money is the

root of all evil. The want of money is so quite as truly. [Samuel Butler, 1835–1902, *Erewhon*, Ch. 20]

10 Doctor – I keep getting these pains in my wallet. [Mel Calman, 1931–94, cartoon caption in *But It's My Turn to Leave You* . . .]

11 In epochs when cash payment has become the sole nexus of man to man. [Thomas Carlyle, 1795–1881, *Critical and Miscellaneous Essays*, 6]

12 I knew once a very covetous, sordid fellow [perhaps William Lowndes], who used to say, 'Take care of the pence, for the pounds will take care of themselves.' [Earl of Chesterfield, 1694–1773, letter to his son, 6 Nov. 1747]

13 To be clever enough to get all that money, one must be stupid enough to want it. [G K Chesterton, 1874–1936, *The Wisdom of Father Brown*, 'Paradise of Thieves']

14 How pleasant it is to have money, heigh-ho! / How pleasant it is to have money. [Arthur Hugh Clough, 1819–61, *Dipsychus*, I, ii]

15 This only grant me, that my means may lie / Too low for envy, for contempt too high. [Abraham Cowley, 1618–67, *Of Myself*]

16 The Best Things in Life are Free. ['Buddy' de Sylva, 1895–1950, and Lew Brown, 1893–1958, title of song, 1927]

17 Annual income twenty pounds, annual expenditure nineteen nineteen six, result happiness. Annual income twenty pounds, annual expenditure twenty pounds ought and six, result misery. [(Mr Micawber) Charles Dickens, 1812–70, *David Copperfield*, Ch. 12]

18 Money doesn't talk, it swears. [Bob Dylan, 1941– , song: *It's Alright, Ma (I'm Only Bleeding)*]

19 Ah, take the Cash, and let the Credit go, / Nor heed the rumble of a distant Drum! [Edward Fitzgerald, 1809–83, *The Rubá'iyát of Omar Khayyám*, Edn 1, 13]

20 Men have a touchstone whereby to try gold, but gold is the touchstone whereby to try men. [Thomas Fuller, 1608–61, *The Holy State*, Bk iv, Ch. 7]

21 Money is a singular thing. It ranks with love as man's greatest source of joy. And with death as his greatest source of anxiety. Money differs from an automobile, a mistress or cancer in being equally important to those who have it and those who do not. [J K Galbraith, 1908– , *The Age of Uncertainty*, TV broadcast version, 6th programme]

22 We're overpaying him but he's worth it. [Samuel Goldwyn, 1882–1974; attr. in A K Adams, *Cassell's Book of Humorous Quotations*]

23 Whenever he saw a dollar in another man's hands he took it as a personal grudge, if he couldn't take it any other way. [O Henry, 1862–1910, *The Octopus Marooned*]

24 A bank is a place that will lend you money if you can prove you don't need it. [Bob Hope, 1903– , in Alan Harrington, *Life in the Crystal Palace*, 'The Tyranny of Forms']

25 By right means, if you can, but by any means make money. [Horace, 65–8 BC, *Epistles*, I, i, 66]

26 We all know how the size of sums of money appears to vary in a remarkable way according as they are being paid in or paid out. [Julian Huxley, 1887–1975, *Essays of a Biologist*, Ch. 5]

27 There are few ways in which a man can be more innocently employed than in getting money. [(To William Strahan) Dr Samuel Johnson, 1709–84, in James Boswell, *Life of J*, 27 Mar. 1775]

28 The importance of money essentially flows from its being a link between the present and the future. [John Maynard Keynes, 1883–1946, *The General Theory of Employment*, Bk v, Ch. 21]

29 It is better that a man should tyrannize over his bank balance than over his fellow citizens. [John Maynard Keynes, 1883–1946, *The General Theory of Employment*, Bk vi, Ch. 24]

30 Clearly money has something to do with life / – In fact, they've a lot in common, if you enquire: / You can't put off being young until you retire. [Philip Larkin, 1922–85, *Money*]

31 For I don't care too much for money, / For money can't buy me love. [John Lennon, 1940–80, and Paul McCartney, 1942– , song: *Can't Buy Me Love*]

32 We have heard it said that five per cent is the natural interest of money. [Lord Macaulay, 1800–1859, *Literary Essays*, 'Southey's Colloquies']

33 What's a thousand dollars? Mere chicken feed. A poultry matter. [Groucho Marx, 1895–1977, in film *The Cocoanuts*, script by George S Kaufman and M Ryskind]

34 I have enough money to last me the rest of my life unless I buy something. [Jackie Mason, 1931– , *Jackie Mason's America*]

35 Money is like a sixth sense, without which you cannot make a complete use of the other five. [W Somerset Maugham, 1874–1965, *Of Human Bondage*, Ch. 51]

36 The chief value of money lies in the fact that one lives in a world in which it is over-estimated. [H L Mencken, 1880–1956, *Chrestomathy*, 30, 'The Mind of Man']

37 Money can't buy friends, but you can get a better class of enemy. [Spike Milligan, 1918– , *Puckoon*, Ch. 6]

38 He must have killed a lot of men to have made so much money. [(Of doctor) Molière, 1622–73, *Le Malade imaginaire*, I. v]

39 Salary is no object. I only want to keep body and soul apart. [(On discussing a job with a prospective employer) Dorothy Parker, 1893–1967, in R E Drennan, *Wit's End*]

40 Happy the man, who, void of cares and strife, / In silken or in leathern purse retains / A Splendid Shilling. [John Philips, 1676–1709, *The Splendid Shilling*, 1]

41 Never invest in anything that eats while you sleep. [Francis Player (advice to sons, Gary Player and his brother), in *Observer*, 24 Feb. 1991]; see 46

42 Said Paterson: / Hath benefit of interest in all / the moneys which it, the bank, creates out of / nothing. [Ezra Pound, 1885–1972, *Cantos*, xlvi]

43 The strength of a war waged without monetary reserves is as fleeting as a breath. Money is the sinews of battle. [François Rabelais, *c.*1492–1553, *Gargantua*, Ch. 46]

44 So you think that money is the root of all evil. Have you ever asked what is the root of money? [Ayn Rand, 1905–82; in *Executive's Quotation Book*, ed. James Charlton]

45 Money is good for bribing yourself through the inconveniences of life. [Gottfried Reinhardt, 1913–94, in Lillian Ross, *Picture*, 'Looks Like We're Still in Business']

46 Never invest your money in anything that eats or needs repainting. [Billy Rose, 1899–1996, in *New York Post*, 1957]; see 41

47 My boy ... always try to rub up against money, for if you rub up against money long enough, some of it may rub off on you. [Damon Runyon, 1884–1946, *Furthermore*, 'A Very Honourable Guy']

48 Finance is the art of passing currency from hand to hand until it finally disappears. [Robert W Sarnoff, 1918– ; in *Executive's Quotation Book*, ed. James Charlton]

49 I can get no remedy against this consumption of the purse: borrowing only lingers and lingers it out, but the disease is incurable. [William Shakespeare, 1564–1616, *2 Henry IV*, I. ii. (268)]

50 Remuneration! O! that's the Latin word for three farthings. [*Love's Labour's Lost*, III. i. (143)]

51 You take my house when you do take the prop / That doth sustain my house; you take my life / When you do take the means whereby I live. [*The Merchant of Venice*, IV. i. (376)]

52 Nothing comes amiss, so money comes withal. [*The Taming of the Shrew*, I. ii. (82)]

53 Nothing links man to man like the frequent passage from hand to hand of cash. [Walter Sickert, 1860–1942, in *New Age*, 28 July 1910]

54 Solvency is entirely a matter of temperament and not of income. [Logan Pearsall Smith, 1865–1946, *Afterthoughts*, 1]

55 But the jingling of the guinea helps the hurt that Honour feels. [Alfred, Lord Tennyson, 1809–92, *Locksley Hall*, 105]

56 Doänt thou marry for munny, but goä wheer munny is! [Alfred, Lord Tennyson, 1809–92, *Northern Farmer; New Style*, 5]

57 Money is used to pay bills and credit is used to delay paying them. [Alan Walters, 1926– ; *Observer*, 'Sayings of the Week', 26 Mar. 1989]

58 Algebra and money are essentially levellers; the first intellectually, the second effectively. [Simone Weil, 1909–43, *Gravity and Grace*, 'Algebra']

59 You can't have money like that and not swell out. [H G Wells, 1866–1946, *Kipps*, Bk II, Ch. 4, ii]

60 Paying for what she doesn't get rankles so dreadfully with Louisa; I can't make her see that it's one of the preliminary steps to getting what you haven't paid for. [Edith Wharton, 1862–1937, *The House of Mirth*, Bk II, Ch. 2]

61 You can be young without money but you

can't be old without it. [Tennessee Williams, 1911–83, *Cat on a Hot Tin Roof*, I]

62 All these financiers, all the little gnomes of Zürich and the other financial centres, about whom we keep on hearing. [Harold Wilson, 1916–95, speech in House of Commons, 12 Nov. 1956]

63 It does not mean, of course, that the pound here in Britain in your pocket or purse or in your bank has been devalued. [Harold Wilson, 1916–95, in prime ministerial broadcast on TV announcing devaluation, 19 Nov. 1967]

See also BUSINESS, GREED, MEANNESS, POVERTY, RICH, THRIFT, WEALTH

MARILYN MONROE

1 Lord, whoever it was that she was going to call up, / she did not call (perhaps it was no one, / perhaps it was Somebody whose name is not in the Los Angeles telephone directory) / answer Thou the telephone! [Ernesto Cardenal, 1925– , *Oración por Marilyn Monroe*]

2 Kissing Marilyn [Monroe] was like kissing Hitler – sure I said that. It wasn't *that* bad. But you can see through that line: there was this woman, beautifully endowed, treating all men like shit. Why did I have to take that? [Tony Curtis, 1925– , in *Game*, Sept. 1975]

3 She was good at playing abstract confusion in the same way that a midget is good at being short. [Clive James, 1939– , *Visions before Midnight*]

4 Goodbye Norma Jean / Though I never knew you at all / You had the grace to hold yourself / While those around you crawled. / They crawled out of the woodwork / And they whispered into your brain / Set you on the treadmill / And made you change your name. [Bernie Taupin, 1950– , song: *Candle in the Wind*, music by Elton John. The lyric was adapted and sung by Elton John to refer to Diana, Princess of Wales at her funeral on 6 Sept. 1997]

See also FILM, FILM STARS, HOLLYWOOD, SHOW BUSINESS

THE MONTHS [in calendar order]

1 Thirty days hath September, / April, June, and November; / All the rest have thirty-one, / Excepting February alone, / And that has twenty-eight days clear / And twenty-nine in each leap-year. [Richard Grafton, *c*.1513–72, *Abridgement of the Chronicles of England*, Introduction (1570)]

2 Snowy, Flowy, Blowy, / Showery, Flowery, Bowery, / Hoppy, Croppy, Droppy, / Breezy, Sneezy, Freezy. [George Ellis, 1753–1815, *The Twelve Months*]

3 February, fill the dyke / With what thou dost like. [Thomas Tusser, 1524?–80, *Five Hundred Points of Good Husbandry*, 'February's Husbandry']

4 Oh, to be in England, / Now that April's there. [Robert Browning, 1812–89, *Home-Thoughts from Abroad*]

5 Whan that Aprille with his shoures soote / The droghte of March hath perced to the roote. [Geoffrey Chaucer, 1340?–1400, *Canterbury Tales*, 'Prologue', 1]

6 April is the cruellest month, breeding / Lilacs out of the dead land. [T S Eliot, 1888–1965, *The Waste Land*, 1]

7 When well-apparelled April on the heel / Of limping Winter treads. [William Shakespeare, 1564–1616, *Romeo and Juliet*, I. ii. 27]

8 From you have I been absent in the spring, / When proud-pied April, dressed in all his trim, / Hath put a spirit of youth in every thing. [*Sonnets*, 98]

9 Sweet April showers / Do spring May flowers. [Thomas Tusser, 1524?–80, *Five Hundred Points of Good Husbandry*, 'April's Husbandry']

10 April, April, / Laugh thy girlish laughter; / Then, the moment after, / Weep thy girlish tears! [William Watson, 1858–1935, *April*]

11 But the merriest month in all the year / Is the merry month of May. [anon. ballad *Robin Hood*]

12 Whan that the month of May / Is comen, and that I here the foules singe, / And that the floures ginnen for to springe, / Farwel my book and my devocioun! [Geoffrey Chaucer, 1340?–1400, *The Legend of Good Women*, Prologue, 36 (second version)]

13 The sun is set, the spring is gone – / We frolic while 'tis May. [Thomas Gray, 1716–71, *Ode on the Spring*]

14 The month of May was come, when every lusty heart beginneth to blossom, and to bring forth fruit. [Thomas Malory, d.1471, *Morte d'Arthur*, Bk xviii, Ch. 25]

15 June is Bustin' Out All Over. [Oscar Hammerstein II, 1895–1960, title of song in musical *Carousel*, music by Richard Rodgers]

16 August for the people and their favourite islands. / Daily the steamers sidle up to meet / The effusive welcome of the pier. [W H Auden, 1907–73, *August for the People*]

17 Since golden October declined into sombre November / And the apples were gathered and stored, and the land became brown sharp points of death in a waste of water and mud. [T S Eliot, 1888–1965, *Murder in the Cathedral*, I]

18 The skies they were ashen and sober; / The leaves they were crispèd and sere – / The leaves they were withering and sere; / It was night in the lonesome October / Of my most immemorial year. [Edgar Allan Poe, 1809–49, *Ulalume*]

19 No shade, no shine, no butterflies, no bees, / No fruits, no flowers, no leaves, no birds, – November! [Thomas Hood, 1799–1845, *No!*]

20 November's sky is chill and drear, / November's leaf is red and sear. [Sir Walter Scott, 1771–1832, *Marmion*, I, Introduction]

See also DAYS, SEASONS, TIME

THE MOON

1 That's one small step for [a] man. One giant leap for mankind. [Neil Armstrong, 1930– , on landing on the moon, 20 July 1969. In the transcript the word 'a' is inaudible]

2 Till clomb above the eastern bar / The hornèd moon, with one bright star / Within the nether tip. [Samuel Taylor Coleridge, 1772–1834, *The Ancient Mariner*, Pt III]

3 who knows if the moon's / a balloon, coming out of a keen city / in the sky – filled with pretty people? [e e cummings, 1894–1962, *Seven Poems*, VII]

4 Slowly, silently, now the moon / Walks the night in her silver shoon. [Walter de la Mare, 1873–1956, *Silver*]

5 So sicken waning moons too near the sun, / And blunt their crescents on the edge of day. [John Dryden, 1631–1700, *Annus Mirabilis*, 125]

6 O the moon shone bright on Mrs Porter / And on her daughter / They wash their feet in soda water. [T S Eliot, 1888–1965, *The Waste Land*, 199]

7 Ah, Moon of my Delight who know'st no wane, / The Moon of Heav'n is rising once again: / How oft hereafter rising shall she look; / Through this same Garden after me – in vain! [Edward Fitzgerald, 1809–83, *The Rubá'iyát of Omar Khayyám*, Edn 1, 74]

8 Part of the moon was falling down the west / Dragging the whole sky with it to the hills. [Robert Frost, 1874–1963, *The Death of the Hired Man*]

9 The moon is nothing / But a circumambulatory aphrodisiac / Divinely subsidized to provoke the world / Into a rising birth-rate. [Christopher Fry, 1907– , *The Lady's Not for Burning*, III]

10 Say, it's only a paper moon, / Sailing over a cardboard sea. ['Yip' Harburg, 1898–1981, song: *Paper Moon*, in musical *Take a Chance*]

11 'What do you think of it, Moon, / As you go? / Is life much or no?' / 'O, I think of it, often think of it / As a show / God ought surely to shut up soon, / As I go.' [Thomas Hardy, 1840–1928, *To the Moon*]

12 I walked abroad, / And saw the ruddy moon lean over a hedge / Like a red-faced farmer. / I did not stop to speak, but nodded, / And round about were the wistful stars / With white faces like town children. [T E Hulme, 1883–1917, *Autumn*]

13 *Cuando sale la luna / de cien rostros iguales, / la moneda de plata / solloza en el bolsillo.* – When the moon of a hundred identical faces comes out, the silver coins sob in the pocket. [Federico García Lorca, 1899–1936, *La luna asoma*]

14 The dews of summer night did fall, / The moon, sweet regent of the sky, / Silvered the walls of Cumnor Hall, / And many an oak that grew thereby. [William Mickle, 1735–88, *Cumnor Hall*]

15 To behold the wandering moon, / Riding near her highest noon, / Like one that had been led astray / Through the heav'n's wide pathless way; / And oft, as if her head she bowed, / Stooping through a fleecy cloud. [John Milton, 1608–74, *Il Penseroso*, 67]

16 This is the greatest week in the history of the world since the creation. [(Of man's first moon-landing) President Nixon, 1913–94, said on board the *Hornet*, 24 July 1969]

17 Ill met by moonlight, proud Titania. [William Shakespeare, 1564–1616, *A Midsummer Night's Dream*, II. i. 60]

18 O! swear not by the moon, the inconstant moon, / that monthly changes in her circled orb, / Lest that thy love prove likewise variable. [*Romeo and Juliet*, II. ii. 109]

19 Art thou pale for weariness / Of climbing heaven and gazing on the earth, / Wandering companionless / Among the stars that have a different birth, – / And ever changing, like a joyless eye / That finds no object worth its constancy? [P B Shelley, 1792–1822, *To the Moon*]

20 And like a dying lady, lean and pale, / Who totters forth, wrapped in a gauzy veil, / Out of her chamber, led by the insane / And feeble wanderings of her fading brain, / The moon arose up in the murky east, / A white and shapeless mass – [P B Shelley, 1792–1822, *The Waning Moon*]

21 With how sad steps, O Moon, thou climb'st the skies! / How silently, and with how wan a face! / What! may it be that even in heavenly place / That busy archer his sharp arrows tries? [Sir Philip Sidney, 1554–86, *Astrophel and Stella*, Sonnet 31]

22 Only the lucid friend to aerial raiders / The brilliant pilot moon, stares down / Upon this plain she makes a shining bone. [Stephen Spender, 1909–95, *Two Armies*]

23 I had had an affair with the moon, in which there was neither sin nor shame. [Laurence Sterne, 1713–68, *A Sentimental Journey*, 'The Monk']

24 The new moon hangs like an ivory bugle / In the naked frosty blue. [Edward Thomas, 1878–1917, *The Penny Whistle*]

25 Small circles glittering idly in the moon, / Until they melted all into one track / Of sparkling light. [William Wordsworth, 1770–1850, *The Prelude*, I, 365]

See also ASTROLOGY, ASTRONOMY, STARS, SUN

MORALS & MORALITY

1 No morality can be founded on authority, even if the authority were divine. [A J Ayer, 1910–89, *Essay on Humanism*]

2 Grub first, then ethics. [Bertolt Brecht, 1898–1956, *The Threepenny Opera*, II. i]

3 A moral (like all morals) melancholy. [Lord Byron, 1788–1824, *Don Juan*, V, 63]

4 Everything's got a moral, if only you can find it. [Lewis Carroll, 1832–98, *Alice in Wonderland*, Ch. 9]

5 The quality of moral behaviour varies in inverse ratio to the number of human beings involved. [Aldous Huxley, 1894–1963, *Grey Eminence*, Ch. 10]

6 Two things fill my mind with ever-increasing wonder and awe, the more often and the more intensely the reflection dwells on them: the starry heavens above me and the moral law within me. [Immanuel Kant, 1724–1804, *Critique of Pure Reason*, conclusion]

7 Morality which is based on ideas, or on an ideal, is an unmitigated evil. [D H Lawrence, 1885–1930, *Fantasia of the Unconscious*, Ch. 7]

8 Leavis demands moral earnestness; I prefer morality . . . I mean I'd sooner live among people who don't cheat at cards than among people who are earnest about not cheating at cards. [C S Lewis, 1898–1963, in Brian Aldiss and Kingsley Amis, *Spectrum IV*]

9 We know no spectacle so ridiculous as the British public in one of its periodical fits of morality. [Lord Macaulay, 1800–1859, *Literary Essays*, 'Moore's Life of Byron']

10 I like a moral issue so much more than a real issue. [Elaine May, 1932– , quoted by Gore Vidal in *New Statesman*, 4 May 1973]

11 Morality in Europe today is animal-morality. [Friedrich Nietzsche, 1844–1900, *Beyond Good and Evil*, Pt 5, sect. 202]

12 One becomes moral as soon as one is unhappy. [Marcel Proust, 1871–1922, *Remembrance of Things Past: Within a Budding Grove*, 'Madame Swann at Home']

13 I wouldn't make the slightest concession for moral leadership. It's much overrated. [Dean Rusk, 1909–94 (said in 1962), in D Halberstam, *The Best and the Brightest*, Ch. 16]

14 Man is not a solitary animal, and so long as social life survives, self-realization cannot be the supreme principle of ethics. [Bertrand Russell, 1872–1970, *A History of Western Philosophy*, 'Romanticism']

15 Without doubt the greatest injury ... was done by basing morals on myth, for sooner or later myth is recognized for what it is, and disappears. Then morality loses the foundation on which it has been built. [Herbert Samuel, 1870–1963, Romanes Lecture, 1947]

16 The so-called new morality is too often the old immorality condoned. [Hartley Shawcross, 1902– , *Observer*, 'Sayings of the Week', 17 Nov. 1963]

17 Personal moral reliability was crucial to business success [in the early nineteenth century]. The warm hassock in the numbered pew and the scrubbed doorstep to the weeded garden were the credit cards of yesterday. [Paul Thompson, 1935– , in *New Society*, 15 May 1987]

18 He [John Middleton Murry] was the type of man who is always trying to live beyond his moral means. [Philip Toynbee, 1916–81, in *Observer*, 12 Jan. 1975]

19 Ethics does not treat of the world. Ethics must be a condition of the world, like logic. [Ludwig Wittgenstein, 1889–1951, in W H Auden, *A Certain World*, 'Hell']

See also BEHAVIOUR, GOOD & EVIL, PUNISHMENTS

MORNING, see DAWN

MORTALITY

1 Who then to frail mortality shall trust, / But limns the water, or but writes in dust. [Francis Bacon, 1561–1626, *The World*]

2 Mortality, behold and fear! / What a change of flesh is here! [Francis Beaumont, 1584–1616, *On the Tombs in Westminster Abbey*]

3 Or ever the silver cord be loosed, or the golden bowl be broken, or the pitcher be broken at the fountain, or the wheel broken at the cistern. Then shall the dust return to the earth as it was: and the spirit shall return unto God who gave it. [Bible, OT, *Ecclesiastes* 12:6]

4 For dust thou art, and unto dust shalt thou return. [Bible, OT, *Genesis* 3:19]

5 Old mortality, the ruins of forgotten times. [Sir Thomas Browne, 1605–82, *Urn Burial*, Preface]

6 Time goes, you say? Ah, no! / Alas, Time stays, *we* go. [Austin Dobson, 1840–1921, *The Paradox of Time*]

7 Can storied urn or animated bust / Back to its mansion call the fleeting breath? / Can honour's voice provoke the silent dust, / Or flattery soothe the dull cold ear of death? [Thomas Gray, 1716–71, *Elegy Written in a Country Churchyard*, 11]

8 And a man who lay with a beast, said the Lord, would surely die. And if he doesn't lie with a beast, I would have countered, he won't die? [Joseph Heller, 1923–99, *God Knows*, Ch. 2]

9 Mortality / Weighs heavily on me like unwilling sleep. [John Keats, 1795–1821, sonnet: *On Seeing the Elgin Marbles*]

10 A heap of dust alone remains of thee; / 'Tis all thou art, and all the proud shall be! [Alexander Pope, 1688–1744, *Elegy to the Memory of an Unfortunate Lady*, 73]

11 We all, we're the one animal that knows that we're going to die, and yet we carry on paying our mortgages, doing our jobs, moving about, behaving as though there's eternity in a sense. And we forget or tend to forget that life can only be defined in the present tense, it is *is* and it is *now* only. I mean, as much as we would like to call back yesterday and indeed yearn to, and ache to sometimes, we can't, it's in us but we can't actually, it's not there in front of us. [Dennis Potter, 1935–94, *Seeing the Blossom*, an interview with Melvyn Bragg, TV Channel 4, April 1994]

12 Fear no more the heat o' the sun, / Nor the furious winter's rages; / Thou thy worldly task hast done, / Home art gone and ta'en thy wages: / Golden lads and girls all must: / As chimney-sweepers, come to dust. [William Shakespeare, 1564–1616, *Cymbeline*, IV. ii. 258]

13 All that live must die, / Passing through nature to eternity. [*Hamlet*, I. ii. 72]

14 A man may fish with the worm that hath eat of a king, and eat of the fish that hath fed of that worm. [*Hamlet*, IV. iii. (29)]

15 Imperious Caesar, dead and turned to clay, / Might stop a hole to keep the wind away. [*Hamlet*, IV. vii. (235)]

16 When that this body did contain a spirit, / A kingdom for it was too small a bound; / But now, two paces of the vilest earth / Is room enough:

this earth, that bears thee dead, / Bears not alive so stout a gentleman. [*1 Henry IV*, V. iv. (88)]

17 GLOUC.: O! Let me kiss that hand!
LEAR: Let me wipe it first, it smells of mortality. [*King Lear*, IV. vi. (136)]

18 There's nothing serious in mortality. / All is but toys; renown and grace is dead, / The wine of life is drawn, and the mere lees / Is left this vault to brag of. [*Macbeth*, II. iii. (100)]

19 Since brass, nor stone, nor earth, nor boundless sea, / But sad mortality o'ersways their power, / How with this rage shall beauty hold a plea, / Whose action is no stronger than a flower? [*Sonnets*, 65]

20 It is a dying lamp, a falling shower, / A breaking billow: – even whilst we speak / Is it not broken? [P B Shelley, 1792–1822, *Adonais*, 284]

21 The glories of our blood and state / Are shadows, not substantial things; / There is no armour against fate; / Death lays his icy hand on kings: / Sceptre and crown / Must tumble down, / And in the dust be equal made / With the poor crooked scythe and spade. [James Shirley, 1596–1666, *The Contention of Ajax and Ulysses*, I, iii]

22 Leave me, O Love, which reachest but to dust; / And thou, my mind, aspire to higher things; / Grow rich in that which never taketh rust; / Whatever fades, but fading pleasure brings. [Sir Philip Sidney, 1554–86, *Astrophel and Stella*, Sonnet 110]

23 One day I wrote her name upon the strand, / But came the waves and washèd it away: / Again, I wrote it with a second hand; / But came the tide, and made my pains his prey. / Vain man, said she, that dost in vain assay, / A mortal thing so to immortalize. [Edmund Spenser, 1552?–99, *Amoretti*, 75]

24 We thank with brief thanksgiving / Whatever gods may be / That no man lives forever, / That dead men rise up never; / That even the weariest river / Winds somewhere safe to sea. [A C Swinburne, 1837–1909, *The Garden of Proserpine*, 11]

25 Oh teach me yet / Somewhat before the heavy clod / Weighs on me, and the busy fret / Of that sharp-headed worm begins / In the gross blackness underneath. [Alfred, Lord Tennyson, 1809–92, *Supposed Confessions of a Second-rate Sensitive Mind*, conclusion]

26 The woods decay, the woods decay and fall, / The vapours weep their burden to the ground, / Man comes and tills the field and lies beneath, / And after many a summer dies the swan. [Alfred, Lord Tennyson, 1809–92, *Tithonus*, 1]

27 Early to rise and early to bed makes a male healthy and wealthy and dead. [James Thurber, 1894–1961, *Fables for Our Time*, 'The Shrike and the Chipmunks']

28 Human deeds have their tears, and mortality touches the heart. [Virgil, 70–19 BC, *Aeneid*, I, 462]

See also AGE, DEATH, LIFE & DEATH, LIFE IS FLEETING, PAST, TIME

MOTHERS

1 We all know Mumsy was vague and clumsy, / Dithering, drunken and dumb. [Morris Bishop, 1893–1973, *There's Money in Mother and Father*]

2 If a mother could be content to be nothing but a mother; but where would you find one who would be satisfied with that part alone? [Elias Canetti, 1905–94, *Auto da Fé*, Pt I, Ch. 1]

3 I love all my children, but some of them I don't like. [Lillian Carter, 1898–1983, in *Woman*, 9 Apr. 1977]

4 I remember my mother, the day that we met, / A thing I shall never entirely forget; / And I toy with the fancy that, young as I am, / I should know her again if we met in a tram. [G K Chesterton, 1874–1936, *Songs of Education*, 3, 'For the Crêche']

5 So for the mother's sake the child was dear, / And dearer was the mother for the child. [Samuel Taylor Coleridge, 1772–1834, *Sonnet to a Friend . . .*]

6 Oh that those lips had language! Life has passed / With me but roughly since I heard thee last. [William Cowper, 1731–1800, *On the Receipt of My Mother's Picture*, 1]

7 I don't think they [her six children] had a deprived childhood, exactly, but I think I had a deprived motherhood. [Alice Thomas Ellis, 1932– , in *The Sunday Times Magazine*, 19 June 1988]

8 Where yet was ever found a mother, / Who'd give her booby for another? [John Gay, 1685–1732, *Fables*, Pt I, iii, 33]

9 She was no different from all other mothers, (how could she be?) in that while she wanted me, in a general way, to be married, she didn't want me, in a specific way, to have a wife. [Howard Jacobson, 1942– , *Peeping Tom*, Pt 1, 7, 5]

10 Behind every beetle you will find a good mother-beetle. [J B Morton ('Beachcomber'), 1893–1979, *The Best of B*, 10]

11 There was an old woman who lived in a shoe, / She had so many children she didn't know what to do. [Nursery rhyme]

12 A mother has an innate ability for aggravating the wounds of her offspring's pride. This is inevitable since the relationship between mother and child is a most unnatural one; other species have the good sense to banish their young at an early age. [John Rae, 1931– , *The Custard Boys*, Ch. 13]

13 It [motherhood] is a dead-end job. You've no sooner learned the skills than you are redundant. [Claire Rayner, 1931– , in *Weekend Guardian*, 15–16 Dec. 1960]

14 As a rule there is only one person an English girl hates more than she hates her eldest sister; and thats her mother. [George Bernard Shaw, 1856–1950, *Man and Superman*, II]

15 No woman can shake off her mother. There should be no mothers, only women. [George Bernard Shaw, 1856–1950, *Too True to be Good*, III]

16 Happy he / With such a mother! faith in womankind / Beats with his blood. [Alfred, Lord Tennyson, 1809–92, *The Princess*, VII, 308]

17 The hand that rocks the cradle / Is the hand that rules the world. [W R Wallace, 1819–81, *John o'London's Treasure Trove*]

18 All women become like their mothers. That is their tragedy. No man does. That's his. [Oscar Wilde, 1854–1900, *The Importance of Being Earnest*, I]

19 Dead! and . . . never called me mother. [Mrs Henry Wood, 1814–87, *East Lynne* (dramatized version)]

See also CHILDHOOD, FAMILY, FATHERS, PARENTS

MOTTOES

1 The scouts' motto is founded on my initials, it is: Be Prepared. [Lord Baden-Powell, 1857–1941, *Scouting for Boys*, Pt 1]

2 Our motto: Life is too short to stuff a mushroom. [Shirley Conran, 1932– , *Superwoman*, epigraph]

3 Let 'Dig for Victory' be the motto for everyone with a garden. [Reginald Dorman-Smith, 1899–1971, BBC radio broadcast to encourage vegetable growing, 3 Oct. 1939]

4 *Fiat justitia et pereat mundus.* – Let justice be done, though the world perish. [Emperor Ferdinand I, 1503–64, motto]

5 Rather suffer than die is man's motto. [Jean de La Fontaine, 1621–95, *Fables*, I, 16, 'Death and the Woodcutter']

6 He profits most who serves best. [A F Sheldon, 1868–1935, *Motto for International Rotary*]

7 Grass will carry you through times of no money better than money through times of no dope. [Gilbert Shelton, 1939– , motto in strip cartoon 'Fabulous Furry Freak Brothers']

8 I've gotter motter – / Always merry and bright! [Arthur Wimperis, 1874–1953, 'My Motter', from *The Arcadians*, III]

See also EPIGRAMS

MOUNTAINS & HILLS

1 Five minutes on even the nicest mountain / Is awfully long. [W H Auden, 1907–73, *Mountains*]

2 The hills, like giants at a hunting, lay, / Chin upon hand, to see the game at bay. [Robert Browning, 1812–89, *Childe Roland to the Dark Tower Came*, 32]

3 Mountains interposed / Make enemies of nations, who had else, / Like kindred drops, been mingled into one. [William Cowper, 1731–1800, *The Task*, Bk II, 17]

4 *Über allen Gipfeln / Ist Ruh'.* – On all the peaks lies peace. [Johann Wolfgang von Goethe, 1749–1832, *Wanderers Nachtlied*]

5 Well, we knocked the bastard off! [Edmund Hillary, 1919– (to George Lowe after the conquest of Everest), *Nothing Venture*, Ch. 10]

6 Here of a Sunday morning / My love and I

would lie, / And see the coloured counties, / And hear the larks so high / About us in the sky. [A E Housman, 1859–1936, *A Shropshire Lad*, 21, 'Bredon Hill']

7 Separate from the pleasure of your company, I don't much care if I never see another mountain in my life. [Charles Lamb, 1775–1834, letter to Wordsworth, 30 Jan. 1801]

8 How beautiful they are, / The lordly ones, / Who dwell in the hills, / In the hollow hills. [Fiona Macleod, 1856–1905, *The Immortal Hour*, ii]

9 Because it's there. [(When asked why he wanted to climb Everest) G H L Mallory, 1886–1924, in John Hunt, *The Ascent of Everest*, Ch. 1]

10 Mountains are the beginning and the end of all natural scenery. [John Ruskin, 1819–1900, *Modern Painters*, Vol. IV, Pt v, Ch. 20, beginning]

11 Be it granted me to behold you again in dying, / Hills of home! [Robert Louis Stevenson, 1850–94, *Songs of Travel*, 45, 'To S. R. Crockett']

12 Whenever I look at a mountain I always expect it to turn into a volcano. [Italo Svevo, 1861–1928, *Confessions of Zeno*]

13 I climbed the roofs at break of day; / Sun-smitten Alps before me lay. / I stood among the silent statues, / And statued pinnacles, mute as they. [Alfred, Lord Tennyson, 1809–92, *The Daisy*, 61]

14 A huge peak, black and huge, / As if with voluntary power instinct / Upreared its head. [William Wordsworth, 1770–1850, *The Prelude*, I, 378]

See also LANDS

MOURNING

1 Stop all the clocks, cut off the telephone, / Prevent the dog from barking with a juicy bone, / Silence the pianos and with muffled drum / Bring out the coffin, let the mourners come. [W H Auden, 1907–73, '*Stop All the Clocks, Cut Off the Telephone*']

2 Would God I had died for thee, O Absalom, my son, my son! [Bible, OT, *2 Samuel* 18:33]

3 They shall grow not old, as we that are left grow old: / Age shall not weary them, nor the years condemn. / At the going down of the sun and in the morning / We will remember them. [Laurence Binyon, 1869–1943, *The Burning of the Leaves*]

4 Blow out, you bugles, over the rich Dead! / There's none of these so lonely and poor of old, / But, dying, has made us rarer gifts than gold. / These laid the world away: poured out the red / Sweet wine of youth. [Rupert Brooke, 1887–1915, *The Dead*]

5 Nature's law, / That man was made to mourn. [Robert Burns, 1759–96, *Man was Made to Mourn*, 31]

6 O! synge untoe mie roundelaie, / O! droppe the brynie teare wythe mee, / Daunce ne moe atte hallie daie, / Lycke a reynynge ryver bee; / Mie love ys dedde, / Gon to hys death-bedde, / Al under the wyllowe-tree. [Thomas Chatterton, 1752–70, *Mynstrelles Songe*]

7 MEDVIENKO: Why do you always wear black? MASHA: I am in mourning for my life. I am unhappy. [Anton Chekhov, 1860–1904, *The Seagull*, I]

8 Toll for the brave – / The brave! that are no more: / All sunk beneath the wave, / Fast by their native shore. [William Cowper, 1731–1800, *On the Loss of the Royal George*]

9 Oh that those lips had language! Life has passed / With me but roughly since I heard thee last. [William Cowper, 1731–1800, *On the Receipt of My Mother's Picture*, 1]

10 She's been thinking of the old 'un! [(Mr Peggotty of Mrs Gummidge) Charles Dickens, 1812–70, *David Copperfield*, Ch. 3]

11 Bombazine would have shown a deeper sense of her loss. [Elizabeth Gaskell, 1810–65, *Cranford*, Ch. 7]

12 One more Unfortunate, / Weary of breath, / Rashly importunate, / Gone to her death. Take her up tenderly, / Lift her with care; / Fashioned so slenderly, / Young, and so fair! [Thomas Hood, 1799–1845, *The Bridge of Sighs*]

13 If a man who turnips cries, / Cry not when his father dies, / 'Tis a proof that he had rather / Have a turnip than a father. [Dr Samuel Johnson, 1709–84, in Mrs Piozzi, *Anecdotes of J*, 'Burlesque of Lines by Lope de Vega']

14 'Mourning is a hard business,' Cesare said. 'If people knew there'd be less death.' [Bernard Malamud, 1914–86, *Idiots First*, 'Life is Better Than Death']

15 What we call mourning for our dead is perhaps not so much grief at not being able to call them back as it is grief at not being able to want to do so. [Thomas Mann, 1875–1955, *The Magic Mountain*, Ch. 7]

16 But O the heavy change, now thou art gone, / Now thou art gone, and never must return! [John Milton, 1608–74, *Lycidas*, 37]

17 In a cavern, in a canyon, / Excavating for a mine / Dwelt a miner, Forty-niner, / And his daughter, Clementine. / Oh, my darling, Oh, my darling, Oh, my darling Clementine! / Thou art lost and gone for ever, dreadful sorry, Clementine. [Percy Montrose, 19th cent., song: *Clementine*]

18 She is far from the land where her young hero sleeps, / And lovers are round her, sighing: / But coldly she turns from their gaze, and weeps, / For her heart in his grave is lying. [Thomas Moore, 1779–1852, *Irish Melodies*, 'She is Far']

19 Whatever mourns when many leave these shores: / Whatever shares / The eternal reciprocity of tears. [Wilfred Owen, 1893–1918, *Insensibility*]

20 A dirge for her, the doubly dead, / In that she died so young. [Edgar Allan Poe, 1809–49, *Lenore*]

21 Seems, madam! Nay, it is; I know not 'seems', / 'Tis not alone my inky cloak, good mother, / Nor customary suits of solemn black . . . [William Shakespeare, 1564–1616, *Hamlet*, I. ii. 76]

22 No longer mourn for me when I am dead / Than you shall hear the surly sullen bell / Give warning to the world that I am fled / From this vile world, with vilest worms to dwell. [*Sonnets*, 71]

23 I weep for Adonais – he is dead! / O, weep for Adonais! though our tears / Thaw not the frost that binds so dear a head! [P B Shelley, 1792–1822, *Adonais*, 1]

24 May there be no moaning of the bar, / When I put out to sea. [Alfred, Lord Tennyson, 1809–92, *Crossing the Bar*]

25 Thy voice is on the rolling air; / I hear thee where the waters run; / Thou standest in the rising sun, / And in the setting thou art fair. [Alfred, Lord Tennyson, 1809–92, *In Memoriam*, 130]

26 Home they brought her warrior dead: / She nor swooned, nor uttered cry: / All her maidens, watching, said, / 'She must weep or she will die.' [Alfred, Lord Tennyson, 1809–92, *The Princess*, VI, song]

27 Deep with the first dead lies London's daughter, / Robed in the long friends, / The grains beyond age, the dark veins of her mother, / Secret by the unmourning water / Of the riding Thames. / After the first death, there is no other. [Dylan Thomas, 1914–53, *A Refusal to Mourn the Death, by Fire, of a Child in London*]

28 When lilacs last in the dooryard bloomed, / And the great star early drooped in the western sky in the night, / I mourned, and yet shall mourn with ever-returning spring. [Walt Whitman, 1819–92, *When Lilacs Last in the Dooryard Bloomed*, I, 1]

29 Not without hope we suffer and we mourn. [William Wordsworth, 1770–1850, *Elegiac Stanzas, Suggested by a Picture of Peele Castle*]

30 Men are we, and must grieve when even the shade / Of that which once was great is passed away. [William Wordsworth, 1770–1850, *On the Extinction of the Venetian Republic*]

See also GRIEF, SORROW, TEARS

MURDER

1 Lizzie Borden took an axe / And gave her mother forty whacks; / When she saw what she had done, / She gave her father forty-one! [anon., on an American trial of the 1890s]

2 And the Lord set a mark upon Cain. [Bible, OT, *Genesis* 4:15]

3 If one denies that there are grounds for suicide one cannot claim them for murder. One cannot be a part-time nihilist. [Albert Camus, 1913–60, *The Rebel*, Introduction]

4 Mordre wol out, that see we day by day. [Geoffrey Chaucer, 1340?–1400, *Canterbury Tales*, 'The Nun's Priest's Tale', 232]

5 Murder Considered as One of the Fine Arts. [Thomas de Quincey, 1785–1859, title of essay]

6 If once a man indulges himself in murder, very soon he comes to think little of robbing; and from robbing he comes next to drinking and sabbath-breaking, and from that to civility and procrastination. [Thomas de Quincey, 1785–1859, *On Murder*]

7 Late last night I slew my wife, / Stretched her on the parquet flooring; / I was loth to take her life, / But I *had* to stop her snoring! [Harry Graham, 1874–1936, *When Grandma Fell off the Boat*, 'Necessity']

8 If we are to abolish the death penalty, let our friends the murderers make the first move. [Alphonse Karr, 1808–90, *Les Guêpes*, 1849]

9 Murder, like talent, seems occasionally to run in families. [G H Lewes, 1817–78, *The Physiology of Common Life*, Ch. 12]

10 Murder most foul, as in the best it is; / But this most foul, strange, and unnatural. [William Shakespeare, 1564–1616, *Hamlet*, I. v. 27]

11 This was the most unkindest cut of all. [*Julius Caesar*, III. ii. (188)]

12 Most sacrilegious murder hath broke ope / The Lord's anointed temple, and stole thence / The life o' the building! [*Macbeth*, II. iii. (72)]

13 What! all my pretty chickens and their dam, / At one fell swoop? [*Macbeth*, IV. iii. 218]

See also DEATH, KILLING

MUSIC

1 Music, the greatest good that mortals know,/ And all of heaven we have below. [Joseph Addison, 1672–1719, *Song for St Cecilia's Day*]

2 A verbal art like poetry is reflective; it stops to think. Music is immediate; it goes on to become. [W H Auden, 1907–73, *The Dyer's Hand*, 8, 'Notes on Music']

3 Music is the best means we have of digesting time. [W H Auden, 1907–73, in Robert Craft, *Stravinsky: Chronicle of a Friendship*]

4 People who attend chamber music concerts are like Englishmen who go to church when abroad. [W H Auden, 1907–73, in Charles Osborne, *W H A: The Life of a Poet*, Ch. 13]

5 The plain fact is that music *per se* means nothing; it is sheer sound, and the interpreter can do no more with it than his own capacities, mental and spiritual, will allow, and the same applies to the listener. [Sir Thomas Beecham, 1879–1961, *A Mingled Chime*, Ch. 33]

6 The English may not like music – but they absolutely love the noise it makes. [Sir Thomas Beecham, 1879–1961, in H Atkins and A Newman, *Beecham Stories*]

7 Silence is the essence of music. It is really the basis. [Alfred Brendel, 1931– , interview in *Observer*, 6 Dec. 1987]

8 *Bang-whang-whang* goes the drum, *tootle-te-tootle* the fife; / No keeping one's haunches still: it's the greatest pleasure in life. [Robert Browning, 1812–89, *Up at a Villa – Down in the City*, 1]

9 Music says nothing to the reason: it is a kind of closely structured nonsense. [Anthony Burgess, 1917–93, in *Observer*, 23 July 1989]

10 O Music! sphere-descended maid, / Friend of Pleasure, Wisdom's aid! [William Collins, 1721–59, *The Passions, An Ode for Music*, 95]

11 Music hath charms to soothe a savage breast, / To soften rocks, or bend a knotted oak. [William Congreve, 1670–1729, *The Mourning Bride*, I. i]

12 If a literary man puts together two words about music, one of them will be wrong. [Aaron Copland, 1900–1990, in Frank Muir, *Frank Muir Book*, 'Music']

13 Recordings are really for people who live in Timbuktu. [Aaron Copland, 1900–1990 (on the necessity of live music), in obituary in *Guardian*, 4 Dec. 1990]

14 Extraordinary how potent cheap music is. [Noël Coward, 1899–1973, *Private Lives*, I. Some versions give 'strange' as the first word]

15 Music is the arithmetic of sounds as optics is the geometry of light. [Claude Debussy, 1862–1918; in Nat Shapiro, *Encyclopedia of Quotations about Music*]

16 When music sounds, all that I was I am / Ere to this haunt of brooding dust I came. [Walter de la Mare, 1873–1956, *Music*]

17 With ravished ears / The monarch hears, / Assumes the god, / Affects to nod, / And seems to shake the spheres. [John Dryden, 1631–1700, *Alexander's Feast*, 37]

18 From harmony, from heavenly harmony / This universal frame began: / From harmony to harmony / Through all the compass of the notes it ran, / The diapason closing full in Man. [John Dryden, 1631–1700, *Song for St Cecilia's Day*, 1]

19 We were none of us musical, though Miss Jenkyns beat time, out of time, by way of appearing to be so. [Elizabeth Gaskell, 1810–65, *Cranford*, Ch. 1]

20 Salvation Army Booth objected to the devil having all the good tunes. I object to jazz and vaudeville having all the best instruments! [Percy Grainger, 1882–1961, Preface to *Spoon River*; in John Bird, *P G*, Appendix C]; see 23

21 The hills are alive with the sound of music / With songs they have sung / For a thousand years. [Oscar Hammerstein II, 1895–1960, title song in musical *The Sound of Music*]

22 I was, however, approached by Chinese journalists, one of whom observed how interesting it was that I combined politics – which is practical, and music – which is fantasy. I replied they had it the wrong way round! [Edward Heath, 1916– , in *The Sunday Times*, 8 Jan. 1989]

23 He did not see any reason why the devil should have all the good tunes. [Rowland Hill, 1744–1833, in E W Broome, *Revd R H*, Ch. 7. Also ascr. to William Booth of the Salvation Army]; see 20

24 Heard melodies are sweet, but those unheard / Are sweeter; therefore, ye soft pipes, play on; / Not to the sensual ear, but, more endeared, / Pipe to the spirit ditties of no tone. [John Keats, 1795–1821, *Ode on a Grecian Urn*, 2]

25 I even think that sentimentally I am disposed to harmony. But organically I am incapable of a tune. [Charles Lamb, 1775–1834, *Essays of Elia*, 'A Chapter on Ears']

26 I can't listen to music too often. It affects your nerves; you want to say nice, stupid things and stroke the heads of people who could create such beauty while living in this vile hell. And now you must not stroke anyone's head – you might get your hand bitten off. You have to hit them on the head, without any mercy. [Vladimir Ilyich Lenin, 1870–1924 (to Maxim Gorky of Beethoven's 'Appassionata' Sonata), in M Lasky, *Utopia and Revolution*, Pt 1, Ch. 2]; see also 37

27 A symphony must be like the world. It must contain everything. [Gustav Mahler, 1860–1911, to Jean Sibelius in Helsingfors, Finland, 1907]

28 Talking about music is like dancing about architecture. [Steve Martin, 1945– , in *Independent*]

29 Music creates order out of chaos; for rhythm imposes unanimity upon the divergent, melody imposes continuity upon the disjointed, and harmony imposes compatibility upon the incongruous. [Yehudi Menuhin, 1916–99, quoted by Anthony Storr in *The Sunday Times*, 10 Oct. 1976]

30 Such sweet compulsion doth in music lie. [John Milton, 1608–74, *Arcades*, 68]

31 Such strains as would have won the ear / Of Pluto, to have quite set free / His half-regained Eurydice. [John Milton, 1608–74, *L'Allegro*, 148]

32 We are the music-makers / And we are the dreamers of dreams, / Wandering by lone sea-breakers, / And sitting by desolate streams; / World-losers and world-forsakers, / On whom the pale moon gleams: / Yet we are the movers and shakers / Of the world forever, it seems. [Arthur O'Shaughnessy, 1844–81, *Ode*]

33 Music is your own experience, your thoughts, your wisdom. If you don't live it, it won't come out of your horn. [Charlie Parker, 1920–55, in Nat Shapiro and Nat Hentoff, *Hear Me Talkin' to Ya*, 'Coda']

34 All art constantly aspires towards the condition of music. [Walter Pater, 1839–94, *The Renaissance*, 'Giorgione']

35 Music and women I cannot but give way to, whatever my business is. [Samuel Pepys, 1633–1703, *Diary*, 9 Mar. 1666]

36 The author's conviction ... is that music begins to atrophy when it departs too far from the dance; that poetry begins to atrophy when it gets too far from music. [Ezra Pound, 1885–1972, *ABC of Reading*, 'Warning']

37 [When asked why he rarely listened to music now] I don't like things ... which interfere with one's heart strings. It doesn't do to awaken longings that can't be fulfilled. [Enoch Powell, 1912– , interview in John Mortimer, *In Character*]; see also 26

38 The basic difference between classical music and jazz is that in the former the music is always greater than its performance – whereas the way jazz is performed is always more important than what is being played. [André Previn, 1929– , in *The Times*, 1967]

39 But I struck one chord of music, / Like the sound of a great Amen. [Adelaide Procter, 1825–64, *A Lost Chord*]

40 To see itself through, music must have an idea or magic. The best has both. Music with neither dies young, though sometimes rich. [Ned Rorem, 1923– , *Pure Contraption*]

41 Not everything in music is audible. [Charles Rosen, 1927– , on BBC Radio 3, 14 May 1997]

42 I don't think there was ever a piece of music that changed a man's decision on how to vote. [Artur Schnabel, 1882–1951, *My Life and Music*, Pt II, Ch. 8]

43 There is still much good music to be written in C major. [Arnold Schoenberg, 1874–1951, in J Machlis, *Introduction to Contemporary Music*]

44 Music, moody food / Of us that trade in love. [William Shakespeare, 1564–1616, *Antony and Cleopatra*, II. v. 1]

45 How sweet the moonlight sleeps upon this bank! / Here will we sit, and let the sounds of music / Creep in our ears: soft stillness and the night / Become the touches of sweet harmony. [*The Merchant of Venice*, V. i. 54]

46 The man that hath not music in himself, / Nor is not moved with concord of sweet sounds, / Is fit for treasons, stratagems, and spoils; / The motions of his spirit are dull as night, / And his affections dark as Erebus: / Let no such man be trusted. [*The Merchant of Venice*, V. i. 83]

47 How sour sweet music is / When time is broke and no proportion kept! / So is it in the music of men's lives. [*Richard II*, V. v. 42]

48 Be not afeard: the isle is full of noises, / Sounds and sweet airs that give delight and hurt not. [*The Tempest*, III. ii. (147)]

49 If music be the food of love, play on; / Give me excess of it, that, surfeiting, / The appetite may sicken, and so die. / That strain again! it had a dying fall: / O! it came o'er my ear like the sweet sound / That breathes upon a bank of violets, / Stealing and giving odour! [*Twelfth Night*, I. i. 1]

50 Hell is full of musical amateurs: music is the brandy of the damned. [George Bernard Shaw, 1856–1950, *Man and Superman*, III]

51 Music, when soft voices die, / Vibrates in the memory. [P B Shelley, 1792–1822, *To —, Music, When Soft Voices Die*]

52 It is not art that rains down upon us in the song of a bird; but the simplest modulation, correctly executed, is already art. [Igor Stravinsky, 1882–1971, *Poetics of Music*, Ch. 2]

53 Film music should have the same relationship to the film drama that somebody's piano-playing in my living-room has on the book I'm reading. [Igor Stravinsky, 1882–1971, in *Music Digest*, Sept. 1946]

54 Teaching music is not my main purpose. I want to make good citizens. If a child hears fine music from the day of his birth, and learns to play it himself, he develops sensitivity, discipline and endurance. He gets a beautiful heart. [Shin'ichi Suzuki, 1898–1998, in *Reader's Digest*, Nov. 1973]

55 Music that gentlier on the spirit lies, / Than tired eyelids upon tired eyes. [Alfred, Lord Tennyson, 1809–92, *The Lotos-Eaters*, 'Choric Song', 1]

56 Music is natural law as related to the sense of hearing. [Anton von Webern, 1883–1945, *The Path to the New Music*]

57 You have Van Gogh's ear for music. [Billy Wilder, 1906– , to Cliff Osmond, attr.]

See also next categories, COMPOSERS, JAZZ

MUSICAL INSTRUMENTS

1 The sound of the cornet, flute, harp, sackbut, psaltery, dulcimer, and all kinds of music. [Bible, OT, *Daniel* 3:5]

2 The trumpet's loud clangour / Excites us to arms. [John Dryden, 1631–1700, *Song for St Cecilia's Day*, 3]

3 I took my harp to a party / But nobody asked me to play. [Gracie Fields, 1898–1979, song: *I Took My Harp*, words and music by Desmond Carter and Noël Gay]

4 Salvation Army Booth objected to the devil having all the good tunes. I object to jazz and vaudeville having all the best instruments! [Percy Grainger, 1882–1961, Preface to *Spoon River*; in John Bird, *P G*, Appendix C]

5 Today unexplored regions of the stringed instruments' fingerboard are non-existent; even the arctic zones of the eternal rosin (near the bridge) have become a habitable abode for fearless climbers. [Paul Hindemith, 1895–1963, *A Composer's World*, Ch. 7, sect. ii]

6 The piano is the easiest instrument to play in the beginning, and the hardest to master in the end. [Vladimir Horowitz, 1904–89, in David Dubal, *Evenings with Horowitz*, Ch. 7]

7 The trumpets came out brazenly with the last post ... Our eyes smarted against our wills. A man hates to be moved to folly by a noise. [T E Lawrence, 1888–1935, *The Mint*, III, 9]

8 Holding a violin is like holding a young bird. It is vibrating under your touch and you must hold it without squeezing it ... It is a good thing to cultivate the feeling of those sympathetic vibrations in dealing with people. [Yehudi Menuhin, 1916–99, in *Daily Mail*, 15 Mar. 1977]

9 The harp that once through Tara's halls / The soul of music shed, / Now hangs as mute as Tara's walls / As if that soul were fled. [Thomas Moore, 1779–1852, *Irish Melodies*, 'The Harp that Once']

10 Seated one day at the organ, / I was weary and ill at ease, / And my fingers wandered idly / Over the noisy keys. [Adelaide Procter, 1825–64, *A Lost Chord*]

11 And the vile squealing of the wry-necked fife. [William Shakespeare, 1564–1616, *The Merchant of Venice*, II. v. (30)]

12 Is it not strange that sheep's guts should hale souls out of men's bodies? [*Much Ado About Nothing*, II. iii. (62)]

See also previous and next categories, COMPOSERS, JAZZ

MUSICIANS

1 A musicologist is a man who can read music but can't hear it. [Sir Thomas Beecham, 1879–1961, in H Proctor-Gregg, *Beecham Remembered*, 'Beecham's Obiter Dicta']

2 There are two golden rules for an orchestra: start together and finish together. The public doesn't give a damn what goes on in between. [Sir Thomas Beecham, 1879–1961, in H Atkins and A Newman, *B Stories*]

3 The rest may reason and welcome; 'tis we musicians know. [Robert Browning, 1812–89, *Abt Vogler*, 11]

4 He [Yehudi Menuhin] never *performs*; he communicates to us, through his fiddle, often in spite of his fiddle, the divinely given best of him. [Sir Neville Cardus, 1889–1975, *Full Score*, 'Menuhin']

5 What we do should only be recognizable to the orchestra, not the audience. We don't conduct the audience. There are too many conductors who mime. These mime what is being heard, whereas the conductor conducts what is not being heard, but will be in the flash of a second. [Antal Dorati, 1906–88, interview at eighty in *Guardian*, 9 Apr. 1986]

6 To hear the latest Pole / transmit the Preludes, through his hair and fingertips. [T S Eliot, 1888–1965, *Portrait of a Lady*]

7 Of all musicians, flautists are most obviously the ones who know something we don't know. [Paul Jennings, 1918–89, *The Jenguin Pennings*, 'Flautists Flaunt Afflatus']

8 Difficult do you call it, Sir? I wish it were impossible. [(Of a violinist's playing) Dr Samuel Johnson, 1709–84, *Anecdotes by William Seward*]

9 Only really very tall conductors can deal adequately with slow music. [Neville Marriner, 1924– , in *Listener*, 14 Mar. 1985]

10 I never used a score when conducting my orchestra ... Does a lion tamer enter a cage with a book on how to tame a lion? [Dimitri Mitropoulos, 1896–1960, said 22 Jan. 1951; in Nat Shapiro, *Encyclopedia of Quotations about Music*]

11 The Minstrel Boy to the war is gone, / In the ranks of death you'll find him; / His father's sword he has girded on, / And his wild harp slung behind him. [Thomas Moore, 1779–1852, *Irish Melodies*, 'The Minstrel Boy']

12 The musician is perhaps the most modest of animals, but he is also the proudest. It is he who invented the sublime art of ruining poetry. [Erik Satie, 1866–1925, in Pierre-Daniel Templier, *Erik Satie*, Ch. 2]

13 I am attracted only to music which I consider to be better than it can be performed. [Artur Schnabel, 1882–1951, *My Life and Music*, Pt II, Ch. 1]

14 Interpretation is a free walk on firm ground. [Artur Schnabel, 1882–1951, *My Life and Music*, Pt II, Ch. 10]

15 The notes I handle no better than many pianists. But the pauses between the notes – ah, that is where the art resides. [Artur Schnabel, 1882–1951, in *Chicago Daily News*, 11 June 1958]

16 It was in Russia that I had all my primary training: I didn't come to the United States till I was ten months old. [Isaac Stern, 1920– , interview in *Guardian*, 16 Feb. 1987]

17 What does von K[arajan]'s conducting really do to Mozart? He opens his bier, unclasps his hands from his bosom, and folds them behind his head. [Igor Stravinsky, 1882–1971, quoted in *Guardian*, 18 July 1989]

18 After I die, I shall return to earth as the doorkeeper of a bordello and I won't let a one of you in. [Arturo Toscanini, 1867–1957 (to his orchestra at rehearsal), in N Lebrecht, *Discord*, Ch. 8]

See also previous categories, COMPOSERS, JAZZ

MYSTICS & THE TRANSCENDENTAL

1 Another Boehme with a tougher book / And subtler meanings of what roses say. [Robert Browning, 1812–89, *Transcendentalism*]

2 Worship is transcendent wonder. [Thomas Carlyle, 1795–1881, *Heroes and Hero-Worship*, i, 'The Hero as Divinity']

3 I've found a perfect description of mysticism – it's the attempt to get rid of mystery. [Roger Fry, 1866–1934, in Virginia Woolf, *R F*, Ch. 11]

4 I don't know whether I believe in God or not. I think, really, I'm some kind of Buddhist. But the essential thing is to put oneself in a frame of mind which is close to that of prayer. [Henri Matisse, 1869–1954, in Françoise Gilot and Carlton Lake, *Life with Picasso*, Pt 6]

5 Nothing to the supernatural sense is really finite; it is founded on a feeling of all in each and each in all. [Sri Aurobindo, 1872–1950, *Synthesis of Yoga*]

6 It is therefore wrong to reproach the mystics, as has been done sometimes, because they use love's language. It is theirs by right. Others only borrow it. [Simone Weil, 1909–43, *Waiting on God*, 'Forms of the Implicit Love of God']

7 Rapt into still communion that transcends / The imperfect offices of prayer and praise. [William Wordsworth, 1770–1850, *The Excursion*, I, 215]

8 Nor less I deem that there are powers / Which of themselves our minds impress; / That we can feed this mind of ours / In a wise passiveness. [William Wordsworth, 1770–1850, *Expostulation and Reply*]

9 We are laid asleep / In body, and become a living soul: / While with an eye made quiet by the power / Of harmony, and the deep power of joy, / We see into the life of things. [William Wordsworth, 1770–1850, *Lines Composed a Few Miles above Tintern Abbey*, 45]

See also PRAYERS, RELIGION

MYTHS

1 Are we the ones who think up myths or is it myths who think us up? [Carlo Ginzburg, 1939– , *Clues, Myths and Emblems*, Ch. 5]

2 Those famous men of old, the Ogres – / They had long beards and stinking armpits, / They were wide-mouthed, long-yarded and great-bellied / Yet of no taller stature, Sirs, than you. [Robert Graves, 1895–1985, *Ogres and Pygmies*]

3 I wonder if we could contrive ... some magnificent myth [also trans. as 'the noble lie'] that would in itself carry conviction to our whole community. [Plato, *c*.428–347 BC, *Republic*, Bk iii, 414]

4 A myth is, of course, not a fairy story. It is the presentation of facts belonging to one category in the idioms appropriate to another. To explode a myth is accordingly not to deny the facts but to re-allocate them. [Gilbert Ryle, 1900–1976, *The Concept of Mind*, Introduction]

5 Without doubt the greatest injury ... was done by basing morals on myth, for sooner or later myth is recognized for what it is, and disappears. Then morality loses the foundation on which it has been built. [Herbert Samuel, 1870–1963, Romanes Lecture, 1947]

6 I was ready to admit – if only I had been old enough to understand them – all the right-wing truths which an old left-wing man taught me through his actions: that Truth and Myth are one and the same thing, that you have to simulate passion to feel it and that man is a creature of ceremony. [Jean-Paul Sartre, 1905–80, *Words*, Pt 1]

See also STORIES

N

NAMES

1 A nickname is the heaviest stone that the devil can throw at a man. [William Hazlitt, 1778–1830, *On Nicknames*]

2 To-day we have naming of parts. Yesterday / We had daily cleaning. And tomorrow morning, / We shall have what to do after firing. But to-day, / To-day we have naming of parts. [Henry Reed, 1914–86, *Lessons of the War*, I, 'Naming of Parts']

3 Nobody ever makes up nicknames, a nickname is your real identity, jumping out from behind you like an afreet. [Robert Robinson, 1927– , *Dog Chairman*, 'Nicknames']

4 What's in a name? that which we call a rose / By any other name would smell as sweet. [William Shakespeare, 1564–1616, *Romeo and Juliet*, II. ii. 43]

5 Rose is a rose is a rose is a rose. [Gertrude Stein, 1874–1946, *Sacred Emily*]

6 Okie use' to mean you was from Oklahoma. Now it means you're scum. Don't mean nothing itself, it's the way they say it. [John Steinbeck, 1902–68, *The Grapes of Wrath*, Ch. 18]

7 'It's giving girls names like that [Euphemia],' said Buggins, 'that nine times out of ten makes 'em go wrong, It unsettles 'em. If ever I was to have a girl, if ever I was to have a dozen girls, I'd call 'em all Jane.' [H G Wells, 1866–1946, *Kipps*, Bk I, Ch. 6, sect. ii]

See also DEFINITIONS

NATIONALISM & INTERNATIONALISM

1 My policy is to be able to take a ticket at Victoria Station and go anywhere I damn well please. [Ernest Bevin, 1881–1951, in *Spectator*, 20 Apr. 1951]

2 A steady patriot of the world alone, / The friend of every country but his own. [George Canning, 1770–1827, *New Morality*, 113]

3 Nationalism is an infantile disease. It is the measles of mankind. [Albert Einstein, 1879–1955, *The World as I See It*]

4 It took man 250,000 years to transcend the hunting pack. It will not take him so long to transcend the nation. [J B S Haldane, 1892–1964, *Daedalus or Science and the Future*]

5 A patriot is a man who loves his country: a nationalist is one who hates everyone else's. [*Listener*, 'Begrudgery: Tall Poppy Syndrome', 1 Dec. 1988]

6 My country is the world, and my religion is to do good. [Thomas Paine, 1737–1809, *The Rights of Man*, Pt I, Ch. 5]

7 I am a citizen, not of Athens or Greece, but of the world. [Socrates, 469–399 BC, quoted in Plutarch, *De Exilio*, v]

8 Nationalism was an economic force before nationality was a political fact. [R H Tawney, 1880–1962, *Religion and the Rise of Capitalism*, Ch. II, i]

9 Nationalism is in this sense like class. To have it, and to feel it, is the only way to end it. If you fail to claim it, or give it up too soon, you will be merely cheated, by other classes and other nations. [Raymond Williams, 1921–88, *Second Generation*]

See also following category, INTERNATIONAL RELATIONS

NATIONS

1 In my view, a nation which eats cheese for breakfast has little room for criticism. [Nancy Banks-Smith, 1929– , in *Guardian*, 6 Feb. 1992]

2 Behold, the nations are as a drop of a bucket, and are counted as the small dust of the balance. [Bible, OT, *Isaiah* 40:15]

3 Nations, like men, have their infancy. [Henry St John, Viscount Bolingbroke, 1678–1751, *On the Study of History*, 4]

4 I do not know the method of drawing up an indictment against a whole people. [Edmund Burke, 1729–97, speech on conciliation with America, 22 Mar. 1775]

5 The unity of a nation consists mainly in its being able to act, when necessary, like a single paranoic. [Elias Canetti, 1905–94, *The Human Province*, '1945']

6 There are few virtues which the Poles do not possess and there are few errors they have ever avoided. [Winston Churchill, 1874–1965, speech in House of Commons after Potsdam Conference, 16 Aug. 1945]

7 Apart from cheese and tulips, the main product of the country is advocaat, a drink made from lawyers. [Alan Coren, 1938– , *The Sanity Inspector*, 'All You Need to Know About Europe']

8 Poor Mexico, so far from God and so near to the United States! [Porfirio Diaz, 1830–1915. Also attr. to Ambrose Bierce]

9 Some people . . . may be Rooshans, and others may be Prooshans; they are born so, and will please themselves. Them which is of other naturs thinks different. [Charles Dickens, 1812–70, *Martin Chuzzlewit*, Ch. 19]

10 'I've never travelled,' Dona Consolation blandly confessed, 'but I dare say, dear, you can't judge Egypt by *Aïda*.' [Ronald Firbank, 1886–1926, *The Eccentricities of Cardinal Pirelli*, 9]

11 [When asked what he thought of New Zealand] I find it hard to say, because when I was there it seemed to be shut. [Clement Freud, 1924– , in BBC radio programme *Quote . . . Unquote*, 12 Apr. 1978. Variants ascr. to other people]

12 Nations, like men, die by imperceptible disorders. We recognize a doomed people by the way they sneeze or pare their nails. [Jean Giraudoux, 1882–1944, *Tiger at the Gates*, II]

13 Some say that the Thais are the nicest people that money can buy, because they like to have fun. [Spalding Gray, 1941– , *Swimming to Cambodia*, Pt 1]

14 A nation is a society united by a delusion about its ancestry and by a common hatred of its neighbours. [W R Inge, 1860–1954, in Sagittarius and D George, *The Perpetual Pessimist*]

15 Authority cannot put up with a nation that gets on its nerves; the nation cannot tolerate an authority it has come to hate. [Ryszard Kapuściński, 1932– , *Shah of Shahs*, 'Dead Flame']

16 The people of the world respect a nation that can see beyond its own image. [President John F Kennedy, 1917–63, in *Saturday Review*, 'Ideas, Attitudes, Purposes from His Speeches and Writings', 7 Dec. 1963]

17 The great nations have always acted like gangsters, and the small nations like prostitutes. [Stanley Kubrick, 1928–99, in *Guardian*, 5 June 1963]

18 'It [Mexico] is a country where men despise sex, and live for it,' said Ramón. 'Which is suicide.' [D H Lawrence, 1885–1930, *The Plumed Serpent*, Ch. 25]

19 The trouble with bridges is that in peacetime the horses crap all over them – and when war comes they're the first things to be blown up. [Jan Masaryk, 1886–1948 (on Czechoslovakia being described as a bridge), in *New Statesman*, 10 Feb. 1981]

20 Austria is Switzerland, speaking pure German and with history added. [J E Morpurgo, 1918– , *The Road to Athens*]

21 We have a sick man – a seriously sick man on our hands. [(Of Turkey) Nicholas I of Russia, 1796–1855, quoted in a letter by Sir G H Seymour, 11 Jan. 1853]

22 No man has a right to fix the boundary of the march of a nation; no man has a right to say to his country – thus far shalt thou go and no further. [Charles Stewart Parnell, 1846–91, speech at Cork, 21 Jan. 1885]

23 Mexicans are descended from the Aztecs, Peruvians from the Incas and Argentinians from the ships. [Octavio Paz, 1914–98, attr. in *Observer*, 16 June 1990]

24 The Japanese have perfected good manners and made them indistinguishable from rudeness. [Paul Theroux, 1941– , *The Great Railway Bazaar*, Ch. 28]

25 In Turkey it was always 1952, in Malaysia 1937; Afghanistan was 1910 and Bolivia 1949. It is twenty years ago in the Soviet Union, ten in Norway, five in France. It is always last year in Australia and next week in Japan. [Paul Theroux, 1941– , *The Kingdom by the Sea*, Ch. 1]

26 Wherever there are three Poles there are four political parties. [Lech Walesa, 1947– , interview in *Independent*, 4 Dec. 1989]

27 If people behaved in the way nations do they would all be put in straitjackets. [Tennessee Williams, 1911–83, BBC interview]

See also previous category, individual countries, FOREIGNERS, INTERNATIONAL RELATIONS, PATRIOTISM

NATURE & THE NATURAL

1 *La nature est un temple où de vivants piliers / Laissent parfois sortir de confuses paroles; / L'homme y passe à travers des forêts de symboles / Qui l'observent avec des regards familiers.* – Nature is a temple in which living columns sometimes emit confused words. Man approaches it through forests of symbols, which observe him with familiar glances. [Charles Baudelaire, 1821–67, *Correspondances*]

2 All things are artificial; for nature is the art of God. [Sir Thomas Browne, 1605–82, *Religio Medici*, Pt 1, 16]

3 There is a pleasure in the pathless woods, / There is a rapture on the lonely shore, / There is society, where none intrudes, / By the deep sea, and music in its roar: / I love not man the less, but Nature more. [Lord Byron, 1788–1824, *Childe Harold's Pilgrimage*, IV, 178]

4 O Lady! we receive but what we give, / And in our life alone does Nature live. [Samuel Taylor Coleridge, 1772–1834, *Dejection: an Ode*, 47]

5 Nature is but a name for an effect, / Whose cause is God. [William Cowper, 1731–1800, *The Task*, Bk VI, 223]

6 Custom, that is before all law; Nature, that is above all art. [Samuel Daniel, 1562–1619, *A Defence of Rhyme*]

7 Nature puts me out. [Henry Fuseli, 1741–1825, quoted in Alexander Gilchrist, *Life of Blake*, Ch. 39]

8 Nature, Mr Allnut, is what we are put into this world to rise above. [Katharine Hepburn, 1907– , to Humphrey Bogart in film *The African Queen*, screenplay by James Agee and John Huston]

9 Though you drive Nature out with a pitchfork, she will still find her way back. [Horace, 65–8 BC, *Epistles*, I, x, 24]

10 In nature there are neither rewards nor punishments – there are consequences. [R G Ingersoll, 1833–99, *Lectures and Essays*, Third Series, 'Some Reasons Why']

11 The flowers at Waterbath would probably go wrong in colour and the nightingales sing out of tune; but she remembered to have heard the place described as possessing those advantages that are usually spoken of as natural. [Henry James, 1843–1916, *The Spoils of Poynton*, Ch. 1]

12 I strove with none; for none was worth my strife; / Nature I loved, and, next to Nature, Art; / I warmed both hands before the fire of life; / It sinks, and I am ready to depart. [Walter Savage Landor, 1775–1864, *I Strove with None*]

13 Nothing prevents us from being natural so much as the desire to appear so. [Duc de La Rochefoucauld, 1613–80, *Maxims*, 431]

14 It is far from easy to determine whether she [Nature] has proved a kind parent to man or a merciless stepmother. [Pliny the Elder, 23–79, *Natural History*, Bk vii, Ch. 1]

15 In Nature's infinite book of secrecy / A little I can read. [William Shakespeare, 1564–1616, *Antony and Cleopatra*, I. ii. (11)]

16 One touch of nature makes the whole world kin. [*Troilus and Cressida*, III. iii. 175]

17 Nature abhors a vacuum. [Benedict Spinoza, 1632–77, *Ethics*, Pt I, 15, note]

18 So careful of the type she [Nature] seems, / So careless of the single life. [Alfred, Lord Tennyson, 1809–92, *In Memoriam*, 55]

19 Nature, red in tooth and claw. [Alfred, Lord Tennyson, 1809–92, *In Memoriam*, 56]

20 We will listen instead to the wind's text / Blown through the roof, or the thrush's song / In the thick bush that proved him wrong, / Wrong from the start, for nature's truth / Is primary and her changing seasons / Correct out of a vaster reason / The vague errors of the flesh. [R S Thomas, 1913– , *The Minister*, final lines]

21 In nature there are no rewards or punishments; there are consequences. [Horace Annesley-Vachell, 1861–1955, *The Face of Clay*, Ch. 10]

22 A dead Nature aims at nothing. It is the essence of life that it exists for its own sake, as the intrinsic reaping of value. [A N Whitehead, 1861–1947, *Nature and Life*, Ch. 1]

23 I believe a leaf of grass is no less than the journey-work of the stars. [Walt Whitman, 1819–92, *Song of Myself*, 31, 663]

24 For Nature then ... / To me was all in all. [William Wordsworth, 1770–1850, *Lines Composed a Few Miles above Tintern Abbey*, 72]

25 I have learned / To look on nature, not as in the hour / Of thoughtless youth: but hearing oftentimes / The still, sad music of humanity. [William Wordsworth, 1770–1850, *Lines Composed a Few Miles above Tintern Abbey*, 88]

26 Nature never did betray / The heart that loved her. [William Wordsworth, 1770–1850, *Lines Composed a Few Miles above Tintern Abbey*, 122]

See also EARTH, ENVIRONMENT, LANDS

THE NAVY, see SAILORS

NECESSITY

1 Necessity hath no law. Feigned necessities, imaginary necessities ... are the greatest cozenage that men can put upon the Providence of God, and make pretences to break known rules by. [Oliver Cromwell, 1599–1658, speech to Parliament, 12 Sept. 1654]

2 The graveyards are full of indispensable men. [General de Gaulle, 1890–1970, attr.]

3 Man wants but little here below, / Nor wants that little long. [Oliver Goldsmith, 1728–74, *The Vicar of Wakefield*, Ch. 8, 'A Ballad', 30]; see 15

4 She was one of those indispensables of whom one makes the discovery, when they are gone, that one can get on quite as well without them. [Aldous Huxley, 1894–1963, *Mortal Coils*, 'Nuns at Luncheon']

5 With necessity, / The tyrant's plea, excused his devilish deeds. [John Milton, 1608–74, *Paradise Lost*, Bk iv, 393]

6 Necessity is the plea for every infringement of human freedom. It is the argument of tyrants; it is the creed of slaves. [William Pitt, the Younger, 1759–1806, speech in House of Commons, 18 Nov. 1783]

7 All places that the eye of heaven visits / Are to a wise man ports and happy havens. / Teach thy necessity to reason thus; / There is no virtue like necessity. [William Shakespeare, 1564–1616, *Richard II*, I. iii. 275]

8 I am sworn brother, sweet, / To grim Necessity, and he and I / Will keep a league till death. [*Richard II*, V. i. 20]

9 Thy necessity is yet greater than mine. [Sir Philip Sidney, 1554–86, on giving his water-bottle to a dying soldier on the battlefield of Zutphen, 22 Sept. 1586. Often misquoted as 'Thy need']

10 *Necessitas dat legem, non ipsa accepit.* – Necessity gives the law, without acknowledging one itself. [Publilius Syrus, 1st cent. BC, *Maxims*, 399. Becomes proverb: *Necessitas non habet legem.* – Necessity has no law.]

11 I find no hint throughout the universe / Of good or ill, of blessing or of curse; / I find alone Necessity Supreme. [James Thomson, 1834–82, *The City of Dreadful Night*, 14]

12 The want of a thing is perplexing enough, but the possession of it is intolerable. [John Vanburgh, 1664–1726, *The Confederacy*, I. ii]

13 Persistent work triumphed, and the stress of need in a hard life. [Virgil, 70–19 BC, *Georgics*, I, 145]

14 There are three things that you need in this world. Respect for all kinds of life, a nice bowel movement on a regular basis and a navy blazer. [Robin Williams, 1952– , in film *The Fisher King*, script by Richard LaGrevenese]

15 Man wants but little, nor that little long. [Edward Young, 1683–1765, *Night Thoughts*, 'Night 4', 118]; see 3

See also FORCE, POWER

NEGLECT

1 The world beats a path past his door. [Guy Bellamy, 1935– , *The Sinner's Congregation*, Ch. 7]

2 A little neglect may breed mischief ... for want of a nail the shoe was lost; for want of a shoe the horse was lost; and for want of a horse the rider was lost. [Benjamin Franklin, 1706–90, *Maxims* ... prefixed to *Poor Richard's Almanac*]

3 No man is well pleased to have his all neglected, be it ever so little. [Dr Samuel Johnson, 1709–84, in James Boswell, *Life of J*, letter to Lord Chesterfield, 7 Feb. 1754]

4 He was but as the cuckoo is in June, / Heard but not regarded. [William Shakespeare, 1564–1616, *1 Henry IV*, III. ii. 75]

NEIGHBOURS

1 Thou shalt love thy neighbour as thyself. [Bible, OT, *Leviticus* 19:18; also *St Matthew* 19:19]

2 Whenever our neighbour's house is on fire, it cannot be amiss for the engines to play a little on our own. [Edmund Burke, 1729–97, *Reflections on the Revolution in France*, Penguin edn, p. 92]; see 6

3 The villas and the chapels where / I learned with little labour / The way to love my fellow-man / And hate my next-door neighbour. [G K Chesterton, 1874–1936, *The World State*]

4 My apple trees will never get across / And eat the cones under his pines, I tell him. / He only says, 'Good fences make good neighbours.' [Robert Frost, 1874–1963, *Mending Wall*]

5 The lady of the house was everyone's neighbour, and knew about half as much as God; and whatever had escaped her she made up out of a fund of experience, gleaned from the purchase and sale of buttons. [Leon Garfield, 1921–96, *The Pleasure Garden*, Ch. 9]

6 When your neighbour's wall is on fire, it becomes your business. [Horace, 65–8 BC, *Epistles*, I, 84]; see 2

7 Do not love your neighbour as yourself. If you are on good terms with yourself it is an impertinence: if on bad, an injury. [George Bernard Shaw, 1856–1950, *Man and Superman*, 'Maxims for Revolutionists', The Golden Rule]

See also FRIENDS

NEUROSIS

1 I am always on at him to get his claustrophobia looked at but it is not easy to find a doctor who will see him in the middle of a field. [Alan Coren, 1938– , *Bumf*, 'No Bloody Fear']

2 Which fiddle-strings is weakness to expredge my nerves this night! [Charles Dickens, 1812–70, *Martin Chuzzlewit*, Ch. 51]

3 My nerves are bad to-night. Yes, bad. [T S Eliot, 1888–1965, *The Waste Land*, 111]

4 Two persons in every one in Woolwich are schizophrenic. [Graffito in lavatory in theatre at Woolwich, in *The Times*, 3 May 1978]

5 For anybody of my generation, so eager for the neurosis, yours if you could manage it, if desperate somebody else's ... [Lillian Hellman, 1905–84, *Pentimento*, 'Theatre']

6 When you suffer an attack of nerves you're being attacked by the nervous system. What chance has a man got against a system? [Russell Hoban, 1925– , *The Lion of Boaz-Jachin and Jachin-Boaz*, Ch. 13]

7 We are born into a world where alienation awaits us. [R D Laing, 1927–89, *The Politics of Experience*, Introduction]

8 It seems to us that *without exception* the experience and behaviour that gets labelled schizophrenic is *a special strategy that a person invents in order to live in an unlivable situation.* [R D Laing, 1927–89, *The Politics of Experience*, Ch. 5]

9 One out of four people in this country is mentally unbalanced. Think of your three closest friends – and if they seem okay then you're the one! [Ann Landers, 1918– , in *Kiss Me Hardy*, ed. Roger Kilroy]

10 A neurotic is the man who builds a castle in the air. A psychotic is the man who lives in it. A psychiatrist is the man who collects the rent. [Jerome Lawrence, 1916– ; in Laurence J Peter, *Peter's Quotations*]

11 Everything we think of as great has come to us from neurotics. It is they and they alone who found religions and create great works of art. The world will never realize how much it owes to them, and what they have suffered in order to bestow their gifts on it. [Marcel Proust, 1871–1922, *Remembrance of Things Past: The Guermantes Way*, 'Decline and Death of My Grandmother']

12 Neurosis has an absolute genius for malingering. There is no illness which it cannot counterfeit perfectly ... If it is capable of deceiving the doctor, how should it fail to deceive the patient? [Marcel Proust, 1871–1922, *Remembrance of Things Past: The Guermantes Way*, 'Decline and Death of My Grandmother']

13 LINUS: You got sort of nervous when she walked by, didn't you, Charlie Brown?
CHARLIE BROWN: What makes you think I got nervous?
LINUS: You tied your peanut butter sandwich in a knot. [Charles Schulz, 1922– , in *Peanuts* strip cartoon]

14 Why don't you get dressed, then, and go to pieces like a man? [James Thurber, 1894–1961, *The Seal in the Bedroom*, cartoon caption]

15 Neurosis is the way of avoiding non-being by avoiding being. [Paul Tillich, 1886–1965, *The Courage to Be*, Pt 2, Ch. 7]

See also ILLNESS, MADNESS, MIND, PSYCHIATRY

NEW YEAR

1 Now the New Year reviving old Desires, / The thoughtful Soul to Solitude retires, / Where the White Hand of Moses on the Bough / Puts out, and Jesus from the Ground suspires. [Edward Fitzgerald, 1809–83, *The Rubá'iyát of Omar Khayyám*, Edn 1, 4]

NEW YORK

1 The cab driver took her to Times Square, which is like hell without the hygiene. [Nancy Banks-Smith, 1929– , in *Guardian*, 8 Dec. 1990]

2 I think that New York is not the cultural centre of America, but the business and administrative centre of American culture. [Saul Bellow, 1915– (radio interview), in *Listener*, 22 May 1969]

3 Manhattan is the home of the bald ego, the American national bird. [Harold Brodkey, 1930–96, *This Wild Darkness*]

4 A city where wise guys peddle gold bricks to each other and Truth, crushed down to earth, rises again as phoney as a glass eye. [Ben Hecht, 1893–1964, screenplay of film *Nothing Sacred*]

5 I don't like the life here in New York. There is no greenery. It would make a stone sick. [Nikita Khrushchev, 1894–1971; in *Barnes and Noble Book of Quotations*, ed. Robert I Fitzhenry, 'America']

6 New York is the perfect model of a city, not the model of a perfect city. [Lewis Mumford, 1895–1990, *My Work and Days*]

7 New York tolerated hypocrisy in private relations; but in business matters it exacted a limpid and impeccable honesty. [Edith Wharton, 1862–1937, *The Age of Innocence*, Bk II, Ch. 26]

8 New York's a small place when it comes to the part of it that wakes up just as the rest is going to bed. [P G Wodehouse, 1881–1975, *My Man Jeeves*, 'The Aunt and the Sluggard']

See also AMERICANS, UNITED STATES OF AMERICA

NEWS

1 News of one day, one afternoon, one time. / If it were possible to take these things / Quite seriously, I believe they might / Curry disorders in the strongest brain, / Immobilize the most resilient will, / Stop trains, break up the city's food supply, / And perfectly demoralize the nation. [John Berryman, 1914–72, *World-Telegram*]

2 As cold waters to a thirsty soul, so is good news from a far country. [Bible, OT, *Proverbs* 25:25]

3 A master-passion is the love of news. [George Crabbe, 1754–1832, *The Newspaper*, 279]

4 When a dog bites a man that is not news, but when a man bites a dog that is news. [Charles A Dana, 1819–97, 'What is News?', *New York Sun*, 1882]

5 The more abhorrent a news item the more comforting it was to be the recipient since the fact that it had happened elsewhere proved that it had not happened here, was not happening here, and would therefore never happen here. [John Fowles, 1926– , *The Ebony Tower*, 'Poor Koko']

6 News is anything that makes a reader say 'Gee whiz!' ... News is whatever a good editor chooses to print. [Arthur McEwen, d.1907, in *Colliers*, 18 Feb. 1911]

7 For evil news rides post, while good news baits. [John Milton, 1608–74, *Samson Agonistes*, 1538]

8 Though it be honest, it is never good / To bring bad news. [William Shakespeare, 1564–1616, *Antony and Cleopatra*, II. v. 85]

9 The report of my death is exaggerated. [Mark Twain, 1835–1910, cable from London to the Associated Press, 1897. Slightly varying versions exist]

10 News is what a chap who doesn't care much about anything wants to read. And it's only news until he's read it. After that it's dead. [Evelyn Waugh, 1903–66, *Scoop*, Bk I, Ch. 1, 4]

See also next category, MEDIA, TELEVISION

NEWSPAPERS

1 What the proprietorship of these papers [referring to Beaverbrook and Rothermere] is aiming at is power, and power without responsibility – the prerogative of the harlot through the ages. [Stanley Baldwin, 1867–1947, by-election speech, 18 Mar. 1931. Lord Birkenhead claims in *Rudyard Kipling*, Ch. 20, that the phrase originated with Kipling and was borrowed by his cousin, Baldwin.]; see 13, 35

2 The wages of sin are increased circulation. [John Beavan, 1910–94; *Independent*, 'Quote Unquote', 29 Apr. 1989]

3 If this paper had covered the crucifixion, Fred thought, it would have had a graph on the front page showing the rising cost of timber. [Guy Bellamy, 1935– , *I Have a Complaint to Make*, Ch. 5]

4 I read the newspaper avidly. It is my one form of continuous fiction. [Aneurin Bevan, 1897–1960; *Observer*, 'Sayings of the Week', 3 Apr. 1960]

5 What on earth is all this stuff about the truth? Truth? Why, when everywhere you go people tell lies. In pubs. To each other. To their husbands. To the children. To the dying – and thank God they do. No one tells the truth. Why single out newspapers? [Howard Brenton, 1942– , and David Hare, 1947– , *Pravda*, II. iv]

6 If you want to make a fortune, don't work on a newspaper: own it. There is absolutely no obligation to read it, even if you can. [James Cameron, 1911–85, *Cameron in the Guardian*, 'Thanks a Million']

7 *The Times* is speechless [over Irish Home Rule] and takes three columns to express its speechlessness. [Winston Churchill, 1874–1965, speech at Dundee, 14 May 1908]

8 Thou god of our idolatry, the Press. [William Cowper, 1731–1800, *The Progress of Error*, 461]

9 [When newspaper artist Frederic Remington cabled to be allowed home since there was no war in Cuba for him to cover] Please remain. You furnish the pictures and I'll furnish the war. [W R Hearst, 1863–1951, cable, 1898]

10 The liberty of the Press is the *Palladium* of all the civil, political, and religious rights of an Englishman. [Junius, 18th cent., *Letters*, dedication]

11 It's the duty of a newspaper to comfort the afflicted and to flick the comfortable. [(Said by Gene Kelly in film *Inherit the Wind*) script by Nathan E Douglas and Harold Jacob Smith, based on play by Jerome Lawrence and Robert E Lee]

12 King over all the children of pride / Is the Press – the Press – the Press! [Rudyard Kipling, 1865–1936, *The Press*]

13 Power without responsibility – the prerogative of the harlot throughout the ages. [Rudyard Kipling, 1865–1936, speech, 14 Feb. 1923]; see 1, 35

14 Newspapers have roughly the same relationship to life as fortune-tellers to metaphysics. [Karl Kraus, 1874–1936, *Half-truths and One-and-a-half Truths*, 'In Hollow Heads']

15 Newspapers always excite curiosity. No one ever lays one down without a feeling of disappointment. [Charles Lamb, 1775–1834, *Last Essays of Elia*, 'Detached Thoughts on Books and Reading']

16 Freedom of the press is guaranteed only to those who own one. [A J Liebling, 1904–63, *The New Yorker*, 14 May 1960]

17 Teenage sex-change priest in mercy dash to Palace. [Magnus Linklater, 1942– (a newspaper editor's dream headline), in BBC radio programme, 18 Sept. 1976]

18 The art of newspaper paragraphing is / to stroke a platitude until it purrs like an epigram. [Don Marquis, 1878–1937, *New York Sun*, 'The Sun Dial']

19 A newspaper does not depend on the names of famous writers; it lives by securing a niche of its own. It must become compulsive reading for a group of people. If enough readers find they cannot do without the paper it will have influence and success; if it merely has brilliant contributors it will die. [Kingsley Martin, 1897–1969, *Father Figures*, Ch. 10]

20 A good newspaper, I suppose, is a nation talking to itself. [Arthur Miller, 1915– ; *Observer*, 'Sayings of the Week', 26 Nov. 1961]

21 SIXTY HORSES WEDGED IN A CHIMNEY – The story to fit this sensational headline has not turned up yet. [J B Morton ('Beachcomber'), 1893–1979, *The Best of B*, 13]

22 Our sages know their onions. [Ken Mullen, 1943– , advertisement for *The Times*, from Leo Burnett Advertising Agency]

23 The Third World never sold a newspaper. [Rupert Murdoch, 1931– , in *Observer*, 1 Jan. 1978]

24 All human life is there. [*News of the World* slogan]

25 All the news that's fit to print. [*The New York Times* slogan, devised by Adolph S Ochs, 1896]

26 They are only ten. [Lord Northcliffe, 1865–1922, said to have been written up in his offices to remind the staff of their readership's mental age]

27 We live under a government of men and morning newspapers. [Wendell Phillips, 1811–84, *Address*, 'The Press']

28 The *New Yorker* will be the magazine which is not edited for the old lady from Dubuque. [(On founding the *New Yorker*, 1925) Harold Ross, 1892–1951, in James Thurber, *The Years with Ross*, Ch. 3. Later she became 'the little old lady']

29 By office boys for office boys. [Lord Salisbury, 1830–1903 (description of the *Daily Mail*), in H Hamilton Fyfe, *Northcliffe, an Intimate Biography*, Ch. 4]

30 Comment is free but facts are sacred. [C P Scott, 1846–1932, in *Manchester Guardian*, 5 May 1921]

31 We cultivate literature on a little oatmeal. [(Proposed motto for the *Edinburgh Review*) Sydney Smith, 1771–1845, *Works*, Vol. i, Preface]

32 It is to be noted that when any part of this paper appears dull, there is a design in it. [Richard Steele, 1672–1729, *The Tatler*, 38]

33 *The Times* has published no rumours; it's only reported the facts, namely that other, less responsible papers are publishing certain rumours. [Tom Stoppard, 1937– , *Dirty Linen*]

34 MILNE: No matter how imperfect things are, if you've got a free press everything is correctable, and without it everything is conceivable.
RUTH: I'm with you on the free press. It's the newspapers I can't stand. [Tom Stoppard, 1937– , *Night and Day*, I]

35 He [Lord Northcliffe] aspired to power instead of influence, and as a result forfeited both. [A J P Taylor, 1906–90, *English History, 1914–1945*, Ch. 1]; see 1, 13

36 The *Pall Mall Gazette* is written by gentlemen for gentlemen. [W M Thackeray, 1811–63, *Pendennis*, Ch. 32]

37 '*The Beast* stands for strong mutually antagonistic governments everywhere,' he said. 'Self-sufficiency at home, self-assertion abroad.' [Evelyn Waugh, 1903–66, *Scoop*, Bk I, Ch. 1, 3]

38 My brother cuts the time it takes to read a newspaper by skipping everything in the future tense; and it's amazing what he doesn't miss. [Katharine Whitehorn, 1926– , *Sunday Best*, 'Never-Never Land']

39 I mean, in my day, in a magazine, you didn't have sex, you had a row of dots. [Victoria Wood, 1953– , *Barmy*, 'No Gossip']

See also MEDIA, NEWS, TELEVISION

NIGHT

1 Watchman, what of the night? The watchman said, The morning cometh, and also the night. [Bible, OT, *Isaiah* 21:11]

2 When the moon is on the wave, / And the glow-worm in the grass, / And the meteor on the grave, / And the wisp on the morass; / When the falling stars are shooting, / And the answered owls are hooting, / And the silent leaves are still / In the shadow of the hill. [Lord Byron, 1788–1824, *Manfred*, I, 1]

3 The tropical night has the companionability of a Roman Catholic cathedral compared to the Protestant churches of the north, which let you in on business only. [Isak Dinesen, 1885–1962, *Out of Africa*, 'The Shooting Accident']

4 The night will never stay, / The night will still go by, / Though with a million stars / You pin it to the sky; / Though you bind it with the blowing wind / And buckle it with the moon, / The night will slip away / Like sorrow or a tune. [Eleanor Farjeon, 1881–1965, *The Night Will Never Stay*]

5 Night makes no difference 'twixt the priest and clerk; / Joan as my lady is as good i' th' dark. [Robert Herrick, 1591–1674, *Hesperides*, 'No Difference i' th' Dark']

6 I wake and feel the fell of dark, not day. / What hours, O what black hours we have spent / This night! [Gerard Manley Hopkins, 1844–89, *I Wake and Feel the Fell*]

7 Sable-vested Night, eldest of things. [John Milton, 1608–74, *Paradise Lost*, Bk ii, 962]

8 'Tis now the very witching time of night, / When churchyards yawn and hell itself breathes out / Contagion to this world. [William Shakespeare, 1564–1616, *Hamlet*, III. ii. (413)]

9 Light thickens; and the crow / Makes wing to the rooky wood; / Good things of day begin to droop and drowse, / Whiles night's black agents to their preys do rouse. [*Macbeth*, III. ii. 50]

10 The iron tongue of midnight hath told twelve; / Lovers to bed; 'tis almost fairy time. [*A Midsummer Night's Dream*, V. i. (372)]

11 Come, civil night, / Thou sober-suited matron, all in black. *Romeo and Juliet*, III. ii. 10]

12 Away! the moor is dark beneath the moon, / Rapid clouds have drunk the last pale beam of even: / Away! the gathering winds will call the darkness soon, / And profoundest midnight shroud the serene lights of heaven. [P B Shelley, 1792–1822, *Stanzas – April 1814*]

13 Swiftly walk o'er the western wave, / Spirit of Night! / Out of the misty eastern cave, / Where, all the long and lone daylight, / Thou wovest dreams of joy and fear. [P B Shelley, 1792–1822, *To Night*]

14 How beautiful is night! / A dewy freshness fills the silent air; / No mist obscures, nor cloud, nor speck, nor stain, / Breaks the serene of heaven. [Robert Southey, 1774–1843, *Thalaba the Destroyer*, I, 1]

15 Now welcome, night, thou night so long expected, / That long day's labour dost at last defray. [Edmund Spenser, 1552?–99, *Epithalamion*, 315]

16 All night have the roses heard / The flute, violin, bassoon; / All night has the casement jessamine stirred / To the dancers dancing in tune; / Till a silence fell with the waking bird, / And a hush with the setting moon. [Alfred, Lord Tennyson, 1809–92, *Maud*, Pt 1, xxii, 3]

17 Out in the dark over the snow / The fallow fawns invisible go / With the fallow doe; / And the winds blow / Fast as the stars are slow. [Edward Thomas, 1878–1917, *Out in the Dark*]

18 Dear night! this world's defeat; / The stop to busy fools; care's check and curb. [Henry Vaughan, 1622–95, *The Night*]

19 Mysterious Night! when our first parent knew / Thee from report divine, and heard thy name, / Did he not tremble for this lovely frame, / This glorious canopy of light and blue? [Joseph Blanco White, 1775–1841, *To Night*]

20 Night, sable goddess! from her ebon throne, / In rayless majesty, now stretches forth / Her leaden sceptre o'er a slumb'ring world. [Edward Young, 1683–1765, *Night Thoughts*, 'Night I', 18]

See also DAWN, DAYS, LIGHT

NINETEENTH CENTURY

1 This strange disease of modern life. [Matthew Arnold, 1822–88, *The Scholar-Gypsy*, 203]

2 They [the Victorians] were lame giants; the strongest of them walked on one leg a little shorter than the other. [G K Chesterton, 1874–1936, *The Victorian Age*, Ch. 3]

3 The characteristic of the present age is a craving credulity. [Benjamin Disraeli, 1804–81, speech at Oxford Diocesan Conference, 25 Nov. 1864]

4 In the nineteenth century the problem was that God is dead; in the twentieth century the problem is that man is dead. [Erich Fromm, 1900–1980, *The Sane Society*, Ch. 9]

5 If the nineteenth century was the age of the editorial chair, ours is the century of the psychiatrist's couch. [Marshall McLuhan, 1911–80, *Understanding Media*, Introduction]

See also TWENTIETH CENTURY

NOISE, see LISTENING

NONSENSE

1 'Twas brillig, and the slithy toves / Did gyre and gimble in the wabe; / All mimsy were the borogoves, / And the mome raths outgrabe. [Lewis Carroll, 1832–98, *Through the Looking Glass*, Ch. 1]

2 'The time has come,' the Walrus said, / 'To talk of many things: / Of shoes – and ships – and sealing-wax – / Of cabbages – and kings – / Of why the sea is boiling hot – / And whether pigs have wings.' [Lewis Carroll, 1832–98, *Through the Looking Glass*, Ch. 4]

3 To die for faction is a common evil, / But to be hanged for nonsense is the Devil. [John Dryden, 1631–1700, *Absalom and Achitophel*, Pt II, 498]

4 It is a far, far better thing to have a firm anchor in nonsense than to put out on the troubled seas of thought. [J K Galbraith, 1908– , *The Affluent Society*, Ch. 11, iv]

5 I never nursed a dear gazelle, / To glad me with its dappled hide, / But when it came to know me well / It fell upon the buttered side. [Thomas Hood the Younger, 1834–74, *Muddled Metaphors*]

6 Sir – In answer to your application regarding my parentage, my mother was a bus-horse, my father a cab-driver, my sister a rough-rider over the Arctic regions. My brothers were all gallant sailors on a steam-roller. [George Joseph Smith, Murderer of the Brides in the Bath, 1872–1915 (letter to father-in-law produced at trial), in Edward Marjoribanks, *Life of Sir Edward Marshall Hall*, Ch. 10]

See also HUMOUR, WIT

NOSTALGIA

1 Stands the Church clock at ten to three? / And is there honey still for tea? [Rupert Brooke, 1887–1915, *The Old Vicarage, Grantchester*]

2 Dear dead women, with such hair, too – what's become of all the gold / Used to hang and brush their bosoms? I feel chilly and grow old. [Robert Browning, 1812–89, *A Toccata of Galuppi's*, 15]

3 The 'good old times' – all times when old are good – / Are gone. [Lord Byron, 1788–1824, *The Age of Bronze*, 1]

4 If only we could go back to Moscow! Sell the house, finish with our life here, and go back to Moscow. [Anton Chekhov, 1860–1904, *The Three Sisters*, I]

5 Montagu Norman , governor of the Bank of England when the Bank of England was as steady as the Bank of England. [Terry Coleman, 1931– , *The Liners*, Ch. 5]

6 What peaceful hours I once enjoyed! / How sweet their memory still! / But they have left an aching void / The world can never fill. [William Cowper, 1731–1800, *Olney Hymns*, 1]

7 Way down upon de Swanee Ribber, / Far, far away, / Dere's where my heart is turning ebber: / Dere's where de old folks stay. / All up and down de whole creation / Sadly I roam, / Still longing for de old plantation, / And for de old folks at home. [Stephen Foster, 1826–64, *Old Folks at Home*]

8 *Les temps héroïques sont passés.* – The heroic times have passed away. [Léon Gambetta, 1838–82, saying]

9 Nostalgia isn't what it used to be. [Graffito]

10 Where once we danced, where once we sang, Gentlemen, / The floors are shrunken, cobwebs hang. [Thomas Hardy, 1840–1928, *An Ancient to Ancients*]

11 I remember, I remember, / The house where I was born, / The little window where the sun / Came peeping in at morn. [Thomas Hood, 1799–1845, *I Remember*]

12 Pale hands I loved beside the Shalimar, / Where are you now? Who lies beneath your spell? [Laurence Hope, 1865–1904, 'Pale Hands I Loved']

13 Testy, querulous and given to praising the way things were when he was a boy. [Horace, 65–8 BC, *Ars Poetica*, 173]

14 Into my heart an air that kills / From yon far country blows: / What are those blue remembered hills, / What spires, what farms are those?

That is the land of lost content, / I see it shining plain, / The happy highways where I went / And cannot come again. [A E Housman, 1859–1936, *A Shropshire Lad*, 40]

15 But were there ever any / Writhed not at passed joy? [John Keats, 1795–1821, *Stanzas In a Drear-nighted December*]

16 Ship me somewhere east of Suez, where the best is like the worst, / I have had playmates, I have had companions, / In my days of childhood, in my joyful school-days, – All, all are gone, the old familiar faces. [Charles Lamb, 1775–1834, *The Old Familiar Faces*]

17 For love that time was not as love is now-adays. [Thomas Malory, d.1471, *Morte d'Arthur*, Bk xx, Ch. 3]

18 Time will run back, and fetch the age of gold. [John Milton, 1608–74, *On the Morning of Christ's Nativity*, 135]

19 Forget six counties overhung with smoke, / Forget the snorting steam and piston stroke, / Forget the spreading of the hideous town; / Think rather of the pack-horse on the down, / And dream of London, small and white and clean, / The clear Thames bordered by its gardens green. [William Morris, 1834–96, *The Earthly Paradise*, 'Prologue, The Wanderers']

20 Before the war, and especially before the Boer War, it was summer all the year round. [George Orwell, 1903–50, *Coming Up for Air*, II, 1]

21 They spend their time mostly looking forward to the past. [John Osborne, 1929–94, *Look Back in Anger*, II. 1]

22 There never was a merry world since the fairies left off dancing, and the parson left conjuring. [John Selden, 1584–1654, *Table Talk*, 99]

23 I was adored once too. [William Shakespeare, 1564–1616, *Twelfth Night*, II. iii. (200)]

24 O world! O life! O time! / On whose last steps I climb, / Trembling at that where I had stood before; / When will return the glory of your prime? / No more – Oh, never more! [P B Shelley, 1792–1822, *A Lament*]

25 For now I see the true old times are dead, / When every morning brought a noble chance, / And every chance brought out a noble knight. [Alfred, Lord Tennyson, 1809–92, *Idylls of the King*, 'The Passing of Arthur', 397]

26 *Mais où sont les neiges d'antan?* – Where are the snows of yesteryear? [François Villon, 1431–65?, *Ballade des dames du temps jadis*]

27 Whither is fled the visionary gleam? / Where is it now, the glory and the dream? [William Wordsworth, 1770–1850, *Ode, Intimations of Immortality*, 4]

See also MEMORY, PAST, REGRET

NOTHING

1 A world where nothing is had for nothing. [Arthur Hugh Clough, 1819–61, *Amours de voyage*, VIII, 5]

2 To whom nothing is given, of him can nothing be required. [Henry Fielding, 1707–54, *Joseph Andrews*, Bk ii, Ch. 8]

3 Nothing can be created out of nothing. [Lucretius, 99–55 BC, *On the Nature of the Universe*, I, 155]

4 Nothink for nothink 'ere, and precious little for sixpence! [*Punch* (1869), lvii, 152]

5 Nothing, thou elder brother ev'n to shade, / Thou hadst a being ere the world was made. [Earl of Rochester, 1647–80, *Upon Nothing*]

6 Nothing will come of nothing: speak again. [William Shakespeare, 1564–1616, *King Lear*, I. i. (92)]

7 God made everything out of nothing. But the nothingness shows through. [Paul Valéry, *Bad Thoughts and Not So Bad*, T]

See also LIMBO

NOVELISTS IN GENERAL

1 No poet or novelist wishes he were the only one who ever lived, but most of them wish they were the only one alive, and quite a number fondly believe their wish has been granted. [W H Auden, 1907–73, *The Dyer's Hand*, 'Writing']

2 You can't get at the truth by writing history; only the novelist can do that. [Gerald Brenan, 1894–1987 (when invited to write the Spanish volume in the *Oxford History of Europe*), in *The Times Literary Supplement*, 28 Nov. 1986]

3 As a novelist he was almost successful. His books were watched for ... but without impatience. [Ronald Firbank, 1886–1926, *Vainglory*, 2]

4 Historians tell the story of the past, novelists the story of the present. [Edmond and Jules de Goncourt, 1822–96, and 1830–70, *Idées et Sensations*]

5 A woman must have money and a room of her own if she is to write fiction. [Virginia Woolf, 1882–1941, *A Room of One's Own*, Ch. 1]

See also following categories, PROSE, STORIES, WRITERS, WRITING

NOVELISTS: INDIVIDUAL (in alphabetical order of subject)

1 The little bit (two inches wide) of ivory on which I work with so fine a brush, as produces little effect after much labour. [Jane Austen, 1775–1817, letter, 16 Dec. 1816]

2 The Big Bow-Wow strain I can do myself like anyone now going; but the exquisite touch, which renders ordinary commonplace things and characters interesting, from the truth of the description and the sentiment, is denied to me. [(Of Jane Austen) Sir Walter Scott, 1771–1832, *Journal*, 14 Mar. 1826]

3 The vital accessories to my work are my reference books, such as the complete Shakespeare and a prayer book, and a large refuse bin. [Beryl Bainbridge, 1934– , interview in *Guardian*, 8 Aug. 1991]

4 Balzac observed all the things that Marx did not see. [Régis Debray, 1941– , *Teachers, Writers, Celebrities*, 'Balzac, or Zoology Today']

5 Bellow says he spent the first third of his life absorbing material, the second third trying to make himself famous, and the last third trying to avoid fame. [Saul Bellow, 1915– , in Edward Hoagland, *Learning to Eat Soup*]

6 She [Charlotte Brontë] does not attempt to solve the problems of human life; she is even unaware that such problems exist; all her force, and it is the more tremendous for being constricted, goes into the assertion, 'I love', 'I hate', 'I suffer'. [Virginia Woolf, 1882–1941, *The Common Reader*, First Series, 'Jane Eyre']

7 We were put to Dickens as children but it never quite took. That unremitting humanity soon had me cheesed off. [Alan Bennett, 1934– , *The Old Country*, II]

8 It does not matter that Dickens' world is not life-like; it is alive. [Lord David Cecil, 1902–86, *Early Victorian Novelists*]

9 Dickens was not the first or the last novelist to find virtue more difficult to portray than the wish for it. [V S Pritchett, 1900–1997, *Books in General*, 'Oliver Twist']

10 Of all the great Victorian writers, he [Dickens] was probably the most antagonistic to the Victorian age itself. [Edmund Wilson, 1895–1972, *The Wound and the Bow*, 'The Two Scrooges']

11 No matter how much of a shabby animal you may be, you can learn from Dostoyevsky and Chekhov, etc., how to have the most tender, unique, coruscating soul on earth. [D H Lawrence, 1885–1930, *Phoenix*, 'Preface to Mastro-don Gesualdo']

12 They are great parables, the novels [Dostoyevsky's], but false art. They are only parables. All the people are *fallen angels* – even the dirtiest scrubs. This I cannot stomach. People are not fallen angels, they are merely people. [D H Lawrence, 1885–1930, letter to J Middleton Murry and Katherine Mansfield, 17 Feb. 1916]

13 Often I think writing is a sheer paring away of oneself leaving always something thinner, barer, more meagre. [F Scott Fitzgerald, 1896–1940, letter to Frances Scott Fitzgerald, 27 Apr. 1940]

14 He [Fitzgerald] knew we pay for everything; this was what he was paid to know. [Andre Le Vot, 1921– , from *F S F: A Biography*, Introduction]

15 As artists they're rot, but as providers they're oil wells; they gush ... And there was that poor sucker Flaubert rolling around on his floor for three days looking for the right word. [Dorothy Parker, 1893–1967, in *Writers at Work*, ed. Malcolm Cowley, First Series]

16 The trouble began with Forster. After him it was considered ungentlemanly to write more than five or six [novels]. [Anthony Burgess, 1917–93, interview in *Guardian*, 24 Feb. 1989]

17 In no book have I got down more than the people I like, the person I think I am, and the people who irritate me. This puts me among the large body of authors who are not really novelists, and have to get on as best they can with these three categories. [E M Forster,

1879–1970, in *Writers at Work* ed. Malcolm Cowley, First Series]

18 E. M. Forster never gets any further than warming the teapot. He's a rare fine hand at that. Feel this teapot. Is it not beautifully warm? Yes, but there ain't going to be no tea. [Katherine Mansfield, 1888–1923, *Journal*, May 1917]

19 The great nineteenth-century English novelists are Gogol, Dostoyevsky, Tolstoy, Stendhal and Balzac in English. [Stephen Vizinczey, 1933– , *Truth and Lies in Literature*, Prologue]

20 I have to watch my characters crossing the room, lighting a cigarette. I have to see everything they do, even if I don't write it down. So my eyes get tired. [Graham Greene, 1904–91 (on his method of writing), interview in John Mortimer, *In Character*]

21 [In reply to Graham Greene, who had said that he intended to write a political novel] I wouldn't give up writing about God at this stage, if I was you. It would be like P. G. Wodehouse dropping Jeeves half-way through the Wooster series. [Evelyn Waugh, 1903–66, in Christopher Sykes, *E W*]

22 I started out very quiet and I beat Mr Turgenev. Then I trained hard and I beat Mr de Maupassant. I've fought two draws with Mr Stendhal, and I think I had an edge in the last one. But nobody's going to get me in any ring with Mr Tolstoy unless I'm crazy or I keep getting better. [Ernest Hemingway, 1899–1961, from the *New Yorker*, 13 May 1950, in Lillian Ross, *Portrait of H*]

23 The work of Henry James has always seemed divisible by a simple dynastic arrangement into three reigns: James I, James II, and the Old Pretender. [Philip Guedalla, 1889–1944, *Supers and Supermen*, 'Some Critics']

24 But then I'm a battered old novelist and it's my business to comprehend. [Henry James, 1843–1916, letter to Edward Marsh, 1915]

25 None of them [the Beat novelists] can write, not even Mr Kerouac. What they do ... isn't writing at all – it's typing. [Truman Capote, 1924–84, on US TV, Feb. 1959]

26 I am a man, and alive ... For this reason I am a novelist. And being a novelist, I consider myself superior to the saint, the scientist, the philosopher, and the poet, who are all great masters of different bits of man alive, but never get the whole hog. [D H Lawrence, 1885–1930, *Phoenix*, 'Why the Novel Matters']

27 Novels don't always come your way ... It's like falling in love. You can't say: 'Oh, gee, I think I'm ready to fall in love,' and then meet some woman who'd be perfect. When a novel comes, it's a grace. Something in the cosmos has forgiven you long enough so that you can start. [Norman Mailer, 1923– , interview in *Weekend Guardian*, 5–6 Oct. 1991]

28 He [Norman Mailer] is now what he wanted to be: the patron saint of bad journalism. [Gore Vidal, 1925– , in *Writers at Work*, ed. George Plimpton, Fifth Series]

29 A whale ship was my Yale College and my Harvard. [Herman Melville, 1819–91, *Moby Dick*, Ch. 24]

30 A novelist is, like all mortals, more fully at home on the surface of the present than in the ooze of the past. [Vladimir Nabokov, 1899–1977, *Strong Opinions*, Ch. 20]

31 Proust is to life as an empty orchestra pit is to music. [John Naughton, 1933– , in *Observer*, 24 Feb. 1991]

32 'And you say it's [Proust's work] about something in particular?' ... 'Well, it's about everything in particular, isn't it?' [Muriel Spark, 1918– , *A Far Cry from Kensington*, Ch. 6]

33 The greatest mind ever to stay in prep school. [(Of J D Salinger) Norman Mailer, 1923– ; in *Oh, What an Awful Thing to Say!*, comp. W Cole and L Phillips]

34 The stories [*The Lord of the Rings*] were made rather to provide a world for the languages than the reverse. To me a name comes first and the story follows. [J R R Tolkien, 1892–1973, letter, in *Observer*, 23 Aug. 1981]

35 Their teacher had advised them not to read Tolstoy's novels, because they were very long and would easily confuse the clear ideas which they had learned from reading critical studies of him. [Alexander Solzhenitsyn, 1918– , *The First Circle*, Ch. 40]

36 I start with characters. I walk around in their shoes for a long time. I stay in my pyjamas all day talking to people who aren't there. [Barbara Trapido, 1941– , interview in *Independent*, 30 July 1994]

37 With all his mastery, Trollope is interested

only in what people are like, not in what they are for. [V S Pritchett, 1900–1997, quoted in obituary in *Guardian*, 22 Mar. 1997]

38 The Old Maid among novelists. [Rebecca West, 1892–1983, review of H G Wells' *Marriage*, 19 Sept. 1912]

See also previous and following categories, PROSE, STORIES, WRITERS, WRITING

NOVELS IN GENERAL

1 What is fictitious in a novel is not so much the story but the method by which thought develops into action, a method which never occurs in daily life. [Alain (Émile Auguste Chartier), 1868–1951, in E M Forster, *Aspects of the Novel*, 3]

2 Hubris clobbered by Nemesis. [Brian Aldiss, 1925– (shortest definition of science fiction), *Science Fiction Art*, Introduction]

3 You can have a men's novel with no women in it except possibly the landlady / or the horse, but you can't have a women's novel with no men in it. / Sometimes men put women in men's novels / but they leave out some of the parts; / the heads, for instance. [Margaret Atwood, 1939– , *Poem*, in Resa Dudovitz, *The Myth of Superwoman*]

4 'And what are you reading, Miss A?' 'Oh! it is only a novel!' ... or, in short, only some work in which the most thorough knowledge of human nature, the happiest delineation of its varieties, the liveliest effusions of wit and humour are conveyed to the world in the best chosen language. [Jane Austen, 1775–1817, *Northanger Abbey*, Ch. 5]

5 History is in the shit sense. You have left it behind you. Fiction is piss: a stream of past events but not behind you, because they never really happened. [Brigid Brophy, 1929–95, *In Transit*, sect. I, 1]

6 Or, my scrofulous French novel / On grey paper with blunt type! / Simply glance at it, you grovel / Hand and foot in Belial's gripe. [Robert Browning, 1812–89, *Soliloquy of the Spanish Cloister*]

7 A good novel tells us the truth about its hero; but a bad novel tells us the truth about its author. [G K Chesterton, 1874–1936, *Heretics*, 15]

8 The novel was invented for the ladies to kill time, / And time was invented to kill the novelist. [Lawrence Durrell, 1912–90, from *Endpapers and Inklings*, in *Antaeus: Journals, Notebooks and Diaries*, ed. D Halpern, p. 93]

9 [A novel is] a machine for generating interpretations. [Umberto Eco, 1932– , from 'Reflections on *The Name of the Rose*', in *Observer*, 7 Apr. 1985]

10 Yes – oh dear, yes – the novel tells a story. [E M Forster, 1879–1970, *Aspects of the Novel*, 2]

11 The novel is born from the very fact that we do not understand one another any longer, because unitary, orthodox language has broken down. [Carlos Fuentes, 1928– , in *Guardian*, 24 Feb. 1989]

12 REG: Just one of those historical romances where the hero shoves his sword into assorted villains and his cock into assorted ladies. It won't get the reviews but it'll make us money.
BEN: If he did it the other way round you might get both. [Simon Gray, 1936– , *Butley*, II]

13 I like a story with a bad moral ... all good stories have a coarse touch or a bad moral, depend on't. If the story-tellers could ha' got decency and good morals from true stories, who'd have troubled to invent parables? [Thomas Hardy, 1840–1928, *Under the Greenwood Tree*, I, Ch. 8]

14 Journalism allows its readers to witness history; fiction gives its readers an opportunity to live it. [John Hersey, 1914–96, in *Time*, 13 Mar. 1950]

15 It is a piece of prose that has something wrong with it. [Randall Jarrell, 1914–65 (defining the novel), in *The Nation*, 25 May 1946]

16 The territory where no one possesses the truth, but where everyone has the right to be understood. [Milan Kundera, 1929– (of the novel), *The Art of the Novel*]

17 According to my calculations there are two or three new fictional characters baptized on earth every second. [Milan Kundera, 1929– , *The Book of Laughter and Forgetting*, Pt 4, 1]

18 Far too many relied on the classic formula of a beginning, a muddle, and an end. [(Of modern novels) Philip Larkin, 1922–85 (speech on judging the Booker Prize, 1977), in *New Fiction*, Jan. 1978]

19 Only in the novel are *all* things given full

play. [D H Lawrence, 1885–1930, *Phoenix*, 'Why the Novel Matters']

20 All art is full of magic and trickery, but in a novel the whole thing can subside into an ocean of reflection and continuous thought – at least in a traditional novel – whereas in theatre you are really jumping from place to place like a mountain goat. [Iris Murdoch, 1919–99, interview in *Weekend Guardian*, 22–23 Apr. 1989]

21 The novel is practically a Protestant form of art; it is a product of the free mind, of the autonomous individual. [George Orwell, 1903–50, *Inside the Whale*, II]

22 People think that because a novel's invented, it isn't true. Exactly the reverse is the case. Biography and memoirs can never be wholly true, since they cannot include every conceivable circumstance of what happened. The novel can do that. [Anthony Powell, 1905– , *Hearing Secret Harmonies*, Ch. 3]

23 The detective novel is the art-for-art's-sake of yawning Philistinism. [V S Pritchett, 1900–1997, *Books in General*, 'The Roots of Detection']

24 What adultery was to the nineteenth century novel espionage is to today's. The sincerity of defection is common to both. [Frederic Raphael, 1931– , in *The Times Literary Supplement*, 3 Apr. 1987]

25 Make 'em laugh; make 'em cry; make 'em wait. [Charles Reade, 1814–84, recipe for novel-writing in serial form]

26 A novel is a mirror walking along a main road. [Stendhal, 1783–1842, *The Red and the Black*, Ch. 49]

27 A novel is a static thing that one moves through; a play is a dynamic thing that moves past one. [Kenneth Tynan, 1927–80, *Curtains*, 1, 'Cards of Identity']

28 I suspect one of the reasons we create fiction is to make sex exciting. [Gore Vidal, 1925– , in *The Times Literary Supplement*, 2 Oct. 1987]

29 Of course we can Learn even from Novels, Nace Novels that is, but it isn't the same thing as serious reading. [H G Wells, 1866–1946, *Kipps*, Bk II, Ch. 2, i]

30 The good ended happily, and the bad unhappily. That is what Fiction means. [Oscar Wilde, 1854–1900, *The Importance of Being Earnest*, II]

31 In the play we recognize the general . . . in the novel, the particular. [Virginia Woolf, 1882–1941, in Kenneth Tynan, *Curtains*, Pt 2]

See also previous and following categories, PROSE, STORIES, WRITERS, WRITING

NOVELS: INDIVIDUAL (in alphabetical order of author of novel)

1 Was there ever yet anything written by mere man that was wished longer by its readers, excepting *Don Quixote*, *Robinson Crusoe*, and the *Pilgrim's Progress*? [Dr Samuel Johnson, 1709–84, in Mrs Piozzi, *Anecdotes of J*]

2 Casting my mind's eye over the whole of fiction, the only absolutely original creation I can think of is Don Quixote. [W Somerset Maugham, 1874–1965, *Ten Novels and their Authors*, Ch. 1, sect. I]

3 *Middlemarch*, the magnificent book which with all its imperfections is one of the few English novels for grown up people. [Virginia Woolf, 1882–1941, *The Common Reader*, First Series, 'George Eliot']

4 The romance of *Tom Jones*, that exquisite picture of human manners, will outlive the palace of the Escurial and the imperial eagle of the house of Austria. [Edward Gibbon, 1737–94, *Autobiography*]

5 An interviewer asked me what book I thought best represented the modern American Woman. All I could think of to answer was: *Madame Bovary*. [Mary McCarthy, 1912–89, *On the Contrary*, 'Characters in Fiction']

6 It [*The Good Soldier*] is the finest French novel in the English language. [John Rodker, quoted by Ford Madox Ford in a dedicatory letter to the novel]

7 The theme defeats structuralism, for it is an emotion. The theme of *Lord of the Flies* is grief, sheer grief, grief, grief. [William Golding, 1911–93, *A Moving Target*, title essay]

8 I understand the hero keeps getting in bed with women, and the war wasn't fought that way. [(On Hemingway's *A Farewell to Arms*) Harold Ross, 1892–1951, in James Thurber, *The Years with Ross*, Ch. 7]

9 All raw, uncooked, protesting. A descendant,

oddly enough, of Mrs [Humphry] Ward: interest in ideas; makes people into ideas. [(Of Aldous Huxley's *Point Counter Point*) Virginia Woolf, 1882–1941, *A Writer's Diary*, 23 Jan. 1935]

10 *Ulysses* ... is a dogged attempt to cover the universe with mud. [E M Forster, 1879–1970, *Aspects of the Novel*, 6]

11 The telephone directory is, because of its rigorous selection and repression, a work of art compared to the wastepaper basket. And [James Joyce's] *Ulysses* is a wastepaper basket. [Gerald Gould, 1885–1936, *The English Novel*]

12 All my good reading, you might say, was done in the toilet ... There are passages of *Ulysses* which can be read only in the toilet – if one wants to extract the full flavour of their content. [Henry Miller, 1891–1980, *Black Spring*, 'Paris and Its Suburbs']

13 Never have I read such tosh. As for the first two chapters we will let them pass, but the 3rd, 4th, 5th, 6th – merely the scratching of pimples on the body of the boot-boy at Claridges. [(Of James Joyce's *Ulysses*) Virginia Woolf, 1882–1941, letter to Lytton Strachey, 24 Aug. 1922]

14 I have only read one book in my life, and that is *White Fang*. It's so frightfully good I've never bothered to read another. [Nancy Mitford, 1904–73, *The Pursuit of Love*, Ch. 2]

15 Nothing odd will do long. *Tristram Shandy* did not last. [Dr Samuel Johnson, 1709–84, in James Boswell, *Life of J*, 20 Mar. 1776]

16 It has been said that a careful reading of *Anna Karenina*, if it teaches you nothing else, will teach you how to make strawberry jam. [Julian Mitchell, 1935– , in *Radio Times*, 30 Oct. 1976]

See also previous categories, PROSE, STORIES, WRITERS, WRITING

NUCLEAR AGE

1 If you carry this resolution and follow out all its implications and do not run away from it, you will send a Foreign Secretary, whoever he was, naked into the conference chamber. [Aneurin Bevan, 1897–1960 (on unilateral disarmament), at Labour Party Conference, 3 Oct. 1957]

2 The way to win an atomic war is to make certain it never starts. [General Omar Bradley, 1893–1981; *Observer*, 'Sayings of the Week', 20 Apr. 1952]

3 Any chortling by officials who have been slothful in pushing this bomb, over the fact that at present it has not succeeded, will be viewed with great disfavour by me. [(To General Ismay) Winston Churchill, 1874–1965, *The Second World War*, Vol. 2, 8]

4 We should have the art [of making atomic bombs] rather than the article [the bombs themselves]. [Winston Churchill, 1874–1965, secret memo to Lord Cherwell, Nov. 1951]

5 Whose finger on the trigger? [*Daily Mirror*, front-page headline on election day, 25 Oct. 1951]; see 13

6 If only I had known. I should have become a watchmaker. [Albert Einstein, 1879–1955, of his making the atom bomb possible (1945)]

7 The release of atom power has changed everything except our way of thinking, and thus we are being driven unarmed towards a catastrophe ... The solution of this problem lies in the heart of humankind. [Albert Einstein, 1879–1955, to US National Commission of Nuclear Scientists, 24 May 1946]

8 Surely the right course is to test the Russians not the bombs. [Hugh Gaitskell, 1906–63; *Observer*, 'Sayings of the Week', 23 June 1957]

9 But God can't want that. [Otto Hahn, 1879–1968 (of the possibility of releasing atomic energy, said in 1939), recalled in *Guardian*, 17 Apr. 1987]

10 We have resolved to endure the unendurable and suffer what is insufferable. [(After dropping of atomic bomb on Hiroshima, Aug. 1945) Emperor Hirohito of Japan, 1901–89, quoted by A J P Taylor in *Listener*, 9 Sept. 1976]

11 Aside from being tremendous it was one of the most aesthetically beautiful things I have ever seen. [Donald Hornig, 1920– (of first atomic test), *The Decision to Drop the Bomb*]

12 At first it [the first atomic explosion] was a giant column that soon took the shape of a supramundane mushroom. [William L Laurence, 1888–1977, in *The New York Times*, 26 Sept. 1945]

13 Fifteen fingers on the safety catch. [Harold Macmillan, 1894–1986, speech in House of Commons, 30 May 1960, on breakdown of summit conference on nuclear disarmament]; see 5

14 The atom bomb is a paper tiger which the United States reactionaries use to scare people. [Mao Zedong, 1893–1976, in conversation with the American correspondent, Anna Louise Strong, Aug. 1946]

15 I say in all sincerity that the nuclear arms race has no military purpose. Wars cannot be fought with nuclear weapons. Their existence only adds to our perils because of the illusions which they have generated. [Lord Mountbatten, 1900–1979, speech at Strasbourg, 11 May 1979]

16 We knew the world would not be the same. [J Robert Oppenheimer, 1904–67 (after first atomic test), in D Hornig, *The Decision to Drop the Bomb*]

17 Some of us may die. / Remember, statistically / It is not likely to be you. / All flags are flying fully dressed / On Government buildings – the sun is shining / Death is the least we have to fear. [Peter Porter, 1929– , *Your Attention Please*]

18 My fellow Americans, I am pleased to tell you I have just signed legislation that will outlaw Russia for ever. We begin bombing in five minutes. [Ronald Reagan, 1911– , rehearsal for TV programme, transmitted in error, 13 Aug. 1984]

19 You may reasonably expect a man to walk a tightrope safely for ten minutes; it would be unreasonable to do so without accident for two hundred years. [(Of the nuclear confrontation of the superpowers) Bertrand Russell, 1872–1970, in D Bagley, *The Tightrope Men*]

20 The energy produced by the breaking down of the atom is a very poor kind of thing. Anyone who expects a source of energy from the transformation of these atoms is talking moonshine. [Ernest Rutherford, 1871–1937, from *Physics Today*, 1970. Often misquoted as 'nuclear power is moonshine']

21 A nuclear holocaust, widely regarded as 'unthinkable' but never as undoable, appears to confront us with an action that we can perform but cannot quite conceive. [Jonathan Schell, 1943– , *The Fate of the Earth*, I]

22 There is no evil in the atom; only in men's souls. [Adlai Stevenson, 1900–1965, speech in Hartford, Connecticut, 18 Sept. 1952]

23 A mushroom of boiling dust up to 20,000 feet. [Col. Paul W Tibbetts, 1915– , description of Hiroshima explosion, 6 Aug. 1945]

24 A bigger bang for a buck. [Charles E Wilson, 1890–1961 (of the H-Bomb tested at Bikini in 1954), in W Safire, *Political Dictionary*]

See also WORLD WAR 2

NUDITY

1 Nakedness is uncomely as well in mind, as body. [Francis Bacon, 1561–1626, *Essays*, 6, 'Of Simulation and Dissimulation']

2 To be naked is to be oneself. To be nude is to be seen naked by others, and yet not recognized for oneself . . . Nudity is a form of dress. [John Berger, 1926– , *et al.*, *Ways of Seeing*]

3 When she raises her eyelids it's as if she were taking off all her clothes. [Colette, 1873–1954, *Claudine and Annie*]

4 No woman so naked as one you can see to be naked underneath her clothes. [Michael Frayn, 1933– , *Constructions*, 25]

5 The naked every day he clad, / When he put on his clothes. [Oliver Goldsmith, 1728–74, *The Vicar of Wakefield*, Ch. 17, 'An Elegy on the Death of a Mad Dog']

6 At the superior nudist camps, a nice class distinction was made: the butlers and maids who brought along the refreshments were forced to admit their lower social standing by wearing loincloths and aprons respectively. [Robert Graves, 1895–1985, and Alan Hodge, 1915–79, *The Long Week-End* (1940), Ch. 16]

7 Then she rode forth, clothed on with chastity. [Alfred, Lord Tennyson, 1809–92, *Godiva*, 53]

8 Nakedness is a luxury in which a man may only indulge without peril to himself when he is warmly surrounded by the multitude of his fellows. [Michel Tournier, 1924– , *Friday or the Other Island*, Ch. 2]

9 There's more enterprise / In walking naked. [W B Yeats, 1865–1939, *A Coat*]

See also CLOTHES

O

OBJECTIVITY

1 Thus I live in the world rather as a spectator of mankind than as one of the species. [Joseph Addison, 1672–1719, *The Spectator*, 1]

2 Sir Roger told them, with the air of a man who would not give his judgement rashly, that much might be said on both sides. [Joseph Addison, 1672–1719, *The Spectator*, 122]

3 You cannot ask us to take sides against arithmetic. You cannot ask us to take sides against the obvious facts of the situation. [Winston Churchill, 1874–1965, speech in House of Commons, 31 Aug. 1926]

4 I am a camera with its shutter open, quite passive, recording, not thinking. [Christopher Isherwood, 1904–86, *Goodbye to Berlin*, 'A Berlin Diary']

5 He reads much; / He is a great observer, and he looks / Quite through the deeds of men. [William Shakespeare, 1564–1616, *Julius Caesar*, I. ii. 200]

See also REALISM

OBSTINACY

1 You are one of those that will not serve God if the devil bid you. [William Shakespeare, 1564–1616, *Othello*, I. i. 108]

2 His whole attitude recalled irresistibly to the mind that of some assiduous hound who will persist in laying a dead rat on the drawing-room carpet, though repeatedly apprised by word and gesture that the market for same is sluggish or even non-existent. [P G Wodehouse, 1881–1975, *The Code of the Woosters*, Ch. 1]

See also CONSTANCY, DECISIONS, INDECISION, RESISTANCE

THE OFFICE

1 A memorandum is written not to inform the reader but to protect the writer. [Dean Acheson, 1893–1971, in *Wall Street Journal*, 8 Sept. 1977]

2 I was a good typist; ... at my high school typing was regarded as a female secondary sex characteristic, like breasts. [Margaret Atwood, 1939– , *Lady Oracle*, Ch. 4]

3 And when at last I'm seated by / The great typewriter in the sky, / Let me type the letters right, / In the morning and at night, / Let the Snopake grow on trees, / Let man's hands stay off me knees, / Let it be a place harmonic, / With no need for gin and tonic, / Thank you in anticipation / Of a favourable reply, / Craving your indulgence, / Yours sincerely. / Goodbye. [Pam Ayres, 1947– , *Some More of Me Poetry*, 'The Secretary's Song']

4 I don't put anything in writing. If it's important enough, you shouldn't, and if it is not important enough, why bother? [Ditta Beard, in Anthony Sampson, *The Sovereign State*, Ch. 9]

5 Whatever was required to be done, the Circumlocution Office was beforehand with all the public departments in the art of perceiving – HOW NOT TO DO IT. [Charles Dickens, 1812–70, *Little Dorrit*, Bk I, Ch. 10]

6 I'll tell you what I don't like about Christmas office parties – looking for a new job afterward.

[Phyllis Diller, 1917– , in *Was It Good for You Too?*, ed. Bob Chieger]

7 Officials are highly educated, but onesided; in his own department an official can grasp whole trains of thought from a single word, but let him have something from another department explained to him by the hour, he may nod politely, but he won't understand a word of it. [Franz Kafka, 1883–1924, *The Castle*, Ch. 15, 'Petitions']

8 So conscious he how short time was / For all he planned to do within it / He nothing did at all, alas, / Save note the hour – and file the minute. [Francis Meynell, 1891–1975, *For a Functionary*]

9 You know how God dictated the Ten Commandments to Moses? Well if, instead of Moses, he had dictated them to a temp – we would now all be working on only Four Commandments. [Denis Norden, 1922– , in Frank Muir and Denis Norden, *Upon My Word!*, 'Old Father Thames']

10 Filing is concerned with the past; anything you actually need to see again has to do with the future. [Katharine Whitehorn, 1926– , *Sunday Best*, 'Sorting Out']

See also CIVIL SERVICE, MANAGERS

OLD AGE

1 We are essentially fragile ... One may go just as easily with the measles or diphtheria, meningitis, colic, influenza or mere hunger. There are so many ways of us dying it's astonishing any of us choose old age. [Beryl Bainbridge, 1934– , *Young Adolf*, Ch. 12]

2 I will never be an old man. To me, old age is always fifteen years older than I am. [Bernard M Baruch, 1870–1965; *Observer*, 'Sayings of the Week', 21 Aug. 1955]

3 The hoary head is a crown of glory, if it be found in the way of righteousness. [Bible, OT, *Proverbs* 16:31]

4 If I'd known I was going to live this long, I'd have taken better care of myself. [Eubie Blake, 1883–1983 (on his 100th birthday, five days before his death), in *Observer*, 20 Feb. 1983]

5 One of the reasons why old people make so many journeys into the past is to satisfy themselves that it is still there. [Ronald Blythe, 1922– , *The View in Winter*, Introduction]

6 Old age takes away from us what we have inherited and gives us what we have earned. [Gerald Brenan, 1894–1987, *Thoughts in a Dry Season*, 'Life']

7 Grow old along with me! / The best is yet to be, / The last of life, for which the first was made: / Our times are in His hand / Who saith, 'A whole I planned, / Youth shows but half; trust God: see all nor be afraid!' [Robert Browning, 1812–89, *Rabbi ben Ezra*, 1]

8 Dear dead women, with such hair, too – what's become of all the gold / Used to hang and brush their bosoms? I feel chilly and grow old. [Robert Browning, 1812–89, *A Toccata of Galuppi's*, 15]

9 Her brood gone from her / And her thoughts as still / As the water / Under a ruined mill. [Joseph Campbell, 1879–1944, *The Old Woman*]

10 'You are old, Father William,' the young man said, / 'And your hair has become very white; / And yet you incessantly stand on your head – / Do you think at your age, it is right?' [Lewis Carroll, 1832–98, *Alice in Wonderland*, Ch. 4]; see 51

11 It is the misfortune of an old man that though he can put things out of his head he can't put them out of his feelings. [Joyce Cary, 1888–1957, *To be a Pilgrim*, Ch. 8]

12 The old are always fond of new things. Young men read chronicles, but old men read newspapers. [G K Chesterton, 1874–1936, *Heretics*, 18]

13 Considering the alternative ... it's not too bad at all. [(Of old age) Maurice Chevalier, 1888–1972, in M Freedland, *M C*, Ch. 20]

14 The awful thing about getting old is that you stay young inside. [Jean Cocteau, 1889–1963, quoted by Lawrence Durrell, in *Guardian*, 28 May 1985]

15 Between 1984 and 1988 the number of centenarian men in Britain had gone up from 100 to 210. According to my pocket calculator, if this alarming trend continues, in a mere sixty-six years' time the entire male population of this country will be over 100. [Alan Coren, 1938– , *Seems Like Old Times*, 'February']

16 Here I am, an old man in a dry month, / Being read to by a boy. [T S Eliot, 1888–1965, *Gerontion*]

17 I grow old . . . I grow old . . . / I shall wear the bottoms of my trousers rolled. [T S Eliot, 1888–1965, *Love Song of J. Alfred Prufrock*]

18 Time walks by your side, ma'am, unwilling to pass. [Christopher Fry, 1907– , *Curtmantle*, II]

19 God doesn't count on his hands, you know. [Lord Hailsham, 1907– (on reaching eighty), in BBC radio programme *Law in Action*, 9 Oct. 1987]

20 To be seventy years young is sometimes far more hopeful than to be forty years old. [Oliver Wendell Holmes, 1809–94, *On the Seventieth Birthday of Julia Ward Howe*]

21 You know you're getting old when the candles cost more than the cake. [Bob Hope, 1903– ; in *Hodder Book of Christian Quotations*, comp. Tony Castle]

22 Hides from himself his state, and shuns to know / That life protracted is protracted woe. [Dr Samuel Johnson, 1709–84, *The Vanity of Human Wishes*, 257]

23 A human being would certainly not grow to be seventy or eighty years old if this longevity had no meaning to the species. The afternoon of human life must also have a significance of its own and cannot be merely a pitiful appendage to life's morning. [C G Jung, 1875–1961, in *Practical Wisdom*, ed. Frederick Ungar, 'Youth and Old Age']

24 Perhaps being old is having lighted rooms / Inside your head, and people in them, acting. / People you know, yet can't quite name. [Philip Larkin, 1922–85, *The Old Fools*]

25 Old age is woman's hell. [Ninon de Lenclos, 1620–1705, attr.]

26 Will you still need me, will you still feed me, / When I'm sixty-four ? [John Lennon, 1940–80, and Paul McCartney, 1942– , song: *When I'm Sixty-four*]

27 [When asked his age at over seventy] I am just turning forty and taking my time about it. [Harold Lloyd, 1893–1971, in *The Times*, 23 Sept. 1970]

28 It is not what old men forget that shadows their senescence, but what they remember. [George Lyttelton, 1883–1962, *Lyttelton–Hart-Davis Letters*, Vol. 2, letter of 27 Oct. 1955]

29 I've been around so long I can remember Doris Day before she was a virgin. [Groucho Marx, 1895–1977 ; in L Halliwell, *The Filmgoer's Book of Quotes*. Also ascr. to Oscar Levant]

30 I am sick of this way of life. The weariness and sadness of old age make it intolerable. I have walked with death in hand, and death's own hand is warmer than my own. I don't wish to live any longer. [W Somerset Maugham, 1874–1965, remarks to the press on his ninetieth birthday ; in M B Strauss, *Family Medical Quotations*]

31 What have I done to achieve longevity? Woken up each morning and tried to remember not to wear my hearing aid in the bath. [Robert Morley, 1908–92, in *London Review of Books*, 20 Mar. 1986]

32 Old people shouldn't eat health foods. They need all the preservatives they can get. [Robert Orben, 1927– ; in *Cook's Quotation Book*, ed. Maria Polushkin Robbins]

33 His golden locks time hath to silver turned ; / O time too swift, O swiftness never ceasing! [George Peele, 1558?–97?, *Polyhymnia*, 'The Old Knight']

34 When men grow virtuous in their old age, they only make a sacrifice to God of the devil's leavings. [Alexander Pope, 1688–1744, *Thoughts on Various Subjects*]

35 Growing old is like being increasingly penalized for a crime you haven't committed. [Anthony Powell, 1905– , *Temporary Kings*, Ch. 1]

36 Old age begins when you realize that forever is not as long as it used to be. [Joseph Prescott, 1913– , *Aphorisms and Other Observations*, Second Series, 'Age']

37 Darling, I am growing old, / Silver threads among the gold. [Eben Rexford, 1848–1916, *Silver Threads among the Gold*]

38 Then old age, and experience, hand in hand, / Lead him to death, and make him understand, / After a search so painful, and so long, / That all his life he has been in the wrong. [Earl of Rochester, 1647–80, *A Satire against Mankind*, 25]

39 First you forget names, then you forget faces, then you forget to pull your zipper up, then you forget to pull your zipper down. [Leo Rosenberg ; in Laurence J Peter, *Peter's Quotations*, 'Old Age']

40 Pissing in his shoe keeps no man warm for long. [Richard Selzer, 1928– , *Confessions of a Knife*, 'In Praise of Senescence']

41 I love long life better than figs. [William Shakespeare, 1564–1616, *Antony and Cleopatra*, I. ii (34)]

42 Lord, Lord, how subject we old men are to this vice of lying! [*2 Henry IV*, III. ii. (329)]

43 I know thee not, old man: fall to thy prayers; / How ill white hairs become a fool and jester! [(Henry V to Falstaff) *2 Henry IV*, IV. v. 52]

44 An old man, broken with the storms of state, / Is come to lay his weary bones among ye; / Give him a little earth for charity. [*Henry VIII*, IV. ii. 21]

45 You are old; / Nature in you stands on the very verge / Of her confine. [*King Lear*, II. ii. (148)]

46 I have lived long enough: my way of life / Is fall'n into the sear, the yellow leaf; / And that which should accompany old age, / As honour, love, obedience, troops of friends, / I must not look to have; but, in their stead, / Curses, not loud but deep, mouth-honour, breath, / Which the poor heart would fain deny and dare not. [*Macbeth*, V. ii. 22]

47 A good old man, sir; he will be talking; as they say, 'when the age is in, the wit is out.' [*Much Ado About Nothing*, III. v. (36)]

48 For I am declined / Into the vale of years. [*Othello*, II. iii. 265]

49 That time of year thou mayst in me behold / When yellow leaves, or none, or few, do hang / Upon those boughs which shake against the cold, / Bare ruined choirs, where late the sweet birds sang. [*Sonnets*, 73]

50 But I grow old always learning many things. [Solon, *c.*640–*c.*558 BC, quoted in Plutarch, *Solon*, xxxi]

51 You are old, Father William, the young man cried, / And pleasures with youth pass away, / And yet you lament not the days that are gone, / Now tell me the reason, I pray. [Robert Southey, 1774–1843, *The Old Man's Comforts*]; see 10

52 There are so few who can grow old with a good grace. [Richard Steele, 1672–1729, *The Spectator*, 263]

53 If you live long enough, the venerability factor creeps in; you get accused of things you never did and praised for virtues you never possessed. [I F Stone, 1907–89, in *International Herald Tribune*, 16 Mar. 1988]

54 I think about death a great deal – almost all the time, but then anyone of my age [93] would. Each morning you open your eyes and you think, what again? [Ben Travers, 1886–1980, in *The Sunday Times Magazine*, 10 Aug. 1980]

55 Old age is the most unexpected of all the things that happen to a man. [Leon Trotsky, 1874–1940, *Diary in Exile*, 15 Feb. 1935]

56 Selfish old age is nothing more than childhood in which there is awareness of death. [Miguel de Unamuno, 1864–1937, *Abel Sanchez*, Ch. 38]

57 For Age, with stealing steps, / Hath clawed me with his clutch. [Thomas, Lord Vaux, 1510–56, *The Aged Lover Renounceth Love*]

58 Is not old wine wholesomest, old pippins toothsomest, old wood burn brightest, old linen wash whitest? Old soldiers, sweethearts, are surest, and old lovers are soundest. [John Webster, 1580?–1625?, *Westward Hoe*, II. ii]

59 Conversation is imperative if gaps are to be filled, and old age, it is the last gap but one. [Patrick White, 1912–90, *The Tree of Man*, Ch. 22]

60 The gods bestowed on Max [Beerbohm] the gift of perpetual old age. [Oscar Wilde, 1854–1900, quoted by R Aldington in his edn of W]

61 AMBROSE: That old man with one foot in the grave!

MRS LEVI: And the other three in the cash box. [Thornton Wilder, 1897–1975, *The Matchmaker*, III]

62 It's never too late to have a fling / For autumn is just as nice as spring, / And it's never too late to fall in love. [Sandy Wilson, 1924– , *The Boy Friend*, III]

63 He was either a man of about a hundred and fifty who was rather young for his years or a man of about a hundred and ten who had been aged by trouble. [P G Wodehouse, 1881–1975, *Blandings Castle*, 'Lord Emsworth Acts for the Best']

64 An aged man is but a paltry thing, / A tattered coat upon a stick, unless / Soul clap its hands and sing, and louder sing / For every tatter in its mortal dress. [W B Yeats, 1865–1939, *Sailing to Byzantium*]

65 What shall I do with this absurdity – / O heart, O troubled heart – this caricature, / Decrepit age that has been tied to me / As to a dog's tail? [W B Yeats, 1865–1939, *The Tower*, 1]

66 When you are old and grey and full of sleep, / And nodding by the fire, take down this book. [W B Yeats, 1865–1939, *When You are Old*]

See also AGE, YOUTH & AGE

OPERA

1 Nothing is capable of being well set to music that is not nonsense. [Joseph Addison, 1672–1719, *The Spectator*, 18]

2 I do not mind what language an opera is sung in so long as it is a language I don't understand. [Edward Appleton, 1892–1965; *Observer*, 'Sayings of the Week', 28 Aug. 1955]; see 11

3 If music in general is an imitation of history, opera in particular is an imitation of human wilfulness. [W H Auden, 1907–73, *A Dyer's Hand*, 8, 'Notes on Music']

4 Opera, next to Gothic architecture, is one of the strangest inventions of Western man. It could not have been foreseen by any logical process. [Kenneth Clark, 1903–83, *Civilization*, Ch. 9]

5 Opera in English, is, in the main, just about as sensible as baseball in Italian. [H L Mencken, 1880–1956, in Frank Muir, *Frank Muir Book*, 'Music']

6 I sometimes wonder which would be nicer – an opera without an interval, or an interval without an opera. [Ernest Newman, 1868–1959, in *Berlioz, Romantic and Classic*, ed. Peter Heyworth]

7 The kind of opera that starts at six o'clock and after it has been going three hours, you look at your watch and it says 6.20. [(Of *Parsifal*) David Randolph, 1914– ; in Frank Muir, *Frank Muir Book*, 'Music']

8 Opera is the theatre of the absurd set to music. [Godfrey Smith, 1926– , in *The Sunday Times*, 15 Nov. 1987]

9 [To a soprano who complained of being left stranded in Massenet's *Don Quixote* by Chaliapin dying too soon] Madam, you are gravely in error. No operatic artist has ever died too soon. [Arturo Toscanini, 1867–1957, in Norman Lebrecht, *Discord*, Ch. 5]

10 Now you have seen what we can do. Now want it! and if you do, we will achieve an art. [Richard Wagner, 1813–83, speech after performance of *Die Götterdämmerung*]

11 An unalterable and unquestioned law of the musical world required that the German text of French operas sung by Swedish artists should be translated into Italian for the clearer understanding of English speaking audiences. [Edith Wharton, 1862–1937, *The Age of Innocence*, Bk I, Ch. 1]; see 2

See also COMPOSERS, MUSIC, MUSICIANS, SONGS

OPINIONS

1 Now, who shall arbitrate? / Ten men love what I hate, / Shun what I follow, slight what I receive; / Ten who in ears and eyes / Match me: we all surmise, / They this thing, and I that: whom shall my soul believe? [Robert Browning, 1812–89, *Rabbi ben Ezra*, 22]

2 He that complies against his will, / Is of his own opinion still. [Samuel Butler, 1612–80, *Hudibras*, III, iii, 547]

3 The wish to spread those opinions that we hold conducive to our own welfare is so deeply rooted in the English character that few of us can escape its influence. [Samuel Butler, 1835–1902, *Erewhon*, 20]

4 The public buys its opinions as it buys its meat, or takes in its milk, on the principle that it is cheaper to do this than to keep a cow. So it is, but the milk is more likely to be watered. [Samuel Butler, 1835–1902, *Notebooks*, Ch. 17, 'Public Opinion']

5 A man's opinion on tramcars matters; his opinion on Botticelli matters; his opinion on all things does not matter. [G K Chesterton, 1874–1936, *Heretics*, Ch. 1]

6 Every man speaks of public opinion, and means by public opinion, public opinion minus his opinion. [G K Chesterton, 1874–1936, *Heretics*, Ch. 8]

7 Bigotry may be roughly defined as the anger of men who have no opinions. [G K Chesterton, 1874–1936, *Heretics*, Ch. 18]

8 'Old girl,' said Mr Bagnet, 'give him my opinion. You know it.' [Charles Dickens, 1812–70, *Bleak House*, Ch. 27]

9 One man's Mede is another man's Persian. [George S Kaufman, 1889–1961; in R E Drennan, *Wit's End*]

10 New opinions are always suspected, and usually opposed, without any other reason but because they are not already common. [John Locke, 1632–1704, *Essay on the Human Understanding*, Dedication]

11 He who knows only his own side of the case knows little of that. [John Stuart Mill, 1806–73, *On Liberty*, Ch. 2]

12 To observations which ourselves we make, / We grow more partial for th' observer's sake. [Alexander Pope, 1688–1744, *Moral Essays*, Epistle I, 11]

13 The average man's opinions are much less foolish than they would be if he thought for himself. [Bertrand Russell, 1872–1970, attr.]

14 [When asked as a young man if he had strongly held left-wing views] No. I have extreme views, weakly held. [A J P Taylor, 1906–90, quoted by R W Johnson in *London Review of Books*, 8 May 1986]

15 *Quot homines tot sententiae: suus cuique mos*. – As many opinions as there are men; each a law to himself. [Terence, *c*.195–159 BC, *Phormio*, 454]

16 I agree with no man's opinion. I have some of my own. [Ivan Turgenev, 1818–83, *Fathers and Sons*, Ch. 13]

17 It is difference of opinion that makes horse races. [Mark Twain, 1835–1910, *Pudd'nhead Wilson*, Ch. 19]

18 A man who wishes to impose his opinions on others is unsure of their value. He has to uphold them by all possible means. He adopts a special tone of voice, thumps the table, smiles on some and browbeats others. In short, he borrows from his body the wherewithal to bolster up his mind. [Paul Valéry, 1871–1945, *Bad Thoughts and Not So Bad*, 'N']

See also IDEAS, JUDGEMENT, THINKING

OPPORTUNITY

1 Never the time and the place / And the loved one all together! [Robert Browning, 1812–89, *Never the Time and the Place*]

2 To the very last, he [Napoleon] had a kind of idea; that, namely, of *La carrière ouverte aux talents*, The tools to him that can handle them. [Thomas Carlyle, 1795–1881, *Critical and Miscellaneous Essays*, 'Sir Walter Scott']

3 It's them that take advantage that get advantage i' this world. [George Eliot, 1819–80, *Adam Bede*, Ch. 32]

4 Why then the world's mine oyster, / Which I with sword will open. [William Shakespeare, 1564–1616, *The Merry Wives of Windsor*, II. ii. 2]

See also AMBITIONS

OPPOSITES

1 Life is itself but the shadow of death, and souls departed but the shadows of the living. All things fall under this name. The sun itself is but the dark *simulacrum*, and light but the shadow of God. [Sir Thomas Browne, 1605–82, *The Garden of Cyrus*, Ch. 4]

2 He did not know that a keeper is only a poacher turned outside in, and a poacher a keeper turned inside out. [Charles Kingsley, 1819–75, *The Water Babies*, Ch. 1]

3 The sublime and the ridiculous are often so nearly related that it is difficult to class them separately. One step above the sublime makes the ridiculous; and one step above the ridiculous makes the sublime again. [Thomas Paine, 1737–1809, *The Age of Reason*, ii, note]

4 O! who can hold a fire in his hand / By thinking on the frosty Caucasus? / Or cloy the hungry edge of appetite / By bare imagination of a feast? / Or wallow naked in December snow / By thinking on fantastic summer's heat? / O, no! the apprehension of the good / Gives but the greater feeling to the worse. [William Shakespeare, 1564–1616, *Richard II*, I. iii. 294]

OPPOSITION

1 And if a house be divided against itself, that house cannot stand. [Bible, NT, *St Mark* 3:25]

2 He that wrestles with us strengthens our nerves, and sharpens our skill. Our antagonist is our helper. [Edmund Burke, 1729–97, *Reflections on the Revolution in France*, Penguin edn, p. 278]

3 A great Whig authority used always to say that the duty of an Opposition was very simple –

it was, to oppose everything, and propose nothing. [Earl of Derby, 1799–1869, speech in House of Commons, 4 June 1841]

4 No Government can be long secure without a formidable Opposition. [Benjamin Disraeli, 1804–81, *Coningsby*, Bk ii, Ch. 1]

5 About one fifth of the people are against everything all the time. [Senator Robert Kennedy, 1925–68, speech at University of Pennsylvania, 6 May 1964]

6 We should support whatever the enemy opposes and oppose whatever the enemy supports. [Mao Zedong, 1893–1976, newspaper interview, 16 Sept. 1939]

7 My real opposition is myself. [Shah of Iran, 1919–80, interview in *Le Monde*, 1 Oct. 1976]

See also GOVERNMENT, PARLIAMENT

OPTIMISM & PESSIMISM

1 I am an old man, but I am profoundly optimistic about nothing. [Francis Bacon, 1909–92, interview on LWT programme *The South Bank Show*, 1985; in *Dictionary of Art Quotations*, comp. Ian Crofton]

2 For why be discouraged, one of the thieves was saved, that is a generous percentage. [Samuel Beckett, 1906–89, *Malone Dies*, slight variant in *Waiting for Godot*, I]; see 24

3 Pessimism, when you get used to it, is just as agreeable as optimism. [Arnold Bennett, 1867–1931, *Things That Have Interested*, 'The Slump in Pessimism']

4 The year's at the spring / And day's at the morn; / Morning's at seven; / The hillside's dew-pearled; / The lark's on the wing; / The snail's on the thorn; / God's in his heaven – / All's right with the world! [Robert Browning, 1812–89, *Pippa Passes*, Pt 1, 222]

5 Let us not always say / 'Spite of this flesh today / I strove, made head, gained ground upon the whole!' / As the bird wings and sings, / Let us cry 'All good things / Are ours, nor soul helps flesh more, now, than flesh helps soul.' [Robert Browning, 1812–89, *Rabbi ben Ezra*, 12]

6 The pessimist is the man who believes things couldn't possibly be worse, to which the optimist replies: 'Oh yes they could!' [Vladimir Bukovsky, 1942– , in *Guardian Weekly*, 10 July 1977]

7 Circumstances break men's bones; it has never been shown that they break men's optimism. [G K Chesterton, 1874–1936, *Charles Dickens*, 2]

8 I came to the conclusion that the optimist thought everything good except the pessimist, and that the pessimist thought everything bad, except himself. [G K Chesterton, 1874–1936, *Orthodoxy*, Ch. 5]

9 Say not the struggle naught availeth, / The labour and the wounds are vain, / The enemy faints not, nor faileth, / And as things have been, things remain. [Arthur Hugh Clough, 1819–61, *Say Not the Struggle Naught Availeth*]

10 'In case anything turned up,' which was his favourite expression. [(Mr Micawber) Charles Dickens, 1812–70, *David Copperfield*, Ch. 11]

11 Said one: 'Folks of a surly Tapster tell, / And daub his Visage with the Smoke of Hell; / They talk of some strict Testing of us – Pish! / He's a Good Fellow, and 'twill all be well.' [Edward Fitzgerald, 1809–83, *The Rubá'iyát of Omar Khayyám*, Edn 1, 64]

12 Gatsby believed in the green light, the orgastic future that year by year recedes before us. It eluded us then, but that's no matter – tomorrow we will run faster, stretch out our arms further . . . And one fine morning – So we beat on, boats against the current, borne back ceaselessly into the past. [F Scott Fitzgerald, 1896–1940, *The Great Gatsby*, Ch. 9]

13 I am a pessimist because of intelligence, but an optimist of will. [Antonio Gramsci, 1891–1937, *Letters from Prison*, 19 Dec. 1929]

14 Sin is behovely, but all shall be well and all shall be well and all manner of thing shall be well. [Juliana of Norwich, 1343–?1416, *Revelations of Divine Love*, Ch. 27]

15 Two men look out through the same bars: / One sees the mud, and one the stars. [Frederick Langbridge, 1849–1923, *A Cluster of Quiet Thoughts*, 1896]

16 There's a good time coming, boys. [Charles Mackay, 1814–89, *There's a Good Time Coming*]; see 21, 30

17 an optimist is a guy / that has never had / much experience [Don Marquis, 1878–1937, *archy and mehitabel*, XII, 'certain maxims of archy']

18 Was I deceived, or did a sable cloud / Turn forth her silver lining on the night? [John Milton, 1608–74, *Comus*, 221]

19 'I'm afraid you've got a bad egg, Mr Jones!' 'Oh no, my Lord, I assure you! Parts of it are excellent!' [*Punch* (1895), cix, 222]

20 I am an idealist. I don't know where I'm going but I'm on my way. [Carl Sandburg, 1878–1967, *The People, Yes*, 'Incidentals']

21 There's a gude time coming. [Sir Walter Scott, 1771–1832, *Rob Roy*, Ch. 32]; see 16, 30

22 The latest definition of an optimist is one who fills up his crossword puzzle in ink. [Clement K Shorter, 1858–1926; *Observer*, 'Sayings of the Week', 22 Feb. 1925]; see MIDDLE AGE, 4

23 I explain my theory of optimo-pessimism. [G M Stonier, 1903–85, *Shaving through the Blitz*, Ch. 5]

24 Do not despair – many are happy much of the time; more eat than starve, more are healthy than sick, more curable than dying; not so many dying as dead; and one of the thieves was saved. [Tom Stoppard, 1937– , *Jumpers*, Coda]; see 2

25 It is not usually our ideas that make us optimists or pessimists, but it is our optimism or pessimism, of physiological or pathological origin ... that makes our ideas. [Miguel de Unamuno, 1864–1937, *The Tragic Sense of Life*, Ch. 1]

26 I am an optimist, unrepentant and militant. After all, in order not to be a fool an optimist must know how sad a place the world can be. It is only the pessimist who finds this out anew every day. [Peter Ustinov, 1921– , *Dear Me*, Ch. 9]

27 In this best of all possible worlds. [Voltaire, 1694–1778, *Candide*, Ch. 1]

28 I'm an optimist, but an optimist who carries a raincoat. [Harold Wilson, 1916–95, in *New Woman*, Sept. 1989]

29 Nor greetings where no kindness is, nor all / The dreary intercourse of daily life, / Shall e'er prevail against us, or disturb / Our cheerful faith, that all which we behold / Is full of blessings. [William Wordsworth, 1770–1850, *Lines Composed a Few Miles above Tintern Abbey*, 130]

30 There's a good time coming, it's almost here, /'Twas a long, long time on the way. [H C Work, 1832–84, *Wake Nicodemus*]; see 16, 21

See also HOPE, PESSIMISM

ORDER & DISORDER

1 Good order is the foundation of all things. [Edmund Burke, 1729–97, *Reflections on the Revolution in France*, Penguin edn, p. 372]

2 Order is heaven's first law. [Alexander Pope, 1688–1744, *An Essay on Man*, IV, 49]

3 Not chaos-like, together crushed and bruised, / But, as the world harmoniously confused: / Where order in variety we see, / And where, though all things differ, all agree. [Alexander Pope, 1688–1744, *Windsor Forest*, 13]

4 The heavens themselves, the planets, and this centre / Observe degree, priority, and place, / Insisture, course, proportion, season, form, / Office, and custom, in all line of order. [William Shakespeare, 1564–1616, *Troilus and Cressida*, I. iii. 85]

5 Take but degree away, untune that string / And hark what discord follows; each thing meets / In mere oppugnancy. [*Troilus and Cressida*, I. iii. 109]

6 A place for everything, and everything in its place. [Samuel Smiles, 1812–1904, *Thrift*, Ch. 5]

See also CHAOS, DIVERSITY, HIERARCHIES

ORDINARY

1 Depend upon it, there is nothing so unnatural as the commonplace. [Arthur Conan Doyle, 1859–1930, *The Adventures of Sherlock Holmes*, 'A Case of Identity']

2 The trivial round, the common task, / Would furnish all we ought to ask; / Room to deny ourselves, a road / To bring us, daily, nearer God. [John Keble, 1792–1866, *The Christian Year*, 'Morning']

3 The Lord prefers common-looking people. That is the reason he makes so many of them. [Abraham Lincoln, 1809–65, speech, 23 Dec. 1863, attr. by J Hay, *Letters*, Vol. i, p. 142]

4 The Normal is the good smile in a child's eyes – all right. It is also the dead stare in a million adults. It both sustains and kills – like a God. It is the Ordinary made beautiful; it is also the Average made lethal. [Peter Shaffer, 1926– , *Equus*, I. xix]

See also MEDIOCRITY, TRIVIALITY

ORIGINALITY

1 An original writer is not one who imitates nobody, but one whom nobody can imitate. [François-René de Chateaubriand, 1768–1848, *The Genius Of Christianity*]

2 Confound the men who have made our remarks before us. [Aelius Donatus, 4th cent. AD, quoted in St Jerome, *Commentary on Ecclesiastes*, Ch. 1]

3 Everything has been said, and we come too late after more than seven thousand years in which man has existed and thought. [Jean de La Bruyère, 1645–96, *Characters*, 'Of Books', 1]

4 Original thought is like original sin: both happened before you were born to people you could not possibly have met. [Fran Lebowitz, ?1948– , *Social Studies*, 'People']

5 Casting my mind's eye over the whole of fiction, the only absolutely original creation I can think of is Don Quixote. [W Somerset Maugham, 1874–1965, *Ten Novels and their Authors*, Ch. 1, sect. i]

6 All good things which exist are the fruits of originality. [John Stuart Mill, 1806–73, *On Liberty*, Ch. 3]

7 Parody is just originality in a second-hand suit. [Eugenio Montale, 1896–1981, in *Listener*, 7 June 1990]

8 The more intelligence one has the more people one finds original. Commonplace people see no difference between men. [Blaise Pascal, 1623–62, *Pensées*, I, 7]

9 One thing about pioneers that you don't hear mentioned is that they are invariably, by their nature, mess-makers. [Robert M Pirsig, 1928– , *Zen and the Art of Motorcycle Maintenance*, Pt III, Ch. 21]

10 All that can be said is, that two people happened to hit on the same thought – and Shakespeare made use of it first, that's all. [R B Sheridan, 1751–1816, *The Critic*, III. i]

11 Born Originals, how comes / it to pass that we die / Copies? [Edward Young, 1879–1960, epigraph to Jacob Golomb, *Inauthenticity and Authenticity*]

See also CREATIVITY, IMITATION

OXFORD & CAMBRIDGE

1 [Oxford] whispering from her towers the last enchantments of the Middle Age . . . Home of lost causes, and forsaken beliefs, and unpopular names, and impossible loyalties! [Matthew Arnold, 1822–88, *Essays in Criticism*, First Series, Preface]

2 That sweet city with her dreaming spires. [(Oxford) Matthew Arnold, 1822–88, *Thyrsis*, 19]; see 11

3 The Oxford Don: 'I don't feel quite happy about pleasure.' [W H Auden, 1907–73, 'Journal of an Airman']

4 For Cambridge people rarely smile, / Being urban, squat, and packed with guile. [Rupert Brooke, 1887–1915, *The Old Vicarage, Grantchester*]

5 It is a secret in the Oxford sense: you may tell it to only one person at a time. [Oliver Franks, 1905–92, quoted by K Rose in the *Sunday Telegraph*, 30 Jan. 1977]

6 To the University of Oxford I acknowledge no obligation; and she will as willingly renounce me for a son, as I am willing to disclaim her for a mother. I spent fourteen months at Magdalen College; they proved the fourteen months the most idle and unprofitable of my whole life. [Edward Gibbon, 1737–94, *Autobiography*]

7 The clever men at Oxford / Know all that there is to be knowed. / But they none of them know one half as much / As intelligent Mr Toad. [Kenneth Grahame, 1859–1932, *The Wind in the Willows*, Ch. 10, song]

8 You will hear more good things on the outside of a stagecoach from London to Oxford than if you were to pass a twelve-month with the undergraduates, or heads of colleges, of that famous university. [William Hazlitt, 1778–1830, *On the Ignorance of the Learned*]

9 Cambridge has seen many strange sights. It has seen Wordsworth drunk, it has seen Porson sober. I am a greater scholar than Wordsworth and I am a greater poet than Porson. So I fall betwixt and between. [A E Housman, 1859–1936 (speech on leaving University College, London, to take up the Chair of Latin at Cambridge, 1911), in R P Graves, *A E H, the Scholar-poet*, Ch. 5]

10 I recollect an acquaintance saying to me that 'the Oriel Common Room stank of Logic'. [Cardinal Newman, 1801–90, *History of My Religious Opinions*]

11 This [Cambridge] is the city of perspiring dreams. [Frederic Raphael, 1931– , *The Glittering Prizes*, 'An Early Life']; see 2

12 Very nice sort of place, Oxford, I should think, for people that like that sort of place. [George Bernard Shaw, 1856–1950, *Man and Superman*, II]

13 The King, observing with judicious eyes / The state of both his universities, / To Oxford sent a troop of horse, and why? / That learned body wanted loyalty; / To Cambridge books, as very well discerning / How much that loyal body wanted learning. [Joseph Trapp, 1679–1747, on George I's donation of a library to Cambridge]

See also UNIVERSITIES

P

PAIN

1 The least pain in our little finger gives us more concern and uneasiness than the destruction of millions of our fellow-beings. [William Hazlitt, 1778–1830, *American Literature*, 'Dr Channing']

2 Tender-handed stroke a nettle, / And it stings you for your pains; / Grasp it like a man of mettle, / And it soft as silk remains. [Aaron Hill, 1685–1750, *Verses Written on a Window*]

3 He might have been a fine young man with a bad toothache, with the first even of his life. What ailed him, above all, she felt, was that trouble was new to him. [Henry James, 1843–1916, *The Spoils of Poynton*, Ch. 8]

4 Pleasure is oft a visitant; but pain / Clings cruelly to us. [John Keats, 1795–1821, *Endymion*, Bk i, 906]

5 Why, all delights are vain; but that most vain / Which, with pain purchased, doth inherit pain. [William Shakespeare, 1564–1616, *Love's Labour's Lost*, I. i. 72]

6 The most intolerable pain is produced by prolonging the keenest pleasure. [George Bernard Shaw, 1856–1950, *Man and Superman*, 'Maxims for Revolutionists', Beauty and Happiness]

7 Nothing begins, and nothing ends, / That is not paid with moan; / For we are born in other's pain, / And perish in our own. [Francis Thompson, 1859–1907, *Daisy*]

See also PLEASURE, SUFFERING, UNHAPPINESS

PAINTERS IN GENERAL

1 Beginning with Van Gogh, however great we may be, we are all, in a measure, auto-didacts – you might almost say primitive painters. Painters no longer live within a tradition and so each one of us must re-create an entire language. [Pablo Picasso, 1881–1973, in Françoise Gilot and Carlton Lake, *Life with Picasso*, Pt 2]

2 That's why painters live so long. While I work I leave my body outside the door, the way Moslems take off their shoes before entering the mosque. [Pablo Picasso, 1881–1973, in Françoise Gilot and Carlton Lake, *Life with Picasso*, Pt 3]

3 A mere copier of nature can never produce anything great. [Joshua Reynolds, 1723–92, *Discourses*, 3]

4 The painter should not paint what he sees, but what will be seen. [Paul Valéry, *Bad Thoughts and Not So Bad*, 'S']

See also next categories, ART, SCULPTURE

PAINTERS: INDIVIDUAL (in alphabetical order of subject)

1 Don't talk to me about Bonnard. That's not painting, what he does. He never goes beyond his own sensibility. He doesn't know how to choose. [Pablo Picasso, 1881–1973, in Françoise Gilot and Carlton Lake, *Life with Picasso*, Pt 6]

2 I do not believe in things: I believe in relationships. [Georges Braque, 1883–1963, in J Culler, *Saussure*, Ch. 4]

3 When I am finishing a picture I hold some God-made object up to it – a rock, a flower, the branch of a tree or my hand – as a kind of final test. If the painting stands up beside a thing man cannot make, the painting is authentic. If there's a clash between the two, it is bad art. [Marc

Chagall, 1889–1985, in *Saturday Evening Post*, 2 Dec. 1962]

4 *Anch'io sono pittore!* – I am a painter too! [Antonio Correggio, 1489?–1534, attr., on seeing Raphael's *St Cecilia* at Bologna, *c.*1525]

5 Picasso is a genius. So am I. Picasso is a Communist. Nor am I. [Salvador Dali, 1904–89, from Jean Cocteau, *Diaries*, Vol. 2, in *The Sunday Times*, 7 Oct. 1990]

6 How to achieve such anomalies, such alterations and re-fashionings of reality so what comes out of it are lies, if you like, but lies that are more than literal truth. [Vincent Van Gogh, 1853–90, letter to his brother Theo, Nuenen, Holland, July 1885]

7 It is no wonder that Hockney, the Cole Porter of figurative painting, should so often and so exaggeratedly have been taken for Mozart. [Robert Hughes, 1938– , *The Shock of the New*, Ch. 8]

8 What I wanted to do was to paint sunlight on the side of a house. [Edward Hopper, 1882–1967, in catalogue to Hayward Gallery exhibition, London, 1981]

9 With what I do the imagery is part of a continuous body. It hasn't rushed in for a quick shout. [(Of his painting) Ken Kiff, 1935– , in *New Statesman*, 17 Jan. 1986]

10 She is older than the rocks among which she sits; like the vampire, she has been dead many times, and learned the secrets of the grave; and has been a diver in deep seas, and keeps their fallen day about her; and trafficked for strange webs with Eastern merchants: and, as Leda, was the mother of Helen of Troy, and, as Saint Anne, the mother of Mary; and all this has been to her but as the sound of lyres and flutes, and lives only in the delicacy with which it has moulded the changing lineaments, and tinged the eyelids and the hands. [(Of Mona Lisa) Walter Pater, 1839–94, *The Renaissance*, 'Leonardo da Vinci']

11 The goitrous torpid and squinting husks provided by Matisse in his sculpture are worthless except as tactful decorations for a mental home. [Percy Wyndham Lewis, 1882–1957, *The Art of Being Ruled*, Pt XII, Ch. 7]

12 Monet's pictures are always too draughty for me. [Edgar Degas, 1834–1917 (in conversation), in *Memoirs of Julie Manet* (Mme Renoir)]

13 Perhaps – I say perhaps because I do not know how to reflect except by opening my mind like a glass-bottomed boat so that I can watch what is swimming below – painting becomes sublime when the artist transcends his personal anguish, when he projects in the midst of a shrieking world an expression of living and its end that is silent and ordered. [Robert Motherwell, 1915–91, *A Tour of the Sublime (The Ides of Art)*, 'Tiger's Eye', 1 Dec. 1948]

14 I mix them with brains, sir. [(When asked how he mixed his colours) John Opie, 1761–1806, quoted in Samuel Smiles, *Self-Help*, Ch. 4]

15 What a genius, that Picasso . . . It's a pity he doesn't paint. [Marc Chagall, 1889–1985, in François Gilot and Carlton Lake, *Life with Picasso*, Pt 6]

16 I never made a painting as a work of art. It's all research. [Pablo Picasso, 1881–1973, quoted by David Hockney in interview in *Observer*, 16 Nov. 1988]

17 If I telegraph one of my canvases to New York . . . any house-painter should be able to do it properly. A painting is a sign – just like the sign that indicates a one-way street. [Pablo Picasso, 1881–1973, in Françoise Gilot and Carlton Lake, *Life with Picasso*, Pt 5]

18 The modern painter begins with nothingness. That is the only thing he copies. The rest he invents. [(Of Jackson Pollock) Harold Rosenberg, 1906–78, in *Guardian*, 23 Nov. 1989]

19 When they talked of their Raphaels, Correggios and stuff, / He shifted his trumpet, and only took snuff. [(Reynolds) Oliver Goldsmith, 1728–74, *Retaliation*, 145]

20 For me, painting is a way to forget life. It is a cry in the night, a strangled laugh. [Georges Rouault, 1871–1958; in Laurence J Peter, *Peter's Quotations*]

21 I have seen, and heard, much of cockney impudence before now; but never expected to hear a coxcomb ask two hundred guineas for flinging a pot of paint in the public's face. [(Of Whistler's *Nocturne in Black and Gold*) John Ruskin, 1819–1900, *Fors Clavigera*, Letter 79]

22 'I only know of two painters in the world,' said a newly introduced feminine enthusiast to Whistler, 'yourself and Velazquez.' 'Why,' answered Whistler in dulcet tones, 'why drag in Velazquez?' [James McNeill Whistler, 1834–1903, in D C Seitz, *W Stories*]

23 No, I ask it for the knowledge of a lifetime. [(Answer to counsel in his case against Ruskin, who had asked, 'For two days' labour you ask two hundred guineas?') James McNeill Whistler, 1834–1903, in D C Seitz, *W Stories*]

24 Yes, madam, Nature is creeping up. [(Answer to a lady who said that a certain landscape reminded her of his pictures) James McNeill Whistler, 1834–1903, in D C Seitz, *W Stories*]

25 With our James vulgarity begins at home, and should be allowed to stay there. [Oscar Wilde, 1854–1900, letter to the *World* on the subject of Whistler]

See also previous and next categories, ART, SCULPTURE

PAINTING

1 Even the dreadful martyrdom must run its course / Anyhow in a corner, some untidy spot / Where the dogs go on with their doggy life. [W H Auden, 1907–73, *Musée des Beaux Arts*]

2 Painting is its own language, and when you try to talk about it, it's like an inferior translation. [Francis Bacon, 1909–92, profile in *Observer*, 19 May 1985]

3 In figure painting, the type of all painting, I have endeavoured to set forth that the principal if not sole source of life enchantments are Tactile Values, Movement and Space Composition. [Bernard Berenson, 1865–1959, *The Decline of Art*]

4 Every painted image of something is also about the absence of the real thing. All painting is about the presence of absence. This is why man paints. The broken pictorial space confesses the art's wishfulness. [John Berger, 1926– , in *New Statesman and Society*, 15 July 1988]

5 Of course all painting, no matter what you're painting, is abstract in that it's got to be organized. [David Hockney, 1937– ; in *Dictionary of Art Quotations*, comp. Ian Crofton]

6 When the Earth's last picture is painted and the tubes are twisted and dried. [Rudyard Kipling, 1865–1936, *When Earth's Last Picture*]

7 It [Post-Impressionist painting] may ... appear ridiculous to those who do not recall the fact that a good rocking-horse has often more of the true horse about it than an instantaneous photograph of a Derby winner. [Desmond MacCarthy, 1877–1952, introduction to exhibition 'Manet and His Contemporaries', 1910]

8 Whoever devotes himself to painting should begin by cutting out his own tongue. [Henri Matisse, 1869–1954, in *Independent*, 2 Oct. 1991]

9 And it's all right in the summer time, / In the summer time it's lovely! / While my old man's painting hard, / I'm posing in the old back yard. / But oh, oh! In the winter-time / It's another thing you know, / With a little red nose, / And very little clothes, / And the stormy winds do blow. [Fred Murray, d.1922, and George Everard, song: *It's All Right in the Summer Time*]

10 A picture has been said to be something between a thing and a thought. [Samuel Palmer, 1805–81, quoted in Arthur Symons, *Life of Blake*]

11 Painting is a blind man's profession. He paints not what he sees, but what he feels, what he tells himself about what he has seen. [Pablo Picasso, 1881–1973, in Jean Cocteau, *Journals*, 'Childhood']

12 For me a painting is a dramatic action in the course of which reality finds itself split apart. [Pablo Picasso, 1881–1973, in Françoise Gilot and Carlton Lake, *Life with Picasso*, Pt 2]

13 Painting is self-discovery. Every good artist paints what he is. [Jackson Pollock, 1912–56, in F V O'Connor, *J P*]

14 It's easier to replace a dead man than a good picture. [George Bernard Shaw, 1856–1950, *The Doctor's Dilemma*, II]

15 Painting is saying 'Ta' to God. [Stanley Spencer, 1891–1959, quoted by his daughter Shirin, in *Observer*, 7 Feb. 1988]

See also previous categories, ART, SCULPTURE

THE PAPACY

1 'It's your audience for 10 a.m., Your Holiness,' murmured the secretary. 'One man?' said the Pope. 'You call that an audience?' [Alan Coren, 1938– , *The Sanity Inspector*, 'Believe Me']

2 The Papacy is not other than the Ghost of the deceased Roman Empire, sitting crowned upon the grave thereof. [Thomas Hobbes, 1588–1679, *Leviathan*, Pt iv, Ch. 47]

3 It often happens that I wake at night and begin to think about a serious problem and decide I must tell the Pope about it. Then I wake up completely and remember I am the Pope. [Pope John XXIII, 1881–1963, in H Fesquet, *Wit and Wisdom of Good Pope John*]

4 I wouldn't take the Pope too seriously. He's a Pole first, a Pope second, and maybe a Christian third. [Muriel Spark, 1918– ; *Observer*, 'Sayings of the Week', 4 June 1989]

5 The Pope! How many divisions has he got? [Joseph Stalin, 1879–1953 (to French Prime Minister, Laval, who asked him to encourage Catholicism to please the Pope, 13 May 1935), in W S Churchill, *The Second World War*, Vol. 1, Ch. 8, but also quoted by President Truman as said to Churchill at Potsdam Conference]

See also CATHOLICS, RELIGION, ROME

PARENTS

1 My parents were very old world. They come from Brooklyn which is the heart of the Old World. Their values in life are God and carpeting. [Woody Allen, 1935– , in Adler and Feinman, *W A: Clown Price of American Humor*, Ch. 2]

2 And my parents finally realize that I'm kidnapped and they snap into action immediately: they rent out my room. [Woody Allen, 1935– , in E Lax, *W A and His Comedy*]

3 The joys of parents are secret, and so are their griefs and fears. [Francis Bacon, 1561–1626, *Essays*, 7, 'Of Parents and Children']

4 Parents are the very last people who ought to be allowed to have children. [H E Bell, speech at University of Reading, Mar. 1977]

5 If one is not going to take the necessary precautions to avoid having parents, one must undertake to bring them up. [Quentin Crisp, 1908–99, *The Naked Civil Servant*, Ch. 5]

6 There are times when parenthood seems nothing but feeding the mouth that bites you. [Peter de Vries, 1910–93, *The Tunnel of Love*, Ch. 5]

7 You don't object to an aged parent, I hope? [Charles Dickens, 1812–70, *Great Expectations*, Ch. 25]

8 Come mothers and fathers / Throughout the land / And don't criticize / What you can't understand. [Bob Dylan, 1941– , song: *The Times They are A-Changin'*]

9 The thing that impresses me most about America is the way parents obey their children. [Edward VIII, 1894–1972, in *Look*, 5 Mar. 1957]

10 Your children are not your children. They are the sons and daughters of Life's longing for itself . . . you may strive to be like them, but seek not to make them like you. [Kahlil Gibran, 1883–1931, *The Prophet*, 'Of Children']

11 One parent is enough to spoil you but discipline takes two. [Clive James, 1939– , *Unreliable Memoirs*, Ch. 1]

12 You Americans do not rear children, you *incite* them; you give them food and shelter and applause. [Randall Jarrell, 1914–65, *Pictures from an Institution*, Pt IV, Ch. 10]

13 Nothing has a stronger influence psychologically on their environment, and especially on their children, than the unlived life of the parents. [C G Jung, 1875–1961, *Paracelsus*]

14 They fuck you up, your mum and dad. / They may not mean to, but they do. / They fill you with the faults they had / And add some extra, just for you. [Philip Larkin, 1922–85, *This be the Verse*]

15 Never allow your child to call you by your first name. He hasn't known you long enough. [Fran Lebowitz, ?1948– , *Social Studies*, 'Parental Guidance']

16 Oh, what a tangled web do parents weave / When they think that their children are naïve. [Ogden Nash, 1902–71, *Baby, What Makes the Sky Blue?*]

17 Children aren't happy with nothing to ignore, / And that's what parents were created for. [Ogden Nash, 1902–71, *The Parent*]

18 My little son, who looked from thoughtful eyes / And moved and spoke in quiet grown-up wise, / Having my law the seventh time disobeyed, / I struck him, and dismissed / With hard words and unkissed, / His mother, who was patient, being dead. [Coventry Patmore, 1823–96, *The Unknown Eros*, Bk i, 10, 'The Toys']

19 All the same, you know parents – especially step-parents – are sometimes a bit of a disappointment to their children. They don't fulfil the promise of their early years. [Anthony Powell, 1905– , *A Buyer's Market*, Ch. 2]

20 How sharper than a serpent's tooth it is / To have a thankless child! [William Shakespeare, 1564–1616, *King Lear*, I. iv. (312)]

21 Parents learn a lot from their children about coping with life. [Muriel Spark, 1918– , *The Comforters*, Ch. 6]

22 You know more than you think you do. [Dr Spock, 1903–98, *Baby and Child Care*, opening words]

23 I have found the best way to give advice to your children is to find out what they want and then advise them to do it. [Harry Truman, 1884–1972, interview with Margaret Truman in TV programme *Person to Person*, 27 May 1955]

24 'Parents are strange,' Amy said, 'for their age.' [Amanda Vail, 1921–66, *Love Me Little*, Ch. 10]

25 Never have children, only grandchildren. [Gore Vidal, 1925– , *Two Sisters*]

26 'I'm a Norfan, both sides,' he would explain, with the air of one who had seen trouble. [H G Wells, 1866–1946, *Kipps*, Bk I, Ch. 6, sect. i]

27 To lose one parent, Mr Worthing, may be regarded as a misfortune; to lose both looks like carelessness. [Oscar Wilde, 1854–1900, *The Importance of Being Earnest*, I]

28 Children begin by loving their parents. After a time they judge them. Rarely, if ever, do they forgive them. [Oscar Wilde, 1854–1900, *A Woman of No Importance*, II]

29 There are no illegitimate children – only illegitimate parents. [Judge Léon Yankwich, 1888–1975, decision in State District Court for the Southern District of California, June 1928, quoting columnist O O McIntyre]

See also CHILDHOOD, FAMILY, FATHERS, MOTHERS

PARIS

1 Good Americans, when they die, go to Paris. [Thomas Appleton, 1812–84, quoted in O W Holmes, *The Autocrat of the Breakfast Table*, Ch. 6. Also used by Oscar Wilde]

2 Every city has a sex and age which have nothing to do with demography. Rome is feminine ... London is a teen-ager and urchin, and, in this, hasn't changed since the time of Dickens. Paris, I believe, is a man in his twenties in love with an older woman. [John Berger, 1926– , in *Guardian*, 27 Mar. 1987]

3 The last time I saw Paris, her heart was warm and gay, / I heard the laughter of her heart in every street café. [Oscar Hammerstein II, 1895–1960, song: *The Last Time I Saw Paris*, in musical *Lady be Good*]

4 I would rather starve where food is good. [Jascha Heifetz, 1901–87 (to his friends on going to Paris in the 1920s), in David Dubal, *Evenings with Horowitz*, Ch. 28]

5 If you are lucky enough to have lived in Paris as a young man, then wherever you go for the rest of your life, it stays with you, for Paris is a moveable feast. [Ernest Hemingway, 1899–1961, to a friend, 1950; used as epigraph to *A Moveable Feast*]

6 Paris is well worth a mass. [Henri IV of France, 1553–1610. Attr. also to his minister Sully]

7 Strether had at this very moment to recognize the truth that wherever one paused in Paris the imagination reacted before one could stop it. [Henry James, 1843–1916, *The Ambassadors*, Bk II, Ch. 2]

8 As an artist, a man has no home in Europe save in Paris. [Friedrich Nietzsche, 1844–1900, *Ecce Homo*]

9 I love Paris in the springtime. [Cole Porter, 1891–1964, song: *I Love Paris*, in musical *Can-Can*]

10 But in Paris, as none kiss each other but the men, I did what amounted to the same thing – I bid God bless her. [Laurence Sterne, 1713–68, *A Sentimental Journey*, 'The Fille de Chambre, Paris']

See also FRANCE, LONDON, ROME, NEW YORK

PARLIAMENT

1 England is the mother of Parliaments. [John Bright, 1811–89, speech at Birmingham, 18 Jan. 1865]

2 A Parliament speaking through reporters to Buncombe and the twenty-seven millions mostly fools. [Thomas Carlyle, 1795–1881, *Latter Day Pamphlets*, 6, 'Parliaments']

3 Parliament is the longest running farce in the West End. [Cyril Smith, 1928– (said in July 1973), in *Big Cyril*, Ch. 8]

See also next two categories

PARLIAMENT: HOUSE OF COMMONS

1 A shiver ran through the Scottish MPs, frantically looking for a spine to run up. [Oliver Brown, *The Extended Tongue*]

2 What the greatest inquest of the nation has begun, its highest Tribunal [the House of Commons] will accomplish. [Edmund Burke, 1729–97, impeachment of Warren Hastings, 15 Feb. 1788]

3 The Commons was the preserve of the upper class who were just bright enough to get the clever middle class to govern and were kept in power by the deferential working-class vote. [(Of the House in the 1960s) Julian Critchley, 1930– , in *Financial Times*, 28 Nov. 1990]

4 You have sat too long here for any good you have been doing. Depart, I say, and let us have done with you. In the name of God, go! [Oliver Cromwell, 1599–1658, speech to the Rump Parliament, 22 Jan. 1654]

5 I think . . . that it is the best club in London. [Charles Dickens, 1812–70, *Our Mutual Friend*, Bk II, Ch. 3]

6 A man may speak very well in the House of Commons, and fail very completely in the House of Lords. There are two distinct styles requisite: I intend, in the course of my career, if I have time, to give a specimen of both. [Benjamin Disraeli, 1804–81, *The Young Duke*, Bk v, Ch. 6]

7 A completely honest answer always gives you the advantage of surprise in the House of Commons. [Jonathan Lynn, 1943– , and Antony Jay, 1930– , *Yes Prime Minister*, Vol. 2, 'The Tangled Web']

8 The Commons, faithful to their system, remained in a wise and masterly inactivity. [Sir James Mackintosh, 1765–1831, *Vindiciae Gallicae*, 1]

9 I never saw so many shocking bad hats in my life. [Duke of Wellington, 1769–1852, on seeing the first Reformed Parliament]

See also previous and next categories, CONSERVATIVES, GOVERNMENT, LIBERALS, SOCIALISTS

PARLIAMENT: HOUSE OF LORDS

1 The House of Lords is like a glass of champagne which has stood for five days. [Clement Attlee, 1883–1967; in *The Fine Art of Political Wit*, ed. Leon A Harris]

2 The British House of Lords is the British Outer Mongolia for retired politicians. [Tony Benn, 1925– (on renouncing his peerage), in *Observer*, 4 Feb. 1962]; see 9

3 My Lord Tomnoddy is thirty-four; / The Earl can last but a few years more. / My Lord in the Peers will take his place: / Her Majesty's councils his words will grace. / Office he'll hold and patronage sway; / Fortunes and lives he will vote away; / And what are his qualifications? ONE / He's the Earl of Fitzdotterel's eldest son. [R B Brough, 1828–60, *My Lord Tomnoddy*]

4 Better than a play! [Charles II, 1630–85, on the Lords' debate on Lord Ross's Divorce Bill, 1670]

5 I am dead: dead, but in the Elysian fields. [(When elevated to the House of Lords in 1876) Benjamin Disraeli, 1804–81, quoted in R Blake, *Disraeli*, Ch. 24]

6 The House of Lords is a model of how to care for the elderly. [Frank Field, 1942– ; *Observer*, 'Sayings of the Week', 24 May 1981]

7 The House of Peers, throughout the war, / Did nothing in particular, / And did it very well. [W S Gilbert, 1836–1911, *Iolanthe*, II]

8 Mr Balfour's Poodle. [David Lloyd George, 1863–1945 (description of House of Lords, in reply to a claim that the Lords were 'the watchdog of the nation'), speech in House of Commons, 26 June 1907]

9 The British Outer Mongolia. [V M Molotov, 1890–1986 (of the House of Lords), in *Listener*, 17/24 Dec. 1987]; see 2

10 There was nowhere else to go. [Emmanuel Shinwell, 1884–1986, attr., on accepting a peerage]

11 The House of Lords, an illusion to which I have never been able to subscribe – responsibility without power, the prerogative of the eunuch throughout the ages. [Tom Stoppard, 1937– , *Lord Malquist and Mr Moon*, Pt VI, 1]

See also previous two categories, CONSERVATIVES, DEMOCRACY, GOVERNMENT, LIBERALS, SOCIALISTS, STATE

PARTIES

1 The sooner every party breaks up the better. [Jane Austen, 1775–1817, *Emma*, 25]

2 No one walks into a party without having a far better party going on inside his head. Every party is going to be that party until we get there. So the key to the boredom and tension at parties is that no one wants to be at the party he's at, he wants to be at the party he's missing. [Jules Feiffer, 1929– , *Ackroyd*, '1965, February 15']

3 For one of the pleasures of having a rout, / Is the pleasure of having it over. [Thomas Hood, 1799–1845, 'Her Dream']

4 Hans Breitmann gife a barty – / Vhere ish dat barty now? / Vhere ish de lofely golden cloud / Dat float on de moundain's prow? [C G Leland, 1824–1903, 'Hans Breitmann's Barty']

5 [When asked whether she had enjoyed a cocktail party] Enjoyed it! One more drink and I'd have been under the host. [Dorothy Parker, 1893–1967, in R E Drennan, *Wit's End*]

See also HOSPITALITY, SOCIABILITY

PASSIONS

1 Where is the thread now? Off again! / The old trick! only I discern – / Infinite passion, and the pain / Of finite hearts that yearn. [Robert Browning, 1812–89, *Two in the Campagna*, 12]

2 The man who is master of his passions is Reason's slave. [Cyril Connolly, 1903–74, in *Turnstile One*, ed. V S Pritchett]

3 A man is to be cheated into passion, but to be reasoned into truth. [John Dryden, 1631–1700, Preface to *Religio Laici*]

4 I rage, I melt, I burn, / The feeble God has stabbed me to the heart. [John Gay, 1685–1732, *Acis and Galatea*, II]

5 A correspondence course of passion was, for her, the perfect and ideal relationship with a man. [Aldous Huxley, 1894–1963, *Point Counter Point*, Ch. 5]

6 A man who has not passed through the inferno of his passions has never overcome them. [C G Jung, 1875–1961, *Memories, Dreams, Reflections*, Ch. 9, iv]

7 Death is the only pure, beautiful conclusion of a great passion. [D H Lawrence, 1885–1930, *Fantasia of the Unconscious*, Ch. 15]

8 It is with our passions as it is with fire and water, they are good servants, but bad masters. [Roger L'Estrange, 1616–1704, *Aesop's Fables*, 38]

9 In tragic life, God wot, / No villain need be! Passions spin the plot: / We are betrayed by what is false within. [George Meredith, 1828–1909, *Modern Love*, 43]

10 Gardens, ponds, palings, the creation, / foamed with the purity of tears, / are only categories of passion, / hoarded by the human heart. [Boris Pasternak, 1890–1960, *Definition of the Creative Power*]

11 And hence one master-passion in the breast, / Like Aaron's serpent, swallows up the rest. [Alexander Pope, 1688–1744, *An Essay on Man*, II, 131]

12 The ruling passion, be it what it will, / The ruling passion conquers reason still. [Alexander Pope, 1688–1744, *Moral Essays*, Epistle III, 153]

13 *Ce n'est plus une ardeur dans mes veines cachée: / C'est Vénus toute entière à sa proie attachée.* – It is no longer a heat concealed in my blood, it is Venus herself grasping her prey. [Jean Racine, 1639–99, *Phèdre*, II. v. 304]

14 Three passions, simple but overwhelmingly strong, have governed my life: the longing for love, the search for knowledge, and unbearable pity for the suffering of mankind. [Bertrand Russell, 1872–1970, *Autobiography*, Vol. I, Prologue]

15 The barbarian is the man who regards his passions as their own excuse for being; who does not domesticate them either by understanding their cause or by conceiving their ideal goal. [George Santayana, 1863–1952, *Egotism in German Philosophy*]

16 Passion, you see, can be destroyed by a doctor. It cannot be created. [Peter Shaffer, 1926– , *Equus*, II. xxxv]

17 Excellent wretch! Perdition catch my soul / But I do love thee! and when I love thee not, / Chaos is come again. [William Shakespeare, 1564–1616, *Othello*, III. iii. 90]

18 So I triumphed ere my passion, sweeping thro' me, left me dry, / Left me with the palsied heart, and left me with the jaundiced eye. [Alfred, Lord Tennyson, 1809–92, *Locksley Hall*, 131]

19 Strange fits of passion have I known: / And I will dare to tell, / But in the lover's ear alone, / What once to me befell. [William Wordsworth, 1770–1850, *Strange Fits of Passion*]

See also EMOTIONS

THE PAST

1 Even God cannot change the past. [Agathon, 447?–401 BC, quoted in Aristotle's *Nicomachean Ethics*, 6]

2 Living in the past has one thing in its favour – it's cheaper. [anon., in *Dramatists' Guild Bulletin*]

3 There is always something rather absurd about the past. [Max Beerbohm, 1872–1956, *1880*]

4 Say not thou, What is the cause that the former days were better than these? for thou dost not enquire wisely concerning this. [Bible, OT, *Ecclesiastes* 7:10]

5 The Moving Finger writes; and, having writ, / Moves on: nor all thy Piety nor Wit / Shall lure it back to cancel half a Line, / Nor all thy Tears wash out a Word of it. [Edward Fitzgerald, 1809–83, *The Rubá'iyát of Omar Khayyám*, Edn 1, 51]

6 All we want is to get to the point where the past can explain nothing about us and we can get on with life. [Richard Ford, 1944– , *The Sportswriter*, 2]

7 It is not only species of animal that die out, but whole species of feeling. And if you are wise you will never pity the past for what it did not know, but pity yourself for what it did. [John Fowles, 1926– , *The Magus*, rev. edn, Ch. 24]

8 We two kept house, the Past and I. [Thomas Hardy, 1840–1928, *The Ghost of the Past*]

9 The past is a foreign country: they do things differently there. [L P Hartley, 1895–1972, *The Go-between*, opening words]

10 If the past cannot teach the present and the father cannot teach the son, then history need not have bothered to go on, and the world has wasted a great deal of time. [Russell Hoban, 1925– , *The Lion of Boaz-Jachin and Jachin-Boaz*, Ch. 1]

11 What we know of the past is mostly not worth knowing. What is worth knowing is mostly uncertain. Events in the past may roughly be divided into those which probably never happened and those which do not matter. [W R Inge, 1860–1954, *Assessments and Anticipations*, 'Prognostications']

12 Trust no Future, howe'er pleasant / Let the dead Past bury its dead! / Act – act in the living Present! / Heart within, and God o'erhead! [H W Longfellow, 1807–82, *A Psalm of Life*]

13 He said that he had learnt to trample on the past. In the beginning it had been like trampling on a garden; later it had been like walking on ground. [V S Naipaul, 1932– , *A Bend in the River*, Ch. 8]

14 One would expect people to remember the past and to imagine the future. But in fact ... they imagine ... [history] in terms of their own experience, and when trying to gauge the future they cite supposed analogies from the past: till, by a double process of repetition, they imagine the past and remember the future. [Lewis Namier, 1888–1969, *Conflicts*, pp. 69–70]

15 The snows of yesterday can't be refreezed. [Denis Norden, 1922– , in BBC radio programme *My Word*, 5 Oct. 1977]

16 Who controls the past controls the future ... Who controls the present controls the past. [George Orwell, 1903–50, *1984*, Pt 1, Ch. 3]

17 They spend their time mostly looking forward to the past. [John Osborne, 1929–94, *Look Back in Anger*, II. i]

18 Now there are fields where Troy once was. [Ovid, 43 BC–AD 17, *Heroides*, I, i, 53]

19 I mean, don't forget the earth's about five thousand million years old, at least. Who can afford to live in the past? [Harold Pinter, 1930– , *The Homecoming*, II]

20 O! call back yesterday, bid time return. [William Shakespeare, 1564–1616, *Richard II*, III. ii. 69]

21 When in the chronicle of wasted time / I see descriptions of the fairest wights, / And beauty making beautiful old rhyme, / In praise of ladies dead and lovely knights. [*Sonnets*, 106]

22 Oh, cease! must hate and death return? / Cease! must men kill and die? / Cease! drain not to the dregs the urn / Of bitter prophecy. / The world is weary of the past, / Oh, might it die or rest at last! [P B Shelley, 1792–1822, *Hellas*, 1096]

23 I met a traveller from an antique land / Who said: Two vast and trunkless legs of stone / Stand in the desert. [P B Shelley, 1792–1822, *Ozymandias*]

24 They don't sell tickets to the past. [Alexander Solzhenitsyn, 1918– , *The First Circle*, Ch. 37]

25 Life is one tenth Here and Now, nine-tenths a history lesson. For most of the time the Here and Now is neither now nor here. [Graham Swift, 1949– , *Waterland*, 8]

26 All are behind, the kind / And the unkind too, no more / To-night than a dream. The stream / Runs softly and drowns the Past, / The dark-lit stream has drowned the Future and the Past. [Edward Thomas, 1878–1917, *The Bridge*]

27 The past, at least, is secure. [Daniel Webster, 1782–1852, second speech on Foot's Resolution, 25 Jan. 1830]

28 I have always said it is a great mistake to prejudge the past. [William Whitelaw, 1918–99, at his first press conference after being appointed Ulster Secretary, 1972]

29 Hindsight is always twenty-twenty. [Billy Wilder, 1906– , in J R Colombo, *Colombo's Hollywood*]

30 Each had his past shut in him like the leaves of a book known to him by heart; and his friends could only read the title. [Virginia Woolf, 1882–1941, *Jacob's Room*, Ch. 5]

See also THE FUTURE, HISTORY, LIFE IS FLEETING, THE PRESENT, TIME

PATIENCE & IMPATIENCE

1 Sad Patience, too near neighbour to despair. [Matthew Arnold, 1822–88, *The Scholar-Gypsy*, 195]

2 A wise man that had it for a by-word, when he saw men hasten to a conclusion, 'Stay a little, that we may make an end the sooner'. [Francis Bacon, 1561–1626, *Essays*, 25, 'Of Dispatch']

3 Tarry at Jericho until your beards be grown. [Bible, OT, *2 Samuel* 10:5]

4 Let every man be swift to hear, slow to speak, slow to wrath. [Bible, NT, *James* 1:19]

5 Ye have heard of the patience of Job. [Bible, NT, *James* 5:11]

6 *Patience*, n. A minor form of despair, disguised as a virtue. [Ambrose Bierce, 1842–1914, *The Devil's Dictionary*]

7 Our patience will achieve more than our force. [Edmund Burke, 1729–97, *Reflections on the Revolution in France*, Penguin edn, p. 281]

8 If that should not be, cousin, I say: patience and shuffle the cards. [Miguel Cervantes, 1547–1616, *Don Quixote*, Pt II, Ch. 23]

9 But the waiting time, my brothers, / Is the hardest time of all. [Sarah Doudney, 1843–1926, *Psalm of Life*, 'The Hardest Time of All']

10 Beware the fury of a patient man. [John Dryden, 1631–1700, *Absalom and Achitophel*, Pt I, 1005]

11 Patience and perseverance at length / Accomplish more than anger and brute strength. [Jean de La Fontaine, 1621–95, *Fables*, II, 11, 'The Lion and the Rat']

12 I very nearly had to wait! [Louis XIV, 1638–1715, attr.]

13 Patience, to prevent / That murmur, soon replies, God doth not need / Either man's work or his own gifts; who best / Bear his mild yoke, they serve him best; his state / Is kingly; thousands at his bidding speed, / And post o'er land and ocean without rest, / They also serve who only stand and wait. [John Milton, 1608–74, sonnet: *On His Blindness*]

14 Your damned nonsense can I stand twice or once, but sometimes always, by God, never! [(To flute player at rehearsal) Hans Richter, 1843–1916, in L Harris, *The Fine Art of Political Wit*, Ch. 12]

15 Though patience be a tired mare, yet she will plod. [William Shakespeare, 1564–1616, *Henry V*, II. i. (25)]

16 I will be the pattern of all patience. [*King Lear*, III. ii. (37)]

17 How poor are they that have not patience! / What wound did ever heal but by degrees? [*Othello*, III. ii. (379)]

18 DUKE: And what's her history?
VIOLA: A blank, my lord. She never told her love, / But let concealment like a worm i' the bud, / Feed on her damask cheek: she pined in thought, / And with a green and yellow melancholy, / She sat like Patience on a monument, / Smiling at grief. [*Twelfth Night*, II. iv. (111)]

19 It is very strange . . . that the years teach us patience; that the shorter our time, the greater our capacity for waiting. [Elizabeth Taylor, 1912–75, *A Wreath of Roses*, Ch. 10]

20 My father [Sir Garfield Todd] taught me a long time ago that you just keep throwing your bread upon the water, and if you're lucky it will come back as ham sandwiches. [Judith Todd, interview in *The Sunday Times Magazine*, 21 Jan. 1990]

21 People will endure their tyrants for years, but they tear their deliverers to pieces if a millennium is not created immediately. [Woodrow Wilson, 1856–1924, in John Dos Passos, *Mr W's War*, heading to Pt V, Ch. 22]

See also ANGER, CALM, PEACE

PATRIOTS & PATRIOTISM

1 Speak for England. [Leo Amery, 1873–1955, to Arthur Greenwood, spokesman for the Labour Party, in House of Commons, 2 Sept. 1939. But Harold Nicolson, in his diary, attr. the words to Robert Boothby]

2 For England, home, and beauty. [Samuel J Arnold, 1774–1852, *The Death of Nelson*]; see 17

3 True patriots we; for be it understood, / We left our country for our country's good. [George Barrington, 1755–?1835, Prologue for the opening of the Playhouse, Sydney, N S W, 1796 (the company being composed of convicts). Also attr. to Henry Carter]

4 The more foreigners I saw, the more I loved my native land. [P-L de Belloy, 1727–75, *The Siege of Calais*, II. iii]

5 If I should die, think only this of me: / That there's some corner of a foreign field / That is for ever England. There shall be / In that rich earth a richer dust concealed. [Rupert Brooke, 1887–1915, *The Soldier*]

6 Give me of Nelson only a touch. [Robert Browning, 1812–89, *Nationality in Drinks*]

7 So to be patriots as not to forget that we are gentlemen. [Edmund Burke, 1729–97, *Thoughts on the Cause of the Present Discontents*]

8 They died to save their country and they only saved the world. [G K Chesterton, 1874–1936, *The English Graves*]

9 'My country, right or wrong', is a thing that no patriot would think of saying except in a desperate case. It is like saying, 'My mother, drunk or sober'. [G K Chesterton, 1874–1936, *The Defendant* (1901), 'Defence of Patriotism']

10 next to of course god america i / love you land of the pilgrims and so forth oh [e e cummings, 1894–1962, *is* 5, 'Two, III']

11 Our country! In her intercourse with foreign nations, may she always be in the right; but our country, right or wrong. [Stephen Decatur, 1779–1820, toast given at Norfolk, Virginia, Apr. 1816.]

12 Upon Saint Crispin's Day / Fought was this noble fray, / Which fame did not delay, / To England to carry. / O when shall English men / With such acts fill a pen, / Or England breed again / Such a King Harry? [Michael Drayton, 1563–1631, *Ballad of Agincourt*]

13 Towards the end of July 1914 . . . I worked out a draft schedule and wrote an advertisement headed 'Your King and Country need you'. [Eric Field of Caxton Advertising Agency, from *Advertising*, Ch. 2]

14 If I had to choose between betraying my *country* and betraying my *friend*, I hope I should have the guts to betray my *country*. [E M Forster, 1879–1970, *Two Cheers for Democracy*, 'What I Believe']

15 Such is the patriot's boast, where'er we roam, / His first, best country ever is at home. [Oliver Goldsmith, 1728–74, *The Traveller*, 73]

16 I came in here in all good faith to help my country. I don't mind giving a reasonable amount [of blood], but a pint . . . why that's very nearly an armful. I'm sorry. I'm not walking around with an empty arm for anybody. [Tony Hancock, 1924–68, BBC TV comedy series *Hancock's Half Hour*, 'The Blood Donor', scripts by Ray Galton and Alan Simpson]

17 Now your country calls you far across the sea, / To do a soldier's duty / For England, home and beauty. [J P Harrington, b.1865, song: *The Girls You Leave Behind You*]; see 2

18 What have I done for you, / England, my England? / What is there I would not do, / England, my own? [W E Henley, 1849–1903, *For England's Sake*, 3]

19 I am happy now that Charles calls on my bedchamber less frequently than of old. As it is, I now endure but two calls a week and when I hear his steps outside my door I lie down on my bed, close my eyes, open my legs and think of England. [Alice, Lady Hillingdon, 1857–1940, *Journal*, 1912]

20 *Deutschland, Deutschland über alles.* – Germany, Germany before all else. [Heinrich Hoffmann von Fallersleben, 1798–1876, poem]

21 *Dulce et decorum est pro patria mori.* – It is a sweet and seemly thing to die for one's country. [Horace, 65–8 BC, *Odes*, III, ii, 13]; see 29

22 Patriotism is the last refuge of a scoundrel. [Dr Samuel Johnson, 1709–84, in James Boswell, *Life of J*, 7 Apr. 1775]

23 And so, my fellow Americans: ask not what your country can do for you – ask what you can do for your country. My fellow citizens of the world: ask not what America will do for you, but what together we can do for the freedom of man. [President John F Kennedy, 1917–63, inaugural address as President, 20 Jan. 1961]

24 I would die for my country but I would never let my country die for me. [Neil Kinnock, 1942– , speech at Labour Party Conference, 30 Sept. 1986]

25 When you've shouted 'Rule Britannia', when you've sung 'God save the Queen', / When you've finished killing Kruger with your mouth. [Rudyard Kipling, 1865–1936, *The Absent-minded Beggar*]

26 An acre in Middlesex is better than a principality in Utopia. [Lord Macaulay, 1800–1859, *Literary Essays*, 'Lord Bacon']

27 They may build their ships, my lads, and think they know the game, / But they can't build boys of the bulldog breed / Who made old England's name. [Felix McGlennon, d.1943, *Sons of the Sea*]

28 Take my drum to England, hang et by the shore. / Strike et when your powder's runnin' low; / If the Dons sight Devon, I'll quit the port o' Heaven, / An' drum them up the Channel as we drummed them long ago. [Henry Newbolt, 1862–1938, *Drake's Drum*]

29 The old Lie: *Dulce et decorum est / Pro patria mori.* [Wilfred Owen, 1893–1918, *Dulce et decorum est*]; see 21

30 These are times that try men's souls. The summer soldier and the sunshine patriot will, in this crisis, shrink from the service of his country; but he that stands it *now* deserves the love and thanks of man and woman. [Thomas Paine, 1737–1809, 'The American Crisis', in the *Pennsylvania Journal*, 23 Dec. 1776]

31 If I were compelled to choose between living in West Bromwich and Florence, I should make straight for West Bromwich. [J B Priestley, 1894–1984, quoted at his memorial service, Westminster Abbey, 2 Oct. 1984]

32 *Allons, enfants de la patrie, / Le jour de gloire est arrivé.* – Come, children of our native land. / The day of glory has arrived. [Rouget de Lisle, 1760–1836, *La Marseillaise*]

33 Patriots always talk of dying for their country, and never of killing for their country. [Bertrand Russell, 1872–1970, attr.]

34 Breathes there the man, with soul so dead, / Who never to himself hath said, / This is my own, my native land! [Sir Walter Scott, 1771–1832, *The Lay of the Last Minstrel*, VI, 1]

35 I vow to thee, my country – all earthly things above – / Entire and whole and perfect, the service of my love. [Cecil Spring-Rice, 1859–1918, *I Vow to Thee, My Country*]

36 Patriotism to the Soviet State is a revolutionary duty, whereas patriotism to a bourgeois state is treachery. [Leon Trotsky, 1874–1940, epigraph to Fitzroy Maclean, *Disputed Barricade*, Pt 1]

37 'Shoot, if you must, this old gray head, / But spare your country's flag,' she said. [John Greenleaf Whittier, 1807–92, *Barbara Frietchie*, 35]

38 I travelled among unknown men, / In lands beyond the sea: / Nor, England! did I know till then / What love I bore to thee. [William Wordsworth, 1770–1850, *I Travelled among Unknown Men*]

See also LOYALTY

PATRONS

1 Catullus, the worst of all poets, gives you his warmest thanks; he being as much the worst of all poets as you are the best of all patrons. [Catullus, 84–54? BC, *Carmina*, 49]

2 I should like to see the custom introduced of readers who are pleased with a book sending the author some small cash token: anything between half-a-crown and a hundred pounds . . . Not more than a hundred pounds – that would be bad for my character – not less than half-a-crown – that would do no good to yours. [Cyril Connolly, 1903–74, *Enemies of Promise*, Ch. 14]

3 *Patron*. Commonly a wretch who supports with insolence, and is paid with flattery. [Dr Samuel Johnson, 1709–84, *Dictionary of the English Language*]

4 Is not a patron, my lord, one who looks with unconcern on a man struggling for life in the water, and when he has reached ground, encumbers him with help?

The notice which you have been pleased to take of my labours, had it been early, had been kind; but it has been delayed till I am indifferent, and cannot enjoy it; till I am solitary, and cannot impart it; till I am known, and do not want it. [Dr Samuel Johnson, 1709–84, in James Boswell, *Life of J*, letter to Lord Chesterfield, 7 Feb. 1754]

5 I was promised on a time, / To have reason for my rhyme; / From that time unto this season, / I received nor rhyme nor reason. [Edmund Spenser, 1552?–99, *Lines on His Promised Pension* (traditional)]

See also CHARITY, GRATITUDE

PEACE

1 Wearily the sentry moves / Muttering the one word: 'Peace.' [Richard Aldington, 1892–1962, *Picket*]

2 Noises at dawn will bring / Freedom for some, but not this peace / No bird can contradict. [W H Auden, 1907–73, *Taller Today*]

3 They shall beat their swords into plowshares, and their spears into pruning-hooks: nation shall not lift up sword against nation, neither shall they learn war any more. [Bible, OT, *Isaiah* 2:4; also *Micah* 4:3 ('a sword' for 'sword')]

4 The wolf also shall dwell with the lamb, and the leopard shall lie down with the kid; and the calf and the young lion and the fatling together; and a little child shall lead them. [Bible, OT, *Isaiah* 11:6]

5 The peace of God, which passeth all understanding. [Bible, NT, *Philippians* 4:7]

6 *Peace*, n. In international affairs, a period of cheating between two periods of fighting. [Ambrose Bierce, 1842–1914, *The Devil's Dictionary*]

7 I believe it is peace for our time ... peace with honour. [Neville Chamberlain, 1869–1940, speech after Munich Agreement, 30 Sept 1938]; see 12

8 Let arms give place to civic robes, laurels to paeans. [Cicero, 106–43 BC, *De Officiis*, I, xxii]

9 So much enamoured on peace that he [Falkland] would have been glad the King should have bought it at any price. [Earl of Clarendon, 1609–74, *Selections from the History of the Rebellion*, 9]

10 *E'n la sua volontade è nostra pace*. – In His will is our peace. [Dante Alighieri, 1265–1321, *The Divine Comedy*, 'Paradiso', iii, 85]

11 What is peace? Is it war? No. Is it strife? No. Is it lovely, and gentle, and beautiful, and pleasant, and serene, and joyful? O yes! [(Mr Chadband) Charles Dickens, 1812–70, *Bleak House*, Ch. 19]

12 Lord Salisbury and myself have brought you back peace – but a peace I hope with honour. [Benjamin Disraeli, 1804–81, speech in House of Commons, 16 July 1878]; see 7

13 Fighting for peace is like fucking for chastity. [*Graffito* magazine, Mar. 1977]

14 When it's a question of peace one must talk to the Devil himself. [Édouard Herriot, 1872–1957; *Observer*, 'Sayings of the Week', 21 Sept. 1953]

15 We love peace, as we abhor pusillanimity; / But not peace at any price. [Douglas Jerrold, 1803–57, *Wit and Opinions*, 'Peace']

16 If peace is a chimaera, I am happy to have caressed her. [Pierre Laval, 1883–1945 (said in 1935); *Observer*, 'Sayings of Our Times', 31 May 1953]

17 They made peace between us; we embraced, and we have been mortal enemies ever since. [Alain René Lesage, 1668–1747, *Le Diable boiteux*, Ch. 3]

18 Peace is indivisible. [Maxim Litvinov, 1876–1951, speech on 22 Feb. 1920, repeated with variants on several occasions]

19 The inglorious arts of peace. [Andrew Marvell, 1621–78, *An Horatian Ode upon Cromwell's Return from Ireland*, 10]

20 I did not shrink, I did not strive, / The deep peace burnt my me alive. [John Masefield, 1878–1967, *The Everlasting Mercy*]

21 Now I see / Peace to corrupt no less than war to waste. [John Milton, 1608–74, *Paradise Lost*, Bk xi, 783]

22 Peace hath her victories / No less renowned than war. [John Milton, 1608–74, sonnet: *To Cromwell*]

23 Give peace in our time, O Lord. [*The Book of Common Prayer*, Morning Prayer]

24 The cankers of a calm world and a long peace. [William Shakespeare, 1564–1616, *1 Henry IV*, IV. ii. (32)]

25 A peace is of the nature of a conquest; / For then both parties nobly are subdued, / And neither party loser. [*2 Henry IV*, IV. ii. 89]

26 And peace proclaims olives of endless age. [*Sonnets*, 107]

27 In the arts of peace Man is a bungler. [George Bernard Shaw, 1856–1950, *Man and Superman*, III]

28 Where they make a desert they call it peace. [Tacitus, *c.*55–*c.*117, *Agricola*, 30]

29 Till the war-drum throbbed no longer, and the battle-flags were furled / In the Parliament of man, the Federation of the world. [Alfred, Lord Tennyson, 1809–92, *Locksley Hall*, 127]

30 Since wars begin in the minds of men, it is in the minds of men that the defence of peace must be constructed. [Unesco Constitution, adopted 16 Nov. 1945, Preamble. Both Clement Attlee and Archibald Macleish credited with authorship]

See also CALM, PATIENCE, QUIETNESS, RESIGNATION, WARS

THE PEOPLE, see MASSES

PERFECTION

1 The pursuit of perfection, then, is the pursuit of sweetness and light. [Matthew Arnold, 1822–88, *Culture and Anarchy*, Ch. 1]

2 What's come to perfection perishes. / Things learned on earth, we shall practise in heaven. / Works done least rapidly, Art most cherishes. [Robert Browning, 1812–89, *Old Pictures in Florence*, 17]

3 On our Pompilia, faultless to a fault. [Robert Browning, 1812–89, *The Ring and the Book*, IX, 1175]

4 American women expect to find in their husbands a perfection that English women only hope to find in their butlers. [W Somerset Maugham, 1874–1965, *A Writer's Notebook*, 1896]

5 Whoever thinks a faultless piece to see, / Thinks what ne'er was, nor is, nor e'er shall be. [Alexander Pope, 1688–1744, *An Essay on Criticism*, 253]

6 Our erected wit maketh us to know what perfection is. [Sir Philip Sidney, 1554–86, *The Defence of Poesy*]

7 A friend who loved perfection would be the perfect friend, did not that love shut his door on me. [Logan Pearsall Smith, 1865–1946, *Afterthoughts*, 3]

8 Finality is death. Perfection is finality. Nothing is perfect. There are lumps in it. [James Stephens, 1882–1950, *The Crock of Gold*, Bk 1, Ch. 4]

9 Faultily faultless, icily regular, splendidly null, / Dead perfection, no more. [Alfred, Lord Tennyson, 1809–92, *Maud*, I, ii]

10 Charity, dear Miss Prism, charity! None of us are perfect. I myself am peculiarly susceptible to draughts. [Oscar Wilde, 1854–1900, *The Importance of Being Earnest*, II]

11 Well nobody's perfect. [Billy Wilder, 1906– , in film *Some Like It Hot*, scripted with I A L Diamond, last lines, as Joe E Brown is told by his bride-to-be, Jack Lemmon, that he is not a woman]

See also MEDIOCRITY

PERSUASION

1 There is a holy mistaken zeal in politics as well as in religion. By persuading others, we convince ourselves. [Junius, 18th cent., *Letters*, 35]

2 Persuade her. Cut her throat but persuade her! [Joe Orton, 1933–67, *Entertaining Mr Sloane*, III]

3 I'll make him an offer he can't refuse. [Mario Puzo, 1920–99, in novel, Ch. 1, and film *The Godfather*, screenplay with Francis Ford Coppola]

4 I come not, friends, to steal away your hearts. / I am no orator, as Brutus is; / But, as you know me all, a plain, blunt man, / That love my friend. [William Shakespeare, 1564–1616, *Julius Caesar*, III. ii. (220)]

See also INFLUENCE

PESSIMISM

1 He is a real pessimist – he could look at a doughnut and only see the hole in it. [anon.; in P and J Holton, *Quote and Unquote*]

2 A pessimist is a man who is never happy unless he is miserable; even then he is not pleased. [anon.; in C Hunt, *The Best Howlers*]

3 A pessimist is just a well-informed optimist. [anon., quoted by Robert Mackenzie in the BBC TV programme *24 Hours*, 18 Mar. 1968, as current Czech aphorism on Dubček's government]

4 She not only expects the worst, but makes the worst of it when it happens. [Michael Arlen, 1895–1956; in A Andrews, *Quotations for Speakers and Writers*]

5 Scratch a pessimist, and you find often a defender of privilege. [Lord Beveridge, 1879–1963; *Observer*, 'Sayings of the Week' 17 Dec. 1943]

6 [Fabricius] finds certain spots and clouds in the sun. [Robert Burton, 1577–1640, *The Anatomy of Melancholy*, II, §2, Memb. 3]

7 The optimist proclaims that we live in the best of all possible worlds; and the pessimist fears this is so. [James Branch Cabell, 1879–1958, *The Silver Stallion*, Bk IV, Ch. 26]

8 There are bad times just around the corner. / We can all look forward to despair, / It's as clear as crystal / From Bridlington to Bristol / That we can't save democracy / And we don't much care. [Noël Coward, 1899–1973, lyric: *There are Bad Times*]

9 Something will come of this. I hope it mayn't be human gore. [Charles Dickens, 1812–70, *Barnaby Rudge*, Ch. 4]

10 This is in the established tradition of social study. Only the man who finds everything wrong and expects it to get worse is thought to have a clear brain. [J K Galbraith, 1908– , *The Age of Uncertainty*, Ch. 10]

11 Nothing to do but work, / Nothing to eat but food, / Nothing to wear but clothes / To keep one from going nude. [Benjamin King, 1857–94, *The Pessimist*]

12 If we see light at the end of the tunnel, / It's the light of the oncoming train. [Robert Lowell, 1917–77, *Day by Day*]

13 Pessimism is a luxury that a Jew never can allow himself. [Golda Meir, 1898–1978; *Observer*, 'Sayings of the Year', 29 Dec. 1974]

14 There are two Newman's Laws. First, it's useless to put on your brakes when you're upside down. Second, just when things look darkest, they go black. [Paul Newman, 1925– , in *Playboy*, Apr. 1983]

15 A pessimist is a man who looks both ways before crossing a one-way street. [Laurence J Peter, 1919–90, *Peter's Quotations*, 'Optimism – Pessimism']

16 The worst is not, / So long as we can say, 'This is the worst.' [William Shakespeare, 1564–1616, *King Lear*, IV. i. 27]

17 Whenever I look at a mountain I always expect it to turn into a volcano. [Italo Svevo, 1861–1928, *Confessions of Zeno*]

See also OPTIMISM

PHILOSOPHERS (in alphabetical order of subject)

1 The great Secretary of Nature and all learning, Sir Francis Bacon. [Izaak Walton, 1593–1683, *Life of Herbert*]

2 Explaining metaphysics to the nation – / I wish he would explain his explanation. [(Of Coleridge) Lord Byron, 1788–1824, *Don Juan*, Dedication, 2]

3 I cannot forgive Descartes; in all his philosophy he did his best to dispense with God. But he could not avoid making Him set the world in motion with a flip of His thumb; after that he had no more use for God. [Blaise Pascal, 1623–62, *Pensées*, II, 77]

4 Hobbes clearly proves that every creature / Lives in a state of war by nature. [Jonathan Swift, 1677–1745, *On Poetry*, 319]

5 Hume seems to me to have been the only one of the great philosophers who wanted to get at the truth. The rest all wanted to get at something else, something that would flatter humanity, or suit their prejudices, or refute their enemies. [Bertrand Russell, 1872–1970, in Kenneth Harris, *K H Talking to . . .*]

6 We are much beholden to Machiavel and others, that write what men do, and not what they ought to do. [Francis Bacon, 1561–1626, *The Advancement of Learning*, II, xxi, 9]

7 Plato is dear to me, but dearer still is truth. [Aristotle, 384–322 BC, attr.]

8 I swear I would rather be wrong with Plato than see the truth with men like these [the Pythagoreans]. [Cicero, 106–43 BC, *Tusculanae Disputationes*, I, 17]

9 So too Plato was, in my view, a very unreliable Platonist. He was too much of a philosopher to think that anything he had said was the last word. It was left to his disciples to identify his footmarks with his destination. [Gilbert Ryle, 1900–1976, *Dilemmas*, Ch. 1]

10 Two godlike faces gazed below; / Plato the wise and large-browed Verulam, / The first of those who know. [Alfred, Lord Tennyson, 1809–92, *The Palace of Art*, 41]

11 The European philosophical tradition ... consists of a series of footnotes to Plato. [A N Whitehead, 1861–1947, *Process and Reality*, Pt 2, Ch. 1]

12 Socrates is guilty of corrupting the minds of the young, and of believing in deities of his own invention instead of the gods recognized by the State. [Plato, *c*.428–347 BC, *Apology*, 24B]

13 *Ein Gott-betrunkener Mensch.* – A God-intoxicated man. [(Of Spinoza) Novalis, 1722–1801]

14 Mock on, mock on, Voltaire, Rousseau; / Mock on, mock on; 'tis all in vain! / You throw the sand against the wind, / And the wind blows it back again. [William Blake, 1757–1827, *Mock On, Mock On, Voltaire, Rousseau*]

15 [Asking whether Ludwig Wittgenstein has made a key contribution to modern philosophy] is like asking whether one can play chess without the queen. [John Wisdom, 1905–93, quoted by Frederic Raphael in *New Society*, 30 May 1985]

See also next category, LOGIC, MIND

PHILOSOPHY

1 I was thrown out of NYU my freshman year ... for cheating on my metaphysics final. You know I looked within the soul of the boy sitting next to me. [Woody Allen, 1935– , in film *Annie Hall*, scripted with Marshall Brickman]

2 The principles of logic and metaphysics are true simply because we never allow them to be anything else. [A J Ayer, 1910–89, *Language, Truth and Logic*]

3 All good moral philosophy is but the handmaid to religion. [Francis Bacon, 1561–1626, *The Advancement of Learning*, II, xxii, 14]

4 A little philosophy inclineth man's mind to atheism; but depth in philosophy bringeth men's minds about to religion. [Francis Bacon, 1561–1626, *Essays*, 16, 'Of Atheism']

5 The Socratic manner is not a game at which two can play. [Max Beerbohm, 1872–1956, *Zuleika Dobson*, Ch. 15]

6 *On a metaphysician:* A blind man in a dark room, looking for a black hat which is not there. [Lord Bowen, 1835–94, attr. in *Notes & Queries*, 182, 123]; see 15

7 Metaphysics is the finding of bad reasons for what we believe upon instinct; but to find these reasons is no less an instinct. [F H Bradley, 1846–1924, *Appearance and Reality*, Preface]

8 To believe only possibilities is not faith, but mere philosophy. [Sir Thomas Browne, 1605–82, *Religio Medici*, Pt 1, 48]

9 For him was lever have at his beddes heed / Twenty bokes, clad in blak or reed, / Of Aristotle and his philosophye, / Than robes riche, or fithele, or gay sautrye. / But al be that he was a philosophre, / Yet hadde he put litel gold in cofre. [Geoffrey Chaucer, 1340?–1400, *Canterbury Tales*, 'Prologue', 293]

10 Nothing so absurd can be said, that some philosopher has not said it. [Cicero, 106–43 BC, *De Divinatione*, ii, 58]

11 'Where would you place yourself philosophically?' ... 'A self-pitying stoic. I founded the school myself.' [Peter de Vries, 1910–93, *Consenting Adults*, Ch. 3]

12 You are a philosopher, Dr Johnson. I have tried too in my time to be a philosopher; but I don't know how, cheerfulness always breaking in. [Oliver Edwards, 1711–91, quoted in James Boswell, *Life of J*, 17 Apr. 1778]

13 This same philosophy is a good horse in the stable, but an arrant jade on a journey. [Oliver Goldsmith, 1728–74, *The Good-Natured Man*, I]

14 If the world were good for nothing else, it is a fine subject for speculation. [William Hazlitt, 1778–1830, *Characteristics*, 302]

15 James was being teased by a theological colleague who said to him: 'A philosopher is like a blind man in a dark cellar, looking for a black cat that isn't there.' 'Yes,' said William James, 'and the difference between philosophy and theology is that theology finds the cat.' [William James, 1842–1910, in A J Ayer, *On Making Philosophy Intelligible*]; see 6

16 Philosophy is concerned with two matters: soluble questions that are trivial and critical questions that are insoluble. [Stephen Kanfer, 1933– , in *Time* magazine, 19 Apr. 1982]

17 Philosophy will clip an angel's wings. [John Keats, 1795–1821, *Lamia*, II, 234]

18 The German philosophers are the most frivolous of all – they count truths like lovers but seldom propose to marry them. [Lin Yutang, 1895–1976, attr.]

19 So the lively force of his mind has broken down all barriers, and he has passed far beyond the fiery walls of the world, and in mind and spirit has traversed the boundless universe. [Lucretius, 99–55 BC, *The Nature of the Universe*, I, 72]

20 How charming is divine philosophy! / Not harsh, and crabbèd as dull fools suppose, / But musical as is Apollo's lute, / And a perpetual feast of nectared sweets, / Where no crude surfeit reigns. [John Milton, 1608–74, *Comus*, 476]

21 In philosophy, if you aren't moving at a snail's pace you aren't moving at all. [Iris Murdoch, 1919–99, *Acastos: Two Platonic Dialogues*]

22 Not to care for philosophy is to be a true philosopher. [Blaise Pascal, 1623–62, *Pensées*, I, 4]

23 There will be no end to the troubles of states, or indeed, my dear Glaucon, of humanity itself, till philosophers become kings in this world, or till those we now call kings and rulers really and truly become philosophers. [Plato, *c.*428–347 BC, *Republic*, Bk v, 473]

24 We thought philosophy ought to be patient and unravel people's mental blocks. Trouble with doing that is, once you've unravelled them, their heads fall off. [Frederic Raphael, 1931– , *The Glittering Prizes*, 'A Double Life']

25 I think that bad philosophers may have a certain influence, good philosophers, never. [Bertrand Russell, 1872–1970; *Observer*, 'Sayings of the Week', 24 Apr. 1955]

26 The collection of prejudices which is called political philosophy is useful provided that it is not called philosophy. [Bertrand Russell, 1872–1970; *Observer*, 'Sayings of the Year', 1962]

27 Philosophy is the replacement of category-habits by category-disciplines. [Gilbert Ryle, 1900–1976, *The Concept of Mind*, Introduction]

28 Philosophy is a battle against the bewitchment of our intelligence by means of language. [Antoine de Saint-Exupéry, 1900–1944, attr.]

29 It is a great advantage for a system of philosophy to be substantially true. [George Santayana, 1863–1952, *The Unknowable*]

30 There are more things in heaven and earth, Horatio, / Than are dreamt of in your philosophy. [William Shakespeare, 1564–1616, *Hamlet*, I. v. 166]

31 For there was never yet philosopher / That could endure the toothache patiently. [*Much Ado About Nothing*, V. i. 35]

32 Philosophy, the lumber of the schools. [Jonathan Swift, 1677–1745, *Ode to Sir W. Temple*, 2]

33 Philosophy is the product of wonder. [A N Whitehead, 1861–1947, *Nature and Life*, Ch. 1]

34 Philosophy, as we use the word, is a fight against the fascination which forms of expression exert upon us. [Ludwig Wittgenstein, 1889–1951, *The Blue Book*, p. 27]

35 Philosophy is not a theory but an activity. [Ludwig Wittgenstein, 1889–1951, *Tractatus Logico-philosophicus*, 4, 112]

See also previous category, LOGIC, MIND

PHOTOGRAPHY

1 Most things in life are moments of pleasure and a lifetime of embarrassment; photography is a moment of embarrassment and a lifetime of pleasure. [Tony Benn, 1925– , in *The Sunday Times*, 31 Dec. 1989]

2 The spectacle creates an eternal present of immediate expectation; memory ceases to be necessary or desirable. With the loss of memory the continuities of meaning and judgement are also lost to us. The camera relieves us of the burden of memory. [John Berger, 1926– , in *New Society*, 17 Aug. 1978]

3 She told me with pride that her husband had photographed her a hundred and twenty-seven times since they had been married. [F Scott Fitzgerald, 1896–1940, *The Great Gatsby*, Ch. 2]

4 What novel – or what else in the world – can have the epic scope of a photograph album ? May our Father in Heaven, the untiring amateur who each Sunday snaps us from above, at an unfortunate angle that makes for hideous foreshortening, and pastes our pictures, properly exposed or not, in his album, guide me safely through this album of mine. [Günter Grass, 1927– , *The Tin Drum*, 'The Photograph Album']

5 All you can do with most ordinary photographs is stare at them – they stare back, blankly – and presently your concentration begins to fade. They stare you down. I mean, photography is all right if you don't mind looking at the world from the point of view of a paralysed cyclops – *for a split second.* [David Hockney, 1937– , in *Cameraworks*, as told to Lawrence Weschler]

6 My interest in the photocopier was philosophical really. Beyond a shadow of doubt, it's that technology that brought down communism. [David Hockney, 1937– , in *Guardian*, 13 Sept. 1990]

7 The picture-papers are more than half-filled with photographs of bathing nymphs – photographs that make one understand the ease with which St Anthony rebuffed his temptations. [Aldous Huxley, 1894–1963, *On the Margin*, 'Beauty in 1920']

8 The modern pantheist not only sees the god in everything, he takes photographs of it. [D H Lawrence, 1885–1930, *St Mawr*]

9 A photograph is not only an image (as a painting is an image), an interpretation of the real; it is also a trace, something directly stencilled off the real, like a footprint or a death mask. [Susan Sontag, 1933– , *On Photography*]

10 What is a photograph? It's something defined, with an edge ... A long time after the event it is still there, and when you look at it you shut out everything else. It becomes an icon, a totem, a curio. A photo is a piece of reality? A fragment of the truth? [Graham Swift, 1949– , *Out of This World*, 'Harry']

PHYSICS & PHYSICISTS

1 A physicist who is able to view any number of partially successful models without favouritism is automatically a bootstrapper. [G F Chew, 1924– , in Fritjof Capra, *The Turning Point*, II, 3]

2 Biology is the study of complicated things that give the appearance of having been designed for a purpose. Physics is the study of simple things that do not tempt us to invoke design. [Richard Dawkins, 1941– , *The Blind Watchmaker*, Ch. 1]

3 You have got the impression that contemporary physics is based on concepts somewhat analogous to the smile of the absent cat. [(Comment on Viscount Samuel) Albert Einstein, 1879–1955, *Essay in Physics*, in John Bowle, *Viscount S*, Ch. 19]

4 If you want to find out anything from the theoretical physicists about the methods they use, I advise you to stick closely to one principle: Don't listen to their words, fix your attention on their deeds. [Albert Einstein, 1879–1955, *The World as I See It*]

5 The most important hypothesis in all of biology, for example, is that everything that animals do, atoms do. In other words, there is nothing that living creatures do that cannot be understood from the point of view that they are made of atoms acting according to the laws of physics. [Richard Feynman, 1918–88, *Lectures on Physics*, Vol. 1]

6 Electricity is of two kinds, positive and negative. The difference is, I presume, that one comes a little more expensive, but is more durable; the other is a cheaper thing, but the moths get into it. [Stephen Leacock, 1869–1944, *Literary Lapses*, 'A Manual of Education']

7 The physicists have known sin; and this is a knowledge which they cannot lose. [J Robert Oppenheimer, 1904–67, lecture at Massachusetts Institute of Technology, 25 Nov. 1947]

8 Nature and Nature's laws lay hid in night: / God said 'Let Newton be!' and all was light. [Alexander Pope, 1688–1744, *Epitaph intended for Sir Isaac Newton*]; see 11

9 Science is divided into two categories, physics and stamp-collecting. [Ernest Rutherford, 1871–1937, in J D Bernal, *The Social Function of Science*]

10 Well, I made the wave, didn't I? [In answer to the jibe 'Lucky fellow, Rutherford, always on the crest of the wave.' [Ernest Rutherford, 1871–1937, in C P Snow, *The Two Cultures and the Scientific Revolution*]

11 It did not last: the Devil howling, 'Ho! / Let Einstein be!' restored the status quo. [J C Squire, 1884–1958, *Answer to Pope's Epitaph on Sir Isaac Newton*]; see 8

12 Modern Physics is an instrument of [world] Jewry for the destruction of Nordic science ... True physics is the creation of the German spirit. [Rudolphe Tomaschek, b.1895, in W L Shirer, *The Rise and Fall of the Third Reich*, Ch. 8]

13 It would be a poor thing to be an atom in a universe without physicists. And physicists are made of atoms. A physicist is an atom's way of knowing about atoms. [George Wald, 1906–97, from Foreword to L J Henderson, *The Fitness of the Environment*]

14 Where the statue stood / Of Newton with his prism and silent face, / The marble index of a mind for ever / Voyaging through strange seas of thought, alone. [William Wordsworth, 1770–1850, *The Prelude*, III, 60]

See also BIOLOGY, MATHEMATICS, SCIENCE, SCIENTISTS

PITY

1 Pity would be no more / If we did not make somebody poor; / And Mercy no more could be / If all were as happy as we. [William Blake, 1757–1827, *Songs of Experience*, 'The Human Abstract']

2 Then cherish pity, lest you drive an angel from your door. [William Blake, 1757–1827, *Songs of Innocence*, 'Holy Thursday']

3 Give both the infinitudes their due – / Infinite mercy, but, I wis, / As infinite a justice too. [Robert Browning, 1812–89, *The Heretic's Tragedy*]

4 I seem forsaken and alone, / I hear the lion roar; / And every door is shut but one, / And that is Mercy's door. [William Cowper, 1731–1800, *Olney Hymns*, 33]

5 Reason to rule but mercy to forgive: / The first is law, the last prerogative. [John Dryden, 1631–1700, *The Hind and the Panther*, 1, 261]

6 We hand folks over to God's mercy, and show none ourselves. [George Eliot, 1819–80, *Adam Bede*, Ch. 42]

7 Pity, like a naked new-born babe, / Striding the blast, or heaven's cherubim, horsed / Upon the sightless couriers of the air, / Shall blow the horrid deed in every eye. [William Shakespeare, 1564–1616, *Macbeth*, I. vii. 21]

8 No ceremony that to great ones 'longs, / Not the king's crown, nor the deputed sword, / The marshal's truncheon, nor the judge's robe, / Become them with one half so good a grace / As mercy does. [*Measure for Measure*, II. ii. 59]

9 The quality of mercy is not strained, / It droppeth as the gentle rain from heaven / Upon the place beneath: it is twice blessed; / It blesseth him that gives and him that takes. [*The Merchant of Venice*, IV. i. (184)]

10 She loved me for the dangers I had passed, / And I loved her that she did pity them. / This only is the witchcraft I have used. [*Othello*, I. iii. 158]

11 No beast so fierce but knows some touch of pity. [*Richard III*, I. ii. 71]

12 A pity beyond all telling / Is hid in the heart of love. [W B Yeats, 1865–1939, *The Pity of Love*]

See also SYMPATHY

PLACES

1 Match me such marvel save in Eastern clime, / A rose-red city – 'half as old as time'! [J W Burgon, 1813–88, *Petra*, l. 132]

2 Aden was a revelation. Until then my belief in God's indifference had been theoretical. [Clive James, 1939– , *Unreliable Memoirs*, Ch. 17]

3 Though the latitude's rather uncertain, / And the longitude also is vague, / The persons I pity who know not the city, / The beautiful city of Prague. [W J Prowse, 1836–70, *The City of Prague*]

4 In this miniature inverted cluster, the British had hit by chance on a perfect symbol of themselves. The Falklands held a mirror up to our own islands, and it reflected, in brilliantly sharp focus, all our injured belittlement, our sense of being beleaguered, neglected and misunderstood. [Jonathan Raban, 1942– , *Coasting*, Ch. 3]

See also specific cities and nations

PLAGIARISM, see IMITATION

PLAYS

1 What the devil does the plot signify, except to bring in fine things? [George Villiers, Second Duke of Buckingham, 1628–87, *The Rehearsal*, III. i]

2 It [a production of Brecht's *The Days of the Commune*] has the depth of a cracker-motto, the drama of a dial-a-recipe service and the eloquence of a conversation between a speak-your-weight machine and a whoopee-cushion. [Bernard Levin, 1928– , in *The Sunday Times*, 6 Nov. 1977]

3 I didn't like the play, but then I saw it under adverse conditions–the curtain was up. [Groucho Marx, 1895–1977; in Laurence J Peter, *Peter's Quotations*]

4 Godot is a play in which nothing happens – twice. [Vivian Mercier, 1919–89, review of text of *Waiting for Godot* in the *Irish Times*, 18 Feb. 1956]; see 11

5 All art is full of magic and trickery, but in a novel the whole thing can subside into an ocean of reflection and continuous thought – at least in a traditional novel – whereas in theatre you are really jumping from place to place like a mountain goat. [Iris Murdoch, 1919–99, interview in *Weekend Guardian*, 22–23 Apr. 1989]

6 Rehearsing a play is making the word flesh. Publishing a play is reversing the process. [Peter Shaffer, 1926– , *Equus*, A Note on the Text]

7 The best actors in the world, either for tragedy, comedy, history, pastoral, pastoral-comical, historical-pastoral, tragical-historical, tragical-comical-historical-pastoral, scene individable or poem unlimited. [William Shakespeare, 1564–1616, *Hamlet*, II. ii. (424)]

8 The play, I remember, pleased not the million; 'twas caviare to the general. [*Hamlet*, II. ii. (465)]

9 Plays work through metaphor. In the end the best play about Vietnam will probably turn out to have been written by Sophocles. [Tom Stoppard, 1937– , interview in *Guardian*, 18 Mar. 1988]

10 A novel is a static thing that one moves through; a play is a dynamic thing that moves past one. [Kenneth Tynan, 1927–80, *Curtains*, 1, 'Cards of Identity']

11 A special virtue attaches to plays which remind the drama of how much it can do without and still exist. By all the known criteria, Samuel Beckett's *Waiting for Godot* is a dramatic vacuum. Pity the critic who seeks a chink in its armour, for it is all chink. [Kenneth Tynan, 1927–80, *Curtains*, 1, 'Waiting for Godot']; see 4

12 In the play we recognize the general ... in the novel, the particular. [Virginia Woolf, 1882–1941, in Kenneth Tynan, *Curtains*, 2]

See also next categories, THEATRE

PLAYWRIGHTS IN GENERAL

1 A gift for dialogue qualifies you to be a playwright no more than a gift for mixing sand and water qualifies you to build cathedrals. [David Hare, 1947– , in *Independent on Sunday*, 26 May 1991]

2 The historian, essentially, wants more documents than he can really use; the dramatist only wants more liberties than he can really take. [Henry James, 1843–1916, *The Aspern Papers*, Preface to 1909 edn]

3 The dramatist changes the props but keeps the players. The Almighty does the reverse. [Thomas McKeown, 1912–88, in *Perspectives in Biology and Medicine*, Spring 1983]

4 All playwrights should be dead for three hundred years. [Joseph Mankiewicz, 1909–93, in film *All about Eve*]

See also previous and next categories, THEATRE

PLAYWRIGHTS: INDIVIDUAL (in alphabetical order of subject)

1 His [Samuel Beckett's] statement of desolation has its own impersonal dignity and you can derive from it whatever comfort you can: otherwise there is always God, economics, or Ibsen. [John Peter, 1938– , on Beckett's death, in *The Sunday Times*, 31 Dec. 1989]

2 I don't regard Brecht as a man of iron-grey purpose and intellect, I think he is a theatrical whore of the first quality. [Peter Hall, 1930– , in Frank Muir, *Frank Muir Book*, 'Theatre']

3 For example, he [Brecht] composed / Plays that staged by us promote / All the values he opposed. [Christopher Logue, 1932– , *C L's A B C*, 'B']

4 Chekhov has the art of showing us farce as inverted poetry. [V S Pritchett, 1900–1997, *Chekhov: A Spirit Set Free*]

5 William Congreve is the only sophisticated playwright England has produced; and like Shaw, Sheridan and Wilde, his nearest rivals, he was brought up in Ireland. [Kenneth Tynan, 1927–80, *Curtains*, 1, 'The Way of the World']

6 Every additional man who learns to read is another reader for Molière. [Charles-Augustin Sainte-Beuve, 1804–69, *Portraits littéraires*, Vol. ii]

7 'But what would you say your plays were *about*, Mr Pinter?' 'The weasel under the cocktail cabinet.' [Harold Pinter, 1930– (exchange at a new writers' brains trust), in J Russell Taylor, *Anger and After*, Ch. 7]

8 Who saw life steadily, and saw it whole: / The mellow glory of the Attic stage. [(Sophocles) Matthew Arnold, 1822–88, *To a Friend*]

9 I depict men as they ought to be, but Euripides portrays them as they are. [Sophocles, 495–406 BC, quoted in Aristotle, *Poetics*, 25]

10 I write fiction because it's a way of making statements I can disown, and I write plays because dialogue is the most respectable way of contradicting myself. [Tom Stoppard, 1937– (TV interview), in *Guardian*, 21 Mar. 1973]

11 I write to get out of jail. [Tom Stoppard, 1937– , in *Observer*, on his fiftieth birthday, 28 June 1987]

12 Webster was much possessed by death / And saw the skull beneath the skin. [T S Eliot, 1888–1965, *Whispers of Immortality*]

13 When I wrote / I always wrote with action in mind / kept sight of the fact / that writing was just a preparation. [Peter Weiss, 1916–82, *The Marat / Sade*, xxviii]

See also previous categories, THEATRE

PLEASURE

1 One half of the world cannot understand the pleasures of the other. [Jane Austen, 1775–1817, *Emma*, 9]

2 A man hath no better thing under the sun than to eat, and to drink and to be merry. [Bible, OT, *Ecclesiastes* 8:15]

3 *Debauchee*, n. One who has so earnestly pursued pleasure that he has had the misfortune to overtake it. [Ambrose Bierce, 1842–1914, *The Devil's Dictionary*]

4 I am convinced that we have a degree of delight, and that no small one, in the real misfortunes and pains of others. [Edmund Burke, 1729–97, *On the Sublime and Beautiful*, I, xiv]

5 But pleasures are like poppies spread – / You seize the flow'r, its bloom is shed; / Or like the snow falls in the river – A moment white, then melts for ever. [Robert Burns, 1759–96, *Tam o' Shanter*, 59]

6 Pleasure after all is a safer guide than either right or duty. [Samuel Butler, 1835–1902, *The Way of All Flesh*, Ch. 19]

7 Though sages may pour out their wisdom's treasure, / There is no sterner moralist than Pleasure. [Lord Byron, 1788–1824, *Don Juan*, III, 64]

8 Rich the treasure, / Sweet the pleasure; / Sweet is pleasure after pain. [John Dryden, 1631–1700, *Alexander's Feast*, 58]

9 We are so made that we can derive intense enjoyment from a contrast and very little from a state of things. [Sigmund Freud, 1856–1939, *Civilization and Its Discontents*, Ch. 2]

10 The art of pleasing consists in being pleased. [William Hazlitt, 1778–1830, *On Manner*]

11 People must not do things for fun. We are not here for fun. There is no reference to fun in any Act of Parliament. [A P Herbert, 1890–1971, *Uncommon Law*, 'Is It a Free Country?']

12 Ever let the fancy roam, / Pleasure never is at home. [John Keats, 1795–1821, *Fancy*, 1]

13 Life would be tolerable, were it not for its amusements. [George Cornewall Lewis, 1806–63, in *The Times*, 18 Sept. 1872]

14 Who loves not wine, woman and song, / Remains a fool his whole life long. [Martin Luther, 1483–1546, inscription at Wartburg, attr.]

15 Openly, yes, / with the naturalness / of the hippopotamus or the alligator / when it climbs out on the bank to / experience the / sun, I do these / things which I do, which please / no one but myself. [Marianne Moore, 1887–1972, *Black Earth*]

16 To strip our pleasures of imagination is to reduce them to their own dimensions, that is to say to nothing. [Marcel Proust, 1871–1922, *Remembrance of Things Past: Within a Budding Grove*, 'Place-names']

17 Pleasure is nothing else but the intermission of pain. [John Selden, 1584–1654, *Table Talk*, 104]

18 Why, all delights are vain; but that most vain / Which, with pain purchased, doth inherit pain. [William Shakespeare, 1564–1616, *Love's Labour's Lost*, I. i. 72]

19 No profit grows where is no pleasure ta'en; / In brief, sir, study what you most affect. [*The Taming of the Shrew*, I. i. 39]

20 Dost thou think, because thou art virtuous, there shall be no more cakes and ale? [*Twelfth Night*, II. iii. (124)]

21 Death said: 'The good is one thing, the pleasant another; these two, having different objects, chain a man. It is well with him who clings to the good; he who chooses the pleasant misses his end.' [Upanishads, 7th cent. BC, *Katha Upanishad*, ii]

22 All the things I really like to do are either illegal, immoral, or fattening. [Alexander Woollcott, 1887–1943, *The Knock at the Stage Door*]

23 Go to your business, I say, pleasure, whilst I go to my pleasure, business. [William Wycherley, 1640?–1716, *The Country Wife*, II]

See also HAPPINESS, JOY, PAIN

POETRY

1 Poetry is more philosophical and of higher value than history. [Aristotle, 384–322 BC, *Poetics*, 9]

2 I think it will be found that the grand style arises in poetry, when a noble nature, poetically gifted, treats with simplicity or with severity a serious subject. [Matthew Arnold, 1822–88, *On Translating Homer*, final words]

3 There is the view that poetry should improve your life. I think people confuse it with the Salvation Army. [John Ashbery, 1927– , in *International Herald Tribune*, Paris, 2 Oct. 1989]

4 A verbal art like poetry is reflective; it stops to think. Music is immediate; it goes on to become. [W H Auden, 1907–73, *A Dyer's Hand*, 8, 'Notes on Music']

5 Poetry, in fact, bears the same kind of relation to Prose, using prose simply in the sense of all those uses of words that are not poetry, that algebra bears to arithmetic. [W H Auden, 1907–73, and J Garrett, 1902–66, *The Poet's Tongue*, Introduction]

6 Oh, love will make a dog howl in rhyme. [Francis Beaumont, 1584–1616, and John Fletcher, 1579–1625, *The Queen of Corinth*, IV. i]

7 The right words in the right order. [Alexander Blok, 1880–1921, in D Burg and G Feifer, *Solzhenitsyn*]

8 *Quelque sujet qu'on traite, ou plaisant, ou sublime, / Que toujours le bon sens s'accorde avec la rime.* – Whether one is treating a light or an exalted subject, let the sense and the rhyme always agree. [Nicholas Boileau, 1636–1711, *L'Art poétique*, I, 27]

9 No poem is ever written for its story line's sake only, just as no life is lived for the sake of an obituary. [Joseph Brodsky, 1940–96, *Less Than One*, 'Keening Music']

10 It looks well enough on the page, but never / well enough. [Basil Bunting, 1900–1985, *Briggflatts*, 2]

11 Would you try it for, say, six months, a poem every week? Preferably set in the form of prose, so as not to offend anyone. [Anthony Burgess, 1917–93, *Inside Mr Enderby*, Pt 1, Ch. 3, ii]

12 The fatal facility of the octosyllabic verse. [Lord Byron, 1788–1824, *The Corsair*, dedication]

13 Nothing so difficult as a beginning / In poesy, unless perhaps the end. [Lord Byron, 1788–1824, *Don Juan*, IV, 1]

14 I have nothing to say /   and I am saying it   and that is / poetry. [John Cage, 1912–92, *Lecture on Nothing*]

15 The poem is not made from these letters that I drive in like nails, but of the white which remains on the paper. [Paul Claudel, 1868–1955, footnote to *Cinq grandes odes*, I, 'Les Muses']

16 That willing suspension of disbelief for the moment, which constitutes poetic faith. [Samuel Taylor Coleridge, 1772–1834, *Biographia Literaria*, Ch. 4]

17 Poetry is not the proper antithesis to prose, but to science. Poetry is opposed to science, and prose to metre. [Samuel Taylor Coleridge, 1772–1834, *Lectures and Notes of 1818*, sect. i]

18 In the hexameter rises the fountain's silvery column; / In the pentameter aye falling in melody back. [Samuel Taylor Coleridge, 1772–1834, *Ovidian Elegiac Metre*]

19 Prose = words in their best order; poetry = the *best* words in the best order. [Samuel Taylor Coleridge, 1772–1834, *Table Talk*, 12 July 1827]

20 Poetry is certainly something more than good sense, but it must be good sense at all events; just as a palace is more than a house, but it must be a house, at least. [Samuel Taylor Coleridge, 1772–1834, *Table Talk*, 9 May 1830]

21 Poetry's unnat'ral; no man ever talked poetry 'cept a beadle on boxin' day. [Charles Dickens, 1812–70, *Pickwick Papers*, Ch. 33]

22 And this unpolished rugged verse I chose / As fittest for discourse and nearest prose. [John Dryden, 1631–1700, *Religio Laici*, 453]

23 Wit will shine / Through the harsh cadence of a rugged line. [John Dryden, 1631–1700, *To the Memory of Mr Oldham*]

24 A poem is what happens when an anxiety meets a technique. [Lawrence Durrell, 1912–90, attr.]

25 Poetry's a mere drug, Sir. [George Farquhar, 1678–1707, *Love and a Bottle*, I. i]

26 All one's inventions are true, you can be sure of that. Poetry is as exact a science as geometry. [Gustave Flaubert, 1821–80, letter to Louise Colet, 14 Aug. 1853]

27 Poetry is a way of taking life by the throat. [Robert Frost, 1874–1963, *Comment*]

28 Writing free verse is like playing tennis with the net down. [Robert Frost, 1874–1963, address at Milton Academy, Massachusetts, 17 May 1935]

29 That which gets left out of verse and prose in translation. [Robert Frost, 1874–1963 (definition of poetry), in *The Times Literary Supplement*, 16 Sept. 1989]

30 Simon, for whom poetry is a closed book in a locked cupbhoard in a high attic in a lonely house in a remote hamlet in a distant land. [Stephen Fry, 1957– , *The Hippopotamus*, 4, iii]

31 Poetry is not an expression of the party line. It's that time of night, lying in bed, thinking what you really think, making the private world public, that's what the poet does. [Allen Ginsberg, 1926–97, in Barry Miles, *Ginsberg*, Ch. 17]

32 I should define a good poem as one that makes complete sense; and says all it has to say memorably and economically, and has been written for no other than poetic reasons. [Robert Graves, 1895–1985, *Steps*, 'Talk on the Legitimate Criticism of Poetry']

33 Only in a world where there are cranes and horses ... can poetry survive. [Robert Graves, 1895–1985, in Derek Walcott, *Sea Cranes*]

34 The language of the age is never the language of poetry, except among the French, whose verse, where the thought or image does not support it, differs in nothing from prose. [Thomas Gray, 1716–71, letter to Richard West, Apr. 1742]

35 I have always disliked the idea of an arts ghetto in which poetry is kept on a life-support system. [Tony Harrison, 1947– , in *Observer*, 23 July 1989]

36 That's the borderline that poetry / Operates on too, always in between / What you would like to happen and what will – / Whether you like it or not. [Seamus Heaney, 1939– , *The Cure at Troy*, p. 2]

37 [Of writing poetry] The movement is from delight to wisdom and not vice versa. [Seamus Heaney, 1939– , *The Redress of Poetry*, title essay]

38 Poetry proper is never merely a higher mode (*melos*) of everyday language. It is rather the reverse: everyday language is a forgotten and therefore used up poem, from which there hardly resounds a call any longer. [Martin Heidegger, 1889–1976, from *Language*, quoted in Bruce Chatwin, *Songlines*, p. 35]

39 A verse may find him who a sermon flies. / And turn delight into a sacrifice. [George Herbert, 1593–1633, *Church Porch*, 1]

40 Who says that fictions only and false hair / Become a verse? Is there in truth no beauty? / Is all good structure in a winding stair? [George Herbert, 1593–1633, *Jordan*]

41 The poetical language of an age should be the current language heightened. [Gerard Manley Hopkins, 1844–89, letter to Robert Bridges, 14 Aug. 1879]

42 Neither men nor gods nor bookstalls have ever allowed poets to be mediocre. [Horace, 65–8 BC, *Ars Poetica*, 372]

43 Good religious poetry ... is likely to be most justly appreciated and most discriminately relished by the undevout. [A E Housman, 1859–1936, *The Name and Nature of Poetry*]

44 If a line of poetry strays into my memory, my skin bristles so that the razor ceases to act. [A E Housman, 1859–1936, *The Name and Nature of Poetry*]

45 Unlearnedly and unreasonably poetry is shaped / Awkwardly but alive in the unmeasured womb. [Patrick Kavanagh, 1905–67, *Art McCooey*]

46 A drainless shower / Of light is poesy; 'tis the supreme power; / 'Tis might half slumbering on his own right arm. [John Keats, 1795–1821, *Sleep and Poetry*, 235]

47 We hate poetry that has a palpable design upon us – and if we do not agree, seems to put its hand in its breeches pocket. Poetry should be great and unobtrusive, a thing which enters into one's soul, and does not startle or amaze it with itself, but with its subject. [John Keats, 1795–1821, letter to J H Reynolds, 3 Feb. 1818]

48 If poetry comes not as naturally as the leaves to a tree it had better not come at all. [John Keats, 1795–1821, letter to John Taylor, 27 Feb. 1818]

49 When power narrows the areas of man's concern, poetry reminds him of the richness and diversity of his existence. When power corrupts, poetry cleanses. [President John F Kennedy, 1917–63, address at dedication of the Robert Frost Library, Amherst College, Massachusetts, 26 Oct. 1963]

50 I can't understand these chaps who go round American universities explaining how they write poems: It's like going round explaining how you sleep with your wife. [Philip Larkin, 1922–85, quoted by John Updike in *The New York Times*, 17 Aug. 1986]

51 I think more of a bird with broad wings flying and lapsing through the air, than anything, when I think of metre. [D H Lawrence, 1885–1930, letter to Edward Marsh, Nov. 1913]

52 As civilisation advances, poetry almost necessarily declines. [Lord Macaulay, 1800–1859, *Literary Essays*, 'Milton']

53 A poem should be palpable and mute / As a globed fruit, / Dumb / As old medallions to the thumb . . . / A poem should be equal to / Not true . . . / A poem should not mean / But be. [Archibald Macleish, 1892–1982, *Ars Poetica*]

54 It's in the margins we'll find the poems. [Osip Mandelstam, 1891–1938, attr.]

55 Poetry is what Milton saw when he went blind. [Don Marquis, 1878–1937, *New York Sun*, 'The Sun Dial']

56 Why is it that the sudden mention of an aunt is so deflating to a poem? [Edward Marsh, 1874–1953, *Ambrosia and Small Beer*, Ch. 5]

57 Poetry is a comforting piece of fiction set to more or less lascivious music. [H L Mencken, 1880–1956, *Prejudices*, Third Series, 'The Poet and his Art']

58 And ever, against eating cares, / Lap me in soft Lydian airs, / Married to immortal verse / Such as the meeting soul may pierce / In notes, with many a winding bout / Of linkèd sweetness long drawn out. [John Milton, 1608–74, *L'Allegro*, 135]

59 Rhyme being no necessary adjunct or true ornament of poem or good verse, in longer works especially, but the invention of a barbarous age, to set off wretched matter with lame metre. [John Milton, 1608–74, *Paradise Lost*, Preface: The Verse]

60 Rhetoric . . . To which poetry would be made subsequent, or indeed rather precedent, as being less subtle and fine, but more simple, sensuous and passionate. [John Milton, 1608–74, *Of Education*]

61 Most people ignore most poetry because most poetry ignores most people. [Adrian Mitchell, 1932– , *Poems* (1964), 'Introduction']

62 Poetry is an extra hand. It can caress or tickle. It can clench and fight. The hand is hot. Take it or leave it. [Adrian Mitchell, 1932– , 'Poetry Lives', in *The Sunday Times*, 13 Feb. 1972]

63 Yea, marry, now it is somewhat, for now it is rhyme; before, it was neither rhyme nor reason. [(To a friend who had versified an indifferent book) Sir Thomas More, 1478–1535, in Francis Bacon, *Apophthegms*, 287]

64 Poetry is an act of peace. Peace goes into the making of a poet as flour goes into the making of bread. [Pablo Neruda, 1904–73, *Memoirs*, Ch. 6]

65 And he whose fustian's so sublimely bad / It is not poetry, but prose run mad. [Alexander Pope, 1688–1744, *Epistle to Dr Arbuthnot*, 187]

66 Rhythm is a form cut into TIME, as a design is determined SPACE. [Ezra Pound, 1885–1972, *ABC of Reading*, 'Treatise on Metre', I]

67 The author's conviction ... is that music begins to atrophy when it departs too far from the dance; that poetry begins to atrophy when it gets too far from music. [Ezra Pound, 1885–1972, *ABC of Reading*, 'Warning']

68 For three years, out of key with his time, / He strove to resuscitate the dead art / Of poetry; to maintain 'the sublime' / In the old sense. Wrong from the start – [Ezra Pound, 1885–1972, *Hugh Selwyn Mauberley*, 'E. P. Ode pour l'élection de son sépulcre', I]

69 And give up verse, my boy, / there's nothing in it. [Ezra Pound, 1885–1972, *Hugh Selwyn Mauberley*, 'Mr Nixon']

70 It [poetry] is a perfectly possible means of overcoming chaos. [I A Richards, 1893–1979, *Science and Poetry*, Ch. 7]

71 Among the Haida Indians of the Pacific Northwest, the verb for 'making poetry' is the same as the verb 'to breathe'. [Tom Robbins, 1936– , *Another Roadside Attraction*]

72 More often than prose or mathematics, poetry is received in a hostile spirit, as if its publication were an affront to the reader. [Michael Roberts, 1902–48, *Faber Book of Modern Verse*, Introduction]

73 A sonnet is a moment's monument, – / Memorial from the Soul's eternity / To one dead deathless hour. [Dante Gabriel Rossetti, 1828–82, *The House of Life*, 1, Introduction]

74 Poetry, surely, is a crisis, perhaps the only actionable one we can call our own. [J D Salinger, 1919– , *Seymour: An Introduction*]

75 Poetry is the achievement of the synthesis of hyacinths and biscuits. [Carl Sandburg, 1878–1967, 'Poetry Considered', in *Atlantic Monthly*, Mar. 1923]

76 Our poesy is as a gum, which oozes / From whence 'tis nourished. [William Shakespeare, 1564–1616, *Timon of Athens*, I. i. 21]

77 Much is the force of heaven-bred poesy. [*The Two Gentlemen of Verona*, III. ii. 72]

78 Not marble, nor the gilded monuments / Of princes shall outlive this powerful rhyme. [*Sonnets*, 55]

79 Poetry is the record of the best and happiest moments of the happiest and best minds. [P B Shelley, 1792–1822, *A Defence of Poetry*]

80 Most wretched men / Are cradled into poetry by wrong, / They learn in suffering what they teach in song. [P B Shelley, 1792–1822, *Julian and Maddalo*, 544]

81 A man does not write poems about what he knows, but about what he does not know. [Robin Skelton, 1925–97, *Teach Yourself Poetry*]

82 Poetry is the supreme fiction, madame. / Take the moral law and make a nave of it / And from the nave build haunted heaven. [Wallace Stevens, 1879–1955, *A High-toned Old Christian Woman*]

83 'Poetry is for women, I suppose?' she said. 'Created by men with women in mind? Like Crimplene.' [Barbara Trapido, 1941– , *Noah's Ark*, 25]

84 A poem is never finished, only abandoned. [Paul Valéry, 1871–1945, *Literature*]

85 Music before all else, and for that choose the irregular, which is vaguer and melts better into the air, having nothing in it that is heavy or emphatic. [Paul Verlaine, 1844–96, *L'Art poétique*, 1]

86 Poetry is to prose as dancing is to walking. [John Wain, 1925–94, talk on BBC radio, 13 Jan. 1976]

87 A lot of contemporary verse sounds like, you know, 'Someone hit me.' Whereas in a narrative you know exactly who hit you. [Derek Walcott, 1930– , interview in *Independent*, 10 Nov. 1990]

88 Poetry is the breath and finer spirit of all knowledge; it is the impassioned expression which is in the countenance of all Science. [William Wordsworth, 1770–1850, *Lyrical Ballads*, Preface]

89 Poetry is the spontaneous overflow of powerful feelings: it takes its origin from emotion recollected in tranquillity. [William Wordsworth, 1770–1850, *Lyrical Ballads*, Preface]

90 'Twas pastime to be bound / Within the sonnet's scanty plot of ground; / Pleased if some souls (for such there needs must be) / Who have felt the weight of too much liberty, / Should find brief solace there, as I have found. [William Wordsworth, 1770–1850, *Miscellaneous Sonnets*, I, 1]

91 We make out of the quarrel with others, rhetoric, but of the quarrel with ourselves, poetry. [W B Yeats, 1865–1939, *Anima Hominis*, 5]

92 Great prose may occur by accident: but not great poetry. [G M Young, 1882–1959, in *Geoffrey Madan's Notebooks*, ed. J A Gere and John Sparrow, 'Extracts and Summaries']

See also next categories, BOOKS, LITERATURE, PROSE, WRITERS, WRITING

POETS IN GENERAL

1 Not deep the poet sees, but wide. [Matthew Arnold, 1822–88, *Resignation*, 214]

2 No poet or novelist wishes he were the only one who ever lived, but most of them wish they were the only one alive, and quite a number fondly believe their wish has been granted. [W H Auden, 1907–73, *The Dyer's Hand*, 'Writing']

3 *Le Poète est semblable au prince des nuées / Qui hante la tempête et se rit de l'archer; / Exilé sur le sol, au milieu des huées, / Ses ailes de géant l'empêchent de marcher.* – The poet is like the prince of the clouds, who rides the tempest and scorns the archer. Exiled on the ground, amidst boos and insults, his giant's wings prevent his walking. [Charles Baudelaire, 1821–67, *L'Albatros*]

4 Or like a poet woo the moon, / Riding an armchair for my steed, / And with a flashing pen harpoon / Terrific metaphors of speed. [Roy Campbell, 1902–57, *The Festivals of Flight*]

5 A poet without love were a physical and metaphysical impossibility. [Thomas Carlyle, 1795–1881, *Critical and Miscellaneous Essays*, 'Burns']

6 Poetry and Religion (and it is really worth knowing) are 'a product of the smaller intestines'. [Thomas Carlyle, 1795–1881, *Critical and Miscellaneous Essays*, 'Signs of the Times']

7 For the godly poet must be chaste himself, but there is no need for his verses to be so. [Catullus, 84–54? BC, *Carmina*, 16]

8 The man who does not look at his change is no true poet. [G K Chesterton, 1874–1936, *The Apostle and the Wild Ducks*, ed. Dorothy E Collins]

9 Who often, but without success, have prayed / For apt Alliteration's artful aid. [Charles Churchill, 1731–64, *The Prophecy of Famine*, 85]

10 A true poet does not bother to be poetical. Nor does a nursery gardener scent his roses. [Jean Cocteau, 1889–1963, *Professional Secrets*]

11 No man was ever yet a great poet, without being at the same time a profound philosopher. [Samuel Taylor Coleridge, 1772–1834, *Biographia Literaria*, Ch. 15]

12 There is a pleasure in poetic pains / Which only poets know. [William Cowper, 1731–1800, *The Task*, Bk II, 285]

13 It is the logic of our times, / No subject for immortal verse – / That we who lived by honest dreams / Defend the bad against the worse. [C Day Lewis, 1904–72, *Where are the War Poets?*]

14 For that fine madness still he did retain / Which rightly should possess a poet's brain. [Michael Drayton, 1563–1631, *To Henry Reynolds, of Poets and Poesy*, 109]

15 Immature poets imitate; mature poets steal. [T S Eliot, 1888–1965, *Selected Essays*, 'Phillip Massinger']

16 We who with songs beguile your pilgrimage / And swear that Beauty lives though lilies die, / We poets of the proud old lineage / Who sing to find your hearts, we know not why, – / What shall we tell you? Tales, marvellous tales / Of ships and stars and isles where good men rest. [James Elroy Flecker, 1884–1915, *The Golden Journey to Samarkand*, Prologue]

17 I knew a very wise man so much of Sir Christopher's sentiment, that he believed if a man were permitted to make all the ballads, he need not care who should make the laws of a nation. [Andrew Fletcher of Saltoun, 1655–1716, *Letter to the Marquis of Montrose and Others*]

18 We all write poems; it is simply that poets are the ones who write in words. [John Fowles, 1926– , *The French Lieutenant's Woman*, Ch. 19]

19 No wonder poets sometimes have to *seem* / So much more business-like than business men. / Their wares are so much harder to get rid of. [Robert Frost, 1874–1963, *New Hampshire*]

20 The poets get a quizzical ahem. / They reflect time, I am the very ticking. [Roy Fuller, 1912–91, *A Wry Smile*]

21 As soon as war is declared it will be impossible to hold the poets back. Rhyme is still the most effective drum. [Jean Giraudoux, 1882–1944, *Tiger at the Gates*, I]

22 To be a poet is a condition rather than a profession. [Robert Graves, 1895–1985, in *Horizon* questionnaire, 1946]

23 Nine-tenths of English poetic literature is the result either of vulgar careerism, or of a poet trying to keep his hand in. Most poets are dead by their late twenties. [Robert Graves, 1895–1985, in *Observer*, 11 Nov. 1962]

24 Take away the rhythm and the metre, and put the first word last and the last first; still the dispersed limbs are those of a poet. [Horace, 65–8 BC, *Satires*, iv. 58–9 and 62]

25 To a poet nothing can be useless. [Dr Samuel Johnson, 1709–84, *Rasselas*, Ch. 10]

26 The business of a poet, said Imlac, is to examine, not the individual but the species; to remark general properties and large appearances. He does not number the streaks of the tulip. [Dr Samuel Johnson, 1709–84, *Rasselas*, Ch. 10]

27 They shall be accounted poet kings / Who simply tell the most heart-easing things. [John Keats, 1795–1821, *Sleep and Poetry*, 267]

28 A poet is the most unpoetical of anything in existence, because he has no identity – he is continually informing and filling some other body. [John Keats, 1795–1821, letter to R Woodhouse, 27 Oct. 1818]

29 The bards sublime, / Whose distant footsteps echo / Through the corridors of Time. [H W Longfellow, 1807–82, *The Day is Done*]

30 Perhaps no person can be a poet, or can even enjoy poetry, without a certain unsoundness of mind. [Lord Macaulay, 1800–1859, *Literary Essays*, 'Milton']

31 'But how divine is utterance,' she said. 'As we to the brutes, poets are to us.' [George Meredith, 1828–1909, *Diana of the Crossways*, Ch. 16]

32 Those who harm simple / people and who laugh at their / injuries will not be safe. / For the poet remembers. [Czeslaw Milosz, 1911– , inscription at the martyrs' monument, Gdansk shipyard, Poland]

33 A poet soaring in the high region of his fancies with his garland and singing robes about him. [John Milton, 1608–74, *The Reason of Church Government*, Bk ii, Introduction]

34 No bad man can be a good poet. [Boris Pasternak, 1890–1960, in Ilya Ehrenburg, *Truce*]

35 While pensive poets painful vigils keep / Sleepless themselves to give their readers sleep. [Alexander Pope, 1688–1744, *The Dunciad*, Bk i, 93]

36 Is there a parson, much bemused in beer, / A maudlin poetess, a rhyming peer, / A clerk foredoomed his father's soul to cross / Who pens a stanza, when he should engross? [Alexander Pope, 1688–1744, *Epistle to Dr Arbuthnot*, 15]

37 Curst be the verse, how well soe'er it flow, / That tends to make one worthy man my foe. [Alexander Pope, 1688–1744, *Epistle to Dr Arbuthnot*, 283]

38 It is the role of the poet to look at what is happening in the world and to know that quite other things are happening. [V S Pritchett, 1900–1997, *The Myth Makers*]

39 For ne'er / Was flattery lost on poet's ear: / A simple race! they waste their toil / For the vain tribute of a smile. [Sir Walter Scott, 1771–1832, *The Lay of the Last Minstrel*, IV, Conclusion]

40 I had rather be a kitten and cry mew / Than one of these same metre ballad-mongers. [William Shakespeare, 1564–1616, *1 Henry IV*, III. i. (128)]

41 As imagination bodies forth / The forms of things unknown, the poet's pen / Turns them to shapes, and gives to airy nothing / A local habitation and a name. [*A Midsummer Night's Dream*, V. i. 14]

42 No, I was not born under a rhyming planet. [*Much Ado About Nothing*, V. ii. (40)]

43 Poets are the unacknowledged legislators of the world. [P B Shelley, 1792–1822, *A Defence of Poetry*]

44 Chameleons feed on light and air: Poets' food is love and fame. [P B Shelley, 1792–1822, *An Exhortation*]

45 Create he can / Forms more real than living man, / Nurslings of immortality! [P B Shelley, 1792–1822, *Prometheus Unbound*, I, 747]

46 There have been many most excellent poets that have never versified, and now swarm many versifiers that need never answer to the name of poets. [Sir Philip Sidney, 1554–86, *The Defence of Poesy*]

47 Ah God! the petty fools of rhyme / That shriek and sweat in pigmy wars. [Alfred, Lord Tennyson, 1809–92, *Literary Squabbles*]

48 The poet from afar has taken speech, / Speech takes the poet far. A poet's speech begins a great way off. / A poet is carried away by speech. [Marina Tsvetayeva, 1892–1941, *The Poet*]

49 The poet is the most defenceless of all beings – for the good reason that he is always walking on his hands. [Paul Valéry, 1871–1945, *Bad Thoughts and Not So Bad*, 'B']

50 The lesson is that dying men must groan; / And poets groan in rhymes that please the ear. / But still it comes expensive, you must own. [John Wain, 1925–94, *Don't Let's Spoil It All, I Thought We Were Going to be Such Good Friends*]

51 Poets that lasting marble seek / Must carve in Latin or in Greek. [Edmund Waller, 1606–87, *Of English Verse*]

52 All poets who, when reading from their own works, experience a choked feeling, are major. For that matter, all poets who read from their own works are major, whether they choke or not. [E B White, 1899–1985, *How to Tell a Major Poet from a Minor Poet*]

53 Oh! many are the poets that are sown / By Nature; men endowed with highest gifts, / The vision and the faculty divine; / Yet wanting the accomplishment of verse. [William Wordsworth, 1770–1850, *The Excursion*, I, 77]

54 By our own spirits are we deified: / We poets in our youth begin in gladness; / But thereof come in the end despondency and madness. [William Wordsworth, 1770–1850, *Resolution and Independence*, 7]

55 Better go down upon your marrow-bones / And scrub a kitchen pavement, or break stones / Like an old pauper, in all kinds of weather; / For to articulate sweet sounds together / Is to work harder than all these. [W B Yeats, 1865–1939, *Adam's Curse*]

56 When I was young, / I had not given a penny for a song / Did not the poet sing it with such airs / That one believed he had a sword upstairs. [W B Yeats, 1865–1939, *All Things Can Tempt Me*]

57 A poet in Russia is more than a poet. [Yevgeny Yevtushenko, 1933– , in *Guardian*, 20 Apr. 1987]

See also previous and next categories, BOOKS, LITERATURE, PROSE, WRITERS, WRITING

POETS: INDIVIDUAL (in alphabetical order of subject)

1 A poet, with the exception of mysterious water-fluent tea-drinking Auden, must be a highly-conscious technical expert. [Cyril Connolly, 1903–74, *Enemies of Promise*, Ch. 16]

2 Auden of the last years, when he had begun to resemble in his own person an ample, flopping, ambulatory volume of the OED in carpet-slippers ... [Seamus Heaney, 1939– , in *London Review of Books*, 4 June 1987]

3 The higher-water mark, so to speak, of Socialist literature is W. H. Auden, a sort of gutless Kipling. [George Orwell, 1903–50, *The Road to Wigan Pier*, Ch. 11]

4 He [W H Auden] had an open mind about sex but a closed one about clocks. [Stephen Spender, 1909–95, *Journals, 1939–83*, 22 Jan. 1975]

5 That William Blake / Who beat upon the wall / Till Truth obeyed his call. [W B Yeats, 1865–1939, *An Acre of Grass*]

6 A man living with English in one room. [(Of Joseph Brodsky) Derek Walcott, 1930– , *Forest of Europe*]

7 [Rupert Brooke] Magnificently unprepared / For the long littleness of life. [Frances Cornford, 1886–1960, *Rupert Brooke*]

8 He [Rupert Brooke] energized the Garden-Suburb ethos with a certain original talent and the vigour of a prolonged adolescence. His verse exhibits ... something that is rather like Keats's vulgarity with a Public School accent. [F R Leavis, 1895–1978, *New Bearings in English Poetry*, Ch. 2]

9 Browning! Since Chaucer was alive and hale, / No man hath walked along our roads with step / So active, so inquiring eye, or tongue / So varied in discourse. [Walter Savage Landor, 1775–1864, *To Robert Browning*]

10 Meredith is a prose Browning, and so is Browning. [Oscar Wilde, 1854–1900, *The Critic as Artist*, Pt I, 'Intentions']

11 Byron! – he would be all forgotten today if he had lived to be a florid old gentleman with iron-grey whiskers, writing very long, very able letters to *The Times* about the Repeal of the Corn Laws. [Max Beerbohm, 1872–1956, *Zuleika Dobson*, Ch. 18]

12 Lord Byron is only great as a poet; as soon as he reflects he is a child. [Johann Wolfgang von Goethe, 1749–1832, *Conversations with Eckermann*, 18 Jan. 1825]

13 Mad, bad, and dangerous to know. [Lady Caroline Lamb, 1785–1828 (of Byron, at their first meeting, Mar. 1812), *Journal*]

14 From the poetry of Lord Byron they drew a system of ethics, compounded of misanthropy and voluptuousness, in which the two great commandments were, to hate your neighbour, and to love your neighbour's wife. [Lord Macaulay, 1800–1859, *Literary Essays*, 'Moore's Life of Byron']

15 Always looking at himself in mirrors to make sure that he was sufficiently outrageous. [(Of Byron) Enoch Powell, 1912–98, in *The Sunday Times* ('Books' section), 8 May 1988]

16 I thought of Chatterton, the marvellous boy, / The sleepless soul that perished in his pride. [William Wordsworth, 1770–1850, *Resolution and Independence*, 7]

17 'Tis sufficient to say [of Chaucer], according to the proverb, that here is God's plenty. [John Dryden, 1631–1700, Preface to *Fables*]

18 Sithe of our language he was the lodesterre. [(Chaucer) John Lydgate, 1370?–1451?, *The Falls of Princes*, Prologue, 252]

19 Dan Chaucer, well of English undefiled, / On Fame's eternal beadroll worthy to be filed. [Edmund Spenser, 1552?–99, *The Faerie Queene*, Bk iv, Canto 2, stanza 32]

20 Dan Chaucer, the first warbler, whose sweet breath / Preluded those melodious bursts that fill / The spacious times of great Elizabeth. [Alfred, Lord Tennyson, 1809–92, *A Dream of Fair Women*, 5]

21 His face when he repeats his verses hath its ancient glory, an Archangel a little damaged. [(Of Coleridge) Charles Lamb, 1775–1834, letter to Wordsworth, 26 Apr. 1816]

22 I would not call that man my friend who should be offended with 'the divine chit-chat of Cowper'. [Charles Lamb, 1775–1834, letter to Coleridge, 5 Dec. 1796]

23 Dante, who loved well because he hated, / Hated wickedness that hinders loving. [Robert Browning, 1812–89, *One Word More*, 5]

24 The majority of poems one outgrows and outlives, as one outgrows and outlives the majority of human passions. Dante's is one of those that one can only just hope to grow up to at the end of life. [T S Eliot, 1888–1965, *Selected Essays*, 'Dante']

25 Here lies a King that ruled, as he thought fit, / The universal monarchy of wit. [Thomas Carew, 1595?–1639, *Elegy on the Death of Dr Donne*]

26 With Donne whose muse on dromedary trots, / Wreathe iron pokers into true-love knots. [Samuel Taylor Coleridge, 1772–1834, *On Donne's Poetry*]

27 Tennyson and Browning are poets, and they think; but they do not feel their thought as immediately as the odour of a rose. A thought to Donne was an experience; it modified his sensibility. [T S Eliot, 1888–1965, *Selected Essays*, 'Metaphysical Poets']

28 Donne, I suppose, was such another / Who found no substitute for sense. / To seize and clutch and penetrate; / Expert beyond experience. [T S Eliot, 1888–1965, *Whispers of Immortality*]

29 Dr Donne's verses are like the peace of God; they pass all understanding. [King James I, 1566–1625, attr. by Archdeacon Plume]

30 The difference between genuine poetry and the poetry of Dryden, Pope, and all their school, is briefly this: their poetry is conceived in their wits, genuine poetry is conceived and composed in the soul. [Matthew Arnold, 1822–88, *Essays in Criticism*, Second Series, 'Gray']

31 Beyond the limits of a vulgar fate, / Beneath the good how far – but far above the great. [(Dryden) Thomas Gray, 1716–71, *The Progress of Poesy*, III, 3]

32 Ev'n copious Dryden wanted, or forgot, / The last and greatest art, the art to blot. [Alexander Pope, 1688–1744, Epistle I, 280]

33 I don't like the word [poet]. I'm a trapeze artist. [Bob Dylan, 1941– ; in J Green, *Book of Rock Quotes*]

34 If Mr Eliot had been pleased to write in demotic English, *The Waste Land* might not have been, as it is to all but anthropologists and literati, so much waste paper. [Charles Powell, in review in *Manchester Guardian*, 31 Oct. 1923]

35 Stirring suddenly from long hibernation, / I knew myself once more a poet / Guarded by timeless principalities / Against the worm of death. [Robert Graves, 1895–1985, *Mid-winter Waking*]

36 Gray, a born poet, fell upon an age of reason. [Matthew Arnold, 1822–88, *Essays in Criticism*, Second Series, 'Gray']

37 The *Churchyard* abounds with images which find a mirror in every mind, and with sentiments to which every bosom returns an echo. [Dr Samuel Johnson, 1709–84, *The Lives of the English Poets*, 'Gray']

38 I would rather have written those lines [Gray's *Elegy*] than take Quebec. [General James Wolfe, 1727–59, on the night before the storming of Quebec]

39 He [Hardy] wrote sometimes overpoweringly well, but always very carelessly; at times his style touches sublimity without ever having passed through the stage of being good. [T S Eliot, 1888–1965, *After Strange Gods*]

40 He's [Seamus Heaney] very popular among his mates. / I think I'm Auden. He thinks he's Yeats. [Gavin Ewart, 1916–95, *Complete Little Ones*, 'Seamus Heaney']

41 I never wrote with an audience in mind. If you're writing poems, you truly forget about an audience – it's the poet himself who *listens in*. [Seamus Heaney, 1939– , interview in *The Sunday Times*, 7 Oct. 1990]

42 He [Seamus Heaney] does address one of the major themes, childhood, in a fabulous way. He puts the shine back on things that I did know once. [Andrew Motion, 1952– , in *Guardian*, 25 June 1987]

43 We can say nothing but what hath been said ... Our poets steal from Homer ... he that comes last is commonly best. [Robert Burton, 1577–1640, *Anatomy of Melancholy*, 'Democritus to the Reader']

44 But if Homer, who is good, nods for a moment, I think it a shame. [Horace, 65–8 BC, *Ars Poetica*, 359]

45 When 'Omer smote 'is bloomin' lyre, / He'd 'eard men sing by land an' sea; / An' what he thought 'e might require, / 'E went an' took – the same as me! [Rudyard Kipling, 1865–1936, *When 'Omer Smote*]

46 Though I've never read a line of Homer I believe the Greek of today is essentially unchanged. If anything he is more Greek than he ever was. [Henry Miller, 1891–1980, *The Colossus of Maroussi*, Ch. 1]

47 It's a bit like talking to the *Encyclopaedia Britannica* – but an unauthorized version, an alternative route to knowledge, well off the main trunk roads. [(Of Ted Hughes) Craig Raine, 1944– , in *The Sunday Times*, 23 Dec. 1984]

48 O then if in my lagging lines you miss / The roll, the rise, the carol, the creation. [Gerard Manley Hopkins, 1844–89, *To R. B.*]

49 Then farewell, Horace; whom I hated so, / Not for thy faults, but mine. [Lord Byron, 1788–1824, *Childe Harold's Pilgrimage*, IV, 77]

50 But if you place me among the lyric bards, I shall touch the stars with my exalted head. [Horace, 65–8 BC, *Odes*, I, i, 35]

51 Hugo – alas! [(When asked to name the greatest French poet) André Gide, 1869–1951, letter to Paul Valéry, in Claude Martin, *La Maturité d'A G*, p. 502]

52 Next these, learn'd Jonson, in this list I bring, / Who had drunk deep of the Pierian spring. [Michael Drayton, 1563–1631, *To Henry Reynolds, of Poets and Poesy*, 129]

53 Now I am almost forty and have a little verse-factory. [Erich Kästner, 1899–1974, *Bei Durchsicht meiner Bücher*, 'Kurzgefasster Lebenslauf']

54 'Tis strange the mind, that very fiery particle, / Should let itself be snuffed out by an article. [(Of John Keats) Lord Byron, 1788–1824, *Don Juan*, XI, 60]

55 I think I shall be among the English poets after my death. [John Keats, 1795–1821, letter to G and G Keats, 14 Oct. 1818]

56 'If I should die', said I to myself, 'I have left no immortal work behind me – nothing to make my friends proud of my memory – but I have loved the principle of beauty in all things, and if I had had time I would have made myself remembered.' [John Keats, 1795–1821, letter to Fanny Brawne, Feb. 1820]

57 Time's printless torrent grew / A scroll of crystal, blazoning the name / Of Adonais! [P B Shelley, 1792–1822, *Fragment on Keats*]

58 Deprivation is for me what daffodils were for Wordsworth. [Philip Larkin, 1922–85, *Required Writing*, 'An Interview with the *Observer*']

59 If poems can teach one anything, Larkin's teach that there is no desolation so bleak that it cannot be made habitable by style. If we live inside a bad joke, it is up to us to learn, at best and worst, to tell it well. [Jonathan Raban, 1942– , *Coasting*, Ch. 6]

60 'How pleasant to know Mr Lear!' / Who has written such volumes of stuff! / Some think him ill-tempered and queer, / But a few think him pleasant enough. [Edward Lear, 1812–88, *Nonsense Songs*, Preface]

61 But in the room of the banished poet / Fear and the Muse stand watch by turn, and the night falls, / without the hope of dawn. [Anna Akhmatova, 1889–1966, *Voronezh* (written after her visit to the banished Osip Mandelstam there)]

62 Now I'm dead in the grave with my lips moving / And every schoolboy repeating my words by heart. [Osip Mandelstam, 1891–1938, *Poems*, No. 306]

63 [Christopher Marlowe] Had in him those brave translunary things / That the first poets had. [Michael Drayton, 1563–1631, *To Henry Reynolds, of Poets and Poesy*, 106]

64 The reason Milton wrote in fetters when he wrote of Angels and God, and at liberty when of Devils and Hell, is because he was a true poet, and of the Devil's party without knowing it. [William Blake, 1757–1827, *The Marriage of Heaven and Hell*, note]

65 Milton's the prince of poets – so we say; / A little heavy, but no less divine. [Lord Byron, 1788–1824, *Don Juan*, III, 91]

66 Three poets, in three distant ages born, / Greece, Italy, and England, did adorn. / The first in loftiness of thought surpassed; / The next in majesty, in both the last. / The force of nature could no further go; / To make a third she joined the former two. [John Dryden, 1631–1700, *Lines Printed under the Engraved Portrait of Milton*]

67 After the erection of the Chinese Wall of Milton, blank verse has suffered not only arrest but retrogression. [T S Eliot, 1888–1965, *Selected Essays*, 'Christopher Marlowe']

68 He passed the flaming bounds of space and time: / The living throne, the sapphire-blaze, / Where angels tremble while they gaze, / He saw; but blasted with excess of light, / Closed his eyes in endless night. [(Of Milton) Thomas Gray, 1716–71, *The Progress of Poesy*, III, 2]

69 Milton ... was a genius that could cut a Colossus from a rock, but could not carve heads upon cherry-stones. [Dr Samuel Johnson, 1709–84, in James Boswell, *Life of J*, 13 June 1784]

70 What in me is dark / Illumine, what is low raise and support; / That to the height of this great argument / I may assert eternal Providence, / And justify the ways of God to men. [John Milton, 1608–74, *Paradise Lost*, Bk i, 22]

71 In quibbles angel and archangel join, / And God the Father turns a school divine. [(On *Paradise Lost*) Alexander Pope, 1688–1744, Epistle I, 101]

72 O mighty-mouthed inventor of harmonies, / O skilled to sing of Time or Eternity, / God-gifted organ voice of England, / Milton, a name to resound for ages. [Alfred, Lord Tennyson, 1809–92, *Experiments in Quantity*, 'Milton, Alcaics']

73 When a damp / Fell round the path of Milton, in his hand / The thing became a trumpet; whence he blew / Soul-animating strains – alas, too few! [(Of the sonnet) William Wordsworth, 1770–1850, *Miscellaneous Sonnets*, II, 1]

74 Milton! thou shouldst be living at this hour: / England hath need of thee: she is a fen / Of stagnant waters. [William Wordsworth, 1770–1850, *National Independence and Liberty*, 14 'London 1802']

75 Dreamer of dreams, born out of my due time, / Why should I strive to set the crooked straight? / Let it suffice me that my murmuring rhyme / Beats with light wing against the ivory gate, / Telling a tale not too importunate. [William Morris, 1834–96, *The Earthly Paradise*, 'An Apology']

76 My subject is war, and the pity of War. The Poetry is in the pity. [Wilfred Owen, 1893–1918, *Poems*, Preface]

77 He [Wilfred Owen] is all blood, dirt and sucked sugar stick. [W B Yeats, 1865–1939, letter, 21 Dec. 1936, *Letters on Poetry to Dorothy Wellesley*]

78 There comes Poe, with his raven, like Barnaby Rudge, / Three fifths of him genius and two fifths sheer fudge. [James Russell Lowell, 1819–91, *A Fable for Critics*]

79 Made poetry a mere mechanic art; / And every warbler has his tune by heart. [(Of Pope) William Cowper, 1731–1800, *Table Talk*, 656]

80 New things are made familiar, and familiar things are made new. [Dr Samuel Johnson, 1709–84, *The Lives of the English Poets*, 'Pope']

81 Too true, too sincere. The Muse prefers the liars, the gay and warty lads. [(Of James Reeves's *The Natural Need*) W B Yeats, 1865–1939, in Robert Graves and Alan Hodge, *The Long Week-end*, Ch. 25]

82 Verse was a special illness of the ear; / Integrity was not enough. [W H Auden, 1907–73, *Rimbaud*]

83 The rest to some faint meaning make pretence, / But Shadwell never deviates into sense. / Some beams of wit on other souls may fall, / Strike through and make a lucid interval. / But Shadwell's genuine night admits no ray, / His rising fogs prevail upon the day. [John Dryden, 1631–1700, *MacFlecknoe*, 19]

84 Your monument shall be my gentle verse, / Which eyes not yet created shall o'er-read; / And tongues to be, your being shall rehearse, / When all the breathers of this world are dead. [William Shakespeare, 1564–1616, *Sonnets*, 81]

85 [Shelley] A beautiful and ineffectual angel beating in the void his luminous wings in vain. [Matthew Arnold, *Essays in Criticism*, Second Series, 'Byron']

86 Ah, did you once see Shelley plain, / And did he stop and speak to you / And did he speak to you again? / How strange it seems and new! [Robert Browning, 1812–89, *Memorabilia*]

87 Shelley and Keats were the last English poets who were at all up to date in their chemical knowledge. [J B S Haldane, 1892–1964, *Daedalus or Science and the Future*]

88 You might curb your magnanimity, and be more of an artist, and load every rift of your subject with ore. [John Keats, 1795–1821, letter to P B Shelley, Aug. 1820]

89 Why does my Muse only speak when she is unhappy?/ she does not, I only listen when I am unhappy. [Stevie Smith, 1902–71, *My Muse*]

90 He [Tennyson] had the finest ear, perhaps, of any English poet; he was also undoubtedly the stupidest. [W H Auden, 1907–73, introduction to his selection of Tennyson's poetry. T S Eliot countered that if Auden had been a better scholar, he would have known many stupider]

91 I do but sing because I must, / And pipe but as the linnets sing. [Alfred, Lord Tennyson, 1809–92, *In Memoriam*, 21]

92 Virgil was no good because Tennyson ran him, and as for Tennyson – well, Tennyson goes without saying. [Samuel Butler, 1835–1902, *Notebooks*, Ch. 12, 'Blake, Dante, etc.']

93 Wielder of the stateliest measure ever moulded by the lips of man. [Alfred, Lord Tennyson, 1809–92, *To Virgil*]

94 Out of us all / That make rhymes, / Will you choose / Sometimes – / As the winds use / A crack in a wall / Or a drain, / Their joy or their pain / To whistle through – / Choose me, / You English words? [Edward Thomas, 1878–1917, *Words*]

95 Our Meistersinger, thou set breath in steel; / And it was thou who on the boldest heel / Stood up and flung the span on even wing / Of that great Bridge, our Myth, whereof I sing. [Hart Crane, 1899–1932, referring to Walt Whitman and Brooklyn Bridge]

96 Walt Whitman who laid end to end words never seen in each other's company before outside of a dictionary ... [David Lodge, 1935– , *Changing Places*, Ch. 5]

97 *Ni un solo momento, viejo hermoso Walt Whitman, / he dejado de ver tu barba llena de mariposas.* – Not for a moment, beautiful aged Walt Whitman, have I failed to see your beard full of butterflies. [Federico García Lorca, 1899–1936, *Oda a Walt Whitman*]

98 His expression may often be called bald ... but it is bald as the bare mountain tops are bald, with a baldness full of grandeur. [Matthew Arnold, 1822–88, *Essays in Criticism*, Second Series, 'Wordsworth']

99 Just for a handful of silver he left us, / Just for a riband to stick in his coat. [(Of Wordsworth)] Robert Browning, 1812–89, *The Lost Leader*]

100 The simple Wordsworth . . . / Who, both by precept and example, shows / That prose is verse, and verse is merely prose. [Lord Byron, 1788–1824, *English Bards and Scotch Reviewers*, 237]

101 It seems that I must bid the Muse go pack, / Choose Plato and Plotinus for a friend / Until imagination, ear and eye, / Can be content with argument and deal / In abstract things; or be derided by / A sort of battered kettle at the heel. [W B Yeats, 1865–1939, *The Tower*, 1]

See also previous categories, BOOKS, LITERATURE, PROSE, WRITERS, WRITING

POLICE

1 The civil guard are a secret hard-hatted race like ghosts with rifles who are really longing to be human. [Anthony Carson, *On to Timbuctoo*, Ch. 2]

2 There *are* no more policemen. Only police dogs. We've eliminated the middle man. [Jules Feiffer, 1929– , in *Observer*, 7 July 1963]

3 When constabulary duty's to be done, / The policeman's lot is not a happy one. [W S Gilbert, 1836–1911, *The Pirates of Penzance*, I]

4 *Con el alma de charol / vienen por la carrera.* – With their patent-leather souls, they [the Civil Guards] come along the road. [Federico García Lorca, 1899–1936, *Romance de la Guardia Civil española*]

5 A thing of duty is a boy for ever. [Flann O'Brien, 1911–66 (on the perennial youthfulness of policemen), in *Listener*, 24 Feb. 1977]

6 The Polis as Polis, in this city, is Null an' Void! [Sean O'Casey, 1880–1964, *Juno and the Paycock*, III]

7 Reading isn't an occupation we encourage among police officers. We try to keep the paper work down to a minimum. [Joe Orton, 1933–67, *Loot*, II]

8 Big Brother is watching you. [George Orwell, 1903–50, *1984*, Pt I, Ch. 1]

9 In the pathology of nervous diseases, a doctor who doesn't talk too much nonsense is a half-cured patient, just as a critic is a poet who has stopped writing verse and a policeman a burglar who has retired from practice. [Marcel Proust, 1871–1922, *Remembrance of Things Past: The Guermantes Way*, 'Decline and Death of My Grandmother']

10 I've never had problems with drugs, only policemen. [Keith Richard, 1943– ; in *Wit and Wisdom of Rock and Roll*, ed. Maxim Jakubowski]

11 The South African Police would leave no stone unturned to see that nothing disturbed the even terror of their lives. [Tom Sharpe, 1928– , *Indecent Exposure*, Ch. 1]

See also CRIME, JUSTICE & INJUSTICE

POLITICIANS IN GENERAL

1 The trouble with this country is that there are too many politicians who believe, with a conviction based on experience, that you can fool all of the people all of the time. [Franklin D Adams, 1881–1960 (disagreeing with Abraham Lincoln's dictum, DECEIT, 8), in *Nods and Becks*]

2 A politician is an animal who can sit on a fence and yet keep both ears to the ground. [anon.; in H L Mencken, *New Dictionary of Quotations*]

3 A political leader must keep looking over his shoulder all the time to see if the boys are still there. If they aren't still there, he's no longer a political leader. [Bernard M Baruch, 1870–1965, quoted in obituary in *The New York Times*, 21 June 1965]

4 I support the left, though I'm leaning to the right. [Pete Brown, 1940– , song: *The Politician*]

5 Your representative owes you, not his industry only, but his judgement; and he betrays instead of serving you if he sacrifices it to your opinion. [Edmund Burke, 1729–97, speech to the electors of Bristol, 3 Nov. 1774]

6 The path of politicians is bestrewn by banana skins, sometimes on ice. [Ronald Butt, 1920– , in *The Times*, 16 Feb. 1989]

7 An honest politician is one who, when he is bought, will stay bought. [Simon Cameron, 1799–1889, in conversation, *c.*1860]

8 It was as dark as the inside of a Cabinet Minister. [Joyce Cary, 1888–1957, *The Horse's Mouth*, 33]

9 Every politician is emphatically a promising politician. [G K Chesterton, 1874–1936, *The Scandal of Father Brown*, 'The Red Moon of Meru']

10 The English statesman is bribed not to be

bribed. He is born with a silver spoon in his mouth, so that he may never afterwards be found with the silver spoons in his pocket. [G K Chesterton, 1874–1936, *What's Wrong with the World*, 'The Unfinished Temple']

11 Statesman all over, in plots famous grown, / He mouths a sentence, as curs mouth a bone. [Charles Churchill, 1731–64, *The Rosciad*, 321]

12 a politician is an arse upon which everyone has sat except a man [e e cummings, 1894–1962, *1x1*, 10]

13 Tricky job being Home Secretary – you've got to keep all your feathers in the air. [William Deedes, 1913– (on receiving life peerage), in *Observer*, 15 June 1986]

14 If you will refrain from telling lies about the Republican Party, I'll promise not to tell the truth about the Democrats. [Senator Chauncey Depuy, 1834–1928, attr. in J F Parker, *If Elected, I Promise...*]

15 For politicians neither love nor hate. [John Dryden, 1631–1700, *Absalom and Achitophel*, Pt I, 223]

16 A politician is a fellow who will lay down your life for his country. [Texas Guinan, 1884–1933; in *Hammer and Tongues*, ed. Michèle Brown and Ann O'Connor, 'Politics']

17 For a politician rises on the backs of his friends (that's probably all they're good for), but it's through his enemies he'll have to govern afterwards. [Richard Hughes, 1900–1976, *The Fox in the Attic*, Bk II, 20]

18 A man with his ears so close to the ground that he cannot hear the words of an upright man. [John Maynard Keynes, 1883–1946 (definition of an American politician), in BBC TV programme *Horizon*, 6 Jan. 1981]

19 Politicians are the same all over. They promise to build a bridge even where there is no river. [Nikita Khrushchev, 1894–1971, impromptu remark on visit to the USA at Glen Cove, NY, Oct. 1960, repeated in Yugoslavia, 21 Aug. 1963]

20 When you're abroad you're a statesman: when you're at home you're just a politician. [Harold Macmillan, 1894–1986 (speech, 1958), in *Observer*, 28 July 1963]

21 did you ever / notice that when / a politician / does get an idea / he usually / gets it all wrong [Don Marquis, 1878–1937, *archys life of mehitabel*, XL, 'archygrams']

22 In modern Britain forward-looking politicians spend much of their time looking back. [Austin Mitchell, 1934– , in *Guardian*, 15 Apr. 1983]

23 He liked to divide politicians into those who want to *be someone* and those who want to *do something*. [(Of Jean Monnet, 1888–1979) Roy Jenkins, 1920– , in *Observer*, 25 Nov. 1990, in reference to Margaret Thatcher, who 'outstandingly' belonged to the second category]

24 Television has devalued politicians of all parties. It has thrown them back on their own merits. [Edward Pearce, 1939– , from *Hummingbirds and Hyenas*, in *Guardian*, 3 Oct. 1985]

25 A statesman is a politician who places himself at the service of the nation. A politician is a statesman who places the nation at his service. [Georges Pompidou, 1911–74; *Observer*, 'Sayings of the Year', 30 Dec. 1973]

26 Statesman, yet friend to truth! of soul sincere / In action faithful, and in honour clear, / Who broke no promise, served no private end, / Who gained no title, and who lost no friend. [Alexander Pope, 1688–1744, *Moral Essays*, Epistle V, 67]

27 A number of anxious dwarfs trying to grill a whale. [(Of politicians) J B Priestley, 1894–1984, *Outcries and Asides*]

28 Bankers sometimes look on politicians as people who, when they see light at the end of the tunnel, order more tunnel. [John Quinton, 1929– , in *Independent*, 15 Apr. 1989]; see also PESSIMISM, 12

29 The most successful politician is he who says what everybody is thinking most often and in the loudest voice. [Theodore Roosevelt, 1858–1919; in *Treasury of Humorous Quotations*, ed. Evan Esar and Nicolas Bentley]

30 Get thee glass eyes; / And, like a scurvy politician, seem / To see the things thou dost not. [William Shakespeare, 1564–1616, *King Lear*, IV. vi. (175)]

31 A politician is a statesman who approaches every question with an open mouth. [Adlai Stevenson, 1835–1914, in Leon A Harris, *The Fine Art of Political Wit*. Also ascr. to Arthur Goldberg describing diplomats]

32 He gave it for his opinion, that whoever could make two ears of corn or two blades of grass to grow upon a spot of ground where only one grew before, would deserve better of mankind, and do more essential service to his country than the whole race of politicians put together. [Jonathan Swift, 1677–1745, *Gulliver's Travels*, 'Voyage to Brobdingnag', Ch. 7]

33 A politician is a man who understands government, and it takes a politician to run a government. A statesman is a politician who's been dead ten or fifteen years. [Harry Truman, 1884–1972, impromptu speech to Reciprocity Club, Washington, 11 Apr. 1958]

34 I'm not a politician and my other habits are good. [Artemus Ward, 1834–67, *A W His Book*, 'Fourth of July Oration']

35 Hence the practised performances of latter-day politicians in the game of musical daggers; never be left holding the dagger when the music stops. [Harold Wilson, 1916–95, *The Governance of Britain*, Ch. 2]

See also next and previous categories

POLITICIANS: INDIVIDUAL (in alphabetical order of subject)

1 Not only did he [Dean Acheson] not suffer fools gladly, he did not suffer them at all. [Lester Pearson, 1897–1972, in *Time* magazine, 25 Oct. 1971]

2 He is a sheep in sheep's clothing. [Winston Churchill, 1874–1965. Usually assumed to be of Clement Attlee, though Churchill told Denis Brogan he had been referring to Ramsay MacDonald and the phrase goes back to Edmund Gosse]

3 It is a fine thing to be honest but it is also very important to be right. [Winston Churchill, 1874–1965, of Stanley Baldwin, attr.]

4 I have always said about Tony [Benn] that he immatures with age. [Harold Wilson, 1916–95, from BBC TV programme *Pebble Mill*, in Jad Williams, *Tony Benn*, Ch. 37]

5 He [Aneurin Bevan] was like a fire in a room on a cold winter's day. [Constance Cummings, 1910– , in Michael Foot, *Aneurin Bevan*, Vol. 1, Ch. 6]

6 [Edmund Burke] Too nice for a statesman, too proud for a wit. [Oliver Goldsmith, 1728–74, *Retaliation*, 38]

7 The unpleasant sound emitting from [Vice-President] Bush as he traipses from one conservative gathering to another is a thin, tinny 'arf' – the sound of a lap-dog. [George F Will, 1941– , in *Washington Post*, 30 Jan. 1986]

8 [Rab Butler] was a sweet man, and very loyal to me. [Pause] Yet I can always see him dressed in a soutane, conspiring in the corridors of the Vatican. [Harold Macmillan, 1894–1986, quoted by Alistair Horne in *The Sunday Times*, 4 Jan. 1987, on Macmillan's death]

9 I met Murder on the way – / He had a mask like Castlereagh. [P B Shelley, 1792–1822, *The Mask of Anarchy*, 5]

10 He [Neville Chamberlain] saw foreign policy through the wrong end of a municipal drainpipe. [David Lloyd George, 1863–1945, in Leon A Harris, *The Fine Art of Political Wit*, Ch. 6]

11 It's easy to be brilliant if you are not bothered about being right. [Hector McNeil, 1907–55 (of Richard Crossman), in Denis Healey, *The Time of My Life*, Ch. 5]

12 In parliamentary life, he [Curzon] was to be one who stayed to get his feet wet before deciding that a ship was sinking. [Leonard Mosley, 1913– , *The Glorious Fault*]

13 The only case I know of a bull who carries his own china shop around with him. [Winston Churchill, 1874–1965 (of John Foster Dulles), in *The Times Higher Education Supplement*, 31 Dec. 1982]

14 He [Anthony Eden] has antennae in all directions, but no brain. He doesn't read papers, he only sniffs them. [Gladwyn Jebb, 1900–1996, in *The Second World War Diary of Hugh Dalton 1940–45*, ed. Ben Pimlott, 2 Sept. 1943]

15 He [Anthony Eden] liked private life punctuated by bursts of public adulation. [Roy Jenkins, 1920– , *A Gallery of Twentieth Century Portraits*]

16 A good man fallen among politicians. [(Of Michael Foot) *Daily Mirror*, editorial, 28 Feb. 1983]

17 I know that the right kind of political leader for the Labour Party is a desiccated calculating machine. [Aneurin Bevan, 1897–1960 (always assumed, though Bevan denied it, to refer to

Hugh Gaitskell), at Labour Party Conference, 29 Sept. 1954]

18 [General de Gaulle is] like a female llama surprised in her bath. [Winston Churchill, 1874–1965, attr.; in Nigel Rees, *Quotable Trivia*]

19 A sophistical rhetorician inebriated with the exuberance of his own verbosity. [(Of Gladstone) Benjamin Disraeli, 1804–81, speech at banquet, 27 July 1878]

20 He [John Hampden] had a head to contrive, a tongue to persuade, and a hand to execute any mischief. [(Quoting a description of Cinna) Earl of Clarendon, 1609–74, *Selections from the History of the Rebellion*, 21]

21 I have a theory about Charles Haughey. Give him enough rope and he'll hang you. [Leo Enright, 1955– , on BBC Radio 4, quoted in the *Guardian*, 31 Jan. 1992]

22 Michael Heseltine cannot see a parapet without ducking below it. [(Before H's resignation from the Cabinet over the Westland affair) Julian Critchley, 1930– , in *Listener*, 2 Jan. 1986]

23 He gave fifty thousand dollars secretly to Henry Kissinger. Imagine – for fifty thousand dollars then you might have bought a small Klee or Bonnard or a large Jackson Pollock, and all he got for his money was a medium-sized Kissinger. [Joseph Heller, 1923–99, *Good as Gold*, 8]

24 Mere ability is not sufficient to explain great destinies. The last yards are run alone. [(Of Henry Kissinger) François Mitterrand, 1916–96, *The Wheat and the Chaff*, Pt 2, 18 Dec. 1975]

25 The right honourable gentleman [Sir Robert Peel] caught the Whigs bathing and walked away with their clothes. [Benjamin Disraeli, 1804–81, speech in House of Commons, 28 Feb. 1845]

26 [When told Ronald Reagan was running for the governorship of California in 1966] No, No! Jimmy Stewart for governor, Reagan for best friend. [Jack L Warner, 1892–1981; in *Morrow Book of Quotations in American History*, ed. Joseph R Conlin]

27 I admire him [Cecil Rhodes], I frankly confess it; and when his time comes I shall buy a piece of the rope for a keepsake. [Mark Twain, 1835–1910, *Following the Equator*, Ch. 7]

28 When they circumcised Herbert Samuel they threw away the wrong bit. [David Lloyd George, 1863–1945, quoted by John Grigg in *Listener*, 7 Sept. 1978]

29 She is so clearly the best man among them. [(On Margaret Thatcher's becoming Conservative Party leader) Barbara Castle, 1911– , *Diaries*, 11 Feb. 1975]

30 Britain's two female figureheads are a woman who can't tell a joke and a woman who can't understand one. [Germaine Greer, 1939– , in *The Sunday Times Magazine*, 19 Jan. 1986]

31 The Iron Maiden. [(Margaret Thatcher) Marjorie Proops, 1911–96), headline in *Daily Mirror*, 5 Feb. 1975]

See also previous and next categories, GOVERNMENT, OPPOSITION, PARLIAMENT, PRIME MINISTERS

POLITICS

1 Man is by nature a political animal. [Aristotle, 384–322 BC, *Politics*, I, 2]

2 Politics is no exact science. [Otto von Bismarck, 1815–98, speech in Prussian Chamber, 18 Dec. 1863]

3 Politics is the art of the possible. [Otto von Bismarck, 1815–98, in conversation with Meyer von Waldeck, 11 Aug. 1867 (used by R A Butler, 1902–82, as epigraph to his memoirs, *The Art of the Possible*]; see 10

4 I always wanted to get into politics, but I was never light enough to make the team. [Art Buchwald, 1925– , 'Fan Letter to Nixon']

5 Magnanimity in politics is not seldom the truest wisdom; and a great empire and little minds go ill together. [Edmund Burke, 1729–97, speech on conciliation with America, 22 Mar. 1775]

6 Either back us or sack us. [James Callaghan, 1912– , speech at Labour Party Conference, Brighton, 5 Oct. 1977]

7 We sit down about two o'clock in the morning around a table in a smoke-filled room. [Harry M Daugherty, 1860–1941 (of presidential campaign), ascr. in *The New York Times*, 21 Feb. 1920, but Daugherty denied he had said 'smoke-filled']

8 Finality is not the language of politics. [Benjamin Disraeli, 1804–81, speech in House of Commons, 28 Feb. 1859]

9 It was Melissa who explained politics to Suzy early on: the Republicans like trees and animals and the countryside, the Democrats like cities and factories and pollution. [Lucy Ellmann, 1956– , *Sweet Desserts*, 'The Heart Operation']

10 Politics is not the art of the possible. It consists in choosing between the disastrous and the unpalatable. [J K Galbraith, 1908– , letter to President Kennedy, 2 Mar. 1962]; see 3

11 I have come to the conclusion that politics are too serious a matter to be left to the politicians. [General de Gaulle, 1890–1970, in Clement Attlee, *A Prime Minister Remembers*, Ch. 4]

12 And I always voted at my party's call, / And I never thought of thinking for myself at all. [W S Gilbert, 1836–1911, *HMS Pinafore*, I]

13 They politics like ours profess, / The greater prey upon the less. [Matthew Green, 1696–1737, *The Grotto*, 69]

14 Politics does not reflect majorities, it constructs them. [Stuart Hall, 1932– , in *Marxism Today*, July 1987]

15 I was, however, approached by Chinese journalists, one of whom observed how interesting it was that I combined politics – which is practical, and music – which is fantasy. I replied they had it the wrong way round! [Edward Heath, 1916– , in *The Sunday Times*, 8 Jan. 1989]

16 Here we are the way politics ought to be in America, the politics of happiness, the politics of purpose and the politics of joy. [Hubert H Humphrey, 1911–78, speech in Washington, 27 Apr. 1968]

17 The politics of the left and centre of this country are frozen in an out-of-date mould which is bad for the economic and political health of Britain and increasingly inhibiting for those who live within the mould. Can it be broken? [Roy Jenkins, 1920– , speech to Parliamentary Press Gallery, 9 June 1980. Also used by others at foundation of the Social Democratic Party, prompting the phrase: 'Breaking the mould of British politics']

18 If you're in politics and you can't tell when you walk into a room who's for you and who's against you, then you're in the wrong line of work. [President Lyndon B Johnson, 1908–73, in B Mooney, *The Lyndon Johnson Story*]

19 Most schemes of political improvement are very laughable things. [Dr Samuel Johnson, 1709–84, in James Boswell, *Life of J*, 26 Oct. 1769]

20 Politics are not my concern ... They impressed me as a dog's life without a dog's decencies. [Rudyard Kipling, 1865–1936, *A Diversity of Creatures*, 'The Village That Voted the Earth was Flat']

21 Politics: Who Gets What, When, How. [Harold Lasswell, 1902–78, title of book]

22 The first rule of politics is Never Believe Anything Until It's Been Officially Denied. [Jonathan Lynn, 1943– , and Antony Jay, 1930– , *Yes Prime Minister*, Vol. 1, 'Party Games']

23 After a long experience of politics I have never found that there is any inhibition caused by ignorance as regards criticism. [Harold Macmillan, 1894–1986, speech in House of Commons, 11 July 1963]

24 Politics is war without bloodshed while war is politics with bloodshed. [Mao Zedong, 1893–1976, *On Protracted War*, May 1938]

25 A man should always be drunk, Minnie, when he talks politics – it's the only way in which to make them important. [Sean O'Casey, 1880–1964, *The Shadow of a Gunman*, I]

26 We are fed up with fudging and mudging, with mush and slush. [David Owen, 1938– , speech at Labour Party Conference, Blackpool, 2 Oct. 1980]

27 I have my own Parkinson's Law: in politics people give you what they think you deserve and deny you what they think you want. [Cecil Parkinson, 1931– ; *Observer*, 'Sayings of the Week', 25 Nov. 1990]

28 It is now known ... that men enter local politics solely as a result of being unhappily married. [C Northcote Parkinson, 1909–93, *Parkinson's Law*, Ch. 10]

29 England elects a Labour Government. When a man goes in for politics over here, he has no time to labour, and any man that labours has no time to fool with politics. Over there politics is an obligation; over here it's a business. [Will Rogers, 1879–1935, *Autobiography*, Ch. 14]

30 The more you read and observe about this Politics thing you got to admit that each party is worse than the other. [Will Rogers, 1879–1935,

The Illiterate Digest, 'Breaking into the Writing Game']

31 And hear poor rogues / Talk of court news; and we'll talk with them too, / Who loses and who wins; who's in, who's out; / And take upon 's the mystery of things. / As if we were God's spies. [William Shakespeare, 1564–1616, *King Lear*, V. iii. 13]

32 He knows nothing; and he thinks he knows everything. That points clearly to a political career. [George Bernard Shaw, 1856–50, *Major Barbara*, III]

33 To listen to some people in politics, you'd think 'nice' was a four-letter word. [David Steel, 1938– (Party Political Broadcast on ITV for the Social Democrats), in *Listener*, 5 Feb. 1987]

34 *Politics* in the middle of things that concern the *imagination* are like a pistol shot in the middle of a concert. [Stendhal, 1783–1842, *Le Rouge et le noir*, Ch. 22]

35 Politics is perhaps the only profession for which no preparation is thought necessary. [Robert Louis Stevenson, 1850–94, *Familiar Studies of Men and Books*, 'Yoshida-Torajiro']

36 Party is the madness of many, for the gain of a few. [Jonathan Swift, 1677–1745, *Thoughts on Various Subjects*]

37 'You have ruined all the graffiti. You can't find anything in a piss-house now but political remarks . . . And just when the spread of popular education was bringing the graffiti lower on the walls.' 'Lower on the walls?' 'Sure. Don't you see the little children were beginning to add their quota, when all this damn politics comes along.' [Thwackhurst, quoted in O St John Gogarty, *As I Was Going Down Sackville Street*, Ch. 4]

38 Politics is the art of preventing people from minding their own business. [Paul Valéry, 1871–1945, *Rhumbs*]

39 My pollertics, like my religion, being of an exceedin accommodatin character. [Artemus Ward, 1834–67, *A W His Book*, 'The Crisis']

40 A week is a long time in politics. [Harold Wilson, 1916–95 (probably said in 1964 at parliamentary lobby after sterling crisis, but variant recorded as early as 1960); in N Rees, *Quote . . . Unquote*]

See also previous categories, GOVERNMENT, OPPOSITION, PARLIAMENT, PRIME MINISTERS

POPULARITY

1 Popularity is a crime from the moment it is sought; it is only a virtue where men have it whether they will or no. [Marquis of Halifax, 1663–95, *Moral Thoughts and Reflections*]

2 Popularity? It's glory's small change. [Victor Hugo, 1802–85, *Ruy Blas*, iii, 4]

3 How I like to be liked, and what I do to be liked! [Charles Lamb, 1775–1834, letter to Dorothy Wordsworth, 8 Jan. 1821]

4 We're more popular than Jesus Christ now. I don't know which will go first. Rock and roll or Christianity. [John Lennon, 1940–80, *The Beatles' Illustrated Lyrics*]

5 He's liked, but he's not well liked. [Arthur Miller, 1915– , *Death of a Salesman*, I]

6 It's better to be wanted for murder than not to be wanted at all. [Marty Winch, *Psychology in the Wry*]

See also FAME, SUCCESS

PORNOGRAPHY

1 I would rather put a phial of prussic acid in the hands of a healthy boy or girl than the book in question. [James Douglas, review of Radclyffe Hall's *The Well of Loneliness* in the *Sunday Express*, 1928]

2 Pornography is the attempt to insult sex, to do dirt on it. [D H Lawrence, 1885–1930, *Phoenix*, 'Pornography and Obscenity']

3 Don't be daft. You don't get any pornography on there, not on the telly. Get filth, that's all. The only place you get pornography is in yer Sunday papers. [Johnny Speight, 1920–98, 'Royal Variety Performance 1972']

4 Pornography was the great vice of the Seventies; plutography – the graphic depiction of the acts of the rich – is the great vice of the Eighties. [Tom Wolfe, 1931– , interview in *The Sunday Times Magazine*, 10 Jan. 1988]

PORTRAITS

1 There he adjusted his hat with care, and regarded himself very seriously, very sternly, from various angles, like a man invited to paint his own portrait for the Uffizi. [Max

Beerbohm, 1872–1956, *Zuleika Dobson*, Ch. 14]

2 Remark all these roughnesses, pimples, warts, and everything as you see me, otherwise I will never pay a farthing for it. [Oliver Cromwell, 1599–1658, instructions to Lely, on the painting of his portrait]

3 I do not paint a portrait to look like the subject, rather does the person grow to look like his portrait. [Salvador Dali, 1904–89, in *Kiss Me Hardy*, ed. Roger Kilroy, 'The Connoisseur']

4 There are two styles of portrait painting; the serious and the smirk. [Charles Dickens, 1812–70, *Nicholas Nickleby*, Ch. 10]

5 A study of family portraits is enough to convert a man to the doctrine of reincarnation. [Arthur Conan Doyle, 1859–1930, *The Hound of the Baskervilles*, Ch. 13]

6 The identifying ourselves with the visual image of ourselves has become an instinct; the habit is already old. The picture of me, the me that is *seen*, is me. [D H Lawrence, 1885–1930, *Phoenix*, 'Art and Morality']

7 I can piss the old boy in the snow. [Max Liebermann, 1847–1935 (to a portrait-painter who complained that he could not draw von Hindenburg's features), in Igor Stravinsky and Robert Craft, *Conversations with Stravinsky*]

8 One never, of course, knows what people in portraits are thinking about. [Penelope Lively, 1933– , *Next to Nature, Art*, Ch. 10]

9 The test of a good portrait is that if you take it down, you have the feeling that somebody has left the room. [Tom Phillips, 1937– , interview in *Observer*, 1 Oct. 1989]

10 A portrait is a picture in which there is just a tiny little something not quite right about the mouth. [John Singer Sargent, 1856–1925, in *Anecdotes of Modern Art*, ed. Donald Hall and Pat Corrington-Wykes. Also ascr. to Eugene Speicher, 1883–1962]

11 Every time I paint a portrait I lose a friend. [John Singer Sargent, 1856–1925; in *Treasury of Humorous Quotations*, ed. Evan Esar and Nicolas Bentley]

12 To 'portray' (used in the best sense) has become synonymous with 'betray'. [Graham Sutherland, 1903–80, in *Guardian*, 9 June 1978]

13 Portraits of famous bards and preachers, all fur and wool from the squint to the kneecaps. [Dylan Thomas, 1914–53, *Under Milk Wood*]

See also PAINTERS, PAINTING

POSSIBLITIES, see IMPOSSIBILITY

POSTERITY

1 Think of your forefathers! Think of your posterity! [John Quincy Adams, 1767–1848, speech, 22 Dec. 1802]

2 'We are always doing', says he, 'something for Posterity, but I would fain see Posterity doing something for us.' [Joseph Addison, 1672–1719, *The Spectator*, 583]; see 5

3 When a man is in doubt about this or that in his writing, it will often guide him if he asks himself how it will tell a hundred years hence. [Samuel Butler, 1835–1902, *Notebooks*, Ch. 7, 'Thought and Word 2', final note]

4 To evoke posterity / Is to weep on your own grave, / Ventriloquizing for the unborn. [Robert Graves, 1895–1985, *To Evoke Posterity*]

5 What has posterity done for us? [Boyle Roche, 1743–1807, speech in Irish Parliament, 1780]; see 2

See also FUTURE

POVERTY

1 To some extent, if you've seen one city slum you've seen them all. [Vice-President Spiro Agnew, 1918–96, speech during election campaign at Detroit, 18 Oct. 1968]

2 She was poor but she was honest, / Victim of the squire's whim: / First he loved her, then he left her, / And she lost her honest name. [anon. song of the 1914–18 War, of which there are many versions]

3 If anyone wants to make himself invisible, there is no surer way than to become poor. [anon., in Simone Weil, 1909–43, *Waiting on God*, 'Forms of the Implicit Love of God']

4 Anyone who has ever struggled with poverty knows how extremely expensive it is to be poor. [James Baldwin, 1924–87, *Nobody Knows My Name*, 'Fifth Avenue, Uptown']

5 Come away; poverty's catching. [Aphra Behn, 1640–89, *The Rover*, Pt Two, I]

6 He raiseth up the poor out of the dust, and lifteth the needy out of the dunghill. [Bible, OT, *Psalms* 113:7]

7 For the poor always ye have with you. [Bible, NT, *St John* 12:8]

8 We were so poor, my mother couldn't afford to have me. The lady next door gave birth to me. [Mel Brooks, 1926– , in *Playboy*, Dec. 1974]

9 The poor are not just living off the crumbs from the rich man's table, they are being asked to put the crumbs back. [David Bryer, 1944– , at 50th anniversary press conference of Oxfam, London, 5 Oct. 1992]

10 'Are you afraid of having your pockets picked?' 'Alas!' replied Mr Beveridge, 'it would take two men to do that.' 'Huh!' snorted the Emperor, 'you are so damned strong are you?' 'I mean,' answered his *vis-à-vis* with his polite smile, 'that it would take one man to put something in and another to take it out.' [J Storer Clouston, 1870–1944, *The Lunatic at Large*, Pt I, Ch. 2]

11 He found it inconvenient to be poor. [William Cowper, 1731–1800, *Charity*, 189]

12 Poverty and oysters always seem to go together. [Charles Dickens, 1812–70, *Pickwick Papers*, Ch. 22]

13 There's no scandal like rags, nor any crime so shameful as poverty. [George Farquhar, 1678–1707, *The Beaux' Stratagem*, I. i]

14 We are not concerned with the very poor. They are unthinkable, and only to be approached by the statistician or the poet. [E M Forster, 1879–1970, *Howards End*, Ch. 6]

15 Let not ambition mock their useful toil, / Their homely joys and destiny obscure; / Nor grandeur hear, with a disdainful smile, / The short and simple annals of the poor. [Thomas Gray, 1716–71, *Elegy Written in a Country Churchyard*, 8]

16 I want there to be no peasant in my kingdom so poor that he cannot have a chicken in his pot every Sunday. [Henri IV of France, 1553–1610, in H de Péréfixe, *Histoire de Henri le Grand*]

17 For the first time in our history it is possible to conquer poverty. [President Lyndon B Johnson, 1908–73; *Observer*, 'Sayings of the Week', 22 Mar. 1964]

18 This mournful truth is ev'rywhere confessed, / Slow rises worth by poverty depressed. [Dr Samuel Johnson, 1709–84, *London*, 176]

19 Poverty is bitter, but it has no harder pang than that it makes men ridiculous. [Juvenal, 60–*c*.130, *Satires*, III, 152]

20 It is not easy for men to emerge from obscurity if their qualities are thwarted by straitened circumstances at home. [Juvenal, 60–*c*.130, *Satires*, III, 164]

21 We're really all of us bottomly broke. I haven't had time to work in weeks. [Jack Kerouac, 1922–69, *On the Road*, Pt I, Ch. 7]

22 May I ask of Protestants and Catholics alike that in these days of rejoicing [Christmas] we shall not forget the pitiful Madonna of the Slums with her pallid children. [David Lloyd George, 1863–1945, speech in London, 18 Dec. 1925]

23 I've worked myself up from nothing to a state of extreme poverty. [Groucho Marx, 1895–1977, in film *Monkey Business*, script by S J Perelman et al.]

24 Poverty of goods is easily cured; poverty of soul, impossible. [Michel de Montaigne, 1533–92, *Essays*, III, 10]

25 I'm a lucky man. I carry the world within me. You see, Salim, in this world beggars are the only people who can be choosers. Everyone else has his side chosen for him. [V S Naipaul, 1932– , *A Bend in the River*, Ch. 9]

26 The forgotten man at the bottom of the economic pyramid. [Franklin D Roosevelt, 1882–1945, broadcast speech, 7 Apr. 1932]

27 The heart of the matter, as I see it, is the stark fact that world poverty is primarily a problem of two million villages, and thus a problem of two thousand million villagers. [E F Schumacher, 1911–77, *Small is Beautiful*, Ch. 13]

28 I am as poor as Job, my lord, but not so patient. [William Shakespeare, 1564–1616, *2 Henry IV*, I. ii. (145)]

29 My poverty, but not my will, consents. [*Romeo and Juliet*, V. i. 75]

30 O world! how apt the poor are to be proud. [*Twelfth Night*, III. i. (141)]

31 CUSINS: Do you call poverty a crime?
UNDERSHAFT: The worst of all crimes. All the other crimes are virtues beside it. [George Bernard Shaw, 1856–1950, *Major Barbara*, III]

32 Our poverty, then, signified chiefly that we were no longer allowed to throw down pennies, done up in screws of paper, to the conductors of German bands. [Osbert Sitwell, 1892–1969, *The Scarlet Tree*, Bk III, Ch. 1]

33 Poverty is no disgrace to a man, but it is confoundedly inconvenient. [Sydney Smith, 1771–1845, *His Wit and Wisdom*]

34 All the nice people were poor; at least, that was a general axiom, the best of the rich being poor in spirit. [Muriel Spark, 1918– , *The Girls of Slender Means*, Ch. 1]

35 He was a gentleman who was generally spoken of as having nothing a-year, paid quarterly. [R S Surtees, 1803–64, *Mr Sponge's Sporting Tour*, Ch. 24]

36 Taäke my word for it, Sammy, the poor in a loomp is bad. [Alfred, Lord Tennyson, 1809–92, *Northern Farmer. New Style*, 12]

37 That eternal want of pence / Which vexes public men. [Alfred, Lord Tennyson, 1809–92, *Will Waterproof's Lyrical Monologue*, 6]

38 There were times my pants were so thin I could sit on a dime and tell if it was heads or tails. [(Of his early struggles) Spencer Tracy, 1900–1967, in L Swindell, *S T*]

39 I was once so poor I didn't know where my next husband was coming from. [Mae West, 1892–1980, in film *She Done Him Wrong*, from West's play *Diamond Lil*]

40 Of course, being fatally poor and dingy, it was wise of Gerty to have taken up philanthropy and symphony concerts. [Edith Wharton, 1862–1937, *The House of Mirth*, Bk I, Ch. 8]

41 As for the virtuous poor, one can pity them, of course, but one cannot possibly admire them. [Oscar Wilde, 1854–1900, *The Soul of Man under Socialism*]

See also RICH, WEALTH

POWER

1 Power tends to corrupt, and absolute power corrupts absolutely. Great men are almost always bad men. [Lord Acton, 1834–1902, *Historical Essays and Studies*, Appendix]

2 [When asked how his party, the Christian Democrats, had remained in government in Italy for over thirty-five years almost continuously without being worn out] Political power wears out those who have not got it. [Giulio Andreotti, 1919– , in *New Statesman*, 19 July 1985]

3 Men in great place are thrice servants: servants of the sovereign or state; servants of fame; and servants of business. [Francis Bacon, 1561–1626, *Essays*, 11, 'Of Great Place']

4 You carry forever the fingerprint that comes from being under someone's thumb. [Nancy Banks-Smith, 1929– , in *Guardian*, 30 Jan. 1991]

5 The strongest poison ever known / Came from Caesar's laurel crown. [William Blake, 1757–1827, *Auguries of Innocence*]

6 The greater the power, the more dangerous the abuse. [Edmund Burke, 1729–97, speech on the Middlesex election, 1771]

7 Why should I run for Mayor when I'm already King? [Walt Disney, 1901–66 (on Ray Bradbury's suggesting that he should run for Mayor of Los Angeles), in *Listener*, 7 Oct. 1982]

8 I repeat . . . that all power is a trust – that we are accountable for its exercise – that, from the people, and for the people, all springs, and all must exist. [Benjamin Disraeli, 1804–81, *Vivian Grey*, Bk vi, Ch. 7]

9 All empire is no more than power in trust. [John Dryden, 1631–1700, *Absalom and Achitophel*, Pt I, 411]

10 Men of power have no time to read; yet the men who do not read are unfit for power. [Michael Foot, 1913– , *Debts of Honour*]

11 You must either conquer and rule or serve and lose, suffer or triumph, be the anvil or the hammer. [Johann Wolfgang von Goethe, 1749–1832, *Der Gross-Cophta*, II]

12 [Hegemony] is the 'spontaneous' consent given by the great masses of the population to the general direction imposed on social life by the dominant . . . group. [Antonio Gramsci, 1891–1937, *Prison Notebooks*, 'The Intellectuals']

13 In the past, those who foolishly sought power by riding on the back of the tiger ended up inside. [President John F Kennedy, 1917–63, inaugural address as President, 20 Jan. 1961]

14 Four things greater than all things are, – / Women and Horses and Power and War. [Rudyard Kipling, 1865–1936, *The Ballad of the King's Jest*]

15 Power is the ultimate aphrodisiac. [Henry Kissinger, 1923– , in *The New York Times*, 19 Jan. 1971]

16 The stronger man's argument is always the best. [Jean de La Fontaine, 1621–95, *Fables* 10, 'The Wolf and the Lamb']

17 I claim not to have controlled events, but confess plainly that events have controlled me. [Abraham Lincoln, 1809–65, letter, 4 Apr. 1864]

18 To leave great themes unfinished is / Perhaps the most satisfying exercise / Of power. [George MacBeth, 1932–92, *The Spider's Nest*]

19 Every Communist must grasp the truth, 'Political power grows out of the barrel of a gun.' [Mao Zedong, 1893–1976, speech to Central Committee, Communist Party, 6 Nov. 1938]

20 A man comes into a great hotel and says, I am a messenger. Who is this man? He disappears walking, there is no noise, nothing. Maybe he will never come back, maybe he will never deliver the message. But a man who rides up on a great machine, this man exists. He will be given messages. [Arthur Miller, 1915– , *A View from the Bridge*, I]

21 God must have loved the People in Power, for he made them so very like their own image of him. [Kenneth Patchen, 1911–72, quoted by Adrian Mitchell in *Guardian*, 1 Feb. 1972]

22 The megalomaniac differs from the narcissist by the fact that he wishes to be powerful rather than charming, and seeks to be feared rather than loved. To this type belong many lunatics and most of the great men of history. [Bertrand Russell, 1872–1970, *The Conquest of Happiness*, Ch. 1]

23 Ye gods, it doth amaze me, / A man of such a feeble temper should / So get the start of the majestic world, / And bear the palm alone. [William Shakespeare, 1564–1616, *Julius Caesar*, I. ii. 128]

24 Why, man, he doth bestride the narrow world / Like a Colossus; and we petty men / Walk under his huge legs, and peep about / To find ourselves dishonourable graves. [*Julius Caesar*, I. ii. 134]

25 We cannot all be masters. [*Othello*, I. i. 43]

26 The good want power, but to weep barren tears. / The powerful goodness want: worse need for them. / ... And all best things are thus confused with ill. [P B Shelley, 1792–1822, *Prometheus Unbound*, I, 625]

27 You only have power over people so long as you don't take *everything* away from them. But when you've robbed a man of everything he's no longer in your power – he's free again. [Alexander Solzhenitsyn, 1918– , *The First Circle*, Ch. 17]

28 Power corrupts, but lack of power corrupts absolutely. [Adlai Stevenson, 1900–1965, in *Observer*, Jan. 1963]; see 1

29 One still strong man in a blatant land, / Whatever they call him, what care I, / Aristocrat, democrat, autocrat – one / Who can rule and dare not lie. [Alfred, Lord Tennyson, 1809–92, *Maud*, Pt 1, x, 5]

30 The man who can dominate a London dinner-table can dominate the world. [Oscar Wilde, 1854–1900, quoted by R Aldington in his edn of W]

31 The good old rule / Sufficeth them, the simple plan, / That they should take, who have the power, / And they should keep who can. [William Wordsworth, 1770–1850, *Rob Roy's Grave*, 37]

32 The wrong sort of people are always in power because they would not be in power if they were not the wrong sort of people. [Jon Wynne-Tyson, 1924– , book review in *The Times Literary Supplement*]

See also INFLUENCE, TYRANTS

PRAISE

1 Through all Eternity to Thee / A joyful song I'll raise, / For oh! Eternity's too short / To utter all Thy praise. [Joseph Addison, 1672–1719, *The Spectator*, 453]

2 Let us now praise famous men, and our fathers that begat us. [Bible, Apocrypha: *Ecclesiasticus* 44:1]

3 Praise him upon the loud cymbals; praise him upon the high-sounding cymbals. [Bible, OT, *Psalms* 150:5]

4 Woe unto you, when all men shall speak well of you! [Bible, NT, *St Luke* 6:26]

5 Out of the mouths of babes and sucklings thou hast perfected praise. [Bible, NT, *St Matthew* 21:16]

6 The advantage of doing one's praising for oneself is that one can lay it on so thick and exactly in the right places. [Samuel Butler, 1835–1902, *The Way of all Flesh*, Ch. 34]

7 In virtues nothing earthly could surpass her, / Save thine 'incomparable oil', Macassar! [Lord Byron, 1788–1824, *Don Juan*, I, 17]

8 Praise the Lord! ye heavens adore Him, / Praise Him, Angels in the height! [John Kempthorne, 1775–1838, hymn]

9 Never praise a sister to a sister, in the hope of your compliments reaching the proper ears. [Rudyard Kipling, 1865–1936, *Plain Tales from the Hills*, 'False Dawn']

10 To refuse praise reveals a desire to be praised twice over. [Duc de La Rochefoucauld, 1613–80, *Maxims*, 149]

11 Praise of one's friends is always more unmixed pleasure than of oneself, because there isn't the slightest discomfort of doubting inwardly whether it is deserved. [Edward Marsh, 1874–1953, letter to Henry James, spring, 1915]

12 Those they praise, but they read the others. [Martial, *c.*40–*c.*104 *Epigrams*, IV, 49]

13 People ask you for criticism, but they only want praise. [W Somerset Maugham, 1874–1965, *Of Human Bondage*, Ch. 50]

14 Of whom to be dispraised were no small praise. [John Milton, 1608–74, *Paradise Regained*, Bk iii, 56]

15 Let us with a gladsome mind / Praise the Lord, for he is kind, / For his mercies ay endure, / Ever faithful, ever sure. [John Milton, 1608–74, *Psalm 136*]

16 They praised him to his face with their courtly foreign grace. [Alfred, Lord Tennyson, 1809–92, *The Revenge*, 13]

17 I can honestly say that I always look on Pauline as one of the nicest girls I was ever engaged to. [P G Wodehouse, 1881–1975, *Thank You, Jeeves*, Ch. 6]

See also BLESSINGS, ENTHUSIASMS

PRAYERS

1 Matthew, Mark, Luke, and John, / The bed be blest that I lie on. / Four angels to my bed, / Four angels round my head, / One to watch, and one to pray, / And two to bear my soul away. [Thomas Ady, 17th cent., *A Candle in the Dark* (1655)]

2 This ae nighte, this ae nighte, / *Every nighte and alle,* / Fire and fleet and candle-lighte, / *And Christ receive thy saule.* [anon., ballad, *A Lyke-wake Dirge*]

3 Now I lay me down to sleep; / I pray the Lord my soul to keep. / If I should die before I wake, / I pray the Lord my soul to take. [anon. prayer, 18th cent.]

4 From ghoulies and ghosties and long-leggety beasties / And things that go bump in the night, / Good Lord, deliver us! [anon. Scottish prayer]

5 From the hag and hungry goblin / That into rage would rend ye, / And the spirit that stands by the naked man / In the book of Moons defend ye! [anon., *Tom o' Bedlam*, 17th cent.]

6 Give me chastity and continency, but not yet. [St Augustine, 354–430, *Confessions*, VIII, 7]

7 The wish to pray is a prayer in itself. [Georges Bernanos, 1888–1948, *The Diary of a Country Priest*, Ch. 4]

8 Keep me as the apple of the eye; hide me under the shadow of thy wings. [Bible, OT, *Psalms* 17:8]

9 Let the words of my mouth, and the meditation of my heart, be acceptable in thy sight, O Lord. [Bible, OT, *Psalms* 19:14]

10 God be merciful unto us, and bless us: and shew us the light of his countenance, and be merciful unto us. [Bible, OT, *Psalms* 67:1 (*Book of Common Prayer* version)]

11 Lord, now lettest thou thy servant depart in peace, according to thy word. [Bible, NT, *St Luke* 2:29]

12 Give us this day our daily bread. Forgive us our trespasses, as we forgive them that trespass against us. Lead us not into temptation, but deliver us from evil. [Bible, NT, *St Matthew* 6:11 (*Book of Common Prayer* version)]

13 Some hae meat, and canna eat, / And some wad eat that want it, / But we hae meat and we can eat, / And sae the Lord be thankit. [Robert Burns, 1759–96, *The Selkirk Grace*]

14 A leap over the hedge is better than good men's prayers. [Miguel Cervantes, 1547–1616, *Don Quixote*, Pt I, Ch. 21]

15 From all that terror teaches, / From lies of

tongue and pen, / From all the easy speeches / That comfort cruel men, / From sale and profanation / Of honour and the sword, / Deliver us, good Lord! [G K Chesterton, 1874–1936, *O God of Earth and Altar*]

16 He prayeth well, who loveth well / Both man and bird and beast. [Samuel Taylor Coleridge, 1772–1834, *The Ancient Mariner*, Pt VII]

17 I think the dying pray at the last not please but thank you as a guest thanks his host at the door. [Annie Dillard, 1945– , *Pilgrim at Tinker Creek*, Ch. 15]

18 Batter my heart, three personed God; for you / As yet but knock, breathe, shine and seek to mend. [John Donne, 1571?–1631, *Holy Sonnets*, 14]

19 Pray for us now and at the hour of our birth. [T S Eliot, 1888–1965, *Animula*]

20 'O God, help me, Dear,' she prayed, 'this little once, O Lord. For Thou knowest my rights.' [Ronald Firbank, 1886–1926, *Caprice*, III]

21 'O, help me heaven,' she prayed, 'to be decorative and to do right.' [Ronald Firbank, 1886–1926, *The Flower beneath the Foot*, Ch. 2]

22 And that inverted Bowl we call The Sky, / Whereunder crawling coop't we live and die, / Lift not thy hands to *It* for help – for It / Rolls impotently on as Thou or I. [Edward Fitzgerald, 1809–83, *The Rubá'iyát of Omar Khayyám*, Edn 1, 52]

23 That still a godly race he ran, / Whene'er he went to pray. [Oliver Goldsmith, 1728–74, *The Vicar of Wakefield*, Ch. 17, 'An Elegy on the Death of a Mad Dog']

24 So many of his prayers had remained unanswered that he had hopes that this one prayer of his had lodged all the time like wax in the Eternal ear. [Graham Greene, 1904–91, *Monsignor Quixote*, Pt 1, Ch. 1]

25 Throw away thy rod, / Throw away they wrath: / O my God. / Take the gentle path. [George Herbert, 1593–1633, *Discipline*]

26 Teach me, my god and King, / In all things Thee to see, / And what I do in anything / To do it as for Thee. [George Herbert, 1593–1633, *The Elixir*]

27 Here a little child I stand, / Heaving up my either hand; / Cold as paddocks though they be, / Here I lift them up to Thee, / For a benison to fall / On our meat, and on us all. Amen. [Robert Herrick, 1591–1674, *Noble Numbers*, 'Another Grace for a Child']

28 And my lament / Is cries countless, cries like dead letters sent / To dearest him that lives alas! Away. [Gerard Manley Hopkins, 1844–89, *I Wake and Feel the Fell*]

29 Oh, I just keep plugging away. At its best it's like being in a dark room with someone you love. You can't see them; but you know they're there. [Cardinal Basil Hume, 1923–99 (of prayer), interview in John Mortimer, *In Character*]

30 Preserve me from unseasonable and immoderate sleep. [Dr Samuel Johnson, 1709–84, *Prayers and Meditations* (1767)]

31 Abide with me from morn to eve, / For without Thee I cannot live: / Abide with me when night is nigh. / For without Thee I dare not die. [John Keble, 1792–1866, *The Christian Year*, 'Evening']

32 Ere yet we loose the legions – / Ere yet we draw the blade, / Jehovah of the Thunders, / Lord God of Battles aid! [Rudyard Kipling, 1865–1936, *Hymn before Action*]

33 The tumult and the shouting dies; / The Captains and the Kings depart: / Still stands thine ancient sacrifice, / An humble and a contrite heart. / Lord God of Hosts, be with us yet, / Lest we forget – lest we forget! [Rudyard Kipling, 1865–1936, *Recessional*]

34 A single grateful thought raised to heaven is the most perfect prayer. [G E Lessing, 1729–81, *Minna von Barnhelm*, vii]

35 To give and not to count the cost; / To fight and not to heed the wounds; / To toil and not to seek for rest; / To labour and not ask for any reward / Save that of knowing that we do Thy will. [St Ignatius Loyola, 1491–1556, *Prayer for Generosity*]

36 Here lie I, Martin Elginbrodde: / Hae mercy o' my soul, Lord God; / As I wod do, were I Lord God, / And ye were Martin Elginbrodde. [George Macdonald, 1824–1905, *David Elginbrod*, Bk i, Ch. 13]

37 Who rises from prayer a better man, his prayer is answered. [George Meredith, 1828–1909, *The Ordeal of Richard Feverel*, Ch. 12]

38 Pray but one prayer for me 'twixt thy closed lips. [William Morris, 1834–96, *Summer Dawn*]

39 God grant me the serenity to accept things I cannot change, courage to change things I can, and wisdom to know the difference. [Reinhold Niebuhr, 1892–1971, attr., but never claimed by him; probably 18th cent. German, if not earlier]

40 Teach me to feel another's woe, / To hide the fault I see; / That mercy I to others show, / That mercy show to me. [Alexander Pope, 1688–1744, *The Universal Prayer*]

41 Lighten our darkness, we beseech thee, O Lord. [*The Book of Common Prayer*, Evening Prayer, third collect]

42 Our Father that art in heaven, stay there and we will stay on earth which is sometimes so pretty. [Jacques Prévert, 1900–1977, *Pater Noster*]

43 O most merciful Redeemer, Friend, and Brother, / May we know Thee more clearly, / Love Thee more dearly, / Follow Thee more nearly: / for ever and ever. Amen. [St Richard of Chichester, 1197–1253, *Prayer*]

44 My words fly up, my thoughts remain below: / Words without thoughts never to heaven go. [William Shakespeare, 1564–1616, *Hamlet*, III. iii. 97]

45 I had most need of blessing, and 'Amen' / Stuck in my throat. [*Macbeth*, II. ii. 33]

46 I am just going to pray for you at St Paul's, but with no very lively hope of success. [Sydney Smith, 1771–1845, letter to R Monckton Milnes, 8 Nov. 1843]

47 Prayers are like those appeals of ours. Either they don't get through or they're returned with 'rejected' scrawled across 'em. [Alexander Solzhenitsyn, 1918– , *One Day in the Life of Ivan Denisovich*]

48 Pray as if everything depended on God, and work as if everything depended upon man. [Cardinal Spellman, 1889–1959; in Lewis C Henry, *Best Quotations for All Occasions*]

49 God bless mother and daddy, my brother and sister, and save the King. And, oh God, do take care of yourself, because if anything happens to you we're all sunk. [(Quoting child's prayer) Adlai Stevenson, 1900–1965, speech at Harvard Business School, 6 June 1959]

50 Pray for my soul. More things are wrought by prayer / Than this world dreams of. [Alfred, Lord Tennyson, 1809–92, *Idylls of the King*, 'The Passing of Arthur', 415]

51 Be near me when my light is low, / When the blood creeps, and the nerves prick / And tingle; and the heart is sick, / And all the wheels of Being slow. [Alfred, Lord Tennyson, 1809–92, *In Memoriam*, 50]

52 Battering the gates of heaven with storms of prayer. [Alfred, Lord Tennyson, 1809–92, *St Simeon Stylites*, 7]

53 The conversation of prayers about to be said / Turns on the quick and the dead, and the man on the stairs / Tonight shall find no dying but alive and warm. [Dylan Thomas, 1914–53, *The Conversation of Prayer*]

54 Whatever a man prays for, he prays for a miracle. Every prayer reduces itself to this: 'Great God, grant that twice two be not four.' [Ivan Turgenev, 1818–83, *Prayer*]

55 O hear us when we cry to Thee / For those in peril on the sea. [William Whiting, 1825–78, hymn: *Eternal Father, Strong to Save*]

See also BLESSINGS

PREJUDICE

1 *Prejudice*, n. A vagrant opinion without visible means of support. [Ambrose Bierce, 1842–1914, *The Devil's Dictionary*]

2 She was anxious to be someone, and, no one ever having voiced a prejudice in her hearing without impressing her, had come to associate prejudice with identity. You could not be a someone without disliking things. [Elizabeth Bowen, 1899–1973, *The House in Paris*, Pt I, Ch. 1]

3 Every man has a House of Lords in his own head. Fears, prejudices, misconceptions – those are the peers, and they are hereditary. [David Lloyd George, 1863–1945, speech at Cambridge, 1927]

4 All seems infected that th'infected spy, / As all looks yellow to the jaundiced eye. [Alexander Pope, 1688–1744, *An Essay on Criticism*, 558]

See also RACES

THE PRESENT

1 Today is the first day of the rest of your life. [Charles Dederich, 1913–97, hippie slogan, late 1960s]

2 The word 'now' is like a bomb through the window, and it ticks. [Arthur Miller, 1915– , *After the Fall*, I]

3 Past and to come seems best; things present, worst. [William Shakespeare, 1564–1616, *2 Henry IV*, I. iii. 108]

4 For we, which now behold these present days, / Have eyes to wonder, but lack tongues to praise. [*Sonnets*, 106]

5 Life could not continue without throwing the past into the past, liberating the present from its burden. [Paul Tillich, 1886–1965, *The Eternal Now*, Pt II, Ch. 1]

6 Everything we see / Teaches the time that we are living in. [Charles Tomlinson, 1927– , *Poem for My Father*]

See also FUTURE, PAST, TIME

PRESENTS

1 They gave it me ... for an un-birthday present. [Lewis Carroll, 1832–98, *Through the Looking Glass*, Ch. 6]

2 He is very fond of making things which he does not want, and then giving them to people who have no use for them. [Anthony Hope, 1863–1933, *The Dolly Dialogues*, 17]

3 'Presents', I often say, 'endear absents.' [Charles Lamb, 1775–1834, *Essays of Elia*, 'A Dissertation upon Roast Pig']

4 Giving presents is one of the most possessive of things we do ... It's the way we keep a hold on other people. Plant ourselves in their lives. [Penelope Lively, 1933– , *Moon Tiger*, Ch. 8]

5 I'm giving him a Useful Pot to Keep Things In. [A A Milne, 1882–1956, *Winnie-the-Pooh*, Ch. 6]

6 Why is it no one ever sent me yet / One perfect limousine, do you suppose? / Ah no, it's always just my luck to get / One perfect rose. [Dorothy Parker, 1893–1967, *One Perfect Rose*]

See also GRATITUDE

PRESIDENTS IN GENERAL

1 I had rather be right than be President. [Henry Clay, 1777–1852, speech, 1850]

2 When I was a boy I was told that anybody could become President: I'm beginning to believe it. [Clarence Darrow, 1857–1938, in I Stone, *C D for the Defence*, Ch. 6]

3 But even the president of the United States / Sometimes must have / To stand naked. [Bob Dylan, 1941– , song: *It's Alright, Ma (I'm Only Bleeding)*]

4 There is one thing about being President – nobody can tell you when to sit down. [Dwight D Eisenhower, 1890–1969; *Observer*, 'Sayings of the Week', 9 Aug. 1953]

5 You know that nobody is strongminded around a President; ... it is always: 'yes sir,' 'no sir' (the 'no sir' comes when he asks whether you're dissatisfied). [George Reedy, 1917– , in *The White House*, ed. R Gordon Hoxie]

6 The buck stops here. [Harry Truman, 1884–1972, notice on his presidential desk]

See also next category, LEADERSHIP, POLITICIANS

PRESIDENTS: INDIVIDUAL (in alphabetical order of subject)

1 At the moment, he [President Bush] would love to save the planet, though not if it means offending General Motors. [Simon Hoggart, 1946– in *Observer*, 10 Dec. 1989]

2 He's the kind of guy you'd like to have around when you want to be alone. With a little effort he could become an anonymity. [(Of George Bush) Richard Little, 1944– , in TV programme on night of US presidential election, 9 Nov. 1988]

3 Eisenhower is the only living unknown soldier. [Senator Robert S Kerr, 1896–1963 (letter to Goodman Ace, 19 July 1960), in Groucho Marx, *The Groucho Letters*]

4 I guess it just proves that in America anyone can be President. [President Gerald Ford, 1913– (on becoming President), in R Reeves, *A Ford, Not a Lincoln*, Ch. 4]

5 Jerry Ford is so dumb that he can't fart and chew gum at the same time. [President Lyndon B Johnson, 1908–73, in R Reeves, *A Ford, Not a Lincoln*, Ch. 1]

6 You [President Gorbachev] have listened to the applause of the West and forgotten whose president you are. [Saji Umaltova, 1953– (speech at Congress of People's Deputies, Moscow), in *Guardian*, 18 Dec. 1990]

7 President Kennedy is a great one for the girls, and during the election his opponents said that if he got to the White House they only hoped he would do for fornication what Eisenhower did for golf. [Rupert Hart-Davis, 1907–99, letter, 25 Feb. 1961, in *Lyttelton–Hart-Davis Letters*, ed. Rupert Hart-Davis, Vol. 3]

8 Spending half his time thinking about adultery, the other half about second-hand ideas passed on by his advisers. [(Of President Kennedy) Harold Macmillan, 1894–1986, quoted by Alistair Horne in *The Sunday Times*, 4 Jan. 1987]

9 I am going to build the kind of nation that President Roosevelt hoped for, President Truman worked for and President Kennedy died for. [President Lyndon B Johnson, 1908–73, speech in Dec. 1964]

10 If Richard Nixon was second-rate, what in the world *is* third-rate? [Joseph Heller, 1923–99, *Good as Gold*, 6]

11 There can be no whitewash at the White House. [President Nixon, 1913–94 (TV address on the Watergate crisis, 30 Apr. 1973), in C Bernstein and B Woodward, *All the President's Men*, 16]

12 I welcome this kind of examination because people have got to know whether or not their President is a crook. Well, I'm not a crook. [President Nixon, 1913–94, at press conference, 11 Nov. 1973]

13 When the President does it, that means it is not illegal. [President Nixon, 1913–94, TV interview with David Frost, 20 May 1977]

14 Would you buy a second-hand car from this man? [Mort Sahl, 1926– , of President Nixon, attr.]

15 [When asked to give an example of an oxymoron] Sincerely, Nixon. [Andrew Salkey, 1928–95, in PBS programme *All Things Considered*, Washington, 1980]

16 Richard Nixon has never been one of my favourite people, anyway. For years I've regarded him as a monument to all the rancid genes and broken chromosomes that corrupt the possibility of the American Dream: he was a foul caricature of himself, a man with no soul, no inner convictions, with the integrity of a hyena and the style of a poison toad. [Hunter S Thompson, 1939– , *The Great Shark Hunt*, 'Presenting: the Richard Nixon Doll']

17 You don't set a fox to watching the chickens just because he has a lot of experience in the hen house. [(Of Vice-President Nixon's candidacy for the presidency) Harry Truman, 1884–1972, speech, 30 Oct. 1960]

18 To listen even briefly to Ronald Reagan is to realize that he is a man upon whose synapses the termites have dined long and well. [Christopher Hitchens, 1949– , *Prepared for the Worst*]

19 Sure, Reagan promised to take senility tests. But what if he forgets? [Lorna Kerr-Walker, in *Pacific Sun*, 21 Mar. 1981]

20 All in all, not bad. Not too bad at all. [President Ronald Reagan, 1911– (verdict on his own presidency), speech on US TV; *Independent*, 'Quote Unquote', 14 Jan. 1989]

21 Washington could not tell a lie; Nixon could not tell the truth; Reagan cannot tell the difference. [Mort Sahl, 1926– ; *Observer*, 'Sayings of the Week', 18 Oct. 1987]

22 Reagan won because he ran against Jimmy Carter. Had he run unopposed he would have lost. [Mort Sahl, 1926– ; *The Other 637 Best Things Anybody Ever Said*, comp. Robert Byrne]

23 He [Ronald Reagan] has achieved a political breakthrough – the Teflon-coated presidency. He sees to it that nothing sticks to him. [Patricia Schroeder, 1940– ; *Oh, What an Awful Thing to Say!*, comp. W Cole and L Phillips]

24 [When asked if he was backing the Republican slate in the 1980 US presidential election] Well, I'm a George Bush man myself. I support the double ticket: Reagan and a heart-attack. [Norman Tebbit, 1931– , in S Hoggart, *Back in the House*]

25 Like much of America [Reagan] contained contradictions, but never experienced them. [Gary Wills, 1934– , *R's America: Innocents at Home*]

26 When Ronald Reagan's career in show business came to an end, he was hired to impersonate, first a California Governor and then an American President. [Gore Vidal, 1925– , *Armageddon*, title essay]

27 The best newspaperman who has ever been President of the United States. [Heywood Broun,

1888–1939 (of Franklin D Roosevelt), in D Boorstin, *The Image*, Ch. 1]

28 In Franklin Roosevelt there died the greatest American friend we have ever known and the greatest champion of freedom who has ever brought help and comfort from the New World to the Old. [Winston Churchill, 1874–1965, *The Second World War*, Vol. 5, 28]

29 Not since Lincoln had there been such an artful manipulator of the good, the bad, and the bewildered in between. I believe he [Roosevelt] saved the capitalist system by deliberately forgetting to balance the books, by transferring the gorgeous resources of credit from the bankers to the government. [Alistair Cooke, 1908– , *America*, Ch. 10]

30 This was the Angel of History! We felt its wings flutter through the room. Was that not the future we awaited so anxiously? [Josef Goebbels, 1897–1945 (on hearing of Roosevelt's death), *Diary*, 12 Apr. 1945]

31 I sit here all day trying to persuade people to do the things they ought to have sense enough to do without my persuading them ... That's all the powers of the President amount to. [Harry Truman, 1884–1972, in R E Neustadt, *Presidential Power*]

32 First in war, first in peace, first in the hearts of his fellow countrymen. [(Of George Washington) Henry Lee, 1756–1818, speech in House of Representatives, 19 Dec. 1799]

33 They say Wilson has blundered. Perhaps he has but I notice he usually blunders forward. [Thomas Edison, 1847–1931, in John Dos Passos, *Mr Wilson's War*, Ch. 2, sect. x]

34 Like Odysseus, the President [Woodrow Wilson] looked wiser when seated. [John Maynard Keynes, 1883–1946, *Economic Consequences of the Peace*, Ch. 3]

35 History buffs probably noted the reunion at a Washington party a few weeks ago of three ex-presidents: Carter, Ford, and Nixon – See No Evil, Hear No Evil, and Evil. [Senator Robert Dole, 1923– ; in *Oh, What an Awful Thing to Say!*, comp. W Cole and L Phillips]

See also previous category, LEADERSHIP, POLITICIANS

THE PRESS, see NEWSPAPERS

PRIDE

1 We'd rather eat grass standing up than eat beef on our knees. [anon. Nicaraguan saying quoted by Charlotte Cornwell in *Time Out*, 22–8 Mar. 1984]

2 Thou art a stiff-necked people. [Bible, OT, *Exodus* 33:3]

3 Pride goeth before destruction, and an haughty spirit before a fall. [Bible, OT, *Proverbs* 16:18]

4 I cannot dig; to beg I am ashamed. [Bible, NT, *St Luke* 16:3]

5 He that is down needs fear no fall, / He that is low no pride. [John Bunyan, 1628–88, *The Pilgrim's Progress*, Pt II, 'Shepherd Boy's Song']

6 We've got a private master comes to teach us at home, but we ain't proud, because ma says it's sinful. [Charles Dickens, 1812–70, *Nicholas Nickleby*, Ch. 16]

7 Pride is faith in the idea that God had, when he made us. A proud man is conscious of the idea, and aspires to realize it. [Isak Dinesen, 1885–1962, *Out of Africa*, 'On Pride']

8 One of the low on whom assurance sits / As a silk hat on a Bradford millionaire. [T S Eliot, 1888–1965, *The Waste Land*, 233]

9 This extraordinary pride in being exempt from temptation that you have not yet risen to the level of. Eunuchs boasting of their chastity. [C S Lewis, 1898–1963, in Brian Aldiss and Kingsley Amis, *Spectrum IV*]

10 I admit I may have seen better days, but I am still not to be had for the price of a cocktail – like a salted peanut. [Joseph Mankiewicz, 1909–93, said by Bette Davis in film *All about Eve*]

11 Yes; I am proud, I must be proud to see/ Men not afraid of God, afraid of me. [Alexander Pope, 1688–1744, *Epilogue to the Satires*, Dialogue II, 208]

12 Pride, the never failing vice of fools. [Alexander Pope, 1688–1744, *An Essay on Criticism*, 204]

13 A confessional passage has probably never been written that didn't stink a little bit of the writer's pride in having given up his pride. [J D Salinger, 1919– , *Seymour: An Introduction*]

14 My pride fell with my fortunes. [William Shakespeare, 1564–1616, *As You Like It*, I. ii. (269)]

15 His nature is too noble for the world: / He would not flatter Neptune for his trident, / Or Jove for's power to thunder. [*Coriolanus*, III. i. 254]

16 But man, proud man, / Drest in a little brief authority, / Most ignorant of what he's most assured, / His glassy essence, like an angry ape, / Plays such fantastic tricks before high heaven / As make the angels weep. [*Measure for Measure*, II. ii. 117]

17 He passed a cottage with a double coach-house, / A cottage of gentility! / And he owned with a grin / That his favourite sin / Is pride that apes humility. [Robert Southey, 1774–1843, *The Devil's Walk* (a poem written in collaboration with Coleridge)]

18 Dust are our frames; and gilded dust, our pride / Looks only for a moment whole and sound. [Alfred, Lord Tennyson, 1809–92, *Aylmer's Field*, 1]

19 There is such a thing as a man being too proud to fight. [Woodrow Wilson, 1856–1924, address at Philadelphia, 10 May 1915]

See also ARROGANCE, HUMILITY, SMUGNESS

PRIME MINISTERS IN GENERAL

1 There are three groups that no British Prime Minister should provoke: the Vatican, the Treasury and the miners. [Stanley Baldwin, 1867–1947, attr. There are variants from other politicians. R A Butler's version, 'Do not run up your nose dead against the Pope and the NUM [National Union of Mineworkers]', in his *The Art of Memory*, p. 110]

2 We had intended you to be / The next Prime Minister but three. [Hilaire Belloc, 1870–1953, *Cautionary Tales*, 'Lord Lundy']

3 Once, when a British Prime Minister sneezed, men half a world away would blow their noses. Now when a British Prime Minister sneezes nobody else will even say 'Bless You'. [Bernard Levin, 1928– , in *The Times*, 8 June 1976]

4 I thought that when I became Prime Minister I'd have power. And what have I got? *Influence!* [Jonathan Lynn, 1943– , and Antony Jay, 1930– , *Yes Prime Minister*, Vol. 2, 'The National Education']

5 Above any other position of eminence that of Prime Minister is filled by fluke. [Enoch Powell, 1912–98; *Observer*, 'Sayings of the Week', 8 Mar. 1987]

6 Most Prime Ministers would not be interesting unless they had been Prime Ministers (and some are not interesting even then). [A J P Taylor, 1906–90, in *New Society*, 17 Oct. 1986]

7 I believe the greatest asset a head of state can have is the ability to get a good night's sleep. [Harold Wilson, 1916–95, BBC radio interview in *The World Tonight*, 16 Apr. 1975]

See also next category, GOVERNMENT, LEADERSHIP, PARLIAMENT, POLITICIANS

PRIME MINISTERS: INDIVIDUAL
(in alphabetical order of subject)

1 He's a modest little man with much to be modest about. [(On Clement Attlee's becoming Prime Minister) Winston Churchill, 1874–1965, in *Chicago Sunday Tribune Magazine of Books*, 27 June 1954]

2 Not even a public figure. A man of no experience. And of the utmost insignificance. [Lord Curzon, 1859–1925 (of Stanley Baldwin's appointment as Prime Minister), in Harold Nicolson, *C: The Last Phase*, Ch. 12]

3 He [Clemenceau] had one illusion – France; and one disillusion – mankind. [John Maynard Keynes, 1883–1946, *Economic Consequences of the Peace*, Ch. 3]

4 In the eighteenth century he would have become Prime Minister before he was thirty; as it was he appeared honourably ineligible for the struggle of life. [(Of Alec Douglas-Home as a schoolboy) Cyril Connolly, 1903–74, *Enemies of Promise*, Ch. 23]

5 After half a century of democratic advance the whole process has ground to a halt with a 14th Earl. [(On Alec Douglas-Home's becoming Prime Minister) Harold Wilson, 1916–95, speech in Manchester, 19 Oct. 1963]

6 He [Anthony Eden] is not only a bore but he bores for England. [Malcolm Muggeridge, 1903–90, 'Boring for England', reprinted in Edward Hyams, *Newstatesmanship*]

7 He [Labouchere] did not object, he once said, to Gladstone's always having the ace of trumps up his sleeve, but only to his pretence that God put it there. [Henry Labouchere, 1831–1912, in A L Thorold, *Life of H L*, Ch. 15]

8 He [Gladstone] spent his declining years trying to guess the answer to the Irish Question; unfortunately whenever he was getting warm, the Irish secretly changed the question. [W C Sellar, 1898–1951, and R J Yeatman, 1897–1968, *1066 and All That*, Ch. 57]

9 He [Gladstone] speaks to Me as if I was a public meeting. [Queen Victoria, 1819–1901, in G W E Russell, *Collections and Recollections*, Ch. 14]

10 He [Lloyd George] could not see a belt without hitting below it. [Margot Asquith, 1865–1945, quoted in introduction to 1962 edition of *Autobiography*]

11 [Lloyd George] did not seem to care which way he travelled provided he was in the driver's seat. [Lord Beaverbrook, 1879–1964, *The Decline and Fall of L G*, Ch. 7]

12 BONHAM CARTER: What do you think happens to Mr Lloyd George when he is alone in the room?
KEYNES: When he is alone in the room there is nobody there. [John Maynard Keynes, 1883–1946, recalled by Lady Violet Bonham Carter in Romanes Lecture, Oxford, 1963]

13 He [Ramsay MacDonald] had sufficient conscience to bother him, but not sufficient to keep him straight. [David Lloyd George, 1863–1945, in A J Sylvester, *Diary*, 29 Aug. 1938]

14 Mr MacDonald has become ... an actor – and that type of actor which the cruel French call a '*m'as-tu vu?*' 'Have you seen me as the Prime Minister? – My greatest role, I assure you,' Mr MacDonald is anxiously asking the nation. Yes, we have seen him. [John Strachey, 1901–63, *The Coming Struggle for Power*, Pt V, 17]

15 I thought the best thing to do was to settle up these little local difficulties, and then turn to the wider vision of the Commonwealth. [Harold Macmillan, 1894–1986, said at London Airport, 7 Jan. 1958, referring to resignation of Treasury Ministers]

16 Macmillan seemed, in his very person, to embody the national decay he supposed himself to be confuting. He exuded a flavour of moth-balls. [Malcolm Muggeridge, 1903–90, *Tread Softly for You Tread on My Jokes*, 'England, Whose England']

17 Greater love hath no man than this, that he lay down his friends for his life. [Jeremy Thorpe, 1929– (of Macmillan's swingeing Cabinet reshuffle on 13 July 1962), in Bernard Levin, *The Pendulum Years*, Ch. 12]

18 It's quite a change to have a Prime Minister who hasn't got any political ideas at all. [(Of John Major) Michael Foot, 1913– ; *Observer*, 'Sayings of the Week', 24 Feb. 1991]

19 He hasn't got the Tebbit touch. I'm afraid you can't turn a spaniel into a Rottweiler. [Denis Healey, 1917– (on John Major's demonstrating aggression during election campaign), to journalists in North Kensington, London, 21 Mar. 1992]

20 I am my own man. [John Major, 1943– , on becoming Prime Minister; *Independent*, 'Quote Unquote', 1 Dec. 1990]

21 We were promised a New Statesman, and what have we got instead? The Spectator. [John Smith, 1938–94 (of John Major's handling of the sterling crisis), speech at Labour Party Conference, Blackpool, 29 Sept. 1992]

22 I'm sure the Government knows best. She usually does. [(Of Margaret Thatcher) Alan Coren, 1938– , *Bumf*, 'The Denmark Factor']

23 She [Margaret Thatcher] has been beastly to the Bank of England, has demanded that the BBC 'set its house in order' and tends to believe the worst of the Foreign and Commonwealth Office. She cannot see an institution without hitting it with her handbag. [Julian Critchley, 1930– , in *The Times*, 21 June 1982]

24 She's got everything she wants and yet she seems furious all day. [(Of Margaret Thatcher) David Hare, 1947– , in *Independent*, 6 Oct. 1988]

25 Mrs Thatcher is doing for monetarism what the Boston Strangler did for door-to-door salesmen. [Denis Healey, 1917– , speech in House of Commons, 15 Dec. 1979]

26 She [Margaret Thatcher] has the mouth of Marilyn Monroe and the eyes of Caligula. [François Mitterrand, 1916–96, in Denis Healey, *The Time of My Life*, Ch. 23]

27 She [Margaret Thatcher] is the best man in England. [Ronald Reagan, 1911– , to reporters, 7 Jan. 1983]; see also POLITICIANS

28 I don't mind how much my ministers talk, as long as they do what I say. [Margaret Thatcher, 1925– ; *Observer*, 'Sayings of the Week', 27 Jan. 1980]

29 You turn if you want to – the lady's not for turning. [Margaret Thatcher, 1925– (denying the possibility of her making a U-turn over economic policy), closing speech at Conservative Party Conference, Brighton, 11 Oct. 1980, phrase ascr. to Ronald Millar as her speech-writer]

30 In Pierre Elliott Trudeau, Canada has at last produced a political leader worthy of assassination. [Irving Layton, 1912– , *The Whole Bloody Bird*, 'Obo II']

31 Walpole ... even when Prime Minister was said to open his gamekeeper's letters first of the batch. [G M Trevelyan, 1876–1962, *History of England*, Bk V, Ch. 2]

32 His [Harold Wilson's] short-term opportunism, allied with a capacity for self-delusion which made Walter Mitty appear unimaginative, often plunged the Government into chaos. [Denis Healey, 1917– , *The Time of My Life*, Ch. 16]

33 One [of the Harolds, Macmillan and Wilson] played the part of the last aristocrat ... advancing through life with a paralysed shuffle, an assortment of facial tics, a voice which was the distilled essence of all the confidence-tricksters who ever went home and entertained the children after the day's work was done. The role assumed by the other was that of the purposive, technologically-equipped, full twentieth-century citizen, leaning forward when he walked, like a man trying not to fall over if the bus starts with a jerk, his voice the ingratiating wheedle of the toucher who wants yet another fiver to tide him over to pay-day, and will do anything to get it. [Bernard Levin, 1928– , *The Pendulum Years*, Ch. 12]

34 No one should have been allowed to become Prime Minister who has made twelve trips to Moscow. [Peter Wright, 1916–95 (of Harold Wilson), in David Leigh, *The Wilson Plot*]

See also previous category, GOVERNMENT, LEADERSHIP, PARLIAMENT, POLITICIANS

PRINCIPLE

1 These are my principles and if you don't like them, I have others. [anon.]

2 I would rather be an opportunist and float than go to the bottom with my principles round my neck. [Stanley Baldwin, 1867–1947, attr.]

3 Olaf (upon what were once knees) / does almost ceaselessly repeat / 'there is some shit I will not eat' [e e cummings, 1894–1962, *Collected Poems* (1938), 204]

4 A precedent embalms a principle. [Benjamin Disraeli, 1804–81, speech in House of Commons, 22 Feb. 1848]

5 Campbell is a good man, a pious man. I am afraid he has not been in the inside of a church for many years; but he never passes a church without pulling off his hat. This shows that he has good principles. [Dr Samuel Johnson, 1709–84, in James Boswell, *Life of J*, 1 July 1763]

6 A man may be very sincere in good principles, without having good practice. [Dr Samuel Johnson, 1709–84, in James Boswell, *Tour of the Hebrides*, 25 Oct. 1773]

7 The Beanstalk Principle – For every animal, object, institution or system there is an optimal limit beyond which it should not grow. [Leopold Kohr 1909– , and Kirkpatrick Sale, 1937– , Manifesto of *The Fourth World*, in the *Guardian*, 25 Nov. 1987]

8 Doctrinaires are the vultures of principle. They feed upon principle after it is dead. [David Lloyd George, 1863–1945, quoted by Dingle Foot in *Guardian*, 17 Jan. 1963]

9 A marciful Providunce fashioned us holler, / O' purpose thet we might our principles swaller. [James Russell Lowell, 1819–91, *The Biglow Papers*, First Series, 4]

10 A precedent embalms a principle. [William Scott, Lord Stowell, 1745–1836, attr. opinion, while Advocate-General]

11 Well, sir, you never can tell. That's a principle in life with me, sir, if you'll excuse my having such a thing, sir. [George Bernard Shaw, 1856–1950, *You Never Can Tell*, II]

See also IDEALS, MORALITY

PRIORITIES

1 Love and a cottage! Eh, Fanny! Ah, give me

indifference and a coach and six! [George Colman the Elder, 1732–94, *The Clandestine Marriage*, I. ii]

2 First things first, second things never. [Shirley Conran, 1932– , *Superwoman*, 'How to be a Working Wife and Mother']

3 'No business before breakfast, Glum!' says the King. 'Breakfast first, business next.' [W M Thackeray, 1811–63, *The Rose and the Ring*, Ch. 11]

PRISON

1 People are capable of doing an awful lot when they have no choice and I had no choice. Courage is when you have choices. [Terry Anderson, 1947– , on being released as hostage in the Lebanon in Paris, 6 May 1992]

2 Prison is an effective deterrent to those who walk past the gate, not through it. [Roger Attrill, prison governor, in *New Statesman*, Sept. 1980]

3 Prisons are built with stones of Law, brothels with bricks of Religion. [William Blake, 1757–1827, *The Marriage of Heaven and Hell*, 'Proverbs of Hell']

4 The formula for prison is lack of space counterbalanced by a surplus of time. [Joseph Brodsky, 1940– , *Less Than One*, title essay]

5 Oh! dreadful is the check – intense the agony – / When the ear begins to hear, and the eye begins to see; / When the pulse begins to throb, the brain to think again; / The soul to feel the flesh, and the flesh to feel the chain. [Emily Brontë, 1818–48, *The Prisoner*]

6 Stone walls do not a prison make / Nor iron bars a cage; / Minds innocent and quiet take / That for an hermitage. [Richard Lovelace, 1618–58, *To Althea, From Prison*]

7 You took away the oceans and all the room. / You gave me my shoe-size in earth and bars around it. [Osip Mandelstam, 1891–1938, *Poems*, No. 307]

8 The singing bird forgets its cage. [Cardinal Mindszenty, 1892–1975, in *Observer*, 5 May 1991]

9 In order to understand birds / You have to be a convict. / And if you share your bread – It means your time is done. [Irina Ratushinskaya, 1954– , *No, I am Not Afraid*, 'The Sparrows of Butyrki']

10 I have been studying how I may compare / The prison where I live unto the world. [William Shakespeare, 1564–1616, *Richard II*, V. v. 1]

11 One of the [zoo] cages had a notice on it: 'White owls do not do well in captivity.' So they know that! And they still lock them up! What sort of degenerate owls, he wondered, did so well in captivity? [Alexander Solzhenitsyn, 1918– , *Cancer Ward*, Pt II, Ch. 14]

12 Anyone who has been to an English public school will always feel comparatively at home in prison. [Evelyn Waugh, 1903–66, *Decline and Fall*, III, 4]

13 I know not whether Laws be right, / Or whether Laws be wrong; / All that we know who lie in gaol / Is that the wall is strong; / And that each day is like a year, / A year whose days are long. [Oscar Wilde, 1854–1900, *The Ballad of Reading Gaol*, Pt V, 1]

14 The vilest deeds like poison-weeds / Bloom well in prison-air; / It is only what is good in Man / That wastes and withers there: / Pale Anguish keeps the heavy gate / And the warder is Despair. [Oscar Wilde, 1854–1900, *The Ballad of Reading Gaol*, Pt V, 5]

See also CRIME, LAW

PRIVACY

1 'If everybody minded their own business,' the Duchess said in a hoarse growl, 'the world would go round a deal faster than it does.' [Lewis Carroll, 1832–98, *Alice in Wonderland*, Ch. 6]

2 Probably one of the most private things in the world is an egg until it is broken. [M F K Fisher, 1908–92, *How to Cook a Wolf*]

3 And now it seems she's on my wavelength. That's all I need. My mind isn't much of a comfort to me but at least I thought it was private. [Russell Hoban, 1925– , *Turtle Diary*, Ch. 21]

4 They do those little personal things people sometimes do when they think they are alone in railway carriages; things like smelling their own armpits. [Jonathan Miller, 1934– , *Beyond the Fringe*]

5 I might have been a gold-fish in a glass bowl for all the privacy I got. [Saki (H H Munro), 1870–1916, *The Innocence of Reginald*]

6 An essentially private man who wished his total indifference to public notice to be universally recognized. [Tom Stoppard, 1937– , *Travesties*, I]

7 This is a free country, madam. We have a right to share your privacy in a public place. [Peter Ustinov, 1921– , *Romanoff and Juliet*, I]

PROBLEMS

1 No problem can be solved. When a situation becomes a problem, it becomes insoluble. No problems can be solved, and all solutions lead to more problems. [William Burroughs, 1914–97 (to Allen Ginsberg over the telephone), in Barry Miles, *Ginsberg*, Ch. 17]

2 It isn't that they can't see the solution. It is that they can't see the problem. [G K Chesterton, 1874–1936, *The Scandal of Father Brown*, 'The Point of a Pin']

3 What we're saying today is that you're either part of the solution or you're part of the problem. [Eldridge Cleaver, 1935–98, speech in San Francisco, 1968]

4 There are two problems in my life. The political ones are insoluble and the economic ones are incomprehensible. [Alec Douglas-Home, 1903–95, speech, Jan. 1964]

5 It is quite a three-pipe problem. [Arthur Conan Doyle, 1859–1930, *The Adventures of Sherlock Holmes*, 'The Red-headed League']

6 The basic problems facing the world today are not susceptible to a military solution. [President John F Kennedy, 1917–63, in *Saturday Review*, 'Ideas, Attitudes, Purposes from His Speeches and Writings', 7 Dec. 1963]

7 The fascination of what's difficult. / Has dried the sap out of my veins, and rent / Spontaneous joy and natural content / Out of my heart. [W B Yeats, 1865–1939, *The Fascination of What's Difficult*]

PROCRASTINATION

1 Right now would be a good time to postpone everything. [Ashley Brilliant, 1933– , *Pot-Shots*, # 3487]

2 Procrastination is the / art of keeping / up with yesterday [Don Marquis, 1878–1937, *archy and mehitabel*, XII, 'certain maxims of archy']

3 Letting 'I dare not' wait upon 'I would', / Like the poor cat i' the adage. [William Shakespeare, 1564–1616, *Macbeth*, I. vii. 44]

4 Make me a beautiful word for doing things tomorrow, for that surely is a great and blessed invention. [George Bernard Shaw, 1856–1950, *Back to Methuselah*, Pt One, I]

5 Be wise today: 'tis madness to defer. [Edward Young, 1683–1765, *Night Thoughts*, 'Night I' 390]

6 Procrastination is the thief of time. [Edward Young, 1683–1765, *Night Thoughts*, 'Night I' 393]

See also LATENESS

PROCREATION

1 I was ever of the opinion, that the honest man who married and brought up a large family, did more service than he who continued single, and only talked of population. [Oliver Goldsmith, 1728–74, *The Vicar of Wakefield*, Ch. 1]

2 A million million spermatozoa, / All of them alive: / Out of their cataclysm but one poor Noah / Dare hope to survive. / And among that billion minus one / Might have chanced to be / Shakespeare, another Newton, a new Donne – / But the One was Me. [Aldous Huxley, 1894–1963, *The Fifth Philosopher's Song*]

3 The command 'Be fruitful and multiply' [was] promulgated according to our authorities, when the population of the world consisted of two persons. [W R Inge, 1860–1954, *More Lay Thoughts of a Dean*, Pt I, 6]

4 Nature's only interest is in having you procreate, then it throws you away. [Fay Weldon, 1931– , in *Guardian*, 15 Jan. 1992]

5 The cat is the offspring of a cat and the dog of a dog, but butlers and lady's maids do not reproduce their kind. They have other duties. [H G Wells, 1866–1946, *Bealby*, Pt I, Ch. 1]

See also PARENTS, SEX

PROFESSIONS & TRADES

1 Charles Robertson is an accountant. If they come any greyer than that they're squirrels. [Nancy Banks-Smith, 1929– , in *Guardian*, 12 Apr. 1989]

2 'Golden hands he's got,' said his father gloomily. 'A pianist's hands. Or a surgeon's hands.' 'Both,' said his mother. She blew her nose fiercely. 'He could have been both. Operating by day, by night playing Bach.' [Alan Coren, 1938– , *The Sanity Inspector*, 'Wholesale War']

3 In every age and clime we see, / Two of a trade can ne'er agree. [John Gay, 1685–1732, *Fables*, Pt I, xxi, 43]

4 In order to prove its phoniness beyond reasonable doubt, a profession has to create grave problems which it then fails to solve. [Hans Keller, 1919–85, *Criticism*, Pt 1, Ch. 1]

5 I went underground as a miner at fourteen and worked fourteen years in a seam which was 1 foot 10 inches high. Even the mice were bow-legged. [Roy Mason, 1924– , maiden speech in House of Lords, Nov. 1987]

6 Our experts describe you as an appallingly dull fellow, unimaginative, timid, spineless, easily dominated, no sense of humour, tedious company and irresistibly drab and awful. And whereas in most professions these would be considered drawbacks, in accountancy they are a positive boon. [Monty Python's Flying Circus, 1969–74, in film *And Now for Something Completely Different*]

7 There are two professions ... whose practitioners are never satisfied with what they do: dentists and photographers. Every dentist would like to be a doctor and every photographer would like to be a painter. [Pablo Picasso, 1881–1973, in Françoise Gilot and Carlton Lake, *Life with P*, Pt 2]

8 All professions are conspiracies against the laity. [George Bernard Shaw, 1856–1950, *The Doctor's Dilemma*, I]

9 People of the same trade seldom meet together, even for merriment and diversion, but the conversation ends in a conspiracy against the public, or in some contrivance to raise prices. [Adam Smith, 1723–90, *The Wealth of Nations*, Vol. ii, Bk i, Ch. 10, Pt ii]

10 Everybody hates house-agents because they have everybody at a disadvantage. All other callings have a certain amount of give and take; the house-agent simply takes. [H G Wells, 1866–1946, *Kipps*, Bk III, Ch. 1, iii]

See also DOCTORS, LAWYERS, WORK

PROGRESS

1 Mr Craven's always been on the side of progress: he had false teeth when he was twenty-seven. [Alan Bennett, 1934– , *Enjoy*, I]

2 Society moves by some degree of parricide, by which the children, on the whole, kill, if not their fathers, at least the beliefs of their fathers, and arrive at new beliefs. This is what progress is. [Isaiah Berlin, 1909–97, in BBC TV programme *Men of Ideas*, 19 Jan. 1978]

3 Without contraries is no progression. [William Blake, 1757–1827, *The Marriage of Heaven and Hell*, 'The Argument']

4 Progress is / The law of life, man is not man as yet. [Robert Browning, 1812–89, *Paracelsus*, V]

5 All progress is based upon a universal innate desire on the part of every organism to live beyond its income. [Samuel Butler, 1835–1902, *Notebooks*, Ch. 1 'Life', 16]

6 As enunciated today, 'progress' is simply a comparative of which we have not settled the superlative. [G K Chesterton, 1874–1936, *Heretics*, Ch. 2]

7 What we call progress is the exchange of one nuisance for another nuisance. [Havelock Ellis, 1859–1939, *Impressions and Comments*, 31 July 1912]

8 The best way out is always through. [Robert Frost, 1874–1963, *A Servant to Servants*]

9 All that is human must be retrograde if it does not advance. [Edward Gibbon, 1737–94, *The Decline and Fall of the Roman Empire*, Ch. 71]

10 It is because nations tend towards stupidity and baseness that mankind moves so slowly; it is because individuals have a capacity for better things that it moves at all. [George Gissing, 1857–1903, *The Private Papers of Henry Ryecroft*, 'Spring', XVI]

11 You'll probably say that progress can be good or bad, like Jews or Germans or films! [Eugene Ionesco, 1912–94, *Maid to Marry*]

12 Time would pass, old empires would fall and new ones take their place, the relations of countries and the relations of classes had to change, before I discovered that it is not quality of goods and utility which matter, but movement; not where you are or what you have, but where you have come from, where you are going and the rate at which you are getting there.

[C L R James, 1901–89, *Beyond a Boundary*, Ch. 8]

13 People fascinated by the idea of progress never suspect that every step forward is also a step on the way to the end. [Milan Kundera, 1929– , *The Book of Laughter and Forgetting*, Pt 6, 17]

14 Is it progress if a cannibal uses knife and fork? [Stanislaw Lec, 1909–66, *Unkempt Thoughts*, p. 78]

15 Nothing is settled, everything can still be altered. What was done but turned out wrong, can be done again. The Golden Age, which blind superstition had placed behind [or ahead of] us, is *in us*. [Claude Lévi-Strauss, 1908– , *Tristes Tropiques*, Ch. 38]

16 The history of England is emphatically the history of progress. [Lord Macaulay, 1800–1859, *Historical Essays*, 'Sir J. Mackintosh's History of the Revolution']

17 There comes a time in a man's life when to get where he has to go – if there are no doors or windows he walks through a wall. [Bernard Malamud, 1914–86, *Rembrandt's Hat*, 'Man in the Drawer']

18 Today, the notion of progress in a single line without goal or limit seems perhaps the most parochial notion of a very parochial century. [Lewis Mumford, 1895–1990, *Technics and Civilization*, Ch. 8, sect. xii]

19 Progress would be wonderful – if only it would stop. [Robert Musil, 1880–1942, attr.]

20 The New Age? It's just the old age stuck in a microwave oven for fifteen seconds. [James Randi, 1928– ; *Observer*, 'Sayings of the Week', 14 Apr. 1991]

21 You can't say civilization don't advance, however, for in every war they kill you a new way. [Will Rogers, 1879–1935, *Autobiography*, Ch. 14]

22 Organic life, we are told, has developed gradually from the protozoon to the philosopher and this development, we are assured, is indubitably an advance. Unfortunately it is the philosopher, not the protozoon, who gives us this assurance. [Bertrand Russell, 1872–1970, *Mysticism and Logic*, Ch. 6]

23 Progress, far from consisting in change, depends on retentiveness ... Those who do not remember the past are condemned to repeat it. [George Santayana, 1863–1952, *The Life of Reason*, Vol. 1, Ch. 12]

24 The reasonable man adapts himself to the world; the unreasonable one persists in trying to adapt the world to himself. Therefore all progress depends on the unreasonable man. [George Bernard Shaw, 1856–1950, *Man and Superman*, 'Maxims for Revolutionists', Reason]

25 Progress, therefore, is not an accident, but a necessity ... It is a part of nature. [Herbert Spencer, 1820–1903, *Social Statics*, I, Ch. 2, 4]

26 All change in history, all advance, comes from the non-conformists. If there had been no troublemakers, no Dissenters, we should still be living in caves. [A J P Taylor, 1906–90, *The Troublemakers*, 1]

27 Yet I doubt not thro' the ages one increasing purpose runs, / And the thoughts of men are widened with the process of the suns. [Alfred, Lord Tennyson, 1809–92, *Locksley Hall*, 137]

28 I say she used to be no better than she ought to be, but she is now. [James Thurber, 1894–1961, *Men, Women and Dogs*, cartoon caption]

See also FUTURE, IMPROVEMENT

PROMISCUITY

1 I see – she's the original good time that was had by all. [Bette Davis, 1908–89, of a starlet; in L Halliwell, *Filmgoer's Book of Quotes*]

2 And, wide as his command, / Scattered his Maker's image through the land. [John Dryden, 1631–1700, *Absalom and Achitophel*, Pt I, 9]

3 Lady Capricorn, he understood, was still keeping open bed. [Aldous Huxley, 1894–1963, *Antic Hay*, 21]

4 You were born with your legs apart. They'll send you to the grave in a Y-shaped coffin. [Joe Orton, 1933–67, *What the Butler Saw*, I]

5 Accursed from their birth they be / Who seek to find monogamy, / Pursuing it from bed to bed – / I think they would be better dead. [Dorothy Parker, 1893–1967, *Reuben's Children*]

6 That woman speaks eighteen languages, and can't say No in any of them. [Dorothy Parker, 1893–1967, in Alexander Woollcott, *While Rome Burns*, 'Our Mrs Parker']

7 If all the girls attending it [a Yale prom] were

laid end to end, I wouldn't be at all surprised. [Dorothy Parker, 1893–1967, in Alexander Woollcott, *While Rome Burns*, 'Our Mrs Parker']

8 Lechery, lechery; still, wars and lechery; nothing else holds fashion. [William Shakespeare, 1564–1616, *Troilus and Cressida*, V. ii. (192)]

9 'I find it rather sad. Mrs Hart had a hard life.' 'You mean she led a hard life,' declared Marion. 'She was a trull before she could toddle.' [Thorne Smith, 1892–1934, *Topper Takes a Trip*, Ch. 14]

See also ADULTERY

PROMISE

1 I do set my bow in the cloud, and it shall be for a token of a covenant between me and the earth. [Bible, OT, *Genesis* 9:13]

2 The rule is, jam to-morrow and jam yesterday – but never jam to-day. [Lewis Carroll, 1832–98, *Through the Looking Glass*, Ch. 5]

3 Work and pray, live on hay. / You'll get pie in the sky when you die. [Joe Hill, 1879–1915, song: *The Preacher and the Slave*]

4 You won't have Nixon to kick around any more, because, gentlemen, this is my last Press Conference. [President Nixon, 1913–94, after losing election for governorship of California, 7 Nov. 1962]

5 I pledge you – I pledge myself – to a new deal for the American people. [Franklin D Roosevelt, 1882–1945, speech at convention, Chicago, 2 July 1932]

6 Promises and pie-crust are made to be broken. [Jonathan Swift, 1677–1745, *Polite Conversation*, Dialogue 1]

PROMOTION

1 Tired of knocking at Preferment's door. [Matthew Arnold, 1822–88, *The Scholar-Gypsy*, 35]

2 He [Halifax] had said that he had known many kicked downstairs, but he never knew any kicked upstairs before. [Bishop Gilbert Burnet, 1643–1715, *Original Memoirs*]

3 And while no doubt talent will find its own level, it remains true that the son-in-law also rises. [(Of promotion in business) Ferdinand Mount, 1939– , from *Spectator*, quoted in *New Statesman*, 12 Oct. 1984]

4 *Lateral Arabesque* – a pseudo-promotion consisting of a new title and a new work place. [Laurence J Peter, 1919–90, and Raymond Hull, 1918–85, *The Peter Principle*, Glossary]

See also AMBITIONS

PROPAGANDA

1 The real struggle is not between East and West, or capitalism and communism, but between education and propaganda. [Martin Buber, 1878–1961, in A Hodes, *Encounter with M B*]

2 Propaganda is that branch of the art of lying which consists in nearly deceiving your friends without quite deceiving your enemies. [F M Cornford, 1874–1943, *Microcosmographia Academica*, preface to 1922 edn]

3 Whoever says the first word to the world is right. [Josef Goebbels, 1897–1945, in *The Media in British Politics*, ed. Ben Pimlott and Jean Seaton]

4 If you feed people just with revolutionary slogans they will listen today, they will listen tomorrow, they will listen the day after tomorrow, but on the fourth day they will say 'To hell with you.' [Nikita Khrushchev, 1894–1971, in *The New York Times*, 4 Oct. 1964]

5 To be effective propaganda has to be confirmation, at some level, of people's desires. [Thomas Kilroy, 1934– , *Double Cross*, Pt 2]

6 Newspeak was the official language of Oceania. [George Orwell, 1903–50, *1984*, Pt 1, Ch. 1, footnote]

See also LIES, NEWS

PROPERTY

1 Well, some people talk of morality, and some of religion, but give me a little snug property. [Maria Edgeworth, 1767–1849, *The Absentee*, Ch. 2]

2 Few rich men own their own property. The property owns them. [R G Ingersoll, 1833–99, address to the McKinley League, New York, 29 Oct. 1896]

3 *La propriété c'est le vol.* – Property is theft. [Pierre-Joseph Proudhon, 1809–65, *Qu'est-ce que la propriété?*]

4 Dosn't thou 'ear my 'erse's legs, as they canters awaäy? / Proputty, proputty, proputty – that's what I 'ears 'em saäy. [Alfred, Lord Tennyson, 1809–92, *Northern Farmer. New Style*, 1]

See also CAPITALISM, RICH, WEALTH

PROPHETS & PROPHECY

1 If there arise among you a prophet, or a dreamer of dreams ... [Bible, OT, *Deuteronomy* 13:1]

2 Prophesy unto the wind. [Bible, OT, *Ezekiel* 37:9]

3 He hath sent me to bind up the broken-hearted, to proclaim liberty to the captives, and the opening of the prison to them that are bound; To proclaim the acceptable year of the Lord, and the day of vengeance of our God; to comfort all that mourn. [Bible, OT, *Isaiah* 61:1]

4 Beware of false prophets, which come to you in sheep's clothing, but inwardly they are ravening wolves. [Bible, NT, *St Matthew* 7:15]

5 A prophet is not without honour, save in his own country. [Bible, NT, *St Matthew* 13:57]

6 It's a habit with prophets to be unhealthy. / Most seers are cripples. [Joseph Brodsky, 1940–96, *Adieu, Mademoiselle Véronique*, V]

7 A hopeful disposition is not the sole qualification to be a prophet. [Winston Churchill, 1874–1965, speech in House of Commons, 30 Apr. 1927]

8 Madame Sosostris, famous clairvoyante, / Had a bad cold, nevertheless / Is known to be the wisest woman in Europe, / With a wicked pack of cards. [T S Eliot, 1888–1965, *The Waste Land*, 43]

9 I was asked in Japan recently not to predict the end of the world – they were nervous it might affect the stock market. [Stephen Hawking, 1942– , in lecture at Royal Albert Hall, London; *Independent*, 'Quote Unquote', 25 Nov. 1995]

10 The Queen of air and darkness / Begins to shrill and cry, / 'O young man, O my slayer, / To-morrow you shall die.' [A E Housman, 1859–1936, *Last Poems*, 3]

11 You can only predict things after they've happened. [Eugene Ionesco, 1912–94, *Rhinoceros*, III]

12 Nothing odd will do long. *Tristram Shandy* did not last. [Dr Samuel Johnson, 1709–84, in James Boswell, *Life of J*, 20 Mar. 1776]

13 I have a dream that my four little children will one day live in a nation where they will not be judged by the colour of their skin but by the content of their character. [Martin Luther King Jr, 1929–68, speech in Washington on completion of civil rights march, 28 Aug. 1963]

14 My gran'ther's rule was safer 'n 't is to crow: / Don't never prophesy – onless ye know. [James Russell Lowell, 1819–91, *The Biglow Papers*, Second Series, 2]

15 Prophets were twice stoned – first in anger; then, after their death, with a handsome slab in the graveyard. [Christopher Morley, 1890–1957, *Where the Blue Begins*, Ch. 11]

16 As I look ahead, I am filled with foreboding. Like the Roman, I seem to see 'the River Tiber foaming with much blood'. [(Of race relations in Britain) Enoch Powell, 1912–98, speech in Birmingham, 20 Apr. 1968]

17 When you are very old and sit at evening beside the fire, by candlelight, carding and spinning, you will say with wonder, as you recite my verses: 'Ronsard sang of me in the time when I was fair.' [Pierre de Ronsard, 1524–85, *Sonnets to Hélène*, II, 43]

18 There's a gude time coming. [Sir Walter Scott, 1771–1832, *Rob Roy*, Ch. 32]; see 24

19 If you can look into the seeds of time, / And say which grain will grow and which will not. [William Shakespeare, 1564–1616, *Macbeth*, I. iii. 58]

20 Methinks I am a prophet new inspired, / And thus expiring do foretell of him: / His rash fierce blaze of riot cannot last, / For violent fires soon burn out themselves; / Small showers last long, but sudden storms are short; / He tires betimes that spurs too fast betimes. [*Richard II*, II. i. 31]

21 Not mine own fears, nor the prophetic soul / Of the wide world dreaming on things to come. [*Sonnets*, 107]

22 The words of the prophets are written / On the subway walls and tenement halls. [Paul Simon, 1942– , song: *Sound of Silence*]

23 The next Augustan age will dawn on the other side of the Atlantic . . . At last some curious traveller from Lima will visit England, and give a description of the ruins of St Paul's, like the editions of Balbec and Palmyra. [Horace Walpole, 1717–97, letter to Horace Mann, 24 Nov. 1774]

24 There's a good time coming, it's almost here, / 'Twas a long, long time on the way. [H C Work, 1832–84, *Wake Nicodemus*]; see 18

See also FUTURE, OPTIMISM

PROSE

1 Yet no one hears his own remarks as prose. [W H Auden, 1907–73, *At a Party*]

2 Poetry, in fact, bears the same kind of relation to Prose, using prose simply in the sense of all those uses of words that are not poetry, that algebra bears to arithmetic. [W H Auden, 1907–73, and J Garrett, 1902–66, *The Poet's Tongue*, Introduction]

3 Prose = words in their best order; poetry = the *best* words in the best order. [Samuel Taylor Coleridge, 1772–1834, *Table Talk*, 12 July 1827]

4 For to write good prose is an affair of good manners. It is, unlike verse, a civil art . . . Poetry is baroque. [W Somerset Maugham, 1874–1965, *The Summing Up*, Ch. 12]

5 What? When I say, 'Nicole, bring me my slippers and give me my nightcap'; that's prose? . . . Gracious me! I've been talking prose for the last forty years and have never known it. [Molière, 1622–73, *Le Bourgeois Gentilhomme*, II. iv]

6 In prose, the worst thing one can do with words is surrender to them. [George Orwell, 1903–50, *Collected Essays*, 'Politics and the English Language']

7 Poetry is to prose as dancing is to walking. [John Wain, 1925–94, talk on BBC radio, 13 Jan. 1976]

8 The poet gives us his essence, but prose takes the mould of the body and mind entire. [Virginia Woolf, 1882–1941, *The Captain's Death Bed*, 'Reading']

9 A good essay must have this permanent quality about it; it must draw its curtain round us, but it must be a curtain that shuts us in not out. [Virginia Woolf, 1882–1941, *The Common Reader*, First Series, 'The Modern Essay']

10 There neither is, nor can be, any *essential* difference between the language of prose and metrical composition. [William Wordsworth, 1770–1850, *Lyrical Ballads*, Preface]

11 O'CONNOR: How are you?
YEATS: Not very well, I can only write prose today. [W B Yeats, 1865–1939, attr.]

12 Great prose may occur by accident: but not great poetry. [G M Young, 1882–1959, in *Geoffrey Madan's Notebooks*, ed. J A Gere and John Sparrow, 'Extracts and Summaries']

See also BOOKS, LITERATURE, NOVELISTS, POETRY, POETS, WRITERS, WRITING

PROSPERITY, see ADVERSITY

PROSTITUTION

1 The harlot's cry from street to street / Shall weave old England's winding-sheet. [William Blake, 1757–1827, *Auguries of Innocence*]

2 When a soldier sees a clean face, there's one more whore in the world. [Bertolt Brecht, 1898–1956, *Mother Courage*, III]

3 Prostitution gives her an opportunity to meet people. It provides fresh air and wholesome exercise, and it keeps her out of trouble. [Joseph Heller, 1923–99, *Catch-22*, Ch. 33]

4 On street corners prostitutes who must have fallen below any standards of dress or appearance set by the EEC stood in their oldest clothes. [Howard Jacobson, 1942– , *Coming from Behind*, Ch. 4]

5 Keeping body and soul together is never as difficult as trying to keep them separate. [Suzanne Lowry, in *Guardian*, 24 May 1974]

6 You can lead a whore to culture but you can't make her think. [Dorothy Parker, 1893–1967, speech to American Horticultural Society, in J Keats, *You Might as Well Live*, Pt 1, Ch. 2]

7 I don't think doing it for money makes it any more moral. I don't think a prostitute is more moral than a wife, but they are doing the same thing. [Philip, Duke of Edinburgh, 1921– , speech in London, 6 Dec. 1988]

8 If you want to buy my wares, / Follow me and climb the stairs. / Love for sale. [Cole Porter, 1891–1964, song: *Love for Sale*, in musical *The New Yorkers*]

9 She chuckled when a bawd was carted: / And thought the nation ne'er would thrive, / Till all the whores were burnt alive. [Matthew Prior, 1664–1721, *Paolo Purganti and his Wife*, 44]

10 She's one of the finest women who ever walked the streets. [Mae West, 1892–1980; in L Halliwell, *Filmgoer's Book of Quotes*]

11 The power to get other people to do things has been the prerogative of the harlot throughout the ages – and of the manager. [Katharine Whitehorn, 1926– , in *Observer*, 26 May 1985]

12 A point of view (I invented this). 'I always give the whores as little as possible: I don't think that prostitution ought to be encouraged.' [Edmund Wilson, 1895–1972, *The Twenties*, 'After the War']

13 Don't take your wife into a brothel, they'll charge you corkage! [In *Wine Graffiti Book*, 'The Four Muscateers']

PROTESTANTS

1 You will be damned if you do – And you will be damned if you don't. [(Definition of Calvinism) Lorenzo Dow, 1777–1834, *Reflections on the Love of God*, 6]

2 She detested Protestantism, from the pneumatic sterility of Milton to the ankle socks and hairy calves of the vicar's wife. [Alice Thomas Ellis, 1932– , *The Sin Eater*, p. 77]

3 Searching the scriptures for hints of things to come, preferably unpleasant, has always been a favourite pastime of extreme Protestantism. [Osbert Lancaster, 1908–86, *With an Eye to the Future*, Ch. 1]

4 The chief contribution of Protestantism to human thought is its massive proof that God is a bore. [H L Mencken, 1880–1956, *Minority Report*, 309]

5 The solitary monk who shook the world. [Robert Montgomery, 1807–55, *Luther, Man's Need and God's Supply*, 68]

See also CATHOLICS, CHRISTIANITY, CHURCHES, CHURCH OF ENGLAND

PSYCHIATRY/PSYCHOANALYSIS

1 In psycho-analysis nothing is true except the exaggerations. [Theodor Adorno, 1903–69, *Minima Memoralia*, Pt 1, 29]

2 I worked with Freud in Vienna. Um yes, we, we broke over the concept of penis envy. Freud felt that it should be limited to women. [Woody Allen, 1935– , in film *Zelig*]

3 The new definition of psychiatry is the care of the id by the odd. [anon.; in M B Strauss, *Familiar Medical Quotations*]

4 To us he is no more a person. / Now but a whole climate of opinion / Under whom we conduct our differing lives. [W H Auden, 1907–73, *In Memory of Sigmund Freud*]

5 Therapy has become what I think of as the tenth American muse. [J Bronowski, 1908–74, in *Radio Times*]

6 Perhaps psychoanalysis could only come about in a Vienna of stiff collars and whalebone corsets. If Freud had worn a kilt in the prescribed Highland manner he might have had a different attitude to genitals. [Anthony Burgess, 1917–93, in *Observer*, 24 Aug. 1986]

7 Psychiatry's chief contribution to philosophy is the discovery that the toilet is the seat of the soul. [Alexander Chase, 1926– , *Perspectives*]

8 Or look at it this way. Psychoanalysis is a permanent fad. [Peter de Vries, 1910–93, *Forever Panting*, opening words]

9 The trouble with Freud is that he never played the Glasgow Empire Saturday night. [Ken Dodd, 1927– (interview in ATV programme *The Laughter Makers*), in *The Times*, 7 Aug. 1965]

10 I do not think our successes can compete with those of Lourdes. There are so many more people who believe in the miracles of the Blessed Virgin than in the existence of the unconscious. [Sigmund Freud, 1856–1939, *New Introductory Lectures*, Lecture 34]

11 Psycho-analysis has revealed to us that the totem animal is really a substitute for the father, and this really explains to us the contradiction that it is usually forbidden to kill the totem animal, that the killing of it results in a holiday, and that the animal is killed and yet mourned. [Sigmund Freud, 1856–1939, *Totem and Taboo*, Ch. 4, sect. v]

12 I am actually not at all a man of science, not

an observer, not an experimenter, not a thinker. I am by temperament nothing but a conquistador – an adventurer. [Sigmund Freud, 1856–1939, letter to Wilhelm Fliess, Feb. 1900]

13 Anybody who goes to see a psychiatrist ought to have his head examined. [Samuel Goldwyn, 1882–1974, attr., but probably invented by one of his staff]

14 'You're crazy,' Clevinger shouted vehemently, his eyes filling with tears. 'You've got a Jehovah complex.' [Joseph Heller, 1923–99, *Catch-22*, Ch. 2]

15 I felt quite funny when Freud died. It was like having a continent disappear. [Randall Jarrell, 1914–65, letter to Allen Tate, Sept. 1939]

16 Among all my patients in the second half of life – that is to say over thirty-five – there has not been one whose problem in the last resort was not that of finding a religious outlook on life. [C G Jung, 1875–1961, *Modern Man in Search of His Soul*]

17 Psychoanalysis is that mental illness for which it regards itself as therapy. [Karl Kraus, 1874–1936, *Half-truths and One-and-a-half Truths*, 'In Hollow Heads']

18 Actually I always loathed the Viennese quack. I used to stalk him down dark alleys of thought, and now we shall never forget the sight of old, flustered Freud seeking to unlock his door with the point of his umbrella. [Vladimir Nabakov, 1899–1977 (TV interview), in *Listener*, 24 Mar. 1977]

19 Psychoanalysis only begins, in any sense, to work when people begin to be impressed by their symptoms. [Adam Phillips, 1954– , in *Mind Readings*, ed. Sarah Dunn et al.]

20 A psychiatrist is a man who goes to the Folies-Bergère and looks at the audience. [Mervyn Stockwood, 1913–95; *Observer*, 'Sayings of the Week', 15 Oct. 1961, but probably of earlier origin]

21 Psychiatrists classify a person as neurotic if he suffers from his problems in living, and as psychotic if he makes others suffer. [Thomas Szasz, 1920– , *The Second Sin*, 'Psychiatry']

22 Like all analysts Randolph is interested only in himself. In fact, I have often thought that the analyst should pay the patient for allowing himself to be used as a captive looking-glass. [Gore Vidal, 1925– , *Myra Breckinridge*, Ch. 37]

See also ILLNESS, MIND, NEUROSIS, UNCONSCIOUS

PSYCHOLOGY

1 Behavioural psychology is the science of pulling habits out of rats. [Dr Douglas Busch; in Laurence J Peter, *Peter's Quotations*]

2 When Dr Watson watches rats in mazes, what he knows, apart from difficult inferences are certain events in himself. [Arthur Eddington, 1882–1944, *Science and the Unseen World*]

3 I am not fond of the word psychological. There is no such thing as psychological. Let us say that one can improve the biography of the person. [Jean-Paul Sartre, 1905–80, in R D Laing, *The Divided Self*, Ch. 8]

4 A large part of the popularity and persuasiveness of psychology comes from its being a sublimated spiritualism: a secular, ostensibly scientific way of affirming the primacy of 'spirit' over matter. [Susan Sontag, 1933– , *Illness as Metaphor*, Ch. 7]

See also BEHAVIOUR, MIND

THE PUB

1 I rarely drink alone where I'm known; they always think you've quarrelled with your wife. [Lincoln Allison, 1946– , in *New Society*, 20 Mar. 1980]

2 When you have lost your inns drown your empty selves, for you will have lost the last of England. [Hilaire Belloc, 1870–1953, *This and That*, 'On Inns']

3 He knew the tavernes wel in every toun. [Geoffrey Chaucer, 1340?–1400, *Canterbury Tales*, 'Prologue', 240]

4 God made the wicked Grocer / For a mystery and a sign, / That men might shun the awful shop / And go to inns to dine. [G K Chesterton, 1874–1936, *The Song against Grocers*]

5 The *incognito* of an inn is one of its striking privileges. [William Hazlitt, 1778–1830, *On Going a Journey*]

6 There is nothing which has yet been contrived by man, by which so much happiness is produced as by a good tavern or inn. [Dr Samuel Johnson,

1709–84, in James Boswell, *Life of J*, 21 Mar. 1776]

7 Souls of poets dead and gone, / What Elysium have ye known, / Happy field or mossy cavern, / Choicer than the Mermaid Tavern? / Have ye tippled drink more fine / Than mine host's Canary wine? [John Keats, 1795–1821, *Lines on the Mermaid Tavern*]

8 In seventy years the one surviving fragment of my knowledge, the only indisputable poor particle of certainty in my entire life is that in a public-house lavatory incoming traffic has the right of way. [Hugh Leonard, 1926– , *Da*]

9 If die I must, let me die drinking in an inn. [Walter Map, *c.*1140–*c.*1209, *De Nugis Curialium*]

10 A fire has destroyed the Chameleon at Strood, / Which makes me exceedingly glad; / For the waitresses there were disgustingly rude / And the food was incredibly bad. [Michael Pope, 1875–1930, *Capital Levities*, 'Epitaph on a Country Inn Destroyed by Fire']

11 'May not the darkness hide it from my face?' / 'You cannot miss that inn.' [Christina Rossetti, 1830–94, *Up-Hill*]

12 Whoe'er has travelled life's dull round, / Where'er his stages may have been, / May sigh to think he still has found / The warmest welcome, at an inn. [William Shenstone, 1714–63, *At an Inn at Henley*]

13 The ship's clock in the bar says half past eleven. Half past eleven is opening time. The hands of the clock have stayed still at half past eleven for fifty years. It is always opening time in the Sailors Arms. [Dylan Thomas, 1914–53, *Under Milk Wood*]

See also DRINK, HOSPITALITY, HOTELS

THE PUBLIC, see MASSES

PUBLISHING, see EDITORS

PUNCTUALITY

1 I meant to be prompt, but it never occurred to me that I had better try to be early. [Clarence Day, 1874–1935, *Life with Father*, 'Father Teaches Me to be Prompt']

2 He was so punctual, you could regulate / The sun by him. [Christopher Fry, 1907– , *A Phoenix Too Frequent*]

3 Sir, Sunday morning, although recurring at regular and well foreseen intervals, always seems to take this railway by surprise. [W S Gilbert, 1836–1911, in a letter of complaint to the stationmaster at Baker Street on the Metropolitan Line, quoted in John Julius Norwich, *A Christmas Cracker*]

4 Punctuality is the politeness of kings. [Louis XVIII, 1755–1824, attr.]

5 Punctuality is the virtue of the bored. [Evelyn Waugh, 1903–66, *Diaries*, ed. M Davie, 'Irregular Notes', 26 Mar. 1962]

See also LATENESS, PROCRASTINATION, TIME

PUNISHMENTS & REWARDS

1 Severity breedeth fear, but roughness breedeth hate. Even reproofs from authority ought to be grave and not taunting. [Francis Bacon, 1561–1626, *Essays*, 11, 'Of Great Place']

2 All punishment is mischief: all punishment in itself is evil. [Jeremy Bentham, 1748–1832, *Principles of Morals and Legislation*, Ch. 13]

3 Having been a little chastised, they shall be greatly rewarded. [Bible, Apocrypha, *Wisdom of Solomon* 3:5]

4 They have sown the wind, and they shall reap the whirlwind. [Bible, OT, *Hosea* 8:7]

5 My father hath chastised you with whips, but I will chastise you with scorpions. [Bible, OT, *1 Kings* 12:11]

6 Unto you that fear my name shall the Sun of righteousness arise with healing in his wings. [Bible, OT, *Malachi* 4:2]

7 He that spareth his rod hateth his son. [Bible, OT, *Proverbs* 13:24]

8 Thou shalt break them with a rod of iron; thou shalt dash them in pieces like a potter's vessel. [Bible, OT, *Psalms* 2:9]

9 Whom the Lord loveth he chasteneth. [Bible, NT, *Hebrews* 12:6]

10 Speak roughly to your little boy, / And beat him when he sneezes: / He only does it to annoy, / Because he knows it teases. [Lewis Carroll, 1832–98, *Alice in Wonderland*, Ch. 6]

11 Far better hang wrong fler [fellow] than no fler. [Charles Dickens, 1812–70, *Bleak House*, 53]

12 Thwackum was for doing justice, and leaving mercy to heaven. [Henry Fielding, 1707–54, *Tom Jones*, Bk iii, 10]

13 My object all sublime / I shall achieve in time – / To let the punishment fit the crime. [W S Gilbert, 1836–1911, *The Mikado*, II]

14 We will hang you, never fear, / Most politely, most politely! [W S Gilbert, 1836–1911, *The Pirates of Penzance*, I]

15 Men are not hanged for stealing horses, but that horses may not be stolen. [Marquis of Halifax, 1663–95, *Political Thoughts and Reflections*, 'Of Punishment']

16 This is the first punishment, that by the verdict of his own heart no guilty man is acquitted. [Juvenal, 60–*c.*130, *Satires*, XIII, 2]

17 If you strike a child, take care that you strike it in anger, even at the risk of maiming it for life. A blow in cold blood neither can nor should be forgiven. [George Bernard Shaw, 1856–1950, *Man and Superman*, 'Maxims for Revolutionists', How to Beat Children]

18 He must have known me if he had seen me and he was wont to see me, for he was in the habit of flogging me constantly. Perhaps he did not recognize me by my face. [Anthony Trollope, 1815–82, *Autobiography*, Ch. 1]

19 I'm all for bringing back the birch, but only between consenting adults. [Gore Vidal, 1925– , on a David Frost TV programme about corporal punishment; in *The Sunday Times Magazine*, 16 Sept. 1973]

See also CRIME, JUSTICE, VICE

PURITANS

1 A puritan's a person who pours righteous indignation into the wrong things. [G K Chesterton, 1874–1936, in *The New York Times*, 30 Nov. 1930]

2 Puritanism in other people we admire is austerity in ourselves. [Cyril Connolly, 1903–74, *Enemies of Promise*, Ch. 9]

3 It was the Puritans who put an end to the practice of dancing, as well as discontinuing the tradition of kings wearing heads on their shoulders. [Mike Harding, 1944– ; in *Apt and Amusing Quotations*, ed. G F Lamb, 'History']

4 To the Puritan all things are impure. [D H Lawrence, 1885–1930, *Etruscan Places*, 'Cerveteri']

5 The Puritan hated bear-baiting, not because it gave pain to the bear, but because it gave pleasure to the spectators. [Lord Macaulay, 1800–1859, *History of England*, I, Ch. 2]

6 Puritanism was the schoolmaster of the English middle classes. It heightened their virtues, sanctified, without eradicating, their convenient vices, and gave them an inexpugnable assurance that, behind virtues and vices alike, stood the inexorable laws of an omnipotent Providence. [R H Tawney, 1880–1962, *Religion and the Rise of Capitalism*, Ch. IV, ii]

See also PROTESTANTS

PURITY

1 I'm as pure as the driven slush. [Tallulah Bankhead, 1903–68; *Observer*, 'Sayings of the Week', 24 Feb. 1957]

2 Purge me with hyssop, and I shall be clean: wash me, and I shall be whiter than snow. [Bible, OT, *Psalms* 51:7]

3 Unto the pure all things are pure. [Bible, NT, *Titus* 1:15]

4 There's a woman like a dew-drop, she's so purer than the purest. [Robert Browning, 1812–89, *A Blot in the 'Scutcheon*, I, iii]

5 Be warm, but pure; be amorous, but be chaste. [Lord Byron, 1788–1824, *English Bards and Scotch Reviewers*, 306]

6 One cannot be precise and still be pure. [Marc Chagall, 1889–1985; *Observer*, 'Sayings of the Week', 3 May 1964]

7 Clear the air! clean the sky! wash the wind! take stone from stone and wash them. [T S Eliot, 1888–1965, *Murder in the Cathedral*, II]

8 Have you seen but a bright lily grow, / Before rude hands have touched it? / Have you marked but the fall o' the snow / Before the soil hath smutched it? . . . O so white! O so soft! O so sweet is she! [Ben Jonson, 1573–1637, *Celebration of Charis*, IV, 'Her Triumph']

9 I can understand why the pure of heart are generally religious people. If you believed that there was a fanlight in your mind, through which an old man with a beard was perpetually peering, taking down notes, you would think twice about throwing orgies in there. [David Lodge, 1935– , *Ginger, You're Barmy*, 4]

10 Wearing the white flower of a blameless life. [Alfred, Lord Tennyson, 1809–92, *Idylls of the King*, Dedication, 24]

11 Blessed are the pure in heart for they have so much more to talk about. [Edith Wharton, 1862–1937, in *John O'London's Weekly*, 10 Apr. 1932]

See also CHASTITY

PURPOSE, see INTENTION

PUT-DOWNS, see INSULTS

Q

QUESTIONS

1 To ask the hard question is simple. [W H Auden, 1907–73, *The Question*]

2 REPORTER: If Mr Stalin dies, what will be the effect on international affairs?
EDEN: That is a good question for you to ask, not a wise question for me to answer. [Anthony Eden, 1897–1977, interview on board *Queen Elizabeth*, 4 Mar. 1953]

3 I keep six honest serving-men / (They taught me all I knew); / Their names are What and Why and When / And How and Where and Who. [Rudyard Kipling, 1865–1936, *Just So Stories* (follows 'The Elephant's Child')]

4 We have learned the answers, all the answers: / It is the question that we do not know. [Archibald Macleish, 1892–1982, *The Hamlet of A. Macleish*]

5 Don't ask *what are* questions, ask *what do* questions, don't ask *why* questions, ask *how* questions. [Karl Popper, 1902–94, quoted by Bernard Levin in *The Sunday Times* ('Books' section), 16 Apr. 1989]

6 It's the little questions from women about tappets that finally push men over the edge. [Philip Roth, 1933– , *Letting Go*, Pt I, Ch. 1]

7 Well, if I called the wrong number, why did you answer the phone? [James Thurber, 1894–1961, *Men, Women and Dogs*, cartoon caption]

8 No question is ever settled / Until it is settled right. [Ella Wheeler Wilcox, 1855–1919, *Settle the Question Right*]

See also ANSWERS

QUIETNESS

1 Study to be quiet, and to do your own business. [Bible, NT, *1 Thessalonians* 4:11]

2 This Quiet, all it hath a mind to do, doth. [Robert Browning, 1812–89, *Caliban upon Setebos*, 138]

3 Anythin' for a quiet life, as the man said wen he took the sitivation at the lighthouse. [(Sam Weller) Charles Dickens, 1812–70, *Pickwick Papers*, Ch. 43]

4 Far from the madding crowd's ignoble strife, / Their sober wishes never learned to stray; / Along the cool sequestered vale of life / They kept the noiseless tenor of their way. [Thomas Gray, 1716–71, *Elegy Written in a Country Churchyard*, 19]

5 Fair quiet, have I found thee here / And innocence thy sister dear? [Andrew Marvell, 1621–78, *The Garden*, 9]

6 He moves from point to point with as little uproar as a jellyfish. [P G Wodehouse, 1881–1975, *My Man Jeeves*, 'Jeeves and the Hard-boiled Egg']

See also CALM, PEACE, SILENCE

QUOTATIONS

1 The surest way to make a monkey of a man is to quote him. [Robert Benchley, 1889–1945, *Quick Quotations*]

2 It is a good thing for an uneducated man to read books of quotations. [(Of himself) Winston Churchill, 1874–1965, *My Early Life*, Ch. 9]

Quotations 3–8

3 I hate quotations. Tell me what you know. [Ralph Waldo Emerson, 1803–82, *Journals*, May 1849]

4 How do people go to sleep? I'm afraid I've lost the knack. I might try busting myself smartly over the temple with the nightlight. I might repeat to myself, slowly and soothingly, a list of quotations beautiful from minds profound; if I can remember any of the damn things. [Dorothy Parker, 1893–1967, *The Little Hours*]

5 A book that furnishes no quotation is, *me judice*, no book – it is a plaything. [T L Peacock, 1785–1866, *Crotchet Castle*, Ch. 9]

6 What a good thing Adam had. When he said a good thing he knew nobody had said it before. [Mark Twain, 1835–1910, *Notebooks*, p. 67]

7 OSCAR WILDE: I wish I had said that.
WHISTLER: You will, Oscar, you will. [James McNeill Whistler, 1834–1903, in L C Ingleby, *Oscar Wilde*]

8 Some for renown, on scraps of learning dote, / And think they grow immortal as they quote. [Edward Young, 1683–1765, *Love of Fame*, Satire I, 89]

R

RACES & RACISM

1 It is a great shock at the age of five or six to find that in a world of Gary Coopers you are the Indian. [James Baldwin, 1924–87, speech at Cambridge Union, 17 Feb. 1965]

2 Everybody's coloured or else you wouldn't be able to see them. [Captain Beefheart, 1941– ; in *Dictionary of Outrageous Quotations*, comp. C R S Marsden]

3 The problem of the twentieth century is the problem of the colour line. [W E B Du Bois, 1868–1963, address to Pan-African Conference, London, 1900]

4 When people like me, they tell me it is in spite of my colour. When they dislike me, they point out that it is not because of my colour. Either way, I am locked into the infernal circle. [Frantz Fanon, 1925–61, *Black Skin, White Masks*, Ch. 1]

5 To be a gringo in Mexico ... ah, that is euthanasia. [Carlos Fuentes, 1928– , *The Old Gringo*, 17]

6 The whole world is run on bluff. No race, no nation, no man has any divine right to take advantage of others. Why allow the other fellow to bluff you? [Marcus Garvey, 1887–1940, *Philosophy and Opinions*, p. 7]

7 We shall never be rough and heartless when it is not necessary, that is clear. We Germans, who are the only people in the world who have a decent attitude towards animals, will also assume a decent attitude towards these human animals. [Heinrich Himmler, 1900–1945, speech, 4 Oct. 1943]

8 All those who are not racially pure are mere chaff. [Adolf Hitler, 1889–1945, *Mein Kampf*, Ch. 2]

9 I have a dream that my four little children will one day live in a nation where they will not be judged by the colour of their skin but by the content of their character. [Martin Luther King Jr, 1929–68, speech in Washington on completion of civil rights march, 28 Aug. 1963]

10 There's times when you'll think that you mightn't, / There's times when you know that you might; / *But the things you will learn from the Yellow and Brown, / They'll 'elp you a lot with the White!* [Rudyard Kipling, 1865–1936, *The Ladies*]

11 Every race which has become self-conscious and idea-bound in the past has perished. [D H Lawrence, 1885–1930, *Fantasia of the Unconscious*, Ch. 7]

12 When a white man in Africa by accident looks into the eyes of a native and sees the human being (which it is his chief preoccupation to avoid), his sense of guilt, which he denies, fumes up in resentment and he brings down the whip. [Doris Lessing, 1919– , *The Grass is Singing*, Ch. 8]

13 A coloured man can tell, in five seconds dead, whether a white man likes him or not. If the white man *says* he does, he is instantly – and usually quite rightly – mistrusted. [Colin MacInnes, 1914–76, *England, Half English*, 'A Short Guide for Jumbles']

14 In this country American means white. Everybody else has to hyphenate. [Toni Morrison, 1931– ; *Observer*, 'Sayings of the Week', 2 Feb. 1992]

15 'But the man is a BA!' 'And LLB. I know, I wouldn't trust an Aryan with my great-grandmother.' [V S Naipaul, 1932– , *A House for Mr Biswas*, Ch. 3]

16 He's really awfully fond of coloured people. Well, he says himself, he wouldn't have white servants. [Dorothy Parker, 1893–1967, *Arrangement in Black and White*]

17 As I look ahead, I am filled with foreboding. Like the Roman, I seem to see 'the River Tiber foaming with much blood'. [Enoch Powell, 1912–98, speech in Birmingham, refering to a future multi-racial Britain resulting from immigration policy, 20 Apr. 1968]

18 Mislike me not for my complexion, / The shadowed livery of the burnished sun. [William Shakespeare, 1564–1616, *The Merchant of Venice*, II. i. 1]

19 The only good Indian is a dead Indian. [Philip H Sheridan, 1831–88, attr., at Fort Cobb, Jan. 1869]

20 Native always means people who belong somewhere else, because they had once belonged somewhere. That shows that the white race does not really think they belong anywhere because they think of everybody else as native. [Gertrude Stein, 1874–1946, *Everybody's Autobiography*, Ch. 1]

21 The law of dislike for the unlike will always prevail. And whereas the unlike is normally situated at a safe distance, the Jews bring the unlike into the heart of *every milieu*, and must there defend a frontier line as large as the world. [Israel Zangwill, 1864–1926, *Speeches, Articles and Letters*, 'The Jewish Race']

See also BLACK CULTURE, PREJUDICE

RADICALS

1 A radical – one who not only knows all the answers but keeps on thinking up new questions. [*New Statesman*, undated]

2 A radical is a man with both feet planted firmly in the air. A reactionary is a somnambulist walking backwards. A conservative is a man with two perfectly good legs who, however, has never learned how to walk forward. A liberal is a man who uses his legs and his hands at the behest of his head. [Franklin D Roosevelt, 1882–1945, radio address, 26 Oct. 1939]

3 Radical: A person whose left hand does not know what his other left hand is doing. [Bernard Rosenberg; in Laurence J Peter, *Peter's Quotations*]

See also LIBERALS, REACTIONARIES

RAILWAYS

1 This is the Night Mail crossing the border, / Bringing the cheque and the postal order, / Letters for the rich, letters for the poor, / The shop at the corner, the girl next door. [W H Auden, 1907–73, 'Night Mail']

2 [Of the parallels between the railways and the Church] Both had their heyday in the mid-nineteenth century; both own a great deal of Gothic-style architecture which is expensive to maintain; both are regularly assailed by critics; and both are firmly convinced that they are the best means of getting man to his ultimate destination. [Revd W Awdry, 1911–97, creator of *Thomas the Tank Engine* children's books, quoted in his obituary in *Independent*, 22 Mar. 1997]

3 Rumbling under blackened girders, Midland, bound for Cricklewood, / Puffed its sulphur to the sunset where that Land of Laundries stood. [John Betjeman, 1906–84, *Parliament Hill Fields*]

4 We travel by plane, oftener than not, and yet the spirit of our country seems to have remained a country of railroads. [John Cheever, 1912–82, *Bullet Park*, Pt I, Ch. 1]

5 One look at the rush-hour jam in the subway and you know why no one rides it any more. [John Ciardi, 1916–86, in *Saturday Review*, 'Manner of Speaking', 8 Aug. 1964]

6 They [railway termini] are our gates to the glorious and the unknown. Through them we pass out into adventure and sunshine, and to them, alas! we return. [E M Forster, 1879–1970, *Howards End*, Ch. 2]

7 Beautiful Railway Bridge of the Silv'ry Tay! / Alas, I am very sorry to say / That ninety lives have been taken away / On the last Sabbath day of 1879, / which will be remember'd for a very long time. [William McGonagall, 1825–1902, *The Tay Bridge Disaster*]

8 They [Sunday evening trains] are full of people going from where they chose to be to where they have to be. [David Nobbs, 1935– , from *Pratt of the Argus*, in *The Times Literary Supplement*, 20 May 1988]

9 But she never, never missed the train. I think she felt that it would not have been sporting to start in time; it would not have given the train a fair chance of getting away without her. [Gwen Raverat, 1885–1957, *Period Piece*, Ch. 5]

10 After the first powerful manifesto / The black statement of pistons, without more fuss / But gliding like a queen, she leaves the station. [Stephen Spender, 1909–95, *The Express*]

11 As we rush, as we rush in the train, / The trees and the houses go wheeling back, / But the starry heavens above the plain / Come flying on our track. [James Thomson, 1834–82, *Sunday at Hampstead*, 10]

12 Commuter – one who spends his life / In riding to and from his wife; / A man who shaves and takes a train, / And then rides back to shave again. [E B White, 1899–1985, *The Commuter*]

See also CARS, TRAVEL

RAIN

1 There ariseth a little cloud out of the sea, like a man's hand. [Bible, OT, *1 Kings* 18:44]

2 The thirsty earth soaks up the rain, / And drinks, and gapes for drink again. / The plants suck in the earth and are / With constant drinking fresh and fair. [Abraham Cowley, 1618–67, *Anacreontic: Drinking*]

3 And then the monsoons came, and they couldn't have come at a worse time, bang in the middle of the rainy season. [Spike Milligan, 1918– , in *Telegraph Sunday Magazine*, 26 June 1977]

4 Rain, rain, go away, / Come again another day. [Nursery rhyme]

5 If you can see the French. coast, it means that it is going to rain; if you can't see it, then it's already raining. [Quinton Pollard, attr.]

6 I wield the flail of the lashing hail, / And whiten the green plains under, / And then again I dissolve it in rain, / And laugh as I pass in thunder. [P B Shelley, 1792–1822, *The Cloud*, 9]

7 Still falls the Rain – / Dark as the world of man, black as our loss – / Blind as the nineteen hundred and forty nails / Upon the Cross. [Edith Sitwell, 1887–1964, *Still Falls the Rain*]

See also SKIES, WEATHER

REACTIONARIES

1 One is always somebody's reactionary. [Georges Clemenceau, 1841–1929, quoted by Ernst Gombrich in *Listener*, 15 Feb. 1979]

2 All reactionaries are paper tigers. [Mao Zedong, 1893–1976, talk with the American correspondent Anna Louise Strong, Aug. 1946]

3 A radical is a man with both feet planted firmly in the air. A reactionary is a somnambulist walking backwards. A conservative is a man with two perfectly good legs who, however, has never learned how to walk forward. A liberal is a man who uses his legs and his hands at the behest of his head. [Franklin D Roosevelt, 1882–1945, radio address, 26 Oct. 1939]

See also CONSERVATIVES, LIBERALS, RADICALS

READING

1 Read not to contradict and confute, nor to believe and take for granted, nor to find talk and discourse, but to weigh and consider. [Francis Bacon, 1561–1626, *Essays*, 50, 'Of Studies']

2 *Hypocrite lecteur! mon semblable, mon frère!* – Hypocritical reader, my double, my brother! [Charles Baudelaire, 1821–67, *Au Lecteur*]

3 The theory these days (or one of them) is that the reader brings as much to the book as the author. So how much more do readers bring who have never managed to get through the book at all? It follows that the books one remembers best are the books one has never read. [Alan Bennett, 1934– , *Kafka's Dick*, Introduction]

4 A good reader is rarer than a good writer. [Jorge Luis Borges, 1899–1986, in Robert Robinson, *Dog Chairman*, 'Arm in Arm with Borges']

5 Read Homer once, and you can read no more, / For all books else appear so mean, so poor, / Verse will seem prose; but still persist to read, / And Homer will be all the books you need. [John Sheffield, 1st Duke of Buckingham and Normanby, 1648–1721, *An Essay on Poetry*]

6 I may have had to make some effort myself, at first, to learn not to read, but now it comes quite naturally to me. The secret is not refusing to look at the written words. On the contrary, you must look at them, intensely, until they disappear. [Italo Calvino, 1923–85, *If on a Winter's Night a Traveller*, Ch. 3]

7 Novel-reading re-enacts the Fall. What keeps the reader going is forbidden fruits, temptation from the tree of knowledge of good and evil. [Valentine Cunningham, 1944– , in *Observer*, 20 Sept. 1987]

8 The reading of all good books is like a conversation with the finest persons of past centuries. [René Descartes, 1596–1650, *Discourse on Method*, 1]

9 Never read any book that is not a year old. [Ralph Waldo Emerson, 1803–82, *Society and Solitude*, 'Books']

10 Do not read, as children do, to amuse yourself, or like the ambitious, for the purpose of instruction. No, read in order to live. [Gustave Flaubert, 1821–80, letter to Mlle de Chantepie, June 1857]

11 Men of power have no time to read; yet the men who do not read are unfit for power. [Michael Foot, 1913– , *Debts of Honour*]

12 As writers become more numerous, it is natural for readers to become more indolent. [Oliver Goldsmith, 1728–74, *The Bee*, No. 175, 'Upon Unfortunate Merit']

13 I read part of it all the way through. [Samuel Goldwyn, 1882–1974, in Philip French, *The Movie Moguls*, Ch. 4]

14 You reading over my shoulder, peering beneath / My writing arm. [Robert Graves, 1895–1985, *The Reader over My Shoulder* (also title of a book of his criticism)]

15 It is not true that we have only one life to live; if we can read, we can live as many more lives and as many kinds of lives as we wish. [S I Hayakawa, 1906–92; in *Writer's Quotation Book*, ed. James Charlton]

16 Reading is sometimes an ingenious device for avoiding thought. [Arthur Helps, 1813–75, *Friends in Council*, Bk ii, Ch. 1]

17 Notes are often necessary, but they are necessary evils. [Dr Samuel Johnson, 1709–84, *Preface to Shakespeare*]

18 A man ought to read just as inclination leads him; for what he reads as a task will do him little good. [Dr Samuel Johnson, 1709–84, in James Boswell, *Life of J*, 14 July 1763]

19 'What (said Elphinston), have you read it through?' ... 'No, Sir, do *you* read books *through?*' [Dr Samuel Johnson, 1709–84, in James Boswell, *Life of J*, 19 Apr. 1773]

20 We read fine things but never feel them to the full until we have gone the same steps as the author. [John Keats, 1795–1821, letter to J H Reynolds, 3 May 1818]

21 Where shall I find the time to do all this non-reading? [Karl Kraus, 1874–1936, *Half-truths and One-and-a-half Truths*, 'Riddles']

22 I love to lose myself in other men's minds. When I am not walking, I am reading; I cannot sit and think. Books think for me. [Charles Lamb, 1775–1834, *Last Essays of Elia*, 'Detached Thoughts on Books and Reading']

23 To read too many books is harmful. [Mao Zedong, 1893–1976, in the *New Yorker*, 7 Mar. 1977]

24 I would sooner read a time-table or a catalogue than nothing at all ... They are much more entertaining than half the novels that are written. [W Somerset Maugham, 1874–1965, *The Summing Up*, Ch. 25]

25 I'd gone to the South of France for six months, to finish my latest book. I'm a very slow reader. [Frank Muir, 1920–98, in foreword to Ronnie Barker, *It's Goodnight from Him*]

26 There are no foreign books; there are only foreign readers. [Joseph Prescott, 1913– , *Aphorisms and Other Observations*, 'Literature']

27 A man who attempts to read all the new productions must do as the fleas do – skip. [Samuel Rogers, 1763–1855, *Table Talk* (1856), p. 199]

28 I never was much on this Book reading, for it takes em too long to describe the colour of the eyes of all the characters. [Will Rogers, 1879–1935, *Autobiography*, Ch. 14]

29 Be sure that you go to the author to get at *his* meaning, not to find yours. [John Ruskin, 1819–1900, *Sesame and Lilies*, 1, §13]

30 In reality, people read because they want to write. Anyway, reading is a sort of rewriting. [Jean-Paul Sartre, 1905–80, *Between Existentialism and Marxism*, 'The Purposes of Writing']

31 POLONIUS: What do you read, my lord?
HAMLET: Words, words, words. [William Shakespeare, 1564–1616, *Hamlet*, II. ii. (195)]

32 People say that life is the thing, but I prefer reading. [Logan Pearsall Smith, 1865–1946, *Afterthoughts*, 6]

33 Live always in the best company when you read. [Sydney Smith, 1771–1845, in Lady Holland, *Memoir*, Vol. i, Ch. 10]

34 Reading is to the mind what exercise is to the body. [Richard Steele, 1672–1729, *The Tatler*, 147]

35 You should only read what is truly good or what is frankly bad. [Gertrude Stein, 1874–1946, in Ernest Hemingway, *A Moveable Feast*, 3]

36 Education ... has produced a vast population able to read but unable to distinguish what is worth reading. [G M Trevelyan, 1876–1962, *English Social History*, Ch. 18]

37 As in the sexual experience, there are never more than two persons present in the act of reading – the writer who is the impregnator, and the reader who is the respondent. [E B White, 1899–1985, *The Second Tree from the Corner*]

38 No two people read the same book. [Edmund Wilson, 1895–1972, quoted by John Russell in *The Sunday Times*, 25 July 1971]

39 Somewhere, everywhere, now hidden, now apparent in whatever is written down, is the form of a human being. If we seek to know him, are we idly occupied? [Virginia Woolf, 1882–1941, *The Captain's Death Bed*, 'Reading']

See also BOOKS, LITERACY

REALISM

1 Be Realistic: Demand the Impossible. [anon. slogan of 1968, quoted in *Listener*, 20 Apr. 1988]

2 Realism doesn't mean copying art back into life. It means making life into art: not just accepting the facts of life but elevating them. [Laurence Olivier, 1907–89, in Kenneth Harris, *K H Talking to . . .*]

3 They said, 'You have a blue guitar, / You do not play things as they are.' / The man replied, 'Things as they are / Are changed upon the blue guitar.' [Wallace Stevens, 1879–1955, *The Man with the Blue Guitar*]

4 Let's talk sense to the American people. Let's tell them the truth, that there are no gains without pains. [Adlai Stevenson, 1900–1965, speech accepting Democratic presidential nomination, Chicago, 26 July 1952]

5 Those who maintain that all is right talk nonsense; they ought to say that all is for the best. [Voltaire, 1694–1778, *Candide*, Ch. 1]

See also OBJECTIVITY

REALITY

1 Reality is what I see, not what you see [Anthony Burgess, 1917–93, in *The Sunday Times Magazine*, 18 Dec. 1983]

2 It's as large as life, and twice as natural! [Lewis Carroll, 1832–98, *Through the Looking Glass*, Ch. 7]

3 Real life seems to have no plots. [Ivy Compton-Burnett, 1884–1969, in review in *Guardian*, Feb. 1973]

4 Everything is a dangerous drug to me except reality, which is unendurable. [Cyril Connolly, 1903–74, *The Unquiet Grave*, Ch. 1]

5 Human kind / Cannot bear very much reality. [T S Eliot, 1888–1965, *Four Quartets*, 'Burnt Norton', 1]

6 I am a man for whom the outside world exists. [Théophile Gautier, 1811–72, *Histoire de Romantisme*]

7 Some people like ping-pong, other people like digging over graves. They're all escapes from now. People will do anything rather than be here now. [John Lennon, 1940–80, in *Playboy Interviews*, ed. G Barry Golson, 12]

8 The interpretation of our reality through patterns not our own serves only to make us ever more unknown, ever less free, ever more solitary. [Gabriel García Márquez, 1928– , epigraph to Rana Kabbani, *Europe's Myths of Orient*]

9 Camerado, this is no book, / Who touches this touches a man. [Walt Whitman, 1819–92, *So Long!*, 53]

REASON

1 Reason is itself a matter of faith. It is an act of faith to assert that our thoughts have any relation to reality at all. [G K Chesterton, 1874–1936, *Orthodoxy*, Ch. 3]

2 I'll not listen to reason ... Reason always means what someone else has got to say. [Elizabeth Gaskell, 1810–65, *Cranford*, Ch. 14]

3 The conservative has but little to fear from the man whose reason is the servant of his passions, but let him beware of him in whom reason has become the greatest and most terrible of passions. [J B S Haldane, 1892–1964, *Daedalus or Science and the Future*]

4 Reason has moons, but moons not hers / Lie mirror'd on her sea, / Confounding her astronomers, / But, O! delighting me. [Ralph Hodgson, 1871–1962, *Reason Has Moons*]

5 A man who does not lose his reason over certain things has none to lose. [G E Lessing, 1729–81, *Emilia Galotti*, IV. vii]

6 God so commanded, and left that command / Sole daughter of his voice; the rest we live / Law to ourselves, our reason is our law. [John Milton, 1608–74, *Paradise Lost*, Bk ix, 652]

7 Pure reason avoids extremes, and requires one to be wise in moderation. [Molière, 1622–73, *Le Misanthrope*, I. i]

8 Reason, an *ignis fatuus* of the mind. [Earl of Rochester, 1647–80, *A Satire against Mankind*, 12]

9 That noble and most sovereign reason, / Like sweet bells jangled, out of tune and harsh; / That unmatched form and figure of blown youth / Blasted with ecstasy. [William Shakespeare, 1564–1616, *Hamlet*, III. i. (166)]

10 What is a man, / If his chief good and market of his time / Be but to sleep and feed? a beast, no more. / Sure he that made us with such large discourse, / Looking before and after, gave us not / That capability and god-like reason / To fust in us unused. [*Hamlet*, IV. iv. 33]

11 Give you a reason on compulsion! If reasons were as plentiful as blackberries, I would give no man a reason upon compulsion, I. [*1 Henry IV*, II. iv. (267)]

12 I have no other but a woman's reason: / I think him so, because I think him so. [*The Two Gentlemen of Verona*, I. ii. 23]

13 If rationality were the criterion of things being allowed to exist, the world would be a gigantic field of soya beans! [Tom Stoppard, 1937–   , *Jumpers*, I]

14 Once the people begin to reason, all is lost. [Voltaire, 1694–1778, letter to Damilaville, 1 Apr. 1766]

See also MIND

REBELLION

1 The surest way to prevent seditions (if the times do bear it) is to take away the matter of them. [Francis Bacon, 1561–1626, *Essays*, 15, 'Of Seditions and Troubles']

2 The people arose as one man. [Bible, OT, *Judges* 20:8]

3 The spirit burning but unbent, / May writhe, rebel – the weak alone repent! [Lord Byron, 1788–1824, *The Corsair*, II, 10]

4 What is a rebel? A man who says no. [Albert Camus, 1913–60, *The Rebel*, Ch. 1]

5 He [Hampden] had a head to contrive, a tongue to persuade, and a hand to execute any mischief. [(Quoting a description of Cinna) Earl of Clarendon, 1609–74, *Selections from the History of the Rebellion*, 21]

6 Plots, true or false, are necessary things, / To raise up commonwealths, and ruin kings. [John Dryden, 1631–1700, *Absalom and Achitophel*, Pt I, 83]

7 No one can go on being a rebel too long without turning into an autocrat. [Lawrence Durrell, 1912–90, *Balthazar*, Pt II]

8 A little rebellion now and then is a good thing. [Thomas Jefferson, 1743–1826, letter to James Madison, 30 Jan. 1787]

9 A riot is at bottom the language of the unheard. [Martin Luther King Jr, 1929–68, *Chaos or Community*, Ch. 4]

10 Your sheep, that were wont to be so meek and tame and so small eaters, now, as I hear say, be become so great devourers, and so wild, that they eat up and swallow down the very men themselves. [Sir Thomas More, 1478–1535, *Utopia*, Bk I]

11 Rebellion lay in his way, and he found it. [William Shakespeare, 1564–1616, *1 Henry IV*, V. i. 28]

12 Unthread the bold eye of rebellion, / And welcome home again discarded faith. [*King John*, V. iv. 11]

13 Open-eyed conspiracy / His time doth take. [*The Tempest*, II. i. (309)]

14 The only possible way there'd be an uprising in this country would be if they banned car boot sales and caravanning. [Victoria Wood, 1953– , stage performance at Strand Theatre, London, Oct. 1990]

15 I have met them at close of day / Coming with vivid faces / From counter or desk among grey / Eighteenth-century houses. / I have passed with a nod of the head / Or polite meaningless words. [W B Yeats, 1865–1939, *Easter 1916*]

See also OPPOSITION, REVOLUTIONS

REFORM

1 All reform except a moral one will prove unavailing. [Thomas Carlyle, 1795–1881, *Critical and Miscellaneous Essays*, 'Corn Law Rhymes']

2 You cannot fight against the future. Time is on our side. [W E Gladstone, 1809–98, speech on the Reform Bill, 1866]

3 All reformers are bachelors. [George Moore, 1852–1933, *The Bending of the Bough*, I]

4 In practice a reformist party considers unshakeable the foundations of that which it intends to reform. [Leon Trotsky, 1874–1940, *History of the Russian Revolution*, Pt III, Ch. 5]

See also IMPROVEMENT

REGRET

1 My one regret in life is that I am not someone else. [Woody Allen, 1935– , in E Lax, *W A and His Comedy*, epigraph]

2 The only thing I regret about my past is the length of it. If I had to live my life again I'd make all the same mistakes – only sooner. [Tallulah Bankhead, 1903–68; in L and M Cowan, *The Wit of Women*]

3 Where there aren't no Ten Commandments, an' a man can raise a thirst: / For the temple-bells are callin', an' it's there that I would be – / By the old Moulmein Pagoda, looking lazy at the sea. [Rudyard Kipling, 1865–1936, *Mandalay*]

4 *Non, je ne regrette rien.* [Edith Piaf, 1915–63, title of song, words by Michel Vaucaire]

5 O! withered is the garland of the war, / The soldier's pole is fallen; young boys and girls / Are level now with men; the odds is gone, / And there is nothing left remarkable / Beneath the visiting moon. [William Shakespeare, 1564–1616, *Antony and Cleopatra*, IV. xiii. 64]

6 When to the sessions of sweet silent thought / I summon up remembrance of things past, / I sigh the lack of many a thing I sought, / And with old woes new wail my dear times' waste: / Then can I drown an eye, unused to flow, / For precious friends hid in death's dateless night, / And weep afresh love's long since cancelled woe, / And moan the expense of many a vanished sight. [*Sonnets*, 30]

7 We look before and after, / And pine for what is not: / Our sincerest laughter / With some pain is fraught; / Our sweetest songs are those that tell of saddest thought. [P B Shelley, 1792–1822, *To a Skylark*, 86]

8 Oh, my grief, I've lost him surely. I've lost the only Playboy of the Western World. [J M Synge, 1871–1909, *The Playboy of the Western World*, closing words]

9 My regret / Becomes an April violet, / And buds and blossoms like the rest. [Alfred, Lord Tennyson, 1809–92, *In Memoriam*, 115]

10 For all sad words of tongue or pen, / The saddest are these: 'It might have been!' [John Greenleaf Whittier, 1807–92, *Maud Muller*, 105]

See also GRIEF, NOSTALGIA, SORROW, UNHAPPINESS

RELATIONSHIPS

1 We don't really go that far into other people, even when we think we do. We hardly ever go in and bring them out. We just stand at the jaws of the cave, and strike a match, and ask quickly if anybody's there. [Martin Amis, 1949– , *Money*, p. 310]

2 I do not believe in things: I believe in relationships. [Georges Braque, 1883–1963, in J Culler, *Saussure*, Ch. 4]

3 If two lives join, there is oft a scar, / They are one and one, with a shadowy third; / One near one is too far. [Robert Browning, 1812–89, *By the Fire Side*, 46]

4 To abuse a man is a lover-like thing and gives him rights. [Joyce Cary, 1888–1957, *Herself Surprised*, Ch. 35]

5 Industrial relations are like sexual relations. It's better between two consenting parties. [Vic

Feather, 1908–76, in *Guardian Weekly*, 8 Aug. 1976]

6 She felt increasingly ... that, though people are important, the relations between them are not. [E M Forster, 1879–1970, *A Passage to India*, Ch. 13]

7 We have flown the air like birds and swum the sea like fishes, but have yet to learn the simple act of walking the earth like brothers. [Martin Luther King Jr, 1929–68, in *Guardian*, 4 Apr. 1983]

8 Before we can ask such an optimistic question as 'What is a personal relationship?', we have to ask if a personal relationship is possible, or, *are persons possible* in our present situation? [R D Laing, 1927–89, *The Politics of Experience*, Ch. 1]

9 Distances are only the relation of space to time and vary with it. [Marcel Proust, 1871–1922, *Remembrance of Things Past: Cities of the Plain*, Pt II, Ch. 3]

10 Moving up the steep hill of a relationship had to be easier on tandem than unicycle, especially if the other person wasn't pedalling in the opposite direction. [Susan Sussman, 1942– , *The Dieter*, Ch. 23]

11 I'm not living with you. We occupy the same cage. [Tennessee Williams, 1911–83, *Cat on a Hot Tin Roof*, I]

See also FAMILY, LOVE

RELIGION

1 We have in England a particular bashfulness in everything that regards religion. [Joseph Addison, 1672–1719, *The Spectator*, 458]

2 The true meaning of religion is thus not simply morality, but morality touched by emotion. [Matthew Arnold, 1822–88, *Literature and Dogma*, Ch. 1, §2]

3 All good moral philosophy is but the handmaid to religion. [Francis Bacon, 1561–1626, *The Advancement of Learning*, II, xxii, 14]

4 A little philosophy inclineth man's mind to atheism; but depth in philosophy bringeth men's minds about to religion. [Francis Bacon, 1561–1626, *Essays*, 16, 'Of Atheism']

5 Art and Religion are, then, two roads by which men escape from circumstance to ecstasy. [Clive Bell, 1881–1964, *Art*, Pt II, 1]

6 Argument, generally speaking in religion, can do no more than clear the track; it cannot make the engine move. [Edwyn Bevan, 1870–1943, *Hellenism and Christianity*]

7 Pure religion and undefiled before God and the Father is this, To visit the fatherless and widows in their affliction, and to keep himself unspotted from the world. [Bible, NT, *James* 1:27]

8 Religions are kept alive by heresies, which are really sudden explosions of faith. Dead religions do not produce them. [Gerald Brenan, 1894–1987, *Thoughts in a Dry Season*, 'Religion']

9 Methinks there be not impossibilities enough in Religion for an active faith. [Sir Thomas Browne, 1605–82, *Religio Medici*, Pt 1, 9]

10 They are for religion when in rags and contempt, but I am for him when he walks in his golden slippers in the sunshine and with applause. [(Mr By-Ends) John Bunyan, 1628–88, *The Pilgrim's Progress*, Pt I]

11 Man is by his constitution a religious animal. [Edmund Burke, 1729–97, *Reflections on the Revolution in France*, Penguin edn, p. 187]

12 Religious persecution may shield itself under the guise of a mistaken and over-zealous piety. [Edmund Burke, 1729–97, impeachment of Warren Hastings, 17 Feb. 1788]

13 Nothing is so fatal to religion as indifference, which is, at least, half infidelity. [Edmund Burke, 1729–97, letter to William Smith, 29 Jan. 1795]

14 One religion is as true as another. [Robert Burton, 1577–1640, *The Anatomy of Melancholy*, III, §4, Memb. 2, 1]

15 To be at all is to be religious more or less. [Samuel Butler, 1835–1902, *Notebooks*, Ch. 22, 'Religion']

16 There's nought, no doubt, so much the spirit calms / As rum and true religion. [Lord Byron, 1788–1824, *Don Juan*, II, 34]

17 Poetry and Religion (and it is really worth knowing) are 'a product of the smaller intestines'. [Thomas Carlyle, 1795–1881, *Critical and Miscellaneous Essays*, 'Signs of the Times']

18 Religion is by no means a proper subject of conversation in a mixed company. [Earl of Chesterfield, 1694–1773, letter to his godson, No. 112 (undated)]

19 Blasphemy itself could not survive religion; if anyone doubts that, let him try to blaspheme

Odin. [G K Chesterton, 1874–1936, in *Daily News*, 24 June 1904]

20 A dying monarchy is always one that has too much power, not too little; a dying religion always interferes more than it ought, not less. [G K Chesterton, 1874–1936, in *Daily News*, 11 Mar. 1911]

21 It's a curious fact that the all-male religions have produced no religious imagery – in most cases have positively forbidden it. The great religious art of the world is deeply involved with the female principle. [Kenneth Clark, 1903–83, *Civilization*, Ch. 7]

22 Men will wrangle for religion; write for it; fight for it; anything but – live for it. [Charles Colton, 1780?–1832, *Lacon*, I, 25]

23 In Mexico the gods ruled, the priests interpreted and interposed, and the people obeyed. In Spain, the priests ruled, the king interpreted and interposed, and the gods obeyed. A nuance in an ideological difference is a wide chasm. [Richard Condon, 1915–96, *A Talent for Loving*, Bk I, Ch. 6]

24 'Sensible men are all of the same religion.' 'And pray, what is that?' inquired the prince. 'Sensible men never tell.' [Benjamin Disraeli, 1804–81, *Endymion*, Bk i, Ch. 81]; see 51

25 We are Buddhists and we have no expectations. If you travel with the river you have to bend with the river. [Dr Ly Va Dong, in *Observer*, 12 Mar. 1989]

26 In pious times, ere priestcraft did begin, / Before polygamy was made a sin. [John Dryden, 1631–1700, *Absalom and Achitophel*, Pt I, 1]

27 Science without religion is lame, religion without science is blind. [Albert Einstein, 1879–1955, paper for conference on science, New York, 9/11 Sept. 1940]

28 To her, religion was mortality and appearance, and she kept it in the same compartment of her mind as her dinner napkins. [Alice Thomas Ellis, 1932– , *The Clothes in the Wardrobe*, p. 50]

29 Religion is far more acute than science, and if it only added judgement to insight, would be the greatest thing in the world. [E M Forster, 1879–1970, *Maurice*, Ch. 44]

30 Ronny approved of religion as long as it endorsed the National Anthem, but he objected when it attempted to influence his life. [E M Forster, 1879–1970, *A Passage to India*, Ch. 5]

31 The various modes of worship, which prevailed in the Roman world, were all considered by the people as equally true; by the philosopher, as equally false; and by the magistrate, as equally useful. [Edward Gibbon, 1737–94, *The Decline and Fall of the Roman Empire*, Ch. 2]

32 As I take my shoes from the shoemaker, and my coat from the tailor, so I take my religion from the priest. [Oliver Goldsmith, 1728–74, quoted in James Boswell, *Life of J*, 9 Apr. 1773]

33 To become a popular religion, it is only necessary for a superstition to enslave a philosophy. [W R Inge, 1860–1954, *Outspoken Essays*, Second Series, 'The Idea of Progress']

34 Religion is a way of walking, not a way of talking. [W R Inge, 1860–1954, attr.]

35 Religion, it might be said, is the term that designates the attitude peculiar to a consciousness which has been altered by the experience of the *numinosum*. [C G Jung, 1875–1961, *Psychology and Religion*, Ch. 1]

36 Religion is the frozen thought of men out of which they build temples. [J Krishnamurti, 1895–1986; *Observer*, 'Sayings of the Week', 22 Apr. 1928]

37 Religion used to try, / That vast moth-eaten musical brocade / Created to pretend we never die. [Philip Larkin, 1922–85, *Aubade*]

38 Such are the heights of wickedness to which men are driven by religion. [Lucretius, 99–55 BC, *On the Nature of the Universe*, I, 101]

39 I count religion but a childish toy, / And hold there is no sin but ignorance. [Christopher Marlowe, 1564–93, *The Jew of Malta*, Prologue, 14]

40 Religion . . . is the opium of the people. [Karl Marx, 1818–83, *Criticism of Hegel's Philosophy of Right*, Introduction]

41 Things have come to a pretty pass when religion is allowed to invade the sphere of private life. [Viscount Melbourne, 1779–1848, attr. by G W E Russell, *Collections and Recollections*, Ch. 6]

42 To sum up: 1. The cosmos is a gigantic flywheel making 10,000 revolutions a minute. 2. Man is a sick fly taking a dizzy ride on it. 3. Religion is the theory that the wheel was designed and set spinning to give him the ride. [H L Mencken, 1880–1956, *Prejudices*, Third Series, 'Ad Imaginem Dei Creavit Illum', Coda]

43 Can the world of God be found in a pool of limelight? [*Observer*, 22 June 1986, 'Profile of Rabbi Julia Neuberger']

44 There's no reason to bring religion into it. I think we ought to have as great a regard for religion as we can, so as to keep it out of as many things as possible. [Sean O'Casey, 1880–1964, *The Plough and the Stars*, I]

45 In my day nobody changed. A man was. Only religion could alter him, and that at least was a glorious misery. [Harold Pinter, 1930– , *No Man's Land*, II]

46 Slave to no sect, who takes no private road, / But looks through nature up to nature's God. [Alexander Pope, 1688–1744, *An Essay on Man*, IV, 331]

47 Religion to me has always been the wound, not the bandage. [Dennis Potter, 1935–94, *Seeing the Blossom*, an interview with Melvyn Bragg, TV Channel 4, Apr. 1994]

48 People are either escapists or Buddhists in this world. [Robert Powell, 1909– , *Zen and Reality*, 'Thoughts on Life']

49 Her religion so well with her learning did suit / That in practice sincere, and in controverse mute, / She shewed she knew better to live than dispute. [Matthew Prior, 1664–1721, *Jinny the Just*]

50 There's nothing in Christianity or Buddhism that quite matches the sympathetic unselfishness of an oyster. [Saki (H H Munro), 1870–1916, *The Match-Maker*]

51 Men of sense are really but of one religion... 'Pray, my lord, what religion is that which men of sense agree in?' 'Madam,' says the earl immediately, 'men of sense never tell it.' [Earl of Shaftesbury, 1621–83, Onslow's note in Bishop Burnet, *History of His Own Time*, Vol. i, Bk ii, Ch. 1]; see 24

52 'Tis mad idolatry / To make the service greater than the god. [William Shakespeare, 1564–1616, *Troilus and Cressida*, II. ii. 56]

53 Beware of the man whose god is in the skies. [George Bernard Shaw, 1856–1950, *Man and Superman*, 'Maxims for Revolutionists', Religion]

54 There is only one religion though there are a hundred versions of it. [George Bernard Shaw, 1856–1950, *Plays Pleasant*, Preface]

55 ALF: That's the one [religion] you got to belong to. No good belonging to any of the others. But who knows which one is His? I mean, that's your problem, annit? 'Cos God ain't said nothing for years, He aint...

MIKE: You ought to join all the religions – don't take any chances... [Johnny Speight, 1920– , BBC TV comedy series *Till Death Us Do Part*, 'Sex before Marriage']

56 We have just enough religion to make us hate, but not enough to make us love one another. [Jonathan Swift, 1677–1745, *Thoughts on Various Subjects*]

57 Educate men without religion and you make them but clever devils. [Duke of Wellington, 1769–1852, attr.]

See also CATHOLICS, CHURCHES, CHURCH OF ENGLAND, GOD

REPENTANCE

1 There is a shame that bringeth sin, and there is a shame which is glory and grace. [Bible, Apocrypha, *Ecclesiasticus* 4:21]

2 Joy shall be in heaven over one sinner that repenteth, more than over ninety and nine just persons, which need no repentance. [Bible, NT, *St Luke* 15:7]

3 That loathsome centipede, Remorse, / Invaded with a stealthy tread / My nasal organ. [H S Leigh, 1837–83, *An Allegory, Written in Deep Dejection*]

4 Ye that do truly and earnestly repent you of your sins, and are in love and charity with your neighbours... [*The Book of Common Prayer*, Holy Communion]

5 If one good deed in all my life I did, / I do repent it from my very soul. [William Shakespeare, 1564–1616, *Titus Andronicus*, V. iii. 189]

See also EMBARRASSMENT, GUILT

REPUTATION

1 It is a maxim with me that no man was ever written out of reputation but by himself. [Richard Bentley, 1662–1742, quoted in Monk, *Life of B*]

2 A good name is better than precious ointment; and the day of death than the day of one's birth. [Bible, OT, *Ecclesiastes* 7:1]

3 Let them cant about decorum / Who have characters to lose. [Robert Burns, 1759–96, *The Jolly Beggars*, 310]

4 Kokoshka at eighty, saying, 'If you last, / you'll see your reputation die three times.' [Robert Lowell, 1917–77, *Notebooks 1967–68*, p. 8]

5 I have bought / Golden opinions of all sorts of people. [William Shakespeare, 1564–1616, *Macbeth*, I. vii. 32]

6 Reputation, reputation, reputation! O! I have lost my reputation, I have lost the immortal part of myself, and what remains is bestial. [*Othello*, II. iii. (264)]

7 Good name in man and woman, dear my lord, / Is the immediate jewel of their souls; / Who steals my purse, steals trash; 'tis something, nothing; / 'Twas mine, 'tis his and has been slave to thousands; / But he that filches from me my good name / Robs me of that which not enriches him, / And makes me poor indeed. [*Othello*, III. iii. 153]

8 'Tis better to be vile than vile esteemed, / When not to be receives reproach of being. [*Sonnets*, 121]

9 There was worlds of reputation in it, but no money. [Mark Twain, 1835–1910, *A Yankee at the Court of King Arthur*, Ch. 9]

See also FAME, SCANDAL

RESEARCH

1 Basic research is like shooting an arrow into the air and, where it lands, painting a target. [Homer Adkins, in *Nature*, 1984, 312, 212]

2 Basic research is when I'm doing what I don't know I'm doing. [Wernher von Braun, 1912–77, in R L Weber, *A Random Walk in Science*]

3 The way to do research is to attack the facts at the point of greatest astonishment. [Celia Green, 1935– , *The Decline and Fall of Science*, 'Aphorisms']

4 No scientist is admired for failing in the attempt to solve problems that lie beyond his competence. The most he can hope for is the kindly contempt earned by the Utopian politician. If politics is the art of the possible, research is surely the art of the soluble. Both are immensely practical-minded affairs. [Peter Medawar, 1915–87 (in *New Statesman*, 19 June 1964), used in *The Art of the Soluble*, Introduction]

5 If you steal from one author it's plagiarism. If you steal from many it's research. [Wilson Mizner, 1876–1933, in Alva Johnston, *The Legendary Mizners*, Ch. 4]

6 You will find it a very good practice always to verify your references, sir. [Martin Routh, 1755–1854, attr. by J W Burgon in *Quarterly Review*, July 1878]

7 The outcome of any serious research can only be to make two questions grow where only one grew before. [Thorstein Veblen, 1857–1929, *The Place of Science in Modern Civilization*]

See also ACADEMICS, KNOWLEDGE, SCIENCE

RESIGNATION

1 Let the long contention cease! / Geese are swans, and swans are geese. [Matthew Arnold, 1822–88, *The Last Word*]

2 Let's contend no more, Love, / Strive nor weep: / All be as before, Love, / – Only sleep! [Robert Browning, 1812–89, *A Woman's Last Word*]

3 Teach us to care and not to care / Teach us to sit still. [T S Eliot, 1888–1965, *Ash Wednesday*, I]

4 Patience is passive, resignation is active. [Penelope Fitzgerald, 1916– , *Innocence*, 32]

5 We are all of us resigned to death: it's life we aren't resigned to. [Graham Greene, 1904–91, *The Heart of the Matter*, Bk 3, Pt 2, Ch. 2, sect. i]

6 But as I raved and grew more fierce and wild / At every word, / Methought I heard one calling, 'Child'; / And I replied, 'My Lord'. [George Herbert, 1593–1633, *The Collar*]

7 Let the world slide, let the world go: / A fig for care, and a fig for woe! / If I can't pay, why I can owe, / And death makes equal the high and the low. [John Heywood, 1497?–1580?, *Be Merry, Friends*]

8 It's our own mediocrity that makes us let go of love, makes us renounce it. True Love doesn't know the meaning of renunciation, is not even aware of that problem, never resigns itself; resignation is for beaten people, as beaten paths are for beaten men. [Eugene Ionesco, 1912–94, *The Hermit*]

9 Let us, then, be up and doing. / With a heart for any fate; / Still achieving, still pursuing, / Learn to labour and to wait. [H W Longfellow, 1807–82, *A Psalm of Life*]

10 There is no good in arguing with the inevitable. The only argument available with an east wind is to put on your overcoat. [James Russell Lowell, 1819–91, *Democracy and Addresses*, 'Democracy']

11 There comes a time in every man's life when he must make way for an older man. [Reginald Maudling, 1917–77 (in Smoking Room of House of Commons on being dropped from Mrs Thatcher's Shadow Cabinet), in *Guardian*, 20 Nov. 1976]

12 Nothing is here for tears, nothing to wail / Or knock the breast, no weakness, no contempt, / Dispraise, or blame; nothing but well and fair, / And what may quiet us in a death so noble. [John Milton, 1608–74, *Samson Agonistes*, 1721]

13 What must the king do now? Must he submit? / The king shall do it: must he be deposed? / The king shall be contented: must he lose / The name of king? o' God's name, let it go: / I'll give my jewels for a set of beads, / My gorgeous palace for a hermitage. [William Shakespeare, 1564–1616, *Richard II*, III. ii. 143]

See also CALM, FATALISM

RESISTANCE

1 It is hard for thee to kick against the pricks. [Bible, NT, *Acts of the Apostles* 9:5]

2 It is better to die on your feet than to live on your knees! [Dolores Ibárruri, 1895–1989 (Republican slogan broadcast in the Spanish Civil War, but coined by Emiliano Zapata in Mexico in 1910), in Hugh Thomas, *The Spanish Civil War*, Ch. 16]

3 *¡no pasarán!* – They shall not pass. [Dolores Ibárruri, 1895–1989, rallying cry to Spanish Republicans in Civil War, 1936. The call echoes the French *Ils ne passeront pas* of 1916 at Verdun]

See also ENDURANCE, OBSTINACY

RESPECT & DISRESPECT

1 I dung on my grandfather's doorstep, / Which is a reasonable and loving due / To hold no taint of spite or vassalage / And understood only by him and me. [Robert Graves, 1895–1985, *Front Door Soliloquy*]

2 We must respect the other fellow's religion, but only in the sense and to the extent that we respect his theory that his wife is beautiful and his children smart. [H L Mencken, 1880–1956, *Minority Report*, 1]

3 He respects Owl, because you can't help respecting anybody who can spell TUESDAY, even if he doesn't spell it right. [A A Milne, 1882–1956, *House at Pooh Corner*, Ch. 5]

4 But I, despite expert advice, / Keep doing things I think are nice, / And though to good I never come – / Inseparable my nose and thumb! [Dorothy Parker, 1893–1967, *Neither Bloody nor Bowed*]

5 I admire him [Cecil Rhodes], I frankly confess it; and when his time comes I shall buy a piece of the rope for a keepsake. [Mark Twain, 1835–1910, *Following the Equator*, Ch. 7]

6 The old-fashioned respect for the young is fast dying out. [Oscar Wilde, 1854–1900, *The Importance of Being Earnest*, I]

RESPONSIBILITY

1 *Fabrum esse suae quemque fortunae.* – Each man the architect of his own fate. [Appius Caecus, 4th cent. BC, quoted by Sallust, *De Civitate*, I, 2]

2 Am I my brother's keeper? [Bible, OT, *Genesis* 4:9]

3 He took water, and washed his hands before the multitude, saying, I am innocent of the blood of this just person. [Bible, NT, *St Matthew* 27:24]

4 Perhaps it is better to be irresponsible and right than to be responsible and wrong. [Winston Churchill, 1874–1965, Party Political Broadcast, London, 26 Aug. 1950]

5 Everyone threw the blame on me. I have noticed that they nearly always do. I suppose it is because they think I shall be able to bear it best. [Winston Churchill, 1874–1965, *My Early Life*, Ch. 17]

6 Whatever you blame, that you have done

yourself. [Georg Groddeck, 1866–1934, *The Book of the It*, Letter 14]

7 It matters not how strait the gate, / How charged with punishments the scroll, / I am the master of my fate: / I am the captain of my soul. [W E Henley, 1849–1903, *Invictus*]

8 Accuse not Nature, she hath done her part; / Do thou but thine. [John Milton, 1608–74, *Paradise Lost*, Bk vii, 561]

9 You become responsible, forever, for what you have tamed. You are responsible for your rose. [Antoine de Saint-Exupéry, 1900–1944, *The Little Prince*, Ch. 21]

10 When one does nothing, one believes oneself responsible for everything. [Jean-Paul Sartre, 1905–80, *Altona*, I]

11 Men at some time are masters of their fates; / The fault, dear Brutus, is not in our stars, / But in ourselves, that we are underlings. [William Shakespeare, 1564–1616, *Julius Caesar*, I. ii. 138]; see 12

12 For man is man and master of his fate. [Alfred, Lord Tennyson, 1809–92, *Idylls of the King*, 'The Marriage of Geraint', 355]; see 11

13 People are responsible for their *opinions*, but Providence is responsible for their morals. [W B Yeats, 1865–1939, in Christopher Hassall, *Edward Marsh*, Ch. 6]

See also POWER

RETIREMENT

1 Absence of occupation is not rest, / A mind quite vacant is a mind distressed. [William Cowper, 1731–1800, *Retirement*, 623]

2 How happy he who crowns in shades like these, / A youth of labour with an age of ease. [Oliver Goldsmith, 1728–74, *The Deserted Village*, 99]

3 Shillin' a day, / Bloomin' good pay – / Lucky to touch it, a shillin' a day. [(Of army pension) Rudyard Kipling, 1865–1936, *Shillin' a Day*]

4 Retire me to my Milan, where / Every third thought shall be my grave. [William Shakespeare, 1564–1616, *The Tempest*, V. i. (310)]

See also WORK

REVENGE

1 Revenge is a kind of wild justice, which the more man's nature runs to, the more ought law to weed it out. [Francis Bacon, 1561–1626, *Essays*, 4, 'Of Revenge']

2 Perish the Universe, provided I have my revenge. [Cyrano de Bergerac, 1620–55, *Agrippine*, IV. iii]

3 Eye for eye, tooth for tooth, hand for hand, foot for foot. [Bible, OT, *Exodus* 21:24; also *Deuteronomy* 19:21]

4 Vengeance is mine; I will repay, saith the Lord. [Bible, NT, *Romans* 12:19]

5 Sweet is revenge – especially to women. [Lord Byron, 1788–1824, *Don Juan*, I, 124]

6 Revenge proves its own executioner. [John Ford, 1586–1639?, *The Broken Heart*, IV. i]

7 We will get everything out of her [Germany] that you can squeeze out of a lemon, and a bit more . . . I will squeeze her until you can hear the pips squeak. [Eric Geddes, 1875–1937, speech at Cambridge, 9 Dec. 1918]

8 What though the field be lost? / All is not lost; th' unconquerable will, / And study of revenge, immortal hate, / And courage never to submit or yield: / And what is else not to be overcome? [John Milton, 1608–74, *Paradise Lost*, Bk i, 105]

9 How all occasions do inform against me, / And spur my dull revenge! [William Shakespeare, 1564–1616, *Hamlet*, IV. iv. 32]

10 Like to the Pontic sea, / Whose icy current and compulsive course / Ne'er feels retiring ebb, but keeps due on / To the Propontic and the Hellespont, / Even so my bloody thoughts, with violent pace, / Shall ne'er look back, ne'er ebb to humble love, / Till that a capable and wide revenge / Swallow them up. [*Othello*, III. iii. 454]

11 Those who offend us are generally punished for the offence they give; but we so frequently miss the satisfaction of knowing that we are avenged! [Anthony Trollope, 1815–82, *The Small House at Allington*, Ch. 50]

12 The vengeance of history is more terrible than the vengeance of the most powerful Secretary General. [Leon Trotsky, 1874–1940, *Final Testament* (written ten days before his murder)]

REVOLUTIONS & REVOLUTIONARIES

1 Revolutionaries don't make revolutions. The revolutionaries are those who know when power is lying in the street and then they can pick it up. Armed uprising by itself has never yet led to a revolution. [Hannah Arendt, 1906–75; in *Woman Talk 2*, comp. Michèle Brown and Ann O'Connor, 'Politics']

2 Revolutions are celebrated when they are no longer dangerous. [Pierre Boulez, 1925– , interview in *Guardian*, 13 Jan. 1989]

3 All modern revolutions have ended in a reinforcement of the power of the state. [Albert Camus, 1913–60, *The Rebel*, Ch. 2]

4 While there is a lower class, I am in it; while there is a criminal element, I am of it; while there is a soul in prison, I am not free. [Eugene Debs, 1855–1926, speech in Cleveland, Ohio, 9 Sept. 1917]

5 They [the generation of 1968] thought of revolution as instant coffee. [Umberto Eco, 1932– (in TV dialogue with Stuart Hall), in *Listener*, 16 May 1985]

6 Here once the embattled farmers stood, / And fired the shot heard round the world. [Ralph Waldo Emerson, 1803–82, *Hymn Sung at the Completion of the Concord Monument*]

7 Even a British revolution could not be made with rose-water. [Michael Foot, 1913– (of Aneurin Bevan), in *Listener*, 18/25 Dec. 1986]; see 18

8 The successful revolutionary is a statesman, the unsuccessful one a criminal. [Erich Fromm, 1900–1980, *The Fear of Freedom*, 7]

9 All successful revolutions are the kicking in of a rotten door. The violence of revolutions is the violence of men who charge into a vacuum. [J K Galbraith, 1908– , *The Age of Uncertainty*, Ch. 1]

10 That was a rotten way to run a revolution. I could have done it better myself. [(Of the General Strike) King George V, 1865–1936, in *The Times*, 8 May 1986]

11 He that goeth about to persuade a multitude that they are not so well governed as they ought to be, shall never want attentive and favourable hearers. [Richard Hooker, 1554?–1600, *Ecclesiastical Polity*, Bk i, §i]

12 The revolution chooses its enemies. [Saddam Hussein, 1937– , in *Guardian*, 10 Dec. 1990]

13 Every revolution evaporates, leaving behind only the slime of a new bureaucracy. [Franz Kafka, 1883–1924, *The Great Wall of China: Aphorisms, 1917–1919*]

14 Castro is without any question a remarkable man. I think it is important for Americans to understand that individuals who go into the mountains to lead a revolution are not motivated by economic considerations. If they were, they would be bank presidents and not revolutionaries. [Henry Kissinger, 1923– , TV interview, May 1975]

15 The revolutionary simpleton is everywhere. [Percy Wyndham Lewis, 1882–1957, *Time and Western Man*, Bk I, Ch. 6]

16 We are fighting for the gates of heaven. [Karl Liebknecht, 1871–1919 (in the abortive German revolution, 1918–19), in Albert Camus, *The Rebel*, Ch. 3]

17 'There won't be any revolution in America,' said Isadore. Nikitin agreed. 'The people are too clean. They spend all their time changing their shirts and washing themselves. You can't feel fierce and revolutionary in a bathroom.' [Eric Linklater, 1889–1974, *Juan in America*, V, 3]

18 Revolutions are not made with rosewater. [Edward Bulwer-Lytton, 1803–73, *The Parisians*, Bk v, Ch. 7]; see 7

19 A revolution only remains victorious through methods which are alien to those that made it. And sometimes even through sentiments which are similarly alien. [André Malraux, 1901–76, from *L'Espoir*, in Fitzroy Maclean, *Back to Bokhara*]

20 The revolt of a population injected with needs they are unable to satisfy. [Herbert Marcuse, 1898–1979 (definition of revolution), 'Warsaw Diary', *Granta*, 16]

21 A revolution is an opinion backed by bayonets. [Napoleon Bonaparte, 1769–1821, *Maxims*]

22 Revolution is not the uprising against pre-existing order, but the setting-up of a new order contradictory to the traditional one. [José Ortega y Gasset, 1883–1955, *The Revolt of the Masses*, Ch. 6]

23 We are dancing on a volcano. [Comte de Salvandy, 1795–1856, said just before the revolution of 1830]

24 In the first days of the revolt you must kill: to shoot down a European is to kill two birds with one stone, to destroy an oppressor and the man he oppresses at the same time: there remain a dead man, and a free man. [Jean-Paul Sartre, 1905–80, in Preface to F Fanon, *The Wretched of the Earth*]

25 We make little revolutions, but there is not a human end, nothing concerning man, only disorders. [Jean-Paul Sartre, 1905–80, last interview before his death, in *Le Nouvel Observateur*, 24 Mar. 1980]

26 The very people who have done the breaking through are themselves often the first to try to put a scab on their achievement. [Igor Stravinsky, 1882–1971, and Robert Craft, 1923– , *Conversations with S*, 'Advice to Young Composers']

27 Revolution by its very nature is sometimes compelled to take in more territory than it is capable of holding. Retreats are possible – when there is territory to retreat from. [Leon Trotsky, 1874–1940, *Diary in Exile*, 15 Feb. 1935]

28 Revolutions are always verbose. [Leon Trotsky, 1874–1940, *History of the Russian Revolution*, Pt 11, Ch. 12]

29 I've always had the impression that real militants are like cleaning women, doing a thankless, daily but necessary job. But you, you're the Ursula Andress of militancy, you make a brief appearance, just enough time for the cameras to flash, you make two or three startling remarks and then you disappear again, trailing clouds of self-serving mystery. [François Truffaut, 1932–84, letter to Jean-Luc Godard, May–June 1973]

30 Revolutions have never succeeded unless the establishment does three-quarters of the work. [Peter Ustinov, 1921– , *Dear Me*, Ch. 15]

31 Where the populace rise at once against the never-ending audacity of elected persons. [Walt Whitman, 1819–92, *Song of the Broad-axe*, 121]

32 And yet, and yet, / These Christs that die upon the barricades, / God knows it I am with them, in some ways. [Oscar Wilde, 1854–1900, *Sonnet to Liberty*]

33 In or about December, 1910, human *character* changed. [Virginia Woolf, 1882–1941, *The Common Reader*, First Series, 'Mr Bennett and Mrs Brown']

34 Thou hast great allies; / Thy friends are exultations, agonies, / And love, and man's unconquerable mind. [William Wordsworth, 1770–1850, *To Toussaint l'Ouverture*]

See also FRENCH REVOLUTION, REBELLION, RUSSIAN REVOLUTION, TYRANTS

THE RICH

1 The rich man has his motor car, / His country and his town estate. / He smokes a fifty-cent cigar / And jeers at Fate. [Franklin P Adams, 1881–1960, *The Rich Man*]

2 Lord Finchley tried to mend the Electric Light / Himself. It struck him dead: And serve him right! / It is the business of the wealthy man / To give employment to the artisan. [Hilaire Belloc, 1870–1953, *Lord Finchley*]

3 He that maketh haste to be rich shall not be innocent. [Bible, OT, *Proverbs* 28:20]

4 It is easier for a camel to go through the eye of a needle, than for a rich man to enter into the kingdom of God. [Bible, NT, *St Matthew* 19:24]

5 A rich man's joke is always funny. [T E Brown, 1830–97, *The Doctor*]

6 The rich are the scum of the earth in every country. [G K Chesterton, 1874–1936, *The Flying Inn*, Ch. 15]

7 Do you sincerely want to be rich? [Bernard Cornfeld, 1927–95, slogan of Investors Overseas Services]

8 Let me tell you about the very rich. They are different from you and me. [F Scott Fitzgerald, 1896–1940, *The Rich Boy*. In *Notebooks*, 'E', Fitzgerald records Hemingway's rejoinder: 'Yes, they have more money'; but elsewhere Hemingway spoke thus of the rich and Mary Colum gave the put-down]

9 Having a rich friend is like drowning and your friend makes lifeboats. But the friend gets touchy if you say one word: lifeboat. [John Guare, 1938– , *Six Degrees of Separation*, opening scene]

10 He considers the lilies, the rewards. / There is no substitute for a rich man. [Geoffrey Hill, 1932– , *To the Supposed Patron*]

11 Few rich men own their own property. The property owns them. [R G Ingersoll, 1833–99, address to the McKinley League, New York, 29 Oct. 1896]

12 The rich are only defeated when running for their lives. [C L R James, 1901–89, *Black Jacobins*, Ch. 3]

13 With the greater part of rich people, the chief enjoyment of riches consists in the parade of riches. [Adam Smith, 1723–90, *The Wealth of Nations*, Bk i, Ch. 11]

14 It is the wretchedness of being rich that you have to live with rich people. [Logan Pearsall Smith, 1865–1946, *Afterthoughts*, 4]

15 If all the rich men in the world divided up their money amongst themselves, there wouldn't be enough to go round. [Christina Stead, 1902–83, *House of All Nations*, 'Credo']

16 One can never be too thin or too rich [Duchess of Windsor, 1896–1986, attr.]

See also next category, MILLIONAIRES, POVERTY, WEALTH

RICH & POOR

1 The rich man in his castle, / The poor man at his gate, / God made them, high or lowly, / And ordered their estate. [Mrs C F Alexander, 1818–95, hymn]

2 It's the same the whole world over, / It's the poor what gets the blame, / It's the rich what gets the pleasure, / Isn't it a blooming shame? [anon. song of 1914–18 war]

3 The rich man's wealth is his strong city: the destruction of the poor is their poverty. [Bible, OT, *Proverbs* 10:15]

4 There are only two families in the world, my old grandmother used to say, the *Haves* and the *Have-nots*. [Miguel Cervantes, 1547–1616, *Don Quixote*, Pt II, Ch. 20]

5 The oligarchic character of the modern English commonwealth does not rest, like many oligarchies, on the cruelty of the rich to the poor. It does not even rest on the kindness of the rich to the poor. It rests on the perennial and unfailing kindness of the poor to the rich. [G K Chesterton, 1874–1936, *Heretics*, 15]

6 Jane is rather like one of those refined persons who go out to sew for the rich because they cannot abide contact with the poor. [Colette, 1873–1954, *The Other One*]

7 People don't resent having nothing nearly as much as too little. I have only just found that out. I am getting the knowledge of the rich as well as their ways. [Ivy Compton-Burnett, 1884–1969, *A Family and a Fortune*, Ch. 2]

8 Art thou poor, yet hast thou golden slumbers? / O sweet content! / Art thou rich, yet is thy mind perplexed? / O punishment! [Thomas Dekker, 1572?–1632, *Patient Grissill*, I]

9 I've been rich and I've been poor; believe me rich is better. [Gloria Grahame, 1925–81, in film *The Big Heat*, 1953, screenplay by S Boehm from novel by W P McGivern]

10 *Enrichissez-vous!* – Enrich yourselves! [François Guizot, 1787–1874, speech, 1 Mar. 1843]

11 In both rich and poor nations consumption is polarized while expectation is equalized. [Ivan Illich, 1926– , *Celebration of Awareness*, Ch. 12]

12 There's nothing surer, / The rich get rich and the poor get poorer, / In the meantime, in between time, / Ain't we got fun. [Gus Kahn, 1886–1941, and Raymond B Egan, 1890–1952, song: *Ain't We Got Fun*, 1921, in film *By the Light of the Silvery Moon*]

13 In a rich country, money is a piece of paper with which you buy goods on the market. You are only a customer. Even a millionaire is only a customer, nothing more. And in a poor country? In a poor country, money is a wonderful thick hedge, dazzling and always blooming, which separates you from everything else. [Ryszard Kapuściński, 1932– , *The Emperor*, 'Throne']

14 Plenty makes me poor. [Ovid, 43 BC–AD 17, *Metamorphoses*, III, 466]

15 Well, whiles I am a beggar, I will rail, / And say there is no sin but to be rich; / And, being rich, my virtue then shall be / To say there is no vice but beggary. [William Shakespeare, 1564–1616, *King John*, II. i. 593]

16 Take physic, pomp; / Expose thyself to feel what wretches feel. [*King Lear*, III. iv. 33]

17 Through tattered clothes small vices do appear; / Robes and furred gowns hide all. [*King Lear*, IV. vi. (169)]

18 I sometimes wished he [his father] would realize that he was poor instead of being that most nerve-racking of phenomena, a rich man without money. [Peter Ustinov, 1921– , *Dear Me*, Ch. 6]

See also previous category, POVERTY, WEALTH

RIGHT

1 This Ariyan Eightfold Path, that is to say: Right view, right aim, right speech, right action, right living, right effort, right mindfulness, right contemplation. [Buddha, *c.*563–*c.*483 BC, in F L Woodward, *Some Sayings of the Buddha*, p. 8]

2 A noisy man is always in the right. [William Cowper, 1731–1800, *Conversation*, 114]

3 But 'twas a maxim he had often tried, / That right was right, and there he would abide. [George Crabbe, 1754–1832, *Tales*, xv, 'The Squire and the Priest', 365]

4 Do well and right, and let the world sink. [George Herbert, 1593–1633, *Priest to the Temple*, Ch. 29]

5 All nature is but art, unknown to thee; / All chance, direction which thou canst not see; / All discord, harmony not understood; / All partial evil, universal good; / And, spite of pride, in erring reason's spite, / One truth is clear, Whatever is, is right. [Alexander Pope, 1688–1744, *An Essay on Man*, I, 289]

6 The right is more precious than peace. [Woodrow Wilson, 1856–1924, address to Congress, 2 Apr. 1917]

See also next category

RIGHT & WRONG

1 Then gently scan your brother man, / Still gentler sister woman; / Tho' they may gang a kennin wrang [a little wrong], / To step aside is human. [Robert Burns, 1759–96, *Address to the Unco Guid*, 49]

2 The word 'orthodoxy' not only no longer means being right; it practically means being wrong. [G K Chesterton, 1874–1936, *Heretics*, Ch. 1]

3 You can create a good impression on yourself by being right, he realizes, but for creating a good impression on others there's nothing to beat being totally and catastrophically wrong. [Michael Frayn, 1933– , *Sweet Dreams*, p. 76]

4 It is not that you do wrong by design, but that you should never do right by mistake. [Junius, 18th cent., *Letters*, 12]

5 There is no harm in being sometimes wrong – especially if one is promptly found out. [John Maynard Keynes, 1883–1946, *Essays in Biography*]

6 I think she must have been very strictly brought up, she's so desperately anxious to do the wrong thing correctly. [Saki (H H Munro), 1870–1916, *Reginald on Worries*]

7 Wrest once the law to your authority: / To do a great right, do a little wrong. [William Shakespeare, 1564–1616, *The Merchant of Venice*, IV. i. (215)]

8 Thus to persist / In doing wrong extenuates not wrong, / But makes it much more heavy. [*Troilus and Cressida*, II. ii. 186]

9 My speciality is being right when other people are wrong. [George Bernard Shaw, 1856–1950, *You Never Can Tell*, IV]

10 Two wrongs don't make a right, but they make a good excuse. [Thomas Szasz, 1920– , *The Second Sin*, 'Social Relations']

See also previous category, GOOD & EVIL

RIGHTS, see JUSTICE

RIVERS

1 Ye banks and braes o' bonnie Doon, / How can ye bloom sae fresh and fair? / How can ye chant, ye little birds, / And I sae weary fu' o' care? [Robert Burns, 1759–96, *Ye Banks and Braes*]

2 I do not know much about gods; but I think that the river / Is a strong brown god. [T S Eliot, 1888–1965, *Four Quartets*, 'Dry Salvages', I]

3 Ol' man river, dat ol' man river, / He must know sumpin', but don't say nothin', / He just keeps rollin', he keeps on rollin' along. [Oscar Hammerstein II, 1895–1960, song: *Ol' Man River*, in musical *Show Boat*, I]

4 The great grey-green, greasy Limpopo River, all set about with fever trees. [Rudyard Kipling, 1865–1936, *Just So Stories*]

5 Then I saw the Congo, creeping through the black, / Cutting through the jungle with a golden track. [Vachel Lindsay, 1879–1931, *The Congo*, 1]

6 Oh Tiber! father Tiber! / To whom the Romans pray, / A Roman's life, a Roman's arms, / Take thou in charge this day! [Lord Macaulay, 1800–1859, *Lays of Ancient Rome*, 'Horatius', 59]

7 Sabrina fair, / Listen where thou art sitting / Under the glassy, cool, translucent wave, / In twisted braids of lilies knitting / The loose train of thy amber-dropping hair. [(Of the River Severn) John Milton, 1608–74, *Comus*, 859]

8 I come from haunts of coot and hern, / I make a sudden sally, / And sparkle out among the fern, / To bicker down a valley. [Alfred, Lord Tennyson, 1809–92, *The Brook*, song, 1]

9 Father Nile, why or in what lands can I say you have hidden your head? On your account your Egypt never sues for showers, nor does the dry grass bow to Jupiter the Rain-bringer. [Tibullus, 54?–18? BC, *Elegies*, I, vii, 23]

10 These waters, rolling from their mountain-springs / With a soft inland murmur. [William Wordsworth, 1770–1850. *Lines Composed a Few Miles above Tintern Abbey*, 3]

11 Still glides the stream, and shall for ever glide; / The form remains, the function never dies. [William Wordsworth, 1770–1850, *The River Duddon*, 34, 'After-Thought']

See also THAMES

ROADS

1 All streets are theatres. [Ronald Blythe, 1922– , *The View in Winter*, Ch. 7]

2 Before the Roman came to Rye or out to Severn strode, / The rolling English drunkard made the rolling English road. [G K Chesterton, 1874–1936, *The Rolling English Road*]

3 The long, laborious road, dry, empty, and white. It was quite open to the heath on each side, and bisected that vast dark surface like the parting-line on a head of black hair, diminishing and bending away on the furthest horizon. [Thomas Hardy, 1840–1928, *The Return of the Native*, Ch. 2]

4 Until thy feet have trod the Road / Advise not wayside folk. [Rudyard Kipling, 1865–1936, *The Comforters*]

5 They shut the road through the woods / Seventy years ago. [Rudyard Kipling, 1865–1936, *The Way through the Woods*]

6 One road leads to London, / One road runs to Wales, / My road leads me seawards / To the white dipping sails. [John Masefield, 1878–1967, *Roadways*]

7 I love roads: / The goddesses that dwell / Far along them invisible / Are my favourite gods. [Edward Thomas, 1878–1917, *Roads*]

8 Where we're going we don't need roads. [Robert Zemeckis, 1952– , in his film *Back to the Future*, 1985. A line much loved and used by President Reagan]

See also TRAVEL

ROME & THE ROMANS

1 Every city has a sex and age which have nothing to do with demography. Rome is feminine ... London is a teen-ager and urchin, and, in this, hasn't changed since the time of Dickens. Paris, I believe, is a man in his twenties in love with an older woman. [John Berger, 1926– , in *Guardian*, 27 Mar. 1987]

2 Everyone soon or late comes round by Rome. [Robert Browning, 1812–89, *The Ring and the Book*, V, 296]

3 *Pax Romana*. Where they made a desolation they called it a peace. What absolute nonsense! It was a nasty, vulgar sort of civilization, only dignified by being hidden and under a lot of declensions. [Anthony Burgess, 1917–93, *Inside Mr Enderby*, Pt 1, Ch. 2, i]

4 Rome's just a city like anywhere else. A vastly overrated city, I'd say. It trades on belief just as Stratford trades on Shakespeare. [Anthony Burgess, 1917–93, *Inside Mr Enderby*, Pt II, Ch. 2, i]

5 While stands the Coliseum, Rome shall stand; / When falls the Coliseum, Rome shall fall; / And when Rome falls – the World. [Lord Byron, 1788–1824, *Childe Harold's Pilgrimage*, IV, 145]

6 I've stood upon Achilles' tomb, / And heard Troy doubted, time will doubt of Rome. [Lord Byron, 1788–1824, *Don Juan*, IV, 101]

7 O happy Rome, born when I was consul! [Cicero, 106–43 BC, quoted in Juvenal, *Satires*, X, 122]

8 Rome shall perish – write that word / In the

blood that she has spilt. [William Cowper, 1731–1800, *Boadicea*]

9 The Roman, like the Englishman who follows in his footsteps, brought to every new shore on which he set his foot (on our shore he never set it) only his cloacal obsession. He gazed about him in his toga and he said: It is meet to be here. Let us construct a water-closet. [James Joyce, 1882–1941, *Ulysses*, Penguin edn, 1992, p. 166]

10 At Rome, all things can be had at a price. [Juvenal, 60–*c.*130, *Satires*, III, 183]

11 Then none was for a party; / Then all were for the state; / Then the great man helped the poor, / And the poor man loved the great. [Lord Macaulay, 1800–1859, *Lays of Ancient Rome*, 'Horatius', 32]

12 Thy Naiad airs have brought me home / To the glory that was Greece, / And the grandeur that was Rome. [Edgar Allan Poe, 1809–49, *To Helen*]

13 He so improved the city that he justly boasted he had found it brick and left it marble. [Suetonius, *c.*70–*c.*140, *The 12 Caesars*, 'Augustus', 28]

14 O Romans, be it your care to rule the nations with imperial sway; these shall be your arts: to impose the rule of peace, to spare the humbled and to crush the proud. [Virgil, 70–19 BC, *Aeneid*, VI, 851]

See also GREECE, ITALY

ROYALTY, see KINGS & QUEENS

RULES

1 He [Algren] shunts aside all rules, regulations, and dicta, except for three laws he says a nice old Negro lady once taught him: Never play cards with any man named 'Doc'. Never eat at any place called 'Mom's'. And never, ever, no matter what else you do in your whole life, *never* sleep with anyone whose troubles are worse than your own. [Nelson Algren, 1909–81, in H E F Donohue, *Conversations with N A*, Foreword]

2 The rule is, jam to-morrow and jam yesterday – but never jam to-day. [Lewis Carroll, 1832–98, *Through the Looking Glass*, Ch. 5]

3 Do not think what you want to think until you know what you ought to know. [John Crow, 1905–70, 'Crow's Law', in R V Jones, *Most Secret War*, Ch. 9]

4 I never make exceptions. An exception disproves the rule. [Arthur Conan Doyle, 1859–1930, *The Sign of Four*, Ch. 2]

5 If anything can go wrong it will. [Capt Ed Murphy, 1918– (Murphy's Law, various versions), in P Dickson, *The Official Rules*. Also ascr. to George Nichols]

6 The golden rule is that there are no golden rules. [George Bernard Shaw, 1856–1950, *Man and Superman*, 'Maxims for Revolutionists', The Golden Rule]

See also ADVICE, WARNINGS

RUSSIA

1 There are only four problems with Soviet agriculture: spring, summer, autumn and winter. [anon. in *The Sunday Times*, 17 Nov. 1985]

2 We pretend to work and they pretend to pay us. [anon., Russian workers' joke, in *Listener*, 16 June 1988]

3 Ambivalence, I think, is the chief characteristic of my nation. [Joseph Brodsky, 1940–96, *Less Than One*, title essay]

4 I cannot forecast to you the action of Russia. It is a riddle wrapped in a mystery inside an enigma; but perhaps there is a key. That key is Russian national interest. [Winston Churchill, 1874–1965, BBC radio broadcast, 1 Oct. 1939]

5 So shall we break up the union because of sausage? [Mikhail Gorbachev, 1931– , responding to Lithuanian complaints about shortages in the shops; *Independent*, 'Quote Unquote', 13 Jan. 1990]

6 Russian circus in town. Do not feed the animals. [Graffito, Czechoslovakia, 1968; in Robert Reisner, *Graffiti*]

7 They [the Soviets] are Communists just as the Victorians were Christians. They attend CP meetings and lectures on Marxism-Leninism at regular intervals in exactly the same way as the Victorians attended church on Sunday . . . And they apply the principles of Marxism in their private lives to just about the same extent as the Victorians applied the principles of the Sermon on the Mount. Neither more nor less. [Fitzroy Maclean, 1911–96, *Back to Bokhara*]

8 Russia has two generals in whom she can trust – Generals Janvier and Février. [Nicholas I of Russia, 1796–1855, *Punch*, 10 Mar. 1853]

9 Russia is an enormous lunatic asylum. There is a heavy padlock on the door, but there are no walls. [Tatyana Tolstaya, 1951– , in *Guardian*, 19 Mar. 1992]

10 You don't understand the Russian spirit. People here do not understand the concept of buying and selling land. The land is like a mother. You don't sell your mother. [Boris Yeltsin, 1931– , in *Guardian*, 7 Dec. 1991]

11 No Jewish blood runs among my blood, / but I am as bitterly and hardly hated / by every anti-semite / as if I were a Jew. By this / I am a Russian. [Yevgeny Yevtushenko, 1933– , *Babiy Yar*]

12 A poet in Russia is more than a poet. [Yevgeny Yevtushenko, 1933– , in *Guardian*, 20 Apr. 1987]

See also next entry

RUSSIAN REVOLUTION

1 Neither can you expect a revolution, because there is no new baby in the womb of our society. He [Lenin] alone could have led Russia into the enchanted quagmire; he alone could have found the way back to the causeway. He saw; he turned; he perished . . . The Russian people were left floundering in the bog. Their worst misfortune was his birth, their next worst – his death. [Winston Churchill, 1874–1965, *The World Crisis*, Ch. 4, 'Aftermath']

2 If there's no dancing count me out. [(Of the Russian Revolution) Emma Goldman, 1869–1940, in *New Statesman*, 1 Mar. 1985]

3 Russia is a collapse, not a revolution. [D H Lawrence, 1885–1930, *Phoenix*, 'Art and Morality']

4 Ten Days That Shook the World. [John Reed, 1887–1920, title of book on Russian Revolution]

5 I have seen the future and it works. [(To Bernard Baruch after a visit to the Soviet Union in 1919) Lincoln Steffens, 1866–1936, *Autobiography*, Ch. 18]

6 It was the supreme expression of the mediocrity of the apparatus that Stalin himself rose to his position. [Leon Trotsky, 1874–1940, *My Life*, Ch. 40]

7 From being a patriotic myth, the Russian people have become an awful reality. [Leon Trotsky, 1874–1940, *History of the Russian Revolution*, Pt III, Ch. 7]

See also FRENCH REVOLUTION, REVOLUTIONS

S

SACRIFICE

1 Bring no more vain oblations; incense is an abomination unto me; the new moons and sabbaths, the calling of assemblies, I cannot away with. [Bible, OT, *Isaiah* 1:13]

2 The good shepherd giveth his life for the sheep. [Bible, NT, *St John* 10:11]

3 Greater love hath no man than this, that a man lay down his life for his friends. [Bible, NT, *St John* 15:13]

4 Bring hither the fatted calf, and kill it. [Bible, NT, *St Luke* 15:23]

5 He that findeth his life shall lose it: and he that loseth his life for my sake shall find it. [Bible, NT, *St Matthew* 10:39]

6 I belong to a generation of men, most of which aren't here any more, and we all did the same thing for the same reason, no matter what we thought about politics. [Noël Coward, 1899–1973, *This Happy Breed*, I. iii]

7 'It is a far, far better thing that I do, than I have ever done; it is a far, far better rest, that I go to, than I have ever known.' [Charles Dickens, 1812–70, *A Tale of Two Cities*, iii, 15]

8 Oh God said to Abraham, 'Kill me a son.' / Abe says, 'Man, you must be puttin' me on.' [Bob Dylan, 1941– , song: *Highway 61 Revisited*]

9 To what green altar, O mysterious priest, / Lead'st thou that heifer lowing at the skies, / And all her silken flanks with garlands drest? / What little town by river or sea shore, / Or mountain-built with peaceful citadel, / Is emptied of this folk, this pious morn? [John Keats, 1795–1821, *Ode on a Grecian Urn*, 4]

10 She's the sort of woman who lives for others – you can always tell the others by their hunted expression. [C S Lewis, 1898–1963, *The Screwtape Letters*, 26]

11 For the sake of the achievement of a specific political goal, it is possible to sacrifice half mankind. [Mao Zedong, 1893–1976 (speech at meeting in Moscow, Nov. 1957), in *Pravda*, 26 Aug. 1973]

12 A woman will always sacrifice herself if you give her the opportunity. It is her favourite form of self-indulgence. [W Somerset Maugham, 1874–1965, *The Circle*, III]

13 I might give my life for my friend, but he had better not ask me to do up a parcel. [Logan Pearsall Smith, 1865–1946, *Afterthoughts*, 6]

See also LOYALTY, MARTYRS, PATRIOTS

SAILORS

1 He that commands the sea is at great liberty, and may take as much and as little of the war as he will. [Francis Bacon, 1561–1626, *Essays*, 29, 'Of the True Greatness of Kingdoms']

2 We joined the Navy to see the world, / And what did we see? We saw the sea. [Irving Berlin, 1888–1989, song: *We Saw the Sea*, in musical *Follow the Fleet*]

3 Ye Mariners of England / That guard our native seas, / Whose flag has braved, a thousand years, / The battle and the breeze. [Thomas Campbell, 1777–1844, *Ye Mariners of England*]

4 My only great qualification for being put in charge of the Navy is that I am very much at sea. [Edward Carson, 1854–1935 (said to senior

Admiralty staff on formation of Coalition, 1916), in H Montgomery Hyde, *Carson*, Ch. 2, i]

5 Don't talk to me about naval tradition. It's nothing but rum, sodomy and the lash. [Winston Churchill, 1874–1965, in P Gretton, *Former Naval Person*, Ch. 1]

6 When I was a lad I served a term / As office-boy to an Attorney's firm; / I cleaned the windows and I swept the floor, / And I polished up the handle of the big front door. / I polished up that handle so carefullee, / That now I am the Ruler of the Queen's Navee! [W S Gilbert, 1836–1911, *HMS Pinafore*, 1]

7 *Oh! combien de marins, combien de capitaines / Qui sont partis joyeux pour des courses lointaines, / Dans ce morne horizon se sont évanouis.* – Oh! how many sailors, how many captains who have gaily set out for long voyages have vanished behind that sad horizon! [Victor Hugo, 1802–85, *Oceano Nox*]

8 'Sailor men 'ave their faults,' said the night-watchman, frankly. 'I'm not denying it. I used to 'ave myself when I was at sea.' [W W Jacobs, 1863–1943, *The Lady of the Barge*, 'Bill's Paper Chase']

9 There were gentlemen and there were seamen in the navy of Charles the Second. But the seamen were not gentlemen: and the gentlemen were not seamen. [Lord Macaulay, 1800–1859, *History of England*, I, Ch. 3]

10 All the Nice Girls Love a Sailor. [A J Mills, b.1872, and Bennett Scott, title of song, 1909]

11 You gentlemen of England / Who live at home at ease, / How little do you think / On the dangers of the seas. [Martin Parker, d.1656, *The Valiant Sailors*]

12 We be three poor mariners / Newly come from the seas. [Thomas Ravenscroft, 1529?–1635?, *Deuteromelia*]

13 A life on the ocean wave, / A home on the rolling deep. [Epes Sargent, 1813–80, *A Life on the Ocean Wave*. These lines were taken from a song by Samuel J Arnold]

14 And last of all an Admiral came, / A terrible man with a terrible name, – / A name which you all know by sight very well, / But which no one can speak, and no one can spell. [Robert Southey, 1774–1843, *The March to Moscow*, 8]

15 Nelson, born in a fortunate hour for himself and for his country, was always in his element and always on his element. [G M Trevelyan, 1876–1962, *History of England*, Bk V, Ch. 5]

16 In this country we find it pays to shoot an admiral from time to time to encourage the others. [Voltaire, 1694–1778, *Candide*, Ch. 23]

17 O hear us when we cry to Thee / For those in peril on the sea. [William Whiting, 1825–78, hymn: *Eternal Father, Strong to Save*]

18 Wrap me up in my tarpaulin jacket, / And say a poor buffer lies low, / And six stalwart lancers shall carry me / With steps solemn, mournful, and slow. [J G Whyte-Melville, 1821–78, song: *The Tarpaulin Jacket*]

19 The Fleet's lit up. It is like fairyland; the ships are covered with fairy lights. [Tommy Woodrooffe, 1899–1978, BBC radio commentary at the Coronation Review of the Royal Navy at Spithead, 20 May 1937]

See also SEA, SHIPS

SAINTS

1 The reason saints wear haloes is so, when they pass the hat round, they don't keep anything for themselves. [Nancy Banks-Smith, 1929– , in *Guardian*, 5 Feb. 1986]

2 St George he was for England, / And before he killed the dragon / He drank a pint of English ale / Out of an English flagon. [G K Chesterton, 1874–1936, *The Englishman*]

3 Saints will aid if men will call: / For the blue sky bends over all! [Samuel Taylor Coleridge, 1772–1834, *Christabel*, Pt 1, 330]

4 O thou undaunted daughter of desires! / By all thy dower of lights and fires; / By all the eagle in thee, all the dove; / By all thy lives and deaths of love; / By thy large draughts of intellectual day. [Richard Crashaw, 1613?–49, *The Flaming Heart upon the Book of Saint Teresa*, 93]

5 The last and greatest herald of Heaven's King, / Girt with rough skins, hies to the deserts wild. [William Drummond, 1585–1649, *For the Baptist*]

6 What after all / Is a halo? It's only one more thing to keep clean. [Christopher Fry, 1907– , *The Lady's Not for Burning*, I]

7 Remote from man, with God he passed the

days, / Prayer all his business, all his pleasure praise. [Thomas Parnell, 1679–1717, *The Hermit*, 5]

8 There may have been disillusionments in the lives of the medieval saints, but they would scarcely have been better pleased if they could have foreseen that their names would be associated nowadays chiefly with racehorses and the cheaper clarets. [Saki (H H Munro), 1870–1916, *Reginald at the Carlton*]

9 Saint George, that swinged the dragon, and e'er since / Sits on his horse back at mine hostess' door. [William Shakespeare, 1564–1616, *King John*, II. i. 288]

10 A man of marvellous mirth and pastimes; and sometime of as sad a gravity; a man for all seasons. [(Of Sir Thomas More) Richard Whittington, *c*.1480–*c*.1530, *Vulgaria: Exercise in School Latin*]

See also MARTYRS

SALVATION

1 Every valley shall be exalted, and every mountain and hill shall be made low: and the crooked shall be made straight, and the rough places plain. [Bible, OT, *Isaiah* 40:4]

2 The harvest is past, the summer is ended, and we are not saved. [Bible, OT, *Jeremiah* 8:20]

3 For he shall give his angels charge over thee, to keep thee in all thy ways. They shall bear thee up in their hands, lest thou dash thy foot against a stone. [Bible, OT, *Psalms* 91:11]

4 Work out your own salvation with fear and trembling. [Bible, NT, *Philippians* 2:12]

5 Strait is the gate, and narrow is the way, which leadeth unto life, and few there be that find it. [Bible, NT, *St Matthew* 7:14]

6 The wounded surgeon plies the steel / That questions the distempered part. [T S Eliot, 1888–1965, *Four Quartets*, 'Burnt Norton', IV]

7 The stars move still, time runs, the clock will strike, / The devil will come, and Faustus must be damned. / Oh, I'll leap up to my God! Who pulls me down? / See, see, where Christ's blood streams in the firmament! / One drop would save my soul, half a drop: ah, my Christ! [Christopher Marlowe, 1564–93, *Doctor Faustus*, 1458]

SATIRE

1 Satire is dependent on strong beliefs, and on strong beliefs wounded. [Anita Brookner, 1938–   , in *Spectator*, 23 Mar. 1989]

2 I'll publish, right or wrong: / Fools are my theme, let satire be my song. [Lord Byron, 1788–1824, *English Bards and Scotch Reviewers*, 5]

3 To hear some people talk, you would think humour was an aspect of satire, instead of the other way round. Satire is simply humour in uniform. [Paul Jennings, 1918–89 (in obituary in the *Guardian*, 1 Jan. 1990)]

4 Satire is something that closes on Saturday night. [George S Kaufman, 1889–1961, in Scott Meredith, *G S K and His Friends*, Ch. 6]

5 The British, he thought, must be gluttons for satire: even the weather forecast seemed to be some kind of spoof, predicting every possible combination of weather for the next twenty-four hours without actually committing itself to anything specific. [David Lodge, 1935–   , *Changing Places*, Ch. 2]

6 He can discover / A selfish motive for anything – and collect / His royalties as recording angel. [Louis MacNeice, 1907–63, *The Satirist*]

7 Satire should, like a polished razor keen, / Wound with a touch that's scarcely felt or seen. [Lady Mary Wortley Montagu, 1689–1762, *To the Imitator of the First Satire of Horace*, Bk ii]

8 Satire is a lesson, parody is a game. [Vladimir Nabakov, 1899–1977, *Strong Opinions*, 6]

9 Satire is a sort of glass, wherein beholders do generally discover everybody's face but their own. [Jonathan Swift, 1677–1745, *The Battle of the Books*, Preface]

10 Yet malice never was his aim; / He lashed the vice, but spared the name; / No individual could resent, / Where thousands equally were meant. [Jonathan Swift, 1677–1745, *On the Death of Dr Swift*, 512]

See also COMEDY, HUMOUR, WIT

SATISFACTION, see CONTENTMENT

SCANDAL

1 They come together like the coroner's inquest, to sit upon the murdered reputations of the week.

[William Congreve, 1670–1729, *The Way of the World*, I. i]

2 Love and scandal are the best sweeteners of tea. [Henry Fielding, 1707–54, *Love in Several Masques*, IV. xi]

3 A great party is not to be brought down because of a scandal by a woman of easy virtue and a proved liar. [Lord Hailsham, 1907–   (on the Profumo affair), in BBC TV interview, 13 June 1963]

4 Well, (said he), we had a good talk.
BOSWELL: Yes, Sir, you tossed and gored several persons. [Dr Samuel Johnson, 1709–84, in James Boswell, *Life of J*, 1768]

5 If you can't say anything good about someone, sit right here by me. [Alice Roosevelt Longworth, 1884–1980, embroidered on a cushion in her sitting-room]

6 At ev'ry word a reputation dies. [Alexander Pope, 1688–1744, *The Rape of the Lock*, III, 16]

7 For greatest scandal waits on greatest state. [William Shakespeare, 1564–1616, *The Rape of Lucrece*, 1006]

8 Here is the whole set! a character dead at every word. [R B Sheridan, 1751–1816, *The School for Scandal*, II. ii]

9 Convey a libel in a frown, / And wink a reputation down. [Jonathan Swift, 1677–1745, *Journal of a Modern Lady*, 192]

10 I am in no need of your God-damned sympathy. I ask only to be entertained by some of your grosser reminiscences. [Alexander Woollcott, 1887–1943, letter to Rex O'Malley, 1942]

See also GOSSIP

SCEPTICISM, see DOUBT

SCHOLARS, see STUDENTS

SCHOOLS

1 What we must look for here is, first, religious and moral principles; secondly, gentlemanly conduct; thirdly, intellectual ability. [Thomas Arnold, 1795–1842, address to his scholars at Rugby]

2 It amazed Ann that Mrs Kershaw, who held such strong views, should send her children to a parochial school with a vicar coming in twice a week to take morning prayers. You'd have thought she might have preferred one of those progressive places where the teachers were called by their christian names and told to shut up. [Beryl Bainbridge, 1934–   , *Sweet William*, Ch. 1]

3 And love levels all, doesn't it? Love and the Board school. [Max Beerbohm, 1872–1956, *Zuleika Dobson*, Ch. 17]

4 The schoolboy, with his satchel in his hand, / Whistling aloud to bear his courage up. [Robert Blair, 1699–1746, *The Grave*, 58]

5 You probably know, the better class of Briton likes to send his children away to school until they're old and intelligent enough to come home again. Then they're too old and intelligent to want to. [Malcolm Bradbury, 1932–   , *Rates of Exchange*, 5, iii]

6 'That's the reason they're called lessons,' the Gryphon remarked: 'because they lessen from day to day.' [Lewis Carroll, 1832–98, *Alice in Wonderland*, Ch. 9]

7 It is arguable that we ought to put the State in order before there can really be such a thing as a State school. [G K Chesterton, 1874–1936, *All I Survey*, 'On Education']

8 Headmasters have powers at their disposal with which Prime Ministers have never yet been invested. [Winston Churchill, 1874–1965, *My Early Life*, Ch. 2]

9 The ape-like virtues without which no one can enjoy a public school. [Cyril Connolly, 1903–74, *Enemies of Promise*, Ch. 2]

10 The art of getting on at school depends on a mixture of enthusiasm with moral cowardice and social sense. The enthusiasm is for personalities and gossip about them, for a schoolboy is a novelist too busy to write. [Cyril Connolly, 1903–74, *Enemies of Promise*, Ch. 21]

11 All schools are hell, nor are we out of them. In a moment you will hear the sound of the second circle: unrestricted boy. [Giles Cooper, 1918–66, radio drama *Unman, Wittering and Zigo*]

12 Girls scream, / Boys shout; / Dogs bark, / School's out. [W H Davies, 1871–1940, *School's Out*]

13 A smattering of everything, and a knowledge of nothing. [(Minerva House) Charles Dickens, 1812–70, *Sketches by Boz*, 'Tales', Ch. 3, 'Sentiment']

14 Sometimes I think I'll not send him to school – but just let his individuality develop. [Ruth Draper, 1889–1956, *The Children's Party*]

15 Twenty years of schoolin' / And they put you on the day shift. [Bob Dylan, 1941– , song: *Subterranean Homesick Blues*]

16 Public schools are the nurseries of all vice and immorality. [Henry Fielding, 1707–54, *Joseph Andrews*, Bk iii, Ch. 5]

17 Greet him like Etonians without a single word, / Absolutely silent and infinitely bored. [Mgr Ronald Knox, 1888–1957, *On the Right Method of Greeting a New Headmaster*]

18 It will be a great day when our schools have all the resources they need and the air force has to hold a cake-sale to buy a bomber. [Lothian Parents Action Group, Scotland (slogan), in *Observer*, 25 May 1986]

19 When I was a boy at school I never minded the lessons. I just resented having to work terribly hard at playing. [John Mortimer, 1923– , *A Voyage round My Father*, I]

20 That deep mistrust of the English upper classes which can best be learned at Harrow. [John Mortimer, 1923– , in *The Sunday Times Magazine*, 31 Aug. 1986]

21 Probably the Battle of Waterloo *was* won on the playing-fields of Eton, but the opening battles of all subsequent wars have been lost there. [George Orwell, 1903–50, *The Lion and the Unicorn*, 'England, Your England']; see 28

22 You can't expect a boy to be depraved until he has been to a good school. [Saki (H H Munro), 1870–1916, *A Baker's Dozen*]

23 Though loaded firearms were strictly forbidden at St Trinian's to all but Sixth-Formers . . . one or two of them carried automatics acquired in the holidays, generally the gift of some indulgent relative. [Ronald Searle, 1920– , and Timothy Shy (D B Wyndham-Lewis), 1891–1961, *The Terror of St Trinian's*, Ch. 3]

24 School is where you go between when your parents can't take you and industry can't take you. [John Updike, 1932– , *The Centaur*, Ch. 4]

25 We class schools, you see, into four grades: Leading School, First-rate School, Good School, and School. [Evelyn Waugh, 1903–66, *Decline and Fall*, I, 1]

26 That's the public-school system all over. They may kick you out, but they never let you down. [Evelyn Waugh, 1903–66, *Decline and Fall*, I, 3]

27 Anyone who has been to an English public school will always feel comparatively at home in prison. [Evelyn Waugh, 1903–66, *Decline and Fall*, III, 4]

28 The battle of Waterloo was won on the playing fields of Eton. [Duke of Wellington, 1769–1852, attr. by Montalembert, *De l'avenir politique de l'Angleterre*]; see 21

29 Mr Polly went into the National School at six, and he left the private school at fourteen, and by that time his mind was in much the same state that you would be in, dear reader, if you were operated on for appendicitis by a well-meaning, boldly enterprising, but rather overworked and underpaid butcher boy, who was superseded towards the climax of the operation by a left-handed clerk of high principles but intemperate habits – that is to say, it was in a thorough mess. [H G Wells, 1866–1946, *The History of Mr Polly*, Ch. I, Pt 2]

See also EDUCATION, LEARNING, TEACHERS

SCIENCE

1 Science knows only one commandment: contribute to science. [Bertolt Brecht, 1898–1956, *The Life of Galileo*, xiv]

2 That is the essence of science: ask an impertinent question, and you are on the way to the pertinent answer. [J Bronowski, 1908–74, *The Ascent of Man*, 4]

3 Science without religion is lame, religion without science is blind. [Albert Einstein, 1879–1955, paper for conference on science, New York, 9/11 Sept. 1940]

4 The process of scientific discovery is, in effect, a continuous flight from wonder. [Albert Einstein, 1879–1955; in Laurence J Peter, *Peter's Quotations*]

5 Science can only state what is, not what should be. [Albert Einstein, 1879–1955, *Out of My Later Years*]

6 A science is any discipline in which the fool of this generation can go beyond the point reached by the genius of the last generation. [Max Gluckman, 1911–75, *Politics, Law and Ritual*, p. 60]

7 Science is all those things which are confirmed to such a degree that it would be unreasonable to withhold one's provisional consent. [Stephen J Gould, 1941– , lecture on evolution, Cambridge, 1984]

8 Natural science does not simply describe and explain nature, it is part of the interplay between nature and ourselves. [Werner Heisenberg, 1901–76, *Physics and Philosophy*]

9 Science is nothing but trained and organized common sense. [T H Huxley, 1825–95, *Collected Essays*, iv, 'The Method of Zadig']

10 Science should leave off making pronouncements: the river of knowledge has too often turned back on itself. [James Jeans, 1887–1946, *The Mysterious Universe*, Ch. 1]

11 Our scientific power has outrun our spiritual power. We have guided missiles and misguided men. [Martin Luther King Jr, 1929–68, *Strength to Love*, Ch. 7]

12 Science is spectral analysis. Art is light synthesis. [Karl Kraus, 1874–1936, *Half-truths and One-and-a-half Truths*, 'Riddles']

13 Scientific discovery is a private event, and the delight that accompanies it, or the despair of finding it illusory does not travel. [Peter Medawar, 1915–87, *Hypothesis and Imagination*]

14 Science, at bottom, is really anti-intellectual. It always distrusts pure reason, and demands the production of objective fact. [H L Mencken, 1880–1956, *Minority Report*, 412]

15 Traditional scientific method has always been at the very *best*, twenty-twenty hindsight. It's good for seeing where you've been. [Robert M Pirsig, 1928– , *Zen and the Art of Motorcycle Maintenance*, Pt III, Ch. 24]

16 Science is built of facts, as a house is built of stones; but an accumulation of facts is no more a science than a heap of stones is a house. [Henri Poincaré, 1854–1912, *Science and Hypothesis*, Ch. 9]

17 Not the *verifiability* but the *falsifiability* of a system is to be taken as a criterion of demarcation ... *It must be possible for an empirical scientific system to be refuted by experience.* [Karl Popper, 1902–94, *The Logic of Scientific Discovery*, Ch. 1, sect. vi]

18 Science must begin with myths, and with the criticism of myths. [Karl Popper, 1902–94, 'Philosophy of Science: A Personal Report', in *British Philosophy in the Mid-century*, ed. C A Mace]

19 It [science] grows out of its past, but never outgrows it, any more than we outgrow our own childhood. [Oliver Sacks, 1933– , in *Hidden Histories of Science*, ed. Robert B Silvers, 'Introduction']

20 Science is organized knowledge. [Herbert Spencer, 1820–1903, *Education*, Ch. 2]

21 The highest wisdom has but one science – the science of the whole – the science explaining the whole creation and man's place in it. [Leo Tolstoy, 1828–1910, *War and Peace*, V, Ch. 2]

22 Nothing holds up the progress of science so much as the right idea at the wrong time. [Vincent de Vignaud, 1901–78, in R V Jones, *Most Secret War*, Ch. 9]

23 Science can find no individual enjoyment in Nature: science can find no aim in Nature; science can find no creativity in Nature; it finds mere rules of succession. [A N Whitehead, 1861–1947, *Nature and Life*, Ch. 2]

24 A science which hesitates to forget its founders is lost. [A N Whitehead, 1861–1947, attr.]

25 Science appears but what in truth she is, / Not as our glory and our absolute boast, / But as a succedaneum, and a prop / To our infirmity. [William Wordsworth, 1770–1850, *The Prelude*, II, 212]

See also next entry, BIOLOGY, MATHEMATICS, PHYSICS

SCIENTISTS

1 When I find myself in the company of scientists, I feel like a shabby curate who has strayed by mistake into a drawing-room full of dukes. [W H Auden, 1907–73, *The Dyer's Hand*, 2, 'The Poet and the City']

2 Scientists, therefore, are responsible for their research not only intellectually but also morally ... the results of quantum mechanics and relativity theory have opened up two very different paths for physics to pursue. They may lead us – to put it in extreme terms – to the Buddha or to the bomb, and it is up to each of us to decide which path to take. [Fritjof Capra, 1939– , *The Turning Point*, II, 3]

3 If an elderly but distinguished scientist says that something is possible, he is almost certainly right, but if he says that it is impossible he is very probably wrong. [Arthur C Clarke, 1917– , in *New Yorker*, 9 Aug. 1969]

4 I believe the souls of five hundred Sir Isaac Newtons would go to the making up of a Shakespeare or a Milton. [Samuel Taylor Coleridge, 1772–1834, letter to Thomas Poole, 23 Mar. 1801]

5 It is a good morning exercise for a research scientist to discard a pet hypothesis every day before breakfast. It keeps him young. [Konrad Lorenz, 1903–89, *On Aggression*, Ch. 2]

6 There is no spiritual copyright in scientific discoveries, unless they should happen to be quite mistaken. Only in making a blunder does a scientist do something which, conceivably, no one might ever do again. [Peter Medawar, 1915–87, *Pluto's Republic*]

7 *Laboratorium est oratorium*. The place where we do our scientific work is a place of prayer. [Joseph Needham, 1900–1995; in *Dictionary of Scientific Quotations*, ed. A L Mackay]

8 Every genuine scientist must be ... a metaphysician. [George Bernard Shaw, 1856–1950, *Back to Methuselah*, Preface]

9 When scientists are faced with an expression of the traditional culture it tends ... to make their feet ache. [C P Snow, 1905–80, *The Two Cultures*, 4]

See also previous entry, BIOLOGY, MATHEMATICS, PHYSICS

SCOTLAND & THE SCOTS

1 A young Scotsman of your ability let loose upon the world with £300, what could he not do? It's almost appalling to think of; especially if he went among the English. [James Barrie, 1860–1937, *What Every Woman Knows*, I]

2 You've forgotten the greatest moral attribute of a Scotsman, Maggie, that he'll do nothing which might damage his career. [James Barrie, 1860–1937, *What Every Woman Knows*, II]

3 The halesome parritch, chief of Scotia's food. [Robert Burns, 1759–96, *The Cotter's Saturday Night*, 92]

4 From scenes like these old Scotia's grandeur springs, / That makes her loved at home, revered abroad: / Princes and lords are but the breath of kings, / 'An honest man's the noblest work of God.' [Robert Burns, 1759–96, *The Cotter's Saturday Night*, 163 (the last line quotes Pope)]

5 My heart's in the Highlands, my heart is not here; / My heart's in the Highlands a-chasing the deer. [Robert Burns, 1759–96, *My Heart's in the Highlands*]

6 Auld Ayr, wham ne'er a town surpasses / For honest men and bonnie lasses. [Robert Burns, 1759–96, *Tam o'Shanter*, 15]

7 Had Cain been Scot, God would have changed his doom / Not forced him wander, but confined him home. [John Cleveland, 1613–58, *The Rebel Scot*]

8 But the great thing about the way Glasgow is now is that if there's a nuclear attack it'll look exactly the same afterwards. [Billy Connolly, 1942– , *Gullible's Travels*, 'Scotland']

9 It's hame and it's hame, hame fain wad I be, / O, hame, hame, hame to my ain countree! [Allan Cunningham, 1784–1842, *It's Hame and It's Hame*]

10 The great benefit of the Scots is that they are the only identifiable, civilized European race who do not have the misfortune to have a government. [Nicholas Fairbairn, 1933–95; *Independent*, 'Quote Unquote', 16 Nov. 1991]

11 I'm only a common old working chap, / As anyone here can see, / But when I get a couple of drinks on a Saturday, / Glasgow belongs to me. [Will Fyffe, 1885–1957, song: *I Belong to Glasgow*]

12 Glasgow, the sort of industrial city where most people live nowadays but nobody imagines living. [Alasdair Gray, 1934– , *Lanark*, Bk 3, Ch. 11]

13 O Knox he was a bad man / he split the Scottish mind. / The one half he made cruel / and the other half unkind. [Alan Jackson, 1938– ; in *Scottish Quotations*, comp. Alan Bold]

14 BOSWELL: I do indeed come from Scotland but I cannot help it ...
JOHNSON: That, Sir, I find, is what a very

great many of your countrymen cannot help. [Dr Samuel Johnson, 1709–84, in James Boswell, *Life of J*, 16 May 1763]

15 Much . . . may be made of a Scotchman, if he be *caught* young. [(On Lord Mansfield) Dr Samuel Johnson, 1709–84, in James Boswell, *Life of J*, 1772]

16 Sir, the noblest prospect that a Scotchman ever sees, is the high road that leads him to London. [Dr Samuel Johnson, 1709–84, in James Boswell, *Tour of the Hebrides*, 10 Nov. 1773]

17 I have been trying all my life to like Scotchmen, and am obliged to desist from the experiment in despair. [Charles Lamb, 1775–1834, *Essays of Elia*, 'Imperfect Sympathies']

18 Hauf his soul a Scot maun use / Indulgin' in illusions, / And hauf in gettin' rid o' them / And comin' to conclusions. [Hugh MacDiarmid, 1892–1978, *A Drunk Man Looks at the Thistle*, 2388]

19 To an Englishman something is what it is called: to a Scotsman something is what it is. [Hugh MacDiarmid, epigraph to, *Scottish Scene*]

20 My wife says I'm Scotch by absorption. [Magnus Magnusson, 1929– , in *Listener*, 21 May 1987]

21 It's ill taking the breeks aff a wild Highlandman. [Sir Walter Scott, 1771–1832, *The Fair Maid of Perth*, Ch. 5]

22 If thou wouldst view fair Melrose aright, / Go visit it by the pale moonlight. [Sir Walter Scott, 1771–1832, *The Lay of the Last Minstrel*, II, 1]

23 O Caledonia! stern and wild, / Meet nurse for a poetic child! / Land of brown heath and shaggy wood, / Land of the mountain and the flood, / Land of my sires! [Sir Walter Scott, 1771–1832, *The Lay of the Last Minstrel*, VI, 2]

24 Stands Scotland where it did? [William Shakespeare, 1564–1616, *Macbeth*, IV. iii. 164]

25 It requires a surgical operation to get a joke well into a Scotch understanding. [Sydney Smith, 1771–1845, in Lady Holland, *Memoir*, Vol. i, Ch. 2]

26 The bitter east, the misty summer / And gray metropolis of the North. [(Of Edinburgh) Alfred, Lord Tennyson, 1809–92, *The Daisy*, 103]

27 The vice of meanness, condemned in every other country, is in Scotland translated into a virtue called 'thrift'. [David Thomson, 1914–88, *Nairn in Darkness and Light*, p. 70]

28 It is never difficult to distinguish between a Scotsman with a grievance and a ray of sunshine. [P G Wodehouse, 1881–1975, *Blandings Castle*, 'The Custody of the Pumpkin']

See also BRITAIN, etc., ENGLAND, NATIONS, WALES

SCULPTURE

1 Sculpture is not for young men. [Constantin Brancusi, 1876–1957, in Ezra Pound, *ABC of Reading*, 'Treatise on Metre', III]

2 Here was art greater than life and not, as with nearly all the art of today, as small as life. [Neville Cardus, 1889–1975 (of Jacob Epstein's sculpture), in *Guardian*, 1961, reprinted 11 Sept. 1986]

3 Of course, I always liked big women. I suppose I was meant to be a sculptor or architect. [Joyce Cary, 1888–1957, *The Horse's Mouth*, 38]

4 The sculptor must himself feel that he is not so much inventing or shaping the curve of a breast or shoulder as delivering the image from its prison. [Anaïs Nin, 1903–77, *Diary of A N*, Vol. 5, Spring 1948]

5 My sculptures are plastic metaphors. It's the same principle as in painting. I've said that a painting shouldn't be a *trompe l'oeil* but a *trompe l'esprit*. I'm out to fool the mind rather than the eye. And that goes for sculpture too. [Pablo Picasso, 1881–1973, in Françoise Gilot and Carlton Lake, *Life with P*, Pt 6]

See also ART, ARTISTS, PAINTING

THE SEA

1 Now the great winds shoreward blow, / Now the salt tides seaward flow; / Now the wild white horses play, / Champ and chafe and toss in the spray. [Matthew Arnold, 1822–88, *The Forsaken Merman*, 4]

2 Oh, pilot! 'tis a fearful night, / There's danger on the deep. [T H Bayly, 1797–1839, *The Pilot*]

3 Quite candidly I've never seen the point of the sea. Except where it meets the land. The shore has point, the sea none. Of course when you say you miss the sea that's what you mean: you miss the shore. [Alan Bennett, 1934– , *The Old Country*, I]

4 They that go down to the sea in ships, that do business in great waters. These see the works of the Lord, and his wonders in the deep. [Bible, OT, *Psalms* 107:23]

5 Roll on, thou deep and dark blue Ocean – roll! / Ten thousand fleets sweep over thee in vain; / Man marks the earth with ruin – his control / Stops with the shore. [Lord Byron, 1788–1824, *Childe Harold's Pilgrimage*, IV, 179]

6 Time writes no wrinkle on thine azure brow: / Such as creation's dawn beheld, thou rollest now. [Lord Byron, 1788–1824, *Childe Harold's Pilgrimage*, IV, 182]

7 What are the wild waves saying / Sister, the whole day long, / That ever amid our playing, / I hear but their low lone song? [J E Carpenter, 1813–85, *What are the Wild Waves Saying?*]

8 For all at last return to the sea – to Oceanus, the ocean river, like the ever-flowing stream of time, the beginning and the end. [Rachel Carson, 1907–64, *The Sea around Us*, last words]

9 Water, water, everywhere, / Nor any drop to drink. [Samuel Taylor Coleridge, 1772–1834, *The Ancient Mariner*, Pt II]

10 for whatever we lose (like a you or a me) / it's always ourselves we find in the sea [e e cummings, 1894–1962, *Poems* 95, 'maggie and milly and molly and may']

11 It is the drawback of all sea-side places that half the landscape is unavailable for purposes of human locomotion, being covered by useless water. [Norman Douglas, 1868–1952, *Alone*, 'Mentone']

12 The dragon-green, the luminous, the dark, the serpent-haunted sea. [James Elroy Flecker, 1884–1915, *The Gates of Damascus*, 'West Gate']

13 A ship, an isle, a sickle moon – / With few but with how splendid stars / The mirrors of the sea are strewn / Between their silver bars. [James Elroy Flecker, 1884–1915, *A Ship, an Isle, a Sickle Moon*]

14 We are as near to heaven by sea as by land. [Humphrey Gilbert, 1539?–83, in Hakluyt, *Voyages*, III, p. 159]

15 On land I am a hero, but on water I am a coward. [Adolf Hitler, 1889–1945 (to von Runstedt), in Milton Shulman, *Defeat in the West*]

16 The snotgreen sea. The scrotumtightening sea. [James Joyce, 1882–1941, *Ulysses*, Penguin edn, 1992, p. 3]

17 It keeps eternal whispering around / Desolate shores. [John Keats, 1795–1821, sonnet: *On the Sea*]

18 We have fed our sea for a thousand years / And she calls us, still unfed, / Though there's never a wave of all her waves / But marks our English dead. [Rudyard Kipling, 1865–1936, *The Coastwise Lights*]

19 What is a woman that you forsake her,/And the hearth-fire and the home-acre,/To go with the old grey Widowmaker? [Rudyard Kipling, 1865–1936, *Harp Song of the Dane Women*]

20 *And the ships shall go abroad / To the Glory of the Lord* / Who heard the silly sailor-folk and gave them back their sea! [Rudyard Kipling, 1865–1936, *The Last Chantey*]

21 'Wouldst thou' – so the helmsman answered. – / 'Learn the secret of the sea? / Only those who brave its dangers / Comprehend its mystery!' [H W Longfellow, 1807–82, *The Secret of the Sea*]

22 I must down to the sea again, for the call of the running tide / is a wild call and a clear call that may not be denied. [John Masefield, 1878–1967, *Sea Fever*]

23 Here, in this little bay, / Full of tumultuous life and great repose, / Where, twice a day, / The purposeless, glad ocean comes and goes. [Coventry Patmore, 1823–96, *The Unknown Eros*, Bk i, 12, 'Magna est Veritas']

24 When I have seen the hungry ocean gain / Advantage on the kingdom of the shore. [William Shakespeare, 1564–1616, *Sonnets*, 64]

25 I will go back to the great sweet mother, / Mother and lover of men, the sea. [A C Swinburne, 1837–1909, *The Triumph of Time*, 33]

26 I will never believe again that the sea was ever loved by anyone whose life was married to it. [H M Tomlinson, 1873–1958, *The Sea and the Jungle*, Ch. 1]

27 From space, the planet is blue. / From space, the planet is the territory / Not of humans, but of the whale. / Blue seas cover seven-tenths of the earth's surface, / And are the domain of the largest brain ever created, / With a fifty-million-year-old smile. [Heathcote Williams, 1941– , *Whale Nation*, opening lines]

See also SAILORS, SHIPS

SEASONS

1 Forget not bees in winter, though they sleep, / For winter's big with summer in her womb. [Victoria Sackville-West, 1892–1962, *The Land*, 'Spring']

2 At Christmas I no more desire a rose / Than wish a snow in May's new-fangled mirth. [William Shakespeare, 1564–1616, *Love's Labour's Lost*, I. i. 105]

3 How many things by season seasoned are / To their right praise and true perfection! [*The Merchant of Venice*, V. i. 107]

4 Thorough this distemperature we see / The seasons alter: hoary headed frosts / Fall in the fresh lap of the crimson rose. [*A Midsummer Night's Dream*, II. i. 106]

See also AUTUMN, SPRING, SUMMER, WEATHER, WINTER

SECRETS

1 Tell it not in Gath, publish it not in the streets of Askelon; lest the daughters of the Philistines rejoice, lest the daughters of the uncircumcised triumph. [Bible, OT, *2 Samuel* 1:20]

2 I waive the quantum o' the sin, / The hazard of concealing; / But oh! it hardens a' within, / And petrifies the feeling! [Robert Burns, 1759–96, *Epistle to a Young Friend*, 45]

3 I know that's a secret, for it's whispered everywhere. [William Congreve, 1670–1729, *Love for Love*, III. iii]

4 It is a secret in the Oxford sense: you may tell it to only one person at a time. [Oliver Franks, 1905–92, quoted by K Rose in *Sunday Telegraph*, 30 Jan. 1977]

5 Once the toothpaste is out of the tube, it is awfully hard to get it back in. [H R Haldeman, 1926–93, comment to John Dean on Watergate affair, 8 Apr. 1973]

6 The Official Secrets Act is not to protect secrets but to protect officials. [Jonathan Lynn, 1943– , and Antony Jay, 1930– , *Yes Minister*, Ch. 7]

SECURITY

1 Whenever our neighbour's house is on fire, it cannot be amiss for the engines to play a little on our own. [Edmund Burke, 1729–97, *Reflections on the Revolution in France*, Penguin edn, p. 92]

2 Being lost in Australia gives you a lovely feeling of security. [Bruce Chatwin, 1940–89, *Songlines*, 10]

3 Security is the mother of danger and the grandmother of destruction. [Thomas Fuller, 1608–61, *The Holy State*, Bk v, Ch. 18, 1]

4 Who is to guard the guards themselves? [Juvenal, 60–*c*.130, *Satires*, VI, 347]

5 It's often safer to be in chains than to be free. [Franz Kafka, 1883–1924, *The Trial*, Ch. 8]

6 It is much safer to obey than to rule. [Thomas à Kempis, *c*.1380–1471, *The Imitation of Christ*, 9]

7 If we cannot now end our differences, at least we can help make the world safe for diversity. [President John F Kennedy, 1917–63, address at American University, Washington, 10 June 1963]

8 Clearly, security without values is like a ship without a rudder. But values without security are like a rudder without a ship. [Henry Kissinger, 1923– , in *Observer*, 9 Mar. 1986]

9 Sweet it is, when on the high seas the winds are lashing the waters, to gaze from the land on another's struggles. [Lucretius, 99–55 BC, *On the Nature of the Universe*, II, 1]

10 Out of this nettle, danger, we pluck this flower, safety. [William Shakespeare, 1564–1616, *1 Henry IV*, II. iii. (11)]

11 There is but one safe thing for the vanquished: not to hope for safety. [Virgil, 70–19 BC, *Aeneid*, II, 354]

See also DANGERS

SEDUCTION

1 She's not so pretty anyone would want to ruin her. [Bertolt Brecht, 1898–1956, *Mother Courage*, 6]

2 A little still she strove, and much repented, / And whispering 'I will ne'er consent' – consented. [Lord Byron, 1788–1824, *Don Juan*, I, 117]

3 The types who make passes at girls who wear glasses – so they can see themselves in the reflection. [Stephanie Calman, 1960– , *Gentlemen Prefer My Sister*, 'Mouth to Mouth Aggravation']; see 13

4 Says he, 'I am a handsome man, but I'm a gay deceiver.' [George Colman the Younger, 1762–1836, *Unfortunate Miss Bailey*]

5 Is not the whole world a vast house of assignation of which the filing system has been lost? [Quentin Crisp, 1908–99, *The Naked Civil Servant*, Ch. 11]

6 She knows her man, and when you rant or swear, / Can draw you to her with a single hair. [John Dryden, 1631–1700, trans. of Persius, *Satires*, v, 246]

7 Seduction is often difficult to distinguish from rape. In seduction, the rapist often bothers to buy a bottle of wine. [Andrea Dworkin, 1946– , speech to New York editors, 1976]

8 He in a few minutes ravished this fair creature, or at least would have ravished her, if she had not, by a timely compliance, prevented him. [Henry Fielding, 1707–54, *Jonathan Wild*, Bk iii, Ch. 7]

9 'Tis woman that seduces all mankind, / By her we first were taught the wheedling arts. [John Gay, 1685–1732, *The Beggar's Opera*, I. ii]

10 You know women as well as I do. They are only willing when you compel them, but after that they're as enthusiastic as you are. [Jean Giraudoux, 1882–1944, *Tiger at the Gates*, I]

11 The trouble with Ian [Fleming] is that he gets off with women because he can't get on with them. [Rosamond Lehmann, 1901–90, in J Pearson, *The Life of I F*, Ch. 8, sect. 1]

12 Had we but world enough, and time, / This coyness, lady, were no crime. [Andrew Marvell, 1621–78, *To His Coy Mistress*]

13 Men seldom make passes / At girls who wear glasses. [Dorothy Parker, 1893–1967, *News Item*]; see 3

14 Lady, Lady, should you meet / One whose ways are all discreet, / One who murmurs that his wife / Is the lodestar of his life, / One who keeps assuring you / That he never was untrue, / Never loved another one . . . / Lady, lady, better run! [Dorothy Parker, 1893–1967, *Social Note*]

15 On a sofa upholstered in panther skin / Mona did researches in original sin. [William Plomer, 1903–73, *Mews Flat Mona*]

16 Even Mr Justin Veezee is not so oldfashioned as to believe any doll will go to his apartment just to look at etchings nowadays. [Damon Runyon, 1884–1946, *Furthermore*, 'What, No Butler?']

17 She is a woman, therefore may be wooed; / She is a woman, therefore may be won, / She is Lavinia, therefore must be loved. / What, man! more water glideth by the mill / Than wots the miller of; and easy it is / Of a cut loaf to steal a shive, we know. [William Shakespeare, 1564–1616, *Titus Andronicus*, II. i. 82]

18 When a man seduces a woman, it should, I think, be termed a *left-handed* marriage. [Mary Wollstonecraft, 1759–97, *A Vindication of the Rights of Women*, 4]

See also SEX, WOMEN & MEN

THE SELF

1 The trouble with self-made men is that they're working with inferior materials. [anon., in *Picking on Men*, comp. Judy Allen]

2 I've always thought you are what you are and you shouldn't pretend to be anyone else. But Oliver used to correct me and explain that you are whoever it is you're pretending to be. [Julian Barnes, 1946– , *Talking It Over*, 2]

3 No, when the fight begins within himself, / A man's worth something. [Robert Browning, 1812–89, *Bishop Blougram's Apology*, 693]

4 I know who I am, and I know too that I am capable of being not only the characters I have named, but all the Twelve Peers of France, and all the Nine Worthies as well. [Miguel Cervantes, 1547–1616, *Don Quixote*, Pt I, Ch. 5]

5 There are two ways of losing oneself: by insulation in the particular or by dilution in the 'universal'. [Aimé Césaire, 1913– , *Letter to Maurice Thorez*, 1956]

6 The men who really believe in themselves are all in lunatic asylums. [G K Chesterton, 1874–1936, *Orthodoxy*, Ch. 2]

7 I have always disliked myself at any given moment; the total of such moments is my life. [Cyril Connolly, 1903–74, *Enemies of Promise*, Ch. 18]

8 We are all serving a life-sentence in the dungeon of self. [Cyril Connolly, 1903–74, *The Unquiet Grave*, Ch. 1]

9 But I do nothing upon myself, and yet I am mine own Executioner. [John Donne, 1571?–1631, *Devotions*, 12]

10 Perhaps the rare and simple pleasure of being seen for what one is compensates for the misery of being it. [Margaret Drabble, 1939– , *A Summer Bird-cage*, Ch. 7]

11 Man's main task in life is to give *birth* to himself. [Erich Fromm, 1900–1980, *Man for Himself*, Ch. 4]

12 I have never agreed with my other self wholly. The truth of the matter seems to lie between us. [Kahlil Gibran, 1883–1931, *Sand and Foam*]

13 It is in self-limitation that a master first shows himself. [Johann Wolfgang von Goethe, 1749–1832, sonnet: *Nature and Art*]

14 What other dungeon is so dark as one's own heart! What jailer so inexorable as one's self! [Nathaniel Hawthorne, 1804–64, *The House of the Seven Gables*, Ch. 11]

15 He was a self-made man who owed his lack of success to nobody. [Joseph Heller, 1923–99, *Catch-22*, Ch. 3]

16 There were times when it seemed to him that the different parts of him were not all under the same management [Russell Hoban, 1925– , *The Lion of Boaz-Jachin and Jachin-Boaz*, Ch. 15]

17 The sign said: 'The Green Turtle, *Chelonia mydas*, is the source of turtle soup . . .' I am the source of William G. soup if it comes to that. Everyone is the source of his or her kind of soup. In a town as big as London that's a lot of soup walking about. [Russell Hoban, 1925– , *Turtle Diary*, Ch. 3]

18 Me, what's that after all? An arbitrary limitation of being bounded by the people before and after and on either side. Where they leave off I begin, and vice versa. [Russell Hoban, 1925– , *Turtle Diary*, Ch. 11]

19 I see / The lost are like this, and their scourge to be / As I am mine, their sweating selves; but worse. [Gerard Manley Hopkins, 1844–89, *I Wake and Feel the Fell*]

20 There's only one corner of the universe you can be certain of improving, and that's your own self. [Aldous Huxley, 1894–1963, *Time Must Have a Stop*, 7]

21 It's all right letting yourself go, as long as you can let yourself back. [Mick Jagger, 1943– ; in J Green, *Book of Rock Quotes*]

22 All censure of a man's self is oblique praise. It is in order to show how much he can spare. [Dr Samuel Johnson, 1709–84, in James Boswell, *Life of J*, 25 Apr. 1778]

23 But what if I should discover that the enemy himself is within me, that I myself am the enemy that must be loved – what then? [C G Jung, 1875–1961, attr.]; see 24

24 We have met the enemy, and he is us. [Walter Kelly, 1913–73, in strip cartoon 'Pogo', parodying Captain Oliver Hazard Perry (1785–1819), 'We have met the enemy and he is ours', at Battle of Lake Erie, 10 Sept. 1813]; see 23

25 If you cannot mould yourself as you would wish, how can you expect other people to be entirely to your liking? [Thomas à Kempis, *c.*1380–1471, *The Imitation of Christ*, 16]

26 One had rather malign oneself than not speak of oneself at all. [Duc de La Rochefoucauld, 1613–80, *Maxims*, 138]

27 Not in the clamour of the crowded street, / Not in the shouts and plaudits of the throng, / But in ourselves, are triumph and defeat. [H W Longfellow, 1807–82, *The Poets*]

28 He that would govern others, first should be / The master of himself. [Philip Massinger, 1583–1640, *The Bondman*, I. iii]

29 I still feel – kind of temporary about myself. [Arthur Miller, 1915– , *Death of a Salesman*, I]

30 The I is hateful. [Blaise Pascal, 1623–62, *Pensées*, VII, 434]

31 I do not see them here; but after death / God knows I know the faces I shall see, / Each one a murdered self, with low last breath. / 'I am thyself, – what hast thou done to me?' / 'And I – and I – thyself' (lo! each one saith,) / 'And thou thyself to all eternity!' [Dante Gabriel Rossetti, 1828–82, *The House of Life*, 86, 'Lost Days']

32 This above all; to thine own self be true, / And it must follow, as the night the day, / Thou canst not then be false to any man. [William Shakespeare, 1554–1616, *Hamlet*, I. iii. 78]

33 It is easy – terribly easy – to shake a man's faith in himself. To take advantage of that to break a man's spirit is devil's work. [George Bernard Shaw, 1856–1950, *Candida*, I]

34 What a bore it is, waking up in the morning always the same person. [Logan Pearsall Smith, 1865–1946, *Trivia*, II, 'Green Ivory']

35 A self-made man is one who believes in luck and sends his son to Oxford. [Christina Stead, 1902–83, *House of All Nations*, 'Credo']

36 What counted was mythology of self, / Blotched out beyond unblotching. [Wallace Stevens, 1879–1955, *The Comedian as the Letter C*, I]

37 I am always with myself, and it is I who am my tormentor. [Leo Tolstoy, 1828–1910, *Memoirs of a Madman*]

38 Not only are selves conditional but they die. Each day we wake slightly altered, and the person we were yesterday is dead. [John Updike, 1932– , *Self-consciousness*, Ch. 6]

39 I celebrate myself, and sing myself. [Walt Whitman, 1819–92, *Song of Myself*, 1, 1]

40 Other people are quite dreadful. The only possible society is oneself. [Oscar Wilde, 1854–1900, *An Ideal Husband*, III]

See also next categories, EGO, INTEGRITY

SELF-DECEPTION

1 I think it's one of the scars in our culture that we have too high an opinion of ourselves. We align ourselves with the angels instead of the higher primates. [Angela Carter, 1940–92, *Marxism Today*, Jan. 1985]

2 Men have been swindled by other men on many occasions. The autumn of 1929 was, perhaps, the first occasion when men succeeded on a large scale in swindling themselves. [J K Galbraith, 1908– , *The Great Crash*, Ch. 7]

3 'And if he never came,' said she, / 'Now what on earth is that to me? / I wouldn't have him back!' / I hope / Her mother washed her mouth with soap. [Dorothy Parker, 1893–1967, *Story*]

SELF-KNOWLEDGE

1 Know thyself. [anon. Greek written up in the temple at Delphi]

2 Why beholdest thou the mote that is in thy brother's eye, but considerest not the beam that is in thine own eye? [Bible, NT, *St Matthew* 7:3]

3 The only effort worth making is the one it takes to learn the geography of one's own nature. [Paul Bowles, 1910–99, in *The Sunday Times*, 'Books' section, 23 July 1989]

4 O wad some Pow'r the giftie gie us / To see oursels as others see us! / It wad frae mony a blunder free us, / And foolish notion. [Robert Burns, 1759–96, *To a Louse*]

5 Look round the habitable world! how few / Know their own good; or knowing it, pursue. [John Dryden, 1631–1700, trans. of Juvenal, x]

6 We should all know what's at the end of our ropes and how it feels to be there. [Richard Ford, 1944– , *The Sportswriter*, 4]

7 Each man in his time plays many parts. And not just for long runs as Shakespeare seems to suggest, but in repertory – one part on Monday night, another on Tuesday, and a third at the Wednesday matinée. [Michael Frayn, 1933– , *Constructions*, 160]

8 Whenever two people meet there are really six people present. There is each man as he sees himself, each man as the other person sees him, and each man as he really is. [William James, 1842–1910; in Laurence J Peter, *Peter's Quotations*]

9 You had to follow the clues inside yourself, even if they led to incoherence, to craziness, and people happened to you on the way. You didn't collect them like stamps. [P J Kavanagh, 1931– , *The Perfect Stranger*, Ch. 5]

10 Know then thyself, presume not God to scan; / The proper study of mankind is man. [Alexander Pope, 1688–1744, *An Essay on Man*, II, 1]

11 We know what we are, but know not what we may be. [William Shakespeare, 1564–1616, *Hamlet*, IV. v. (43)]

12 I am the only person in the world I should like to know thoroughly. [Oscar Wilde, 1854–1900, *Lady Windermere's Fan*, II]

13 I have met a great many people on their way towards God and I wonder why they have chosen to look for him rather than themselves. [Jeanette Winterson, 1959– , *Sexing the Cherry*, p. 102]

SELF-LOVE

1 [When he heard that an egocentric had fallen in love] Against whom? [Alfred Adler, 1870–1937, in J Bishop, *Some of My Best Friends*, 'Exponent of the Soul']

2 He is, after all, the reflection of the tenderness I bear for myself. It is always ourselves we love. [Beryl Bainbridge, 1934– , *A Weekend with Claud*, 'Maggie']

3 Self-esteem is the most voluble of the emotions. [Frank Moore Colby, 1865–1925, *Essays*, in C Fadiman, *Reading I Have Liked*]

4 The affair between Margot Asquith and Margot Asquith will live as one of the prettiest love stories in all literature. [Dorothy Parker, 1893–1967 (review of Margot Asquith, *Autobiography*), in *New Yorker*, 22 Oct. 1927]

5 That true self-love and social are the same. [Alexander Pope, 1688–1744, *An Essay on Man*, IV, 396]

6 He fell in love with himself at first sight and it is a passion to which he has always remained faithful. Self-love seems so often unrequited. [Anthony Powell, 1905– , *The Acceptance World*, Ch. 1]

7 We have always known that heedless self-interest was bad morals; we know now that it is bad economics. [Franklin D Roosevelt, 1882–1945, second inaugural address, 20 Jan. 1937]

8 One of the great drawbacks to self-centred passions is that they afford so little variety in life. The man who loves only himself cannot, it is true, be accused of promiscuity in his affections, but he is bound in the end to suffer intolerable boredom from the inevitable sameness of the object of his devotion. [Bertrand Russell, 1872–1970, *Autobiography*, Vol. II, Ch. 17]

9 He loved himself only as much as self-respect required, and the reason why he saw himself so clearly was that he looked not often, but suddenly, so catching himself unawares. [Elizabeth Taylor, 1912–75, *A Wreath of Roses*, Ch. 9]

10 I like my face in the mirror, / I like my voice when I sing. / My girl says it's just infatuation – / I know it's the real thing. [Kit Wright, 1944– , *Every Day in Every Way*]

See also EGO

SELF-PRESERVATION

1 The gods help them that help themselves. [Aesop, *fl.* *c.*550 BC, *Fables*, 'Hercules and the Waggoner']

2 For, those that fly, may fight again, / Which he can never do that's slain. [Samuel Butler, 1612–80, *Hudibras*, III, iii, 243]

3 If a madman were to come into this room with a stick in his hand, no doubt we should pity the state of his mind; but our primary consideration would be to take care of ourselves. We should knock him down first, and pity him afterwards. [Dr Samuel Johnson, 1709–84, in James Boswell, *Life of J*, 3 Apr. 1776]

4 Our remedies oft in ourselves do lie, / Which we ascribe to heaven. [William Shakespeare, 1564–1616, *All's Well that Ends Well*, I. i. (235)]

5 *Cet animal est très méchant. Quand on l'attaque il se défend.* – This creature is very wicked. He defends himself when attacked. [Théodore P K, *La Ménagerie* (1868)]

SELLING, see BUYING

SENSE

1 Take care of the sense, and the sounds will take care of themselves. [Lewis Carroll, 1832–98, *Alice in Wonderland*, Ch. 9]

2 Common sense is the most widely distributed commodity in the world, for everyone thinks himself so well endowed with it that those who are hardest to please in every other respect generally have no desire to possess more of it than they have. [René Descartes, 1596–1650, *Discourse on Method*, I]

3 Common sense is the collection of prejudices acquired by age eighteen. [Albert Einstein, 1879–1955, in *Scientific American*, Feb. 1976]

4 We seldom attribute common sense except to those who agree with us. [Duc de La Rochefoucauld, 1613–80, *Maxims*, 347]

5 That rarest gift / To Beauty, Common Sense. [George Meredith, 1828–1909, *Modern Love*, 32]

6 For fools admire, but men of sense approve. [Alexander Pope, 1688–1744, *An Essay on Criticism*, 391]

7 What is known as common sense, whose virtue, uniquely among virtues, is that everybody has it. [Tom Stoppard, 1937– , *Jumpers*, I]

See also INTELLIGENCE, REASON

SENTIMENTALITY

1 Sentimentality – that's what we call the sentiment we don't share. [Graham Greene, 1904–91; in A Andrews, *Quotations for Speakers and Writers*]

2 Sentimentalism is the working off on yourself of feelings you haven't really got. [D H Lawrence, 1885–1930, *Phoenix*, 'John Galsworthy']

3 Sentimentality is the emotional promiscuity of those who have no sentiment. [Norman Mailer, 1923– , *Cannibals and Christians*, p. 51]

4 Sentimentality is only sentiment that rubs you up the wrong way. [W Somerset Maugham, 1874–1965, *A Writer's Notebook*, 1941]

SERVANTS & SERVICE

1 In my opinion butlers ought / To know their place, and not to play / The Old Retainer night and day. [Hilaire Belloc, 1870–1953, *Cautionary Tales*, 'Lord Lundy']

2 We are unprofitable servants: we have done that which was our duty to do. [Bible, NT, *St Luke* 17:10]

3 No man is a hero to his valet. [Mme de Cornuel, 1605–94, *Lettres de Mlle Aïssé à Mme C*, 13 Aug. 1728]

4 No! I am not Prince Hamlet, nor was meant to be; / Am an attendant lord. [T S Eliot, 1888–1965, *Love Song of J. Alfred Prufrock*]

5 Many a man has been a wonder to the world, whose wife and valet have seen nothing in him that was even remarkable. Few men have been admired by their servants. [Michel de Montaigne, 1533–92, *Essays*, III, 2]

6 If your honour disna ken when ye hae a gude servant, I ken when I hae a gude master. [Sir Walter Scott, 1771–1832, *Rob Roy*, Ch. 24]

7 I don't like to give offence by giving notice – in a servant it looks presumptuous. [Tom Stoppard, 1937– , *On the Razzle*, I (adapted from Johann Nestroy)]

8 Live? Our servants will do that for us. [Auguste Villiers de l'Isle Adam, 1838–89, *Axel*, IV. ii]

9 A very large part of English middle-class education is devoted to the training of servants ... In so far as it is, by definition, the training of upper servants, it includes, of course, the instilling of that kind of confidence which will enable the upper servants to supervise and direct the lower servants. [Raymond Williams, 1921–88, *Culture and Society*, Ch. 3, Conclusion]

10 '... you can't stick lighted matches between the toes of an English butler. He would raise his eyebrows and freeze you with a glance. You'd feel as if he had caught you using the wrong fork.' [P G Wodehouse, 1881–1975, *The Old Reliable*, 17]

11 Small service is true service, while it lasts. [William Wordsworth, 1770–1850, *To a Child, Written in Her Album*]

SEX

1 Is sex dirty? Only if it's done right. [Woody Allen, 1935– , in film *All You've Ever Wanted to Know about Sex*]

2 Fun? that was the most fun I've ever had without laughing. [Woody Allen, 1935– , of sex, in film *Annie Hall*, scripted with Marshall Brickman]

3 Hey, don't knock masturbation! It's sex with someone I love. [Woody Allen, 1935– , in film *Annie Hall*, scripted with Marshall Brickman]

4 If S-E-X ever rears its ugly head, close your eyes before you see the rest of it. [Alan Ayckbourn, 1939– , *Bedroom Farce*, III]

5 Erotic practices have become diversified. Sex used to be single-crop farming, like cotton or wheat; now people raise all kinds of things. [Saul Bellow, 1915– , *More Die of Heartbreak*, p. 317]

6 In Slaka, sex is just politics with the clothes off. [Malcolm Bradbury, 1932– , *Rates of Exchange*, 4, III]

7 Sex without using someone is as difficult as eating without chewing. [Julie Burchill, 1960– , in *Observer*, 2 Mar. 1986]

8 It doesn't matter what you do in the bed-room

as long as you don't do it in the street and frighten the horses. [Mrs Patrick Campbell, 1865–1940, in Daphne Fielding, *The Duchess of Jermyn Street*, Ch. 2]

9 Sex is only the liquid centre of the great Newberry Fruit of friendship. [Jilly Cooper, 1937– , *Super-Jilly*, jacket]

10 I'm sure you'd never exploit one; / I expect you'd rather be dead; / I'm thoroughly convinced of it – / Now can we go to bed? [Wendy Cope, 1945– , *From June to December*]

11 For flavour, Instant Sex will never supersede the stuff you had to peel and cook. [Quentin Crisp, 1908–99, *The Sayings of Q C*]

12 Sex suppressed will go berserk, / But it keeps us all alive. / It's a wonderful change from wives and work / And it ends at half past five. [Gavin Ewart, 1916–95, *Office Friendships*]

13 Industrial relations are like sexual relations. It's better between two consenting parties. [Vic Feather, 1908–76, in *Guardian Weekly*, 8 Aug. 1976]

14 Personally I know nothing about sex because I've always been married. [Zsa Zsa Gabor, 1919– ; *Observer*, 'Sayings of the Year', 27 Dec. 1987]

15 Sex? – I'd rather have a cup of tea – any day! [Boy George, 1961– , attr. in 1983. With variants]

16 Why are women – most women – more interested in a man after he has made love to them than before? Why are men – most men – more interested in a woman before they have made love to her than after? . . . Men have to *unload*, he thought. The rubbish doesn't care about the feelings of the skip. [Victoria Glendinning, 1937– , *The Grown-ups*, Ch. 11]

17 But did thee feel the earth move? [Ernest Hemingway, 1899–1961, *For Whom the Bell Tolls*, Ch. 13]

18 Sex and taxes are in may ways the same. Tax does to cash what males do to genes. It dispenses assets among the population as a whole. Sex, not death, is the great leveller. [Steve Jones, 1944– , speech to the Royal Society, London, 23 Jan. 1997]

19 The zipless fuck is the purest thing there is. And it is rarer than the unicorn. And I have never had one. [Erica Jong, 1942– , *Fear of Flying*, Ch. 1]

20 KOLLONTAI: I regard sex like a glass of water, from which I drink when I am thirsty.
LENIN: But who wants to drink a glass of dirty water? [Alexandra Kollontai, 1879–1950, in Georgie Anne Geyer, *The Young Russians*, Ch. 15]

21 Sexual intercourse began / in nineteen sixty-three / – (Which was rather late for me) – / Between the end of the *Chatterley* ban / And the Beatles' first LP. [Philip Larkin, 1922–85, *Annus Mirabilis*]

22 It's all this cold-hearted fucking that is death and idiocy. [D H Lawrence, 1885–1930, *Lady Chatterley's Lover*, Ch. 14]

23 You know the worst thing about oral sex? The view. [Maureen Lipman, 1946– ; in *Dictionary of Outrageous Quotations*, comp. C R S Marsden]

24 The Duke returned from the wars today and did pleasure me in his top-boots. [Sarah, Duchess of Marlborough, 1660–1744, attr., with variants]

25 Continental people have sex life; the English have hot-water bottles. [George Mikes, 1912–87, *How to be an Alien*]

26 Sex is one of the nine reasons for reincarnation . . . The other eight are unimportant. [Henry Miller, 1891–1980, *Big Sur and the Oranges of Hieronymus Bosch*]

27 When she saw the sign 'Members only' she thought of him. [Spike Milligan, 1918– , *Puckoon*, Ch. 3]

28 The orgasm has replaced the Cross as the focus of longing and the image of fulfilment. [Malcolm Muggeridge, 1903–90, *The Most of M M*, 'Down with Sex']

29 And his cheques, I fear, / Mean that sex is here / To stay. [Cole Porter, 1891–1964, song: *Sex is Here to Stay*]

30 Sex is something I really don't understand too hot. You never know *where* the hell you are. I keep making up these sex rules for myself, and then I break them right away. [J D Salinger, 1919– , *The Catcher in the Rye*, Ch. 9]

31 The wren goes to 't, and the small gilded fly / Does lecher in my sight. / Let copulation thrive. [William Shakespeare, 1564–1616, *King Lear*, IV. vi. (115)]

32 Your daughter and the Moor are now making the beast with two backs. [*Othello*, I. i. (117)]

33 It would be much better if young women should stop being raped much earlier in the proceedings than some of them do. [Mr Justice Stable, 1923– ; *Observer*, 'Sayings of the Week', 8 Jan. 1961]

34 If sex were all, then every trembling hand / Could make us squeak, like dolls, the wished-for words. [Wallace Stevens, 1879–1955, *Le Monocle de mon oncle*]

35 Masturbation: the primary sexual activity of mankind. In the nineteenth century it was a disease; in the twentieth, it's a cure. [Thomas Szasz, 1920– , *The Second Sin*, 'Sex']

36 She said he proposed something on their wedding night her own brother wouldn't have suggested. [James Thurber, 1894–1961; in *Kiss Me Hardy*, ed. Roger Kilroy, 'Family Circle']

37 If sex is so personal, why are we expected to share it with someone else? [Lily Tomlin, 1939– , in *Was It Good for You Too?*, ed. Bob Chieger]

38 Sex is like money; only too much is enough. [John Updike, 1932– , *Couples*, Ch. 5]

39 All this fuss about sleeping together. For physical pleasure I'd sooner go to my dentist any day. [Evelyn Waugh, 1903–66, *Vile Bodies*, Ch. 6]

40 Most women know that sex is good for headaches. [Richard Wilbur, 1921– ; *Observer*, 'Sayings of the Week', 1 Nov. 1987]

See also next category, HOMOSEXUALS, LOVE, SEDUCTION, WOMEN & MEN

SEXUALITY

1 It is better to marry than to burn. [Bible, NT, *1 Corinthians* 7:9]

2 To be carnally minded is death. [Bible, NT, *Romans* 8:6]

3 People will insist ... on treating the *mons Veneris* as though it were Mount Everest. [Aldous Huxley, 1894–1963, *Eyeless in Gaza*, Ch. 30]

4 At thirty-three ... Lilian Aldwinkle appealed to all the instinctive bigamist in one. She was eighteen in the attics and widow Dido on the floors below. [Aldous Huxley, 1894–1963, *Those Barren Leaves*, Pt 1, Ch. 2]

5 Be a good animal, true to your animal instincts. [D H Lawrence, 1885–1930, *The White Peacock*, Pt II, Ch. 2]

6 This is a boy, sir. Not a girl. If you're baffled by the difference it might be as well to approach both with caution. [Joe Orton, 1933–67, *What the Butler Saw*, II]

7 Every kind of destructive action by itself is the reaction of the organism to the denial of the gratification of a vital need, especially the sexual. [Wilhelm Reich, 1897–1957, *The Function of the Orgasm*]

8 You cannot call it love; for at your age / The hey-day in the blood is tame, it's humble / And waits upon the judgement. [William Shakespeare, 1564–1616, *Hamlet*, III. iii. 68]

9 There's language in her eye, her cheek, her lip, / Nay, her foot speaks, her wanton spirits look out / At every joint and motive of her body. [*Troilus and Cressida*, IV. v. 55]

See also previous category, HOMOSEXUALS, LOVE, SEDUCTION, WOMEN & MEN

WILLIAM SHAKESPEARE

1 Others abide our question. Thou art free. / We ask and ask: Thou smilest and art still, / Out-topping knowledge. [Matthew Arnold, 1822–88, *Shakespeare*]

2 Shake was a dramatist of note; / He lived by writing things to quote. [H C Brunner, 1855–96, *Shake, Mulleary and Go-ethe*]

3 Shakespeare was with us, Milton was for us / Burns, Shelley, were with us, – they watch from their graves. [Robert Browning, 1812–89, *The Lost Leader*]

4 Our *myriad-minded* Shakespeare. [Samuel Taylor Coleridge, 1772–1834, *Biographia Literaria*, Ch. 15]

5 He [Shakespeare] was the man who of all modern, and perhaps ancient poets, had the largest and most comprehensive soul ... He was naturally learned; he needed not the spectacles of books to read nature; he looked inwards, and found her there. [John Dryden, 1631–1700, *Essay of Dramatic Poesy*]

6 We can say of Shakespeare, that never has a

man turned so little knowledge to such a great account. [T S Eliot, 1888–1965, lecture: 'The Classics and the Man of Letters']

7 I saw Hamlet Prince of Denmark played; but now the old plays begin to disgust this refined age. [John Evelyn, 1620–1706, *Diary*, 26 Nov. 1661]

8 'Was there ever,' cried he, 'such stuff as great part of Shakespeare? Only one mustn't say so!' [King George III, 1738–1820, in Fanny Burney, *Diary*, 19 Dec. 1785]

9 Far from the sun and summer-gale, / In thy green lap was Nature's darling laid. [Thomas Gray, 1716–71, *The Progress of Poesy*, III, 1]

10 For there is an upstart crow, beautified with our feathers, that with his tiger's heart wrapped in a player's hide, supposes he is as well able to bumbast out a blank verse as the best of you; and being an absolute *Iohannes fac totum*, is in his own conceit the only Shake-scene in a country. [Robert Greene, 1560?–92, *Groatsworth of Wit*]

11 Playing Shakespeare is very tiring. You never get to sit down unless you're a King. [Josephine Hull, 1886–1957, in *Time* magazine, 16 Nov. 1953]

12 In his tragic scenes there is always something wanting. [Dr Samuel Johnson, 1709–84, *Preface to Shakespeare*]

13 Shakespeare never has six lines together without a fault. [Dr Samuel Johnson, 1709–84, in James Boswell, *Life of J*, 19 Oct 1769]

14 Shakespeare that in his writing (whatsoever he penned) he never blotted out a line. My answer hath been, 'Would he had blotted a thousand.' [Ben Jonson, 1573–1637, *Timber, or Discoveries*, 64]

15 For I loved the man, and do honour his memory, on this side idolatry, as much as any. [Ben Jonson, 1573–1637, *Timber, or Discoveries*, 64]

16 And though thou hadst small Latin, and less Greek. [Ben Jonson, 1573–1637, *To the Memory of Shakspeare*]

17 Shakespeare led a life of allegory; his works are the comments on it. [John Keats, 1795–1821, letter to G and G Keats, 14 Feb. – 3 May 1819]

18 We do not know very much about Shakespeare but we do know he was dealing with an audience of, like, 3000 drunks and his competition was bear-baiting and prostitution. [Baz Luhrmann, 1962– , interview in *Observer*, 23 Mar. 1997]

19 What needs my Shakespeare, for his honoured bones, / The labour of an age in pilèd stones? [John Milton, 1608–74, *On Shakespeare*]

20 Shakespeare – the nearest thing in incarnation to the eye of God. [Laurence Olivier, 1907–89, in Kenneth Harris, *Kenneth Harris Talking to . . .*, 'Sir Laurence Olivier']

21 Shakespeare . . . / For gain not glory, winged his roving flight, / And grew immortal in his own despite. [Alexander Pope, 1688–1744, *Epistle* I, 69]

22 You might say he [Shakespeare's Henry V] was a cold bath king, that he was a scoutmaster, yes. But you must remember he is the *exaltation* of scoutmasters. [(To Laurence Olivier) Ralph Richardson, 1902–83, in Gary O'Connor, *Ralph Richardson: An Actor's Life*, Pt II, Ch. 22]

23 The play-bill, which is said to have announced the tragedy of Hamlet, the character of the Prince of Denmark being left out. [Sir Walter Scott, 1771–1832, *The Talisman*, Introduction]

24 With the single exception of Homer, there is no eminent writer, not even Sir Walter Scott, whom I can despise so entirely as I despise Shakespear when I measure my mind against his . . . It would positively be a relief to me to dig him up and throw stones at him. [George Bernard Shaw, 1856–1950, *Dramatic Opinions and Essays*, Vol. ii, p. 52]

25 Scorn not the Sonnet; Critic, you have frowned, / Mindless of its just honours; with this key / Shakespeare unlocked his heart. [William Wordsworth, 1770–1850, *Miscellaneous Sonnets*, II, 1]

SHAME, see REPENTANCE

GEORGE BERNARD SHAW

1 He cannot see beyond his own nose. Even the fingers he outstretches from it to the world are (as I shall suggest) often invisible to him. [Max Beerbohm, 1872–1956, *Around Theatres*, 'A Conspectus of G.B.S.']

2 This bright, nimble, fierce, and comprehending being – Jack Frost dancing bespangled in the sunshine. [Winston Churchill, 1874–1965, *Great Contemporaries*]

3 He is a good man fallen among Fabians. [Vladimir Ilyich Lenin, 1870–1924, in Arthur Ransome, *Six Weeks in Russia in 1919*, 'Notes of Conversations with Lenin']

4 Sherard Blaw, the dramatist who had discovered himself, and who had given so ungrudgingly of his discovery to the world. [Saki (H H Munro), 1870–1916, *The Unbearable Bassington*, Ch. 13]

5 Shaw's characters are himself: mere puppets stuck up to spout Shaw. [George Bernard Shaw, 1856–1950, *Fanny's First Play*, Epilogue]

6 It does not follow . . . that the right to criticize Shakespear involves the power of writing better plays. And in fact . . . I do not profess to write better plays. [George Bernard Shaw, 1856–1950, *Three Plays for Puritans*, Preface]

7 It is disappointing to report that George Bernard Shaw appearing as George Bernard Shaw is sadly miscast in the part. Satirists should be heard and not seen. [Robert E Sherwood, 1896–1955, review of Shaw play]

8 He hasn't an enemy in the world, and none of his friends like him. [Oscar Wilde, 1854–1900, quoted in G B Shaw, *Sixteen Self Sketches*, Ch. 17]

SHIPS

1 My experience of ships is that on them one makes an interesting discovery about the world. One finds one can do without it completely. [Malcolm Bradbury, 1932– , *Stepping Westward*, Bk I, Ch. 2]

2 What is a ship but a prison? [Robert Burton, 1577–1640, *Anatomy of Melancholy*, Pt II, §3, Memb. 4]

3 As idle as a painted ship / Upon a painted ocean. [Samuel Taylor Coleridge, 1772–1834, *The Ancient Mariner*, Pt II]

4 The wooden walls are the best walls of this kingdom. [Lord Coventry, 1578–1640, speech to the Judges, 17 June 1635]

5 A wet sheet and a flowing sea, / A wind that follows fast / And fills the white and rustling sail / And bends the gallant mast. [Allan Cunningham, 1784–1842, *A Wet Sheet and a Flowing Sea*]

6 It was so old a ship – who knows, who knows? / And yet so beautiful, I watched in vain / To see the mast burst open with a rose / And the whole deck put on its leaves again. [James Elroy Flecker, 1884–1915, *The Old Ships*]

7 Oh, I am a cook and captain bold, / And the mate of the *Nancy* brig, / And a bo'sun tight, and a midshipmite, / And the crew of the captain's gig. [W S Gilbert, 1836–1911, *The Bab Ballads*, 'The Yarn of the Nancy Bell']

8 With lack of sleep and too much understanding I grow a little crazy, I think, like all men at sea who live too close to each other and too close thereby to all that is monstrous under the sun and moon. [William Golding, 1911–93, *Rites of Passage*, final words]

9 There is nothing – absolutely nothing – half so much worth doing as simply messing about in boats. [Kenneth Grahame, 1859–1932, *The Wind in the Willows*, Ch. 11]; see 10

10 Coarse sailing is not mucking around in boats, but boating around in muck. [Michael Green, 1927– , *The Art of Coarse Sailing*, blurb]; see 9

11 When stately ships are twirled and spun / Like whipping tops and help there's none / And mighty ships ten thousand ton / Go down like lumps of lead. [Ralph Hodgson, 1871–1962, *The Song of Honour*]

12 His heart was mailed with oak and triple brass who first committed a frail ship to the wild seas. [Horace, 65–8 BC, *Odes*, iii, 9]

13 Even a luxury liner is really just a bad play surrounded by water. [Clive James, 1939– , *Unreliable Memoirs*, Ch. 17]

14 No man will be a sailor who has contrivance enough to get himself into a jail; for being in a ship is being in a jail, with the chance of being drowned. . . . A man in a jail has more room, better food and commonly better company. [Dr Samuel Johnson, 1709–84, in James Boswell, *Life of J*, Mar. 1759]

15 Oh, where are you going to, all you Big Steamers, / With England's own coal, up and down the salt seas? [Rudyard Kipling, 1865–1936, *Big Steamers*]

16 Build me straight, O worthy Master! / Staunch and strong, a goodly vessel, / That shall laugh at all disaster, / And with wave and whirlwind wrestle! [H W Longfellow, 1807–82, *The Building of the Ship*]

17 Quinquireme of Nineveh from distant Ophir / Rowing home to haven in sunny Palestine, / With a cargo of ivory, / And apes and peacocks, / Sandalwood, cedarwood and sweet white wine. [John Masefield, 1878–1967, *Cargoes*]

18 Dirty British coaster with a salt-caked smoke stack, / Butting through the Channel in the mad March days, / With a cargo of Tyne coal, / Road-rail, pig-lead, / Firewood, iron-ware, and cheap tin-trays. [John Masefield, 1878–1967, *Cargoes*]

19 I must down to the seas again, to the lonely sea and the sky, / And all I ask is a tall ship and a star to steer her by, / And the wheel's kick and the wind's song and the white sail's shaking, / And a grey mist on the sea's face and a grey dawn breaking. [John Masefield, 1878–1967, *Sea Fever*]

20 A baby Sardine / Saw her first submarine: / She was scared and watched through a peephole. / 'Oh, come, come, come,' / Said the Sardine's mum, / 'It's only a tin full of people.' [Spike Milligan, 1918– , *A Book of Milliganimals*, 'Sardines']

21 A rotten carcass of a boat, not rigged, / Nor tackle, sail, nor mast; the very rats / Instinctively have quit it. [William Shakespeare, 1564–1616, *The Tempest*, I. ii. 146]

22 A ship is floating in the harbour now, / A wind is hovering o'er the mountain's brow; / There is a path on the sea's azure floor, / No keel has ever ploughed that path before; / The halcyons brood around the foamless isles; / The treacherous ocean has forsworn its wiles; / The merry mariners are bold and free: / Say, my heart's sister, wilt thou sail with me? [P B Shelley, 1792–1822, *Epipsychidion*, 408]

23 O Captain! my Captain! our fearful trip is done, / The ship has weathered every rack, the prize we sought is won, / The port is near, the bells I hear, the people all exulting. [Walt Whitman, 1819–92, *O Captain! My Captain!*]

See also SAILORS, SEA

SHOW BUSINESS

1 Showbusiness is worse than dog eat dog, it's dog doesn't return other dog's phone calls. [Woody Allen, 1935– , in film *Crimes and Misdemeanours*]

2 It's far easier to become a star again than become one. [Josephine Baker, 1906–75, in Bruce Chatwin, *What am I Doing Here*, 'André Malraux']

3 There's No Business Like Show Business. [Irving Berlin, 1888–1989, title of song]

4 I've been making a comeback but nobody ever tells me where I've been. [Billie Holiday, 1915–59, in *New Woman*, July 1989]

5 That's what show business is for – to prove that it's not what you are that counts, it's what they *think* you are. [Andy Warhol, 1927–87, *POPism*, '1967']

See also FILM, HOLLYWOOD, STARS

SIGHT & INSIGHT

1 Where there is no vision, the people perish. [Bible, OT, *Proverbs* 29:18]

2 When I was a child, I spake as a child, I understood as a child, I thought as a child: but when I became a man, I put away childish things. For now we see through a glass, darkly; but then face to face. [Bible, NT, *1 Corinthians* 13:11]

3 This life's five windows of the soul / Distorts the Heavens from pole to pole, / And leads you to believe a lie / When you see with, not thro', the eye. [William Blake, 1757–1827, *The Everlasting Gospel*, γ]

4 If the doors of perception were cleansed, everything would appear to man as it is, infinite. [William Blake, 1757–1827, *The Marriage of Heaven and Hell*, 'The ancient tradition . . .']

5 The dwarf sees farther than the giant, when he has the giant's shoulder to mount on. [Samuel Taylor Coleridge, 1772–1834, *The Friend*, I, 8]; see 7

6 A moment's insight is sometimes worth a life's experience. [Oliver Wendell Holmes, 1809–94, *The Professor at the Breakfast Table*, Ch. 10]

7 If I have seen further, it is by standing on the shoulders of giants. [Isaac Newton, 1642–1727, letter to Robert Hooke, 5 Feb. 1675/76. Variants of the phrase in Lucan, Robert Burton]; see 5

8 It is our noticing them that puts things in a room, our growing used to them that takes them away again and clears a space for us. [Marcel

Proust, 1871–1922, *Remembrance of Things Past: Within a Budding Grove*, 'Place-names']

9 A falseness in all our impressions of external things, which I would generally characterize as the 'pathetic fallacy'. [John Ruskin, 1819–1900, *Modern Painters*, Vol. III, Pt iv, Ch. 12]

10 Not only is there but one way of *doing* things rightly, but there is only one way of *seeing* them, and that is seeing the whole of them. [John Ruskin, 1819–1900, *The Two Paths*, Lecture II]

11 When thy seeing blindeth thee / To what thy fellow-mortals see; / When thy sight to thee is sightless; / Their living, death; their light, most lightless; / Search no more – / Pass the gates of Luthany, tread the region Elenore. [Francis Thompson, 1859–1907, *The Mistress of Vision*, 20]

12 There was a time when meadow, grove, and stream, / The earth, and every common sight, / To me did seem / Apparelled in celestial light, / The glory and the freshness of a dream. / It is not now as it hath been of yore; – / Turn wheresoe'er I may, / By night or day, / The things which I have seen I now can see no more. [William Wordsworth, 1770–1850, *Ode, Intimations of Immortality*, 1]

13 Visionary power / Attends the motions of the viewless winds, / Embodied in the mystery of words. [William Wordsworth, 1770–1850, *The Prelude*, V, 595]

See also EYES, VISIONS

SILENCE

1 When he had opened the seventh seal, there was silence in heaven about the space of half an hour. [Bible, NT, *Revelation* 8:1]

2 How much one has to say in order to be heard when silent. [Elias Canetti, 1905–94, *The Human Province*, '1943']

3 Silence is deep as Eternity; speech is shallow as Time. [Thomas Carlyle, 1795–1881, *Critical and Miscellaneous Essays*, 'Sir Walter Scott']

4 Dumb's a sly dog. [Colley Cibber, 1671–1757, *Love Makes the Man*, IV. i]

5 No voice; but oh! the silence sank / Like music on my heart. [Samuel Taylor Coleridge, 1772–1834, *The Ancient Mariner*, Pt VI]

6 When you have nothing to say, say nothing. [Charles Colton, 1780?–1832, *Lacon*, 183]

7 Deep is the silence, deep/ On moon-washed apples of wonder. [John Drinkwater, 1882–1937, *Moonlit Apples*]

8 An horrid stillness first invades the ear, / And in that stillness we the tempest fear. [John Dryden, 1631–1700, *Astraea Redux*, 7]

9 You cannot be absolutely dumb when you live with a person unless you are an inhabitant of the North of England or the State of Maine. [Ford Madox Ford, 1873–1939, *The Good Soldier*, Pt III, Ch. 5]

10 Silence is become his mother tongue. [Oliver Goldsmith, 1728–74, *The Good-Natured Man*, II]

11 Silent? ah, he is silent! He can keep silence well. That man's silence is wonderful to listen to. [Thomas Hardy, 1840–1928, *Under the Greenwood Tree*, II, Ch. 5]

12 And silence, like a poultice, comes / To heal the blows of sound. [Oliver Wendell Holmes, 1809–94, *The Music Grinders*]

13 Elected Silence, sing to me / And beat upon my whorlèd ear. [Gerard Manley Hopkins, 1844–89, *Habit of Perfection*]

14 And silence sounds no worse than cheers / After death has stopped the ears. [A E Housman, 1859–1936, *A Shropshire Lad*, 19, 'To an Athlete Dying Young']

15 'Isn't that lovely?' she sighed. 'It's my favourite programme – fifteen minutes of silence – and after that there's a half hour of quiet and then an interlude of lull.' [Norton Juster, 1929– , *The Phantom Tollbooth*, Ch. 12]

16 And suddenly she craved again for the more absolute silence of America. English stillness was so soft, like an inaudible murmur of voices, of presences. [D H Lawrence, 1885–1930, *St Mawr*]

17 The silence went straight from rapt to fraught without pausing at pregnant. [Bernard Levin, 1928– , in *The Times*, 17 Oct. 1974]

18 Silence is the real crime against humanity. [Nadezhda Mandelstam, 1899–1980, *Hope against Hope*, 11]

19 Darkness more clear than noonday holdeth her, / Silence more musical than any song. [Christina Rossetti, 1830–94, *Rest*]

20 'Tis visible silence, still as the hour-glass, / Deep in the sun-searched growths the dragon-fly / Hangs like a blue thread loosened from the sky: – / So this winged hour is dropped to us from above. [Dante Gabriel Rossetti, 1828–82, *The House of Life*, 19, 'Silent Noon']

21 Silence is the perfectest herald of joy: I were but little happy if I could say how much. [William Shakespeare, 1564–1616, *Much Ado About Nothing*, II. i. (319)]

22 The silence often of pure innocence / Persuades when speaking fails. [*The Winter's Tale*, II. ii. 41]

23 *Seul le silence est grand; tout le reste est faiblesse.* – Only silence is great; all else is weakness. [Alfred de Vigny, 1797–1863, *La Mort du loup*]

24 Whereof one cannot speak, thereof one must be silent. [Ludwig Wittgenstein, 1889–1951, *Tractatus Logico-philosophicus*, 7]

25 The silence that is in the starry sky, / The sleep that is among the lonely hills. [William Wordsworth, 1770–1850, *Song at the Feast of Brougham Castle*, 163]

See also QUIETNESS, SPEECH

SIMPLICITY

1 Everything should be made as simple as possible, but not simpler. [Albert Einstein, 1879–1955; in *Reader's Digest*, Oct. 1977]

2 For him light labour spread her wholesome store, / Just gave what life required, but gave no more: / His best companions, innocence and health; / And his best riches, ignorance of wealth. [Oliver Goldsmith, 1728–74, *The Deserted Village*, 59]

3 Teach us delight in simple things, / And mirth that has no bitter springs. [Rudyard Kipling, 1865–1936, *The Children's Song*]

4 Any intelligent fool can make things bigger, more complex, and more violent. It takes a touch of genius – and a lot of courage – to move in the opposite direction. [E F Schumacher, 1911–77, in obituary in *Guardian*, 6 Sept. 1977]

5 Our life is frittered away by detail . . . Simplify, simplify. [H D Thoreau, 1817–62, *Walden*, 'Where I Lived, and What I Lived For']

See also SINCERITY, TRIVIALITY

SINCERITY

1 I don't think you want too much sincerity in society. It would be like an iron girder in a house of cards. [W Somerset Maugham, 1874–1965, *The Circle*, I]

2 Unlearn'd, he knew no schoolman's subtle art, / No language, but the language of the heart. [Alexander Pope, 1688–1744, *Epistle to Dr Arbuthnot*, 398]

3 He hath a heart as sound as a bell, and his tongue the clapper; for what his heart thinks his tongue speaks. [William Shakespeare, 1564–1616, *Much Ado About Nothing*, III. ii. (12)]

4 But I will wear my heart upon my sleeve / For daws to peck at. [*Othello*, I. i. 64]

5 Words, words, mere words, no matter from the heart. [*Troilus and Cressida*, V. iii. (109)]

6 It is dangerous to be sincere unless you are also stupid. [George Bernard Shaw, 1856–1950, *Man and Superman*, 'Maxims for Revolutionists', Stray Sayings]

7 A little sincerity is a dangerous thing, and a great deal of it is absolutely fatal. [Oscar Wilde, 1854–1900, *The Critic as Artist*, Pt II]

See also HONESTY, INTEGRITY

SINGERS, see SONGS

SINS

1 His was the sort of career that made the Recording Angel think seriously about taking up shorthand. [Nicholas Bentley, 1908–78; in *Treasury of Humorous Quotations*, ed. Evan Esar and Nicolas Bentley]

2 Though your sins be as scarlet, they shall be as white as snow. [Bible, OT, *Isaiah* 1:18]

3 All we like sheep have gone astray. [Bible, OT, *Isaiah* 53:6]

4 Be sure your sin will find you out. [Bible, OT, *Numbers* 32:23]

5 The way of transgressors is hard. [Bible, OT, *Proverbs* 13:15]

6 If we say that we have no sin, we deceive ourselves, and the truth is not in us. [Bible, NT, *1 John* 1:8]

7 The wages of sin is death. [Bible, NT, *Romans* 6:23]

8 He that is without sin among you, let him first cast a stone at her. [Bible, NT, *St John* 8:7]

9 Around his part of town even original sin is secondhand. [Edward Blishen, 1920–96 (quoting a backstreet teacher), from *A Nest of Teachers*, in *Guardian*, 31 Jan. 1980]

10 Pleasure's a sin, and sometimes sin's a pleasure. [Lord Byron, 1788–1824, *Don Juan*, I, 133]

11 When you confess your sins before a parson, / You find it no great effort to disclose / Your crimes of murder, bigamy and arson, / But can you tell him that you pick your nose? [Norman Cameron, 1905–53, *Punishment Enough*]

12 There are different kinds of wrong. The people sinned against are not always the best. [Ivy Compton-Burnett, 1884–1969, *The Mighty and Their Fall*, Ch. 7]

13 [When asked what a clergyman had said in a sermon on sin] He said he was against it. [Calvin Coolidge, 1872–1933, attr. in J H McKee, *C: Wit and Wisdom*]

14 There is a fountain filled with blood / Drawn from Emmanuel's veins; / And sinners, plunged beneath that flood, / Lose all their guilty stains. [William Cowper, 1731–1800, *Olney Hymns*, 15]

15 Did wisely from expensive sins refrain, / And never broke the Sabbath, but for gain. [John Dryden, 1631–1700, *Absalom and Achitophel*, Pt I, 587]

16 There was really no joy in pouring out one's sins while he sat assiduously picking his nose. [Ronald Firbank, 1886–1926, *Valmouth*, Ch. 6]

17 Though guiltless, you must expiate your fathers' sins. [Horace, 65–8 BC, *Odes*, III, vi, 1]

18 For the sin ye do by two and two ye must pay for one by one! [Rudyard Kipling, 1865–1936, *Tomlinson*]

19 There's nothing so artificial as sinning nowadays. I suppose it once was real. [D H Lawrence, 1885–1930, *St Mawr*]

20 It is a public scandal that offends; to sin in secret is no sin at all. [Molière, 1622–73, *Tartuffe*, IV. v]

21 We have erred and strayed from thy ways like lost sheep. [*The Book of Common Prayer*, 'General Confession']

22 We have left undone those things which we ought to have done; And we have done those things which we ought not to have done; And there is no health in us. [*The Book of Common Prayer*, 'General Confession']

23 Miniver loved the Medici, / Albeit he had never seen one; / He would have sinned incessantly / Could he have been one. [Edwin Arlington Robinson, 1869–1935, *Miniver Cheevy*]

24 At such an hour the sinners are still in bed resting up from their sinning of the night before, so they will be in good shape for more sinning a little later on. [Damon Runyon, 1884–1946, *Runyon à la Carte*, 'The Idyll of Miss Sarah Brown']

25 Cut off even in the blossoms of my sin, / Unhouseled, disappointed, unaneled, / No reckoning made, but sent to my account / With all my imperfections on my head. [William Shakespeare, 1564–1616, *Hamlet*, I. v. 76]

26 O! my offence is rank, it smells to heaven. [*Hamlet*, III. iii. 36]

27 Commit / The oldest sins the newest kind of ways. [*2 Henry*, IV. v. 124]

28 I am a man / More sinned against than sinning. [*King Lear*, III. ii. (59)]

29 Few love to hear the sins they love to act. [*Pericles*, I. i. 92]

30 He passed a cottage with a double coach-house, / A cottage of gentility! / And he owned with a grin / That his favourite sin / Is pride that apes humility. [Robert Southey, 1774–1843, *The Devil's Walk* (a poem written in collaboration with Coleridge)]

31 Even stroking a cat may be regarded by strict Presbyterians as a carnal sin. [David Thomson, 1914–88, *Nairn in Darkness and Light*, p. 185]

32 All sins are attempts to fill voids. [Simone Weil, 1909–43, *Gravity and Grace*, 'To Desire . . .']

See also EVIL, VICE, WICKEDNESS

SKIES

1 The spacious firmament on high, / And all the blue ethereal sky, / And spangled heavens, a shining frame, / Their great Original proclaim. [Joseph Addison, 1672–1719, *The Spectator*, 465, Ode]

2 I do set my bow in the cloud, and it shall be for a token of a covenant between me and the earth. [Bible, OT, *Genesis* 9:13]

3 There's heaven above, and night by night / I look right through its gorgeous roof. [Robert Browning, 1812–89, *Johannes Agricola in Meditation*]

4 Oh! 'darkly, deeply, beautifully blue', / As someone somewhere sings about the sky. [Lord Byron, 1788–1824, *Don Juan*, IV, 110]

5 Than these November skies / Is no sky lovelier. The clouds are deep; / Into their grey the subtle spies / Of colour creep, / Changing their high austerity to delight, / Till ev'n the leaden interfolds are bright. [John Freeman, 1880–1929, *November Skies*]

6 Without a wish, without a will, / I stood upon that silent hill / And stared into the sky until / My eyes were blind with stars and still / I stared into the sky. [Ralph Hodgson, 1871–1962, *The Song of Honour*]

7 When I behold, upon the night's starred face, / Huge cloudy symbols of a high romance. [John Keats, 1795–1821, sonnet: *When I have Fears*]

8 Up in the heavenly saloon / Sheriff sun and rustler moon / Gamble, stuck in the sheriff's mouth / The fag end of an afternoon. [James Michie, 1889–1952, *Arizona Nature Myth*]

9 I never saw a man who looked / With such a wistful eye / Upon that little tent of blue / Which prisoners call the sky. [Oscar Wilde, 1854–1900, *The Ballad of Reading Gaol*, Pt I, 3]

10 My heart leaps up when I behold / A rainbow in the sky. [William Wordsworth, 1770–1850, *My Heart Leaps Up*]

11 The clouds that gather round the setting sun / Do take a sober colouring from an eye / That hath kept watch o'er man's mortality. [William Wordsworth, 1770–1850, *Ode, Intimations of Immortality*, 11]

12 Suddenly I saw the cold and rook-delighting heaven / That seemed as though ice burned and was but the more ice. [W B Yeats, 1865–1939, *The Cold Heaven*]

See also MOON, NIGHT, STARS, SUN, WEATHER

SLANG

1 All slang is metaphor and all metaphor is poetry. [G K Chesterton, 1874–1936, *The Defendant*, 'Defence of Slang']

2 His slang ... was always a little out of date as though he had studied in a dictionary of popular usage, but not in the latest edition. [Graham Greene, 1904–91, *The Comedians*, Pt 1, Ch. 1, sect. i]

3 Slang is a language that rolls up its sleeves, spits on its hands and goes to work. [Carl Sandburg, 1878–1967, in *The New York Times*, 13 Feb. 1959]

See also LANGUAGE, SPEECH

SLAVERY

1 Slavery they can have anywhere. It is a weed that grows in every soil. [Edmund Burke, 1729–97, speech on conciliation with America, 22 Mar. 1775]

2 I am in earnest – I will not equivocate – I will not excuse – I will not retreat a single inch – and I will be heard! [William Lloyd Garrison, 1805–79, salutatory address of the anti-slavery newspaper *The Liberator*, 1 Jan. 1831]

3 Servitude that hugs her chain. [Thomas Gray, 1716–71, *Ode for Music*]

4 In giving freedom to the slave, we assure freedom to the free, – honourable alike in what we give and what we preserve. [Abraham Lincoln, 1809–65, speech, 1 Dec. 1862]

5 So every bondman in his own hand bears / The power to cancel his captivity. [William Shakespeare, 1564–1616, *Julius Caesar*, I. iii. 101]

6 Being your slave, what should I do but tend / Upon the hours and times of your desire? [*Sonnets*, 57]

7 Am I not a man and a brother? [Josiah Wedgwood, 1730–95, inscription on a medal, and afterwards the motto of the Anti-Slavery Society]

8 Among men, a slave does not become like his master by obeying him. On the contrary, the more he obeys the greater is the distance between them. [Simone Weil, 1909–43, *Waiting on God*, 'Forms of the Implicit Love of God']

See also EXPLOITATION, SERVANTS

SLEEPING & WAKING

1 Care-charming Sleep, thou easer of all woes, / Brother to Death. [Francis Beaumont, 1584–

1616, and John Fletcher, 1579–1625, *Valentinian*, V. ii]

2 If thou wilt ease thine heart / Of love and all its smart, / Then sleep, dear, sleep. [T L Beddoes, 1798–1815, *Death's Jest Book*, II. ii]

3 The sleep of a labouring man is sweet. [Bible, OT, *Ecclesiastes* 5:12]

4 Sleep is a death; O make me try, / By sleeping, what it is to die; / And as gently lay my head / On my grave, as now my bed. [Sir Thomas Browne, 1605–82, *Urn Burial*, 12]

5 O earth, so full of dreary noises! / O men, with wailing in your voices! / O delvèd gold, the wailers heap! / O strife, O curse, that o'er it fall! / God strikes a silence through you all, / And giveth his beloved, sleep. [Elizabeth Barrett Browning, 1806–61, *The Sleep*]

6 God bless the inventor of sleep, the cloak that covers all men's thoughts, the food that cures all hunger ... the balancing weight that levels the shepherd with the king and the simple with the wise. [Miguel Cervantes, 1547–1616, *Don Quixote*, Pt II, Ch. 68]

7 Oh sleep! it is a gentle thing, / Beloved from pole to pole! [Samuel Taylor Coleridge, 1772–1834, *The Ancient Mariner*, Pt V]

8 Care-charmer Sleep, son of the sable Night, / Brother to Death, in silent darkness born. [Samuel Daniel, 1562–1619, *Sonnets to Delia*, 44]

9 Golden slumbers kiss your eyes, / Smiles awake you when you rise. / Sleep, pretty wantons, do not cry, / And I will sing a lullaby. [Thomas Dekker, 1572?–1632, *Patient Grissill*, IV. ii]

10 Too tired to yawn, too tired to sleep: / Poor tired Tim! It's sad for him. [Walter de la Mare, 1873–1956, *Tired Tim*]

11 It is not true that some people need less sleep than others. They simply sleep faster. [Peter de Vries, 1910–93, *Consenting Adults*, Ch. 7]

12 Try thinking of love, or something, / Amor vincit insomnia. [Christopher Fry, 1907– , *The Sleep of Prisoners*]

13 Sleep is when all the unsorted stuff comes flying out as from a dustbin upset in a high wind. [William Golding, 1911–93, *Pincher Martin*, Ch. 6]

14 Counting the beats, / Counting the slow heart beats, / The bleeding to death of time in slow heart beats, / Wakeful they lie. [Robert Graves, 1895–1985, *Counting the Beats*]

15 Preserve me from unseasonable and immoderate sleep. [Dr Samuel Johnson, 1709–84, *Prayers and Meditations* (1767)]

16 My heart aches, and a drowsy numbness pains / My sense, as though of hemlock I had drunk. [John Keats, 1795–1821, *Ode to a Nightingale*, 1]

17 O soft embalmer of the still midnight, / Shutting, with careful fingers and benign / Our gloom-pleased eyes. [John Keats, 1795–1821, sonnet: *To Sleep*]

18 What hath night to do with sleep? [John Milton, 1608–74, *Comus*, 122]

19 How do people go to sleep? I'm afraid I've lost the knack. I might try busting myself smartly over the temple with the nightlight. I might repeat to myself, slowly and soothingly, a list of quotations beautiful from minds profound; if I can remember any of the damn things. [Dorothy Parker, 1893–1967, *The Little Hours*]

20 It is said that the effect of eating too much lettuce is 'soporific'. [Beatrix Potter, 1866–1943, *The Tale of the Flopsy Bunnies*]

21 I remarked that his eyes were open so he must be awake. 'The one on your side is,' said a backer, 'but the one on the other side is closed. He is sleeping one-eyed.' [Damon Runyon, 1884–1946, *Short Takes*, 'Bed-Warmers']

22 O sleep! O gentle sleep! / Nature's soft nurse, how have I frighted thee, / That thou no more wilt weigh mine eyelids down / And steep my senses in forgetfulness? [William Shakespeare, 1564–1616, *2 Henry IV*, III. i. 5]

23 Sleep so soundly as the wretched slave / Who with a body filled and vacant mind / Gets him to rest, crammed with distressful bread. [*Henry V*, IV. i. (288)]

24 Sleep shall neither night nor day / Hang upon his pent-house lid; / He shall live a man forbid: / Weary se'nnights nine times nine / Shall he dwindle, peak and pine. [*Macbeth*, I. iii. 19]

25 Methought I heard a voice cry, 'Sleep no more! / Macbeth does murder sleep', the innocent sleep, / Sleep that knits up the ravelled sleave of care, / The death of each day's life, sore labour's bath, / Balm of hurt minds, great nature's second course, / Chief nourisher in life's feast. [*Macbeth*, II. ii. 36]

26 Come sleep! O sleep, the certain knot of peace, / The baiting place of wit, the balm of woe, / The poor man's wealth, the prisoner's release, / Th' indifferent judge between the high and low. [Sir Philip Sidney, 1554–86, *Astrophel and Stella*, Sonnet 39]

27 Sleep after toil, port after stormy seas, / Ease after war, death after life, does greatly please. [Edmund Spenser, 1552?–99, *The Faerie Queene*, Bk i, Canto 9, stanza 40]

28 Sleep, Death's twin-brother, knows not Death, / Nor can I dream of thee as dead. [Alfred, Lord Tennyson, 1809–92, *In Memoriam*, 68]

29 I have come to the borders of sleep, / The unfathomable deep / Forest where all must lose / Their way. [Edward Thomas, 1878–1917, *Lights Out*]

30 There are two gates of Sleep, whereof one is said to be of horn, through which the spirits of truth find an easy passage, the other made of gleaming white ivory, through which the gods send up false dreams to the upper world. [Virgil, 70–19 BC, *Aeneid*, VI, 893]

31 I haven't been to sleep for over a year. That's why I go to bed early. One needs more rest if one doesn't sleep. [Evelyn Waugh, 1903–66, *Decline and Fall*, II, 3]

32 A flock of sheep that leisurely pass by, / One after one; the sound of rain and bees / Murmuring; the fall of rivers, winds and seas, / Smooth fields, white sheets of water, and pure sky; / I have thought of all by turns, and yet do lie / Sleepless! [William Wordsworth, 1770–1850, *Miscellaneous Sonnets*, 1, 14, 'To Sleep']

33 Tired Nature's sweet restorer, balmy sleep! / He, like the world, his ready visit pays / Where fortune smiles; the wretched he forsakes. [Edward Young, 1683–1765, *Night Thoughts*, 'Night I', 1]

See also DAWN, DREAMS, NIGHT, TIREDNESS

SMELLS

1 I counted two and seventy stenches, / All well defined, and several stinks! [Samuel Taylor Coleridge, 1772–1834, *Cologne*]

2 And anon there came in a dove at a window, and in her mouth there seemed a little censer of gold, and therewithal there was such a savour as all the spicery of the world had been there. [Thomas Malory, d.1471, *Morte d'Arthur*, Bk xi, Ch. 2]

3 You may break, you may shatter the vase, if you will, / But the scent of the roses will hang round it still. [Thomas Moore, 1779–1852, *Irish Melodies*, 'Farewell! But Whenever']

4 And as the soldiers bore dead bodies by, / He called them untaught knaves, unmannerly, / To bring a slovenly unhandsome corpse / Betwixt the wind and his nobility. [William Shakespeare, 1564–1616, *1 Henry IV*, I. iii. 42]

5 Here's the smell of the blood still: all the perfumes of Arabia will not sweeten this little hand. [*Macbeth*, V. i. (55)]

6 The rankest compound of villanous smell that ever offended nostril. [*The Merry Wives of Windsor*, III. iv. (95)]

7 A very ancient and fish-like smell. [*The Tempest*, II. ii. (27)]

8 Odours when sweet violets sicken, / Live within the sense they quicken. [P B Shelley, 1792–1822, *To —, Music, When Soft Voices Die*]

SMOKING

1 Tobacco, divine, rare, superexcellent tobacco, which goes far beyond all their panaceas, potable gold, and philosopher's stones, a sovereign remedy to all diseases . . . But, as it is commonly abused by most men, which take it as tinkers do ale, 'tis a plague, a mischief, a violent purger of goods, lands, health, hellish, devilish, and damned tobacco, the ruin and overthrow of body and soul. [Robert Burton, 1577–1640, *Anatomy of Melancholy*, II, §4, Memb. 2, 1]

2 All grow by slow degrees / Brainless as chimpanzees, / Meagre as lizards; / Go mad, and beat their wives; / Plunge (after shocking lives) / Razors and carving knives / Into their gizzards. [C S Calverley, 1831–84, *Ode to Tobacco*]

3 Pernicious weed! whose scent the fair annoys, / Unfriendly to society's chief joys, / Thy worst effect is banishing for hours / The sex whose presence civilizes ours. [William Cowper, 1731–1800, *Conversation*, 251]

4 But when I don't smoke I scarcely feel as if I'm

living. I don't feel as if I'm living unless I'm killing myself. [Russell Hoban, 1925– , *Turtle Diary*, Ch. 7]

5 Herein is not only a great vanity, but a great contempt of God's good gifts, that the sweetness of man's breath, being a good gift of God, should be wilfully corrupted by this stinking smoke. [King James I, 1566–1625, *A Counterblast to Tobacco*]

6 Neither do thou lust after that tawny weed tobacco. [Ben Jonson, 1573–1637, *The Alchemist*, II. vi]

7 I do hold it, and will affirm it before any prince in Europe, to be the most sovereign and precious weed that ever the earth rendered to the use of man. [Ben Jonson, 1573–1637, *Every Man in His Humour*, III. ii]

8 And a woman is only a woman, but a good cigar is a smoke. [Rudyard Kipling, 1865–1936, *The Betrothed*]

9 It is now proved beyond doubt that smoking is one of the leading causes of statistics. [Fletcher Knebel, 1911–93, in *Reader's Digest*, Dec. 1961]

10 For thy sake, Tobacco, I / Would do anything but die. [Charles Lamb, 1775–1834, *A Farewell to Tobacco*, 122]

11 What this country needs is a really good five-cent cigar. [Vice-President T R Marshall, 1854–1925 (supposedly said to Henry M Rose), in *New York Tribune*, 4 Jan. 1920]

12 There's nothing like tobacco; it is the passion of all decent people; someone who lives without tobacco does not deserve to live. [Molière, 1622–73, *Don Juan*, I. i]

13 My doctor has always told me to smoke. He even explains himself: 'Smoke, my friend. Otherwise someone else will smoke in your place.' [Erik Satie, 1866–1925, *Memoirs of an Amnesiac*]

14 I have every sympathy with the American who was so horrified by what he had read of the effects of smoking that he gave up reading. [Henry G Strauss, 1892–1974; in A Andrews, *Quotations for Speakers and Writers*]

15 There's no sweeter tobacco comes from Virginia, and no better brand than the Three Castles. [W M Thackeray, 1811–63, *The Virginians*, Ch. 1]

SMUGNESS

1 Although he [David Ben-Gurion] did not believe in God himself, he somehow gave the impression that God believed in him. [Chaim Bermant, 1929– , in *Observer*, 4 Sept. 1983]

2 Woe unto them that are wise in their own eyes, and prudent in their own sight! [Bible, OT, *Isaiah* 5:21]

3 God, I thank thee, that I am not as other men are. [Bible, NT, *St Luke* 18:11]

4 Of all the horrid, hideous notes of woe, / Sadder than owl-songs or the midnight blast, / Is that portentous phrase, 'I told you so'. [Lord Byron, 1788–1824, *Don Juan*, V, 50]; see 12

5 Where he falls short, 'tis Nature's fault alone; / Where he succeeds, the merit's all his own. [Charles Churchill, 1731–64, *The Rosciad*, 1025]

6 Oh gracious, why wasn't I born old and ugly? [(Miss Miggs) Charles Dickens, 1812–70, *Barnaby Rudge*, Ch. 70]

7 I've never any pity for conceited people, because I think they carry their comfort about with them. [George Eliot, 1819–80, *The Mill on the Floss*, Bk v, Ch. 4]

8 I can trace my ancestry back to a protoplasmal primordial atomic globule. Consequently, my family pride is something inconceivable. I can't help it. I was born sneering. [W S Gilbert, 1836–1911, *The Mikado*, I]

9 And when I'm finally called, by the Great Architect, and he says 'What did you do?' I shall just bring me book out and say, 'Here you are, add that lot up.' [Tony Hancock, 1924–68, BBC TV comedy series *Hancock's Half Hour*, 'The Blood Donor', scripts by Ray Galton and Alan Simpson]

10 Try not to despise yourself too much – it's only conceit. [P J Kavanagh, 1931– , *A Song and Dance*, Ch. 6]

11 Jehovah's Witnesses, awaiting the Last Day with the quiet kind of satisfaction that a man gets in the dry season when he knows his neighbour's house is not insured against fire. [Bernard Levin, 1928– , *The Pendulum Years*, Ch. 1]

12 He seemed the incarnate 'Well, I told you so!' [H W Longfellow, 1807–82, *Tales of a Wayside Inn*, Pt I, 'The Poet's Tale']; see 4

See also ARROGANCE, HUMILITY, PRIDE

SNOBS & SNOBBERY

1 We mean to live very quietly, only seeing the King and a few friends. [(On her husband's fall from power) Margot Asquith, 1865–1945, quoted in *Observer*, 20 Dec. 1981]

2 Phone for the fish-knives, Norman, / As Cook is a little unnerved; / You kiddies have crumpled the serviettes / And I must have things daintily served. [John Betjeman, 1906–84, *How to Get on in Society*]

3 Yet it is better to drop thy friends, O my daughter, than to drop thy 'H.s'. [C S Calverley, 1831–84, *Proverbial Philosophy*, 'Of Friendship']

4 I never knew that the lower classes had such white skins. [Lord Curzon, 1859–1925 (when seeing troops bathing), attr. in K Rose, *Superior Person*, Ch. 12]

5 He calls the knaves, Jacks, this boy! ... And what coarse hands he has! And what thick boots! [Charles Dickens, 1812–70, *Great Expectations*, Ch. 8]

6 He would certainly have despised Christ for being the son of a carpenter, if the New Testament had not proved in time to be such a howling commercial success. [Graham Greene, 1904–91, *Dr Fischer of Geneva*, Ch. 7]

7 There are few who would not rather be taken in adultery than in provincialism. [Aldous Huxley, 1894–1963, *Antic Hay*, 10]

8 Tomorrow every Duchess in London will be wanting to kiss me! [Ramsay MacDonald, 1866–1917 (on forming the national government, 25 Aug. 1931), in Viscount Snowden, *Autobiography*]

9 But let a lord once own the happy lines, / How the wit brightens! how the style refines! [Alexander Pope, 1688–1744, *An Essay on Criticism*, 420]

10 Just as there are OK-words in conversationship so there are OK-*people to mention* in Newstatesmanship. [Stephen Potter, 1900–1969, *Lifemanship*, 5]

11 His hatred of snobs derived from his snobbishness, but made the simple-minded (in other words, everyone) believe that he was immune from snobbishness. [Marcel Proust, 1871–1922, *Remembrance of Things Past: The Guermantes Way*, 'The Wit of the Guermantes', Ch. 2]

12 You can be in the Horse Guards and still be common, dear. [Terence Rattigan, 1911–77, *Separate Tables*, 'Table Number Seven']

13 It is impossible, in our condition of society, not to be sometimes a snob. [W M Thackeray, 1811–63, *The Book of Snobs*, Ch. 3]

14 Whenever he met a great man he grovelled before him, and my-lorded him as only a free-born Briton can do. [W M Thackeray, 1811–63, *Vanity Fair*, Ch. 13]

15 Laughter would be bereaved if snobbery died. [Peter Ustinov, 1921– ; *Observer*, 'Sayings of the Week', 13 Mar. 1955]

16 You breed babies and you eat chips with everything. [Arnold Wesker, 1932– , *Chips with Everything*, I. ii]

17 CECILY: When I see a spade I call it a spade. GWENDOLEN: I am glad to say I have never seen a spade. It is obvious that our social spheres have been widely different. [Oscar Wilde, 1854–1900, *The Importance of Being Earnest*, II]

See also ARISTOCRACY, CLASS, MANNERS

SOCIABILITY

1 I do not want people to be very agreeable, as it saves me the trouble of liking them a great deal. [Jane Austen, 1775–1817, *Letters*, 24 Dec. 1798]

2 A crowd is not company, and faces are but a gallery of pictures. [Francis Bacon, 1561–1626, *Essays*, 27, 'Of Friendship']

3 Society, friendship, and love, / Divinely bestowed upon man, / Oh, had I the wings of a dove, / How soon would I taste you again! [William Cowper, 1731–1800, *Verses Supposed to be Written by Alexander Selkirk*]

4 Ez shoshubble ez a baskit er kittens. [Joel Chandler Harris, 1848–1908, *Nights with Uncle Remus*, Ch. 3]

5 Some people can stay longer in an hour than others can in a week. [William Dean Howells, 1837–1920; attr. in *Treasury of Humorous Quotations*, ed. Evan Esar and Nicolas Bentley]

6 My life is spent in a perpetual alternation between two rhythms, the rhythm of attracting people for fear I may be lonely and the rhythm of trying to get rid of them because I know that I am bored. [C E M Joad, 1891–1953; *Observer*, 'Sayings of the Week', 12 Dec. 1948]

7 There are people whom one should like very well to drop, but would not wish to be dropped by. [Dr Samuel Johnson, 1709–84, in James Boswell, *Life of J*, Mar. 1781]

8 Where two or three / are gathered together, that / is about enough. [Les Murray, 1938– , *Company*]

9 Go very light on vices such as carrying on in society. The social ramble ain't restful. [Satchel Paige, *c.*1906–82, *Six Rules for a Long Life*]

10 I've sometimes regretted living so close to Marie . . . because although I'm very fond of her, I'm not quite so fond of her company. [Marcel Proust, 1871–1922, *Remembrance of Things Past: Cities of the Plain*, Pt II, Ch. 1]

11 FALSTAFF: Company, villanous company, hath been the spoil of me. [William Shakespeare, 1564–1616, *1 Henry IV*, III. iii. (10)]

12 One's impossible, two is dreary, / Three is company, safe and cheery. [Stephen Sondheim, 1930– , song: *Side by Side by Side*]

13 I love good creditable acquaintance; I love to be the worst of the company. [Jonathan Swift, 1677–1745, *Journal to Stella*, 17 May 1711]

14 Thus was I reconverted to the world; / Society became my glittering bride, / And airy hopes my children. [William Wordsworth, 1770–1850, *The Excursion*, III, 734]

See also FRIENDS, HOSPITALITY, SOCIETY

SOCIALISTS

1 Making capitalism out of socialism is like making eggs out of an omelette. [Vadim Bakatin (first candidate in Russian presidential election), 1937– , said in May 1991; in *Hutchinson Gallup Info 92*]

2 Then raise the scarlet standard high! / Beneath its shade we'll live and die! / Though cowards flinch, and traitors jeer, / We'll keep the Red Flag flying here! [James Connell, 1852–1929, *The Red Flag*]

3 Socialism with a Human Face. [Alexander Dubček, 1921–92 (motto of the Prague Spring), in *Rudé Právo*, 19 July 1968. Coined by Radovan Richta, according to *Penguin Dictionary of Political Quotations*, comp. Robert Stewart]; see 9

4 We are all Socialists nowadays. [Edward VII, 1841–1910, speech at Mansion House, 5 Nov. 1895]

5 Vote Labour and you build castles in the air. Vote Conservative and you can live in them. [David Frost, 1939– , from BBC TV programme *That Was the Week That Was*, 31 Dec. 1962]

6 There are some of us, Mr Chairman, who will fight and fight and fight again to save the party we love. [Hugh Gaitskell, 1906–63, speech at Labour Party Conference, Scarborough, 3 Oct. 1960]

7 To wait until one has grown to half the voters plus one is the programme of cowardly souls who wait for socialism by a royal decree countersigned by two ministers. [Antonio Gramsci, 1891–1937, in A Pozzolini, *A G: An Introduction to His Thought*, Ch. 2]

8 The Fabians are 100 years old. In many ways they always have been. [Roy Hattersley, 1932– (on centenary of the Fabian Society), in *Guardian*, 17 Mar. 1984]

9 What we need now is socialism with a human *head*. [Miroslav Holub, 1923–98, quoted by W L Webb in *Guardian*, 13 July 1987]; see 3

10 Fair Shares for All is Labour's Call. [Douglas Jay, 1907–96, slogan at North Battersea by-election, London, June 1946]

11 Under socialism *all* will govern in turn and will soon become accustomed to no one governing. [Vladimir Ilyich Lenin, 1870–1924, *The State and Revolution*, Ch. 6, iii]

12 If my friend cannot ride two horses – what's he doing in the bloody circus? [(On the political difficulties of straddling the Independent Labour Party and Labour Party, at Scottish ILP Conference, Jan. 1931) James Maxton, 1885–1946, in G McAllister, *J M*, Ch. 14]

13 Too much thinking, in my opinion, is not becoming to Toryism. It ought not to be encouraged. Thought is a Socialist temptation, not a Tory one. [Shiva Naipaul, 1945–85, in *Spectator*, 28 May 1983]

14 As with the Christian religion, the worst advertisement for Socialism is its adherents. [George Orwell, 1903–50, *The Road to Wigan Pier*, Ch. 11]

15 The underlying motive of many Socialists, I believe, is simply a hypertrophied sense of order. The present state of affairs offends them not because it causes misery, still less because it makes freedom impossible, but because it is untidy; what they desire, basically, is to reduce the world to something resembling a chessboard. [George Orwell, 1903–50, *The Road to Wigan Pier*, Ch. 11]

16 We are the masters at the moment – and not only for the moment, but for a very long time to come. [Hartley Shawcross, 1902– , said in House of Commons in a debate on the trade unions, 2 Apr. 1946]

17 Many people consider the things which government does for them to be social progress, but they consider the things government does for others as socialism. [Earl Warren, 1891–1974, in Laurence J Peter, *Peter's Quotations*]

18 This party is a moral crusade, or it is nothing. [Harold Wilson, 1916–95, at Labour Party Conference, 1 Oct. 1962]

19 Yes, the labour movement was truly religious, like Judaism itself. It was one of those things you believed in for all mankind and didn't care about for a second in your own life. [Tom Wolfe, 1931– , *The Bonfire of the Vanities*, Ch. 8]

See also COMMUNISM, CONSERVATIVES, LIBERALS

SOCIETY

1 This great society is going smash; / They cannot fool us with how fast they go, / How much they cost each other and the gods! / A culture is no better than its woods. [W H Auden, 1907–73, *Winds*]

2 The good is better than the best, else what does society mean? [Alan Bennett, 1934 , *The Old Country*, II]

3 Society is indeed a contract . . . it becomes a partnership not only between those who are living, but between those who are living, those who are dead, and those who are to be born. [Edmund Burke, 1729–97, *Reflections on the Revolution in France*, Penguin edn, p. 194]

4 The people I'm used to just have more marriages and more Matisses than the people you're used to. [Randall Jarrell, 1914–65, *Pictures from an Institution*, Pt III, Ch. 6]

5 For in your time we have the opportunity to move not only toward the rich society and the powerful society, but upward to the Great Society. [President Lyndon Johnson, 1908–73, speech at University of Michigan, Ann Arbor, 22 May 1964]

6 Society is based on the assumption that everyone is alike and no one is alive. [Hugh Kingsmill, 1889–1949, *The Best of Hugh Kingsmill*, ed. Michael Holroyd, Introduction]

7 Our own society is the only one which we can transform and yet not destroy, since the changes which we should introduce would come from within. [Claude Lévi-Strauss, 1908– , *World on the Wane*, Ch. 35]

8 The whole trouble with Western society today is the lack of anything worth concealing. [Joe Orton, 1933–67, diary, 11 July 1966]

9 If the (First World) war didn't happen to kill you it was bound to start you thinking. After that unspeakable idiotic mess you couldn't go on regarding society as something eternal and unquestionable, like a pyramid. You knew it was just a balls-up. [George Orwell, 1903–50, *Coming up for Air*, II, 8]

10 This civilization has not yet fully recovered from the shock of its birth – the transition from the tribal or 'closed society', with its submission to magical forces, to the 'open society' which sets free the critical powers of man. [Karl Popper, 1902–94, *The Open Society and Its Enemies*, Introduction]

11 Man is not a solitary animal, and so long as social life survives, self-realization cannot be the supreme principle of ethics. [Bertrand Russell, 1872–1970, *A History of Western Philosophy*, 'Romanticism']

12 Polite Society believed in God so that it need not talk of Him. [Jean-Paul Sartre, 1905–80, *Words*, Pt 1]

13 3RD FISHERMAN: I marvel how the fishes live in the sea.
1ST FISHERMAN: Why, as men do a-land; the great ones eat up the little ones. [William Shakespeare, 1564–1616, *Pericles*, II. i. (29)]

14 Physically there is nothing to distinguish human society from the farm-yard except that children are more troublesome and costly than chickens and women are not so completely enslaved as farm stock. [George Bernard Shaw, 1856–1950, *Getting Married*, Preface]

15 As long as men are men, a poor society cannot be too poor to find a right order of life, nor a rich society too rich to have need to seek it. [R H Tawney, 1880–1962, *The Acquisitive Society*]

16 There is no such thing as society. There are individual men and women and there are families. [Margaret Thatcher, 1925– , in *Woman's Own*, 31 Oct. 1987]

17 The Social Contract is nothing more nor less than a vast conspiracy of human beings to lie to and humbug themselves and one another for the general Good. Lies are the mortar that binds the savage individual man into the social masonry. [H G Wells, 1866–1946, *Love and Mr Lewisham*, Ch. 23]

18 Never speak disrespectfully of Society, Algernon. Only people who can't get into it do that. [Oscar Wilde, 1854–1900, *The Importance of Being Earnest*, III]

19 There is / One great society alone on earth: / The noble living and the noble dead. [William Wordsworth, 1770–1850, *The Prelude*, XI, 393]

See also STATE

SOLDIERS IN GENERAL

1 Over the heather the west wind blows, / I've lice in my tunic and a cold in my nose. / The rain comes pattering out of the sky, / I'm a Wall soldier and I don't know why. [W H Auden, 1907–73, *Roman Wall Blues*]

2 The Guards die, but do not surrender. [Baron de Cambronne, 1770–1842, when called on to surrender at Waterloo. Attr. to Cambronne but always disclaimed by him; he insisted that he just said '*Merde*' ('Shit'). Elsewhere attr. to Col. Michel]

3 In my experience ... officers with high athletic qualifications are not usually successful in the higher ranks. [Winston Churchill, 1874–1965, *The Second World War*, Vol. 2, Appendix C, 4 Feb. 1941]

4 The uncontrolled licentiousness of a brutal and insolent soldiery. [Lord Erskine, 1750–1823, *In Defence of William Stone*]

5 Old soldiers never die; / They only fade away! [John Foley, song of 1914–18 War; ascr. to Foley in *Oxford Dictionary of Modern Quotations*, ed. Tony Augarde]

6 He led his regiment from behind – / He found it less exciting. [W S Gilbert, 1836–1911, *The Gondoliers*, I]

7 I am the very model of a modern Major-General. [W S Gilbert, 1836–1911, *The Pirates of Penzance*, I]

8 Ask any soldier. To kill a man is to merit a woman. [Jean Giraudoux, 1882–1944, *Tiger at the Gates*, I]

9 What of the faith and fire within us / Men who march away / Ere the barncocks say / Night is growing gray, / Leaving all that here can win us? [Thomas Hardy, 1840–1928, *Men Who March away*]

10 Ben Battle was a soldier bold, / And used to war's alarms: / But a cannon-ball took off his legs, / So he laid down his arms. [Thomas Hood, 1799–1845, *Faithless Nelly Gray*]

11 The love that loves a scarlet coat / Should be more uniform. [Thomas Hood, 1799–1845, *Faithless Nelly Gray*]

12 Every man thinks meanly of himself for not having been a soldier, or not having been at sea. [Dr Samuel Johnson, 1709–84, in James Boswell, *Life of J*, 10 Apr. 1778]

13 Oh, it's Tommy this, an' Tommy that, an' 'Tommy, go away'; / But it's 'Thank you, Mr Atkins', when the band begins to play. [Rudyard Kipling, 1865–1936, *Tommy*]

14 They're changing guard at Buckingham Palace – / Christopher Robin went down with Alice. / Alice is marrying one of the guard. / 'A soldier's life is terrible hard,' / Says Alice. [A A Milne, 1882–1956, *When We Were Very Young*, 'Buckingham Palace']

15 The soldier who never admits that he has been defeated is always right. [Charles Péguy, 1873–1914, quoted in *Independent*, 1 Sept. 1995]

16 I saw him stab / And stab again / A well-killed Boche. / This is the happy warrior. / This is he ... [Herbert Read, 1893–1968, *The Happy Warrior*]

17 Soldiers are citizens of death's grey land, / Drawing no dividend from time's tomorrows. [Siegfried Sassoon, 1886–1967, *Dreamers*]

18 'He's a cheery old card,' grunted Harry to Jack / As they slogged up to Arras with rifle and pack ... / But he did for them both by his plan of attack. [Siegfried Sassoon, 1886–1967, *The General*]

19 Soldier, rest! thy warfare o'er, / Dream of fighting fields no more: / Sleep the sleep that knows not breaking. / Morn of toil, nor night of waking. [Sir Walter Scott, 1771–1832, *The Lady of the Lake*, I, 31]

20 He made me mad / To see him shine so brisk and smell so sweet / And talk so like a waiting-gentlewoman / Of guns, and drums, and wounds, – God save the mark! – / And telling me the sovereign'st thing on earth / Was parmaceti for an inward bruise; / And that it was great pity, so it was, / This villainous salt-petre should be digged / Out of the bowels of the harmless earth, / Which many a good tall fellow had destroyed / So cowardly; and but for these vile guns, / He would himself have been a soldier. [William Shakespeare, 1564–1616, *1 Henry IV*, I. iii. 53]

21 On, on, you noblest English, / Whose blood is fet from fathers of war-proof! / Fathers that, like so many Alexanders, / Have in these parts from morn till even fought, / And sheathed their swords for lack of argument. [*Henry V*, III. i. 17]

22 The painful warrior famousèd for fight, / After a thousand victories once foiled, / Is from the book of honour razèd quite, / And all the rest forgot for which he toiled. [*Sonnets*, 25]

23 The British soldier can stand up to anything except the British War Office. [George Bernard Shaw, 1856–1950, *The Devil's Disciple*, III]

24 Someone had blundered: / Theirs not to make reply, / Theirs not to reason why, / Theirs but to do and die. [Alfred, Lord Tennyson, 1809–92, *The Charge of the Light Brigade*]

25 Dead battles, like dead generals, hold the military mind in their dead grip. [Barbara Tuchman, 1912–89, *The Guns of August*, Ch. 2]

26 As for being a General, well at the age of four with paper hats and wooden swords we're all Generals. Only some of us never grow out of it. [Peter Ustinov, 1921–   , *Romanoff and Juliet*, I]

27 I don't know what effect these men will have upon the enemy, but, by God, they terrify me. [Duke of Wellington, 1769–1852, on a draft sent out to him in Spain, 1809]

28 Who is the happy warrior? Who is he / That every man in arms should wish to be? . . . Who doomed to go in company with pain, / And fear, and bloodshed, miserable train! / Turns his necessity to glorious gain. [William Wordsworth, 1770–1850, *Character of the Happy Warrior*]

See also next category, ARMY, BATTLES, WAR, WARS

SOLDIERS: INDIVIDUAL (in alphabetical order of subject)

1 It is not the job of the general to be winning. It is his job to win. [(Of General Eisenhower and his relationship with General Montgomery) Nancy Banks-Smith, 1929–   , in *Guardian*, 9 May 1990]

2 He [Field-Marshal Lord Haig] was brilliant to the top of his army boots. [David Lloyd George, 1863–1945, attr. in J Wintle, *Dictionary of War Quotations*]

3 I didn't fire him [General MacArthur] because he was a dumb son of a bitch, although he was, but that's not against the law for generals. If it was, half to three-quarters of them would be in gaol. [Harry Truman, 1884–1972, interview; in Merle Miller, *Plain Speaking*, 24]

4 In defeat unbeatable; in victory unbearable. [Winston Churchill, 1874–1965 (of Field-Marshall Montgomery), in Edward Marsh, *Ambrosia and Small Beer*, Ch. 5, sect. ii]

5 I used to say of him [Napoleon] that his presence on the field made the difference of forty thousand men. [Duke of Wellington, 1769–1852, P H Stanhope, *Notes on Conversations with the Duke of W*, 2 Nov. 1831]

6 Rude am I in my speech, / And little blessed with the soft phrase of peace, / For since these arms of mine had seven years' pith, / Till now some nine moons wasted, they have used / Their dearest action in the tented field. [William Shakespeare, 1564–1616, *Othello*, I. iii. 81]

7 This is England's greatest son, / He that gained a hundred fights, / Nor ever lost an English gun. [Alfred, Lord Tennyson, 1809–92, *Ode on the Death of the Duke of Wellington*, 6]

See also previous category, ARMY, BATTLES, WAR, WARS

SOLITUDE

1 Dotting the shoreless watery wild, / We mortal millions live *alone*. [Matthew Arnold, 1822–88, *To Marguerite, Isolation*]

2 It had been hard for him that spake it to have put more truth and untruth together, in few words, than in that: 'Whosoever is delighted in solitude is either a wild beast, or a god'. [Francis Bacon, 1561–1626, *Essays*, 27, 'Of Friendship']

3 To fly from, need not be to hate, mankind: / All are not fit with them to stir and toil, / Nor is it discontent to keep the mind / Deep in its fountain. [Lord Byron, 1788–1824, *Childe Harold's Pilgrimage*, III, 69]

4 Then stirs the feeling infinite, so felt / In solitude, where we are *least* alone. [Lord Byron, 1788–1824, *Childe Harold's Pilgrimage*, III, 90]

5 I long for scenes where man has never trod; / A place where woman never smiled or wept; / There to abide with my Creator, God, / And sleep as I in childhood sweetly slept: / Untroubling and untroubled where I lie; – The grass below – above the vaulted sky. [John Clare, 1793–1864, *I Am*]

6 We live, as we dream – alone. [Joseph Conrad, 1857–1924, *Heart of Darkness*, Ch. 1]

7 I am monarch of all I survey, / My right there is none to dispute; / From the centre all round to the sea / I am lord of the fowl and the brute. / Oh, solitude, where are the charms / That sages have seen in thy face? / Better dwell in the midst of alarms, / Than reign in this horrible place. [William Cowper, 1731–1800, *Verses Supposed to be Written by Alexander Selkirk*]

8 I want to be alone. [Greta Garbo, 1905–90, attr., but she always insisted she had said, 'I want to be left alone.' Subsequently used in her film *Grand Hotel*, script by William A Drake]

9 Solitude is for me a fount of healing which makes my life worth living. Talking is often a torment for me and I need many days of silence to recover from the futility of words. [C G Jung, 1875–1961, *Letters*, Vol. 2, 1951–61]

10 Solitude would be an ideal state if one were able to pick the people one avoids. [Karl Kraus, 1874–1936, *Half-truths and One-and-a-half Truths*, 'Lord, Forgive the . . .']

11 Alas, solitude is not very likely, there is so little of it in life, so what can we expect after death! After all, the dead far outnumber the living! [Milan Kundera, 1929– , *Immortality*, Pt 1, 3]

12 Ships that pass in the night, and speak each other in passing; / Only a signal shown and a distant voice in the darkness; / So on the ocean of life we pass and speak one another, / Only a look and a voice; then darkness again and a silence. [H W Longfellow, 1807–82, *Tales of A Wayside Inn*, Pt III, 'The Theologian's Tale']

13 But 'twas beyond a mortal's share / To wander solitary there: / Two paradises 'twere in one, / To live in paradise alone. [Andrew Marvell, 1621–78, *The Garden*, 61]

14 For solitude sometimes is best society, / And short retirement urges sweet return. [John Milton, 1608–74, *Paradise Lost*, Bk ix, 249]

15 Any time you see him he is generally by himself because being by himself is not apt to cost him anything. [Damon Runyon, 1884–1946, *Furthermore*, 'Little Miss Marker']

16 To be alone is the fate of all great minds – a fate deplored at times, but still always chosen as the less grievous of two evils. [Arthur Schopenhauer, 1788–1860, *Aphorisms: Parerga and Paralipomena*]

17 Duty and dereliction guide thee back to solitude. [P B Shelley, 1792–1822, *Stanzas – April 1814*]

18 I never found the companion that was so companionable as solitude. [H D Thoreau, 1817–62, *Walden*, 'Solitude']

19 We're all of us sentenced to solitary confinement inside our own skins, for life! [Tennessee Williams, 1911–83, *Orpheus Descending*, II. i]

20 They [daffodils] flash upon that inward eye / Which is the bliss of solitude. [William Wordsworth, 1770–1850, *I Wandered Lonely as a Cloud*]

21 When from our better selves we have too long / Been parted by the hurrying world, and droop, / Sick of its business, of its pleasures tired, / How gracious, how benign, is solitude. [William Wordsworth, 1770–1850, *The Prelude*, IV, 354]

See also LONELINESS

SONGS & SINGERS

1 *Aujourd-hui, ce qui ne vaut pas la peine d'être dit, on le chante.* – Today when something is not worth saying, they sing it. [Pierre de Beaumarchais, 1732–99, *The Barber of Seville*, I. ii]

2 It is the best of all trades, to make songs, and the second best to sing them. [Hilaire Belloc, 1870–1953, *On Everything*, 'On Song']

3 Sing unto him a new song; play skilfully with a loud noise. [Bible, OT, *Psalms* 33:3]

4 And I made a rural pen, / And I stained the water clear, / And I wrote my happy songs /

Every child may joy to hear. [William Blake, 1757–1827, *Songs of Innocence*, Introduction]

5 I guess all songs is folk songs. I never heard no horse sing 'em. ['Big Bill' Broonzy, 1893–1958, in C Keil, *Urban Blues*]

6 Swans sing before they die – 'twere no bad thing / Did certain persons die before they sing. [Samuel Taylor Coleridge, 1772–1834, *Epigram on a Volunteer Singer*]

7 Thou needst not make new songs, but say the old. [Abraham Cowley, 1618–67, *On the Death of Mr Crashaw*]

8 Most of them think: 'Well he [Crosby] sings about like I do, you know, when I'm in the bathroom, or in the shower, and feel good and wake up with a gay feeling.' Why they think I'm one of the fellas. [Bing Crosby, 1901–77, epigraph to C Thompson, *Bing*]

9 I sang as one / Who on a tilting deck sings / To keep men's courage up, though the wave hangs / That shall cut off their sun. [C Day Lewis, 1904–72, *The Conflict*]

10 Admirable, but what language was he singing in? [Frederick Delius, 1862–1934 (after a recital of his own songs), in Sir Thomas Beecham, *A Mingled Chime*, Ch. 19]

11 A song is anything that can walk by itself. [Bob Dylan, 1941– , *Bringing It All Back Home*, sleeve notes]

12 [When asked whether he knew what his songs were about] Yeah, some of them are about ten minutes long, others five or six. [Bob Dylan, 1941– , interview, *c*.1965]

13 A German singer! I should as soon expect to get pleasure from the neighing of my horse. [Frederick the Great, 1712–86; quoted in Evan Esar, ed., *Treasury of Humorous Quotations*]

14 I'm singing in the rain, just singing in the rain; What a wonderful feeling, I'm happy again. [Arthur Freed, 1894–1973, song: *Singing in the Rain*, from musical, *Hollywood Review of 1929*]

15 She was a singer who had to take any note above A with her eyebrows. [Montague Glass, 1877–1934, in Frank Muir, *Frank Muir Book*, 'Music']

16 Good people all, of every sort, / Give ear unto my song; / And if you do find it wondrous short, / It cannot hold you long. [Oliver Goldsmith, 1728–74, *The Vicar of Wakefield*, Ch. 17, 'An Elegy on the Death of a Mad Dog']

17 The songs I had are withered / Or vanished clean, / Yet there are bright tracks / Where I have been. [Ivor Gurney, 1890–1937, *The Songs I Had*]

18 She [Bessie Smith] showed me the air and taught me how to fill it. [Janis Joplin, 1943–70, in C Albertson, *Bessie*]

19 All people that on earth do dwell, / Sing to the Lord with cheerful voice. [William Kethe, d.1608, hymn]

20 There is delight in singing, tho' none hear / Beside the singer. [Walter Savage Landor, 1775–1864, *To Robert Browning*]

21 And the song, from beginning to end, / I found again in the heart of a friend. [H W Longfellow, 1807–82, *The Arrow and the Song*]

22 Blest pair of Sirens, pledges of Heav'n's joy, / Sphere-born harmonious sisters, voice and verse. [John Milton, 1608–74, *At a Solemn Music*, 1]

23 Or bid the soul of Orpheus sing / Such notes as, warbled to the string, / Drew iron tears down Pluto's cheek. [John Milton, 1608–74, *Il Penseroso*, 105]

24 The most despairing songs are the most beautiful, and I know some immortal ones that are pure tears. [Alfred de Musset, 1810–57, *La Nuit de mai*]

25 And the rightful owner of the music, / tiny and no longer timid, sang, / for the rightful owners of the song. [Brian Patten, 1946– , *Interruption at the Opera House*]

26 You know that cheap songs so-called actually do have something of the Psalms of David about them. They do say the world is other than it is. [Dennis Potter, 1935–94, *Seeing the Blossom*, an interview with Melvyn Bragg, TV Channel 4, April 1994]

27 Odds life! must one swear to the truth of a song? [Matthew Prior, 1664–1721, *A Better Answer*]

28 Of course, we've all dreamed of reviving the castrati; but it's needed Hilda to take the first practical steps towards making them a reality ... She's drawn up a list of well-known singers who she thinks would benefit from ... treatment ... It's only a question of getting them to agree. [Henry Reed, 1914–86, BBC radio drama *The Private Life of Hilda Tablet*]

29 A love song is just a caress set to music. [Sigmund Romberg, 1887–1951; in Nat Shapiro, *Encyclopedia of Quotations about Music*]

30 *Souvent j'écoute encor quand le chant a cessé.* – Often I am still listening when the song is over. [Marquis de Saint-Lambert, 1716–1803, *Les Saisons*, 'Le Printemps']

31 The way was long, the wind was cold, / The Minstrel was infirm and old; / His withered cheek and tresses grey / Seemed to have known a better day. [Sir Walter Scott, 1771–1832, *The Lay of the Last Minstrel*, Introduction]

32 Orpheus with his lute made trees, / And the mountain tops that freeze, / Bow themselves when he did sing. [William Shakespeare, 1564–1616, *Henry VIII*, III. i. 3]

33 Warble, child; make passionate my sense of hearing. [*Love's Labour's Lost*, III. i. 1]

34 Since once I sat upon a promontory, / And heard a mermaid on a dolphin's back, / Uttering such dulcet and harmonious breath, / That the rude sea grew civil at her song, / And certain stars shot madly from their spheres, / To hear the sea-maid's music. [*A Midsummer Night's Dream*, II. i. 149]

35 It gives a very echo to the seat / Where Love is throned. [*Twelfth Night*, II. iv. 21]

36 The spinsters and the knitters in the sun, / And the free maids that weave their thread with bones, / Do use to chant it: it is silly sooth, / And dallies with the innocence of love, / Like the old age. [*Twelfth Night*, II. iv. 44]

37 Such harmonious madness / From my lips would flow / The world should listen then – as I am listening now. [P B Shelley, 1792–1822, *To a Skylark*, 103]

38 Certainly, I must confess mine own barbarousness, I never heard the old song of Percy and Douglas, that I found not my heart moved more than with a trumpet. [Sir Philip Sidney, 1554–86, *A Defence of Poesy*]

39 I too have written songs. I too have heard the shepherds call me bard. But I am incredulous of them: I have the feeling that I cannot yet compare with Varius or Cinna, but cackle like a goose among melodious swans. [Virgil, 70–19 BC, *Eclogue* IX, 33]

40 Will no one tell me what she sings?– / Perhaps the plaintive numbers flow / For old, unhappy, far-off things / And battles long ago. [William Wordsworth, 1770–1850, *The Solitary Reaper*]

See also JAZZ, MUSIC

SORROW

1 But such a woe, believe me, as wins more hearts, / Than Mirth can do with her enticing parts. [anon. song, *I Saw My Lady Weep*, set by John Dowland]

2 Weep you no more, sad fountains; / What need you flow so fast? / Look how the snowy mountains / Heaven's sun doth gently waste. [anon. song, *Weep You No More*, set by John Dowland]

3 Nothing's so dainty sweet as lovely melancholy. [Francis Beaumont, 1584–1616, and John Fletcher, 1579–1625, *The Nice Valour*, III. iii, song]

4 Is it nothing to you, all ye that pass by? behold, and see if there be any sorrow like unto my sorrow. [Bible, OT, *Lamentations* 1:12]

5 And God shall wipe away all tears from their eyes; and there shall be no more death, neither sorrow, nor crying, neither shall there be any more pain: for the former things are passed away. [Bible, NT, *Revelation* 21:4]

6 Can I see another's woe, / And not be in sorrow too? [William Blake, 1757–1827, *Songs of Innocence*, 'On Another's Sorrow']

7 All my joys to this are folly, / Naught so sweet as melancholy. [Robert Burton, 1577–1640, *Anatomy of Melancholy*, 'The Author's Abstract']

8 But Life will suit / Itself to Sorrow's most detested fruit, / Like to the apples on the Dead Sea's shore, / All ashes to the taste. [Lord Byron, 1788–1824, *Childe Harold's Pilgrimage*, III, 34]

9 With eyes upraised, as one inspired, / Pale Melancholy sat retired; / And from her wild sequestered seat, / In notes by distance made more sweet, / Poured through the mellow horn her pensive soul. [William Collins, 1721–59, *The Passions, An Ode for Music*, 57]

10 *A raconter ses maux, souvent on les soulage.* – One often calms one's grief by recounting it. [Pierre Corneille, 1606–84, *Polyeucte*, I. iii]

11 Only with beauty wake wild memories – / Sorrow for where you are, for where you would be. [Walter de la Mare, 1873–1956, *The Cage*]

12 Nought but vast sorrow was there – / The sweet cheat gone. [Walter de la Mare, 1873–1956, *The Ghost*]

13 It is a good thing to have a great sorrow. Or should human beings allow Christ to have died on the Cross for the sake of their toothaches? [Isak Dinesen, 1885–1962, *Last Tales*, 'Of Hidden Thoughts and Heaven']

14 *Adieu tristesse / Bonjour tristesse / Tu es inscrite dans les lignes du plafond.* – Farewell sadness, / Good day sadness. / You are written in the lines on the ceiling. [Paul Éluard, 1895–1952, *La Vie immédiate*]

15 Between grief and nothing I will take grief. [William Faulkner, 1897–1962, *The Wild Palms*, p. 228]

16 *Ich weiss nicht, was soll es bedeuten, / Dass ich so traurig bin; / Ein Märchen aus alten Zeiten, / Das kommt mir nicht aus dem Sinn.* – I do not know why it should be, but I am so sad; there is an old-time story which I cannot get out of my head. [Heinrich Heine, 1797–1856, *Die Lorelei*]

17 To Sorrow / I bade good-morrow, / And thought to leave her far away behind; / But cheerly, cheerly, / She loves me dearly; / She is so constant to me, and so kind. [John Keats, 1795–1821, *Endymion*, Bk iv, 173]

18 But when the melancholy fit shall fall / Sudden from heaven like a weeping cloud, / That fosters the droop-headed flowers all, / And hides the green hill in an April shroud; / Then glut thy sorrow on a morning rose. [John Keats, 1795–1821, *Ode on Melancholy*, 2]

19 Ay, in the very temple of delight / Veiled Melancholy has her sovran shrine, / Though seen of none save him whose strenuous tongue / Can burst Joy's grape against his palate fine; / His soul shall taste the sadness of her might, / And be among her cloudy trophies hung. [John Keats, 1795–1821, *Ode on Melancholy*, 3]

20 We cannot help the birds of sadness flying over our heads, / But we need not let them build their nests in our hair. [George Mathew (alleged Chinese saying), in James Agate, *Ego 1*, 1933]

21 Hence loathèd Melancholy, / Of Cerberus and blackest Midnight Sorrow is tranquillity remembered in emotion. [Dorothy Parker, 1893–1967, *Sentiment*]

22 Happiness is beneficial for the body, but it is grief that develops the powers of the mind. [Marcel Proust, 1871–1922, *Remembrance of Things Past: Time Regained*, Ch. 2]

23 I can suck melancholy out of a song, as a weasel sucks eggs. [William Shakespeare, 1564–1616, *As You Like It*, II. v. (12)]

24 It is a melancholy of mine own, compounded of many simples, extracted from many objects, and indeed the sundry contemplation of my travels, which by often rumination, wraps me in a most humorous sadness. [*As You Like It*, IV. i. (16)]

25 When sorrows come, they come not single spies, / But in battalions. [*Hamlet*, IV. v. (78)]

26 Here I and sorrows sit; / Here is my throne, bid kings come bow to it. [*King John*, III. i. 73]

27 Affliction may one day smile again; and till then, sit thee down, sorrow! [*Love's Labour's Lost*, I. i (312)]

28 Ah! do not, when my heart hath 'scaped this sorrow, / Come in the rearward of a conquered woe; / Give not a windy night a rainy morrow, / To linger out a purposed overthrow. [*Sonnets*, 90]

29 We are not sure of sorrow, / And joy was never sure. [A C Swinburne, 1837–1909, *The Garden of Proserpine*, 10]

30 O Sorrow, wilt thou live with me / No casual mistress, but a wife. [Alfred, Lord Tennyson, 1809–92, *In Memoriam*, 59]

31 Tis held that sorrow makes us wise. [Alfred, Lord Tennyson, 1809–92, *In Memoriam*, 113]

32 She only said, 'My life is dreary, / He cometh not,' she said: / She said, 'I am aweary, aweary, / I would that I were dead.' [Alfred, Lord Tennyson, 1809–92, *Mariana*]

33 Pure and complete sorrow is as impossible as pure and complete joy. [Leo Tolstoy, 1828–1910, *War and Peace*, XV, Ch. 1]

See also GRIEF, REGRET, UNHAPPINESS

SOULS

1 I was thrown out of NYU my freshman year . . . for cheating on my metaphysics final. You know I looked within the soul of the boy sitting next to me. [Woody Allen, 1935– , in film *Annie Hall*, scripted with Marshall Brickman]

2 And see all sights from pole to pole, / And glance, and nod, and bustle by; / And never once possess our soul / Before we die. [Matthew Arnold, 1822–88, *A Southern Night*, 69]

3 We see the envelope they are / but the soul of things stays shut, / like a library on Sundays. [John Ash, 1948– , *Disbelief*, 'Unsentimental Journey']

4 As the hart panteth after the water brooks, so panteth my soul after thee, O God. [Bible, OT, *Psalms* 42:1]

5 My soul doth magnify the Lord, And my spirit hath rejoiced in God my Saviour. [Bible, NT, *St Luke* 1:46]

6 What is a man profited, if he shall gain the whole world, and lose his own soul? [Bible, NT, *St Matthew* 16:26]

7 Every wolf's and lion's howl / Raises from Hell a human soul. [William Blake, 1757–1827, *Auguries of Innocence*]

8 Man has no Body distinct from his Soul; for that called Body is a portion of Soul discerned by the five Senses, the chief inlets of Soul in this age. [William Blake, 1757–1827, *The Marriage of Heaven and Hell*, 'The Voice of the Devil']

9 THE SCHOLAR: Whither goes the soul when the body dies?

THE MASTER: There is no necessity for it to go anywhere. [Jacob Böhme, 1575–1624, *Of Heaven and Hell, A Dialogue*]

10 Ages past the soul existed, / Here an age 'tis resting merely. [Robert Browning, 1812–89, *Cristina*]

11 The souls of women are so small, / That some believe they've none at all. [Samuel Butler, 1612–80, *Miscellaneous Thoughts*]

12 Whither depart the souls of the brave that die in the battle, / Die in the lost, lost fight, for the cause that perishes with them? [Arthur Hugh Clough, 1819–61, *Amours de voyage*, V, 6]

13 I believe the souls of five hundred Sir Isaac Newtons would go to the making up of a Shakespeare or a Milton. [Samuel Taylor Coleridge, 1772–1834, letter to Thomas Poole, 23 Mar. 1801]

14 So must pure lovers' souls descend / T'affections, and to faculties, / Which sense may reach and apprehend, / Else a great Prince in prison lies. [John Donne, 1571?–1631, *The Extasie*, 65]

15 If they be two, they are two so / As stiff twin compasses are two, / Thy soul the fixt foot makes no show / To move, but doth, if the other do.

And though it in the centre sit, / Yet when the other far doth roam, / It leans, and hearkens after it, / And grows erect, as that comes home. [John Donne, 1571?–1631, *Valediction: Forbidding Mourning*]

16 I am aware of the damp souls of housemaids / Sprouting despondently at area gates. [T S Eliot, 1888–1965, *Morning at the Window*]

17 Little soul, wandering and pleasant guest and companion of the body, into what places will you now depart, pale, stiff, and naked; and you will sport no longer as you did! [Emperor Hadrian, 76–138, poem]

18 Out of the night that covers me, / Black as the pit from pole to pole, / I thank whatever gods may be / For my unconquerable soul. [W E Henley, 1849–1903, *Invictus*]

19 Love bade me welcome; yet my soul drew back / Guilty of dust and sin. [George Herbert, 1593–1633, *Love (3)*]

20 Only a sweet and virtuous soul, / Like seasoned timber, never gives; / But though the whole world turn to coal, / Then chiefly lives. [George Herbert, 1593–1633, *Virtue*]

21 Is the soul greater than the hum of its parts? [Douglas R Hofstadter, 1945– , *The Mind's I*, composed with Daniel C Dennett, 11, 'Reflections']

22 For him in vain the envious seasons roll / Who bears eternal summer in his soul. [Oliver Wendell Holmes, 1809–94, *The Old Player*]

23 A man should have the fine point of his soul taken off to become fit for this world. [John Keats, 1795–1821, letter to J H Reynolds, 22 Nov. 1817]

24 'Ye have scarce the soul of a louse,' he said, / 'But the roots of sin are there.' [Rudyard Kipling, 1865–1936, *Tomlinson*]

25 No matter how much of a shabby animal you may be, you can learn from Dostoyevsky and Chekhov, etc., how to have the most tender, unique, coruscating soul on earth. [D H Lawrence, 1885–1930, *Phoenix*, 'Preface to Mastro-don Gesualdo']

26 The soul started at the knee-cap and ended at the navel. [Percy Wyndham Lewis, 1882–1957, *The Apes of God*, Pt XII]

27 Life is real! Life is earnest! / And the grave is not its goal. / Dust thou art, to dust returnest, / Was not spoken of the soul. [H W Longfellow, 1807–82, *A Psalm of Life*]

28 Two souls with but a single thought, / Two hearts that beat as one. [Marie Lovell, 1803–77, *Ingomar the Barbarian*, II (trans. of Friedrich Halm)]

29 O soul, be changed into little waterdrops, / And fall into the ocean, ne'er be found! [Christopher Marlowe, 1564-93, *Doctor Faustus*, 1502]

30 Earth cannot show so brave a sight, / As when a single soul does fence / The batteries of alluring sense / And Heaven views it with delight. [Andrew Marvell, 1621–78, *A Dialogue between the Resolved Soul and Created Pleasure*, 45]

31 Go, Soul, the body's guest, / Upon a thankless arrant: / Fear not to touch the best; / The truth shall be thy warrant: / Go, since I needs must die, / And give the world the lie. [Sir Walter Raleigh, *c.*1552–1618, *The Lie*]

32 My soul's a trampled duelling ground where Sade, / the gallant marquis, fences for his life / against the invulnerable retrograde / Masoch, his shade, more constant than a wife. [Edgell Rickword, 1898–1982, *Chronique scandaleuse*]

33 Mount, mount my soul! thy seat is up on high, / Whilst my gross flesh sinks downward, here to die. [William Shakespeare, 1564–1616, *Richard II*, V. v. 112]

34 Poor soul, the centre of my sinful earth, / Fooled by these rebel powers that thee array, / Why dost thou pine within and suffer dearth, / Painting thy outward walls so costly gay? [*Sonnets*, 146]

35 My soul is an enchanted boat, / Which, like a sleeping swan, doth float / Upon the silver waves of thy sweet singing. [P B Shelley, 1792–1822, *Prometheus Unbound*, II. v. 72]

36 Most people sell their souls, and live with a good conscience on the proceeds. [Logan Pearsall Smith, 1865–1946, *Afterthoughts*, 3]

37 I am positive I have a soul; nor can all the books with which materialists have pestered the world ever convince me of the contrary. [Laurence Sterne, 1713–68, *A Sentimental Journey*, 'Maria, Moulines']

38 I am that which began: / Out of me the years roll; / Out of me God and man; / I am equal and whole; / God changes, and man, and the form of them bodily; I am the soul. [A C Swinburne, 1837–1909, *Hertha*, 1]

39 A little soul for a little bears up this corpse which is man. [A C Swinburne, 1837–1909, *Hymn to Proserpine*]

40 I ask around all Paris, for it's / only in stories or pictures / that people rise to the skies: / where is your soul gone, where? [Marina Tsvetayeva, 1892–1941, *Epigraph*]

41 My soul, like to a ship in a black storm, / Is driven, I know not whither. [John Webster, 1580?–1625?, *The White Devil*, V. vi. 248]

42 Body and soul are not two substances but one. They are man becoming aware of himself in two different ways. [C F Von Weizsäcker, 1912– ; in *Hodder Book of Christian Quotations*, comp. Tony Castle]

43 The gods approve / The depth, and not the tumult, of the soul. [William Wordsworth, 1770–1850, *Laodamia*, 74]

See also MYSTICS, SPIRIT

SOUNDS, see LISTENING

SPACE

1 What odds / Whether the couples walk on the campus and look at / The moon or walk on the moon and look at the earth? / Just so long as there's somewhere left to walk, to sit, to cycle, / And something left to look at. [D J Enright, 1920– , *Addictions*]

2 Is it seemly that I, at my age, should be hurled with my books of reference, and bed-clothes, and hot-water bottle, across the sky at the unthinkable rate of nineteen miles a second? As I say, I don't like it at all. [Logan Pearsall Smith, 1865–1946, *Trivia*, I, 'Vertigo']

3 The astronauts! . . . Rotarians in outer space. [Gore Vidal, 1925– , *Two Sisters*]

4 Really, to spend millions of pounds of public money in letting off invisible fireworks. [(Of space travel) Evelyn Waugh, 1903–66, from *Letters*, ed. Mark Amory]

See also UNIVERSE

SPAIN & THE SPANISH

1 The French are wiser than they seem, and the Spaniards seem wiser than they are. [Francis Bacon, 1561–1626, *Essays*, 26, 'Of Seeming Wise']

2 Every Spaniard is like a man-of-war, armed cap-à-pie to defend himself. That is why so much restraint and good manners are necessary. One man-of-war must reassure the other man-of-war that its guns will not be wanted. [Gerald Brenan, 1894–1987, *Thoughts in a Dry Season*, 'People and Places']

3 There is never any doubt, then, that one has arrived in Spain ... There is a faint sound of drums, a smell of crude olive-oil, and current of strong, leaking electricity. [Anthony Carson, *A Train to Tarragona*, Pt I, Ch. 2]

4 In Mexico the gods ruled, the priests interpreted and interposed, and the people obeyed. In Spain, the priests ruled, the king interpreted and interposed, and the gods obeyed. A nuance in an ideological difference is a wide chasm. [Richard Condon, 1915–96, *A Talent for Loving*, Bk I, Ch. 6]

5 Do you believe that since the earth is round, you will find landscapes everywhere? Does a round face have several noses? There are very few landscapes. They all converge here. Catalonia is the nose of the earth. [Salvador Dali, 1904–89, in Robert Descharnes and Clovis Prévost, *Gaudi, the Visionary*, Preface]

6 The master illusion of Spain is the conviction that the Spaniards are a people different, when they are only a people separate. [Jan Morris, 1926– , *The Presence of Spain*]

See also BRITAIN, FRANCE, ITALY, NATIONS

SPEECH

1 The stroke of the whip maketh marks in the flesh; but the stroke of the tongue breaketh bones. [Bible, Apocrypha, *Ecclesiasticus* 28:17]

2 Let thy speech be short, comprehending much in few words. [Bible, Apocrypha, *Ecclesiasticus* 32:8]

3 A word spoken in due season, how good is it! [Bible, OT, *Proverbs* 15:23]

4 Let your speech be alway with grace, seasoned with salt. [Bible, NT, *Colossians* 4:6]

5 The tongue can no man tame; it is an unruly evil. [(Commonly misquoted as 'The tongue is an unruly member') Bible, NT, *James* 3:8]

6 Not that which goeth into the mouth defileth a man; but that which cometh out of the mouth, this defileth a man. [Bible, NT, *St Matthew* 15:11]

7 Free speech is about as good a cause as the world has ever known ... Everybody favours free speech in the slack moments when no axes are being ground. [Heywood Broun, 1888–1939, in *New York World*, 23 Oct. 1926]

8 Tongue; well, that's a wery good thing when it ain't a woman's. [Charles Dickens, 1812–70, *Pickwick Papers*, Ch. 19]

9 A sharp tongue is the only edged tool that grows keener with constant use. [Washington Irving, 1783–1859, *The Sketch Book*, 'Rip Van Winkle']

10 There are some who speak one moment before they think. [Jean de La Bruyère, 1645–96, *Characters*, 'Of Society and Conversation', 15]

11 Speech is the small change of silence. [George Meredith, 1828–1909, *The Ordeal of Richard Feverel*, Ch. 34]

12 You've a sharp tongue in your head, Mr Essick. Look out it doesn't cut your throat. [S J Perelman, 1904–79, *The Rising Gorge*, 'All Out ...']

13 One way of looking at speech is to say it is a constant stratagem to cover nakedness. [Harold Pinter, 1930– ; in *Barnes and Noble Book of Quotations*, ed. Robert I Fitzhenry, 'Words']

14 The most precious things in speech are pauses. [Ralph Richardson, 1902–83, attr.]

15 Men of few words are the best men. [William Shakespeare, 1564–1616, *Henry V*, III. ii. (40)]

16 Speak low, if you speak love. [*Much Ado About Nothing*, II. i. (104)]

17 I dont want to talk grammar. I want to talk like a lady. [George Bernard Shaw, 1856–1950, *Pygmalion*, II]

18 He [Macaulay] has occasional flashes of silence that make his conversation perfectly delightful. [Sydney Smith, 1771–1845, in Lady Holland, *Memoir*, Vol. i, Ch. 11]

19 Speech was given to man to disguise his thoughts. [Charles-Maurice de Talleyrand, 1754–1838. Also attr. to many others]

20 *Prends l'éloquence et tords-lui son cou!* – Take eloquence and wring its neck. [Paul Verlaine, 1844–96, *L'Art poétique*, 21]

21 Everything that can be said can be said clearly. [Ludwig Wittgenstein, 1889–1951, *Tractatus Logico-philosophicus*, 4, 116]

See also next category, CONVERSATION, LANGUAGE, TALK

SPEECHES

1 Our two rhetoricians [Churchill and Lloyd George] ... have good brains of different types. But they can only think talking, just as some people can only think writing. Only the salt of the earth can think inside, and the bulk of mankind cannot think at all! [H H Asquith, 1852–1928, in *The Wit of the Asquiths*, comp. Mary Tester, 'The Imperialists']

2 [When asked his opinion of Anthony Eden's speeches] Clitch, clitch, clitch. [Ernest Bevin, 1881–1951, attr.]; see 6

3 I take the view, and always have done, that if you cannot say what you have to say in twenty minutes, you should go away and write a book about it. [Lord Brabazon, 1884–1964, speech in House of Lords, 21 June 1955]

4 He [Lord Charles Beresford] is one of those orators of whom it was well said, 'Before they get up they do not know what they are going to say; when they are speaking, they do not know what they are saying; and when they sit down they do not know what they have said.' [Winston Churchill, 1874–1965, speech in House of Commons, 20 Dec. 1912]

5 We know that he [Ramsay MacDonald] has, more than any other man, the gift of compressing the largest amount of words into the smallest amount of thought. [Winston Churchill, 1874–1965, speech in House of Commons, 23 Mar. 1933]

6 They consist entirely of clichés – clichés old and new – everything from 'God is Love' to 'Please adjust your dress before leaving'. [Winston Churchill, 1874–1965 (of Anthony Eden's speeches), attr. in *Life*, 9 Dec. 1940, but disclaimed by him.]; see 2

7 A bigot is a stone-deaf orator. [Kahlil Gibran, 1883–1931, *Sand and Foam*]

8 I absorb the vapour and return it as a flood. [W E Gladstone, 1809–98 (on public speaking), in Lord Riddell, *Some Things that Matter*, p. 69]

9 That part of his speech was rather like being savaged by a dead sheep. [Denis Healey, 1917– , on being attacked in a parliamentary debate by Geoffrey Howe over his Budget proposals, House of Commons, 14 June 1978]

10 It was the speech a vain average would make to an audience of means. [Randall Jarrell, 1914–65, *Pictures from an Institution*, Pt VI, Ch. 4]

11 The object of oratory alone is not truth but persuasion. [Lord Macaulay, 1800–1859, *Essay on Athenian Orators*]

12 Ward has no heart, they say; but I deny it: / He has a heart, and gets his speeches by it. [Samuel Rogers, 1763–1855, *Epigram upon Lord Dudley*]

13 Friends, Romans, countrymen, lend me your ears; / I come to bury Caesar, not to praise him. / The evil that men do lives after them, / The good is oft interrèd with their bones. [William Shakespeare, 1564–1616, *Julius Caesar*, III. ii. (79)]

14 I always say that if you want a speech made you should ask a man, but if you want something done you should ask a woman. [Margaret Thatcher, 1925– , at AGM of Townswomen's Guild, 26 July 1982]

15 It just shows, what any Member of Parliament will tell you, that if you want real oratory, the preliminary noggin is essential. Unless pie-eyed, you cannot hope to grip. [P G Wodehouse, 1881–1975, *Right Ho, Jeeves*, Ch. 17]

See also previous category

SPELLS, see MAGIC SPELLS

SPIRIT

1 The letter killeth, but the spirit giveth life. [Bible, NT, *2 Corinthians* 3:6]

2 Leave the flesh to the fate it was fit for! the

spirit be thine! [Robert Browning, 1812–89, *Saul*, 13]

3 Sir, the pretending to extraordinary revelations and gifts of the Holy Ghost is a horrid thing, a very horrid thing. [Bishop Joseph Butler, 1692–1752 (to John Wesley), quoted in John Wesley, *Works*, xiii, 449]

4 The dove descending breaks the air / With flame of incandescent terror. [T S Eliot, 1888–1965, *Four Quartets*, 'Little Gidding', IV]

5 At one with the One, it didn't mean a thing beside a glass of Guinness on a sunny day. [Graham Greene, 1904–91, *Brighton Rock*, Pt 1, Ch. 1]

6 Spirits are not finely touched / But to fine issues. [William Shakespeare, 1564–1616, *Measure for Measure*, I. i. 35]

7 Thou canst not soar where he is sitting now. – / Dust to the dust! but the pure spirit shall flow / Back to the burning fountain whence it came, / A portion of the eternal. [P B Shelley, 1792–1822, *Adonais*, 337]

8 All spirits are enslaved that serve things evil. [P B Shelley, 1792–1822, *Prometheus Unbound*, II, iv, 110]

See also MYSTICS, SOULS

SPORTS

1 Float like a butterfly, sting like a bee. [anon. career slogan. Muhammed Ali, 1942– . Ascr. to Drew 'Bundini' Brown at weigh-in for his heavyweight title fight with Sonny Liston, at Miami Beach Convention Center, Florida, 25 Feb. 1964]

2 Th' athletic fool, to whom what Heaven denied / Of soul, is well compensated in limbs. [John Armstrong, 1709–79, *The Art of Preserving Health*, III, 206]

3 Pam, I adore you, Pam, you great big mountainous sports girl / Whizzing them over the net, full of the strength of five. [John Betjeman, 1906–84, *Pot Pourri from a Surrey Garden*]

4 The dread of beatings! Dread of being late! / And, greatest dread of all, the dread of games! [John Betjeman, 1906–84, *Summoned by Bells*, 7]

5 Boxing's just show business with blood. [Frank Bruno, 1961– ; *Observer*, 'Sayings of the Week', 24 Nov. 1991]

6 And I have loved thee, Ocean! and my joy / Of youthful sports was on thy breast to be / Borne, like thy bubbles, onward: from a boy / I wantoned with thy breakers. [Lord Byron, 1788–1824, *Childe Harold's Pilgrimage*, IV, 184]

7 His blade struck the water a full second before any other . . . until . . . as the boats began to near the winning-post, his was dipping into the water twice as often as any other. [(Popularly amended to 'All rowed fast but none so fast as stroke') Desmond Coke, 1879–1931, *Sandford of Merton*, Ch. 12]

8 Jolly boating weather, / And a hay harvest breeze, / Blade on the feather, / Shade off the trees. [W J Cory, 1823–92, *Eton Boating Song*]

9 The most important thing in the Olympic Games is not to win but to take part, just as the most important thing in life is not the triumph but the struggle. [Pierre de Coubertin, 1863–1937, speech at banquet at close of games, 24 July 1908, London]

10 Honey, I forgot to duck. [Jack Dempsey, 1895–1983, to his wife after losing his World Heavyweight title to Gene Tunney, 23 Sept. 1926. Borrowed by President Reagan when he survived an assassination attempt, 1981]

11 The bigger they come, the harder they fall. [Bob Fitzsimmons, 1862–1917, before fight with J Jeffries, San Francisco, 9 June 1899]

12 Who foremost now delight to cleave / With pliant arm thy glassy wave? [Thomas Gray, 1716–71, *Ode on a Distant Prospect of Eton College*, 3]

13 It didn't demoralize us, but it moralized them. [Dick Greenwood (England Rugby Union coach), 1941– (on a mistake that led to defeat by Wales), in *Guardian*, 'Sporting Life 1985', 24 Dec. 1985]

14 Any cyclist will confirm that in hilly country the slope is always steeper the side you are going up. This is one of the great mysteries of Nature. [Philippa Gregory, 1954– , in *Guardian*, 12 Oct. 1985]

15 We was robbed! [Joe Jacobs, 1896–1940, after Max Schmeling (whose manager he was) was declared loser in heavyweight-boxing title fight with Jack Sharkey, 21 June 1932]

16 Get your retaliation in first. [Carwyn James, 1929–83 (to British Lions team, 1971), in *Guardian*, 7 Nov. 1989]

17 The only athletic sport I ever mastered was backgammon. [Douglas Jerrold, 1803–57, *Wit and Opinions*, quoted in W Jerrold, *D J*, Vol. i, Ch. 1]

18 Limits the Romans' anxieties to two things – bread and games. [Juvenal, 60–*c.*130, *Satires*, X, 80]

19 Don't you think it's going to be rather wet for the horses? [(On having the Boat Race course described to him) Spike Milligan, 1918– , attr.]; see 23

20 Serious sport has nothing to do with fair play. It is bound up with hatred, jealousy, boastfulness, disregard of all rules and sadistic pleasure in witnessing violence. In other words, it is war minus the shooting. [George Orwell, 1903–50, *Shooting an Elephant*, 'The Sporting Spirit']

21 Jogging is very beneficial. It's good for your legs and your feet. It's also very good for the ground. It makes it feel needed. [(Snoopy) Charles Schulz, 1922– , in *Peanuts* strip cartoon]

22 I have often observed in women of her type a tendency to regard all athletics as inferior forms of fox-hunting. [Evelyn Waugh, 1903–66, *Decline and Fall*, I, 10]

23 MARILYN MONROE: Water polo? Isn't that terribly dangerous?
TONY CURTIS: I'll say! I had two ponies drown under me. [Billy Wilder, 1906– , in film *Some Like It Hot*, scripted with I A L Diamond]; see 19

24 One of the foulest cross-country runs that ever occurred outside Dante's *Inferno*. [P G Wodehouse, 1881–1975, *Psmith Journalist*, Ch. 30]

See also CRICKET, FOOTBALL, GAMES, GOLF

SPRING

1 Lenten ys come with love to toune, with blosmen and with briddes roune. [anon., *Lenten is Come with Love to Town*, 13th cent.]

2 Rise up, my love, my fair one, and come away. For, lo, the winter is past, the rain is over and gone; The flowers appear on the earth; the time of the singing birds is come, and the voice of the turtle is heard in our land. [Bible, OT, *Song of Solomon* 2:10]

3 Spring goeth all in white, / Crowned with milk-white may: / In fleecy flocks of light / O'er heaven the white clouds stray. [Robert Bridges, 1844–1930, *Spring Goeth All in White*]

4 For spring bade the sparrows pair, / And the boys and girls gave guesses, / And stalls in our street looked rare / With bulrush and water-cresses. [Robert Browning, 1812–89, *Youth and Art*, 9]

5 And the Spring comes slowly up this way. [Samuel Taylor Coleridge, 1772–1834, *Christabel*, Pt I, 22]

6 While you and i have lips and voices which / are for kissing and to sing with / who cares if some oneeyed son of a bitch / invents an instrument to measure Spring with? [e e cummings, 1894–1962, *is* 5, 'One, XXIII']

7 Sweet spring, full of sweet days and roses, / A box where sweets compacted lie. [George Herbert, 1593–1633, 'Virtue']

8 I sing of brooks, of blossoms, birds, and bowers: / Of April, May, of June, and July-flowers. / I sing of maypoles, hock-carts, wassails, wakes, / Of bridegrooms, brides, and of their bridal cakes. [Robert Herrick, 1591–1674, *Hesperides*, 'The Argument']

9 The snows have fled; already the grass is returning to the fields and the leaves to the trees. [Horace, 65–8 BC, *Odes*, III, vii, 1]

10 Spring, the sweet spring, is the year's pleasant king; / Then blooms each thing, then maids dance in a ring, / Cold doth not sting, the pretty birds do sing: / Cuckoo, jug-jug, pu-we, to-witta-woo! [Thomas Nashe, 1567–1601, *Spring*]

11 Spring has returned. The earth is like a child that knows poems. [Rainer Maria Rilke, 1875–1926, *Sonnets to Orpheus*, I, 21]

12 The country habit has me by the heart, / For he's bewitched for ever who has seen, / Not with his eyes but with his vision, Spring / Flow down the woods and stipple leaves with sun. [Victoria Sackville-West, 1892–1962, *The Land*, 'Winter']

13 When daisies pied and violets blue / And lady-smocks all silver-white / And cuckoo-buds of yellow hue / Do paint the meadows with delight, / The cuckoo then, on every tree, / Mocks married men; for thus sings he, / Cuckoo, / Cuckoo, cuckoo: O word of fear, / Unpleasing to a married ear. [William Shakespeare, 1564–1616, *Love's Labour's Lost*, V. ii. (902)]

14 When daffodils begin to peer, / With heigh! the doxy, over the dale, / Why, then comes in the sweet o' the year; / For the red blood reigns in the winter's pale. [*The Winter's Tale*, IV. ii. 1]

15 O, Wind, / If Winter comes, can Spring be far behind? [P B Shelley, 1792–1822, *Ode to the West Wind*, 69]

16 I dreamed that, as I wandered by the way, / Bare winter suddenly was changed to spring. [P B Shelley, 1792–1822, *The Question*]

17 Fresh spring the herald of love's mighty king. [Edmund Spenser, 1552?–99, *Amoretti*, 70]

18 The soote season, that bud and bloom forth brings, / With green hath clad the hill and eke the vale. [Henry Howard, Earl of Surrey, 1517?–47, *Spring*]

19 When the hounds of spring are on winter's traces, / The mother of months in meadow or plain / Fills the shadows and windy places / With lisp of leaves and ripple of rain. [A C Swinburne, 1837–1909, *Atalanta in Calydon*, Chorus, 'When the Hounds of Spring', 1]; see 24

20 And in green underwood and cover / Blossom by blossom the spring begins. [A C Swinburne, 1837–1909, *Atalanta in Calydon*, 4]

21 I dreamed there would be Spring no more, / That Nature's ancient power was lost. [Alfred, Lord Tennyson, 1809–92, *In Memoriam*, 69]

22 Now fades the long last streak of snow, / Now burgeons every maze of quick / About the flowering squares, and thick / By ashen roots the violets grow. [Alfred, Lord Tennyson, 1809–92, *In Memoriam*, 115]

23 In the spring a young man's fancy lightly turns to thoughts of love. [Alfred, Lord Tennyson, 1809–92, *Locksley Hall*, 20]

24 I said the hounds of Spring are on Winter's traces – but let it pass, let it pass! [James Thurber, 1894–1961, *Men, Women and Dogs*, cartoon caption]; see 19

See also AUTUMN, SEASONS, SUMMER, WINTER

STARS

1 Canst thou bind the sweet influences of the Pleiades, or loose the bands of Orion? [Bible, OT, *Job* 38:31]

2 One star differeth from another star in glory. [Bible, NT, *1 Corinthians* 15:41]

3 Oh, never star / Was lost here, but it rose afar! / Look East, where whole new thousands are! / In Vishnu-land what Avatar? [Robert Browning, 1812–89, *Waring*, II, 3]

4 Ye stars! which are the poetry of heaven! [Lord Byron, 1788–1824, *Childe Harold's Pilgrimage*, III, 88]

5 Star that bringest home the bee, / And settest the weary labourer free! [Thomas Campbell, 1777–1844, *Song to the Evening Star*]

6 *Cette obscure clarté qui tombe des étoiles.* – This dark brightness that falls from the stars. [Pierre Corneille, 1606–84, *Le Cid*, IV. iii]

7 Stars scribble on our eyes the frosty sagas, / The gleaming cantos of unvanquished space. [Hart Crane, 1899–1932, *The Bridge*, 'Cape Hatteras']

8 A star looks down at me, / And says: 'Here I and you / Stand, each in our degree: / What do you mean to do?' [Thomas Hardy, 1840–1928, *Waiting Both*]

9 Look at the stars! look, look up at the skies! / O look at all the fire-folk sitting in the air! / The bright boroughs, the circle-citadels there! [Gerard Manley Hopkins, 1844–89, *The Starlight Night*]

10 Bright star, would I were steadfast as thou art – / Not in lone splendour hung aloft the night / And watching, with eternal lids apart, / Like Nature's patient, sleepless Eremite, / The moving waters at their priestlike task / Of pure ablution round earth's human shores. [John Keats, 1795–1821, sonnet: *Bright Star*]

11 Silently one by one, in the infinite meadows of heaven / Blossomed the lovely stars, the forget-me-nots of the angels. [H W Longfellow, 1807–82, *Evangeline*, I, 3]

12 Not till the fire is dying in the grate, / Look we for any kinship with the stars. [George Meredith, 1828–1909, *Modern Love*, 4]

13 The stars, / That nature hung in heaven, and filled their lamps / With everlasting oil, to give due light / To the misled and lonely traveller. [John Milton, 1608–74, *Comus*, 197]

14 I often looked up at the sky an' assed meself the question – what is the stars, what is the stars? [Sean O'Casey, 1880–1964, *Juno and the Paycock*, I]

15 The stars are in one's brain. [Bertrand Russell, 1872–1970, in R D Laing, *Politics of Experience*, Ch. 1]

16 Look how the floor of heaven / Is thick inlaid with patines of bright gold: / There's not the smallest orb which thou behold'st / But in his motion like an angel sings. [William Shakespeare, 1564–1616, *The Merchant of Venice*, V. i. 58]

17 When he shall die, / Take him and cut him out in little stars, / And he will make the face of heaven so fine / That all the world will be in love with night, / And pay no worship to the garish sun. [*Romeo and Juliet*, III. ii. 21]

18 Twinkle, twinkle, little star, / How I wonder what you are! / Up above the world so high, / Like a diamond in the sky! [Anne and Jane Taylor, 1782–1866 and 1783–1827, *The Star*]

19 You meaner beauties of the night, / That poorly satisfy our eyes, / More by your number than your light; / You common people of the skies, / What are you when the sun shall rise? [Henry Wotton, 1568–1639, *Upon his Mistress, the Queen of Bohemia*]

20 When shall the stars be blown about the sky, / Like the sparks blown out of a smithy, and die? [W B Yeats, 1865–1939, *The Secret Rose*]

21 Stars lay like yellow pollen / That from a flower has fallen; / And single stars I saw / Crossing themselves in awe; / Some stars in sudden fear / Fell like a falling tear. [Andrew Young, 1885–1971, *The Stars*]

See also ASTROLOGY, ASTRONOMY, MOON, NIGHT, SKIES, SUN

THE STATE

1 A state without the means of some change is without the means of its conservation. [Edmund Burke, 1729–97, *Reflections on the Revolution in France*, Penguin edn, p. 106]

2 The State, in choosing men to serve it, takes no notice of their opinions. If they be willing faithfully to serve it, that satisfies. [Oliver Cromwell, 1599–1658, before Marston Moor, 2 July 1644]

3 The welfare state is perhaps the greatest altruistic system the animal kingdom has ever known. [Richard Dawkins, 1941– , *The Selfish Gene*, Ch. 7]

4 The state is not 'abolished', it withers away. [Friedrich Engels, 1820–95, *Anti-Dühring*]; see 7

5 *Les états sont les monstres froids.* – States are frigid monsters. [General de Gaulle, 1890–1970, in *Listener*, 19 Jan. 1989]

6 It has been calculated by the ablest politicians that no State, without becoming soon exhausted, can maintain above the hundredth part of its members in arms and idleness. [Edward Gibbon, 1737–94, *The Decline and Fall of the Roman Empire*, Ch. 5]

7 To proclaim in advance the dying away of the state will be a violation of historical perspective. [Vladimir Ilyich Lenin, 1870–1924, at 7th Party Congress, Mar. 1918]; see 4

8 *L'État c'est moi.* – I am the state. [Louis XIV, 1638–1715, attr. to speech, 13 Apr. 1655]

9 The worth of a State, in the long run, is the worth of the individuals composing it. [John Stuart Mill, 1806–73, *On Liberty*, Ch. 5]

10 The state is an instrument in the hands of the ruling class for suppressing the resistance of its class enemies. [Joseph Stalin, 1879–1953 (on 'Proletarian democracy'), *Foundations of Leninism*, sect. 4/6]

11 A land of settled government, / A land of just and old renown, / Where Freedom slowly broadens down / From precedent to precedent. [Alfred, Lord Tennyson, 1809–92, *You Ask Me Why*]

12 For two decades the State, whether Conservative or Labour administrations, has been taking liberties, and these liberties were once ours. [E P Thompson, 1924–93, *Writing by Candlelight*, Introduction]

13 As there was no form of government common to the peoples thus segregated, nor tie of language, history, habit, or belief, they were called a Republic. [Evelyn Waugh, 1903–66, *Scoop*, Bk II, Ch. 1, 1]

See also GOVERNMENT, NATIONS, SOCIETY

STATISTICS

1 One to mislead the public, another to mislead the Cabinet, and the third to mislead itself. [(On the War Office's keeping three sets of figures) H H Asquith, 1852–1928, in Alistair Horne, *The Price of Glory*, Ch. 2]

2 A witty statesman said, you might prove anything by figures. [Thomas Carlyle, 1795–1881, *Critical and Miscellaneous Essays*, 'Chartism', Ch. 2]

3 There are three kinds of lies – lies, damned lies and statistics. [Benjamin Disraeli, 1804–81, quoted in Mark Twain, *Autobiography*, Pt V, Ch. 1, but also ascr. to others]

4 Statistics show that of those who contract the habit of eating, very few ever survive. [William Wallace Irwin; in *The Cook's Quotation Book*, ed. Maria Polushkin Robbins]

5 He uses statistics as a drunken man uses lamp-posts – for support rather than illumination. [Andrew Lang, 1844–1912; in *A Dictionary of Scientific Quotations*, ed. A L Mackay]

6 You cannot feed the hungry on statistics. [David Lloyd George, 1863–1945 (speech on Tariff Reform, 1904), in Malcolm Thomson, *D L G*, Ch. 8]

7 You mean, your statistics are facts, but my facts are just statistics. [Jonathan Lynn, 1943– , and Antony Jay, 1930– , *Yes Prime Minister*, Vol. 1, 'The Smokescreen']

8 There are two kinds of statistics, the kind you look up and the kind you make up. [Rex Stout, 1886–1975, *Death of a Doxy*, Ch. 9]

STORIES

1 Does the blind man own his escort? No, neither do we the story; rather it is the story that owns us and directs us. It is the thing that makes us different from cattle; it is the mark on the face that sets one people apart from their neighbours. [Chinua Achebe, 1930– , *Anthills of the Savannah*, 9]

2 All stories, before they are narrated, begin with the end. [John Berger, 1926– , *Story for Aesop*]

3 It is a foolish thing to make a long prologue, and to be short in the story itself. [Bible, Apocrypha, *2 Maccabees* 2:32]

4 Listen, little Elia, draw your chair up close to the edge of the precipice and I'll tell you a story. [F Scott Fitzgerald, 1896–1940, *Notebooks*, 'N']

5 If a nation loses its storytellers it loses its child-hood. [Peter Handke, 1942– , in *Independent*, 9 June 1988]

6 A man is always a teller of tales, he lives surrounded by his stories and the stories of others, he sees everything that happens to him through them; and he tries to live his life as if he were recounting it. [Jean-Paul Sartre, 1905–80, *Nausea*, Saturday, noon]

7 Your tale, sir, would cure deafness. [William Shakespeare, 1564–1616, *The Tempest*, I. ii. 106]

8 A sad tale's best for winter. / I have one of sprites and goblins. [*The Winter's Tale*, II. i. 24]

9 With a tale, forsooth, he cometh unto you; with a tale which holdeth children from play, and old men from the chimney corner. [Sir Philip Sidney, 1554–86, *A Defence of Poesy*]

10 'The story is like the wind,' the Bushman prisoner said. 'It comes from a far off place, and we feel it.' [Laurens van der Post, 1906–96, *A Story Like the Wind*]

See also BOOKS, NOVELS, NOVELISTS

STRENGTH

1 In quietness and in confidence shall be your strength. [Bible, OT, *Isaiah* 30:15]

2 Out of the eater came forth meat, and out of the strong came forth sweetness. [Bible, OT, *Judges* 14:14]

3 We then that are strong ought to bear the infirmities of the weak. [Bible, NT, *Romans* 15:1]

4 It is the characteristic excellence of the strong man that he can bring momentous issues to the fore and make a decision about them. The weak are always forced to decide between alternatives they have not chosen themselves. [Dietrich Bonhoeffer, 1906–45, *Letters and Papers from Prison*, 'Miscellaneous Thoughts']

5 He who did most, shall bear most; the strongest shall stand the most weak. [Robert Browning, 1812–89, *Saul*, 18]

6 The General spoke again, slowly, using his strength as carefully as an out-of-work showgirl uses her last good pair of stockings. [Raymond Chandler, 1888–1959, *The Big Sleep*, Ch. 2]

7 The strongest man upon earth is the man who stands most alone. [Henrik Ibsen, 1828–1906, *An Enemy of the People*, V]

8 This is the Law of the Yukon, that only the Strong shall thrive; / That surely the Weak shall perish, and only the Fit survive. [Robert Service, 1874–1958, *The Law of the Yukon*]

9 Life persists in the vulnerable, the sensitive ... They carry it on. The invulnerable, the too heavily armoured perish. [Elizabeth Taylor, 1912–75, *A Wreath of Roses*, Ch. 5]

10 My strength is as the strength of ten, / Because my heart is pure. [Alfred, Lord Tennyson, 1809–92, *Sir Galahad*, 1]

11 Strongest minds / Are often those of whom the noisy world / Hears least. [William Wordsworth, 1770–1850, *The Excursion*, I, 91]

See also POWER, WEAKNESS

STRIKES

1 I decline to be impartial as between the fire brigade and the fire. [Winston Churchill, 1874–1965, speech in House of Commons on General Strike, 7 July 1926]

2 Not a penny off the pay; not a second on the day. [A J Cook, 1885–1931, slogan of coal strike, 1926]

3 There is no right to strike against the public safety by anybody, anywhere, anytime. [Calvin Coolidge, 1872–1933, telegram to President of American Federation of Labor, 14 Sept. 1919]

STUDENTS

1 I would live to study and not study to live. [Francis Bacon, 1561–1626, *Memorial of Access*]

2 But I'm such a bad scholar, I feel like a man with a white cane knocking into knowledge. [Peter Carey, 1943–   , interview in *The Sunday Times*, 20 Mar. 1988]

3 And let a scholar all Earth's volumes carry, / He will be but a walking dictionary. [George Chapman, 1559?–1634, *Tears of Peace*, 266]

4 The gretteste clerkes been noght the wysest men. [Geoffrey Chaucer, 1340?–1400, *Canterbury Tales*, 'The Reeve's Tale', 134]

See also ACADEMICS, LEARNING, UNIVERSITIES

STUPIDITY

1 I am more stupid about some things than about others; not equally stupid in all directions; I am not a well-rounded person. [Saul Bellow, 1915–   , *Mr Sammler's Planet*, Ch. 2]

2 Much malice mingles with a little wit. [John Dryden, 1631–1700, *The Hind and the Panther*, III, 1]

3 Often the cockloft is empty in those which nature hath built many stories high. [Thomas Fuller, 1608–61, *Holy State*, Bk v, Ch. 18, 9]

4 Against stupidity the gods themselves struggle in vain. [Friedrich von Schiller, 1759–1805, *The Maid of Orleans*, III. vi]

5 You can stay stupid in a village, but if you take your stupidity to the town, the traffic runs you over. [Tom Vernon, 1939–   , *Fat Man in the Kitchen*]

6 There is no sin except stupidity. [Oscar Wilde, 1854–1900, *The Critic as Artist*, Pt II]

See also CLEVERNESS, FOOLS, IGNORANCE, WISDOM, WIT

STYLE

1 *Le style est l'homme même.* – Style is the man himself. [George-Louis de Buffon, 1707–88, *Discours sur le style*]

2 I am well aware that an addiction to silk underwear does not necessarily imply that one's feet are dirty. None the less, style, like sheer silk, too often hides eczema. [Albert Camus, 1913–60, *The Fall*]

3 Rococo even spread to England, although the native good sense of a fox-hunting society prevented its more extravagant flights. [Kenneth Clark, 1903–83, *Civilization*, Ch. 9]

4 With charm you've got to get up close to see it; style slaps you in the face. [John Cooper Clarke, 1949–   , interview in *Observer*, 19 May 1985]

5 I shall christen this style the Mandarin, since it is beloved by literary pundits. It is the style of all those writers whose tendency is to make their language convey more than they mean or more than they feel, it is the style of most artists and all humbugs. [Cyril Connolly, 1903–74, *Enemies of Promise*, Ch. 2]

6 O could I flow like thee, and make thy stream / My great example, as it is my theme! / Though deep, yet clear, though gentle, yet not dull, / Strong without rage, without o'er-flowing full. [John Denham, 1615–69, *Cooper's Hill*, 189]

7 Merely corroborative detail, intended to give artistic verisimilitude to an otherwise bald and unconvincing narrative. [W S Gilbert, 1836–1911, *The Mikado*, II]

8 To me style is just the outside of content, and content the inside of style, like the outside and inside of the human body – both go together, they can't be separated. [Jean-Luc Godard, 1930– , in Richard Roud, *G*, Introduction]

9 Often a purple patch or two is tacked on to a serious work of high promise, to give an effect of colour. [Horace, 65–8 BC, *Ars Poetica*, 14]

10 The inflated style is itself a kind of euphemism. A mass of Latin words falls upon the facts like soft snow, blurring the outlines and covering up all the details. The great enemy of clear language is insincerity. [George Orwell, 1903–50, *Collected Essays*, 'Politics and the English Language']

11 When one finds a natural style, one is amazed and delighted, for where one expected to see an author, one discovers a man. [Blaise Pascal, 1623–62, *Pensées*, I, 29]

12 Effectiveness of assertion is the alpha and omega of style. [George Bernard Shaw, 1856–1950, *Man and Superman*, Preface]

13 Proper words in proper places, make the true definition of style. [Jonathan Swift, 1677–1745, *Letter to a Young Clergyman*, 9 Jan. 1720]

14 All styles are good except the tiresome sort. [Voltaire, 1694–1778, *L'Enfant prodigue*, Preface to edn of 1738]

15 Style is the dress of thought; a modest dress, / Neat, but not gaudy, will true critics please. [Samuel Wesley, 1662–1735, *An Epistle to a Friend concerning Poetry*]

16 In matters of grave importance, style, not sincerity, is the vital thing. [Oscar Wilde, 1854–1900, *The Importance of Being Earnest*, III]

See also FASHION, LANGUAGE, TASTE

SUBURBS

1 I come from suburbia, Dan, personally, I don't ever want to go back. It's the one place in the world that's further away than anywhere else. [Frederic Raphael, 1931– , *The Glittering Prizes*, 'A Sex Life']

2 She was more than ever proud of the position of the bungalow, so almost in the country. [Angus Wilson, 1913–91, *A Bit off the Map*, 'A Flat Country Christmas']

See also CITY, COUNTRY

SUCCESS

1 'Tis not in mortals to command success, / But we'll do more, Sempronius; we'll deserve it. [Joseph Addison, 1672–1719, *Cato*, I. ii. 43]

2 One's religion is whatever he is most interested in, and yours is Success. [James Barrie, 1860–1937, *The Twelve-pound Look*, I]

3 For thence – a paradox / Which comforts while it mocks, – / Shall life succeed in that it seems to fail: / What I aspired to be, / And was not, comforts me: / A brute I might have been, but would not sink i' the scale. [Robert Browning, 1812–89, *Rabbi ben Ezra*, 7]

4 The only infallible criterion of wisdom to vulgar minds – success. [Edmund Burke, 1729–97, *Letter to a Member of the National Assembly*]

5 The trouble with Cecil [B de Mille, his brother] is that he always bites off more than he can chew – and then chews it. [William de Mille, 1878–1955, in L Halliwell, *Halliwell's Filmgoer's Companion*]

6 A great social success is a pretty girl who plays her cards as carefully as if she were plain. [F Scott Fitzgerald, 1896–1940, undated letter to Frances Scott Fitzgerald]

7 We never do anything well till we cease to think about the manner of doing it. [William Hazlitt, 1778–1830, *On Prejudice*]

8 The moral flabbiness born of the bitch-goddess Success. [William James, 1842–1910, letter to H G Wells, 11 Sept. 1906]

9 The race is not always to the swift, but that is where to look. [Hugh E Keough, d.1912 ?, quoted by F P Adams in the *Atlantic Monthly*, Aug. 1942]

10 To establish oneself in the world one has to do all one can to appear established. [Duc de La Rochefoucauld, 1613–80, *Maxims*, 56]

11 Nothing succeeds like the appearance of success. [Christopher Lasch, 1932–94, *The Culture of Narcissism*, Ch. 3]

12 The worst part of having success is to try finding someone who is happy for you. [Bette Midler, 1945– ; attr. in *Penguin Dictionary of Modern Humorous Quotations*, comp. Fred Metcalf]

13 He [Dr Smart-Allick of Narkover] said it was not always the timid fellow, with four conventional aces in his hand, who won the highest honours. 'It is often,' he said, 'the fifth ace that makes all the difference between success and failure.' [J B Morton ('Beachcomber'), 1893–1979, *The Best of B*, 8]

14 To burn always with this hard, gem-like flame, to maintain this ecstasy, is success in life. [Walter Pater, 1839–94, *The Renaissance*, Conclusion]

15 No pain, no palm; no thorns, no throne; no gall, no glory; no cross, no crown. [William Penn, 1644–1718, *No Cross, No Crown*]

16 The only place where success comes before work is in a dictionary. [Vidal Sassoon, 1928– , on BBC radio, quoting one of his teachers]

17 This proverb flashes thro' his head, / 'The many fail, the one succeeds'. [Alfred, Lord Tennyson, 1809–92, *The Day-Dream*, 'The Arrival', 15]

18 Whenever a friend succeeds, a little something inside me dies. [Gore Vidal, 1925– , in *The Sunday Times Magazine*, 16 Sept. 1973]

19 Success nourished them; they seemed to be able, and so they were able. [Virgil, 70–19 BC, *Aeneid*, V, 231]

20 It's just as difficult to overcome success as it is to overcome failure. [William Walton, 1902–83 (on receiving the Order of Merit, 1967), in Susanna Walton, *W W: Behind the Façade*, Ch. 16]

21 To journey is better than to arrive – or so say those who have already arrived. [Fay Weldon, 1931– , *The Heart of the Country*, 'Doing It All Wrong']

22 I started at the top and worked my way down. [Orson Welles, 1915–85; in L Halliwell, *The Filmgoer's Book of Quotes*]

23 She's the kind of girl who climbed the ladder of success, wrong by wrong. [Mae West, 1892–1980, in film *I'm no Angel*]

24 Success is paralysing only to those who have never wished for anything else. [Thornton Wilder, 1897–1975, *Journals, 1939–61*, ed. Donald Gallup]

See also ACHIEVEMENT, FAILURE, REPUTATION

SUFFERING

1 About suffering they were never wrong, / The Old Masters: How well they understood / Its human position; how it takes place / While someone else is eating or opening a window / Or just walking along. [W H Auden, 1907–73, *Musée des Beaux Arts*]

2 Man that is born of a woman is of few days, and full of trouble. [Bible, OT, *Job* 14:1]

3 Come unto me, all ye that labour and are heavy laden, and I will give you rest. [Bible, NT, *St Matthew* 11:28]

4 *Wer nie sein Brot mit Tränen ass, / Wer nie die kummervollen Nächte / Auf seinem Bette weinend sass, / Der kennt euch nicht, ihr himmlischen Mächte.* – Who never ate his bread with tears, who never sat through the sorrowful night, weeping upon his bed, does not know you, O heavenly powers. [Johann Wolfgang von Goethe, 1749–1832, *Wilhelm Meister*, ii, 13]

5 Eighteen is a good time for suffering. One has all the necessary strength, and no defences. [William Golding, 1911–93, *The Pyramid*, p. 12]

6 How small, of all that human hearts endure, / That part which laws or kings can cause or cure. [Oliver Goldsmith, 1728–74, *The Traveller*, 429]

7 To each his suff'rings: all are men, / Condemned alike to groan; / The tender for another's pain, / Th' unfeeling for his own. / Yet ah! why should they know their fate? / Since sorrow never comes too late, / And happiness too swiftly flies. [Thomas Gray, 1716–71, *Ode on a Distant Prospect of Eton College*, 10]

8 Smile out; but still suffer: / The paths of love are rougher / Than thoroughfares of stones. [Thomas Hardy, 1840–1928, *The End of the Episode*]

9 'Law, Brer Tarrypin!' sez Brer Fox, sezee, 'you ain't see no trouble yit. Ef you wanter see sho' nuff trouble, you des oughter go 'longer me; I'm de man w'at kin show you trouble', sezee. [Joel Chandler Harris, 1848–1908, *Nights with Uncle Remus*, Ch. 17]

10 Fade far away, dissolve, and quite forget / What thou among the leaves hast never known, / The weariness, the fever, and the fret / Here, where men sit and hear each other groan. [John Keats, 1795–1821, *Ode to a Nightingale*, 2]

11 *The Two Ways*: One is to suffer; the other is to become a professor of the fact that another suffered. [Søren Kierkegaard, 1813–55, in W H Auden, *A Kierkegaard Anthology*, p. 20]

12 'How are you, sir?' 'Loungin' round and sufferin', my son.' [Rudyard Kipling, 1865–1936, *Debits and Credits*, 'The United Idolaters']

13 Rather suffer than die is man's motto. [Jean de La Fontaine, 1621–95, *Fables*, I, 16, 'Death and the Woodcutter']

14 It is not true that suffering ennobles the character; happiness does that sometimes, but suffering, for the most part, makes men petty and vindictive. [W Somerset Maugham, 1874–1965, *The Moon and Sixpence*, Ch. 17]

15 A man who fears suffering is already suffering from what he fears. [Michel de Montaigne, 1533–92, *Essays*, III, 13]

16 People who haven't red hair don't know what trouble is. [L M Montgomery, 1874–1942, *Anne of Green Gables*, Ch. 7]

17 One nail drives out another. But four nails make a cross. [Cesare Pavese, 1908–50, *This Business of Living: A Diary 1935–1950*, 16 Aug. 1950]

18 But yet the pity of it, Iago! [William Shakespeare, 1564–1616, *Othello*, III. iii. (205)]

19 Oh, lift me as a wave, a leaf, a cloud! / I fall upon the thorns of life! I bleed! [P B Shelley, 1792–1822, *Ode to the West Wind*, 53]

20 *J'aime la majesté des souffrances humaines.* – I love the majesty of human sufferings. [Alfred de Vigny, 1797–1863, *La Maison du berger*]

21 He groaned slightly and winced, like Prometheus watching his vulture dropping in for lunch. [P G Wodehouse, 1881–1975, in Richard Usborne, *Wodehouse at Work to the End*, Ch. 10]

22 Action is transitory – a step, a blow. / The motion of a muscle – this way or that – / 'Tis done, and in the after-vacancy / We wonder at ourselves like men betrayed: / Suffering is permanent, obscure and dark, / And shares the nature of infinity. [William Wordsworth, 1770–1850, *The Borderers*, III, 1539]

See also GRIEF, SORROW, UNHAPPINESS, WORRY

SUICIDE

1 I would have killed myself but I was in analysis with a strict Freudian and if you kill yourself . . . they make you pay for the sessions you miss. [Woody Allen, 1935– , in film *Annie Hall*, scripted with Marshall Brickman]

2 There have been times when I've thought about suicide – but with my luck it would probably turn out to be only a temporary solution. [Woody Allen, 1935– ; in *Apt and Amusing Quotations*, ed. G F Lamb, 'Death']

3 After all / I think I will not hang myself today. [G K Chesterton, 1874–1936, *A Ballade of Suicide*]

4 Without the possibility of suicide, I would have killed myself long ago. [E M Cioran, 1911–95; *Independent*, 'Quote Unquote', 2 Dec. 1989]

5 To commit suicide was invading the prerogative of the Almighty, by rushing into his presence uncalled for. [Lord Denning, 1899–1999 (quoting Sir William Blackstone, an 18th cent. lawyer), speech in House of Lords, 2 Mar. 1961]; see 7

6 I am a demd villain! . . . I will fill my pockets with change for a sovereign in half-pence and drown myself in the Thames . . . who for her sake will become a demd, damp, moist, unpleasant body! [Charles Dickens, 1812–70, *Nicholas Nickleby*, Ch. 34]

7 Then the eighty-year-old lady with a sparkle, / A Cambridge lady, hearing of the latest / Suicide, said to her friend, turning off / TV for tea, 'Well, my dear, doesn't it seem / A little like going where you haven't been invited?' [Richard Eberhart, 1904– , *How It Is*]; see 5

8 However great a man's fear of life . . . suicide remains the courageous act, the clear-headed act of a mathematician. The suicide has judged by the laws of chance – so many odds against one, that to live will be more miserable than to die. His sense of mathematics is greater than his sense of survival. [Graham Greene, 1904–91, *The Comedians*, Pt 1, Ch. 1, 4, i]

9 Why kill time when you can kill yourself? [Tony Hancock, 1924–68, in film *The Rebel*, script by Ray Galton and Alan Simpson]

10 Done because we are too menny. [Thomas Hardy, 1840–1928, *Jude the Obscure*, Pt VI, Ch. 2]

11 But, merciful God! People don't do such things! [Henrik Ibsen, 1828–1906, *Hedda Gabler*, IV]

12 Death hath a thousand doors to let out life: / I shall find one. [Philip Massinger, 1583–1640, *A Very Woman*, V. iv]

13 A suicide kills two people, Maggie, that's what it's for! [Arthur Miller, 1915– , *After the Fall*, II]

14 Guns aren't lawful; / Nooses give; / Gas smells awful; / You might as well live. [Dorothy Parker, 1893–1967, *Résumé*]

15 Let's do it after the high Roman fashion, / And make death proud to take us. [William Shakespeare, 1564–1616, *Antony and Cleopatra*, IV. xiii. 87]

16 O! that this too too solid flesh would melt, / Thaw, and resolve itself into a dew; / Or that the Everlasting had not fixed / His canon 'gainst self-slaughter! O God! O God! / How weary, stale, flat, and unprofitable / Seem to me all the uses of this world. / Fie on't! O fie! 'tis an unweeded garden, / That grows to seed; things rank and gross in nature / Possess it merely. [*Hamlet*, I. ii. 129]

17 To be or not to be: that is the question: / Whether 'tis nobler in the mind to suffer / The slings and arrows of outrageous fortune, / Or to take arms against a sea of troubles, / And by opposing end them? [*Hamlet*, III. i. 56]

18 Caesar, now be still; / I killed not thee with half so good a will. [*Julius Caesar*, V. v. 50]

19 Why should I play the Roman fool, and die / On mine own sword? [*Macbeth*, V. vii. 30]

20 They remind me of a very tired rich man who said to his chauffeur 'Drive off that cliff, James, I want to commit suicide.' [Adlai Stevenson, 1900–1965; in A Andrews, *Quotations for Speakers and Writers*]

See also DEATH, KILLING

SUMMER

1 Sumer is icumen in. / Lhude sing cuccu! / Groweth sed and bloweth med / And springth the wude nu. [anon., *Sumer is Icumen In*, 13th cent.]

2 *J'ai bu l'été comme un vin doux.* – I drank summer like a sweet wine. [Louis Aragon, 1897–1982, *Zone libre*]

3 All the live murmur of a summer's day. [Matthew Arnold, 1822–88, *The Scholar Gypsy*, 20]

4 For I have seyne, of a ful misty morwe / Folwen ful ofte a mery someres day. [Geoffrey Chaucer, 1340?–1400, *Troilus and Criseyde*, iii, 1060]

5 Summer has set in with its usual severity. [Samuel Taylor Coleridge, 1772–1834, remark quoted in Charles Lamb's letter to V Novello, 9 May 1826]

6 Summertime, and the living is easy. [Ira Gershwin, 1896–1983, and Du Bose Heyward, 1885–1940, song: *Summertime*, in *Porgy and Bess*]

7 Children are dumb to say how hot the day is, / How hot the scent is of the summer rose. [Robert Graves, 1895–1985, *The Cool Web*]

8 It was not in the winter / Our loving lot was cast! / It was the time of roses, / We plucked them as we passed! [Thomas Hood, 1799–1845, ballad: *It was Not in the Winter*]

9 There's a whisper down the field where the year has shot her yield, / And the ricks stand grey to the sun, / Singing: – 'Over then, come over, for the bee has quit the clover, / And your English summer's done'. [Rudyard Kipling, 1865–1936, *The Long Trail*]

10 In a somer seson whan soft was the sonne. [William Langland, 1330?–1400?, *Piers Plowman*, B Text, Prologue, 1]

11 The oldest griefs of summer seem less sad / than drone of mowers on suburban lawns / and girls' thin laughter, to the ears that hear / the soft rain falling of the failing stars. [Edgell Rickword, 1898–1982, *Regrets*, II]

12 The summer's flower is to the summer sweet, / Though to itself it only live and die. [William Shakespeare, 1564–1616, *Sonnets*, 94]

See also AUTUMN, SEASONS, SPRING, WINTER

THE SUN

1 Truly the light is sweet, and a pleasant thing it is for the eyes to behold the sun. [Bible, OT, *Ecclesiastes* 11:7]

2 The sun was shining on the sea, / Shining with all his might: / He did his very best to make / The billows smooth and bright – / And this was odd because it was / The middle of the night. [Lewis Carroll, 1832–98, *Through the Looking Glass*, Ch. 4]

3 The sun came up upon the left, / Out of the sea came he! / And he shone bright, and on the right / Went down into the sea. [Samuel Taylor Coleridge, 1772–1834, *The Ancient Mariner*, Pt 1]

4 Busy old fool, unruly Sun, / Why dost thou thus, / Through windows, and through curtains call on us? / Must to thy motions lovers' seasons run? [John Donne, 1571?–1631, *The Sun Rising*]

5 Phoebus arise, / And paint the sable skies / With azure, white, and red. [William Drummond, 1585–1649, song: *Phoebus Arise*]

6 I said to the First Officer, 'Gad, that sun's hot,' to which he replied, 'Well, you shouldn't touch it.' [Spike Milligan, 1918– , *A Dustbin of Milligan*, 'Letters to Harry Secombe', I]

7 So sinks the day-star in the ocean bed, / And yet anon repairs his drooping head, / And tricks his beams, and with new-spangled ore, / Flames in the forehead of the morning sky. [John Milton, 1608–74, *Lycidas*, 168]

8 So when the sun in bed, / Curtained with cloudy red, / Pillows his chin upon an orient wave. [John Milton, 1608–74, *On the Morning of Christ's Nativity*, 229]

9 In dim eclipse disastrous twilight sheds / On half the nations, and with fear of change / Perplexes monarchs. [John Milton, 1608–74, *Paradise Lost*, Bk i, 597]

10 I have a horror of sunsets, they're so romantic, so operatic. [Marcel Proust, 1871–1922, *Remembrance of Things Past: Cities of the Plain*, Pt II, Ch. 2]

11 Thank heavens, the sun has gone in, and I don't have to go out and enjoy it. [Logan Pearsall Smith, 1865–1946, *Last Words*]

See also MOON, SKIES

SUNDAY

1 Sunday clears away the rust of the whole week. [Joseph Addison, 1672–1719, *The Spectator*, 112]

2 Suffolk used to worship Sunday, not God ... Bugger Sunday, I say, and praise God when you can. [Ronald Blythe, 1922– , *Akenfield*, 6, 'Gregory Gladwell']

3 Hail, Sabbath, thee I hail, the poor man's day. [James Grahame, 1765–1811, *The Sabbath*, 29]

4 Sometimes there's nothing but Sundays for weeks on end. Why can't they move Sunday to the middle of the week so you could put it in the OUT tray on your desk? [Russell Hoban, 1925– , *The Lion of Boaz-Jachin and Jachin-Boaz*, Ch. 32]

5 The feeling of Sunday is the same everywhere, heavy, melancholy, standing still. Like when they say, 'As it was in the beginning, is now, and ever shall be, world without end.' [Jean Rhys, 1894–1979, *Voyage in the Dark*, Ch. 4]

6 I always love to begin a journey on Sundays, because I shall have the prayers of the church, to preserve all that travel by land, or by water. [Jonathan Swift, 1677–1745, *Polite Conversation*, Dialogue 2]

See also DAYS

SUPERSTITIONS

1 There is a superstition in avoiding superstition. [Francis Bacon, 1561–1626, *Essays*, 17, 'Of Superstition']

2 For my part, I have ever believed, and do now know, that there are witches. [Sir Thomas Browne, 1605–82, *Religio Medici*, Pt 1, 30]

3 Superstition is the religion of feeble minds. [Edmund Burke, 1729–97, *Reflections on the Revolution in France*, Penguin edn, p. 269]

4 Foul Superstition! howsoe'er disguised, / Idol, saint, virgin, prophet, crescent, cross, / For whatsoever symbol thou art prized, / Thou sacerdotal gain, but general loss! / Who from true worship's gold can separate thy dross? [Lord Byron, 1788–1824, *Childe Harold's Pilgrimage*, II, 44]

5 And some of the bigger bears try to pretend / That they came round the corner to look for a friend; / And they'll try to pretend that nobody cares / Whether you walk on the lines or the squares. [A A Milne, 1882–1956, *When We Were Very Young*, 'Lines and Squares']

6 Yesterday the bird of night did sit. / Even at noon-day, upon the market place, / Hooting and shrieking. [William Shakespeare, 1564–1616, *Julius Caesar*, I. iii. 26]

7 There is a divinity in odd numbers, either in nativity, chance or death. [*The Merry Wives of Windsor*, V. i. (3)]

8 I read somewhere of a shepherd who, when asked why he made, from within fairy rings, ritual observances to the moon to preserve his flocks, replied: 'I'd be a damn' fool if I didn't!' [Dylan Thomas, 1914–53, *Collected Poems*, Author's Note]

9 Whatever you do crush that infamous thing [superstition], and love those who love you. [Voltaire, 1694–1778, letter to M. d'Alembert, 28 Nov. 1762]

See also MAGIC, MYTHS, PROPHETS

SURPRISE, see ASTONISHMENT

SURVIVAL

1 It isn't important to come out on top, what matters is to be the one who comes out alive. [Bertolt Brecht, 1898–1956, *In the Jungle of the Cities*, x]

2 Philip is a living example of natural selection. He was as fitted to survive in this modern world as a tapeworm in an intestine. [William Golding, 1911–93, *Free Fall*, Ch. 2]

3 A man can be destroyed but not defeated. [Ernest Hemingway, 1899–1961, *The Old Man and the Sea*]

4 Nothing is wasted, nothing is in vain: / The seas roll over but the rocks remain. [A P Herbert, 1890–1971, *Tough at the Top*]

5 I bend but do not break. [Jean de La Fontaine, 1621–95, *Fables*, I, 22, 'The Oak and the Reed']

6 To prove / Our almost-instinct almost true: / What will survive of us is love. [Philip Larkin, 1922–85, *An Arundel Tomb*]

7 You know, of course, that the Tasmanians, who never committed adultery, are now extinct. [W Somerset Maugham, 1874–1965, *The Breadwinner*, III]

8 Oh, don't worry about Alan ... Alan will always land on somebody's feet. [(Of her husband on the day their divorce became final) Dorothy Parker, 1893–1967; in J Keats, *You Might as Well Live*, Pt IV, 1]

9 The human race's prospects of survival were considerably better when we were defenceless against tigers than they are today when we have become defenceless against ourselves. [Arnold Toynbee, 1889–1975; *Observer*, 'Sayings of the Year,' 1963]

See also ENDURANCE, EVOLUTION

SUSPICION

1 Suspicions amongst thoughts are like bats amongst birds, they ever fly by twilight. [Francis Bacon, 1561–1626, *Essays*, 31, 'Of Suspicion']

2 There is death in the pot. [Bible, OT, *1 Kings* 4:40]

3 Caesar's wife must be above suspicion. [Julius Caesar, 102?–44 BC, traditional, based on Plutarch's *Life of Julius Caesar*, x, 6]

4 It was a maxim with Foxey – our revered father, gentlemen – 'Always suspect everybody'. [Charles Dickens, 1812–70, *The Old Curiosity Shop*, Ch. 66]

5 If he were / To be made honest by an act of parliament, / I should not alter in my faith of him. [Ben Jonson, 1573–1637, *The Devil is an Ass*, IV. i]

6 Let me remind you of the old maxim: people under suspicion are better moving than at rest, since at rest they may be sitting in the balance without knowing it, being weighed together with their sins. [Franz Kafka, 1883–1924, *The Trial*, Ch. 8]

7 Ye diners-out from whom we guard our spoons. [Lord Macaulay, 1800–1859, *Political Georgics* (letter to Hannah Macaulay, 29 June 1831)]

8 If [your wife] happens to be travelling anywhere without you and you want her back in a hurry, send her a copy of your local newspaper with a little paragraph cut out. [Lord Mancroft, 1914–87, in *Punch*, 27 Jan. 1971]

9 Mr Speaker I smell a rat; I see him forming in the air and darkening the sky; but I'll nip him in the bud. [Boyle Roche, 1743–1807, attr.]

10 Suspicion of one's own motives is especially necessary for the philanthropist and the executive. [Bertrand Russell, 1872–1970, *The Conquest of Happiness*, Ch. 8]

11 The lady doth protest too much, methinks. [William Shakespeare, 1564–1616, *Hamlet*, III. ii (242)]

12 Mistrust first impulses; they are nearly always good. [Charles-Maurice de Talleyrand, 1754–1838. Also attr. to Count Montrond]

13 *Timeo Danaos et dona ferentes.* – I fear the Greeks, even though they offer gifts. [Virgil, 70–19 BC, *Aeneid*, II, 49]

See also FEAR, TRUST

SWEARING

1 Some guy hit my fender the other day, and I said unto him, 'Be fruitful, and multiply.' But not in those words. [Woody Allen, 1935– , in Adler and Feinman, *W A: Clown Prince of American Humor*, Ch. 2]

2 Oaths are but words, and words but wind. [Samuel Butler, 1612–80, *Hudibras*, II, ii, 107]

3 No one is ever capable of swearing properly in any language other than their own. [Ben Elton, 1959– , *Stark*, 'Love among the Radicals']

4 Today I pronounced a word which should never come out of a lady's lips it was that I called John a Impudent Bitch. [Marjorie Fleming, 1803–11, *Journal*, 2]

5 When you're lying awake with a dismal headache, and repose is tabooed by anxiety, / I conceive you may use any language you choose to indulge in without impropriety. [W S Gilbert, 1836–1911, *Iolanthe*, II]

6 Nowadays, to curse effectively one cannot rely merely on breaches of religious or semi-religious taboos; a reality or at least a plausibility must be invoked. [Robert Graves, 1895–1985, *Occupation: Writer*, 'Lars Porsena']

7 Ethelberta breathed a sort of exclamation, not right out, but stealthily, like a parson's damn. [Thomas Hardy, 1840–1928, *The Hand of Ethelberta*, Ch. 26]

8 Lars Porsena of Clusium / By the nine gods he swore / That the great house of Tarquin / Should suffer wrong no more. / By the Nine Gods he swore it, / And named a trysting day, / And bade his messengers ride forth, / East and west and south and north, / To summon his array. [Lord Macaulay, 1800–1859, *Lays of Ancient Rome*, 'Horatius', 1]

9 That in the captain's but a choleric word, / Which in the soldier is flat blasphemy. [William Shakespeare, 1564–1616, *Measure for Measure*, II. ii. 130]

10 'He shall not die, by G—,' cried my uncle Toby. – The Accusing Spirit which flew up to heaven's chancery, blushed as he gave it in: – and the Recording Angel, as he wrote it down, dropped a tear upon the word, and blotted it out for ever. [Laurence Sterne, 1713–68, *Tristram Shandy*, Vol. vi, Ch. 8]

11 'Before she came,' said a soldier, 'there was cussin' and swearin', but after that it was as 'oly as a church.' The most cherished privilege of the fighting man was abandoned for the sake of Miss Nightingale. [Lytton Strachey, 1880–1932, *Eminent Victorians*, 'Florence Nightingale']

12 A foreign swear-word is practically inoffensive except to the person who has learnt it early in life and knows its social limits. [Paul Theroux, 1941– , *Saint Jack*, Ch. 12]

See also CURSES

SWITZERLAND

1 Since both its national products, snow and chocolate, melt, the cuckoo clock was invented solely in order to give tourists something solid to remember it by. [Alan Coren, 1938– , *The Sanity Inspector*, 'And Though They Do Their Best']

2 The Swiss who are not a people so much as a neat clean quite solvent business ... [William Faulkner, 1897–1962, *Intruder in the Dust*, Ch. 7]

3 Switzerland is a country where very few things begin, but many things end. [F Scott Fitzgerald, 1896–1940, *Notebooks*, 'E']

4 I think the Swiss have sublimated their sense of time into clock-making. [Glynis Johns, 1923– , attr.]

5 The Swiss managed to build a lovely country around their hotels. [George Mikes, 1912–87, *Down with Everybody*]

6 I look upon Switzerland as an inferior sort of Scotland. [Sydney Smith, 1771–1845, letter to Lord Holland, 1815]

7 What a bloody country, even the cheese has got holes in it! [Tom Stoppard, 1937– , *Travesties*, I]

8 They say that if the Swiss had designed these mountains [the Alps], they'd be rather flatter. [Paul Theroux, 1941– , *The Great Railway Bazaar*, Ch. 2]

9 In Italy for thirty years under the Borgias they had warfare, terror, murder, bloodshed – they produced Michelangelo, Leonardo da Vinci and the Renaissance. In Switzerland they had brotherly love, five hundred years of democracy and peace, and what did they produce ...? The cuckoo clock. [Orson Welles, 1915–85, Harry Lime's parting speech in film *The Third Man*]

10 The immeasurable height / Of woods decaying, never to be decayed, / The stationary blasts of waterfalls. [(The Simplon Pass) William Wordsworth, 1770–1850, *The Prelude*, VI, 624]

See also FRANCE, GERMANY, ITALY, NATIONS

SYMBOLS

1 Of course, that's only a symbol, but we need symbols to protect us from ourselves. [Edward Bond, 1934– , *Narrow Road to the Deep North*, I. iv]

2 All the eagles and other predatory creatures that adorn our coats of arms seem to me to be apt psychological representations of our true nature. [C G Jung, 1875–1961, *Memories, Dreams, Reflections*, Ch. 9, ii]

SYMPATHY

1 All you're supposed to do is every once in a while give the boys a little tea and sympathy. [Robert Anderson, 1917– , *Tea and Sympathy*, I]

2 Human nature is so well disposed towards those who are in interesting situations, that a young person, who either marries or dies, is sure to be kindly spoken of. [Jane Austen, 1775–1817, *Emma*, 22]

3 A fellow-feeling makes one wondrous kind. [David Garrick, 1717–79, *Occasional Prologue on Quitting the Theatre*]

4 Our sympathy is cold to the relation of distant misery. [Edward Gibbon, 1737–94, *The Decline and Fall of the Roman Empire*, Ch. 49]

5 She was a machine-gun riddling her hostess with sympathy. [Aldous Huxley, 1894–1963, *Mortal Coils*, 'The Gioconda Smile', ii]

6 Personalize your sympathies, depersonalize your antipathies. [W R Inge, 1860–1954, *More Lay Thoughts of a Dean*, Pt IV, 1]

7 We all need someone we can bleed on. [Mick Jagger, 1943– , and Keith Richard, 1943– , song: *Let It Bleed*]

8 He bit his lip in a manner which immediately awakened my maternal sympathy, and I helped him bite it. [S J Perelman, 1904–79, *Crazy Like a Fox*, 'The Love Decoy']

See also KINDNESS

T

TACT

1 A word spoken in due season, how good is it! [Bible, OT, *Proverbs* 15:23]

2 One shouldn't talk of halters in the hanged man's house. [Miguel Cervantes, 1547–1616, *Don Quixote*, Pt I, Ch. 25]

3 The essential tact in daring is to know how far one can go too far. [Jean Cocteau, 1889–1963, *Le Coq et l'arlequin*]

4 Men must be taught as if you taught them not, / And things unknown proposed as things forgot. [Alexander Pope, 1688–1744, *An Essay on Criticism*, 574]

See also DISCRETION

TALENT

1 Whom the gods wish to destroy they first call promising. [Cyril Connolly, 1903–74, *Enemies of Promise*, Ch. 13]

2 I believe that since my life began / The most I've had is just / A talent to amuse. [Noël Coward, 1899–1973, *Bitter Sweet*, II. i, 'If Love were All']

3 Mediocrity knows nothing higher than itself, but talent instantly recognizes genius. [Arthur Conan Doyle, 1859–1930, *The Sign of Four*, Ch. 1]

4 If a man can write a better book, preach a better sermon, or make a better mouse-trap than his neighbour, though he build his house in the woods, the world will make a beaten path to his door. [Ralph Waldo Emerson, 1803–82, lecture noted down by Sarah Yule, quoted in her *Borrowings*. Also ascr. to Elbert Hubbard]

5 Talent is formed in quiet, character in the stream of human life. [Johann Wolfgang von Goethe, 1749–1832, *Torquato Tasso*, I. ii]

6 When a person dies who does any one thing better than anyone else in the world, which so many others are trying to do well, it leaves a gap in society. [(On the death of John Cavanagh, the fives-player) William Hazlitt, 1778–1830, *The Indian Jugglers*]

7 I think it's the most extraordinary collection of talent, of human knowledge, that has ever been gathered together at the White House – with the possible exception of when Thomas Jefferson dined alone. [President John F Kennedy, 1917–63, at a dinner for Nobel prizewinners, 29 Apr. 1962]

8 Genius does what it must, and Talent does what it can. [Owen Meredith, 1831–91, *Last Words of a Sensitive Second-rate Poet*]

9 If you have great talents, industry will improve them: if you have but moderate abilities, industry will supply their deficiency. [Joshua Reynolds, 1723–92, *Discourses*, 2]

10 Talent without genius comes to little. Genius without talent is *nothing*. [Paul Valéry, 1871–1945, *At Moments*, 'The Beautiful is Negative']

See also GENIUS

TALK

1 In all labour there is profit: but the talk of the lips tendeth only to penury. [Bible, OT, *Proverbs* 14:23]

2 'Let me not live,' said Aretine's Antonia, 'if I had not rather hear thy discourse than see a play.' [Robert Burton, 1577–1640, *Anatomy of Melancholy*, III, §1, Memb. 1, 1]

3 In me the need to talk is a primary impulse, and I can't help saying right off what comes to my tongue. [Miguel Cervantes, 1547–1616, *Don Quixote*, Pt I, Ch. 30]

4 For most good talkers, when they have run down, are miserable; they know that they have betrayed themselves, that they have taken material which should have a life of its own to dispense it in noises upon the air. [Cyril Connolly, 1903–74, *Enemies of Promise*, Ch. 13]

5 Oh – I listen a lot and talk less. You can't learn anything when you're talking. [Bing Crosby, 1901–77, BBC TV interview with Michael Parkinson, 1975]

6 But far more numerous was the herd of such, / Who think too little, and who talk too much. [John Dryden, 1631–1700, *Absalom and Achitophel*, Pt I, 533]

7 In the room the women come and go / Talking of Michelangelo. [T S Eliot, 1888–1965, *The Love Song of J. Alfred Prufrock*]

8 Nothing is more despicable than a professional talker who uses his words as a quack uses his remedies. [François de Fénelon, 1651–1715, letter to the Academy]

9 The meaning doesn't matter if it's only idle chatter of a transcendental kind. [W S Gilbert, 1836–1911, *Patience*, I]

10 He [Coleridge] talked on for ever; and you wished him to talk on for ever. [William Hazlitt, 1778–1830, *Lectures on the English Poets*, 8]; see 13

11 The men, the young and the clever ones, find it a house ... with intellectual elbow-room, with freedom of talk. Most English talk is a quadrille in a sentry-box. [Henry James, 1843–1916, *The Awkward Age*, V, 19]

12 It does not always pay to have a golden tongue unless one has the ability to hold it. [(Of Lord Curzon) Paul Johnson, 1928– , in *Listener*, 5 June 1986]

13 The fear of every man that heard him was, lest he should make an end. [(Of Bacon) Ben Jonson, 1573–1637, *Timber, or Discoveries*, 78]; see 10

14 Great people talk about ideas, average people talk about things, and small people talk about wine. [Fran Lebowitz, ?1948– , *Social Studies*, 'People']

15 You know you haven't stopped talking since I came here? You must have been vaccinated with a phonograph needle. [Groucho Marx, 1895–1977, in film *Duck Soup*, script by Bert Kalmar et al.]

16 Now speak, / Or be for ever silent. [Philip Massinger, 1583–1640, *The Duke of Milan*, IV. iii]

17 Most people have a furious itch to talk about themselves and are restrained only by the disinclination of others to listen. Reserve is an artificial quality that is developed in most of us as the result of innumerable rebuffs. [W Somerset Maugham, 1874–1965, *The Summing Up*, Ch. 19]

18 Beware of the conversationalist who adds 'in other words'. He is merely starting afresh. [Robert Morley, 1908–92, in *Observer*, 6 Dec. 1964]

19 They never taste who always drink; / They always talk, who never think. [Matthew Prior, 1664–1721, *Upon This Passage in Scaligerana*]

20 A gentleman, nurse, that loves to hear himself talk, and will speak more in a minute than he will stand to in a month. [William Shakespeare, 1564–1616, *Romeo and Juliet*, II. iii. (156)]

21 We talked a lot about life. There was nothing else to talk about. [Amanda Vail, 1921–66, *Love Me Little*, Ch. 8]

22 A good listener is not someone who has nothing to say. A good listener is a good talker with a sore throat. [Katharine Whitehorn 1926– ; in Herbert V Prochnow, *The Public Speaker's Treasure Chest*]

23 With skill she vibrates her eternal tongue, / For ever most divinely in the wrong. [Edward Young, 1683–1765, *Love of Fame*, Satire VI, 105]

24 We have ways of making men talk. [Waldemar Young, et al., in film *The Lives of a Bengal Lancer*, 1935]

See also CONVERSATION, GOSSIP, SPEECH

TASTE

1 Between thirty and forty a man may have reached the height of discretion without having tumbled over the top into the feather-bed of correctitude. [Arnold Bennett, 1867–1931, in *Evening Standard Years*, 29 May 1930]

2 It is a common error to think of bad taste as sterile; rather, it is good taste, and good taste alone, that possesses the power to sterilize and is always the first handicap to any creative functioning. One has only to consider the good taste of the French: it has encouraged them not to do anything. [Salvador Dali, 1904–89, in Robert Descharnes and Clovis Prévost, *Gaudi, the Visionary*, Preface]

3 What is food to one man is bitter poison to others. [Lucretius, 99–55 BC, *On the Nature of the Universe*, IV, 637]

4 Things sweet to taste prove in digestion sour. [William Shakespeare, 1564–1616, *Richard II*, I. iii. 236]

See also FASHION, STYLE

TAXATION

1 There is one difference between a tax collector and a taxidermist – the taxidermist leaves the hide. [Mortimer Caplin, 1916– , in *Time* magazine, 1 Feb. 1963]

2 Why shouldn't the American people take half my money from me? I took all of it from them. [Edward Filene, 1860–1937, in Arthur M Schlesinger Jr, *The Coming of the New Deal*, Pt 7, Ch. 2, sect. iv]

3 In this world nothing can be said to be certain, except death and taxes. [Benjamin Franklin, 1706–90, letter to Jean-Baptiste Le Roy, 13 Nov. 1789]

4 All taxes must, at last, fall upon agriculture. [Edward Gibbon, 1737–94, *The Decline and Fall of the Roman Empire*, Ch. 8]

5 Sex and taxes are in many ways the same. Tax does to cash what males do to genes. It dispenses assets among the population as a whole. Sex, not death, is the great leveller. [Steve Jones, 1944– , speech to the Royal Society, London, 23 Jan. 1997]

6 If once you have paid him the Dane-geld / You never get rid of the Dane. [Rudyard Kipling, 1865–1936, *Dane-geld*]

7 Taxation without representation is tyranny. [James Otis, 1725–83, watchword of the American Revolution. Attr., but probably apocryphal]

8 It [income tax] has made more liars out of the American people than golf. [Will Rogers, 1879–1935, *The Illiterate Digest*, 'Warning to Jokers']

TEA & COFFEE

1 The infusion of a China plant sweetened with the pith of an Indian cane. [Joseph Addison, 1672–1719, *The Spectator*, 69]

2 Tea, although an Oriental, / Is a gentleman at least; / Cocoa is a cad and coward, / Cocoa is a vulgar beast. [G K Chesterton, 1874–1936, *The Song of Right and Wrong*]

3 The slavery of the tea and coffee and other slop-kettle. [William Cobbett, 1762–1835, *Advice to Young Men*, Letter 1]

4 Now stir the fire, and close the shutters fast, / Let fall the curtains, wheel the sofa round, / And, while the bubbling and loud-hissing urn / Throws up a steamy column, and the cups, / That cheer but not inebriate, wait on each, / So let us welcome peaceful evening in. [William Cowper, 1731–1800, *The Task*, Bk IV, 36]

5 When I makes tea I makes tea, as old mother Grogan said. And when I makes water I makes water. [James Joyce, 1882–1941, *Ulysses*, Penguin edn, 1992, p. 13]

6 We had finished our coffee, which was loathsome, as in all countries . . . where the accent of the word for coffee falls on the first syllable. [Primo Levi, 1919–87, *The Wrench*]

7 The trouble with tea is that originally it was quite a good drink. [George Mikes, 1912–87, *How to be an Alien*]

8 Coffee, which makes the politician wise, / And see through all things with his half-shut eyes. [Alexander Pope, 1688–1744, *The Rape of the Lock*, III, 117]

9 Our trouble is that we drink too much tea. I see in this the slow revenge of the Orient, which has diverted the Yellow River down our throats. [J B Priestley, 1894–1984; *Observer*, 'Sayings of the Week', 15 May 1949]

10 Look here, Steward, if this is coffee, I want tea; but if this is tea, then I wish for coffee. [*Punch* (1902), cxxiii, 44]

11 Why do they always put mud into coffee on board steamers? Why does the tea generally taste of boiled boots? [W M Thackeray, 1811–63, *The Kickleburys on the Rhine*]

12 'Tea' to the English is really a picnic indoors. [Alice Walker, 1944– , *The Color Purple*, p. 116]

See also DRINK: WEAK

TEACHERS

1 The most formidable headmaster I ever knew was a headmistress ... She had X-ray pince-nez and that undivided bust popularized by Queen Mary. I think she was God in drag. [Nancy Banks-Smith, 1929– , in *Guardian*, 8 Jan. 1977]

2 The schoolmaster is abroad, and I trust more to him, armed with his primer, than I do to the soldier in full military array, for upholding and extending the liberties of his country. [Lord Brougham, 1778–1868, speech in House of Commons, 29 Jan. 1828]

3 That is the difference between good teachers and great teachers: good teachers make the best of a pupil's means: great teachers foresee a pupil's ends. [Maria Callas, 1923–77, in Kenneth Harris, *Talking to ...*]

4 And gladly wolde he lerne and gladly teche. [Geoffrey Chaucer, 1340?–1400, *Canterbury Tales*, 'Prologue', 308]

5 If he [a teacher] is indeed wise he does not bid you enter the house of his wisdom, but rather leads you to the threshold of your own mind. [Kahlil Gibran, 1883–1931, *The Prophet*, 'Of Teaching']

6 A man severe he was, and stern to view, / I knew him well, and every truant knew; / Well had the boding tremblers learned to trace / The day's disasters in his morning face; / Full well they laughed with counterfeited glee, / At all his jokes, for many a joke had he; / Full well the busy whisper, circling round, / Conveyed the dismal tidings when he frowned; / Yet he was kind, or if severe in aught, / The love he bore to learning was in fault. [Oliver Goldsmith, 1728–74, *The Deserted Village*, 197]

7 A Guru is far more than a teacher in the ordinary sense of the word. A teacher gives knowledge, but a Guru gives himself. [Ana Angarika Govinda, 1898–1985, *The Way of the White Clouds*, 6]

8 Sixth-form teachers are something like firemen called in to quench flames that are already out. [Simon Gray, 1936– , *Butley*, II]

9 The headmaster said you ruled with a rod of iron. He called you the Himmler of the lower fifth. [Terence Rattigan, 1911–77, *The Browning Version*]

10 For every person wishing to teach there are thirty not wanting to be taught. [W C Sellar, 1898–1951, and R J Yeatman, 1897–1968, *And Now All This*, Introduction]

11 He who can, does. He who cannot, teaches. [George Bernard Shaw, 1856–1950, *Man and Superman*, 'Maxims for Revolutionists', Education]

12 Give me a girl at an impressionable age, and she is mine for life. [Muriel Spark, 1918– , *The Prime of Miss Jean Brodie*, Ch. 1]

13 A teacher should have maximal authority and minimal power. [Thomas Szasz, 1920– , *The Second Sin*, 'Education']

14 I expect you'll be becoming a schoolmaster, sir. That's what most of the gentlemen does, sir, that gets sent down for indecent behaviour. [Evelyn Waugh, 1903–66, *Decline and Fall*, Prelude]

15 Culture ... is an instrument manipulated by teachers for manufacturing more teachers, who when their turn comes will manufacture still more teachers. [Simone Weil, 1909–43, *The Need for Roots*, Pt 2, 'Uprootedness in the Towns']

See also EDUCATION, LEARNING, SCHOOLS, STUDENTS

TEARS

1 Tears may be intellectual, but they can never be political. They save no man from being shot, no child from being thrown alive into the furnace. [Saul Bellow, 1915– , *The Dean's December*, 12]

2 Every tear from every eye / Becomes a babe in Eternity. [William Blake, 1757–1827, *Auguries of Innocence*]

3 For a tear is an intellectual thing; / And a sigh is the sword of an angel king; / And the bitter groan of a martyr's woe / Is an arrow from the Almighty's bow. [William Blake, 1757–1827, *Jerusalem*, f. 52]

4 Does the day-star rise? / Still thy stars do fall and fall. / Does day close his eyes? / Still the fountain weeps for all. / Let night or day do what they will, / Thou hast thy task; thou weepest still. [Richard Crashaw, 1613?–49, *Saint Mary Magdalene, or The Weeper*, 23]

5 Tears were to me what glass beads are to African traders. [Quentin Crisp, 1908–99, *The Naked Civil Servant*, Ch. 2]

6 Bid me to weep, and I will weep, / While I have eyes to see. [Robert Herrick, 1591–1674, *Hesperides*, 'To Anthea, Who May Command Him Anything']

7 She couldn't possibly go back to the gentleman's flat; she had no right to cry in strangers' houses. [Katherine Mansfield, 1888–1923, *The Garden Party*, 'Life of Ma Parker']

8 What's Hecuba to him or he to Hecuba / That he should weep for her? [William Shakespeare, 1564–1616, *Hamlet*, II. ii. (593)]

9 If you have tears, prepare to shed them now. [*Julius Caesar*, III. ii. (174)]

10 No, I'll not weep: / I have full cause of weeping, but this heart / Shall break into a hundred thousand flaws / Or ere I'll weep. O fool! I shall go mad. [*King Lear*, II. ii. (286)]

11 Some pretty match with shedding tears? / As thus; to drop them still upon one place / Till they have fretted us a pair of graves. [*Richard II*, III. ii. 165]

12 When in disgrace with fortune and men's eyes / I all alone beweep my outcast state. [*Sonnets*, 29]

13 Ah! but those tears are pearl which thy love sheds, / And they are rich and ransom all ill deeds. [*Sonnets*, 34]

14 Her tears fell with the dews at even; / Her tears fell ere the dews were dried. [Alfred, Lord Tennyson, 1809–92, *Mariana*]

15 Tears, idle tears, I know not what they mean, / Tears from the depth of some divine despair. [Alfred, Lord Tennyson, 1809–92, *The Princess*, IV, second song]

16 *Il pleure dans mon cœur / Comme il pleut sur la ville.* – Tears fall in my heart like the rain on the town. [Paul Verlaine, 1844–96, *Romances sans paroles*, 3]

17 Laugh and the world laughs with you; / Weep, and you weep alone; / For the sad old earth must borrow its mirth, / But has trouble enough of its own. [Ella Wheeler Wilcox, 1855–1919, *Solitude*]

See also GRIEF, LAUGHTER, SORROW

TECHNOLOGY

1 Give me a firm spot on which to stand, and I will move the earth. [Archimedes, 287–212 BC, on the lever]

2 Technology is not the mastery of nature but of the relation between nature and man. [Walter Benjamin, 1892–1940, *One-way Street*, 'To the Planetarium']

3 Either you're on the steamroller, or you're part of the road. [Stewart Brand, of the digital revolution, quoted in internet magazine *Feed*, Oct. 1995]

4 The easiest place in which to carry technology is in the mind. [Hugh Brody, 1943– , *Living Arctic*, Ch. 6]

5 Man is a tool-using animal ... Without tools he is nothing, with tools he is all. [Thomas Carlyle, 1795–1881, *Sartor Resartus*, Bk 1, Ch. 5]

6 Any sufficiently advanced technology is indistinguishable from magic. [Arthur C Clarke, 1917– , *Profiles of the Future*]

7 Soon shall thy arm, unconquered steam! afar / Drag the slow barge, or drive the rapid car; / Or on wide-waving wings expanded bear / The flying chariot through the field of air. [Erasmus Darwin, 1731–1802, *The Botanic Garden*, I, i, 289]

8 Man is a tool-making animal. [Benjamin Franklin, 1706–90, quoted in James Boswell, *Life of J*, 7 Apr. 1778]

9 Technology ... the knack of so arranging the world that we don't have to experience it. [Max Frisch, 1911–91, *Homo Faber*, 'Second Stop']

10 The thing with high-tech is that you always end up using scissors. [David Hockney, 1937– ; *Observer* 'Sayings of the Week', 10 July 1994]

11 This is not the age of pamphleteers. It is the age of engineers. The spark-gap is mightier than the pen. Democracy will not be salvaged by men who talk fluently, debate forcefully and quote aptly. [Lambert Hogben, 1895–1975, *Science for the Citizen*, 'Epilogue']

12 One machine can do the work of fifty ordinary men. No machine can do the work of one extraordinary man. [Elbert Hubbard, 1856–1915, *Roycroft Dictionary and Book of Epigrams*]

13 If you fall in love with a machine there is something wrong with your love life. If you worship a machine there is something wrong with your religion. [Lewis Mumford, 1895–1990, *Art and Technics*]

14 The machine threatens all achievement. [Rainer Maria Rilke, 1875–1926, *Sonnets to Orpheus*, II, 10]

15 The Britain that is going to be forged in the white heat of this revolution will be no place for restrictive practices or outdated methods on either side of industry. [Harold Wilson, 1916–95, speech at Labour Party Conference, 1 Oct. 1963]

TEETH

1 Oh, I wish I'd looked after me teeth, / And spotted the perils beneath, / All the toffees I chewed, / And the sweet sticky food, / Oh, I wish I'd looked after me teeth. [Pam Ayres, 1947– , 'Oh, I Wish I'd Looked After Me Teeth']

2 For years I have let dentists ride roughshod over my teeth; I have been sawed, hacked, chopped, whittled, bewitched, bewildered, tattooed, and signed on again; but this is cuspid's last stand. [S J Perelman, 1904–79, *Crazy Like a Fox*, 'Nothing but the Tooth']

3 Certain people are born with natural false teeth. [Robert Robinson, 1927– , in BBC radio programme *Stop the Week*, 1977]

4 He had one peculiar weakness; he had faced death in many forms but he had never faced a dentist. The thought of dentists gave him just the same sick horror as the thought of Socialism. [H G Wells, 1866–1946, *Bealby*, Pt VIII, 1]

5 Notice the smug suppressions of his face. In his mouth are Lies in the shape of false teeth. [H G Wells, 1866–1946, *Love and Mr Lewisham*, Ch. 23]

6 To lose a lover or even a husband or two during the course of one's life can be vexing. But to lose one's teeth is a catastrophe. [Hugh Wheeler, 1912– , musical, *A Little Night Music*]

See also BODY PARTS

TELEVISION & RADIO

1 TV – a clever contraction derived from the words Terrible Vaudeville. However, it is our latest medium – we call it a medium because nothing's well done. [Goodman Ace, 1899–1982, letter to Groucho Marx, *The Groucho Letters*]

2 Some television programmes are so much chewing gum for the eyes. [John Mason Brown, 1900–1969, interview, 28 July 1955]

3 If it weren't for Philo T. Farnsworth, inventor of television, we'd still be eating frozen radio dinners. [Johnny Carson, 1925– ; in *The 637 Best Things Anybody Ever Said*, comp. Robert Byrne]

4 After all the public is entitled to what it wants, isn't it? The Romans knew that and even they lasted four hundred years after they started to putrefy. [(Of TV) Raymond Chandler, 1888–1959, letter to Carl Brandt, 15 Nov. 1951]

5 Television is a form of soliloquy. [Kenneth Clark, 1903–83, in *Guardian*, 26 Nov. 1977]

6 Working for the BBC is like working for a cross between the Church and the Post Office; it seldom fails to live down to expectations. [Tom Clarke, 1918–93, quoted by Richard Eyre in *Listener*, 12 Dec. 1987]

7 Television: the key to all minds and hearts because it permits people to be entertained by their government without ever having to participate in it. [Richard Condon, 1915–96; *Observer*, 'Sayings of the Week', 10 June 1990]

8 Television is more interesting than people. If it were not, we should have people standing in the corners of our rooms. [Alan Coren, 1938– , in *The Times*]

9 Television is for appearing on, not watching. [Noël Coward, 1899–1973, in *Guardian*, 28 Nov. 1988]

10 The finger that turns the dial rules the air. [Will Durant, 1885–1981, *What is Civilization?*]

11 Television is an invention that permits you to be entertained in your living room by people you wouldn't have in your home. [David Frost, 1939– , from CBC TV programme *David Frost Revue*, 1971; in Jonathon Green, *Says Who?*]

12 Generally speaking, the only way of getting any feeling from a TV set is to touch it when you're wet. [Larry Gelbart, 1928– , in *Listener*, 17/24 Dec. 1987]

13 The box they buried entertainment in. [Bob Hope, 1903– , in *New Society*, 10 Jan. 1985]

14 It's television, you see. If you are not on the thing every week, the public think you are either dead or deported. [Frankie Howerd, 1922–92; *Independent*, 'Quote Unquote', 16 Mar. 1991]

15 It's the tragedy of TV that instead of drawing upon new experience and fresh sources of comedy it cannibalizes old pop culture. When movies do the same now, they aren't even imitating movies, they're imitating TV. The result is too infantile to be called decadent; it's pop culture for those with bad memories for pop culture, or so young they have no memories. [Pauline Kael, 1919– , *Deeper into Movies*, 'Collaboration and Resistance']

16 A medium, so called because it is neither rare nor well done. [Ernie Kovacs, 1919–62, of television; in L Halliwell, *Filmgoer's Book of Quotes*]

17 In front of the small screen, life becomes fiction, and fiction life. [John Lahr, 1941– , in *Independent on Sunday*, 29 Sept. 1991]

18 Television has devalued politicians of all parties. It has thrown them back on their own merits. [Edward Pearce, 1939– , from *Hummingbirds and Hyenas*]

19 It was always possible to measure the distance between so-called management and the so-called creative by the time it took for a memo to go in one direction and a half-brick in the other. [(Of the BBC) Dennis Potter, 1935–94, James MacTaggart Memorial Lecture, Edinburgh Film Festival, 1993]

20 Nation shall speak peace unto nation. [M J Rendall, 1862–1950, motto of BBC, 1927]

21 Television? No good will come of this device. The word is half Greek and half Latin. [C P Scott, 1846–1932, attr.]

22 We don't have television. It stops you from doing anything useful – you watch other people live instead of living yourself. [John Seymour, 1914– , in *The Sunday Times Magazine*, 12 Feb. 1989]

23 A stake in commercial television is the equivalent of having a licence to print money. [Roy Thomson, 1894–1976 (on the profit in commercial TV in Britain, Aug. 1957), in R Braddon, *Roy Thomson*, Ch. 32]

24 My video recorder records programmes I don't want to see, and then plays them back when I'm out. [Ernie Wise, 1925– ; in *Apt and Amusing Quotations*, ed. G F Lamb, 'Television']

See also MEDIA, NEWS, NEWSPAPERS

TEMPTATION

1 To Carthage I came, where there sang all around my ears a cauldron of unholy loves. [St Augustine, 354–430, *Confessions*, III, 1]

2 My son, if thou come to serve the Lord, prepare thy soul for temptation. [Bible, Apocrypha, *Ecclesiasticus* 2:1]

3 God is faithful, who will not suffer you to be tempted above that ye are able. [Bible, NT, *1 Corinthians* 10:13]

4 Why comes temptation but for man to meet / And master and make crouch beneath his foot, / And so be pedestaled in triumph? [Robert Browning, 1812–89, *The Ring and the Book*, X, 1184]

5 I find I always have to write SOMETHING on a steamed mirror. [Elaine Dundy, 1927– , *The Dud Avocado*, Ch. 1]

6 The last temptation is the greatest treason: / To do the right deed for the wrong reason. [T S Eliot, 1888–1965, *Murder in the Cathedral*, I]

7 Many a dangerous temptation comes to us in gay, fine colours, that are but skin-deep. [Matthew Henry, 1662–1714, *Commentaries, Genesis*, 3, 1]

8 There must be several young women who would render the Christian life intensely difficult to him if only you could persuade him to marry one of them. [C S Lewis, 1898–1963, *The Screwtape Letters*, 19]

9 This extraordinary pride in being exempt from temptation that you have not yet risen to the level of. Eunuchs boasting of their chastity. [C S Lewis, 1898–1963, in Brian Aldiss and Kingsley Amis, *Spectrum IV*]

10 Temptation came to him, in middle age, tentatively and without insistence, like a neglected butcher-boy who asks for a Christmas box in February for no more hopeful reason than that he didn't get one in December. [Saki (H H Munro), 1870–1916, *The Reticence of Lady Anne*]

11 I never resist temptation, because I have found that things that are bad for me do not tempt me. [George Bernard Shaw, 1856–1950, *The Apple Cart*, II]

12 I can resist everything except temptation. [Oscar Wilde, 1854–1900, *Lady Windermere's Fan*, I]

See also SINS

THAMES

1 Crossing the stripling Thames at Bablock-hithe, / Trailing in the cool stream thy fingers wet, / As the slow punt swings round. [Matthew Arnold, 1822–88, *The Scholar-Gypsy*, 74]

2 Every drop of the Thames is liquid 'istory. [John Burns, 1858–1943 (to transatlantic visitors), attr. by Frederick Whyte; in *Daily Mail*, 25 Jan. 1943]

3 Against the bridal day, which is not long: / Sweet Thames! run softly, till I end my song. [Edmund Spenser, 1552?–99, *Prothalamion*, 17]

See also RIVERS

THEATRE

1 The theatre must start to take its audience seriously. It must stop telling them stories they can understand. [Howard Barker, 1946– , in *Guardian*, 10 Feb. 1986]

2 What things have we seen, / Done at the Mermaid! heard words that have been / So nimble, and so full of subtle flame, / As if that every one from whence they came / Had meant to put his whole wit in a jest, / And had resolved to live a fool, the rest / Of his dull life. [Francis Beaumont, 1584–1616, *Letter to Ben Jonson*]

3 All drama is a form of anthropology. [Michael Billington, 1939– , in *Guardian*, 30 Nov. 1987]

4 'Why, what the D—l,' cried the Captain, 'do you come to the play, without knowing what it is?' 'O yes, Sir, yes, very frequently; I have no time to read play-bills; one merely comes to meet one's friends, and show that one's alive.' [Fanny Burney, 1752–1840, *Evelina*, Letter 20]

5 Dear Doctor, I have read your play, / Which is a good one in its way, – / Purges the eyes and moves the bowels, / And drenches handkerchiefs like towels. [Lord Byron, 1788–1824, *Epistle from Mr Murray to Dr Polidori*]

6 Theatre is like operating with a scalpel. Film is operating with a laser. [Michael Caine, 1933– , in BBC TV programme *Acting*, 28 Aug. 1987]

7 You know, I go to the theatre to be entertained ... I don't want to see plays about rape, sodomy and drug addiction ... I can get all that at home. [Peter Cook, 1937–95, caption to cartoon by Roger Law in *Observer*, 8 July 1962]

8 Don't put your daughter on the stage, Mrs Worthington. [Noël Coward, 1899–1973, lyric: *Don't Put Your Daughter on the Stage*]

9 The theatre is the best way of showing the gap between what is said and what is seen to be done, and that is why, ragged and gap-toothed as it is, it has still a far healthier potential than some poorer, abandoned arts. [David Hare, 1947– , in *The Sunday Times Magazine*, 26 Nov. 1978, 'The Playwright as Historian']

10 Drama is life with the dull bits left out. [Alfred Hitchcock, 1899–1980; in L Halliwell, *The Filmgoer's Book of Quotes*]

11 I am unable to pass a theatre without wanting to walk in, and am unable to listen to a single word from an actor without wanting to walk out again. [Howard Jacobson, 1942– , in *Listener*, 23 Jan. 1986]

12 The drama's laws, the drama's patrons give, / For we that live to please, must please to live. [Dr Samuel Johnson, 1709–84, *Prologue at the Opening of Theatre in Drury Lane*]

13 A first night was notoriously distracting owing to the large number of people who stand about looking famous. [Denis Mackail, 1892–1971, *How Amusing*]

14 Then to the well-trod stage anon, / If Jonson's learnèd sock be on, / Or sweetest Shakespeare, Fancy's child, / Warble his native wood-notes wild. [John Milton, 1608–74, *L'Allegro*, 131]

15 In the theatre, the director is God – but unfortunately, the actors are atheists. [Zarko Petan, in *The Times*, 15 June 1977]

16 To make mankind in conscious virtue bold, / Live o'er each scene, and be what they behold. [Alexander Pope, 1688–1744, *Prologue to Mr Addison's 'Cato'*, 3]

17 A nice, respectable, middle-class, middle-aged maiden lady, with time on her hands and the money to help her pass it ... Let us call her

Aunt Edna ... Aunt Edna is universal, and to those who may feel that all the problems of the modern theatre might be solved by her liquidation, let me add that ... she is also immortal. [Terence Rattigan, 1911–77, *Collected Plays*, Vol. II, Preface]

18 One of the thousand reasons I quit going to the theatre when I was about twenty was that I resented like hell filing out of the theatre just because some playwright was forever slamming down his silly curtain. [J D Salinger, 1919– , *Seymour: An Introduction*]

19 Can this cockpit hold / The vasty fields of France? or may we cram / Within this wooden O the very casques / That did affright the air at Agincourt? [William Shakespeare, 1564–1616, *Henry V*, Chorus, 11]

20 As in a theatre, the eyes of men, / After a well-graced actor leaves the stage, / Are idly bent on him that enters next, / Thinking his prattle to be tedious. [*Richard II*, IV. ii. 23]

21 A good drama critic is one who perceives what is happening in the theatre of his time. A great drama critic also perceives what is not happening. [Kenneth Tynan, 1927–80, *Tynan Right and Left*, Foreword]

See also ACTING, ACTORS, PLAYS, PLAYWRIGHTS

THEFT

1 What is robbing a bank compared to founding one? [Bertolt Brecht, 1898–1956, *The Threepenny Opera*, III. i]

2 He that first cries out stop thief, is often he that has stolen the treasure. [William Congreve, 1670–1729, *Love for Love*, III. xiv]

3 Some will rob you with a six gun, / And some with a fountain pen. [Woody Guthrie, 1912–67, song: *Pretty Boy Floyd*]

4 A burglar who respects his art always takes his time before taking anything else. [O Henry, 1862–1910, *Makes the Whole World Kin*]

5 The traveller with empty pockets will sing in the thief's face. [Juvenal, 60–*c.*130, *Satires*, X, 22]

6 It has become the fashion here [Moscow] to stick your hand in someone else's pocket and when they catch you, you say, 'Ah, you don't understand market relations.' [Viktor Khavkin, in *Guardian*, 22 May 1992]

7 He doesn't want to let his left hand know whose pocket the right one is picking. [Charles Laughton, in film *The Big Clock*, script Jonathan Latimer, from novel by Kenneth Fearing]

8 For de little stealin' dey gits you in jail soon or late. For de big stealin' dey makes you emperor and puts you in de Hall o' Fame when you croaks. [Eugene O'Neill, 1888–1953, *The Emperor Jones*]

9 'Convey' the wise it call. 'Steal!' foh! a fico for the phrase. [William Shakespeare, 1564–1616, *The Merry Wives of Windsor*, I. iii. (30)]

10 The robbed that smiles steals something from the thief. [*Othello*, I. iii. 208]

11 He that is robbed, not wanting what is stolen, / Let him not know't and he's not robbed at all. [*Othello*, III. iii. 343]

See also CRIME

THEOLOGY

1 [James] was being teased by a theological colleague who said to him: 'A philosopher is like a blind man in a dark cellar, looking for a black cat that isn't there.' 'Yes,' said William James, 'and the difference between philosophy and theology is that theology finds the cat.' [William James, 1842–1910, in A J Ayer, *On Making Philosophy Intelligible*]

2 Now it is on the whole more convenient to keep history and theology apart. [H G Wells, 1866–1946, *A Short History of the World*, Ch. 37]

See also RELIGION

THEORY

1 A theory can be proved by experiment; but no path leads from experiment to the birth of a theory. [Albert Einstein, 1879–1955, in *The Sunday Times*, 18 July 1976]

2 You know very well that unless you're a scientist, it's much more important for a theory to be shapely, than for it to be true. [Christopher Hampton, 1946– , *The Philanthropist*, i]

3 Resistentialism is concerned with what Things think about men. [Paul Jennings, 1918–89, *Even Oddlier*, 'Developments in Resistentialism']

4 A first-rate theory predicts; a second-rate theory forbids; and a third-rate theory explains after the event. [A I Kitaigorodski, 1914– , lecture in Amsterdam, Aug. 1975; in *Dictionary of Scientific Quotations*, ed. A L Mackay]

5 Theory is often just practice with the hard bits left out. [J M Robson, ?1900–1982, in *The Library*, 1985, VI, 7]

THIN, see FAT

THINKING & THOUGHT

1 True thoughts are those alone which do not understand themselves. [Theodor Adorno, 1903–69, *Memoralia Minima*, Pt 3, 122]

2 Our two rhetoricians [Churchill and Lloyd George] . . . have good brains of different types. But they can only think talking, just as some people can only think writing. Only the salt of the earth can think inside, and the bulk of mankind cannot think at all! [H H Asquith, 1852–1928, in *The Wit of the Asquiths*, comp. Mary Tester, 'The Imperialists']

3 The universe is transformation; our life is what our thoughts make it. [Marcus Aurelius, 121–80, *Meditations*, IV, 3]

4 I have always found that the man whose second thoughts are good is worth watching. [James Barrie, 1860–1937, *What Every Woman Knows*, III]

5 Which of you by taking thought can add one cubit unto his stature? [Bible, NT, *St Matthew* 6:27]

6 Somebody not prepared to use induction would have to drink all the water in the sea before being prepared to admit that the sea is salty. [Richard Casement, 1942–82, *Man Suddenly Sees to the Edge of the Universe*]

7 I wonder if a single thought that has helped forward the human spirit has ever been conceived or written down in an enormous room: except, perhaps, in the reading room of the British Museum. [Kenneth Clark, 1903–83, *Civilization*, Ch. 7]

8 Do not think what you want to think until you know what you ought to know. [John Crow, 1905–70, 'Crow's Law', in R V Jones, *Most Secret War*, Ch. 9]

9 The highest possible stage in moral culture is when we recognize that we ought to control our thoughts. [Charles Darwin, 1809–82, *The Descent of Man*, Ch. 4]

10 *Cogito, ergo sum.* – I think, therefore I am. [René Descartes, 1596–1650, *Discourse on Method*, IV]

11 Tenants of the house, / Thoughts of a dry brain in a dry season. [T S Eliot, 1888–1965, *Gerontion*]

12 Beware when the great God lets loose a thinker on this planet. [Ralph Waldo Emerson, 1803–82, *Essays*, 'Circles']

13 Only when we turn thoughtfully toward what has already been thought, will we be turned to use for what must still be thought. [Martin Heidegger, 1889–1976, *Identity and Difference*, p. 41]

14 Don't think too much youwl grow hair on the in side of your head. [Russell Hoban, 1925– , *Riddley Walker*, 10]

15 But men at whiles are sober / And think by fits and starts, / And if they think, they fasten / Their hands upon their hearts. [A E Housman, 1859–1936, *Last Poems*, 10]

16 Think no more; 'tis only thinking / Lays lads underground. [A E Housman, 1859–1936, *A Shropshire Lad*, 49]

17 Sooner or later, false thinking brings wrong conduct. [Julian Huxley, 1887–1975, *Essays of a Biologist*, Ch. 7]

18 A great many people think they are thinking when they are merely rearranging their prejudices. [William James, 1842–1910; attr. in Clifton Fadiman, *American Treasury*]

19 Whatever withdraws us from the power of our senses; whatever makes the past, the distant, or the future predominate over the present, advances us in the dignity of thinking beings. [Dr Samuel Johnson, 1709–84, *Journey to the Western Islands*, 'Inch Kenneth']

20 Solitary thinkings; such as dodge / Conception to the very bourne of heaven, / Then leave the naked brain. [John Keats, 1795–1821, *Endymion*, Bk i, 294]

21 The father of the arrow is the thought: how do I expand my reach? [Paul Klee, 1879–1940, *Pedagogical Sketchbook*, IV, 37]

22 A man able to think isn't defeated – even when he is defeated. [Milan Kundera, 1929– , interview with Philip Roth in *The Sunday Times Magazine*, 20 May 1984]

23 Thought is not a trick, or an exercise, or a set of dodges. / Thought is a man in his wholeness wholly attending. [D H Lawrence, 1885–1930, *Thought*]

24 I must not think of thee; and, tired yet strong, / I shun the thought that lurks in all delight – / The thought of thee – and in the blue heaven's height, / And in the sweetest passage of a song. [Alice Meynell, 1847–1922, *Renouncement*]

25 Thoughts pay no duty. [Martin Luther, 1483–1546, motto of *Von weltlicher Obrigkeit*]

26 His thoughts, few that they were, lay silent in the privacy of his head. [Spike Milligan, 1918– , *Puckoon*, Ch. 1]

27 Him that yon soars on golden wing, / Guiding the fiery-wheelèd throne, / The Cherub Contemplation. [John Milton, 1608–74, *Il Penseroso*, 52]

28 A second thought is never an odd thought. [Flann O'Brien, 1911–66, *At Swim-Two-Birds*, Ch. 1]

29 An Englishman thinks seated; a Frenchman, standing; an American, pacing; an Irishman afterward. [Austin O'Malley, 1858–1932, in A Andrews, *Quotations for Speakers and Writers*]

30 Mental reflection is so much more interesting than TV it's a shame more people don't switch over to it. They probably think what they hear is unimportant but it never is. [Robert M Pirsig, 1928– , *Zen and the Art of Motorcycle Maintenance*, Pt III, 17]

31 Thought is only a flash in the midst of a long night. But it is this flash which is everything. [Henri Poincaré, 1854–1912, *The Value of Science*, p. 142]

32 With too much quickness ever to be taught; / With too much thinking to have common thought. [Alexander Pope, 1688–1744, *Moral Essays*, Epistle II, 97]

33 I think that nought is worth a thought, / And I'm a fool for thinking. [W M Praed, 1802–39, *The Chant of the Brazen Head*]

34 Better the world should perish than that I or any other human being should believe a lie ... that is the religion of thought, in whose scorching flames the dross of the world is being burnt away. [Bertrand Russell, 1872–1970, *Mysticism and Logic*, Ch. 10]

35 Many people would sooner die than think. In fact they do. [Bertrand Russell, 1872–1970, epigraph to A Flew, *Thinking about Thinking*]

36 This seems to be the nature of thought that it leads to its own starting point, the timeless home of the mind. [Oliver Sacks, 1933– , *A Leg to Stand On*, final words]

37 My thought is *me*: that is why I can't stop. I exist by what I think ... and I can't prevent myself from thinking. [Jean-Paul Sartre, 1905–80, *Nausea*, 'Monday']

38 Still are the thoughts to memory dear. [Sir Walter Scott, 1771–1832, *Rokeby*, I, 33]

39 But now behold, / In the quick forge and working-house of thought. [William Shakespeare, 1564–1616, *Henry V*, V. Chorus, 22]

40 Yond Cassius has a lean and hungry look; / He thinks too much: such men are dangerous. [*Julius Caesar*, I. ii. 193]

41 He gave man speech, and speech created thought, / Which is the measure of the universe. [P B Shelley, 1792–1822, *Prometheus Unbound*, II, iv, 72]

42 I am gone into the fields / To take what this sweet hour yields; – / Reflection, you may come to-morrow, / Sit by the fireside with Sorrow. [P B Shelley, 1792–1822, *To Jane: The Invitation*]

43 I don't know any business you have to think at all. Thought does not become a young woman. [R B Sheridan, 1751–1816, *The Rivals*, I. ii]

44 Interviews are funny things because I keep having to improvise what I think I think I think. In fact I never give it a thought. [Tom Stoppard, 1937– , interview in *Observer*, 29 July 1990]

45 It has been one of the great errors of our time to think that by thinking about thinking, and then talking about it, we could possibly straighten out and tidy up our minds ... It is all very well to be aware of your awareness, even proud of it, but never try to operate it. You are not up to the job. [Lewis Thomas, 1913–93, *Late Night Thoughts*, 'The Attic of the Brain']

46 Cognition reigns but does not rule. [Paul Valéry, 1871–1945, *Bad Thoughts and Not so Bad*, 'D']

47 *Variation on Descartes:* Sometimes I think; and sometimes I *am*. [Paul Valéry, 1871–1945, *Odds and Ends*, VIII]

48 'Thinkers' are people who re-think; who think that what was thought before was never thought *enough*. [Paul Valéry, 1871–1945, *Suite*, 'Thinkers']

49 Great thoughts come from the heart. [Marquis de Vauvenargues, 1715–47, *Reflexions and Maxims*, 127]

50 [Men] use thought only to justify their wrong-doings, and words only to conceal their thoughts. [Voltaire, 1694–1778, *Dialogue du chapon et de la poularde*]

51 The little girl had the makings of a poet in her who, being told to be sure of her meaning before she spoke, said: 'How can I know what I think till I see what I say?' [Graham Wallas, 1858–1932, *The Art of Thought*, Ch. 4]

52 In order to draw a limit to thinking, we should have to be able to think both sides of this limit. [Ludwig Wittgenstein, 1889–1951, *Tractatus Logico-philosophicus*, Preface]

53 I heard a thousand blended notes / While in a grove I sate reclined, / In that sweet mood when pleasant thoughts / Bring sad thoughts to the mind. [William Wordsworth, 1770–1850, *Lines Written in Early Spring*]

See also INTELLECT, MIND

THRIFT

1 We could have saved sixpence. We have saved fivepence. (*Pause*) But at what cost? [Samuel Beckett, 1906–89, *All That Fall*]

2 O'erjoyed was he to find / That, though on pleasure she was bent, / She had a frugal mind. [William Cowper, 1731–1800, *John Gilpin*, 8]

3 For loss of time, / Although it grieved him sore, / Yet loss of pence, full well he knew, / Would trouble him much more. [William Cowper, 1731–1800, *John Gilpin*, 14]

4 I have enough money to last me the rest of my life unless I buy something. [Jackie Mason, 1931– , *J M's America*]

5 The vice of meanness, condemned in every other country, is in Scotland translated into a virtue called 'thrift'. [David Thomson, 1914–88, *Nairn in Darkness and Light*, p. 70]

See also MEANNESS, MONEY

TIME

1 To choose time is to save time. [Francis Bacon, 1561–1626, *Essays*, 25, 'Of Dispatch']

2 We live in deeds, not years; in thoughts, not breaths; / In feelings, not in figures on a dial. / We should count time by heart-throbs. He most lives / Who thinks most – feels the noblest – acts the best. [P J Bailey, 1816–1902, *Festus*, 5]

3 VLADIMIR: That passed the time.
ESTRAGON: It would have passed in any case.
VLADIMIR: Yes, but not so rapidly. [Samuel Beckett, 1906–89, *Waiting for Godot*, 1]

4 A French five minutes is ten minutes shorter than a Spanish five minutes, but slightly longer than an English five minutes which is usually ten minutes. [Guy Bellamy, 1935– , *Comedy Hotel*, Ch. 12]

5 I see the dragon of years is almost done, / Its claws loosen, its eyes / Crust now with tears, lust and a scale of lies. [John Berryman, 1914–72, *New Year's Eve*]

6 To every thing there is a season, and a time to every purpose under the heaven. A time to be born, and a time to die; a time to plant, and a time to pluck up that which is planted. [Bible, OT, *Ecclesiastes* 3:1]

7 Time, the avenger! unto thee I lift / My hands, and eyes, and heart, and crave of thee a gift. [Lord Byron, 1788–1824, *Childe Harold's Pilgrimage*, IV, 130]

8 Time is what prevents everything from happening at once. [Marvin Cohen, 1931– , in *Guardian*, 21 Apr. 1981]

9 'Dear me,' said Mr Grewgious, peeping in, 'it's like looking down the throat of Old Time.' [Charles Dickens, 1812–70, *Edwin Drood*, Ch. 9]

10 Time is the great physician. [Benjamin Disraeli, 1804–81, *Endymion*, Bk vi, 9]

11 Jesus, who's got time to keep up with the times? [Bob Dylan, 1941– , interview in *The Sunday Times*, 1 July 1984]

12 Time present and time past / Are both perhaps present in time future, / And time future contained in time past. [T S Eliot, 1888–1965, *Four Quartets*, 'Burnt Norton', I]

13 Come, fill the Cup, and in the Fire of Spring / The Winter Garment of Repentance fling: / The Bird of Time has but a little way / To fly – and Lo! the Bird is on the Wing. [Edward Fitzgerald, 1809–83, *The Rubá'iyát of Omar Khayyám*, Edn 1, 7]

14 Remember that time is money. [Benjamin Franklin, 1706–90, *Advice to a Young Tradesman*]

15 Ah, *now*! That odd time – the oddest time of all times; the time it always is ... by the time we've reached the 'w' of 'now' the 'n' is ancient history. [Michael Frayn, 1933– , *Constructions*, 126]

16 *Werd ich zum Augenblicke sagen: / Verweile doch! Du bist so schön!* – / If I say to the moment: 'Stay now! You are so beautiful!' [Johann Wolfgang von Goethe, 1749–1832, *Faust*, Pt I, 'Faust's Study']

17 Time, you old gipsy man, / Will you not stay, / Put up your caravan / Just for one day? [Ralph Hodgson, 1871–1962, *Time, You Old Gipsy Man*]

18 The years as they pass plunder one thing after another. [Horace, 65–8 BC, *Epistles*, II, ii, 55]

19 Some people wear a watch – on the one hand. On the other hand they don't look at it very often. [Garrison Keillor, 1942– , *Lake Wobegon Days*, 'Summer']

20 We must use time as a tool not as a couch. [President John F Kennedy, 1917–63; *Observer*, 'Sayings of the Week', 10 Dec. 1961]

21 In time the savage bull sustains the yoke, / In time all haggard hawks will stoop to lure. / In time small wedges cleave the hardest oak, / In time the flint is pierced with softest shower. [Thomas Kyd, 1557–95?, *The Spanish Tragedy*, I. vi]

22 O time, suspend your flight, and you, happy hours, stay your feet! Let us savour the swift delights of our life's loveliest days! [Alphonse de Lamartine, 1790–1869, *Le Lac*, 21]

23 Nothing puzzles me more than time and space; and yet nothing troubles me less, as I never think about them. [Charles Lamb, 1775–1834, letter to T Manning, 2 Jan. 1810]

24 Gratitude looks to the past and love to the present; fear, avarice, lust and ambition look ahead. [C S Lewis, 1898–1963, *The Screwtape Letters*, 15]

25 For tribal man space was the uncontrollable mystery. For technological man it is time that occupies the same role. [Marshall McLuhan, 1911–80, *The Mechanical Bride*, 'Magic That Changes Mood']

26 Now hast thou but one bare hour to live / And then thou must be damned perpetually! / Stand still, you ever-moving spheres of heaven, / That time may cease and midnight never come. [Christopher Marlowe, 1564–93, *Doctor Faustus*, 1450]

27 Time wounds all heels. [Groucho Marx, 1895–1977, in *Sunday Telegraph*, 21 Aug. 1977]

28 *Tempus edax rerum.* – Time the devourer of things. [Ovid, 43 BC–AD 17, *Metamorphoses*, XXV, 234]

29 The difference between a gun and a tree is a difference of tempo. The tree explodes every spring. [Ezra Pound, 1885–1972, in *Criterion*, July 1937]

30 We have at any rate one advantage over Time and Space. We think *them* whereas it is extremely doubtful whether *they* think *us*! [John Cowper Powys, 1872–1963, *Art of Happiness*, 1929, p. 39]

31 In theory one is aware that the earth revolves, but in practice one does not perceive it, the ground upon which one treads seems not to move, and one can live undisturbed. So it is with Time in one's life. [Marcel Proust, 1871–1922, *Remembrance of Things Past: Within a Budding Grove*, 'Madame Swann at Home']

32 How goes the enemy? [(Said by Mr Ennui, 'the time-killer') Frederic Reynolds, 1764–1841, *The Dramatist*, I. i]

33 Half our life is spent trying to find something to do with the time we have rushed through life trying to save. [Will Rogers, 1879–1935, *Autobiography*, Ch. 15]

34 Never before have we had so little time in which to do so much. [Franklin D Roosevelt, 1882–1945, *Fireside Chat*, radio address, 23 Feb. 1942]

35 Time travels in divers paces with divers persons. I'll tell you who Time ambles withal, who Time trots withal, who Time gallops withal and who he stands still withal. [William

Shakespeare, 1564–1616, *As You Like It*, III. ii. (328)]

36 But thought's the slave of life, and life's time's fool; / And time, that takes survey of all the world, / Must have a stop. [*1 Henry IV*, V. iv. (81)]

37 Spite of cormorant devouring Time. [*Love's Labour's Lost*, I. i. 4]

38 Come what come may, / Time and the hour runs through the roughest day. [*Macbeth*, I. iii. 146]

39 Time hath, my lord, a wallet at his back, / Wherein he puts alms for oblivion, / A great-sized monster of ingratitudes: / Those scraps are good deeds past: which are devoured / As fast as they are made, forgot as soon / As done. [*Troilus and Cressida*, III. iii. 145]

40 Time is like a fashionable host / That slightly shakes his parting guest by the hand, / And with his arms outstretched, as he would fly, / Grasps in the comer: welcome ever smiles, / And farewell goes out sighing. [*Troilus and Cressida*, III. iii. 165]

41 And thus the whirligig of time brings in his revenges. [*Twelfth Night*, V. i. (388)]

42 When I do count the clock that tells the time, / I see the brave day sunk in hideous night; / When I behold the violet past prime, / And sable curls all silvered o'er with white; / When lofty trees I see barren of leaves, / Which erst from heat did canopy the herd, / And summer's green all girded up in sheaves, / Borne on the bier with white and bristly beard. [*Sonnets*, 12]

43 When I have seen by Time's fell hand defaced / The rich-proud cost of outworn buried age. [*Sonnets*, 64]

44 She did not recognize her enemy, / She thought him Dust: / But what is Dust, / Save Time's most lethal weapon, / Her faithful ally and our sneaking foe? [Osbert Sitwell, 1892–1969, *Mrs Southern's Enemy*]

45 Time: That which man is always trying to kill, but which ends in killing him. [Herbert Spencer, 1820–1903, *Definitions*]

46 Time turns the old days to derision, / Our loves into corpses or wives. [A C Swinburne, 1837–1909, *Dolores*, 20]

47 As on this whirligig of Time / We circle with the seasons. [Alfred, Lord Tennyson, 1809–92, *Will Waterproof's Lyrical Monologue*, 8]

48 As if you could kill time without injuring eternity. [H D Thoreau, 1817–62, *Walden*, 'Economy']

49 Time is but the stream I go a-fishing in. [H D Thoreau, 1817–62, *Walden*, 'Where I Lived, and What I Lived For']

50 *Sed fugit interea, fugit inreparabile tempus.* – Meanwhile time is flying – flying never to return. [Virgil, 70–19 BC, *Georgics*, III, 284]

51 Time like an ever-rolling stream / Bears all its sons away; / They fly forgotten as a dream / Dies at the opening day. [Isaac Watts, 1674–1748, *Psalms*, xc]

52 An instant of time, without duration, is an imaginative logical construction. Also each duration of time mirrors in itself all temporal durations. [A N Whitehead, 1861–1947, *Science and the Modern World*, Ch. 4]

53 For time is the longest distance between two places. [Tennessee Williams, 1911–83, *The Glass Menagerie*, vii]

54 The years like great black oxen tread the world, / And God the herdsman goads them on behind, / And I am broken by their passing feet. [W B Yeats, 1865–1939, *The Countess Cathleen*, IV]

55 Time drops in decay, / Like a candle burnt out. [W B Yeats, 1865–1939, *The Moods*]

56 The bell strikes one. We take no note of time / But from its loss. [Edward Young, 1683–1765, *Night Thoughts*, 'Night I', 55]

See also AGE, FUTURE, HISTORY, LIFE IS FLEETING, PAST, PRESENT

TIREDNESS

1 With fingers weary and worn, / With eyelids heavy and red, / A woman sat in unwomanly rags, / Plying her needle and thread – / Stitch! stitch! stitch! [Thomas Hood, 1799–1845, *The Song of the Shirt*]

2 Fatigue makes women talk more and men less. [C S Lewis, 1898–1963, *The Screwtape Letters*, 30]

3 A small man can be just as exhausted as a great man. [Arthur Miller, 1915– , *Death of a Salesman*, I]

4 I am worn to a ravelling. [Beatrix Potter, 1866–1943, *The Tailor of Gloucester*]

5 Weariness / Can snore upon the flint, when resty sloth / Finds the down pillow hard. [William Shakespeare, 1564–1616, *Cymbeline*, III. vi. 33]

6 Weary with toil I haste me to my bed. [*Sonnets*, 27]

7 Ask me no more : thy fate and mine are sealed : / I strove against the stream and all in vain : / Let the great river take me to the main : / No more, dear love, for at a touch I yield ; / Ask me no more. [Alfred, Lord Tennyson, 1809–92, *The Princess*, VII, Song]

See also SLEEPING

TOLERANCE

1 For ye suffer fools gladly, seeing ye yourselves are wise. [Bible, NT, *2 Corinthians* 11:19]

2 There is, however, a limit at which forbearance ceases to be a virtue. [Edmund Burke, 1729–97, *Observations on 'The Present State of the Nation'*]

3 As I know more of mankind I expect less of them, and am ready now to call a man *a good man*, upon easier terms than I was formerly. [Dr Samuel Johnson, 1709–84, in James Boswell, *Life of J*, Sept. 1783]

4 Stevens' mind was so tolerant that he could have attended a lynching every day without becoming critical. [Thorne Smith, 1892–1934, *The Jovial Ghosts*, Ch. 11]

5 Laissez faire and let laissez faire is what I believe in. [James Thurber, 1894–1961, *Men, Women and Dogs*, cartoon caption]

See also INTOLERANCE

TOWN & COUNTRY, see COUNTRY

TRADITION

1 Tradition may be defined as an extension of the franchise. Tradition means giving votes to the most obscure of all classes, our ancestors. It is the democracy of the dead. [G K Chesterton, 1874–1936, *Orthodoxy*, Ch. 4]

2 See this word *tradition* / it'll squeak if you touch it / then break up like a baked turd / into tiny wee bits. [Tom Paulin, 1949– , *The Good Lord Must Persecute Me*]

3 But to my mind, – though I am native here, / And to the manner born, – it is a custom / More honoured in the breach than the observance. [William Shakespeare, 1564–1616, *Hamlet*, I. iv. 14]

4 A renewal is fruitful only when it goes hand in hand with tradition. [Igor Stravinsky, 1882–1971, *Poetics of Music*, Ch. 5]

See also HABIT

TRAGEDY

1 A perfect tragedy is the noblest production of human nature. [Joseph Addison, 1672–1719, *The Spectator*, 39]

2 Tragedy is an imitation of a whole and complete action of some amplitude. . . . Now a whole is that which has a beginning, a middle, and an end. [Aristotle, 384–322BC, *Poetics*, 7]

3 Tragedy is if I cut my finger . . . Comedy is if you walk into an open sewer and die. [Mel Brooks, 1926– , in Kenneth Tynan, *Show People*]

4 All tragedies are finished by a death, / All comedies are ended by a marriage. [Lord Byron, 1788–1824, *Don Juan*, III, 9]

5 Tragedie is to seyn a certeyn storie, / As olde bokes maken us memorie, / Of him that stood in greet prosperitee / And is y-fallen out of heigh degree / Into miserie, and endeth wrecchedly. [Geoffrey Chaucer, 1340?–1400, *Canterbury Tales*, 'The Monk's Prologue', 85]

6 The actual tragedies of life bear no relation to one's preconceived ideas. In the event, one is always bewildered by their simplicity, their grandeur of design, and by that element of the bizarre which seems inherent in them. [Jean Cocteau, 1889–1963, *Les Enfants terribles*]

7 Of course in nature the only end is death, but death hardly ever happens when people are at their best. That is why we like tragedies. They show men ending energetically with their wits about them and deserving to do it. [Alasdair Gray, 1934– , *Lanark*, Bk 1, Interlude]

8 I think avoiding humiliation is the core of tragedy and comedy. [John Guare, 1938– , in *Independent*, 17 Oct. 1988]

9 We participate in a tragedy; at a comedy we only look. [Aldous Huxley, 1894–1963, *The Devils of Loudun*, Ch. 11]

10 Willy Loman never made a lot of money. His name was never in the paper. He's not the finest character that ever lived. But he's a human being, and a terrible thing is happening to him. So attention must be paid. [Arthur Miller, 1915– , *Death of a Salesman*, I]

11 Sometime let gorgeous Tragedy / In sceptred pall come sweeping by, / Presenting Thebes, or Pelops' line, / Or the tale of Troy divine. [John Milton, 1608–74, *Il Penseroso*, 97]

12 You're familiar with the tragedies of antiquity, are you? The great homicidal classics? [Tom Stoppard, 1937– , *Rosencrantz and Guildenstern are Dead*, I]

13 The bad end unhappily, the good unluckily. That is what tragedy means. [Tom Stoppard, 1937– , *Rosencrantz and Guildenstern are Dead*, II]

14 *Il faut tout prendre au sérieux, mais rien au tragique.* – Everything must be taken seriously, nothing tragically. [Adolphe Thiers, 1797–1877, speech in National Assembly, 24 May 1873]

15 And killing time is perhaps the essence of comedy, just as the essence of tragedy is killing eternity. [Miguel de Unamuno, 1864–1937, *San Manuel Bueno*, Prologue]

16 The world is a comedy to those that think, a tragedy to those that feel. [Horace Walpole, 1717–97, letter to the Countess of Upper Ossory, 16 Aug. 1776]

17 In this world there are only two tragedies. One is not getting what one wants, and the other is getting it. [Oscar Wilde, 1854–1900, *Lady Windermere's Fan*, III]

See also COMEDY

TRAINS, see RAILWAYS

TRANSLATION

1 Translation is at best an echo. [George Borrow, 1803–81, *Lavengro*, 25]

2 Translations (like wives) are seldom faithful if they are in the least attractive. [Roy Campbell, 1902–57, in *Poetry Review*, June/July 1949]

3 Some hold translations not unlike to be / The wrong side of a Turkish tapestry. [James Howell, 1594?–1666, *Familiar Letters*, Bk i, 6]

4 It is difficult to decide whether translators are heroes or fools. They must surely know that the Afrikaans for 'Hamlet, I am thy father's ghost' sounds something like 'Omlet, ek is de papa spook.' [Paul Jennings, 1918–89; in Stephen Potter, *The Sense of Humour*, Ch. 3]

TRAVEL

1 Travel, in the younger sort, is a part of education; in the elder, a part of experience. [Francis Bacon, 1561–1626, *Essays*, 18, 'Of Travel']

2 In America there are two classes of travel – first class, and with children. [Robert Benchley, 1889–1945, *Pluck and Luck*]

3 I often think of making a geographical change but in my experience it just does not work. If you went to the South Pole the first person you would meet there would be yourself. [Jeffrey Bernard, 1932–97, *More Low Life*, 'Dead End']

4 Wouldn't it be better to stay peacefully at home, and not roam about the world seeking better bread than is made of wheat, never considering that many go for wool and come back shorn? [Miguel Cervantes, 1547–1616, *Don Quixote*, Pt I, Ch. 7]

5 One voyage to India is enough; the others are merely repletion. [Winston Churchill, 1874–1965, *My Early Life*, Ch. 10]

6 But why, oh why, do the wrong people travel, / When the right people stay at home? [Noël Coward, 1899–1973, *Sail Away*, 'Why Do . . . ?']

7 Travelling is almost like talking with those of other centuries. [René Descartes, 1596–1650, *Discourse on Method*, 1]

8 One of the pleasantest things in the world is going a journey; but I like to go by myself. [William Hazlitt, 1778–1830, *On Going a Journey*]

9 They change their skies but not their souls who run across the sea. [Horace, 65–8 BC, *Epistles*, I, xi, 27]

10 I prefer a bike to a horse. The brakes are more easily checked. [Lambert Jeffries; in *Apt and Amusing Quotations*, ed. G F Lamb, 'Horse']

11 Much have I travelled in the realms of gold, / And many goodly states and kingdoms seen; / Round many western islands have I been / Which bards in fealty to Apollo hold. [John Keats, 1795–1821, sonnet: *On First Looking into Chapman's Homer*]

12 He travels the fastest who travels alone. [Rudyard Kipling, 1865–1936, *The Winners*]

13 For sheer pleasure few methods of progression can compare with the perambulator. The motion is agreeable, the range of vision extensive, and one has always before one's eyes the rewarding spectacle of a grown-up maintaining prolonged physical exertion. [Osbert Lancaster, 1908–86, in *The Times Literary Supplement*, 12 June 1981]

14 Whenever I prepare for a journey I prepare as though for death. Should I never return, all is in order. This is what life has taught me. [Katherine Mansfield, 1888–1923, *Journal*, 1922]

15 Writing about travels is nearly always tedious, travelling being, like war and fornication, exciting but not interesting. [Malcolm Muggeridge, 1903–90, review of *Diaries of Evelyn Waugh*, in *Observer*, 5 Sept. 1976]

16 The trouble with many travellers is that they take themselves along. [Joseph Prescott, 1913– , *Aphorisms and Other Observations*, 'Travel']

17 Travelling broadens the mind ... [No] it narrows it. Jesus never travelled; not more than a hundred miles; Michelangelo, Rembrandt, Milton: they are people who made a journey of scarcely any consequence at all and subsequently never travelled further. Travel is for people without imagination: dullards, clods; those who need to animate the landscape, otherwise they see nothing there at all. [Ralph Richardson, 1902–83, in Gary O'Connor, *R R: An Actor's Life*, Pt II, Ch. 20]

18 In the middle ages people were tourists because of their religion, whereas now they are tourists because tourism is their religion. [Robert Runcie, 1921– ; *Observer*, 'Sayings of the Week', 11 Dec. 1988]

19 A man should know something of his own country, too, before he goes abroad. [Laurence Sterne, 1713–68, *Tristram Shandy*, Bk vii, Ch. 2]

20 Give to me the life I love, / Let the lave go by me, / Give the jolly heaven above / And the byway nigh me. [Robert Louis Stevenson, 1850–94, *Songs of Travel*, 1, 'The Vagabond']

21 For my part, I travel not to go anywhere, but to go. I travel for travel's sake. The great affair is to move. [Robert Louis Stevenson, 1850–94, *Travels with a Donkey*, 'Cheylard and Luc']

22 There's nothing under Heaven so blue / That's fairly worth the travelling to. [Robert Louis Stevenson, 1850–94, *Underwoods*, I, 2, 'A Song of the Road']

23 To travel hopefully is a better thing than to arrive, and the true success is to labour. [Robert Louis Stevenson, 1850–94, *Virginibus Puerisque*, 'El Dorado']

24 I always love to begin a journey on Sundays, because I shall have the prayers of the church, to preserve all that travel by land, or by water. [Jonathan Swift, 1677–1745, *Polite Conversation*, Dialogue 2]

25 Extensive travelling induces a feeling of encapsulation, and travel, so broadening at first, contracts the mind. [Paul Theroux, 1941– , *The Great Railway Bazaar*, Ch. 21]

26 Unanticipated invitations to travel are dancing lessons from God. [Kurt Vonnegut, 1922– , quoted by David Mamet in interview in *Guardian*, 16 Feb. 1989]

See also CARS, RAILWAYS

TREACHERY & TREASON

1 During his office, treason was no crime. / The sons of Belial had a glorious time. [John Dryden, 1631–1700, *Absalom and Achitophel*, Pt I, 597]

2 T' abhor the makers, and their laws approve, / Is to hate traitors, and the treason love. [John Dryden, 1631–1700, *The Hind and the Panther*, 1, 706]

3 A desperate disease requires a dangerous remedy. [Guy Fawkes, 1570–1606, of Gunpowder Plot, 5 Nov. 1605, echoing Hippocrates]

4 Treason doth never prosper: what's the reason? / For if it prosper, none dare call it treason. [John Harington, 1561–1612, *Epigrams*, 'Of Treason']

5 There's such divinity doth hedge a king, / That treason can but peep to what it would. [William Shakespeare, 1564–1616, *Hamlet*, IV. v. (123)]

6 *Et tu, Brute!* [*Julius Caesar*, III. i. 77]

7 Thou art a traitor: / Off with his head! [*Richard III*, III. iv. 74]

See also LOYALTY, PATRIOTISM

TREES

1 When sycamore leaves wer a spreadèn, / Green-ruddy, in hedges, / Bezide the red doust o' the ridges, / A-dried at Woak Hill. [William Barnes, 1801–86, *Woak Hill*]

2 When the green woods laugh with the voice of joy. [William Blake, 1757–1827, *Songs of Innocence*, 'Laughing Song']

3 Your ghost will walk, you lover of trees / (If our loves remain) / In an English lane, / By a cornfield-side a-flutter with poppies. [Robert Browning, 1812–89, *De Gustibus –*]

4 Spare, woodman, spare the beechen tree. [Thomas Campbell, 1777–1844, *The Beech-Tree's Petition*]

5 I like trees because they seem more resigned to the way they have to live than other things do. [Willa Cather, 1873–1947, *O Pioneers!*, Pt 2, Ch. 8]

6 The one red leaf, the last of its clan, / That dances as often as dance it can, / Hanging so light, and hanging so high, / On the topmost twig that looks up at the sky. [Samuel Taylor Coleridge, 1772–1834, *Christabel*, Pt 1, 49]

7 Hail, old patrician trees, so great and good! [Abraham Cowley, 1618–67, *Of Solitude*]

8 The poplars are felled, farewell to the shade, / And the whispering sound of the cool colonnade! [William Cowper, 1731–1800, *The Poplar Field*]

9 For pines are gossip pines the wide world through. [James Elroy Flecker, 1884–1915, *Brumana*]

10 Fair pledges of a fruitful tree, / Why do ye fall so fast? [Robert Herrick, 1591–1674, *Hesperides*, 'Blossoms']

11 Loveliest of trees, the cherry now / Is hung with bloom along the bough. [A E Housman, 1859–1936, *A Shropshire Lad*, 2]

12 In a drear-nighted December, / Too happy, happy tree, / Thy branches ne'er remember / Their green felicity. [John Keats, 1795–1821, *Stanzas in a Drear-nighted December*]

13 I think that I shall never see / A poem lovely as a tree. [Joyce Kilmer, 1888–1918, *Trees*]

14 Of all the trees that grow so fair, / Old England to adorn, / Greater are none beneath the Sun, / Than Oak and Ash and Thorn. [Rudyard Kipling, 1865–1936, *A Tree Song*]

15 As beautiful as woman's blush, – / As evanescent too. [Letitia Landon, 1802–38, *Apple Blossoms*]

16 Fig-tree, for a long time now I have found meaning in the way you almost entirely overleap the stage of blossom and thrust your pure mystery, unsung, into the early set fruit. [Rainer Maria Rilke, 1875–1926, *Duino Elegies*, 6]

17 *O Tannenbaum, O Tannenbaum, / Wie grün sind deine Blätter*. – O pine-tree, O pine-tree, / How green are your leaves! [Louis Schneider, 1805–78, *Der Kurmärker und die Picarde*. Modernization of lines from a folk-song, previously rendered by August Zarnack (1777–1827): '*Wie treu sind deine Blätter*']

18 There is a willow grows aslant a brook, / That shows his hoar leaves in the glassy stream. [William Shakespeare, 1564–1616, *Hamlet*, IV. vii. (167)]

19 I frequently tramped eight or ten miles through the deepest snow to keep an appointment with a beech-tree, or a yellow birch, or an old acquaintance among the pines. [H D Thoreau, 1817–62, *Walden*, 'Winter Visitors']

See also FLOWERS, WOODS

TRIVIALITY

1 My own idear is that these things are as piffle before the wind. [Daisy Ashford, 1881–1972, *The Young Visiters*, 5]

2 Little things affect little minds. [Benjamin Disraeli, 1804–81, *Sybil*, Bk iii, Ch. 2]

3 You know my method. It is founded upon the observance of trifles. [Arthur Conan Doyle, 1859–1930, *The Adventures of Sherlock Holmes*, 'The Boscombe Valley Mystery']

4 It has long been an axiom of mine that the little things are infinitely the most important. [Arthur Conan Doyle, 1859–1930, *The Adventures of Sherlock Holmes*, 'A Case of Identity']

5 It might be termed the Law of Triviality. Briefly stated, it means that the time spent on any item of the agenda will be in inverse proportion to the sum involved. [C Northcote Parkinson, 1909–93, *Parkinson's Law*, Ch. 3]

6 The man who is denied the opportunity of taking decisions of importance begins to regard as important the decisions he is allowed to take.

He becomes fussy about filing, keen on seeing that pencils are sharpened, eager to ensure that the windows are open (or shut) and apt to use two or three different-coloured inks. [C Northcote Parkinson, 1909–93, *Parkinson's Law*, Ch. 10]

7 What dire offence from am'rous causes springs, / What mighty contests rise from trivial things. [Alexander Pope, 1688–1744, *The Rape of the Lock*, I, 1]

8 It's not catastrophes, murders, deaths, diseases, that age and kill us; it's the way people look and laugh, and run up the steps of omnibuses. [Virginia Woolf, 1882–1941, *Jacob's Room*, Ch. 6]

9 Let a man get up and say, 'Behold, this is the truth', and instantly I perceive a sandy cat filching a piece of fish in the background. Look, you have forgotten the cat, I say. [Virginia Woolf, 1882–1941, *The Waves*]

See also ORDINARY

TRUST

1 Never trust men with short legs. Brains too near their bottoms. [Noël Coward, 1899–1973; in Nancy McPhee, *Book of Insults*]

2 Thrust ivrybody, but cut th' ca-ards. [Finley Peter Dunne, 1867–1936, *Mr Dooley's Opinions*, 'Casual Observations']

3 Never trust the man who hath reason to suspect that you know he hath injured you. [Henry Fielding, 1707–54, *Jonathan Wild*, Bk iii, Ch. 4]

4 Man who trust woman walk on duckweed over pond. [Alan Ladd, 1913–64, in film *Calcutta*, scripted by Seton I Miller]

5 After all, one never trusts anyone that one has deceived. [Jonathan Lynn, 1943– , and Antony Jay, 1930– , *Yes Prime Minister*, Vol. 1, 'The Smokescreen']

6 There are three kinds of man you must never trust: a man who hunts south of the Thames, a man who has soup for lunch, and a man who waxes his moustache. [James Richards, 1907–92, quoting his father in *Memoirs of an Unjust Fella*]

7 Trust thou thy Love: if she be proud, is she not sweet? / Trust thou thy Love: if she be mute, is she not pure? / Lay thou thy soul full in her hands, low at her feet; – / Fail, sun and breath! – Yet for thy peace, she shall endure. [John Ruskin, 1819–1900, *Trust Thou Thy Love*]

8 Trust none; / For oaths are straws, men's faiths are wafer-cakes, / And hold-fast is the only dog, my duck. [William Shakespeare, 1564–1616, *Henry V*, II. iii. 53]

9 I wonder men dare trust themselves with men. [*Timon of Athens*, I. ii. (45)]

10 *Experto credite*. – Trust one who has experienced it. [Virgil, 70–19 BC, *Aeneid*, XI, 283]

See also DOUBT, FAITHS

TRUTH

1 The truth that makes men free is for the most part the truth which men prefer not to hear. [Herbert Agar, 1897–1980, *A Time for Greatness*, Ch. 7]

2 'But the Emperor has nothing on at all!' said a little child. [Hans Christian Andersen, 1805–75, *The Emperor's New Clothes*]

3 *Se non è vero, è molto ben trovato*. – If it is not true, it is a very happy invention. [anon. common Italian saying, quoted by Giordano Bruno, 1585]

4 Plato is dear to me, but dearer still is truth. [Aristotle, 384–322 BC, attr.]

5 It contains a misleading impression, not a lie. It was being economical with the truth. [Sir Robert Armstrong, 1927– , of his evidence at the Peter Wright–MI5 trial in Melbourne; *Observer*, 'Sayings of the Year', 28 Dec. 1986. The phrase dates back to Edmund Burke *Letters on a Regicide Peace*]; see 64

6 What is truth? said jesting Pilate; and would not stay for an answer. [Francis Bacon, 1561–1626, *Essays*, 1, 'Of Truth']

7 What I claim is to live to the full the contradiction of my time, which may well make sarcasm the condition of truth. [Roland Barthes, 1915–80, *Mythologies*, Preface]

8 A man may say, 'From now on I'm going to speak the truth.' But the truth hears him and runs away and hides before he's even done speaking. [Saul Bellow, 1915– , *Herzog*, p. 271]

9 Women are strongest: but above all things Truth beareth away the victory. [Bible, Apocrypha, *1 Esdras* 13:12]

10 The truth shall make you free. [Bible, NT, *St John* 8:32]

11 Pilate saith unto him, What is truth? [Bible, NT, *St John* 18:38]

12 A truth that's told with bad intent / Beats all the lies you can invent. [William Blake, 1757–1827, *Auguries of Innocence*]

13 Truth can never be told so as to be understood, and not be believed. [William Blake, 1757–1827, *The Marriage of Heaven and Hell*, 'Proverbs of Hell']

14 Two sorts of truth: trivialities, where opposites are obviously absurd, and profound truths, recognized by the fact that the opposite is also a profound truth. [Niels Bohr, 1885–1962, in *N B: His Life and Work*, ed. S Rozental, p. 328]

15 Truth lies within a little and certain compass, but error is immense. [Henry St John, Viscount Bolingbroke, 1678–1751, *Reflections upon Exile*]

16 Truth that peeps / Over the glasses' edge when dinner's done, / And body gets its sop and holds its noise / And leaves soul free a little. [Robert Browning, 1812–89, *Bishop Blougram's Apology*, 17]

17 He said true things, but called them by wrong names. [Robert Browning, 1812–89, *Bishop Blougram's Apology*, 995]

18 I would give my life for a man who is looking for the truth. But I would gladly kill a man who thinks that he has found the truth. [Luis Buñuel, 1900–1983, quoted by Carlos Fuentes in *Guardian*, 24 Feb. 1989]

19 Agree to a short armistice with truth. [Lord Byron, 1788–1824, *Don Juan*, III, 83]

20 'Tis strange – but true; for truth is always strange; / Stranger than fiction. [Lord Byron, 1788–1824, *Don Juan*, XIV, 101]

21 What I tell you three times is true. [Lewis Carroll, 1832–98, *The Hunting of the Snark*, Fit 1]

22 Trouthe is the hyeste thing that man may kepe. [Geoffrey Chaucer, 1340?–1400, *Canterbury Tales*, 'The Franklin's Tale', 751]

23 And diff'ring judgements serve but to declare, / That truth lies somewhere, if we knew but where. [William Cowper, 1731–1800, *Hope*, 423]

24 'It is,' says Chadband, 'the ray of rays, the sun of suns, the moon of moons, the star of stars. It is the light of Terewth.' [Charles Dickens, 1812–70, *Bleak House*, Ch. 25]

25 'It was as true,' said Mr Barkis, . . . as taxes is. And nothing's truer than them.' [Charles Dickens, 1812–70, *David Copperfield*, Ch. 21]

26 I wonder if it is really possible to be absolutely truthful when you are alone. Truth, like time, is an idea arising from, and dependent upon, human intercourse. What is the truth about a mountain in Africa that has no name and not even a footpath across it? [Isak Dinesen, 1885–1962, *Seven Gothic Tales*, 'The Roads Round Pisa']

27 It is an old maxim of mine that when you have excluded the impossible, whatever remains, however improbable, must be the truth. [Arthur Conan Doyle, 1859–1930, *The Adventures of Sherlock Holmes*, 'The Beryl Coronet']

28 Errors, like straws, upon the surface flow; / He who would search for pearls must dive below. [John Dryden, 1631–1700, *All for Love*, Prologue, 25]

29 For truth has such a face and such a mien / As to be loved needs only to be seen. [John Dryden, 1631–1700, *The Hind and the Panther*, I, 33]

30 A man is to be cheated into passion, but to be reasoned into truth. [John Dryden, 1631–1700, preface to *Religio Laici*]

31 Saddest tale told on land or sea / Is the tale they told / When they told the truth on me. [Duke Ellington, 1899–1974, *Saddest Tale*]

32 An exaggeration is a truth that has lost its temper. [Kahlil Gibran, 1883–1931, *Sand and Foam*]

33 It's easy to make a man confess the lies he tells to himself; it's far harder to make him confess the truth. [Geoffrey Household, 1900–1988, *Rogue Male*]

34 Irrationally held truths may be more harmful than reasoned errors. [T H Huxley, 1825–95, *Collected Essays*, xii, 'The Coming of Age of the Origin of Species']

35 It is the customary fate of new truths to begin as heresies and to end as superstitions. [T H Huxley, 1825–95, *Collected Essays*, xii, 'The Coming of Age of the Origin of Species']

36 The first casualty when war comes is truth.

[Hiram Johnson, 1866–1945, speech in US Senate, 1918. Can be traced back to Aeschylus]

37 'Beauty is truth, truth beauty,' – That is all / Ye know on earth, and all ye need to know. [John Keats, 1795–1821, *Ode on a Grecian Urn*, 5]

38 I have never yet been able to perceive how anything can be known for truth by consecutive reasoning – and yet it must be. [John Keats, 1795–1821, letter to Benjamin Bailey, 22 Nov. 1817]

39 But it's the truth even if it didn't happen. [Ken Kesey, 1935– , *One Flew over the Cuckoo's Nest*, Pt I]

40 Two half-truths do not make a truth, and two half-cultures do not make a culture. [Arthur Koestler, 1905–83 (on the 'Two Cultures'), *The Ghost in the Machine*, Preface]; see 68

41 I maintain that Truth is a pathless land, and you cannot approach it by any path whatsoever, by any religion, by any sect. [J Krishnamurti, 1895–1986 (speech in Holland, 3 Aug. 1929), in *Guardian* at his death, 19 Feb. 1986]

42 Absolute truth belongs to Thee alone. [G E Lessing, 1729–81, *Wolfenbüttler Fragmente*]

43 It is notorious that we speak no more than half-truths in our ordinary conversation, and even a soliloquy is likely to be affected by the apprehension that walls have ears. [Eric Linklater, 1889–1974, *Juan in America*, II, 4]

44 There are no new truths, but only truths that have not been recognized by those who have perceived them without noticing. A truth is something that everyone can be shown to know and to have known, as people say, all along. [Mary McCarthy, 1912–89, *On the Contrary*, 'The Vita Activa']

45 A great truth is a truth whose opposite is also a great truth. [Thomas Mann, 1875–1955, *Essay on Freud*]

46 In the long run a harmful truth is better than a useful lie. [Thomas Mann, 1875–1955 (quoted by Arthur Koestler on leaving the Communist Party), in Koestler's obituary in *Guardian*, 4 Mar. 1983]

47 Exactitude is not truth. [Henri Matisse, 1869–1954 (essay title), in *Matisse on Art*, ed. J D Flam]

48 The man who boasts that he habitually tells the truth is simply a man with no respect for it. It is not a thing to be thrown about loosely, like small change; it is something to be cherished and hoarded, and disbursed only when absolutely necessary. [H L Mencken, 1880–1956, *Prejudices*, Third Series, 'Types of Men', 10]

49 Let us begin by committing ourselves to the truth, to see it like it is and to tell it like it is, to find the truth, to speak the truth and live with the truth. That's what we'll do. [President Richard Nixon, 1913–94, speech accepting Republican nomination in presidential election, Miami, 8 Aug. 1968]

50 Truths that become old become decrepit and unreliable; sometimes they may be kept going artificially for a certain time, but there is no life in them ... Ideas can be too old. [P D Ouspensky, 1878–1947, *A New Model of the Universe*, Preface to 2nd edn]

51 For want of me the world's course will not fail; / When all its work is done, the lie shall rot; / The truth is great, and shall prevail, / When none cares whether it prevail or not. [Coventry Patmore, 1823–96, *The Unknown Eros*, Bk i, 12, 'Magna est Veritas']

52 The truth being rather a current which flows from what people say to us, and which we pick up, invisible though it is, than the actual thing they have said. [Marcel Proust, 1871–1922, *Remembrance of Things Past: Cities of the Plain*, Pt II, Ch. 3]

53 The truth, which is a standard for the naturalist, for the poet is only a stimulus. [George Santayana, 1863–1952, *Soliloquies in England*, 'Ideas']

54 I was ready to admit – if only I had been old enough to understand them – all the right-wing truths which an old left-wing man taught me through his actions: that Truth and Myth are one and the same thing, that you have to simulate passion to feel it and that man is a creature of ceremony. [Jean-Paul Sartre, 1905–80, *Words*, Pt 1]

55 Like all dreamers, I mistook disenchantment for truth. [Jean-Paul Sartre, 1905–80, *Words*, Pt 2]

56 O! while you live, tell truth, and shame the devil! [William Shakespeare, 1564–1616, *1 Henry IV*, III. I. (62)]

57 And simple truth miscalled simplicity, / And captive good attending captain ill. [*Sonnets*, 66]

58 All great truths begin as blasphemies. [George Bernard Shaw, 1856–1950, *Annajanska*]

59 When truth is discovered by someone else, it loses something of its attractiveness. [Alexander Solzhenitsyn, 1918– , *Candle in the Wind*, iii]

60 I would make a proposition to my Republican friends ... That if they will stop telling lies about the Democrats, we will stop telling the truth about them. [Adlai Stevenson, 1900–1965, campaign remark, Fresno, California, 10 Sept.; in *Respectfully Quoted*, ed. Suzy Platt. Described as a favourite line of Stevenson, it in fact reverses original of Senator Chauncey Depew]

61 It's deadly commonplace, but, after all, the commonplaces are the great poetic truths. [Robert Louis Stevenson, 1850–94, *Weir of Hermiston*, Ch. 6]

62 A truth is always a compound of two half-truths, and you never reach it, because there is always something more to say. [Tom Stoppard, 1937– (TV interview), in *Guardian*, 21 Mar. 1973]

63 It takes two to speak the truth,– one to speak, and another to hear. [H D Thoreau, 1817–62, *A Week on the Concord and Merrimack Rivers*, 'Wednesday']

64 Truth is the most valuable thing we have. Let us economize it. [Mark Twain, 1835–1910, *Following the Equator*, Ch. 7]; see 5

65 Truth is not victorious; truth is simply what is left when everything else has gone to pot. [Ludvík Vaculík, 1926– , *A Cup of Coffee with My Interrogator*]

66 Truth is naked; but under the skin lies the anatomy. [Paul Valéry, *Bad Thoughts and Not so Bad*, 'M']

67 It is more important that a proposition be interesting than that it be true. [A N Whitehead, 1861–1947, *Adventures of Ideas*, Ch. 16]

68 There are no whole truths; all truths are half-truths. It is trying to treat them as whole truths that plays the devil. [A N Whitehead, 1861–1947, *Dialogues*, Prologue]; see 40

69 Truth is rarely pure, and never simple. [Oscar Wilde, 1854–1900, *The Importance of Being Earnest*, I]

70 It is a terrible thing for a man to find out suddenly that all his life he has been speaking nothing but the truth. [Oscar Wilde, 1854–1900, *The Importance of Being Earnest*, III]

71 Let a man get up and say, 'Behold, this is the truth', and instantly I perceive a sandy cat filching a piece of fish in the background. Look, you have forgotten the cat, I say. [Virginia Woolf, 1882–1941, *The Waves*]

72 I believe that in the end the truth will conquer. [John Wycliffe, *c.*1320–84, to the Duke of Lancaster, 1381; quoted in J R Green, *Short History of the English People*]

73 When I try to put all into a phrase I say 'Man can embody truth, but he cannot know it.' [W B Yeats, 1865–1939, Letter, 4 Jan. 1939, just before his death]

74 Truth is on the march; nothing will stop it now. [Émile Zola, 1840–1902, *La Vérité en marche*, article on the Dreyfus case]

See also FAULTS, LIES, MISTAKES

TWENTIETH CENTURY

1 Though the Jazz Age continued, it became less and less of an affair of youth. The sequel was like a children's party taken over by the elders. [F Scott Fitzgerald, 1896–1940, *The Crack-up*, 'Echoes of the Jazz Age']

2 In the nineteenth century the problem was that God is dead; in the twentieth century the problem is that man is dead. [Erich Fromm, 1900–1980, *The Sane Society*, Ch. 9]

3 The twentieth century is only the nineteenth speaking with a slight American accent. [Philip Guedalla, 1889–1944, attr.]

4 Nothing happened in the sixties except that we all dressed up. [John Lennon, 1940–80; in *Wit and Wisdom of Rock and Roll*, ed. Maxim Jakubowski]

5 If the nineteenth century was the age of the editorial chair, ours is the century of the psychiatrist's couch. [Marshall McLuhan, 1911–80, *Understanding Media*, Introduction]

6 The horror of the Twentieth Century was the size of each event, and the paucity of the reverberation. [Norman Mailer, 1923– , *Fire on the Moon*, Pt 1, Ch. 2]

See also MODERN AGE, NINETEENTH CENTURY

TYRANTS & TYRANNY

1 Under conditions of tyranny, it is far easier to act than to think. [Hannah Arendt, 1906–75, in W H Auden, *A Certain World*, 'Tyranny']

2 He knew human folly like the back of his hand, / And was greatly interested in armies and fleets; / When he laughed, respectable senators burst with laughter, / And when he cried the little children died in the streets. [W H Auden, 1907–73, *Epitaph on a Tyrant*]

3 Everyone knows there is no fineness or accuracy of suppression; if you hold down one thing you hold down the adjoining. [Saul Bellow, 1915– , *The Adventures of Augie March*, 6]

4 What mean ye that ye beat my people to pieces, and grind the faces of the poor? [Bible, OT, *Isaiah* 3:15]

5 The most potent weapon in the hands of the oppressor is the mind of the oppressed. [Steve Biko, 1946–77, address to Cape Town Conference, 1971]

6 Lenin was literate, Stalin was literate, so was Hitler. As for Mao Zedong, he even wrote verse. What all these men had in common, though, was that their hit list was longer than their reading list. [Joseph Brodsky, 1940–96, *On Grief and Reason*, lecture, 1987]

7 I wish the Roman people had only one neck! [Caligula, 12–41, in Suetonius, *Lives of the Caesars*, 'Caligula', 30]

8 Tyranny sets up its own echo-chamber; a void where confused signals buzz about at random; where a murmur or innuendo causes panic: so, in the end, the machinery is more likely to vanish, not with war or revolution, but with a puff, or the voice of falling leaves. [Bruce Chatwin, 1940–89, *Utz*, p. 120]

9 Dictators ride to and fro upon tigers which they dare not dismount. And the tigers are getting hungry. [Winston Churchill, 1874–1965, *While England Slept*]

10 All men would be tyrants if they could. [Daniel Defoe, 1661?–1731, *The Kentish Petition*, addenda, 11]

11 A man may build himself a throne of bayonets, but he cannot sit on it. [W R Inge, 1860–1954, *The Philosophy of Plotinus*, Lect. 22]; see 18

12 The cry of the Little Peoples goes up to God in vain, / For the world is given over to the cruel sons of Cain. [Richard Le Gallienne, 1866–1947, *The Cry of the Little Peoples*]

13 But whenever there's a snatch of talk / it turns to the Kremlin mountaineer, / the ten thick worms his fingers, / his words like measures of weight, / the huge laughing cockroaches on his top lip, / The glitter of his boot-rims. [Osip Mandelstam, 1891–1938, *Poems*, No. 286, 'Stalin Epigram']

14 Those who harm simple / people and who laugh at their / injuries will not be safe. / For the poet remembers. [Czeslaw Milosz, 1911– , inscription at the martyrs' monument, Gdansk shipyard, Poland]

15 With necessity, / The tyrant's plea, excused his devilish deeds. [John Milton, 1608–74, *Paradise Lost*, Bk iv, 393]

16 In Germany, the Nazis came for the Communists and I didn't speak up because I was not a Communist. Then they came for the Jews and I didn't speak up because I was not a Jew. Then they came for the trade unionists and I didn't speak up because I was not a trade unionist. Then they came for the Catholics and I was a Protestant so I didn't speak up. Then they came for me . . . By that time there was no one to speak up for anyone. [Martin Niemöller, 1892–1984. Attr. in *Congressional Record*, 14 Oct. 1968]

17 O! it is excellent / To have a giant's strength, but it is tyrannous / To use it like a giant. [William Shakespeare, 1564–1616, *Measure for Measure*, II. ii. 107]

18 You can make a throne from bayonets, but you can't sit on it for long. [Boris Yeltsin, 1931– (from the top of a tank during the coup against Gorbachev); *Independent*, 'Quote Unquote', 24 Aug. 1991]; see 11

See also FASCISM

U

UGLINESS

1 It can hardly be a coincidence that no language on Earth has ever produced the expression 'as pretty as an airport'. [Douglas Adams, 1952– , *The Long Dark Tea-time of the Soul*, opening words]

2 A woman who cannot be ugly is not beautiful. [Karl Kraus, 1874–1936, *Half-truths and One-and-a-half Truths*, 'Not for Women']

3 It is for homely features to keep home, / They had their name thence; coarse complexions / And cheeks of sorry grain will serve to ply / The sampler, and to tease the housewife's wool. / What need a vermeil-tinctured lip for that, / Love-darting eyes, or tresses like the morn? [John Milton, 1608–74, *Comus*, 748]

4 All things uncomely and broken, all things worn out and old, / The cry of a child by the roadway, the creak of a lumbering cart, / The heavy steps of the ploughman, splashing the wintry mould, / Are wronging your image that blossoms a rose in the deeps of my heart. [W B Yeats, 1865–1939, *The Lover Tells of the Rose in His Heart*]

See also BEAUTY

THE UNCONSCIOUS

1 Every man contains within himself a ghost continent – a place circled as warily as Antarctica was circled two hundred years ago by Captain James Cook. [Loren Eiseley, 1907–77, *The Unexpected Universe*, Ch. 1]

2 We are like icebergs in the ocean: one-eighth part consciousness and the rest submerged beneath the surface of articulate apprehension. [William Gerhardie, 1895–1977, *The Polyglots*, Ch. 14]

3 The deep well of unconscious cerebration. [Henry James, 1843–1916, *The American*, Preface]

4 A more or less superficial layer of the unconscious is undoubtedly personal. I call it the personal unconscious. But this personal unconscious rests upon a deeper layer, which does not derive from personal experience and is not a personal acquisition but is inborn. The deeper layer I call the collective unconscious. [C G Jung, 1875–1961, *Archetypes and the Collective Unconscious*]

5 It'll do him good to lie there unconscious for a bit. Give his brain a rest. [N F Simpson, 1919– , *One-way Pendulum*, I]

See also DREAMS, ILLNESS, MIND, PSYCHIATRY

UNDERSTANDING

1 I shall light a candle of understanding in thine heart, which shall not be put out. [Bible, Apocrypha, *2 Esdras* 14:25 (quoted by Bishop Latimer at the stake)]

2 If ye had not plowed with my heifer, ye had not found out my riddle. [Bible, OT, *Judges* 14:18]

3 She understood, as women often do more easily than men, that the declared meaning of a spoken sentence is only its overcoat, and the real meaning lies underneath its scarves and buttons. [Peter Carey, 1943– , *Oscar and Lucinda*, 43]

4 I discovered the secret of the sea in meditation upon the dewdrop. [Kahlil Gibran, 1883–1931, *Spiritual Sayings*]

5 Unless one is a genius, it is best to aim at being intelligible. [Anthony Hope, 1863–1933, *The Dolly Dialogues*, 15]

6 Sir, I have found you an argument; but I am not obliged to find you an understanding. [Dr Samuel Johnson, 1709–84, in James Boswell, *Life of J*, 13 June 1784]

7 God and I both knew what it [a passage in one of his poems] meant once; now God alone knows. [Friedrich Klopstock, 1724–1803, attr. by Cesare Lombroso, *The Man of Genius*, Pt I, Ch. 2. Also ascr. to Browning]

8 Be sure that you go to the author to get at *his* meaning, not to find yours. [John Ruskin, 1819–1900, *Sesame and Lilies*, 1, §13]

9 *Tout comprendre c'est tout pardonner*. – To understand all is to forgive all. [Mme de Staël, 1766–1817. Common misquotation of *Corinne*, XVIII, Ch. 5]; see 11

10 All, everything that I understand, I understand only because I love. [Leo Tolstoy, 1828–1910, *War and Peace*, VII, Ch. 16]

11 *Tout comprendre, c'est tout pardonner*, and *tout pardonner* makes very dull copy. [Nicholas Tomalin, 1931–73, quoted by James Cameron on BBC radio, Nov. 1976]; see 9

12 There are, I have discovered, two kinds of people in this world, those who long to be understood and those who long to be misunderstood. It is the irony of life that neither is gratified. [Carl van Vechten, 1880–1964, *The Blind Bow-boy*]

13 The human crisis is always a crisis of understanding: what we genuinely understand we can do. [Raymond Williams, 1921–88, *Culture and Society*, Ch. 3, Conclusion]

UNEMPLOYMENT

1 Gizza job, go on, gizzit! [Alan Bleasdale, 1946– , Yosser Hughes in *Boys from the Blackstuff*, 'Jobs for the Boys' and *passim*]

2 Something must be done. [Edward VIII, 1894–1972, speech during tour of unemployment areas in South Wales, 18 Nov. 1936]

3 Whenever you save 5s. you put a man out of work for a day. [John Maynard Keynes, 1883–1946, *Essays in Persuasion*, II, 'Inflation and Deflation']

4 He [Tebbit's father] didn't riot. He got on his bike and he looked for work. And he kept on looking until he found it. [Norman Tebbit, 1931– , speech at Conservative Party Conference, Blackpool, 15 Oct. 1981. Commonly misquoted as 'On your bike']

5 It's a recession when your neighbour loses his job; it's a depression when you lose your own. [Harry Truman, 1884–1972; *Observer*, 'Sayings of the Week', 6 Apr. 1958]

See also WORK

UNHAPPINESS

1 In the morning thou shalt say, Would God it were even! and at even thou shalt say, Would God it were morning! [Bible, OT, *Deuteronomy* 28:67]

2 For in all adversity of fortune the worst sort of misery is to have been happy. [Boethius, 480?–524, *The Consolation of Philosophy*, Bk ii, Prose 4]

3 Man's unhappiness, as I construe, comes of his greatness; it is because there is an Infinite in him, which with all his cunning he cannot quite bury under the Finite. [Thomas Carlyle, 1795–1881, *Sartor Resartus*, Bk ii, Ch. 9]

4 But misery still delights to trace / Its semblance in another's case. [William Cowper, 1731–1800, *The Castaway*]

5 Unhappiness is best defined as the difference between our talents and our expectations. [Edward de Bono, 1933– ; *Observer*, 'Sayings of the Week', 12 June 1977]

6 He recognizes that there is a real divergence of expert opinion between those that believe that men are happy because they are miserable, and those that believe that men are miserable because they are happy; and wisely arrives at a synthesis of both views. [Michael Frayn, 1933– , *Sweet Dreams*, p. 88]

7 The majority of men devote the greater part of their lives to making their remaining years unhappy. [Jean de La Bruyère, 1645–96, *Characters*, 'Of Man', 102]

8 Man hands on misery to man, / It deepens like a coastal shelf. / Get out as early as you can, / And don't have any kids yourself. [Philip Larkin, 1922–85, *This be the Verse*]

9 We have all enough strength to bear other people's troubles. [Duc de La Rochefoucauld, 1613–80, *Maxims*, 19]

10 Men are the only animals who devote themselves assiduously to making one another unhappy. It is, I suppose, one of their godlike qualities. Jahweh, as the Old Testament shows, spends a large part of His time trying to ruin the business and comfort of all other gods. [H L Mencken, 1880–1956, *Minority Report*, 93]

11 Years ago a person, he was unhappy, didn't know what to do with himself – he'd go to church, start a revolution – *something*. Today you're unhappy? Can't figure it out? What is the salvation? Go shopping. [Arthur Miller, 1915– , *The Price*, I]

12 Why, after all, should readers never be harrowed? Surely there is enough happiness in life without having to go to books for it. [Dorothy Parker, 1893–1967, attr.]

13 Gertie recommended her to adopt the habit of not magnifying grievances; if you wanted to view trouble, you could take opera-glasses, but you should be careful to hold them the wrong way round. [W Pett Ridge, 1857–1930, *Love at Paddington Green*, Ch. 4]

14 He's simply got the instinct for being unhappy highly developed. [Saki (H H Munro), 1870–1916, *The Match-Maker*]

15 The secret of being miserable is to have leisure to bother about whether you are happy or not. [George Bernard Shaw, 1856–1950, *Misalliance*, Preface]

16 I was told I am a true cosmopolitan: I am unhappy everywhere. [Stephen Vizinczey, 1933– , in *Guardian*, 7 Mar. 1968]

17 Those who are unhappy have no need for anything in this world but people capable of giving them their attention. [Simone Weil, 1909–43, *Waiting on God*, 'Reflections on the Right Use of School Studies']

18 He spoke with a certain what-is-it in his voice, and I could see that, if not actually disgruntled, he was far from being gruntled. [P G Wodehouse, 1881–1975, *The Code of the Woosters*, Ch. 1]

See also GRIEF, HAPPINESS, REGRET, SORROW

UNITED STATES IN GENERAL

1 God bless the USA, so large, / So friendly, and so rich. [W H Auden, 1907–73, *On the Circuit*]

2 Consider the history of labour in a country [USA] in which, spiritually speaking, there are no workers, only candidates for the hand of the boss's daughter. [James Baldwin, 1924–87, *The Fire Next Time*, 'Down at the Cross']

3 America is so big, and everyone is working, making, digging, bulldozing, trucking, loading, and so on, and I guess the sufferers suffer at the same rate. [Saul Bellow, 1915– , *Henderson the Rain King*, Ch. 3]

4 History had created something new in the USA, namely crookedness with self-respect or duplicity with honour. [Saul Bellow, 1915– , *Humboldt's Gift*, p. 217]

5 America is never wholly herself unless she is engaged in high moral principle. We as a people have such a purpose today. It is: to make kinder the face of the nation, and gentler the face of the world. [George Bush, 1924– , inaugural presidential address, Washington, 20 Jan. 1989]

6 I called the New World into existence, to redress the balance of the Old. [George Canning, 1770–1827, speech, 12 Dec. 1826]

7 America has a new delicacy, a coarse, rank refinement. [G K Chesterton, 1874–1936, *Charles Dickens*, 6]

8 America is the only nation in history which miraculously has gone directly from barbarism to degeneration without the usual interval of civilization. [Georges Clemenceau, 1841–1929, attr. in *Saturday Review*, 1 Dec. 1945]

9 The chief business of the American people is business. [Calvin Coolidge, 1872–1933, speech in Washington, 17 Jan. 1925. Commonly misquoted as 'The business of America is business']

10 In England you have to know people very intimately indeed before they tell you about the rust in their Volvo. It has never surprised me that there are fifty million Roman Catholics in America, and nearly as many psychiatrists: bean-spilling is the national mania. [Alan Coren, 1938– , review of Kurt Vonnegut's *Palm Sunday* in *The Sunday Times*, 21 June 1981]

11 I was given a bed in which four people could have slept without ever being introduced. Everything in America is on wide screen. [Quentin Crisp, 1908– , *How to Become a Virgin*, 'America']

12 It seems that in the United States, Englishmen are regarded as pets, like budgies, that can almost speak American. [Quentin Crisp, 1908–99, *The Wit and Wisdom of Q C*, ed. Guy Kettelhack, Pt 7]

13 In England, the system is benign and the people are hostile. In America, the people are friendly – and the system is brutal! [Quentin Crisp, 1908–99, interview in *Guardian*, 23 Oct. 1985]

14 in every language even deafanddumb / thy sons acclaim your glorious name by gorry / by jingo by gee by gosh by gum [e e cummings, 1894–1962, *is* 5, 'Two, III']

15 Whatever America hopes to bring to pass in this world must first come to pass in the heart of America. [Dwight D Eisenhower, 1890–1969, inaugural presidential address, 20 Jan. 1953]

16 America is a country of young men. [Ralph Waldo Emerson, 1803–82, *Society and Solitude*, 'Old Age']

17 America, I'm putting my queer shoulder to the wheel. [Allen Ginsberg, 1926–97, *America*]

18 Go West, young man, and grow up with the country. [Horace Greeley, 1811–72, *Hints towards Reform*. Originally said by J B L Soule]

19 The United States is like a gigantic boiler. Once the fire is lighted under it there is no limit to the power it can generate. [Sir Edward Grey, 1862–1933, in Winston S Churchill, *Their Finest Hour*, Ch. 32]

20 Ours is the only country deliberately founded on a good idea. [John Gunther, 1901–70, *Inside America*]

21 This Land is Your Land, this Land is My Land. [Woody Guthrie, 1912–67, song: *This Land is Your Land*]

22 In the United States, there one feels free ... Except from the Americans – but every pearl has its oyster. [Randall Jarrell, 1914–65, *Pictures from an Institution*, Pt IV, Ch. 10]

23 I believe in an America that is on the march. [President John F Kennedy, 1917–63, in *Saturday Review*, 'Ideas, Attitudes, Purposes from His Speeches and Writings', 7 Dec. 1963]

24 'Tis the star-spangled banner, O! long may it wave / O'er the land of the free and the home of the brave! [Francis Scott Key, 1779–1843, *The Star-Spangled Banner*]

25 The trouble with us in America isn't that the poetry of life has turned to prose, but that it has turned to advertising copy. [Louis Kronenberger, 1904–80, *Company Manners*, 'The Spirit of the Age']

26 Give me your tired, your poor, / Your huddled masses yearning to breathe free. [Emma Lazarus, 1849–87, inscription on the Statue of Liberty, New York harbour]

27 'There won't be any revolution in America,' said Isadore. Nikitin agreed. 'The people are too clean. They spend all their time changing their shirts and washing themselves. You can't feel fierce and revolutionary in a bathroom.' [Eric Linklater, 1889–1974, *Juan in America*, V, 3]

28 Thou, too, sail on, O Ship of State! / Sail on, O Union, strong and great! / Humanity with all its fears, / With all the hopes of future years, / Is hanging breathless on thy fate! [H W Longfellow, 1807–82, *The Building of the Ship*]

29 American life, in large cities at any rate, is a perpetual assault on the senses and the nerves; it is out of asceticism, out of unworldliness, precisely, that we bear it. [Mary McCarthy, 1912–89, *On the Contrary*, 'America the Beautiful']

30 The immense popularity of American movies abroad demonstrates that Europe is the unfinished negative of which America is the proof. [Mary McCarthy, 1912–89, *On the Contrary*, 'America the Beautiful']

31 First the sweetheart of the nation, then the aunt, woman governs America because America is a land of boys who refuse to grow up. [Salvador de Madariaga, 1886–1978; in Sagittarius and D George, *The Perpetual Pessimist*]

32 But then the country is our religion. The true religion of America has always been America. [Norman Mailer, 1923– , interview in *Time Out*, 27 Sept.–3 Oct. 1984]

33 Instead of leading the world, America appears to have resolved to buy it. [Thomas Mann, 1875–1955, letter, 1947; in *Morrow Book of Quotations in American History*, ed. Joseph R Conlin]

34 So everyone's a fool outside their own country. America, having emerged from World War II as the only country with any money left, got a twenty-year head start on being fools overseas. [P J O'Rourke, 1947– , interview in *Observer*, 15 Jan. 1989]

35 If I were an American, as I am an Englishman, while a foreign troop was landed in my country, I never would lay down my arms – never – never – never! [(Of the American Revolution) William Pitt, the Elder, 1708–78, speech in House of Lords, 18 Nov. 1777]

36 There is nothing wrong with America that together we can't fix. [Ronald Reagan, 1911– ; in Robert Andrews, *Routledge Dictionary of Quotations*, 'America']

37 And furthermore did you know that behind the discovery of America there was a Jewish financier? [Mordechai Richler, 1931– , *Cocksure*, Ch. 24]

38 I see one-third of a nation ill-housed, ill-clad, ill-nourished. [Franklin D Roosevelt, 1882–1945, second presidential inaugural address, 20 Jan. 1937]

39 In America everything goes and nothing matters, while in Europe nothing goes and everything matters. [Philip Roth, 1933– , interview in *Time* magazine, Nov. 1983]

40 America became top nation and history came to a full stop. [W C Sellar, 1898–1951, and R J Yeatman, 1897–1968, *1066 and All That*, Ch. 62]

41 England and America are two countries separated by the same language. [George Bernard Shaw, 1856–1950, attr. in *Reader's Digest*, Nov. 1942]

42 My country, 'tis of thee, / Sweet land of liberty, / Of thee I sing. [Samuel F Smith, 1808–95, *America*]

43 In the United States there is more space where nobody is than where anybody is. That is what makes America what it is. [Gertrude Stein, 1874–1946, *The Geographical History of America*]

44 America is a large, friendly dog in a very small room. Every time it wags its tail it knocks over a chair. [Arnold Toynbee, 1889–1975, broadcast news summary, 14 July 1954]

45 I have seen the future and it does not work. [(Of the USA) Philip Toynbee, 1916–81 in *Observer*, 27 Jan. 1974]; see RUSSIAN REVOLUTION, 5

46 It's a country evenly divided between conservatives and reactionaries. [(Of the USA) Gore Vidal, 1925– , interview in *Observer*, 16 Sept. 1984]

47 That impersonal insensitive friendliness that takes the place of ceremony in that land of waifs and strays. [Evelyn Waugh, 1903–66, *The Loved One*]

48 What a horror it is for a whole nation to be developing without the sense of beauty, and eating bananas for breakfast. [Edith Wharton, 1862–1937, letter to Sara Norton, 19 Aug. 1904, *Letters of E W*, ed. R W B and Nancy Lewis]

49 America ... is the prize amateur nation of the world. Germany is the prize professional nation. [Woodrow Wilson, 1856–1924, speech to officers of the fleet, Aug. 1917]

50 There are a great many hyphens left in America. For my part, I think the most un-American thing in the world is a hyphen. [(Of double-barrelled names) Woodrow Wilson, 1856–1924, speech at St Paul, Minnesota, 9 Sept. 1919]

51 For we must consider that we shall be as a City upon a hill. The eyes of all people are upon us. So that if we shall deal falsely with our God in this work we have undertaken, and so cause him to withdraw his present help from us, we shall be made a story and a byword throughout the world. [John Winthrop, 1588–1649, discourse written on board the *Arbella*, 1630, as the Pilgrim Fathers approached America]

52 America is God's Crucible, the great Melting Pot where all the races of Europe are melting and re-forming. [Israel Zangwill, 1864–1926, *The Melting Pot*, I]

See also next category, CANADA

UNITED STATES: PARTICULAR PLACES (in alphabetical order of place)

1 Beverly Hills is very exclusive. For instance, their fire department won't make house calls. [Mort Sahl, 1926– , attr. in *Penguin Dictionary of Modern Humorous Quotations*, comp. Fred Metcalf]

2 And this is good old Boston, / The home of the bean and the cod, / Where the Lowells talk to the Cabots, / And the Cabots talk only to God. [J C Bossidy, 1860–1928, toast proposed at Holy Cross Alumni dinner, Boston, Massachusetts, 1910]

3 I guess God made Boston on a wet Sunday. [Raymond Chandler, 1888–1959, letter to Bernice Baumgarten, 21 Mar. 1949]

4 California, the department-store state. The most of everything and the best of nothing. [Raymond Chandler, 1888–1959, *The Little Sister*, Ch. 13]

5 I met a Californian who would / Talk California – a state so blessed, / He said, in climate, none had ever died there / A natural death. [Robert Frost, 1874–1963, *New Hampshire*]

6 There's the big advantage of backwardness. By the time the latest ideas reach Chicago, they're worn thin and easy to see through. You don't have to bother with them and it saves lots of trouble. [Saul Bellow, 1915– , *The Dean's December*, 6]

7 Hog Butcher for the World. [(Of Chicago) Carl Sandburg, 1878–1967, in *Chicago*]

8 A big hard-boiled city with no more personality than a paper cup. [(Of Los Angeles) Raymond Chandler, 1888–1959, *The Little Sister*, Ch. 26]

9 There are two modes of transport in Los Angeles: car and ambulance. Visitors who wish to remain inconspicuous are advised to choose the latter. [Fran Lebowitz, ?1948– , *Social Studies*, 'Lesson One']

10 Seventy-two suburbs in search of a city. [(Of Los Angeles) Dorothy Parker, 1893–1967; in L Halliwell, *The Filmgoer's Book of Quotes*, but others are attr. with the description]

11 It's like paradise, with a lobotomy. [(Of Los Angeles) Neil Simon, 1927– , said by Jane Fonda in film *California Suite*]

12 The difference between Los Angeles and yogurt is that yogurt has real culture. [Tom Taussik, from *Legless in Gaza*; in *Contradictory Quotations*, ed. M Rogers]

13 The most serious charge which can be brought against New England is not Puritanism but February. [Joseph Wood Krutch, 1893–1970, *Twelve Seasons*, 'February']

14 Okie use' to mean you was from Oklahoma. Now it means you're scum. Don't mean nothing itself, it's the way they say it. [John Steinbeck, 1902–68, *The Grapes of Wrath*, Ch. 18]

15 The beaten, ignorant, Bible-ridden, white South. [Sherwood Anderson, 1876–1941, in Arthur M Schlesinger Jr, *The Politics of Upheaval*, Pt I, Ch. 4, sect. v]

16 Out where the smile dwells a little longer, / That's where the West begins. [Arthur Chapman, 1873–1935, *Out Where the West Begins*]

See also previous category, HOLLYWOOD, NEW YORK

THE UNIVERSE

1 The Answer to the Great Question of . . . Life, the Universe and Everything . . . Is . . . Forty-two. [Douglas Adams, 1952– , *The Hitch-hiker's Guide to the Galaxy*, Ch. 27]

2 If I had been present at the creation, I would have given some useful hints for the better arrangement of the Universe. [Alfonso the Wise, King of Castile, 1221–84, attr.]

3 The universe is transformation; our life is what our thoughts make it. [Marcus Aurelius, AD 121–80, *Meditations*, IV, 3]

4 The visible universe was an illusion or, more precisely, a sophism. Mirrors and fatherhood are abominable because they multiply it and extend it. [Jorge Luis Borges, 1899–1986, *Ficciones*, 'Tlön, Uqbar, Orbis, Tertius']

5 But perhaps it is this same distrust of our senses that prevents us from feeling comfortable in the universe. [Italo Calvino, 1923–85, *Mr Palomar*, 'the eye and the planets']

6 I laid my heart open to the benign indifference of the universe. [Albert Camus, 1913–60, *The Outsider*, II, 5]

7 I don't pretend to understand the Universe – it's a great deal bigger than I am . . . People ought to be modester. [Thomas Carlyle, 1795–1881 (remark to William Allingham), quoted in D A Wilson and D Wilson McArthur, *Carlyle in Old Age*]

8 The cosmos is about the smallest hole that a man can hide his head in. [G K Chesterton, 1874–1936, *Orthodoxy*, Ch. 2]

9 I am very interested in the Universe – I am specializing in the universe and all that surrounds it. [Peter Cook, 1937–95, *Beyond the Fringe*]

10 We doctors know / a hopeless case if – listen: there's a hell / of a good universe next door, let's go. [e e cummings, 1894–1962, *1×1*, 14]

11 Anyone informed that the universe is expanding and contracting in pulsations of eighty billion years has a right to ask, 'What's in it for me?' [Peter de Vries, 1910–93, *The Glory of the Hummingbird*, Ch. 1]

12 My own suspicion is that the universe is not only queerer than we suppose, but queerer than we *can* suppose. [J B S Haldane, 1892–1964, *Possible Worlds*, title essay]

13 The universe is not hostile, nor yet is it friendly. It is simply indifferent. [Revd J H Holmes, 1879–1964, *The Sensible Man's View of Religion*]

14 The universe begins to look more like a great thought than a great machine. [James Jeans, 1887–1946, *The Mysterious Universe*, Ch. 1]

15 Ventre offers us a grand vision of the Universe as One Thing – the Ultimate Thing (Dernière Chose). And it is against us. [Paul Jennings, 1918–89, *The Jenguin Pennings*, 'Report on Resistentialism']

16 To sum up: 1. The cosmos is a gigantic flywheel making 10,000 revolutions a minute. 2. Man is a sick fly taking a dizzy ride on it. 3. Religion is the theory that the wheel was designed and set spinning to give him the ride. [H L Mencken, 1880–1956, *Prejudices*, Third Series, '*Ad Imaginem dei creavit illum*', Coda]

17 My theology, briefly, is that the universe was dictated but not signed. [Christopher Morley, 1890–1957, in A Andrews, *Quotations for Speakers and Writers*]

18 All are but parts of one stupendous whole, / Whose body nature is, and God the soul. [Alexander Pope, 1688–1744, *An Essay on Man*, I, 267]

19 I saw the flaring atom-streams / And torrents of her myriad universe, / Ruining along the illimitable inane. [Alfred, Lord Tennyson, 1809–92, *Lucretius*, 38]

20 The spirit within nourishes, and the mind, diffused through all the members, sways the mass and mingles with the whole frame. [(Of the universe) Virgil, 70–19 BC, *Aeneid*, VI, 726]

See also SPACE

UNIVERSITIES

1 Undergraduates owe their happiness chiefly to the consciousness that they are no longer at school. The nonsense which was knocked out of them at school is all put gently back at Oxford or Cambridge. [Max Beerbohm, 1872–1956, *Going Back to School*]; see 9

2 The true University of these days is a collection of books. [Thomas Carlyle, 1795–1881, *Heroes and Hero-Worship*, i, v, 'The Hero as Man of Letters']

3 Tis well enough for a servant to be bred at an university: but the education is a little too pedantic for a gentleman. [William Congreve, 1670–1729, *Love for Love*, V. iii]

4 I am not impressed by the Ivy League establishments. Of course they graduate the best – it's all they'll take, leaving to others the problem of educating the country. They will give you an education the way the banks will give you money – provided you can prove to their satisfaction that you don't need it. [Peter de Vries, 1910–93, *The Vale of Laughter*, Pt 1, Ch. 4]

5 A University should be a place of light, of liberty, and of learning. [Benjamin Disraeli, 1804–81, speech in House of Commons, 11 Mar. 1873]

6 There are as many fools at a university as elsewhere ... But their folly, I admit, has a certain stamp – the stamp of university training, if you like. It is trained folly. [William Gerhardie, 1895–1977, *The Polyglots*, Ch. 7]

7 As to our universities, I've come to the conclusion that they are élitist where they should be egalitarian and egalitarian where they should be élitist. [David Lodge, 1935–   , *Nice Work*, 5, 4]

8 I don't think one 'comes down' from Jimmy's university. According to him, it's not even red brick, but white tile. [John Osborne, 1929–94, *Look Back in Anger*, II. i]

9 He was sent, as usual, to a public school, where a little learning was painfully beaten into him, and from thence to the university, where it was carefully taken out of him. [T L Peacock, 1785–1866, *Nightmare Abbey*, Ch. 1]; see 1

10 Degrees are like false teeth. You'd rather not be without them, but you don't flaunt the fact you've got them to the world. [Godfrey Smith, 1926–   , in *Directory of Opportunities for Graduates*, 1957]

See also ACADEMICS, EDUCATION, LEARNING, RESEARCH, STUDENTS

UNMARRIED

1 I would be married, but I'd have no wife, / I would be married to a single life. [Richard Crashaw, 1613?–49, *On Marriage*]

2 I pray thee, good Lord, that I may not be married. But if I am to be married, that I may not be a cuckold. But if I am to be a cuckold, that I may not know. But if I am to know, that I may not mind. [Isak Dinesen, 1885–1962, *Seven Gothic Tales*, 'The Poet'. A saying described as 'the bachelors' prayer']

3 Being an old maid is like death by drowning, a really delightful sensation after you cease to struggle. [Edna Ferber, 1887–1968; in R E Drennan, *Wit's End*, 'Completing the Circle']

4 She would have liked for instance ... to marry; and nothing in general is more ridiculous, even when it has been pathetic, than a woman who has tried and has not been able. [Henry James, 1843–1916, *The Golden Bowl*, Bk I, Pt ii, Ch. 10]

5 Marriage has many pains, but celibacy has no pleasures. [Dr Samuel Johnson, 1709–84, *Rasselas*, Ch. 26]

6 Nothing is to me more distasteful than that entire complacency and satisfaction which beam in the countenances of a new-married couple. [Charles Lamb, 1775–1834, *Essays of Elia*, 'A Bachelor's Complaint of Married People']

7 When married people don't get on they can separate, but if they're not married it's impossible. It's a tie that only death can sever. [W Somerset Maugham, 1874–1965, *The Circle*, III]

8 Shall I never see a bachelor of three-score again? [William Shakespeare, 1564–1616, *Much Ado About Nothing*, I. i. (209)]

9 The world must be peopled. When I said I would die a bachelor, I did not think I should live till I were married. [*Much Ado About Nothing*, II. iii. (262)]

10 I can't mate in captivity. [(On why she has never married) Gloria Steinem, 1934– ; in *The Other 637 Best Things Anybody Ever Said*, comp. Robert Byrne]

11 Bachelor's fare; bread and cheese, and kisses. [Jonathan Swift, 1677–1745, *Polite Conversation*, Dialogue 1]

See also DIVORCE, MARRIAGE

USSR, see RUSSIA

UTOPIAS

1 *Et in Arcadia ego.* – I too am in Arcadia. [anon. inscription on a tomb, the subject of paintings by Nicolas Poussin and others]; see also DEATH, 4

2 Political utopias are a form of nostalgia for an imagined past projected on to the future as a wish. [Michael Ignatieff, 1947– , *The Needs of Strangers*, Ch. 4]

3 Not in Utopia, – subterranean fields, – / Or some secreted island, Heaven knows where! / But in the very world, which is the world / Of all of us, – the place where, in the end, / We find our happiness, or not at all! [(Of French Revolution) William Wordsworth, 1770–1850, *The Prelude*, XI, 140]

See also PERFECTION

V

VANITY

1 It beareth the name of Vanity Fair, because the town where 'tis kept, is lighter than vanity. [John Bunyan, 1628–88, *The Pilgrim's Progress*, Pt I]

2 She felt sexual urgings towards Yvonne in the manner that politicians feel an enormous sexual pull toward mirrors. [Richard Condon, 1915–96, *Bandicoot*, Ch. 21]

3 Wich is your partickler wanity? Wich wanity do you like the flavour on best, sir? [Charles Dickens, 1812–70, *Pickwick Papers*, Ch. 45]

4 He [Thomas E. Dewey] is just about the nastiest little man I've ever known. He struts sitting down. [Lillian Dykstra, in J T Patterson, *Mr Republican*, Ch. 35]

5 Vanity is other people's pride. [Sacha Guitry, 1885–1957, *Jusqu'à nouvel ordre*]

6 What is your sex's earliest, latest care, / Your heart's supreme ambition? – To be fair. [George Lyttelton, 1709–73, *Advice to a Lady*]

7 Pull down thy vanity / Thou art a beaten dog beneath the hail, / A swollen magpie in a fitful sun, / Half black half white / Nor knowst'ou wing from tail / Pull down thy vanity. [Ezra Pound, 1885–1972, *Cantos*, LXXXI]

8 There was never yet fair woman but she made mouths in a glass. [William Shakespeare, 1564–1616, *King Lear*, III. ii. (35)]

See also HUMILITY, PRIDE

VEGETARIANS

1 You will find me drinking gin / In the lowest kind of inn, / Because I am a rigid Vegetarian. [G K Chesterton, 1874–1936, *The Logical Vegetarian*]

2 I'm all for killing animals and turning them into handbags, I just don't want to have to eat them. [Victoria Wood, 1953– , interview in *Independent*, 7 Oct. 1987]

See also FOOD

VICE

1 Vice itself lost half its evil, by losing all its grossness. [Edmund Burke, 1729–97, *Reflections on the Revolution in France*, Penguin edn, p. 170]

2 Vice ... is a creature of such heejus mien ... that the more ye see it th' better ye like it. [Finley Peter Dunne, 1867–1936, *Mr Dooley's Opinions*, 'The Crusade against Vice']; see 5

3 If he does really think that there is no distinction between virtue and vice, why, Sir, when he leaves our houses let us count our spoons. [Dr Samuel Johnson, 1709–84, in James Boswell, *Life of J*, 14 July 1793]

4 Saint Augustine! well hast thou said, / That of our vices we can frame / A ladder, if we will but tread / Beneath our feet each deed of shame! [H W Longfellow, 1807–82, *The Ladder of St Augustine*]

5 Vice is a monster of so frightful mien, / As to be hated needs but to be seen; / Yet seen too oft, familiar with her face, / We first endure, then pity, then embrace. [Alexander Pope, 1688–1744, *An Essay on Man*, II, 217]; see 2

6 Men's evil manners live in brass; their virtues / We write in water. [William Shakespeare, 1564–1616, *Henry VIII*, IV. ii. 45]

7 Change in a trice! The lilies and languors of virtue / For the raptures and roses of vice. [A C Swinburne, 1837–1909, *Dolores*, 9]

8 Vice and virtues are products like sulphuric acid and sugar. [Hippolyte Taine, 1828–93, *Histoire de la littérature anglaise*, Introduction, iii]

See also EVIL, GOOD, SINS, VIRTUE

VICTIM

1 As some day it may happen that a victim must be found, / I've got a little list – I've got a little list / Of society offenders who might well be underground, / And who never would be missed / who never would be missed! [W S Gilbert, 1836–1911, *The Mikado*, I]

2 Though England prefers victims who begin by being restive, / They taste better afterwards – like birds / Cooked while their blood is still warm. [Hugh MacDiarmid, 1892–1978, *England's Double Knavery*]

3 Every reformation must have its victims. You can't expect the fatted calf to share the enthusiasm of the angels over the prodigal's return. [Saki (H H Munro), 1870–1916, *Reginald on the Academy*]

4 I hate victims who respect their executioners. [Jean-Paul Sartre, 1905–80, *Altona*, I]

See also TYRANTS

VICTORY

1 Anybody can Win unless there Happens to be a Second Entry. [George Ade, 1866–1944, *Thirty Fables in Slang*, 'The Fable of the Brash Drummer']

2 Let the victors, when they come, / When the forts of folly fall, / Find thy body by the wall. [Matthew Arnold, 1822–88, *The Last Word*]

3 *Veni, vidi, vici.* – I came, I saw, I conquered. [Julius Caesar, 102 ?–44 BC, in Suetonius *Lives of the Caesars*, 'Divus Julius', 37, 2]

4 In war, whichever side may call itself the victor, there are no winners, but all are losers. [Neville Chamberlain, 1869–1940, speech at Kettering, 3 July 1938]

5 You ask: 'What is our aim?' I can answer in one word: 'Victory!' Victory at all costs, victory in spite of all terror, victory however long and hard the road may be: for without victory there is no survival. [Winston Churchill, 1874–1965, first speech in House of Commons as Prime Minister, 13 May 1940]

6 We must be very careful not to assign to this deliverance [Dunkirk] the attributes of a victory. Wars are not won by evacuations. [Winston Churchill, 1874–1965, *The Second World War*, Vol. II, 5]

7 As always, victory finds a hundred fathers, but defeat is an orphan. [Count Ciano, 1903–44, Diary entry, 9 Sept. 1942]

8 *Victoire, c'est la Volonté!* – The will to conquer is the first condition of victory. [Marshal Foch, 1851–1929, in B Tuchman, *The Guns of August*, Ch. 3]

9 The victor will not be asked afterwards whether he told the truth or not. In starting and waging a war it is not right that matters, but victory. [Adolf Hitler, 1889–1945, in W L Shirer, *The Rise and Fall of the Third Reich*, Ch. 16]

10 'NIGHT BATTLE ON MEADOW BORDER RESULTS IN ...' He paused and flew lower, in some confusion as to who had won and who had lost. 'VICTORY!' he concluded. [Russell Hoban, 1925– , *The Mouse and His Child*, Ch. 3]

11 We Shall Overcome. [Ziphia Horton, 1907–57, title of song, original version. Later additions by Pete Seeger, Frank Hamilton, Guy Carawan]

12 They see nothing wrong in the rule that to the victors belong the spoils of the enemy. [Senator William Marcy, 1786–1857, speech in US Senate, 25 Jan. 1832]

13 Westminster Abbey or victory! [(At Battle of Cape St Vincent) Horatio, Lord Nelson, 1758–1805, quoted in R Southey, *Life of Nelson*, Ch. 4]

14 'And everybody praised the Duke, / Who this great fight did win.' / 'But what good came of it at last?' / Quoth little Peterkin. / 'Why, that I cannot tell,' said he, / 'But 'twas a famous victory.' [Robert Southey, 1774–1843, *The Battle of Blenheim*]

15 Nobody wins unless everybody wins. [Bruce Springsteen, 1949– (catchphrase), in Dave Marsh, *Glory Days*, Ch. 12]

16 They [the Franco rebels] will conquer, but they will not convince. [Miguel de Unamuno, 1864–1937, said at the end of his life]

See also DEFEAT, FIGHTS, WAR, WARS

VIETNAM

1 The last crusade. [Chester Cooper, 1917– (of USA's war in Vietnam), in *Daily Telegraph*, 4 Apr. 1975]

2 You have a row of dominoes set up. You knock over the first one, and what will happen to the last one is a certainty that it will go over very quickly. [Dwight D Eisenhower, 1890–1969 (on the strategic importance of Indochina), at press conference, 7 Apr. 1954]

3 You've got to forget about this civilian. Whenever you drop bombs, you're going to hit civilians. [Barry Goldwater, 1909–98 (of Vietnam), speech in New York, 23 Jan. 1967]

4 Hey, hey, L.B.J., how many kids did you kill today? [Graffito at period of Vietnam War, in Robert Reisner, *Graffiti*]

5 We are not about to send American boys 9 or 10,000 miles away from home to do what Asian boys ought to be doing for themselves. [President Lyndon B Johnson, 1908–73, speech at Akron University, Ohio, 21 Oct. 1964]

6 My solution to the problem [of North Vietnam] would be to tell them frankly that they've got to draw in their horns and stop their aggression, or we're going to bomb them back into the Stone Age. [General Curtis Le May, 1906–90, *Mission with Le May*, p. 565]

7 To win in Vietnam, we will have to exterminate a nation. [Dr Spock, 1903–98, *Dr Spock on Vietnam*, Ch. 7]

VIOLENCE

1 Keep violence in the mind / Where it belongs. [Brian Aldiss, 1925– , *Barefoot in the Head*]

2 All they that take the sword shall perish with the sword. [Bible, NT, *St Matthew* 26:52]

3 The wish to hurt, the momentary intoxication with pain, is the loophole through which the pervert climbs into the minds of ordinary men. [J Bronowski, 1908–74, *The Face of Violence*, Ch. 5]

4 Violence is as American as cherry pie. [H Rap Brown, 1943– , speech in Washington, 27 July 1967]

5 Ay me! what perils do environ / The man that meddles with cold iron! [Samuel Butler, 1612–80, *Hudibras*, I, iii, 1]

6 I suppose nobody has ever been struck a direct blow by a rabbit. At least, not deliberately. ['Cassandra', 1909–67, in *Daily Mirror*]

7 Violence is man re-creating himself. [Frantz Fanon, 1925–61, *The Wretched of the Earth*, Ch. 1]

8 All terrorists, at the invitation of the Government, end up with drinks at the Dorchester. [Hugh Gaitskell, 1906–63, quoted by Dora Gaitskell in letter to *Guardian*, 23 Aug. 1977]

9 We are effectively destroying ourselves by violence masquerading as love. [R D Laing, 1927–89, *The Politics of Experience*, Ch. 4]

10 In London town a man gets mugged every twenty minutes. He's getting very sick of it. ['Suggs' McPherson, 1961– , in *New Musical Express*, 20/27 Dec. 1986]

11 I distrust the incommunicable; it is the source of all violence. [Jean-Paul Sartre, 1905–80, *What is Literature?*]

12 These violent delights have violent ends. [William Shakespeare, 1564–1616, *Romeo and Juliet*, II. vi. 9]

13 We must try to find ways to starve the terrorist and the hijacker of the oxygen [publicity] on which they depend. [Margaret Thatcher, 1925– , speech to London branch of American Bar Association, 15 July 1985]

14 The man that lays his hand upon a woman, / Save in the way of kindness, is a wretch / Whom 'twere gross flattery to name a coward. [John Tobin, 1770–1804, *The Honeymoon*, II. i]

See also AGGRESSION

VIRTUE

1 The eternal *not ourselves* that makes for righteousness. [Matthew Arnold, 1822–88, *Literature and Dogma*, Ch. 8, §1]

2 As in nature things move violently to their place and calmly in their place, so virtue in ambition is violent, in authority settled and calm. [Francis Bacon, 1561–1626, *Essays*, 11, 'Of Great Place']

3 A man's nature runs either to herbs, or to weeds; therefore let him seasonably water the one, and destroy the other. [Francis Bacon, 1561–1626, *Essays*, 43, 'Of Beauty']

4 All our righteousnesses are as filthy rags;

and we all do fade as a leaf. [Bible, OT, *Isaiah* 64:6]

5 The path of the just is as the shining light, that shineth more and more unto the perfect day. [Bible, OT, *Proverbs* 4:18]

6 Who can find a virtuous woman? for her price is far above rubies. [Bible, OT, *Proverbs* 31:10]

7 I have been young, and now am old; yet have I not seen the righteous forsaken, nor his seed begging bread. [Bible, OT, *Psalms* 37:25]

8 The righteous shall flourish like the palm-tree: he shall grow like a cedar in Lebanon. [Bible, OT, *Psalms* 92:12]

9 There is no road or ready way to virtue. [Sir Thomas Browne, 1605–82, *Religio Medici*, Pt 1, 55]

10 Caesar's wife must be above suspicion. [Julius Caesar, 102?–44 BC, traditional, based on Plutarch, *Life of JC*, x, 6]

11 My virtue's still far too small, I don't trot it out and about yet. [Colette, 1873–1954, *Claudine at School*]

12 The only reward of virtue is virtue; the only way to have a friend is to be one. [Ralph Waldo Emerson, 1803–82, *Essays*, 'Friendship']

13 I said that virtue was the weakness of strong generals, and the strength of weak magistrates. [Jean Giraudoux, 1882–1944, *Duel of Angels*, 1]

14 To flee vice is a virtue, and the beginning of wisdom is to be done with folly. [Horace, 65–8 BC, *Epistles*, I, i, 41]

15 He had cured her, he remembered, of a passion for Burne-Jones, but never, alas, of her prejudice in favour of virtue. [Aldous Huxley, 1894–1963, *Point Counter Point*, Ch. 4]

16 Virtue is the one and only nobility. [Juvenal, 60–*c*.130, *Satires*, VIII, 20]

17 To be discontented with the divine discontent, and to be ashamed with the noble shame, is the very germ of the first upgrowth of all virtue. [Charles Kingsley, 1819–75, *Health and Education*, 'The Science of Health']

18 We need greater virtues to bear good fortune than bad. [Duc de La Rochefoucauld, 1613–80, *Maxims*, 25]

19 Most usually our virtues are only vices in disguise. [Duc de La Rochefoucauld, 1613–80, added to the fourth edn of *Maxims*]

20 I cannot praise a fugitive and cloistered virtue, unexercised and unbreathed, that never sallies out and sees her adversary, but slinks out of the race, where that immortal garland is to be run for, not without dust and heat. [John Milton, 1608–74, *Areopagitica*]

21 Virtue could see to do what Virtue would / By her own radiant light, though sun and moon / Were in the flat sea sunk. [John Milton, 1608–74, *Comus*, 373]

22 Virtue may be assailed, but never hurt, / Surprised by unjust force, but not enthralled. [John Milton, 1608–74, *Comus*, 589]

23 Mortals, that would follow me, / Love virtue, she alone is free, / She can teach ye how to climb / Higher than the sphery chime; / Or if virtue feeble were, / Heav'n itself would stoop to her. [John Milton, 1608–74, *Comus*, 1018]

24 Her virtue and the conscience of her worth, / That would be wooed, and not unsought be won. [John Milton, 1608–74, *Paradise Lost*, Bk vii, 502]

25 Most men admire / Virtue, who follow not her lore. [John Milton, 1608–74, *Paradise Regained*, Bk i, 482]

26 Those strong dislikes that vice should inspire in virtuous souls. [Molière, 1622–73, *Le Misanthrope*, I. i]

27 Virtue will have nothing to do with ease ... It demands a steep and thorny road. [Michel de Montaigne, 1533–92, *Essays*, II, 11]

28 Let them look upon virtue and pine because they have lost her. [Persius, 34–62, *Satires*, III, 38]

29 Charms strike the sight, but merit wins the soul. [Alexander Pope, 1688–1744, *The Rape of the Lock*, V, 34]

30 When men grow virtuous in their old age, they only make a sacrifice to God of the devil's leavings. [Alexander Pope, 1688–1744, *Thoughts on Various Subjects*]

31 Assume a virtue, if you have it not. [William Shakespeare, 1564–1616, *Hamlet*, III. iii. 160]

32 Men's evil manners live in brass; their virtues / We write in water. [*Henry VIII*, IV. ii. 45]

33 Some rise by sin, and some by virtue fall. [*Measure for Measure*, II. i. 38]

34 Virtue is bold, and goodness never fearful. [*Measure for Measure*, III. i. (214)]

35 Virtue! a fig! 'tis in ourselves that we are thus, or thus. [*Othello*, I. iii. (323)]

36 Virtue itself turns vice, being misapplied; / And vice sometime's by action dignified. [*Romeo and Juliet*, II. iii. 21]

37 The rarer action is / In virtue than in vengeance. [*The Tempest*, V. i. 27]

38 What is virtue but the Trade Unionism of the married? [George Bernard Shaw, 1856–1950, *Man and Superman*, III]

39 Self-denial is not a virtue; it is only the effect of prudence on rascality. [George Bernard Shaw, 1856–1950, *Man and Superman*, 'Maxims for Revolutionists', Virtues and Vices]

40 Woman's virtue is man's greatest invention. [Cornelia Otis Skinner, 1901–79, attr.]

41 Will Honeycomb calls these over-offended ladies the outrageously virtuous. [Richard Steele, 1672–1729, *The Spectator*, 266]

42 Virtue is the roughest way, / But proves at night a bed of down. [Henry Wotton, 1568–1639, *Upon the Sudden Restraint of the Earl of Somerset*]

See also EVIL, GOOD, SINS, VICE

VISIONS

1 Write the vision, and make it plain upon tables, that he may run that readeth it. [Bible, OT, *Habbakuk* 2:2]

2 Every valley shall be exalted, and every mountain and hill shall be made low: and the crooked shall be made straight, and the rough places plain. [Bible, OT, *Isaiah* 40:4]

3 To see a World in a grain of sand, / And a Heaven in a wild flower, / Hold Infinity in the palm of your hand, / And Eternity in an hour. [William Blake, 1757–1827, *Auguries of Innocence*]

4 A sight to dream of, not to tell! [Samuel Taylor Coleridge, 1772–1834, *Christabel*, Pt 1, 253]

5 In Xanadu did Kubla Khan / A stately pleasure-dome decree; / Where Alph, the sacred river, ran / Through caverns measureless to man / Down to a sunless sea.

So twice five miles of fertile ground / With walls and towers was girdled round: / And there were gardens bright with sinuous rills, / Where blossomed many an incense-bearing tree; / And here were forests ancient as the hills, / Enfolding sunny spots of greenery. [Samuel Taylor Coleridge, 1772–1834, *Kubla Khan*]

6 A faire felde ful of folke fonde I there bitwene, / Of alle manner of men, the mene and the riche, / Worching and wandring as the worlde asketh. [William Langland, 1330?–1400?, *Piers Plowman*, B Text, Prologue, 17]

7 Methought I saw my late espousèd saint / Brought to me like Alcestis, from the grave. [John Milton, 1608–74, sonnet: *On His Deceased Wife*]

8 My soul looked down from a vague height with Death. / As unremembering how I rose or why, / And saw a sad land, weak with sweats of dearth. [Wilfred Owen, 1893–1918, *The Show*]

9 Our revels now are ended. These our actors, / As I foretold you, were all spirits and / Are melted into air, into thin air: / And, like the baseless fabric of this vision, / The cloud-capped towers, the gorgeous palaces, / The solemn temples, the great globe itself, / Yea, all which it inherit, shall dissolve / And, like this insubstantial pageant faded, / Leave not a rack behind. [William Shakespeare, 1564–1616, *The Tempest*, IV. i. 148]

10 After it, follow it, / Follow The Gleam. [Alfred, Lord Tennyson, 1809–92, *Merlin and The Gleam*]

11 The Men! O what venerable and reverend creatures did the aged seem! Immortal Cherubims! And young men glittering and sparkling angels, and maids strange seraphic pieces of life and beauty! Boys and girls tumbling in the street, and playing, were moving jewels. [Thomas Traherne, 1637?–74, *Centuries of Meditations*, iii, 3]

12 There was a time when meadow, grove, and stream, / The earth, and every common sight, / To me did seem / Apparelled in celestial light, / The glory and the freshness of a dream. / It is not now as it hath been of yore; – / Turn wheresoe'er I may, / By night or day, / The things which I have seen I now can see no more. [William Wordsworth, 1770–1850, *Ode, Intimations of Immortality*, 1]

13 A slumber did my spirit seal; / I had no human fears: / She seemed a thing that could not feel / The touch of earthly years.

No motion has she now, no force; / She neither hears nor sees; / Rolled round in earth's diurnal course, / With rocks, and stones, and trees. [William Wordsworth, 1770–1850, *A Slumber Did My Spirit Seal*]

14 Nothing can stay my glance / Until that glance run in the world's despite / To where the damned have howled away their hearts, / And where the blessed dance. [W B Yeats, 1865–1939, *All Souls' Night*]

15 Yet always when I look death in the face, / When I clamber to the heights of sleep, / Or when I grow excited with wine, / Suddenly I meet your face. [W B Yeats, 1865–1939, *A Deep-Sworn Vow*]

See also DREAMS, ILLUSION, IMAGINATION

VOICE

1 There was nothing wrong with her that a vasectomy of the vocal cords wouldn't fix. [Lisa Alther, 1944– , *Kinflicks*, Ch. 4]

2 Her voice is full of money. [F Scott Fitzgerald, 1896–1940, *The Great Gatsby*, Ch. 7]

3 he had a voice / that used to shake / the ferry-boats / on the north river [Don Marquis, 1878–1937, *archy and mehitabel*, XXX, 'the old trouper']

4 A shout that tore hell's concave, and beyond / Frightened the reign of Chaos and old Night. [John Milton, 1608–74, *Paradise Lost*, Bk i, 542]

5 The higher the voice the smaller the intellect. [Ernest Newman, 1868–1959, attr. by Peter Heyworth]

6 Her voice was ever soft, / Gentle and low, an excellent thing in woman. [William Shakespeare, 1564–1616, *King Lear*, V. iii. (274])

7 I will aggravate my voice so that I will roar you as gently as any sucking dove; I will roar you as 'twere any nightingale. [*A Midsummer Night's Dream*, I. ii. (84)]

8 What music is more enchanting than the voices of young people, when you can't hear what they say? [Logan Pearsall Smith, 1865–1946, *Afterthoughts*, 2]

9 A good voice but too autocratic for oratorio. [Gwyn Thomas, 1913–81, *The Keep*, II]

10 Her voice trailed away in a sigh that was like the wind blowing through the cracks in a broken heart. [P G Wodehouse, 1881–1975, *Full Moon*, Ch. 10]

11 A voice so thrilling ne'er was heard / In spring-time from the cuckoo-bird, / Breaking the silence of the seas / Among the farthest Hebrides. [William Wordsworth, 1770–1850, *The Solitary Reaper*]

See also SONGS, SPEECH

VOID, see LIMBO

VULGARITY

1 The vulgar mind always mistakes the exceptional for the important. [W R Inge, 1860–1954, *More Lay Thoughts of a Dean*, Pt IV, 1]

2 That fellow would vulgarize the day of judgement. [Douglas Jerrold, 1803–57, *Wit and Opinions*, 'A Comic Author']

3 All except the best men would rather be called wicked than vulgar. [C S Lewis, 1898–1963, in *Guardian*, 21 Aug. 1980]

WALES & THE WELSH

1 The Welsh are all actors. It's only the bad ones who become professionals. [Richard Burton, 1925–84, in *Listener*, 9 Jan. 1986]

2 The flag of morn in conqueror's state / Enters at the English gate: / The vanquished eve, as night prevails, / Bleeds upon the road to Wales. [A E Housman, 1859–1936, *A Shropshire Lad*, 28, 'The Welsh Marches']

3 Eddy was a tremendously tolerant person, but he wouldn't put up with the Welsh. He always said, surely there's enough English to go round. [John Mortimer, 1923– , *Two Stars for Comfort*, I. ii]

4 The land of my fathers. My fathers can have it. [Dylan Thomas, 1914–53, *Adam*, Dec. 1953]

5 Too many of the artists of Wales spend too much time talking about the position of the artists of Wales. There is only one position for an artist anywhere: and that is upright. [Dylan Thomas, 1914–53, *Quite Early One Morning*, Pt 2, 'Wales and the Artist']

6 I wanted a play that would paint the full face of sensuality, rebellion and revivalism. In South Wales these three phenomena have played second fiddle only to Rugby Union which is a distillation of all three. [Gwyn Thomas, 1913–81, *Jackie the Jumper*, Introduction]

7 We were a people taut for war; the hills / Were no harder, the thin grass / Clothed them more warmly than the coarse / Shirts our small bones. [R S Thomas, 1913– , *Welsh History*]

8 An impotent people, / Sick with inbreeding, / Worrying the carcase of an old song. [R S Thomas, 1913– , *Welsh Landscape*]

9 We can trace almost all the disasters of English history to the influence of Wales. [Evelyn Waugh, 1903–66, *Decline and Fall*, I, 8]

10 The Welsh as a people have lived by making and remaking themselves in generation after generation, usually against the odds, usually in a British context. Wales is an artefact which the Welsh produce. If they want to ... But that people who are my people and no mean people, are now nothing but a naked people under an acid rain. [Gwyn A Williams, 1925–95, *When was Wales?*, concluding words]

See also BRITAIN, ENGLAND, IRELAND, SCOTLAND

WAR & PEACE

1 Mark! where his carnage and his conquests cease! / He makes a solitude, and calls it – peace! [Lord Byron, 1788–1824, *The Bride of Abydos*, I, 20]

2 Those who can win a war well can rarely make a good peace and those who could make a good peace would never have won the war. [Winston Churchill, 1874–1965, *My Early Life*, Ch. 26]

3 Moral of the Work. In war: resolution. In defeat: defiance. In victory: magnanimity. In peace: goodwill. [Winston Churchill, 1874–1965, *The Second World War*, Vol. I, epigraph, but originally used to describe 1914–18 War]

4 Peace with Germany and Japan on our terms will not bring much rest ... As I observed last time, when the war of the giants is over the wars of the pygmies will begin. [Winston Churchill, 1874–1965, *The Second World War*, Vol. V, 25]

5 There never was a good war or a bad peace. [Benjamin Franklin, 1706–90, letter to Josiah Quincy, 11 Sept. 1783]

6 The opposite of peaceful coexistence is warlike non-existence. [Jonathan Lynn, 1943– , and Antony Jay, 1930– , *Yes Prime Minister*, Vol. 1, 'A Victory for Democracy']

7 The peaceful population is the sea in which the guerrilla swims like a fish. [Mao Zedong, 1893–1976, in R Taber, *The War of the Flea*]

8 War is Peace / Freedom is Slavery / Ignorance is Strength. [George Orwell, 1903–50, *1984*, Pt 1, Ch. 1]

9 Once more unto the breach, dear friends, once more; / Or close the wall up with our English dead. / In peace there's nothing so becomes a man / As modest stillness and humility: / But when the blast of war blows in our ears, / Then imitate the action of the tiger; / Stiffen the sinews, summon up the blood, / Disguise fair nature with hard-favoured rage. [William Shakespeare, 1564–1616, *Henry V*, III. i. 1]

10 Our stern alarums changed to merry meetings; / Our dreadful marches to delightful measures. [*Richard III*, I. i. 7]

11 Let him who desires peace prepare for war. [Vegetius, 4th cent., *De Re Mil.*, 3, Prologue]

12 When you're at war you think about a better life; when you're at peace you think about a more comfortable one. [Thornton Wilder, 1897–1975, *The Skin of Our Teeth*, I]

See also PEACE, WARS

WARNINGS

1 Beware the Jabberwock, my son! / The jaws that bite, the claws that catch! / Beware the Jubjub bird, and shun / The frumious Bandersnatch! [Lewis Carroll, 1832–98, *Through the Looking Glass*, Ch. 1]

2 If you don't know where you are going, you will probably end up somewhere else. [Laurence J Peter, 1919–90, and Raymond Hull, 1918–85, *The Peter Principle*, Ch. 15]

3 You may go into the field or down the lane, but don't go into Mr McGregor's garden. [Beatrix Potter, 1866–1943, *The Tale of Peter Rabbit*]

4 Do not on any account attempt to write on both sides of the paper at once. [W C Sellar, 1898–1951, and R J Yeatman, 1897–1968, *1066 and All That*, Test Paper 5]

5 Beware the ides of March. [William Shakespeare, 1564–1616, *Julius Caesar*, I. ii. 18]

6 Beware of the man whose god is in the skies. [George Bernard Shaw, 1856–1950, *Man and Superman*, 'Maxims for Revolutionists', Religion]

See also PROPHETS

WARS IN GENERAL

1 *Ah Dieu! que la guerre est jolie / Avec ses chants ses longs loisirs.* – Ah God, how pretty war is with its songs, its long rests! [Guillaume Apollinaire, 1880–1918, *L'Adieu du cavalier*]

2 And on the issue of their charm depended / A land laid waste, with all its young men slain, / The women weeping, and its towns in terror [W H Auden, 1907–73, *In Time of War*, xix]

3 The only defence is in offence, which means that you have to kill more women and children more quickly than the enemy if you want to save yourselves. [Stanley Baldwin, 1867–1947, speech in House of Commons, 10 Nov. 1932]

4 When the guns begin to rattle / And the men to die / Does the Goddess of the Battle / Smile or sigh? [George Barker, 1916–91, *Battle Hymn of the New Republic*]

5 I have never understood this liking for war. It panders to instincts already catered for within the scope of any respectable domestic establishment. [Alan Bennett, 1934– , *Forty Years On*, I]

6 One knows what a war is about only when it is over. [H N Brailsford, 1873–1958, *The Levellers and the English Revolution*, Ch. 1]

7 What they could do with round here is a good war. What else can you expect with peace running wild all over the place. You know what the trouble with peace is? No organization. [Bertolt Brecht, 1898–1956, *Mother Courage*, i]

8 War is like love, it always finds a way. [Bertolt Brecht, 1898–1956, *Mother Courage*, vi]

9 War knows no power. Safe shall be my going, / Secretly armed against all death's endeavour; / Safe though all safety's lost; safe where men fall; / And if these poor limbs die, safest of all. [Rupert Brooke, 1887–1915, *Safety*]

10 Usually, when a lot of men get together it's called a war. [Mel Brooks, 1926– , in *Listener*, 1978]

11 War, war is still the cry, 'War even to the knife!' [Lord Byron, 1788–1824, *Childe Harold's Pilgrimage*, I, 86]

12 Earth will grow worse till men redeem it, / And wars more evil, ere all wars cease. [G K Chesterton, 1874–1936, *A Song of Defeat*]

13 The wars of the peoples will be more terrible than those of kings. [Winston Churchill, 1874–1965 (speech in House of Commons on Army Estimates, 1901), in *Maxims and Reflections*, sect. v]

14 I have always been against the Pacifists during the quarrel, and against the Jingoes at its close. [Winston Churchill, 1874–1965, *My Early Life*, Ch. 26]

15 No one can guarantee success in war, but only deserve it. [Winston Churchill, 1874–1965, *The Second World War*, Vol. II, 27]

16 Laws are dumb in time of war. [Cicero, 106–43 BC, *Pro Milone*, IV, xi]

17 War is nothing more than the continuation of politics by other means. [Karl von Clausewitz, 1780–1831, *On War*, I, 1]; see 38

18 War is much too important a thing to be left to the generals. [Georges Clemenceau, 1841–1929 (said in 1886), in G Suarez, *Clemenceau*, but also attr. to Talleyrand, among others]; see 56

19 But war's a game, which, were their subjects wise, / Kings would not play at. [William Cowper, 1731–1800, *The Task*, Bk V, 187]

20 War, he sung, is toil and trouble; / Honour but an empty bubble; / Never ending, still beginning, / Fighting still, and still destroying. / If all the world be worth thy winning, / Think, oh think, it worth enjoying. [John Dryden, 1631–1700, *Alexander's Feast*, 99]

21 Men were made for war. Without it they wandered greyly about, getting under the feet of the women, who were trying to organize the really important things of life. [Alice Thomas Ellis, 1932– , *The Sin Eater*, p. 70]

22 Even the wars were girly after the Vikings left. [Ben Elton, 1959– , Rik Mayall, 1958– , Lise Mayer, *The Young Ones Book*]

23 In guerrilla war the struggle no longer concerns the place where you are, but the place where you are going. Each fighter carries his warring country between his toes. [Frantz Fanon, 1925–61, *The Wretched of the Earth*, Ch. 2]

24 What, then, was war? No mere discord of flags / But an infection of the common sky / That sagged ominously upon the earth / Even when the season was the airiest May? [Robert Graves, 1895–1985, *Recalling War*]

25 Frankly, I'd like to see the government get out of war altogether and leave the whole field to private industry. [Joseph Heller, 1923–99, *Catch-22*, Ch. 24]

26 Never think that war, no matter how necessary nor how justified, is not a crime. [Ernest Hemingway, 1899–1961, in *The Norton Book of Modern War*, ed. Paul Fussell, Introduction]

27 Older men declare war. But it is youth that must fight and die. And it is youth that must inherit the tribulation, the sorrow, and the triumphs that are the aftermath of war. [President Herbert Hoover, 1874–1964, speech at Republican National Convention, Chicago, 27 June 1944]

28 The first casualty when war comes is truth. [Hiram Johnson, 1866–1945, speech in US Senate, 1918. Can be traced back to Aeschylus]

29 In short . . . we must be constantly prepared for the worst, and constantly acting for the best . . . strong enough to win a war and . . . wise enough to prevent one. [President Lyndon B Johnson, 1908–73, Annual Message to Congress on the State of the Union, 8 Jan. 1964]

30 *Kennst Du das Land, wo die Kanonen blühn? Du kennst es nicht? Du wirst es kennen lernen.* – Do you know the land where the cannon flower grew? You don't? But you will. [Erich Kästner, 1899–1974, *Bei Durchsicht meiner Bücher*, '*Kennst Du das Land, wo die Kanonen blühn?*']

31 Four things greater than all things are, – / Women and Horses and Power and War. [Rudyard Kipling, 1865–1936, *The Ballad of the King's Jest*]

32 The most persistent sound which reverberates through men's history is the beating of war drums. [Arthur Koestler, 1905–83, *Janus: A Summing Up*, Prologue]

33 How is the world ruled and how do wars start? Diplomats tell lies to journalists and then believe what they read. [Karl Kraus, 1874–1936, *Half-truths and One-and-a-half Truths*, 'In This War']

34 Wars are fought by children – conceived by their mad demonic elders and fought by boys. [Penelope Lively, 1933– , *Moon Tiger*, Ch. 8]

35 Gad, sir, Lord Coot is right. War brings out the best in a man – and it stays out. [David Low, 1891–1963, Colonel Blimp in cartoon in *Evening Standard*]

36 It is not armaments that cause war, but wars ... that cause armaments. [Salvador de Madariaga, 1886–1978, *Morning without Noon*, Pt 1, Ch. 9]

37 The enemy advances, we retreat; the enemy camps, we harass; the enemy tires, we attack; the enemy retreats, we pursue. [Mao Zedong, 1893–1976, letter, 5 Jan. 1930, but in fact quoting a letter from the Front Committee to the Central Committee of the Chinese Communist Party]

38 Politics is war without bloodshed while war is politics with bloodshed. [Mao Zedong, 1893–1976, *On Protracted War*, May 1938]; see 17

39 Accursed be he that first invented war. [Christopher Marlowe, 1564–93, *Tamburlaine the Great*, Pt One, II. iv. 1]

40 War will never cease until babies begin to come into the world with larger cerebrums and smaller adrenal glands. [H L Mencken, 1880–1956, *Minority Report*, 164]

41 War hath no fury like a non-combatant. [C E Montague, 1867–1928, *Disenchantment*, Ch. 16]

42 The Doctor is said to have invented an extraordinary weapon which will make war less brutal. It is described as a very powerful liquid which rots braces at a distance of a mile. [J B Morton ('Beachcomber'), 1893–1979, *The Best of B*, 5]

43 In war, moral considerations account for three-quarters, the balance of actual forces only for the other quarter. [Napoleon Bonaparte, 1769–1821, letter, 27 Aug. 1808]

44 One does not fight with men against material; it is with material served by men that one makes war. [Marshal Pétain, 1856–1951, in Alistair Horne, *The Price of Glory*, Ch. 27]

45 War ... does not escape the laws of our old Hegel. It is a state of perpetual becoming. [Marcel Proust, 1871–1922, *Remembrance of Things Past: Time Regained*, Ch. 2]

46 The strength of a war waged without monetary reserves is as fleeting as a breath. Money is the sinews of battle. [François Rabelais, *c.*1492–1553, *Gargantua*, Ch. 46]

47 War is, after all, the universal perversion. We are all tainted: if we cannot experience our perversion at first hand we spend our time reading war stories, the pornography of war; or seeing war films, the blue films of war; or titillating our senses with the imagination of great deeds, the masturbation of war. [John Rae, 1931– , *The Custard Boys*, Ch. 13]

48 From the accountants' point of view, war was simply a speeded up kind of peace, with conspicuously increased consumption. [Frederic Raphael, 1931– , in *New Society*, 10 May 1984]

49 And the various holds and rolls and throws and breakfalls / Somehow or other I always seemed to put / In the wrong place. And as for war, my wars / Were global from the start. [Henry Reed, 1914–86, *Lessons of the War*, III, 'Unarmed Combat']

50 Sometimes they'll give a war and nobody will come. [Carl Sandburg, 1878–1967, *The People, Yes*]

51 O! now for ever / Farewell the tranquil mind; farewell content! / Farewell the plumèd troop and the big wars / That make ambition virtue! O farewell! / Farewell the neighing steed and the shrill trump, / The spirit-stirring drum, the ear-piercing fife, / The royal banner, and all quality, / Pride, pomp, and circumstance of glorious war! [William Shakespeare, 1564–1616, *Othello*, III. iii. 348]

52 I am tired and sick of war. Its glory is all moonshine ... War is hell. [General Sherman, 1820–91, attr. words in address at Michigan Military Academy, 19 June 1879. Phrase repeated, Columbus, Ohio, 11 Aug. 1880]

53 They start bloody wars they can't afford ... That old fool Chamberlain that was ... 'Peace in our time' ... Didn't give a thought to the cost of it – didn't enter his head to go into a few figures – get an estimate – soppy old sod. [Johnny Speight, 1920–98, BBC TV comedy series *Till Death Us Do Part*, 'The Bird Fancier']

54 War is capitalism with the gloves off and many who go to war know it but they go to war because they don't want to be a hero. [Tom Stoppard, 1937– , *Travesties*, I]

55 The guerrilla fights the war of the flea, and his military enemy suffers the dog's disadvantages: too much to defend; too small, ubiquitous, and agile an enemy to come to grips with. [Robert Taber, 1921– , *The War of the Flea*, Ch. 2]

56 War is much too serious a thing to be left to military men. [Charles-Maurice de Talleyrand, 1754–1838, attr. to him and others. Quoted by Aristide Briand to Lloyd George]; see 18

57 That war is an evil is something that we all know, and it would be pointless to go on cataloguing all the disadvantages involved in it. No one is forced into war by ignorance, nor, if he thinks he will gain from it, is he kept out of it by fear. [Thucydides, *c.*471–*c.*400 BC, *History*, IV, 4]

58 One of the main effects of war, after all, is that people are discouraged from being characters. [Kurt Vonnegut, 1922– , *Slaughterhouse 5*, Ch. 7]

59 What a country calls its vital economic interests are not the things which enable its citizens to live, but the things which enable it to make war. Petrol is more likely than wheat to be a cause of international conflict. [Simone Weil, 1909–43, in *Nouveaux Cahiers*, 1 and 15 Apr. 1937]

60 The third peculiarity of aerial warfare was that it was at once enormously destructive and entirely indecisive. [H G Wells, 1866–1946, *The War in the Air* (1908), Ch. 8]

61 As long as war is regarded as wicked, it will always have its fascination. When it is looked upon as vulgar, it will cease to be popular. [Oscar Wilde, 1854–1900, *The Critic as Artist*, Pt II]

62 Once lead this people into war and they'll forget there ever was such a thing as tolerance. [Woodrow Wilson, 1856–1924, in John Dos Passos, *Mr W's War*, Pt III, Ch. 2, sect. xii]

See also next category, WAR, WORLD WAR 1, WORLD WAR 2

WARS: INDIVIDUAL (in chronological order)

1 They now *ring* the bells, but they will soon *wring* their hands. [Robert Walpole, 1676–1745, remark on the declaration of war with Spain, 1739]

2 Another year! – another deadly blow! / Another mighty empire overthrown. [William Wordsworth, 1770–1850, *Nov. 1806*]

3 [The Russians] dash on towards the thin red line tipped with steel. [W H Russell, 1820–1907, *The British Expedition to the Crimea*]

4 My opinion is that the Northern States will manage somehow to muddle through. [John Bright, 1811–89, said during the American Civil War]

5 Out of that bungled, unwise war / An alp of unforgiveness grew. [William Plomer, 1903–73, *The Boer War*]

6 The stars are dead; the animals will not look: / We are left alone with our day, and the time is short and / History to the defeated / May say Alas but cannot help or pardon. [W H Auden, *Spain 1937*, stanza 23]

7 The wrong war, at the wrong place, at the wrong time, and with the wrong enemy. [General Omar Bradley, 1893–1981, at the Senate inquiry over General MacArthur's proposal to carry the Korean conflict into China, 15 May 1951]

8 If we lose this war, I'll start another in my wife's name. [Moshe Dayan, 1915–81, of Six Day War, 1967, attr.]

9 The Falklands thing [war of 1982] was a fight between two bald men over a comb. [Jorge Luis Borges, 1899–1986, in *Time* magazine, 14 Feb. 1983]

10 [To heckler who said, 'At least Mrs Thatcher has got guts' in reference to Falklands War] And it's a pity people had to leave theirs on the ground at Goose Green in order to prove it. [Neil Kinnock, 1942– , in TV election programme, 5 June 1983]

11 The great, the jewel and the mother of battles has begun. [Saddam Hussein, 1937– , at the outset of the Gulf War, 17 Jan. 1991]

See also previous category, VIETNAM, WAR, WORLD WAR 1, WORLD WAR 2

WASTE

1 Neither cast ye your pearls before swine. [Bible, NT, *St Matthew* 7:6]

2 Some seeds fell by the way side. [Bible, NT, *St Matthew* 13:4]

3 I don't particularly mind waste, but I think it's a pity not to know what one is wasting. Some old ladies use pound notes as bookmarks: this is silly only if it is absent-minded. [Peter Brook, 1925– , *The Empty Space*, Ch. 1]

4 Slowly the poison the whole blood stream fills ... / The waste remains, the waste remains and kills. [William Empson, 1906–84, *Missing Dates*]

5 Full many a gem of purest ray serene / The dark unfathomed caves of ocean bear: / Full many a flower is born to blush unseen, / And waste its sweetness on the desert air. [Thomas Gray, 1716–71, *Elegy Written in a Country Churchyard*, 14]

WATER

1 And Noah he often said to his wife when he sat down to dine, / 'I don't care where the water goes if it doesn't get into the wine'. [G K Chesterton, 1874–1936, *Wine and Water*]

2 [When asked whether the Niagara Falls looked the same as when he first saw them] Well, the principle seems the same. The water still keeps falling over. [Winston Churchill, 1874–1965, *The Second World War*, Vol. V, 5]

3 *O fons Bandusiae splendidior vitro.* – O spring of Bandusia, brighter than glass. [Horace, 65–8 BC, *Odes*, III, xiii, 1]

4 It's not the taste of water I object to. It's the after-effects. [Mgr Ronald Knox, 1888–1957, in *Geoffrey Madan's Notebooks*, ed. J A Gere and John Sparrow, 'Extracts and Summaries']

5 The biggest waste of water in the country by far. You spend half a pint and flush two gallons. [Philip, Duke of Edinburgh, 1921– , attr., speech, 1965]

6 Water is best. [(Inscription over the Pump Room, Bath) Pindar, 518–*c*.437 BC, *Olympian Odes*, I]

See also DRINK: WEAK, RIVERS, SEA

WEAKNESS

1 Achilles only had one Achilles heel, I have a whole Achilles body. [Woody Allen, 1935– , in film *Mighty Aphrodite*]

2 He wist not that the Lord was departed from him. [(Of Samson) Bible, OT, *Judges* 16:20]

3 The weak have one weapon: the errors of those who think they are strong. [Georges Bidault, 1899–1983; *Observer*, 'Sayings of the Week', 15 July 1962]

4 The concessions of the weak are the concessions of fear. [Edmund Burke, 1729–97, speech on conciliation with America, 22 Mar. 1775]

5 The spirit burning but unbent, / May writhe, rebel – the weak alone repent! [Lord Byron, 1788–1824, *The Corsair*, II, 10]

6 We are the hollow men / We are the stuffed men / Leaning together. [T S Eliot, 1888–1965, *The Hollow Men*, I]

7 Like the feather pillow he bears the mark of the last person who sat on him. [Earl Haig, 1861–1928 (of the Earl of Derby), letter to Lady Haig, 14 Jan. 1918]

8 Like all weak men he laid an exaggerated stress on not changing one's mind. [W Somerset Maugham, 1874–1965, *Of Human Bondage*, Ch. 37]

9 Men always try to make virtues of their weaknesses. Fear of death and fear of life become piety. [H L Mencken, 1880–1956, *Minority Report*, 54]

10 To be weak is miserable / Doing or suffering. [John Milton, 1608–74, *Paradise Lost*, Bk i, 157]

11 Yet do I fear thy nature; / It is too full o' the milk of human kindness / To catch the nearest way. [William Shakespeare, 1564–1616, *Macbeth*, I. v. (17)]

12 I am a tainted wether of the flock, / Meetest for death: the weakest kind of fruit / Drops earliest to the ground. [*The Merchant of Venice*, IV. i. 114]

13 'Tis not enough to help the feeble up, / But to support him after. [*Timon of Athens*, I. i. 108]

14 Life persists in the vulnerable, the sensitive ... They carry it on. The invulnerable, the too heavily armoured perish. [Elizabeth Taylor, 1912–75, *A Wreath of Roses*, Ch. 5]

15 Never support two weaknesses at the same time. It's your combination sinners – your lecherous liars and your miserly drunkards – who dishonour the vices and bring them into bad repute. [Thornton Wilder, 1897–1975, *The Matchmaker*, III]

See also POWER, STRENGTH

WEALTH

1 Riches are a good handmaiden, but the worst mistress. [Francis Bacon, 1561–1626, *De Dignitate et Augmentis Scientiarium*, Pt I, vi, 3, 6]

2 Riches are for spending. [Francis Bacon, 1561–1626, *Essays*, 28, 'Of Expense']

3 Riches certainly make themselves wings. [Bible, OT, *Proverbs* 23:5]; see 7

4 If riches increase, set not your heart upon them. God hath spoken once; twice have I heard this; that power belongeth unto God. [Bible, OT, *Psalms* 62:10]

5 If we command our wealth, we shall be rich and free; if our wealth commands us, we are poor indeed. [Edmund Burke, 1729–97, *Letters on a Regicide Peace*, 1]

6 To a shower of gold most things are penetrable. [Thomas Carlyle, 1795–1881, *French Revolution*, Pt I, Bk iii, Ch. 7]

7 Riches have wings, and grandeur is a dream. [William Cowper, 1731–1800, *The Task*, Bk III, 263]; see 3

8 In every state wealth is a sacred thing: in democracies it is the only sacred thing. [Anatole France, 1844–1924, *Penguin Island*, Bk 6, Ch. 2]

9 Wealth has never been a sufficient source of honour in itself. It must be advertised and the normal medium is obtrusively expensive goods. [J K Galbraith, 1908– , *The Affluent Society*, Ch. 7, v]

10 If you can actually count your money then you are not a really rich man. [Paul Getty, 1892–1976, in Bernard Levin, *The Pendulum Years*, Ch. 1]

11 Ill fares the land, to hastening ills a prey, / Where wealth accumulates, and men decay; / Princes and lords may flourish, or may fade; / A breath can make them, as a breath has made; / But a bold peasantry, their country's pride, / When once destroyed, can never be supplied. [Oliver Goldsmith, 1728–74, *The Deserted Village*, 51]

12 As their wealth increaseth, so enclose / Infinite riches in a little room. [Christopher Marlowe, 1564–93, *The Jew of Malta*, I. i. 36]

13 Let none admire / That riches grow in hell; that soil may best / Deserve the precious bane. [John Milton, 1608–74, *Paradise Lost*, Bk i, 690]

14 Spend, spend, spend. [(When asked what she was going to do with record football pools win) Vivian Nicholson, 1936– , in *Daily Herald*, Sept. 1961. Also used as title of her autobiography]

15 There is no wealth but Life. [John Ruskin, 1819–1900, *Unto This Last*, IV, §77]

16 If Heaven had looked upon riches to be a valuable thing, it would not have given them to such a scoundrel. [Jonathan Swift, 1677–1745, letter to Miss Vanhomrigh, 12 Aug. 1720]

17 It is not the creation of wealth that is wrong, but love of money for its own sake. [Margaret Thatcher, 1925– , speech to the General Assembly of the Church of Scotland, Edinburgh, 21 May 1988]

See also MILLIONAIRES, MONEY, POVERTY, RICH

WEATHER

1 What dreadful hot weather we have! It keeps me in a continual state of inelegance. [Jane Austen, 1775–1817, *Letters*, 18 Sept. 1796]

2 This is a London particular ... A fog, miss. [Charles Dickens, 1812–70, *Bleak House*, Ch. 3]

3 The yellow fog that rubs its back upon the windowpanes. [T S Eliot, 1888–1965, *Love Song of J. Alfred Prufrock*]

4 This is the weather the cuckoo likes / And so do I. [Thomas Hardy, 1840–1928, *Weathers*]

5 Wherever you go, the weather is, without exception, exceptional. [Kingsley Martin, 1897–1969, quoted by Katharine Whitehorn in *Observer*, 26 June 1988]

See also AUTUMN, RAIN, SEASONS, SPRING, SUMMER, WINDS, WINTER

WEDDINGS

1 A woman seldom asks advice before she has bought her wedding clothes. [Joseph Addison, 1672–1719, *The Spectator*, 475]

2 Says John, It is my wedding-day, / And all the world would stare, / If wife should dine at Edmonton, / And I should dine at Ware. [William Cowper, 1731–1800, *John Gilpin*, 49]

3 Walter! Walter! Lead me to the altar, / I'll make a better man of you. [Gracie Fields, 1898–1979, song: *Walter, Walter*, words and music by W Haines et al.]

4 Same old slippers, / Same old rice, / Same old glimpse of / Paradise. [W J Lampton, 1859–1917, *June Weddings*]

5 Pussy said to the Owl, 'You elegant fowl! / How charmingly sweet you sing! / O let us be married! too long we have tarried: / But what shall we do for a ring?' / They sailed away for a year and a day, / To the land where the Bong-Tree grows, / And there in a wood a Piggy-wig stood, / With a ring at the end of his nose. [Edward Lear, 1812–88, *Nonsense Songs*, 'The Owl and the Pussy-Cat']

6 There was I, waiting at the church, / Waiting at the church, waiting at the church, / When I found he'd left me in the lurch, / Lor', how it did upset me . . . / Can't get away to marry you today – / My wife won't let me! [Fred Leigh, d.1924, song: *Waiting at the Church* (1906)]

7 I'm getting married in the morning, / Ding dong! the bells are gonna chime. / Pull out the stopper! / Let's have a whopper! / But get me to the church on time! [Alan Jay Lerner, 1918–86, *My Fair Lady*, I. iii]

8 It has been said that a bride's attitude towards her betrothed can be summed up in three words: Aisle. Altar. Hymn. [Frank Muir, 1920–98, in Frank Muir and Denis Norden, *Upon My Word!*, 'A Jug of Wine', but perhaps of earlier origin]

9 The trouble / with being best man is, you doon't get a chance to prove it. [Les Murray, 1938–   , *The Boy Who Stole the Funeral*]

10 If any of you know cause, or just impediment. [*The Book of Common Prayer*, Solemnization of Matrimony, Banns]

11 First, it was ordained for the procreation of children. [*The Book of Common Prayer*, Solemnization of Matrimony]

12 To have and to hold from this day forward, for better for worse, for richer for poorer, in sickness and in health, to love and to cherish, till death us do part. [*The Book of Common Prayer*, Solemnization of Matrimony]

13 A happy bridesmaid makes a happy bride. [Alfred, Lord Tennyson, 1809–92, *The Bridesmaid*]

See also MARRIAGE

WICKEDNESS

1 I myself have seen the ungodly in great power: and flourishing like a green bay-tree. [Bible, OT, *Psalms* 37:36 (*The Book of Common Prayer* version)]

2 If thou, Lord, shouldest mark iniquities, O Lord, who shall stand? [Bible, OT, *Psalms* 130:3]

3 The wickedness of the world is so great you have to run your legs off to avoid having them stolen from under you. [Bertolt Brecht, 1898–1956, *The Threepenny Opera*, I. iii]

4 For every inch that is not fool is rogue. [John Dryden, 1631–1700, *Absalom and Achitophel*, Pt II, 463]

5 I have observed, in the course of a dishonest life, that when a rogue is outlining a treacherous plan, he works harder to convince himself than to move his hearers. [George Macdonald Fraser, 1925–   , *Flashman*, p. 135]

6 In every deed of mischief he [Comenus] had a heart to resolve, a head to contrive, and a hand to execute. [Edward Gibbon, 1737–94, *The Decline and Fall of the Roman Empire*, Ch. 48]

7 When they spoke of the mammon of iniquity / The coins in my pockets reddened like stove-lids. [Seamus Heaney, 1939–   , *Terminus*]

8 Wickedness is always easier than virtue; for it takes the short cut to everything. [Dr Samuel Johnson, 1709–84, in James Boswell, *Tour of the Hebrides*, 17 Sept. 1773]

9 No one ever reached the depths of wickedness all at once. [Juvenal, 60–*c.*130, *Satires*, II, 83]

10 O villain, villain, smiling, damned villain! / My tables, – meet it is I set it down, / That one may smile, and smile, and be a villain, / At least I'm sure it may be so in Denmark. [William Shakespeare, 1564–1616, *Hamlet*, I. v. 106]

11 Now am I, if a man should speak truly, little better than one of the wicked. [*1 Henry IV*, I. ii. (105)]

12 How oft the sight of means to do ill deeds / Makes ill deeds done! [*King John*, IV. ii. 219]

13 The villany you teach me I will execute, and it shall go hard but I will better the instruction. [*The Merchant of Venice*, III. i. [(76)]

14 If a man is going to be a villain, in heaven's name let him remain a fool. [Archbishop William Temple, 1881–1944, *Mens Creatrix*]

See also EVIL, GOOD, VICE, VIRTUE

WIDOWS & WIDOWERS

1 These widows, sir, are the most perverse creatures in the world. [Joseph Addison, 1672–1719, *The Spectator*, 335]

2 Take example by your father, my boy, and be wery careful o' vidders all your life, specially if they've kept a public house, Sammy. [Charles Dickens, 1812–70, *Pickwick Papers*, Ch. 20]

3 When widows exclaim loudly against second marriage, I would always lay a wager that the man, if not the wedding-day, is absolutely fixed on. [Henry Fielding, 1707–54, *Amelia*, vi, 8]

4 Do like other widows – buy yourself weeds, and be cheerful. [John Gay, 1685–1732, *The Beggar's Opera*, II. xi]

5 What is a woman that you forsake her, / And the hearth-fire and the home-acre, / To go with the old grey Widowmaker? [Rudyard Kipling, 1865–1936, *Harp Song of the Dane Women*]

6 Well, a widow, I see, is a kind of sinecure. [William Wycherley, 1640?–1716, *The Plain Dealer*, V. iii]

See also MOURNING

WILLS, see INHERITANCE

WINDS

1 O Western Wind, when wilt thou blow / That the small rain down can rain? / Christ, that my love were in my arms / And I in my bed again! [anon., 16th cent.]

2 The wind bloweth where it listeth, and thou hearest the sound thereof, but canst not tell whence it cometh, and whither it goeth. [Bible, NT, *St John* 3:8]

3 The south-wind strengthens to a gale, / Across the moon the clouds fly fast, / The house is smitten as with a flail, / The chimney shudders to the blast. [Robert Bridges, 1844–1930, *Low Barometer*]

4 Of a' the airts the wind can blaw, / I dearly like the west. [Robert Burns, 1759–96, *Of A' the Airts*]

5 There came a wind like a bugle; / It quivered through the grass. [Emily Dickinson, 1830–86, *There Came a Wind*]

6 It's a warm wind, the west wind, full of birds' cries. [John Masefield, 1878–1967, *The West Wind*]

7 Wind, wind! thou art sad, art thou kind? / Wind, wind, unhappy! thou art blind, / Yet still thou wanderest the lily-seed to find. [William Morris, 1834–96, *The Wind*]

8 Who has seen the wind? / Neither you nor I; / But when the trees bow down their heads / The wind is passing by. [Christina Rossetti, 1830–94, *Sing-Song*]

9 Blow, winds, and crack your cheeks! rage! blow! / You cataracts and hurricanoes spout / Till you have drenched our steeples, drowned the cocks! [William Shakespeare, 1564–1616, *King Lear*, III. ii. 1]

10 West wind, wanton wind, wilful wind, womanish wind, false wind from over the water, will you never blow again? [George Bernard Shaw, 1856–1950, *St Joan*, III]

11 O wild West Wind, thou breath of Autumn's being, / Thou, from whose unseen presence the leaves dead / Are driven, like ghosts from an enchanter fleeing, / Yellow, and black, and pale, and hectic red, / Pestilence-stricken multitudes. [P B Shelley, 1792–1822, *Ode to the West Wind*, 1]

12 Scatter, as from an unextinguished hearth / Ashes and sparks, my words among mankind! / Be through my lips to unawakened earth / The trumpet of a prophecy! O, Wind. [P B Shelley, 1792–1822, *Ode to the West Wind*, 66]

13 Yet true it is, as cow chews cud, / And trees at spring do yield forth bud, / Except wind stands as never it stood, / It is an ill wind turns none to good. [Thomas Tusser, 1524?–80, *Five Hundred Points of Good Husbandry*, 'A Description of the Properties of Winds']

14 The wind blows out of the gates of the day, / The wind blows over the lonely of heart, / And the lonely of heart is withered away. [W B Yeats, 1865–1939, *The Land of Heart's Desire*]

See also WEATHER, WIND

WINE

1 For when the wine is in, the wit is out. [Thomas Becon, 1512–67, *Catechism*, 375]

2 Look not upon the wine when it is red. [Bible, OT, *Proverbs* 23:31]

3 And wine that maketh glad the heart of man, and oil to make his face to shine, and bread which strengtheneth man's heart. [Bible, OT, *Psalms* 104:15]

4 Drink no longer water, but use a little wine for thy stomach's sake and thine often infirmities. [Bible, NT, *1 Timothy* 5:23]

5 Go fetch to me a pint o' wine, / An' fill it in a silver tassie. [Robert Burns, 1759–96, *Go Fetch to me a Pint o' Wine*]

6 Let us have wine and women, mirth and laughter, / Sermons and soda-water the day after. [Lord Byron, 1788–1824, *Don Juan*, I. 178]

7 The wine they drink in Paradise / They make in Haute Lorraine. [G K Chesterton, 1874–1936, *A Cider Song*]

8 If an angel out of heaven / Brings you other things to drink, / Thank him for his kind attentions, / Go and pour them down the sink. [G K Chesterton, 1874–1936, *The Song of Right and Wrong*]

9 The Duke of Clarence ... a prisoner in the Tower, was secretly put to death and drowned in a barrel of Malmesey wine. [Robert Fabyan, d.1513, *Chronicles* (1477; early edns give 'malvesye')]

10 The Grape that can with Logic absolute / The Two-and-Seventy jarring Sects confute. [Edward Fitzgerald, 1809–83, *The Rubá'iyát of Omar Khayyám*, Edn 1, 43]

11 I often wonder what the Vintners buy / One half so precious as the Goods they sell. [Edward Fitzgerald, 1809–83, *The Rubá'iyát of Omar Khayyám*, Edn 1, 71]

12 Fill ev'ry glass, for wine inspires us, / And fires us / With courage, love and joy. / Women and wine should life employ. / Is there aught else on earth desirous? [John Gay, 1685–1732, *The Beggar's Opera*, II. i]

13 He said that few people had intellectual resources sufficient to forgo the pleasures of wine. They could not otherwise contrive how to fill the interval between dinner and supper. [Dr Samuel Johnson, 1709–84, in James Boswell, *Life of J*, 1772]

14 O for a draught of vintage! that hath been / Cooled a long age in the deep delvèd earth, / Tasting of flora and the country green, / Dance, and Provençal song, and sunburnt mirth! / O for a beaker full of the warm South, / Full of the true, the blushful Hippocrene, / With beaded bubbles winking at the brim, / And purple-stainèd mouth; / That I might drink, and leave the world unseen, / And with thee fade away into the forest dim. [John Keats, 1795–1821, *Ode to a Nightingale*, 1]

15 Frenchmen drink wine just like we used to drink water before Prohibition. [Ring Lardner, 1885–1933; in R E Drennan, *Wit's End*]

16 Wine experts are of two kinds, gastronomic and intellectual, distinguishable according to whether on sight of the bottle they reach for their glass or their glasses. [Thomas McKeown, 1912–88, in *Perspectives in Biology and Medicine*, Summer 1981, 'It Has Been Said']

17 Bacchus, that first from out the purple grape, / Crushed the sweet poison of misusèd wine. [John Milton, 1608–74, *Comus*, 46]

18 *In vino veritas.* – Truth comes out in wine. [Pliny the Elder, 23–79. Proverbial adaptation of *Natural History*, xiv, 28]

19 A good general rule is to state that the bouquet is better than the taste, and vice versa. [Stephen Potter, 1900–1969, *One-upmanship*, Ch. 14]

20 If I had a thousand sons, the first human principle I would teach them should be, to forswear thin potations and to addict themselves to sack. [William Shakespeare, 1564–1616, *2 Henry IV*, IV. ii. (133)]

21 Good wine is a good familiar creature if it be well used. [*Othello*, II. iii. (315)]

22 Pour out the wine without restraint or stay, / Pour not by cups, but by the bellyful, / Pour out to all that wull. [Edmund Spenser, 1552?–99, *Epithalamion*, 18]

23 It's a naïve domestic Burgundy without any breeding, but I think you'll be amused by its presumption. [James Thurber, 1894–1961, *Men, Women and Dogs*, cartoon caption]

See also BEER, DRINK : STRONG

WINTER

1 Many human beings say that they enjoy the winter, but what they really enjoy is feeling proof against it. [Richard Adams, 1920– , *Watership Down*, Ch. 50]

2 In seed time learn, in harvest teach, in winter enjoy. [William Blake, 1757–1827, *The Marriage of Heaven and Hell*, 'Proverbs of Hell']

3 When men were all asleep the snow came flying, / In large white flakes falling on the city brown, / Stealthily and perpetually settling and loosely lying, / Hushing the latest traffic of the drowsy town. [Robert Bridges, 1844–1930, *London Snow*]

4 Winter is an abstract season; it is low on colours . . . and big on the imperatives of cold and brief daylight . . . beauty at low temperatures *is* beauty. [Joseph Brodsky, 1940– , *Watermark*, p. 27]

5 The English winter – ending in July, / To recommence in August. [Lord Byron, 1788–1824, *Don Juan*, XIII, 42]

6 Whether the eave-drops fall / Heard only in the trances of the blast, / Or if the secret ministry of frost / Shall hang them up in silent icicles, / Quietly shining to the quiet moon. [Samuel Taylor Coleridge, 1772–1834, *Frost at Midnight*, 70]

7 O Winter, ruler of th' inverted year. [William Cowper, 1731–1800, *The Task*, Bk IV, 120]

8 The winter evening settles down / With smell of steaks in passage ways. [T S Eliot, 1888–1965, *Preludes*, I]

9 Winter has been sacked / for negligence / It appears he left / the sun on all day. [Roger McGough, 1937– , *Sky in the Pie*, 'March Ingorders']

10 I, singularly moved / To love the lovely that are not beloved, / Of all the seasons, most / Love winter. [Coventry Patmore, 1823–96, *The Unknown Eros*, Bk i, 3, 'Winter']

11 Winter is for women – / The woman still at her knitting, / At the cradle of Spanish walnut, / Her body a bulb in the cold and too dumb to think. [Sylvia Plath, 1932–63, *Wintering*]

12 Winter is icummen in, / Lhude sing Goddamm. / Raineth drop and staineth slop, / And how the wind doth ramm! / Sing: Goddamm. [Ezra Pound, 1885–1972, *Ancient Music*]; see SUMMER, 1

13 Snow had fallen, snow on snow, / Snow on snow, / In the bleak mid-winter, / Long ago. [Christina Rossetti, 1830–94, *Mid-Winter*]

14 When icicles hang by the wall / And Dick the shepherd blows his nail, / And Tom bears logs into the hall / And milk comes frozen home in pail, / When blood is nipped, and ways be foul, / Then nightly sings the staring owl / Tu-who; / Tu-whit, tu-who – a merry note, / While greasy Joan doth keel the pot. [William Shakespeare, 1564–1616, *Love's Labour's Lost*, V. ii. (920)]

15 A widow bird sate mourning for her love / Upon a wintry bough; / The frozen wind crept on above, / The freezing stream below. [P B Shelley, 1792–1822, *Charles I*, v]

16 O, Wind, / If Winter comes, can Spring be far behind? [P B Shelley, 1792–1822, *Ode to the West Wind*, 69]

17 In winter, when the dismal rain / Came down in slanting lines, / And Wind, that grand old harper, smote / His thunder-harp of pines. [Alexander Smith, 1830–67, *A Life Drama*, ii]

18 For winter's rains and ruins are over, / And all the season of snows and sins; / The days dividing lover and lover, / The light that loses,the night that wins. [A C Swinburne, 1837–1909, *Atalanta in Calydon*, 4]

19 It is a winter's tale / That the snow blind twilight ferries over the lakes / And floating fields from the farm in the cup of the vales. [Dylan Thomas, 1914–53, *A Winter's Tale*]

See also AUTUMN, SEASONS, SPRING, SUMMER

WISDOM

1 A wise man will make more opportunities than he finds. [Francis Bacon, 1561–1626, *Essays*, 52, 'Of Ceremonies and Respects']

2 Nothing doth more hurt in a state than that cunning men pass for wise. [Francis Bacon, 1561–1626, *Essays*, 22, 'Of Cunning']

3 The wise man thinks once before he speaks twice. [Robert Benchley, 1889–1945, *Maxims from the Chinese*]

4 How can he get wisdom . . . whose talk is of bullocks? [Bible, Apocrypha, *Ecclesiasticus* 38:25]

5 The price of wisdom is above rubies. [Bible, OT, *Job* 28:18]

6 Wisdom is the principal thing; therefore get wisdom: and with all thy getting get understanding. [Bible, OT, *Proverbs* 4:7]

7 Out of the mouth of babes and sucklings hast thou ordained strength. [Bible, OT, *Psalms* 8:2]

8 So teach us to number our days, that we may apply our hearts unto wisdom. [Bible, OT, *Psalms* 90:12]

9 The fear of the Lord is the beginning of wisdom. [Bible, OT, *Psalms* 111:10]

10 The wisdom of this world is foolishness with God. [Bible, NT, *1 Corinthians* 3:19]

11 When I was a child, I spake as a child, I understood as a child, I thought as a child: but when I became a man, I put away childish things. For now we see through a glass, darkly; but then face to face. [Bible, NT, *1 Corinthians* 13:11]

12 Wisdom is justified of her children. [Bible, NT, *St Matthew* 11:19]

13 The sage left nothing in his ink-horn. [Miguel Cervantes, 1547–1616, *Don Quixote*, Pt II, Ch. 3]

14 The gretteste clerkes been noght the wysest men. [Geoffrey Chaucer, 1340?–1400, *Canterbury Tales*, 'The Reeve's Tale', 134]

15 Be wiser than other people if you can, but do not tell them so. [Earl of Chesterfield, 1694–1773, letter to his son, 19 Nov. 1745]

16 When all philosophies shall fail, / This word alone shall fit; / That a sage feels too small for life, / And a fool too large for it [G K Chesterton, 1874–1936, *The Ballad of the White Horse*, 8]

17 I was never tired of listening to his wisdom or imparting my own. [Winston Churchill, 1874–1965, *My Early Life*, Ch. 7]

18 A sadder and a wiser man, / He rose the morrow morn. [Samuel Taylor Coleridge, 1772–1834, *The Ancient Mariner*, Pt VII]

19 History teaches us that men and nations behave wisely once they have exhausted all other alternatives. [Abba Eban, 1915– , speech in London, 16 Dec. 1970]

20 The wise through excess of wisdom is made a fool. [Ralph Waldo Emerson, 1803–82, *Essays*, 'Experience']

21 We are wiser than we know. [Ralph Waldo Emerson, 1803–82, *Essays*, 'The Over-Soul']

22 Some are weather-wise, some are otherwise. [Benjamin Franklin, 1706–90, *Poor Richard's Almanac*, Feb. 1735]

23 *Three* wise men – are you serious? [Graffito from *c.*1984; used as epigraph to Julian Barnes, *Staring at the Sun*, Pt 2]

24 Wisdom denotes the pursuing of the best ends by the best means. [Francis Hutcheson, 1694–1746, *Inquiry into the Original of Our Ideas of Beauty and Virtue*, I, v]

25 The art of being wise is the art of knowing what to overlook. [William James, 1842–1910, *The Principles of Psychology*, Ch. 22]

26 With these celestial Wisdom calms the mind, / And makes the happiness she does not find. [Dr Samuel Johnson, 1709–84, *The Vanity of Human Wishes*, 367]

27 With grave / Aspect he rose, and in his rising seemed / A pillar of state; deep on his front engraven / Deliberation sat and public care; / And princely counsel in his face yet shone, / Majestic though in ruin. [John Milton, 1608–74, *Paradise Lost*, Bk ii, 300]

28 The first and wisest of them all professed / To know this only, that he nothing knew. [John Milton, 1608–74, *Paradise Regained*, Bk iv, 293]

29 Be wisely worldly, be not worldly wise. [Francis Quarles, 1592–1644, *Emblems*, Bk II, ii, 46]

30 So wise so young, they say, do never live long. [William Shakespeare, 1564–1616, *Richard III*, III. i. 79]

31 To be wise, and love, / Exceeds man's might. [*Troilus and Cressida*, III. ii. (163)]

32 Knowledge comes, but wisdom lingers. [Alfred, Lord Tennyson, 1809–92, *Locksley Hall*, 143]

33 Be wise today: 'tis madness to defer. [Edward Young, 1683–1765, *Night Thoughts*, 'Night I', 390]

See also next category, FOOLS, INTELLECT, MIND

WIT

1 One cannot be always laughing at a man without now and then stumbling on something witty. [Jane Austen, 1775–1817, *Pride and Prejudice*, 40]

2 Conquered people tend to be witty. [Saul Bellow, 1915– , *Mr Sammler's Planet*, Ch. 2]

3 The loudest wit I e'er was deafened with. [Lord Byron, 1788–1824, *Don Juan*, XVI, 81]

4 I never in my life said anything merely because I thought it funny; though, of course, I have an ordinary human vainglory, and may have thought it funny because I had said it. [G K Chesterton, 1874–1936, *Orthodoxy*, Ch. 1]

5 What he has is wit, not humour, and wit alone never turns inwards. [Robertson Davies, 1913–95, *The Rebel Angels*, 'Second Paradise, VI']

6 A man who could make so vile a pun would not scruple to pick a pocket. [John Dennis, 1657–1734, in *Gentleman's Magazine*, 1781]

7 Great wits are sure to madness near allied, / And thin partitions do their bounds divide. [John Dryden, 1631–1700, *Absalom and Achitophel*, Pt I, 156]

8 A thing well said will be wit in all languages. [John Dryden, 1631–1700, *Essay of Dramatic Poesy*]

9 [Wit] involves, probably, a recognition, implicit in the expression of every experience, of other kinds of experience that are possible. [T S Eliot, 1888–1965, *Selected Essays*, 'Andrew Marvell']

10 It [a pun] is a pistol let off at the ear; not a feather to tickle the intellect. [Charles Lamb, 1775–1834, *Last Essays of Elia*, 'Popular Fallacies', 9]

11 Impropriety is the soul of wit. [W Somerset Maugham, 1874–1965, *The Moon and Sixpence*, Ch. 4]

12 The English are very fond of humour, but they are afraid of wit. For wit is like a sword, but humour is like a jester's bladder. [J B Morton ('Beachcomber'), 1893–1979, from *Spectator*; in *The Sunday Times*, 27 Sept. 1987]

13 A wit with dunces, and a dunce with wits. [Alexander Pope, 1688–1744, *The Dunciad*, Bk iv, 90]

14 True wit is nature to advantage dressed, / What oft was thought but ne'er so well expressed. [Alexander Pope, 1688–1744, *An Essay on Criticism*, 297]

15 And wit's the noblest frailty of the mind. [Thomas Shadwell, 1642?–92, *A True Widow*, II. i]

16 I shall ne'er be ware of mine own wit till I break my shins against it. [William Shakespeare, 1564–1616, *As You Like It*, II. iv. (59)]

17 Brevity is the soul of wit. [*Hamlet*, II. ii. 90]

18 FALSTAFF: I am not only witty in myself, but the cause that wit is in other men. I do here walk before thee like a sow that hath overwhelmed all her litter but one. [*2 Henry IV*, I. ii. (10)]

19 Methinks sometimes I have no more wit than a Christian or an ordinary man has; but I am a great eater of beef, and I believe that does harm to my wit. [*Twelfth Night*, I. iii. (90)]

See also CLEVERNESS, COMEDY, FOOLS, HUMOUR, IRONY, SATIRE

WIVES

1 Basically my wife was immature. I'd be at home in the bath and she'd come in and sink my boats. [Woody Allen, 1935– , in *Nudge Nudge, Wink Wink*, ed. Nigel Rees, 12]

2 It is a truth universally acknowledged, that a single man in possession of a good fortune, must be in want of a wife. [Jane Austen, 1775–1817, *Pride and Prejudice*, Ch. 1]

3 Wives are young men's mistresses; companions for middle age; and old men's nurses. [Francis Bacon, 1561–1626, *Essays*, 8, 'Of Marriage and Single Life']

4 What is it then to have or have no wife, / But single thraldom, or a double strife? [Francis Bacon, 1561–1626, *The World*]

5 A virtuous woman is a crown to her husband: but she that maketh ashamed is as rottenness in his bones. [Bible, OT, *Proverbs* 12:4]

6 It is better to dwell in a corner of the housetop, than with a brawling woman in a wide house. [Bible, OT, *Proverbs* 21:9]

7 Giving honour unto the wife, as unto the weaker vessel. [Bible, NT, *1 Peter* 3:7]

8 The starring role of Housewife – a woman who married a house. [Maeve Binchy, 1940– , in *Guardian*, 5 Feb. 1985]

9 When a man has married a wife, he finds out whether / Her knees and elbows are only glued together. [William Blake, 1757–1827, *Miscellaneous Epigrams*]

10 A man's friend likes him but leaves him as he is: his wife loves him and is always trying to turn him into somebody else. [G K Chesterton, 1874–1936, *Orthodoxy*, Ch. 5]

11 Wife, spouse, my dear, joy, jewel, love, sweet-heart and the rest of that nauseous cant, in which men and their wives are so fulsomely familiar. [William Congreve, 1670–1729, *The Way of the World*, IV. v]

12 There is no fury like an ex-wife searching for a new lover. [Cyril Connolly, 1903–74, *The Unquiet Grave*, Ch. 1]

13 The true index of a man's character is the health of his wife. [Cyril Connolly, 1903–74, *The Unquiet Grave*, Ch. 1]

14 He knows little, who tells his wife all he knows. [Thomas Fuller, 1608–61, *The Holy State*, Bk i, Ch. 3]

15 One wife is too much for most husbands to hear, / But two at a time there's no mortal can bear. [John Gay, 1685–1732, *The Beggar's Opera*, III. xi]

16 I . . . chose my wife, as she did her wedding gown, not for a fine glossy surface, but such qualities as would wear well. [Oliver Goldsmith, 1728–74, *The Vicar of Wakefield*, Ch. 1]

17 [When asked why he had never married] Why the hell should I get a wife when the man next door's got one? ['Furry' Lewis, 1893–1981, at age eighty-seven in 1980; in *Was It Good for You Too?*, ed. Bob Chieger]

18 I've been married six months. She looks like a million dollars, but she only knows a hundred and twenty words and she's only got two ideas in her head. The other one's hats. [Eric Linklater, 1889–1974, *Juan in America*, II, 5]

19 The Duke returned from the wars today and did pleasure me in his top-boots. [Sarah, Duchess of Marlborough, 1660–1744, attr., and various versions]

20 Best image of myself and dearer half. [John Milton, 1608–74, *Paradise Lost*, Bk v, 95]

21 My wife, who, poor wretch, is troubled with her lonely life. [Samuel Pepys, 1633–1703, *Diary*, 19 Dec. 1662]

22 She who ne'er answers till a husband cools, / Or if she rules him, never shows she rules; / Charms by accepting, by submitting sways, / Yet has her humour most when she obeys. [Alexander Pope, 1688–1744, *Moral Essays*, Epistle II, 261]

23 Dwell I but in the suburbs / Of your good pleasure? If it be no more, / Portia is Brutus' harlot, not his wife. [William Shakespeare, 1564–1616, *Julius Caesar*, II. ii. 285]

24 For a light wife doth make a heavy husband. [*The Merchant of Venice*, V. i. 130]

25 This is the way to kill a wife with kindness. [*The Taming of the Shrew*, IV. i. (211)]

26 Such duty as the subject owes the prince, / Even such a woman oweth to her husband. [*The Taming of the Shrew*, V. ii. 156]

27 Let still the woman take / An elder than herself, so wears she to him, / So sways she level in her husband's heart: / For, boy, however we do praise ourselves, / Our fancies are more giddy and unfirm, / More longing, wavering, sooner lost and worn, / Than women's are. [*Twelfth Night*, II. iv. 29]

28 As thro' the land at eve we went, / And plucked the ripened ears, / We fell out, my wife and I, / O we fell out I know not why, / And kissed again with tears. [Alfred, Lord Tennyson, 1809–92, *The Princess*, II, song]

29 Some respite to husbands the weather may send, / But housewives' affairs have never an end. [Thomas Tusser, 1524?–80, *Five Hundred Points of Good Husbandry*, 'Preface to the Book of Housewifery']

30 'But you married?' 'Yes, mum, but it was in the war, and he was very drunk.' [Evelyn Waugh, 1903–66, *Decline and Fall*, II, 5]

31 Bricklayers kick their wives to death, and dukes betray theirs; but it is among the small clerks and shopkeepers nowadays that it comes most often to the cutting of throats. [H G Wells, 1866–1946, *Short Stories*, 'The Purple Pileus']

32 The amount of women in London who flirt with their own husbands is perfectly scandalous. It looks so bad. It is simply washing one's clean linen in public. [Oscar Wilde, 1854–1900, *The Importance of Being Earnest*, I]

See also next category, HUSBANDS, MARRIAGE

WOMEN

1 The weaker sex, to piety more prone. [William Alexander, Earl of Stirling, 1567?–1640, *Doomsday*, Hour V, 45]

2 Martina is not a woman of the world. She is a woman of somewhere else. [Martin Amis, 1949– , *Money*, p. 134]

3 All the privilege I claim for my own sex ... is that of loving longest, when existence or when hope is gone. [Jane Austen, 1775–1817, *Persuasion*, 23]

4 One is not born, but rather becomes, a woman. [Simone de Beauvoir, 1908–86, *The Second Sex*, opening words]

5 'After all,' as a pretty girl once said to me, 'women are a sex by themselves, so to speak.' [Max Beerbohm, 1872–1956, *The Pervasion of Rouge*]

6 You will find that the woman who is really kind to dogs is always one who has failed to inspire sympathy in men. [Max Beerbohm, 1872–1956, *Zuleika Dobson*, Ch. 6]

7 Green grow the rashes O; / The sweetest hours that e'er I spend, / Are spent among the lasses O! [Robert Burns, 1759–96, *Green Grow the Rashes*]

8 Brigands demand money or your life, whereas women require both. [Samuel Butler, 1835–1902, *Notebooks, Further Extracts*, Vol. iv, 'Women and Brigands']

9 Alas! the love of women! it is known / To be a lovely and a fearful thing. [Lord Byron, 1788–1824, *Don Juan*, II, 199]

10 I thought it would appear / That there had been a lady in the case. [Lord Byron, 1788–1824, *Don Juan*, V, 19]

11 There is a tide in the affairs of women, / Which, taken at the flood, leads – God knows where. [Lord Byron, 1788–1824, *Don Juan*, VI, 12]

12 Certain women should be struck regularly, like gongs. [Noël Coward, 1899–1973, *Private Lives*, III]

13 *Il y a une femme dans toutes les affaires; aussitôt qu'on me fait un rapport, je dis: 'Cherchez la femme'.* – There is a woman in every case; as soon as they bring me a report, I say, 'Look for the woman'. [Alexandre Dumas, 1802–70, *Les Mohicans de Paris*, II. iii]

14 She takes just like a woman, yes, she does / She makes love just like a woman, yes, she does / And she aches just like a woman / But she breaks just like a little girl. [Bob Dylan, 1941– , song: *Just Like a Woman*]

15 The happiest women, like the happiest nations, have no history. [George Eliot, 1819–80, *The Mill on the Floss*, Bk vi, Ch. 3]

16 When lovely woman stoops to folly and / Paces about her room again, alone, / She smoothes her hair with automatic hand, / And puts a record on the gramophone. [T S Eliot, 1888–1965, *The Waste Land*, 253]

17 How a little love and good company improves a woman! [George Farquhar, 1678–1707, *The Beaux' Stratagem*, IV. i]

18 A woman is like an elephant – I like to look at 'em, but I wouldn't want to own one. [W C Fields, 1879–1946, in film *Mississippi*]

19 The great question ... which I have not been able to answer, despite my thirty years of research into the feminine soul, is 'What does a woman want?' [Sigmund Freud, 1856–1939, letter to Marie Bonaparte, in Ernest Jones, *S F: Life and Work*, Vol. 2, Pt 3, Ch. 16]

20 And when a lady's in the case, / You know, all other things give place. [John Gay, 1685–1732, *Fables*, Pt I, 1, 41]

21 *Das Ewig-Weibliche, / Zieht uns hinan.* – The eternal in woman draws us on. [Johann Wolfgang von Goethe, 1749–1832, *Faust*, Pt Two, V]

22 Of all the plagues with which the world is cursed, / Of every ill, a woman is the worst. [George Granville, Baron Lansdowne, 1667–1735, *The British Enchanters*, II. i]

23 Women are reputed never to be disgusted. The sad fact is that they often are, but not with men, they are most often disgusted with themselves. [Germaine Greer, 1939– , *The Female Eunuch*, 'Loathing and Disgust']

24 He seldom errs / Who thinks the worst he can of womankind. [John Home, 1722–1808, *Douglas*, III. iii]

25 A woman's whole life is a history of the affections. [Washington Irving, 1783–1859, *The Sketch Book*, 'The Broken Heart']

26 Sir, a woman's preaching is like a dog's walking on his hind legs. It is not done well; but you are surprised to find it done at all. [Dr Samuel Johnson, 1709–84, in James Boswell, *Life of J*, 31 July 1763]

27 There is hardly a case in which the dispute was not caused by a woman. [Juvenal, 60–*c*.130, *Satires*, VI, 242]

28 Four things greater than all things are, – / Women and Horses and Power and War. [Rudyard Kipling, 1865–1936, *The Ballad of the King's Jest*]

29 The First Blast of the Trumpet Against the Monstrous Regiment of Women. [John Knox, 1505–72, title of pamphlet, 1558]

30 Being a woman is of special interest only to aspiring male transsexuals. To actual women, it is simply a good excuse not to play football. [Fran Lebowitz, ?1948– , *Metropolitan Life*, 'Letters']

31 'Now women are mostly troublesome cattle to deal with mostly,' said Goggins. [Samuel Lover, 1797–1868, *Handy Andy*, Ch. 36]

32 Shall there be womanly times, or shall we die? [Ian McEwan, 1948– , *Or Shall We Die?*]

33 Store of ladies, whose bright eyes / Rain influence, and judge the prize. [John Milton, 1608–74, *L'Allegro*, 121]

34 God is thy law, thou mine: to know no more / Is woman's happiest knowledge, and her praise. [John Milton, 1608–74, *Paradise Lost*, Bk iv, 637]

35 I am quite agreeable that a woman shall be informed about everything, but I cannot allow her the shocking passion for acquiring learning in order to be learned. When she is asked questions, I like her often to know how not to know the things she does know. [Molière, 1622–73, *Les Femmes savantes*, I. iii]

36 Disguise our bondage as we will, / 'Tis woman, woman, rules us still. [Thomas Moore, 1779–1852, *Sovereign Woman*]

37 I think being a woman is like being Irish . . . Everyone says you're important and nice but you take second place all the same. [Iris Murdoch, 1919–99, *The Red and the Green*, Ch. 2]

38 Women would rather be right than reasonable. [Ogden Nash, 1902–71, *Frailty, Thy Name is a Misnomer*]

39 If women could be fair and yet not fond. [Edward de Vere, Earl of Oxford, 1550–1604, *Women's Changeableness*]

40 Music and women I cannot but give way to, whatever my business is. [Samuel Pepys, 1633–1703, *Diary*, 9 Mar. 1666]

41 Most women have no characters at all. [Alexander Pope, 1688–1744, *Moral Essays*, Epistle II, 2]

42 Woman's at best a contradiction still. [Alexander Pope, 1688–1744, *Moral Essays*, Epistle II, 270]

43 *Elle flotte, elle hésite; en un mot, elle est femme.* – She wavers, she hesitates; in one word, she is a woman. [Jean Racine, 1639–99, *Athalie*, II. v. 490]

44 A woman is like a teabag. It's only when she's in hot water that you realize how strong she is. [Nancy Reagan, 1921– , address to US Women's Congress; *Observer*, 'Sayings of the Week', 29 Mar. 1981]

45 The woman who can sacrifice a clean unspoiled penny stamp is probably unborn. [Saki (H H Munro), 1870–1916, *The Unbearable Bassington*, Ch. 1]

46 The fundamental fault of the female character is that it has no sense of justice. [Arthur Schopenhauer, 1788–1860, *Essays and Aphorisms*, 'On Women']

47 O Woman! In our hours of ease, / Uncertain, coy, and hard to please, / And variable as the shade / By the light quivering aspen made; / When pain and anguish wring the brow, / A ministering angel thou! [Sir Walter Scott, 1771–1832, *Marmion*, VI, 30]

48 Do you not know I am a woman? When I think, I must speak. [William Shakespeare, 1564–1616, *As You Like It*, III. ii. (265)]

49 Frailty, thy name is woman! [*Hamlet*, I. ii. 146]

50 The one thing that made her content to be a woman was that she would never have to marry one. [R S Surtees, 1803–64, *Mr Facey Romford's Hounds*, Ch. 40]

51 Women are like teeth. Some tremble and never fall and some fall and never tremble. [Edith Templeton, 1916– , *The Surprise of Cremona*, 'Urbino']

52 Woman, a sick child and twelve times unclean. [Alfred de Vigny, 1797–1863, *La Colère de Samson*]

53 *Varium et mutabile semper / Femina.* – Woman is always fickle and changing. [Virgil, 70–19 BC, *Aeneid*, IV, 569]

54 The female woman is one of the greatest institooshuns of which this land can boste. [Artemus Ward, 1834–67, *A W His Book*, 'Woman's Rights']

55 One should never trust a woman who tells one her real age. A woman who would tell one that would tell one anything. [Oscar Wilde, 1854–1900, *A Woman of No Importance*, I]

56 I do not wish them to have power over men; but over themselves. [Mary Wollstonecraft, 1759–97, *A Vindication of the Rights of Women*, 4]

57 A woman must have money and a room of her own if she is to write fiction. [Virginia Woolf, 1882–1941, *A Room of One's Own*, Ch. 1]

See also next category, FEMINISM, MOTHERS

WOMEN & MEN

1 People knew a man by the company he kept, but they generally knew a woman by the man who kept her. [Lisa Alther, 1944– , *Kinflicks*, Ch. 2]

2 You can have a men's novel with no women in it except possibly the landlady / or the horse, but you can't have a women's novel with no men in it. / Sometimes men put women in men's novels / but they leave out some of the parts; / the heads, for instance. [Margaret Atwood, 1939– , from *Poem*, in Resa Dudovitz, *The Myth of Superwoman*]

3 Women were brought up to believe that men were the answer. They weren't. They weren't even one of the questions. [Julian Barnes, 1946– , *Staring at the Sun*, Pt 2]

4 Zuleika, on a desert island, would have spent most of her time in looking for a man's footprint. [Max Beerbohm, 1872–1956, *Zuleika Dobson*, Ch. 2]

5 Women who love the same man have a kind of bitter freemasonry. [Max Beerbohm, 1872–1956, *Zuleika Dobson*, Ch. 4]

6 The social presence of a woman is different in kind from that of a man ... A man's presence suggests what he is capable of doing to you or for you ... A woman's presence ... defines what can and cannot be done to her. [John Berger, 1926– , *et al.*, *Ways of Seeing*]

7 Anything You Can Do, I Can Do Better. [Irving Berlin, 1888–1989, title of song in musical *Annie Get Your Gun*, II]

8 One man among a thousand have I found; but a woman among all those have I not found. [Bible, OT, *Ecclesiastes* 7:28]

9 So God created man in his own image, in the image of God created he him; male and female created he them. [Bible, OT, *Genesis* 1:27]

10 The sons of God saw the daughters of men, that they were fair. [Bible, OT, *Genesis* 6:2]

11 It amuses me, you know, the way you seem to see women. You think of them as sort of loose-fitting men. [Malcolm Bradbury, 1932– , *Eating People is Wrong*, Ch. 6]

12 My theory is that mature woman is physically polygamous but emotionally monogamous, while mature man is emotionally polygamous but physically monogamous. [Alan Brien, 1925– , in *New Statesman*, 6 Dec. 1968]

13 The whole world was made for man; but the twelfth part of man for woman: man is the whole world, and the breath of God; woman the rib and crooked piece of man. I could be content that we might procreate like trees, without conjunction, or that there were any way to perpetuate the world without this trivial and vulgar way of union. [Sir Thomas Browne, 1605–82, *Religio Medici*, Pt II, 9]

14 What signifies the life o' man, / An' 'twere na for the lasses O. [Robert Burns, 1759–96, *Green Grow the Rashes*]

15 Wommen desyren to have sovereyntee / As wel over hir housbond as hir love. [Geoffrey Chaucer, 1340?–1400, *Canterbury Tales*, 'The Tale of the Wife of Bath', 182]

16 A man of sense only trifles with them [women], plays with them, humours and flatters them, as he does with a sprightly and forward child; but he neither consults them about, nor trusts them with, serious matters. [Earl of Chesterfield, 1694–1773, letter to his son, 5 Sept. 1748]

17 Women are much more like each other than men: they have, in truth, but two passions, vanity and love; these are their universal characteristics. [Earl of Chesterfield, 1694–1773, letter to his son, 19 Dec. 1749]

18 There is more difference within the sexes

than between them. [Ivy Compton-Burnett, 1884–1969, *Mother and Son*, 10]

19 But what is woman? – only one of Nature's agreeable blunders. [Hannah Cowley, 1743–1809, *Who's the Dupe?*, II. ii]

20 Women never have young minds. They are born three thousand years old. [Shelagh Delaney, 1939– , *A Taste of Honey*, I. i]

21 Most women set out to try to change a man, and when they have changed him they do not like him. [Marlene Dietrich, 1901–92; in A Andrews, *Quotations for Speakers and Writers*]

22 Man and woman are two locked caskets, of which each contains the key to the other. [Isak Dinesen, 1885–1962, *Winter's Tales*, 'A Consolatory Tale']

23 Now, Watson, the fair sex is your department. [Arthur Conan Doyle, 1859–1930, *The Return of Sherlock Holmes*, 'The Second Stain']

24 You can't live with men but you can't chop them up into little pieces and boil them either – because that would be cooking. [Jenny Eclair, 1960– , in comedy show *Prozac and Tantrums*]

25 I'm not denyin' the women are foolish: God Almighty made 'em to match the men. [George Eliot, 1819–80, *Adam Bede*, Ch. 53]

26 When a woman behaves like a man, why doesn't she behave like a nice man? [Edith Evans, 1888–1976; *Observer*, 'Sayings of the Week', 30 Sept. 1956]; see 52

27 She was one of those people who would just as soon starve in a garret with a man – if she didn't have to. [F Scott Fitzgerald, 1896–1940, *Notebooks*, 'E']

28 'What kind of man was he?' 'Well, he was one of those men who come in a door and make any woman with them look guilty.' [F Scott Fitzgerald, 1896–1940, *Notebooks*, 'E']

29 A man has every season while a woman only has the right to spring. That disgusts me. [Jane Fonda, 1937– , in *Daily Mail*, 13 Sept. 1989]

30 If women like them like men like those, / Then why don't women like me? [George Formby, 1905–61, song]

31 That is the great distinction between the sexes. Men see objects, women see the relationship between objects. Whether the objects need each other, love each other, match each other. It is an extra dimension of feeling we men are without and one that makes war abhorrent to all real women – and absurd. [John Fowles, 1926– , *The Magus*, rev. edn, Ch. 52]

32 If the heart of a man is depressed with cares, / The mist is dispelled when a woman appears. [John Gay, 1685–1732, *The Beggar's Opera*, I. iii]

33 O Polly, you might have toyed and kissed. / By keeping men off, you keep them on. [John Gay, 1685–1732, *The Beggar's Opera*, I. ix]

34 Man may escape from rope and gun; / Nay, some have out-lived the doctor's pill; / Who takes a woman must be undone, / That basilisk is sure to kill. [John Gay, 1685–1732, *The Beggar's Opera*, II. viii]

35 When lovely woman stoops to folly, / And finds too late that men betray, / What charm can soothe her melancholy, / What art can wash her guilt away? [Oliver Goldsmith, 1728–74, *The Vicar of Wakefield*, Ch. 29]

36 Women have very little idea of how much men hate them. [Germaine Greer, 1939– , *The Female Eunuch*, 'Loathing and Disgust']

37 My mother said it was simple to keep a man, you must be a maid in the living room, a cook in the kitchen and a whore in the bedroom. I said I'd hire the other two and take care of the bedroom bit. [Jerry Hall, 1956– ; *Observer*, 'Sayings of the Year', 29 Dec. 1985]

38 About the only job left that a woman can beat a man in is female impersonator in vaudeville. [O Henry, 1862–1910, *The Hand That Rules the World*]

39 Man has his will – but woman has her way. [Oliver Wendell Holmes, 1809–94, *The Autocrat of the Breakfast Table*, Ch. 1]

40 'Dealing with a man,' said the night-watchman thoughtfully, 'is as easy as a teetotaller walking along a nice wide pavement; dealing with a woman is like the same teetotaller, arter four or five whiskies, trying to get up a step that ain't there.' [W W Jacobs, 1863–1943, *Deep Water*, 'Husbandry']

41 Follow a shadow, it still flies you, / Seem to fly it, it will pursue. / So court a mistress, she denies you; / Let her alone, she will court you. / Say, are not women truly, then / Styled but the shadows of us men? [Ben Jonson, 1573–1637, song: *That Women are But Men's Shadows*]

42 I sometimes think that whenever men want to cool down their lives women instinctively want to hot them up, and vice versa. [P J Kavanagh, 1931– , *A Happy Man*, Ch. 13]

43 For the female of the species is more deadly than the male. [Rudyard Kipling, 1865–1936, *The Female of the Species*]

44 There be triple ways to take, of the eagle or the snake, / Or the way of a man with a maid. [Rudyard Kipling, 1865–1936, *The Long Trail*]

45 Women don't look for handsome men, they look for men with beautiful women. [Milan Kundera, 1929– , *The Book of Laughter and Forgetting*, Pt 1, 8]

46 Women run to extremes; they are either better or worse than men. [Jean de La Bruyère, 1645–96, *Characters*, 'Of Women', 53]

47 When Eve ate this particular apple, she became aware of her own womanhood, mentally. And mentally she began to experiment with it. She has been experimenting ever since. So has man. To the rage and horror of both of them. [D H Lawrence, 1885–1930, *Fantasia of the Unconscious*, Ch. 7]

48 My destiny has been cast among cocksure women. Perhaps when man begins to doubt himself, woman, who should be nice and peacefully hen-sure, becomes instead insistently cocksure. She develops convictions, or she catches them. And then woe betide everybody. [D H Lawrence, 1885–1930, *Phoenix*, 'Women are So Cocksure']

49 I'm not sure if a mental relation with a woman doesn't make it impossible to love her. To know the *mind* of a woman is to end in hating her. Love means the pre-cognitive flow ... it is the honest state before the apple. [D H Lawrence, 1885–1930, letter to Dr Trigant Burrow, 3 Aug. 1927]

50 Men aren't attracted to me by my mind. They're attracted by what I don't mind. [Gypsy Rose Lee, 1914–70; in *Woman Talk*, comp. Michèle Brown and Ann O'Connor]

51 As unto the bow the cord is, / So unto the man is woman; / Though she bends him, she obeys him, / Though she draws him, yet she follows; / Useless each without the other! [H W Longfellow, 1807–82, *The Song of Hiawatha*, 10]

52 Women do not find it difficult nowadays to behave like men; but they often find it extremely difficult to behave like gentlemen. [Compton Mackenzie, 1883–1972, *On Moral Courage*]; see 26

53 First the sweetheart of the nation, then the aunt, woman governs America because America is a land of boys who refuse to grow up. [Salvador de Madariaga, 1886–1978, in Sagittarius and D George, *The Perpetual Pessimist*]

54 Happy is the man with a wife to tell him what to do and a secretary to do it. [Lord Mancroft, 1914–87: *Observer*, 'Sayings of the Week', 18 Dec. 1966]

55 Any man who says he can see through a woman is missing a lot. [Groucho Marx, 1895–1977; in P and J Holton, *Quote and Unquote*]

56 I can't remember a single masculine figure created by a woman who is not, at bottom, a booby. [H L Mencken, 1880–1956, *In Defence of Women*, Ch. 1, sect. i]

57 I expect that Woman will be the last thing civilized by Man. [George Meredith, 1828–1909, *The Ordeal of Richard Feverel*, Ch. 1]

58 For contemplation he and valour formed; / For softness she and sweet attractive grace, / He for God only, she for God in him: / His fair large front and eye sublime declared / Absolute rule. [John Milton, 1608–74, *Paradise Lost*, Bk iv, 297]

59 Nature has not placed us in an inferior rank to men, no more than the females of other animals, where we see no distinction of capacity, though I am persuaded if there was a commonwealth of rational horses ... it would be an established maxim among them that a mare could not be taught to pace. [Lady Mary Wortley Montagu, 1689–1762, letter to Lady Bute, 6 Mar. 1753]

60 O woman! lovely woman! Nature made thee / To temper man: we had been brutes without you; / Angels are painted fair, to look like you. [Thomas Otway, 1652–85, *Venice Preserved*, I. i]

61 Some men break your heart in two, / Some men fawn and flatter, / Some men never look at you; / And that cleans up the matter. [Dorothy Parker, 1893–1967, *Experience*]

62 The man she had was kind and clean / And well enough for every day, / But oh, dear friends, you should have seen / The one that got away!

[Dorothy Parker, 1893–1967, *Tombstones in the Starlight*, 'The Fisherwoman']

63 A woman is a foreign land, / Of which, though there he settle young, / A man will ne'er quite understand / The customs, politics, and tongue. [Coventry Patmore, 1823–96, *The Angel in the House*, Bk II, ix, Prelude 2]

64 Men, some to business, some to pleasure take; / But every woman is at heart a rake. [Alexander Pope, 1688–1744, *Moral Essays*, Epistle II, 215]

65 In his younger days a man dreams of possessing the heart of the woman whom he loves; later, the feeling that he possesses a woman's heart may be enough to make him fall in love with her. [Marcel Proust, 1871–1922, *Remembrance of Things Past: Swann's Way*, 'Swann in Love']

66 It's the little questions from women about tappets that finally push men over the edge. [Philip Roth, 1933– , *Letting Go*, Pt I, Ch. 1]

67 Women always want to be our last love, and we their first. [Arthur Schnitzler, 1862–1931; in *Practical Wisdom*, ed. Frederick Ungar]

68 Is there no way for men to be, but women / Must be half-workers? [William Shakespeare, 1564–1616, *Cymbeline*, II. v. 1]

69 Let still the woman take / An elder than herself, so wears she to him, / So sways she level in her husband's heart: / For, boy, however we do praise ourselves, / Our fancies are more giddy and unfirm, / More longing, wavering, sooner lost and worn, / Than women's are. [*Twelfth Night*, II. iv. 29]

70 Like all young men, you greatly exaggerate the difference between one young woman and another. [George Bernard Shaw, 1856–1950, *Major Barbara*, III]

71 Give women the vote, and in five years there will be a crushing tax on bachelors. [George Bernard Shaw, 1856–1950, *Man and Superman*, Preface]

72 The one certain way for a woman to hold a man is to leave him for religion. [Muriel Spark, 1918– , *The Comforters*, Ch. 1]

73 A woman without a man is like a fish without a bicycle. [Gloria Steinem, 1934– ; attr. in *Quotable Women*, comp. Elaine Partnow]

74 For men at most differ as Heaven and Earth, / But women, worst and best, as Heaven and Hell. [Alfred, Lord Tennyson, 1809–92, *Idylls of the King*, 'Merlin and Vivien', 812]

75 Man is the hunter; woman is his game: / The sleek and shining creatures of the chase, / We hunt them for the beauty of their skins. [Alfred, Lord Tennyson, 1809–92, *The Princess*, V, 147]

76 The woman's cause is man's: they rise or sink / Together. [Alfred, Lord Tennyson, 1809–92, *The Princess*, VII, 243]

77 'Tis strange what a man may do, and a woman yet think him an angel. [W M Thackeray, 1811–63, *Henry Esmond*, Bk i, Ch. 7]

78 I always say that if you want a speech made you should ask a man, but if you want something done you should ask a woman. [Margaret Thatcher, 1925– , at AGM of Townswomen's Guild, 26 July 1982]

79 The cocks may crow, but it's the hen that lays the egg. [Margaret Thatcher, 1925– (at a private dinner party, 1987), quoted by Robert Skidelsky in *The Sunday Times*, 'Books' section, 9 Apr. 1989]

80 It is great glory in a woman to show no more weakness than is natural to her sex, and not be talked of, either for good or evil by men. [Thucydides, *c.*471–*c.*400 BC, *History*, II, 45, ii]

81 Sometimes I think if there was a third sex men wouldn't get so much as a glance from me. [Amanda Vail, 1921–66, *Love Me Little*, Ch. 6]

82 But lasting joys the man attend / Who has a polished female friend! [Cornelius Whur, 1782–1853, *The Accomplished Female Friend*]

83 Women represent the triumph of matter over mind, just as men represent the triumph of mind over morals. [Oscar Wilde, 1854–1900, *The Picture of Dorian Gray*, Ch. 4]

84 Women have served all these centuries as looking-glasses possessing the magic and delicious power of reflecting the figure of man at twice its natural size. [Virginia Woolf, 1882–1941, *A Room of One's Own*, Ch. 2]

See also previous categories, FEMINISM, MEN

WOODS

1 This great society is going smash; / They cannot fool us with how fast they go, / How much they cost each other and the gods! / A culture is no better than its woods. [W H Auden, 1907–73, *Winds*]

2 I am for the woods against the world, / But are the woods for me? [Edmund Blunden, 1896–1974, *The Kiss*]

3 Keep cold, young orchard. Goodbye and keep cold. / Dread fifty above more than fifty below. [Robert Frost, 1874–1963, *Goodbye and Keep Cold*]

4 The woods are lovely, dark and deep. / But I have promises to keep, / And miles to go before I sleep. [Robert Frost, 1874–1963, *Stopping by Woods on a Snowy Evening*]

5 Where once the number 2 bus used to stop / They'd set a kind of pristine jungle up / And apes – orang-outangs – hung on the trees. [Erich Kästner, 1899–1974, *Doktor Erich Kästners Lyrische Hausapotheke*, 'Dangerous Establishment']

6 As when, upon a trancèd summer-night, / Those green-robed senators of mighty woods, / Tall oaks, branch-charmèd by the earnest stars, / Dream, and so dream all night without a stir. [John Keats, 1795–1821, *Hyperion*, Bk i, 72]

7 Now this is the Law of the Jungle – as old and as true as the sky. [Rudyard Kipling, 1865–1936, *The Law of the Jungle*]

8 Enter these enchanted woods, / You who dare. [George Meredith, 1828–1909, *The Woods of Westermain*]

9 When these old woods were young / The thrushes' ancestors / As sweetly sung / In the old years. [Edward Thomas, 1878–1917, *Under the Woods*]

10 One impulse from a vernal wood / May teach you more of man, / Of moral evil and of good, / Than all the sages can. [William Wordsworth, 1770–1850, *The Tables Turned*]

See also TREES

WORDS

1 Let mortals beware / Of words, for / With words we lie, / Can we say peace / When we mean war. [W H Auden, 1907–73, *United Nations Hymn*]

2 A word spoken in due season, how good is it! [Bible, OT, *Proverbs* 15:23]

3 Of all the words in all languages I know, the greatest concentration is in the English word *I*. [Elias Canetti, 1905–94, *The Human Province*, '1943']

4 Personally I like short words and vulgar fractions. [Winston Churchill, 1874–1965, speech in Margate, 10 Oct. 1953]

5 We must use words as they are used or stand aside from life. [Ivy Compton-Burnett, 1884–1969, *Mother and Son*, Ch. 9]

6 The only sort of four-letter words I use are 'good', 'love', 'warm' and 'kind'. [Catherine Cookson, 1906–98, interview in John Mortimer, *In Character*]

7 Some of them words got syllables all over 'em. [Alan Coren, 1938– , *The Cricklewood Diet*, 'Zuleika Capp']

8 Philologists who chase / A panting syllable through time and space, / Start it at home, and hunt it in the dark, / To Gaul, to Greece, and into Noah's ark. [William Cowper, 1731–1800, *Retirement*, 691]

9 Until we learn the use of living words we shall continue to be waxworks inhabited by gramophones. [Walter de la Mare, 1873–1956; *Observer*, 'Sayings of the Week', 12 May 1929]

10 Papa, potatoes, poultry, prunes and prism, are all very good words for the lips; especially prunes and prism. [Charles Dickens, 1812–70, *Little Dorrit*, Bk ii, Ch. 5]

11 The intolerable wrestle / With words and meanings. [T S Eliot, 1888–1965, *Four Quartets*, 'East Coker', II]

12 A sentence is a sound in itself on which sounds called words may be strung. [Robert Frost, 1874–1963, letter to John Bartlett, 22 Feb. 1914]

13 Some word that teems with hidden meaning – like 'Basingstoke'. [W S Gilbert, 1836–1911, *Ruddigore*, II]

14 *Denn eben, wo Begriffe fehlen, / Da stellt ein Wort zur rechten Zeit sich ein.* – For just when ideas fail, a word comes in to save the situation. [Johann Wolfgang von Goethe, 1749–1832, *Faust*, Pt I, 'Faust's Study']

15 Everyone knows that it is much harder to turn word into deed than deed into word. [Maxim Gorky, 1868–1936, from 'On Plays'; in *USSR in Construction*, Apr. 1937]

16 Words are wise men's counters, they do but

reckon with them, but they are the money of fools. [Thomas Hobbes, 1588–1679, *Leviathan*, Pt I, Ch. 4]

17 Once a word has been allowed to escape, it cannot be recalled. [Horace 65–8 BC, *Epistles*, I, xviii, 71]

18 Summer afternoon – summer afternoon; to me those have always been the two most beautiful words in the English language. [Henry James, 1843–1916, in Edith Wharton, *A Backward Glance*, Ch. 10]

19 Words that open our eyes to the world are always the easiest to remember. [Ryszard Kapuściński, 1932– , *Shah of Shahs*, 'Daguerreotypes']

20 Words are, of course, the most powerful drug used by mankind. [Rudyard Kipling, 1865–1936, speech, 14 Feb. 1923]

21 I am a Bear of Very Little Brain and long words Bother Me. [A A Milne, 1882–1956, *Winnie-the-Pooh*, Ch. 4]

22 Words are like leaves; and where they most abound, / Much fruit of sense beneath is rarely found. [Alexander Pope, 1688–1744, *An Essay on Criticism*, 309]

23 One of our defects as a nation is a tendency to use what have been called 'weasel words'. When a weasel sucks eggs the meat is sucked out of the egg. If you use a 'weasel word' after another there is nothing left of the other. [Theodore Roosevelt, 1858–1919, speech in St Louis, Missouri, 31 May 1916]

24 Immodest words admit of no defence, / For want of decency is want of sense. [Earl of Roscommon, 1637–88, *Essay on Translated Verse*, 113]

25 Zounds! I was never so bethumped with words / Since I first called my brother's father dad. [William Shakespeare, 1564–1616, *King John*, II. i. 466]

26 Scatter, as from an unextinguished hearth / Ashes and sparks, my words among mankind! / Be through my lips to unawakened earth / The trumpet of a prophecy! O, Wind. [P B Shelley, 1792–1822, *Ode to the West Wind*, 66]

27 Thy words are like a cloud of wingèd snakes; / And yet I pity those they torture not. [P B Shelley, 1792–1822, *Prometheus Unbound*, I, 632]

28 Some of his words were not Sunday-school words. [Mark Twain, 1835–1910, *A Tramp Abroad*, Ch. 20]

29 Of two possible words always choose the lesser. [Paul Valéry, *Odds and Ends*, 'Advice to the Writer']

30 [Men] use thought only to justify their wrong-doings, and words only to conceal their thoughts. [Voltaire, 1694–1778, *Dialogue du chapon et de la poularde*]

31 One forgets words as one forgets names. One's vocabulary needs constant fertilizing or it will die. [Evelyn Waugh, 1903–66, *Diaries*, ed. M Davie, 'Irregular Notes', 25 Dec. 1962]

See also LANGUAGE, SPEECH

WORK & WORKERS

1 Work was like cats were supposed to be: if you disliked and feared it and tried to keep out of its way, it knew at once and sought you out and jumped on your lap and climbed all over you to show how much it loved you. Please God, he thought, don't let me die in harness. [Kingsley Amis, 1922–95, *Take A Girl Like You*, Ch. 5]

2 *Arbeit macht frei*. – Work Sets You Free. [Slogan above Auschwitz (1940–45) concentration camp's main gate]

3 The pleasantness of an employment does not always evince its propriety. [Jane Austen, 1775–1817, *Sense and Sensibility*, 13]

4 Consider the history of labour in a country [USA] in which, spiritually speaking, there are no workers, only candidates for the hand of the boss's daughter. [James Baldwin, 1924–87, *The Fire Next Time*, 'Down at the Cross']

5 For years I thought my work was in front of me, and now it is behind me: at no moment was it with me. [Simone de Beauvoir, 1908–86, in obituary in *Observer*, 20 Apr. 1986]

6 I do most of my work sitting down; that's where I shine. [Robert Benchley, 1889–1945; in R E Drennan, *Wit's End*]

7 Man goeth forth to his work, and to his labour until the evening. [Bible, OT, *Psalms* 104:23]

8 The labourer is worthy of his hire. [Bible, NT, *St Luke* 10:7]

9 If any would not work, neither should he eat. [Bible, NT, *2 Thessalonians* 3:10]

10 We labour soon, we labour late, / To feed the titled knave, man; / And a' the comfort we're to get / Is that ayont the grave, man. [*The Tree of Liberty*, attr. to Robert Burns, 1759–96]

11 Blessed is he who has found his work; let him ask no other blessedness. [Thomas Carlyle, 1795–1881, *Past and Present*, Bk i, 11]

12 Work is the grand cure of all the maladies and miseries that ever beset mankind. [Thomas Carlyle, 1795–1881, Rectorial Address at Edinburgh University, 2 Apr. 1886]

13 The time's come: there's a terrific thundercloud advancing upon us, a mighty storm is coming to freshen us up ... It's going to blow away all this idleness and indifference, and prejudice against work ... I'm going to work, and in twenty-five or thirty years' time every man and woman will be working. [Anton Chekhov, 1860–1904, *Three Sisters*, I]

14 Your work parallels your life, but in the sense of a glass full of water where people look at it and say, 'Oh, the water's the same shape as the glass!' [Francis Ford Coppola, 1939– , interview in *Guardian*, 15 Oct. 1988]

15 Work is much more fun than fun. [Noël Coward, 1899–1973; *Observer*, 'Sayings of the Week', 21 June 1963]

16 Honest labour bears a lovely face. [Thomas Dekker, 1572?–1632, *Patient Grissill*, I. i]

17 One of the best ways of avoiding necessary and even urgent tasks is to seem to be busily employed on things that are already done. [J K Galbraith, 1908– , *The Affluent Society*, Ch. 1, sect. ii]

18 I've got a whole day's work ahead of me. I'm going to change the ribbon on my typewriter. [Ira Gershwin, 1896–1983, on his careful craftsmanship]

19 I like work: it fascinates me. I can sit and look at it for hours. I love to keep it by me: the idea of getting rid of it nearly breaks my heart. [Jerome K Jerome, 1859–1927, *Three Men in a Boat*, Ch. 15]

20 Each in his place, by right, not grace, / Shall rule his heritage – / The men who simply do the work / For which they draw the wage. [Rudyard Kipling, 1865–1936, *The Wage-slaves*]

21 Who first invented work and bound the free / And holiday-rejoicing spirit down? [Charles Lamb, 1775–1834, *Work*]

22 Why should I let the toad *work* / Squat on my life? [Philip Larkin, 1922–85, *Toads*]

23 In an English ship, they say, it is poor grub, poor pay, and easy work; in an American ship, good grub, good pay, and hard work. And this is applicable to the working populations of both countries. [Jack London, 1876–1916, *The People of the Abyss*, Ch. 20]

24 The workers have nothing to lose but their chains. They have a world to gain. Workers of the world, unite. [Karl Marx, 1818–83, and Friedrich Engels, 1820–95, *The Communist Manifesto*, closing words]

25 Work expands so as to fill the time available for its completion. General recognition of this fact is shown in the proverbial phrase. 'It is the busiest man who has time to spare.' [C Northcote Parkinson, 1909–93, *Parkinson's Law*, Ch. 1]

26 Work is accomplished by those employees who have not yet reached their level of incompetence. [Laurence J Peter, 1919–90, and Raymond Hull, 1918–85, *The Peter Principle*, Ch. 1]

27 They say hard work never hurt anybody, but I figure why take the chance! [Ronald Reagan, 1911– , speech in Washington, 22 Apr. 1987]

28 Which of us ... is to do the hard and dirty work for the rest – and for what pay? Who is to do the pleasant and clean work, and for what pay? [John Ruskin, 1819–1900, *Sesame and Lilies*, 1, §30, note]

29 The hand of little employment hath the daintier sense. [William Shakespeare, 1564–1616, *Hamlet*, IV. vii. (75)]

30 The labour we delight in physics pain. [*Macbeth*, II. iii. (56)]

31 All things have rest: why should we toil alone, / We only toil, who are the first of things. [Alfred, Lord Tennyson, 1809–92, *The Lotos-Eaters*, 'Choric Song', 2]

32 There is, of course, a certain amount of drudgery in newspaper work, just as there is in teaching classes, tunnelling into a bank, or being President of the United States. I suppose that even the most pleasurable of imaginable occupations, that of batting baseballs through the windows of the RCA Building, would pall a little as the days ran on. [James Thurber, 1894–1961, *The Thurber Carnival*, 'Memoirs of a Drudge']

33 It's dogged as does it. It ain't thinking about it. [Anthony Trollope, 1815–82, *The Last Chronicle of Barset*, Ch. 61]

34 Work banishes those three great evils, boredom, vice, and poverty. [Voltaire, 1694–1778, *Candide*, Ch. 30]

35 It is necessary to be somewhat underemployed if you want to do something significant. [James D Watson, 1928– , in H Judson, *The Eighth Day of Creation*]

36 Work is the curse of the drinking classes. [Oscar Wilde, 1854–1900, quoted in Hesketh Pearson, *Life of O W*, Ch. 12]

37 That's not a friend, that's an employer I'm trying out for a few days. [Thornton Wilder, 1897–1975, *The Matchmaker*, III]

See also LEISURE, PROFESSIONS, UNEMPLOYMENT

WORLD

1 The earth is the Lord's, and the fulness thereof; the world, and they that dwell therein. [Bible, OT, *Psalms* 24:1; NT, *1 Corinthians* 10:26]

2 For the world, I count it not an inn, but an hospital; and a place not to live but to die in. [Sir Thomas Browne, 1605–82, *Religio Medici*, Pt II, 11]

3 The world and its way have a certain worth. [Robert Browning, 1812–89, *The Statue and the Bust*, 46]

4 There may be heaven; there must be hell; / Meantime, there is our earth here – well! [Robert Browning, 1812–89, *Time's Revenges*]

5 The Earth is one, but the world is not. [Brundtland Report, 1987– , World Commission on Environment and Development, *Our Common Future*, opening words]

6 As I walked through the wilderness of this world . . . [John Bunyan, 1628–88, *The Pilgrim's Progress*, Pt I]

7 I have not loved the world, nor the world me; / I have not flattered its rank breath, nor bowed / To its idolatries a patient knee, / Nor coined my cheek to smiles, nor cried aloud / In worship of an echo. [Lord Byron, 1788–1824, *Childe Harold's Pilgrimage*, III, 113]

8 This world is very odd we see, / We do not comprehend it; / But in one fact we all agree, / God won't, and we can't mend it. [Arthur Hugh Clough, 1819–61, *Dipsychus*, II, ii]

9 Well then; I now do plainly see, / This busy world and I shall ne'er agree. [Abraham Cowley, 1618–67, *The Wish*]

10 What a world of gammon and spinnage it is, though, ain't it! [(Miss Mowcher) Charles Dickens, 1812–70, *David Copperfield*, Ch. 22]

11 How much can come / And much can go, / And yet abide the world! [Emily Dickinson, 1830–86, *There Came a Wind*]

12 Of this fair volume which we world do name / If we the sheets and leaves could turn with care. [William Drummond, 1585–1649, *The World*]

13 The worlds revolve like ancient women / Gathering fuel in vacant lots. [T S Eliot, 1888–1965, *Preludes*, IV]

14 It's a funny old world – a man's lucky if he gets out of it alive. [W C Fields, 1879–1946, in film *You're Telling Me*]

15 The world is not black and white. More like black and grey. [Graham Greene, 1904–91; *Observer*, 'Sayings of the Year', Dec. 1982]

16 The world has shown me what it has to offer . . . it's a nice place to visit, but I wouldn't want to live there. [Arlo Guthrie, 1947– ; in *Wit and Wisdom of Rock and Roll*, ed. Maxim Jakubowski]

17 To persons standing alone on a hill during a clear midnight such as this, the roll of the world eastward is almost a palpable movement. [Thomas Hardy, 1840–1928, *Far from the Madding Crowd*, Ch. 2]

18 Well, World, you have kept faith with me, / Kept faith with me; / Upon the whole you have proved to be / Much as you said you were. [Thomas Hardy, 1840–1928, *He Never Expected Much*]

19 The world is charged with the grandeur of God. [Gerard Manley Hopkins, 1844–89, *God's Grandeur*]

20 Call the world if you please 'The Vale of Soul-making'. [John Keats, 1795–1821, letter to G and G Keats, 14 Feb. – 3 May 1819]

21 I see the world as a football, kicked about by the higher powers, with me clinging on by my teeth and toenails to the laces. [Dan Leno, 1860–1904, in Desmond MacCarthy, *Theatre*]

22 The world is an oyster, but you don't crack it open on a mattress. [Arthur Miller, 1915– , *Death of a Salesman*, I]

23 The world does seem to become one, however much its component elements may resist. Indeed, the stronger the resistance the more certain is the outcome. *We resist only what is inevitable.* [Henry Miller, 1891–1980, *Big Sur and the Oranges of Hieronymus Bosch*]

24 The world is but a school of inquiry. [Michel de Montaigne, 1533–92, *Essays*, III, 8]

25 Stop the World, I Want to Get Off. [Anthony Newley, 1931–99, and Leslie Bricusse, 1931– , title of musical]

26 The whole worl's in a state o' chassis. [Sean O'Casey, 1880–1964, *Juno and the Paycock*, I]

27 The earth is nobler than the world we have put upon it. [J B Priestley, 1894–1984, *Johnson over Jordan*, III]

28 The world itself is but a large prison, out of which some are daily led to execution. [Sir Walter Raleigh, *c.*1552–1618, when returning to prison from his trial]

29 *Die Könige der Welt sind alt / und werden keine Erben haben.* – The kings of the earth are old and will have no heirs. [Rainer Maria Rilke, 1875–1926, *Book of Hours*, 'The Kings of the Earth are Old']

30 In my family we've always found the world's air hard to breathe; we arrive hoping for somewhere better. [Salman Rushdie, 1937– , *The Moor's Last Sigh*, 4]

31 O, how full of briers is this working-day world! [William Shakespeare, 1564–1616, *As You Like It*, I. iii. (12)]

32 All the world's a stage, / And all the men and women merely players: / They have their exits and their entrances; / And one man in his time plays many parts. [*As You Like It*, II. vii. (139)]

33 I hold the world but as the world, Gratiano; / A stage where every man must play a part, / And mine a sad one. [*The Merchant of Venice*, I. i. 77]

34 This world to me is like a lasting storm, / Whirring me from my friends. [*Pericles*, IV. i. 19]

35 Search well another world; who studies this, / Travels in clouds, seeks manna, where none is. [Henry Vaughan, 1622–95, *The Search*, last lines]

36 The world is everything that is the case. [Ludwig Wittgenstein, 1889–1951, *Tractatus Logico-philosophicus*, I, 1]

See also EARTH, ENVIRONMENT, UNIVERSE

WORLD WAR I

1 Kill winter with your cannon / Hold back Orion with your bayonets / And crush the spring leaf with your armies. [Richard Aldington, 1892–1962, *In the Trenches*]

2 We are Fred Karno's Army, / The ragtime infantry; / We cannot fight, we cannot shoot, / What bloody good are we! [anon. song of 1914–18 war, sung to hymn tune]

3 A lot of hard-faced men who look as if they had done well out of the war ... [Stanley Baldwin, 1867–1947 (of the House of Commons returned in the 1918 election), in J M Keynes, *Economic Consequences of the Peace*, Ch. 5]

4 Just for a word – 'neutrality', a word which in wartime has so often been disregarded, just for a scrap of paper – Great Britain is going to make war. [Theobald von Bethmann Hollweg, 1856–1921, to Sir Edward Goschen, 4 Aug. 1914]

5 Now, God be thanked who has matched us with His hour, / And caught our youth, and wakened us from sleeping. [Rupert Brooke, 1887–1915, *Peace*]

6 The maxim of the British people is 'Business as usual'. [Winston Churchill, 1874–1965, speech at Guildhall, London, 9 Nov. 1914]

7 Come on, you sons of bitches! Do you want to live for ever? [Sergeant Dan Daly, US Marines, 1874–1937, attr., Battle of Belleau Wood, 6 June 1918. Echoes Frederick the Great]

8 The lamps are going out all over Europe; we shall not see them lit again in our lifetime. [Sir Edward Grey, 1862–1933, on the eve of war, 3 Aug. 1914]

9 Viewed as drama, the [Great] War is somewhat disappointing. [D W Griffith, 1874–1933; in L Halliwell, *The Filmgoer's Book of Quotes*]

10 Every position must be held to the last man: there must be no retirement. With our backs to the wall, and believing in the justice of our cause, each one of us must fight on to the end. [Earl Haig, 1861–1928, order to the British troops, 12 Apr. 1918]

11 LUDENDORFF: The English soldiers fight like lions.
HOFFMAN: True. But don't we know that they are lions led by donkeys. [General Max Hoffman, 1869–1927 (of 1915 battles), in A Clark, *The Donkeys*]

12 We have all lost the war. All Europe. [D H Lawrence, 1885–1930, *The Ladybird*, title story]

13 In Flanders fields the poppies blow / Between the crosses, row on row. [John McCrae, 1872–1918, *In Flanders Fields*]

14 If the war didn't happen to kill you it was bound to start you thinking. After that unspeakable idiotic mess you couldn't go on regarding society as something eternal and unquestionable, like a pyramid. You knew it was just a balls-up. [George Orwell, 1903–50, *Coming Up for Air*, II, 8]

15 What passing-bells for those who die as cattle? / Only the monstrous anger of the guns. / Only the stuttering rifles' rapid rattle / Can patter out their hasty orisons. [Wilfred Owen, 1893–1918, *Anthem for Doomed Youth*]

16 Red lips are not so red / As the stained stones kissed by the English dead. / Kindness of wooed and wooer / Seems shame to their love pure. [Wilfred Owen, 1893–1918, *Greater Love*]

17 There died a myriad, / And of the best, among them, / For an old bitch gone in the teeth, / For a botched civilization. [Ezra Pound, 1885–1972, *Hugh Selwyn Mauberley*, 'E P Ode pour l'élection de son sépulcre', V]

18 I saw him stab / And stab again / A well-killed Boche. / This is the happy warrior. / This is he ... [Herbert Read, 1893–1968, *The Happy Warrior*]

19 I'd like to see a Tank come down the stalls, / Lurching to rag-time tunes, or 'Home, sweet Home', / And there'd be no more jokes in Music-halls / To mock the riddled corpses round Bapaume. [Siegfried Sassoon, 1886–1967, *Blighters*]

20 I am making this statement as a wilful defiance of military authority because I believe that the War is being deliberately prolonged by those who have the power to end it. [Siegfried Sassoon, 1886–1967, letter in *Memoirs of an Infantry Officer*, Pt X, 3]

21 When you march into France, let the last man on the right brush the Channel with his sleeve. [Field Marshal von Schlieffen, 1833–1913, in B Tuchman, *The Guns of August*, Ch. 2]

22 That's what you all are ... All of you young people who served in the war. You are a lost generation. [Gertrude Stein, 1874–1946, in Ernest Hemingway, *A Moveable Feast*, 3]

23 You will be home before the leaves have fallen from the trees. [Kaiser Wilhelm II, 1859–1941 (to troops leaving for the Front, Aug. 1914), in B Tuchman, *The Guns of August*, Ch. 9]

24 The war we have just been through, though it was shot through with terror, is not to be compared with the war we would have to face next time. [Woodrow Wilson, 1856–1924, in John Dos Passos, *Mr W's War*, Pt V, Ch. 22]

See also next category, WARS IN GENERAL, WARS: INDIVIDUAL

WORLD WAR II

1 How horrible, fantastic, incredible it is that we should be digging trenches and trying on gas-masks here because of a quarrel in a faraway country between people of whom we know nothing! [Neville Chamberlain, 1869–1940, radio broadcast, 27 Sept. 1938]

2 We shall defend our island, whatever the cost may be, we shall fight on the beaches, we shall fight on the landing grounds, we shall fight in the fields and in the streets, we shall fight in the hills; we shall never surrender. [Winston Churchill, 1874–1965, speech in House of Commons, 4 June 1940]

3 Let us therefore brace ourselves to our duties, and so bear ourselves that, if the British Empire and its Commonwealth last for a thousand years, men will still say: 'This was their finest hour.' [Winston Churchill, 1874–1965, speech in House of Commons, 18 June 1940]

4 Never in the field of human conflict was so much owed by so many to so few. [(Of Battle of Britain) Winston Churchill, 1874–1965, speech in House of Commons, 20 Aug. 1940]

5 Give us the tools, and we will finish the job. [Winston Churchill, 1874–1965, BBC radio broadcast, addressed to President Roosevelt, 9 Feb. 1941]; see 14

6 This is not the end. It is not even the beginning of the end. But it is, perhaps, the end of the beginning. [(Of the victory in Egypt) Winston Churchill, 1874–1965, speech at Mansion House, London, 10 Nov. 1942]

7 A splendid moment in our great history and in our small lives. [(On the unconditional surrender of Germany, 1945) Winston Churchill, 1874–1965, speech in House of Commons]

8 One day President Roosevelt told me that he was asking publicly for suggestions about what the war should be called. I said at once 'the Unnecessary War'. [Winston Churchill, 1874–1965, *The Second World War*, Vol. I, Preface]

9 In the midst of our defeat glory came to the Island people, united and unconquerable; and the tale of the Dunkirk beaches will shine in whatever records are preserved of our affairs. [Winston Churchill, 1874–1965, *The Second World War*, Vol. II, 5]

10 Before Alamein we never had a victory. After Alamein we never had a defeat. [Winston Churchill, 1874–1965, *The Second World War*, Vol. IV, 33]

11 I'm glad we've been bombed. It makes me feel I can look the East End in the face. [Queen Elizabeth, the Queen Mother, 1900– , to policeman, 13 Sept. 1940]

12 France has lost a battle but France has not lost the war. [General de Gaulle, 1890–1970, broadcast from London after the fall of France, probably composed on 18 June 1940 but not issued until July]

13 We can be prepared, without butter, but not without guns, for example. [Josef Goebbels, 1897–1945, speech in Berlin, 17 Jan. 1936. Echoed later that year by Goering]

14 We have finished the job, what shall we do with the tools? [Emperor Haile Selassie of Abyssinia, 1892–1975 (telegram in 1941 to Winston Churchill), in Edward Marsh, *Ambrosia and Small Beer*, Ch. 4]; see 5

15 And we who have been brought up to think of 'Gallant Belgium' / As so much blague / Are now prepared again to essay good through evil / For the sake of Prague. [Louis MacNeice, 1907–63, *Autumn Journal*, VII]

16 I have told you once and I will tell you again – your boys will not be sent into any foreign wars. [Franklin D Roosevelt, 1882–1945, election speech, 30 Oct. 1940]

17 The tasks of the party are . . . to be cautious and not allow our country to be drawn into conflicts by warmongers who are accustomed to have others pull the chestnuts out of the fire for them. [Joseph Stalin, 1879–1953, speech to the 8th Congress of the Communist Party, 6 Jan. 1941]

18 If we see that Germany is winning the war we ought to help Russia, and if Russia is winning we ought to help Germany, and in that way let them kill as many as possible. [Harry Truman, 1884–1972, in *The New York Times*, 24 July 1941, the day the Nazis invaded Russia]

19 I fear we have only awakened a sleeping giant, and his reaction will be terrible. [(After Japanese attack on Pearl Harbor, 1941) Isoruku Yamamoto, 1884–1943, quoted by A J P Taylor in *Listener*, 9 Sept. 1976]

See also previous category, WARS IN GENERAL, WARS: INDIVIDUAL

WORRY

1 Begone, dull care! I prithee begone from me! / Begone, dull care, you and I shall never agree. [anon., *Begone Dull Care*]

2 What's the use of worrying? / It never was worth while, / So, pack up your troubles in your old kit-bag, / And smile, smile, smile. [Georg Asaf, 1880–1951, *Pack up Your Troubles in Your Old Kit-bag*]

3 Irks care the crop-full bird? Frets doubt the maw-crammed beast? [Robert Browning, 1812–89, *Rabbi ben Ezra*, 4]

4 When I look back on all these worries I remember the story of the old man who said on his deathbed that he had had a lot of trouble in his life, most of which had never happened. [Winston Churchill, 1874–1965, *The Second World War*, Vol. II, 23]

5 If I have not fretted myself till I am pale again, there's no veracity in me. [William Congreve, 1670–1729, *The Way of the World*, III. i]

6 But Jesus, when you don't have any money, the problem is food. When you have money, it's sex. When you have health, you worry about getting ruptured or something. If everything is simply jake then you're frightened of death. [J P Donleavy, 1926– , *The Ginger Man*, Ch. 5]

7 Don't worry me – I am an 8 Ulcer Man on 4

Ulcer Pay. [Stephen Early, 1889–1951 (letter to President Truman, to whom line sometimes attr.), in W Hillman, *Mr President*, Pt 5, p. 222]; see 20

8 Cliff had been worrying about all the things kids worry about – unemployment, the pigs, high rise, spray-on boredom. [Ben Elton, 1959– , Rik Mayall, 1958– , Lise Mayer, *The Young Ones Book*]

9 One has two duties – to be worried and not to be worried. [E M Forster, 1879–1970; *Observer*, 'Sayings of the Week', 4 Jan. 1959]

10 The reason why worry kills more people than work is that more people worry than work. [Robert Frost, 1874–1963; in Barbara Rowes, *Book of Quotes*]

11 Black Care takes her seat behind the horseman. [Horace, 65–8 BC, *Odes*, III, i, 40]

12 Worry is the interest paid on trouble before it falls due. [W R Inge, 1860–1954; *Observer*, 'Sayings of the Week', 14 Feb. 1932]

13 Our ingress into the world / Was naked and bare; / Our progress through the world / Is trouble and care. [H W Longfellow, 1807–82, *Tales of a Wayside Inn*, Pt II, 'The Student's Tale']

14 Care / Sat on his faded cheek. [John Milton, 1608–74, *Paradise Lost*, Bk i, 601]

15 To make a union with Great Britain would be fusion with a corpse. [(On Churchill's proposal for Anglo-French union, 1940) Marshal Pétain, 1856–1951, in W S C, *Their Finest Hour*, Ch. 10]

16 Care to our coffin adds a nail no doubt; / And ev'ry grin, so merry, draws one out. [Peter Pindar, 1738–1819, *Expostulatory Odes*, 15]

17 I've developed a new philosophy – I only dread one day at a time. [Charles Schulz, 1922– ; in *Barnes and Noble Book of Quotations* ed. Robert I. Fitzhenry, 'Philosophy']

18 There is some ill a-brewing towards my rest, / For I did dream of money-bags to-night. [William Shakespeare, 1564–1616, *The Merchant of Venice*, II. v. 17]

19 I am sure care's an enemy to life. [*Twelfth Night*, I. iii. (2)]

20 An eight-ulcer man on a four-ulcer job, and all four ulcers working. [President Harry Truman, 1884–1972, letter to the *Washington Post* on unflattering reviewer of his daughter's song recital, 5 Dec. 1950. The remark was originally made by Stephen Early in a letter to Truman]; see 7

21 If you don't like the heat, get out of the kitchen. [Major-General Harry Vaughan, 1893–1981, in *Time* magazine, 28 Apr. 1952. Often quoted by President Truman and wrongly ascr. to him; elsewhere phrase described as proverbial]

22 He looked haggard and careworn, like a Borgia who has suddenly remembered that he has forgotten to shove cyanide in the consommé, and the dinner-gong due any moment. [P G Wodehouse, 1881–1975, *Carry On, Jeeves*, 'Clustering around Young Bingo']

See also RESIGNATION

WRITERS IN GENERAL

1 Writers don't give prescriptions . . . They give head-aches! [Chinua Achebe, 1930– , *Anthills of the Savannah*, 12]

2 Someone watches over us when we write. Mother. Teacher. Shakespeare. God. [Martin Amis, 1949– , *London Fields*, Ch. 20]

3 When success happens to an English writer, he acquires a new typewriter. When success happens to an American writer, he acquires a new life. [Martin Amis, 1949– , *The Moronic Inferno*, 'Kurt Vonnegut']

4 Most writers need a wound, either physical or spiritual. [Martin Amis, 1949– , interview with John Updike in *Observer*, 30 Aug. 1987]

5 The greatest writer cannot see through a brick wall but unlike the rest of us he does not build one. [W H Auden, 1907–73, *The Dyer's Hand*, 'Writing']

6 Writers are usually in the unfortunate predicament of having to speak the truth without the authority to speak it. [W H Auden, 1907–73, in Charles Osborne, *W H A: The Life of a Poet*, Ch. 13]

7 It is easy, after all, not to be a writer. Most people aren't writers, and very little harm comes to them. [Julian Barnes, 1946– , *Flaubert's Parrot*, 9]

8 One who gets paid per word, per piece, or perhaps. [Robert Benchley, 1889–1945 (definition of a freelance writer), quoted by James Thurber in letter to Frances Glennon, 24 June

1959, *Selected Letters*, ed. Helen Thurber and Edward Weeks]

9 Like every writer, he measured the virtues of other writers by their performances, and asked that they measure him by what he conjectured or planned. [Jorge Luis Borges, 1899–1986, *The Secret Miracle*]

10 There were moments when Henry was glad he was a writer, for writers could live in their own minds and didn't have to go out at all. [Malcolm Bradbury, 1932– , *Cuts*, 5]

11 A good writer, in my experience, is a good writer who does not write a large number of books but works back over the first one and gets it more or less right. [Malcolm Bradbury, 1932– , *Unsent Letters*]

12 You, for example, clever to a fault, / The rough and ready man that write apace, / Read somewhat seldomer, think perhaps even less – [Robert Browning, 1812–89, *Bishop Blougram's Apology*, 420]

13 It is from the moment when I shall no longer be more than a writer that I shall cease to write. [Albert Camus, 1913–60, quoted by Nadine Gordimer in *Guardian*, 4 Oct. 1991]

14 True writers encounter their characters only *after* they've created them. [Elias Canetti, 1905–94, *The Human Province*, '1946']

15 Most of the basic material a writer works with is acquired before the age of fifteen. [Willa Cather, 1873–1947; in *Writer's Quotation Book*, ed. James Charlton]

16 An original writer is not one who imitates nobody, but one whom nobody can imitate. [François-René de Chateaubriand, 1768–1848, *The Genius of Christianity*]

17 The faults of great authors are generally excellences carried to an excess. [Samuel Taylor Coleridge, 1772–1834, *Miscellanies*, 149]

18 I believe the souls of five hundred Sir Isaac Newtons would go to the making up of a Shakespeare or a Milton. [Samuel Taylor Coleridge, 1772–1834, letter to Thomas Poole, 23 Mar. 1801]

19 A great writer creates a world of his own and his readers are proud to live in it. A lesser writer may entice them in for a moment, but soon he will watch them filing out. [Cyril Connolly, 1903–74, *Enemies of Promise*, Ch. 1]

20 If, as Dr Johnson said, a man who is not married is only half a man, so a man who is very much married is only half a writer. [Cyril Connolly, 1903–74, *Enemies of Promise*, Ch. 14]

21 The best that can happen for a writer is to be taken up very late or very early, when either old enough to take its measure, or so young that when dropped by society he has all his life before him. [Cyril Connolly, 1903–74, *Enemies of Promise*, Ch. 15]

22 The health of a writer should not be too good, and perfect only in those periods of convalescence when he is not writing. [Cyril Connolly, 1903–74, *Enemies of Promise*, Ch. 16]

23 The more books we read, the clearer it becomes that the true function of a writer is to produce a masterpiece and that no other task is of any consequence. [Cyril Connolly, 1903–74, *The Unquiet Grave*, Ch. 1]

24 The self-esteem of the quality writer depends on his belief that those readers who care about good stuff cannot afford to buy it. [Alan Coren, 1938– , *Seems Like Old Times*, 'January']

25 I love being a writer. What I can't stand is the paperwork. [Peter de Vries, 1910–93; in *Writer's Quotation Book*, ed. James Charlton]

26 That is one last thing to remember: *writers are always selling somebody out*. [Joan Didion, 1934– , *Slouching towards Bethlehem*, Preface]

27 An author who speaks about his own books is almost as bad as a mother who talks about her own children. [Benjamin Disraeli, 1804–81, speech at banquet in Glasgow, 19 Nov. 1873]

28 Talent alone cannot make a writer. There must be a man behind the book. [Ralph Waldo Emerson, 1803–82, *Representative Men*, 'Goethe']

29 If a writer has to rob his mother, he will not hesitate; the 'Ode to a Grecian Urn' is worth any number of old ladies. [William Faulkner, 1897–1962, in *Writers at Work*, ed. Malcolm Cowley, First Series]

30 An author ought to write for the youth of his own generation, the critics of the next, and the schoolmasters of ever afterwards. [F Scott Fitzgerald, 1896–1940, *Author's Apology*]

31 Writers aren't people exactly. Or, if they're

any good, they're a whole *lot* of people trying so hard to be one person. [F Scott Fitzgerald, 1896–1940, *The Last Tycoon*, Ch. 1]

32 How rare, how precious is frivolity! How few writers can prostitute all their powers! They are always implying 'I am capable of higher things.' [E M Forster, 1879–1970, *Abinger Harvest*, 'Ronald Firbank']

33 I always try to tell my critics: Don't classify me, read me. I'm a writer, not a genre. [Carlos Fuentes, 1928– , from *Myself with Others*, 'How I Started to Write']

34 A writer needs a desert island in the morning and the big city at night. As William Faulkner once declared, the perfect home for a writer is a brothel – because in the morning hours it's always calm and in contrast at night there's always a party atmosphere. [Gabriel García Márquez, 1928– , in *Observer*, 24 Oct. 1982]

35 A serious writer is not to be confounded with a solemn writer. A serious writer may be a hawk or a buzzard or even a popinjay, but a solemn writer is always a bloody owl. [Ernest Hemingway, 1899–1961, in Cyril Connolly, *Enemies of Promise*, Ch. 8]

36 He always hurries to the issue, rushing his readers into the middle of the story as if they knew it already. [Horace, 65–8 BC, *Ars Poetica*, 148]

37 He has won every vote who mingles profit with pleasure, by delighting and instructing the reader at the same time. [Horace, 65–8 BC, *Ars Poetica*, 343]

38 For her there were two species: writers and people; and the writers were really people, and the people weren't. [Randall Jarrell, 1914–65, *Pictures from an Institution*, Pt I, Ch. 9]

39 Authors are easy enough to get on with – if you are fond of children. [Michael Joseph, 1897–1958; *Observer*, 'Sayings of the Week', 29 May 1949]

40 A writer's ambition should be to trade a hundred contemporary readers for ten readers in ten years' time and for one reader in a hundred years' time. [Arthur Koestler, 1905–83, interview in *The New York Times Book Review*, 1 Apr. 1951]

41 Liking a writer and then meeting the writer is like liking goose liver and then meeting the goose. [Arthur Koestler, 1905–83, in *International Herald Tribune*, 24–25 Apr. 1982]

42 One must read all writers twice – the good as well as the bad. The one will be recognized; the other, unmasked. [Karl Kraus, 1874–1936, *Half-truths and One-and-a-half Truths*, 'Riddles']

43 Authors and uncaptured criminals ... are the only people free from routine. [Eric Linklater, 1889–1974, *Poet's Pub*, Ch. 23]

44 I'm happy the great ones are thriving, / But what puzzles my head / Is the thought that they need reviving. / I had never been told they were dead. [Phyllis McGinley, 1905–78, *On the Prevalence of Literary Revivals*]

45 He who would not be frustrate of his hope to write well hereafter in laudable things ought himself to be a true poem. [John Milton, 1608–74, *Apology for Smectymnuus*]

46 Any writer overwhelmingly honest about pleasing himself is almost sure to please others. [Marianne Moore, 1887–1972; in *Writer's Quotation Book*, ed. James Charlton]

47 The shelf life of the modern hard-back author is somewhere between the milk and the yoghurt. [John Mortimer, 1923– , when opening the Antiquarian Book Fair, London, 23 June 1987]

48 Writers tend to hang around the edges of society, designated court jesters who know they've landed the best job in the court. They also know that they win in the end. [Alan Plater, 1935– , in *Listener*, 2 Mar. 1989]

49 A dead writer can at least be illustrious without any strain on himself. [Marcel Proust, 1871–1922, *Remembrance of Things Past: The Guermantes Way*, 'Decline and Death of My Grandmother', Ch. 2]

50 What I like in a good author is not what he says, but what he whispers. [Logan Pearsall Smith, 1865–1946, *Afterthoughts*, 5]

51 For a country to have a great writer is like having a second government. That is why no regime has ever loved great writers, only minor ones. [Alexander Solzhenitsyn, 1918– , *The First Circle*, Ch. 57]

52 Those big-shot writers ... could never dig the fact that there are more salted peanuts consumed than caviar. [Mickey Spillane,

1918– ; in *Writer's Quotation Book*, ed. James Charlton]

53 Writers are the engineers of human souls. [Joseph Stalin, 1879–1953; in *Barnes and Noble Book of Quotations*, ed. Robert I Fitzhenry, 'Writers and Writing']; see also ARTISTS, 23

54 Great writers are not those who tell us we shouldn't play with fire but those who make our fingers burn. [Stephen Vizinczey, 1933– , *Truth and Lies in Literature*, p. 161]

55 I would never read a book if it were possible to talk half an hour with the man who wrote it. [Woodrow Wilson, 1856–1924, advice to his students at Princeton, 1900]

56 Every great and original writer, in proportion as he is great and original, must himself create the taste by which he is to be relished. [William Wordsworth, 1770–1850, *Lyrical Ballads*, Preface]

See also next categories, NOVELISTS, POETS

WRITERS: INDIVIDUAL (in alphabetical order of subject)

1 *Vous créez un frisson nouveau.* – You create a new shiver of horror. [Victor Hugo, 1802–85, letter to Charles Baudelaire, 6 Oct. 1859]

2 To give an accurate and exhaustive account of that period would need a far less brilliant pen than mine. [Max Beerbohm, 1872–1956, *1880*]

3 The gods bestowed on Max [Beerbohm] the gift of perpetual old age. [Oscar Wilde, 1854–1900, quoted by R Aldington in his edn of W]

4 When I am dead, I hope it may be said: / 'His sins were scarlet, but his books were read'. [Hilaire Belloc, 1870–1953, *Epigrams*, 'On His Books']

5 Tom Birch is as brisk as a bee in conversation; but no sooner does he take a pen in his hand, than it becomes a torpedo to him, and benumbs all his faculties. [Dr Samuel Johnson, 1709–84, in James Boswell, *Life of J*, 1743]

6 For Boswell stumbled soon upon the vital discovery that experience is three parts hallucination. [V S Pritchett, 1900–1997, quoted in P's obituary, *Guardian*, 22 Mar. 1997]

7 You will see Coleridge – he who sits obscure / In the exceeding lustre and the pure / Intense irradiation of a mind, / Which, with its own internal lightning blind, / Flags wearily through darkness and despair. [P B Shelley, 1792–1822, *Letter to Maria Gisborne*, 146]

8 He [T S Eliot] likes to look on the bile when it's black. [Aldous Huxley, 1894–1963, in Edward Marsh, *Ambrosia and Small Beer*, Ch. 5, sect. i]

9 He [T S Eliot] is without pose and full of poise. He makes one feel that all cleverness is an excuse for thinking hard. [Harold Nicolson, 1886–1968, *Diaries and Letters, 1930–1939*, 2 Mar. 1932]

10 I once told Fordie [Ford Madox Ford] that if he were placed naked and alone in a room without furniture, I would come back in an hour and find total confusion. [Ezra Pound, 1885–1972, in V S Pritchett, *The Working Novelist*]

11 Another damned, thick, square book! Always scribble, scribble, scribble! Eh! Mr Gibbon? [William Henry, Duke of Gloucester, 1743–1805, quoted in note to James Boswell, *Life of Johnson*]

12 Though we are mighty fine fellows nowadays, we cannot write like Hazlitt. [Robert Louis Stevenson, 1850–94, *Virginibus Puerisque*, 'Walking Tours']

13 Every word she [Lillian Hellman] writes is a lie, including 'and' and 'the'. [Mary McCarthy, 1912–89, discussing the 1930s in TV interview on *Dick Cavett Show*, 25/26 Jan. 1980]

14 So, in this way of writing without thinking, / Thou hast a strange alacrity in sinking. [Thomas Sackville, Earl of Dorset, 1536–1608, *Satire on Edward Howard*]

15 Hugo was a madman who believed himself to be Victor Hugo. [Jean Cocteau, 1889–1963, *Opium*, p. 51]

16 Indeed, the freedom with which Dr Johnson condemns whatever he disapproves is astonishing. [Fanny Burney, 1752–1840, *Diary*, 23 Aug. 1778]

17 If you were to make little fishes talk, they would talk like whales. [(Said to Johnson) Oliver Goldsmith, 1728–74, quoted in James Boswell, *Life of J*, 27 Apr. 1773]

18 Dr Johnson's morality was as English an article as a beefsteak. [Nathaniel Hawthorne, 1804–64, *Our Old Home*, 'Lichfield and Uttoxeter']

19 Dr Johnson's sayings would not appear so

extraordinary were it not for his *bow-wow way*. [Earl of Pembroke, 1734–94, in James Boswell, *Life of J*, 27 Mar. 1775, note]

20 That great Cham of literature, Samuel Johnson. [Tobias Smollett, 1721–71, letter to John Wilkes, 16 Mar. 1759, quoted in James Boswell, *Life of J*]

21 Write it, damn you, write it! What else are you good for? [James Joyce, 1882–1941, *Giacomo Joyce*]

22 Kipling is our first American writer. [V S Pritchett, 1900–1997, quoted in P's obituary in the *Independent*, 22 Mar. 1997]

23 His sayings are generally like women's letters; all the pith is in the postscript. [(Of Charles Lamb) William Hazlitt, 1778–1830, *Conversations of Northcote*, 'Boswell Redivivus']

24 I like to write when I feel spiteful: it's like having a good sneeze. [D H Lawrence, 1885–1930, letter to Lady Cynthia Asquith, Nov. 1913]

25 The ordinary novel would trace the history of the diamond – but I say, 'Diamond, what! This is carbon.' And my diamond may be coal or soot and my theme is carbon. [D H Lawrence, 1885–1930, letter to Edward Garnett, 5 June 1914]

26 Here is a man who questioned life, but did not know in what name he questioned life. [(Of T E Lawrence) André Malraux, 1901–76, in Bruce Chatwin, *What am I Doing Here*, 'André Malraux']

27 If it sounds like writing, I rewrite it. [Elmore Leonard, 1925– , in *Newsweek*, 22 Apr. 1985]

28 Macaulay is well for a while, but one wouldn't *live* under Niagara. [Thomas Carlyle, 1795–1881, remark quoted in R M Milnes, *Notebook*]

29 I shall not be satisfied unless I produce something that shall for a few days supersede the last fashionable novel on the tables of young ladies. [Lord Macaulay, 1800–1859, letter to Macvey Napier, 5 Nov. 1841]

30 I wish that I was as cocksure of anything as Tom Macaulay is of everything. [Viscount Melbourne, 1779–1848, attr. by Earl Cowper, in preface to *Lord Melbourne's Papers*]

31 He had just one illusion about them and that was that they were no good. [(Of Somerset Maugham's boast that he had no illusions about his fellow men) Noël Coward, 1899–1973, in Frederic Raphael, *S M and His World*]

32 Meredith is a prose Browning, and so is Browning. [Oscar Wilde, 1854–1900, *The Critic as Artist*, Pt I, 'Intentions']

33 I suffer from the disease of writing books and being ashamed of them when they are finished. [Baron de Montesquieu, 1689–1755, *Pensées diverses*, 'Portrait de Montesquieu par lui-même']

34 Everything I write probably is *Hamlet* in disguise. [Iris Murdoch, 1919–99, interview in *Guardian*, 15 Sept. 1980]

35 I think like a genius, I write like a distinguished author, and I speak like a child. [Vladimir Nabokov, 1899–1977, *Strong Opinions*, Foreword]

36 His fine wit / Makes such a wound, the knife is lost in it. [(Of T L Peacock) P B Shelley, 1792–1822, *Letter to Maria Gisborne*, 240]

37 Just before they made S. J. Perelman, they broke the mould [Dorothy Parker, 1893–1967, quoted by Alan Coren in *Observer*, 29 Nov. 1987]

38 'Poe,' I said, 'was perhaps the first great nonstop literary drinker of the American nineteenth century. He made the indulgences of Coleridge and De Quincey seem like a bit of mischief in the kitchen with the cooking sherry.' [James Thurber, 1894–1961, *Alarms and Diversions*, 'The Moribundant Life . . .']

39 A village explainer, excellent if you were a village, but if you were not, not. [(Of Ezra Pound) Gertrude Stein, 1874–1946, in Malcolm Cowley, *Exile's Return*, Part IV.2]

40 And he [J. B. Priestley] gives us what only the rare ones give us: a sense that we are collaborating, rather than simply paying to go in. He admits us to the country of ourselves. [Robert Robinson, 1927– , *Dog Chairman*, 'Priestley']

41 Thou large-brained woman and large-hearted man. [Elizabeth Barrett Browning, 1806–61, *To George Sand, A Desire*]

42 His works (taken together) are almost like a new edition of human nature. [(Of Sir Walter Scott) William Hazlitt, 1778–1830, *English Literature*, Ch. 14]

43 Doeg, though without knowing how or why, / Made still a nonsense, never out nor in; / Free from all meaning, whether good or bad, / And in one word, heroically mad. [(Of Elkanah Settle) John Dryden, 1631–1700, *Absalom and Achitophel*, Pt II, 412]

44 O let my books be then the eloquence / And dumb presagers of my speaking breast. [William Shakespeare, 1564–1616, *Sonnets*, 23]

45 Smollett's temper was, in some respects, a new, frost-bitten bud of civilization, of which sick, divided and impossible men are frequently the growing point. [V S Pritchett, 1900–97, *Books in General*, 'The Unhappy Traveller']

46 He had written much blank verse, and blanker prose. [(Of Southey) Lord Byron, 1788–1824, *The Vision of Judgement*, 98]

47 Writing, when properly managed, (as you may be sure I think mine is) is but a different name for conversation. [Laurence Sterne, 1713–68, *Tristram Shandy*, Bk ii, Ch. 11]

48 I have thus played the sedulous ape to Hazlitt, to Lamb, to Wordsworth, to Sir Thomas Browne, to Defoe, to Hawthorne, to Montaigne, to Baudelaire and to Obermann. [Robert Louis Stevenson, 1850–94, *Memories and Portraits*, Ch. 4]

49 First I write one sentence: then I write another. That's how I write. And so I go on. But I have a feeling writing ought to be like running through a field. [Lytton Strachey, 1880–1932 (in conversation with Max Beerbohm), in Virginia Woolf, *A Writer's Diary*, 1 Nov. 1938]

50 Good God! What a genius I had when I wrote that book. [Jonathan Swift, 1677–1745 (of *The Tale of A Tub*), attr.]

51 Thurber is the greatest unlistener I know. [Harold Ross, 1892–1951, in James Thurber, *The Years with Ross*, Ch. 5]

52 Thurber wrote the way a child skips rope, the way a mouse waltzes. [E B White, 1899–1985 (from the *New Yorker*, on Thurber's death in 1961), in *Guardian*, 29 Jan. 1982]

53 One cannot really be a Catholic and grown-up. [(Of Evelyn Waugh) George Orwell, 1903–50, Notebook, undated, before Mar. 1949]

54 I put the words down and push them a bit. [Evelyn Waugh, 1903–66, in obituary in *The New York Times*, 11 Apr. 1966]

55 I have put my genius into my life; all I've put into my works is my talent. [Oscar Wilde, 1854–1900, in André Gide, *Journals*, 13 June 1889]

56 He [Thornton Wilder] arranges flowers beautifully, but he does not grow them. [Harold Clurman, 1901–80, *Lies Like Truth*]

57 English literature's performing flea. [(Of P G Wodehouse) Sean O'Casey, 1880–1964, in Wodehouse, *Performing Flea*, 'Postscript']

58 Every phrase and gesture was studied. Now and again when she said something a little out of the ordinary she wrote it down herself in a notebook. *It was like watching someone organizing her own immortality.* [(On sitting next to Virginia Woolf at lunch) Harold Laski, 1893–1950, in letter of George Lyttelton, 27 Oct. 1955, *Lyttelton–Hart-Davis Letters*, Vol. 1]

59 Virginia Woolf, I enjoyed talking to her, but thought *nothing* of her writing. I considered her 'a beautiful little knitter'. [Edith Sitwell, 1887–1964, letter to G Singleton, 11 July 1955]

60 Woollcott himself used to brag that he was the best writer in America, but had nothing to say. [Alexander Woollcott, 1887–1943, in James Thurber, *The Years with Ross*, Ch. 15]

61 I refuse to be famous for a book on Wordsworth, although after all it was all Wordsworth was famous for. [Cyril Connolly, 1903–74, *A Romantic Friendship, Letters to Noel Blakiston*, letter of 27 Aug. 1962]

See also previous and next categories, NOVELS, NOVELISTS, POETRY, POETS, PROSE

WRITING

1 No iron can stab the heart with such force as a full stop put just at the right place. [Isaac Babel, 1894–?1939, *Guy de Maupassant*]

2 The biggest obstacle to professional writing today is the necessity for changing a typewriter ribbon. [Robert Benchley, 1889–1945, *Chips off the Old Benchley*, 'Learn to Write']

3 *Qui ne sait se borner ne sut jamais écrire.* – No one who cannot limit himself has ever been able to write. [Nicholas Boileau, 1636–1711, *L'Art poétique*, I, 63]

4 *Vingt fois sur le métier remettez votre ouvrage; / Polissez-le sans cesse et le repolissez.* – Bring your work back to the workshop twenty times. Polish it continuously, and polish it again. [Nicholas Boileau, 1636–1711, *L'Art poétique*, I, 172]

5 Writing is nothing more than a guided dream. [Jorge Luis Borges, 1899–1986, *Doctor Brodie's Report*, Preface]

6 When I write a page that reads badly I know that it is myself who has written it. When it reads well it has come through from somewhere else. [Gerald Brenan, 1894–1987, *Thoughts in a Dry Season*, 'Writing']

7 In the business of writing what one accumulates is not expertise but uncertainties. [Joseph Brodsky, 1940–96, *Less Than One*, title essay]

8 Because writing always means hiding something in such a way that it then is discovered. [Italo Calvino, 1923–85, *If on a Winter's Night a Traveller*, 8]

9 Better to write for yourself and have no public, than write for the public and have no self. [Cyril Connolly, 1903–74, in *Turnstile One*, ed. V S Pritchett]

10 All good writing is *swimming under water* and holding your breath. [F Scott Fitzgerald, 1896–1940, undated letter to Frances Scott Fitzgerald]

11 You start by writing to live. You end by writing so as not to die. [Carlos Fuentes, 1928– , *Myself with Others*, 'How I Started to Write']

12 You must write for children in the same way as you do for adults, only better. [Maxim Gorky, 1868–1936, attr.]

13 Between my finger and my thumb / The squat pen rests; snug as a gun. [Seamus Heaney, 1939– , *Digging*]

14 A man may write at any time, if he will set himself doggedly to it. [Dr Samuel Johnson, 1709–84, in James Boswell, *Life of J*, Mar. 1750]

15 A man will turn over half a library to make one book. [Dr Samuel Johnson 1709–84, in James Boswell, *Life of J*, 6 Apr. 1775]

16 No man but a blockhead ever wrote, except for money. [Dr Samuel Johnson 1709–84, in James Boswell, *Life of J*, 5 Apr. 1776]

17 An inveterate and incurable itch for writing besets many and grows old with their sick hearts. [Juvenal, 60–*c*.130, *Satires*, VII, 51]

18 Beneath the rule of men entirely great, / The pen is mightier than the sword. [Edward Bulwer-Lytton, 1803–73, *Richelieu*, II. ii]

19 I wish I wrote books like other people do, from beginning to end . . . For me, writing a book is like doing a jigsaw puzzle under house arrest. [Brenda Maddox, 1932– , in *Listener*, 16 Oct. 1986]

20 If you want to get rich from writing, write the sort of thing that's read by persons who move their lips when reading to themselves. [Don Marquis, 1878–1937; in *Writer's Quotation Book*, ed. James Charlton]

21 Writing is like getting married. One should never commit oneself until one is amazed at one's luck. [Iris Murdoch, 1919–99, *The Black Prince*, 'Bradley Pearson's Foreword']

22 The last thing one discovers in writing a book is what to put first. [Blaise Pascal, 1623–62, *Pensées*, I, 19]

23 True ease in writing comes from art, not chance, / As those move easiest who have learned to dance. / 'Tis not enough no harshness gives offence, / The sound must seem an echo to the sense. [Alexander Pope, 1688–1744, *An Essay on Criticism*, 362]

24 If you don't spend every morning of your life writing, it's awfully difficult to know what to do otherwise. [Anthony Powell, 1905– , interview in *Observer*, 3 Apr. 1984]

25 The acid test of a good piece of writing, even if it is of violence and cruelty, is that it must make one's ears water. [Bernice Rubens, 1928– , in *The Sunday Times*, 3 Apr. 1988]

26 You write with ease, to show your breeding, / But easy writing's curst hard reading. [R B Sheridan, 1751–1816, *Clio's Protest*]

27 'Fool,' said my Muse to me, 'look in thy heart and write.' [Sir Philip Sidney, 1554–86, *Astrophel and Stella*, Sonnet 1]

28 All writing, even the clumsy kind, exposes in its loops and slants a yearning deeper than an intention, the soul of the writer flopping on the clothes-peg of his exclamation mark. [Paul Theroux, 1941– , *Saint Jack*, Ch. 1]

29 Three hours a day will produce as much as a man ought to write. [Anthony Trollope, 1815–82, *Autobiography*, Ch. 15]

30 Of two possible words always choose the lesser. [Paul Valéry, *Odds and Ends*, 'Advice to the Writer']

31 It is wisest to write in 'B-natural'. But many write in 'B-sharp'. [Paul Valéry, 1871–1945, *Rhumbs*]

32 Every drop of ink in my pen ran cold. [Horace Walpole, 1717–97, letter to George Montagu, 3 July 1752]

33 I think if you had ever written a book you were absolutely pleased with, you'd never write another. The same probably goes for having children. [Fay Weldon, 1931– , interview in *Guardian*, 28 Nov. 1991]

See also previous categories, LITERACY, NOVELS, NOVELISTS, POETRY, POETS, PROSE, READING

Y

YOUTH

1 *Gaudeamus igitur, / Iuvenes dum sumus.* – Let us live then and be glad / While young life's before us. [anon. medieval students' song]

2 Youth would be an ideal state if it came a little later in life. [H H Asquith, 1852–1928, in *Observer*, 15 Apr. 1923]

3 Remember now thy Creator in the days of thy youth, while the evil days come not, nor the years draw nigh, when thou shalt say, I have no pleasure in them. [Bible, OT, *Ecclesiastes* 12:1]

4 Alas! our young affections run to waste, / Or water but the desert. [Lord Byron, 1788–1824, *Childe Harold's Pilgrimage*, IV, 120]

5 'Whom the gods love die young' was said of yore. [Lord Byron, 1788–1824, *Don Juan*, IV, 12]; see 17

6 They try to tell us we're too young / Too young to really be in love. [Sylvia Dee, song: *Too Young*]

7 Youth's the season made for joys, / Love is then our duty. [John Gay, 1685–1732, *The Beggar's Opera*, I. iv]

8 No young man believes he shall ever die. [William Hazlitt, 1778–1830, *On the Feeling of Immortality in Youth*]

9 Only the young die good. [Oliver Herford, 1863–1935; in A Andrews, *Quotations for Speakers and Writers*]

10 They carry back bright to the coiner the mintage of man, / The lads that will die in their glory and never be old. [A E Housman, 1859–1936, *A Shropshire Lad*, 23]

11 Some day, youth will come here and thunder on my door, and force its way in to me. [Henrik Ibsen, 1828–1906, *The Master Builder*, I]

12 In her position – that of a young person spending, in framed and wired confinement, the life of a guinea-pig or a magpie. [Henry James, 1843–1916, *In the Cage*, Ch. 1]

13 When all the world is young, lad, / And all the trees are green; / And every goose a swan, lad / And every lass a queen; / Then hey for boot and horse, lad, / And round the world away: / Young blood must have its course, lad, / And every dog his day. [Charles Kingsley, 1819–75, *The Water Babies*, 'Young and Old']

14 In this way I spent youth, / Tracing the trite untransferable / Truss-advertisement, truth. [Philip Larkin, 1922–85, *Send No Money*]

15 In the lexicon of youth, which fate reserves / For a bright manhood, there is no such word / As – *fail*. [Edward Bulwer-Lytton, 1803–73, *Richelieu*, II. ii]

16 The atrocious crime of being a young man . . . I shall attempt neither to palliate nor to deny. [William Pitt, the Elder, 1708–78, speech in reply to Robert Walpole, 27 Jan. 1741]

17 He whom the gods favour dies young. [Plautus, 254–184 BC, *Bacchides*, IV. 816]; see 5

18 There is a strong disposition in youth, from which some individuals never escape, to suppose that everyone else is having a more enjoyable time than we are ourselves. [Anthony Powell, 1905–   , *A Buyer's Market*, Ch. 4]

19 My salad days, / When I was green in judgement. [William Shakespeare, 1564–1616, *Antony and Cleopatra*, I. v. 73]

20 Then come kiss me, sweet and twenty, / Youth's a stuff will not endure. [*Twelfth Night*, I. v. (54)]

21 One would think his mother's milk were scarce out of him. [*Twelfth Night*, I. v. (171)]

22 Home-keeping youth have ever homely wits. [*The Two Gentlemen of Verona*, I. i. 2]

23 I would there were no age between sixteen and three-and-twenty, or that youth would sleep out the rest; for there is nothing in the between but getting wenches with child, wronging the ancientry, stealing, fighting. [*The Winter's Tale*, III. iii. 58]

24 Give me the young man who has brains enough to make a fool of himself [Robert Louis Stevenson, 1850–94, *Virginibus Puerisque*, 'Crabbed Age and Youth']

25 Oh as I was young and easy in the mercy of his means, / Time held me green and dying / Though I sang in my chains like the sea. [Dylan Thomas, 1914–53, *Fern Hill*]

26 The force that through the green fuse drives the flower / Drives my green age. [Dylan Thomas, 1914–53, *The Force that through the Green Fuse*]

27 We're none of us infallible – not even the youngest among us. [W H Thompson, 1810–86 (remark to a junior fellow, when Master of Trinity College, Cambridge), quoted in G W E Russell, *Collections and Recollections*, Ch. 18]

28 The old-fashioned respect for the young is fast dying out. [Oscar Wilde, 1854–1900, *The Importance of Being Earnest*, I]

29 The youth who daily farther from the east / Must travel, still is Nature's priest, / And by the vision splendid / Is on his way attended: / At length the man perceives it die away, / And fade into the light of common day. [William Wordsworth, 1770–1850, *Ode, Intimations of Immortality*, 5]

See also next category, ADOLESCENCE, AGE, CHILDHOOD, MIDDLE AGE

YOUTH & AGE

1 Youth is a blunder; Manhood a struggle; Old Age a regret. [Benjamin Disraeli, 1804–81, *Coningsby*, Bk iii, Ch. 1]

2 Ah, but I was so much older then, / I'm younger than that now. [Bob Dylan, 1941– , song: *My Back Pages*]

3 If youth knew, if age could. [Henri Estienne, 1531–98, *Les Prémices*, 191]

4 I never dared be radical when young / For fear it would make me conservative when old. [Robert Frost, 1874–1963, *Precaution*]

5 Now, of my threescore years and ten, / Twenty will not come again. [A E Housman, 1859–1936, *A Shropshire Lad*, ii]

6 From the earliest times the old have rubbed it into the young that they are wiser than they, and before the young had discovered what nonsense this was they were old too, and it profited them to carry on the imposture. [W Somerset Maugham, 1874–1965, *Cakes and Ale*, Ch. 9]

7 The old get old, the young get stronger, / They've got the guns but we got the numbers. [Jim Morrison, 1943–71, song: *Five to One*]

8 Behold the child, by nature's kindly law / Pleased with a rattle, tickled with a straw: / Some livelier plaything gives his youth delight, / A little louder, but as empty quite: / Scarfs, garters, gold, amuse his riper stage, / And beads and prayer-books are the toys of age: / Pleased with this bauble still, as that before; / Till tired he sleeps, and life's poor play is o'er. [Alexander Pope, 1688–1744, *An Essay on Man*, II, 275]

9 See how the world its veterans rewards! / A youth of frolics, an old age of cards. [Alexander Pope, 1688–1744. *Moral Essays*, Epistle II, 243]

10 The young have aspirations that never come to pass, the old have reminiscences of what never happened. [Saki (H H Munro), 1870–1916, *Reginald at the Carlton*]

11 The young man who has not wept is a savage, and the old man who will not laugh is a fool. [George Santayana, 1863–1952, *Dialogues in Limbo*, Ch. 3]

12 I came to this world very young at a very old time. [Erik Satie, 1866–1925, in Pierre-Daniel Templier, *E S*, Ch. 1]

13 For in my youth I never did apply / Hot and rebellious liquors to the blood . . . Therefore my age is as the lusty winter, / Frosty, but kindly. [William Shakespeare, 1564–1616, *As You Like It*, II. iii. 48]

14 The oldest hath borne most: we that are

young / Shall never see so much, nor live so long. [*King Lear*, V. iii. (327)]

15 Crabbed age and youth cannot live together: / Youth is full of pleasance, age is full of care. [*The Passionate Pilgrim*, xii]

16 Old and young, we are all on our last cruise. [Robert Louis Stevenson, 1850–94, *Virginibus Puerisque*, 4, 'Crabbed Age and Youth']

17 O man, that from thy fair and shining youth / Age might but take the things youth needed not! [William Wordsworth, 1770–1850, *The Small Celandine*]

18 That is no country for old men. The young / In one another's arms, birds in the trees / – Those dying generations – at their song, / The salmon-falls, the mackerel-crowded seas. [W B Yeats, 1865–1939, *Sailing to Byzantium*]

19 Much did I rage when young, / Being by the world oppressed, / But now with flattering tongue / It speeds the parting guest. [W B Yeats, 1865–1939, *Youth and Age*]

See also previous category, ADOLESCENCE, AGE, CHILDHOOD, MIDDLE AGE

Z

ZED

1 Thou whoreson zed! thou unnecesssary letter! [William Shakespeare, 1564–1616, *King Lear*, II. ii. (68)]

Index of authors

Abbreviations: (I) = Individual; (G) = In General; (P) = Particular

Index of authors

Index of authors

Index of authors

Bampfylde, J C, 1754–96, English poet, BEAUTY 1

Bankhead, Tallulah, 1903–68, US actress, CRITICISM 2, DRUGS 1, PURITY 1, REGRET 2

Banks-Smith, Nancy, 1929– , English journalist, ARCHITECTURE 1, ENGLISH 2, EYES 2, NATIONS 1, NEW YORK 1, POWER 4, PROFESSIONS 1, SAINTS 1, SOLDIERS (I) 1, TEACHERS 1

Barbauld, Anna Laetitia, 1743–1825, English poet and hymn-writer, DEATH 10

Barber, Lynn 1944– , English journalist, ADULTERY 2

Barbour, John, 1316?–95, Scottish poet, cleric and scholar, LIBERTY 2

Barham, Revd R H, 1788–1845, English comic poet, author of *Ingoldsby Legends*, CURSES 1, FAMILY 2

Baring, Maurice, 1874–1945, English writer and diplomat, GENIUS 3, MONEY 4

Baring-Gould, S, 1834–1924, English cleric, CHRISTIANITY 2

Barker, George, 1916–91, English poet, WARS (G) 4

Barker, Howard, 1946– , English playwright, THEATRE 1

Barker, Ronnie, 1929– , English comedian, JOKES 1

Barnes, Binnie, 1905–98, British actress, BORES & BOREDOM 1

Barnes, Julian, 1946– , English novelist, COUNTRY & TOWN 2, ENGLISH 3, FEMINISM 2, SELF 2, WOMEN & MEN 3, WRITERS (G) 7

Barnes, William, 1801–86, English poet, TREES 1

Barnfield, Richard, 1574–1627, English poet, CERTAIN 2, LUCK 1

Barnum, Phineas T, 1810–91, US showman, FOOLS 2

Barrie, James, 1860–1937, Scottish playwright and novelist, especially famous for *Peter Pan*, BOYS 1, CHARM 1, COMFORT 1, DAUGHTERS 1, DEATH 11, EQUALITY 1, FAIRIES 2, HEAVEN & HELL 2, KNOWLEDGE 3, MATHEMATICS 2, SCOTLAND 1, 2, SUCCESS 2, THINKING 4

Barrington, George, 1755–?1835, Irish pick-pocket, transported to Botany Bay, writer of historical works on Australia, PATRIOTISM 3

Barrow, John D, 1952– , English astronomer, EXISTENCE 2

Barth, Karl, 1886–1968, Swiss theologian, COMPOSERS (I) 12, GOOD & GOODNESS 1

Barthes, Roland, 1915–80, French writer, semiologist, critic and teacher, CARS 1, MODERN AGE 3, TRUTH 7

Baruch, Bernard, 1870–1965, US financier and government adviser, OLD AGE 2, POLITICIANS (G) 3

Barzun, Jacques, 1907– , French-born US cultural historian and scholar, INTELLECT 1

Baudelaire, Charles, 1821–67, French poet, translator and critic, CITY 1, DEATH 12, EVENING 1, MEMORY 3, NATURE 1, POETS (G) 3, READING 2

Baum, Vicki, 1888–1960, German novelist, MARRIAGE 6

Bax, Sir Arnold, 1883–1953, English composer, EXPERIENCE 1

Bayfield, Anthony, 1946– , English rabbi, JEWS 2

Bayley, Stephen, 1951– , British design critic, CIVILIZATION 1

Baylis, Lilian, 1874–1937, English theatrical manager, ACTORS & ACTRESSES (G) 1

Bayly, T H, 1797–1839, English poet and playwright, DREAMS 2, SEA 2

Beatty, Warren, 1937– , US film actor, MARRIAGE 7

Beaumont, Francis, 1584–1616, English playwright and poet, EXERCISE 1, HELP 1, MORTALITY 2, POETRY 6, SLEEPING & WAKING 1, SORROW 3, THEATRE 2

Beaumarchais, Pierre-Augustin de, 1732–99, French playwright, ARISTOCRACY 3, HUMAN BEINGS 5, LAUGHTER 1, SONGS & SINGERS 1

Beauvoir, Simone de, 1908–86, French feminist, socialist and writer, WOMEN 4, WORK 5

Beavan, John, [Lord Ardwick], 1910–94, English newspaper editor, NEWSPAPERS 2

Beaverbrook, Lord, 1879–1964, Canadian-born British newspaper proprietor, AGGRESSION 2, LAST WORDS 2, PRIME MINISTERS (I) 11

Beckett, Samuel, 1906–89, Irish-born playwright who lived mainly in France, AFTERLIFE 1, ART 3, CHANGE 3, ENDURANCE 2, FATHERS 1, GRAVE 1, HELL 2, LIFE IS FLEETING 5, MADNESS & SANITY 3, MEANNESS 1, OPTIMISM & PESSIMISM 2, THRIFT 1, TIME 3

Beckford, William, 1759–1844, English writer, art collector and eccentric, HEAVEN & HELL 3

Becon, Thomas, 1512–67, English cleric, chaplain to Thomas Cranmer, WINE 1

Beddoes, T L, 1798–1815, English poet and playwright, DREAMS 3, SLEEPING & WAKING 2

Bede, The Venerable, 673–735, English historian, scholar and monk, LIFE IS FLEETING 6

Bedell, Geraldine, 1956– , English journalist, FEMINISM 3

Beebe, William, 1877–1962, US ornithologist and zoo curator, EXISTENCE 3

Beecham, Sir Thomas, 1879–1961, English conductor, COMPOSERS (I) 23, MUSIC 5, 6, MUSICIANS 1, 2

Beefheart, Captain, 1941– , US musician, RACES 2

Beer, Patricia, 1924–99, English poet, HELL 3

Beerbohm, Max, 1872–1956, English writer and critic, CHAOS 2, DAYS 2, EXPERIENCE 2, FOOLS 3, GOLF 1, LEARNING 3, MASSES 2, PAST 3, PHILOSOPHY 5, POETS (I) 11, PORTRAITS 1, SCHOOLS 3, UNIVERSITIES 1, WOMEN 5, 6, WOMEN & MEN 4, 5, WRITERS (I) 2

Behan, Brendan, 1923–64, Irish playwright, ABSENCE 2, IRELAND 3, 4

Behn, Aphra, 1640–89, English playwright and novelist, CHOICE 2, LOVE 8, MONEY 5, POVERTY 5

Bei, Dao, 1949– , Chinese poet, LIBERTY 3

Bell, Clive, 1881–1964, English art critic, ART 4, ARTISTS 2, 3, COMFORT 2, CRITICISM 3, LIBERTY 4, RELIGION 5

Bell, H E, English educationist, PARENTS 4

Bellah, James Warner, 1899–1976, US screenwriter, JOURNALISM 3

Bellamy, Guy, 1935– , English novelist, BRITISH EMPIRE 1, HUMAN BEINGS 6, JOURNALISM 4, NEGLECT 1, NEWSPAPERS 3, TIME 4

Bellay, Joachim du, 1515–60, French poet, FRANCE 13

Belloc, Hilaire, 1870–1953, French-born, English poet, essayist and biographer, ACADEMICS 3,

Index of authors

Index of authors

Connolly, Billy, 1942– , Scottish comedian and actor, ADVICE 8, BEER 4, FUTURE 10, MARRIAGE 32, SCOTLAND 8

Connolly, Cyril, 1903–74, English writer and editor of magazine, *Horizon*, ADOLESCENCE 2, ARISTOCRACY 7, ART 13, ARTISTS 10, BEGINNINGS 3, BOOKS (G) 10, BOYS 5, CHARM 3, CITY 3, CIVILIZATION 5, DISASTERS 2, FAT & THIN 3, FEAR 8, HUMOUR 9, INSULTS 6, JOURNALISM 12, LIFE 19, LITERATURE 6, MEMORY 5, PASSIONS 2, PATRONS 2, POETS (I) 1, PRIME MINISTERS (I) 4, PURITANS 2, REALITY 4, SCHOOLS 9, 10, SELF 7, 8, STYLE 5, TALENT 1, TALK 4, WIVES 12, 13, WRITERS (G) 19–23, WRITERS (I) 61, WRITING 9

Conrad, Joseph, 1857–1924, Polish-born English novelist, ACHIEVEMENT 4, ENGLAND (G) 11, MEMORY 6, SOLITUDE 6

Conran, Shirley, 1932– , English journalist and writer, EFFORT 2, HOUSEWORK 1, LAZINESS 6, MOTTOES 2, PRIORITIES 2

Conservative Party, British Parliamentary party, ECONOMICS 3

Constantine, Emperor, 274?–337, Roman Emperor from 306, CHRISTIANITY 9

Cook, A J, 1885–1931, Welsh miners' leader, STRIKES 2

Cook, Dan, 1926– , US sports editor, ENDS 3

Cook, Eliza, 1818–89, English poet, COMFORT 6

Cook, Peter, 1937–95, English comedian, LANGUAGES 5, THEATRE 7, UNIVERSE 9

Cooke, Alistair, 1908– , English-born US journalist and broadcaster of weekly *Letter from America* from 1946, DEMOCRACY 7, FRANCE 9, PRESIDENTS (I) 29

Cookson, Catherine, 1906–98, English novelist, WORDS 6

Coolidge, Calvin, 1872–1933, 30th US President, BUSINESS 3, DEMOCRACY 8, SINS 13, STRIKES 3, USA (G) 9

Cooper, Chester, 1917– , US political commentator, VIETNAM 1

Cooper, Giles, 1918–66, English writer, ACHIEVEMENT 5, FAILURE 2, SCHOOLS 11

Cooper, Jilly, 1937– , English novelist and journalist, SEX 9

Cooper, Tommy, 1921–84, Welsh comedian, DREAMS 10

Cooper, William, 1910– , English novelist and civil servant, GIRLS 4, HITLER 6

Cope, Wendy, 1945– , English poet, LOVERS 6, MEN 2, MISTAKES 4, SEX 10

Copeland, Robert, 1945– , US music critic, COMMITTEES 3

Copland, Aaron, 1900–90, US composer, MUSIC 12, 13

Coppola, Francis Ford, 1939– , US film-director, WORK 14

Corbet, Richard, 1582–1635, English poet and cleric, FAIRIES 3

Coren, Alan, 1938– , English journalist and humorist, BOOKS (I) 1, DOGS 5, PAPACY 1, PROFESSIONS 2, SWITZERLAND 1, TELEVISION 8, USA (G) 10, WORDS 7, WRITERS (G)24

Corneille, Peter, ANIMALS 11

Corneille, Pierre, 1606–84, French playwright, BATTLES 2, DUTY 5, SORROW 10, STARS 6

Cornfeld, Bernard, 1927–95, US businessman, RICH 7

Cornford, F M, 1874–1943, English academic, ACTION 6, PROPAGANDA 2

Cornford, Frances, 1886–1960, English poet, POETS (I) 7

Cornford, John, 1915–36, poet and writer on politics, killed in Spanish Civil War, INFLUENCE 2

Correggio, Antonio, 1489?–1534, Italian painter, PAINTERS (I) 4

Corrigan, Dame Felicitas, 1908– , British nun and biographer, LIFE 20

Cory, W J, 1823–92, English poet and school teacher, CONVERSATION 1, DEATH 38, SPORTS 8

Coué, Emil, 1857–1926, French psychologist, ILLNESS 5

Coubertin, Pierre de, 1863–1937, French educationist who revived the Olympic Games, SPORTS 9

Coulson, R, MARRIAGE 33

Cousin, Victor, 1792–1867, French philosopher, ART 14

Coventry, Lord, 1578–1640, English judge, SHIPS 4

Coward, Noël, 1899–1973, English playwright, actor and song-writer, ACTORS & ACTRESSES (G) 4, ADVICE 9, AFTERLIFE 4, ARISTOCRACY 8, BRITISH EMPIRE 6, CHARACTER 4, CLASS 3, DANCING 6, ENGLISH 12, EQUALITY 4, FRANCE 10, GERMANY 6, GHOSTS 1, HYPOCRISY 11, MASSES 9, MUSIC 14, PESSIMISM 8, SACRIFICE 6, TALENT 2, TELEVISION 9, THEATRE 8, TRAVEL 6, TRUST 1, WOMEN 12, WORK 15, WRITERS (I) 31

Cowley, Abraham, 1618–67, English poet, CHANGE 5, CITY 4, CONSTANCY 3, DRINK: STRONG 15, GARDENS 5, LIFE 21, 23, MONEY 15, RAIN 2, SONGS & SINGERS 7, TREES 7, WORLD 9

Cowley, Hannah, 1743–1809, English playwright, LATENESS 1, WOMEN & MEN 19

Cowper, William, 1731–1800, English poet, ABSENCE 4, ANIMALS 12, ARGUMENT 6, ART 15, BIBLE 7, BRITISH EMPIRE 7, CHOICE 4, CLERGY 8, 9, COUNTRY & TOWN 7, CRUELTY 3, DOGS 6, DRUNKENNESS 3, ENGLAND (G) 12, FISH 2, FLATTERY 4, FLOWERS 10, FOOD 10, FOOLS 14, 15, FRIENDS 15, GAMBLING 3, GARDENS 6, GOD 40, 41, GRIEF 2, GUILT 2, HONESTY 5, HORSES & RACING 7, HUMAN NATURE 7, HUNTING 2, ILLNESS 6, LAWYERS 2, LAZINESS 7, LIBERTY 14, LOSS 5, MOTHERS 6, MOUNTAINS 3, MOURNING 8, 9, NATURE 5, NEWSPAPERS 8, NOSTALGIA 6, PITY 4, POETS (G) 12, POETS (I) 79, POVERTY 11, RETIREMENT 1, RIGHT 2, ROME 8, SINS 14, SMOKING 3, SOCIABILITY 3, SOLITUDE 7, TEA & COFFEE 4, THRIFT 2, 3, TREES 8, TRUTH 23, UNHAPPINESS 4, WARS (G) 19, WEALTH 7, WEDDINGS 2, WINTER 7, WORDS 8

Crabbe, George, 1754–1832, English poet, BOOKS (G) 11, CHURCHES 10, GOOD & GOODNESS 3, HABIT 2, NEWS 3, RIGHT 3

Crabtree, Tom, 1924– , British psychologist, MISFORTUNES 3

Craig, Edward Gordon, 1872–1966, English actor, stage designer and director, ARTISTS 11, COMEDY 7

Crane, Hart, 1899–1932, US poet, CHRISTIANITY 10, POETS (I) 95, STARS 7

Cranmer, Thomas, 1489–1556, Anglican archbishop and martyr, MARTYRS 5

Crashaw, Richard, 1613?–49, English poet, LIFE & DEATH 2, LOVE 36, SAINTS 4, TEARS 4, UNMARRIED 1

Craster, Mrs, d. 1874, English comic poet, ANIMALS 13

Creelman, James, 1901–4, US screen-writer, BEAUTY 10

Crick, Francis, 1916– , British molecular biologist, DISCOVERY 4

Crisp, Quentin, 1908–99, English humorist, ABROAD 1, BIOGRAPHY 6, BRITAIN & OTHERS 6, CHILDHOOD 16, COMPETITION 4, EXTREMISM 1, FRANCE 11, GOD 42, HOMOSEXUALS 1–3, HOUSEWORK 2, LIFE 24, LUCK 4, PARENTS 5, SEDUCTION 5, SEX 11, TEARS 5, USA (G) 11–13

Critchley, Julian, 1930– , British Conservative politician and journalist, PARLIAMENT: COMMONS 3, POLITICIANS (I) 22, PRIME MINISTERS (I) 23

Crofton, John 1912– , Scottish scientist, DRINK: STRONG 14

Croker, J W, 1780–1857, Irish politician and essayist, CONSERVATIVES 5, DECEPTION 3

Cromwell, Oliver, 1599–1658, English soldier and Puritan politician in Civil War, HONESTY 6, LAST WORDS 8, MISTAKES 5, NECESSITY 1, PARLIAMENT: COMMONS 4, PORTRAITS 2, STATE 2

Crosby, Bing, 1901–77, US singer and film actor, FRIENDS 16, LISTENING 1, TALK 5

Crossman, Richard, 1907–74, British Labour politician and diarist, CIVIL SERVICE 2, LEADERSHIP 1

Crow, John, 1905–70, British thinker, RULES 3, THINKING 8

Cruise, Tom, 1962– , US film actor, ACTING 2

Cumberland, Bishop Richard, 1631–1718, English cleric AGE 5

Cummings, Constance, 1910– , British actress, POLITICIANS (I) 5

cummings, e e, 1894–1962, US poet, BODY PARTS 4, DEATH 39, DREAMS 11, GIRLS 5, HUMAN BEINGS 20, 21, LIBERTY 15, MIND 9, MOON 3, PATRIOTISM 10, POLITICIANS (G) 12, PRINCIPLE 3, SEA 10, SPRING 6, UNIVERSE 10, USA (G) 14

Cunningham, Allan, 1784–1842, Scottish poet, SCOTLAND 9, SHIPS 5

Cunningham, Valentine, 1944– , British academic and journalist, READING 7

Cuppy, Will, 1884–1949, British humorist, GOOD & GOODNESS 4

Curran, John Philpot, 1750–1817, Irish judge, LIBERTY 16

Curtis, Tony, 1925– , film actor, MARILYN MONROE 2

Curtiz, Michael, 1888–1962, Hungarian-born film-director, COMEDY 8, FILM DIRECTORS & WRITERS 3

Curzon, Lord, 1859–1925, British Conservative politician, Viceroy of India, CLASS 4, PRIME MINISTERS (I) 2, SNOBBERY 4

Dahlberg, Edward, 1900–77, US novelist and critic, CARS 3

Dali, Salvador, 1904–89, Spanish surrealist painter, PAINTERS (I) 5, PORTRAITS 3, SPAIN 5, TASTE 2

Dahrendorf, Ralf, 1920– , German-born British sociologist, LIBERALS 6

Daly, Sergeant Dan, 1874–1937, US soldier, WORLD WAR I 7

Dana, Charles A, 1819–97, US newspaper editor, NEWS 4

Daniel, Samuel, 1562–1619, English poet and playwright, AMBITIONS 3, HUMAN BEINGS 22, LOVE 37, NATURE 6, SLEEPING & WAKING 8

Dante, Alghieri, 1265–1321, Italian poet, GRIEF 3, HELL 4, LOVE 38, MIDDLE AGE 2, PEACE 10

Danton, Georges, 1759–94, French revolutionary, COURAGE 8

Dark, Ian, 1950– , British broadcaster, FAME 9

Darling, Mr Justice, 1849–193, English judge, LAW 10

Darrow, Clarence, 1857–1938, US lawyer, PRESIDENTS (G) 2

Darwin, Charles, 1809–82, English naturalist, famous for his *Origin of Species*, EVOLUTION 3, 4, HUMAN BEINGS 23, THINKING 9

Darwin, Charles Galton, 1887–1962, English physicist, grandson of Charles, EVOLUTION 5, HUMAN BEINGS 24

Darwin, Erasmus, 1731–1802, English doctor and poet, TECHNOLOGY 7

Daugherty, Harry M, 1860–1941, US politician, POLITICS 7

Davenant, Charles, 1656–1714, English playwright and political economist, HABIT 3

Davenant, William, 1606–68, English playwright and poet, DAWN 1

Davenport, Walter, 1889–1971, US writer, EDITORS 5

Davies, Sir John, 1569–1626, English poet, ENDS 4, MARRIAGE 34

Davies, Robertson, 1913–95, Canadian novelist and essayist, ACADEMICS 6, WIT 5

Davies, W H, 1871–1940, Welsh poet, BIRDS 11, 12, LEISURE 1, SCHOOLS 12

Davis, Bette, 1908–89, US film actress, ACTING 3, CONTENTMENT 5, HOLLYWOOD 5, HOME & HOUSES 5, PROMISCUITY 1

Davis, Miles, 1926–91, US jazz trumpeter and band leader, FAME 10

Davis Jr, Sammy, 1925–90, US comedian, actor and musician, DISABILITIES 1, FILM STARS (I) 9

Davis, T O, 1814–45, Irish poet and politician, INVITATIONS 1

Davy, Humphrey, 1862–1944, DOCTORS 17

Dawkins, Richard, 1941– , English biologist, BIOLOGY 1, EVOLUTION 6, PHYSICS 2, STATE 3

Day, Clarence, 1874–1935, US humorist, BOOKS (G) 12, FUNERALS 4, LANGUAGES 6, PUNCTUALITY 1

Day Lewis, C, 1904–72, Irish-born poet, translator and detective story writer, DISAPPOINTMENTS 2, ENDS 5, POETS (G) 13, SONGS & SINGERS 9

Dayan, Moshe, 1915–81, Israeli soldier and politician, AGREEMENT 6, WARS (I) 8

Feldman, Marty, 1933–83, British comedian, CANNIBALS 2, COMEDY 9

Fellini, Frederico, 1920–93, Italian film director, FILM STARS (I) 15

Fénelon, François de, 1651–1715, HISTORY 19, TALK 8

Fenton, James, 1949– , English poet and critic, CRIME 7, DESTRUCTION 4

Ferber, Edna, 1887–1968, US novelist, UNMARRIED 3

Ferdinand I, 1503–64, Holy Roman Emperor from 1558, JUSTICE 12, MOTTOES 4

Ferrier, Kathleen, 1912–53, English contralto, LAST WORDS 13

Feuerbach, Ludwig, 1804–72, German philosopher, FOOD 16

Feynman, Richard, 1918–88, US physicist, BIOLOGY 2, BODY PARTS 8, PHYSICS 5

Ffrangcon-Davies, Gwen, 1891–1992, Welsh actress, DEATH 55

Field, Eric, of Caxton Advertising Agency, PATRIOTISM 13

Field, Frank, 1942– , British Labour politician, PARLIAMENT: LORDS 6

Fielding, Gabriel, 1916–86, English novelist, FIGHTING 8

Fielding, Henry, 1707–54, English novelist and playwright, CLERGY 12, COURTSHIP 6, DOCTORS 9, ENVY 4, HUNTING 5, HUSBANDS 7, NOTHING 2, PUNISHMENTS 12, SCANDAL 2, SCHOOLS 16, SEDUCTION 8, TRUST 3, WIDOWS 3

Fields, Gracie, 1898–1979, English variety artist and singer, HITLER 7, MUSICAL INSTRUMENTS 3, WEDDINGS 3

Fields, W C, 1879–1946, US comedian and screenwriter, CHILDHOOD 20, DRINK: STRONG 22, DRINK: WEAK 2, EPITAPHS 17, FAILURE 4, FILM STARS (I) 23, WOMEN 18, WORLD 14

Filene, Edward, 1860–1937, US businessman, TAXATION 2

Finney, Albert, 1936– , English film and stage actor, BRITISH 7

Firbank, Ronald, 1886–1926, English novelist, AGE 10, BOOKS (G) 14, CLERGY 13, ENGLISH 13, ILLNESS 7, JEALOUSY 5, LANGUAGES 7, MANAGERS 2, MILLIONAIRES 1, NATIONS 10, NOVELISTS (G) 3, PRAYERS 20, SINS 16

Fisher, Carrie, 1956– , US film actress and writer, HOLLYWOOD 6

Fisher, H A L, 1856–1940, English historian, HISTORY 20

Fisher, Lord John, 1841–1920, British admiral, CHURCHILL 5, HAPPINESS 8

Fisher, M F K, 1908–92, US writer, especially on cookery, PRIVACY 2

Fishman, Melvin, US humorist, FOOD 17

Fitzgerald, Edward, 1809–83, English poet, critic and translator, particularly famous for the *Rubá'iyát of Omar Khayyám*, ARGUMENT 7, CONTENTMENT 6, DAWN 3, DESTINY 7, 8, DREAMS 15, EXISTENCE 7, FLOWERS 12, FORGIVENESS 8, FUTURE 11, HOPE 8, IMPROVEMENT 2, LIFE IS FLEETING 26–8, MEMORY 10, MONEY 19, MOON 7, NEW YEAR 1, OPTIMISM & PESSIMISM 11, PAST 5, PRAYERS 22, TIME 13, WINE 10, 11

Fitzgerald, F Scott, 1896–1940, US novelist, ACTIVITY 5, AGE 11, AGGRESSION 6, AMERICANS 6, ARISTOCRACY 9, ARTISTS 15, BORES & BOREDOM 9, DESPAIR 3, DRINK: STRONG 23, 24, DRUNKENNESS 5, GIRLS 6, GREATNESS 4, HEROISM 8, HONESTY 8, HOSPITALITY 3, 4, KISSING 7, LIFE 29, 30, MILLIONAIRES 2, NOVELISTS (I) 13, OPTIMISM & PESSIMISM 12, PHOTOGRAPHY 3, RICH 8, STORIES 4, SUCCESS 6, SWITZERLAND 3, TWENTIETH CENTURY 1, VOICE 2, WOMEN & MEN 27, 28, WRITERS (G) 30, 31, WRITING 10

Fitzgerald, Penelope, 1916– , English novelist, ABILITY 1, DUTY 8, RESIGNATION 4

Fitzsimmons, Bob, 1862–1917, US boxer, SPORTS 11

Flanders, Michael, 1922–75, English song-writer, CANNIBALS 3

Flaubert, Gustave, 1821–80, French novelist, ARTISTS 16, IDEAS 3, LANGUAGE 9, POETRY 26, READING 10

Flecker, James Elroy, 1884–1915, English poet, CURIOSITY 2, DEATH 56, DISCOVERY 6, LIFE IS FLEETING 29, MEN 7, POETS (G) 16, SEA 12, 13, SHIPS 6, TREES 9

Fleming, Ian, 1908–64, English novelist, creator of secret service agent, James Bond – 007, DRINK: STRONG 25, HORSES & RACING 9

Fleming, Marjorie, 1803–11, Scottish child writer, DEATH 54, SWEARING 4

Fletcher, Andrew of Saltoun, 1655–1716, Scottish patriot, POETS (G) 17

Fletcher, Cyril, 1913– , British comedian, BORES & BOREDOM 10, FOOLS 17, MIDDLE AGE 4

Fletcher, John, 1579–1625, English playwright, EXERCISE 1, HELP 1, POETRY 6, SORROW 3

Fletcher, Phineas, 1582–1650, English poet and cleric, COWARDICE 6, EYES 8, LOVE 47

Florio, John, 1553?–1625, English lexicographer and translator, ENGLAND (G) 13

Flynn, Errol, 1909–59, Australian-born US film actor, DEBT 2, EXTRAVAGANCE 3

Foch, Marshal, 1851–1929, French soldier, VICTORY 8

Foley, John, 1914–18, English song-writer, SOLDIERS (G) 5

Fonda, Jane, 1937– , US film actress, AGE 12, WOMEN & MEN 29

Fonda, Henry, 1905–82, US film actor, ACTORS & ACTRESSES (G) 5

Foot, Michael, 1913– , British Labour politician, POWER 10, PRIME MINISTERS (I) 18, READING 11, REVOLUTIONS 7

Foote, Samuel, 1720–77, English actor and playwright, BORES & BOREDOM 11, LEARNING 8

Ford, Ford Madox, 1873–1939, English writer and editor, SILENCE 9

Ford, Gerald, 1913– , 38th US President, PRESIDENTS (I) 4

Ford, Henry, 1863–1947, US car manufacturer, CHOICE 5, EVIL 6, EXERCISE 2, HISTORY 21

Index of authors

Index of authors

15, FLOWERS 14, 15, KISSING 8, LIFE IS FLEETING 33, LOVE 56, NIGHT 5, PRAYERS 27, SPRING 8, TEARS 6, TREES 10

Herriot, James, 1916–95, Scottish-born veterinary surgeon and writer of popular books based on experiences of country vet, ANIMALS 20

Hersey, John, 1914–96, US writer and reporter, particularly of eye-witness account of the aftermath of bombing of Hiroshima, JOURNALISM 16, NOVELS (G) 14

Hervey, James, 1714–58, English poet, BLESSINGS 8

Herzog, Werner, 1942– , German film-director, FILM 9

Hesse, Hermann, 1877–1962, German novelist and poet, BODY 2, 3, DESTRUCTION 6, HATE 8, MIDDLE CLASS 4

Hewart, Lord Justice, 1870–1943, British lawyer, JUSTICE 15

Heyward, Du Bose, 1885–1940, US novelist and playwright, HUMILITY 7, SUMMER 6, WEALTH 10

Heywood, John, 1497?–1580?, English playwright, RESIGNATION 7

Hicks, Seymour, 1871–1949, English writer, AGE 15

Hickson, William Edward, 1803–70, British teacher and writer on singing, ENDURANCE 6

Higgins, George V, 1939–99, US novelist, MIDDLE AGE 5

Higley, Brewster, 19th-century US song-writer, HOME & HOUSES 12

Hill, Aaron, 1685–1750, English poet and playwright, PAIN 2

Hill, Christopher, 1912– , English historian, LIBERTY 29

Hill, Geoffrey, 1932– , English poet, RICH 10

Hill, Joe, 1879–1915, US labour leader and song-writer, AFTERLIFE 6, LAST WORDS 22, PROMISE 3

Hill, Rowland, 1744–1833, English cleric, MUSIC 23

Hillary, Edmund, 1919– , New Zealand mountaineer, MOUNTAINS 5

Hillingdon, Lady Alice, 1857–1940, English aristocrat and diarist, PATRIOTISM 19

Hilton, James, 1900–54, English novelist, famous for *Goodbye Mr Chips* [1934], AGE 16

Himmler, Heinrich, 1900–45, German Nazi leader, GERMANY 8, RACES 7

Hindemith, Paul, 1895–1963, German composer, MUSICAL INSTRUMENTS 5

Hippocrates, *c.* 460–*c.* 357 BC, Greek physician, the 'father of medicine', LIFE IS FLEETING 34, MEDICINE 3

Hirohito, Emperor of Japan, 1901–89, NUCLEAR AGE 10

Hitchcock, Alfred, 1899–1980, English film-director, ACTORS & ACTRESSES (G) 10, FEAR 12, FILM 10, THEATRE 10

Hitchens, Christopher, 1949– , British journalist and writer, PRESIDENTS (I) 18

Hitler, Adolf, 1889–1945, German Nazi dictator, AMERICANS 9, ARTISTS 20, COMPARISONS 3, DESTINY 12, ENGLISH 23, LEADERSHIP 3, LIES 16, MASSES 14, 15, RACES 8, SEA 15, VICTORY 9

Hoagland, Edward, 1932– , US novelist and essayist, MIDDLE AGE 6

Hoban, Russell, 1925– , US novelist and children's writer, ANIMALS 21, DISCOVERY 8, EYES 11, FEAR 13, INDIVIDUAL 5, KNOWLEDGE 18, LANGUAGES 9, LOSS 6, NEUROSIS 6, PAST 10, PRIVACY 3, SELF 16, 18, SMOKING 4, SUNDAY 4, THINKING 14, VICTORY 10

Hobbes, Thomas, 1588–1679, English philosopher, HUMAN BEINGS 35, LAST WORDS 23, LAUGHTER 17, LIFE & DEATH 11, PAPACY 2, WORDS 16

Hobsbawm, Eric 1917– , British historian, FUTURE 12, INSULTS 8

Hoch, Edward Wallis, 1849–1925, US politician, GOOD & EVIL 11

Hockney, David, 1937– , British painter and photographer, ART 25, COMMUNISM 7, PAINTING 5, PHOTOGRAPHY 5, 6, TECHNOLOGY 10

Hodgson, Ralph, 1871–1962, English poet, BIRDS 19, HEAVEN 15, REASON 4, SHIPS 11, SKIES 6, TIME 17

Hoffenstein, Samuel, 1890–1947, US comic poet, FEAR 14, FLOWERS 16, HOLLYWOOD 9, LIFE IS FLEETING 35

Hoffer, Eric, 1902–83, US social philosopher, IMITATION 3, LOVE 57

Hoffman, Elisha B, 1776–1822, US hymn-writer, JESUS CHRIST 18

Hoffman, Heinrich, 1809–74, German children's writer, BEHAVIOUR 5, FOOD 18

Hoffman, General Max, 1869–1927, German soldier, WORLD WAR I 11

Hoffmann von Fallersleben, Heinrich, 1798–1876, German poet, PATRIOTISM 20

Hofstadter, Douglas R, 1945– , US cognitive scientist, SOULS 21

Hogben, Lancelot, 1895–1975, English physiologist and popularizer of science and maths, TECHNOLOGY 11

Hoggart, Richard, 1918– , British teacher, critic and cultural historian, COMMUNICATION 3

Holford, William, 1907–75, British architect, ARCHITECTURE 9

Holiday, Billie, 1915–59, US jazz singer, SHOW BUSINESS 4

Holland, Revd Henry Scott, 1847–1914, English cleric famous as a preacher, DEATH 66

Holmes, Revd J H, 1879–1964, US Unitarian minister, UNIVERSE 13

Holmes, Larry, 1949– , US boxer, BLACK CULTURE 7

Holmes, Oliver Wendell, 1809–94, US essayist, poet and doctor, ACADEMICS 8, DRINK: STRONG 34, EVENING 7, HUMOUR 13, OLD AGE 20, SIGHT & INSIGHT 6, SILENCE 12, SOULS 22, WOMEN & MEN 39

Holst, Gustav, 1874–1934, British composer and music teacher of Swedish origin, COMPOSERS (I) 11

Holtby, Winifred, 1898–1935, English novelist, EPITAPHS 25

Holub, Miroslav, 1923–98, Czech poet and scientist, ABILITY 2, BODY PARTS 10, SOCIALISTS 9

Home, John, 1722–1808, Scottish playwright, WOMEN 24

Jefferson, Thomas, 1743–1826, 3rd US President, EQUALITY 9, INDEPENDENCE 2, LIBERTY 33, MISTAKES 8, REBELLION 8
Jeffrey, Revd Edward, 1932– , English cleric, CLERGY 16
Jeffries, Lambert, English humorist, TRAVEL 10
Jellicoe, Ann, 1927– , English playwright, ILLUSION 9
Jenkins, Roy, 1920– , British Liberal politician, POLITICIANS (G) 23, POLITICIANS (I) 15, POLITICS 17
Jenkins, Rt Revd David, 1925– , English theologian and bishop, BELIEF 7, GOD 66
Jennings, Elizabeth, 1926– , English poet, BEDS 5
Jennings, Paul, 1918–89, English journalist and author, MUSICIANS 7, SATIRE 3, THEORY 3, TRANSLATION 4, UNIVERSE 15
Jerome, Jerome K, 1859–1927, English humorous writer, playwright, famous for *Three Man in a Boat* [1900], HOME & HOUSES 13, ILLNESS 10, 11, LAZINESS 14, LOVE 59, WORK 19
Jerrold, Douglas, 1803–57, English playwright and journalist, AUSTRALIA 2, PEACE 15, SPORTS 17, VULGARITY 2
Joad, C E M, 1891–1953, English philosopher and broadcaster, CONSCIENCE 4, ENGLAND (G)14, KNOWLEDGE 19, SOCIABILITY 6
John XXIII, 1881–1963, Pope 1958–63, DEATH 71, HUMAN BEINGS 39, PAPACY 3
John Paul I, 1912–78, Pope for only 33 days, ADULTERY 9, CLERGY 17
John Paul II, 1920–, Polish-born Pope from 1978, ADULTERY 9
John, Augustus, 1878–1961, Welsh painter, LIFE 39
Johns, Glynis, 1923– , Welsh film actress, SWITZERLAND 4
Johnson, Hiram, 1866–1945, US politician, TRUTH 36, WARS (G) 28
Johnson, Paul, 1928– , English journalist and historian, DISCRETION 8, JEWS 10, TALK 12
Johnson, Lyndon B, 1908–73, 36th US President, ADVICE 13, LOYALTY 4, POLITICS 18, POVERTY 17, PRESIDENTS (I) 5, 9, SOCIETY 5, VIETNAM 5, WARS (G) 29
Johnson, Dr Samuel, 1709–84, English poet, lexicographer and critic, ACADEMICS 9, ACTORS & ACTRESSES (G) 11, 12, AFTERLIFE 7, AGE 17, AMERICANS 11, ANTICIPATION 7, COMPETITION 8, CRITICISM 19, DEFINITIONS 1, DESTINY 14, DOUBT 18, DRINK: STRONG 37, EDITORS 8, 9, ENGLISH 25, EPITAPHS 28–30, EQUALITY 10, EXPERIENCE 12, FOOD 19, 20, FOOLS 23, FRIENDS 24, GAMBLING 6, GENIUS 13, GREATNESS 7, GREECE 5, GRIEF 6, HAPPINESS 19, HATE 9, HOSPITALITY 6, HYPOCRISY 13, IGNORANCE 7, INEQUALITY 4, 5, IRELAND 13, ITALY 8, JUSTICE 17, KINGS & QUEENS (G) 18, KNOWLEDGE 20, 21, LANGUAGES 10, LAWYERS 7, LAZINESS 15, 16, LETTERS 5, 6, LIBERALS 10, LIFE & DEATH 14, LIFE 40, 41, LONDON 13, 14, LOVE 60, MARRIAGE 55–7, MASSES 16, MIND 21, MONEY 27, MOURNING 13, MUSICIANS 8, NEGLECT 3, NOVELS (I) 1, 15, OLD AGE 22, PATRIOTISM 22, PATRONS 3, POETS (G) 25, 26, POETS (I) 37, 69, 80, POLITICS 19, POVERTY 18, PRAYERS 30, PRINCIPLE 5, 6, PROPHETS 12, PUB 6, READING 17–19, SCANDAL 4, SCOTLAND 14–16, SELF 22, SELF-PRESERVATION 3,SHAKESPEARE 12, 13, SHIPS 14, SLEEPING & WAKING 15, SOCIABILITY 7, SOLDIERS (G) 12, THEATRE 12, THINKING 19, TOLERANCE 3, UNDERSTANDING 6, UNMARRIED 5, VICE 3, WICKEDNESS 8, WINE 13, WISDOM 26, WOMEN 26, WRITERS (I) 5, WRITING 14–16
Johnston, Alva, 1880–1950, US journalist and writer, INSULTS 9
Johnston, Jill, 1929– , US feminist writer, HOMOSEXUALS 6
Johst, Hanns, 1890–1978, German playwright, CULTURE 7
Jolson, Al, 1886–1950, Russian-born US actor and singer, FILM 12
Jones, R V, 1911–97, British Director of Intelligence, writer and academic, ARMY 6
Jones, Steve, 1944– , Welsh geneticist and academic, SEX 18, TAXATION 5
Jones, William, 1746–94, English lawyer, LAW 17
Jong, Erica, 1942– , US novelist and poet famous for novel *Fear of Flying* [1973], SEX 19
Jonson, Ben, 1573–1637, English playwright and poet, APPEARANCE 10, BELLS 2, EPITAPHS 31, EVENING 8, FAT & THIN 5, FEAR 16, GREED 7, PURITY 8, SHAKESPEARE 14–16, SMOKING 6, 7, SUSPICION 5, TALK 13, WOMEN & MEN 41
Joplin, Janis, 1943–70, US rhythm and blues singer, LONELINESS 7, SONGS 18
Joseph, Michael, 1897–1958, English publisher, WORRY 39
Joseph, Sir Keith, 1918–94, British Conservative politician, INEQUALITY 6
Jowett, Benjamin, 1817–93, British classicist and academic, LIES 17
Joyce, James, 1882–1941, Irish novelist, CLOTHES 11, DEVIL 14, FACES 21, HISTORY 30, INSPIRATION 3, IRELAND 14, 15, KINGS & QUEENS (I) 7, ROME 9, SEA 16, TEA & COFFEE 5, WRITERS (I) 21
Julian the Apostate, Emperor, 331–63, Roman Emperor from 360, LAST WORDS 28
Juliana of Norwich, ?1343–?1416, English anchoress, who spent much of her life enclosed in a cell, OPTIMISM & PESSIMISM 14
Jung, C G, 1875–1961, Swiss psychiatrist, CONVERSATION 3, DRUGS 4, ENEMIES 4, EXISTENCE 11, FAITH 20, HUMAN NATURE 11, IMPROVEMENT 3, LEADERSHIP 4, MADNESS & SANITY 16, MIND 22, PARENTS 13, PASSIONS 6, PSYCHIATRY 16, RELIGION 35, SELF 23, SOLITUDE 9, SYMBOLS 2, UNCONSCIOUS 4
Jünger, Ernst, 1895–1998, German novelist, EVOLUTION 9
'Junius', 18th cent Political pseudonymous correspondent whose identity was never established, JUSTICE 18, NEWSPAPERS 10, PERSUASION 1, RIGHT & WRONG 4
Juster, Norton, 1929– , US children's writer, ANSWERS 2, INFINITY 2, SILENCE 15

Index of authors

Lee, Gypsy Rose, 1914–70, US actress, GOD 71, WOMEN & MEN 50

Lee, Harper, 1926– , US novelist, BIRDS 27

Lee, Henry, 1756–1818, US politician and soldier, PRESIDENTS (I) 32

Lee, Laurie, 1914–97, English writer, famous for *Cider with Rosie* [1959], COURTSHIP 7

Lee, Nathaniel, 1655–92, English playwright, HUMAN NATURE 14

Le Gallienne, Richard, 1866–1947, English poet, TYRANTS 12

Lehmann, Rosamond, 1901–90, SEDUCTION 11

Lehrer, Tom, 1928– , US song-writer and academic, COMPOSERS (I) 13, DRUGS 6, GERMANY 14, LIFE 47

Leigh, Fred, d. 1924, British song-writer, WEDDINGS 6

Leigh, H S, 1837–83, English writer, REPENTANCE 3

Leland, C G, 1824–1903, US comic writer, PARTIES 4

Lenclos, Ninon de, 1620–1705, French writer, OLD AGE 25

Lenin, Vladimir Ilyich, 1870–1924, Russian revolutionary, CAPITALISM 9, COMMUNISM 10, DEMOCRACY 14, GOVERNMENT 16, HISTORY 31, LIBERTY 37, 38, MUSIC 26, SHAW 3, SOCIALISTS 11, STATE 7

Lennon, John, 1940–80, British pop singer and song-writer, AUDIENCES 4, BEAUTY 21, CARS 6, FRIENDS 30, LIFE 48, LONELINESS 8, MONEY 31, OLD AGE 26, POPULARITY 4, REALITY 7, TWENTIETH CENTURY 4

Leno, Dan, 1860–1904, English comedian, WORLD 21

Leonard, Elmore, 1925– , US thriller writer, WRITERS (I) 27

Leonard, Hugh, 1926– , Irish dramatist and critic, IRELAND 17, LIFE & DEATH 21, PUB 8

Lerner, Alan Jay, 1918–86, US librettist, song-writer, ENGLISH 32, GOOD & GOODNESS 11, INSULTS 10, MEN 13, WEDDINGS 7

Lesage, Alain René, 1668–1747, French playwright and novelist, JUSTICE 21, PEACE 17

Lessing, Doris, 1919– , Rhodesian writer who has lived much of her life in Britain, INTOLERANCE 2, RACES 12

Lessing, G E, 1729–81, German playwright and critic, PRAYERS 34, REASON 5, TRUTH 42

Lester, Alfred, 1874–1925, English song-writer, COWARDICE 7

Lestrange, Roger, 1616–1704, English journalist, PASSIONS 8

Lethaby, W R, 1857–1931, English architect, designer and teacher, ART 31

Levant, Oscar, 1906–72, US composer, pianist and wit, FILM STARS (I) 13, HOLLYWOOD 10

Lever, Harold, 1914–95, MARRIAGE 59

Leverhulme, Lord, 1851–1925, English soap-maker and philanthropist, ADVERTISING 4

Leverson, Ada, 1865–1936, English novelist and journalist, CHARM 6, LETTERS 7

Levi, Primo, 1919–87, Italian writer, TEA & COFFEE 6

Levin, Bernard, 1928– , British journalist, DESTRUCTION 8, MILLIONAIRES 3, PRIME MINISTERS (G) 3, PRIME MINISTERS (I) 33, SILENCE 17, SMUGNESS 11

Leviné, Eugen, 1883–1919, Russian-born German Communist, COMMUNISM 11

Lévi-Strauss, Claude 1908– , French social anthropologist, HISTORY 33, LANGUAGE 13, SOCIETY 7

Lévis, Duc de, 1764–1830, French soldier and writer, ARISTOCRACY 13, 19

Le Vot, Andrew, 1921– , NOVELISTS (I) 14

Lewes, G H, 1817–78, English writer, life-long partner of George Eliot, MURDER 9

Lewis, C S, 1898–1963, English scholar, writer on Christianity and for children, BOOKS (G) 26, COURAGE 17, FEAR 19, GOD 72, GRATITUDE 3, HELL 5, HUMAN BEINGS 40, MORALS 8, PRIDE 9, SACRIFICE 10, TEMPTATION 8, 9, TIME 24, TIREDNESS 2, VULGARITY 3

Lewis, George Cornewall, 1806–63, British Liberal politician and writer, LIFE 49, PLEASURE 13

Lewis D B Wyndham, 1891–1961, English writer, EXCUSES 2

Lewis, Percy Wyndham, 1882–1957, English novelist, painter and critic, ACTIVITY 9, COMEDY 16, IDEAS 7, IMITATION 4, PAINTERS (I) 11, REVOLUTIONS 15, SOULS 26

Lewis, Sinclair, 1885–1951, US novelist, ACADEMICS 10, ARTISTS 26, BUYING 6, CARS 7

Ley, Robert, 1890–1945, German Nazi, FASCISM 3

Liberace, 1919–87, US pianist and entertainer, CRITICISM 23

Liebermann, Max, 1847–1935, German painter and graphic artist, PORTRAITS 7

Liebknecht, Karl, 1871–1919, German lawyer and revolutionary, REVOLUTIONS 16

Liebling, A J, 1904–63, US writer and journalist, NEWSPAPERS 16

Lillie, Beatrice, 1894–1989, Canadian comic actress, BIRTH 9

Lin Yutang, 1895–1976, Chinese author and philologist, PHILOSOPHY 18

Lincoln, Abraham, 1809–65, 16th US President, AMBIVALENCE 9, CONSERVATIVES 18, CRITICISM 24, DECEPTION 8, DEMOCRACY 15, ELECTIONS 2, INTENTION 5, LIBERTY 39, ORDINARY 3, POWER 17, SLAVERY 4

Lindsay, Vachel, 1879–1931, US poet, FAITHS 21, RIVERS 5

Linklater, Eric, 1889–1974, Scottish journalist and writer, REVOLUTIONS 17, TRUTH 43, USA (G) 27, WIVES 18, WRITERS (G) 43

Linklater, Magnus, 1942– , Scottish journalist, NEWSPAPERS 17

Linton, W J, 1812–98, English engraver and poet, GENTLEMEN 8

Lipman, Maureen, 1946– , British actress and comedian, HOLLYWOOD 11, SEX 23

Little, Richard, 1944– , US political commentator, PRESIDENTS (I) 2

Litvinov, Maxim, 1876–1951, Russian diplomat, PEACE 18

Lively, Penelope, 1933– , English novelist, PORTRAITS 8, PRESENTS 4, WARS (G) 34

Livingstone, Ken, 1945– , British Labour politician, BRITAIN & OTHERS 10

Livy, 59 BC–17 AD, Roman historian, DEFEAT 4

MacCarthy, Desmond, 1877–1952, British critic and essayist, ART 33, JOURNALISM 20, PAINTING 7

McCarthy, Senator Joseph, 1908–57, US politician, AMERICANS 13

McCarthy, Mary, 1912–89, US writer, AMERICANS 14, AMERICANS & OTHERS 5–7, CARS 8, CITY 5, EUROPE 7, 8, MATERIALISM 6, NOVELS (I) 5, TRUTH 44, USA (G) 29, 30, WRITERS (I) 13

McCartney, Paul, 1942– , British pop singer and song-writer, member of The Beatles, BEAUTY 21, CARS 6, FRIENDS 30, LONELINESS 8, MONEY 31, OLD AGE 26

McCrae, John, 1872–1918, English poet, WORLD WAR I 13

McCullough, Revd Joseph, 1908–90, British cleric, CHURCH OF ENGLAND 4

McCullough, W D H, 1901–78, English humorist, GAMBLING 10

MacDiarmid, Hugh, 1892–1978, Scottish poet, EXTREMISM 5, KILLING 5, LANDS 6, LIGHT 8, SCOTLAND 18, 19, VICTIM 2

Macdonald, George, 1824–1905, Scottish poet and novelist, BABIES 6, PRAYERS 36

MacDonald, Ramsay, 1866–1917, British Labour Prime Minister, 1924 and 1929–35 SNOBBERY 8

MacDonald, William, Scottish cleric, BRITISH EMPIRE 12

McEwan, Ian, 1948– , English novelist, CHILDHOOD 29, FACES 22, WOMEN 32

McEwen, Arthur, d. 1907, English journalist, NEWS 6

McGinley, Phyllis, 1905–78, US poet, WRITERS (G) 44

McGlennon, Felix, d. 1943, British song-writer, PATRIOTISM 27

McGonagall, William, 1825–1902, Scottish writer of doggerel, DISASTERS 3, RAILWAYS 7

McGough, Roger, 1937– , English poet, DEATH 78, GUILT 11, WINTER 9

McIlvanney, William, 1936– , Scottish writer, LAUGHTER 22

MacInnes, Colin, 1914–76, English novelist, ART 34, BUILDINGS 9, RACES 13

Mackail, Denis, 1892–1971, English writer, THEATRE 13

Mackay, Charles, 1814–89, Scottish song-writer, OPTIMISM & PESSIMISM 16

Mackenzie, Compton, 1883–1972, English writer, WOMEN & MEN 52

McKeown, Thomas, 1912–88, British biologist, GOD 74, PLAYWRIGHTS (G) 3, WINE 16

Mackintosh, Sir James, 1765–1831, Scottish philosopher and historian, PARLIAMENT: COMMONS 8

Maclaine, Shirley, 1934– , US film actress, FILM STARS (I) 18

Maclean, Fitzroy, 1911–96, COMMUNISM 13, RUSSIA 7

Macleish, Archibald, 1892–1982, US poet, HISTORY 34, 35, POETRY 53, QUESTIONS 4

Macleod, Fiona, 1856–1905, Scottish writer, HEART 11, MOUNTAINS 8

Macleod, Iain, 1913–70, British Conservative politician, HISTORY 36

McLuhan, Marshall, 1911–80, Canadian academic and writer, AMERICANS 15, CARS 9, COMMUNICATION 5, EDITORS 12, MEDIA 1, 2, NINETEENTH CENTURY 5, TIME 25, TWENTIETH CENTURY 5

Macmillan, Harold, 1894–1986, British Conservative Prime Minister 1957–63, ADVERSITY 6, AFRICA 3, AMERICANS 8,CAPITALISM 10, CONSERVATIVES 19, DIPLOMACY 9, ECONOMICS 14, EUROPE 9,GOVERNMENT 19, NUCLEAR AGE 13, POLITICIANS (G) 20, POLITICIANS (I) 8, POLITICS 23, PRESIDENTS (I) 8, PRIME MINISTERS (I) 15

MacNeice, Louis, 1907–63, Northern Irish poet, DEFINITIONS 2, DESTRUCTION 9, EMBARRASSMENT 4, FIRE 2, LIBRARIES 2, LUXURY 3, SATIRE 6 WORLD WAR II 15

McNeil, Hector, 1907–55, British Labour politician, POLITICIANS (I) 11

McPherson, 'Suggs', 1961– , British pop-singer, VIOLENCE 10

Madariaga, Salvador de, 1886–1978, Spanish writer and diplomat, BEHAVIOUR 7, FASCISM 4, LIBERTY 42, USA (G) 31, WARS (G) 36, WOMEN & MEN 53

Maddow, Ben 1909–92, US screen-writer, CRIME 12

Maddox, Brenda, 1932– , US biographer, WRITING 19

Magnusson, Magnus, 1929– , Icelandic-Scottish journalist, writer and broadcaster, SCOTLAND 20

Mahler, Gustav, 1860–1911, Austrian composer and conductor, CANADA 3, MARRIAGE 61, MUSIC 27

Mahood, Molly, 1919– , British university teacher, CRITICISM 26

Mailer, Norman, 1923– , US writer, FILM STARS (I) 5, HEROISM 16, KISSING 11, NOVELISTS (I) 27, 33, SENTIMENTALITY 3, TWENTIETH CENTURY 6, USA (G) 32

Major, John, 1943– , British Conservative Prime Minister 1990–7, PRIME MINISTERS (I) 20

Malamud, Bernard, 1914–86, US novelist, BIOGRAPHY 10, FRIENDS 31, MOURNING 14, PROGRESS 17

Malcolm X, 1925–65, US Black nationalist leader, BLACK CULTURE 10

Mallaby, George, 1902–78, English writer, BEHAVIOUR 8

Mallory, G H L 1886–1924, British mountaineer, MOUNTAINS 9

Malo, Mae, US humorist, MISFORTUNES 7

Malory, Thomas, d. 1471, English writer, ACHIEVEMENT 10, CHIVALRY 5, KINGS & QUEENS (G) 19, LOVERS 15, MONTHS 14, NOSTALGIA 17, SMELLS 2

Malraux, André, 1901–76, French writer and art critic, BRITAIN & OTHERS 11, FRANCE 20, INTELLECTUALS 9, REVOLUTIONS 19, WRITERS (I) 26

Malthus, Thomas, 1766–1834, English economist and cleric, EXISTENCE 12

Mamet, David, 1947– , US screen-writer and playwright, FILM 15

Mancroft, Lord, 1914–87, British Conservative politician, SUSPICION 8, WOMEN & MEN 54

Mandela, Nelson, 1918– , South African lawyer, and first Black President from 1994, LIBERTY 43

Mandelstam, Nadezhda, 1899–1980, Russian writer and wife of Osip, SILENCE 18

Maurois, André, 1885–1967, French novelist and biographer, ENGLAND (G) 21
Maxton, James, 1885–1946, Scottish politician, SOCIALISTS 12
May, Elaine, 1932– , US actress and screen-writer, MORALS 10
Mayakovsky, Vladimir, 1893–1930, Russian poet, ART 35, COMMITTEES 5, JOY 10
Mayall, Rick, 1958– , TV actor and comedian, FEMINISM 5, WARS (G) 22, WORRY 8
Mayer, Louis B, 1885–1957, US film producer, BIBLE 11, COMMITTEES 6
Mayo, Charles, 1865–1939, US surgeon, EXPERTS 6
Mearns, Hughes, 1875–1965, US writer, ABSENCE 6
Medawar, Peter, 1915–87, British zoologist, RESEARCH 4, SCIENCE 13, SCIENTISTS 6
Mehta, Gita, 1943– , Indian writer, COMMUNICATION 6
Meir, Golda, 1898–1978, Israeli politician and Prime Minister 1969–74, JEWS 13, PESSIMISM 13
Melbourne, Viscount, 1779–1848, British Whig Prime Minister, 1834, 1835–41, RELIGION 41, WRITERS (I) 30
Mellon, Andrew, 1855–1937, US financier and philanthropist, ECONOMICS 15
Melville, Herman, 1819–91, US novelist and poet, DRUNKENNESS 10, NOVELISTS (I) 29
Mencken, H L, 1880–1956, US journalist and critic, ARTISTS 30, BORES & BOREDOM 15, BUSINESS 11, CLERGY 19, CONTRACEPTION 6, DRINK: STRONG 38, EGOTISM 13, FAITHS 23, FAMILY 11, GOD 75, IDEALS 3, LITERATURE 15, MARRIAGE 63, MONEY 36, OPERA 5, POETRY 57, PROTESTANTS 4, RELIGION 42, RESPECT & DISRESPECT 2, SCIENCE 14, TRUTH 48, DRUNKENNESS 10, UNHAPPINESS 10, UNIVERSE 16, WARS (G) 40, WEAKNESS 9, WOMEN & MEN 56
Mendès-France, Pierre, 1907–82, French politician and Prime Minister, 1954–5, GOVERNMENT 21
Menninger, Karl, 1893–1990, US psychiatrist, ILLNESS 16
Menuhin, Yehudi, 1916–99, British violinist and conductor, MUSIC 29, MUSICAL INSTRUMENTS 8
Mercer, David, 1928–80, English playwright, AUDIENCES 5
Mercer, Johnny, 1909–76, US song-writer, BABIES 7
Mercier, Louis-Sébastien, 1740–1814, French writer, EXTREMISM 6
Mercier, Vivian, 1919–89, Irish academic and critic, PLAYS 4
Meredith, George, 1828–1909, English novelist and poet, CERTAIN 9, COOKERY 4, CYNICS 3, FORGETTING 7, 8, IRELAND 18, LOVE 65, LOVERS 17, PASSIONS 9, POETS (G) 31, PRAYERS 37, SENSE 5, SPEECH 11, STARS 12, WOMEN & MEN 57, WOODS 8
Meredith, Owen, 1831–91, English poet and Viceroy of India, GENIUS 15, TALENT 8
Merrill, Bob, 1921–98, US song-writer, HUMAN BEINGS 44
Merritt, Dixon, 1879–1972, US comic poet, BIRDS 29
Metternich, Prince, 1773–1859, Austrian politician, ITALY 11
Meyerstein, E H W, 1889–1952, British critic, COMPOSERS (I) 4
Meyer, Lise, co-script-writer of TV series *The Young Ones*, FEMINISM 5, WARS (G) 22, WORRY 8
Meynell, Alice, 1847–1922, English poet and essayist, MEMORY 16, THINKING 24
Meynell, Francis, 1891–1975, English poet, COMPARISONS 4, OFFICE 8
Michie, James, 1889–1952, US poet, SKIES 8
Mickle, William, 1735–88, Scottish poet, MOON 14
Middleton, Thomas, 1570?–1627, English playwright, HATE 10, HONESTY 10
Midler, Bette, 1945– , US comedian and actress, LONDON 17, SUCCESS 12
Mies van der Rohe, Ludwig, 1886–1969, German-born US architect, ARCHITECTURE 11
Mikes, George, 1912–87, Hungarian-born humorous writer, CLASS 10, CLEANLINESS 3, ENGLAND (G) 22, SEX 25, SWITZERLAND 5, TEA & COFFEE 7
Mill, John Stuart, 1806–73, English philosopher and economist, HAPPINESS 25, LIBERTY 45, 46, OPINIONS 11, ORIGINALITY 6, STATE 9
Millay, Edna St Vincent, 1892–1950, US poet, BEAUTY 24, DEATH 80, EXTRAVAGANCE 5, LIFE 53
Miller, Alice Duer, 1874–1942, US writer, ENGLAND (G) 23
Miller, Arthur, 1915– , US playwright, BUYING 7, CHURCHES 19, EXPERTS 7, FIGHTING 11, FUNERALS 9, HUMOUR 14, JUSTICE 23, NEWSPAPERS 20, POPULARITY 5, POWER 20, PRESENT 2, SELF 29, SUICIDE 13, TIREDNESS 3, TRAGEDY 10, UNHAPPINESS 11, WORLD 22
Miller, Henry, 1891–1980, US writer, ARTISTS 31, LITERATURE 16, NOVELS (I) 12, POETS (I) 46, SEX 26, WORLD 23
Miller, Jonathan, 1934– , British doctor, broadcaster, theatre director, BODY 4, ENGLAND (G) 24, JEWS 14, PRIVACY 4
Miller, Max, 1895–1963, English comedian, GIRLS 11
Milligan, Spike, 1918– , Indian-born British humorist, BODY PARTS 15, CLASS 11, CONTRACEPTION 7, ELECTIONS 3, ENGLISH 36, HEROISM 18, MATERIALISM 7, MATHEMATICS 7, MIND 29, MONEY 37, RAIN 3, SEX 27, SHIPS 20, SPORTS 19, SUN 6, THINKING 26
Mills, A J, b. 1872, English song-writer, SAILORS 10
Milne, A A, 1882–1956, English children's writer, FOOD 26, GLUTTONY 3, IDEAS 9, INHERITANCE 6, INSPIRATION 4, KINGS & QUEENS (G) 20, LANGUAGES 13, MIND 30, PRESENTS 5, RESPECT & DISRESPECT 3, SOLDIERS (G) 14, SUPERSTITIONS 5, WORDS 21
Milner, Lord, 1854–1925, British colonial administrator, DUTY 11
Milosz, Czeslaw, 1911– , Lithuanian-born Polish poet, CRUELTY 5, KINDNESS 4, POETS (G) 32, TYRANTS 14
Milton, John, 1608–74, English poet, ACADEMICS 11, AGE 18, AMBITIONS 8, BEAUTY 25–7, BIRDS 30–2, BLINDNESS 3–5, BOOKS (G) 28, BRITAIN 8, CENSORSHIP 4, CHANCE 5, CHASTITY 2, CHILDHOOD 32, CHRISTMAS

Mordaunt, Thomas, 1730–1809, British soldier and poet, GLORY 3
More, Sir Thomas, 1478–1535, English statesman, saint and martyr, LAST WORDS 30, POETRY 63, REBELLION 10
Morehead, J M, 1796–1866, Governor of North Carolina, DRINK: STRONG 40
Morell, Thomas, 1703–84, English librettist, HEROISM 19
Morgenstern, Christian, 1871–1914, German poet, ARCHITECTURE 12, BODY PARTS 16, FACTS 6
Morley, Christopher, 1890–1957, US writer, BIBLE 12, HUMAN BEINGS 45, LIFE 58, 59, PROPHETS 15, UNIVERSE 17
Morley, Robert, 1908–92, English actor and humorist, BRITAIN & OTHERS 12, FOOD 29, FRANCE 23, OLD AGE 31, TALK 18
Morpurgo, J E, 1918– , British historian, NATIONS 20
Morris, Charles, 1745–1838, English song-writer, LONDON 18
Morris, Desmond, 1928– , British ecologist, artist and writer, CITY 7, HUMAN BEINGS 46
Morris, Jan, 1926– , English journalist and travel writer, SPAIN 6
Morris, William, 1834–96, English writer, artist and designer, DEATH 84, FRIENDS 34, GARDENS 13, HOME & HOUSES 17 KISSING 14, LOVE 68, NOSTALGIA 19, POETS (I) 75, PRAYERS 38, WINDS 7
Morrison, Jim, 1943–71, US rock-singer and song-writer, YOUTH & AGE 7
Morrison, Toni, 1931– , US writer, LAUGHTER 27, RACES 14
Mortimer, John, 1923– , English novelist, playwright and barrister, CENSORSHIP 5, COMEDY 17, CONTENTMENT 11, HOMOSEXUALS 9, IMMORTALITY 12, LANGUAGES 15, LAW 21, LIFE 60, MARRIAGE 67, SCHOOLS 19, 20, WALES 3, WORRY 47
Morton, J B, 'Beachcomber', 1893–1979, English journalist and humorist, ABILITY 4, AMBITIONS 9, ANIMALS 27, ARISTOCRACY 18, COMPOSERS (I) 31, DEFINITIONS 3, FISH 5, GAMBLING 11, INSULTS 12, MOTHERS 10, NEWSPAPERS 21, WARS (G) 42, WIT 12
Moser, Claus, 1922– , German-born British statistician, EDUCATION 20, IGNORANCE 8
Mosley, Leonard, 1913– , son of Oswald, English writer, POLITICIANS (I) 12
Mosley, Oswald, 1896–1980, British Fascist leader, BRITISH EMPIRE 13, FASCISM 5
Motherwell, Robert, 1915–91, US painter, PAINTERS (I) 13
Motion, Andrew, 1952– , English poet and biographer, POETS (I) 42
Motley, J L, 1814–77, US historian, EPITAPHS 43, LUXURY 4
Motteux, Peter, 1660–1718, English translator, DEVIL 20
Mount, Ferdinand, 1939– , English writer, PROMOTION 3
Mountbatten, Lord, 1900–79, British naval commander and statesman, INDIA 4, NUCLEAR AGE 15
Muggeridge, Malcolm, 1903–90, British journalist and writer, DEVIL 21, EXAGGERATION 5, GOD 78, PRIME MINISTERS (I) 6, 16, SEX 28, TRAVEL 15
Muir, Edwin, 1887–1959, Scottish poet, GOOD & EVIL 16, LIFE 61
Muir, Frank, 1920–98, English writer, broadcaster and humorist, DOGS 11, READING 25, WEDDINGS 8
Muldoon, Paul, 1951– , Irish poet, MIND 32
Mullen, Ken, 1943– , British advertising copywriter, MODESTY 8, NEWSPAPERS 22
Muller, Herbert J, 1905–80, US writer, INVENTIONS 4
Mumford, Lewis, 1895–1990, US sociologist and writer, CITY 8, GENERATIONS 8, NEW YORK 6, PROGRESS 18, TECHNOLOGY 13
Murdoch, Iris, 1919–99, Irish-born, English novelist, and philosopher, ART 37, GOOD & GOODNESS 13, LITERATURE 17, MARRIAGE 68, NOVELS (G) 20, PHILOSOPHY 21, PLAYS 5, WOMEN 37, WRITERS (I) 34, WRITING 21
Murdoch, Rupert, 1931– , Australian-born US newspaper proprietor, NEWSPAPERS 23
Murphy, Capt Ed, 1918– , US soldier, RULES 5
Murray, David, 1888–1962, British journalist, JOURNALISM 21
Murray, Fred, d. 1922, US song-writer, PAINTING 9
Murray, Gilbert, 1866–1957, Australian-born classical scholar and translator, EXPERIENCE 17
Murray, Les, 1938– , Australian poet and critic, SOCIABILITY 8, WEDDINGS 9
Murrow, Edward, 1908–65, US journalist and broadcaster, WINSTON CHURCHILL 7
Musil, Robert, 1880–1942, Austrian novelist, PROGRESS 19
Musset, Alfred de, 1810–57, French poet and playwright, ARTISTS 32, INFINITY 3, SONGS & SINGERS 24
Mussolini, Benito, 1883–1945, Italian Fascist dictator, FASCISM 6, 7, GERMANY 16, LIFE 62

Nabokov, Vladimir, 1899–1977, Russian-born US novelist, BELIEF 11, CULTURE 11, EDUCATION 21, EPIGRAMS 3, IMITATION 5, INTELLECTUALS 11, KNOWLEDGE 25, LAUGHTER 28, LUST 3, NOVELISTS (I) 30, PSYCHIATRY 18, SATIRE 8, WRITERS (I) 35
Naipaul, Shiva, 1945–85, Trinidadian writer, CONSERVATIVES 20, SOCIALISTS 13
Naipaul, V S, 1932– , Trinidadian writer, AFRICA 4, PAST 13, POVERTY 25, RACES 15
Nairne, Lady, 1766–1845, Scottish song-writer, FISH 6, LOYALTY 8
Namier, Lewis, 1888–1969, FUTURE 15, PAST 14
Nansen, Fridtjof, 1861–1930, Norwegian explorer and scientist, IMPOSSIBILITY 4
Narayan, R K, 1906– , Indian writer, INDIA 5
Nash, Ogden, 1902–71, US comic poet, ACCIDENTS 5, ADVERTISING 3, ANIMALS 28–30, BABIES 8, BIRDS 34, CATS 9, DREAMS 19, DRINK: STRONG 41, EPITAPHS 44, EYES 15, FACTS 7, FAMILY 12, FISH 7, 8, FORGETTING 9, HUSBANDS 12, INSECTS 2, MIDDLE AGE 9, MIND 33, PARENTS 16, 17, WOMEN 38
Nashe, Thomas, 1567–1601, English playwright, BEAUTY 28, LIFE IS FLEETING 45, SPRING 10

Plath, Sylvia, 1932–63, US poet, DEATH 87, LOVE 71, WINTER 11

Plato, 428–347 BC, Greek philosopher, DEMOCRACY 19, MYTHS 3, PHILOSOPHERS 12, PHILOSOPHY 23

Plautus, *c.* 254–184 BC, Roman comic playwright, YOUTH 17

Player Francis, father of Gary, the golfer, MONEY 41

Pliny the Elder, 23–79, Roman statesman and scholar, AFRICA 5, NATURE 14, WINE 18

Plomer, William, 1903–73, South African-born English poet, AGE 21, LIBERALS 11, MANNERS 6, SEDUCTION 15, WARS (I) 5

Plotinus, *c.* 205–70, Greek philosopher, founder of Neoplatonism, ETERNITY 9

Plummer, Christopher, 1927– , FILM STARS (I) 1

Poe, Edgar Allan, 1809–49, US poet and short-story writer, BELLS 3, BIRDS 36, DREAMS 20, 21, GREECE 7, LIFE & DEATH 24, LIFE IS FLEETING 46, MONTHS 18, MOURNING 20, ROME 12

Poincaré, Henri, 1854–1912, French mathematician and philosopher of science, MATHEMATICS 8, SCIENCE 16, THINKING 31

Pollard, A W, 1859–1944, English historian, FUTURE 16

Pollard, Quinton, RAIN 5

Pollock, Channing, 1880–1946, US humorist, COURAGE 18

Pollock, Jackson, 1912–56, US painter, PAINTING 13

Pompidou, Georges, 1911–74, French President from 1969–74, POLITICIANS (G) 25

Pope, Alexander, 1688–1744, English poet, AMBITIONS 12, CHAOS 3, CHARITY 20, CHASTITY 3, CHURCHES 23, CLASS 15, CLERGY 22, 23, COMFORT 10, CONSISTENCY 4, CRITICISM 29, DEATH 88, DISAPPOINTMENTS 7, DIVERSITY 5, DOCTORS 14, DOGS 13, DUTY 12, EDUCATION 24, EPITAPHS 49, EYES 16, FACES 27, FAITHS 25, FAME 19, FASHION 8, FOOLS 28–30, FOREIGNERS 5, FORGIVENESS 13, 14, FRIENDS 36, GOOD & EVIL 18, HAPPINESS 28–30, HEART 13, 14, HONESTY 11, HOPE 16, HUMAN BEINGS 52, HUMILITY 8, ILLNESS 18, INSULTS 14, INTEGRITY 11, JEALOUSY 8, JUDGEMENT 13, 14, JUSTICE 24, KINGS & QUEENS (G) 21, KNOWLEDGE 27, LAUGHTER 30, LEARNING 12, LIFE 64, LOVE 72, LOVERS 21, MASSES 23, MEDIOCRITY 3, MIND 35, MISFORTUNES 10, MODESTY 10, MORTALITY 10, OLD AGE 34, OPINIONS 12, ORDER & DISORDER 2, 3, PASSIONS 11, 12, PERFECTION 5, PHYSICS 8, POETRY 65, POETS (G) 35, 36, 37, POETS (I) 32, 71, POLITICIANS (G) 26, PRAYERS 40, PREJUDICE 4, PRIDE 11, 12, RELIGION 46, RIGHT 5, SCANDAL 6, SELF-KNOWLEDGE 10, SELF-LOVE 5, SENSE 6, SHAKESPEARE 21, SINCERITY 2, SNOBBERY 9, TACT 4, TEA & COFFEE 8, THEATRE 16, THINKING 32, TRIVIALITY 7, UNIVERSE 18, VICE 5, VIRTUE 29, 30, WIT 13, 14, WIVES 22, WOMEN 41, 42, WOMEN & MEN 64, WORDS 22, WRITING 23, YOUTH & AGE 8, 9

Pope, Michael, 1875–1930, English comic poet, PUB 10

Popper, Karl, 1902–94, Austrian-born British philosopher, DESTINY 17, HISTORY 39, IGNORANCE 9, LIBERTY 54, QUESTIONS 5, SCIENCE 17, 18, SOCIETY 10

Porter, Cole, 1891–1964, US song-writer, CONSTANCY 7, FASHION 9, FATHERS 10, LAZINESS 20, LOVE 73, MILLIONAIRES 4, PARIS 9, PROSTITUTION 8, SEX 29

Porter, Peter, 1929– , Australian poet and critic, LOVE & HATE 7, NUCLEAR AGE 17

Porter, Roy, 1946– , English historian particularly of medicine, HISTORY 40

Potter, Beatrix, 1866–1943, English children's writer, SLEEPING & WAKING 20, TIREDNESS 4, WARNINGS 3

Potter, Dennis, 1935–94, English playwright, mostly for TV, DESPAIR 9, GOD 80, MEMORY 20, MORTALITY 11, RELIGION 47, SONGS & SINGERS 26, TELEVISION 19

Potter, Stephen, 1900–69, English humorous writer, ACADEMICS 12, COMPETITION 11, GAMBLING 12, SNOBBERY 10, WINE 19

Pound, Ezra, 1885–1972, US poet, EDUCATION 25, HISTORY 41, LANGUAGE 16, LIFE IS FLEETING 47, LITERATURE 18, 19, MONEY 42, MUSIC 36, POETRY 66–9, TIME 29, VANITY 7, WINTER 12, WORLD WAR I 17, WRITERS (I) 10

Powell, Anthony, 1905– , English novelist, FAMILY 13, GOOD & EVIL 19, GOSSIP 6, HOSPITALITY 9, INSULTS 15, NOVELS (G) 22, OLD AGE 35, PARENTS 19, SELF-LOVE 6, WRITING 24, YOUTH 18

Powell, Charles, British reviewer, POETS (I) 34

Powell, Enoch, 1912–98, British Conservative politician, IMAGINATION 10, MUSIC 37, POETS (I) 15, PRIME MINISTERS (G) 5, PROPHETS 16, RACES 17

Powell, Robert, 1918– , religious writer, RELIGION 48

Pownall, David, 1938– , English novelist, FOOTBALL 1

Powys, John Cowper, 1872–1963, English novelist and essayist, CERTAIN 12, TIME 30

Praed, W M, 1802–39, English comic poet, THINKING 33

Prayer, Book of Common, CHILD 37, FORGIVENESS 15, FUNERALS 11, LIFE IS FLEETING 48, MARRIAGE 72, PEACE 23, PRAYERS 41, REPENTANCE 4, SINS 21, 22, WEDDINGS 10–12

Prescott, Joseph, 1913– , US academic and epigrammatist, ACADEMICS 13, BIRTH 10, OLD AGE 36, READING 26, TRAVEL 16

Prévert, Jacques, 1900–77, French poet and screenwriter, PRAYERS 42

Previn, André, 1929– , German-born US conductor and composer, JAZZ 4, MUSIC 38

Priestley, J B, 1894–1984, English novelist, playwright and critic, CHURCH OF ENGLAND 5, COMEDY 18, CRICKET 5, EARS 5, HEROISM 21, HOLIDAYS 1, MASSES 24, MEANNESS 2, PATRIOTISM 31, POLITICIANS (G) 27, TEA & COFFEE 9, WORLD 27

Prior, Matthew, 1664–1721, English poet, AGE 22, DEBT 5, DOCTORS 15, EPITAPHS 50, HOPE 17, MIND 36, PROSTITUTION 9, RELIGION 49, SONGS & SINGERS 27, TALK 19

Reed, Henry, 1914–86, English playwright and poet, BIRTHDAYS 2, CIVIL WAR 4, DREAMS 22, HELL 9, NAMES 2, SONGS & SINGERS 28, WARS (G) 49

Reed, John, 1887–1920, US war correspondent and revolutionary, RUSSIAN REVOLUTION 4

Reed, Rex, 1938– , US humorist, HOLLYWOOD 16

Reedy, George, 1917– , US politician, PRESIDENTS (G) 5

Rees, C B, British music critic, COMPOSERS (I) 5

Rees, Leonard, 1856–1932, British newspaper editor, EDITORS 13

Reich, Wilhelm, 1897–1957, Austrian psychoanalyst, SEXUALITY 7

Reinhardt, Gottfried, 1913–94, US film-director and producer, HOLLYWOOD 17, INTELLIGENCE 7, MONEY 45

Reith, Lord, 1889–1971, Scottish engineer and first Director General of the British Broadcasting Corporation, GOVERNMENT 25

Rendall, M J, 1862–1950, member of the first British Broadcasting Corporation board, TELEVISION 20

Rexford, Eben, 1848–1916, US song-writer, OLD AGE 37

Reynolds, Burt, 1936– , US film actor, ACTORS & ACTRESSES (G) 16

Reynolds, Frederic, 1764–1841, prolific English playwright, TIME 32

Reynolds, Joshua, 1723–92, English painter, PAINTERS (G) 3, TALENT 9

Reynolds, Malvina, 1900–78, US song-writer, HOME & HOUSES 19

Reynolds, Oliver, 1957– , English poet, MISFORTUNES 11

Rhodes, Cecil, 1853–1902, British-born South African statesman, ENGLISH 40, LAST WORDS 40

Rhys, Jean, 1894–1979, English novelist born in West Indies, SUNDAY 5

Ricciardi, Mirella, MARRIAGE 74

Rice, Grantland, 1880–1954, US sports writer, FOOTBALL 2

Rice-Davies, Mandy, 1944– , Welsh showgirl, LIES 22

Richard, St, 1197–1253, Bishop of Chichester from 1245, PRAYERS 43

Richard, Keith, 1943– , member of Rolling Stones pop group, POLICE 10, SYMPATHY 7

Richards, Frank, 1876–1961, English boys' writer, famous for creating Billy Bunter, GRATITUDE 5

Richards, I A, 1893–1979, English literary critic, DESIRES 9, POETRY 70

Richards, James, 1907–92, English architectural writer, TRUST 6

Richardson, Ralph, 1902–83, English stage and film actor, ACTING 12–14, ACTORS & ACTRESSES (G) 17, ACTORS & ACTRESSES: (I) 4, FILM STARS (I) 8, GOD 85, SPEECH 14, TRAVEL 17

Richelieu, Cardinal, 1585–1642, French priest and statesman, JUSTICE 25

Richler, Mordechai, 1931– ,Canadian writer, CANADA 4, USA (G) 37

Richter, Hans, 1843–1916, German conductor, PATIENCE & IMPATIENCE 14

Ricks, Christopher, 1933– , British academic and critic, EXCUSES 3

Rickword, Edgell, 1898–1982, English poet and critic, SOULS 32, SUMMER 11

Ridge, W Pett, 1857–1930, English writer, MANNERS 8, UNHAPPINESS 13

Ridgeway, William, 1853–1926, Irish classical scholar, DEAFNESS 1

Ridley, Nicholas, 1929–93, British Conservative politician, GERMANY 17

Rilke, Rainer Maria, 1875–1926, German poet, ANGELS 11, CHANGE 19, CHILDHOOD 38, FAREWELLS 20, 21, GOD 86, HEROISM 22, IMMORTALITY 14, INSECTS 4, LIFE & DEATH 25, LOVE & HATE 9, MARRIAGE 75, SPRING 11, TECHNOLOGY 14, TREES 16, WORLD 29

Rimbaud, Arthur, 1854–91, French poet, COLOUR 5

Rimsky-Korsakov, Nikolai, 1849–1908, Russian composer, COMPOSERS (I) 7

Rivarol, Antoine de, 1753–1801, French writer, FRANCE 27

Rivers, Joan, 1933– , US humorist, JEWS 16

Robbins, Tom, 1936– , US novelist, HAPPINESS 32, HUMAN BEINGS 56, POETRY 71

Roberts, Michael, 1902–48, English writer, POETRY 72

Robey, George, 1869–1954, British comedian, LETTERS 8

Robin, Leo, 1900–84, US song-writer, JEWELLERY 5

Robinson, Edwin Arlington, 1869–1935, US poet, FRIENDS 37, SINS 23

Robinson, Joan, 1903–83, British economist, ECONOMICS 19

Robinson, Mary, 1944– , Irish President 1990–97, INTERDEPENDENCE 10

Robinson, Robert, 1927– , English writer and broadcaster, CARS 13, COUNTRY & TOWN 15, EDITORS 14, FOOD 32, LEISURE 2, NAMES 3, TEETH 3, WRITERS (I) 40

Robson, J M, ?1900–82, British academic, THEORY 5

Roche, Boyle, 1743–1807, Irish politician, POSTERITY 5, SUSPICION 9

Rochester, John Wilmot, Earl of, 1647–80, English poet, CONSTANCY 8, COWARDICE 9, EPITAPHS 53, HUMAN BEINGS 57, KINGS & QUEENS (I) 2, NOTHING 5, OLD AGE 38, REASON 8

Rodgers, James, ?–1960, US criminal, LAST WORDS 41

Rodker, John, NOVELS (I) 6

Roethke, Theodore, 1908–63, US poet, EYES 18, FUNERALS 12

Rogers, Richard, 1933– , British architect, BUILDINGS 10

Rogers, Samuel, 1763–1855, English poet, ACTION 12, BOOKS (G) 31, EPITAPHS 54, LONELINESS 11, MARRIAGE 76, READING 27, SPEECHES 12

Rogers, Will, 1879–1935, US actor and humorous writer, ANCESTRY 3, BIRTH 11, COLD WAR 8, COMEDY 19, GOSSIP 7, GOVERNMENT 26, GREATNESS 11, HEROISM 23, HUMOUR 15, IGNORANCE 10, POLITICS

Russell, Bertrand – *cont*
INTELLECTUALS 12, LIFE IS FLEETING 50, MATHEMATICS 9, 10, MODESTY 11, MORALS 14, NUCLEAR AGE 19, OPINIONS 13, PASSIONS 14, PATRIOTISM 33, PHILOSOPHERS 5, PHILOSOPHY 25, 26, POWER 22, PROGRESS 22, SELF-LOVE 8, SOCIETY 11, STARS 15, SUSPICION 10, THINKING 34, 35

Russell, Claude, 1919– , university teacher and linguist, CLOTHES 17

Russell, George W (A E), 1867–1935, Irish writer, LITERATURE 23

Russell, Lord John, 1792–1878, British Whig Prime Minister 1846–52, 65–6, EPIGRAMS 5

Russell, Willy, 1947– , English playwright, MARRIAGE 78

Rutherford, Ernest, 1871–1937, New Zealand physicist, NUCLEAR AGE 20, PHYSICS 9, 10

Ryle, Gilbert, 1900–76, British philosopher, MYTHS 4, PHILOSOPHERS 9, PHILOSOPHY 27

Sacks, Oliver, 1933– , British neurologist and writer, HEALTH 8, ILLNESS 21, SCIENCE 19, THINKING 36

Sackville, Thomas, 1536–1608, English poet and statesman, WRITERS (I) 14

Sackville-West, Victoria, 1892–1962, English poet, novelist and gardener, CATS 11, EXPERIENCE 19, KNOWLEDGE 28, SEASONS 1, SPRING 12

Sagan, Françoise, 1935– , French novelist, MARRIAGE 79, MEN 16

Sagittarius (Olga Katzin), English writer and anthologist, 1896–1987, LIBERTY 24

Sahl, Mort, 1926– , US journalist and humorist, LONELINESS 13, PRESIDENTS (I) 14, 21, 22, USA: PLACES 1

Sainte-Beuve, Charles-Augustin, 1804–69, French writer, PLAYWRIGHTS (I) 6

Saint-Exupéry, Antoine de, 1900–44, French writer and aviator, ADULTS 3, CHILDHOOD 40, HEART 16, JUDGEMENT 16, PHILOSOPHY 28, RESPONSIBILITY 9

Saint-Lambert, Marquis de, 1716–1803, French poet, SONGS & SINGERS 30

Saki (H.H Munro), 1870–1916, Scottish short-story writer and novelist, ADVICE 19, AGE 23, BEAUTY 33, CHINA 2, CHRISTIANITY 16, CLOTHES 18, CONSCIENCE 5, COOKERY 6, DEATH 92, EXTRAVAGANCE 6, FASHION 10, FOOD 34, GENEROSITY 4, GREECE 8, HIDING 3, HIERARCHIES 4, HISTORY 42, KNOWLEDGE 29, PRIVACY 5, RELIGION 50, RIGHT & WRONG 6, SAINTS 8, SCHOOLS 22, SHAW 4, TEMPTATION 10, UNHAPPINESS 14, VICTIM 3, WOMEN 45, YOUTH & AGE 10

Sale, Kirkpatrick, 1937– , US environmental activist, PRINCIPLES 7

Salinger, J D, 1919, US novelist and short-story writer, ACTORS & ACTRESSES (G) 18, CARS 14, CHARACTER 16, COMPETITION 12, GIRLS 15, 16, HORSES & RACING 16, JESUS CHRIST 26, POETRY 74, PRIDE 13, SEX 30, THEATRE 18

Salisbury, Lord, 1830–1903, British Conservative Prime Minister, 1855–56, 1886–92, 1895–1902, EUROPE 15, NEWSPAPERS 29

Salkey, Andrew, 1928–95, Jamaican novelist and poet, CULTURE 12, PRESIDENTS (I) 15

Sallust, 86–34 BC, Roman historian, FRIENDS 38

Salvandy, Comte de, 1795–1856, French writer and minister, REVOLUTIONS 23

Sampson, Anthony, 1926– , British journalist and writer, HIERARCHIES 5, JOURNALISM 24

Sampson, Geoffrey, 1944– , British linguist and academic, ACADEMICS 14

Sampson, George, 1873–1950, British educationist, EDUCATION 26

Samuel, Herbert, 1870–1963, British Liberal politician, CIVIL SERVICE 3, DEMOCRACY 21, FRIENDS 39, LIBRARIES 3, MORALS 15, MYTHS 5

Sandburg, Carl, 1878–1967, US poet, MASSES 26, OPTIMISM & PESSIMISM 20, POETRY 75, SLANG 3, USA: PLACES 7, WARS (G) 50

Sanders, George, 1906–72, British film actor, HOME & HOUSES 20

Sankey, Ira D, 1840–1908, US hymn-writer, ETERNITY 10

Santayana, George, 1863–1952, Spanish-born US philosopher and critic, ACTION 13, BIBLE 14, EMOTIONS 11, ENGLAND (G) 29, FANATICS 5, FRIENDS 40, HAPPINESS 36, LIFE 66, 67, PASSIONS 15, PHILOSOPHY 29, PROGRESS 23, TRUTH 53, YOUTH & AGE 11

Sargent, Epes, 1813–80, British song-writer, SAILORS 13

Sargent, John Singer, 1856–1925, US painter, PORTRAITS 10, 11

Sarnoff, Robert W, 1918– , US humorist, MONEY 48

Sartre, Jean-Paul, 1905–80, French existentialist philosopher, playwright, novelist and critic, AMERICANS & OTHERS 10, APPEARANCE 14, BELIEF 15, DEATH 93, DESPAIR 11, DOUBT 20, EMOTIONS 12, EVIL 13, EXISTENCE 16, FAMILY 15, FUTURE 17, HELL 10, 11, HUMAN BEINGS 59, ILLNESS 22, LATENESS 4, LIBERTY 60, LIFE 68, LITERATURE 24, MIDDLE CLASS 10, MYTHS 6, PSYCHOLOGY 3, READING 30, RESPONSIBILITY 10, REVOLUTIONS 24, 25, SOCIETY 12, STORIES 6, THINKING 37, TRUTH 54, 55, VICTIM 4, VIOLENCE 11

Sassoon, Siegfried, 1886–1967, English poet and autobiographer, GHOSTS 3, IMMORTALITY 15, SOLDIERS (G) 17, 18, WORLD WAR I 19, 20

Sassoon, Vidal, 1928– , British hairdresser, SUCCESS 16

Satie, Erik, 1866–1925, French composer, COMPOSERS (I) 17, MUSICIANS 12, SMOKING 13, YOUTH & AGE 12

Saville, Victor, 1897–1979, British film producer, FILM STARS (I) 19

Sayers, Dorothy L, 1893–1957, English detective-story writer and translator, INSULTS 16

Sayle, Alexei, 1952– , British comedian, LONDON 20

Scalpone, Al, 1913– , US Catholic evangelist, FAMILY 16

Scanlon, Hugh, 1913– , British trade unionist, ILLUSION 12, LIBERTY 61

Smith, Alexander, 1830–67, English poet, WINTER 17
Smith, Cyril, 1928– , British Liberal politician, PARLIAMENT 3
Smith, F E, Earl of Birkenhead, 1872–1930, British Conservative politician and lawyer, INSULTS 18
Smith, George Joseph, 1872–1915, Murderer of the Brides in the Bath, NONSENSE 6
Smith, Godfrey, 1926– , British journalist, OPERA 8, UNIVERSITIES 10
Smith, Harold Jacob, US screen-writer, NEWSPAPERS 11
Smith, James, 1775–1839, English poet, HOME & HOUSES 22, LAST WORDS 44
Smith, John, 1938–94, British Labour politician, PRIME MINISTERS (I) 21
Smith, Logan Pearsall, 1865–1946, US-born British writer and anthologist, AMBITIONS 22, BALDNESS 3, BOOKS (G) 35, DEATH 115, FRIENDS 50, MIND 41, MONEY 54, PERFECTION 7, READING 32, RICH 14, SACRIFICE 13, SELF 34, SOULS 36, SPACE 2, SUN 11, VOICE 8, WRITERS (G) 50
Smith, Maggie, 1933– , British actress, ACTORS & ACTRESSES: (I) 8
Smith, Samuel F, 1808–95, US poet and cleric, USA (G) 42
Smith, Stevie, 1902–71, English poet and novelist, ADOLESCENCE 7, DANGERS 3, DESPAIR 15, FUTURE 18, POETS (I) 89
Smith, Revd Sydney, 1771–1845, English journalist, cleric and preacher, BEER 8, BOOKS (G) 36, BRITAIN 10, CHURCH OF ENGLAND 8, CLERGY 26, COUNTRY & TOWN 17, 18, CRITICISM 35, GLUTTONY 7, HEALTH 10, HEAVEN 21, HOT & COLD 2, IGNORANCE 11, JOKES 5, KNOWLEDGE 31, MARRIAGE 94, NEWSPAPERS 31, POVERTY 33, PRAYERS 46, READING 33, SCOTLAND 25, SWITZERLAND 6
Smith, Thorne, 1892–1934, British comic novelist, PROMISCUITY 9, TOLERANCE 4
Smollett, Tobias, 1721–71, Scottish novelist, CRIME 18, WRITERS (I) 20
Snow, C P, 1905–80, English novelist and physicist, FACES 37, HUMOUR 17, SCIENTISTS 9
Snowden, Philip, 1864–1937, British Labour politician, GOVERNMENT 27
Snyder, Gary, 1930– , US poet, KNOWLEDGE 32
Socrates, 469–399 BC, Greek philosopher, DEATH 116, FOOD 39, GOOD & GOODNESS 16, LAST WORDS 45, LIFE 74, NATIONALISM & INTERNATIONALISM 7
Soderbegh, Steven, 1963– , US screen-writer and film-director, FILM 17
Solon, *c.* 640–*c.* 558 BC, Athenian statesman, HAPPINESS 41, LEARNING 14, OLD AGE 50
Solzhenitsyn, Alexander, 1918– , Russian novelist, ANIMALS 37, CAPITALISM 13, CRITICISM 36, LIBERTY 64, LIES 28, LIFE & DEATH 32, NOVELISTS (I) 35, PAST 24, POWER 27, PRAYERS 47, PRISON 11, TRUTH 59, WRITERS (G) 51
Somerville, William, 1675–1742, English poet, HUNTING 9
Somoza, Anastasio, 1925–80, Nicaraguan dictator, ELECTIONS 4
Sondheim, Stephen, 1930– , US composer and lyricist, FOOD 40, MARRIAGE 95, SOCIABILITY 12
Sontag, Susan, 1933– , US writer and critic, ILLNESS 23, PHOTOGRAPHY 9, PSYCHOLOGY 4
Sophocles, *c.* 495–*c.* 406 BC, Greek playwright, HUMAN BEINGS 68, PLAYWRIGHTS (I) 9
Sorley, Charles, 1895–1915, English poet, DEATH 117
Southey, Robert, 1774–1843, English poet, AFTERLIFE 14, CURSING 6, DEVIL 26, MEMORY 30, NIGHT 14, OLD AGE 51, PRIDE 17, SAILORS 14, SINS 30, VICTORY 14
Southwell, Robert, 1561?–95, English poet and Roman Catholic martyr, CHRISTMAS 16
Spaeth, Duncan, British wit, BRITISH EMPIRE 17
Spain, Nancy, 1917–64, English writer, BEDS 12
Spark, Muriel, 1918– , Scottish novelist, FOOD 41, INTELLECTUALS 14, LISTENING 7, MIND 42, NOVELISTS (I) 32, PAPACY 4, PARENTS 21, POVERTY 34, TEACHERS 12, WOMEN & MEN 72
Speight, Johnny, 1920–98, English comedy screen-writer, KINGS & QUEENS (I) 16, LANGUAGE 22, PORNOGRAPHY 3, WARS (G) 53
Spellman, Cardinal, 1889–1959, US churchman, PRAYERS 48
Spencer, Herbert, 1820–1903, English philosopher, EDUCATION 30, GAMBLING 13, INTERDEPENDENCE 13, PROGRESS 25, SCIENCE 20, TIME 45
Spencer, Stanley, 1891–1959, English painter, HUMAN NATURE 20, PAINTING 15
Spender, Stephen, 1909–95, English poet and critic, CHILDHOOD 42, EVIL 16, GREATNESS 16, LIFE 75, MOON 22, POETS (I) 4, RAILWAYS 10
Spenser, Edmund, 1552?–99, English poet, ANGELS 15, BIRDS 44, CALM 7, COURAGE 24, LONDON 22, LOVE 102, MANNERS 10, MIND 43, MORTALITY 23, NIGHT 15, PATRONS 5, POETS (I) 19, SLEEPING & WAKING 27, SPRING 17, THAMES 3, WINE 22
Spiel, Hilde, 1911–90, Austrian-born journalist and novelist, HATE 15
Spillane, Mickey, 1918– , US crime novelist, WRITERS (G) 52
Spinoza, Benedict, 1632–77, Dutch philosopher, ETERNITY 12, HUMAN NATURE 21, IMMORTALITY 19, NATURE 17
Spock, Dr, 1903–98, US paediatrician, writer for parents, and political activist, PARENTS 22, VIETNAM 7
Spooner, Revd W A, 1844–1930, English cleric and academic, creator of legendary slips of the tongue, FAREWELLS 31, MEMORY 31
Spring-Rice, Cecil, 1859–1918, British diplomat and hymn-writer, PATRIOTISM 35
Springsteen, Bruce, 1949– , US rock singer and guitarist, VICTORY 15
Squire, J C, 1884–1958, English poet, anthologist, editor, DRUNKENNESS 13, PHYSICS 11
Sri Aurobindo, 1872–1950, Indian religious teacher and writer, MYSTICS 5

Index of authors

Tolstoy, Leo, 1828–1910, Russian novelist, and social reformer, ARMY 13, FAMILY 22, GOOD & GOODNESS 20, HISTORY 51, IGNORANCE 12, LOVE OF GOD 7, SCIENCE 21, SELF 37, SORROW 33, UNDERSTANDING 10

Tomalin, Nicholas, 1931–73, British journalist, UNDERSTANDING 11

Tomaschek, Rudolphe, b. 1895, PHYSICS 4

Tomblin, David, British film and TV director, LIBERTY 44

Tomlin, Lily, 1939– , US comedian, BEAUTY 44, INTERDEPENDENCE 15, LOVE 109, SEX 37

Tomlinson, Charles, 1927– , English poet, PRESENT 6

Tomlinson, H M, 1873–1958, English writer, SEA 26

Toole, John Kennedy, 1937–69, US novelist, CIVIL SERVICE 4, COOKERY 8, FOOD 42

Torrijos Herrera, Omar, 1929–81, Panamanian general and politician, GRAVE 19

Tortelier, Paul, 1914–90, French cellist, COMPOSERS (I) 28

Toscanini, Arturo, 1867–1957, Italian conductor, COMPOSERS (I) 24, MUSICIANS 18, OPERA 9

Tourneur, Cyril, 1575?–1626, English playwright, HELL 13

Tournier, Michel, 1924– , French writer, NUDITY 8

Toynbee, Arnold, 1889–1975, English historian, SURVIVAL 9, USA (G) 44

Toynbee, Philip, 1916–81, English journalist and writer, MORALS 18, USA (G) 45

Tracy, Spencer, 1900–67, US film actor, POVERTY 38

Traherne, Thomas, 1637?–74, English poet and mystic, ETERNITY 15, JOY 15, VISIONS 11

Trapido, Barbara, 1941, English novelist, ECCENTRICS 3, NOVELISTS (I) 36, POETRY 83

Trapp, Joseph, 1679–1747, English poet and pamphleteer, OXFORD & CAMBRIDGE 13

Travers, Ben, 1886–1980, English playwright, EPITAPHS 68, OLD AGE 54

Travis, Merle, 1917–83, US country singer and songwriter, DEBT 7

Tree, Herbert Beerbohm, 1853–1917, British actor-manager, ACTING 20, BORES & BOREDOM 20, FAME 26, GOD 96, HATE 17

Tremain, Rose, 1951– , English novelist, ASTONISHMENT 4

Trench, R V, 1807–86, Irish poet and playwright, ENGLAND (G) 32

Trevelyan, G M, 1876–1962, English historian, LITERACY 5, PRIME MINISTERS (I) 31, READING 36, SAILORS 15

Trevor-Roper, Hugh, 1914– , British historian, KINGS & QUEENS (I) 23

Trilling, Lionel, 1905–75, US literary critic, AMERICANS 20, EQUALITY 16, HEALTH 11

Trollope, Anthony, 1815–82, English novelist, CHILDHOOD 46, FAME 27, GENTLEMEN 19, HUMILITY 11, PUNISHMENTS 18, REVENGE 11, WORK 33, WRITING 29

Trotsky, Leon, 1874–1940, Ukraine-born Russian revolutionary, CIVILIZATION 14, DEATH 126, DEMOCRACY 26, ENDS 12, GERMANY 19, IDEAS 13, INDIA 10, MIDDLE CLASS 11, PATRIOTISM 36, REFORM 4, REVENGE 12, REVOLUTIONS 27, 28, RUSSIAN REVOLUTION 6, 7

Truffaut, François, 1932–84, French film-director, REVOLUTIONS 29

Truman, Harry S, 1884–1972, 33rd US President, BOOKS (I) 3, ECONOMICS 22, PARENTS 23, POLITICIANS (G) 33, PRESIDENTS (G) 6, PRESIDENTS (I) 17, 31, SOLDIERS (I) 3, UNEMPLOYMENT 5, WORLD WAR II 18, WORRY 20

Trumbull, John, 1750–1831, English playwright, EYES 25

Tsvetayeva, Marina 1892–1941, Russian poet, HUNGER 11, POETS (G) 48, SOULS 40

Tuchman, B, 1912–89, US historian, BRITISH 14, SOLDIERS (G) 25

Tucker, Sophie, 1884–1966, Russian-born US singer and vaudeville entertainer, MIDDLE AGE 14

Tupper, Martin, 1810–89, English writer, BOOKS (G) 38

Turenne, Marshal, 1611–75, French soldier, ARMY 14, GOD 97

Turgenev, Ivan, 1818–83, Russian novelist, DEATH 127, OPINIONS 16, PRAYERS 54

Tusser, Thomas, 1524?–80, English instructional poet, BORROWERS & LENDERS 6, CHANGE 23, CHRISTMAS 18, HOME & HOUSES 26, MONTHS 3, 9, WINDS 13, WIVES 29

Tutu, Desmond, 1931– , South African, first black Bishop of Johannesburg, AFRICA 6

Tuwim, Julian, 1894–1954, Polish writer, BLOOD 5

Twain, Mark, 1835–1910, US writer, BOOKS (G) 39, BOOKS (I) 4, EDUCATION 31, FAMILIARITY 4, FOOD 43, FOREIGNERS 7, GAMBLING 3, ITALY 14, JOKES 6, JUSTICE 30, KINGS & QUEENS (G) 36, LIBERTY 66, LIFE & DEATH 36, NEWS 9, OPINIONS 17, POLITICIANS (I) 27, QUOTATIONS 6, REPUTATION 9, RESPECT 5, TRUTH 64, WORDS 28

Tynan, Kenneth, 1927–80, English theatre critic, ACTORS & ACTRESSES: (I) 1, 3, 7, CRITICISM 45, FILM STARS (I) 17, NOVELS (G) 27, PLAYS 10, 11, PLAYWRIGHTS (I) 5, THEATRE 21

Ufford, Edward Smith, 1851–1928, English hymnwriter, HELP 6

Umaltova Saji, 1953– , PRESIDENTS (I) 6

Umberto I, 1844–1900, King of Italy from 1878, ASSASSINATION 7

Unamuno, Miguel de, 1864–1937, Spanish philosopher and writer, COMEDY 24, DOUBT 25, FAITHS 29, GLORY 8, OLD AGE 56, OPTIMISM & PESSIMISM 25, TRAGEDY 15, VICTORY 16

Unesco Constitution, [1946] PEACE 30

Upanishads, 7th cent BC, Hindu scriptures, EARS 6, GOOD & GOODNESS 21, KNOWLEDGE 34, PLEASURE 21

Updike, John, 1932– , US novelist, ADVICE 23, AFTERLIFE 17, AMERICANS 21, BORES & BOREDOM 21, CHRISTIANITY 20, CHURCHES 27, COMFORT 13, HUMOUR 21, MARRIAGE 102, SCHOOLS 24, SELF 38, SEX 38

Usborne, Richard, 1907– , English writer, COMEDY 25, EPITAPHS 69, MEMORY 37

Ustinov, Peter, 1921– , English stage and film actor, playwright and director, ACTORS & ACTRESSES: (I) 6, DEMOCRACY 27, DIPLOMACY 12, FRIENDS 54, JEWS 21, LAUGHTER 33, LOVE 110, LOYALTY 14, MIND 44, OPTIMISM & PESSIMISM 26, PRIVACY 7, REVOLUTIONS 30, RICH & POOR 18, SNOBBERY 15, SOLDIERS (G) 26

Vachell, Horace Annesley, 1861–1955, English writer, NATURE 21

Vaculík, Ludvík, 1926– , Czech novelist, TRUTH 65

Vadim, Roger, 1928– , FILM STARS (I) 4

Vail, Amanda, 1921–66, US writer, GIRLS 17, PARENTS 24, TALK 21, WOMEN & MEN 81

Valéry, Paul, 1871–1945, French poet and critic, ABILITY 6, ENTHUSIASMS 5, GENIUS 17, GREATNESS 19, HUMAN BEINGS 77, HUMAN NATURE 24, IDEAS 14, NOTHING 7, OPINIONS 18, PAINTERS (G) 4, POETRY 84, POETS (G) 49, POLITICS 38, TALENT 10, THINKING 46–8, TRUTH 66, WORDS 29, WRITING 30–1

Vanburgh, John, 1664–1726, English playwright and architect, GOOD & EVIL 29, INCONSTANCY 4, MATERIALISM 9, NECESSITY 12

Van der Post, Laurens, 1906–96, South African explorer, writer and soldier, HEAVEN & HELL 13, STORIES 10

Van Gogh, Vincent 1853–90, Dutch post-Impressionist artist, PAINTERS (I) 6

Vaughan, Henry, 1622–95, English religious poet, AFTERLIFE 18, BIRTH 16, CHILDHOOD 47, DEATH 128, ETERNITY 16, GOD 98, HEAVEN 24, HUMAN BEINGS 78, IMMORTALITY 20, LIFE & DEATH 37, NIGHT 18, WORLD 35

Vaughan, Major-General Harry, 1893–1981, US soldier, WORRY 21

Vaughan Williams, Ralph, 1872–1958, British composer, COMPOSERS (I) 29

Vauvenargues, Marquis de, 1715–47, French writer, ACHIEVEMENT 14, THINKING 49

Vaux, Lord Thomas, 1510–56, English writer and courtier, OLD AGE 57

Veblen, Thorstein, 1857–1929, US social scientist, BUSINESS 19, MATERIALISM 10, RESEARCH 7

Vechten, Carl van, 1880–1964, US critic and novelist, UNDERSTANDING 12

Vegetius, 4th cent AD, Roman military writer, WAR & PEACE 11

Vergniaud, Pierre, 1753–93, French revolutionary, FRENCH REVOLUTION 11

Verlaine, Paul, 1844–96, French poet, AUTUMN 9, LITERATURE 27, POETRY 85, SPEECH 20, TEARS 16

Vernon, Tom, 1939– , English broadcaster and humorist, STUPIDITY 5

Vian, Boris, 1920–59, French playwright, novelist and poet, HAPPINESS 46

Victoria, 1819–1901, Queen of United Kingdom and Ireland 1837–1901, DEFEAT 7, LAUGHTER 34, PRIME MINISTERS (I) 9

Vidal, Gore, 1925– , US novelist and essayist ACTORS & ACTRESSES (G) 22, AMERICANS 11, ARTISTS 40, BORES & BOREDOM 22, BRITAIN 19, BUSINESS 20, CHILDHOOD 48, ELECTIONS 6, FILM 18, FIRE 4, LIES 34, LITERATURE 28, MIDDLE AGE 15, NOVELS (G) 28, NOVELISTS (I) 28, PARENTS 25, PRESIDENTS (I) 26, PSYCHIATRY 22, PUNISHMENTS 19, SPACE 3, SUCCESS 18, USA (G) 46

Vignaud, Vincent de 1901–78, Canadian biochemist, SCIENCE 22

Vigny, Alfred de, 1797–1863, French poet, ARMY 15, GOD 99, HUNTING 11, SILENCE 23, SUFFERING 20, WOMEN 52

Villiers de l'Isle Adam, Philippe-Auguste, 1838–89, French writer, LIFE & DEATH 38, SERVANTS 8

Villon, François, 1431–65 ?, French poet, NOSTALGIA 26

Virgil, 70–19 BC, Roman poet, ABILITY 7, AGRICULTURE 5, BOYS 14, BRITAIN & OTHERS 20, COMPARISONS 10, ENDURANCE 16, GREECE 12, GREED 9, HELL 14, HEROISM 25, IMMORTALITY 21, INSECTS 6, KNOWLEDGE 35, LEISURE 4, LOVE 111, MEMORY 38, MORTALITY 28, NECESSITY 13, ROME 14, SECURITY 11, SLEEPING & WAKING 30, SONGS & SINGERS 39, SUCCESS 19, SUSPICION 13, TIME 50, TRUST 10, UNIVERSE 20, WOMEN 53

Vizinczey, Stephen, 1933– , Hungarian novelist and critic NOVELISTS (I) 19, UNHAPPINESS 16, WRITERS (G) 54

Voinovich, Vladimir, 1932– , Russian novelist, COMMITTEES 7

Voltaire, 1694–1778, French philosopher and writer, ART 49, DEATH 129, EMPIRE 4, EXAGGERATION 12, FAILURE 11, GARDENS 20, GOD 100–2, GOOD & GOODNESS 22, HISTORY 52, 53, IRONY 5, LIBERTY 67, MASSES 29, OPTIMISM & PESSIMISM 27, REALISM 5, REASON 14, SAILORS 16, STYLE 14, SUPERSTITIONS 9, WORDS 30, WORK 34

Vonnegut, Kurt, 1922– , HATE 18, US novelist, TRAVEL 26, WARS (G) 58

Voznesensky, Andrei, 1933– , Russian poet, CREATION 12, GENIUS 18

Vreeland, Diana, 1903–89, US fashion editor, COLOUR 8

Wagner, Jane, 1927– , US humorist, AMBITIONS 23

Wagner, Richard, 1813–83, German composer, OPERA 10

Wain, John, 1925–94, English writer, POETS (G) 50, POETRY 86, PROSE 7

Walcott, Derek, 1930– , West Indian poet and playwright, CREATIVITY 6, FISH 9, HISTORY 54, MATURITY 4, POETRY 87, POETS (I) 6

Wald, George, 1906–97, US biochemist, EVOLUTION 11, PHYSICS 13

Walesa, Lech, 1947– , Polish trade-unionist and President, NATIONS 26

Waley, Arthur, 1889–1965, English translator from the Chinese, CENSORSHIP 7

Walker, Alice, 1944– , US writer, CHURCHES 28, FEMINISM 13, GOD 103, 104, TEA & COFFEE 12

Walker, Walter, 1912– , English soldier, CIVIL SERVICE 5

Wall, Max, 1908–90, British comedian and actor, BIRTH 17

Wallace, Vice-President Henry, 1888–1965, US democratic politician, MASSES 30

Wallace, W R, 1819–81, US poet, MOTHERS 17

Wallas, Graham, 1858–1932, British political psychologist, THINKING 51

Waller, Edmund, 1606–87, English poet AGE 27, CALM 9, CLOTHES 25, COMPARISONS 11, POETS (G) 51

Walpole, Horace, 1717–97, English writer, politician and correspondent, COMEDY 26, FASHION 11, MASSES 31, PROPHETS 23, TRAGEDY 16, WRITING 32

Walpole, Robert, 1676–1745, British Whig Prime Minister 1721–42, CYNICS 4, HISTORY 55, WARS (I) 1

Walsh, William, 1663–1708, English poet, DESPAIR 17

Walters, Alan, 1926– , British economist, MONEY 57

Walton, Izaak, 1593–1683, English angler and writer, BUSINESS 21, EPITAPHS 70, FISH 10, FOOD 44, HEALTH 12, LAUGHTER 35, LOSS 8, PHILOSOPHERS 1

Walton, William, 1902–83, British composer, COMPOSERS (I) 32, SUCCESS 20

Warburton, William, 1698–1779, English cleric, Bishop of Gloucester from 1759, BELIEF 19

Ward, Artemus, 1834–67, US humorist, BORROWERS & LENDERS 7, CLEVERNESS 7, EMOTIONS 14, HOTELS 4, POLITICIANS (G) 34, POLITICS 39, WOMEN 54

Ward, Thomas, 1577–1639, English poet, CHOICE 11

Ward, Wendy, British wit, ATHEISM 11

Warhol, Andy, 1927–87, US pop artist, ARTISTS 41, ASSASSINATION 8, EPITAPHS 71, FAME 28, FOOD 45, HEAVEN & HELL 14, LOVE 112, SHOW BUSINESS 5

Warner, Jack L, 1892–1981, US film mogul, POLITICIANS (I) 26

Warner, Susan, 1819–85, US novelist and hymn-writer, BIBLE 16

Warren, Earl, 1891–1974, US politician and lawyer, GOVERNMENT 31, SOCIALISTS 17

Warren, Samuel, 1807–77, English writer, ABILITY 8

Washburn, H S, 1813–1903, English poet, ABSENCE 13

Washington, George, 1732–99, 1st US President, INTERNATIONAL RELATIONS 11, LIES 35

Waterhouse, Keith, 1929– , English journalist, novelist, playwright and humorist, ANIMALS 39, FACES 39, INDEPENDENCE 7, LOVERS 32

Watkyns, Rowland, 1616–64, English poet, HATE 19

Watson, James D, 1928– , US biologist, AGE 28, FEMINISM 14, WORK 35

Watson, William, 1858–1935, English poet, CONSERVATIVES 24

Watts, Isaac, 1674–1748, English hymn-writer, CHILDHOOD 49, CHRISTIANITY 21, CLOTHES 26, GOD 105, HEAVEN 25, HELL 15, INSECTS 7, JESUS CHRIST 33, LAZINESS 26, 27, TIME 51

Waugh, Arthur, 1866–1943, LITERATURE 29

Waugh, Evelyn, 1903–66, English novelist, AGE 29, AGREEMENT 14, AMERICANS & OTHERS 12, BIOGRAPHY 13, BRITISH 15, CANNIBALS 7, CHOICE 12, CHURCHES 29, CLERGY 29, CRIME 20, DREAMS 31, ELECTIONS 7, 8, ENGLISH 49, FAT & THIN 11, FOOD 46, FORGETTING 16, FRANCE 32, GENTLEMEN 21, HUMAN NATURE 25, LITERATURE 30, NEWS 10, NEWSPAPERS 37, NOVELISTS (I) 22, PRISON 12, PUNCTUALITY 5, SCHOOLS 25–7, SEX 39, SLEEPING & WAKING 31, SPACE 4, SPORTS 22, STATE 13, TEACHERS 14, USA (G) 47, WALES 9, CHURCHILL 9, WIVES 30, WORDS 31, WRITERS (I) 54

Wavell, Lord, 1883–1950, English soldier and Viceroy of India, INSULTS 19

Webb, Beatrice, 1858–1943, English socialist, social historian and diarist, CLEVERNESS 8

Webb, Sidney, 1859–1947, English socialist, social historian and economist, CHANGE 24

Webern, Anton von, 1883–1945, Austrian composer, MUSIC 56

Webster, Daniel, 1782–1852, US poet and lawyer, AMBITIONS 24, PAST 27

Webster, John, 1580?–1625, English playwright, ASTROLOGY 5, BIRDS 49, DEATH 130, GLORY 9, GRAVE 20, OLD AGE 58, SOULS 41

Wedgwood, C V, 1910–97, English historian, HISTORY 56

Wedgwood, Josiah, 1730–95, English potter, SLAVERY 7

Weil, Simone, 1909–43, French philosopher and mystic, ATTENTION 7, CERTAIN 15, CREATION 13, CULTURE 15, EVIL 17, FAITHS 30, FRIENDS 55, GIVING & TAKING 8, GOD 106, HUMAN BEINGS 79, JUSTICE 31, LOVE OF GOD 8, MATHEMATICS 11, MONEY 58, MYSTICS 6, SINS 32, SLAVERY 8, TEACHERS 15, UNHAPPINESS 17, WARS (G) 59

Weinreich, Max, LANGUAGES 20

Weiss, Peter, 1916–82, German playwright, FRENCH REVOLUTION 12, PLAYWRIGHTS (I) 13

Weizmann, Chaim, 1874–1952, Russian-born first President of Israel, IMPOSSIBILITY 6

Weizsäcker, C F von, 1912– , German physicist, SOULS 42, BODY 5

Weizsäcker, Richard von, 1920– , President of Germany, ENGLAND (G) 33

Welch, Raquel, 1940– , US film actress, MIND 45

Weldon, Fay, 1931– , English novelist, and screenwriter, CHRISTIANITY 22, FEMINISM 15, MEN 17, PROCREATION 4, SUCCESS 21, WRITING 33

Welles, Orson, 1915–85, US film-director and actor, ART 50, FILM DIRECTORS & WRITERS 14, SUCCESS 22, SWITZERLAND 9

Wellington, Duke of, 1769–1852, Irish-born soldier and statesman, British Prime Minister from 1829, ARMY 16, BATTLES 10, 11, EDITORS 17, IMPOSSIBILITY 7, KNOWLEDGE 36, PARLIAMENT: COMMONS 9, RELIGION 57, SCHOOLS 28, SOLDIERS (G) 27, SOLDIERS (I) 5

Wells, H G, 1866–1946, English novelist, BOOKS (G) 40, CHRISTIANITY 23, CHURCHES 30, COMMUNISM 20, CRIME 21, CYNICS 5, EDEN 5, EDUCATION 32, EPITAPHS 72, EVOLUTION 12, FACES 40, GOOD & GOODNESS 23, HISTORY 57, LITERATURE 31, MONEY 59, NAMES 7, NOVELS (G) 29, PARENTS 26, PROCREATION 5, PROFESSIONS 10, SCHOOLS 29, SOCIETY 17, TEETH 4, 5, THEOLOGY 2, WARS (G) 60, WIVES 31

Wesker, Arnold, 1932– , English playwright, SNOBBERY 16